PSYCHOLOGY

Perspectives and Connections

PSYCHOLOGY
PERSPECTIVES AND CONNECTIONS 3E

McGraw Hill Education

GREGORY J. FEIST

ERIKA L. ROSENBERG

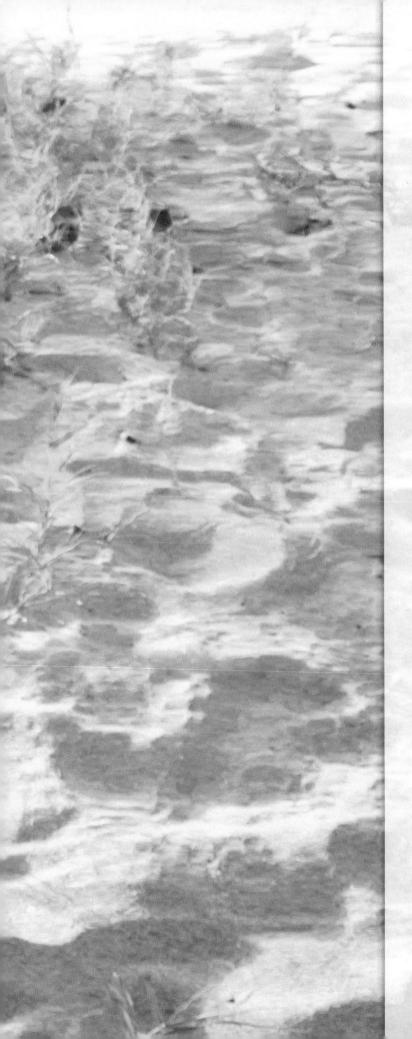

THIRD EDITION

PSYCHOLOGY
Perspectives and Connections

Gregory J. Feist
San Jose State University

Erika L. Rosenberg
University of California, Davis

Mc
Graw
Hill
Education

PSYCHOLOGY: PERSPECTIVES AND CONNECTIONS, THIRD EDITION

2 3 4 5 6 7 8 9 0 DOW/DOW 1 0 9 8 7 6 5

ISBN 978-0-07-786187-2
MHID 0-07-786187-6

Senior Vice President, Products & Markets: *Kurt L. Strand*
Vice President, General Manager, Products & Markets: *Michael Ryan*
Vice President, Content Design & Delivery: *Kimberly Meriwether David*
Managing Director: *William Glass*
Executive Director: *Krista Bettino*
Senior Brand Manager: *Nancy Welcher*
Director, Product Development: *Meghan Campbell*
Product Developer: *Betty Chen*
Marketing Managers: *Ann Helgerson; AJ Laferrera*
Lead Product Developer: *Dawn Groundwater*
Digital Product Analyst: *Neil Kahn*

Director, Content Design & Delivery: *Terri Schiesl*
Program Manager: *Debra Hash*
Content Project Manager: *(core) Sandy Wille; (assessment) Jodi Banowetz*
Buyer: *Laura M. Fuller*
Design: *Trevor Goodman*
Content Licensing Specialists: *John Leland (photo); Shirley Lanners (text)*
Cover Image: *Getty RM © Matthias Clamer*
Compositor: *MPS Limited*
Printer: *R. R. Donnelley*

Library of Congress Cataloging-in-Publication Data

Feist, Gregory J.
  Psychology: perspectives and connections/Gregory J. Feist, San Jose State University;
Erika L. Rosenberg, University of California, Davis.--Third edition.
     pages cm
  Includes index.
  ISBN 978-0-07-786187-2 (alk. paper)
     1. Psychology. I. Rosenberg, Erika L. II. Title.
  BF121.F32 2015
  150--dc23
        2014022576

To our most precious collaborative work,
Jerry and Evan

About the Authors

Gregory J. Feist

Gregory J. Feist is Associate Professor of Psychology in Personality and Adult Development at San Jose State University. He has also taught at the College of William & Mary and the University of California, Davis. He received his PhD from the University of California, Berkeley, and his undergraduate degree from the University of Massachusetts–Amherst.

Dr. Feist is widely published in the psychology of creativity, the psychology of science, and the development of scientific talent. One of his major goals is establishing the psychology of science as a healthy and independent study of science, along the lines of history, philosophy, and sociology of science.

Toward this end, Dr. Feist has published a book titled *Psychology of Science and the Origins of the Scientific Mind* (2006, Yale University Press), which was awarded the 2007 William James Book Prize by the Division of General Psychology, American Psychological Association (APA). In addition, he is the founding president of the International Society for the Psychology of Science and Technology.

A second major focus for Dr. Feist is the identification and development of scientific talent, as seen in finalists of the Westinghouse and Intel Science Talent Search. His paper (co-authored with Frank Barron) "Predicting Creativity from Early to Late Adulthood: Intellect, Potential, and Personality" won Article of the Year for 2003 in the *Journal of Research in Personality* and *Psychology of Aesthetics, Creativity and the Arts.* His teaching efforts have been recognized by outstanding teaching awards at both UC Berkeley and UC Davis. Dr. Feist is also co-author with his father, Jess Feist (and Tomi-Ann Roberts), of the undergraduate text *Theories of Personality.* In his spare time, Dr. Feist enjoys cycling and skiing.

Married to Erika Rosenberg, Dr. Feist is the father of Jerry and Evan.

Erika L. Rosenberg

Erika L. Rosenberg is an emotions researcher, health psychologist, and teacher of meditation. Her research on emotion has examined how feelings are revealed in facial expressions, how social factors influence emotional signals, and how anger affects cardiovascular health. Dr. Rosenberg received her PhD in psychology from the University of California, San Francisco, where she studied with Paul Ekman. Dr. Rosenberg served on the faculties at the University of Delaware and the College of William & Mary, and currently is at the Center for Mind and Brain at the University of California, Davis, where she is a senior investigator on the Shamatha Project, a multidisciplinary study of how intensive meditation affects cognition, emotion, and neurophysiology. She is a co-author of studies from this project, which are published in *Psychological Science, Emotion, and Psychoneuroendocrinology.*

Dr. Rosenberg is a world-renowned expert in facial expressions measurement using the Facial Action Coding System (FACS). She consults with scientists, artists, and the entertainment industry on the use of FACS in a variety of contexts, including her role as scientific consultant on the Fox TV show *Lie to Me.* She teaches FACS workshops worldwide.

A longtime practitioner of meditation, Erika Rosenberg serves on the faculty of Nyingma Institute of Tibetan Studies in Berkeley, where she teaches meditation courses and workshops for working with emotions in daily life. Recently, Erika helped develop a secular compassion-training program with Geshe Thupten Jinpa, PhD, at the Center for Compassion and Altruism Research and Education at Stanford University, where she is a senior teacher. Dr. Rosenberg has presented this program to His Holiness the Dalai Lama and taught the program at Google and throughout the Bay Area, and she now co-directs the Compassion Cultivation Teacher Training Program. Dr. Rosenberg is also a Senior Fellow at the Mind and Life Institute.

Dr. Rosenberg and her husband, Greg Feist, have two sons, Jerry and Evan. They live in the San Francisco Bay Area.

Brief Contents

1 Introduction to Psychology 2

2 Conducting Research in Psychology 32

3 The Biology of Behavior 70

4 Sensing and Perceiving Our World 116

5 Human Development 158

6 Consciousness 208

7 Memory 248

8 Learning 284

9 Language and Thought 322

10 Intelligence, Problem Solving, and Creativity 356

11 Motivation and Emotion 394

12 Stress and Health 442

13 Personality: The Uniqueness of the Individual 476

14 Social Behavior 512

15 Psychological Disorders 548

16 Treatment of Psychological Disorders 588

Contents

Foreword by Paul Ekman xxi

Preface: Don't Believe Everything You Think xxii

1 Introduction to Psychology 2

What Is Psychology? 5

Psychology Defined 5

Why Should You Study Psychology? 6

Psychology in the Real World: Why Psychology Is Important to My Life 7

Subdisciplines of Psychology 8

The Origins of Psychology 11

A Brief History of the Practice of Clinical Psychology 11

A Brief History of Scientific Psychology 14

Ways of Thinking about Mind, Body, and Experience 20

The Nature-Nurture Debate 20

Mind-Body Dualism 21

The Evolution of Human Behavior 22

No One Perspective Tells the Whole Story in Psychology 26

Challenge Assumptions: Don't Believe Everything You Think 26

Connections within and between Chapters 27

Bringing It All Together: Making Connections in Psychology 28

Chapter Review 30

2 Conducting Research in Psychology 32

The Nature of Science 35

Common Sense and Logic 35

The Limits of Observation 35

What Is Science? 36

The Scientific Method 38

Research Process 39

What Science Is Not: Pseudoscience 40

Research Methods in Psychology 41

    Principles of Research Design 41

    Descriptive Studies 42

    Meta-Analysis 46

    Correlational Studies 47

    Experimental Studies 49

Challenging Assumptions in the Objectivity of Experimental Research 53

Commonly Used Measures of Psychological Research 54

    Self-Report Measures 54

    Behavioral Measures 56

    Physiological Measures 57

Making Sense of Data with Statistics 57

    Descriptive Statistics 58

    Inferential Statistics 59

Psychology in the Real World: Challenge the Assumptions of Advertisers' Statistics 60

Research Ethics 62

    Ethical Research with Humans 62

    Ethical Research with Animals 64

Bringing It All Together: Making Connections in Psychological Research 66

Chapter Review 67

3 The Biology of Behavior 70

Genes and Behavior 73

    The Complex Connection between Genes and Behavior 74

    Polygenic Influence on Behavior 75

    Genes and the Environment 75

    Epigenetics: How the Environment Changes Gene Expression 76

The Nervous System 78

    Organization of the Nervous System 78

    The Cells of the Nervous System: Glial Cells and Neurons 79

    Common Neurotransmitters 85

    Summary of the Steps in Neural Transmission 89

The Brain 90

    Evolution of the Human Brain 90

    Overview of Brain Regions 92

Psychology in the Real World: Brain-Computer and
Brain-Machine Interfaces 99

Brain Plasticity and Neurogenesis 100

**Challenging Assumptions about Neural
Growth in the Adult Brain 104**

Early Evidence of Neurogenesis in Adults 104

Key Figures in the Discovery of Neural Growth
in Adults 104

Measuring the Brain 106

Electroencephalography 106

Magnetic Resonance Imaging (MRI) and Functional
MRI (fMRI) 106

Positron Emission Tomography (PET) 107

Research Process 108

The Endocrine System 109

Bringing It All Together: Making Connections in the Biology
of Behavior 111

Chapter Review 113

4 Sensing and Perceiving Our World 116

The Long, Strange Trip from Sensation to Perception 119

Basic Sensory Processes 119

Principles of Perception 119

Vision 123

Sensing Visual Stimuli 123

Perceiving Visual Stimuli 130

Organizing Visual Information: The Gestalt Laws
of Grouping 134

Perceiving Color 138

Hearing 140

The Physics of Sound and the Psychology
of Hearing 140

The Ear 142

Psychology in the Real World: Hearing Loss Can Happen
in Young People Too 143

Hearing in the Brain 143

The Bodily Senses 144

Touch 145

Pain 145

The Chemical Senses: Smell and Taste **148**

Smell (Olfaction) 148

Taste 149

Synesthesia 151

Bringing It All Together: Making Connections in Sensation and Perception 152

Research Process 154

Chapter Review 156

5 Human Development 158

The Developing Fetus 161

Stages of Prenatal Development 161

Brain and Sensory Development before Birth 162

Nature and Nurture Influences on Fetal Development 165

Prenatal Personality Development 166

The Developing Infant and Child 167

Physical Development in Infancy and Childhood 167

Early Cognitive Development 171

Psychology in the Real World: Musical Training Changes the Brain 172

Development of Moral Reasoning 178

Research Process 179

Personality Development during Infancy 181

Early Socioemotional Development 181

The Developing Adolescent 187

Physical Development in Adolescence 188

Cognitive and Brain Development in Adolescence 188

Social Development in Adolescence 191

The Developing Adult 193

Early Adulthood 193

Middle Adulthood 197

Late Adulthood 198

Death and Dying 201

Bringing It All Together: Making Connections in Human Development 202

Chapter Review 206

6 Consciousness 208

What Is Consciousness? 210

Two Dimensions of Consciousness: Wakefulness and Awareness 211

    Minimal Consciousness 212

    Moderate Consciousness 213

    Full Consciousness 213

Attention: Focusing Consciousness 214

    Selective Attention 214

    Sustained Attention 216

    Multitasking: The Implications of Shifting Attention 217

Psychology in the Real World: Hazards of Using a Mobile Device or Texting While Driving 218

Training Consciousness: Meditation 220

    Meditation and Conscious Experience 221

    Meditation Training and the Brain 221

Sleeping and Dreaming 222

    Sleeping 222

Research Process 223

    Dreaming 231

Hypnosis 233

Altering Consciousness with Drugs 236

    Depressants 236

    Stimulants 240

    Hallucinogens 242

Bringing It All Together: Making Connections in Consciousness 245

Chapter Review 246

7 Memory 248

Three Types of Memory 251

    Sensory Memory 253

    Short-Term, or Working, Memory 254

    Long-Term Memory 257

The Biological Basis of Memory 264

    The Neural Basis of Memory 265

Psychology in the Real World: Manipulating Memory with Drugs and Drinks 266

    Challenging Assumptions in Brain Stimulation and Memory 268

    The Sensory Cortexes 269

Research Process 270

    Pathways of Short-Term Memory in the Hippocampus and Prefrontal Cortex 271

    Long-Term Memory Storage in the Cortex 271

    Emotion, Memory, and the Brain 273

Forgetting and Memory Loss 276

    Forms of Forgetting 276

    Memory Loss Caused by Brain Injury and Disease 279

Bringing It All Together: Making Connections in Memory 280

Chapter Review 282

8 Learning 284

Basic Processes of Learning 287

    Association 287

Conditioning Models of Learning 287

    Classical Conditioning 288

    Operant Conditioning 292

    Challenging Assumptions about Conditioning Models of Learning 301

Social Learning Theory 306

The Interaction of Nature and Nurture in Learning 310

    Imprinting 311

    Imitation, Mirror Neurons, and Learning 312

Research Process 313

Psychology in the Real World: Sleep Facilitates Learning 314

    Synaptic Change during Learning 314

    Experience, Enrichment, and Brain Growth 316

Bringing It All Together: Making Connections in Learning 317

Chapter Review 319

9 Language and Thought 322

Language 325

The Nature of Language 325

The Evolution of Language in Humans 326

Language Development in Individuals 326

Theories of Language Acquisition 329

Can Other Species Learn Human Language? 333

Language, Culture, and Thought 335

Thinking, Reasoning, and Decision Making 337

Research Process 338

How Do We Represent Thoughts in Our Minds? 339

How Do We Reason about Evidence? 342

Critical Thinking 344

How Do We Make Judgments and Decisions? 345

Psychology in the Real World: Applying Critical Thinking beyond the Classroom 346

Bringing It All Together: Making Connections in Language and Thought 352

Chapter Review 354

10 Intelligence, Problem Solving, and Creativity 356

Intelligence 358

Defining Intelligence 359

Theories of Intelligence 359

Measuring Intelligence 363

Psychology in the Real World: Bringing Multiple Intelligences to School 364

Extremes of Intelligence 369

The Nature and Nurture of Human Intelligence 373

Group Differences in Intelligence Scores 377

Non-Western Views of Intelligence 378

Problem Solving 379

Types of Problems 380

Solution Strategies 381

Obstacles to Solutions 382

Creativity 383

What Is Creativity? 383

Stages of Creative Problem Solving 384

Creativity and the Brain 384

Research Process 386

Cognitive Processes in Creative Thinking 387

The Creative Personality 388

Bringing It All Together: Making Connections in Intelligence, Problem Solving, and Creativity 389

Chapter Review 391

11 Motivation and Emotion 394

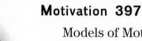

Motivation 397

Models of Motivation 397

Hunger: Survival of the Individual 401

Sex: Survival of the Species 407

Research Process 410

The Needs to Belong and to Excel 413

Motivation in the Workplace 415

Emotion 418

What Are Emotions? 418

Emotion as a Process 422

Psychology in the Real World: Botox and Emotion 430

Emotion and the Brain 431

How Culture Impacts Emotion Expression 433

Gender and Emotion 434

Emotional Intelligence 435

Bringing It All Together: Making Connections in Motivation and Emotion 437

Chapter Review 439

12 Stress and Health 442

Stress 444

Stress as Stimulus or Response 445

The Physiology of Stress 447

Coping 453

Coping Strategies 453

The Positive Psychology of Coping 456

Psychology in the Real World: Does Stress Cause Aging? 458

How Stress and Coping Affect Health 459

    The Birth of Psychoneuroimmunology 461

    Psychological Risk Factors for Heart
    Disease 464

    Research on Health-Relevant Behavior 466

Research Process 470

Bringing It All Together: Making Connections
in Stress and Health 472

Chapter Review 473

13 Personality: The Uniqueness of the Individual 476

Defining Personality 478

The Nature and Nurture of Personality 480

    The Evolution of Personality Traits 480

    Genetics and Personality 481

    Temperament and the Fetal Environment 483

    Personality and Culture: Universality
    and Differences 483

    Challenging Assumptions in Animal
    Personality 485

How Do Theorists Explain Personality? 487

    Psychoanalytic Theories 487

    Humanistic-Positive Psychological
    Theories 494

    Social-Cognitive Learning Theories 496

    Trait Theories 496

    Biological Theories 498

How Is Personality Measured? 500

    Behavioral Observation 500

    Interviewing 501

    Projective Tests 501

    Personality Questionnaires 501

    Social Network Measurement of Personality 502

Psychology in the Real World: Personality and Career Interest
and Job Performance 504

Bringing It All Together: Making Connections
in Personality 506

Research Process 509

Chapter Review 510

14 Social Behavior 512

Group Living and Social Influence 515

Conformity 515

Minority Social Influence 517

Obedience 518

Social Perception 521

Attribution 521

Detecting Deception 522

Schemas 523

Stereotypes 523

Exclusion and Inclusion 524

Psychology in the Real World: The Social Psychology
of Social Networks 526

Prejudice and Discrimination 526

Challenging Assumptions in Social
Behavior 528

Attitudes and Behavior 529

The Nature and Nurture of Attitudes 530

Attitude Change 530

Social Relations 533

The Nature and Nurture of Aggression 533

Prosocial Behavior 535

Liking, Attraction, and Love 539

Research Process 540

Bringing It All Together: Making Connections
in Social Behavior 544

Chapter Review 546

15 Psychological Disorders 548

Defining Psychological Disorders 551

Neurodevelopmental Disorders 555

Subtypes of Neurodevelopmental Disorders 555

Causes of Neurodevelopmental Disorders 556

Schizophrenia 558

Major Symptoms of Schizophrenia 558

Nature and Nurture Explanations of Schizophrenia 559

Depressive Disorders 563

Nature and Nurture Explanations of Depression 565

Research Process 566

Bipolar Disorder 567

Causes of Bipolar Disorder 568

Anxiety Disorders 569

Generalized Anxiety Disorder 570

Panic Disorder 570

Social Phobia (Social Anxiety Disorder) 571

Agoraphobia 571

Specific Phobias 572

Nature and Nurture Explanations of Anxiety Disorders 572

Obsessive-Compulsive Disorder 574

Causes of Obsessive-Compulsive Disorder 575

Post-Traumatic Stress Disorder 575

Dissociative Disorders 576

Dissociative Identity Disorder 576

Causes of Dissociative Disorders 577

Somatic Symptom Disorders 577

Personality Disorders 578

Odd-Eccentric Personality Disorders 578

Dramatic-Emotional Personality Disorders 579

Anxious-Fearful Personality Disorders 580

Nature and Nurture Explanations of Personality Disorders 580

Psychology in the Real World: Can Internet Use Become an Addiction? 582

Bringing It All Together: Making Connections in Psychological Disorders 583

Chapter Review 585

16 Treatment of Psychological Disorders 588

Biomedical Treatments for Psychological Disorders 590

Drug Therapies 591

Psychosurgery 595

Electric and Magnetic Therapies 595

Challenging Assumptions in the Treatment of Severe Depression 597

Effectiveness of Biomedical Treatments 598

Psychological Treatments for Psychological Disorders 600

Psychoanalytic Therapy 600

Humanistic/Positive Therapy 602

Behavior Therapies 603

Cognitive and Cognitive-Behavioral Treatments 603

Group Therapy 605

Effectiveness of Psychological Treatments 607

Research Process 608

Technology-Based Treatments for Psychological Disorders 609

Effectiveness of Technology-Based Therapy 610

Combined Approaches 610

Drugs and Psychotherapy 610

Integrative Therapy 610

Mindfulness Training and Psychotherapy 611

Effectiveness of Combined Approaches 612

Psychology in the Real World: How to Choose a Therapist 614

Emerging Therapies 614

Preventing Disorders 617

Bringing It All Together: Making Connections
in the Treatment of Psychological Disorders 618

Chapter Review 620

■ connect· McGraw-Hill Psychology's APA Style
Documentation Guide

Glossary G-1

References R-1

Credits C-1

Name Index NI-1

Subject Index SI-1

Foreword by Paul Ekman

Perhaps it was because I had never taken Introductory Psychology that I became a psychologist—or so I used to quip at the start of undergraduate lectures. Fifty years ago the textbooks for introductory courses were a turn-off. Most were dry and segmented. The only reason to read them was to pass Introductory Psychology in order to get to the higher-level courses you really wanted to take. It was an obstacle you had to jump over. Things have changed!

This textbook—I hesitate to use the word—is fun to read, enlightening, useful, and provocative. I recommend it to anyone—not just undergraduates—who wants a contemporary overview of psychology. In fact, people with no intentions of studying psychology will find this book engaging and interesting and useful to their life. Wow.

Make no mistake—this is not a how-to book. It is not going to tell you how to get rid of whatever bothers you or find a mate or choose a career or become the most charming person in the world. But it will fascinate you; in each chapter, you will learn about the cutting edge of knowledge, how science is done, what it means, and why it is important to understand that most complex of all subjects—why we do what we do and when and how we do it.

My own specialty for 40 years has been the study of facial expressions, and in the last decade or so I have reached out to develop a theory about emotion itself and how to lead a better emotional life. So I was surprised to find that when I read Chapter 11, "Motivation and Emotion," I learned something new. This is a comprehensive book; the coverage, even from a specialist's view, is amazing. And in each chapter the reader learns about both the breakthrough discoveries that have fundamentally altered the field of psychology and those scientists responsible for them.

I still find it a bit amazing that I should be ending a foreword to a textbook with the phrase "have fun."

Don't Believe Everything

Virtually all of our students enter Introductory Psychology with a full set of preconceived notions—many of them incorrect. *Psychology: Perspectives and Connections* is designed to move students beyond what may seem obvious to them, to have them reevaluate the thoughts and beliefs they bring to the course.

Students often think they already "know" psychology. They sometimes *think* "psychology is just common sense." Perhaps they *believe* that human behavior is simply a by-product of heredity. Or perhaps they think that all they need to know about psychology is best learned by reading words on a page or a screen.

With this in mind, we challenge our students: *Don't believe everything you think*. We encourage students to question preconceived notions, putting their ideas—and the ideas of others—to the test. Through text that is one component of a rich, digital environment, we *engage* students in thinking critically. We continually demonstrate the importance of challenging assumptions and experiences—whether as a student or as a researcher—to understand that *no one perspective tells the whole story*.

CHALLENGING ASSUMPTIONS

Psychology: Perspectives and Connections helps students understand the path to discovery by challenging their assumptions, moving beyond "black-and-white" thinking. With this in mind, each chapter begins with **Challenge Your Assumptions**. We pose assertions such as "Pulling an all-nighter is a good way to study for an exam" or "Eyewitness memories are usually accurate," prompting students to question their own perspective and begin to understand the importance of thinking critically. Responses to these assertions can be found in call-outs throughout the chapter.

Challenge Your Assumptions
True or False? Craving sweet, fatty, and salty foods is a socially and culturally determined preference.
False: The fact that we crave basic foodstuffs is very much a product of evolution.

were scarce during ancestral times: sugar, salt, and fat. The fast-food industry capitalizes on this fact by creating foods that are rich in these substances (Moss, 2013). Companies conduct research to determine precisely the optimal levels of flavors that people crave—the so-called bliss point. Sweets and fats are no longer scarce in industrialized society, and their easy access and overconsumption contribute to increasing problems of obesity.

Our choice of what we eat is also driven by culture. That some people eat cows and others worms is, for the most part, culturally determined. Different cultures expose children to different flavors. Different cultures expose children to unique flavor combinations or shape food preferences while people are young. For instance, people in very cold climates commonly eat raw animal fat: Icelanders eat raw whale blubber pickled in whey; the Inuit eat raw seal fat. In contrast, cow brains and tongue are commonly eaten in Mexico. Exposure does not immediately lead to preference, however (Pliner, 1982; Rozin, 1996). It often takes multiple exposures before children will come to like a food that they initially disliked (Birch & Fisher, 1996; Birch & Martin, 1982). The more often people eat certain foods, the more they like them. Once people develop a preference for a kind of food, they are motivated and even driven to eat that kind of food. If you develop a strong liking for Mexican food, but then spend a year studying in

METACOGNITION

How many students *think* they know what they know but struggle on the first exam? McGraw-Hill's adaptive technology uses continual assessment and artificial intelligence to personalize the learning experience for each student.

LearnSmart® maximizes learning productivity and efficiency by identifying the most important learning objectives for each student to master at a given point in time. It knows when students are likely to forget specific information and revisits that content to advance knowledge from their short-term to long-term memory. Data-driven reports highlight the concepts with which individual students—or the entire class—is struggling. LearnSmart is proven to improve academic performance—including higher retention rates and better grades.

LEARNSMART®

BETTER DATA, SMARTER REVISION, IMPROVED RESULTS

For this new edition, data were analyzed to identify the concepts students found to be the most difficult, allowing for expansion on the discussion, practice, and assessment of the challenging topics. The revision process for a new edition used to begin with gathering information from instructors about what they would change and what they would keep. Experts in the field were asked to provide comments that pointed out new material to add and dated material to remove. Using all these reviews, authors revised the material. But now, a new tool has revolutionized that paradigm.

McGraw-Hill Education authors now have access to student performance data to analyze and to inform their revisions. These data are anonymously collected from the many students who use LearnSmart. Because virtually every text paragraph is tied to several questions that students answer while using LearnSmart, the specific concepts with which students are having the most difficulty are easily pinpointed through empirical data in the form of a "heat map" report.

You Think

SmartBook™ is the first and only adaptive reading experience designed to change the way students read and learn. It creates a personalized reading experience by highlighting the most impactful concepts a student needs to learn at that moment in time. As a student engages with SmartBook, the reading experience continuously adapts by highlighting content based on what the student knows and doesn't know. This ensures that the focus is on the content he or she needs to learn while simultaneously promoting long-term retention of material. Use SmartBook's real-time reports to quickly identify the concepts that require more attention from individual students—or the entire class. The end result? Students are more engaged with course content, can better prioritize their time, and come to class ready to participate.

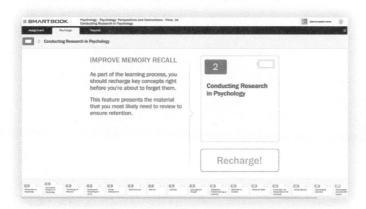

MOVING BEYOND BLACK-AND-WHITE THINKING

Psychology: Perspectives and Connections pays careful attention to multiple causality, moving students beyond "black-and-white" or "either/or" thinking.

> **Connection**
>
> The prefrontal cortex plays a key role in working memory by evaluating sensory information and designating it for storage or disposal.
>
> See "Pathways of Short-Term Memory in the Hippocampus and Prefrontal Cortex," Chapter 7, "Memory," p. 271.

Connections annotations appear throughout the text, reinforcing the interrelatedness of subfields of psychology. In Chapter 8, for example, we explore the relationship among mirror neurons, learning, and socio-emotional development.

Coverage of psychological disorders, such as categories and definitions, has been updated to reflect the publication of the fifth edition of the *Diagnostic and Statistical Manual of Mental Disorders (DSM-5)*. Along with the updates are discussions surrounding the changes in categories, the impact on diagnoses and treatments, and the role of biology.

FOSTERING EXPERIENTIAL LEARNING

Connect Psychology includes assignable and assessable videos, quizzes, exercises, and interactivities, all associated with learning objectives for *Psychology: Perspectives and Connections,* third edition. Videos, interactive assessments, and simulations invite engagement and add real-world perspective to the introductory psychology course. With Connect Psychology, students can study whenever and wherever they choose.

PSYCHOLOGY IN EVERYDAY LIFE

By connecting psychology to students' own lives, concepts become more relevant and understandable.

Powered by McGraw-Hill's Connect, **Newsflash** exercises tie current news stories to key psychological principles and learning objectives. After interacting with a contemporary news story, students are assessed on their ability to make the connection between real life and research findings. Many cases are revisited across chapters, encouraging students to consider multiple perspectives. In Chapter 3, students visit the case of Congresswoman Gabrielle Giffords, who suffered a brain injury in a 2011 shooting. The case is revisited in Chapter 9, "Language and Thought."

Concept Clips, designed to help students comprehend some of the most difficult concepts in introductory psychology, include colorful graphics and stimulating animations to break down core concepts in a step-by-step manner, to engage students, and to increase their retention. Powered by Connect Psychology, Concept Clips can be used as both a lively presentation tool for the classroom and student assessment.

TESTING ASSUMPTIONS THROUGH THE RESEARCH PROCESS

Overcoming preconceptions through an understanding of the research process is often one of the biggest challenges students face in Introductory Psychology. **Research Process,** appearing in Chapters 2 through 16, demystifies research by providing a step-by-step, visual approach to the scientific method. Students are presented with the basic structure of a contemporary study, walking through the "story" of how the research was conducted. In Chapter 3, for example, students are led through the methodology chosen by a researcher exploring whether different parts of the brain are responsible for imagining and seeing faces versus only imagining.

Research Process

1 Research Question

Are there differences between men and women in their interest in casual sex? The researchers hypothesized that men are more eager for casual sex than are women.

2 Method

Clark and Hatfield (1989) developed a brief survey to address the research question. Research assistants who were college students approached students of the opposite sex. After a brief introduction, the research assistant would ask each student one of these questions: "Would you go out with me tonight?" "Would you come over to my apartment tonight?" or "Would you go to bed with me tonight?"

3 Results

This table gives responses to the various questions, by gender.

4 Conclusion

Men and women were equally likely to agree to go on a date with someone they didn't really know. As the proposal became increasingly intimate, however, women backed off. Consistent with the hypothesis, men were much more likely than women to agree to have sex. This finding would be predicted by potential investment theory, which states that the aim of having sexual relationships is to pass on one's genes.

CHAPTER-BY-CHAPTER CHANGES

Psychology: Perspectives and Connections includes over 2,300 research citations, with one-quarter of them coming from 2012 or later.

But research is only part of the story. *Psychology: Perspectives and Connections* also reflects substantial chapter-by-chapter contents and begins with "Challenge Your Assumptions" questions.

Chapter 1: Introduction to Psychology

- new chapter-opening vignette on the effects of technology
- new material on applying the field of psychology to real life
- new material on how introductory psychology can change your life
- updated material on studying electronic social interactions
- updated material on industrial/organizational psychology

Chapter 2: Conducting Research in Psychology

- expanded and reorganized coverage of descriptive statistics and inferential statistics
- new coverage of IQ and normal distribution
- new material that applies the notion "Don't believe everything you think" to student lives
- new meaningful graphic on independent and dependent variables

Chapter 3: The Biology of Behavior

- expanded coverage of brain-computer and brain-machine interfaces, including new material on robotics
- new coverage of gray matter and white matter
- new coverage of diffusion tensor imaging
- new coverage of genes, environment, and family
- new coverage of transcranial direct current and magnetic stimulation
- new coverage of "softwiring"—for example, human brains are softwired and predisposed to certain traits
- expanded coverage of epigenetics

Chapter 4: Sensing and Perceiving Our World

- new coverage of synesthesia
- new research on how physical and emotional pain are processed the same way in the brain
- new material on the association between pain threshold and depression
- new material on color vision in humans and other animals

Chapter 5: Human Development

- new opening vignette on the power of the environment to shape genetic influence in twins
- expanded coverage on how musical training shapes brain development over the life span and its association with intelligence

- new material on distracted driving in teens
- new research on neural pruning during brain development
- expanded coverage of middle adulthood
- updated coverage of digital technology's impact across every stage of human development
- expanded coverage of the positive benefits of regular exercise on learning and memory in teens, adults, and the elderly
- new coverage of the development of dementias, especially Alzheimer's disease

Chapter 6: Consciousness

- reorganized coverage of hypnosis
- expanded and updated section on the functions of sleep
- updated research on meditation and the brain
- new coverage of sleep deprivation and daily functioning
- new coverage of sleep and neural growth
- new material on nightmares
- expanded and updated coverage of multitasking
- new research on the therapeutic applications of certain psychedelic drugs

Chapter 7: Memory

- new coverage on how electrical and magnetic brain stimulation can enhance memory
- new research on how psychologists are developing methods to interfere with and even block painful memories
- new discussion of the extent to which drinks and over-the-counter drugs can enhance memory (and whether stimulants actually help memory formation)

Chapter 8: Learning

- new opening on how behavior is shaped by learning
- updated coverage of the Little Albert story
- updated coverage of how sleeping facilitates learning
- updated research throughout the chapter

Chapter 9: Language and Thought

- new chapter opening on language learning and thought
- new coverage of language and nature and nurture
- new coverage of hormones and thinking
- new coverage of the long-term effects of family environment on language learning
- updated research on the cognitive benefits of bilingualism
- updated and expanded coverage of nonrational decision making
- expanded coverage of the brain and language development

Chapter 10: Intelligence, Problem Solving, and Creativity

- new research on the genetic influence on intelligence
- expanded coverage of different forms of intelligence

- new coverage of intelligence and nature and nurture
- new coverage of brain activity and creativity
- new research on and discussion of whether intelligence is a necessary and sufficient condition for creative achievement
- new meaningful graphic on creativity and intelligence

Chapter 11: Motivation and Emotion

- new research on sleep and weight loss
- new discussion of an evolutionary revision to Maslow's hierarchy of needs
- new research on gender differences in sexual behavior
- reorganized coverage of Ekman's expression research
- new feature on the effects of Botox on facial expression and mood
- new coverage of flourishing, positive emotion, and well-being
- additional coverage of emotion and gender differences
- new meaningful graphic on needs and drives

Chapter 12: Stress and Health

- expanded coverage on how adverse experiences in childhood have lasting impacts on personality and health
- revised coverage of immune system
- new coverage of stressors
- new material on the role of "grit" (perseverance) and hardiness as qualities of successful people
- updated research on stress and cellular aging
- presentation of new models of "good stress" versus "bad stress" and coverage of the benefits of acute stress on health

Chapter 13: Personality: The Uniqueness of the Individual

- new material on assessing personality traits via social media, such as Facebook "likes"
- new discussion of how personality influences how we use social network sites
- revised coverage of personality and Alzheimer's disease
- new coverage on the evolution of personality traits
- new coverage of cross-cultural findings in personality
- new meaningful graphic on how personality traits both change and remain stable over the life span

Chapter 14: Social Behavior

- updated coverage of cyberbullying and social acceptance/exclusion
- expanded discussion of critical analysis of the Zimbardo and Milgram studies
- updated coverage of media violence and aggression
- new discussion of applied research on cognitive dissonance
- major research updates throughout the chapter
- new research on the role of electronic social networks on lived experience

- new text on the benefits of kindness, altruism, and giving in the sections on prosocial behavior
- new text section, "Sexual Attraction and Mate Selection," on electronic dating sites

Chapter 15: Psychological Disorders

- extensive revision incorporating all the new diagnoses of psychological disorders according to *Diagnostic and Statistical Manual-5 (DSM-5)*
- updated coverage of autism spectrum disorder
- new research process feature on gene-environment interaction in depression
- new coverage of the prevalence of psychological disorders
- new meaningful graphic on brain size and neglect

Chapter 16: Treatment of Psychological Disorders

- new coverage of electrical and magnetic brain stimulation and depression
- updated coverage of schizophrenia treatments
- new material on optogenetic therapy for chemical dependency and obsessive-compulsive disorder

 **Personalized Grading, On the Go, Made Easier.** The first and only analytics tool of its kind, Connect Insight™ is a series of visual data displays—each framed by an intuitive question—to provide at-a-glance information regarding how a class is doing: *How are my students doing? How is this student doing? How is this assignment doing? How are my assignments doing? How is my section doing?*

Instructors receive instant student performance matched with student activity, view real-time analytics so instructors can take action early and keep struggling students from falling behind, and are empowered with a more valuable and productive connection between themselves and their students with the transparency Connect Insight™ provides in the learning process.

 Easily rearrange chapters, combine material from other content sources, and quickly upload content you have written, such as your course syllabus or teaching notes, using McGraw-Hill Create. Find the content you need by searching through thousands of leading McGraw-Hill textbooks. Arrange your book to fit your teaching style. Create even allows you to personalize your book's appearance by selecting the cover and adding your name, school, and course information. Order a Create book, and you will receive a complimentary print review copy in 3 to 5 business days or a complimentary electronic review copy via email in about an hour. Experience how McGraw-Hill empowers you to teach *your* students *your* way. **http://create.mheducation.com**

 Capture lessons and lectures in a searchable format for use in traditional, hybrid, "flipped classes," and online courses by using Tegrity. Its personalized learning features make study time efficient, and its affordability brings this benefit to every student on campus. Patented search technology and real-time Learning Management System (LMS) integrations make Tegrity the market-leading solution and service.

 McGraw-Hill Campus (**www.mhcampus.com**) provides faculty with true single sign-on access to all of McGraw-Hill's course content, digital tools, and other high-quality learning resources from any LMS. This innovative offering allows for secure and deep integration, enabling seamless access for faculty and students to any of McGraw-Hill's course solutions, such as McGraw-Hill Connect® (all-digital teaching and learning platform), McGraw-Hill Create (state-of-the-art custom-publishing platform), McGraw-Hill LearnSmart (online adaptive study tool), and Tegrity (fully searchable lecture-capture service).

McGraw-Hill Campus includes access to McGraw-Hill's entire content library, including eBooks, assessment tools, presentation slides and multimedia content, among other resources, providing faculty open, unlimited access to prepare for class, create tests/quizzes, develop lecture material, integrate interactive content, and more.

REVIEWERS

William Adler, Collin County College

Jessica Alexander, Concord University

Clarissa Arms-Chavez, Auburn University at Montgomery

Irwin J. Badin, Montclair State University

Justin Bailey, Limestone College

Jane Bardal, Central New Mexico Community College

Dave Baskind, Delta College

Arlin James Benjamin Jr, University of Arkansas–Fort Smith

Richard Bernstein, Broward College

Jennifer E. Breneiser, Valdosta State University

Victor Broderick, Lincoln Land Community College

Elaine H. Cassel, Lord Fairfax Community College

Chrystal Christman-Hennel, University of Cincinnati

Wanda Clark, South Plains College

Abby Coats, Westminster College

Jill Cohen, Los Angeles Pierce College

Deborah Conway, Community College of Allegheny County

Kimberly Cummings, University of Tampa

Deanna DeGidio, Northern Virginia Community College

Meliksah Demir, Northern Arizona University

Katherine Demitrakis, Central New Mexico Community College

Susan Dutch, Westfield State University

Sam Ehrenreich, University of Texas at Dallas

Nolen Embry-Bailey, Bluegrass Community and Technical College

James Feger, Somerset Community College

Lisa M. Fosbender, Gulf Coast State College

Patricia S. Foster, Stephen F. Austin State University

Suzanne Gibson, Meridian Community College

Adam Goodie, University of Georgia

Jennifer Grewe, Utah State University

Mark Hauber, Hunter College

John Haworth, Chattanooga State Community College

Jeff Henriques, University of Wisconsin–Madison

Becky Hester, Western Carolina University

Michael Himle, University of Utah

Jameson Hirsch, East Tennessee State University

Lindsay Holland, Chattanooga State Community College

Jason Hortin, Olney Central College

Scott Husband, University of Tampa

Charles Jones, Wayne County Community College

Lance Jones, University of Toledo

Veronika Karpenko, University of Central Oklahoma

Don Kates, College of Dupage

Norman Kinney, Southeast Missouri State University

Michael Kitchens, Lebanon Valley College

Sandra Knode, Anne Arundel Community College

Erin Koterba, University of Tampa

Tyson Kreiger, Utica College

William J. Loftus, Big Sandy Community and Technical College

Cynthia Lonsbary, SUNY Jefferson Community College

Jeffrey Love, Penn State University

David Ludden, Lindsey Wilson College

Mark Mach, Dodge City Community College

Noah MacKenzie, University of Cincinnati, Clermont College

Tammy Mahan, College of the Canyons

Deborah Maher, Orange Coast College

Michael Mangan, University of New Hampshire

Donna B. Mantooth, Georgia Highlands College

Marion Mason, Bloomsburg University of Pennsylvania

Sean Meegan, University of Utah

Steven Mewaldt, Marshall University

Stephanie Moore, Northeast Mississippi Community College

Lisa Murphy, York County Community College

Margaret Nauta, Illinois State University

Arthur Olguin, Santa Barbara City College

Haley Orthel, Northern Arizona University

Tori Norris, Owensboro Community and Technical College

William Price, North Country Community College

Adam Privitera, Chemeketa Community College

Douglas L. Pruitt, Western Kentucky Community and Technical College

Meera Rastogi, University of Cincinnati, Clermont College

Heather Rice, Washington University in St. Louis

Mark Rittman, Cuyahoga Community College

Vicki Ritts, St. Louis Community College, Meramec

Alan Roberts, Indiana University

Ronnie Rothschild, Broward College

Jeffrey Rudski, Muhlenberg College

Michael Sauro, Adirondack Community College

Peggy Skinner, South Plains College

Randyl Smith, Metropolitan State University of Denver

Lynn Sprott, SUNY Jefferson Community College

Barry Stennett, University of North Georgia

Rachelle Tannenbaum, Anne Arundel Community College

Lara Tedrow, Tidewater Community College

Eloise Thomas, Ozarks Technical Community College

Jeremy Tost, Valdosta State University

Terry Trepper, Purdue University Calumet

Tommy Turner, Snead State Community College

Denise Wallace, Wayne County Community College

Emily Wickelgren, California State University, Sacramento

Thomas Williams, Bowling Green Technical College

Ralph Worthing, Delta College

Dawn Wright, Meridian Community College

John W. Wright, Washington State University

Jennifer Yanowitz, Utica College

Acknowledgments

Writing *Psychology: Perspectives and Connections* has been an enormous undertaking of hard work and love. We have felt privileged by the opportunity to delve into the literature of so many areas of psychology in depth, something for which career academics rarely have time. We have also been fortunate to have had the commitment of a vast team of collaborators, to whom we offer our profound gratitude. We thank the wonderful professionals at McGraw-Hill who have had utter confidence in this project from day one: Krista Bettino, our executive director, jump-started our new vision for the second edition and shepherded it through the intense revision schedule. Betty Chen, as our product developer, has been invaluable in helping shape new and crisper language and updating concepts. We also want to acknowledge the developmental editor on the first edition, Judith Kromm, who acted as a third author in crafting text, interpreting reviews, and helping us learn that strong substance can co-exist with simple and clear writing. Sheryl Adams, as executive market development manager, always has her finger on the pulse of the people for whom we wrote the book—instructors and students. As midcareer authors, we sometimes forget how 19- and 20-year-old students think and will respond to the information we are presenting. Sheryl always kept us in line in this regard. Dawn Groundwater, as lead product developer, was instrumental in keeping the project on task and developing new ideas for how to best package the unique qualities of the book. Nancy Welcher, the brand manager at McGraw-Hill, has been a tremendous help. We would like to thank Sarah Colwell, digital development editor, who was instrumental in developing Newsflash and Concept Clip. Finally, although no longer with McGraw-Hill, we want to still acknowledge Mike Sugarman, our original publisher, who was a man of vision and always said the right things when we needed encouragement and support the most on earlier editions.

Our thanks also go to the Editing, Design, and Production team: Sandy Wille, who guided us through the copyediting and composition stages of production; designers Trevor Goodman and Preston Thomas; and Content Licensing Specialists John Leland and Shirley Lanners. We also must thank copyeditor Deb DeBord, who offered invaluable advice in helping craft the language and clarify text. We also have been honored to have the invaluable input of our friends and colleagues—all experts in their fields—on various topics in the book. In particular, we are grateful to Paul Ekman, Elissa Epel, Jess Feist, David Galin, Mary Gomes, Lee Huntington, Allen Kanner, Alan Kaufman, James Kaufman, Lee Kirkpatrick, Katherine MacLean, Clifford Saron, Valerie Stone, and especially Mary True, who contributed her expertise to important revisions in Chapter 5 on both the second and third editions of this book.

We have also benefited from having research support from our students Sarah Greene, Adam Larson, Spencer James, and Yvette Szabo. Yvette wrote a wonderful new piece for Chapter 1 on what Introduction to Psychology has meant for her. Our colleague Rebecca Jedel also caught some inaccuracies in the chapters on Learning and Personality in the previous edition, and we are thankful for that feedback. We extend our thanks also to Dean Simonton, who pointed out historical inaccuracies in the two-string problem discussion and graphic. We also thank our parents—Sandra Rosenberg and Jess and Mary Jo Feist—for their love and unending support throughout the writing of the first edition. Mary

Jo, unfortunately, passed away in September 2009 and was not around to see the second and third editions. We also want to give our special and heartfelt thanks to our two wonderful boys, Jerry and Evan. They have been real troopers throughout our work on all the editions. Although they sometimes lost us both for weekends or evenings, they also came to appreciate the positives of this project, like getting to attend sales meetings in New Orleans, team meetings in New York, and a national teaching of psychology conference at a beach resort in Florida.

Erika would also like to extend a very heartfelt "THANKS!" to our local café, Bica Coffeehouse, for their superb coffees and the lovely space that served as her office during her writing of the third edition.

We are in an unusual situation for ending this acknowledgments section. Often, authors end by thanking their spouses or partners. In this case, spouse also means co-author. More than one person we have told about this project has said, "Wow! And you're still married?" Projects as big, complex, and difficult as this one test the mettle of any relationship. By affording us the opportunity to work creatively together, this project has challenged and strengthened the bond between us. We learned how to play to each other's strengths, balance viewpoints and expertise, and compromise. We were able to work through things late at night, even when one of us did not feel like it. We wonder how other coauthors of introductory psychology textbooks manage to work out the complex problems that arise while writing something this big without such convenience and intimacy as our relationship provides. We are grateful for each other.

PSYCHOLOGY
Perspectives and Connections

1 Introduction to Psychology

Chapter Outline

What Is Psychology?

Subdisciplines of Psychology

The Origins of Psychology

Ways of Thinking about Mind, Body, and Experience

No One Perspective Tells the Whole Story in Psychology

Chapter Review

Challenge Your Assumptions

True or False?

- Psychology is all about curing mental illness. (see page 6)

- Psychology is made up of many different subfields. (see page 9)

- Genetic influence on our thoughts and actions is set at birth and can't be changed. (see page 18)

- Psychologists agree that most of human thought and behavior cannot be explained by one perspective. (see page 26)

I n the spring of 2011 revolution spread throughout Egypt. After decades of violent oppression and despotic rule, everyday Egyptians wanted change. Revolutions have existed as long as rulers and governments have, but something new accelerated the spread of these uprisings: social networking sites. Organized protests were planned and carried out over Twitter, Facebook, and YouTube. Eighteen days after the revolution started, it successfully and relatively bloodlessly disposed the government.

In another instance of online social interaction, Tonya was skeptical of online dating. She had already been married, had a 12-year-old daughter, and was not finding anyone to date (Schipani, 2014). Her parents offered to buy her a subscription to an online dating service and at first she resisted. Within a few weeks she was matched with Frank, who had had no luck after a year of online dating. After exchanging emails for some time, Tonya and Frank finally went on their first date and immediately hit it off: Their date lasted 9 hours, and they talked about everything from children to religion. Tonya now says, "There really is someone out there who is so good for me—so smart, funny. He's never let me down. We're just so stinkin' happy" (Schipani, 2014). They soon got married and now are expecting their first child.

These two events give just a small hint of the wide-ranging ways that online technologies have changed social interaction and human behavior. Here are some others:

- Millions of people have free or very inexpensive access to online learning through massive open online courses (MOOCs), such as Udacity and Coursera.

- We can immediately be in contact with friends and family via texting and email, and with wider circles of people via Twitter, Facebook, Tumblr, and Reddit, to name a few.

- Online psychotherapies have helped many individuals and couples dealing with mental illness and broken relationships.

- Sexting photos have had traumatic effects on people's lives and even ruined politicians' careers.

- A baby died of malnutrition and neglect by a couple in South Korea who were spending 14–16 hours a day raising a virtual baby on the online site Prius Online.

- Distracted driving (much of which involves mobile device use) kills more than 3,000 Americans a year (more than 10 each day; *Distracted driving,* 2013).

In many ways, people behave online much the way they do in everyday life, but with the capacity to affect more people, both known and unknown, and potentially with more widespread impact. What happens to social interactions when they become primarily electronic? Do the depths of our friendships increase or decrease through social media? Does technology make our attention scattered, or does it improve our ability to do more than one thing at a time? These are important questions; our interactions and social connections, or *networks,* can influence everything from opinion to eating patterns to one's likelihood of quitting smoking (Christakis & Fowler, 2007, 2008). Do Facebook and other social networks operate in ways that resemble real-world networks? What are the consequences of electronic interaction for our social lives? Each of these questions centers on understanding the effects of technology on thought, feeling, and behavior.

You might assume that social networks only enhance social life. The surprise from psychological science is that social networking both improves and impairs our relationships (Garrett & Danziger, 2008). People use "friending" on social networks to widen their social circles, which can translate into real-life social benefits (P. G. Lange, 2008). These media help us reach people we might not otherwise communicate with at all (such as long-lost cousins). Yet social networking can also reduce interactions with close friends to short electronic statements and lessen the amount of face-to-face time. In addition, technology in general increases our likelihood to multitask, which makes it harder for us to engage in any one task deeply (Bowman et al., 2010; Foerde, Knowlton, & Poldrack, 2006). As psychology begins to identify the pros and cons of this overlap between real and virtual worlds, the ways to navigate this realm in a healthy manner become clearer.

You may be wondering why we are opening a text about psychology with a discussion of people's use of technology. The answer is that technology involves people thinking, behaving, and interacting, which is what psychology is all about.

WHAT IS PSYCHOLOGY?

In one sense, you have been a psychologist for most of your life. Every time you ponder why you think and feel in particular ways, you are thinking psychologically. Every time you try to explain what someone else is doing—and why—you are thinking psychologically. You do it when you say your friend dominates conversations because he is self-absorbed. You also do it when you conclude that your big sister is bossy because she is older and always gets what she wants. We think and live psychology every day.

Psychology Defined

Many fields of study aim to understand people's thoughts and actions. Literature helps us understand people through storytelling, character exploration, development of setting, and use of imagery. History helps us understand people through description and analysis of past events and artifacts. Anthropology is the study of human culture and origins. Sociology seeks to understand people in terms of large-scale social forces and group membership rather than individuals. Psychology is unique in that it is the *science* of understanding individuals—animals as well as people. Formally defined, **psychology** is the scientific study of thought and behavior. The root word *psyche* comes from the Greek for "mind," but modern psychology is as likely to study the brain and behavior as it is the "mind."

psychology
The scientific study of thought and behavior.

You might be thinking, Don't psychologists treat people with mental illness or try to help us figure out how our parents messed us up? Yes, they do these things too. Some professional psychologists practice, or *apply*, psychology to diagnose and treat problems of thought and behavior. In fact, psychology is both a clinical practice and a science. The clinical practice side encompasses the services provided in therapists' offices, schools, hospitals, and businesses. Without fail, when we (the authors of this text) tell people that we are psychologists, they immediately think we are clinical psychologists and are analyzing their every move, looking for hidden meaning in everything they do.

You can also find popular psychology in homes, on radio talk shows, on Internet news sites, and in TV news reports. What sets scientific psychology apart from popular psychology—known as *folk* or *pop psychology*—are the methods used in each. As you will see in Chapter 2, "Conducting Research in Psychology," and again in Chapter 16, "Treatment of Psychological Disorders," the methods of scientific and clinical psychologists are quite different from those of lay folk, who sometimes draw from an unreliable body of knowledge known as *common sense*.

Perhaps because of the ubiquity of popular psychology, most people you talk to on the street don't think of psychology as a science; rather, they probably think of it only as a clinical practice. The editors of *Scientific American*, for instance, commented that "whenever we run articles on social topics, some readers protest that we should stick to 'real science'" ("The Peculiar Institution," 2002, p. 8).

As we will see throughout this text, not only is psychology a science, but it is also considered a core science, along with medicine, earth science, chemistry, physics, and math (Boyack, Klavans, & Börner, 2005). Core sciences are those that have many other disciplines organized around them.

Why Should You Study Psychology?

Reasons for studying psychology vary from person to person. Maybe your advisor suggested it would be a good course to take, or maybe you're taking the course because it satisfies a general education requirement. Psychology is considered part of a good general education because its content is useful to many fields. It is also relevant to your life.

Adopting a scientific perspective on human behavior helps you develop a curiosity for how behavior works. It also fosters an appreciation for how much of human thought and behavior cannot be explained from one perspective. As you move through this text, you will find that many of the concepts you learn, such as memory, have several definitions depending on how you look at them. *Memory*, for instance, can refer either to a specific recalled event (such as your memory of last summer's vacation) or to the process by which we recall such information.

Studying psychology not only makes you more aware of how people work in general, but it also makes you more aware of how *you* work—very practical knowledge to have in many settings. Understanding others' thoughts, feelings, and motives—as well as your own—may help you be a more effective doctor, lawyer, businessperson, or friend. Understanding how children learn, think, reason, and play will help you if you become a parent or a teacher. To learn how one recent college graduate has applied her knowledge of psychology in her life, read the "Psychology in the Real World" feature on p. 7.

The study of psychology is as old as the human species. Before people wondered about the stars, rocks, and planets, no doubt they tried to figure out themselves and others. They did, after all, form relationships, have children, and protect

Psychology in the Real World

Why Psychology Is Important to My Life

Yvette Szabo, *University of Louisville*

For me, studying psychology has meant so much more than learning concepts for an exam. Every day I see how it applies to my life. Material from class and the textbook come alive in my daily encounters. For instance, I now understand what affects my own productivity and what increases my motivation. I know that stress sometimes serves as a major stimulant for me and activates me to work, but it also wears down my immune system. Also, too much stress impairs the quality of my work. From Intro Psych, I learned that these experiences are consistent with what research on motivation, stress, and health tells us.

I have also noticed how patterns of behavior repeat themselves within families or groups of friends. When I learned about the effects of birth order on personality, for example, I was able to connect the concept to my sister and me. I am the younger sister, and I am more rebellious and open to new ideas. In contrast, my elder sister is more agreeable and has a more cautious personality. When I learned in Intro Psych that younger-born children are "born to rebel" [see Chapter 13], I was amazed to discover that the pattern I see with my sister and me is a common one. This has helped put my own life in a larger context of human behavior.

As a curious student, I always enjoy understanding something new. One thing I appreciated with this class is how all of the fields of psychology overlap and interconnect. For example: Different people see and perceive events differently. In other words, social and personality psychology are closely connected to memory, sensation, and perception. What we perceive and remember overlaps with our social environment and our personality. Perceiving and remembering is almost like a camera lens, but the lens has filters—your personality and previous experiences filter what you take in, what sense you make of it, and what you recall.

Additionally, for me, connections between the subfields are clearer when I look at an area that interests me—diagnoses and treatments for depression. In order to understand both the causes of and treatments for depression, you need to appreciate how the biological origins of depression, such as hormones and neurotransmitters, are affected by life experiences, such as stress and trauma. If we don't integrate the biological and social approaches to understanding disorders, then we won't be very successful at diagnosing and treating them.

Moreover, psychology often explores the roles of nature and nurture in shaping behavior and personality. This book in particular does a great job of emphasizing how nature and nurture work together to create who we are and who we become. I have seen this firsthand. My cousin, adopted by my uncle and his wife, developed mannerisms similar to those of her family members. And yet, I've also learned in class that twins separated at birth will likely have similar interests and characteristics. These examples both show that nature and nurture are intertwined.

My knowledge of psychology provides constant explanations for the kinds of relationships I see all around me. For example, as I learned in my psychology courses, research shows that children who were bullied at home will be more likely to befriend someone meek so they can achieve dominance. Sure enough, a close friend of mine recently admitted she was a bully in grade school because it was the one place she was tougher than those around her. At home she was picked on, and so she wanted to dominate when she could at school. Psychology allowed me to better understand this not-so-desirable behavior in my friend. Similarly, I learned that people who do not receive much human contact and were not held as children will likely have difficulty forming bonds and close attachments as adults. I have seen this play out among numerous friends and acquaintances. Both of these cases show the importance of caregiving behavior in the formation of social relationships.

By turning what I learn in my classes outward, I can better understand the actions of others. I am more effective at motivating others and myself, because I better understand individual differences and different types of motivation that stem from internal and environmental sources. I am more conscious about what motivates me. Sometimes I am more motivated by an internal source, such as when I participate in a sport because I enjoy the game. Other times, I am more motivated by external sources, such as when I work to earn a high grade in a class.

Most importantly, the things I learned in Introductory Psychology have laid a foundation for all my future studies in psychology and even other courses. As I have studied more about the clinical applications of psychology, I have become more conscious of the role of a listener and speaker and have greatly improved my listening skills. Psychology has taught me techniques for learning, like scheduling study time over several days, getting a good night's sleep, rehearsing material, and making information personal and relevant. Intro Psych can help you not only to understand other people but also to do well in college.

Psychology has helped me so much in my everyday life that I want to continue to take as many psychology classes as I can and then pursue a doctoral degree in psychology. My motivation to learn more than what is required originated from the sampling of fields covered in introductory psychology. It is only in Intro Psychology where you learn about everything in psychology—from the brain and genetics to learning, memory, and perception; from development and aging to social groups and disorders of the mind. Intro Psych has been a wonderful foundation for understanding my own and other people's thought and behavior—and after all, isn't that what psychology is all about?

their families. Human babies could not survive without others to care for them. Perhaps that is why people fascinate us. From our very first days, we humans are inherently interested in other humans—for survival. Newborns prefer faces to almost any other object. Our very existence is social, and as you will learn, our brains have evolved mechanisms and structures that allow us to understand others in a remarkably complex way (Dunbar, 1996; Frith & Frith, 2010).

As you begin your study of psychology, you will learn just how broad the field is. You may even find a subfield that dovetails with another interest you have already developed.

Quick Quiz 1.1: What Is Psychology?

1. Psychology is best defined as the scientific study of
   a. human behavior.
   b. mental illness.
   c. neuroses.
   d. human thought and behavior.
2. As a field, psychology is
   a. a social science.
   b. the practice of diagnosing and treating mental illness.
   c. a biological science.
   d. all of the above.

3. How does psychology differ from the related field of sociology?
   a. Psychology studies systems; sociology studies cultures.
   b. Psychology studies cultures; sociology studies people.
   c. Psychology studies individuals; sociology studies groups.
   d. Psychology studies groups and cultures; sociology studies human behavior.

Answers can be found at the end of the chapter.

SUBDISCIPLINES OF PSYCHOLOGY

As a science and a practice, psychology is divided into various areas of investigation. Just as this book consists of chapters on different topics in psychology, the field of psychology is divided into more than 25 distinct, but increasingly interrelated, subdisciplines. Figure 1.1 gives a breakdown of the percentages of doctorates awarded in 2008 in each of the major subdisciplines we discuss.

Cognitive psychology is the study of how we perceive information, how we learn and remember, how we acquire and use language, and how we solve problems. For example, a researcher who is concerned with how people visualize objects in their minds is studying cognitive psychology. Those who do research on cognition and learning are often referred to as *experimental psychologists,* because they conduct laboratory experiments to address their research questions.

Developmental psychology explores how thought and behavior change and show stability across the life span. This developmental perspective allows us to appreciate that organisms—human or otherwise—change and grow. Developmental psychologists ask such questions as these: How do our reasoning skills or emotional skills change as we age? How does parent-infant bonding affect adult relationships? Does old age bring wisdom?

Behavioral neuroscience studies the links among brain, mind, and behavior. Neuroscience cuts across various disciplines and subdisciplines of psychology. One can study the brain functions involved in learning, emotion, social behavior, and mental illness, to name just a few areas. The more general subdiscipline of **biological psychology** includes research on all areas of connection between bodily systems and chemicals and their relationship to behavior and thought. An example of research in biological psychology

cognitive psychology
The study of how people perceive, remember, think, speak, and solve problems.

developmental psychology
The study of how thought and behavior change and remain stable across the life span.

behavioral neuroscience
The study of the links among brain, mind, and behavior.

biological psychology
The study of the relationship between bodily systems and chemicals and how they influence thought and behavior.

appears in Chapter 12, where we discuss the effects of stress on hormones and behavior. Neuroscience and biological psychology overlap substantially. The latter is an older term that is being replaced by *behavioral neuroscience* in contemporary psychology. Using noninvasive advanced imaging techniques and electrical recordings, behavioral neuroscientists study the structure and functions of the living brain.

Personality psychology considers what makes people unique, as well as the consistencies in people's behavior across time and situations. Personality research addresses questions such as whether our personal traits and dispositions change or stay the same from infancy to childhood to adulthood. A question from this area, for example, might be whether the tendency to be friendly, anxious, or hostile affects one's health, career choice, or interpersonal relationships or whether a friendly or anxious child will necessarily have the same characteristics as an adult.

Social psychology considers how the real or imagined presence of others influences thought, feeling, and behavior. Research on prejudice and racism, for example, looks at how a person of one group perceives and treats people in other groups. Social psychologists ask such questions as these: How does the presence of other people change an individual's thoughts, feelings, or perceptions? Why is someone less likely to help a person in need when there are many people around than when there is no one else around? Why are we attracted to particular kinds of people?

Clinical psychology focuses on the diagnosis and treatment of mental, emotional, and behavioral disorders and ways to promote psychological health.

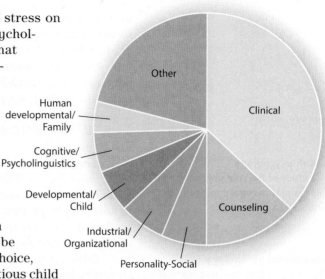

FIGURE **1.1**

PERCENTAGE OF PhDs AWARDED IN THE SUBFIELDS OF PSYCHOLOGY IN 2008. (Adapted from Mulvey & Grus, 2010)

Some clinical psychologists also conduct research and teach. Clinical psychologists work in universities, medical settings, or private practice. As you can see from Figure 1.1, clinical psychology is the single largest subdiscipline in psychology. In the United States, since the late 1940s, the main approach to training in psychology has been the scientist-practitioner model, in which people with PhDs in clinical psychology should be both therapists and researchers—or at least be trained to be both (Benjamin, 2007). Psychology is a practice as well as a science.

A related field is *counseling psychology.* Counseling psychologists tend to work with less severe psychological disorders than clinical psychologists. They treat and assess relatively healthy people and assist them with career

personality psychology
The study of what makes people unique and the consistencies in people's behavior across time and situations.

social psychology
The study of how living among others influences thought, feeling, and behavior.

clinical psychology
The diagnosis and treatment of mental, emotional, and behavioral disorders and the promotion of psychological health.

Challenge Your Assumptions

True or False? Psychology is made up of many different subfields.

True: Psychology has many subfields and is not just one overall discipline. Each subfield examines an important component of thought and behavior, such as cognition, personality, or social influence.

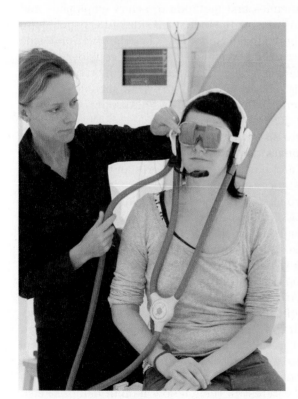

The woman wearing goggles and headgear is being prepared for a neuroimaging exam in a neuroscience lab.

and vocational interests. Training for counseling psychologists is more likely to occur in schools of education than in psychology departments (Norcross et al., 1998).

Other professionals who provide therapy include clinical psychologists who have obtained a PsyD (a professional degree oriented toward nonresearch clinical careers); social workers; marriage and family therapists (who generally have master's degrees); and psychiatrists. Psychiatrists have training in medicine and an MD degree; in addition to offering therapy, they can prescribe drugs.

Health psychology examines the role of psychological factors in physical health and illness. Topics in health psychology range from studies of how stress is linked to illness and immune function to studies on the role of social factors in how people interact with health care professionals. Some health psychologists work in disease prevention, treatment, and rehabilitation; thus, this area involves clinical practice as well as research.

Educational psychology draws on several other areas of psychology to study how students learn, the effectiveness of particular teaching techniques, the dynamics of school populations, and the psychology of teaching. This field also attempts to understand special populations of students, such as the academically gifted and those with special needs. Educational psychologists are usually academics, theorists, or researchers. *School psychology* is a related field generally practiced by counselors in school settings. Approximately 9% of the doctorates in psychology were awarded in school psychology in 2005–2006.

Industrial/organizational (I/O) psychology is an applied science, meaning that it involves understanding real-world rather than laboratory behavior (Aamodt, 2010). The industrial and organizational sides focus on two distinct sets of problems. The *industrial* side involves matching employees to their jobs and uses psychological principles and methods to select employees and evaluate job performance. For this reason, the industrial side of I/O psychology is also sometimes referred to as personnel psychology. The *organizational* side of I/O aims to make workers more productive and satisfied by considering how work environments and management styles influence worker motivation, satisfaction, and productivity. I/O is one of the fastest-growing subdisciplines in psychology, with a nearly 50% increase in the number of PhD programs between 1986 and 2004 (Rogelberg & Gill, 2006).

Two of the smaller and newer disciplines in psychology are sports psychology and forensic psychology. **Sports psychology** examines the psychological factors that affect performance and participation in sports and exercise (R. S. Weinberg & Gould, 2007). For instance, sports psychologists might focus on improving athletic performance through techniques such as relaxation and visualization. **Forensic psychology** is a blend of psychology, law, and criminal justice (J. Adler, 2004). Forensic psychologists make legal evaluations of a person's mental competency to stand trial, the state of mind of a defendant at the time of a crime, the fitness of a parent to have custody of children, and allegations of child abuse. Occasionally, they develop criminal profiles of the type of person who might have committed a particular crime.

As you study the chapters of this text, you may find that one area of psychology especially excites you. Keep in mind, however, that psychology is about how humans think and behave. Thus, all of the topics are useful, many of them are closely intertwined, and there are many reasons for studying psychology, even if you don't become a psychologist. The field of psychology is the outcome of millions of years of humans' interest in their fellow human beings (Feist, 2006). As we will see next, however, the formal history of the field is not quite so old.

health psychology
The study of the role psychological factors play in regard to health and illness.

educational psychology
The study of how students learn, the effectiveness of particular teaching techniques, the social psychology of schools, and the psychology of teaching.

industrial/organizational (I/O) psychology
The application of psychological concepts and questions to work settings.

sports psychology
The study of psychological factors in sports and exercise.

forensic psychology
The field that blends psychology, law, and criminal justice.

1. What subdiscipline of psychology examines how thoughts, feelings, and behaviors change over the life span?
   a. developmental psychology
   b. cognitive psychology
   c. personality psychology
   d. educational psychology

2. A psychologist has conducted a series of studies on which part of the brain is most active during a memory task. She is probably
   a. a developmental psychologist.
   b. a behavioral neuroscientist.
   c. a cognitive psychologist.
   d. an industrial/organizational psychologist.

3. The main difference between a clinical and a counseling psychologist is that counseling psychologists treat
   a. people with more severe psychological disorders.
   b. more children than adults.
   c. people with less severe psychological disorders.
   d. people with learning disabilities only.

Answers can be found at the end of the chapter.

THE ORIGINS OF PSYCHOLOGY

In this section, we look briefly at the origins of the two main forms of psychology: clinical practice and science. The practice of psychology has deeper roots in human history than does the science of psychology. The prehistoric record offers evidence of efforts to heal people's suffering from disturbances of the mind, often in ways we now find alarming. The foundations for psychology as a science date back to the ancient Greeks, and the modern science of psychology originated in the 1870s (D. N. Robinson, 1995). First, we consider the practice of psychology.

shamans
Medicine men or women who treat people with mental problems by driving out their demons with elaborate rituals, such as exorcisms, incantations, and prayers.

A Brief History of the Practice of Clinical Psychology

Disorders of thought and behavior are no doubt as old as humans—indeed, there is evidence that primates (monkeys and apes) are afflicted with psychological disorders such as depression, anxiety, repetitive and functionless behaviors, and self-injuries (Maestripieri et al., 2006; Novak, 2003; Troisi, 2003). Thus, research suggests that these behaviors go back to the ancestors of both species, in this case approximately 6 million years.

Prehistoric Views   As far back as the Stone Age (7,000 years ago and maybe even as long as 50,000 years ago), humans tried to cure one another of various mental problems. Most prehistoric cultures had medicine men or women, known as **shamans,** who treated the possessed by driving out demons with elaborate rituals, such as exorcisms, incantations, and prayers. Some of these shamans appeared to have practiced the oldest of all known surgical procedures, trephination.

Trephination involves drilling a small hole in a person's skull, usually less than an inch in diameter (Alt et al., 1997; Weber & Wahl, 2006). Some of these surgeries may have been for medical reasons, such as an attempt to heal a brain injury. Some may also have been performed for psychological reasons, to release the spirits and demons they believed possessed the afflicted person. Anthropological evidence suggests that a surprisingly large percentage of people survived such surgeries—which today's scientists can confirm by identifying bone growth after the procedure—and the surgeons must have had moderately sophisticated knowledge and understanding of the brain (Alt et al., 1997; Weber & Wahl, 2006).

Ancient Views   Around 2600 BCE (Before the Common Era), the ancient Chinese moved away from supernatural explanations of psychological disorders toward

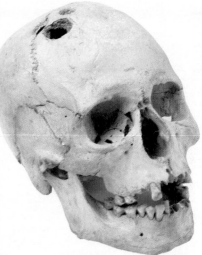

The hole in this skull may have been created by trephination, a prehistoric practice believed to release spirits or demons responsible for psychological disturbances.
What do you think actually happens to those who undergo such a procedure?

natural and physiological explanations (Tseng, 1973). Specifically, they made connections between a person's bodily organs and emotions. The heart housed the mind; the liver, the spiritual soul; the lung, the animal soul; the spleen, ideas and intelligence; and the kidneys, will and vitality. The ancient Egyptians and Greeks also sought natural explanations for psychological disorders. In the second century BCE, the ancient Egyptians apparently used narcotics to treat pain (Finger, 1994). The Greek physician Hippocrates (460–377 BCE) was the first to write about a man suffering from a phobia of heights—now called acrophobia.

Medieval to Early Modern Views   In medieval Europe from approximately 400 to 1400 CE (Common Era), psychological disorders were again attributed to supernatural causes. In the worldview that dominated this era and the Renaissance (from about 1400 to the early 1600s), people were thought to be possessed by demons, spirits, and the devil—not by physical disorders. These views were taken to an extreme during the Inquisition, when the Catholic Church investigated witchcraft and heresy as part of a broad campaign to eliminate dissent from established Church dogma. Some witchcraft practices were viewed as harmless and even beneficial, but others were branded as the work of the devil. In order to distinguish good witchcraft from bad, Church officials held inquisitions and trials, using several techniques to determine whether a person was a witch (D. N. Robinson, 1995). Sometimes the accused was prodded with a metal pole and spears; if she felt no pain, she was protected by the devil and therefore was a witch. In another common method, the *float test*, the woman's hands and feet were tied, and she was thrown into a lake or river. If she floated, she had to be guilty, because only the devil could make someone float; if she sank, she was innocent—but had drowned (D. N. Robinson, 1995). The most common punishment for the infrequent survivor of the float test—deemed to be a witch—was being burned at the stake. To be fair, numerous writers during the 14th to 16th centuries argued that witchery was caused not by spirits and supernatural elements but rather by natural ones, such as hallucinations or "melancholia"—what we would now call depression (D. N. Robinson, 1995; Veith, 1965).

In the Middle Ages, people who were judged to be witches could be burned at the stake. Some of them may have had psychological disorders that caused them to behave strangely.

Although we see these as very outdated reactions to those who may be mentally ill, can you think of modern-day reactions that one day may also seem as outdated?

During the witch hunts of the 16th and 17th centuries, the first facilities for the mentally ill—called **asylums**—were built throughout Europe. The most famous, or infamous, of these was located at St. Mary of Bethlehem in London, England. Although it had served as a hospital for the mentally ill and others since the 1300s, Henry VIII designated it as a hospital for the insane in 1547. It was really no more than a storage house for the mentally ill and other social castaways. For the most part, early efforts to "treat" mental illness focused on removing afflicted people from society rather than helping them adjust to society. The conditions were deplorable and chaotic—patients were put in windowless and filthy rooms and were chained and shackled to the walls. The local population, including William Shakespeare, called the place *Bedlam*, a shortened version of *Bethlehem*, and that is how the term came to be associated with chaotic and noisy conditions.

In response to these inhumane conditions, reform movements in support of **moral treatment** emerged in Europe and the United States. The main idea was to provide a relaxing place where patients would be treated with dignity and care. The first major proponent of humane therapies was the Frenchman Philippe Pinel in 1783. Dorothea Dix pioneered moral treatment in the United States. After visiting a prison in 1841 and witnessing the abhorrent and inhumane treatment of the inmates, some of them suffering from psychological disorders, Dix vowed to change these conditions. Over the next 40 years, she helped open 30 homes throughout North America (Nolen-Hoeksema, 2007). Moral therapies were among the first forms of treatment that regularly helped people get better.

Modern Views   The last decades of the 1800s also saw the emergence of the first truly modern view of psychological disorders—the idea that they are simply one form of illness and should be treated as medical conditions, with appropriate diagnosis and therapy. This view is now known as the "medical model" perspective in clinical psychology. In the 1880s and 1890s, the German psychiatrist Emil Kraepelin collected data on the various kinds of psychological disorders and began systematically classifying and diagnosing them (Shepard, 1995). He popularized the term *dementia praecox* (premature dementia), which he later changed to *schizophrenia*, to refer to the major thought disorder known previously as "split mind." He was also the first to distinguish thought disorders (schizophrenia) from the mood disorders of melancholia (depression) and manic depression (bipolar disorder; Jablensky & Woodbury, 1995). In short, his views were a major influence on diagnostic categories formulated during the 20th century.

Around the turn of the 20th century in Austria, Sigmund Freud developed a form of therapy called psychoanalysis. A clinical approach to understanding and treating psychological disorders, **psychoanalysis** assumes that the unconscious mind is the most powerful force behind thought and behavior and that dreams have meaning and are the most direct route to the unconscious mind (Freud, 1900/1953). It also assumes that our experiences during childhood are a powerful force in the development of our adult personality. Psychoanalysis assumes that people use psychological defenses to protect themselves against threatening impulses, thoughts, feelings, and fantasies. Last, it assumes that the unconscious blocking, or repression, of disturbing thoughts and impulses—especially sexual and aggressive impulses—is at the heart of all maladaptive adult behavior.

By the mid-20th century, three of the major modern developments in clinical psychology had emerged: psychotherapy, drug therapy, and modern criteria for diagnosing mental disorders. For example, one common form of modern therapy—cognitive-behavioral—focuses on changing a person's maladaptive thought and behavior patterns by discussing and rewarding more appropriate ways of thinking and behaving. Although we will consider the modern diagnostic criteria in detail in Chapter 15 and *psychotherapy* (psychological assessment and treatment by a trained therapist) and drug therapy in detail in Chapter 16, it is appropriate to conclude our discussion of the history of psychology as a clinical

asylums
Facilities for treating the mentally ill in Europe during the Middle Ages and into the 19th century.

moral treatment
The 19th-century approach to treating the mentally ill with dignity in a caring environment.

Connection

Disturbance, dysfunction, distress, and deviance must be present for the diagnosis of psychological disorders. The *DSM-5* describes specific symptoms of more than 250 different disorders.

See "Defining Psychological Disorders," Chapter 15, "Psychological Disorders," p. 551.

psychoanalysis
A clinically based approach to understanding and treating psychological disorders; it assumes that the unconscious mind is the most powerful force behind thought and behavior.

Sigmund Freud

practice with a brief introduction to the classification system that guides the diagnosis of psychological disorders today.

When diagnosing psychological disorders, psychologists use the *Diagnostic and Statistical Manual*. Currently in its fifth edition, this standardized reference is referred to as the *Diagnostic and Statistical Manual–5*, or *DSM-5* (American Psychiatric Association, 2013). Originally published in 1952, the *DSM* includes diagnoses for more than 250 psychological disorders. The various editions of the *DSM* have incorporated new findings and added new disorders, objectively describing the behaviors and symptoms of each disorder, so that psychologists from all perspectives can agree on a single diagnosis for an individual with a given set of symptoms. You might find it surprising to know, however, that this goal of universal agreement often is not achieved, so different clinicians hold different views about what constitutes a mental disorder. Occasionally, the *DSM* authors have removed behavior patterns (such as homosexuality, which was deleted from the list of disorders recognized by the American Psychiatric Association in 1973) that do not meet updated diagnostic criteria. Further, practitioners from the various subfields do not always agree with each other about the definitions of a given disorder. Cognitive-behavioral practitioners view depression, for example, as the patient's distorted thinking ("I am worthless"), whereas psychodynamic practitioners might consider the same person's depression (and expressed thoughts) to be the result of unconscious disturbing family relationship patterns that need to be made conscious. Clearly, perspective matters when it comes to psychological treatment, and we must continually question what we know from the perspective we are adopting.

A Brief History of Scientific Psychology

As with all sciences, scientific psychology can claim philosophy as one of its parent disciplines. By the middle of the 1800s, however, psychology had grown away from philosophy to become a science. Let's look briefly at this history.

The Philosophy of Empiricism   Perhaps the most important philosophical question for psychology is the nature of knowledge and how human beings create knowledge. Does knowledge come from reflection and thinking or from experience? In the 4th century BCE, the Greek philosopher Plato argued for the former and his student Aristotle for the latter. In 17th-century Europe, however, the English philosopher John Locke established the view that knowledge and thoughts come from experience, a point of view known as **empiricism**. Specifically, Locke argued that the mind begins as a *tabula rasa*, or blank slate, onto which experience writes the contents of the mind (Locke, 1690/1959).

empiricism
The view that all knowledge and thoughts come from experience.

This view that the mind simply receives what our sensory organs—eyes, ears, nose, skin, and tongue—take in from the outside world is very important in philosophy and psychology. In contrast to scientists, however, philosophers do not collect data to test their ideas. Psychology gained its independence from philosophy when researchers started to examine and test human sensations and perception using scientific methods. Psychology as a modern empirical science tests predictions about behavior with systematic observations and gathered data. In the mid- to late 1800s, many German universities were starting scientific laboratories in physics, chemistry, and medicine. In the 1870s, they opened the first laboratories in psychology.

The Psychophysics of Human Perception   The starting point for empiricism is that we know and experience the world through our five senses of seeing, hearing, tasting, smelling, and touching. Because of the profound influence of the empiricists, the first researchers in psychological science developed the field of **psychophysics** to examine the subjective experience of physical sensations. If the mind consists only of what we sense, then understanding the senses will lead to a direct understanding of the mind. German psychophysics researchers in the 1860s focused on the sensations of touch, vision, hearing, and smell. Whereas physicists study the physical properties of light and sound, psychophysicists study human perception of light and sound.

One important principle of psychophysics is that the perception of physical properties is not the same as the physical properties themselves. To demonstrate, let's consider the classic question, What weighs more, a pound of feathers or a pound of bricks? You might be thinking, How dumb do they think I am? I've heard that so many times. They weigh the same! A pound is a pound. Maybe, for that answer is true only for the objective, physical property of weight. The *perceived* weight of the two—a psychological property—would be very different. Researchers found that, when people's estimates of the weights of both items are empirically tested, contrary to common sense, people think a pound of bricks weighs two to three times as much as a pound of feathers (Benjamin, 2007). If you don't believe us, try it for yourself. *Psychophysics* is all about this relationship between the physical and psychological worlds.

In essence, the scientists who first developed psychophysics were the first experimental psychologists. Ernst Weber (1795–1878) did some of the first research in perception and laid the groundwork for what later became known as psychophysics. For instance, he investigated the smallest change in weight or length that people could discern. Then, in 1850, building on Weber's work, his mentor, Gustav Fechner (1801–1889), had a sudden realization that one could study the psychological and physical worlds. Fechner coined the term *psychophysics* for this new discipline, and he went on to refine some of Weber's principles of perception (Fancher, 1996).

A physician and physicist, Hermann von Helmholtz (1821–1894), not only made important contributions to the study of memory, physiology, and color vision but also made key contributions to the laws of conservation in physics and to music theory, meteorology, and geometry; he designed a workable telephone years before Alexander Graham Bell (Benjamin, 2007). In addition, he was the first to calculate the speed of a nerve impulse at about 90 feet per second. With the work of these pioneers, psychophysics took the first steps toward establishing psychology as a science.

Psychology blossomed into a full-fledged science with the help of Wilhelm Wundt (1832–1920). In 1879 (remember this date!), Wundt set up a psychology laboratory in Leipzig, Germany, now considered the birthplace of experimental psychology. Although others went before Wundt, he is credited with giving psychology its independence from philosophy and physiology (Benjamin, 2007; Fancher, 1996). He did so by applying the scientific methods of physiology and physics to questions of philosophy (Benjamin, 2007). Before Wundt, people evaluated the question of how the mind worked only by way of argument, not by scientific investigation. By establishing a laboratory, Wundt created a place where the best young minds could learn the science of psychology, and come to learn they did. Wundt single-handedly trained more than 180 students in his laboratory. Of these, more than 100 came from countries other than Germany and then returned to their native countries, taking their knowledge of experimental psychology with them.

An American, G. Stanley Hall (1844–1924), went to Germany to learn from Wundt. At Harvard, Hall also studied with William James, who is considered the founder of American psychology. Hall holds the distinction of earning the first PhD (1878) in psychology in the United States as James's student. He opened the first psychology laboratory in the United States at Johns Hopkins University in Baltimore, officially establishing psychology as a science in this country. He also founded the American Psychological Association (APA) and became its first

psychophysics
The study of how people psychologically perceive physical stimuli, such as light, sound waves, and touch.

Wilhelm Wundt

William James

president in 1892. Hall started the first scientific journal in American psychology, the *American Journal of Psychology*. Finally, he was able to persuade both Sigmund Freud and his famous protégé, Carl Jung, to make their only journey to the United States and give lectures at Clark University in Massachusetts in 1909. G. Stanley Hall was also the teacher and mentor of Francis Cecil Sumner (1895–1954), the first African American to earn a PhD in psychology (1920). From 1928 until his death in 1954, Sumner chaired the psychology department at Howard University, where he conducted research on equality and justice.

Another of William James's students, Mary Whiton Calkins (1863–1930), became the first female president of APA in 1905. Harvard was an all-male university until 1920, and the male students did not want to have a woman in class, so she and James had to conduct their coursework in James's home. Calkins went on to complete the requirements for the PhD, although Harvard would not grant her the degree, simply because she was a woman (Benjamin, 2007). Nevertheless, Calkins had an accomplished academic career. She taught at Wellesley College and conducted research on dreaming, gender issues, and self-image (Furumoto, 1981). James acknowledged her to be among the best students he had ever encountered (Benjamin, 2007).

Structuralism and Functionalism   What is the best way to understand the human mind, by examining its parts or its function? In the last decades of the 1800s, psychology weathered its first major scientific debate, with two different perspectives on how to study thought and behavior. The field was divided over whether it was more important to study the *elements* or the *functions* behind human thought and behavior. Focus on the elements of mind led to the school of thought known as structuralism, whereas focus on the functions of mind led to the school of thought known as functionalism. Edward Titchener (1867–1927), a British American psychologist trained by Wilhelm Wundt, coined both terms.

According to **structuralism,** breaking down experience into its elemental parts offered the best way to understand thought and behavior. Structuralists believed that a detailed analysis of experience as it happened provided the most accurate glimpse into the workings of the human mind. Their method was **introspection,** looking into one's own mind for information about the nature of conscious experience. Structuralists divided each experience into its smallest elements. Wundt, the chief proponent of structuralism, wanted to describe human experience in terms of the elements that combined to produce it (Benjamin, 2007). For example, structuralists, like chemists describing elements, would not describe a peach as "a good peach" but rather would describe their experience with the peach as sweet, round, slightly orange, fuzzy, wet, and juicy.

Influenced by Charles Darwin's theory of natural selection, psychologists who supported **functionalism** thought it was better to look at why the mind worked the way it did rather than to describe its parts. The functionalists asked, "Why do people think, feel, or perceive, and how did these abilities come to be?" Functionalists used introspection as well. William James, the most famous functionalist, relied on introspection as a primary method of understanding how the mind worked.

James's and Wundt's methods of introspection were impressive attempts to describe the conscious mind. Eventually, however, introspection failed as a method of science because of difficulties in reaching a consensus as to the nature of certain experiences. Moreover, the rise of psychology as the science of *observable* behavior led to complete rejection of the study of the mind. It also gave way to the rise of behaviorism.

Behaviorism   In 1913, a little-known 34-year-old psychologist, John Watson, directly challenged the use of introspection. He founded **behaviorism,** which asserts that psychology can be a true science only if it examines observable

structuralism
A 19th-century school of psychology that argued that breaking down experience into its elemental parts offered the best way to understand thought and behavior.

introspection
The main method of investigation for structuralists; it involves looking into one's own mind for information about the nature of conscious experience.

functionalism
A 19th-century school of psychology that argued it was better to look at why the mind works the way it does than to describe its parts.

behaviorism
A school of psychology that proposed that psychology could be a true science only if it examines observable behavior, not ideas, thoughts, feelings, or motives.

behavior, not ideas, thoughts, feelings, or motives. In Watson's view, mental experiences are hypothetical concepts, for they cannot be directly measured. As long as psychology focused on such internal states, it would forever be a false science. Behaviorism is an extreme form of environmentalism, the view that all behavior comes from experience interacting with the world. It is the school of psychology that most clearly expresses John Locke's ideas about our minds being a blank slate at birth.

A decade or so after behaviorism emerged, it became the dominant force in experimental psychology. Its most famous figure, B. F. Skinner (1904–1990), was largely responsible for making behaviorism the major approach in experimental psychology, a position it held for nearly 50 years. Skinner modified Watson's ideas and argued that consequences shape behavior.

This dolphin is being trained by means of shaping, a behaviorist technique that rewards animals for small changes in behavior as they learn a desired behavior pattern, such as leaping out of the water on cue.

 Can you think of undesirable human behaviors that could be shaped with rewards to lessen them or to make them go away?

Humanistic and Positive Psychology During the first half of the 20th century, the two major schools of thought in psychology were split along the divide between practice and science. On the therapeutic side were psychoanalysis and Freud, and on the scientific side were behaviorism and Skinner. In the 1940s and 1950s, Abraham Maslow and Carl Rogers presented an alternative to both of these perspectives. They argued that both psychoanalysis and behaviorism ignored people at their best, and neither approach considered what it meant to be psychologically healthy. Maslow and Rogers proposed an alternative called **humanistic psychology,** which promoted personal growth and meaning as a way of reaching one's highest potential.

The humanistic movement had waned by the late 1970s, mostly because it had moved away from its research and scientific base. It surfaced again in the late 1990s, however, when Martin Seligman and Mihaly Csikszentmihalyi started the positive psychology movement (Seligman & Csikszentmihalyi, 2000). **Positive psychology** shares with humanism a belief that psychology should focus on studying, understanding, and promoting healthy and positive psychological functioning. It does so with a better appreciation than humanistic psychology for the importance of studying well-being from a scientific perspective. As you will see in this text, much of contemporary psychology embraces the positive psychological view.

humanistic psychology
A theory of psychology that focuses on personal growth and meaning as a way of reaching one's highest potential.

positive psychology
A scientific approach to studying, understanding, and promoting healthy and positive psychological functioning.

Gestalt psychology
A theory of psychology that maintains that we perceive things as wholes rather than as a compilation of parts.

Cognitivism After Watson banished thoughts, feelings, and motives as the focal point of the modern science of psychology in the 1910s, research into these topics nearly disappeared from the field for almost 50 years. Two events kept them in the minds of psychologists, however. First, in the 1920s and 1930s, a movement in Germany called Gestalt psychology attracted worldwide attention. Led by Max Wertheimer (1880–1943), **Gestalt psychology**—after the German word for "whole form"—proposed that perception occurs in unified wholes, where the whole is more than the sum of its parts. As the Gestaltists suspected, our brains actively shape sensory information into perceptions. For an example of this phenomenon, look at Figure 1.2. You see a triangle within three circles, but no triangle actually exists. The brain, however, organizes your perception of the markings on the page into the shape of a triangle.

Second, mental processes returned to psychology full force in the 1950s and 1960s—just when the influence of behaviorism was at its peak. The new

FIGURE **1.2**

A DEMONSTRATION OF GESTALT PSYCHOLOGY.

 Why do you see a triangle even though no triangle actually exists?

emphasis was really a forgotten focus on the processes that fascinated Fechner, Wundt, and Helmholtz in the 19th century: sensation, perception, and mental processes. The term *mental*, however, had lost its appeal. Instead, a new word for thought and mental processes appeared: *cognition* (Benjamin, 2007; H. Gardner, 1987).

By the 1960s, the field of cognitive science had been born, with a focus on the scientific study of thought (H. Gardner, 1987). In addition to freeing itself from the label *mental*, cognitive science made use of a new modern metaphor for the human mind—the computer. A fairly recent innovation at the time, the computer seemed to have a lot in common with the human mind. Computers store, retrieve, and process information, just as the brain stores, retrieves, and processes sensations, memories, and ideas. Sensation was the input; perception was the interpretation and processing of the input; and behavior and thoughts were the output. By the 1980s, cognitive science had combined many disciplines in addition to psychology—namely, linguistics, philosophy, anthropology, artificial intelligence, and neuroscience (H. Gardner, 1987).

Some of the thinking in this new cognitive movement was based on a book by the British psychologist Frederick Bartlett (1886–1969). Bartlett wrote that memory is not an objective and accurate representation of events but rather a highly personal reconstruction based on one's own beliefs, ideas, and point of view. For example, racial-ethnic stereotypes are frameworks that can alter memory (Graham & Lowery, 2004). If a witness to a crime holds a bias about how likely a crime is to be perpetrated by a person of a certain racial-ethnic background, the witness may misremember the appearance of the accused. This example illustrates that, as Bartlett argued, when people remember, they reconstruct experience in terms of what is most relevant to them rather than providing an unbiased account of events. Bartlett showed that our cognitive frameworks organize how we experience the world. This view is now well accepted in psychology, though Bartlett's insights were unappreciated in the United States for decades (Benjamin, 2007).

Behavioral Genetics, Behavioral Neuroscience, and Evolutionary Psychology By the 1980s, more and more psychologists had become receptive to the ideas that who we are and what we do and think are very much influenced by genetic factors (behavioral genetics) and brain activity (behavioral neuroscience), with a long evolutionary past (evolutionary psychology). The roots of this approach lie in many related fields. Recent behavioral genetic research has overturned a long-held notion that genetic influence is set at birth and is unchanging. We now know that genes get turned on and off by experience—that is, genetic influence changes how we think and behave over the course of our lives. Similarly, evolutionary psychology was jump-started in 1992 when John Tooby and Leda Cosmides (1992) published "The Psychological Foundations of Culture" in a seminal book on evolutionary psychology. These developments all began to shift psychology toward a more complex view of the origins of human thought and behavior as products of nature and nurture, enhanced by new brain imaging techniques and the sequencing of the human genome.

Our review of the history of psychological science, summarized in Figure 1.3, has only scratched the surface of how psychologists think about human thought and behavior, about mind, body, and experience. Debates and theories about how and why we think and act the way we do go back thousands of years. Some of the key debates remain unresolved to this day, primarily because in many cases no one perspective explains the whole story of how things work. These systems of thought have profoundly influenced the development of psychology. Let's now consider the major ways of thinking about mind, body, and experience that have shaped modern psychological science.

Connection

Our genetic code is not set in stone at birth. Genes are turned on or off by experiences we have, foods we eat, and even foods our mothers ate while pregnant with us.

See "Epigenetics: How the Environment Changes Gene Expression," Chapter 3, "The Biology of Behavior," p. 76.

Challenge Your Assumptions

True or False? Genetic influence on our thoughts and actions is set at birth and can't be changed.
False: Experience can and does change how and when genes get expressed.

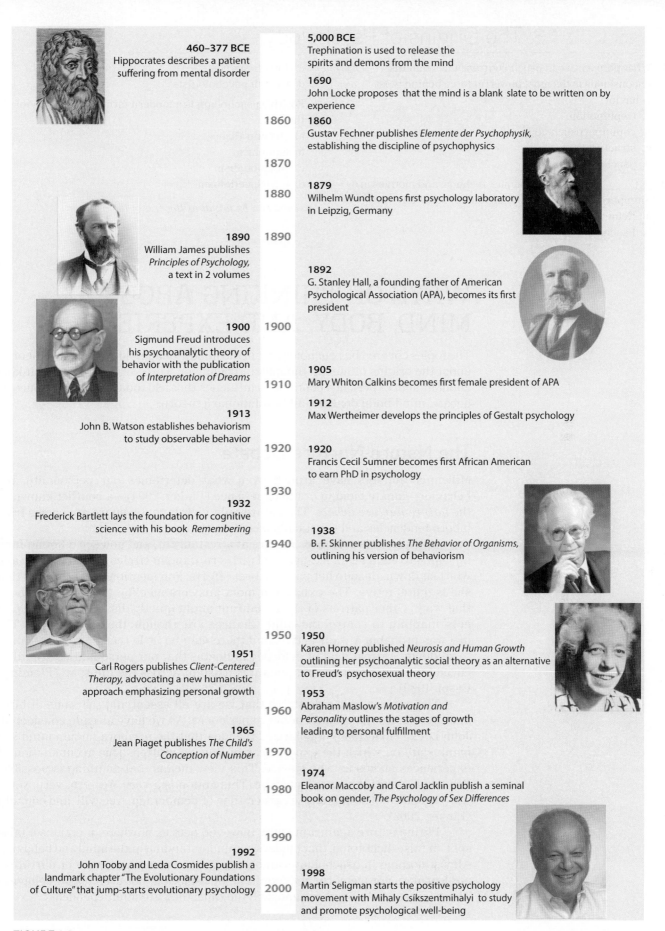

460–377 BCE
Hippocrates describes a patient suffering from mental disorder

5,000 BCE
Trephination is used to release the spirits and demons from the mind

1690
John Locke proposes that the mind is a blank slate to be written on by experience

1860
Gustav Fechner publishes *Elemente der Psychophysik*, establishing the discipline of psychophysics

1879
Wilhelm Wundt opens first psychology laboratory in Leipzig, Germany

1890
William James publishes *Principles of Psychology*, a text in 2 volumes

1892
G. Stanley Hall, a founding father of American Psychological Association (APA), becomes its first president

1900
Sigmund Freud introduces his psychoanalytic theory of behavior with the publication of *Interpretation of Dreams*

1905
Mary Whiton Calkins becomes first female president of APA

1912
Max Wertheimer develops the principles of Gestalt psychology

1913
John B. Watson establishes behaviorism to study observable behavior

1920
Francis Cecil Sumner becomes first African American to earn PhD in psychology

1932
Frederick Bartlett lays the foundation for cognitive science with his book *Remembering*

1938
B. F. Skinner publishes *The Behavior of Organisms*, outlining his version of behaviorism

1950
Karen Horney published *Neurosis and Human Growth* outlining her psychoanalytic social theory as an alternative to Freud's psychosexual theory

1951
Carl Rogers publishes *Client-Centered Therapy*, advocating a new humanistic approach emphasizing personal growth

1953
Abraham Maslow's *Motivation and Personality* outlines the stages of growth leading to personal fulfillment

1965
Jean Piaget publishes *The Child's Conception of Number*

1974
Eleanor Maccoby and Carol Jacklin publish a seminal book on gender, *The Psychology of Sex Differences*

1992
John Tooby and Leda Cosmides publish a landmark chapter "The Evolutionary Foundations of Culture" that jump-starts evolutionary psychology

1998
Martin Seligman starts the positive psychology movement with Mihaly Csíkszentmihalyi to study and promote psychological well-being

FIGURE **1.3**
KEY FIGURES AND EVENTS IN THE HISTORY OF PSYCHOLOGY.

1. What perspective in psychology assumes that the unconscious is the most powerful force behind most behavior?
   a. trephination
   b. cognitive psychology
   c. structuralism
   d. psychoanalysis

2. _____ argued that thoughts, feelings, and motives are unimportant in understanding human behavior.
   a. Behaviorists
   b. Psychoanalysts
   c. Functionalists
   d. Gestalt psychologists

3. Positive psychology is a modern form of which school of thought?
   a. structuralism
   b. humanism
   c. functionalism
   d. introspectionism

Answers can be found at the end of the chapter.

WAYS OF THINKING ABOUT MIND, BODY, AND EXPERIENCE

The topics covered by psychology sit in the middle of age-old debates and theories about the origins of human thought and behavior. Three major ways of thinking about human experience continue to influence the field today: the nature-nurture debate, mind-body dualism, and evolutionary theory.

The Nature-Nurture Debate

Millennia thinkers have argued over what determines our personality and behavior—innate biology or life experience (Pinker, 2004)—a conflict known as the *nature-nurture debate*. The nature-only view is that who we are comes from inborn tendencies and genetically based traits.

Consider this scenario. You are at a restaurant, and you see a young family trying to eat a meal. A 2-year-old girl is running in circles around a table and won't sit down, despite her parents' best efforts. You mention to the parents that she is quite active. The exhausted mom answers meekly, "Yes, she was born that way." Other patrons of the restaurant might quietly disapprove of the parents' inability to control the child. Chances are, though, the mom is right. The girl was probably always active, and there may be little they can do to get her to sit down. A great deal of evidence indicates that our personalities are influenced by genetic factors and remain consistent across the life span (Plomin & Caspi, 1999).

The nurture-only side states that we are all essentially the same at birth and that we are the product of our experiences. As we have already considered, John Locke (1690/1959) popularized the idea that the newborn human mind is a blank slate on which the experiences of life are written. This accumulation of experiences makes us who we are. This view means that anything is possible. You can be anything you want to be. This notion is a very Western, very North American idea. It stands as the cornerstone of democracy, free will, and equality (Pinker, 2002).

Pitting nature against nurture, however, gets us nowhere. It creates a false split, or false dichotomy, that hinders our understanding of the mind and behavior. Almost nothing in psychology can be categorized as either nature or nurture—not learning, not memory, not cognition, not emotion, not even social behavior! These forces work together almost all the time; they are interdependent.

Throughout this text, we will point out many cases in which environmental and genetic forces work together to shape who we are (Rutter, 2002). For example, in the processes of learning and remembering, certain genes in the brain are turned on or off by what happens to us (Kandel, 2006). New connections between brain cells result from these changes in the genes. Consequently, the brains of people and animals reared in richly stimulating environments differ from the brains of people reared in understimulating, neglectful, or abusive environments.

Given how much biological and environmental forces interact and influence each other, we introduce the term *softwire* to reflect this new way of thinking about nature and nurture. **Softwiring,** in contrast to hardwiring, means that biological systems involved in thought and behavior—genes, brain structures, brains cells, and so on—are inherited yet are still open to modification from the environment (Herbert & Rich, 1999; Ottersen, 2010). Much of who we are is more softwired than hardwired.

softwiring
In contrast to hardwiring, biological systems—genes, brain structures, and brain cells—are inherited but open to modification from the environment.

Here's an example of softwiring: Research reveals that people whose mothers developed certain infections during pregnancy are more likely to develop schizophrenia than people whose mothers were healthy during pregnancy (A. S. Brown, 2006). Risks of this disorder in offspring increase sevenfold in mothers infected with the flu virus and 10- to 12-fold in mothers infected with rubella, the virus that causes German measles (Boska, 2008; A. S. Brown, 2006). Evidence suggests that the crucial event may be that the mothers are mounting an immune response against an infectious agent during key stages of neural development in pregnancy (Fruntes & Limosin, 2008). A baby of the same genetic makeup who was not exposed to the virus and immune response would be less likely to develop the disorder.

These examples illustrate how what we are born with and what we are exposed to interact to create thought and behavior. For decades, many psychologists have shied away from the idea of an interrelationship, clinging to the nature-nurture debate. Old habits die hard. To fully appreciate human behavior, we must take a broader view. All creatures are born with genetic instructions, but even before birth environmental factors alter the ways in which genes are expressed. Throughout life, genetic factors, such as a familial predisposition toward anxiety, assert themselves. Rather than pitting nature against nurture, we prefer the phrase **nature through nurture,** whereby the environment—be it the womb or the world outside—interacts continuously with biology to shape who we are and what we do (Begley, 2007; Pinker, 2004; Ridley, 2003).

nature through nurture
The position that the environment constantly interacts with biology to shape who we are and what we do.

Mind-Body Dualism

How is the mind related to the body and brain? Are they one and the same or two distinct entities? Since its inception, psychology has been burdened by that question, known as *mind-body dualism*. In the 17th century René Descartes, a French philosopher and mathematician, offered proofs of many important concepts in mathematics (Crump, 2001). He proposed one idea that crippled the social sciences for years, stating that the mind and the body are separate entities, an idea often referred to as *mind-body dualism*. From this perspective, the mind controls the body. The body can occasionally control the mind, too, but mainly when we abandon good judgment, such as in the throes of passion. Mostly, in Descartes's view, mind and body are separate.

Dualism, the separation of mind and body, allows for many ideas central to Western thinking: For example, a soul survives bodily death, the mind is separate from the brain, and humans are superior to animals. Like nature versus nurture, mind-body dualism represents a false dichotomy—in the sense of being either-or. Mind and body are both useful concepts, but they are exquisitely intertwined. That which we call *mind,* our thoughts, feelings, and ideas—our entire mental world—results from the functioning of the *brain,* which is indeed part of the body.

Both the nature-nurture and mind-body dichotomies have influenced Western thought and the development of psychology as a field. Notice that we have been talking about *Western* thinking. Indeed, modern psychological science grew from the marriage of Western philosophy and physiology, with Wundt's laboratory in Leipzig as the first child. In contrast, systems of thought from elsewhere in the world—especially Eastern philosophy—have long emphasized the interdependence of body and mind (Begley, 2007; Tulku, 1984). There are other perspectives still. In much of Eastern thought, body and mind are very much seen as part of a whole. Psychological science is, at last, beginning to arrive at this same conclusion, but it has taken over a century to get there.

The Evolution of Human Behavior

One principle that plays an important role in understanding human behavior is evolution. The basics of this theory are more complex than most of us realize. Here we briefly explain the fundamental processes of evolution.

Evolution means "change." With respect to biological species, **evolution** is the change over time in the frequency with which specific genes occur within a breeding species (D. M. Buss, 1999). What does the frequency of gene transmission have to do with behavior? Our genes contain instructions for making all the

evolution
The change over time in the frequency with which specific genes occur within a breeding species.

In Industrial England in the 1800s, the peppered moth, which was originally mostly white, blended into the white lichen on trees. Pollution killed the white lichen on trees and put the original white moth in danger of being easy prey. Some started to become darker to blend in with the lichenless trees. Can you see both moths in each image? The white one on the right is so well camouflaged that a red circle had to be drawn to show its location.

⚙️ **How does this exemplify Darwin's idea of natural selection?**

FIGURE **1.4**

HOW NATURAL SELECTION WORKS. Natural selection is one of the basic mechanisms of evolution. This hypothetical example shows how natural selection might change the predominant color of a population of beetles from green to brown.

To understand how Darwin's idea of evolution works, consider a population of beetles:

1 There is variation in traits.

Some beetles are green and some are brown.

3 There is heredity.

The surviving brown beetles have brown baby beetles because this trait has a genetic basis.

4 There is the end result.

The more advantageous trait, brown coloration, allows the beetle to have more offspring and becomes more common in the population. If this process continues, eventually, all individuals in the population will be brown.

2 There is differential reproduction.

Since the environment can't support unlimited population growth, not all individuals get to reproduce to their full potential. In this example, green beetles tend to be eaten by birds and thus do not reproduce, while brown beetles survive to reproduce. There are now fewer green beetles.

proteins in our bodies. Proteins in turn make up a lot of what we are: cell membranes, hormones, enzymes, and muscle tissue, for instance. These constituents carry out our intentions, in our brains and in our bodies. Thus, behaviors have genetic bases that are affected by many environmental factors. Human interaction with the world influences which genes are passed on to future generations, and these in turn shape human behavior. These changes take place by *natural selection.*

First described by the 19th-century English naturalist Charles Darwin (1809–1882), **natural selection** is formally defined as a feedback process whereby nature favors one design over another, depending on whether it has an impact on reproduction. This process takes a long time to work, but it ultimately shapes who we are and how species evolve. Charles Darwin's great contribution was not the theory of evolution itself but rather his explanation of *how evolution works*—that is, by natural selection.

Natural selection occurs by chance. Every once in a while, genes change for no apparent reason. Spontaneous changes in genes, called *chance mutations,* can alter the design of a structure or a set of behaviors. Let's suppose that a chance mutation in a population of green beetles results in a brown beetle. If the brown beetle is less visible to predators, it might have more success in surviving and reproducing, as Figure 1.4 shows. When it reproduces, the brown beetle passes on its "brown" genes to its offspring.

The brown offspring have a better survival rate, which means they are more likely to reproduce. Eventually, this physiological trait becomes common among members of the species. The complete change takes many generations, but eventually the entire beetle species will be brown (Tooby & Cosmides, 1992). The key in natural selection is that the behaviors have to increase reproductive success, because reproduction and gene transmission drive the whole process.

The accumulation of chance mutations underlies evolutionary change. Each generation is a product of beneficial modifications from its evolutionary

natural selection
A feedback process whereby nature favors one design over another because it has an impact on reproduction.

adaptations
Inherited solutions to ancestral problems that have been selected for because they contribute in some way to reproductive success.

evolutionary psychology
The branch of psychology that studies human behavior by asking what adaptive problems it may have solved for our early ancestors.

past. Natural selection creates structures and behaviors that solve adaptive problems. Among the adaptive problems that our early human ancestors faced were avoiding predators, choosing nutritious foods, finding a mate, and communicating effectively with others. **Adaptations** are inherited solutions to ancestral problems that have been naturally selected because they directly contribute in some way to reproductive success (Tooby & Cosmides, 1992). Adaptations evolved to solve problems in past generations, not current ones. In other words, we are living with traits and tendencies that benefited our ancestors. Even though these tendencies might not seem to enhance our fitness in today's world, eons spent in harsher environments have left us predisposed to perform certain social behaviors when a situation calls forth ancient patterns. Consider our preference for fatty foods. In our evolutionary past, eating fat was a good strategy. Early humans, as hunter-gatherers, did not know when they would find food. If they found fat, they ate it, because fat could be stored in the body and used later when food might be scarce. For this reason, humans evolved to like fat. Modern society, however, offers easy access to food. Now eating fat is not the best strategy, because we don't need to store it for future use. More food will be available when we need it. So we eat fat, store it up, and carry it around as extra weight. Human cravings have not changed much, even though our environments have.

Evolutionary psychology is the branch of psychology that aims to uncover the adaptive problems the human mind may have solved in the distant past and the effect of evolution on behavior today. Rather than just describing what the mind does, evolutionary psychologists are interested in the functions of the human mind (Tooby & Cosmides, 1992). Evolutionary changes in organs and bodily structures—or color, as in our beetle example—are not difficult to understand, but how do human behaviors evolve?

Let's consider the emotions as an example of a behavioral adaptation. In Chapter 11, we discuss emotions in detail and explore the feelings that move us powerfully. For now, imagine that you are driving on the highway and the car in

Early hunters, like the ones portrayed in this ancient rock painting from the Tadrart Acacus of Libya, ate fat when it was available, and their bodies stored the excess in order to survive when food was scarce. This adaptation has persisted for thousands of years, even though for most people access to food is not a problem.

the lane next to you has just cut you off. You have to slam on your brakes to keep from smashing into it, and you are shaking with fright. The possible car accident is an immediate cause of your fear.

Why do you experience this intense bodily reaction called fear in the first place? The answer, from an evolutionary perspective, is that fear was naturally selected to solve an adaptive problem. What we call fear—including the way it moves our bodies, impels us to act, and makes our hearts race—evolved because it helps us deal quickly and efficiently with danger (Ekman, 2003). Eons ago, a genetic variation occurred in a human that somehow led to a specific way of responding to threatening circumstances—quick action to avoid being killed—and the human was able to avoid harm and reproduce more readily; that is, it had an advantage. Without thinking about it, the ancestor who recognized a beast that could kill her while she was picking berries just wanted to get out of harm's way. Experiencing fear, she was more likely to escape death. This woman survived, reproduced, and passed on a genetic tendency to experience fear to the next generation. Thus, emotions are behavioral adaptations. They are quick and ready response patterns that tell us whether something is good or bad for our well-being (Ekman, 2003; R. S. Lazarus, 1991).

Not all products of evolution are adaptations. Sometimes things evolve because they solve one problem and just happen to solve another one too. These structures or features that perform a function that did not arise through natural selection are often called *by-products* or, more technically, *exaptations* (Buss, 1999; S. J. Gould & Vrba, 1982). An example of a by-product is feathers. Feathers probably evolved for insulation in flightless dinosaurs, but they turned out to be useful for flight in birds, the dinosaurs' descendants. Because feathers did not evolve for that purpose, they are considered by-products ("Exaptations," 2006). Evolutionary changes in bodies and brains are prime examples of how nature and nurture interact to shape the psychology of human thought and behavior.

Similarly, humans didn't evolve to speak in fully grammatical sentences or to do scientific research, but once they started doing so, there were legitimate adaptive reasons to continue. Thus, language and science are not adaptations but are by-products of adaptations (Feist, 2006b; Pinker, 1994).

Nothing illustrates more vividly than evolution how nature and nurture work together. Depending on how they enable organisms to respond to their environment, certain characteristics of animals predominate or not—such as the brown color of a beetle and the fear response in humans. Nature and nurture work together to create our bodies (including our brains) and behavior. They are interdependent—they depend on and interact with each other.

Quick Quiz 1.4: Ways of Thinking about Mind, Body, and Experience

1. Which phrase most accurately reflects a modern perspective in psychology?
   a. nature versus nurture
   b. nature over nurture
   c. nurture over nature
   d. nature through nurture

2. Charles Darwin's great contribution was the theory of
   a. how evolution works (natural selection).
   b. evolution.
   c. psychoanalysis.
   d. adaptations.

3. Mind-body dualism proposes that
   a. the mind and body are one.
   b. the mind influences the body and the body influences the mind.
   c. the mind and body are separate.
   d. the mind and body are both adaptations.

Answers can be found at the end of the chapter.

NO ONE PERSPECTIVE TELLS THE WHOLE STORY IN PSYCHOLOGY

Challenge Your Assumptions

True or False? Psychologists agree that most of human thought and behavior cannot be explained by one perspective.

True: Human thought and behavior are so complex and determined by so many different factors that no one perspective can fully capture the richness of human psychology.

As we have seen in this chapter, in order to fully appreciate the complexity of human thought and behavior, one must consider a wide variety of perspectives—no one perspective tells the whole story. Throughout this text we highlight diverse explanations of human thought and behavior. This variety of perspectives raises the question, How does one resolve the various views? There are two strategies for answering this question: by using science and critical thinking and by making connections.

Challenge Assumptions: Don't Believe Everything You Think

First, the methods of science and critical thinking help us choose among various explanations for thought and behavior. Science tests our assumptions against observation from the real world. Think about it: People thought the world was flat until explorers began to map out the surface of the Earth. Because it is based on skepticism, the scientific view encourages critical thinking—that is, not believing everything we think. By comparing our assumptions with real-world observation, science helps us choose among competing explanations of behavior. For example, one recent popular theory has been that something in childhood vaccines causes autism. Over the last 10 years, scientists have conducted many studies of the vaccine-autism explanation and have found no support for it. As we discuss in the research ethics section of Chapter 2, the original study on which the argument had been based turned out to be fraudulent, consisting of false data.

Although collecting observations and conducting research help us choose one viewpoint over another, sometimes more than one perspective can be correct. Consider the psychological disorder of schizophrenia. For years people attributed the development of this disorder mostly to upbringing, arguing for a pure "nurture" explanation. Then biological explanations, such as an imbalance of particular neurotransmitters, became fashionable. The most recent research suggests that schizophrenia emerges from an interaction of biological and environmental influences—in a very real sense, elements of both explanations are correct (Moffitt, Caspi, & Rutter, 2005). The more open we are to diverse perspectives, the better able we will be to explain the whole and often surprising picture of human behavior.

We believe strongly that modern psychological science tells us that we must combine multiple perspectives in order to come to a complete understanding of human thought and behavior. One of the overarching themes of multiple perspectives is the proverbial nature-nurture question. Psychological science shows that almost every fundamental aspect of human behavior—whether it is brain development, learning, intelligence, perception, personality, social behavior, or psychological disorders—develops from a complex interplay of biological and environmental forces, of nature and nurture.

Research can also lead us to surprising findings, sometimes challenging our most basic assumptions. For example, a young neuroscientist named Helen Mayberg parted paths with most of her colleagues and did not focus on drug therapies to treat depression. She focused instead directly on the brain. In so doing she stumbled on a surprising and counterintuitive discovery: A particular part of the brain is overactive in depressed people (Mayberg, 1997, 2003). She went on to pioneer treatment for depression by stimulating the part of the brain that was overactive.

There is a psychology behind the science of psychology, and there are personal stories for every discovery (Feist, 2006b). Seeing the dynamic and often personal side of psychological science leads to a better appreciation of how psychological science came about and may help you challenge assumptions to break new ground.

Connections within and between Chapters

To bring together the various perspectives, we also explicitly connect theories and findings throughout the text. Seeing connections is a creative act, and psychological ideas and research findings are connected sometimes in obvious ways and sometimes in surprising ways. Learning to bring together ideas is an important part of learning to think critically. To facilitate this skill, we connect concepts both within and between chapters, as we just did with deep brain stimulation and depression. We do so by means of a "Connection" note in the margin, in which we provide section, chapter, and page number to facilitate easy access to these related ideas. By regularly returning to ideas from the same or different chapters, we can put them in a different context.

As a way of reviewing and connecting all of the important topics in each chapter, but in an applied way, we end each chapter with a section titled "Bringing It All Together." In this section, we explore one topic that brings together most of the main concepts and ideas in the chapter. For example, in this chapter, we consider how psychologists in different subfields of psychology have begun to study the effects of electronic social interactions on human behavior.

Connection

Area 25 is a region in the front of the brain; it is overly active in people with depression. A therapy known as "deep brain stimulation" can calm this area down and lead to a sudden decrease in depressed symptoms for some people.

See "Challenging Assumptions in the Treatment of Severe Depression," Chapter 16, "Treatment of Psychological Disorders," p. 597.

Quick Quiz 1.5: No One Perspective Tells the Whole Story in Psychology

1. Which of the following is a technique we argue for integrating the many perspectives in psychology?
   a. using not believing everything you think
   b. using the scientific method
   c. making connections within and between chapters
   d. all of the above

2. Research on the association between vaccines and autism has shown
   a. no connection between the two.
   b. a weak connection between the two.
   c. a strong connection between the two.
   d. inconclusive results.

Answers can be found at the end of the chapter.

Bringing It All Together

Making Connections in Psychology

Studying Electronic Social Interactions

There are nearly a dozen ways a person can interact with others electronically—via email, blogs, cell phones, chat rooms, texting, instant messaging, audio or video chats, gaming (either solo or multiplayer), videos, photos, bulletin boards, and social network sites (SNSs). Humans have taken to electronic forms of interaction like fish to water. As a form of behavior that is evolving at a rapid pace, electronic social interaction holds great interest for psychologists in all of the subfields you read about in this chapter. Let's consider how psychologists from some of these areas might study electronic communication and its effects on human behavior and thought.

Cognitive Psychology

Cognitive scientists typically are interested in how we learn, remember, think, and reason. They are also interested in attention. The widespread use of mobile devices has sparked a number of research questions. The most obvious one concerns how drivers can pay attention to driving while talking on a mobile device. Researchers who have examined the effect of talking on a hands-free mobile device while driving report that a person's ability to operate a car while doing so is significantly impaired and is even similar to the ability to drive while drunk (Caird et al., 2008; Strayer, Drews, & Couch, 2006). In addition, attitudes and beliefs about how dangerous and how common mobile phone use is while driving predict using phones while driving (Hafetz et al., 2010; Zhou et al., 2009): Those who think most about receiving phone calls and think about their phones while they are off are most likely to have accidents while driving (O'Connor et al., 2013).

Developmental Psychology

Developmental psychologists study how we change over the life span. They might ask questions like these: At what age is a person too young to form electronic social networks? At what age does participation in Internet social networks peak? Will they always be for the younger generation, or will people 60 and older use them? Does gender affect interest and participation in SNSs? How have mobile phones and other electronic methods of communicating changed the way teenagers interact with others?

Researchers have already given us answers to some of these questions. Some suggest that older teenage girls

How does technology change how we learn, think, feel, and behave with others?

and young women are more likely to participate in social networking sites than are boys and young men (Boyd, 2007; Hargittai, 2008). College men are more likely to use SNSs to begin new relationships, whereas college women are more likely to use them to maintain existing relationships (Muscanell & Guadagno, 2012). Electronic interactions are popular with adolescents because of psychological factors: identity, autonomy, intimacy, and sexuality (Subrahmanyam & Greenfield, 2008; Walsh, White, & Young, 2009). One reason the popularity of electronic interactions declines with age may be that these issues decline in importance as one moves from early adulthood to middle and late adulthood (Erikson, 1982; Harris Interactive, 2008).

Social Psychology

More than just about any other area of psychology, social psychology lends itself to a rich set of research questions regarding electronic interactions. Texting in particular and mobile device use in general are the primary tools for staying connected to friends and peers (Harris Interactive, 2008; Walsh et al., 2009). One of the first Internet applications for social purposes was online dating services. Such forms of electronic interaction may be a preferred method of contact for people with high social anxiety (Stevens & Morris, 2007). Although most people who use online dating services tend to be over 30, college-age teens and young adults are increasingly using them as well (Stevens & Morris, 2007; Valkenburg & Peter, 2007b). Contrary to what some people originally thought, however, electronic interactions cannot easily be used to hide one's "real personality" and to avoid ever having real face-to-face contact with others. Research on this phenomenon suggests that people use the Internet not simply to interact with others from afar but also to arrange real face-to-face meetings (Couch & Liamputtong, 2008).

Electronic interactions have led to new behaviors and language as the boundaries between public and private have broken down. For instance, being *privately public* means connecting with many other people while being relatively non-public about revealing who you are. Being *publicly private* means you disclose a lot of details of your private life and may or may not limit access to your site (P. G. Lange, 2008).

Another electronic behavior is "friending," which raises ancient issues of being "popular," socially excluded, rejected, or accepted. In one tragic case of online rejection, a 13-year-old girl was so distraught over being rejected by a boy online that she committed suicide. The even greater tragedy, however, was that the boy did not exist: A neighbor's mother allegedly had made him up to get back at the girl for making disparaging remarks about her daughter.

Personality Psychology

A personality psychologist could ask many questions about electronic interaction and presentation—such as "Are people who interact extensively with other people via Facebook more or less outgoing than those who do not?" Moreover, how much of people's personality is reflected in their Facebook profiles? Scientific literature consistently finds that people who are extraverted are more likely than introverts to use Facebook and have a wider network of social relationships (Amichai-Hamburger & Vinitzky, 2010; Nadkarni & Hofmann, 2012). Yet introverts are likely than extraverts to spend more time on Facebook and have a more favorable attitude toward it (Orr et al., 2009).

Health Psychology

A very innovative and at least partially successful application of electronic media is using a mobile device to access health information and symptoms of various diseases. A program in San Francisco, California, has phone numbers for people to call if they suspect they have a particular disease, often a sexual disease. The embarrassment of having to ask questions face-to-face is taken away when one can call or text to obtain a health diagnosis anonymously.

Clinical Psychology

Clinical psychologists can diagnose disorders of technology use but also use the same technologies to help treat people with various kinds of disorders. When do SNSs and other electronic interactions become a problem? Can one become "addicted" to such behavior, and can such interactions become dangerous to those involved? One of the main criteria for a mental illness is that it interferes with everyday life and functioning. If one is online for 10–12 hours a day, is that healthy? What about the danger involved in meeting someone in person whom you know only from online interaction? Sexual predators use these connections to meet victims. They contact potential victims through chat rooms, instant messages, and email. According to one study, one in seven teens (ages 10–17) have been sexually solicited online (Ybarra & Mitchell, 2008).

There is also the psychologically interesting phenomenon of creating an alternative personality, or avatar, in the gaming world. People sometimes take on personalities that are very different from their own in an online world that allows them to say things they would not in direct, face-to-face contact. This ability to be people we are not has allowed psychotherapists to use avatar personality games, such as Second Life®, to help people overcome their social anxieties in real life (Gottschalk, 2010; Lisetti et al., 2009). Similarly, video services such as SKYPE and GoogleChat are increasingly used to connect psychotherapist and patient, who can now be in different states if need be.

We hope this chapter has helped you appreciate the richness and excitement of psychology as a clinical practice and science. More than that, we hope it encourages you to become an active and critical student of human behavior: Don't believe everything you think, and question how conclusions are drawn—even conclusions in this text. We hope that at this point, as a first step toward active learning and investigating, you are asking, How do psychologists know all this? How do they do research? In the next chapter, we discuss the techniques by which psychological scientists study mental processes and behavior. Welcome to the fascinating world of psychology.

Chapter Review

WHAT IS PSYCHOLOGY?

- Psychology is the scientific study of thought and behavior. We can see psychology all around us—in our own thoughts and feelings, in the behavior of our friends and relatives, and in how we interpret others' behaviors. As a field, it prepares us well not only for life in general but also for a wide variety of professions in which social interaction plays a key role.

- As a discipline, psychology is both a practice and a science. Clinical psychologists and counselors treat mental, emotional, and behavioral disorders and promote psychological health. Clinical psychologists also conduct research on psychological disorders and health. They practice psychology. As a science, psychology is the field of study in which researchers examine how the mind works and the rules that govern behavior within and between individuals.

SUBDISCIPLINES OF PSYCHOLOGY

- As a broad field, psychology comprises several subdisciplines, or areas of focused study, including cognitive, developmental, social, personality, health, educational, and industrial/organizational psychology.

- Neuroscience explores the links among brain, mind, and behavior and thus cuts across other subdisciplines.

THE ORIGINS OF PSYCHOLOGY

- The practice of psychology goes back to prehistoric times. Thousands of years ago, humans drilled holes in the skull to treat brain injury and perhaps mental anguish.

- In the Middle Ages, the mentally ill were often treated as if possessed by demons. A few hundred years later, asylums served as storage houses for the severely mentally disabled.

- The late 1800s and early 1900s witnessed the beginning of more humane and more sophisticated treatment of people with psychological disorders.

- Around the turn of the 20th century, Sigmund Freud developed psychoanalysis to treat people suffering from disorders. By the middle of the 20th century, modern diagnostic criteria for mental disorders, psychotherapy, and drug therapy had emerged.

- The history of psychology as a science is not nearly as old as that of clinical practice, although its origins in philosophy go back to the ancient Greeks. Psychological science emerged from a tradition of empiricism and observations of the world.

- John Locke's 17th-century view of the mind as a blank slate on which experience writes the contents influences psychology to this day.

- The first psychological scientists did experimental work in perception and laid the groundwork for psychophysics. Only when laboratories started to empirically examine and test human sensations and perception did psychology gain its independence from philosophy and become a science.

- Wilhelm Wundt opened the first laboratory in experimental psychology in Leipzig, Germany, in 1879. Key figures in the birth of scientific psychology in the United States include William James and G. Stanley Hall.

- The biggest development in psychological research in the United States was the birth of behaviorism in the early 20th century. According to behaviorism, all behavior comes from experience. Founded by John Watson, behaviorism reached its pinnacle with B. F. Skinner.

- Behaviorism proved a very useful model for developing methods of studying learning in humans and animals, but it left the unobservable world of the mind unexplained. This all changed with the cognitive revolution of the 1950s and 1960s. Initially, cognitive science used the computer as a model for the way the human mind processes and stores sensations, memories, and ideas.

- Many fields that have older origins came together in the psychology of the 1980s and 1990s: neuroscience, behavioral genetics, and evolutionary psychology.

WAYS OF THINKING ABOUT MIND, BODY, AND EXPERIENCE

- Psychological science in the 21st century has reintegrated biological and environmental explanations of human thought and behavior.

- The fully modern view squares explanations of behavior with the principles of evolution. It also surpasses old absolutes, such as the nature-nurture debate and mind-body dualism.

NO ONE PERSPECTIVE TELLS THE WHOLE STORY IN PSYCHOLOGY

- Multiple perspectives are often needed to fully explain the complexity of human thought and behavior.

- To integrate these multiple perspectives, it helps to use the methods of science and critical thinking and to integrate and connect related ideas and concepts.

BRINGING IT ALL TOGETHER: MAKING CONNECTIONS IN PSYCHOLOGY

- The world of electronic interaction provides a context for research in many subdisciplines of psychology. For example, personality psychologists have examined which types of people are more likely to use social networking sites (SNSs); social psychologists have studied whether SNSs operate as real-life social networks do; and developmental psychologists have begun to explore how the use of email, SNSs, and texting varies by age and gender.

Key Terms

adaptations, p. 24
asylums, p. 13
behavioral neuroscience, p. 8
behaviorism, p. 16
biological psychology, p. 8
clinical psychology, p. 9
cognitive psychology, p. 8
developmental psychology, p. 8
educational psychology, p. 10
empiricism, p. 14
evolution, p. 22

evolutionary psychology, p. 24
forensic psychology, p. 10
functionalism, p. 16
Gestalt psychology, p. 17
health psychology, p. 10
humanistic psychology, p. 17
industrial/organizational (I/O) psychology, p. 10
introspection, p. 16
moral treatment, p. 13
natural selection, p. 23

nature through nurture, p. 21
personality psychology, p. 9
positive psychology, p. 17
psychoanalysis, p. 13
psychology, p. 5
psychophysics, p. 15
shamans, p. 11
social psychology, p. 9
softwiring, p. 21
sports psychology, p. 10
structuralism, p. 16

Quick Quiz Answers

Quick Quiz 1.1: 1. d 2. d 3. c **Quick Quiz 1.2:** 1. a 2. b 3. c **Quick Quiz 1.3:** 1. d 2. a 3. b **Quick Quiz 1.4:** 1. d 2. a 3. c **Quick Quiz 1.5:** 1. d 2. a

2 Conducting Research in Psychology

Chapter Outline

The Nature of Science

Research Methods in Psychology

Challenging Assumptions in the Objectivity of Experimental Research

Commonly Used Measures of Psychological Research

Making Sense of Data with Statistics

Research Ethics

Chapter Review

Challenge Your Assumptions

True or False?

- Psychology is not a science. (see page 36)

- Doubt and skepticism activate the same brain region as disgust. (see page 37)

- Knowing what you're looking for in an experiment has no effect on the outcome. (see page 54)

- Eating sugar makes children hyperactive. (see page 60)

You are at your apartment near campus one summer day when the police knock at your door. After they confirm your identity, they arrest you on suspicion of armed robbery. The cops handcuff your hands, put you in the police car, and take you down to the police station. There you are booked, fingerprinted, and placed in a detention cell. You are then blindfolded and driven to a nearby prison, where you are stripped, sprayed with a delousing agent, and made to stand nude and alone in the cell yard. Finally, you are given a uniform, photographed, and assigned to a prison cell. But you have done nothing, and the people who arrested you knew this.

This scenario may seem far-fetched, but it actually happened to 10 male college students in the summer of 1971 in Palo Alto, California. They had previously agreed to participate in a "psychological study on 'prison life' in return for payment of $15 a day" (Haney, Banks, & Zimbardo, 1973, p. 73). Yet the officers who arrested them said nothing about a connection between their arrest and their agreement to participate. Philip Zimbardo conducted this study—now known as the Stanford Prison Experiment—to examine whether normal people might behave in extreme ways when thrust into situations that place extreme demands on them. In this case, they readily took on roles that made them either powerful or powerless (Haney et al., 1973). Zimbardo chose 21 carefully screened male student volunteers and assigned them to be either "guards" or "prisoners" in a simulated prison environment for 2 weeks. All were briefed beforehand about what conditions would be like in the mock prison. All the students signed a form, consenting to participate. Six days into the simulation, however, the experiment had taken such an unexpected turn that Zimbardo had to end the study—the students were playing their roles too well. Prisoners went back and forth between plotting riots and having emotional breakdowns—getting sick and crying, for instance. Guards became extremely authoritarian, restricting the prisoners' personal freedom almost completely. They dehumanized the prisoners by referring to each one only by his assigned number, never by name. They put anyone suspected of "disobeying" and being "a bad prisoner" in solitary confinement. The line between fiction and reality, between assigned role and true identity, blurred. In fact, half of the "prisoners" had to be released ahead of schedule, because they were experiencing extreme emotional distress as a result of their "incarceration."

Zimbardo's study served as a springboard for additional research on group behavior, and it provided a strong incentive for prison reform. Interest in this study continues today, and it takes on new significance in light of more recent cases of prisoner abuse, such as the mistreatment of Iraqi prisoners by American soldiers following the 2003 U.S. invasion (Zimbardo, 2007). Still, the Stanford Prison Experiment also provoked great concern about the treatment of human participants in research. What hypothesis was Zimbardo testing? Were the scientific gains worth the trauma caused to these young men? These are questions of research ethics, one of many topics of research methods in psychology covered in this chapter. We will first look, however, at psychology as a science and the methods of scientific inquiry applied in psychological research. We will then turn to the subject of how psychologists collect, analyze, and interpret data—processes that become the building blocks of knowledge in the field.

THE NATURE OF SCIENCE

Science is about testing intuitive assumptions regarding how the world works, observing the world, and being open-minded to unexpected findings. Some of science's most important discoveries happened only because the scientists were open to surprising and unexpected results. Fundamentally, science entails collecting observations, or *data*, from the real world and evaluating whether the data support our ideas or not. The Stanford Prison Experiment fulfilled these criteria, and we will refer to this example several times in our discussion of research methods, measures, and ethics.

Common Sense and Logic

Science involves more than common sense, logic, and pure observation. Although reason and sharp powers of observation can lead to knowledge, they have limitations. Consider common sense, the intuitive ability to understand the world. Often common sense is quite useful: Don't go too close to that cliff. Don't rouse that sleeping bear. Don't eat food that smells rotten. Sometimes, though, common sense leads us astray. In psychology, our intuitive ideas about people's behavior are often contradictory or flat-out wrong. For example, most of us intuitively believe that who we are is influenced by our parents, family, friends, and society. It is equally obvious, especially to parents, that children come into the world as unique people, with their own temperaments, and people who grow up in similar environments do not have identical personalities. To what extent are we the products of our environment, and how much do we owe to heredity? Common sense cannot answer that question, but science can.

Logic is also a powerful tool in the scientist's arsenal, but it can tell us only how the world *should* work, not how the world actually works. Sometimes the world is not logical. A classic example of the shortcoming of logic is seen in the work of the ancient Greek philosopher Aristotle. He argued that heavier objects should fall to the ground at a faster rate than lighter objects. Sounds reasonable, right? Unfortunately, it's wrong. For 2,000 years, however, the argument was accepted simply because the great philosopher Aristotle wrote it and it made intuitive sense. It took the genius of Galileo to say, "Wait a minute. Is that really true? Let me do some tests to see whether it is true." He did and discovered that Aristotle was wrong (Crump, 2001); the weight of an object does not affect its rate of speed when falling. Science combines logic with research and experimentation.

The Limits of Observation

Science relies on observation, but even observation can lead us astray. Our knowledge of the world comes through our five senses, but they can be fairly easily fooled, as any good magician or artist can demonstrate—as we explore in some detail in Chapter 4, "Sensing and Perceiving Our World." Even when we are not being intentionally fooled, the way in which our brains organize and interpret sensory experiences may vary from person to person.

Another problem with observation is that people tend to generalize from their observations and assume that what they witness in one situation applies to all similar situations. Imagine you are visiting another country for the first time. Let's say the first person you have any extended interaction with is rude, and a second, briefer interaction goes along the same lines. Granted, you have lots of language difficulties; nevertheless, you might conclude that all people from that country are rude. After all, that has been your experience. Those, however, were only two interactions, and after a couple of days you might meet other people who

Connection

How do psychologists tease apart the question of how much of a trait is due to genetics and how much is due to environment? A common approach is to study twins (both identical and fraternal) who are reared apart or reared together.

See "Genes and the Environment," Chapter 3, "The Biology of Behavior," p. 75.

Reality can be different from what we think. Our perceptions are not the same as what is really out there. Camouflaged animals are just one example.

⚙️ **Can you think of other common examples of perceptions that don't reflect reality?**

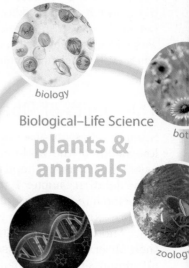

are quite nice. The point is that one or two cases are not a solid basis for a generalization. Scientists must collect numerous observations and conduct several studies on a topic before generalizing their conclusions.

What Is Science?

Is physics a science? Few would argue that it is not. What about biology? Psychology? Astrology? How does one decide? Now that we have looked at some of the components of science and explored their limitations, let's consider the larger question: What *is* science? People often think only of the physical sciences as "science," but science comes in at least three distinct flavors: physical, biological, and social (Feist, 2006b). As we mentioned in Chapter 1, psychology is a social science (see Figure 2.1).

The physical sciences study the world of things—the inanimate world of stars, light, waves, atoms, the Earth, compounds, and molecules. These sciences include physics, astronomy, chemistry, and geology. The biological sciences study plants and animals in the broadest sense. These sciences include biology, zoology, genetics, and botany. Finally, the social sciences study humans, both as individuals and as groups. These sciences include anthropology, sociology, economics, and psychology.

FIGURE **2.1**
SIMPLIFIED MAP OF THE SCIENCES: THE STUDY OF THINGS, PLANTS, ANIMALS, AND PEOPLE.

In 1998, Dr. Andrew Wakefield published a scientific paper claiming that autism spectrum disorder was often caused by vaccines for measles, mumps, and rubella. There were many problems with the paper from the outset, not the least of which was its small, unrepresentative sample size (12 children). Many scientists and medical panels could not confirm the results and were highly skeptical of Dr. Wakefield's findings. Unfortunately, the paper created quite a bit of publicity, and many parents ignored standard vaccination schedules, leading to numerous deaths from preventable diseases. In January 2011, the original 1998 paper was deemed fraudulent in a 7-year investigation by the *British Medical Journal*. The investigation concluded that Dr. Wakefield had altered the results of his study to make vaccines appear to be the cause of autism spectrum disorder.

Science is as much a way of thinking or a set of attitudes as it is a set of procedures. **Scientific thinking** involves the cognitive skills required to generate, test, and revise theories (Koslowski, 1996; Kuhn, Amsel, & O'Loughlin, 1988; Zimmerman, 2007). What we believe or theorize about the world and what the world is actually like, in the form of evidence, are two different things. Scientific thinking keeps these two things separate. In other words, scientists remember that belief is not the same as reality.

The first attitude of science, therefore, is to *question authority*—including scientific authority. Be skeptical (see Figure 2.2). Don't just take the word of an expert; test ideas yourself. The expert might be right, or not. That advice extends to textbooks—including this one. Wonder. Question. Ask for the evidence. Be a critical thinker. Also question your *own* ideas. Our natural inclination is to really like our own ideas, especially if they occur to us in a flash of insight. As one bumper sticker extols, "Don't believe everything you think." Believing something does not make it true.

As expressed by cosmologist and astrophysicist Carl Sagan (1987), the second attitude of science is open skepticism. Doubt and skepticism are hallmarks of critical and scientific reasoning. The French philosopher Voltaire put scientific skepticism most bluntly: "Doubt is uncomfortable, certainty is ridiculous"; however, skepticism for skepticism's sake is also not scientific, but stubborn. Scientists are ultimately open to accepting whatever the evidence reveals, however bizarre it may be and however much they may not like it or want it to be the case. For example, could placing an electrical stimulator deep in the brain, as if it were a switch, turn off depression? That sounds like a far-fetched treatment, worthy of skepticism, but it does work for some people (Mayberg et al., 2005). Be skeptical, but let the evidence speak for itself. Confirming Voltaire's assertion that doubt is uncomfortable, recent brain imaging evidence suggests that doubt and skepticism are associated with areas of the brain involved in the sensation of taste and disgust (and belief with reward and pleasure), so doubt is a less pleasant state than belief (Harris, Sheth, & Cohen, 2008; Harris et al., 2009; Shermer, 2011).

The third scientific attitude is *intellectual honesty*. When the central tenet of knowing is not what people think and believe, but rather how nature behaves, then we must accept the data and follow them wherever they take us. If a researcher falsifies results or interprets them in a biased way, then other scientists will not arrive at the same results if they repeat the study. Every so often we hear of a scientist who faked data in order to gain fame or funding. For the most part, however, the fact that scientists must submit their work to the scrutiny of other scientists helps ensure the honest and accurate presentation of results.

All sciences—whether physics, chemistry, biology, or psychology—share the general properties of open inquiry that we have discussed. Let's now turn to the specific methods scientists use to acquire new and accurate knowledge of the world.

scientific thinking
The process of using the cognitive skills required to generate, test, and revise theories.

Don't believe everything you think

FIGURE **2.2**
Science is an attitude that requires we keep open eyes and questioning minds.

Can you think of some ideas you've had that you no longer believe?

Challenge Your Assumptions
True or False? Doubt and skepticism activate the same brain region as disgust.

True: When we disbelieve a statement, the same region of the anterior cingulate cortex (ACC), also involved in perceptions of taste and disgust, is activated.

The Scientific Method

scientific method
The procedures by which scientists conduct research, consisting of the five basic processes of observation, prediction, testing, interpretation, and communication.

theory
A set of related assumptions from which scientists can make testable predictions.

hypothesis
A specific, informed, and testable predication of the outcome of a particular set of conditions in a research design.

Science depends on the use of sound methods to produce trustworthy results that can be confirmed independently by other researchers. The **scientific method** by which scientists conduct research consists of five basic processes: **O**bserve, **P**redict, **T**est, **I**nterpret, and **C**ommunicate (O-P-T-I-C; see the Research Process for this chapter, Figure 2.3). In the *observation* and *prediction* stages of a study, researchers develop expectations about an observed phenomenon. Often, these expectations stem from reading and reviewing the current and past scientific literature. They express their expectations as a **theory**, defined as a set of related assumptions from which testable predictions can be made. Theories organize and explain what we have observed and guide what we will observe (Popper, 1965). To put it simply, theories are not facts—they explain facts. Our observations of the world are always either unconsciously or consciously theory-driven, if you understand that theory in this broader sense means little more than "having an expectation." In science, however, a theory is more than a guess. Scientific theories must be tied to real evidence, they must organize observations, and they must generate expectations that can be tested systematically.

A **hypothesis** is a specific, informed, and testable prediction of what kind of outcome should occur under a particular condition. For example, consider the real-life study that suggests that caffeine increases sex drive in female rats (Guarraci & Benson, 2005). The hypothesis may have been phrased this way: "Female rats that consume caffeine will seek more couplings with male rats than female rats that do not consume caffeine." This hypothesis predicts that a particular form of behavior (coupling with male rats) will occur in a specific group (female rats) under particular conditions (the influence of caffeine). The more specific a hypothesis is, the more easily each component can be changed to determine what effect it has on the outcome.

To *test* their hypotheses (the third stage of the scientific method), scientists select one of a number of established research methods, along with the appropriate measurement techniques. Selecting the methods involves choosing a design for the study, the tools that will create the conditions of the study, and the tools for measuring responses (such as how often each female rat allows a male to mount her). We will examine each of these elements in the section "Research Methods in Psychology" on page 41.

In the fourth step of the scientific method, scientists use mathematical techniques to *interpret* the results and determine whether they are significant (not just a matter of chance) and whether they closely fit the prediction. Do psychologists' ideas of how people behave hold up, or must they be revised? Let's say that the caffeine-consuming female rats coupled more frequently with males than did nonconsuming females. Might this enhanced sexual interest hold for all rats or just those few we studied? Statistics, a branch of mathematics we will discuss shortly, helps answer that question.

The fifth stage of the scientific method is to *communicate* the results. Generally, scientists publish their findings in a peer-reviewed professional journal. Following a standardized format, the researchers report their hypotheses, describe their research design and the conditions of the study, summarize the results, and share their conclusions. In their reports, researchers also consider the broader implications of their results. What might the effects of caffeine on sexuality in female rats mean for our understanding of caffeine, arousal, and sex in female humans? Publication also serves an important role in making research findings part of the public domain. Such exposure not only indicates that colleagues who reviewed the study found it to be credible but also allows other researchers to repeat and/or build on the research.

replication
The repetition of a study to confirm the results; it is essential to the scientific process.

Replication is the repetition of a study to confirm the results. The advancement of science hinges on replication. No matter how interesting and exciting results are, if they cannot be duplicated, the original findings may have been accidental. Whether a result holds or not, new predictions can be generated from the data, leading in turn to new studies. This is why the process of scientific discovery is cumulative. Previous knowledge builds on older knowledge.

Research Process

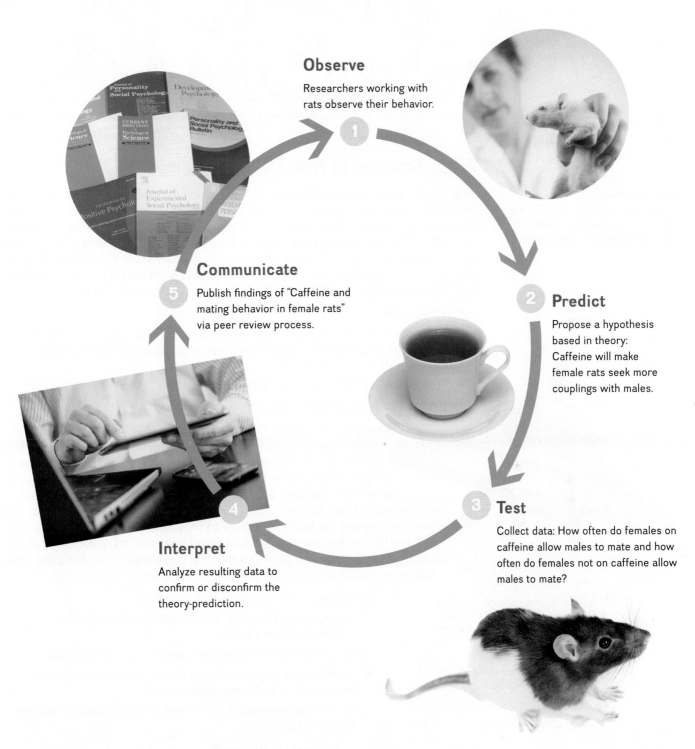

Observe

Researchers working with rats observe their behavior.

Communicate

Publish findings of "Caffeine and mating behavior in female rats" via peer review process.

Predict

Propose a hypothesis based in theory: Caffeine will make female rats seek more couplings with males.

Interpret

Analyze resulting data to confirm or disconfirm the theory-prediction.

Test

Collect data: How often do females on caffeine allow males to mate and how often do females not on caffeine allow males to mate?

FIGURE **2.3**

THE SCIENTIFIC METHOD. The scientific method consists of an ongoing cycle of observation, prediction, testing, interpretation, and communication (OPTIC). Research begins with observation, but it doesn't end with communication. Publishing the results of a study allows other researchers to repeat the procedure and confirm the results.

What Science Is Not: Pseudoscience

pseudoscience
Claims presented as scientific that are not supported by evidence obtained with the scientific method.

Do you believe that the planets and stars determine our destiny, that aliens have visited Earth, or that the human mind is capable of moving or altering physical objects? Astrology, unidentified flying objects (UFOs), and extrasensory perception (ESP) are certainly fascinating topics to ponder. As thinking beings, we try to understand things that science may not explain to our satisfaction. Many of us are willing to believe things that science and skeptics easily dismiss. For example, a Harris poll of 2,303 American adults in 2009 found the following (*What people*, 2009):

- Seventy-two percent believed in angels.
- Forty percent believed in creationism (that is, the Earth was created by God in 6 days about 6,000 years ago); by comparison, 45% believed in Darwin's theory of evolution.
- Thirty-two percent believed in UFOs.
- Twenty-six percent believed in astrology.

Similarly, a Gallup Poll in 2005 reported that 55% believed in spiritual or psychic healing, 42% in demonic possession, and 41% in extrasensory perception (ESP; *Three in four*, 2005). People often claim there is "scientific evidence" for certain unusual phenomena, but that does not mean the evidence is truly scientific. There is also false science, or *pseudo*science. **Pseudoscience** refers to practices that appear to be and claim to be science but, in fact, do not use the scientific method to come to their conclusions. What makes something pseudoscientific comes more from the way it is studied than from the content area. Pseudoscience practitioners (Derry, 1999)

1. make no real advances in knowledge,
2. disregard well-known and established facts that contradict their claims,
3. do not challenge or question their own assumptions,
4. tend to offer vague or incomplete explanations of how they came to their conclusions, and
5. tend to use unsound logic in making their arguments (see Figure 2.4).

Philosophy, art, music, and religion, for instance, are not pseudosciences because they do not claim to be science. Pseudoscientific claims have been made for alchemy, creation science, intelligent design, attempts to create perpetual motion machines, astrology, alien abduction, psychokinesis, and some forms of mental telepathy.

1 Lacks the cumulative progress seen in science

2 Disregards real-world observations and established facts/results and contradicts what is already known

3 Lacks internal skepticism

4 Only vaguely explains how conclusions are reached

5 Uses loose and distorted logic

FIGURE 2.4

THE CHARACTERISTICS OF PSEUDOSCIENCE. It is wise to be skeptical of claims that aren't supported by scientific evidence.

 What makes something a false science, or pseudoscience?

Perhaps the most pervasive pseudoscience is astrology, which uses the positions of the sun, moon, and planets to explain an individual's personality traits and to predict the future. There simply is no credible scientific evidence that the positions of the moon, planets, and stars and one's time and place of birth have any influence on personality or life course (Shermer, 1997), yet about one in four American adults believe in astrology.

Overall, telekinesis, astrology, alien abduction explanations of UFOs, and creation science, to name a few, meet the criteria for pseudoscience. In all fairness, there have been some reliable observations of UFOs and some scientifically sound evidence for telepathy (Bem & Horonton, 1994; Rosenthal, 1986). Reading the scientific literature on these two topics, one has little choice but to conclude that some of these experiences have some validity. Remember, open skepticism is the hallmark of science. If there is scientifically sound evidence for something—even if it is difficult to explain—and it has been replicated, then we have to accept it. The key is to know how to distinguish sound from unsound evidence.

Quick Quiz 2.1: The Nature of Science

1. The scientific method consists of
   a. observing, predicting, testing.
   b. observing, predicting, trying.
   c. observing, predicting, testing, communicating.
   d. observing, predicting, testing, interpreting, communicating.

2. Which of the following is NOT a characteristic of science?
   a. It is cumulative.
   b. It is a search for truth.
   c. It is an attitude.
   d. It requires intellectual honesty.

3. Scientific theories are
   a. a set of related assumptions that guide and explain observations and allow testable predictions to be made.
   b. educated guesses.
   c. hunches.
   d. hypotheses.

4. What distinguishes science from pseudoscience?
   a. the use of statistics
   b. the content area studied
   c. open skepticism
   d. the search for truth

Answers can be found at the end of the chapter.

RESEARCH METHODS IN PSYCHOLOGY

Science involves testing ideas about how the world works, but how do we design studies that test our ideas? This question confronts anyone wanting to answer a psychological question scientifically.

Principles of Research Design

Like other sciences, psychology makes use of several types of **research designs**—plans for how to conduct a study. The design chosen for a given study depends on the question being asked. Some questions can best be answered by randomly placing people in different groups in a laboratory to see whether a treatment causes a change in behavior. Other questions have to be studied by questionnaires or surveys. Still other questions can best be answered simply by making initial observations and seeing what people do in the real world. Sometimes researchers analyze the results of many studies on the same topic to look for trends.

In this section, we examine variations in research designs, along with their advantages and disadvantages. We begin by defining a few key terms common to all research designs in psychology.

A general goal of psychological research is to measure change in behavior, thought, or brain activity. A **variable** is anything that changes, or varies, within

research designs
Plans of action for how to conduct a scientific study.

variable
A characteristic that changes, or "varies," such as age, gender, weight, intelligence, anxiety, and extraversion.

Researchers often work with a small sample of the population they're interested in studying. **Can a small sample represent the larger population? If so, how is that done?**

or between individuals. People differ from one another on age, gender, weight, intelligence, and level of anxiety and extraversion, to name a few psychological variables. Psychologists do research by predicting how and when variables influence each other. For instance, a psychologist who is interested in whether girls develop verbal skills at a different rate than boys focuses on two variables: gender and vocabulary.

All researchers must pay careful attention to how they obtain participants for a study. The first step is for the researchers to decide the makeup of the entire group, or **population**, in which they are interested. In psychology, populations can be composed of, for example, animals, adolescents, boys or girls of any age, college students, or students at a particular school. How many are older than 50 or younger than 20? How many are European American, African American, Asian American, Pacific Islander, or Native American? How many have high school educations, and how many have college educations?

Can you think of a problem that would occur if a researcher tried to collect data directly on an entire population? Because most populations are too large to survey or interview directly, researchers draw on small subsets of each population, called **samples**. A sample of a population of college students, for instance, might consist of students enrolled in one or more universities in a particular geographic area. Research is almost always conducted on samples, not populations. If researchers want to draw valid conclusions or make accurate predictions about a population, it is important that their samples accurately represent the population in terms of age, gender, ethnicity, or any other variables of interest. When a poll is wrong in predicting who will win an election, it is often because the polled sample did not accurately represent the population.

Descriptive Studies

Many, if not most, creative ideas for studies start with specific experiences or events—one person being painfully shy; someone rushing onto train tracks to rescue a person who had fallen in front of an ongoing train; or, as actually happened

population
The entire group a researcher is interested in—for example, all humans, all adolescents, all boys, all girls, or all college students.

samples
Subsets of the population studied in a research project.

in a famous case, of Kitty Genovese, who was attacked, stabbed and raped over the course of 30 minutes and numerous witnesses heard the attack. To be fair, many witnesses did not realize a murder was taking place and one woman went to help her out as she lay dying. Near the end of the attack one witness called the police. But only one call to the police out of a dozen or more witnesses. The Genovese case was so shocking that it drove two psychologists—Bibb Latané and John Darley—to conduct research on what they later called "the bystander effect."

The point is that single events and single cases often lead to new ideas and new lines of research. When a researcher is interested in a question or topic that is relatively new to the field, often the wisest approach may be to use a descriptive design. In **descriptive designs** the researcher makes no prediction and does not try to control any variables. She simply defines a problem of interest and describes as carefully as possible the variable of interest. The basic question in a descriptive design is, What is variable X? For example, What is love? What is genius? What is apathy? The psychologist makes careful observations, often in the real world outside the research lab. Descriptive studies usually occur during the exploratory phase of research, in which the researcher is looking for meaningful patterns that might lead to predictions later on; they do not involve testing hypotheses. The researcher then notes possible relationships or patterns that may be used in other designs as the basis for testable predictions (see Figure 2.5). Three of the most common kinds of descriptive methods in psychology are case studies, naturalistic observations, and interviews/surveys.

Case Study   Psychotherapists have been making use of insights gained from individual cases for more than 100 years. A **case study** involves the observation

descriptive designs
Study designs in which the researcher defines a problem and variable of interest but makes no prediction and does not control or manipulate anything.

case study
A study design in which a psychologist, often a therapist, observes one person over a long period of time.

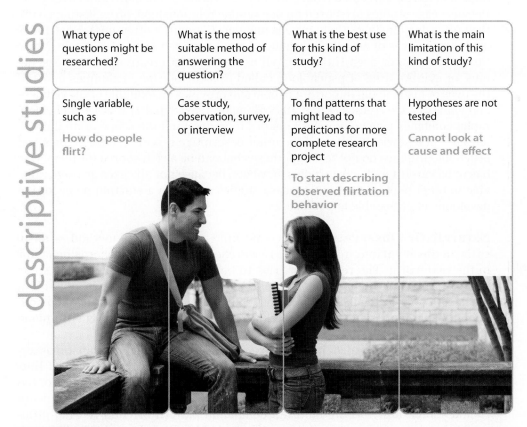

descriptive studies	What type of questions might be researched?	What is the most suitable method of answering the question?	What is the best use for this kind of study?	What is the main limitation of this kind of study?
	Single variable, such as _How do people flirt?_	Case study, observation, survey, or interview	To find patterns that might lead to predictions for more complete research project _To start describing observed flirtation behavior_	Hypotheses are not tested _Cannot look at cause and effect_

FIGURE **2.5**
CHARACTERISTICS OF DESCRIPTIVE STUDIES. In descriptive studies, researchers look for patterns that might help them create testable hypotheses.

Primatologist Jane Goodall is famous for her observational studies of chimpanzees in the wild.

of one person, often over a long period of time. Much wisdom and knowledge of human behavior can come from careful observation of one individual over time. Because case studies are based on one-on-one relationships, often lasting years, they offer deep insights that surveys and questionnaires often miss. Sometimes studying the lives of extraordinary individuals, such as van Gogh, Lincoln, Marie Curie, Einstein, or even Hitler can tell us much about creativity, greatness, genius, or evil. An area of psychology called *psychobiography* examines in detail the lives of historically important people and provides an example of the richness and value of case studies (Elms, 1993; Runyan, 1982; Schultz, 2005). Psychobiography combines psychology with history to understand the scope of an individual's life in historical context. Like other descriptive research, case studies and psychobiographies do not test hypotheses but can be a rich source for them. One has to be careful with case studies, however, because not all cases are generalizable to other people. That is why case studies are often a starting point for the development of testable hypotheses.

naturalistic observation
A study in which the researcher unobtrusively observes and records behavior in the real world.

Naturalistic Observation   A second kind of descriptive method is **naturalistic observation,** in which the researcher observes and records behavior in the real world. The researcher tries to be as unobtrusive as possible so as not to influence the behavior of interest. Naturalistic observation is more often the design of choice in comparative psychology by researchers who study nonhuman behavior (especially primates) to determine what is and is not unique about our species.

Developmental psychologists occasionally also conduct naturalistic observations. For example, the developmental psychologist Edward Tronick of Harvard University has made detailed naturalistic observations of the infants of the Efe people in Zaire. He has tracked these children from 5 months through 3 years to understand how the Efe culture's communal pattern of child rearing influences social development in children (Tronick, Morelli, & Ivey, 1992). Although the traditional Western view is that having a primary caregiver is best for the social and emotional well-being of a child, Tronick's research suggests that the use of multiple, communal caregivers can also foster children's social and emotional well-being.

The advantage of naturalistic observation is that it gives researchers a look at real behavior in the real world rather than in a controlled setting—such as in a laboratory, where people might not behave naturally. Few psychologists use naturalistic observation, however, because conditions cannot be controlled and cause-and-effect relationships between variables cannot be demonstrated.

Interview and Survey   From a research participant's point of view, it's often much more enjoyable and engaging to sit down and talk to a researcher than to complete a questionnaire. In fact, two related and widely used techniques for gaining information about people's thoughts and behaviors are interviews and surveys. They both involve asking people directly or indirectly what they think, feel, or have done. They also both involve specific questions, usually asked in precisely the same way to each respondent. Answers can be completely open-ended, allowing the person to answer however she or he wants. More often than not, however, the possible answers are restricted to some kind of rating scale, such as 1 for "completely disagree," 3 for "neither disagree nor agree," and 5 for "completely agree." Historically, interviews were conducted mostly face-to-face, but now both interviews and surveys are more often carried out over the phone or the Internet. Researchers may thus survey thousands of individuals on almost any topic, such as abortion, sex, capital punishment, voting, or gay marriage.

Collecting data via large-scale interviews and surveys has two obvious pitfalls:

- The inclusion of people who are not representative of the group at large
- Biased responses

Think about your own response when you are contacted via phone or email about participating in a scientific survey. Many of us don't want to participate and ignore the request. So how does a researcher know that people who participate are not different from people who don't participate? Maybe those who participate are older or younger, have more education or less education. In other words, we need to know that the information we collect comes from people who represent the group we are interested in, which is known as a **representative sample** (see Figure 2.6).

representative sample
A research sample that accurately reflects the population of people one is studying.

Representative sample

population

Unrepresentative sample

FIGURE **2.6**

SAMPLING. For practical reasons, research is typically conducted with small samples of the population of interest. If a psychologist wanted to study a population of 2,200 people (each face in the figure represents 100 people), he or she would aim for a sample that represented the makeup of the whole group. Thus, if 27% of the population were blue, the researcher would want 27% of the sample population to be blue, as shown in the pie chart on the left. Contrary to what many students think, *representative* does *not* mean that all groups have the same numbers.

Americans were shocked by Alfred Kinsey's initial reports on male and female sexual behavior. Kinsey was the first researcher to survey people about their sexual behavior. For better or worse, his publications changed attitudes about sex.

The well-known Kinsey surveys of male and female sexual behavior provide good examples of the strengths and weaknesses of survey research (Kinsey, Pomeroy, & Martin, 1948; Kinsey et al., 1953). Make no mistake—just publishing such research caused an uproar in both the scientific community and the general public at the time. Kinsey reported, for instance, that up to 50% of the interviewed men but only about half as many (26%) of the women had had extramarital affairs. Another widely cited finding was that approximately 10% of the population could be considered homosexual. The impact of Kinsey's research has been profound. By itself it began the science of studying human sexuality and permanently changed people's views. For example, Kinsey was the first to consider sexual orientation on a continuum from 0 (completely heterosexual) to 6 (completely homosexual) rather than as an either-or state with only two options. This approach remains a lasting contribution of his studies.

By today's standards, Kinsey's techniques for interviewing and collecting data were rather primitive. He didn't use representative sampling and oversampled people in Indiana (his home state) and in prisons, for example. In addition, he interviewed people face-to-face about the most personal and private details of their sex lives, making it more likely they would not be perfectly honest in their responses.

Meta-Analysis

As powerful as results may be from an individual study, the real power of scientific results comes from the cumulative overall findings from all studies on a given topic. If a topic or question has been sufficiently studied, researchers may choose to stand back and analyze all the results of the numerous studies on a given topic. For example, a researcher interested in the effects of media violence on children's aggressive behavior might want to know what all of the research—not just one or two studies—suggests. **Meta-analysis** is a quantitative method for combining the results of all the published and even unpublished results on one question and drawing a conclusion based on the entire set of studies on the topic. To do a meta-analysis, the researcher converts the findings of each study into a standardized statistic known as effect size. **Effect size** is a measure of the strength of the relationship between two variables or the magnitude of an experimental effect. The average effect size across all studies reflects what the literature overall says on a topic or question. In short, meta-analysis tells us whether all of the research on a topic has or has not led to consistent findings and what the size of the effect is.

meta-analysis
A research technique for combining all research results on one question and drawing a conclusion.

effect size
A measure of the strength of the relationship between two variables or the extent of an experimental effect.

Correlational Studies

Once an area of study has developed far enough that predictions can be made, but for various reasons people cannot be randomly assigned to groups or variables cannot be manipulated, a researcher might choose to test hypotheses by means of a correlational study. **Correlational designs** measure two or more variables and their relationship to one another. In this design, the basic question is, Is X related to Y? For instance, "Is sugar consumption related to increased activity levels in children?" If so, how strong is the relationship, and is increased sugar consumption associated (correlated) with increased activity levels, as we would predict, or does activity decrease as sugar consumption increases? Or is there no clear relationship?

correlational designs
Studies that measure two or more variables and their relationship to one another; they are not designed to show causation.

Correlational studies are useful when the experimenter cannot manipulate or control the variables. For example, it would be unethical to raise one group of children one way and another group another way in order to study parenting behavior. We could use a good questionnaire to find out whether parents' scores related to their parenting behavior are consistently associated with particular behavioral outcomes in children. In fact, many questions in developmental psychology, personality psychology, and even clinical psychology are examined with correlational techniques.

Do you think sugar makes kids hyperactive? What does the evidence show?

The major limitation of the correlational approach is that it does not establish whether one variable actually causes the other. Parental neglect in childhood might be associated with antisocial behavior in adolescence, but that does not necessarily mean that neglect causes antisocial behavior. Some other variable (e.g., high levels of testosterone, poverty, antisocial friends) might be the cause of the behavior. We must always be mindful that correlation is necessary for causation but is not sufficient by itself to establish causation (see Figure 2.7).

Psychologists often use a statistic called the correlation coefficient to draw conclusions from their correlational studies. **Correlation coefficients** tell us whether two variables relate to each other and the direction of the relationship. Correlations range between −1.00 and +1.00, with coefficients near 0.00 indicating that there is no relationship between the two variables. A 0.00 correlation means that knowing about one variable tells us nothing about the other. As a correlation approaches +1.00 or −1.00, the strength of the relationship increases.

correlation coefficients
Statistics that range from −1.00 to +1.00 and assess the strength and direction of associations between two variables.

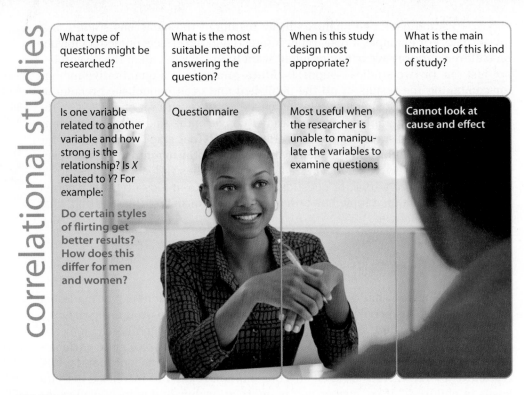

correlational studies

What type of questions might be researched?	What is the most suitable method of answering the question?	When is this study design most appropriate?	What is the main limitation of this kind of study?
Is one variable related to another variable and how strong is the relationship? Is *X* related to *Y*? For example: Do certain styles of flirting get better results? How does this differ for men and women?	Questionnaire	Most useful when the researcher is unable to manipulate the variables to examine questions	**Cannot look at cause and effect**

FIGURE **2.7**

CHARACTERISTICS OF CORRELATIONAL STUDIES. These studies measure two or more variables and their relationship to one another.

Correlation coefficients can be positive or negative. If the relationship is positive, then as a group's score on variable *X* increases, its score on variable *Y* also increases. Height and weight are positively correlated—taller people generally weigh more than shorter people. For negative correlations, as one variable increases, the other decreases. Alcohol consumption and motor skills are negatively correlated—the more alcohol people consume, the less physically coordinated they become.

To further demonstrate correlation, let's consider the positive correlation between students' scores on midterm and final exams. By calculating a correlation, we know whether students who do well on the midterm are likely to do well on the final. Based on a sample of 76 students in one of our classes, we found a correlation of +.57 between midterm and final exam grades. This means that, generally, students who did well on the midterm did well on the final. Likewise, those who did poorly on the midterm tended to do poorly on the final. The correlation, however, was not extremely high (.80 or .90), so there was some inconsistency. Some people performed differently on the two exams. When we plot these scores, we see more clearly how individuals did on each exam (see Figure 2.8). Each dot represents one student's scores on both exams. For example, one student scored an 86 on the midterm but only a 66 on the final.

When interpreting correlations, it is important to remember that a correlation does not mean there is a causal relationship between the two variables. *Correlation is necessary but not sufficient for causation.* When one variable causes another, it must be correlated with it, but just because variable *X* is correlated with variable *Y*, it does not mean that *X* causes *Y*. The supposed cause may be an effect, or a third variable may be the cause. What if hairiness and

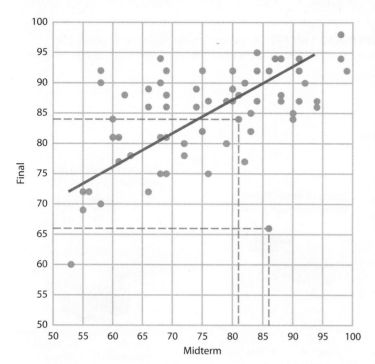

FIGURE **2.8**

EXAMPLE OF A SCATTERPLOT OF POSITIVE CORRELATION: STUDENTS' SCORES ON A MIDTERM AND A FINAL EXAM. The correlation between scores on the midterm and final is +.57, which means that in general the students who do well on the midterm tend to do well on the final. It also means that students who do poorly on the midterm tend to do poorly on the final. Each circle is a particular student's scores on the midterm and final. For example, one student scored an 81 on the midterm (vertical dashed line) and an 84 on the final (horizontal dashed line). Students above the diagonal line did better on the final than expected. Students below the diagonal line performed worse on the final than expected. For example, one student scored an 86 on the midterm but only a 66 on the final.

aggression in men were positively correlated? Would that imply that being hairy makes a man more aggressive? No. In fact, both hairiness and aggressiveness are related to a third variable, the male sex hormone testosterone (Simpson, 2001; see Figure 2.9).

Experimental Studies

Often people use the word *experiment* to refer to any research study, but in science an experiment is something quite specific. A true **experiment** has two crucial characteristics:

1. Experimental manipulation of a predicted cause, the independent variable, and measurement of the response, or dependent variable

2. Random assignment of participants to control and experimental groups or conditions, meaning that each participant has an equal chance of being placed in each group

The **independent variable** in an experiment is an attribute the experimenter manipulates under controlled conditions. The independent variable is the condition the researcher predicts will cause a particular outcome. The **dependent variable** is the outcome, or response to the experimental manipulation. You can think of the independent variable as the "cause" and the dependent variable as the "effect," although reality is not always so simple. If there is a causal connection between the two, then the responses *depend* on the treatment, hence the name *dependent variable.*

Earlier we mentioned the hypothesis that sugar consumption makes kids overly active. In this example, sugar levels consumed would be the independent variable and behavioral activity level the dependent variable. Recall the study of the effect of caffeine on sex drive in rats. Is caffeine the independent or dependent variable? What about sex drive? Figure 2.10 features other examples of independent and dependent variables.

experiment
A research design that includes independent and dependent variables and random assignments of participants to control and experimental groups or conditions.

independent variable
A property that is manipulated by an experimenter under controlled conditions to determine whether it caused the predicted outcome of an experiment.

dependent variable
In an experiment, the outcome of or response to an experimental manipulation.

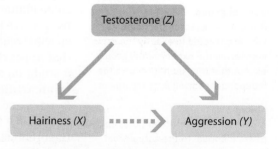

FIGURE **2.9**

CORRELATION IS NOT CAUSATION. Hairiness (*X*) and aggression (*Y*) may be correlated, but that does not mean hairiness causes aggression. In reality, a third variable (testosterone, *Z*) is the cause of both of them (Simpson, 2001). The solid lines imply cause; the dashed line implies correlation.

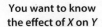

You want to know
the effect of X on Y

FIGURE **2.10**

INDEPENDENT AND DEPENDENT VARIABLES. Remember: The response, or dependent variable (DV), depends on the treatment. It is the treatment, or independent variable (IV), that the researcher manipulates.

Number of people present *(X)*
and likelihood of helping
someone in distress *(Y)*

Hours of sleep *(X)* and
performance on a test *(Y)*

Relaxation training *(X)*
and blood pressure *(Y)*

Independent
variable:
Number of
people present

Dependent
variable:
Likelihood of
helping

Independent
variable:
Number of
hours asleep

Dependent
variable:
Test grade

Independent
variable:
Relaxation
training

Dependent
variable:
Blood
pressure

random assignment
The method used to assign participants to different research conditions, so that all participants have the same chance of being in any specific group.

experimental group
A group consisting of those participants who will receive the treatment or whatever is predicted to change behavior.

control group
A group of research participants who are treated in exactly the same manner as the experimental group, except that they do not receive the independent variable, or treatment.

placebo
A substance or treatment that appears identical to the actual treatment but lacks the active substance.

Random assignment is a method used to assign participants to different research conditions to guarantee that each person has the same chance of being in one group as another. Random assignment is achieved with either a random numbers table or some other unbiased technique. Random assignment is critical, because it ensures that *on average* the groups will be similar with respect to all possible variables, such as gender, intelligence, motivation, and memory, when the experiment begins. If the groups are the same on these qualities at the beginning of the study, then any differences between the groups at the end are likely to be the result of the independent variable.

Experimenters randomly assign participants to either an experimental group or the control group. An **experimental group** consists of participants who receive the treatment or whatever is thought to change behavior. In the sugar consumption and activity study, for example, the experimental group would receive a designated amount of sugar.

The **control group** consists of participants who are treated in exactly the same manner as the experimental group but with one crucial difference: They do not receive the independent variable, or treatment. Instead, they often receive no special treatment or, in some cases, they get a **placebo**, a substance or treatment that appears identical to the actual treatment but lacks the active substance. In a study on sugar consumption and activity level, an appropriate placebo could be an artificial sweetener. The experimental group would receive the treatment (sugar), and the control group would be treated exactly the same way but would not receive the actual treatment. Instead, the control group could receive a food flavored with an artificial sweetener.

Experimental and control groups must be equivalent at the outset of an experimental study so as to minimize the possibility that other characteristics could explain any difference found after the administration of the treatment. If two groups of children are similar at the start and if one group differs from the other on activity level after receiving different amounts of sugar, then we can conclude that the treatment caused the observed effect. That is, different levels of sugar consumption caused the differences in activity level.

In our hypothetical study on sugar and activity, for instance, we would want to include equal numbers of boys and girls in the experimental and control groups and match them with respect to age, ethnicity, and other characteristics, so that we could attribute differences in activity level following treatment to differences in sugar consumption only. Suppose we didn't do a good job of randomly assigning participants to our two conditions and the experimental group ended up with 90% boys but the control group had 90% girls. If, after administering the sugar to the experimental group and the placebo (sugar substitute) to the control group, we found a difference in activity, then we would have two possible explanations for the difference: gender and sugar. Either being male or female caused the difference or consuming large amounts of sugar did. In this case, gender would be a **confounding variable**—an additional variable whose influence cannot be separated from the independent variable being examined (sugar consumption). Because most of the people in the experimental group were male and consumed sugar, we do not know whether male gender or sugar consumption was responsible for the difference in active behavior. These two variables are confounded and cannot be teased apart.

The power of the experimental design is that it allows us to say that the independent variable (treatment) caused changes in the dependent variable, as long as everything other than the independent variable was held constant (see Figure 2.11). Random assignment guarantees group equivalence on a number of variables and prevents ambiguity over whether effects might be due to other differences between the groups.

In addition to random assignment to control and experimental groups, a true experiment requires experimental control of the independent variable.

confounding variable
A variable whose influence on the dependent variable cannot be separated from the independent variable being examined.

experimental studies

What type of questions might be researched?	What is the most suitable method of answering the question?	What is the best use for this kind of study?	What is the main limitation of this kind of study?
Does the independent variable cause the dependent variable? Does *X* cause *Y*? Do smiles with raised eyebrows versus those without lead to more offers of dates?	Random assignments of participants, controlled experimental conditions in a lab setting	Most useful for the researcher to infer cause	Results cannot always be applied to the real world

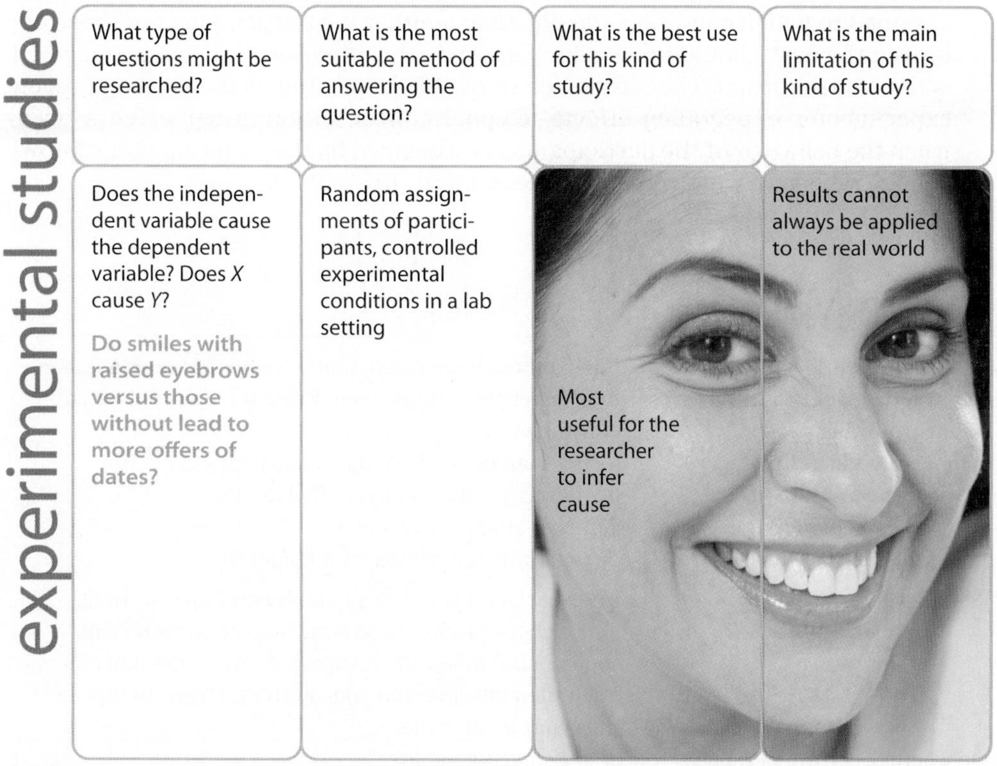

FIGURE **2.11**

CHARACTERISTICS OF EXPERIMENTAL STUDIES. Only in true experimental designs, in which researchers manipulate the independent variable and measure its effects on the dependent variable, can researchers determine cause and effect.

Thus, researchers must make sure that all environmental conditions (such as noise level and room size) are equivalent for the two groups. Again, the goal is to make sure that nothing affects the dependent variable besides the independent variable.

In our experiment on sugar consumption and activity level, we first must randomly assign participants to either the experimental group (in which participants receive some amount of sugar) or the control group (in which participants receive some sugar substitute). The outcome of interest is activity level, so each group might be videotaped for a short period 30 minutes after eating the sugar or sugar substitute. What if the room where the experimental group was given the sugar were several degrees warmer than the room where the control group received the sugar substitute, and our results showed that the participants in the warmer room were more active? Could we feel confident that sugar led to increased activity level? No, because the heat in that room may have caused the increase in activity level. In this case, room temperature would be the confounding variable.

Any knowledge that participants and experimenters have about the experimental conditions to which participants have been assigned can also affect outcome. In **single-blind studies,** participants do not know the experimental condition to which they have been assigned. This is a necessary precaution in all studies to avoid the possibility that participants will behave in a biased way. For example, if participants know they have been assigned to a group that receives a new training technique on memory, then they might try harder to perform well. This would confound the results.

Another possible problem can come from the experimenter knowing who is in which group and unintentionally treating the two groups somewhat differently. This could lead to the predicted outcome simply because the experimenter has biased the results. In **double-blind studies,** neither the participants nor the researchers (at least the ones administering the treatment) know who has been assigned to which condition. Ideally, then, neither the participants nor those collecting the data should know which group is the experimental group and which is the control group. The advantage of double-blind studies is that they prevent experimenter expectancy effects. **Experimenter expectancy effects** occur when the behavior of the participants is influenced by the experimenter's knowledge of who is in which condition (Rosenthal, 1976, 1994).

single-blind studies
Studies in which participants do not know the experimental condition (group) to which they have been assigned.

double-blind studies
Studies in which neither the participants nor the researchers administering the treatment know who has been assigned to the experimental or control group.

experimenter expectancy effects
Results that occur when the behavior of the participants is influenced by the experimenter's knowledge of who is in the control group and who is in the experimental group.

Quick Quiz 2.2: Research Methods in Psychology

1. Dr. Lovejoy wanted to do research on real-world conditions that lead to aggression in 10-year-old children, defining aggression as "intent to harm another person." She went to a local elementary school and videotaped a 10-minute recess period. She and her trained coders then coded the behavior of every child and counted the number of times each child acted aggressively. This is an example of what kind of research design?
   a. descriptive
   b. correlational
   c. case study
   d. experimental

2. If Dr. Lovejoy wanted to examine whether certain personality traits make aggression more likely, she would probably use what kind of research design?
   a. descriptive   c. interview
   b. correlational   d. experimental

3. Researchers have consistently found that married men live longer than single men. From this finding, we can conclude that
   a. if a man gets married he adds years to his life.
   b. marriage causes men to live longer.
   c. being single causes men to die earlier.
   d. marriage correlates with longer life.

4. In research on whether sugar causes hyperactivity, researchers randomly assign children to receive no sugar, small amounts of sugar, or large amounts of sugar. They then observe and code activity levels. In this case, the sugar level is the
   a. outcome variable.
   b. dependent variable.
   c. independent variable.
   d. control condition.

5. In contrast to other kinds of research designs, a true experimental design must have two things:
   a. random assignment of participants to conditions and statistical analysis.
   b. random assignment of participants to conditions and manipulation of an independent variable.
   c. manipulation of an independent variable and a dependent variable.
   d. hypothesis testing and observation.

   Answers can be found at the end of the chapter.

CHALLENGING ASSUMPTIONS IN THE OBJECTIVITY OF EXPERIMENTAL RESEARCH

You don't have to be a scientist to understand that it would be wrong and unethical for an experimenter to tell participants how to behave and what to do. Even for the participants to know what group they are in or what the hypotheses of the study are is bad science and biases behavior. Can what the experimenter knows change the behavior of the participants?

Robert Rosenthal

In a classic case of scientific serendipity, Robert Rosenthal's PhD thesis challenged the assumption that experimenters who randomly assign animals or people to conditions and manipulate an independent variable are being quite objective—that is, these procedures assure objective results. He discovered the assumption of objectivity was wrong when he set out to conduct a study on perceived success and intelligence. Rosenthal hypothesized that people who believed they were successful would be more likely to see success in others. To test this idea, he conducted an experiment in which he told one group of participants they had done well on an intelligence test and another group they had done poorly on an intelligence test. Rosenthal randomly assigned participants to be in one of these conditions (there was also a neutral control condition in which participants received no feedback on the intelligence test). Then he asked all groups to look at photographs of people doing various tasks and rate how successful they thought the people in the photos were. He reasoned that people who are told they did well on an intelligence test should see more success in photographs of people doing various tasks than people who are told they did not do well on the test.

As a good scientist, Rosenthal compared the average test scores of the participants assigned to different conditions before giving them any feedback on their performance—that is, before the experimental treatment. The reason is simple: If the treatment causes a difference in behavior for the different groups, the researcher needs to make sure the groups started out behaving the same way before treatment. To Rosenthal's dismay, the groups did differ before receiving treatment. They were also different in exactly the way that favored his hypothesis!

Given random assignment, the only difference in the groups at the outset was Rosenthal's knowledge of who was in which group. Somehow, by knowing who was in which group, he created behaviors that favored his hypothesis. He was forced to conclude that, even when trying to be "scientific" and "objective," researchers bias results unintentionally in their favor by subtle voice changes or gestures. Instead of having a wonderful "aha moment" of scientific discovery, Rosenthal had more of an "oh no" moment: "What I recall was a panic experience when I realized I'd ruined the results of my doctoral dissertation by unintentionally influencing my research participants to respond in a biased manner because of my expectations" (Rosenthal, personal communication, April 18, 2010).

Challenge Your Assumptions

True or False? Knowing what you're looking for in an experiment has no effect on the outcome.

False: Even when being careful, if the researcher is aware of the hypothesis, he or she may unconsciously act differently and unintentionally affect the behavior of the participants.

Rosenthal decided to systematically study what he came to call experimenter expectancy effects. Through several experiments, he confirmed that experimenter expectancies can ruin even the best-designed studies. Also, he discovered that two other surprising factors can change the outcome of the study as well. First, if the study involves direct interaction between an experimenter and participants, the experimenter's age, ethnicity, personality, and gender can influence the participants' behavior (Rosenthal, 1976). Second, Rosenthal stumbled upon a more general phenomenon known as **self-fulfilling prophecy.** A self-fulfilling prophecy is a statement that changes events to cause a belief or prediction to become true. If you say, "I am going to fail this exam" and then do not study, that belief becomes self-fulfilling when you do fail the exam.

Ten years after Rosenthal's first publication on experimenter expectancy effect, more than 300 other studies confirmed his results (Rosenthal & Rubin, 1978). Such expectancies affect animal participants as well as humans (Jussim & Harber, 2005; Rosenthal & Fode, 1963). Rosenthal's demonstration of experimenter expectancy effects and self-fulfilling prophecies also led to the development of double-blind procedures in science. Think about it: If what experimenters know about a study can affect the results, then they'd better be as blind to experimental conditions as the participants are. All of this came to be because Rosenthal "messed up" his dissertation and unintentionally challenged the assumptions of the best way to conduct scientific experiments.

Quick Quiz 2.3: Challenging Assumptions in the Objectivity of Experimental Research

1. One explanation for experimenter expectancy effect is
   a. double-blind studies.
   b. self-fulfilling prophecy.
   c. confounding variables.
   d. experimental manipulation.

2. The best way to lessen the effects of experimenter expectancy is to design a study that uses
   a. single-blind methods.
   b. double-blind methods.
   c. triple-blind methods.
   d. quasi-experimental methods.

Answers can be found at the end of the chapter.

COMMONLY USED MEASURES OF PSYCHOLOGICAL RESEARCH

When psychologists conduct research, they rely on a vast array of tools to measure variables relevant to their research questions. The tools and techniques they use to assess thought and behavior are called **measures.** Measures in psychological science tend to fall into three categories: self-report, behavioral, and physiological. To study complex behaviors, researchers may employ multiple measures (see Figure 2.12).

Self-Report Measures

Self-reports are people's written or oral accounts of their thoughts, feelings, or actions. Two kinds of self-report measures are commonly used in psychology:

- Interviews
- Questionnaires

	Description	Use	Limitations
self-reports	Participants' written or oral accounts of thoughts, actions, feelings	Interviews and questionnaires	Social desirability bias Lack of clear insight into one's own behavior
behavioral measures	Objective observation of actions in either natural or lab settings	Small-scale studies on behavior	Time required to train coders and conduct coding Participants may modify their behavior
physiological measures	Data collection of bodily responses under certain conditions	Studies to determine the magnitude of physiological change	Specialized training on expensive equipment, on how to collect measurements, and on data interpretation
multiple measures	Several measures combined to acquire data on one aspect of behavior	Offset limitation of any single measurement Complex behaviors to study	Expensive and time-consuming

FIGURE **2.12**

COMMONLY USED MEASURES IN PSYCHOLOGY.

 Why does the best research strategy involve using as many techniques as possible to study the same question?

In an interview, a researcher asks a set of questions, and the respondent usually answers in any way he or she feels is appropriate. The answers are often open-ended and not constrained by the researcher. (See the section "Descriptive Studies," p. 42, for additional discussion on interviews.)

In a questionnaire, responses are limited to the choices given in the questionnaire. In the Stanford Prison Experiment, for example, the researchers used several questionnaires to keep track of the psychological states of the prisoners and guards. They had participants complete mood questionnaires many times during the study, so that the researchers could track any emotional changes the participants experienced. The participants also completed forms that assessed personality characteristics, such as trustworthiness and orderliness, that might be related to how they acted in a prison environment (Haney et al., 1973).

Self-report questionnaires are easy to use, especially in the context of collecting data from a large number of people at once. They are also relatively inexpensive. If designed carefully, questionnaires can provide important information on key psychological variables. A major problem with self-reports, however, is that people are not always the best sources of information about themselves. Why? Sometimes, as a reflection of the tendency toward social desirability, called **social desirability bias,** people present themselves more favorably than they really are, not wanting to reveal what they are really thinking or feeling to others for fear of looking bad. Presented with questions about social prejudice, for example, respondents might try to avoid giving answers that suggest they are prejudiced against a particular group. Another problem with self-reports is that we have to assume that people are accurate witnesses to their own experiences.

social desirability bias
The tendency toward favorable self-presentation, which could lead to inaccurate self-reports.

Of course, there is no way to know exactly what a person is thinking without asking that person, but people do not always have clear insight into how they might behave (Nisbett & Wilson, 1977).

Behavioral Measures

Behavioral measures involve the systematic observation of people's actions either in their normal environment (that is, naturalistic observation) or in a laboratory setting. A psychologist interested in aggression might bring people into a laboratory, place them in a situation that elicits aggressive behavior, and videotape the responses. Afterward, trained coders observe the videos and, using a prescribed method, code the level of aggressive behavior exhibited by each person. Training is essential for the coders, so that they can evaluate the video and apply the codes in a reliable, consistent manner.

Behavioral measures are less susceptible to social desirability bias than are self-report measures. They also provide more objective measurements, because they come from a trained outside observer, rather than from the participants themselves. This is a concern for researchers on topics for which people are not likely to provide accurate information in self-report instruments. In the study of emotion, for example, measuring facial expressions from video reveals things about how people are feeling that they might not reveal on questionnaires (Rosenberg & Ekman, 2000).

One drawback of behavioral measures is that people may modify their behavior if they know they are being observed and/or measured. The major drawback of behavioral measurement, however, is that it can be time-intensive; it takes time to train coders to use the coding schemes, to collect behavioral data, and to prepare the coded data for analysis. As a case in point, one of the most widely used methods for coding facial expressions of emotion requires intensive training, on the order of 100 hours, for people to be able to use it

What are some advantages and disadvantages to collecting data via observation?

correctly (Ekman, Friesen, & Hager, 2002)! Moreover, researchers can collect data on only a few participants at once, and therefore behavioral measures are often impractical for large-scale studies.

Physiological Measures

Physiological measures provide data on bodily responses. For years, researchers relied on physiological information to index possible changes in psychological states—for example, to determine the magnitude of a stress reaction. Research on stress and anxiety often measures electrical changes in involuntary bodily responses, such as heart rate, sweating, and respiration, as well as hormonal changes in the blood that are sensitive to changes in psychological states. Some researchers measure brain activity while people perform certain tasks to determine the speed and general location of cognitive processes in the brain.

We will look at specific brain imaging technologies in Chapter 3. Here we note simply that they have enhanced our understanding of the brain's structure and function tremendously. However, these technologies, and even more simple ones, such as the measurement of heart rate, often require specialized training in the use of equipment, collection of measurements, and interpretation of data. Further, some of the equipment is expensive to buy and maintain. Outside the health care delivery system, only major research universities with medical schools tend to have them. In addition, researchers need years of training and experience in order to use these machines and interpret the data they generate.

physiological measures
Measures of bodily responses, such as blood pressure or heart rate, used to determine changes in psychological state.

Quick Quiz 2.4: Commonly Used Measures of Psychological Research

1. An advantage of self-report questionnaires is that they are easy to administer to large numbers of participants. A disadvantage of questionnaires is that
   a. they cost too much.
   b. people do not always accurately report their true thoughts or feelings.
   c. scoring responses is subjective.
   d. they have low reliability.

2. One advantage of behavioral measures compared with self-reported measures is that they
   a. are less prone to social desirability bias.
   b. are less time-intensive.

   c. are always more valid.
   d. cost less.

3. A psychologist who is interested in how brain activity relates to behavior will most likely use which kind of measure?
   a. interview
   b. questionnaire
   c. behavioral
   d. physiological

Answers can be found at the end of the chapter.

MAKING SENSE OF DATA WITH STATISTICS

Once researchers collect data, they must make sense of them. Raw data are difficult to interpret. They are, after all, just a bunch of numbers. It helps to have some way to organize the information and give it meaning. To make sense of information, scientists use **statistics,** mathematical procedures for collecting, analyzing, interpreting, and presenting numeric data. For example, researchers use statistics to describe and simplify data and to understand how variables relate to one another. There are two classes of statistics: descriptive and inferential.

statistics
The collection, analysis, interpretation, and presentation of numeric data.

Descriptive Statistics

descriptive statistics
Measures used to describe and summarize research.

mean
The arithmetic average of a series of numbers.

median
The score that separates the lower half of scores from the upper half.

mode
A statistic that represents the most commonly occurring score or value.

standard deviation
A statistical measure of how much scores in a sample vary around the mean.

frequency
The number of times a particular score occurs in a set of data.

normal distribution
A bell curve; a plot of how frequent data are that is perfectly symmetrical, with most scores clustering in the middle and only a few scores at the extremes.

The first step in understanding research results involves calculating **descriptive statistics,** which simply tell researchers the range, average, and variability of the scores. For instance, one useful way to describe data is by calculating the center, or average, of the scores. There are three ways to calculate an average—the mean, median, and mode. The **mean** is the arithmetic average of a series of numbers. It is calculated by adding all the numbers together and dividing by the number of scores in the series. An example of a mean is your GPA, which averages the numeric grade points for all of the courses you have taken. The **median** is the middle score, which separates the lower half of scores from the upper half. The **mode** is the most frequently occurring score.

Sometimes scores vary widely among participants, but the mean, median, and mode do not reveal anything about how spread out—or how varied—scores are. For example, one person's 3.0 GPA could come from getting B's in all his courses, while another person's 3.0 could result from getting A's in half her classes and C's in the other half. The second student has much more variable grades than the first. The most common way to represent variability in data is to calculate the **standard deviation,** a statistical measure of how much scores in a sample vary around the mean. A higher standard deviation indicates more variability (more spread); a lower one indicates less variability (less spread). In the example, the student with all B's would have a lower standard deviation than the student with A's and C's.

Another useful way of describing data is by plotting, or graphing, their frequency. **Frequency** is the number of times a particular score occurs in a set of data. A graph of frequency scores is known as a distribution. To graph a distribution, we place the scores on the horizontal axis, or X-axis, and their frequencies on the vertical axis, or Y-axis. When we do this for many psychological variables, such as intelligence or personality, we end up with a very symmetrical shape to our distribution, which is commonly referred to as either a **normal distribution** or a "bell curve"—because it looks like a bell (see Figure 2.13).

Let's look at a concrete example of a normal distribution with the well-known intelligence quotient (IQ). If we gave 1,000 children an IQ test and plotted all 1,000 scores, we would end up with something very close to a symmetrical,

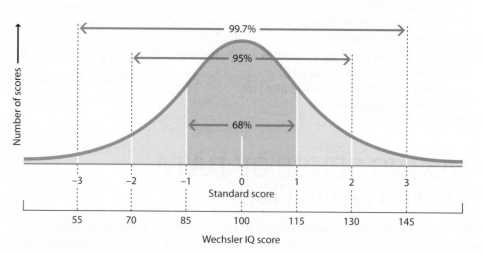

FIGURE 2.13

BELL CURVE. Psychological variables, such as intelligence, show a normal distribution, which is represented by a bell curve.

 In a bell curve, what percentage of the population falls within **1** standard deviation (plus or minus) from the mean?

bell-shaped distribution. Very few children would score 70 or below, and very few children would score 130 or above. The majority of children would be right around the average, or mean, of 100. In fact, two-thirds (68%, to be exact) would be within 1 standard deviation (15 points) of the mean. Moreover, about 95% would be within 2 standard deviations, or between 70 and 130.

How do we know this? We know it because we know the exact shape of a normal distribution in the population. Knowing the shape of the distribution allows us to make inferences from our specific sample to the general population. For example, because a normal distribution has a precise shape, we know exactly what percentage of scores is within 1 standard deviation of the mean (68%) and how many are within 2 standard deviations of the mean (95%). This is why we know that a mean IQ score of 70 or lower or 130 or higher occurs only 5 times in 100—neither is very unlikely to occur by chance. This quality of allowing conclusions or inferences to be drawn about populations is the starting point for the second class of statistics, inferential statistics.

Inferential Statistics

We do not draw any conclusions from descriptive results. We just describe the scores with them. **Inferential statistics,** however, allow us to test hypotheses and draw a conclusion (that is, make an inference) as to how likely a sample score is to occur in a population. They also allow us to determine how likely it is that two or more samples came from the same population. In other words, inferential statistics use probability and the normal distribution to rule out chance as an explanation for why group scores are different.

What is an acceptable level of chance before we say that a score is not likely to occur by chance? Five in 100 (5%) is the most frequent choice made by psychological researchers and is referred to as the *probability level.* So if we obtain two means and our statistical analysis tells us there is only a 5% or less chance that these means come from the same population, we conclude that the numbers are not just different but statistically different and not likely by chance.

Researchers use many kinds of statistical analyses to rule out chance, but the most basic ones involve the comparison of two or more means. To compare just two means, we use a statistic known as the **t-test.** The basic logic of t-tests is to determine whether the means for your two groups are so different that they are not likely to come from the same population. If our two groups are part of an experiment and one is the experimental group and the other the control group, then we are determining whether our treatment caused a significant effect, seen in different means. In short, t-tests allow us to test our hypotheses and rule out chance as an explanation.

Let's look at an example, by returning to a question we considered earlier: Does sugar cause hyperactive behavior in children? We will make the common-sense prediction that sugar does cause hyperactive behavior. We randomly assign 100 children to consume sugar (experimental group); another 100 children do not consume sugar (control group). We then wait 30 minutes—to let the sugar effect kick in—and observe their behavior for an additional 30 minutes. We video record each child's behavior and code it on number of "high activity acts." If sugar causes activity levels to increase, then the sugar groups number of high activity acts should be higher than those of the no-sugar group. Our data show that the experimental (sugar) group exhibited an average of 9.13 high activity behaviors in the 30 minutes after eating the sugar; the control (no-sugar) group exhibited an average of 7.91 such behaviors. On the face of it, our hypothesis seems to be supported. After all, 9.13 is higher than 7.91. However, we need to conduct a statistical test to determine whether the difference in the number of hyperactive behaviors between our groups of kids who ate sugar versus those who did not really represents a true difference between these two different populations of kids in the real world.

inferential statistics
Analyses of data that allow us to test hypotheses and make an inference as to how likely a sample score is to occur in a population.

t-test
A statistic that compares two means to see whether they could come from the same population.

Psychology in the Real World

Challenge the Assumptions of Advertisers' Statistics

Learning about research methods plays a crucial role in understanding psychological science, but it offers huge practical advantages as well. You can learn how to look at claims in the news and advertisements with a critical eye to challenge your assumptions about things that matter to you in your own life. Much of what you learn in this class may be forgotten not long after you leave college, but you are bombarded with advertisements dozens of times each day, something that will continue throughout your life. So let's look briefly at three scenarios that will help you be a more critical and intelligent consumer of information.

Scenario 1
A billboard advertising a popular hybrid vehicle: "The car more people would buy again"

That sounds great! Not only is the car good for the environment (which is one reason to get it), but it also gets great mileage (which will save you money) and people like it (they must, if they say they would buy it again). Are you sold yet?

Wait a minute. What does the ad actually say? The car more people would buy again. More than what? The meaning of this claim depends entirely on what this vehicle is being compared to. The implication is that more people would buy this car again than would buy any other car. What did they actually compare it to?

Other hybrids?
All other cars?
A horse and buggy?

These are things you need to know. Otherwise, you can't judge what the statement means. Advertisers regularly leave out such information and hope you will fill in the blank with what helps them most. In this case, they hope and assume you fill in the blank with "all other cars."

Scenario 2
In an ad in the morning paper, Company B reports on a recent lab study showing that just a half ounce of its new drug—let's call it No-Cold—killed 37,202 germs in a test tube in less than 15 seconds! (adapted from Huff, 1954)

The implication is that No-Cold is a great cold medicine—perhaps better than others—on the basis of these hard scientific data. Let's take this claim apart, though. Can you see what is wrong with this statement? Here are a few things to consider:

1. Just because a substance works well in a test tube does not mean it will work in the human throat or respiratory tract. The test tube is a controlled environment, whereas a host of factors interact in the human body. Temperature, moisture, other bacteria, the human immune system, and phlegm are just a few examples of such factors.
2. The ad doesn't say what kind of germs No-Cold killed. Were they the ones that cause colds? (The common cold is caused by a variety of viruses.) Medical researchers still have little idea of the specific viruses

The t-test is the test to use in this case, the purpose of which is to determine whether the difference between the two means ($9.23 - 7.61 = 1.62$) is a chance occurrence or not. If we calculate our t-test and find out that the probability (p-level) that these two means came from the same population is .55, then we cannot rule out chance as an explanation. Because there is a 55% chance our two means came from the same population, we conclude the means are not significantly different from each other; children who eat sugar are no more active than those who do not. In this case, our hypothesis is *not* supported, and we are forced to conclude that we have no evidence that sugar increases activity level. These figures are hypothetical but completely consistent with the actual literature on the topic of sugar and activity level (Kanarek, 1994; Krummel, Seligson, & Guthrie, 1996).

Rejecting a hypothesis is never fun. We may have really wanted sugar to be a cause of activity level and, in fact, most parents believe this; however, it is not what the evidence shows, and we have to conclude that sugar does not cause hyperactive behavior, regardless of what we want to believe. This is a perfect example of a very widely held assumption being false. Scientists keep a distance

Challenge Your Assumptions

True or False? Eating sugar makes children hyperactive.

False: There is no evidence supporting the belief that sugar intake directly affects hyperactivity.

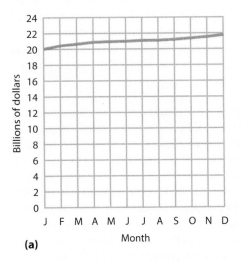

(a)

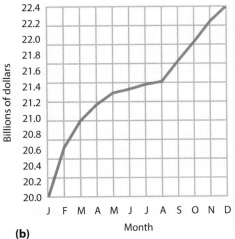

(b)

FIGURE **2.14**

BILLIONS OF DOLLARS SPENT ON EDUCATION.

If you wanted to persuade someone that education spending is out of control, which graph would you use to make your case?

(germs) that cause colds, though some of them have been isolated. Were these germs even relevant to colds? Were they even viruses? Can you identify any other problems with the ad?

Scenario 3

Graphic displays of data can be misleading.

Consider Figures 2.14a and 2.14b, both of which depict the billions of dollars spent on education over a 1-year period. Figure 2.14b seems to show a much bigger increase in spending on education than Figure 2.14a. If you look

closely, however, both depict a $2 billion increase in spending over a 1-year period. The information contained in each picture is exactly the same, but the slopes of the lines differ dramatically. This difference stems from how the illustrations' vertical axes are segmented. If you want to imply that the spending increases in education are insufficient, then you might graph them as shown in Figure 2.14a, which has $2 billion increments, so it shows a gradual increase across the year. Figure 2.14b, on the other hand, uses $0.2 billion increments. Businesses, journalists, and politicians can mislead people by graphically distorting data.

from their ideas; they don't believe what they think, at least not until it can be confirmed and replicated.

As useful and helpful as statistics are to help us understand our results, be aware that they also can be and are used to mislead people.

Quick Quiz 2.5: Making Sense of Data with Statistics

1. If two sets of scores have the same mean, then
   a. they must have the same variability.
   b. they must have similar variabilities.
   c. they must have different variabilities.
   d. their variabilities could be the same or they could be different.

2. Why is GPA a good example of the statistic *mean*?
   a. It is calculated by adding scores and dividing by the number of scores.
   b. It is a good measure of how well a student is doing.

   c. It measures the spread, or variability, of a student's performance.
   d. We can plot it on a graph.

3. Scores that are widely spread apart have a
   a. high standard deviation.
   b. low standard deviation.
   c. high mean.
   d. low reliability.

Answers can be found at the end of the chapter.

RESEARCH ETHICS

Due to current ethical guidelines, some of the most important and classic studies in psychology could not be performed today. One of them is the Stanford Prison Experiment, which you read about at the beginning of this chapter. This experiment subjected participants to conditions that so altered their behavior the researchers had to intervene and end the study early. In 1971, there were few ethical limitations on psychological research. Since then, and partly as a consequence of studies like the Stanford Prison Experiment, professional organizations and universities have put in place strict ethical guidelines to protect research participants from physical and psychological harm.

ethics
The rules governing the conduct of a person or group in general or in a specific situation—or more simply, standards of right and wrong.

Ethics are the rules governing the conduct of a person or group in general or in a specific situation; stated more simply, ethics are standards of right and wrong. What are the ethical boundaries of the treatment of humans and animals in psychological research? In psychology today, nearly every study conducted with humans and animals must pass through a rigorous review of its methods by a panel of experts. If the proposed study does not meet the standards, it cannot be approved.

Another notable example of research that would violate current ethics guidelines was a classic series of studies by Stanley Milgram in the early 1960s. Milgram's landmark research on obedience is discussed in more detail in Chapter 14, but we mention it here for its pivotal role in the development of ethical guidelines for human psychological research. Milgram, like many other social psychologists of the mid-20th century, was both fascinated and horrified by the atrocities of the Holocaust and wondered to what extent psychological factors influenced people's willingness to carry out the orders of the Nazi regime. Milgram predicted that most people are not inherently evil and argued that there might be powerful aspects of social situations that make people obey orders from authority figures. He designed an experiment to test systematically the question of whether decent people could be made to inflict harm on others.

Briefly, Milgram's studies of obedience involved a simulation in which participants were misled about the true nature of the experiment. Thinking that they were part of an experiment on learning, they administered what they thought were electrical shocks to punish the "learner," who was in another room, for making errors. In spite of protests from the learner when increasingly intense shocks occurred, the experimenter pressured the "teachers" to continue administering shocks. Some people withdrew from the study, but most of the participants continued to shock the learner. After the study, Milgram fully explained to his participants that the learner had never been shocked or in pain at all (Milgram, 1974).

In the Stanford Prison Experiment, college students assigned to the role of either a prison guard or a prisoner acted their parts so well that they blurred the distinction between reality and the world created for this study. The extreme distress experienced by some of the prisoners forced the researchers to end the simulation earlier than planned.

 Do you think the experimenter pushed the participants too far?

Milgram's study provided important data on how easily decent people could be persuaded by the sheer force of a situation to do cruel things. What is more, Milgram conducted many replications and variations of his findings, which helped build knowledge about human social behavior. Was it worth the distress it exerted on the participants? One could ask the same of the Stanford Prison Experiment. The prison study, though dramatic, created much publicity but did not generate a great deal of scientific research. Although the prison experiment led to some reform in U.S. prisons, it is hard to know whether the deception of the participants and the emotional breakdowns some of them experienced was worth it. What do you think?

Ethical Research with Humans

The Milgram study is one of the most widely discussed studies in the history of psychology. A number of psychologists protested it on ethical grounds (Baumrind, 1964). The uproar led to the creation of explicit guidelines for the ethical treatment of human subjects. Today all psychological and medical researchers must adhere to the following guidelines:

1. *Informed consent:* Tell participants in general terms what the study is about, what they will do and how long it will take, what the known risks and benefits are, and whom to contact with questions. They must also be told that they have the right to withdraw at any time without penalty. This information is provided in written form and the participant signs it, signifying consent. If a participant is under the age of 18, informed consent must be granted by a legal guardian. Informed consent can be omitted only in situations such as completely anonymous surveys.

2. *Respect for persons:* Safeguard the dignity and autonomy of the individual and take extra precautions when dealing with study participants, such as children, who are less likely to understand that their participation is voluntary.

3. *Beneficence:* Inform participants of costs and benefits of participation; minimize costs for participants and maximize benefits. For example, many have argued that the Milgram study was worth the distress (cost) it may have caused participants, for the benefit of the knowledge we have gained about how readily decent people can be led astray by powerful social situations. In fact, many of the participants said that they were grateful for this opportunity to gain knowledge about themselves that they would have not predicted (Milgram, 1974).

4. *Privacy and confidentiality:* Protect the privacy of the participant, generally by keeping all responses confidential. Confidentiality ensures that participants' identities are never directly connected with the data they provide in a study.

5. *Justice:* Benefits and costs must be distributed equally among participants.

In Milgram's study, participants were led to believe they were taking part in a learning study when, in fact, they were participating in a study on obedience to authority. Is this kind of deception ever justified? The answer (according to the American Psychological Association, APA) is that deception is to be avoided whenever possible, but it is permissible if these conditions are met: It can be fully justified by its significant potential scientific, educational, or applied value; it is part of the research design; there is no alternative to deception; and full debriefing occurs afterward. **Debriefing** is the process of informing participants of the exact purposes of the study—including the hypotheses—revealing any and all deceptive practices and explaining why they were necessary to conduct the study and ultimately what the results of the study were.

debriefing
An explanation of the purposes of a study following data collection.

Debriefing is required to minimize any negative effects (e.g., distress) experienced as a result of the deception. Deception comes in different shades and degrees. In the Stanford Prison Experiment, all participants were fully informed about the fact that they would be assigned the roles of a prisoner or a guard. In that sense there was no deception. They were not informed of the details and the extent to which being in this study would be like being in a real prison world. They were not told upfront that, if they were assigned to the "prisoner" role, they would be strip-searched. When they were taken from their homes, the "prisoners" were not told this was part of the study. Not informing participants of the research hypotheses may be deceptive but necessary to prevent biased and invalid responses. Not telling participants that they might experience physical pain or psychological distress is a much more severe form of deception and is not ethically permissible.

Today, to ensure adherence to ethical guidelines, **institutional review boards (IRBs)** evaluate proposed research before it is conducted to make sure

institutional review boards (IRBs)
Organizations that evaluate research proposals to make sure research involving humans does not cause undue harm or distress.

research involving humans does not cause undue harm or distress. Should Milgram's study have been permitted? Were his procedures ethical by today's standards? To this day, there are people who make strong cases both for and against the Milgram study on ethical grounds, as we have discussed. It is harder to justify what Zimbardo did in the prison experiment.

Ethical Research with Animals

Human participants are generally protected by the ethical guidelines itemized in the previous section. What about animals? They cannot consent, so how do we ethically treat animals in research?

The use of nonhuman species in psychological research is even more controversial than is research with humans. There is a long history in psychology of conducting research on animals. Typically, such studies concern topics that are harder to explore in humans. We cannot, for instance, isolate human children from their parents to see what effect an impoverished environment has on brain development. Researchers have done so with animals. The subfields of biological psychology and learning most often use animals for research. For instance, to determine what exactly a particular brain structure does, one needs to compare individuals who have healthy structures to those who do not. With humans this might be done by studying the behavior of individuals with accidental brain injury or disease and comparing it to the behavior of normal humans. Injury and disease, however, never strike two people in precisely the same way, so it is not possible to reach definite conclusions about the way the brain works by just looking at accidents and illness. Surgically removing

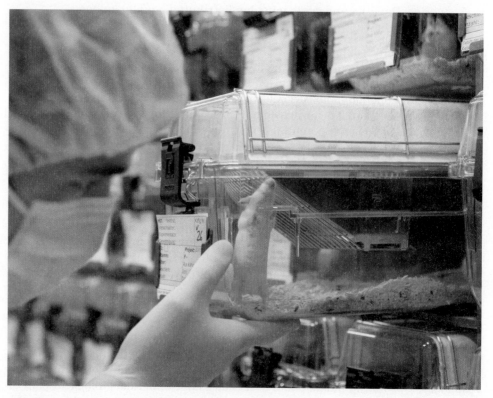

Strict laws and ethical standards govern the treatment of animals used in research.
What are the pros and cons of using animals for scientific research?

the brain structure is another way to determine function, but this approach is obviously unethical with humans. In contrast, nonhuman animals, usually laboratory rats, offer the possibility of more highly controlled studies of selective brain damage. For example, damage could be inflicted on part of a brain structure in one group of rats while another group is left alone. Then the rats' behaviors and abilities could be observed to see whether there were any differences between the groups.

Animals cannot consent to research, and if they could, they would not likely agree to any of this. Indeed, it is an ongoing debate as to how much animal research should be permissible at all. Because animal research has led to many treatments for disease (e.g., cancer, heart disease), as well as advances in understanding basic neuroscientific processes (such as the effects of environment on brain cell growth), it is widely considered to be acceptable. Animal research is acceptable, that is, as long as the general conditions and treatment of the animals is humane.

If informed consent is the key to ethical treatment of human research participants, then humane treatment is the key to the ethical use of animal subjects. The standards for humane treatment of research animals involve complex legal issues. State and federal laws generally require housing the animals in clean, sanitary, and adequately sized structures. In addition, separate IRBs evaluate proposals for animal research. They require researchers to ensure the animals' comfort, health, and humane treatment, which also means keeping discomfort, infection, illness, and pain to an absolute minimum at all times. If a study requires euthanizing the animal, it must be done as painlessly as possible.

Despite the existence of legal and ethical safeguards and the importance for medical research in humans, some animal rights groups argue that any and all animal research should be discontinued, unless it directly benefits the animals. These groups contend that computer modeling can give us much of the knowledge sought in animal studies and eliminates the need for research with animals. In addition, current brain-imaging techniques, which allow researchers to view images of the living human brain, reduce the need to sacrifice animals to examine their brain structures (P. M. Thompson et al., 2000).

As is true of all ethical issues, complex and legitimate opposing needs must be balanced in research. The need to know, understand, and treat illness must be balanced against the needs, well-being, and rights of participants and animals. Consequently, the debate and discussion about ethical treatment of humans and animals must be ongoing and evolving.

Quick Quiz 2.6: Research Ethics

1. When conducting research with humans, researchers
   a. never have to obtain informed consent if it interferes with the research.
   b. almost always must obtain informed consent.
   c. always must obtain informed consent.
   d. used to be required to obtain informed consent, but this requirement has been discontinued.

2. Current guidelines on research ethics state that, when studying humans, deception
   a. must be avoided whenever possible.
   b. can be used only if it's part of the research design.
   c. must be followed by debriefing.
   d. must be fully justified.
   e. all of the above.

3. Ethical guidelines for research with nonhuman animals state that
   a. informed consent is always required.
   b. ethical and humane conditions must exist throughout the research process.
   c. computer modeling must always be tried before research with animals.
   d. deception can be used if fully justified.

Answers can be found at the end of the chapter.

Bringing It All Together

Making Connections in Psychological Research

Can Experience Change the Brain?

Can enriching experiences actually improve brain function and/or make the brain grow faster? By looking at different research approaches to answering this question and at some of the ethical issues involved, we can see why certain methods are chosen over others and get a sense of the cumulative nature of science.

In the early 1960s a group at the University of California, Berkeley, decided to study the effects of different environments on the brains of rats (Bennett et al., 1964; Rosenzweig et al., 1962). In numerous experimental studies, the researchers randomly assigned genetically similar rats to either enriched or impoverished environments for up to 30 days. The enriched environments included many opportunities and apparatuses for play and activity, such as running wheels and climbing tubes, as well as food and water. The impoverished environments provided only food and water. As you might have guessed, the independent variable in these experiments was how enriched the environment was; the dependent variables were change in brain size and/or changes in the growth of brain cells. The researchers found that rats raised in enriched environments showed evidence of growth in brain tissue compared to the animals reared in the impoverished environments. Using an experimental design with random assignment (the groups of rats were equivalent at the beginning of each experiment), the researchers

replicated their basic finding many times. By doing so, they established that rats raised in the enriched conditions did indeed develop more brain tissue and thicker cortexes.

These experiments all involved true experimental designs, in which the animals were randomly assigned to different environmental conditions, all aspects of the study were tightly controlled, and the animals were euthanized afterward to allow for detailed study of brain structure. One of the main reasons we study these phenomena in animals is to learn how these processes work in humans, but ethical limitations prevent human research. Thus, the animals serve as models for how human brain organization and function might be modified by experience.

Do rats serve as good models for how things happen in humans? Although rat and human brains have many similarities, they also have a multitude of anatomical differences. This suggests that rat brain organization is not a perfect model for understanding human brain organization.

Research on humans is necessary to know whether environmental enrichment causes changes in the human brain, but the ways in which we can study such processes in humans are limited. Clearly, it would be unethical even to randomly assign babies to live in either enriched or impoverished environments for several years so that we

Early musical training not only develops a child's appreciation for music but also correlates with increases in brain size relative to children who don't learn to play an instrument at a young age.

How does training actually change the brain?

could assess differences in their behavior or brain activity. Which research designs might be appropriate to address these questions with humans?

Probably the most rigorous design that one could apply in this context is a **quasi-experimental design,** which is much like an experimental design except that it makes use of naturally occurring groups rather than randomly assigned ones. For example, some humans grow up in more enriched environments than others, benefiting perhaps from specialized training or unique experiences. Instead of assigning people to these conditions, quasi-experimental designs take advantage of the fact that people are in different groups in the real world. In order to lessen confounds, however, it is important to make sure these naturally occurring groups are very similar on other traits except for the ones being studied.

Several quasi-experimental studies have focused on people who had received intensive musical training—something beyond the normal level of experience or enrichment. According to studies of brain images, people who have received intensive musical training, especially those who started it before age 7, have a thicker corpus callosum (the band of nerve fibers that connects the two halves of the brain) than nonmusicians (Schlaug et al., 1995). This finding means that musicians have more communication between the two sides of the brain than people who have not had such training. Further, brain imaging studies comparing the brains of experienced musicians with those of nonmusicians reveal increased brain growth relative to control subjects in regions associated with music-related skills (Schlaug et al., 1995). A more recent study reported that musicians have a larger cerebellum (an area involved in motor coordination) than nonmusicians (Hutchinson et al., 2003).

quasi-experimental design
Research method similar to an experimental design except that it makes use of naturally occurring groups rather than randomly assigning subjects to groups.

These findings suggest that musical training can change the brain, but because the researchers relied on naturally occurring groups and the groups were not matched, the results are correlational *rather than* causal. That is, we cannot conclude that musical training causes brain growth in particular areas of the brain. Only true experiments, with random assignment, allow us to draw conclusions about cause and effect, so any group differences observed in a quasi-experimental design cannot be attributed to a specific cause. Remember that correlation is not causation, although causation does require correlation.

Chapter Review

THE NATURE OF SCIENCE

- Science is about empirically testing our ideas and learning whether our understanding of the world is correct.

- The key attitudes of science are skepticism, openness to new ideas based on evidence, and intellectual honesty.

- The scientific method by which research is conducted can be summed up by OPTIC: Observing, Predicting, Testing, Interpreting, and Communicating. Scientists start with observations of the world, make predictions once they see a pattern, devise a study to test predictions, interpret results with the aid of statistics and decide whether the prediction was correct, and publish their work to clearly describe findings to others. These new findings lead to new predictions, and the whole process begins anew.

- Pseudoscience lacks cumulative progress, disregards empirical facts, lacks skepticism of its own assumptions, and vaguely describes how it came to its conclusions, which often stem from loose and distorted logic.

- In experimental designs, researchers randomly assign participants to conditions and carefully manipulate the predicted cause (independent variable), then look for differences in outcome (dependent variables). True experiments address the question "Does X cause Y?"

RESEARCH METHODS IN PSYCHOLOGY

- Psychologists use three types of research designs to test their ideas: descriptive designs, correlational designs, and experimental designs.

- In descriptive designs, researchers simply observe and describe what they see. They address the question "What is X?" They don't manipulate anything or have any predictions to test.

- In correlational designs, researchers measure two or more things carefully to see whether or not they are related. They address the question "Is X related to Y?" These designs use correlational statistics to interpret the results and to make and test hypotheses, but they do not allow researchers to draw any conclusions about causality.

- Researchers use correlation coefficients to assess the strength and direction of association between two variables.

- In experimental designs, researchers randomly assign participants to conditions and carefully manipulate the predicted cause (independent variable), then look for differences in outcome (dependent variables). True experiments address the question "Does X cause Y?"

CHALLENGING ASSUMPTIONS IN THE OBJECTIVITY OF EXPERIMENTAL RESEARCH

- Researchers can unintentionally affect the outcome of results if they are aware of the study's hypotheses.

- In order to lessen these effects, double-blind procedures, in which both the participant and the experimenter are blind to the study's hypotheses, need to be implemented.

COMMONLY USED MEASURES OF PSYCHOLOGICAL RESEARCH

- Psychological researchers draw on several types of tools to measure variables relevant to their research questions. These measures fall into three major categories: self-report, behavioral, and physiological.

- Self-reports are people's written or oral accounts of their thoughts, feelings, or actions.

- Behavioral measurements involve systematic observation of people's actions in either their normal life situations (naturalistic observation) or laboratory situations.

- Physiological measures include various types of measures of bodily responses. Each measure has strengths and weaknesses. By employing multiple measures, researchers offset the limitations of any given measure.

MAKING SENSE OF DATA WITH STATISTICS

- Descriptive statistics organize data for interpretation and help researchers evaluate their hypotheses. The mean is the arithmetic average of a set of data. The median is the score that separates the lower half of scores from the upper half.

- Variability is the spread between the lowest and highest values in a set of data; it is measured in terms of the standard deviation around the mean.

- Inferential statistics go beyond describing data and allow researchers to test hypotheses and rule out chance as an explanation for the findings.

RESEARCH ETHICS

- Ethics are standards of right and wrong that guide people's behavior.

- Professional ethics have been developed to protect the rights of humans and animals that participate in psychological research. Researchers must obtain informed consent from human participants before a study begins. Animals cannot provide informed consent, but strict ethical guidelines ensure humane living conditions and treatment.

BRINGING IT ALL TOGETHER: MAKING CONNECTIONS IN PSYCHOLOGICAL RESEARCH

- Research on environmental enrichment and brain growth using experimental designs with animal models and correlational studies with humans illustrates how numerous methodological issues unfold in a given research area.

Key Terms

behavioral measures, p. 56
case study, p. 43
confounding variable, p. 51
control group, p. 50
correlation coefficients, p. 47
correlational designs, p. 47
debriefing, p. 63
dependent variable, p. 49
descriptive designs, p. 43
descriptive statistics, p. 58
double-blind studies, p. 52
effect size, p. 47
ethics, p. 62
experiment, p. 49
experimental group, p. 50
experimenter expectancy effects, p. 52
frequency, p. 58

hypothesis, p. 38
independent variable, p. 49
inferential statistics, p. 59
institutional review boards (IRBs), p. 63
mean, p. 58
measures, p. 54
median, p. 58
meta-analysis, p. 47
mode, p. 58
naturalistic observation, p. 44
normal distribution, p. 58
physiological measures, p. 57
placebo, p. 50
population, p. 42
pseudoscience, p. 40
quasi-experimental design, p. 67
random assignment, p. 50

replication, p. 38
representative sample, p. 45
research designs, p. 41
samples, p. 42
scientific method, p. 38
scientific thinking, p. 37
self-fulfilling prophecy, p. 54
self-reports, p. 54
single-blind studies, p. 52
social desirability bias, p. 55
standard deviation, p. 58
statistics, p. 57
theory, p. 38
t-test, p. 59
variable, p. 41

Quick Quiz Answers

Quick Quiz 2.1: 1. d 2. b 3. a 4. c   **Quick Quiz 2.2:** 1. a 2. b 3. d 4. c 5. b   **Quick Quiz 2.3:** 1. b. 2. b

Quick Quiz 2.4: 1. b 2. a 3. d   **Quick Quiz 2.5:** 1. d 2. a 3. a   **Quick Quiz 2.6:** 1. c 2. e 3. b

3 The Biology of Behavior

Chapter Outline

Genes and Behavior
The Nervous System
The Brain
Challenging Assumptions about Neural Growth in the Adult Brain
Measuring the Brain
The Endocrine System
Chapter Review

Challenge Your Assumptions

True or False?

- Traits that are genetically influenced are set and unchanged after conception. (see page 77)

- Learning increases the number and structure of neurons in your brain. (see page 95)

- In people who are blind, vision areas of the brain do not function. (see page 103)

- New neurons grow in children but not adults. (see page 105)

See the painting in Figure 3.1. It is pleasing, colorful, and nicely done. It features realistic color, perspective, and shadowing. It seems, perhaps, not extraordinary—except by virtue of its maker. He cannot see at all.

Born blind to an impoverished family in Turkey, Esref Armagan started drawing at a young age; later he began painting with oils and acrylics. Armagan has been actively painting for over 35 years. His work strikes us not only for its beauty but also for how it depicts objects in a way that a sighted person would see them. How can someone who has never seen anything in his life create beautiful paintings that depict realistic images? It seems as if his brain is doing something that his eyes cannot.

You can experience how this is possible at the Tactile Dome, part of the Exploratorium in San Francisco. Once there, you enter a room full of common, recognizable objects, such as a cheese grater, an egg carton, and a sieve. You look at them and feel them.

Then you proceed through a pitch-black tunnel. As you find your way through it by touch, you feel the common objects you saw earlier. When you reach the end, you are prompted to think back and remember your way through the tunnel. Surprisingly, the memory of what you encountered along the path in the dark with your hands is visual! Your brain has taken a tactile experience and unwittingly converted it into a visual memory. How?

The Tactile Dome and the skills of Esref Armagan both suggest that our experience of the world is not a direct representation of what is out there. The brain can change our experiences—give us visual memories for tactile experiences. The brain is both fixed and flexible in how it acts. While most of us use the rear portion of our brains to process visual information, Esref Armagan uses that area when he paints by the feel of his hands.

In this chapter and the next, we will explore what is known about how the brain works, supports behavior, and is transformed by experience. Our main task in this chapter is to introduce the biological systems that are most relevant to a basic understanding of psychology. We will look at the role of heredity and evolution in shaping the brain and behavior, explore the workings of the nervous system, and learn of the relationship between behavior and chemicals called hormones. Given how much biological and environmental forces interact and influence each other, we use the term *softwire* to reflect this new way of thinking. As mentioned in Chapter 1, softwiring, in contrast to hardwiring, means that biological systems involved in thought and behavior—genes, brain structures, brain cells, and so on—are inherited but open to modification from the environment (Herbert & Rich, 1999; Ottersen, 2010). Much of who we are is more softwired than hardwired.

FIGURE **3.1**

PAINTING BY ESREF ARMAGAN, A BLIND PAINTER. Besides being beautiful to look at, Armagan's vivid, realistic paintings and drawings challenge conventional thinking about the brain and its ability to adapt and overcome limitations imposed on it.

 Can you think of how Armagan is able to paint with color, shadow, and perspective, even though he has never seen any of these?

GENES AND BEHAVIOR

We seldom have trouble accepting the idea that heredity is responsible for outward family resemblances, such as the shape of the nose and face, height, and the color of hair and skin. But when it comes to behavior, many of us are uncomfortable with the idea that heredity might determine what we think and do. Research has revealed that heredity strongly influences our behavior and experience, although it does not operate in a simple, deterministic way.

Before we can explore how our hereditary material and behavior are linked, we must first determine the structures and mechanisms involved in heredity. Your genetic material is composed mainly of **DNA (deoxyribonucleic acid)** and is passed down in the form of chromosomes from both your mother and your father. A **chromosome** is a very long thread of DNA wrapped around proteins to hold it all together. You inherit 23 chromosomes from one parent and 23 chromosomes from the other parent such that you end up with *23 pairs* of chromosomes (46 individual chromosomes) in every cell of your body. The main ingredients of DNA are called nucleotides, of which there are four, symbolized with letters: A for adenine, G for guanine, T for thymine, and C for cytosine. A DNA molecule wrapped up in one of your chromosomes can have hundreds of millions of these letters attached end to end, forming a sequence (for example, . . . AGTGAGGTCAC . . .). These four letters are arranged in a unique sequence in every individual human on the planet—this is what makes you genetically unique (unless you have an identical twin brother or sister). Together, the total amount of your unique DNA is referred to as your **genome.**

Within your genome, some of the letters code for information that will be turned into a working component of your cell, such as a protein. **Genes** are what we call the segments of DNA that contain this coding information. The proteins that are coded from genes in turn make up most chemicals and structures in the body (see Figure 3.2). As a result, genes have a profound

DNA (deoxyribonucleic acid)
A large molecule that contains genes.

chromosome
A coiled-up thread of DNA.

genome
All the genetic information in DNA.

genes
Small segments of DNA that contain information for producing proteins.

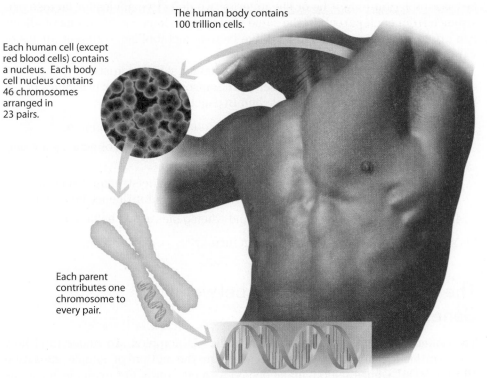

The human body contains 100 trillion cells.

Each human cell (except red blood cells) contains a nucleus. Each body cell nucleus contains 46 chromosomes arranged in 23 pairs.

Each parent contributes one chromosome to every pair.

Each chromosome contains numerous genes, segments of DNA that contain instructions to make proteins—the building blocks of life.

FIGURE **3.2**
DNA, CHROMOSOMES, AND THE HUMAN CELL. Every cell in the human body contains the same genetic material distributed in 23 pairs of chromosomes.

control over physical characteristics, such as height or hair color, by directing the synthesis of proteins. In addition, there are genes that code for proteins responsible for making up your brain and the chemicals it needs to make you feel happy or sad. Thus, genes play an important role in shaping how you think and feel.

Individuals in a population are different from one another with regard to a given trait—such as eye color, height, or personality—because of genetic differences, however small those differences may be. For example, the ability to digest dairy products (such as milk) as an adult can depend on a single letter change in the vast sequence of your genome. Every human can metabolize lactose (digest milk) as an infant, but most people lose this ability with age, because the activity of lactase (the protein that breaks down lactose) decreases. Some humans, however, have a change, or **mutation,** in their genetic sequence that allows lactase activity to persist into adulthood, so they can eat and drink dairy products without getting an upset stomach. This means that some people have one form of the gene, which allows lactase persistence (they are lactose tolerant), and some people have another form, which results in lactase nonpersistence (they are lactose intolerant). These different forms of a gene are known as **alleles** (W. R. Clark & Grunstein, 2000; Starr & Taggart, 2004).

Remember that you have *two* copies of every gene, one from your mom and one from your dad. Sometimes the genes have the same form, or allele. You could receive the allele for lactase persistence from your mom and the same allele from your dad. This would allow you to digest dairy products easily in adulthood. However, what if your mom gave you the same allele but your dad gave you the "bad" allele of lactase that prevents metabolism of dairy products? The lactase persistence allele is dominant to the defective allele. **Dominant alleles** show their effect even if there is only one copy of that allele in the pair. So if you have one lactase persistence allele and one defective allele, chances are you will still be able to digest some dairy products. Alternatively, **recessive alleles** show their effects only when both alleles are the same. Consequently, a person will be lactose intolerant only if he or she inherits two defective alleles for lactose persistence from each parent. In the same way that various combinations of alleles can affect something physiological like lactose metabolism, different alleles of various genes can also affect behavior.

To understand how heredity affects behavior, psychologists turn to the science of **behavioral genetics** (Fuller & Thompson, 1960). Four principles of behavioral genetics are especially relevant in psychology:

1. The relationship between specific genes and behavior is complex.
2. Most specific behaviors derive from dozens or hundreds of genes—not one or two.
3. By studying twins and adoptees, behavioral geneticists may disentangle the contributions of heredity and environment that influence behavior.
4. The environment influences how and when genes affect behavior.

Let's consider each of these principles in turn.

The Complex Connection between Genes and Behavior

The connection between genes and behavior is complex. To understand how genes influence behavior, we must abandon the notion of simple causation (Rutter, 2006). Genes seldom make behaviors a certainty. For example, no single gene causes anxiety. Both genetic and environmental factors make anxiety more likely to trouble some people than others.

mutation
A change in genetic sequence.

alleles
Different forms of a gene.

dominant alleles
Alleles that show their effect even if there is only one allele for that trait in the pair.

recessive alleles
Alleles that show their effects only when both alleles are the same.

behavioral genetics
The scientific study of the role of heredity in behavior.

In a few cases, having a specific gene guarantees an outcome—such as the incurable neuromuscular disease called Huntington's—but these outcomes are primarily physical, not behavioral. Typically, a specific gene plays only a small part in creating a given behavior, and genetic influence is only part of the story. Environmental events such as smoking during pregnancy, early childhood experiences, stress or trauma, and enriched environments all interact with genes to make specific behaviors more or less likely.

Polygenic Influence on Behavior

The second principle of behavioral genetics states that traits tend to be influenced by many genes (W. R. Clark & Grunstein, 2000; Hamer & Copeland, 1998). Relatively few human traits result from single genes. As stated earlier, they tend to be physical rather than behavioral characteristics. Traits that are determined by a single gene, such as Huntington's disease, are referred to as **monogenic.**

However, the number of potential outcomes for most traits and behaviors is not small. For example, there is wide variation in intelligence because numerous genes contribute to it. Traits that are determined by the interaction of many genes are referred to as **polygenic.** Other examples of polygenic traits are skin color, mental disorders, personality traits (such as whether a person is likely to be adventurous), height, and weight (W. R. Clark & Grunstein, 2000; Ebstein, 2006; L. M. Evans et al., 2007).

Genes and the Environment

The third principle of behavioral genetics is that teasing apart and identifying genetic and environmental influences on behavior require special techniques. The extent to which a characteristic is influenced by genetics is known as **heritability.** Researchers use twin-adoption studies and gene-by-environment studies to study heritability.

In order to tease apart the role of genes and environment on behavior experimentally, researchers would have to hold one of these factors constant while varying the other one. That is hard to do, because for obvious ethical reasons researchers cannot assign people to grow up in the same or different environments. Nor can researchers assign people to be either genetically alike or different. Fortunately, nature does both of these things for us. Researchers take advantage of genetically similar and different people by studying twins, siblings, and unrelated individuals reared together or apart.

Twin-Adoption Studies **Fraternal twins** develop from two different eggs fertilized by two different sperm, as are any two siblings born at separate times. Thus, genetically speaking, fraternal twins are no more alike or different than are nontwin brothers and sisters. **Identical twins** develop from a single fertilized egg, which splits into two independent cells. As a result, identical twins develop from two embryos with identical genetic information. Fraternal and identical twins provide a natural population for researchers to determine how much of a trait is due to genetics and how much is due to environment. The best way to untangle

Connection

Genetic influence accounts for about 50% of the differences in performance on intelligence tests, leaving about the same amount to be explained by nongenetic influences.

See "The Nature and Nurture of Human Intelligence," Chapter 10, "Intelligence, Problem Solving, and Creativity," p.373.

monogenic
The hereditary passing on of traits determined by a single gene.

polygenic
The process by which many genes interact to create a single characteristic.

heritability
The extent to which a characteristic is influenced by genetics.

fraternal twins
Twins that develop from two different eggs fertilized by two different sperm.

identical twins
Twins that develop from a single fertilized egg that splits into two independent cells.

Actors Maggie and Jake Gyllenhaal inherited their blue eyes from their parents. Blue eyes are a recessive trait, which means that each parent must possess at least one allele for blue eyes.

Twins form a natural population for teasing apart the influences of genetics and environment on development.

the effects of genetics and environment is to study twins who are adopted, which is what **twin-adoption studies** do. The logic of the twin-adoption approach is simple yet powerful. Identical twins are 100% alike genetically, whereas fraternal twins, like all siblings, share only 50% of their genes.

Adopted children and their adoptive parents and siblings share no genes. If heredity strongly influences a trait, then the greater the genetic similarity, the greater the similarity on the trait should be. Similarity should be strongest in identical twins reared together and next in identical twins reared apart. It should be modest in siblings reared together and biological parent-offspring. Similarity should be weakest in adopted siblings and adoptive parent-offspring. As we will see in later chapters, this pattern holds for intelligence, mental disorders, and even personality, suggesting a moderately strong genetic component to these outcomes.

twin-adoption studies
Research into hereditary influence on twins, both identical and fraternal, who were raised apart (adopted) and who were raised together.

gene-by-environment interaction research
The method of studying heritability by comparing genetic markers; it allows researchers to assess how genetic differences interact with the environment to produce certain behaviors in some people but not in others.

Gene-by-Environment Studies   The second technique in the study of heritability, **gene-by-environment interaction research,** allows researchers to assess how genetic differences interact with the environment to produce certain behavior in some people but not in others (Moffitt, Caspi, & Rutter, 2005; Thapar, Langley, & Asherson, 2007).

Instead of using twins, family members, and adoptees to vary genetic similarity, gene-by-environment studies directly measure genetic variation in parts of the genome itself and examine how such variation interacts with different kinds of environments to produce different behaviors. Individuals do not differ in whether they have a gene but rather in the form, or allele, that gene takes. For example, the same gene in different people might vary in the number of particular DNA sequences it has.

Some DNA sequences are long in some people but short in others. Differences in the length of DNA sequences represent a *genetic marker*. Through gene-by-environment studies, researchers have learned that genetic markers interact with a stressful environment to make depression more likely in some people (short DNA sequence) than in others (long DNA sequence; Caspi, Sugden, et al., 2003; Kendler et al., 2005).

Epigenetics: How the Environment Changes Gene Expression

genotype
The entire genetic makeup of an organism.

epigenetics
The study of changes in the way genes are turned on or off without a change in the sequence of DNA.

The fourth—and, in many ways, the most important—principle of behavioral genetics is a relatively new one: The unique and incomparable **genotype,** or genetic makeup, that each of us is born with is not the end point but the starting point of gene expression. Genes are switched on and off by many different factors, and our experiences and environmental exposure, starting in the womb, contribute to these factors. This principle is seen most clearly in **epigenetics** (Meaney, 2010; Rutter, 2006). Epigenetics is the study of changes in the way genes are expressed—that is, are activated (turned "on") or deactivated (turned "off")—without changing the sequence of DNA. Put differently, epigenetics involves heritable changes to DNA that are independent of the genetic sequence yet influence its expression. This means that experience (nurture) shapes our nature.

Currently, the most well understood mechanism of epigenetic change involves the *methylation process* of DNA. Remarkably, when we eat or drink certain things, exercise, or are exposed to particular chemicals in the environment, molecular tags known as methyl groups can get attached to specific nucleotides in the DNA, often targeting cytosines (see Figure 3.3). These tags turn off particular genes, regardless of the actual genetic sequence around them.

The food we eat, the drugs we take, and our exposure to certain chemicals in the environment, among other things, can have epigenetic consequences. Contrary to what many people think, genes are not destiny. They are simply the starting point for biological structures. Many things—including experience—can turn genes on or off. Epigenetic effects have been demonstrated in a host of psychological traits—including attention deficit hyperactivity disorder (ADHD), aggression, dementia, obesity, and anxiety, just to name a few (Curley et al., 2011; Gluckman & Hanson, 2008; Mill & Petronis, 2008; Sweatt, 2010).

What is even more amazing is that these environmentally produced tags can be inherited—passed on from parent to offspring. In other words, genetics is not the only way inheritance works. It also works via epigenetics (Meaney, 2010; Zimmer, 2008). An activated gene in your grandparent that gets turned off environmentally in one of your parents can be inherited by you as a deactivated gene. This secondary form of inheritance via epigenetics is sometimes referred to as *soft inheritance* to contrast it with traditional genetically based inheritance (Graff & Mansury, 2008). The term *soft inheritance* is similar and related to *softwiring*—both express how nature and nurture work side-by-side.

Epigenetics offers one explanation for why identical twins—whose genomes are 100% alike—end up being not completely identical on numerous traits. For instance, they do not have identical fingerprints. Recent longitudinal research shows that differences in epigenetic tags in identical twins already exist in early to middle childhood and that these differences can be related to personality differences in twins (Kaminsky et al., 2008; Wong et al., 2010). In short, although identical twins share 100% of their genotype, their **phenotype**—or their observed characteristics—may be subtly (even strikingly) different because different epigenetic tags are turning different genes on or off.

Obesity is one behavioral and genetic problem that has been the focus in much epigenetic research. Obese mothers are more likely to have overweight children with an increased risk of Type II diabetes, likely due to both nature and nurture factors (Whitaker et al., 2010). Environmental factors, such as diet or gastric bypass surgery, may modify genetic expression of obesity and prevent the "transmission" of obesity to their offspring (Kral et al., 2006; Patti, 2013; Smith et al., 2009). A large-scale study of the effects of maternal weight surgery on offspring found that obesity-related genes were expressed differently in the offspring of the women who had had gastric bypass surgery before pregnancy compared to the offspring of those who had not (Guénard et al., 2013). These changes in the genes (methylation) correlated with hormonal factors that should regulate weight gain. So by taking this step to reduce their weight, these mothers also changed the future of their children. Genes are not destiny.

Much of the research findings in epigenetics have focused on maternal factors that impact gene expression. Recently, scientists have reported evidence of *paternal* epigenetic effects, at least in rodents. Specifically, chronic stress during the father's

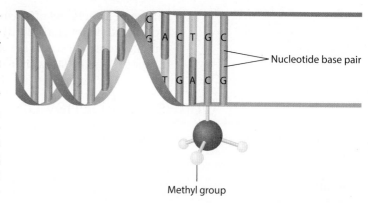

Nucleotide base pair

Methyl group

FIGURE **3.3**

THE EPIGENOME: METHYL GROUPS TAG DNA TO TURN GENES OFF. Methyl groups are tags that attach to DNA itself. These tags act as off switches and silence a particular gene. Incredibly, these methyl group tags come about purely by what happens to us—our diet, drugs, or exposure to certain chemicals. Genes, therefore, are not destiny but simply a starting point for biological structures.

Challenge Your Assumptions

True or False? Traits that are genetically influenced are set and unchanging after conception.

False: Genes continue to get turned on or off throughout our lives by what we eat, drink, or are exposed to.

phenotype
An organism's observed characteristics.

The field of study known as epigenetics examines how experience can turn genes on or off.
What implications does this have for what we eat, drink, and are exposed to?

life span affects the offspring by selectively changing the genetic material in the sperm (Rodgers et al., 2013). Both male and female offspring of mice fathers that endured chronic stress across the life span showed a suppressed responsiveness of the HPA axis (stress hormone system; see Chapter 12) under the stress.

Quick Quiz 3.1: Genes and Behavior

1. Genes occur in pairs, or alternate forms of each other, called
   a. chromosomes.
   b. alleles.
   c. base-pairs.
   d. ribosomes.

2. Why are twin-adoption studies powerful ways to untangle the effects of genes and the environment on thought and behavior?
   a. They allow both genetic and environmental similarity to be compared and contrasted.
   b. Twins share genes.

   c. They allow for understanding epigenetic influences.
   d. They allow researchers to experimentally manipulate genetic and environmental similarity.

3. Nurturing behavior in rats can produce calmer, less stressed offspring because genes that are involved in stress reactions are turned off. This is an example of
   a. epigenetics.
   b. genetic engineering.
   c. recessive genes.
   d. dominant genes.

Answers can be found at the end of the chapter.

THE NERVOUS SYSTEM

The human genome contains an estimated 20,000 to 25,000 genes (National Human Genome Research Institute, 2010). At least half of these genes code for proteins in the brain, where they play a central role in seeing, hearing, thinking, memory, learning, movement, and all other behavior. The brain mediates all of our experiences and orchestrates our responses to those experiences.

The nervous system controls all the actions and automatic processes of the body. Ultimately, everything we experience and do results from the activity of nerve cells, which are organized in a net of circuits far more complex than any electrical system you could imagine.

Organization of the Nervous System

central nervous system (CNS)
The part of the nervous system that comprises the brain and spinal cord.

peripheral nervous system
The part of the nervous system that comprises all the nerve cells in the body outside the central nervous system.

somatic nervous system
The nerve cells of the peripheral nervous system that transmit sensory information to the central nervous system (CNS) and those that transmit information from the CNS to the skeletal muscles.

autonomic nervous system (ANS)
All the nerves of the peripheral nervous system that serve involuntary systems of the body, such as the internal organs and glands.

sympathetic nervous system
The branch of the autonomic nervous system that activates bodily systems in times of emergency.

parasympathetic nervous system
The branch of the autonomic nervous system that usually relaxes or returns the body to a less active, restful state.

The human nervous system has two main parts and several components, as depicted in Figure 3.4. It is divided into the **central nervous system (CNS),** which includes the brain and spinal cord, and the **peripheral nervous system,** which consists of all the other nerve cells in the body. The peripheral nervous system includes the somatic nervous system and the autonomic nervous system. The **somatic nervous system** transmits sensory information to the brain and spinal cord and from the brain and spinal cord to the skeletal muscles. The **autonomic nervous system (ANS)** serves the involuntary systems of the body, such as the internal organs and glands.

Autonomic means "self-governing," and to a large extent the structures served by the autonomic nervous system control bodily processes over which we have little conscious control, such as changes in heart rate and blood pressure. The ANS has two main branches: the **sympathetic nervous system** and the **parasympathetic nervous system.** The nerves of these systems control muscles in organs such as the stomach, small intestine, and bladder and in glands such as the sweat glands. The sympathetic branch of the ANS is responsible for what the physiologist Walter Cannon (1939) labeled the *fight-or-flight response;* it activates bodily systems in times of emergency by increasing the heart rate, dilating the pupils of the eyes, or inhibiting digestion. The function of the parasympathetic branch of the ANS is largely one of relaxation, returning the body to a less active, restful state. All of the systems that are aroused by the sympathetic

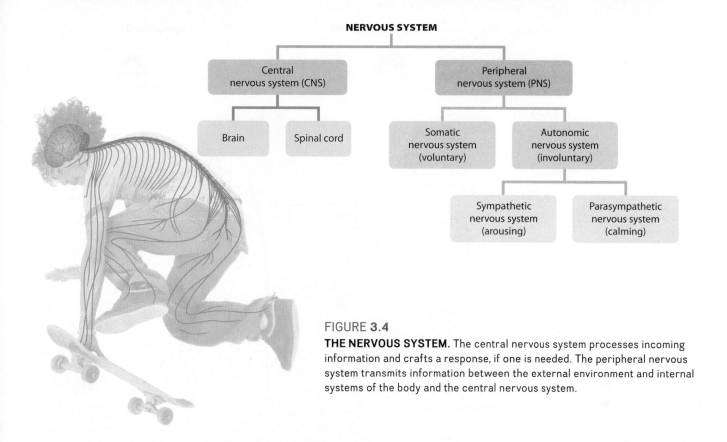

NERVOUS SYSTEM

- Central nervous system (CNS)
  - Brain
  - Spinal cord
- Peripheral nervous system (PNS)
  - Somatic nervous system (voluntary)
  - Autonomic nervous system (involuntary)
    - Sympathetic nervous system (arousing)
    - Parasympathetic nervous system (calming)

FIGURE **3.4**

THE NERVOUS SYSTEM. The central nervous system processes incoming information and crafts a response, if one is needed. The peripheral nervous system transmits information between the external environment and internal systems of the body and the central nervous system.

nervous system are relaxed by the parasympathetic nervous system (see Figure 3.5). Because of its effects on these various bodily systems, the ANS produces many of the physical sensations we experience during emotional arousal, such as a racing heart or sweaty palms.

The Cells of the Nervous System: Glial Cells and Neurons

Without a nervous system, we would have no sensory experiences—no seeing, hearing, touching, tasting, smelling, or feeling. We would also have no thoughts, memories, or emotions. Everything we sense or do is accomplished by means of nerve cells.

The central nervous system is made up of two types of cells: glial cells and neurons. *Glia* is the Greek word for "glue." Indeed, **glial cells** serve the primary function of holding the CNS together. For years their primary functions were thought to be structural support for the CNS and the removal of cellular debris (Kandel, 2000b). We now know that glial cells also play an important role in communication between neurons, produce the material that insulates neurons (myelin), aid cell metabolism, help form the blood-brain barrier, play a key role in the control of breathing, regulate neuronal transmission, and may play an important role in repair after brain injury (Ballanyi, Panaitescu, & Ruangkittisakul, 2010; Benner et al., 2013; Eroglu & Barres, 2010; Parpura & Verkhratsky, 2012; Verkhratsky, Rodrıguez, & Parpura, 2012).

Neurons are the cells that process and transmit information throughout the nervous system. Within the brain, neurons receive, integrate, and generate messages. By most estimates, there are more than 10 billion neurons in the human brain. Each neuron has approximately 10,000 connections to other neurons, making for trillions of neural connections in the human brain (Hyman, 2005; Nauta & Feirtag, 1979). Thus, it is understandable why some

glial cells
Central nervous system cells that provide structural support, promote efficient communication between neurons, and serve as scavengers, removing cellular debris.

neurons
The cells that process and transmit information in the nervous system.

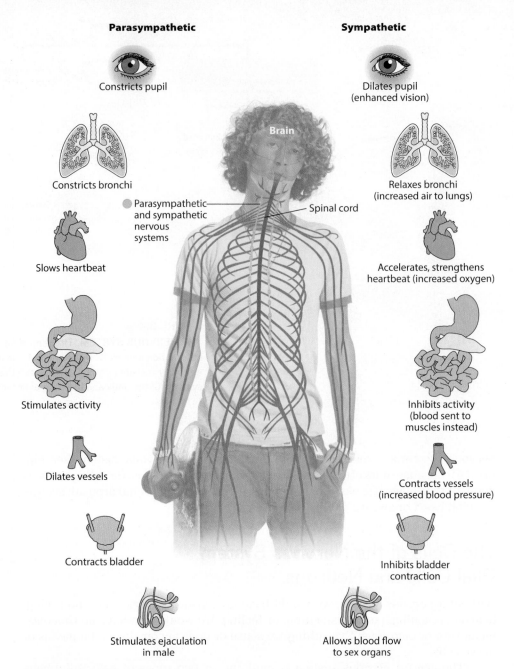

Parasympathetic

Constricts pupil

Constricts bronchi

Slows heartbeat

● Parasympathetic and sympathetic nervous systems

Stimulates activity

Dilates vessels

Contracts bladder

Stimulates ejaculation in male

Sympathetic

Dilates pupil (enhanced vision)

Relaxes bronchi (increased air to lungs)

Accelerates, strengthens heartbeat (increased oxygen)

Inhibits activity (blood sent to muscles instead)

Contracts vessels (increased blood pressure)

Inhibits bladder contraction

Allows blood flow to sex organs

Brain

Spinal cord

FIGURE 3.5

THE SYMPATHETIC AND PARASYMPATHETIC NERVOUS SYSTEMS. The sympathetic nervous system prepares the body for action, whereas the parasympathetic nervous system returns it to a relaxed and resting state.

scientists consider the human brain to be one of the most complex structures in the known universe. Over the last 125 years, three major principles of neuroscience have emerged concerning the neuron and how it communicates with other neurons (Kandel, 2006):

1. Neurons are the building blocks of the nervous system. All the major structures of the brain are composed of neurons.

2. Information travels within a neuron in the form of an electrical signal by action potentials.

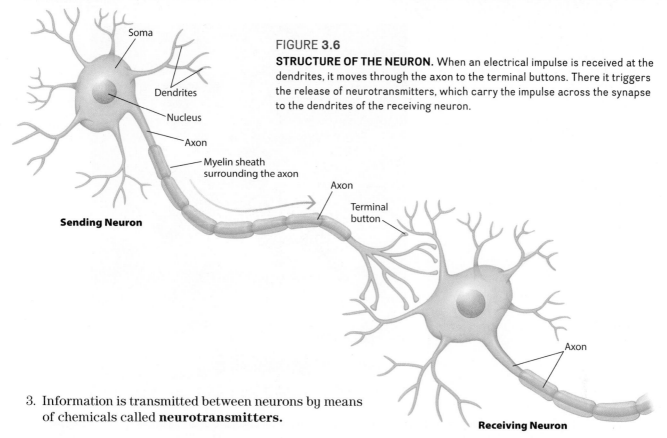

Soma

Dendrites

Nucleus

Axon

Myelin sheath
surrounding the axon

Sending Neuron

Axon

Terminal
button

Axon

Receiving Neuron

FIGURE **3.6**

STRUCTURE OF THE NEURON. When an electrical impulse is received at the dendrites, it moves through the axon to the terminal buttons. There it triggers the release of neurotransmitters, which carry the impulse across the synapse to the dendrites of the receiving neuron.

3. Information is transmitted between neurons by means of chemicals called **neurotransmitters.**

Let's explore each of these principles to better understand the mechanisms of brain function and behavior.

The Structure and Types of Neurons   Whereas most cells in the body have a round shape, neurons are spidery, with long branches and projections. Neurons are so small that they cannot be seen with the naked eye; only a strong microscope can magnify them enough to be viewed and described. In the late 1800s, the Spanish anatomist Santiago Ramón y Cajal deciphered the precise nature and structure of nerve cells, which he named neurons. It was Ramón y Cajal who identified the three major parts of the neuron: cell body, dendrites, and axon.

As in other cells, the cell body, or **soma,** of the neuron contains a *nucleus* and other components needed for cell maintenance and function (see Figure 3.6). The genes that direct neural change and growth lie within the nucleus itself. Extending from one side of the soma is a long projection called an **axon,** which transmits electrical impulses toward the adjacent neuron. On the other side of the soma are **dendrites,** fingerlike projections that receive incoming messages from other neurons.

The axons of some neurons are wrapped in a fatty **myelin sheath.** Just like rubber around an electrical wire, the myelin sheath insulates the axon, so that the impulse travels more efficiently, strengthening the connection to adjacent neurons. The process of *myelination* is a gradual one that starts before birth, is facilitated in breast-fed babies, and continues into early adulthood (Deoni et al., 2013; R. D. Fields, 2008). The glial cells myelinate axons throughout the nervous system (Nave, 2010). The junction between the axon and the adjacent neuron is known as the **synapse.** At the end of the axon, at each synapse, is a **terminal button** containing tiny sacs of neurotransmitters. When an electrical impulse reaches the terminal button, it triggers the release of neurotransmitter molecules into the gap between neurons, known as the *synaptic cleft.* The neurotransmitter carries the signal across the synaptic cleft to the next neuron.

neurotransmitters
Chemicals that transmit information between neurons.

soma
The cell body of the neuron.

axon
A long projection that extends from a neuron's soma; it transmits electrical impulses toward the adjacent neuron and stimulates the release of neurotransmitters.

dendrites
Fingerlike projections from a neuron's soma that receive incoming messages from other neurons.

myelin sheath
The fatty substance wrapped around some axons, which insulates the axon, making the nerve impulse travel more efficiently.

synapse
The junction between an axon and the adjacent neuron, where information is transmitted from one neuron to another.

terminal button
A little knob at the end of an axon; it contains tiny sacs of neurotransmitters.

Sensory and motor neurons working in concert with the brain make this sprinter's elegant strides possible.

Connection

Mirror neurons support learning by imitation as well as empathy.

See "The Developing Infant and Child," Chapter 5, "Human Development," p. 167; "Imitation, Mirror Neurons, and Learning," Chapter 8, "Learning," p. 312; and "Prosocial Behavior," Chapter 14, "Social Behavior," p. 535.

sensory neurons
Nerve cells that receive incoming sensory information from the sense organs (eye, ear, skin, tongue, nose).

motor neurons
Nerve cells that carry commands for movement from the brain to the muscles of the body.

mirror neurons
Nerve cells that are active when we observe others performing an action, as well as when we are performing the same action.

interneurons
Neurons that communicate only with other neurons.

There are three kinds of neurons: sensory neurons, motor neurons, and interneurons. **Sensory neurons** receive incoming sensory information from the sense organs (eyes, ears, skin, tongue, and nose). Any sensation you receive—anything you see, hear, touch, taste, or smell—activates sensory neurons, which take the message to the brain for processing.

Motor neurons take commands from the brain and carry them to the muscles of the body. Each time you move any muscle in your body, intentionally or not, motor neurons are at work. Researchers have identified motor neurons that are active when monkeys observe others performing an action, as well as when the monkeys undertake the same action (Rizzolatti et al., 1996). Neurons that behave this way, called **mirror neurons,** appear to play an important role in learning (Rizzolatti & Craighero, 2004).

The most definitive work on mirror neurons has been conducted on monkeys because it has been possible to record directly from single neurons deep in their brains. So far, this has not been done with humans, but there is indirect evidence of systems of neurons acting as mirrors in humans (Debes, 2010). Preliminary evidence shows that mirror neuron systems are activated when we process social cues from others (Mainieri et al., 2013). The discovery of mirror neurons has changed the way we understand a wide range of human experience, including how we feel empathy toward others.

Interneurons communicate only with other neurons. Most interneurons connect neurons in one part of the brain with neurons in another part. Others receive information from sensory neurons and transmit it to motor neurons for action. If you touched a sharp object, interneurons in your spinal cord would receive pain information from sensory neurons in your fingers and communicate it to motor neurons in the muscles of your arm, so that you could pull away. Interneurons are the most common kind of neuron in the brain, outnumbering sensory and motor neurons by at least 10 to 1 (Nauta & Feirtag, 1979). They play a crucial role in the inhibition of impulses between one brain region and another (Haider et al., 2006). Dysfunction in these important inhibitory circuits has been implicated in disorders associated with overexcitation in the brain, such as epilepsy and schizophrenia (Marin, 2012).

Neural Communication   Neural communication is a two-step process: action potential and neurotransmission.

The Action Potential   The **action potential,** an electrical and chemical process, is the positively charged impulse that moves one way down an axon. This happens by virtue of changes in the neuron itself. The neuron, like all cells in the body, is surrounded by a membrane that is somewhat permeable, letting only certain particles move through it. The fluid inside and outside the cell contains electrically charged particles called **ions.** Positively charged sodium and potassium ions and negatively charged chloride ions are the most common. Channels in the membrane of the neuron allow ions to flow between the inside and outside of the cell. Some of these channels are always open. Others, called *voltage-dependent channels,* open only when certain electrical conditions are met.

Due to the flow of ions into and out of the neuron, there is a difference in charge inside the cell compared to outside at all times. In the resting state, there is an excess of negatively charged particles inside the axon, whereas the fluid outside the axon has a positive charge. When a neuron is at rest, the charge difference, known as a *potential,* between the inside and the outside of the axon is -70 millivolts (mV). This value is the **resting potential** of the neuronal membrane (see Figure 3.7a).

Neurons do not stay at rest, however. An incoming impulse—which may have been stimulated by events as different as pressure to the skin and the thought of a loved one—can temporarily change the potential. How does this happen? A message received from sense receptors in the skin or from other neurons changes the axonal membrane's permeability, especially to positively charged sodium ions. If an incoming impulse increases the positive charge inside the neuron to a certain threshold, the neuron becomes *depolarized* and fires an action potential, a surge in positive charge (see Figure 3.7b). The sodium channels at the top of the axon fly open, and positively charged sodium ions pour into the cell. The influx of sodium leads to a brief spike in positive charge, raising the membrane potential from -70 mV to $+40$ mV.

Once initiated, the action potential causes sodium channels to close and potassium voltage-dependent channels to open (see Figure 3.7c). As positively charged potassium ions flow out of the cell, the membrane potential returns to its resting state of -70 mV. While the neuron is returning to its resting state, it temporarily becomes supernegatively charged. During this brief period, known as the **refractory period,** the neuron cannot generate another action potential.

We can summarize the electrical changes in the neuron from resting to action potential to refractory period and back to the resting state as follows (see Figure 3.7d):

1. Resting potential is -70 mV.

2. If an incoming impulse causes sufficient depolarization, voltage-dependent sodium channels open and sodium ions flood into the neuron.

3. The influx of positively charged sodium ions quickly raises the membrane potential to $+40$ mV. This surge in positive charge inside the cell is the action potential.

4. When the membrane potential reaches $+40$ mV, the sodium channels close and potassium channels open. The outward flow of positively charged potassium ions restores the negative charge inside the cell.

This process repeats all along the axon, as the impulse moves toward the synapse. As the action potential subsides in one area, it immediately depolarizes the

action potential
The impulse of positive charge that runs one way down an axon.

ions
Chemically charged particles that predominate in bodily fluids; they are found both inside and outside cells.

resting potential
The difference in electrical charge between the inside and outside of an axon when the neuron is at rest.

refractory period
The span of time, after an action potential has been generated, when the neuron is returning to its resting state and the neuron cannot generate an action potential.

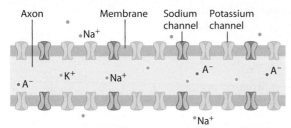

(a) Resting potential: Time 1.
In the resting neuron, the fluid outside the axon contains a higher concentration of positive ions than the inside of the axon, which contains many negatively charged anions (A–).

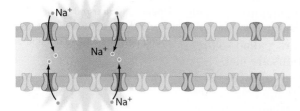

(b) Action potential: Time 2.
An action potential occurs in response to stimulation of the neuron. Sodium channels in the axonal membrane open, and positively charged sodium ions (NA+) pour into the axon, temporarily raising the charge inside the axon up to +40 mV.

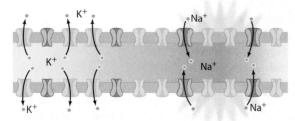

(c) Resting potential restored: Time 3.
As the impulse moves on down the axon, potassium (K+) channels open, allowing more K+ to flood out of the cell, restoring the negative resting potential (–70 mV).

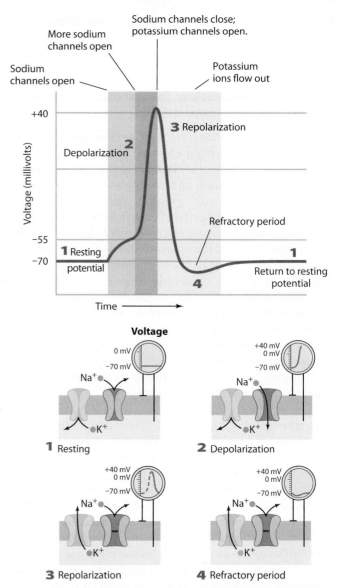

(d) This graph depicts the electrical changes that occur during each stage of an action potential (resting, depolarization, repolarization, refractory period). The top portion shows changes in voltage over time as measured by direct recording from single neurons in animal research. The lower four pictures show the membrane changes that correspond to each stage. The electrical changes of an action potential occur in a few thousandths of a second. During the refractory period, no new action potential can be generated.

FIGURE **3.7**

HOW NEURONS FIRE: MEMBRANES AND VOLTAGE CHANGES IN ACTION POTENTIALS.
What does a baby's grip of our fingers feel like? Thousands of sensory neurons fire and send signals to the sensory cortex, where the touch sense is processed. How does a neural firing (action potential) happen?

next portion of membrane, causing sodium channels to open there, continuing (*propagating*) the action potential. Like a wave, the action potential travels along the axon, until it reaches the terminal buttons. In myelinated neurons, the action potential travels faster still, as depolarization occurs only at gaps in the myelin sheath and the action potential jumps from gap to gap (see Figure 3.6).

How fast are action potentials? In the 1920s, Edgar Douglas Adrian recorded individual action potentials of sensory neurons and confirmed a speed of about

100 feet per second (Kandel, 2006). Adrian's work also confirmed the existence of a threshold—a point of no return. Once the charge inside the neuron exceeds threshold (and *only* if it exceeds threshold), the action potential fires. This is known as the **all-or-none principle;** that is, either an action potential fires or it does not.

Neurotransmission The arrival of an action potential at the terminal buttons of a neuron triggers the second phase in neural communication—the release of neurotransmitters into the synaptic cleft to pass on the impulse to other neurons. Neurotransmitters are packaged in sacs called **synaptic vesicles** in the terminal button. When an action potential reaches the terminal button, the vesicles fuse with the cell membrane of the terminal and release neurotransmitter molecules into the synaptic cleft, where they may be taken up by receptors in the dendrites of adjacent neurons (J. H. Schwartz, 2000).

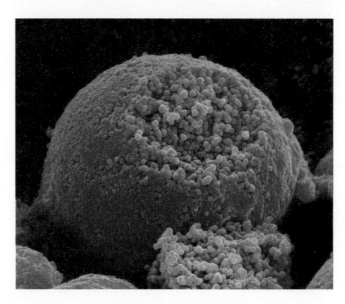

In this image taken by a scanning electron microscope, we see a terminal button that has been broken to show vesicles (colored balls). Neurotransmitters reside in the vesicles.

Neurotransmitters bind with receptors in the receiving, or *postsynaptic*, neuron in a lock-and-key type of arrangement (see Figure 3.8). There are different types of neurotransmitters, each of which binds only with a specific receptor. For example, some receptors bind only with the neurotransmitter acetylcholine. If other neurotransmitters come in contact with acetylcholine receptors, they will not bind and no signal will be transmitted.

Not all of the neurotransmitter molecules that are released into the synaptic cleft bind with receptors. Usually, excess neurotransmitter remains in the synaptic cleft and needs to be removed. There are two removal methods: (1) **enzymatic degradation,** in which enzymes specific to that neurotransmitter bind with the neurotransmitter and destroy it, and (2) **reuptake,** which returns excess neurotransmitter to the sending, or *presynaptic*, neuron for storage in vesicles and future use. Even the neurotransmitter that binds to the dendrites of the *postsynaptic* neuron does not stay there. Eventually, it disengages from the receptor and floats away.

After a neurotransmitter binds to a receptor on the postsynaptic neuron, a series of changes occurs in that neuron's cell membrane. These small changes in membrane potential are called **graded potentials.** Unlike action potentials, these are not "all-or-none." Rather, they affect the likelihood that an action potential will occur in the receiving neuron. Some neurotransmitters, called *inhibitory* neurotransmitters, create graded potentials that decrease the likelihood of a neuron firing. One such neurotransmitter is GABA (gamma-aminobutyric acid). In contrast, *excitatory* neurotransmitters create graded potentials that increase the likelihood of an action potential. **Glutamate** is the most common excitatory neurotransmitter in the brain.

The excitatory potentials bring the neuron closer to threshold, while the inhibitory potentials bring it further away from threshold. The soma in the postsynaptic neuron *integrates* the various graded potentials. If the integrated message from these graded potentials depolarizes the axon enough to cross the threshold, then an action potential will occur.

Common Neurotransmitters

Within the past century, researchers have discovered at least 60 distinct neurotransmitters and have learned what most of them do. Of the known neurotransmitters, the most relevant for the study of human thought and behavior

all-or-none principle
The idea that, once the threshold has been crossed, either an action potential fires or it does not.

synaptic vesicles
Tiny sacs in the terminal buttons that contain neurotransmitters.

enzymatic degradation
A way of removing excess neurotransmitter from the synapse, in which enzymes specific for that neurotransmitter bind with the neurotransmitter and destroy it.

reuptake
A way of removing excess neurotransmitter from the synapse, in which excess neurotransmitter is returned to the sending, or presynaptic, neuron for storage in vesicles and future use.

graded potentials
Small changes in membrane potential that by themselves are insufficient to trigger an action potential.

glutamate
A major excitatory neurotransmitter in the brain that increases the likelihood that a postsynaptic neuron will fire; it is important in learning, memory, neural processing, and brain development.

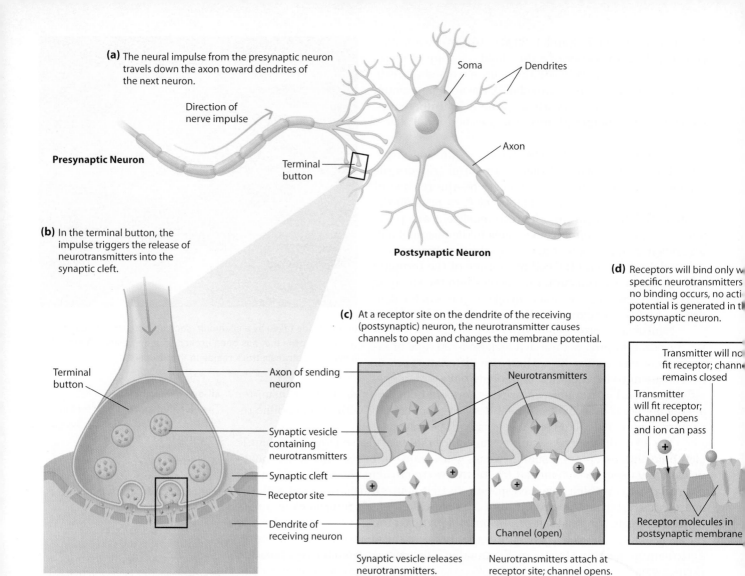

(a) The neural impulse from the presynaptic neuron travels down the axon toward dendrites of the next neuron.

Direction of nerve impulse

Presynaptic Neuron

Soma

Dendrites

Axon

Terminal button

Postsynaptic Neuron

(b) In the terminal button, the impulse triggers the release of neurotransmitters into the synaptic cleft.

Terminal button

Axon of sending neuron

Synaptic vesicle containing neurotransmitters

Synaptic cleft

Receptor site

Dendrite of receiving neuron

(c) At a receptor site on the dendrite of the receiving (postsynaptic) neuron, the neurotransmitter causes channels to open and changes the membrane potential.

Neurotransmitters

Synaptic vesicle releases neurotransmitters.

Channel (open)

Neurotransmitters attach at receptor site; channel opens.

(d) Receptors will bind only w specific neurotransmitters no binding occurs, no acti potential is generated in t postsynaptic neuron.

Transmitter will no fit receptor; chann remains closed

Transmitter will fit receptor; channel opens and ion can pass

Receptor molecules in postsynaptic membrane

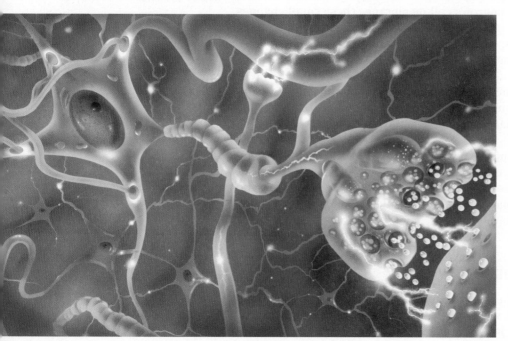

FIGURE **3.8**

HOW SYNAPSES AND NEUROTRANMSITTERS WORK. In (a), two neurons connect, a presynaptic neuron and a postsynaptic neuron. They do not touch, but terminal buttons in the presynaptic neuron form a synaptic cleft with the postsynaptic neuron. In (b), the synaptic cleft has been enlarged to show the synaptic vesicles that carry neurotransmitters. They release neurotransmitter into the cleft where they bind to receptor sites on the postsynaptic neuron. In (c), we see a further enlargement of the neurotransmitters being released into the synaptic cleft and binding to receptor sites in the postsynaptic neuron. In (d), each receptor site binds to only one specific kind neurotransmitter. To the left is a three-dimensiona artistic interpretation of neurons in the brain.

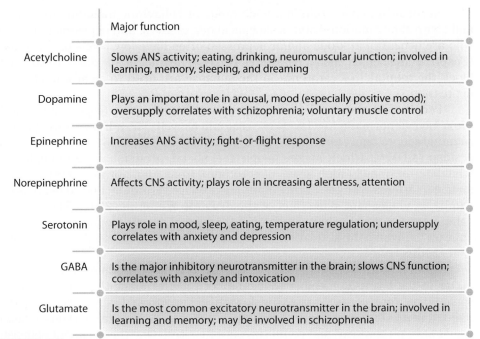

	Major function
Acetylcholine	Slows ANS activity; eating, drinking, neuromuscular junction; involved in learning, memory, sleeping, and dreaming
Dopamine	Plays an important role in arousal, mood (especially positive mood); oversupply correlates with schizophrenia; voluntary muscle control
Epinephrine	Increases ANS activity; fight-or-flight response
Norepinephrine	Affects CNS activity; plays role in increasing alertness, attention
Serotonin	Plays role in mood, sleep, eating, temperature regulation; undersupply correlates with anxiety and depression
GABA	Is the major inhibitory neurotransmitter in the brain; slows CNS function; correlates with anxiety and intoxication
Glutamate	Is the most common excitatory neurotransmitter in the brain; involved in learning and memory; may be involved in schizophrenia

FIGURE 3.9

NEUROTRANSMITTERS AND THEIR FUNCTIONS. Neurotransmitters can be excitatory, increasing the likelihood of an action potential, or inhibitory, decreasing the likelihood of an action potential.

are acetylcholine, dopamine, epinephrine, norepinephrine, serotonin, GABA, and glutamate (see Figure 3.9). Neurotransmitters are found only in the brain. They are synthesized inside the neuron for the purpose of neurotransmission.

The neurotransmitter **acetylcholine (ACh)** controls muscle movement and plays a role in mental processes such as learning, memory, attention, sleeping, and dreaming. Whether ACh excites muscles or slows them down depends on what kind of receptor receives it. Furthermore, researchers have discovered that the degenerative memory disorder called Alzheimer's disease results at least partly from a decrease in ACh activity and that ACh drug enhancers aid memory. ACh enhancers are now used to treat memory disorders, such as Alzheimer's disease, and they seem to slow the progression of memory loss (Czech & Adessi, 2004; Selkoe, 2002).

Dopamine is involved in voluntarily controlling your muscles and is released during feelings of pleasure or reward. Eating a good meal, doing well on an exam, having an orgasm, or drinking a glass of water when really thirsty—each of these behaviors stimulates dopamine activity in the brain (Hamer & Copeland, 1998). Because dopamine activity makes us feel good, many drug addictions involve increased dopamine activity. For instance, cocaine blocks the reuptake of dopamine into the presynaptic neuron, leaving it in the synaptic cleft for a longer period of time before it binds to receptors in the postsynaptic neuron (Bradberry, 2007). The result is a feeling of euphoria and pleasure.

Epinephrine and **norepinephrine** primarily have energizing and arousing properties. (Epinephrine was formerly called *adrenaline*, a term that is still widely used in everyday speech—"Wow! What an adrenaline rush!") Both are produced in the brain and by the adrenal glands that rest atop the kidneys. Epinephrine tends not to affect mental states, whereas norepinephrine increases mental arousal and alertness. Norepinephrine activity also leads to physical arousal—increased heart rate and blood pressure. People who suffer from ADHD have unusually low norepinephrine levels, and treatment sometimes includes drugs to increase norepinephrine levels (Barr et al., 2002).

acetylcholine (ACh)
A neurotransmitter that controls muscle movement and plays a role in mental processes such as learning, memory, attention, sleeping, and dreaming.

dopamine
A neurotransmitter released in response to behaviors that feel good or are rewarding to the person or animal; it is also involved in voluntary motor control.

epinephrine
Also known as adrenaline, a neurotransmitter that arouses bodily systems (such as increasing heart rate).

norepinephrine
A neurotransmitter that activates the sympathetic response to stress, increasing heart rate, rate of respiration, and blood pressure in support of rapid action.

Serotonin plays a role in a wide range of behaviors, including dreaming and controlling emotional states such as anger, anxiety, and depression. People who are generally anxious and/or depressed often have low levels of serotonin (Caspi, Sugden, et al., 2003; Frokjaer et al., 2009; Kendler et al., 2005). Drugs that block the reuptake of serotonin in the synapse are used to treat anxiety and depression.

People who are consistently angry and/or aggressive (especially males) often have abnormally low levels of serotonin as well. The administration of serotonin reduces aggressive behavior in monkeys (Suomi, 2005). The street drug ecstasy (MDMA), which makes people feel social, affectionate, and euphoric, stimulates extremely high levels of serotonin. Ironically, however, ecstasy ultimately interferes with the brain's ability to produce serotonin, and so depression can be an unpleasant side effect of the drug (de Win et al., 2004). The psychedelic state created by hallucinogenic drugs, such as psilocybin mushrooms, appears to involve the activation of serotonergic systems (Muthukumaraswamy et al., 2013).

Gamma-aminobutyric acid, or **GABA,** is a major inhibitory neurotransmitter in the brain. Remember that inhibitory neurotransmitters tell the postsynaptic neurons *not* to fire. GABA slows CNS activity and is necessary for the regulation and control of neural activity. Without it, the central nervous system would have no "brakes" and could run out of control. One theory about epilepsy is that GABA does not function properly in people who suffer from the disorder (Laschet et al., 2007). Many drugs classified as depressants, such as alcohol, increase GABA activity in the brain and lead to relaxing yet ultimately uncoordinated states. Because GABA inhibits much of the CNS activity that keeps us conscious, alert, and able to form memories, large amounts of alcohol consumption can lead to memory lapses, blackouts, loss of consciousness, and even death (A. M. White, 2003).

Glutamate, the brain's major excitatory neurotransmitter, is important in learning, memory, neural processing, and brain development. More specifically,

The street drug known as ecstasy stimulates the release of high levels of the neurotransmitter serotonin, which makes people temporarily feel euphoric and affectionate. By interfering with the body's ability to produce serotonin, however, ecstasy eventually may cause depression in some people.

glutamate facilitates growth and change in neurons and the migration of neurons to different sites in the brain, all of which are basic processes of early brain development (Nadarajah & Parnavelas, 2002). It also amplifies some neural transmissions, so that a person can tell the difference between important and less important information. For example, is it more important to notice that a car is skidding out of control in front of you or that your shoes are still the same color they were when you put them on this morning? Glutamate boosts the signals about the car. The physiologically stimulating effects of nicotine in tobacco stem from glutamate synapses (Guillem & Peoples, 2010).

Summary of the Steps in Neural Transmission

We have considered the complex phenomena of action potentials and neurotransmission and described the neurotransmitters involved in human thought and behavior. Before we discuss the major structures of the brain, let's take time to summarize the process of neural communication.

- The information in neural transmission always travels in one direction in the neuron—from the dendrites to the soma to the axon to the synapses. This process begins with information received from the sense organs or other neurons, which generate a nerve impulse.

- The dendrites receive a message from other neurons. That message, in the form of an electrical and chemical impulse, is then integrated in the soma.

- If the excitatory messages pass the threshold intensity, an action potential will occur, sending the nerve impulse down the axon. If the inhibitory messages win out, the likelihood that the postsynaptic neuron will fire goes down.

- The nerve impulse, known as the action potential, travels down the axon, jumping from one space in the axon's myelin sheath to the next, because channels are opening and closing in the axon's membrane. Ions, mostly sodium and potassium, pass in and out of the membrane.

- This impulse of opening and closing channels travels like a wave down the length of the axon, where the electrical charge stimulates the release of neurotransmitter molecules in the cell's synapses and terminal buttons.

- The neurotransmitters are released into the space between neurons, known as the synaptic cleft. Neurotransmitters released by the presynaptic neuron then bind with receptors in the membrane of the postsynaptic neuron.

- This binding of neurotransmitter to receptor creates electrical changes in the postsynaptic neuron's cell membrane, at its dendrites. Some neurotransmitters tend to be excitatory and increase the likelihood of an action potential. Others tend to be inhibitory and decrease the likelihood of an action potential.

- The transmission process is repeated in postsynaptic neurons, which now become presynaptic neurons.

Quick Quiz 3.2: The Nervous System

1. Which branch of the nervous system is responsible for the fight-or-flight response?
   a. the parasympathetic nervous system
   b. the somatic nervous system
   c. the sympathetic nervous system
   d. the central nervous system

2. The fingerlike projections on neurons that receive input from other neurons are called
   a. dendrites.
   b. nuclei.
   c. axons.
   d. terminal buttons.

3. What property of the neuron is most directly responsible for the changes that lead up to an action potential?
   a. sodium ions outside the cell
   b. its permeable membrane
   c. chloride ions inside the cell
   d. the flux of potassium ions

4. What is the most common excitatory neurotransmitter in the brain?
   a. GABA
   b. serotonin
   c. glutamate
   d. acetylcholine

Answers can be found at the end of the chapter.

THE BRAIN

The brain is a collection of neurons and glial cells that controls all the major functions of the body; produces thoughts, emotions, and behavior; and makes us human. This jellylike mass at the top of the spine has been mapped and described in astonishing detail. Here we consider the evolution of the brain, look at key brain regions, and explore what is currently known about their specialized functions. At this point, the picture is still far from complete, and neuroscientists continue to piece it together.

Evolution of the Human Brain

Evolution provides a fundamental example of how biology and environment interact. As we discussed in Chapter 1, over long periods of time, nature selects traits and behaviors that work well in a given environment. Recall the example of the beetle population becoming more brown than green as brown beetles blended into their surroundings better and were more likely to survive and reproduce. This natural selection process gradually leads to big changes in living forms and structures—from cells to muscles to brains to new species.

The human brain has been shaped, via natural selection, by the world in which humans have lived. It is worth noting that brains do not fossilize to allow a present-day analysis, but the skulls that hold them do. By looking at the size and shape of skulls from all animals and over very long time periods, scientists can glean something about how and when human brains evolved. The evolution of the human brain is a fascinating story. Although the details lie well beyond the scope of this book, we can consider a general outline of brain evolution (Dunbar, 2001; Jerison, 2000; R. G. Klein, 1999; Striedter, 2005).

Arthropods, which have no backbone and external skeleton, were probably the first organisms with a central nervous system (brain) about 520 million years ago (Ma et al., 2012). Within a few million years, the first primitive vertebrates (animals with backbones) appeared. They were jawless fish, and they had a bigger mass of nerve cells than flatworms (Jerison, 2000). The first land animals came into existence around 450 million years ago and the first mammals around 200 million years ago. Land animals had more than a bundle of neurons above the spinal cord; they had complex brains with numerous structures.

The first primates lived around 55 million years ago—10 million years after the dinosaurs went extinct (Jerison, 2000). Compared to other mammals, birds and reptiles, and fish, primates have relatively large amounts of brain cortex, allowing more complex thinking and problem solving. The earliest

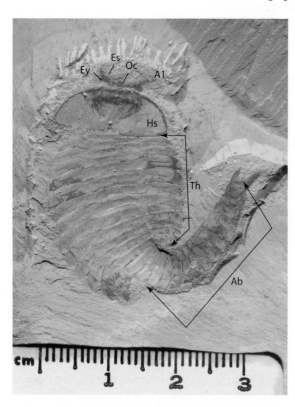

The arthropod from 520 million years ago had the first known central nervous system. Notes: Ey = eye; Es = eye stalk; Oc = optic capsule; A1 = antenna; Hs = head stalk; Th = thorax; Ab = abdomen

Neanderthals had larger but less complex brains than modern humans do.
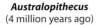 **Can you think of how this is the case—that is, what makes a brain complex?**

ancestors of humans appeared in Africa about 6 million years ago. One of our closest evolutionary relatives, the Neanderthals (*Homo neanderthalensis*), lived from about 350,000 to 28,000 years ago, when they were replaced by our species (*Homo sapiens*). Neanderthals had brains slightly larger, on average, than those of modern humans (see Figure 3.10).

Nevertheless, these early humans did not produce highly complex tools, may have possessed very rudimentary language, and never made symbolic pieces of art, at least none that have been found. Their brains were modern in size but not modern in function. It is possible, therefore, that the modern human brain took up to 100,000 years to become fully wired and complex, all the while staying the same overall size.

Australopithecus (4 million years ago)	*Homo erectus* (1.6 million to 100,000 years ago)	Neanderthal (350,000 to 28,000 years ago)	*Homo sapiens* (200,000 years ago to present)

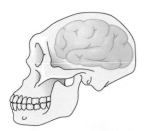 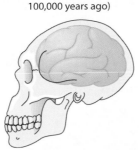 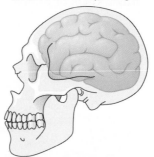 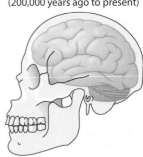

The brain capacity ranges from 450 to 650 cubic centimeters (cc).	Further development of skull and jaw are evident and brain capacity is 900 cc.	The human skull has now taken shape: The skull case has elongated to hold a complex brain of 1,450 cc.	The deeply convoluted brain reflects growth in areas concerned with higher mental processes (1,300 cc).

FIGURE 3.10

EVOLUTION OF THE HUMAN BRAIN OVER THE LAST 4 MILLION YEARS. An early form of prehuman, *Australopithecus,* had a brain about one-third the size of the modern human (*H. sapiens*) brain. In general, the overall brain size has grown over the course of 4 million years. But note that Neanderthal's brain was slightly larger than ours. Just as important as overall size for modern human thought and behavior is the relative enlargement of the frontal lobe area. This can be seen in the less-sloped forehead of modern humans compared to their earlier ancestors.

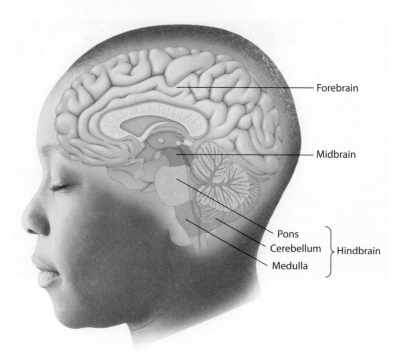

FIGURE **3.11**

THREE MAIN BRAIN STRUCTURES: HINDBRAIN, MIDBRAIN, AND FOREBRAIN. The hindbrain regulates breathing, heart rate, arousal, and other basic survival functions. The midbrain controls eye muscles, processes auditory and visual information, and initiates voluntary movement. The forebrain controls cognitive, sensory, and motor function and regulates temperature, reproductive function, eating, sleeping, and emotions.

Overview of Brain Regions

In evolutionary terms, then, the human brain is the result of a few hundred million years of natural selection. The three major regions of the brain, in order from earliest to develop to newest, are the hindbrain, the midbrain, and the forebrain (see Figure 3.11). By comparing the relative size of each region in distinct kinds of animals that vary in evolutionary age (see Figure 3.12), we gain

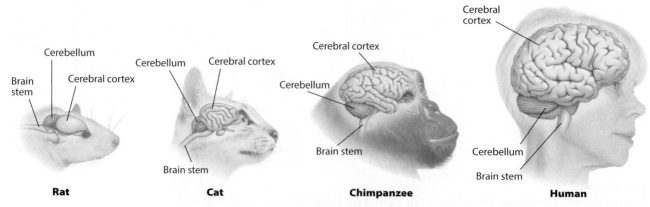

FIGURE **3.12**

THE BRAIN STRUCTURE OF MAMMALS. Mammals have many of the same brain structures, but of different relative sizes. Notice how much larger the cerebral cortex is in humans than in chimpanzees, cats, and rats. Also notice the increase in brain folds in primates.

What are the main differences you notice in these brains?

an appreciation of how these regions evolved. When we compare brains from these different groups, we see an increase in size of the forebrain in humans and other primates (Jerison, 2000).

Hindbrain The oldest brain region is the hindbrain, the region directly connected to the spinal cord. Hindbrain structures regulate breathing, heart rate, arousal, and other basic functions of survival. There are three main parts of the hindbrain: the medulla, the pons, and the cerebellum.

Extending directly from the spinal cord, the **medulla** regulates breathing, heart rate, and blood pressure. It is also involved in various kinds of reflexes, such as coughing, swallowing, sneezing, and vomiting.

Reflexes are inborn, involuntary behaviors that are elicited by very specific stimuli (Amaral, 2000). **Pons** means "bridge," and the pons indeed serves as a bridge between lower brain regions and higher midbrain and forebrain activity. For instance, information about body movement and various sensations is relayed from the cortex via the pons to the cerebellum.

The **cerebellum,** or "little brain," contains more neurons than any other single part of the brain. It is responsible for body movement, balance, coordination, and fine motor skills such as typing and piano playing. The cerebellum is also important in cognitive activities such as learning and language (Amaral, 2000; Stroodley & Schmahmann, 2009).

Midbrain The next brain region to evolve after the hindbrain was the smallest of the three major areas, the midbrain. Different parts of the midbrain control the eye muscles, process auditory and visual information, and initiate voluntary movement of the body. People with Parkinson's disease have problems with midbrain functioning, due to the loss of neurons that use dopamine there, and so they shake uncontrollably. The midbrain, the medulla, and the pons together are sometimes referred to as the *brain stem.*

A network of nerves called the **reticular formation** runs through both the hindbrain and the midbrain (*reticular* means "netlike"). The reticular formation plays a key role in wakefulness. Among the first neuroscientists to study the reticular formation were Giuseppe Moruzzi and Horace Magoun. In a classic study, Moruzzi and Magoun electrically stimulated the reticular formation of a sleeping cat, and it immediately awoke. When they *lesioned,* or damaged, its connection to higher brain systems, the cat went into a deep coma, from which it never recovered. No kind of pinching or loud noises would arouse the cat (Moruzzi & Magoun, 1949).

Forebrain The last major region to evolve was the largest part of the human brain, the forebrain. It consists of the cerebrum and numerous other structures, including the thalamus and the limbic system. Collectively, the structures of the forebrain control cognitive, sensory, and motor function and regulate temperature, reproductive functions, eating, sleeping, and the display of emotions. Most forebrain structures are *bilateral;* that is, there are two of them, one on each side of the brain.

From the bottom up, the first forebrain structure is the **thalamus,** which receives input from the ears, eyes, skin, or taste buds and relays sensory information to the part of the cerebral cortex most responsible for processing that specific kind of sensory information. For this reason, the thalamus is often called

Swallowing is one of a number of inborn reflexes; it is controlled by the medulla.

medulla
A hindbrain structure that extends directly from the spinal cord; it regulates breathing, heart rate, and blood pressure.

reflexes
Inborn and involuntary behaviors—such as coughing, swallowing, sneezing, or vomiting—that are elicited by very specific stimuli.

pons
The hindbrain structure that serves as a bridge between lower brain regions and higher midbrain and forebrain activity.

cerebellum
A hindbrain structure involved in body movement, balance, coordination, fine-tuning of motor skills, and cognitive activities such as learning and language.

reticular formation
A network of nerve fibers that runs up through both the hindbrain and the midbrain; it is crucial to waking up and falling asleep.

thalamus
A forebrain structure that receives information from the senses and relays it to the cerebral cortex for processing.

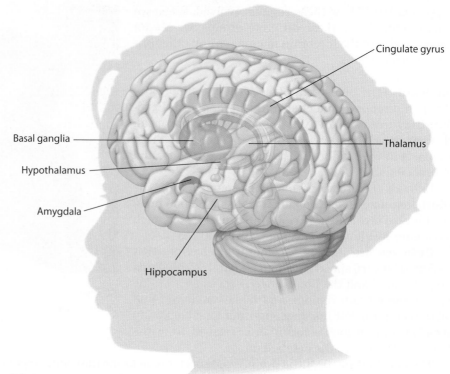

Cingulate gyrus

Basal ganglia

Thalamus

Hypothalamus

Amygdala

Hippocampus

FIGURE **3.13**

THE LIMBIC SYSTEM. The limbic system controls motivation and emotion. It includes the hypothalamus, hippocampus, amygdala, and cingulate gyrus.

 Can you think of certain kinds of drives and emotions that result from activation of the limbic system?

How does this picture make you feel? The structures of the limbic system play a key part in emotion and motivation.

hypothalamus
The limbic structure that is the master regulator of almost all major drives and motives we have, such as hunger, thirst, temperature, and sexual behavior; it also controls the pituitary gland.

hippocampus
The limbic structure that wraps itself around the thalamus; it plays a vital role in learning and memory.

a sensory relay station. Olfaction (the sense of smell) appears to be the only sense that does not have a thalamic relay (Kay & Sherman, 2007).

The Limbic System   In the middle of the brain, directly around the thalamus, lies a set of structures, traditionally referred to as the *limbic system* (see Figure 3.13). These are the hypothalamus, the hippocampus, the amygdala, and the cingulate gyrus. Together, the limbic system structures are important in emotion and motivation. However, there is some debate as to whether these structures work together as a system, so some neuroscientists suggest that the term *limbic system* should be abandoned altogether (LeDoux, 2003).

The structure directly below the thalamus is the hypothalamus (*hypo* means "below"). The **hypothalamus** regulates almost all of our major drives and motives, including hunger, thirst, temperature, and sexual behavior. It also controls the pituitary gland, which is responsible for producing and controlling the hormones our bodies produce. Researchers in the 1940s discovered the hypothalamus's role in eating: Lesioning one part of it produced overeating and obesity in animals, whereas lesioning another part of the hypothalamus led to undereating (Kupfermann, Kandel, & Iversen, 2000). The hypothalamus is also involved in sexual arousal (Brunetti et al., 2008; Karama et al., 2002).

Wrapped around the thalamus is the **hippocampus,** which plays a vital role in learning and memory. Sensory information from the sense organs goes to the hippocampus. If these events are important enough, they are processed in the hippocampus and eventually established as lasting memories.

As we will see throughout this text, learning and memory change the brain, another example of softwiring. The brain structure most open to such change is the hippocampus. To get a feel for the kind of research that demonstrates this capacity, let's look at recent research conducted with taxicab drivers in London. Why study taxi drivers? Their work requires a tremendous amount of spatial and geographic knowledge, and they have to pass a difficult driving test (Maguire, Woollett, & Spiers, 2006). They must know where all the streets are relative to other streets. Neuroscientists examined images of the hippocampus and found that the hippocampi of taxi drivers were larger than that of other drivers. Moreover, the stress and frequency of driving did not account for these hippocampal size differences. Compared to bus drivers, taxi drivers had larger hippocampi (Maguire et al., 2006). Why? Bus drivers drive the same route every day, so they need to learn much less about the spatial layout of the city than taxi drivers. As this study suggests, learning changes the brain.

The **amygdala** is a small, almond-shaped structure directly in front of the hippocampus. Anatomically, the amygdala connects with many other areas of the brain, including the structures involved in emotion and memory: the hypothalamus, which controls the autonomic nervous system; the hippocampus, which plays a crucial role in memory; the thalamus, which contains neurons that receive information from the sense organs; and the cerebral cortex. By virtue of its prime location, the amygdala plays a key role in determining the emotional significance of stimuli, especially when they evoke fear (Öhman, 2002; Phelps & LeDoux, 2005).

Studies in animals and humans show how important the amygdala is to emotions, especially fear. Electrical stimulation of the amygdala in cats makes them arch their backs in an angry-defensive manner, a response suggesting that anger and aggression involve the amygdala. Moreover, when aggressive monkeys had this region of the brain surgically lesioned, they became tame and nonaggressive. They also became fearless; for instance, rather than fleeing from snakes, they approached them (Klüver & Bucy, 1939; Meunier & Bachevalier, 2002). Similarly, in cases of disease, injury, or surgery to the human amygdala, people often lose their aggressive tendencies. They become mild-mannered yet also fearless. Additionally, our ability to recognize certain emotional expressions on other people's faces— especially fear—involves the amygdala (Adolphs, Gosselin, et al., 2005; J. S. Morris et al., 1996). Without the amygdala, we cannot learn appropriate emotional responses, especially to potentially dangerous situations. The amygdala, along with the hypothalamus and other brain structures, is also activated during sexual arousal (Fonteille & Stoléru, 2011; Hamann et al., 2004; Karama et al., 2002).

The **cingulate gyrus** is a beltlike structure in the middle of the brain. Portions of the cingulate gyrus, in particular the front part, play an important role in attention and cognitive control (Botvinick, Cohen, & Carter, 2004). When people are first trying to figure out a difficult problem and preparing to solve it, parts of the cingulate gyrus are activated (Kounios et al., 2006; Qiu et al., 2010). In contrast, this area seems to malfunction in people with schizophrenia, who have major difficulties in focusing their attention (Carter et al., 1997).

The **basal ganglia** are a collection of structures surrounding the thalamus; they are involved in voluntary motor control. Several movement-related

amygdala
A small, almond-shaped structure directly in front of the hippocampus; it has connections with many important brain regions and is important for processing emotional information, especially that related to fear.

One of the special functions of the amygdala is to recognize situations for which fear is an appropriate response.
What would happen if humans were not able to experience fear?

cingulate gyrus
A beltlike structure in the middle of the brain that plays an important role in attention and cognitive control.

basal ganglia
A collection of structures surrounding the thalamus; they are involved in voluntary motor control.

Lobes of the brain

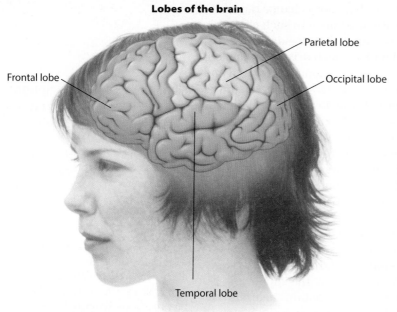

Parietal lobe

Frontal lobe

Occipital lobe

Temporal lobe

FIGURE 3.14

FOUR LOBES OF THE CEREBRAL CORTEX. Each of the four lobes has a counterpart on the opposite side of the brain. Most important for thinking, planning, and integrating the brain's activity are the frontal lobes. The parietal lobes integrate the sensation and perception of touch. Visual information is processed in the occipital lobes, whereas hearing is processed in the temporal lobes.

cerebrum
Each of the large halves of the brain, covered with convolutions (folds).

cerebral cortex
The thin, outer layer of the cerebrum, in which much of human thought, planning, perception, and consciousness takes place.

neurological disorders, including Parkinson's disease and Huntington's disease, affect the functioning of neurons in this region. Individuals who have these disorders suffer from jerky, often uncontrollable movements. Often considered part of the limbic system, the basal ganglia reside on both sides of the thalamus and above the limbic system. They connect with the cerebral cortex, thalamus, and brain stem (Kopell et al., 2006).

The Cerebrum and Cerebral Cortex The uppermost portion of the brain, the **cerebrum,** is folded into convolutions and divided into two large hemispheres. When most of us think about the human brain, we typically envision the outer layer, with all of its convolutions. This outer layer is called the **cerebral cortex.** The cortex is only about one-tenth to one-fifth of an inch thick, yet it is in this very thin layer of brain that much of human thought, planning, perception, and consciousness takes place. In short, it is the site of all brain activity that makes us most human.

The cerebrum is composed of four large areas called *lobes,* each of which carries out distinct functions. These lobes are bilateral, which means they are located on both the left and right sides of the brain. The four lobes are the frontal, temporal, parietal, and occipital (see Figure 3.14). The *frontal lobes,* in the front of the brain, make up one-third of the area of the cerebral cortex. One important region of the frontal lobe, descending from the top of the head toward the center of the brain, is the *primary motor cortex.* One of the earliest discoveries about the brain's frontal lobes involved the motor cortex. In the 1860s, while caring for wounded soldiers, the German physiologist Eduard Hitzig noticed that touching the surface of a specific side of the brain caused a soldier's body to twitch on the opposite side.

Hitzig then discovered that, as he moved the stimulation along this strip of cortex and stimulated one small region at a time, different parts of the soldier's body moved. More importantly, he was the first researcher to discover and study something that few believed: Different parts of the cortex are responsible for different functions—a phenomenon known as *cortical localization* (Finger, 1994).

The frontal lobe carries out many important functions, including attention, holding things in mind while we solve problems, planning, abstract thinking, control of impulses, creativity, and social awareness (B. L. Miller & Cummings, 1999). The frontal lobes are more interconnected with other brain regions than any other part of the brain and therefore are able to integrate much brain activity. This integration allows for insight and creative problem solving (Fuster, 1999). For example, connections between the frontal lobes and the hippocampus and temporal lobe facilitate tasks involving language and memory, respectively. More than any other part of the brain, the frontal lobes are what make humans human. They are also the "youngest" brain systems to evolve and the last to fully develop in individuals. The frontal lobes continue to develop until the early 20s. Children and teenagers act more impulsively than adults partially because their frontal lobes are not fully developed.

Probably the most famous story in neuroscience comes from the first case study of frontal lobe involvement in impulse control and personality (Macmillan, 2000). In September 1848, a 25-year-old railroad foreman, Phineas Gage, was laying railroad ties. While hammering a tamping iron (an iron bar), Gage accidentally ignited gun powder used to lay the track, and it exploded. The iron bar shot upward, entered Gage's left cheek, and exited through the top of his skull after passing through his frontal lobe (see Figure 3.15). The iron bar was traveling so fast that it moved cleanly through Gage's head and landed 25 feet away. Miraculously, not only did Gage survive, but he never even lost consciousness!

Although not mortally wounded, Gage suffered immediate and obvious changes to his personality. Before the accident, he had been a mild-mannered but clever businessman. After the accident, he was stubborn, impulsive, and argumentative, and at times he said offensive things. Gage's accident was one of the first documented cases of marked personality change following an injury to the frontal lobes, suggesting that these areas play a key role in regulating social behavior.

The *parietal lobes,* which make up the top and rear sections of the brain, are important in the sensation and perception of touch. The frontmost portion of the parietal lobes is the *somatosensory cortex.* When different parts of the body are touched, different parts of this strip of cortex are activated. The somatosensory cortex lies directly behind the motor cortex of the frontal lobe. In fact, these two regions are "twins." The areas of the motor and somatosensory cortexes that govern specific parts of the body are parallel to and directly next to each other (see Figure 3.16). For example, the part of the motor cortex involved in moving the lips

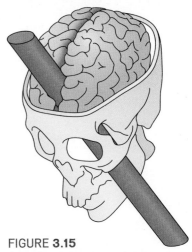

FIGURE **3.15**
PHINEAS GAGE'S ACCIDENT.
Miraculously, Gage survived, but his personality changed dramatically as a result of the injury to his frontal lobe.

From what you have learned about the frontal lobes, can you predict what effects the accident had on Gage's personality?

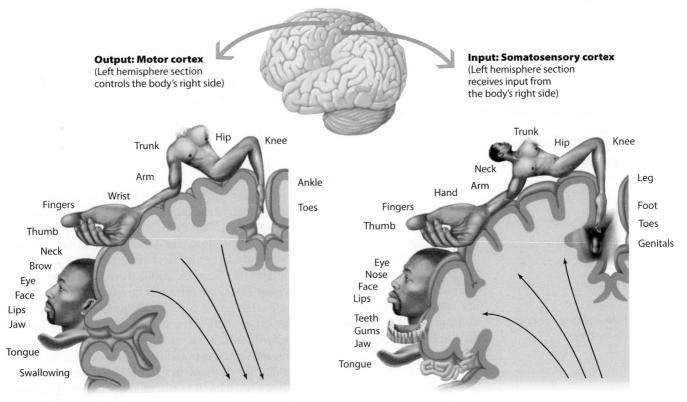

Output: **Motor cortex**
(Left hemisphere section controls the body's right side)

Input: **Somatosensory cortex**
(Left hemisphere section receives input from the body's right side)

FIGURE **3.16**
MOTOR AND SOMATOSENSORY CORTEXES OF THE BRAIN. Note that the regions of the motor and somatosensory cortexes are "twins." The face, lips, or toes, for example, activate the same areas of both cortexes. The arrows going down into the lower brain region represent motor neurons, and the arrows coming up into the somatosensory cortex correspond to sensory neurons.

Can you think of why the distorted size differences are shown in various body parts?

is directly opposite the region of the sensory cortex where we sense that our lips are being touched. Neural signals from the motor cortex can communicate with computers to control robotic arms or artificial limbs, as explained in "Psychology in the Real World."

The *temporal lobes* lie directly below the frontal and parietal lobes and right behind the ears. The temporal lobes have many different functions, but the main one is hearing. The temporal lobes house the *auditory cortex,* where sound information arrives from the thalamus for processing. Here, we "hear" our mother's voice, a symphony, an approaching car, or any other sound. The temporal lobes also house and connect with the hippocampus and amygdala and, so, are also involved in memory and emotion.

The *occipital lobes* occupy the rear of the brain. The optic nerve travels from the eye to the thalamus and then to the occipital lobes—specifically, to the *primary visual cortex.* Visual information is processed in the visual cortex, where we "see" and "imagine." Neuroscientists have discovered that different neurons in the visual cortex are activated when we see horizontal lines, diagonal lines, and vertical lines. In other words, individual neurons are specialized for the many different aspects of vision, including shape, color, shadow, light, and orientation (Wurtz & Kandel, 2000a).

The **insula** is a small structure deep inside the cerebrum, in the area that separates the temporal lobe from the parietal lobe. The insula is active in the perception of bodily sensations, emotional states, empathy, and addictive behavior (Damasio, 2000; Naqvi et al., 2007). It communicates with structures of the limbic system and higher brain areas involved in decision making. The insula also plays a key role in our awareness of our bodies as our own (Tsakiris et al., 2007).

Cerebral Hemispheres The human cerebrum is divided into two equal *hemispheres.* Although they look similar, the hemispheres differ in shape, size, and function. In general terms, the left hemisphere processes information in a more focused and analytic manner, whereas the right hemisphere integrates information in a more holistic, or broader, manner (Beeman & Bowden, 2000; Beever & Chiarello, 2009). Insights and solutions to problems are more likely to occur in the right hemisphere.

The hemispheres do not operate independently, however. The **corpus callosum,** the thick band of nerve fibers connecting the two hemispheres, provides a channel for extensive communication between the hemispheres in both logical and creative tasks.

Perhaps the best-known and biggest functional difference between the cerebral hemispheres is in language. Speech and language comprehension involve two separate regions in the left hemisphere. The French physician Paul Broca is credited with being the first "neuropsychologist." He deserves this title because his work in the early 1860s demonstrated for the first time that specific parts of the brain control particular behaviors (Kandel, 2006). Broca studied a man who had suffered a stroke. This man could understand language, but he could not speak in grammatical sentences. He had a type of **aphasia,** a deficit in the ability to speak or comprehend language. After the man died, Broca performed an autopsy and found that a cyst had damaged a small region in the left frontal lobe. Broca inferred that this area must be responsible for a person's ability to speak, and he went on to discover similar damage in eight other aphasia patients (Pinker, 1994). These clinical findings have been confirmed by modern brain imaging techniques: People with aphasia often have damage or lesions in the same region of the left frontal lobe. This region, responsible for the ability to produce speech, is commonly referred to as **Broca's area,** and this type of aphasia is known as Broca's aphasia.

About 20 years after Broca found the area of the brain now named for him, a German physiologist, Carl Wernicke, discovered that damage to another region

insula
A small structure inside the cerebrum that plays an important role in the perception of bodily sensations, emotional states, empathy, and addictive behavior.

corpus callosum
A group of nerve fibers that connect the two hemispheres of the brain.

aphasia
A deficit in the ability to speak or comprehend language.

Broca's area
The area in the left frontal lobe responsible for the ability to produce speech.

Psychology in the Real World

Brain-Computer and Brain-Machine Interfaces

Think about how incredible it is that we can use our thoughts to control voluntary movement. We think, I want to scratch my nose, and then we can almost instantaneously lift an arm and move a finger to scratch the nose. When injury cuts connections between the CNS and the skeletal muscles, a person's intention to move a limb—say, to pick up a coffee cup—cannot affect the muscles needed to lift the cup. Thoughts cannot lead to action.

Researchers now combine technology and neuroscience to help people who are not able to move their limbs. With the development of brain-computer interfaces and brain-machine interfaces, people can learn to control computers or machinery with only their thoughts. How does this work? These machines convert neural activity (action potentials, see p. 84) into digital signals that can control a prosthetic or paralyzed limb (Fetz, 2007; Hargrove, 2013). These machines can then execute the neural instructions, such as "lift the arm."

What would be needed so that thoughts can control an artificial limb that cannot be felt? First, we'd need to know which neurons in the motor cortex control intentional movement. Such mapping of individual neurons can be done in a surgical lab setting (most of these cases have been done in monkeys; Pohlmeyer et al., 2009). Also, it would be important to know that some kind of mental representation of an action—such as imagining a movement—activates the same motor neurons necessary to make the movement happen. This creates the thought-action link. Neurons in the motor cortex that are instrumental in generating movement can also be activated when people simply imagine movement but do not actually move (Jeannerod, 1995).

Once we've identified the neurons that control movement and that we can mentally activate, we would need a device for translating neural signals into instructions to be sent to a machine that can move a prosthetic or paralyzed limb. Computers convert neural signal information into instructions, which can then be sent to an artificial limb or a robotic arm. The computer is the *interface* between the thoughts and the arm. The computer can control either an external device (an artificial or robotic arm) or a device that can electrically activate paralyzed muscles. In laboratory studies, paralyzed patients—including tetraplegics—can use their intentional thoughts toward movement to control a robotic arm, which may prove to be a help for quality of life if these changes can move out into their daily lives (Hochberg et al., 2012).

Forearm electrical stimulation (FES) is used to stimulate forearm muscles with fixed instructions from a computer (Peckham et al., 2001). FES can create movements in paralyzed limbs, but the actions generated are fixed and limited to only the actions that the computer can instruct the arm to do. Ideally, one would have flexibility, as with a normally functioning arm; that is, people could choose which movements to make.

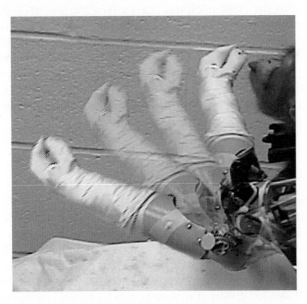

The monkey's real arms are constrained below (white cover at bottom), and a prosthetic arm is attached next to the shoulder and to microelectrodes in the motor cortex of the brain. The monkey learns to control the prosthetic arm much the same way it does its real arm—by sending neural signals from the motor cortex to the arm. Here the monkey is using the prosthetic arm to feed itself. (Velliste et al., 2008)

Pohlmeyer and his colleagues (2009) took an important step toward creating more flexibility in moving paralyzed limbs. After putting implants deep into the brains of two monkeys to record signals from neurons in the motor cortex, they used nerve-blocking drugs to temporarily paralyze the animals' arms. Then they wanted to see whether they could use a brain-machine interface to have these neural signals stimulate muscles in the monkeys. The monkeys—in spite of almost completely paralyzed wrists—were able to use this cortically controlled FES system to control the contraction of four forearm muscles.

Recent research uses less invasive techniques—such as brain imaging—to control machines (Doud et al., 2011; Min, Marzelli, & Yoo, 2010; Yuan et al., 2010). These new systems allow for a bidirectional line of communication between the brain and the computer; that is, feedback from a computer can be used to modulate brain activity. Such computer-to-brain interfaces might even make possible brain-to-brain interfaces in the future (Min et al., 2010).

of the left hemisphere creates a different language problem. This area of the left temporal lobe, now called **Wernicke's area,** is responsible for speech comprehension. Wernicke's aphasia, in contrast to Broca's aphasia, results in fluent, grammatical streams of speech that lacks meaning. A patient with this disorder who was asked why he was in the hospital responded, "Boy, I'm sweating. I'm awfully nervous, you know, once in awhile I get caught up, I can't mention the tarripoi, a month ago, quite a little, I've done a lot well, I impose a lot, while, on the other hand, you know what I mean, I have to run around, look it over, trebbin and all that sort of stuff" (as quoted in Pinker, 1994, p. 316).

Communication between the Hemispheres   As we have seen, the two hemispheres of the brain do not operate independently. All communication between one side of the brain and the other travels across the corpus callosum.

In the early 1960s, a former prisoner of war from World War II developed epileptic seizures as a result of a failed parachute jump. The seizures were so severe that his doctor approached Roger Sperry, a local researcher who had begun to do research on the corpus callosum, for help (Finger, 1994). Previous medical evidence had suggested that cutting the bundle of nerves between the two hemispheres could stop epileptic seizures. Because the war veteran's seizures had become life threatening, Sperry recommended surgery, which was very successful. Not only did the man's seizures stop, but there was also no noticeable change in his personality or intelligence. However, Sperry and his colleagues soon discovered a fascinating problem. The man could not name things that were presented to his left visual field, but he could do so with things presented to his right visual field. Why?

Recall that language—both speech and comprehension—resides in the left hemisphere of the human brain. In addition, information from our right visual field (the right portion of the visual scope of each eye) goes to the left occipital cortex, whereas information from the left visual field (the left portion of the visual scope of each eye) goes to the right occipital cortex (see Figure 3.17). But because the war veteran had had his corpus callosum cut, the information from the left visual field could not get transferred to the language centers in the left hemisphere. He could, however, consistently pick up with his *left* hand the image he saw! Thus, because the right hemisphere (where the image was projected) controls the left side of the body, he could move his hand to the correct object (see Figure 3.18). This *split-brain research* shows that we can know something even if we cannot name it (Sperry, Gazzaniga, & Bogen, 1969).

Brain Plasticity and Neurogenesis

When scientists began mapping the brain in the late 19th century, they did so by stimulating various brain regions in animals and observing the behavioral changes that such stimulation caused; they then diagrammed the locations of functions in the cerebral cortex (Kandel, 2006). Such mapping contributed to the notion that brain function was fixed: Certain brain regions had certain functions. But as far back as the early 20th century, researchers had stimulated different places on the motor cortex in several different monkeys and had found that maps generated from such stimulation varied from monkey to monkey. They were as individual as fingerprints.

In the early 20th century, other neuroscientists mapped the motor cortexes of several monkeys many times during a 4-month period. They found that neural areas corresponding to the movement of specific fingers changed to reflect changes in the animal's patterns of movement over that time period (Jenkins et al., 1990). By the 1970s, there was evidence that learning occurs through synaptic change. These findings were only the tip of the iceberg. Since the 1990s,

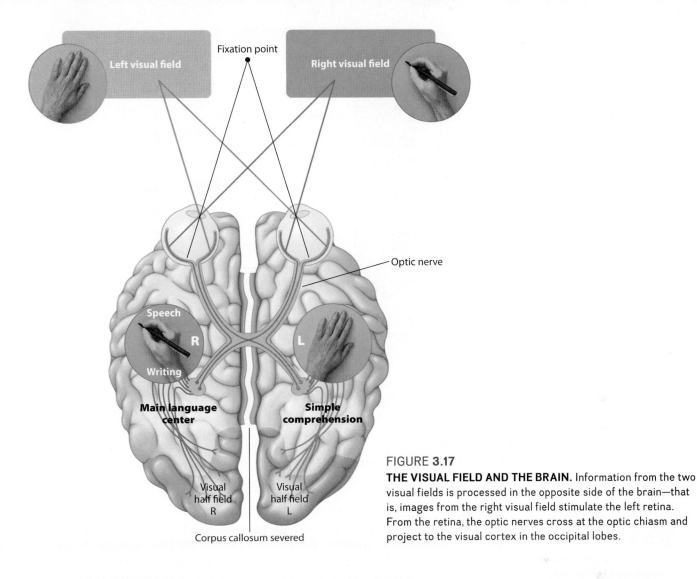

Fixation point

Left visual field

Right visual field

Optic nerve

Speech

R

L

Writing

Main language center

Simple comprehension

Visual half field R

Visual half field L

Corpus callosum severed

FIGURE **3.17**

THE VISUAL FIELD AND THE BRAIN. Information from the two visual fields is processed in the opposite side of the brain—that is, images from the right visual field stimulate the left retina. From the retina, the optic nerves cross at the optic chiasm and project to the visual cortex in the occipital lobes.

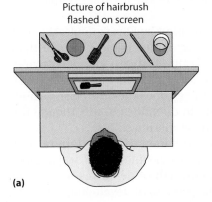

Picture of hairbrush flashed on screen

(a)

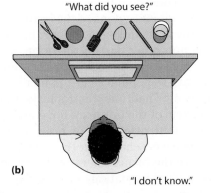

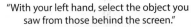

"What did you see?"

"I don't know."

(b)

"With your left hand, select the object you saw from those behind the screen."

(c)

FIGURE **3.18**

PERCEPTION AND LANGUAGE IN A SPLIT-BRAIN PATIENT. In (a), a person who has had an operation to cut the corpus callosum is shown an object (hairbrush) to his left visual field. In (b), when asked what he saw, he cannot say, because his language production center (Broca's area) is in his left hemisphere. Because the image is shown to his left visual field, only his right visual cortex perceives it. With a split corpus callosum, there is no way for that information to cross from the right hemisphere to the left. So he is unable to say what he saw. In (c), however, he is able to pick up the object he saw with his *left* hand. Why his left hand? Because it is controlled by his right hemisphere, which did, in fact, perceive the brush.

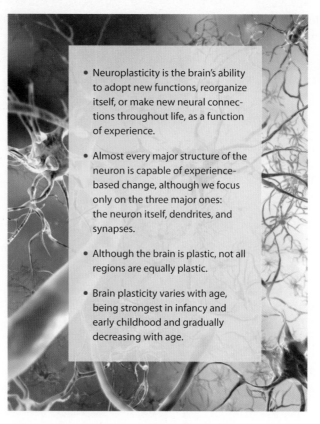

- Neuroplasticity is the brain's ability to adopt new functions, reorganize itself, or make new neural connections throughout life, as a function of experience.

- Almost every major structure of the neuron is capable of experience-based change, although we focus only on the three major ones: the neuron itself, dendrites, and synapses.

- Although the brain is plastic, not all regions are equally plastic.

- Brain plasticity varies with age, being strongest in infancy and early childhood and gradually decreasing with age.

FIGURE **3.19**

FOUR PRINCIPLES OF BRAIN PLASTICITY.

neuroplasticity
The brain's ability to adopt new functions, reorganize itself, or make new neural connections throughout life, as a function of experience.

neurogenesis
The development of new neurons.

arborization
The growth and formation of new dendrites.

synaptogenesis
The formation of entirely new synapses or connections with other neurons.

numerous principles of brain plasticity have emerged (B. D. Perry, 2002). First and most generally, **neuroplasticity** is the brain's ability to adopt new functions, reorganize itself, or make new neural connections throughout life, as a function of experience. Second, almost every major structure of the neuron is capable of experience-based change.

Third, not all regions of the brain are equally plastic. For example, the part of the brain most involved in learning, the hippocampus, is more plastic than just about any other part of the brain. Finally, brain plasticity varies with age, being strongest in infancy and early childhood and gradually decreasing with age. Contrary to popular belief, at no time in our lives does the brain lose its ability to grow new neurons. Neuroplasticity occurs in all stages of life, though the different parts of the brain are not equally plastic at all times.

These four principles of brain plasticity are summarized in Figure 3.19. Experience-based change in the nervous system occurs in several ways. Most common are the formation of new neurons, the growth of dendrites in existing neurons, and the formation of new synapses. The process of developing new neurons is known as **neurogenesis.** The growth and formation of new dendrites is called **arborization** (from the Latin *arbor,* meaning "tree"), because dendrites are like branches on a tree. Probably the best-known example of neuroplasticity, however, is **synaptogenesis,** the formation of entirely new synapses or connections with other neurons—the basis of learning. All of these neuroplasticity examples are forms of softwiring—biological systems being modified by input from the environment.

Although these principles of neuroplasticity are universal—that is, they apply to everyone—some of the strongest evidence for them comes out of research on people with different kinds of sensory deficits, such as blindness or deafness. It is in deafness and blindness that we see most clearly how flexible the brain really is. Brain function and localization vary considerably on the basis of the experience of the individual brain.

In most hearing people, the area called the *auditory cortex* processes sound. Although labeled by its function, anatomically the auditory cortex is actually a section of the temporal lobe. It is called the auditory cortex because the sensory neurons from the inner ear go there. But if those neurons don't pick up any sounds, what does this area of the brain do?

For centuries, scientists and others have observed that deaf people see better than hearing people and that blind people hear better than sighted people. The neuroscientist Helen Neville always thought there must be truth to these observations. In the process of testing these assumptions, she discovered that, overall, blind people are not better at hearing. They are not more sensitive to softer sounds than sighted people. Similarly, deaf people do not excel at all kinds of vision, nor are they able to see fainter images than do hearing people.

What Neville found, however, was that deaf and blind people are more expert in peripheral sensory experiences. Deaf people have better *peripheral* vision than sighted people—they are better at seeing things "out of the corner of their eyes" (Bavelier et al., 2000). They have better motion detection as well, and this seems to be processed by the auditory cortex. Just as deaf people see better at the periphery, those who are blind don't hear better overall, but their *peripheral* hearing—hearing for things around the edges of a sound field (rather than the center)—is better than that of sighted people. These peripheral sounds are processed by the visual cortex (Bavelier et al., 2000). According to Neville, "This was some of the first evidence that brain specializations such as auditory cortex are not anatomically determined" (Neville, as quoted in Begley, 2007, p. 84). In short, by virtue of natural plasticity and softwiring, the brain compensates for deficits in one sensory modality by reorganizing and rewiring unused regions to take on new functions. Once again, we see how forces of nature and nurture interact to shape human thought and behavior and how psychological research leads to startling changes in our assumptions.

To compensate for deafness or blindness, the brain reorganizes and rewires the part normally dedicated to hearing or vision for other uses. Marlee Matlin, shown here with her dance partner from *Dancing with the Stars,* is an Oscar-winning actress with limited hearing.

Challenge Your Assumptions

True or False? In people who are blind, the vision areas of the brain do not function.

False: The visual cortex takes on new functions, such as processing auditory information, in blind people.

Quick Quiz 3.3: The Brain

1. This region of the brain was the last to evolve. It is also the biggest part of the brain.
   a. cerebellum
   b. forebrain
   c. hindbrain
   d. pons

2. Which limbic structure plays a crucial role in fear?
   a. hypothalamus
   b. basal ganglia
   c. amygdala
   d. hippocampus

3. Where is the somatosensory cortex?
   a. in the occipital lobes
   b. in the frontal lobes
   c. in the temporal lobes
   d. in the parietal lobes

Answers can be found at the end of the chapter.

CHALLENGING ASSUMPTIONS ABOUT NEURAL GROWTH IN THE ADULT BRAIN

Neurons are unique cells in the body. Unlike many other cells, including hair, blood, and skin cells, nerve cells do not grow and die on an hourly basis. Nor do they divide. Because of these two facts, discovered by the Spanish physician and Nobel Prize winner Santiago Ramón y Cajal more than 100 years ago, the prevailing wisdom was that neurons were incapable of growth, at least after early childhood.

These observations led Ramón y Cajal to put forth the *neuron doctrine*, which declared that neurons do not regenerate. Until the 1990s, researchers and physicians alike accepted the idea that, once a region of the brain was damaged, its function was lost forever. All neural growth and change were understood to be limited to fetal and childhood development, and the adult brain did not change.

Early Evidence of Neurogenesis in Adults

By the early 1960s, however, an accumulation of evidence began to suggest that adult brains do change. Perhaps the first empirical demonstration of neural growth (neurogenesis) occurred when neuroscientists detected evidence of cell division (evidence of growth) in the brains of adult rats (Bryans, 1959).

In the early 1960s, Joseph Altman published a series of groundbreaking studies with adult rats and cats. Armed with a new cell-labeling technique, Altman found evidence of the growth of new neurons in several brain areas that are crucial for learning and memory (Altman & Das, 1966; C. G. Gross, 2000). Even though his reports appeared in prestigious journals, Altman's findings were almost completely ignored or discounted. Why? He was working alone, and he was a little-known researcher who violated the dogma, or strongly accepted view.

As often happens with ideas that radically challenge basic assumptions and long-held beliefs, neuroscientists and others either trivialized or ignored Altman's findings of adult neurogenesis. What does it take for a movement to change a well-entrenched, century-old idea? In this case, three scientific events took place during the 1980s and 1990s that finally turned the tide of disbelief.

First, a series of studies on birds showed exceptional neural growth in many areas of the adult avian brain, including the hippocampus (Nottebohm, 1985). Second, there was increasing evidence for the formation of new synaptic connections in the brains of rats when they were raised in enriched environments, more so than normally occurs with development (Comery et al., 1996). For example, rats that lived in cages with playmates, wheels to run on, and toys showed more dendritic growth than those that lived alone in sparse cages (Rosenzweig & Bennett, 1969). Third, in the 1990s, researchers began to find solid evidence for neurogenesis in one region of the hippocampus in adult rats, monkeys, and humans. Neurogenesis was no longer something seen only in birds and rats. There was no more denying that neural growth occurs in humans.

Key Figures in the Discovery of Neural Growth in Adults

The person most responsible for demonstrating neurogenesis in humans is Fred "Rusty" Gage (ironically, a cousin of the famous Phineas Gage who had an iron rod blast through his skull; Gage, 2002; Gage, Kemperman, & Song, 2008). How is this research done in humans if researchers cannot train humans and then slice open their brains to see if neural growth has occurred? Current brain imaging techniques cannot detect the growth of new cells. Gage and his researchers, some of whom did medical research, hit upon the solution that allowed them to detect new neural growth in humans. It involves injecting people with a substance called BrdU, which is incorporated into dividing cells so that they can be identified.

However, there is a problem with BrdU: You can't simply inject humans with it, because it is radioactive, but—here was the big breakthrough—some people have to have it injected for medical reasons. Gage and his colleague Peter Erikkson knew that some cancer patients receive this injection as part of their therapy. Because it identifies new cells, it is used to track how aggressively cancerous tumors are growing. After some patients who had been injected with BrdU died, Gage and Erikkson examined their hippocampus tissue. Based on the presence of BrdU, they found new cells in the adult human hippocampus (Begley, 2007; Erikkson et al., 1998). It was the same part of the hippocampus that earlier had shown the greatest neuronal growth in rats and monkeys.

Another of the key figures in demonstrating new neural growth in adult primates has been Elizabeth Gould (Glasper, Leuner, & Gould, 2008). She and her colleagues have compared rates of neurogenesis and synaptic growth in the brains of primates living in naturalistic settings with those living in lab cages. The naturalistic settings simulated a wild environment, with natural vegetation where the animals could search for food, among other activities. The brains of the animals that lived in these environmentally complex settings showed brain growth in areas important for thinking and feeling. They also had higher rates of neurogenesis and more connections between neurons than the animals reared in cages. In other studies, Gould and her colleagues found that stress and impoverished environments resulted in less neurogenesis in mammals (Mirescu & Gould, 2006; Mirescu et al., 2006).

Because of the onslaught of findings demonstrating neurogenesis in adult animals during the 1990s, the dogma of no new neural growth finally died. Now we know that neurons and their dendrites and synapses change, grow, and die in both young and old animals—including humans—depending on the kind of stimulation they receive from the outside world. When we learn anything, and even when we exercise, neurons in the brain are changed.

Animals reared in naturalistic settings have higher rates of neurogenesis than those reared in cages.

 Why is that?

Challenge Your Assumptions

True or False? New neurons grow in children but not adults.

False: Neural growth slows with age but never completely stops.

Connection

Learning results in new synapses, dendrites, and even neurons in certain regions of the brain. Regular exercise also stimulates neural growth.

See "Synaptic Change during Learning," Chapter 8, "Learning," p. 314, and "Research on Health-Relevant Behavior," Chapter 12, "Stress and Health," p. 466.

Quick Quiz 3.4: Challenging Assumptions about Neural Growth in the Adult Brain

1. The brain's ability to adopt new functions, reorganize itself, and make new neural connections is known as
   a. neuroplasticity.
   b. neurogenesis.
   c. the neuron doctrine.
   d. localization of function.

2. In what region of the human brain is there the most evidence of neurogenesis?
   a. frontal cortex
   b. hypothalamus
   c. amygdala
   d. hippocampus

Answers can be found at the end of the chapter.

MEASURING THE BRAIN

To be able to look into the brain as it is working was a long-time dream of philosophers and scientists. In the last few decades, realizing this wish has become possible. At least three techniques are now commonly used to measure brain activity in psychological research.

FIGURE **3.20**
ELECTROENCEPHALOGRAPHY (EEG). One of the authors (Erika) in an EEG cap for a study on brain activity and facial expression of emotion: The dots on her face allow for video motion capture of facial expression changes.

 Do measurements taken from the scalp determine precisely where in the brain activity is happening for different tasks such as whether the amygdala or hippocampus is activated? Explain.

electroencephalography (EEG)
A method for measuring brain activity in which the electrical activity of the brain is recorded from electrodes placed on a person's scalp.

event-related potential (ERP)
A technique that extracts electrical activity from raw EEG data to measure cognitive processes.

magnetic resonance imaging (MRI)
A brain imaging technique that uses magnetic fields to produce detailed images of the structure of the brain and other soft tissues.

functional MRI (fMRI)
A brain imaging technique that uses magnetic fields to produce detailed images of activity in areas of the brain and other soft tissues.

Electroencephalography

Researchers use **electroencephalography (EEG)** to record the electrical activity of the brain. The procedure involves placing electrodes, metal disks attached to wires, on a person's scalp. The electrodes are usually mounted in a fabric cap that fits snugly over the head. Typically, the person is performing certain tasks while the electrical activity is recorded. EEG is superior to other brain imaging techniques in showing *when* brain activity occurs. It is not very accurate, however, at indicating precisely *where* activity occurs (see Figure 3.20).

Event-related potential (ERP) is a special technique that extracts electrical activity from raw EEG data to measure cognitive processes. To examine ERPs, one gathers electrical recordings from an EEG cap on research participants who are performing cognitive or emotional tasks, such as trying to attend to an object on a computer screen, remember a list of words, or view emotionally charged slides. Typically, raw EEG data provide a summary of all the electrical activity in the brain that happens at a particular time. Generally, this level of detail is fine for measuring states of wakefulness, for example, but more temporal precision is needed to see a brain reaction to a particular stimulus, such as a flashing light or a line. To examine ERPs, researchers use an averaging process that allows them to filter out all electrical activity except the activity related to the stimulus the person is processing in a controlled experiment.

Because they are based on EEG, ERPs provide excellent temporal resolution (they show brain activity linked with psychological tasks almost immediately in time) but poor spatial resolution. Spatial resolution involves how tiny an area can be pinpointed as being active at a certain time. Two other techniques provide better spatial resolution than EEG: MRI and PET.

Magnetic Resonance Imaging (MRI) and Functional MRI (fMRI)

MRI stands for **magnetic resonance imaging.** MRI uses magnetic fields to produce very finely detailed images of the structure of the brain and other soft tissues. In MRI, the patient lies on a platform or bed, which slides into a tube surrounded by a circular magnet. The magnet, along with radio waves, is used to produce a signal, which is then processed by computer. The computer then produces an image with an amazing level of detail (see Figure 3.21). MRI provides static pictures, very useful for looking at *structures*, such as when someone is injured, but MRI does not tell us anything about *activity*.

A variation on MRI, **functional MRI (fMRI),** does tell us about brain activity. fMRI produces indirect, high-resolution images of activity based on how the brain uses oxygen, rather than a direct "readout" of nerve impulses. The images show where brain activity is occurring during particular tasks by tracking blood oxygen use in brain tissue, as shown in Figure 3.21. In this way, researchers can see which areas of the brain are using the most oxygen (and presumably are most

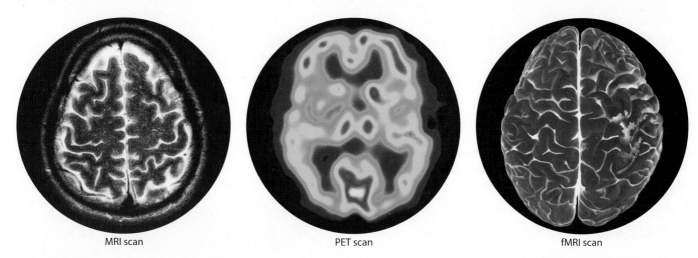

MRI scan   PET scan   fMRI scan

FIGURE 3.21

BRAIN IMAGING TECHNOLOGY. MRI equipment takes very clear, detailed images of soft tissue, including the brain, but it doesn't record brain activity. Both PET scans and fMRI, in contrast, highlight brain activity.

Which of these techniques gives the most precise location of brain activity?

active) during certain tasks (Casey, Davidson, & Rosen, 2002; Lagopoulos, 2007). When people perform various tasks while being scanned, the researchers can distinguish which areas are active during each task.

Although fMRI provides a much better measure of *where* activity occurs than EEG does, it is not without drawbacks. For one thing, it is very expensive. Also, it does not provide very precise measures of *when* activation occurs in response to a particular stimulus or task. It is not entirely clear exactly how directly fMRI images reflect underlying neural activity (Lagopoulos, 2007). Some studies suggest a fairly direct correlation with processing in certain cortical areas (Logothetis et al., 2001). As a result, fMRI findings should always be interpreted with care. The Research Process for this chapter illustrates the use of fMRI to study how people perceive faces (see Figure 3.22).

Positron Emission Tomography (PET)

Positron emission tomography (PET) measures blood flow to brain areas in the active brain (see Figure 3.21). From these measurements, researchers and doctors can determine which brain areas are active during certain situations. PET involves injecting the participant or patient with a radioactive form of oxygen (or glucose). The brain then takes up the oxygen during cell metabolism. Thanks to the radioactive *label* on the oxygen, scanners and computers can be used to create images of the brain regions using that oxygen during a certain task. Although the results are very informative, the use of radioactive substances means PET is not completely riskfree. fMRI is a much safer way to image metabolism in the brain.

The imaging techniques we have discussed so far focus on measuring the structure or activity of clusters of somas of neurons. What is known as the *gray matter* is the brain tissue composed of neuron cell bodies, because the soma or cell body is where cell metabolism takes place and thus oxygen is used by the cell. Information, however, is communicated among different areas of the brain via long fibers of myelinated axons, which are not typically well imaged by MRI or PET. Because these fibers are covered with myelin, they are called *white matter.* Several methods have been developed for better imaging white matter, or neural

positron emission tomography (PET)

A brain imaging technique that measures blood flow to active areas in the brain.

Research Process

1 **Research Questions**

Is any part of the brain dedicated to seeing faces and no other object? Likewise, is there a part of the brain dedicated exclusively to perceiving places (such as buildings)? If so, are these brain regions equally active when you imagine a face or place and when you actually see one?

2 **Method**

Previous research had found one distinct part of the brain activated when we see a face (the fusiform face area, FFA) and a different area of the brain (the parahippocampal place area, PPA) activated when we see a place or a building. O'Craven and Kanwisher (2000) wanted to confirm this result and extend it by seeing whether the activity was as strong when just imagining faces or places as it was when seeing these images.

Eight participants were placed inside an fMRI machine (see image) and then viewed images of either famous faces or familiar buildings on their university campus. For the imagining condition, participants were read the names of famous people and places and asked to close their eyes and form a "vivid mental image" of each one.

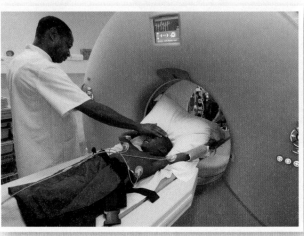

A young boy being prepped for a brain imaging procedure in an fMRI machine.

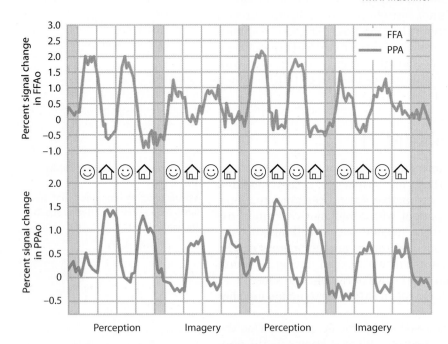

3 **Results**

Results confirmed the FFA showed high activity (% signal change) for faces but low activity for places, whereas the PPA showed the opposite (see graph). Moreover, the results for imagining faces and places showed the same pattern of results, only less strongly.

4 **Conclusion**

Different regions of the brain are dedicated to very specific kinds of visual stimuli. We know this only because fMRI technology allows us to see specific areas of brain activity when we are shown different kinds of objects and given different kinds of tasks.

FIGURE **3.22**

DISTINCT BRAIN REGIONS INVOLVED IN IMAGINING AND PERCEIVING FACES AND PLACES. ("Mental Imagery of Faces and Places Activates Corresponding Stimulus-Specific Brain Regions," by K. M. O'Craven and N. N. Kanwisher, 2000, *Journal of Cognitive Neuroscience, 12,* 1013–1023. doi:10.1162/08989290051137549.)

fibers. One such method is *diffusion tensor imaging,* which is a kind of MRI adapted for better imaging of myelinated fibers and *tracts* (collections of myelinated fibers). This type of imaging shows promise in studying the connectivity among brain areas (Hua et al., 2009; Jones, Knösche, & Turner, 2012).

Quick Quiz 3.5: Measuring the Brain

1. Which brain measurement technique best shows *when* neural activity has occurred?
   a. PET
   b. MRI
   c. EEG
   d. fMRI

2. Betty has an injury to a particular part of her brain and suddenly has trouble imagining, recognizing, and interpreting faces. What region of the brain was likely affected and which technology told us this?
   a. parahippocampal place area (PPA); MRI
   b. parahippocampal place area (PPA); fMRI
   c. fusiform face area (FFA); MRI
   d. fusiform face area (FFA); fMRI

Answers can be found at the end of the chapter.

THE ENDOCRINE SYSTEM

In the nervous system, neurons communicate information electrochemically by means of membrane changes and neurotransmitters released into the synaptic cleft. In the **endocrine system,** glands secrete chemicals called **hormones,** which travel through the bloodstream to tissues and organs all over the body and regulate body functions. Hormones also play a crucial role in regulating metabolism, growth, reproduction, mood, and other processes.

Figure 3.23 depicts some of the major endocrine glands of the body. The hypothalamus is a brain structure that controls the **pituitary gland,** known as the master gland of the body because it secretes hormones that control the release of hormones from glands elsewhere in the body. The *thyroid* gland sits in the neck region and releases hormones that control the rate of metabolism, the process by which the body converts nutritional substances into energy. The *pancreas* releases hormones, including insulin, that play a vital role in regulating blood sugar levels. The sex glands (ovaries and testes) release sex hormones, which lead to the development of sex characteristics (such as body hair and breast development), sex drive, and other aspects of sexual maturation.

The **adrenal glands,** which sit atop the kidneys, release hormones in response to stress and emotions. They also help regulate heart rate, blood pressure, and blood sugar. In addition, the adrenal glands produce **catecholamines,** a class of chemicals that includes the neurotransmitters dopamine, norepinephrine, and epinephrine, which control ANS activation. Norepinephrine activates the sympathetic nervous system, increasing the heart rate, rate of respiration, and blood pressure in order to support rapid action of the body. The adrenal glands also release stress hormones, such as **cortisol,** which is responsible for maintaining the activation of bodily systems during prolonged stress.

The endocrine system works in conjunction with the nervous system and in a dynamic relationship with the brain. An example is its control of the female menstrual cycle. Each month, the hypothalamus sends signals to the pituitary to release hormones that stimulate a woman's ovaries to develop (mature) an egg. As part of the process, the ovary itself releases hormones that prepare the womb to receive a fertilized egg. If the egg is fertilized, the ovaries send hormonal feedback to the hypothalamus, so that it will not stimulate further egg development.

endocrine system
A system of glands that secrete and regulate hormones in the body.

hormones
Chemicals, secreted by glands, that travel in the bloodstream and carry messages to tissues and organs all over the body.

pituitary gland
The master endocrine gland of the body; it controls the release of hormones from glands throughout the body.

adrenal glands
Endocrine structures that release hormones important in regulating the stress response and emotions.

catecholamines
Chemicals released from the adrenal glands that function as hormones and as neurotransmitters to control ANS activation.

cortisol
A stress hormone produced by the body to ensure that the body gets enough fuel during emotional arousal and stress.

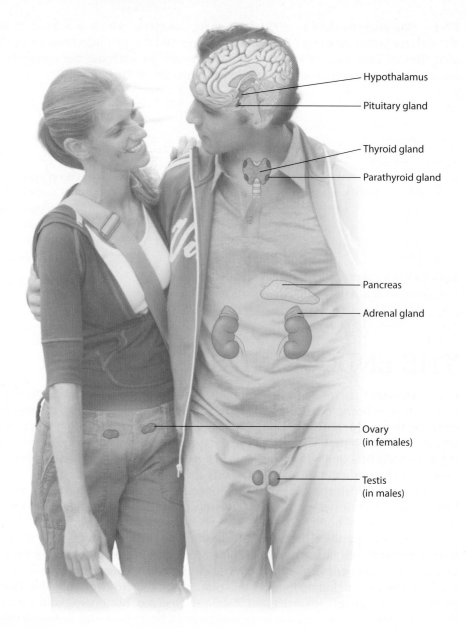

Hypothalamus

Pituitary gland

Thyroid gland

Parathyroid gland

Pancreas

Adrenal gland

Ovary
(in females)

Testis
(in males)

FIGURE **3.23**

THE ENDOCRINE SYSTEM. The endocrine system consists of numerous glands throughout the body. The pancreas, for example, releases insulin, which is important in transporting sugars (glucose) from the bloodstream into the cells. Cells then use the glucose as their energy source. The thyroid gland regulates metabolism.

Quick Quiz 3.6: The Endocrine System

1. How do hormones differ from neurotransmitters?
   a. Hormones are proteins; neurotransmitters are fats.
   b. Hormones carry messages in the bloodstream; neurotransmitters carry messages across synapses.
   c. Hormones have no effect on mood; neurotransmitters do.
   d. All of the above are correct.

2. What is the name of the stress hormone released by the adrenal glands?
   a. catecholamine
   b. insulin
   c. thyroxin
   d. cortisol

Answers can be found at the end of the chapter.

Bringing It All Together

Making Connections in the Biology of Behavior

What Esref Armagan's Story Reveals about the Brain

This chapter opened with a profile of the blind artist Esref Armagan. Besides being a fine example of someone creatively overcoming a disability, Armagan's story offers us a way to connect much of the material in this chapter.

When Armagan paints, he uses a Braille stylus (writing instrument) to sketch out his drawing by laying down bumps on paper. With his other hand, he follows the raised bumps to "see" what he has put down (Motluk, 2005). He then transfers this sketch to canvas and applies acrylic paint with his fingers, one color at a time. Armagan waits for each color to dry before applying another, so that they will not blend or smear too much. No one helps him when he paints, and his paintings are entirely his own creations.

Armagan has learned much from talking with other people, such as what the typical colors of certain objects are. He always keeps his paints lined up in the same order, so that he can find the right color. His sense of perspective is harder to explain. He portrays perspective with uncanny realism, far beyond what any other blind painter has ever achieved (Kennedy & Juricevic, 2006). He says he learned this from talking with others, as well as from feeling his way in the world ("Biography," n.d.).

Armagan's skill appears to have at least some inborn basis, given how early he started without receiving any instruction. Before age 6, he drew in the dirt and scratched drawings on the furniture in his home. His parents, wanting to save their furniture, finally gave him drawing materials (Kennedy & Juricevic, 2006; Motluk, 2005)—something not usually offered to blind children. This early, automatic, and almost compulsive behavior suggests that something about how his brain is wired drove young Esref to draw, and genetics likely played a role.

What senses does Armagan use while painting? Like many blind people, Armagan relies mostly on his sense of touch. Interestingly, he needs total silence while working. In many blind people, the so-called visual centers of the brain are used to process hearing (Röder, 2006).

How can we explain Armagan's act of painting in the context of the nervous system? As Armagan moves the stylus to create bumps on paper and moves his fingers over those bumps, the sensations from his fingertips stimulate his sensory neurons. These neurons in turn stimulate interneurons in different regions of the brain, which eventually stimulate motor neurons to move his hands and fingers in precise ways to execute his painting.

Throughout this process, millions of neurons are firing. As Armagan moves his hands and fingers and begins to paint, the neurons send impulses to other neurons.

Esref Armagan with some of his paintings

Some of the messages are excitatory; some are inhibitory. If a neuron receives a preponderance of excitatory impulses and the membrane potential changes sufficiently, it will fire in an all-or-none fashion. At this point, the cell membrane opens channels, letting potassium out and sodium in. The wave of opening and closing channels moves the impulse down the axon and stimulates the release of neurotransmitters in vesicles in the terminal buttons. The neurotransmitters are released into the synaptic cleft, where they bind with receptor sites in postsynaptic neurons, get taken back up into the presynaptic neuron, or degrade. The message is then relayed to the next (postsynaptic) neurons.

What neurotransmitters are most likely to be involved in painting? As Armagan sketches and paints, he voluntarily moves his arms, hands, and fingers. Voluntary motor movements of muscles use synapses involving dopamine and acetylcholine. His attention and focus while painting, and his blocking out of auditory stimulation, increase his levels of norepinephrine as well. Additionally, the learning and memory needed for his artistry involve the effects of acetylcholine and glutamate in various parts of the brain.

There is activity throughout his brain, in brain stem structures as well as in the forebrain. As Armagan paints, as is true for anything he does, his breathing, heart rate, body temperature, and even consciousness are regulated by his medulla (see Figure 3.24). Armagan's thalamus transfers and relays most of the sensory information coming into various parts of his brain for different kinds of processing. As he develops new ideas for what he wants to paint, his hippocampus is active in sending those ideas to the frontal lobes for memory or to various cortexes for more permanent storage.

In order to paint, Armagan needs to plan and execute the actions of painting. The frontal lobes play a key role in planning and keeping in mind the tasks needed to paint. His motor cortex controls the movement of his legs, arms, hands, and fingers. His basal ganglia help carry out the commands to move the various parts of his body. Perhaps Armagan decides to put his fingers in the paint container to his left. The parietal lobes get involved in orienting his body in space, and the frontal lobes plan the action to reach for the paint pot to his left. When he is ready to move his hand, the signal from these cortical areas travels to the cerebellum to control fine movement, then to the pons, the medulla, and finally the spinal cord to the nerves that control the muscles in his hand and arm. All this occurs in an instant. His brain gets feedback on the position of his hand and makes needed adjustments: a complex interplay among the somatosensory cortex (which receives sensory input from his fingers and arms as he paints), the insula, and the cerebellum.

Armagan is one of the few blind people with the ability to accurately portray depth and perspective in his drawings and paintings. When asked to draw a cube and then rotate it once and then once again, he draws it in perfect perspective, with horizontal and vertical lines converging at imaginary points in the distance (Kennedy & Juricevic, 2006). This ability to render perspective accurately in three dimensions is processed in the parietal lobes near the top and back of his brain. The visual images that Armagan forms from his sense of touch activate the occipital lobe.

When sighted people imagine something, their visual cortex (in the occipital lobe) is active, but in a much weaker way than when they actually look at something. When Armagan imagines an object, his visual cortex is even less active than that. But when he paints, his occipital cortex

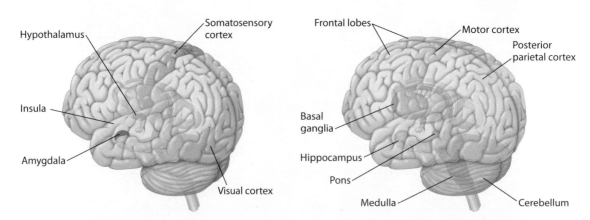

FIGURE **3.24**
SOME OF THE BRAIN REGIONS INVOLVED WHEN ESREF ARMAGAN PAINTS. When he is drawing or painting, Armagan uses many different regions of the brain. Most interestingly, Armagan's visual cortex is active in forming images of what he paints. These images do not stem from his visual system (eyes) but rather from his sense of touch (fingers). When Armagan touches something, his occipital lobes are as active as a sighted person's occipital lobes are when seeing something. In other words, he forms visual images, but they come from touching rather than seeing.

Touring the Nervous System and the Brain

The Neuron and Synapse ■ The Resting Potential and Action Potential
Structures and Functions of the Human Brain ■ Lobes of the Cerebral Cortex
Visual Information in the Split Brain ■ Central and Peripheral Nervous Systems

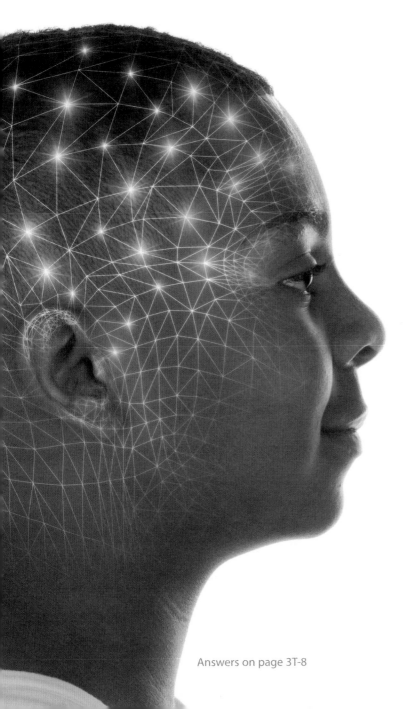

GOALS OF THE TOUR

1 **The Neuron and Synapse.** You will be able to identify parts of the neuron and synapse and describe how they communicate information.

2 **The Resting Potential and Action Potential.** You will be able to describe the membrane changes involved in maintaining the resting potential and in producing the action potential.

3 **Structures and Functions of the Human Brain.** You will be able to identify the brain's key structures and functions.

4 **Lobes of the Cerebral Cortex.** You will be able to identify the location and describe the function of the four lobes of the cerebral cortex.

5 **Visual Information in the Split Brain.** You will be able to describe hemispheric lateralization and communication in the brain.

6 **Central and Peripheral Nervous Systems.** You will be able to identify the parts of the central and peripheral nervous systems and describe the body functions they control.

Answers on page 3T-8

The Neuron and the Synapse

1 Identify parts of the neuron and synapse and describe how they communicate information.

Presynaptic Neuron

1a **Neuron**
Stimulus to a neuron causes a neural impulse to travel down the axon toward dendrites of the next neuron.

Direction of nerve impulse

Postsynaptic Neuron

1b **Synapse**
In the terminal button, the impulse triggers the release of neurotransmitters into the synaptic cleft.

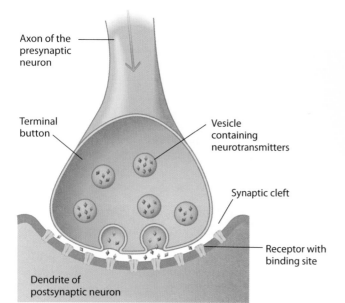

Axon of the presynaptic neuron

Terminal button

Vesicle containing neurotransmitters

Synaptic cleft

Receptor with binding site

Dendrite of postsynaptic neuron

The Resting Potential and Action Potential

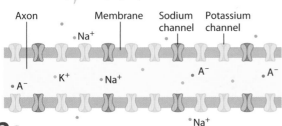

Direction of nerve impulse

Describe the membrane changes involved in maintaining the resting potential and in producing the action potential.

2

2a Resting Potential

Axon | Membrane | Sodium channel | Potassium channel

Na⁺ — Na^+

A^- — K^+ — Na^+ — A^- — A^-

Na^+

In the resting neuron, the fluid outside the axon contains a higher concentration of positive ions than the inside of the axon, which contains many negatively charged anions (A–).

2a Action Potential

The action potential is an impulse of positive charge that sweeps down the axon.

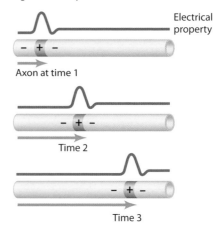

Electrical property

– + –
Axon at time 1

– + –
Time 2

– + –
Time 3

The graph below depicts the electrical changes that occur during each stage of an action potential (**1** resting potential, **2** depolarization, **3** repolarization, and **4** refractory period).

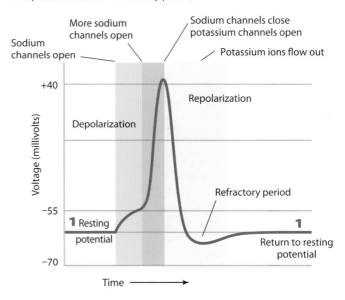

Sodium channels open

More sodium channels open

Sodium channels close potassium channels open

Potassium ions flow out

Voltage (millivolts)

+40

Depolarization

Repolarization

–55

1 Resting potential

Refractory period

1

Return to resting potential

–70

Time

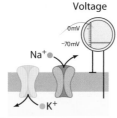

Voltage

0mV
–70mV

Na^+

K^+

1 Resting potential

Structures and Functions of the Human Brain

3 Identify the brain's key structures and functions.

3a Brain Stem Structures

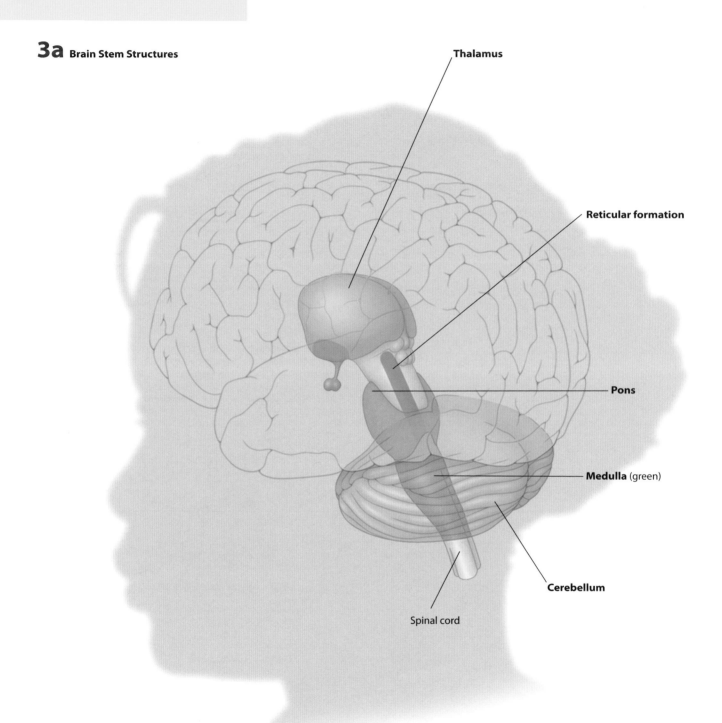

Thalamus

Reticular formation

Pons

Medulla (green)

Cerebellum

Spinal cord

Lobes of the Cerebral Cortex

Identify the location of the lobes of the cerebral cortex and describe their primary function.

4

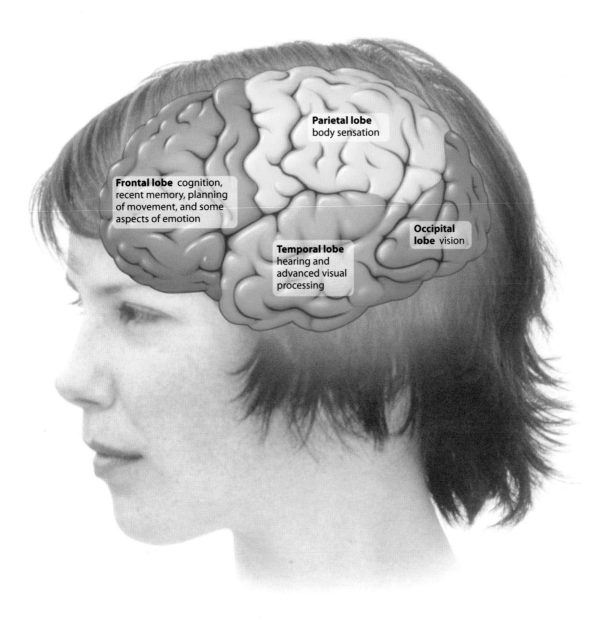

Parietal lobe body sensation

Frontal lobe cognition, recent memory, planning of movement, and some aspects of emotion

Temporal lobe hearing and advanced visual processing

Occipital lobe vision

Visual Information in the Split Brain

5 Describe hemispheric lateralization and communication in the brain.

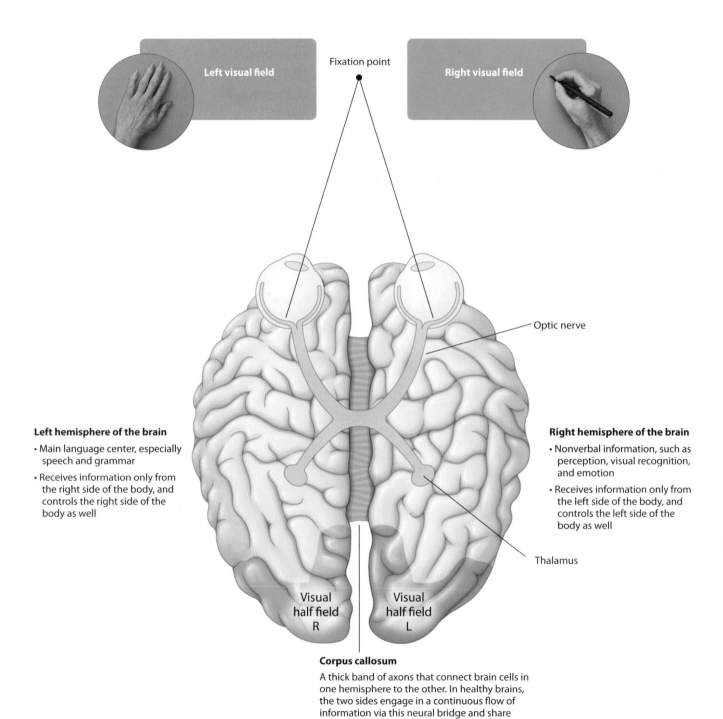

Left visual field

Fixation point

Right visual field

Optic nerve

Left hemisphere of the brain
- Main language center, especially speech and grammar
- Receives information only from the right side of the body, and controls the right side of the body as well

Right hemisphere of the brain
- Nonverbal information, such as perception, visual recognition, and emotion
- Receives information only from the left side of the body, and controls the left side of the body as well

Thalamus

Visual half field R

Visual half field L

Corpus callosum
A thick band of axons that connect brain cells in one hemisphere to the other. In healthy brains, the two sides engage in a continuous flow of information via this neural bridge and share information.

Central and Peripheral Nervous Systems

a The Central Nervous System

⬤ Central nervous system

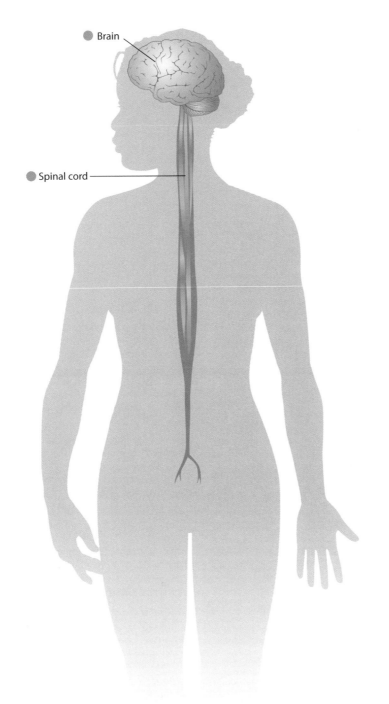

⬤ Brain

⬤ Spinal cord

Identify the parts of the central and peripheral nervous systems and describe the body functions they control.

6

1. THE NEURON AND SYNAPSE

The *neuron* consists of a *soma, dendrites,* and an *axon.* The soma is the structure of the neuron that contains the nucleus, which consists of the genetic material including the chromosomes. The dendrites are branches of the neuron that receive information from other neurons. The axon sends information away from the soma to other neurons or cells.

When a neuron fires, it sends an electrical impulse down the axon, known as the *action potential.* When the impulse arrives at the axon terminal buttons, it causes the release of *neurotransmitter* molecules into the *synapse.* The synapse is the gap junction between two neurons. Neurons communicate with one another by means of chemical signals provided by neurotransmitters that cross the synapse.

The neurotransmitter released by the sending neuron enters the synaptic gap and attaches to a *receptor* on the postsynaptic neuron. The receptor site contains a channel that is typically closed when the receiving neuron is in the resting state (*resting potential*). When the neurotransmitter binds to the receptor site, the receptor channel opens to allow a particular *ion* to enter or leave the neuron. If a neurotransmitter causes channels for a positively charged ion like sodium (Na^+) to open, the postsynaptic neuron will become less negative in charge. The entry of sodium will cause a change in the electrical charge (potential) of the receiving neuron that may make it more likely to generate its own action potential.

2. THE RESTING POTENTIAL AND ACTION POTENTIAL

The neuron maintains electrical properties called an *electrical potential,* which is a difference in the electrical charge inside and outside of the cell. This charge difference is maintained because the membrane of the neuron is *selectively permeable.* This means some molecules can pass through the membrane more freely than others. The membrane is not permeable to large negatively charged protein molecules that are trapped inside the neuron. Inside and outside the neuron are electrically charged particles called *ions* that vary in concentrations. The ions that play an important role in the function of the neuron are sodium (Na^+), potassium (K^+), and chloride (Cl^-). These ions enter or leave the neuron through special channels provided by protein molecules that line the neuron.

The *resting potential* is the electrical property of the neuron when it is not stimulated or not sending a nerve impulse. In a typical neuron this is seen as a -70 mV charge inside relative to the outside of the membrane. During the resting potential, the sodium channels are closed, leaving a higher concentration of sodium ions outside of the neuron membrane. The negative charge of a neuron during the resting state is largely maintained by the negatively charged protein molecules trapped inside the neuron and by the inability of positively charged sodium ions to cross the membrane into the neuron.

If the neuron receives enough excitatory messages to surpass the threshold level, an *action potential* will occur, sending the nerve impulse down the axon. Positively charged sodium ions enter the neuron, and potassium ions move out. The action potential jumps from one space in the axon's myelin sheath to the next, changing membrane qualities at each space. Membrane channels for sodium close to keep sodium ions out of the neuron and potassium channels open to allow potassium to move into the neuron, restoring the resting potential.

3. STRUCTURES AND FUNCTIONS OF THE HUMAN BRAIN

The brain stem structures are embedded within the core of the brain and provide a number of vital functions for survival. These include the medulla, pons, cerebellum, reticular formation, and the thalamus.

The *medulla* is a brain structure just above the spinal cord. It controls a number of life-sustaining reflexes and functions including breathing, coughing, vomiting, and heart rate. The *pons* lies just above the medulla and is particularly involved in sleep and arousal. The *cerebellum* is a large structure at the base of the brain with many folds. It is traditionally known to be involved in motor coordination and balance but also plays a role in attention of visual and auditory stimuli and the timing of movements. The *reticular formation* is an elaborate diffuse network of neurons that runs through the core of the medulla and pons to the base of the thalamus. It plays a role in arousal, attention, sleep patterns, and stereotyped patterns such as posture and locomotion. The *thalamus* is a central structure in the brain that relays auditory, visual, and somatosensory (body senses) information to the cerebral cortex.

The limbic system comprises a number of brain structures involved in m vation, emotion, and memory. The *hypothalamus* is a small structure th located just below the thalamus. It controls the autonomic nervous sys as well as the release of hormones from the pituitary gland. It is involve a number of functions including eating, drinking, and sexual behavior, plays an important role in the expression of emotions and stress respo The *hippocampus* is located in the temporal lobe and plays a role in lear and memory. Adjacent to the hippocampus is the amygdala, which is invo in fear and anxiety. The *cingulate gyrus,* a beltlike structure in the middl the brain, is involved in attention and cognitive control.

The *cerebral cortex* is the outer layer of the brain and is involved in hig order functions such as thinking, learning, consciousness, and memory.

4. LOBES OF THE CEREBRAL CORTEX

The *cerebral cortex* is anatomically divided into four lobes: occipital l parietal lobe, temporal lobe, and frontal lobe. The *occipital lobe* is loc in the posterior end (back region) of the cortex and is involved in proces *visual information.* The *parietal lobe* makes up the top rear section of cortex. The parietal lobe is involved in *bodily senses.* The area just in fron the parietal lobe is the *somatosensory cortex.* It is the primary target for *touch senses* of the body and information for muscle-stretch receptors joint receptors. The *temporal lobe* is the large portion of each hemisp near the temples and lies behind the frontal lobe and below the *lateral fiss* It is the primary region of the cortex that processes *auditory information. frontal lobe* extends from the central sulcus to the anterior limit (forw region) of the brain. The region of the frontal lobe immediately adjacen the central sulcus is called the *motor cortex* because it controls *fine mo* ments. The most anterior region is called the *prefrontal cortex;* it is invo in higher brain functions including *cognition* (thought processes), re *memory,* the *planning of movement,* and some aspects of *emotion.*

5. VISUAL INFORMATION IN THE SPLIT BRAIN

Lateralization refers to the division of labor between the two cerebral he spheres of the brain. The *left hemisphere* receives sensory information fr and controls the movements in the right side of the body. Likewise, ima of objects in the right visual field are projected to the left half of the re of each eye, which in turn sends the information to the visual cortex in left hemisphere. The left hemisphere also contains the main language a involved in the comprehension and production of language.

The *right hemisphere* receives sensory information from and controls movements in the left side of the body. Likewise, images of objects in the visual field are projected to the right half of the retina of each eye, which turn sends the information to the visual cortex in the right hemisphere. right hemisphere processes nonverbal information, such as perception, vis recognition, and emotion.

In the healthy brain the two cerebral hemispheres share information w each other across the broad band of axons called the *corpus callosum.* some instances the corpus callosum is surgically cut, resulting in wha called a *split brain.* In the split brain, information in one cerebral hemisph is confined to that side of the brain.

6. CENTRAL AND PERIPHERAL NERVOUS SYSTEMS

The nervous system is made up of the *central nervous system* and the *peri eral nervous system.* The central nervous system is comprised of the br and the spinal cord. The peripheral nervous system consists of all nerve fib outside of the brain and spinal cord. The peripheral nervous system is m up of two major divisions: the *somatic nervous system* and the *autono nervous system.*

The *somatic nervous system* consists of nerve fibers conveying informat from the brain and spinal cord to skeletal muscles; this information contr movement and sends information back to the brain via the spinal cord fr sensory receptors located in various parts of the body.

The *autonomic nervous system* controls the glands and muscles of the in nal organs such as the heart, digestive system, lungs, and salivary glan and it consists of the sympathetic and the parasympathetic branches. T *sympathetic branch* arouses the body, mobilizes its energy during physi exercise and in stressful situations, and activates the adrenal gland to re epinephrine into the bloodstream. The *parasympathetic branch* calms body and conserves and replenishes energy.

becomes so active that it cannot easily be distinguished from a sighted person's visual cortex as the person actually sees something (Begley, 2007; Motluk, 2005). Armagan's brain appears to be seeing.

Because Armagan has been blind since birth, his visual cortex has never received any visual input (light), but that part of his brain didn't merely die or stop functioning. In many blind people, the visual cortex takes on hearing functions, enabling them to hear certain types of sounds better than sighted people can (Röder, 2006). Armagan's occipital cortex indeed is very active when he paints, but he is receiving tactile (touch) and not visual input.

Furthermore, in most blind people who read Braille, the visual cortex is active in processing tactile and verbal memory function, but Armagan can't read Braille and his visual cortex is not recruited for any aspect of language. His memory for language is rather poor. He is a very "visual" person, but his visual images are built from tactile information. There is evidence from neuroscientists that this plasticity of the occipital lobes is the norm—it usually processes tactile information, verbal information, or both for blind people (Amedi et al., 2005). Armagan's life, abilities, and brain illustrate that the brain is both highly plastic *and* specialized (Begley, 2007). The so-called visual part of his brain found something to do.

Chapter Review

GENES AND BEHAVIOR

- At least four principles of behavioral genetics are important for psychology: (1) The relationship between specific genes and behavior is complex. (2) Most specific behaviors derive from many genes. (3) Behavioral genetics employs studies of twins and adoptees to disentangle the contributions of heredity and environment to behavior. (4) The environment influences how and when genes affect behavior.

- The extent to which a characteristic is influenced by genetics is known as heritability. Researchers use twin-adoption studies and gene-by-environment designs to study heritability.

THE NERVOUS SYSTEM

- There are two kinds of cells in the central nervous system: glial cells and neurons.

- Glial cells provide structural support, among other important functions.

- Neurons transmit information throughout the nervous system by means of action potentials. Messages are received by the branchlike dendrites and cell bodies of neighboring neurons; these messages create changes in the membrane of the receiving neuron. If the right conditions are met, then neurons fire in an all-or-none fashion.

- Action potentials move down the length of the axon as channels in the membrane open and close, allowing ions to move into and out of the axon. The action potential stimulates the release of neurotransmitters from the terminal buttons into the synaptic cleft.

- Neurotransmitters bind to receptor sites on the dendrites of postsynaptic neurons, allowing an action potential to be generated if the charge threshold is surpassed. Excess neurotransmitter is either taken back into the original neuron or broken down in the synaptic cleft.

THE BRAIN

- The brain is divided into three major regions: the hindbrain, midbrain, and forebrain.

- The topmost brain structures are the cerebrum and cerebral cortex, which are the seat of abstract reasoning, planning, and higher-order thought.

- The cerebrum comprises four lobes: The frontal lobes are involved in abstract reasoning, self-control, and motor control; the temporal lobes house the auditory cortex; the parietal lobes process tactile and spatial information; and the occipital lobes house the visual cortex.

- The left and right hemispheres of the brain carry out somewhat different functions. The biggest difference between the hemispheres is language, which is usually controlled by the left hemisphere.

- One major shift in our understanding of the brain over the last 15–20 years is how much neurons and brain structures are shaped by experience. New neurons form, new dendrites grow, and new synapses are created across the life span, especially in infancy and early childhood.

CHALLENGING ASSUMPTIONS ABOUT NEURAL GROWTH IN THE ADULT BRAIN

- Although first uncovered in the 1960s, evidence for neural growth in adult brains was not fully appreciated and accepted until the 1990s and 2000s.

MEASURING THE BRAIN

- Various methods offer glimpses into the brain and its functions.

- Electroencephalography (EEG) measures electrical activity from scalp readings.

- Magnetic resonance imaging (MRI) measures blood flow changes in the brain without the added risk of the radioactive dyes used in PET scans. The adaptation of MRI to functional MRIs (fMRI) allows researchers to determine which brain areas are active during specific tasks.

THE ENDOCRINE SYSTEM

- In the endocrine system, glands secrete chemicals called hormones, which travel in the bloodstream to tissues and organs all over the body.

- The pituitary gland, called the master gland of the body, controls the release of hormones from other glands in the body.

- The adrenal glands secrete hormones involved in sympathetic nervous system responses and stress.

BRINGING IT ALL TOGETHER: MAKING CONNECTIONS IN THE BIOLOGY OF BEHAVIOR

- The story of Esref Armagan offers a glimpse of the brain in action.

- As Armagan moves his hands and fingers and begins to paint, the neurons send impulses to other neurons. Activation occurs in many regions of the brain. The cerebellum fine-tunes his movements by attending to whether his body is moving appropriately with the right amount of effort.

- The visual images that Armagan forms from his sense of touch activate the same region of the brain that is active when seeing people see something: the occipital lobe.

Key Terms

acetylcholine (ACh), p. 87
action potential, p. 83
adrenal glands, p. 109
alleles, p. 74
all-or-none principle, p. 85
amygdala, p. 95
aphasia, p. 98
arborization, p. 102
autonomic nervous system (ANS), p. 78
axon, p. 81
basal ganglia, p. 95
behavioral genetics, p. 74
Broca's area, p. 98
catecholamines, p. 109
central nervous system (CNS), p. 78
cerebellum, p. 93
cerebral cortex, p. 96
cerebrum, p. 96

chromosome, p. 73
cingulate gyrus, p. 95
corpus callosum, p. 98
cortisol, p. 109
dendrites, p. 81
DNA (deoxyribonucleic acid), p. 73
dominant alleles, p. 74
dopamine, p. 87
electroencephalography (EEG), p. 106
endocrine system, p. 109
enzymatic degradation, p. 85
epigenetics, p. 76
epinephrine, p. 87
event-related potential (ERP), p. 106
fraternal twins, p. 75
functional MRI (fMRI), p. 106
GABA (gamma-aminobutyric acid), p. 88

gene-by-environment interaction research, p. 76
genes, p. 73
genome, p. 73
genotype, p. 76
glial cells, p. 79
glutamate, p. 85
graded potentials, p. 85
heritability, p. 75
hippocampus, p. 94
hormones, p. 109
hypothalamus, p. 94
identical twins, p. 75
insula, p. 98
interneurons, p. 82
ions, p. 83
magnetic resonance imaging (MRI), p. 106
medulla, p. 93

mirror neurons, p. 82
monogenic, p. 75
motor neurons, p. 82
mutation, p. 74
myelin sheath, p. 81
neurogenesis, p. 102
neurons, p. 79
neuroplasticity, p. 102
neurotransmitters, p. 81
norepinephrine, p. 87
parasympathetic nervous system,
    p. 78
peripheral nervous system, p. 78

phenotype, p. 77
pituitary gland, p. 109
polygenic, p. 75
pons, p. 93
positron emission tomography
    (PET), p. 107
recessive alleles, p. 74
reflexes, p. 93
refractory period, p. 83
resting potential, p. 83
reticular formation, p. 93
reuptake, p. 85
sensory neurons, p. 82

serotonin, p. 88
soma, p. 81
somatic nervous system, p. 78
sympathetic nervous system,
    p. 78
synapse, p. 81
synaptic vesicles, p. 85
synaptogenesis, p. 102
terminal button, p. 81
thalamus, p. 93
twin-adoption studies, p. 76
Wernicke's area, p. 100

Quick Quiz Answers

Quick Quiz 3.1: 1. b 2. a 3. a   **Quick Quiz 3.2:** 1. c 2. a 3. b 4. c   **Quick Quiz 3.3:** 1. b 2. c 3. d
Quick Quiz 3.4: 1. a 2. d   **Quick Quiz 3.5:** 1. c 2. d   **Quick Quiz 3.6:** 1. b 2. d

4 Sensing and Perceiving Our World

Chapter Outline

The Long, Strange Trip from Sensation to Perception
Vision
Hearing
The Bodily Senses
The Chemical Senses: Smell and Taste
Synesthesia
Chapter Review

Challenge Your Assumptions

True or False?

- Seeing is done as much with the brain as with the eyes. (see page 129)

- Some visual neurons fire only when presented with images of the actress Halle Berry. (see page 129)

- Color is a property of objects in the world. (see page 138)

- Different regions of the tongue contain taste buds for specific types of taste, such as sweet or bitter. (see page 149)

- The experience of "seeing sounds" or "hearing colors" occurs only under the influence of drugs. (see page 151)

When Ben Underwood was 3 years old, he had both eyes removed. He had a rare and malignant eye cancer, and removing the eyes altogether was his best shot at survival. When he woke up from the surgery, he said, "Mom, I can't see you anymore, Mom." But his mother said, "Yes you can see me. You can see me with your hands. You can see me with your ears. You can see me with your nose. I said baby, you can still see" ("Extraordinary People," 2007). Ben's mother wanted him to think of himself as normal, and he did. He learned to ride a bike, played basketball, and walked everywhere. He did all of these things without any aid whatsoever, other than a clicking tongue and his ability to "echolocate" (use differences in pitch when sounds bounce off objects of different sizes and distances), which he taught himself. When he was 4, he was in the car with the window rolled down, listening to the passing sounds. He astonished his mother by saying, "Mom, do you see that big building out there?" She said, "Yeah, I can see that big building but how can you see it?" ("Extraordinary People," 2007). He was "seeing" the buildings by the different sounds the building made compared to open spaces or other kinds of buildings.

Tragically, when Ben was 16 the cancer returned, and he died in 2009, yet Ben's legacy lives on. Inspired by Ben, and with the aid of echolocation proponent Daniel Kish, schools for the blind in Scotland and Israel are teaching their students to use echolocation to help them maneuver and get around (Kloosterman, 2009; Macaskill, 2008).

Ben's ability to "see" with sound is but one fascinating example of the flexibility in how humans sense and perceive their world. Every moment of every day we are bombarded with stimulation— sights, sounds, tastes, smells, and textures. In this chapter we examine the interface between the outer world and our inner experience by looking at how we sense and perceive external stimuli. Sometimes there is a one-to-one correspondence between the kind of stimulation our sense organs receive (such as light) and our perceptual experience (sight). Other times, one sense can replace another (as in Ben's case). For each of the major sensory systems, we will examine how physical information is transformed into neural signals, how the brain processes that information, and how our knowledge and expectations can shape our sensory experiences.

After just a few seconds' viewing, the centers of these circles appear to be moving.

Are they? Obviously not, but how do our brains perceive movement when none is there?

THE LONG, STRANGE TRIP FROM SENSATION TO PERCEPTION

How does the outer world become the inner world that we perceive, understand, and make sense out of? The better that animals can sense what is happening in the world around them, the better they can survive and reproduce. Yet the apparently simple act of interpreting the sound vibrations hitting your ear as someone's calling your name, for example, is a complex process involving both the sense organs and the brain. The sense organs transform information from its physical form (light or sound waves or chemicals) into a nerve impulse and transmit it to the brain, which organizes that information, interprets it, and then initiates a response. It all happens in an instant and without effort on our part. Think about that for a second: Vibrations in your ear become your friend's voice; light waves that hit your retina become images of your home. How does sensation become perception?

This interplay between taking in information from the outside world and interpreting it is what sensation and perception are all about. **Sensation** is the stimulation of our sense organs by the outer world. Eyes are sensitive to light waves, ears to sounds, skin to touch and pressure, tongues to tastes, and noses to odors.

Perception is the act of organizing and interpreting sensory experience. It is how our psychological world represents our physical world. If you had not been taught to read, the words on this page would not be words. You read and make sense of the marks on the page because you spent years learning to speak and read English, and your brain transforms the raw sensory experience into meaningful concepts. We can have different experiences of the real world because individuals can experience the same physical object in different ways.

As we mentioned in Chapter 3, the brain organizes and interprets sensory experience to give it meaning. Before the brain can create meaning from sensory information, our sense organs transform physical stimuli from the outer world to a form that the brain can use—action potentials. Let's consider how basic sensory processes transform stimuli into neural information.

Basic Sensory Processes

Imagine if you were constantly aware of the sensations that bombard your sense organs, such as the sound of the air conditioner and traffic; the sight of the chair you're sitting on and the rug on the floor; the smells in the air; and the feel of your clothing against your skin. If you were constantly sensing all this, you would suffer from sensory overload. Our sensitivity diminishes when we have constant stimulation, a process known as **sensory adaptation.** Sensory adaptation ensures that we notice changes in stimulation more than stimulation itself.

The sense organs convert physical stimuli into neural impulses. This conversion of physical into neural information is called **transduction,** such as when cells in the retina change light waves to neural energy, when hair cells in the inner ear change sound waves to neural energy, when chemicals in the air bind to receptors in the nose, when food chemicals stimulate taste buds on the tongue, and when pressure and temperature stimulate nerve cells in the skin. In short, transduction is when the outer world becomes the inner world.

Principles of Perception

Some of the earliest experiments in psychology were in the field of *psychophysics,* the study of how people psychologically perceive (*psycho-*) physical stimuli ("physics") such as light, sound waves, and touch (see Chapter 1). Some basic principles of perception have emerged from over a century of research in this

sensation
A physical process, the stimulation of our sense organs by features of the outer world.

perception
A psychological process, the act of organizing and interpreting sensory experience.

sensory adaptation
The process by which our sensitivity diminishes when an object constantly stimulates our senses.

transduction
The conversion of physical into neural information.

area, including absolute threshold, signal detection theory, difference threshold, and perceptual set. We outline these principles briefly in this section.

Absolute Threshold When do we go from not sensing an object or event to sensing it? For example, what is the softest sound you can hear? These questions concern **absolute threshold,** the lowest intensity level of a stimulus we can detect half of the time. A common way to assess absolute thresholds is for a researcher to present stimuli, such as light, of different intensities to a research participant. The intensity level that a participant can see 50% of the time is that person's absolute threshold for light. Imagine that six light intensities, whose values are 150, 160, 170, 180, 190, and 200, are presented 10 times each. Of these values, a participant detects the 180 value 50% of the time. Then 180 is this person's absolute threshold for this light stimulus (Goldstein, 2007).

Psychologists have made some general conclusions about thresholds of perception (see Figure 4.1). Classic research from the 1960s reported that, under ideal laboratory conditions, an average person on a very clear night can detect a single candle from 30 miles away or can distinguish 2 gallons of water with only 1 teaspoon of sugar as being different from 2 gallons of pure water (Galanter, 1962). Interestingly, more recent research has reported that, compared to nondepressed people, depressed individuals have higher thresholds (requiring more stimulus) for pain and cold perception (Boettger, Grossman, & Bär, 2013; Dickens, McGowan, & Dale, 2003).

Absolute thresholds, however, are not constant; they change depending on the cost of making an error, motivation, and even personality. There are a few problems with measuring general absolute thresholds. Detecting sensations is a matter not only of the intensity of the stimulus but also of the person's decision-making process in a particular context. **Signal detection theory** attempts to separate "signal" from "noise" and takes into account both stimulus intensity and the decision-making processes people use in detecting a stimulus.

Consider situations in which there are serious consequences if you miss detecting a visual or auditory stimulus. A nurse in emergency medicine would not want to miss a slight change (signal) in a vital sign of a severely injured patient.

absolute thresholds
The lowest intensity levels of stimuli a person can detect half of the time.

signal detection theory
The viewpoint that both stimulus intensity and decision-making processes are involved in the detection of a stimulus.

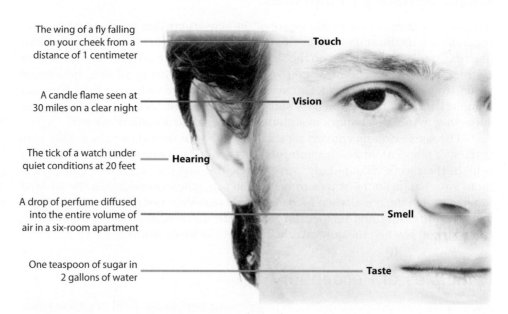

The wing of a fly falling on your cheek from a distance of 1 centimeter — Touch

A candle flame seen at 30 miles on a clear night — Vision

The tick of a watch under quiet conditions at 20 feet — Hearing

A drop of perfume diffused into the entire volume of air in a six-room apartment — Smell

One teaspoon of sugar in 2 gallons of water — Taste

FIGURE **4.1**

ABSOLUTE SENSORY THRESHOLDS. How much of a stimulus must be present for us to notice it? These are the smallest amounts of a stimulus that most humans can perceive. (Smith, 1998)

Why is it important for certain jobs to have people with more awareness of low-intensity signals, and what does it say about how we measure absolute thresholds?

An air traffic controller would not want to miss a bleep on the screen to avert a midair collision. In such situations, people may be more sensitive to sensory input, so much so that they might say they saw or heard something that was not there.

In signal detection research, a low-intensity stimulus is presented on some occasions but not presented on other occasions (Green & Swets, 1974; Swets, 1964; Wickens, 2002). Instead of having a 50% detection line, which is at threshold, signal detection experiments present only a single, low-intensity stimulus. Let's use the air traffic controller example. In signal detection research, a controller has 100 chances to detect a faint signal on the radar. During the 100 chances, the signal is present only about half the time. There are two kinds of correct responses: A *hit* correctly detects a stimulus that is present; a *correct rejection* is not to believe a signal is there when it is not present. There are also two kinds of errors the controller wants to avoid: A *false alarm* ("false positive") is the belief that something is there when it is not; a *miss* ("false negative") is not to detect something when it is present). In this example, a miss is often a more serious mistake than a false alarm, so controllers tend to have sensitive absolute thresholds. Figure 4.2 summarizes the possible outcomes in signal detection theory.

In a signal detection study, the participant's responses create a profile of hits, misses, false alarms, and correct rejections. Using the classic method of absolute threshold, a person's threshold is assumed to be constant (for example, light intensity of 180). But in signal detection, it is assumed that a person's absolute threshold fluctuates, sometimes being more sensitive and other times being less sensitive, depending on the cost of failing to detect the stimulus.

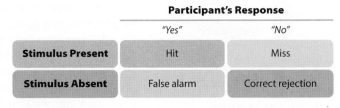

	Participant's Response	
	"Yes"	"No"
Stimulus Present	Hit	Miss
Stimulus Absent	False alarm	Correct rejection

FIGURE **4.2**

POSSIBLE OUTCOMES IN SIGNAL DETECTION RESEARCH. In signal detection theory, the participant's responses create a profile of hits, misses, false alarms, and correct rejections.

Difference Threshold   Absolute thresholds involve the line between perceiving and not perceiving a stimulus. But what about perceiving a change in a stimulus? Once we already perceive a stimulus, how much does it have to change before we notice the change? This threshold is known as a **difference threshold.** Difference thresholds are relative thresholds and are also referred to as *just*

difference threshold
The smallest amount of change between two stimuli that a person can detect half of the time.

noticeable differences (JND) because they involve the smallest difference that is noticeable. For example, being able to perceive slight differences is essential to a piano tuner, who has to be able to distinguish the slightest change in pitch to tune the instrument.

The laws of just noticeable differences in sensory perception go back to Ernst Weber, who in 1834 discovered that the size of the JND is a constant fraction of the intensity of the stimulus, a finding that came to be known as **Weber's law.** To explain Weber's law more concretely, if you are given two weights, one at 100 grams and the other at 103 grams, you would probably be able to say, "Yes, these two objects are different in weight." But you might not be able to detect the difference between a 100-gram object and a 102-gram object. In this case, 3 grams, or 3%, is the JND. In fact, classic research demonstrated that 3% is the JND for weight perception (Canter & Hirsch, 1955). Even if you had much heavier objects—say, of 100 and 102 *kilo*grams—you would not perceive a difference in their weight.

Weber's law
The size of a just noticeable difference is a constant fraction of the intensity of the stimulus.

perceptual set
The effect of frame of mind on perception, or a tendency to perceive stimuli in a certain manner.

Perceptual Set   We have already made clear that perception happens in the brain, after transduction of the stimulus at the sense organ. So our experience of seeing, hearing, or tasting is primarily a result of brain processing.

Other things going on in the brain at the time of sensory processing can influence perceptual experience. In particular, our frame of mind, which is ultimately coded in the brain, can impact how we perceive things. The effect of frame of mind on perception is known as **perceptual set.** Perceptual set makes us more likely to perceive one thing than another and explains the adage "we see what we want to see and hear what we want to hear." Figure 4.3 reproduces an image from a classic study of perceptual set. Bruner and Minturn (1955) showed two groups of research participants this image. However, each of the groups saw a different set of items before viewing the image. One group saw a series of numbers; the other saw a series of letters. Of those who saw the numbers first, the vast majority said that this image was the number "13." For those who saw letters first, the vast majority saw the figure as a "B." Thus, what people had seen prior to the test image created an expectation, or perceptual set, for how they perceived what came next. Beliefs, motives, culture, and emotions all act as perceptual sets when we perceive events in the world.

People who hold particular political beliefs will perceive any one event in a way that is consistent with those beliefs (Blais et al., 2010; Munro, Lasane, & Leary, 2010; Richardson, Huddy, & Morgan, 2008). Political jokes, airport security, presidential debates, and news releases are among the many situations that are perceived one way by liberals and another way by conservatives. In one study, people differed in their perceptions of a biracial candidate's skin color depending on whether they were likely to vote for that candidate or not (Caruso, Mead, & Balcetis, 2009). As we will discuss in Chapter 14 ("Social Behavior"), many of the attitudes and opinions we hold can influence how we perceive and interpret information that we bring in from the world around us.

FIGURE **4.3**
A DEMONSTRATION OF PERCEPTUAL SET. On a quick look, what do you see here?
What conditions might lead to people having different perceptions of this image?

Quick Quiz 4.1: The Long, Strange Trip from Sensation to Perception

1. The conversion of physical into neural information is called
   a. conduction.
   b. transduction.
   c. perception.
   d. adaptation.

2. Which of the following may act as a perceptual set in constructing our visual experience?
   a. mood
   b. expectation
   c. knowledge of how the world works
   d. all of the above

Answers can be found at the end of the chapter.

VISION

Most mammals rely on smell over all other senses, but humans are visual creatures. We rely so much on our sense of sight that we often ignore other types of information. Why is vision so important? In terms of evolution, being able to see helps us know where we are, what other people might want from us, and whether there is danger nearby. As hunter-gathers, our vision is critical for locating prey and avoiding danger, as well as for finding the foods we can eat. We also rely on hearing, the second most important sense, and smelling. But vision is king, and it starts with the eye.

Sensing Visual Stimuli

What does the eye do? It bends light, converts light energy to neural energy, and sends that information to the brain for further processing. The eye is the gateway to vision, but very little of what we experience as vision actually happens in the eye. Visual experience happens in the brain, with input from the eye. Before we explore the more complicated matter of how the brain sees, let's look briefly at the eye organ and how it converts light energy to neural energy.

Vision and the Eye   Light enters the eye at the **cornea,** a clear, hard covering that protects the lens. It then passes through liquid until it reaches a hole called the **pupil.** Light enters the interior of the eye through the pupil. The colored part of the eye, the **iris,** adjusts the pupil to control the amount of light entering. The light then passes through the **lens,** which bends the light rays. Through a process known as **accommodation,** muscles around the lens alter its shape to adjust to viewing objects at different distances and to allow the lens to focus light on the retina.

The **retina** is a thin layer of nerve tissue that lines the back of the eye. As indicated in Figure 4.4, the light that hits the retina travels through several cell layers before processing begins. Note how the image hits the retina upside down. The brain reorients the inverted image, so that our world is right side up. The deepest layer of cells, where processing of light energy begins, is made up of **photoreceptors.** The two types of photoreceptors in the retina—rods and cones—convert light energy into neural impulses.

Rods play a key role in night vision, as they are most responsive to dark-and-light contrast. They work well at low illumination. We have all experienced rods in action. Consider what happens when someone turns out the lights. At first, everything is completely dark. Then, with a bit of time, we begin to see shapes and forms, although we cannot really see colors. The process of adjustment to seeing in the dark, known as **dark adaptation,** can take up to 30 minutes and reflects the rods at work (Rushton, 1961). Rods are very sensitive, however, and sudden exposure to light can quickly cancel out their effectiveness.

Cones, on the other hand, are responsible for color vision and are most functional in conditions of bright light. They act much more quickly than rods. On exposure to light, cones reach maximum effectiveness in about 5 minutes, because the chemicals involved in their function replenish quickly (Rushton, 1961). The **fovea,** a spot on the back of the retina, contains the highest concentration of cones in the retina. We see images with the greatest clarity when they are focused on the fovea. So **visual acuity,** or our ability to see clearly, depends on our cones. Animals that have the most cones have the best acuity.

Humans and other primates are unique when it comes to vision in mammals. Primates—humans included—have three kinds of cones: those that are sensitive to red, to green, or to blue wavelengths of light (G. H. Jacobs & Nathans, 2009).

cornea
The clear, hard covering that protects the lens of the eye.

pupil
The opening in the iris through which light enters the eye.

iris
The muscle that forms the colored part of the eye; it adjusts the pupil to regulate the amount of light that enters the eye.

lens
The structure that sits behind the pupil; it bends the light rays that enter the eye to focus images on the retina.

accommodation
The process by which muscles control the shape of the lens to adjust to viewing objects at different distances.

retina
The thin layer of nerve tissue that lines the back of the eye.

photoreceptors
Cells in the retina (called rods and cones) that convert light energy into nerve energy.

rods
Photoreceptors that function in low illumination and play a key role in night vision; they are responsive to dark and light contrast.

dark adaptation
The process of adjustment to seeing in the dark.

cones
Photoreceptors that are responsible for color vision and are most functional in conditions of bright light.

fovea
A spot on the back of the retina; it contains the highest concentration of cones in the retina and is the place of clearest vision.

visual acuity
The ability to see clearly.

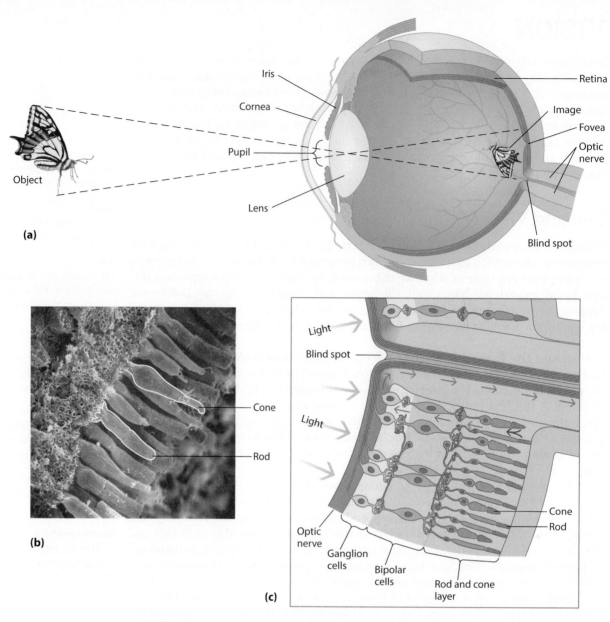

(a)

(b)

(c)

FIGURE **4.4**

THE EYE AND ITS RECEPTOR CELLS. In (a), we see all the main structures of the eye. Notice that the image of the butterfly is projected upside down on the retina in the back of the eye. In (b), we see the layers of cells in the retina, including the photoreceptors (rods and cones). In (c), an enlarged view of the retina shows the layers of the cells involved in processing light. Light hits the retina and is processed first by the photoreceptors (deepest layers), then by the *bipolar cells,* which send the light to the ganglion cells.

Humans therefore are trichromatic (sensitive to three colors; see Figure 4.5). The millions of colors we see are simply combinations of different intensities of these three wavelengths. All mammals other than primates are sensitive to only two pigments—they are dichromatic, sensitive only to blue (short) and green (medium) wavelengths. Most nocturnal animals are sensitive to only one wavelength. Birds, reptiles, and many fish, however, have cones sensitive to four different wavelengths of light (Goldsmith, 2006; G. H. Jacobs & Nathans, 2009). They are usually sensitive to wavelengths longer than red—that is, infrared light. So not only do birds see more colors than we do but they also far surpass our visual acuity.

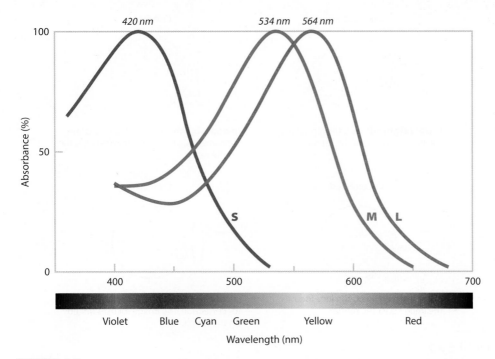

FIGURE **4.5**

THREE TYPES OF CONES IN HUMAN COLOR VISION. Humans have three different cones, sensitive to different wavelengths of light: blue (short), green (medium), and yellow-red (long). The long-wavelength cone is actually most sensitive in the yellow range of the wavelength (about 565 nm) but is referred to as red.

 Why do some people have color blindness, and why do most mammals view colors differently than we do?

Vision and the Brain After transduction at the photoreceptor layer, visual information is processed by different layers of cells in the retina. One of these layers is made up of *ganglion cells*, the axons of which make up the optic nerve. The **optic nerve** transmits signals from the eye to the brain. The point at which the optic nerve exits the eye is called the *blind spot* of the retina because this location has no receptor cells and therefore nothing is seen. Figure 4.6 offers a demonstration of the blind spot.

Another interesting detail about the focusing of the visual image on the retina concerns how well we see. In people with normal vision, the lens projects the

optic nerve
A structure composed of the axons of ganglion cells from the retina that carry visual information from the eye to the brain.

FIGURE **4.6**

TEST YOUR BLIND SPOT. Locate the blind spot in your left eye by shutting your right eye and looking at the upper cross with your left eye. Hold the book about 15 inches from your eye and move it slightly closer to and away from your eye until the circle on the left disappears. At this point the circle occupies the blind spot on your left eye. If you then look at the lower cross, the gap in the black line falls on the blind spot and the black line will appear to be continuous. (Wurtz & Kandel, 2000a, adapted from Hurvich, 1981)

Uncorrected

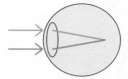

In **nearsightedness,** the lens focuses
the image in front of the retina.

Corrected

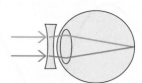

In **nearsightedness** with a minus lens
for correction, the image focuses directly
on the retina.

Uncorrected

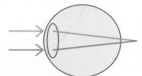

In **farsightedness,** the lens focuses
the image past the retina.

Corrected

In **farsightedness** with a plus lens
for correction, the image focuses directly
on the retina.

FIGURE **4.7**

NEARSIGHTEDNESS AND FARSIGHTEDNESS. In nearsightedness, the uncorrected lens of the
eye focuses the image short of the retina. In farsightedness, the uncorrected lens focuses the
image past the retina. With corrective lenses, the image is accurately projected on the retina.

image to hit just on the retina. In people who are nearsighted (myopic), the image
focuses slightly in front of the retina (see Figure 4.7). Nearsighted people can see
close objects clearly, but distant objects are fuzzy. In people who are farsighted
(hyperopic), the image focuses behind the retina. They can see distant objects
clearly, but close objects are fuzzy. As people age, the lens becomes less flexible,
and it is more likely that the visual image will focus behind the retina. This is an
age-related form of farsightedness (presbyopia).

Exactly what happens when visual information arrives in the brain? The
optic nerve carries impulses to the thalamus and, ultimately, to the visual cortex
of the occipital lobes. This journey is *not* straightforward: As you can see in Figure 4.8, the information from the left visual field is processed in the brain's right
hemisphere, and the information from the right visual field is processed in the
brain's left hemisphere. How the visual information gets to these hemispheres is
a bit complicated. Let's look at this process more closely.

In Figure 4.8, notice that, in each eye, each half of the retina (the area at
the back) sends out its own axons. Thus, each optic nerve has two strands. One
strand contains axons that travel from the retina to the thalamus and on to the
visual cortex of the *same* side of the brain as the eye from which the axons come.
The other strand crosses to the *opposite* side of the brain in an area called the
optic chiasm.

The first stop in the brain for most of the optic nerve fibers is the thalamus. If the pathways to the thalamus are cut, visual perception is not possible,
beyond some crude ability to detect the presence of a stimulus (Wurtz & Kandel,
2000a). As we discussed in Chapter 3, the thalamus serves as a relay station for
most of the major sense inputs to the brain, taking information from the sense
organs and sending it to the relevant area of the cerebral cortex for processing.
The thalamus does more than just relay information, though. Real visual processing occurs there. A cluster of the neuron cell bodies in the thalamus forms the
lateral geniculate nucleus (LGN). Visual information creates a point-by-point

optic chiasm
The point at which strands of the
optic nerve from half of each eye
cross over to the opposite side of
the brain.

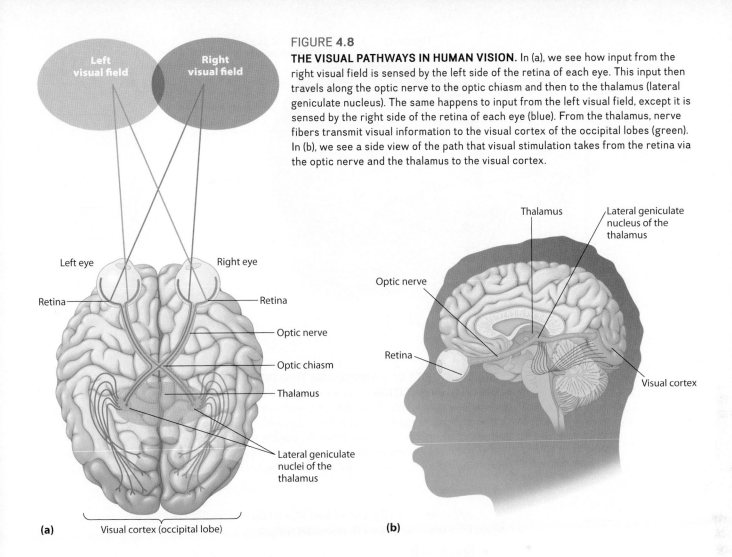

FIGURE 4.8

THE VISUAL PATHWAYS IN HUMAN VISION. In (a), we see how input from the right visual field is sensed by the left side of the retina of each eye. This input then travels along the optic nerve to the optic chiasm and then to the thalamus (lateral geniculate nucleus). The same happens to input from the left visual field, except it is sensed by the right side of the retina of each eye (blue). From the thalamus, nerve fibers transmit visual information to the visual cortex of the occipital lobes (green). In (b), we see a side view of the path that visual stimulation takes from the retina via the optic nerve and the thalamus to the visual cortex.

representation on the tissue of the LGN. Patterns of neural firing that correspond to the shape projected on a specific region of the retina affect a similar layout of cells in the LGN. So the retina and the LGN represent visual information in similar ways (Wurtz & Kandel, 2000a).

Fibers from the LGN in the thalamus then travel to the visual cortex in the occipital lobes. Neurons in the visual cortex analyze the retinal image in terms of its various patterns, contrasts, lines, and edges. Different cortical cells handle different aspects of this analysis, as a breakthrough discovery by Hubel and Wiesel demonstrated.

Vision and Specific Neurons Researchers had known for decades that, after leaving the retina, optic fibers go to the visual portion of the thalamus (the LGN) and then travel to the visual cortex in the occipital lobes. The work, however, of Hubel and Wiesel—for which they won the Nobel Prize in 1981—showed something astounding and challenged all the science of the day: Individual neurons fire only because of very specific visual information. Some neurons fire only to angled lines; some only to movement; and some only to edges. Hubel and Wiesel were able to record specialized activity of individual cells in the brain's vision area by implanting electrodes into the visual cortex of cats. As a result, in the visual cortex they discovered neurons called **feature detectors,** which analyze the retinal image and respond to specific aspects of shapes, such as angles and movements (Hubel & Wiesel, 1962, 1979).

feature detectors
Neurons in the visual cortex that analyze the retinal image and respond to specific aspects of shapes, such as angles and movements.

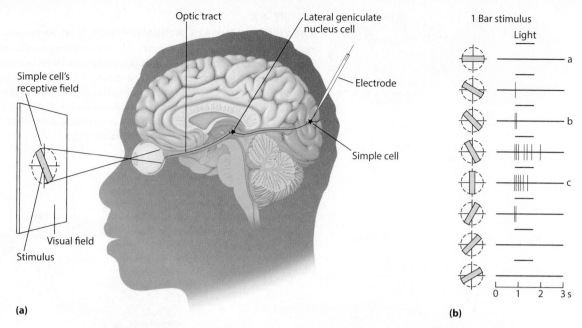

(a)

(b)

FIGURE 4.9

NEURAL ACTIVITY OF A SIMPLE CELL THAT IS RECEPTIVE TO ONE PARTICULAR DIAGONAL ORIENTATION. In (a), we see the stimulus on a visual field and how this simple cell is receptive to lines tilted from about 11 o'clock to 5 o'clock as if it were a clock face. In (b), each vertical line to the right of the stimulus represents a neural impulse. The cell begins to fire more often as the stimulus (line) approaches the angle to which the cell is the most responsive. As the stimulus passes that orientation on its way back to horizontal, the cell fires less and less frequently. Otherwise, this cell does not fire. (Adapted from Wurtz & Kandel, 2000a, p. 534)

More specifically, Hubel and Wiesel discovered three types of neurons in the visual cortex that act as feature detectors:

- Simple cells
- Complex cells
- Hypercomplex cells

Simple cells respond to very specific information, such as a bar of light oriented at a particular angle. Some simple cells respond to only one angle or orientation, while others respond to other angles of orientation or to edges, shapes, and sizes of lines. As seen in Figure 4.9a, a particular simple cell might be receptive only to a diagonal line of a particular orientation. As seen in Figure 4.9b, recordings from this one simple cell show activity only to lines that match its receptive field, which in this case is a diagonal line from about 11 o'clock to 5 o'clock (\). The cell begins to fire more often as the stimulus (line) approaches the angle to which the cell is most responsive. As the stimulus passes that orientation on its way back to horizontal, the cell fires less and less often. This is the activity of just one simple cell, which responds only to visual stimuli that stay still or are in the middle of its receptive field.

Other cells, called *complex cells*, receive input from many different simple cells and are receptive to particular stimuli in different parts of the receptive field. Unlike simple cells, complex cells are also sensitive to the movement of an image and respond if the image appears anywhere in the visual field.

Finally, *hypercomplex cells* receive inputs from many complex cells, so they fire in response to patterns of lines. If some simple cells are responsive to / and others to \, then the hypercomplex cells are sensitive to the entire configuration of \/ \/. Hypercomplex cells, therefore, are partially involved in integrating pieces of visual information into whole parts. Much of the integration into whole parts occurs when the visual cortex sends the images to other parts of the brain, such as the frontal or parietal lobes (Perry & Zeki, 2000; Wurtz & Kandel, 2000b). The cortex does not passively accept the nerve impulses from the retina and thalamus; it actively transforms the signals by first breaking them down and then putting them back together.

Hubel and Wiesel made an even more monumental early discovery of neuroplasticity when they closed one eye of a newborn cat. In the first weeks in a cat's life, when its brain is growing most rapidly, visual experience is critical for brain structures to develop all the neural connections needed to see well. If a cat is blinded or has its eyes closed for a week or more during this important stage of development, its visual cortex does not develop properly and the animal's vision is forever stunted. If one eye is closed early in life for an extended period of time, the part of the brain receiving messages from the closed eye soon begins to receive and process visual messages from the one good eye. Moreover, it is not merely light that the developing brain needs if vision is to properly develop but also lines, shapes, and colors—the full visual experience. Eyes alone are not enough to see. We need neural growth in our brains to really see; we have to learn to see.

A dramatic demonstration in humans of the principle neuroplasticity of the brain and how it needs to develop in order to see comes from the case of Mike May and others like him. May lost his vision at age 3. Four decades later, he had surgery to repair his eyes, in which doctors replaced the corneas (the clear outer layer of the eye) and other tissues. The surgery gave May working eyes, but he could not miraculously "see" right after his surgery. He could barely make out vague shapes, colors, and light. It took him months to learn how to see again. Finally, 3 years after the surgery, Mike's vision started to approach normal. Many formerly blind people never fully recover their vision; if they have been blind since birth, they never quite obtain normal vision (Kurson, 2007). Seeing requires the right environmental stimulation (in this case, light) and neurons specialized for vision. It requires both sensation and perception, which involve a complex dance of environmental input and biology, of nature and nurture. In short, visual perception is softwired and requires input from the environment in order to develop.

Challenging Assumptions in How Neurons "Recognize" Human Faces

After Hubel and Wiesel's groundbreaking work, other researchers continued to find different cortical cells that fire in response to certain visual stimuli. Some neurons, for example, respond only to faces. What happens when cells are stimulated with a specific face? The answer may surprise you.

Some of the first evidence for a specific region of the brain being dedicated to face recognition came from Kanwisher and O'Craven (2000). As we can see in Figure 4.10, simply imagining a face compared to a physical place activates different regions of the brain. Imaging a face activates neurons in the fusiform face area, whereas imaging a place activates neurons in the parahippocampal place area. In 2005 Rodrigo Quian Quiroga and his colleagues decided to test how selective individual neurons really are (Quiroga et al., 2005). They took advantage of surgical procedures already being conducted on people with epileptic seizures to test the activity of individual neurons. The brains of these patients were being probed with electrodes that measured the activity of single neurons, so Quiroga and colleagues piggybacked onto that procedure to examine whether single neurons fire to specific images of famous and nonfamous people, animals, and buildings. The famous people included Bill Clinton, Jennifer Aniston, and Halle Berry. The results of the study were stunning and surprising. As Quiroga put it, "The first time we saw a neuron firing to seven different pictures of Jennifer Aniston—and nothing else—we literally jumped out of our chairs" (Martindale, 2005, p. 22).

This finding has been dubbed the "Halle Berry neuron," even though it applies to more than just Halle Berry. Recent research has extended this finding and has demonstrated that just thinking about Halle Berry (not actually seeing a picture of her) is enough to stimulate the "Halle Berry neuron" (Sanders, 2009).

Challenge Your Assumptions

True or False? Seeing is done as much with the brain as with the eyes.

True: We integrate and make sense of visual information only if our brains have been stimulated with visual information. In this sense, we "see" as much with our brains as with our eyes.

Challenge Your Assumptions

True or False? Some visual neurons fire only when presented with images of the actress Halle Berry.

True: Believe it or not, single neurons learn specific objects and fire only when those objects are perceived.

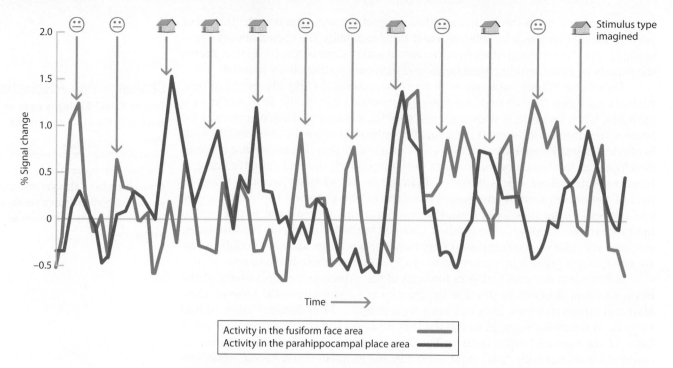

Stimulus type imagined

% Signal change

Time →

Activity in the fusiform face area
Activity in the parahippocampal place area

FIGURE **4.10**

FACE/PLACE RECOGNITION IN THE BRAIN. In this figure we see the amount of change in neural activity in different regions of the brain when people have been instructed to simply imagine either a face or a place. The icon of either a face or a place is what the participant was asked to image at that time (one every 12 seconds). As you can see, imaging a face activates neurons in the fusiform face area, whereas imaging a place activates neurons in the parahippocampal place area.

Does that mean we are born with Halle Berry neurons? No. What it does mean is that, based on our exposure and interest in certain things or people, *single cells* can come to represent a category of things, such as all things Halle Berry-ish. It also means that neurons are not passive switches but rather are more like computers or even "thinking" cellular organisms.

Perceiving Visual Stimuli

So far, we have followed visual information from light entering the eye to impulses sent to the thalamus and then on the visual cortex, where cells fire in response to very specific features of a visual stimulus. How do we move from detecting edges to perceiving shapes, from noticing lines to identifying objects? A number of processes, involving motion, depth, size, grouping, and color perception, work together to help us recognize objects in the world. Neurons are shaped by experience and "learn" to respond only to very specific faces, buildings, or animals—demonstrating once again the interplay between nature and nurture.

Perceiving Motion Feature detectors play a role in how we perceive movement and form. We perceive movement when an image moves across the retina. Simple and complex cells respond to either the orientation or the direction of moving images. Sometimes these moving images truly reflect movement in the world around us.

As we view any scene, at least two factors contribute to how we perceive movement: (1) the background against which an object moves and (2) the size of

Do you have a Halle Berry neuron?

the object. When an object moves across a complex background, it appears to move faster than when it moves across a simple background. For example, a deer running across a field, with mountains and trees in the background, will seem to move faster than one running across a wide open plain, simply because the background objects provide references that help us note the change of position in the deer. The human visual system is quite sensitive to changes in the position of objects, a sensitivity that appears to decline a bit with age (P. J. Bennett, Sekuler, & Sekuler, 2007).

Size matters too. Smaller objects appear to move faster than larger objects, when all else is equal. If we see a domestic rabbit and a mule deer run across a wide open plain, the rabbit will appear to be running faster because of its size, even though these two animals run at about the same speed.

We can also be fooled into thinking something is moving when it is not. We refer to this illusion as *apparent motion* because our brains interpret images that move across our retinas as movement. The "moving" lights on a movie theater marquee are a rapid succession of bulbs lighting up in a row. Even though we know the lights are not moving, we still interpret this illusion as movement.

Depth Perception We take for granted that we see things in three dimensions and can discriminate what is near from what is far; this is called **depth perception,** a remarkable skill, given that the image projected on the retina is two-dimensional. How does this work? Two major aspects of human visual anatomy and processing allow for depth perception: binocular and monocular depth cues.

Binocular Depth Cues **Binocular depth cues** rely on input from both eyes. One key binocular cue to depth comes from the fact that the eyes are separated by a few inches, so the images from each eye provide slightly different viewpoints. The difference, or *binocular disparity*, in these retinal images plays a key role in our ability to perceive depth. To see how this works, hold a finger out in front of you. Close one eye, open it, and then close the other eye: You will see how the image shifts slightly to one side, depending on which eye is closed and which eye is opened. The brain integrates these two slightly different two-dimensional images into a single three-dimensional image. Many animals are capable of depth perception, but this quality depends on the location of the eyes in the head.

Three-dimensional TV and movies make use of binocular depth cues for their effect. Just as humans have two eyes slightly apart, 3-D movies are filmed with two cameras slightly apart. Traditionally, one camera films with a red filter and the other camera with a blue filter. On the screen both images are projected, but when the moviegoer puts on red and blue glasses, each eye sees only one of the two separate images (see Figure 4.11). The brain then integrates these two images into one, and the effect is perceived as three-dimensional. Rather than using color to filter the images, modern 3-D technology in movie theaters uses polarizing filters to do the same. The effect is the same: Each eye sees only one perspective, which is merged in the brain as three-dimensional.

depth perception
The ability to see things in three dimensions and to discriminate what is near from what is far.

binocular depth cues
Aids to depth perception that rely on input from both eyes.

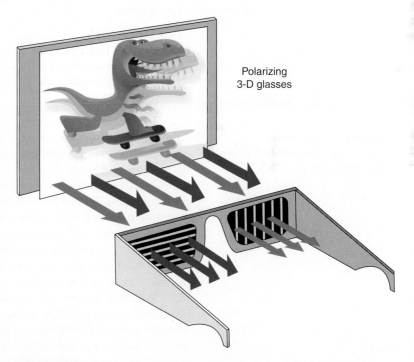

Polarizing
3-D glasses

FIGURE **4.11**

MODERN TECHNOLOGY FOR THREE-DIMENSIONAL TELEVISION AND MOVIES. Two cameras are needed for modern 3-D technology. Each camera records with a differently angled polarizing filter—either horizontal or vertical. Once a movie is made and projected, the moviegoer wears polarizing glasses. One lens filters out the vertical image and leaves only the horizontal one; the other eyeglass lens filters out the horizontal image and leaves only the vertical one. Each eye, therefore, sees only one image. The brain then integrates these two slightly different images, so that we see them as being three-dimensional. (Adapted from: id work/iStock Exclusive/Getty Images.)

(a) linear perspective

(b) texture gradient

(c) atmospheric perspective

(d) interposition

FIGURE **4.12**

MONOCULAR CUES TO DEPTH.

 What characteristics of these images allow for depth perception, even in people who do not have binocular vision?

monocular depth cues
Aids to depth perception that do not require two eyes.

Monocular Depth Cues   We derive a great deal of information about depth from the numerous **monocular depth cues** (*monocular* means "one eye") that do not require two eyes to be effective. These cues allow people who are blind in one eye to perceive some depth. Our knowledge of many of these cues derives from the seminal work of James Gibson (1950, 1966). Let's discuss some of the most common ones. *Linear perspective* involves parallel lines that converge, or come together, the farther away they are from the viewer. The more they converge, the greater distance we perceive. See Figure 4.12a for this classic effect in railroad tracks. *Texture gradient* is a monocular depth cue that causes the texture of a surface to appear more tightly packed together as the surface moves to the background. These changes in textural information help us judge depth.

Notice in Figure 4.12b that the red poppies are more tightly packed at the top of the picture, which makes us think that those flowers are farther away. Another cue, *atmospheric perspective*, comes from looking across a vast space into the distance in the outdoors. Anyone who has stood at the edge of the Grand Canyon has seen atmospheric perspective at work. We look through air and particles in the air (more so when the air is polluted). Objects farther away appear more blurred and bluish as a result (see Figure 4.12c). Another monocular depth cue is *interposition*, the partial blocking of objects farther away from the viewer by objects closer to the viewer, which overlap those farther away. This is a reliable cue to depth. Look at the image in Figure 4.12d. The closer lemons hide part of the one behind them, which is farther away.

Perceptual Constancy   We know what familiar objects look like. We also know that, when they change position or distance in relation to us, they remain the

(a)

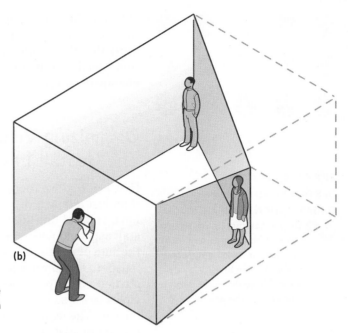

(b)

FIGURE **4.13**

THE AMES ROOM.

 These two children are about the same size, so why does the child on the right appear enormous compared to the child on the left? What does the Ames room demonstration show about perceptual constancy?

same. Nevertheless, the images on our retinas change shape and size as objects move through space. The brain's ability to preserve perception of such objects in spite of the changes in retinal image is known as **perceptual constancy.** We will look at two types: constancy of size and of shape.

Size Constancy   We see things as the same size regardless of the changing size of the image on the retina, because we know what the size of the object is. If you see your friend Jayson, who is about 6 feet tall, walking away from you, the size of his image on your retina shrinks, yet you do not suddenly think, Oh no, Jayson is shrinking! Your knowledge of Jayson's height and your knowledge that people maintain their height even when they move away from you prevent you from interpreting the smaller retinal image as a smaller person. Also, distance cues, such as linear perspective, indicate that the road Jayson is walking on is in the distance, and your brain makes use of this information *plus* your knowledge of Jayson's size to keep his size constant in your mind.

A stunning demonstration of distortions in the perception of size is the Ames room. In the photograph in Figure 4.13a, the child on the right looks enormous compared to the one on the left. It turns out, however, that the room is not rectangular (as we expect it to be) but rather trapezoidal, and the girl on the right is standing much closer to the peephole through which the viewer looks (Figure 4.13b). So the distance cues we tend to rely on are not available, and we perceive the two people as equally far away, which makes the child on the right appear enormous.

Shape Constancy   People know the shapes of common things, just as they know their sizes. The brain uses this knowledge to override changing retinal images that might make the world very confusing. Take a look at Figure 4.14. When we see a door that is closed,

perceptual constancy
The brain's ability to preserve perception of objects in spite of changes in retinal image when an object changes in position or distance from the viewer.

FIGURE **4.14**

SHAPE CONSTANCY. Even though the two-dimensional retinal image of the door changes in shape from rectangular to trapezoidal when the door is opened, we know the door's shape hasn't changed.

FIGURE 4.15

GESTALT LAWS OF ORGANIZATION: SIMILARITY.

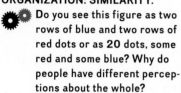

Do you see this figure as two rows of blue and two rows of red dots or as 20 dots, some red and some blue? Why do people have different perceptions about the whole?

similarity
A Gestalt law that says we tend to group like objects together in visual perception.

continuity
A Gestalt law that says we see points or lines in such a way that they follow a continuous path.

proximity
A Gestalt law that says we tend to group objects together that are near one another.

law of closure
The tendency to perceive a whole object in the absence of complete information.

FIGURE 4.16

GESTALT LAWS OF ORGANIZATION: CONTINUITY.

it looks like a rectangle (and this is what the 2-D image on our retina looks like). A door that is partially open looks like a trapezoid. Still, we would not think that the door has suddenly changed shape. The brain corrects our perception based on our previous knowledge that doors retain their shape when they change position.

Organizing Visual Information: The Gestalt Laws of Grouping

How is it that we recognize a set of marks on a page as a letter or a shape rather than just a bunch of markings? We know that the letter *E* is more than just one long, vertical line segment plus three shorter, horizontal line segments. The Gestalt psychologists recognized that often we perceive wholes as more than merely the sum of their parts. *Gestalt* is a German word that means "form," "pattern," or "shape." German researchers Max Wertheimer, Kurt Koffka, and Wolfgang Köhler studied visual perception in the early 20th century and described a set of principles or laws by which people organize elements of figures or scenes into whole objects. The major Gestalt laws of visual organization are similarity, continuity, proximity, closure, and figure-ground.

What do you see when you look at Figure 4.15? Most people with normal color vision would report seeing two lines of blue dots alternating with two lines of red dots. You would not say, "Oh, 20 dots; some are red and some are blue." Instead, you group the elements that are like one another together into a perceptual unit—the red dots go together and the blue dots go together. This Gestalt tendency to group like objects together is known as **similarity.**

According to the Gestalt law of **continuity,** we see points or lines in such a way that they follow a continuous path. For example, consider the first drawing in Figure 4.16. We see a straight line running through a curved line. We do *not* see the first drawing as a result of combining the two pieces from the second drawing.

The Gestalt law of **proximity** says that we tend to group together objects that are near one another. Figure 4.17 shows a series of blue boxes. Most people say they see four pairs of boxes, rather than eight boxes, because of the spacing. The first two are closer together than the second and third, and the third and fourth are closer together than the fourth and fifth, and so on.

Take a look at Figure 4.18a. Most observers see these figures as distinct shapes (a circle and two triangles) rather than lines, curves, and spheres, even though they are incomplete. The **law of closure** occurs when we perceive a whole object in the absence of complete information. The drawing in Figure 4.18b provides another example of how our perceiving brain completes the drawing to see a duck.

Another key Gestalt notion concerns how we separate things into *figure* and *ground*, where the figure is the thing that stands in front of a somewhat unformed background. Gestalt psychologists pointed out that we readily separate

FIGURE 4.17

GESTALT LAWS OF ORGANIZATION: PROXIMITY.

How would you describe what you see here? Four pairs or eight single boxes? Which do you think most people see, and why?

(a)

(b)

FIGURE **4.18**

GESTALT LAWS OF ORGANIZATION: CLOSURE. Challenge your perceptions: There really is no circle, triangle, or duck in the images—the "whole" appears only in your mind.

⚙ **How and why do you view these images as whole?**

(a)

(b)

FIGURE **4.19**

FIGURE-GROUND EFFECTS.

⚙ In (a), is it a vase or two faces? In (b), **M. C. Escher's** *Sky and Water I,* do you see fish or geese?

a figure from its background in order to perceive it. Perhaps the most famous example of figure-ground effects is the face-vase figure, a version of which is shown in Figure 4.19a. Notice that you can view the figure either as a blue vase against a light background or as two facial profiles (with blue space between them). It is impossible to see both the vase and the faces at the same moment. Dutch painter M. C. Escher regularly used figure-ground effects in his paintings (Figure 4.19b).

Numerous visual illusions stem from Gestalt figure-ground principles, many of which have hidden figures, as in Figure 4.20. Once you know what to look for in the picture, the hidden object becomes figural and you cannot help but see it. Try it for yourself.

Other visual illusions make use of the way the brain interprets depth cues. In Figure 4.21, which line is longer, the one on the right or the one on the left? If you take a ruler to the page, you find that both line segments are identical in length, but many people report that the one on the right looks longer. Why do we

FIGURE 4.20
FIGURE-GROUND EFFECTS IN SCENE PERCEPTION.
What do you see in this image? See p. 157 to find out what you may have missed.

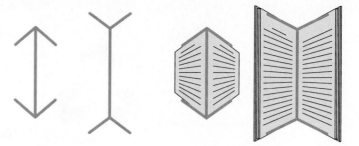

FIGURE 4.21
THE MÜLLER-LYER ILLUSION. Which line is longer?

see it that way? This illusion, known as the Müller-Lyer illusion, results from our tendency to see the right line as the inside corner of a room and the left one as the outside corner of a room or building, making use of the monocular depth cue of linear perspective.

Another commonly experienced illusion results from monocular depth cues. Take a look at Figure 4.22. Distance cues (horizon) make objects look bigger than they are. More famously, the *moon illusion* occurs when the moon is closer to the horizon (see Figure 4.23). At that time, it appears to be much larger than when it is farther from the horizon. Of course, the moon is not any larger, so why does this happen? Scientists offer several explanations for the moon illusion, and although

FIGURE 4.22
ANOTHER ILLUSION OF SIZE AND DEPTH PERCEPTION.
 Is the figure in the front smaller than the one in the back? No. Both are exactly the same size. Measure them and see for yourself. Why don't you believe they are all the same size? Like the moon illusion in Figure 4.23, this illusion comes about by our brain believing objects nearer the horizon are larger than those closer to us.

FIGURE **4.23**

MOON ILLUSION. Distance cues make the moon look bigger on the horizon.

no answer provides one true cause for the illusion, nearly all explanations involve cues to depth perception (E. B. Goldstein, 2007).

One explanation is that, when the moon is near the horizon, we see it against other cues that indicate we are looking off into the distance (such as buildings interposed on the moon, possibly roads that offer cues to linear perspective, and so on). Another way to look at it is this: When the moon is in the middle of the night sky, there are no cues to distance, no objects with which to compare it, and a huge sky surrounds it. Relative to the sky, the moon does not look so big. When the moon is on the horizon, however, we view it against objects whose size we know. Relative to those earthly objects, the moon looks enormous, as it is (Baird, Wagner, & Fuld, 1990).

Visual Perception: Bottom Up or Top Down?   One question long asked by philosophers and now neuroscientists is, Does perception of our world happen from the bottom up or the top down? Does brain activity (perception) occur only after we perceive the world and try to understand it, or does it shape and influence what we actually sense?

We have explored two answers to this question. On the one hand, feature detection research suggests that visual perception is a process of building a visual experience from smaller pieces. We put the pieces together, and then we "see" the whole, which is known as **bottom-up processing.** On the other hand, we have also looked at how the brain's perceptual set and Gestalt principles can guide how we make visual sense of information. An implied familiar shape, such as "13" in Figure 4.3, overrides our perception of the elements. Processing in which perception of the whole guides perception of smaller elemental features is called **top-down processing.**

These two processes seem to work in opposition, so which is correct? It depends on the nature of the information being processed. Reading relies on both bottom-up and top-down processing. To recognize a vertical line segment intersected by a shorter line segment as a *t*, some building up of elemental features is required. To make sense of the meaning of a *t* next to an *o* as the word *to*, some top-down processing takes over, including your knowledge of English and the function of a preposition in a sentence (Johnston & McClelland, 1974; Pelli, Farell, & Moore, 2003).

bottom-up processing
The idea that perception is a process of building a perceptual experience from smaller pieces.

top-down processing
Perception of the whole based on our experience and expectations, which guide our perception of smaller, elemental features of a stimulus.

Perceiving Color

Challenge Your Assumptions
True or False? Color is a property of objects in the world.

False: Color is perceived because of the specific length of light wave that reflects off objects, and the visible light spectrum consists of light waves from 350 nanometers (violet) to 750 nanometers (red).

We tend to think of color as a property of the objects we see: "That rose is red" or "the sky is blue." You may be surprised to learn that color is not a property of objects—it is a property of us. Our perception of color depends on our photoreceptors, our brains, and the physical characteristics of the stimulus we look at. Let's start with the physical stimulus. Color perception is partly determined by wavelength, measured in billionths of a meter, or nanometers (nm). The spectrum of color visible to humans ranges from 350 nm, which most of us perceive to be the color violet, to 750 nm, which most of us perceive as red. Light that we perceive as green is at 550 nm. Figure 4.24 shows the spectrum of light visible to humans.

Two Theories of Color Vision Psychological science has offered two main theories of color perception that explain different aspects of how most humans see color. Let's consider the aspects of each perception.

Young and Helmholtz developed their theory of color vision around the idea that people have three kinds of cones: red, green, and blue. We now know this is anatomically correct, but Young and Helmholtz did not. They inferred it from their experiments on color perception. Their **trichromatic color theory** reasoned that all the color we experience must result from a mixing of these three colors of light, but mixing light is not like mixing paints. Mix red, green, and blue light together in equal amounts and you get white; with paints, you get a brownish muck. Light color mixing actually occurs inside the eye, in terms of how different kinds of cones respond to different wavelengths of light.

The human retina contains three kinds of receptor cones, each sensitive to different wavelengths of light. The red cones fire in response to longer-wavelength light. Green cones respond to medium-wavelength light, and blue cones respond to shorter-wavelength light. The different firing patterns of these photoreceptors combine to help us experience a wide array of colors. How much each cone is stimulated determines the color we see. For most people, the perception of yellow occurs with equal stimulation of red and green cones, plus a smidgen of blue cone stimulation. So trichromatic color theory went a long way toward explaining how humans see color, but it has limitations.

trichromatic color theory
The theory that all the color we experience results from a mixing of three colors of light (red, green, and blue).

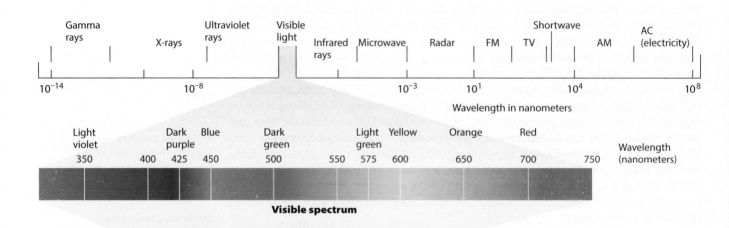

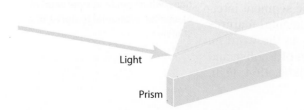

FIGURE 4.24

LIGHT WAVES AND THE ELECTROMAGNETIC SPECTRUM. The entire electromagnetic spectrum ranges from gamma waves at the shortest end to AC current at the longest end. Between these two extremes is a very narrow band of wavelengths visible to the human eye. Visible light ranges from about 350 nanometers (violet) to about 750 nanometers (red).

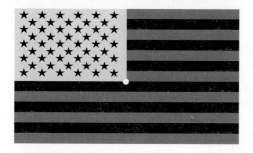 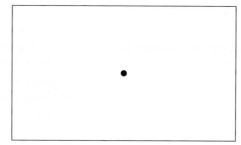

FIGURE **4.25**

COLOR AFTERIMAGE. Stare at the white spot in the middle of the green and black flag for about 10 seconds, and then stare at the black dot in the white rectangle on the right. You will see, very briefly, a regular red, white, and blue American flag. Trichromatic color theory cannot account for this afterimage, but opponent-process theory can.

Even though trichromatic color explains how photoreceptors process colored light, it cannot explain some aspects of color vision, such as **afterimages,** visual images that remain after removal of the stimulus. Figure 4.25 demonstrates a popular color afterimage.

Ewald Hering (1878) proposed **opponent-process theory** to explain color vision. He said that cones are linked together in three opposing color pairs: blue/yellow, red/green, and black/white. The members of the color pairs oppose one another, whereby activation of one member of the pair inhibits activity in the other. Opponent-process theory can account for the color afterimage of the American flag, and it helps explain some types of color blindness, as well as why we never experience some colors, such as reddish-green or yellowish-blue.

Current research indicates that both theories account for how human color vision works. The trichromatic theory better explains color processing at the red, blue, and green cones in the retina. Opponent-process theory better explains how cells in the LGN of the thalamus and visual cortex process color information. In these brain areas, some cells are excited by red and inhibited by green stimuli (Lennie, 2000). Also, opponent-process theory can explain color afterimages, whereas trichromatic theory cannot.

afterimages
Visual images that remain after removing or looking away from a stimulus.

opponent-process theory
The theory that color vision results from cones linked together in three pairs of opposing colors, so that activation of one member of the pair inhibits activity in the other.

Deficiencies in Color Vision There are many types of color blindness. Only about 10 people in a million actually fail to see color at all (Goldstein, 2007). More commonly, *color blindness* refers to a weakness or deficiency in the perception of certain colors, usually resulting from an inherited pigment deficiency in the photoreceptors. The most common form, often seen in men and boys due to the pattern of inheritance, occurs from a deficiency in cones sensitive to red (long-wavelength) and green (medium-wavelength) light. People with this disorder have trouble distinguishing some shades of green from red, may see green and brown as similar, or might have difficulty distinguishing blue and purple (purple has more red in it, so when a person cannot pick up on the red, purple and blue look alike).

Color blindness may be an evolutionary vestige of mammals most commonly being sensitive to only short and medium wavelengths rather than long (G. H. Jacobs & Nathans, 2009). When mice had a gene introduced to them that made them trichromatic (sensitive to long wavelengths as well as short and medium wavelengths), they could suddenly distinguish colors the way trichromatic humans do (Smallwood et al., 2003). Figure 4.26 presents a color blindness test that taps into red-green weaknesses. Yellow-blue deficiencies are less common.

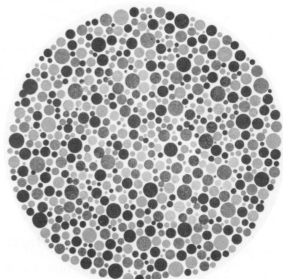

FIGURE **4.26**

EXAMPLES OF THE ISHIHARA COLOR BLINDNESS TEST. People with normal color vision can see the numbers embedded among the dots of both pictures. People with red-green color blindness cannot see the "74" embedded in the circle.

1. Neurons called _____ in the visual cortex analyze the retinal image and respond to aspects of shapes, such as angles and movements.
   a. subjective contours
   b. shape-responsive cells
   c. feature detectors
   d. horizontal cells

2. How did Hubel and Wiesel discover that some cortical neurons respond to seeing lines of a specific orientation?
   a. by using fMRI to study cat brain function during visual tasks
   b. by inserting electrodes into single cells in the visual cortex
   c. through surgical removal of cortical tissue
   d. with EEG

3. After leaving the retina, what is the first stop in the brain for processing of visual information?
   a. the occipital cortex
   b. the parietal lobe
   c. the hypothalamus
   d. the thalamus

4. Which of the following is NOT a monocular depth cue?
   a. linear perspective
   b. 3-D movies
   c. texture gradient
   d. interposition

5. The brain's ability to preserve perception of objects in spite of the changes in retinal image is known as
   a. interrelative consistency.
   b. proximity.
   c. visual stability.
   d. perceptual constancy.

Answers can be found at the end of the chapter.

HEARING

We could clearly make the case that sight is the most important sense for humans. So much of our lives revolves around what we see. The science of vision is much more developed than the science of any other sense, but people who are both blind and deaf beg to differ, as the American author Helen Keller put it eloquently when she wrote

> I am just as deaf as I am blind. The problems of deafness are deep and more complex, if not more important, than those of blindness. Deafness is a much worse misfortune. For it means the loss of the most vital stimulus—the sound of the voice that brings language, sets thoughts astir and keeps us in the intellectual company of man. (Helen Keller, as quoted in Ackerman, 1990, p. 191)

Just as vision starts when we sense light waves, hearing begins when we sense sound waves. Sound waves must travel through a medium, or we cannot hear them. Sound waves can move through fluid or air, but most of the time we hear sound waves that travel through air. Sound waves travel much more slowly than light waves, which is why you hear thunder after you have seen lightning.

The Physics of Sound and the Psychology of Hearing

We perceive different shapes and sizes of sound waves as different sounds. Hearing is affected by three physical properties of the sound wave: its amplitude, frequency, and purity. The height, or *amplitude*, of the sound wave determines what we perceive as loudness. The taller the wave is, the louder the sound. The scale for a sound's loudness is decibels (dB), starting with 0, which is the threshold for normal human hearing. The scale has no upper limit, but sounds above 150–170 dB are seldom registered anywhere.

Theaters and concert halls are designed to reflect and absorb sound, so that wherever you sit you can hear the performance. For musicians, however, constant exposure to loud music can cause hearing loss.

A whisper is about 30 dB, a regular human conversation is about 55–60 dB, a jackhammer is about 90 dB, a very loud bar or nightclub is around 100–110 dB, a very loud rock concert is about 110–120 dB, and a jet airplane is about 130–140 dB. If you ever were to hear a sound at 160 dB, your eardrum would burst. Believe it or not, car sound system competitions, such as "dB Drag Racing," regularly achieve sound in the 150–160 dB range. The record stands at 171 dB, about as loud as the Space Shuttle at launch! Needless to say, these levels are strictly for competition, and no one is in the car during the competition. Blue whales produce the loudest sound of any living animal ever recorded, reaching up to 188 dB (Cummings & Thompson, 1971).

The *frequency* of a sound wave, or how many waves occur in a given period of time, is what we perceive as the sound's pitch. Frequency is measured in units called *hertz (Hz),* which is how many times the wave cycles per second. The higher the frequency, the higher the pitch. For example, the higher keys on a piano—those farther to the right—are of higher pitch than the lower keys. The range for human pitch perception is from about 20 Hz to about 20,000 Hz, but most people cannot hear sounds at either extreme. Sounds below 20 Hz are called *subsonic* and above 20,000 are called *ultrasonic.* Most sounds we hear are in the range of 400 to 4,000 Hz. The human voice generally produces sounds ranging from 200 to 800 Hz, and a piano plays notes ranging from 30 to 4,000 Hz.

The third property of sound waves, *purity,* is the complexity of the wave. Some sound waves are pretty simple, made of only one frequency (see Figure 4.27). Most waves are *complex;* that is, they contain a mixture of frequencies. A sound's purity, which we perceive as timbre (pronounced "tamber"), is defined by how many frequencies are present in the wave. Musicians often refer to timbre as the "color" of sound. Timbre allows us to distinguish a middle C (256 Hz) as being from either a piano or a violin. They both are 256 Hz and may even be of equal loudness, but we have no trouble telling them apart because they produce waves of different purities.

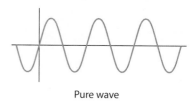

Pure wave

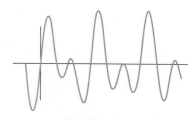

Complex wave

FIGURE **4.27**
PURE AND COMPLEX SOUND WAVES. A pure sound wave consists of only one wave, whereas a complex wave is a mixture of more than one wave.

The Ear

As the structures on the sides of our head, our ears have very little to do with hearing itself. These external structures, called *pinnae*, collect and funnel sounds into the passage called the *auditory canal*. Once inside this canal, sound vibrations travel to the eardrum, or **tympanic membrane.** The auditory canal and tympanic membrane make up the *outer ear*. The sound waves on the tympanic membrane set into motion the bones of the *middle ear*: the hammer, anvil, and stirrup (see Figure 4.28). These bones do more than just vibrate, however: They amplify the waves, so that they have more than 20 times the energy they had entering the ear. The hammer hits the anvil, and the anvil moves the stirrup. The vibration of the stirrup in turn sets into motion a series of important changes in the *inner ear*.

The inner ear includes the cochlea and semicircular canals. The **semicircular canals** play a key role in maintaining a sense of balance. As the stirrup vibrates, it moves a membrane that covers the inner ear, called the *oval window*. The vibrations on the oval window send movement through the fluid-filled cavity of the **cochlea,** a bony tube, curled like a snail's shell and filled with fluid. The **basilar membrane** runs through the cochlea. Within the basilar membrane of the cochlea are **hair cells,** which are the sensory receptors for sound, just as the photoreceptors are for vision. As the vibrations move through the cochlear fluid, the basilar

tympanic membrane
The eardrum.

semicircular canals
The structures of the inner ear involved in maintaining balance.

cochlea
A bony tube of the inner ear, which is curled like a snail's shell and filled with fluid.

basilar membrane
A membrane that runs through the cochlea; it contains the hair cells.

hair cells
Inner ear sensory receptors for sound that transduce sound vibrations into neural impulses.

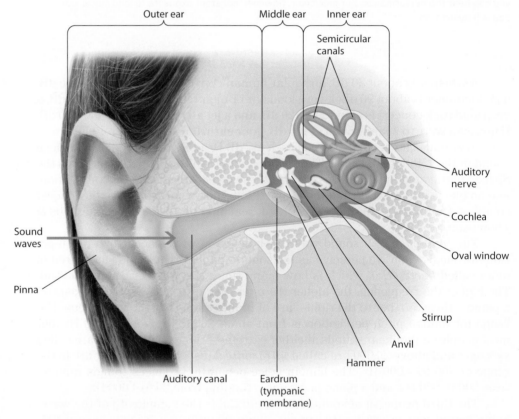

FIGURE **4.28**

ANATOMY OF THE HUMAN EAR. Sound waves hit the outer ear and travel down the auditory canal, where they hit the eardrum and cause vibrations, setting in motion the bones of the middle ear (hammer, anvil, and stirrup). The bones vibrate and amplify the waves, where they vibrate the oval window. The vibrations cause fluid in the cochlea to bend the hair cells. Stimulation of the hair cells transduces sound vibrations into electrical impulses, which can generate an action potential in the auditory nerve. An electrical impulse is then sent to the brain's auditory cortex for processing and interpretation.

Psychology in the Real World

Hearing Loss Can Happen in Young People Too

Most people take their hearing for granted, but there is a good chance that at some point in your lifetime you will suffer some degree of hearing loss. Studies often divide the causes of hearing loss into the categories of age-related and noise exposure, but these two are related. Being exposed to loud noise levels over long periods of time leads to a loss of hearing after 10–15 years.

Noise often leads to age-related hearing loss, especially in the high-frequency range of 5,000–15,000 Hz (Lutman & Spencer, 1991). In a large-scale study of exposure to noise at work, it was found that middle-aged to older men (ages 45 to 70) have their threshold for hearing high-frequency sounds (4,000 Hz and higher) raised by 10 dB compared to men not exposed to such noise at work (Tambs et al., 2006). A 10 dB increase translates to sound that is 10 times as intense, which we perceive as twice as loud. Factory or machine workers exposed to noise at the 90 dB level for 8 hours a day, 5 days a week suffer permanent hearing loss after 10 years on the job (F. Bauer et al., 1991; Lutman & Spencer, 1991). Similarly, rock musicians exposed to noise levels 95–107 dB, when tested before and after concerts, showed both temporary and permanent hearing loss (Gunderson, Moline, & Catalano, 1997).

Don't think that hearing loss affects only older people. MP3 players have maximum decibel levels of around 115–120 dB, about the loudness of a rock concert. It is not a coincidence that since the first iPod was released in late 2001 hearing loss of any kind in teens had increased from 15% in 1988–1994 to 19.5% by 2005–2006 (Shargorodsky et al., 2010). As with older adults, hearing loss in teens is also most likely in the high-frequency range (National Institute on Deafness, 2008). Earbud-style headphones are the most problematic, as they let in the most ambient noise (Hodgetts, Szarko, & Rieger, 2009). Ambient noise comes from your surrounding environment and when that is louder, you have to turn the volume up to hear the music. Most young people claim to understand the risks of hearing loss due to frequent MP3 player use, but it is not clear whether they act in accordance with that information (Danhauer et al., 2009). The following are some guidelines for listening to an MP3 player without causing long-term damage to your ears (Knox, 2007):

- Limit earphone listening to an hour a day, at a setting no greater than 6 on a 10-notch scale.
- If someone can hear earphone "leakage" from several feet away, it is too loud.
- If someone has ringing in the ears or a feeling of fullness in the ear, or if speech sounds are muffled after a listening session, the music was too loud.
- Try over-the-ear headphones rather than earbuds.

---

membrane vibrates, making the hair cells bend. As they bend, they transduce the sound vibrations into electrical impulses, which may generate an action potential in the **auditory nerve.**

Hair cells vary in size depending on their location in the cochlea. The smallest hair cells are nearest the oval window, and the largest hair cells are in the coiled-up center part of the cochlea. There is a one-to-one connection between the size of a hair cell and its sensitivity to different frequencies of sound. The smallest cells are sensitive to the highest frequencies (up to 20,000 Hz), and the largest hair cells are sensitive to the lowest frequencies (down to 20 Hz; see Figure 4.29). The louder the sound, the bigger the vibration in the cochlear fluid, the more stimulation of the hair cells, the faster the rate of action potentials in the auditory nerve, and the louder the sound we perceive. If the hair cells in the inner ear become damaged, as can happen when a person is exposed to very loud noises once or moderately loud noises (such as machines) over long periods of time, the person can suffer irreparable hearing loss. For more information about hearing loss, see "Psychology in the Real World."

auditory nerve
The nerve that receives action potentials from the hair cells and transmits auditory information to the brain.

Hearing in the Brain

After sound energy is changed to neural energy in the cochlea, the hair cells synapse with the auditory neurons that transmit the sound impulses to the thalamus in the brain. From there, the neural impulses are relayed to various parts of the

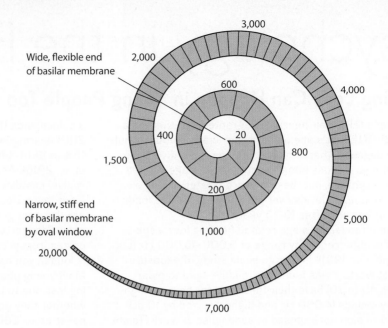

FIGURE 4.29

DIFFERENT PARTS OF THE COCHLEA PROCESS DIFFERENT FREQUENCIES OF SOUND. The highest frequencies of sound stimulate the narrowest region of the cochlea. The small hair cells here are sensitive to high-frequency (higher-pitch) sounds in the range of 15,000 to 20,000 cycles per second (Hertz). The largest hair cells are in the wide center portion of the cochlea. These hair cells respond to low-frequency (low-pitch) sounds in the range of 20 to 100 cycles per second.

brain, including the brain stem and the temporal lobes, home of the auditory cortex. Recall that the visual pathways go through the LGN. The auditory pathways go from the cochlea to the *inferior colliculus* in the brain stem and from there to the *medial (middle) geniculate nucleus (MGN)* of the thalamus. It is in the brain that we organize and interpret sounds from the outside world, and where hearing takes place.

Quick Quiz 4.3: Hearing

1. The _____ of a sound wave determines what we perceive as loudness.
   a. frequency
   b. shape
   c. amplitude
   d. width

2. Which structure is responsible for the transduction of sound vibrations into action potentials?
   a. tympanic membrane
   b. cochlea
   c. stapes
   d. hair cells

Answers can be found at the end of the chapter.

THE BODILY SENSES

We feel things on our skin and in our organs. The largest contact surface area any sensory input has with our bodies is the skin, and it is carefully mapped in the somatosensory cortex in the parietal lobe of the brain (Blakeslee & Blakeslee, 2007). The senses based in the skin, body, or any membrane surfaces are known as the **bodily senses,** which include knowing where our body parts are. We also sense things inside our bodies—organ pain, levels of heart rate, depth of breathing, to name a few. There are at least six distinct bodily or somatic senses: touch, temperature, pain, position/motion, balance, and interoception (perception of bodily sensations). Of these six senses, we will discuss touch and pain.

bodily senses
The senses based in the skin, body, or any membrane surfaces.

Touring the Senses

GOALS OF THE TOUR

1 Parts of the Eye. You will be able to identify the structures of the human eye and describe their functions.

2 Visual Pathways. You will be able to identify the pathways for visual stimulation and describe the brain's role in visual information processing.

3 Parts of the Ear. You will be able to identify the three areas of the ear and describe the key structures of the inner ear.

4 Parts of the Nose. You will be able to describe how the nose (olfactory sense) processes a smell.

Parts of the Eye and Visual Pathways

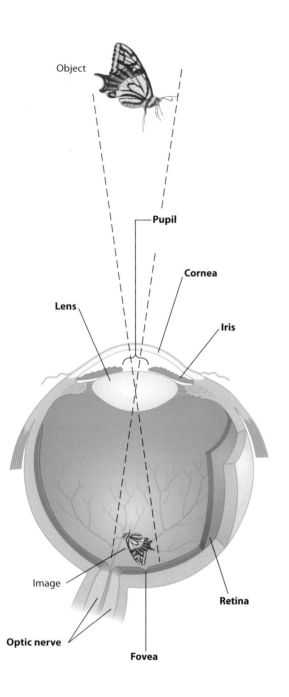

Object

Pupil

Cornea

Lens

Iris

Image

Retina

Optic nerve

Fovea

2 Identify the pathways for visual stimulation and describe the brain's role in visual information processing.

Left visual field

Right visual field

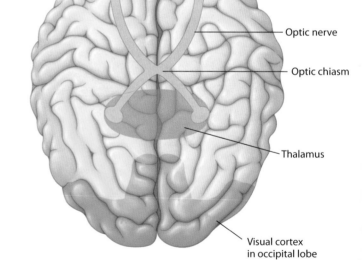

Optic nerve

Optic chiasm

Thalamus

Visual cortex in occipital lobe

Parts of the Ear and Parts of the Nose

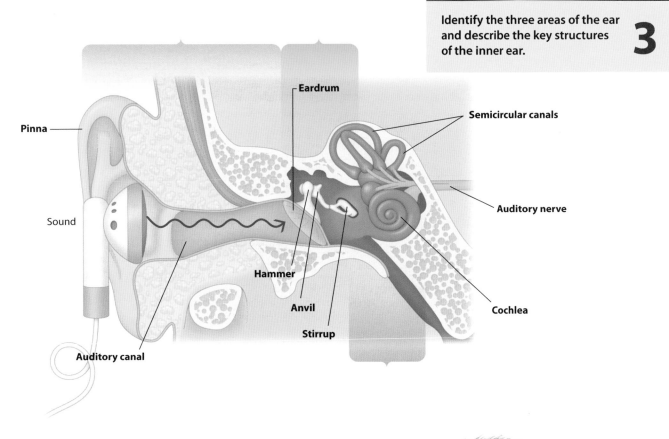

3 Identify the three areas of the ear and describe the key structures of the inner ear.

Pinna

Eardrum

Semicircular canals

Auditory nerve

Sound

Hammer

Anvil

Stirrup

Cochlea

Auditory canal

4 Describe how the nose (olfactory sense) processes a smell.

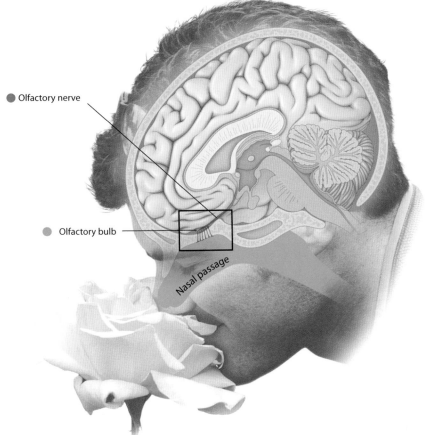

● Olfactory nerve

● Olfactory bulb

Nasal passage

1. PARTS OF THE EYE

The *retina* is made up of a layer of cells in the interior of the eye that contain the *photoreceptors*, the rods and the cones.

The *cornea* is the transparent membrane in the front of the eye that protects the eye and bends light to provide focus.

The *pupil* is the opening that allows light to enter the eye.

The *iris* is the colored muscle that surrounds the pupil and adjusts the amount of light entering into the eye through the pupil. It dilates (opens) or constricts (closes) in response to the intensity (brightness) of the light. It also dilates in response to certain emotions.

The *lens* focuses the image onto the retinal layer on the back surface of the eye. As in a camera, the image projected by the lens onto the retina is reversed.

The *fovea* is the region of the retina that is directly in line with the pupil and contains mostly cones, which are involved in color perception and visual acuity (sharpness).

The *optic nerve* receives inputs from the photoreceptors and sends information to the brain.

2. VISUAL PATHWAYS

Images of objects in the right visual field are projected to the left half of the retina of each eye, which in turn sends the information first to the thalamus for initial processing and then to the visual cortex in the left hemisphere where perception takes place. Likewise, images of objects in the left visual field are projected to the right half of the retina of each eye, which in turn sends the information to the thalamus and then to the visual cortex in the right hemisphere.

3. PARTS OF THE EAR

The *outer ear* is the visible portion of the ear and the auditory canal (ear canal) that funnels sound waves to the eardrum.

The *middle ear* includes the eardrum and three tiny bones (hammer, anvil, and stirrup) that transmit the eardrum's vibrations to a membrane on the cochlea called the oval window.

The *inner ear* includes the snail-shaped tube called the cochlea, which translates sound waves into fluid waves, and the semicircular canals, which sense equilibrium.

4. PARTS OF THE NOSE

Airborne molecules (olfactory chemicals) enter the nasal passage and reach receptor cells located in the olfactory epithelium of the upper nasal passage. The receptors send messages to the brain's olfactory bulb and then onward to the primary smell cortex located in the temporal lobes.

ANSWERS

Touch

Imagine that your eyes are closed and someone puts an object in your left hand. For a minute, you feel its weight, shape, hardness, and temperature. Then the person puts something in your right hand. You conclude, with eyes still shut, that the first is a screwdriver and the second is a pen. How are you able to do this?

The top layers of skin have receptor cells that are sensitive to different tactile qualities—some to shape, some to grooves, some to vibrations and movements. These receptor cells are known as **mechanoreceptors,** and they are like the photoreceptors in the eye and the hair cells in the ear. There are four kinds of mechanoreceptors; each kind has a unique profile of sensitivity. Some of the mechanoreceptors are slow to change, and others are fast with variations in tactile stimulation. Some are sensitive to fine details, whereas others are not. For example, slowly drag your fingertip over a quarter. You can feel the bumps and grooves, thanks to fine-detail receptors in your skin. Some mechanoreceptors also sense movement and vibration, such as when someone runs fingers over your forearm. You have far fewer mechanoreceptors on the soles of your feet than on your fingertips, probably a good thing—it would be overwhelmingly uncomfortable to have extremely sensitive soles.

Women have finer tactile sensitivity in their fingertips than men, but this appears to be due to smaller fingertip size in women (Peters, Hackeman, & Goldreich, 2009). The cells for tactile sensation are more densely packed in smaller fingers. When men and women with equal-sized fingertips are compared, their tactile sensitivity is the same.

Like photoreceptors in the eye, mechanoreceptors mark only the beginning of the journey from sensation to perception. The sensory qualities (shape, size, hardness, and temperature) of the screwdriver and pen stimulate different kinds of mechanoreceptors in the skin, but the resulting sensory impulses must travel to the brain to be processed and interpreted. When something touches our fingertips, forearm, or shoulder, a dedicated region of cortex becomes active, and we perceive the sensation of being touched. Tactile sensations from our skin travel via sensory neurons to the spinal cord and up to the brain. The first major structure involved in processing bodily sensations is the thalamus, which relays the impulses to the somatosensory cortex in the parietal lobes.

Repeated sensory and motor tactile experience changes the amount of cortex involved in processing a particular sensation or movement. The general location in the somatosensory cortex stays the same, but the areas of the cortex devoted to that experience or function grow (Jenkins et al., 1990; Ostry et al., 2010). The more one body region is touched or stimulated, the more sensory or motor cortex is used to process information from the mechanoreceptors. Musicians who play stringed instruments, such as a violin, use the right hand to bow and the left hand to play the notes. Researchers have found that experienced violinists have larger representations, or *brain maps,* of the hand and finger regions of the somatosensory cortex than do nonmusicians (Pantev et al., 2001).

Connection

The part of the brain involved in the sense of touch is the somatosensory cortex and is shown in **Figure 3.16.**

See "Overview of Brain Regions," Chapter 3, "The Biology of Behavior," p. 92.

mechanoreceptors
Receptor cells in the skin that are sensitive to different tactile qualities, such as shape, grooves, vibrations, and movements.

Pain

We need pain to survive. People born with no pain receptors can be severely injured or killed, because they don't know they have been harmed (Watkins & Maier, 2003). **Pain** is a complex emotional and sensory experience associated with actual or potential tissue damage (Merskey & Bogduk, 1994). It is usually very unpleasant, but people vary widely in their experiences of pain, what they think is painful, and whether they might even enjoy pain (Schwerdtfeger, 2007). Some people feel no pain during great injury (such as soldiers in battle situations), and others feel pain when no tissue damage is present. The latter situation occurs

pain
A complex emotional and sensory experience associated with actual or potential tissue damage.

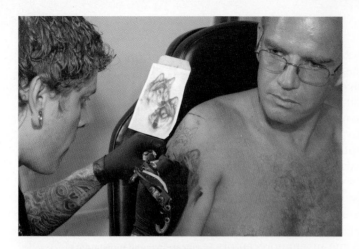

Pain is subjective, and the perception of pain varies from one person to another. Some people may perceive the experience of getting a tattoo as moderately uncomfortable. Others might find it to be quite painful.

with *phantom limb pain,* when people who have lost a limb feel pain in the missing arm or leg. Such cases dramatically show how pain is not just a direct result of tissue damage, but an experience in the brain as well. Pain also is enhanced by one's reaction to the injury. Often the emotional reaction to pain creates as much suffering as the actual tissue damage.

Pain Perception How do we sense and perceive pain? It's not merely touch gone too far. Damage to the skin is only one kind of pain. Other forms include organ tissue and nerve damage, as well as joint inflammation. Pain from skin damage is called *nociceptive pain.* The skin has pain receptors that are sensitive to heat, cold, chemical irritation, and pressure; all these pain receptors are kinds of *nociceptors* (Basbaum & Jessell, 2000). Getting frostbite, suffering from chemical burns, and hitting your thumb with a hammer all hurt because these events stimulate nociceptors in the skin. The nociceptors send signals to the spinal cord and then to the brain, signaling that damage has occurred. The brain can then initiate an appropriate response, such as pulling your hand away from a hot burner. You can now see why not experiencing pain would be so dangerous!

Many brain structures are involved in the perception of skin damage alone. A partial list of brain structures activated by skin-based pain includes the thalamus, hypothalamus, limbic system, insula, and anterior cingulate cortex (see Figure 4.30; Goldstein, 2007). A somewhat surprising finding is that some of the same brain regions and neurochemicals activated when we experience physical pain are also activated during emotional pain—especially when we are rejected by others or see others receive shocks (Eisenberger, 2013; Singer et al., 2004). For example, the class of drugs known as opiates relieves both physical and emotional pain, which is one reason they can be so easily abused (Crain, Crain, & Crain, 2013; Panksepp, 1998). Moreover, the brain regions active in both physical and emotional pain are the anterior cingulate cortex (ACC) and the insula (see Figure 4.30). Even more fascinating, as Singer and colleagues (2004) showed, when we observe a loved one being given a mild shock, only the ACC and the insula become active, not the somatosensory cortex, which is activated when we ourselves are shocked. So when we see someone we love hurt, the aspects of the pain circuit involved with emotion are active, but not the entire circuit.

Emotion and pain systems interact considerably, as indicated by the well-established observation that emotional states can influence pain perception. Certain negative emotions—such as sadness—worsen the pain experience, whereas positive emotions can lessen it (Berna et al., 2010; Villemure & Schweinhardt, 2010). Scientists are just beginning to understand the brain mechanisms involved in emotional modulation of pain. Apparently, in the transmission of pain signals between the spinal cord and brain, there are many opportunities for communication with the brain systems involved in emotion (Roy et al., 2009).

Explaining Pain One of the more influential explanations for pain comes from Ronald Melzack and Patrick Wall (1965, 1988). Their **gate control theory of pain** proposes that the spinal cord regulates the experience of pain by either

gate control theory of pain
The theory that the spinal cord regulates the experience of pain by either opening or closing neural channels, called gates, which transmit pain sensations to the brain.

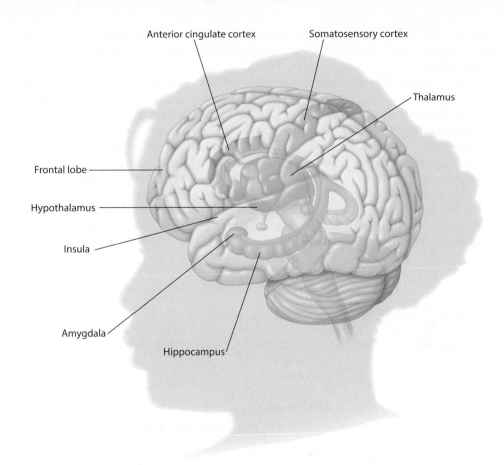

Anterior cingulate cortex

Somatosensory cortex

Thalamus

Frontal lobe

Hypothalamus

Insula

Amygdala

Hippocampus

FIGURE **4.30**

THE BRAIN AND PAIN. What structures are activated during the perception of physical pain? Which of these are involved in emotional pain?

opening or closing the neural channels, called *gates,* involved in pain sensations that are sent to the brain. Smaller neural channels are dedicated to pain sensations, and when they are activated, pain messages get sent to the brain. Activation of larger neural channels that are involved in the sensation of pain can inhibit the transmission of pain impulses to the brain, which explains why certain kinds of stimulation—such as acupuncture or even rubbing one's skin—can relieve sensations of pain. The signals from acupuncture may override other, even more intense sensations of pain, such as chronic pain from injury (P. White, 2006).

What is most interesting about the gate control theory of pain is the idea that inhibitory channels can come from the brain as well as the body. Messages sent by the brain itself can close the channels in the spinal cord that are involved in pain sensations. Thoughts, feelings, and beliefs can affect pain sensations, which is one reason people vary so much in their perception of pain. Different people experiencing the same level of pain may have completely different experiences of their pain.

Controlling Pain   In addition to thoughts and feelings that control the experience of pain, our bodies have natural painkillers called *endorphins (endogenous morphines).* When we are hurt, our bodies respond by releasing these substances (H. L. Fields, 2009). Endorphins work by stimulating the release of neurotransmitters that interfere with pain messages in the spinal cord and brain. Endorphin release may explain why some people, such as soldiers and automobile accident victims, report no immediate sensations of pain after a horrible injury

(Warga, 1987). Only hours afterward or maybe the next day while in a hospital does the pain begin. Endorphins also play a role in acupuncture-based pain relief (Han, 2004).

If thoughts, feelings, and endorphins are not enough to control pain, there are drug treatments. For small aches and pains, many people take aspirin, acetaminophen, ibuprofen, or other similar drugs. Generally, these drugs work to control inflammation (Loeser & Melzack, 1999). For more severe pain, doctors may prescribe opioids, which are a class of drugs known as *analgesics,* meaning "without pain." Morphine, heroin, oxycodone, and hydrocodone are all opioids. All but heroin are commonly prescribed for pain relief. They deaden or lessen pain by blocking the neural activity involved in pain perception (Crain et al., 2013). Morphine, for example, is widely used before and after medical procedures and in the care of terminally ill patients. There is a high risk of dependency on opioids, so their use must be carefully monitored.

Quick Quiz 4.4: The Bodily Senses

1. The receptor cells for touch that reside in the skin are called
   a. tactile cilia.
   b. mechanoreceptors.
   c. interoceptors.
   d. receptive fields.

2. Our bodies have natural painkillers called
   a. analgesics.
   b. opioids.
   c. endorphins.
   d. acetaminophens.

Answers can be found at the end of the chapter.

THE CHEMICAL SENSES: SMELL AND TASTE

Smell and taste are chemical senses, because they respond to contact with molecules from objects we encounter in the world. Smell and taste are very important survival-related senses, for they govern our choices about what we take into our bodies. As such, these senses are very sensitive, are heightened during pregnancy, and can trigger emotional reactions (Profet, 1992; Rolls, 2004).

Unlike receptors for other senses, receptors for chemical molecules are regularly replaced, because they are constantly exposed not only to the chemicals in food but also to dirt and bacteria that can impair function (Goldstein, 2007). Smell and taste receptors are replaced every few weeks.

Smell (Olfaction)

olfactory sensory neurons
The sensory receptors for smell that reside high up inside the nose.

olfactory bulb
A forebrain structure that sends information either directly to the smell-processing areas in the cortex or indirectly to the cortex by way of the thalamus.

A small area high in the lining of the nasal cavity contains the **olfactory sensory neurons,** which are the receptors for smell (see Figure 4.31). These neurons contain hairlike projections called *cilia,* which are similar to the hair cells in the inner ear. The cilia convert the chemical information in odor molecules into neural impulses.

When chemicals come in contact with the cilia, transduction occurs, and the olfactory message travels to the **olfactory bulb** in the forebrain. The olfactory bulb sends information either directly to the smell-processing areas in the cortex or indirectly to the cortex by way of the thalamus (Buck, 2000).

The *primary olfactory cortex* resides in the temporal lobe; the *secondary olfactory cortex* is in the frontal lobe near the eyes.

Some fibers from the olfactory bulb go directly to the amygdala, which sends smell information to the hypothalamus, thalamus, and frontal cortex. You may recall that the amygdala plays a key role in emotional responses and connects to memory areas such as the hippocampus. These connections may explain why smells can instantly evoke an emotional memory (Herz, 2004). The smell of cedar wood, for example, immediately transports one of the authors (Greg) to his grandmother's attic in Kansas.

Just as there are specific photoreceptors for different primary colors, different odors stimulate different olfactory neurons. Most mammals have hundreds of different types of olfactory sensory neurons; these account for their highly discriminating sense of smell (Fleischer, Breer & Strotmann, 2009). Greater concentrations of odors stimulate a greater number of sensory neurons; as a result, we perceive the same odor presented at different concentrations as entirely different smells. People differ considerably in their ability to sense odors. Some people lose the ability to sense smell with infection or injury, but usually this is short-term.

Animals have a heightened sense of smell compared to humans: We rely on dogs to sniff out suspects and bombs. Grizzly bears can locate dead animals from miles away and will readily feed on them ("Brown/Grizzly Bear facts," n.d.). Sharks can detect one drop of blood in 25 gallons of water (R. Marks, 2006).

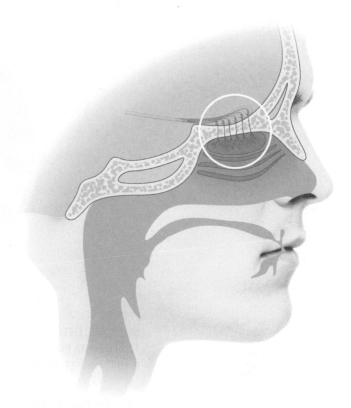

FIGURE **4.31**
OLFACTORY RECEPTORS IN THE NASAL CAVITY. The receptors in the nasal cavity, called cilia, are like the hair cells in the ear. They change chemical stimulation received from smells to nerve signals that are sent to the brain for processing and interpreting.

Taste

A close look at the human tongue reveals all kinds of ridges and bumps. These textured structures, called **papillae,** contain about 10,000 **taste buds.** Dozens of **taste receptor cells** on each bud process taste information. The papillae in the central part of the tongue contain very few taste buds and taste receptor cells, so we do not taste from that region. Human experience of taste results primarily from the stimulation of taste buds throughout the tongue, not in specific regions as was once thought (Figure 4.32). When chemicals from food or liquid come in contact with the tips of these taste buds, a chain of events unfolds, leading to the experience of taste.

Humans distinguish among five basic taste qualities: bitter, sweet, salty, sour, and savory. There is increasing evidence that a sixth taste quality—fattiness—may exist as well, but further research is needed (Garcia-Bailo et al., 2009). Researchers once thought that receptors for the different tastes resided only in certain regions of the tongue, but we now know that these taste receptor cells are distributed in many regions (Buck, 2000; Chaudhari & Roper, 2010; Huang et al., 2006). Although specific receptors exist for each type of taste, the savory experience—also known as *umami* from the Japanese word for "good flavor"—comes from the combined sensory experience of monosodium glutamate (MSG; a flavor enhancer, traditionally used in many Asian foods) and the perception of savory odors (Kawamura & Kare, 1987; McCabe & Rolls, 2007). The combined

papillae
Textured structures on the surface of the tongue; they contain thousands of taste buds.

taste buds
Structures inside the papillae of the tongue; they contain taste receptor cells.

taste receptor cells
Sensory receptors for taste that reside in the taste buds.

Challenge Your Assumptions

True or False? Different regions of the tongue contain taste buds for specific types of taste, such as sweet or bitter.

False: Recent evidence shows taste receptor cells are distributed throughout the tongue.

FIGURE 4.32

UNTIL RECENTLY, IT WAS THOUGHT THAT DISTINCT REGIONS OF THE TONGUE HAD TASTE BUDS FOR SPECIFIC TYPES OF TASTE. We now know that the entire tongue is involved in each taste sensation.

factors that produce the savory flavor point to the important roles both taste and smell play in our experiences of flavor in general.

Simply put, the experience of flavor results from the combination of taste plus smell (Goldstein, 2007). Have you ever noticed how dull food tastes when you have a cold? This is because your sense of smell is impaired. Try squeezing your nostrils shut while tasting an apple or any other food. Notice the flavor. Then release your nostrils and take another bite. You will notice more intense "appleness" with your nostrils open, because food aromas contribute greatly to the experience of flavor (Lawless et al., 2004). When the nose is shut, olfactory receptors in the passage that connects the oral and nasal cavities do not get stimulated. As a result, less olfactory information is available, and taste is impaired. Also, the region of the brain most involved in flavor perception—the orbitofrontal cortex (OFC)—receives inputs from brain areas involved in olfaction and taste, as well as from areas involved in touch and vision (Rolls, 2000). The OFC is where signals from taste and smell meet (Rolls, 2006).

The experience of flavor showcases the brain's ability to combine sensory information to produce a unique sensory experience. In some people, sensory experiences sometimes combine in even more unusual ways. The next section, on synesthesia, focuses on these cases.

Because dogs have a keen sense of smell, humans often employ them to locate illegal drugs, explosives, criminals, and missing people.

1. The primary olfactory cortex resides in which lobe of the brain?
   a. temporal
   b. frontal
   c. parietal
   d. occipital

2. Humans have taste receptor cells for what flavors?
   a. sweet, sour, salty, sharp, savory
   b. sweet, sour, bitter, salty, sharp
   c. sweet, sour, bitter, salty, savory
   d. sweet, sour, salty, sharp

Answers can be found at the end of the chapter.

SYNESTHESIA

Many of us use expressions such as "he was green with envy" or "her anger was red hot." We use these colors metaphorically, knowing full well he is not really green and her anger is not really red, but what if we literally experienced numbers as colors or touch as tastes? A surprisingly large segment of the population—about 4%–5%—can do just that (Simner et al., 2006). They experience what is known as **synesthesia,** which occurs when a person experiences sensations in one sense when a different sense is stimulated (Cytowic, 1989; Ramachandran & Hubbard, 2003; Spector & Maurer, 2009; Ward, 2013). In short, synesthesia occurs when the senses get mixed up and don't stay separate. Some people with this condition experience yellow when they hear a tone such as middle C. Others taste shapes. In one recent case, a man saw colored halos around human faces (Ramachandran et al., 2011). Still others experience numbers as colors, such as 5s as green and 2s as red.

The most common form of synesthesia is the one in which people experience numbers or sometimes letters as colors (Ramachandran & Hubbard, 2003; Spector & Maurer, 2009). One way that scientists were able to discover that synesthesia is a real perceptual phenomenon and not just a learned association or merely an overly active sense of metaphor was to administer perceptual tests such as the one in Figure 4.33 (5s and 2s). In the figure on the left, there are a few 5s within the 2s. For most of us, they are hard to pinpoint, and it takes us a while to determine how many there are, but a person who sees 5s as blue and 2s as red, as shown on the right, has no trouble seeing that there are six 5s, forming a triangle.

synesthesia
An unusual sensory experience in which a person experiences sensations in one sense when a different sense is stimulated.

Challenge Your Assumptions

True or False? The experience of "seeing sounds" or "hearing colors" occurs only under the influence of drugs.

False: About 4% of the population regularly has a crossover of sensory experience where they "see sounds" or "hear colors." This is known as synesthesia.

The way a person without synesthesia sees it

The way a person with synesthesia sees it

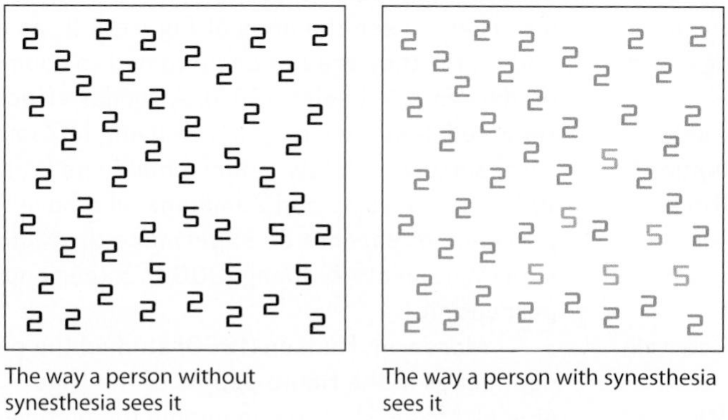

FIGURE **4.33**

SYNESTHESIA. People who perceive numbers as colors would have no trouble distinguishing the numbers 5 and 2 in the square on the left. They would see the numbers in color, as shown in the example on the right.

How does synesthesia happen? The most well-established explanation is that synesthesia results from a cross-wiring or cross-activation of sensory neurons in various parts of the brain (Hubbard & Ramachandran, 2005; Spector & Maurer, 2009; Tomson et al., 2013; van Leeuwen et al., 2011). Cross-activation occurs when two areas of the brain, normally kept separate, become activated at the same time by the same stimulus. In synesthesia, the brain regions involved in color perception cross-activate with sensations of numbers. As it turns out, one region of the temporal lobe is active in processing both color sensations and numbers and is therefore the most likely area of cross-activation in this form of synesthesia (Hubbard & Ramachandran, 2005; Ramachandran & Hubbard, 2003). Some evidence suggests that this sensory cross-wiring is a result of unusual neural development, including a failure to prune synaptic connections that are temporary in early stages of development (Spector & Maurer, 2009; Ward, 2013). Many infants have these cross-wired neurons connecting different sensory systems, but with age and experience they get pruned or eliminated. They do not appear to be pruned in people with synesthesia. Finally, certain hallucinogenic drugs can temporarily create synesthetic experiences, such as when people see musical sounds as colors. The brain mechanisms responsible for this kind of synesthesia are not well described (Weil & Rosen, 1998).

Bringing It All Together

Making Connections in Sensation and Perception

Differences across Cultures

Throughout this chapter we have touched on ways in which people differ in sensory perception. For example, some people are more sensitive to bitter tastes than others. Individual differences in perception may result from differences in perceptual set, or frame of mind. Thus, it stands to reason that growing up in a certain environment, with particular beliefs, ways of viewing things, and physical settings, might impact how one perceives the world. Culture and place can serve as perceptual sets. Most research on the cultural influences on perception has focused on three sense systems: vision, olfaction, and pain.

Cultural Variation in Visual Perception

Differences exist across cultures in response to certain visual images that use monocular cues to depth. Look again at the Müller-Lyer line illusion in Figure 4.21. Recall that linear perspective explains why people see the line on the right as longer than the one on the left when the lines are, in fact, equal. Do people who grow up in a world with no corners view these drawings the same way we do? Researchers have studied the effects of living in a *carpentered world*—an environment with constructed buildings with many right angles—on various people's perceptions of depth. Navajos who have lived at least 10 years in round huts are much less likely to see the lines of Figure 4.21 as differing in length, for they are not accustomed to rooms with edges (Pedersen & Wheeler, 1983). A similar effect has been reported in studies of children living in Zambia, in a rural setting with few modern buildings (V. M. Stewart, 1973), but Navajos and Zambians who have lived in the presence of corners do experience the Müller-Lyer illusion (Matsumoto & Juang, 2004). Experience modifies perception.

Moreover, Hudson (1960) studied the perception of depth cues in the Bantu people of the Niger-Congo region of Africa. He showed people the picture depicted in Figure 4.34 and others similar to it. He then asked them to explain what was going on in the scene. When people from the United States, Europe, and India viewed such a picture, they said the hunter was going after the gazelle,

FIGURE **4.34**

A PICTURE FOR DEPTH PERCEPTION TASKS TESTED ON BANTU.

 Is the hunter after the elephant or the gazelle? How might your explanation of this scene depend on your cultural perspective? (Based on Hudson, 1960)

as the elephant was clearly in the distance. Bantu people, however, said the hunter was attacking the elephant. So the Bantu do not appear to use relative size differences as cues to depth because they don't see the elephant as being in the background. Why? The Bantu people's response may result from not having much experience with two-dimensional drawings like the figure. Interestingly, Bantu who had been educated in European schools said the hunter was going for the gazelle (Matsumoto & Juang, 2004).

As we have just seen, different cultural backgrounds can impact not only illusions and depth perception but also foreground and background. People from Eastern cultures tend to perceive the world more as a whole, with people, objects, and the context being connected and belonging together. Westerners, however, tend to focus most on foreground objects and less on the background and periphery (Nisbett et al., 2001). The Research Process for this chapter (see Figure 4.35) focuses on cultural influences on how people perceive and recall figural versus background information in visual scenes (Masuda & Nisbett, 2001). The findings are consistent with the more established observation that Eastern people view themselves as embedded in the larger world rather than as independent entities (Markus & Kitayama, 1991). In another example of top-down processing, one's orientation toward life and the world can shape visual perception and memory.

Cultural Variation in Olfactory Experience

Smell is an interesting sense to compare across cultures, in part because it is a highly emotional sense. Because smells elicit emotions so readily, cultures often develop strong rules or norms about which smells are okay and which ones aren't and differ widely on the acceptability of odors based on experience, climate, and cuisine. Also, different places vary in their standards for cleanliness and for what is acceptable body odor (Hannigan, 1995). Do people who are raised so differently with respect to what is typical to smell or what it is okay to smell like show differences in scent detection in controlled experiments?

A highly controlled experiment on scent detection with participants from the United States and Japan suggests remarkable similarity across these two cultures in ability to recognize a wide variety of scents (Kobayashi et al., 2006). A few distinct differences, however, appear to be culturally based. Japanese were much better than Americans at detecting 3 of the 13 smells in final testing, because each of these scents (such as condensed milk) is more common in Japan, and therefore these results help us understand that smell recognition is a perceptual process guided by experience with the substances to which we are exposed.

Other aspects of smell may be less susceptible to cultural effects. Consider gender differences in smell perception. Women tend to be more sensitive to smells than men (G. Brand & Millot, 2001). Scientists at the University of Pennsylvania wanted to know whether such gender differences in smell perception hold across cultures and ethnic backgrounds. They tested how well native Japanese and Americans of African, European, and Korean descent could identify odors in a controlled laboratory setting (Doty et al., 1985). Korean Americans performed better than African Americans and White Americans on the odor detection tasks, and both of these groups performed better than native Japanese. Across all the groups, however, women outperformed men.

Cultural Variation in Pain

Given the large role that subjective factors play in pain perception, many researchers have looked at cultural, gender, and ethnic differences in pain (Al-Atiyyat, 2009; Wickelgren, 2009). There are big differences among people in pain tolerance, and we can even experience pain in the absence of any real tissue damage—remember phantom limb pain? One general finding is that women tend to have a lower pain threshold than men; that is, they more quickly say a stimulus is painful as it becomes more intense (Wickelgren, 2009). Moreover, there are clear cultural differences in tolerance for pain. In one of the most painful of human experiences, childbirth, we see widely differing perceptions of how painful it is.

For example, the Yap who live in the South Pacific consider childbirth to be simply a part of everyday life. Yap women routinely work in the fields right up until childbirth and are often back at work the next day. What

Research Process

 Research Question

Do people from an Eastern culture (Japan) focus more on and have better recall for objects in the background and periphery of a scene than people from a Western culture (United States)?

 Method

For this quasi-experimental study by Masuda and Nisbett (2001), participants came into the laboratory individually and sat down at a computer. They watched a 20-second video of the scene depicted here. The large fish are considered foreground. Plants, small fish, and the other nonmoving animals (rocks and snail) are considered background. Arrows indicate the direction in which the fish and other objects moved during the scene. After viewing the video, participants orally described what they had seen. Trained coders rated the number of statements they made about various aspects of the scene, such as foreground and background fish, the small stationary animals, and the plants.

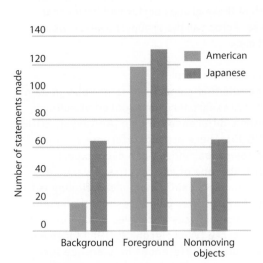

 Results

As predicted, and consistent with cultural values and attitudes, the Japanese commented much more on the background and nonmoving animals (snail and frog) than the Americans did. There was no significant difference in how much people from each culture commented on the large fish in the foreground.

Conclusion

How we perceive everyday scenes is influenced by our culture. Our brains have been shaped by the assumptions and values of our society. In this case, people in Eastern cultures, such as Japan, tend to focus on background, foreground, and nonmoving objects, whereas those in Western cultures, such as the United States, tend to focus more on the foreground and moving objects only. This research is consistent with the more established observation that Eastern people view themselves as rooted in the larger world rather than as independent individuals.

FIGURE **4.35**

HOW CULTURE AFFECTS PERCEPTION OF FOREGROUND-BACKGROUND. How does culture influence the way we perceive visual information? ("Attending Holistically versus Analytically: Comparing the Context Sensitivity of Japanese and Americans," by T. Masuda and R. E. Nisbett, 2001, *Journal of Personality and Social Psychology, 81,* 922–934)

Cultural differences in pain perception are evident in this photo, taken during the Hindu festival of Thaipusam in Malaysia.

is even more interesting is that Yap fathers experience the pain of childbirth, and they are the ones who stay in bed to recover after the birth of the child (Kroeber, 1948). In the Huichol tribe of Mexico, so that fathers-to-be would go through their own painful birth process along with the mothers in labor, a string would be tied around the man's testicles. The woman in labor would hold the other end of the string, and with each contraction she experienced, she would pull on the string (Cassidy, 2006)!

Chapter Review

THE LONG, STRANGE TRIP FROM SENSATION TO PERCEPTION

- Sensation is the stimulation of our sense organs by the external world. Perception is the process by which the brain organizes and interprets sensory experience.

- Stimulation of the sense organs involves taking in sensory energy from the outside world, whether it be sound waves, light waves, chemicals, or pressure. Our sensory system transforms the physical energy into neural energy in a process known as transduction. The brain then organizes the transformed information, interprets it, and initiates a response.

- Absolute thresholds are the lowest levels of a stimulus that humans sense. Difference thresholds are the smallest amounts of change in stimulus that a person detects.

- According to Weber's law, the smallest detectable change is a constant proportion of the intensity of the original stimulus.

- Our frame of mind affects our perception of objects and is known as our perceptual set.

VISION

- The eye bends light, converts light energy into electrical energy, and sends that information to the brain for further processing.

- Vision happens in the brain, in the lateral geniculate nucleus (LGN) of the thalamus and in the visual cortex in the occipital lobes.

- Hubel and Wiesel demonstrated that single cells in the visual cortex act as feature detectors, and there are three kinds for vision: simple cells, complex cells, and hypercomplex cells. Integration of this feature information occurs in the parietal and temporal cortexes.

- Depth perception is the ability to figure out how far or near objects are. One cue for depth perception is binocular disparity, the fact that our two eyes provide slightly different viewpoints, which our brains integrate into a single 3-D image. Monocular depth cues include linear perspective, texture gradient, atmospheric perspective, and interposition.

- The brain organizes visual sensations with Gestalt laws of similarity, continuity, proximity, and closure.

- Separating figures from backgrounds helps us organize visual sensations, but it also makes us vulnerable to illusions.

HEARING

- Humans respond to three different properties of sound waves: We perceive amplitude as loudness, frequency as pitch, and purity as timbre.

- The receptor hair cells in the cochlea are sensitive to different frequencies of sound waves and convert the mechanical energy of sound into neural energy for processing in the auditory cortex.

THE BODILY SENSES

- The bodily senses include sensations of touch, temperature, pain, balance, position/motion, and interoception.

- The brain regions most involved in touch are the thalamus and the somatosensory cortex in the parietal lobes. Pain sensations are processed mainly by the insula and the anterior cingulate cortex in the frontal lobes.

THE CHEMICAL SENSES: SMELL AND TASTE

- The retina contains two types of photoreceptor cells, called rods and cones. Cones are sensitive to red, green, and blue light waves, whereas rods are sensitive to light and are responsible for dark adaptation.

- The trichromatic theory of color vision states that we perceive the full range of colors as different combinations of three colors. The opponent-process theory says that cones are linked together in three opposing color pairs: blue/yellow, red/green, and black/white.

- Smell receptors in the nose contain olfactory sensory neurons, which convert chemical information into neural information. The olfactory message goes to the olfactory bulb and then to the primary olfactory cortex in the temporal lobe.

- Information about taste is processed in the taste buds of the tongue. Humans distinguish among five basic taste qualities: bitter, sweet, salty, sour, and savory.

SYNESTHESIA

- Synesthesia occurs when one sensory system is activated by the stimulation of a different sensory system, and the neurons are cross-activated in the brain.

- In the most common form of synesthesia, people experience letters or numbers as colors.

BRINGING IT ALL TOGETHER: MAKING CONNECTIONS IN SENSATION AND PERCEPTION

- Variations in experience across cultures influence the way people see, smell, and feel pain.

- Ethnic and cultural differences aside, women are more sensitive to smells than are men.

Key Terms

absolute threshold, p. 120
accommodation, p. 123
afterimages, p. 139
auditory nerve, p. 143
basilar membrane, p. 142
binocular depth cues, p. 131
bodily senses, p. 144
bottom-up processing, p. 137
cochlea, p. 142
cones, p. 123
continuity, p. 134
cornea, p. 123
dark adaptation, p. 123
depth perception, p. 131
difference threshold, p. 121
feature detectors, p. 127
fovea, p. 123
gate control theory of pain, p. 146

hair cells, p. 142
iris, p. 123
law of closure, p. 134
lens, p. 123
mechanoreceptors, p. 145
monocular depth cues, p. 132
olfactory bulb, p. 148
olfactory sensory neurons, p. 148
opponent-process theory, p. 139
optic chiasm, p. 126
optic nerve, p. 125
pain, p. 145
papillae, p. 149
perception, p. 119
perceptual constancy, p. 133
perceptual set, p. 122
photoreceptors, p. 123
proximity, p. 134

pupil, p. 123
retina, p. 123
rods, p. 123
semicircular canals, p. 142
sensation, p. 119
sensory adaptation, p. 119
signal detection theory, p. 120
similarity, p. 134
synesthesia, p. 151
taste buds, p. 149
taste receptor cells, p. 149
top-down processing, p. 137
transduction, p. 119
trichromatic color theory, p. 138
tympanic membrane, p. 142
visual acuity, p. 123
Weber's law, p. 122

Quick Quiz Answers

Quick Quiz 4.1: 1. b 2. d   **Quick Quiz 4.2:** 1. c 2. b 3. d 4. b 5. d   **Quick Quiz 4.3:** 1. c 2. d
Quick Quiz 4.4: 1. b 2. c   **Quick Quiz 4.5:** 1. a 2. c   **Solution to Figure 4.20 on p. 136:**

5 Human Development

Chapter Outline

The Developing Fetus
The Developing Infant and Child
The Developing Adolescent
The Developing Adult
Chapter Review

Challenge Your Assumptions

True or False?

- The heart is the first major organ to develop. (see page 161)

- Schizophrenia in an offspring is more likely if the mother is exposed to a virus while pregnant. (see page 165)

- Differences in human temperament already show in the womb. (see page 166)

- Babies are born able to see and hear as well as adults. (see page 168)

- All babies are emotionally attached to their caregivers. (see page 182)

- Being regularly touched as a newborn increases both physical and mental health later in life. (see page 184)

- Parents are the main social influence on development up through late adolescence. (see page 191).

- Alzheimer's disease is limited to problems of memory. (see page 200)

I dentical twins are "identical" because they start from one fertilized egg (monozygotic), which for reasons unknown splits into two developing fetuses with identical genetic information.

Why might one "identical" twin look slightly different from the other, or why might one develop schizophrenia as a young adult whereas the other does not? Genotype is not phenotype. Many events can occur between the time genotype is established at conception and the time traits get expressed as phenotypes over the course of a lifetime. These events define development, shaping somewhat different paths for identical twins before and after birth:

- Genetic mutations (copy errors) lead to slightly less than 100% genetic similarity between identical twins (Bruder et al., 2008).

- In the womb, up to 40% of identical twins develop in their own placenta (a saclike organ in which the fetus lives; Segal, 1999).

- Even if they are raised in the same house, they nevertheless have different experiences and sometimes different friends and teachers.

- If raised in separate houses, their experiences and upbringing are even more different.

- Epigenetic processes turn off or on different genes as different life experiences accumulate over time, leading to greater and greater epigenetic differences over the life course (Fraga et al., 2005).

Even with these numerous sources of biological and environmental differences, identical twins often turn out to be amazingly similar in all kinds of ways: not only in how they look but also in their personalities, intelligence, illness and disease histories, and even careers and marriage patterns.

Many cases abound of long-lost identical twins being reunited to discover uncanny similar personality traits (Segal, 1999). Oskar Stohr and Jack Yufe, for example, were identical twins given up for adoption who could have hardly been raised in more different environments (Holden, 1980). Oskar was raised by a German Catholic family and was headed toward a Hitler Youth program when World War II ended, whereas Jack was raised Jewish in the Caribbean and lived some time in Israel on a kibbutz. Despite these extreme differences in upbringing, when reunited in their 40s, they discovered similarities in their personalities, such as similar patterns of speech and thought, cravings for spicy foods and sweet liqueurs, absent-mindedness, and domineering relationships with women. They even had the habit of flushing the toilet prior to using it.

Similarly, identical twins Elyse and Paula did not even know about each other until age 35, when they were reunited, and hence were dubbed "identical strangers" (Schein & Bernstein, 2007). Both studied film and are writers. Their favorite director is the German director Wim Winders and their favorite film is *Wings of Desire*. They also both suffer from depression and have very similar mannerisms.

human development
The study of change and continuity in an individual across the life span.

Twins, of course, are just a special case of sibling. We all are changing and growing from the moment of conception to the moment of death. How we change and yet remain stable over the entire life course is the story of **human development.** Developmental psychology examines any and all influences of change over the life span—genetic, epigenetic, neurological, cognitive, social, emotional, and personality.

THE DEVELOPING FETUS

From conception until birth, we grow from a single cell to a fully formed, but still developing, human. The brain is the first major organ to form. The heart develops about a week later. (It is strange to think we have a brain before we have a heart!) A little more than 8 months later, when we are born, the brain has more than 100 billion cells.

We pass more biological milestones before birth than we will during the rest of our lives. Development in the womb is incredibly fast and complex and includes not only physical growth but psychological development as well. Personality and cognitive traits are already being shaped before we are born.

Stages of Prenatal Development

Life before birth is commonly divided into three distinct stages: germinal, embryonic, and fetal. The **germinal stage** begins at conception and lasts for 2 weeks. At conception, the fertilized egg is a single-celled **zygote,** which starts dividing rapidly around 36 hours after conception. By day 7, the multicelled organism—now called a blastocyst—travels down the mother's fallopian tube and attaches to the uterine wall (see Figure 5.1). This process is far from risk-free: Between 30% and 50% of blastocysts do not implant properly, and the pregnancy ends without the woman's having known she was pregnant (Gupta et al., 2007).

germinal stage
The first prenatal stage of development, which begins at conception and lasts 2 weeks.

zygote
The single cell that results when a sperm fertilizes an egg.

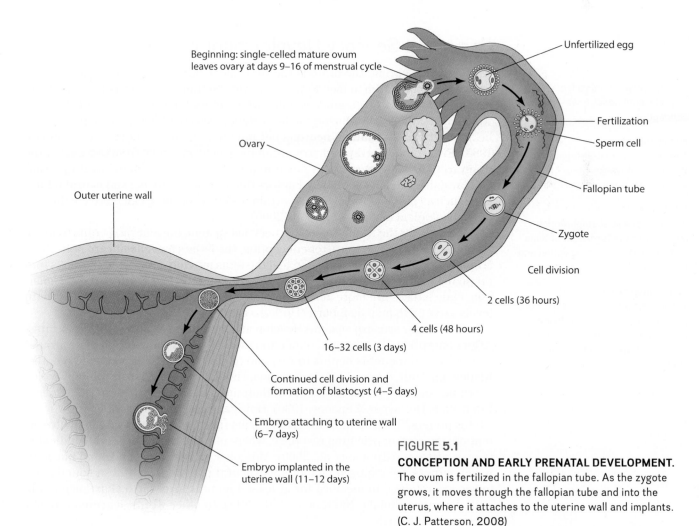

Beginning: single-celled mature ovum leaves ovary at days 9–16 of menstrual cycle

Unfertilized egg

Ovary

Fertilization

Sperm cell

Outer uterine wall

Fallopian tube

Zygote

Cell division

2 cells (36 hours)

4 cells (48 hours)

16–32 cells (3 days)

Continued cell division and formation of blastocyst (4–5 days)

Embryo attaching to uterine wall (6–7 days)

Embryo implanted in the uterine wall (11–12 days)

FIGURE **5.1**

CONCEPTION AND EARLY PRENATAL DEVELOPMENT.
The ovum is fertilized in the fallopian tube. As the zygote grows, it moves through the fallopian tube and into the uterus, where it attaches to the uterine wall and implants. (C. J. Patterson, 2008)

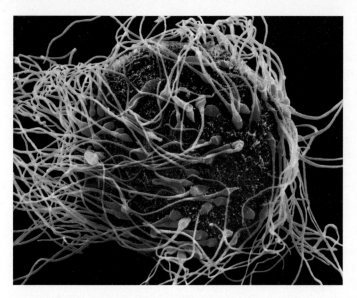

Life begins with the fertilization of an egg. In this highly magnified image, many sperm surround a single egg. Only one sperm will succeed in penetrating the egg.

If implantation is successful, the second stage of prenatal development begins, at about 2 weeks after conception. At this point, the growing bundle of cells is officially an **embryo.** The **embryonic stage** is marked by the formation of the major organs: the nervous system, heart, eyes, ears, arms, legs, teeth, palate, and external genitalia. Embryonic development continues until about 8 weeks after conception.

In Figure 5.2, we see the timetable for prenatal development. Each bar in Figure 5.2 shows when major structures develop and how long it takes. Notice that the central nervous system (brain and spinal cord) takes the longest amount of time to develop. Most major abnormalities occur only in the early stages of development, when exposure to environmental hazards, such as drugs or illness, can cause serious defects.

The key event that distinguishes the embryonic stage from the third stage, the **fetal stage,** is the formation of bone cells at 8 weeks after conception. By this time, all the major organs have already begun to form. Between 8 and 12 weeks into development, the heartbeat can be detected with a stethoscope. Organs continue to grow and mature while the fetus rapidly increases in size.

Brain and Sensory Development before Birth

As mentioned earlier, the brain is the first major organ to develop, and it is still growing rapidly at birth (see Figure 5.3). By the time an infant is born, its head has grown to 25% of its adult weight, whereas its body is only 5% of its adult weight (see Figure 5.4). During the fetal stage, the rate of new neural growth can be approximately 3 million neurons per minute at its peak (Purves & Lichtman, 1985). From months 3 through 5 of pregnancy, neurons move from one part of the brain to their more permanent home in a process known as **neural migration** (Nadarajah & Parnavelas, 2002). Factors that interfere with normal neural migration, such as prenatal exposure to certain toxins or viruses, can increase the risk of psychological disorders (Kandel, 2006).

Soon after the formation of the nervous system, the embryo begins to move its limbs. By 4 to 6 months after conception, the fetus's movements are noticeable (DiPietro et al., 1996). Mothers can feel the fetus moving as early as 16 weeks into pregnancy, although it may feel a little like abdominal gas or "butterflies." Generally, male fetuses are more active than females, suggesting their greater activity levels after birth may be inborn (DiPietro et al., 1996).

The major sensory systems develop at different times and at different rates. After conception, the neurons connecting the ear to the brain are complete around 18 weeks, and the fetus begins to respond to sound around 26 weeks (6 months; Kisilevsky, Muir, & Low, 1992). A few weeks later, fetuses find their mother's voice soothing, and they prefer the sound of their mother's voice to others (DeCasper & Fifer, 1980; DeCasper & Spence, 1986). How can researchers possibly know what a fetus prefers? They monitor the fetus's heart rate. Slowed heart rate indicates attention, interest, or orienting response, whereas an increased heart rate indicates fear or distress (Groome et al., 2000). Moreover, particular sounds and music to which fetuses are exposed change their neural networks and these sounds and music are retained in memory for at least 4 months after birth (Partanen et al., 2013; Partanen, Kujala, Näätänen, et al., 2013). In other words, learning already occurs prior to birth!

embryo
A developing organism from 2 weeks until about 8 weeks after conception.

embryonic stage
The second prenatal stage, from 2 weeks to 8 weeks after conception, when all the major organs form.

fetal stage
The third prenatal stage, which begins with the formation of bone cells 8 weeks after conception and ends at birth.

neural migration
The movement of neurons from one part of the fetal brain to their more permanent destination; this occurs during months 3–5 of the fetal stage.

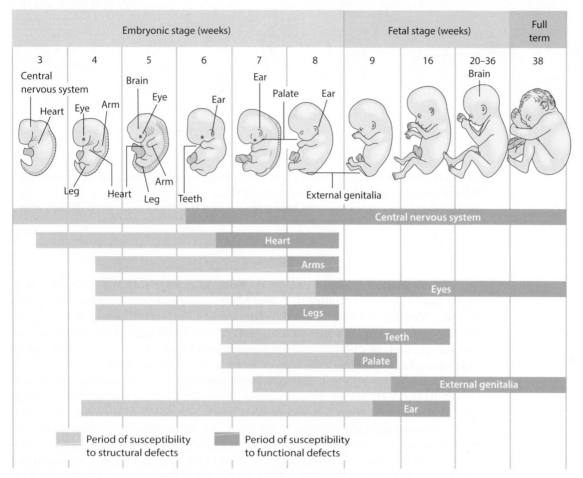

FIGURE **5.2**

PRENATAL DEVELOPMENT TIMELINE. Does the brain develop before or after the heart completes its development? Review the graph to find out. Each bar shows when major structures develop and how long it takes for development to be completed. Note that the central nervous system begins developing in the third week after conception and continues to develop nearly the entire time we are in the womb. The blue section of each bar indicates when major abnormalities can occur if growth goes awry. After that crucial period, minor abnormalities can still occur.

Kanye West or Mozart—can a fetus hear the difference? How so, and what would be its reactions to the different music styles?

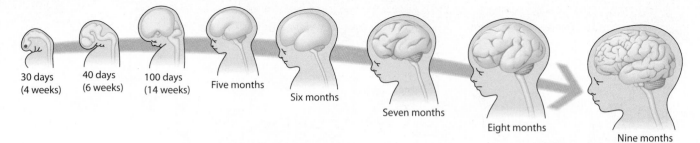

30 days
(4 weeks)

40 days
(6 weeks)

100 days
(14 weeks)

Five months

Six months

Seven months

Eight months

Nine months

FIGURE **5.3**

PRENATAL BRAIN DEVELOPMENT. The size and complexity of the brain increase dramatically in the weeks and months following conception.

What do you notice about the head in the drawing that shows the brain at 40 days after conception?

Taste- and odor-related chemicals from the mother's diet are present in amniotic fluid (Mennella, Johnson, & Beauchamp, 1995). In turn, fetuses are sensitive to odors in the amniotic fluid before birth, and they remember these smells. When pregnant women consumed anise-flavored foods during the last stages of pregnancy, their newborns liked the smell of anise more than babies whose moms did not consume the flavor (Schaal, Marlier, & Soussignan, 2000).

Such studies suggest that our taste preferences may start in the womb (Beauchamp & Mennella, 2009; Hopson, 1998). By 13 to 15 weeks after conception, the taste buds of a fetus look very much like those of an adult (Bradley, 1972). Researchers do not know whether the fetus uses the taste buds, but babies born prematurely—who would otherwise still be developing in the womb—prefer sweet flavors, suggesting that this taste preference exists in the womb (Beauchamp & Mennella, 2009; Mennella & Beauchamp, 1996).

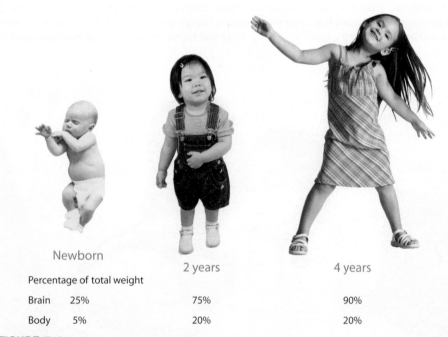

Newborn

2 years

4 years

Percentage of total weight

Brain	25%	75%	90%
Body	5%	20%	20%

FIGURE **5.4**

NEWBORN AND CHILD BRAIN AND BODY AS A PERCENTAGE OF ADULT WEIGHT. The size and complexity of the brain increase dramatically in the weeks and months following conception.

The sense that is least well developed in the fetus is vision (Hopson, 1998). Fetuses do not open their eyes. Also, as discussed in Chapters 3 and 4, vision perception occurs in the brain, which needs visual stimulation to develop the sense of sight (Ptito & Desgent, 2006). Because it is not receiving visual stimulation, the fetus's brain is not developing the appropriate neural connections in the visual cortex to respond to visual imagery. Thus, at birth, infants cannot see things clearly unless the objects are close to the face. Infants cannot see as well as adults until they are at least 6 months old, whereas their hearing is almost adultlike soon after birth.

Nature and Nurture Influences on Fetal Development

To a fetus, the mother's womb is its only "environment." Thus, what a pregnant mother eats, drinks, smokes, feels, and experiences play an important role in fetal development, such as both subtle and profound effects on biological systems in the developing fetus. Nature and nurture work together to shape who we are and who we become. Specifically, **prenatal programming** is the process by which events in the womb alter the development of physical and psychological health (Coe & Lubach, 2008). Of particular concern in this context are **teratogens,** or substances that can cause permanent damage to the developing embryo or fetus.

prenatal programming
The process by which events in the womb alter the development of physical and psychological health.

teratogens
Substances that can disrupt normal prenatal development and cause lifelong deficits.

Maternal Nutrition and Teratogens   Doctors know that what a pregnant woman eats and drinks affects the health of the fetus and even of the infant and child for years after birth. Both schizophrenia and antisocial personality disorder are more likely to occur if the mother is malnourished during pregnancy (Neugebauer, Hoek, & Susser, 1999; Wahlbeck et al., 2001). Similarly, if pregnant women smoke, the risk of the child developing bipolar disorder later in life doubles (Talati et al., 2013).

As it turns out, the body may have a built-in toxin detector called pregnancy sickness, commonly referred to as "morning sickness." Pregnant women often develop aversions to certain foods, and some get nauseated and even vomit regularly (Profet, 1992). Pregnancy sickness is worst during the first 3 months, when the fetus's major organs develop and the embryo is most vulnerable to teratogens, and it occurs most commonly with exposure to foods susceptible to molds (such as aged cheeses) and to bitter substances (such as coffee), possibly because these foods can cause birth defects (Keeler, 1983).

Maternal nutrition—a key part of the developing baby's environment—provides one of the most important examples of epigenetics, the study of how the environment affects gene expression (see Chapter 3). Certain kinds of maternal diet during pregnancy can lead to obesity in offspring—whether or not the mother is obese. In one study, researchers randomly assigned two genetically identical strands of female laboratory mice to receive two kinds of diet while pregnant (Dolinoy & Jirtle, 2008). Group A received a diet rich in substances that activate a gene that causes weight gain, while Group B received a diet rich in nutritional supplements (folic acid and B$_{12}$) that protect against such weight gain. The results showed that the *offspring* of the Group A mice became obese. The diet of the pregnant mother led to obesity in the offspring, and not the child's diet after birth. Equally noteworthy is that the diet of the Group B mice appeared to protect against obesity in their offspring (Dolinoy & Jirtle, 2008; Waterland & Jirtle, 2003).

Challenge Your Assumptions
True or False? Schizophrenia in an offspring is more likely if the mother is exposed to a virus while pregnant.
True: The odds increase four-fold (from 1% to 4%) of developing schizophrenia if the mother is afflicted with a viral illness, such as the flu, while pregnant.

Teratogens   Substances from the external environment impact fetal and infant development. Because all major body parts are forming and growing during the embryonic and fetal stages, the fetus is quite susceptible to birth defects.

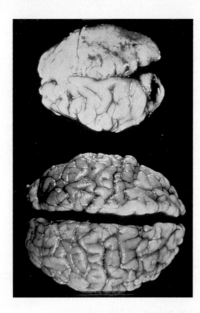

Compared with the brain of a typical child (bottom), what does the brain of a child with **FASD** (top) look like? What would cause such underdevelopment?

fetal alcohol spectrum disorder (FASD)
A consequence of prenatal alcohol exposure that causes multiple problems, notably brain damage.

Connection

How does having the flu while pregnant influence the way neurons grow in the developing fetus and increase its vulnerability to schizophrenia later in life?

See "Schizophrenia," Chapter 15, "Psychological Disorders," p. 558.

Challenge Your Assumptions

True or False? Differences in human temperament already show in the womb.

True: Fetuses in the last trimester are already exhibiting physiological and behavioral differences that are related to temperament (arousal and activity).

temperament
The biologically based tendency to behave in particular ways from very early in life.

personality
The unique and relatively enduring set of behaviors, feelings, thoughts, and motives that characterize an individual.

Known teratogens include viruses, such as those that cause rubella (measles) and the flu; alcohol; nicotine; prescription drugs, such as the antidepressants Prozac and Zoloft; and radiation. Viruses may have a major impact early in pregnancy and relatively little effect toward the end of pregnancy. If a pregnant woman develops an infection, such as the flu, especially during months 4–6 of pregnancy, the risk of schizophrenia increases for the child later in life (A. S. Brown, 2006; Khandaker, Dibben, & Jones, 2012; Koenig, 2006).

Maternal substance use can also cause serious prenatal and postnatal problems. Pregnant women who drink alcohol take chances with their developing baby, as there is no known safe level of alcohol consumption during pregnancy (Centers for Disease Control and Prevention [CDC], 2007). The most serious effect of prenatal alcohol exposure is **fetal alcohol spectrum disorder (FASD),** which causes damage to the brain and central nervous system; mental retardation; low birth weight; physical abnormalities in the face, head, heart, and joints; and behavioral problems (Burd et al., 2007; May & Gossage, 2001; Medina & Krahe, 2008; E. S. Moore et al., 2007; Sen & Swaminathan, 2007; Uylings, 2006).

Another teratogen is nicotine; exposure from maternal smoking interferes with the oxygen supply to the fetus. Such exposure can lead to premature and low-birth-weight babies as well as increased risk for stillbirth, the delivery of a dead fetus (CDC, 2007; Zigler, Finn-Stevenson, & Hall, 2002).

Prescription drugs pose other potential risks for the developing fetus. Many women take prescription drugs during pregnancy, especially if they were taking them before they learned they were pregnant. Research on animals and humans generally indicates that the antidepressants Zoloft and Prozac can cause respiratory problems, increased risk of preterm birth, and short-lasting effects on motor development (Huang et al., 2013; Maschi et al., 2008; Moses-Kolko et al., 2005). The safest course of action is to avoid these drugs prior to pregnancy, if at all possible.

Prenatal Personality Development

Before the 1990s, most people, including psychologists, thought that personality was something that starts to develop only after birth, maybe not until one is a toddler. A finding that challenged these assumptions revealed that temperament begins before birth. **Temperament** is the biologically based tendency to behave in particular ways from very early in life. In one study, Janet DiPietro and her colleagues (1996) showed that fetal activity and fetal heart rate predict temperament differences over the first year of life. In particular, a high heart rate in a 36-week-old fetus foreshadowed less predictable eating and sleeping habits at 3 and 6 months after birth. A high heart rate also predicted a less emotional infant at 6 months after birth.

What happens to the mother while pregnant may affect not only the temperament of the fetus but the temperament and personality later of the infant as well. As we discuss in more detail in Chapter 13, **personality** stems from temperament and is the consistently unique way in which an individual behaves over time and in many different situations. Mothers who are depressed or anxious or who experience a lot of stress during pregnancy are more likely to have infants who are temperamentally "difficult" and "fussy" (Austin et al., 2004; Gutteling et al., 2005). Thus, temperament and sensitivity to stress are set not only by our genes (nature) but also by our mothers' experiences (nurture).

Quick Quiz 5.1: The Developing Fetus

1. Life before birth is commonly divided into three distinct stages: the _____, embryonic, and fetal stages.
   a. gestational
   b. seminal
   c. germinal
   d. cellular

2. How can researchers tell which sounds a fetus prefers to hear?
   a. by measuring the position of the fetus in the womb
   b. by measuring changes in fetal heart rate in response to sounds
   c. by taking a reading of fetal respiration
   d. It is not possible to measure fetal preferences.

3. Teratogens are
   a. substances that can cause birth defects.
   b. genes that turn on or off with exposure to viruses.
   c. inborn fetal taste preferences.
   d. factors that influence the generation of fetal brain tissue.

Answers can be found at the end of the chapter.

THE DEVELOPING INFANT AND CHILD

Because it's still developing, the newborn human brain is more responsive than that of other animals to its surroundings. This distinction allows nurture to shape human nature more than is the case for most animals.

Physical Development in Infancy and Childhood

Adults take for granted the ability to act at will, yet when first born, humans are completely incapable of acting intentionally. Motor and sensory systems develop substantially in newborns. In this section, we explore how physical growth, motor skills, and sensory capacities develop in infancy and early childhood. We examine how experience and the brain interact to shape early human experience.

Early Motor Development   When we speak of motor development, we are referring to changes in physical movement and body control. Figure 5.5 outlines

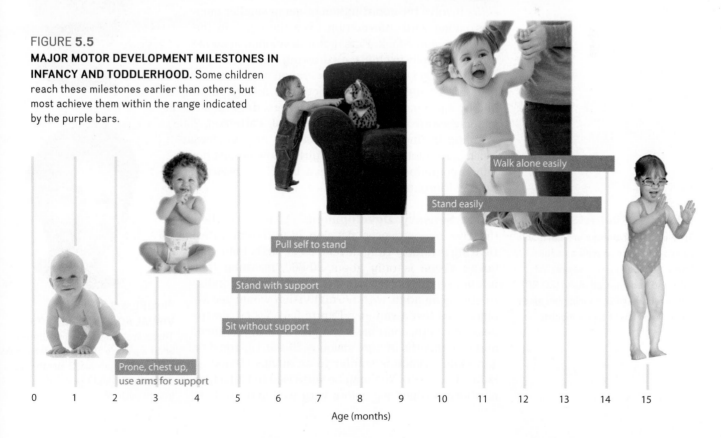

FIGURE **5.5**

MAJOR MOTOR DEVELOPMENT MILESTONES IN INFANCY AND TODDLERHOOD. Some children reach these milestones earlier than others, but most achieve them within the range indicated by the purple bars.

Walk alone easily

Stand easily

Pull self to stand

Stand with support

Sit without support

Prone, chest up, use arms for support

Age (months)

0 1 2 3 4 5 6 7 8 9 10 11 12 13 14 15

the major milestones of motor development during the first 15 months. Although the sequence is predictable, the exact age at which children reach each milestone varies. For example, our son Jerry did not crawl until he was 9 months old, but he walked at 10 months. Our son Evan, on the other hand, crawled at 7½ months and then started walking at about 12 months.

Early in infancy, babies start to show intentional movements. First, they look at their mother with an unfocused gaze, and then they turn their head to look at her. By about 2 months of age, babies lying on their stomach can lift their head. A 3-month-old who is fascinated by a stuffed ring dangling in front of him will suddenly, though not very smoothly, grab for it. At 4 months, babies can hold objects. By 6 months, many can sit by themselves, without any help. By 7 months, babies can pull themselves up and hold on to furniture, and at about 8 to 9 months, they walk from sofa to coffee table by holding on to the furniture. Many babies take their first steps around their first birthday, though it may be some time—at about 17 months of age—before they settle into walking on their own (C. J. Patterson, 2008).

Other motor responses are more specific. If you give a newborn baby your finger, she will grasp it tightly. If you stroke her cheek, she will turn her head, open-mouthed in expectation of a breast, a reflex called *rooting*. Grasping and rooting are among several reflexes—involuntary responses to very specific stimuli—present at birth.

It takes a while before young children can turn knobs and pick up tiny objects. These *fine motor skills* involve the coordination of many smaller muscles, along with information from the eyes, in the service of some task. Fine motor development shows up, for example, in children's drawing skills. Two-year-olds typically show very crude crayon scribbles, but by age 3 or 4 children can make crude drawings of people, and by age 5 most kids can print letters, dress alone, and use silverware (H. Gardner, 1980; C. J. Patterson, 2008). Training in fine motor skills actually aids kindergarteners' attention, especially in girls, showing just how joined cognition and action can be (R. A. Stewart, Rule, & Giordano, 2007).

Challenge Your Assumptions

True or False? Babies are born able to see and hear as well as adults.

False: Newborn vision is only 20-600 and becomes adultlike (20-20) only around age 3; hearing becomes adultlike by about age 6 months.

Early Sensory Development As noted earlier, the five major senses develop at different rates. Hearing is almost fully developed at birth, but a newborn's vision is only about 20-600, meaning that infants see an object that is 20 feet away as indistinctly as an adult with normal vision would see an object 600 feet away (see Figure 5.6). Visual sharpness, or acuity, continues to improve during infancy, and by 6 months of age, vision is 20-100. By age 3 or 4, a child's vision is similar to an adult's (Banks & Salapatek, 1983). You may be surprised to learn that newborns do not see colors very well and are best

FIGURE **5.6**
VISUAL ACUITY IN INFANTS.
These are computer simulations of what a picture of a human face looks like to a 1-month-old, 2-month-old, 3-month-old, and 1-year-old (top to bottom).

FIGURE **5.7**

THE VISUAL CLIFF.

In what appears to be a cliff by using a clear sheet of plastic, do you think babies will stop at the edge? Explain.

able to see black and white edges and patterns (Fantz, 1963). Color vision approximates that of adults by 4 months of age (Kellman & Arterberry, 2006).

Experience is crucial in the development of vision, as it is in all aspects of human development. The occipital cortex of the brain has to be stimulated by visual input, so that it can develop the proper synaptic connections needed to process visual information. It is for this reason that young infants respond chiefly to visual stimuli within 8 to 12 inches of their faces.

Can all babies who have normal vision in both eyes and can crawl see the world in three dimensions? In a study that has become a classic, Gibson and Walk (1960) tested this question by creating a *visual cliff* to test depth perception in babies who have learned to crawl (see Figure 5.7). They placed clear Plexiglas (hard plastic) over one end of a crawl area to make it look as though there was a steep drop in the middle. They put a baby on one end of the crawl area and asked the mother to stand at the end with the drop. The mother's role was to encourage the baby to crawl across the clear plastic surface to her. In this study, babies stopped crawling when they reached the visual cliff, indicating that, at least by the time they learn to crawl, babies can perceive depth.

Early Brain Development   Experiences such as eating, exercising, and learning mold our brains throughout life, but especially in infancy and childhood. With learning and experience, certain synaptic connections strengthen, whereas those that don't receive stimulation from the environment die off—a process known as **pruning,** nature's way of making the brain more efficient (Baltes, Reuter-Lorenz,

pruning
The degradation of synapses and dying off of neurons that are not strengthened by experience.

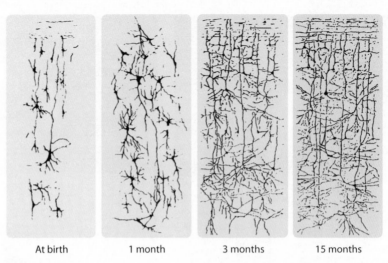

| At birth | 1 month | 3 months | 15 months |

FIGURE **5.8**

NEURAL GROWTH DURING THE FIRST 6 MONTHS OF LIFE.

Describe what happens during neural growth and what happens to neurons and synapses not reinforced by learning. Adapted from *The postnatal development of the human cerebral cortex, Vols. I–VIII*, by Jesse LeRoy Conel. (Harvard University Press, **1939**).

Connection

Experience is crucial in the formation of synaptic connections and the growth of neurons in the brain throughout the life span. Unused synapses are left to die. Pruning is nature's way of making the brain function more efficiently.

See "The Nervous System," Chapter 3, "The Biology of Behavior," p. 78.

& Rösler, 2006; Greenough, Volkmar, & Juraska, 1973; B. D. Perry, 2002). Pruning is not only about creating a more efficient brain but is also required for normal brain development. Research shows that problems with neural pruning may result in neurological disorders, such as autism or schizophrenia (Cusack et al., 2013; Rapoport et al., 2009).

After birth, the brain continues to grow new neurons (see Figure 5.8). Contrary to scientific thought as recently as 15 years ago, brain growth continues throughout the life span. The rate of change slows down considerably after the age of 6, increases in early adolescence, and then settles again after adolescence (Chechik, Meilijson, & Ruppin, 1999; Sakai, 2005).

In some 9-year-old children showing early signs of puberty, gray matter in the prefrontal and parietal regions of the brain surprisingly *decreases* somewhat in volume (Giedd et al., 1999; Peper et al., 2009). Such decreases in gray matter volume suggest that pruning—in which unused neurons die—is still occurring late in childhood. Recall that gray matter consists of the cell bodies and is a measure of the number of neurons; white matter is made up of the axons and myelin (see Figure 5.9). The number of neurons (gray matter) starts to decline in adolescence, but white matter (axons and connectivity) continues to grow into one's 40s (Westlye et al., 2010).

Because pruning is based on input from the environment, the quality of the environments in which we are raised influences how our brains develop. Normal and enriched environments create more complex neural connections, whereas abusive, neglectful, and impoverished environments create less developed neural connections and fewer of them (Mirescu & Gould, 2006). An example of how experience can positively shape the brain is seen in the findings that physically fit children are also more cognitively fit; that is, they do better in reasoning tasks and school in general (Castelli et al., 2007; Hillman et al., 2009). "Psychology in the Real World" looks at another type of experience—musical training—that influences brain growth and cognitive development.

Neglect exists when caregivers fail to provide basic sensory experience and stimulation to a child during key periods of development (B. D. Perry, 2002). Timing is critical. A dramatic instance of the effect

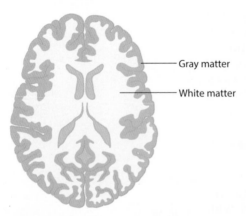

— Gray matter

— White matter

FIGURE **5.9**

WHITE AND GRAY MATTER IN THE HUMAN BRAIN.

of neglect and abuse on the development of the human brain comes from research on children who spent their early years in Romanian orphanages, where they were confined much of the time to cribs and had very limited stimulation. Figure 5.10 shows a PET scan from one of the orphans alongside one from a typically developing child. The red to yellow areas in Figure 5.10a represent the active regions in the brain of a normal child. Figure 5.10b shows the brain activity of a Romanian orphan who was neglected from birth. As you can see, brain activity is greatly diminished in the orphan (Cicchetti, 2001). Similarly, research shows decreases in brain size in children raised in severely neglectful homes. These deficits can be overcome if the children are removed from the neglectful environment—sooner rather than later, however. The longer they stay in the deprived environment, the less likely it is that they will recover (B. D. Perry, 2002).

Findings in neuroscience suggest that children's brains are more plastic and more sensitive to stimulation from the outside world than are the brains of older people. Part of the reason is that young brains are more flexible because they have less myelin, which makes neural transmission more efficient but at a cost to neuroplasticity. In Chapter 3 we noted that many axons are covered with a myelin sheath, the fatty insulation that allows nerve impulses to travel faster. Few neurons are myelinated at birth; with age, myelination increases (R. D. Fields, 2008; Peper et al., 2009). Figure 5.11 shows the relative increases in myelin over time from age 4 to age 20.

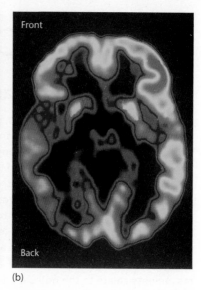

(a) (b)

FIGURE 5.10

BRAIN DEVELOPMENT IN A NORMAL CHILD COMPARED TO A DEPRIVED AND NEGLECTED CHILD.

 If red represents high levels of brain activity and blue relatively less brain activity, what do these two images tell you about the brain of (a) a typically developing child and (b) a child who experienced deprivation and neglect in an orphanage? (Cicchetti, 2001)

Early Cognitive Development

With brain growth come advances in the ability to think, pay attention, reason, remember, learn, and solve problems. How do cognitive skills grow, and how can we study them in babies who cannot speak yet? The answer is that infants look at things longer when they are interested in them, and such looking can indicate

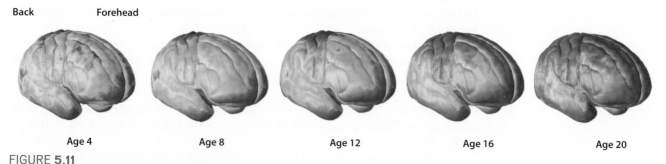

Back   Forehead

Age 4   Age 8   Age 12   Age 16   Age 20

FIGURE 5.11

MYELINATION IN THE DEVELOPING BRAIN. In the figure, unmyelinated neurons appear yellow and orange. Myelinated neurons appear purple.

What does myelin do for developing brains?
(R. D. Fields, 2008)

Psychology in the Real World

Musical Training Changes the Brain

The brain develops throughout life, yet it is most responsive to stimulation during infancy and childhood. In other words, early in life there is more opportunity for experience to leave its mark on the brain (Cicchetti, 2001).

Learning to play a musical instrument is a fascinating example of how experience changes the brain, or of how nature and nurture work together to create who we are. If you want to learn guitar, you must learn how to finger on the neck, how to hold your fingers and press the strings firmly enough to get a clear sound, and how the fingering movements relate to the notes on different musical scales. In Chapter 3, "The Biology of Behavior," we discussed how monkeys trained in a finger-tapping task showed substantial increases in the amount of somatosensory cortex devoted to the fingertips compared to both the amount they had before training and the amount in untrained monkeys (Jenkins et al., 1990). Can we see similar effects in the brains of string instrument players?

Researchers who were curious about this question applied a slight pressure to each finger on each hand of right-handed musicians and nonmusicians of various ages. Using fMRI, they mapped the brain's responses to this pressure. For musicians, the area on the somatosensory cortex devoted to those fingers on the side of the brain that controls the fingering left hand was bigger than the area that controls the nonfingering right hand, and musicians who started playing before the age of 12 showed the most pronounced differences. The somatosensory maps did not differ between sides in the brains of nonmusicians (Elbert et al., 1995). So musical training may change brain organization, especially for people who start training as children.

Musical training appears to shape the structure of the brain as well. People who have had intensive musical training have a thicker corpus callosum and more brain growth in regions associated with music-related skills than do nonmusicians, and the difference is even greater if they started their training before age 7 (Schlaug et al., 1995). A thicker corpus callosum makes for greater communication between the two sides of the brain. Also, musicians have larger cerebellums (an area involved in motor coordination) than do nonmusicians (Hutchinson et al., 2003). Other research shows that, the earlier musical training begins, the greater the degree of activation of the music-processing areas of the brain (left auditory cortex) when listening to music (Ohnishi et al., 2001), and evidence indicates significant growth in brain regions of 6-year-old children after just 15 months of musical training compared to those without training (K. L. Hyde et al., 2009).

Moreover, as the brain regions involved in moving muscles and processing sound grew, the better the children's musical performance became. Recent evidence points to musical training enhancing neural activity in the hippocampus, which is the brain region most involved in learning and memory (Herdener et al., 2010). Most impressive, perhaps, is the finding that these neuroplastic effects of musical training last well into adulthood (Skoe & Kraus, 2012).

The findings discussed so far are correlational. Recall a lesson from Chapter 2: Correlation is necessary but not sufficient for causation. Correlational findings

---

preference. Researchers who study infants have come to rely on visual preference as their primary means of studying infant thought and attention (J. E. Richards, Reynolds, & Courage, 2010).

When infants from 4 to 7 months of age pay attention to something for more than a few seconds, brain activity narrows from many brain regions to more specific brain regions (J. E. Richards et al., 2010). This finding suggests that the brain is becoming more organized and efficient during the first 6 months of life, and this increased brain organization leads to increased ability to pay attention and focus on one thing during the first year of life (J. E. Richards et al., 2010).

If there is one important thing developmental psychologists have learned about infants over the last 20 years, it is that infants are smarter than we ever thought. Alison Gopnik summarized these findings in her book *The Philosophical Baby* (2009). Infant perception, knowledge of the world, and even problem-solving skills are much more sophisticated than previously thought.

suggest that musical training can shape the brain, but they do not lead to the conclusion that musical training necessarily *causes* brain growth. One way to address the problem of correlation is to do an experiment, which is what Alvaro Pascual-Leone, professor of neurology at Harvard University, did. He taught people who had never before played piano a one-hand, five-finger exercise. They repeated the exercise in 2-hour practice sessions for 5 days, and then they were given a test involving 20 repetitions of the exercise (responses measured by computer for speed, etc.). As skill improved, cortical representation for the finger muscles involved in the task increased (Pascual-Leone, 2001). Next, participants were randomly assigned either to continue daily practice of the exercise for 4 more weeks or to stop practicing. For those who stopped practicing, within 1 week, brain maps returned to the way they were before training. For those who continued practicing, brain map changes continued. In short, if you don't use it, you lose it!

Your parents may have wanted you to take music lessons "because it would be good for you." Well, there is evidence, as difficult as it may be for you to believe, that your parents were correct about this. Musical training enhances cognitive skills beyond those directly related to music, such as verbal memory, verbal reasoning, nonverbal reasoning, and mathematical reasoning, as well as IQ in general (Forgeard et al., 2008; Ho, Cheung, & Chan, 2003; Rodrigues, Loureiro, & Caramelli, 2010; Schellenberg, 2004, 2006, 2011; Spelke, 2008). For example, music training is positively correlated with intelligence test

scores in children and college students, and this relationship is strongest for people who have trained longer (Schellenberg, 2006). Recent evidence, however, suggests that high intelligence is more of a cause than an effect of musical training, with high cognitive ability children more likely to take music lessons than average or low cognitive ability children (Schellenberg, 2011). High intelligence extends neuroplasticity and the sensitivity periods for learning, meaning that musical training can shape the brain even more and for a longer period of time in those with high intelligence (Brant et al., 2013).

For example, 8-month-old infants understand the basics of statistics and probability. To arrive at this finding, a researcher put mostly white but a few red Ping-Pong balls into a box, then reached into the box and pulled out a few white but many red balls (Xu & Garcia, 2008). The babies registered that this was very unlikely; they looked a lot longer at this situation than when the researcher pulled out many white and only a few red balls (Xu & Garcia, 2008). Psychologists therefore call babies "intuitive statisticians"—without any training, they know some events are very unlikely.

So we have learned from developmental science that infants and young children have many perceptual and cognitive skills that develop rapidly over time. Are there any limits on how and when these skills develop? Jean Piaget's (1954) principles of cognitive development from birth throughout childhood outline stages at which certain cognitive capacities appear. Relying primarily on observations of his own three children, Piaget outlined four phases of cognitive development from birth through adolescence, which he called the sensorimotor,

Jean Piaget

	Approximate age (years)	Core cognitive capacities
Sensorimotor	0–2	Knowledge is through senses (tasting, seeing, smelling, touching, hearing) Object permanence develops between 4 and 9 months
Preoperational	2–5	Verbal and egocentric thinking develop Can do mentally what once could only do physically Conservation of shape, number, liquid not yet possible
Concrete operational	6–11	Conservation of shape, number, liquid are now possible Logic and reasoning develop, but are limited to appearance and what is concretely observed
Formal operational	12 and up	Abstract reasoning—principles and ideals develop Systematic problem solving is now possible (no longer just trial and error) Ability to think about and reflect upon one's thinking (metacognition) Scientific reasoning

FIGURE **5.12**
PIAGET'S STAGES OF COGNITIVE DEVELOPMENT.

sensorimotor stage
Piaget's first stage of cognitive development (ages 0–2), when infants learn about the world by using their senses and moving their bodies.

object permanence
The ability to realize that objects still exist when they are not being sensed.

preoperational, concrete operational, and formal operational stages. Figure 5.12 summarizes Piaget's theory of cognitive development.

Piaget called the first stage of cognitive development the **sensorimotor stage** because it characterizes the way infants learn about the world through their senses and their own movements. Young children sense more than they "think" and come to understand the world by manipulating and moving through it. Piaget also observed that, during the first 8 or 9 months, a child has no concept of **object permanence,** which is the ability to realize that objects still exist when they are not being sensed (Piaget, 1954). In other words, it is "out of sight, out of mind" for young infants. When an object is hidden from them, they will not look for it, even if they see someone hide it. Around 9 months of age, however, infants will move a cloth or look under something to find the hidden object, because they have begun to remember that objects continue to exist even when they are not directly sensed. Mastering object permanence is a hallmark of the sensorimotor stage.

Renée Baillargeon and colleagues conducted intriguing research using a different technique that challenged Piaget's argument that infants develop object permanence at about 9 months (Baillargeon & DeVos, 1991). They measured infants' responses to both expected and impossible events (see Figure 5.13). First, infants were shown an inclined track and a screen that was lowered or raised in front of the track. They learned that, when a car rolls down the track, the car keeps rolling behind the lowered screen and appears on the other side of it. They were not surprised to see the car, even though it was hidden for a short time by the lowered screen. They were shown this event many times, until they got used to it—that is, until it became expected. In the next sequence, everything was the same except that the researchers placed a toy mouse *behind* the track while the babies watched. Again, they were not surprised to see the car roll behind the lowered screen and appear on the other side of it.

Then something impossible happened. The researchers placed the mouse *on* the track while the infants watched. When the screen was down, hiding the mouse from the infants' view, the experimenters removed the mouse. The researchers

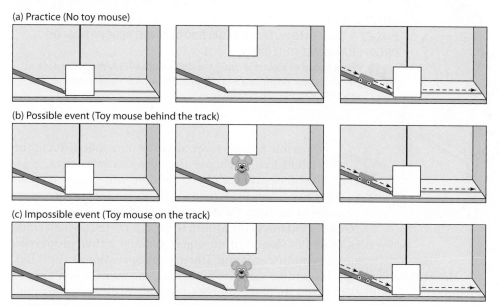

(a) Practice (No toy mouse)

(b) Possible event (Toy mouse behind the track)

(c) Impossible event (Toy mouse on the track)

FIGURE **5.13**

THE DEVELOPMENT OF OBJECT PERMANENCE. In the practice sessions (a), children learn that cars can still roll all the way to the wall, because the screen is in front of the track, not blocking the car's path. In the possible session (b), they are not surprised to again see the car roll all the way to the wall, because the mouse was behind, not on, the track. But in the impossible session (c), the infants were surprised to see the car roll all the way to the wall, because the mouse should have blocked it (unbeknownst to the children, the mouse had been removed while the screen was down).

 How do the researchers know whether the young child was surprised or not? (Baillargeon and DeVos, 1991)

found that, when the car rolled down the track and kept rolling (impossible if the mouse were still on the track), the infants were quite surprised, which Baillargeon and DeVos were able to tell by studying the infants' eyes. When things go as expected, infants get bored and stop looking at the event, but when they witness an impossible event, their eyes widen and they keep looking. Infants as young as 4 months of age, not 9 months, realize objects still exist even when they do not see them. Piaget was right about object permanence but wrong about the age at which it first happens.

At around age 2, with the emergence of symbolic thought, children move into Piaget's second stage of cognitive development—the **preoperational stage,** a period that lasts until about age 5 or 6. Symbolic thinking involves using symbols, such as words or letters, to represent ideas or objects. The cognitive limitations of the preoperational stage include animistic thinking, egocentrism, and lack of conservation.

Animistic thinking refers to the idea that inanimate objects are alive. For example, Piaget reported on a child in this stage who was asked whether the sun moved. The child answered, "Yes, when one walks, it follows." When the child was asked why it moves, he responded, "Because when one walks, it goes too." Finally, when the child was asked whether the sun was alive, he responded, "Of course, otherwise it wouldn't follow us; it couldn't shine" (Piaget, 1972b, p. 215).

Egocentrism is the tendency to view the world only from one's own perspective. Piaget and Inhelder (1967) designed the *three mountains task* to measure young children's egocentrism (see Figure 5.14). For this demonstration, three mountains are placed on a small table. The child sits on one side of the table, and a doll is placed in a chair on the other side of the table. The experimenter asks the child to describe how the doll sees the three mountains. Typically, the three

preoperational stage
The second major stage of cognitive development (ages 2–5), which begins with the emergence of symbolic thought.

animistic thinking
A belief that inanimate objects are alive.

egocentrism
Viewing the world from one's own perspective and not being capable of seeing things from another person's perspective.

FIGURE 5.14

PIAGET'S THREE MOUNTAINS TASK: EGOCENTRIC PERCEPTION OF PREOPERATIONAL CHILDREN.

When asked to describe what the doll can see from the other side of the table, how do children in the preoperational stage respond, and why? (C. J. Patterson, 2008)

possible perspectives are drawn on a board and the child has to choose the correct perspective. Egocentric, preoperational children will choose the perspective from which *they* see the mountains; they cannot visualize them from the doll's point of view.

Conservation is the ability to recognize that, when some properties (such as shape) of an object change, other properties (such as volume) remain constant. During preoperational thinking, the child cannot yet recognize that amounts stay the same when shapes change. Psychologists say that they are unable to conserve. Piaget used many objects and situations to examine conservation. Figure 5.15 shows a number of them.

Let's look at conservation of liquid as an example. This task involves filling two glasses of the same shape and size with equal amounts of water. The

conservation
The recognition that, when some properties (such as shape) of an object change, other properties (such as volume) remain constant.

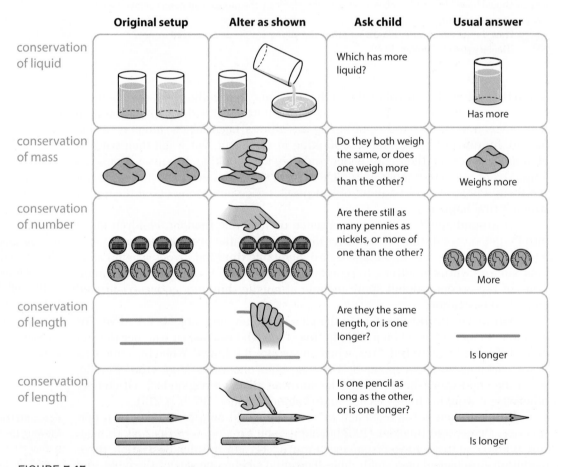

	Original setup	Alter as shown	Ask child	Usual answer
conservation of liquid			Which has more liquid?	Has more
conservation of mass			Do they both weigh the same, or does one weigh more than the other?	Weighs more
conservation of number			Are there still as many pennies as nickels, or more of one than the other?	More
conservation of length			Are they the same length, or is one longer?	Is longer
conservation of length			Is one pencil as long as the other, or is one longer?	Is longer

FIGURE 5.15
DIFFERENT KINDS OF CONSERVATION TASKS. Children in the preoperational stage don't realize that the quantity of something doesn't change if it is rearranged. (Seifert, Hoffnung, & Hoffnung, 2000)

child confirms that the two glasses contain the same amount of water. Then the child pours one of the glasses of water into a third container, which is wider but shorter than the first two. The child does nothing to the second. When asked whether the two glasses contain the same amount of water, the child will say no if he or she lacks the ability to conserve. Usually, the child will say that the tall, thin container has more water than the short, wide one.

During Piaget's third stage, called the **concrete operational stage** (ages 6–11), children can perform mental operations on real, or concrete, objects and events—but they still have trouble with abstract ideas and reasoning. The ability to reverse events is one type of operation a child masters in this stage. One of the yardsticks that measures whether a child has moved from preoperational to concrete operational thinking is the ability to conserve, such as when the child realizes that an amount of liquid doesn't change when pouring it from one container into another of different shape. In this stage, logic remains concrete and limited to objects that a child directly observes. The child can reason that the amount of liquid she or he sees go from one glass into the other must remain the same but would have trouble solving a problem of this type: "If Susan is half as old as Robert, and Robert is twice as old as Samantha, then how old is Samantha compared to Susan?"

With the onset of adolescence, children gain the ability to reason about abstract concepts and problems. Piaget called this phase of cognitive development the **formal operational stage** (Inhelder & Piaget, 1958; Piaget, 1972a). During this stage, formal logic becomes possible. Here is an example: "If Maria is a woman, and all women are mortal, then Maria is mortal." In addition, adolescents develop scientific reasoning and hypothesis-testing skills. We'll go into more detail about this stage of cognitive development in the section on adolescence.

After a 4- or 5-year-old child (preoperational) sees liquid poured from a short, fat container to a tall, thin one, does the child think the amount of liquid is more than or is the same as when it was in the short container? What did Piaget's research tell us?

concrete operational stage
Piaget's third stage of cognitive development, which spans ages 6–11, during which the child can perform mental operations, such as reversing, on real objects or events.

formal operational stage
Piaget's final stage of cognitive development, from age 11 or 12 through adulthood, when formal logic is possible.

CALVIN AND HOBBES © 1986 Watterson. Dist. by Universal Uclick. Reprinted with permission. All rights reserved.

The Russian psychologist Lev Vygotsky developed a more social view of cognitive development than Piaget. Vygotsky (1978), for instance, argued that cognitive development does not happen in a vacuum but rather must be understood in its social context. Other people can and do affect what we learn. Vygotsky coined the phrase **zone of proximal development** and defined it as the distance between what a child can learn alone and what that child can learn assisted by someone else, usually an adult. The idea of a zone of proximal development is that, when a child is near his or her potential (in the zone), a more experienced person can aid the child in learning more and learning faster than the child would alone. Learning, therefore, is best understood as a social process.

zone of proximal development
The distance between what a child can learn alone and what that child can learn assisted by someone else, usually an adult.

theory of mind
Ideas and knowledge about how other people's minds work.

Theory of Mind   Knowing and understanding what other people are thinking, wanting, or feeling is a critical skill in human society. The term **theory of mind** refers to our knowledge and ideas of how other people's minds work. The important questions from a development perspective are when and how does such a skill emerge and how does it change with age?

Most adults—especially those who learn to think critically—know that people believe things that sometimes are not true. They may even come to realize that their own beliefs may not always be true. Children under the age of 4 are cognitively incapable of understanding that people may believe things that are not true. Psychologists created the *false-belief* task to explore children's theory of mind and the stage at which they come to know that others may hold false beliefs (Wimmer & Perner, 1983). They discovered that age 4 is commonly when children understand that other people can believe something different from their own beliefs (see Research Process, Figure 5.16).

Development of Moral Reasoning

As children develop cognitive skills, social skills, and theory of mind, they also develop a sense of right and wrong. Most likely, social and cognitive skills work together to help the child make sense of the workings of the world.

The most well-known account of the development of moral reasoning comes from Lawrence Kohlberg (1981), who studied the development of moral reasoning in children and adults by giving them a moral dilemma and recording the reasons they provided for their responses. Their responses were less important to him than was the reasoning behind them.

The dilemma Kohlberg commonly presented to his participants was the "Heinz Dilemma," as follows:

> A woman was near death from a special kind of cancer. There was one drug that the doctors thought might save her. It was a form of radium that a druggist in the same town had recently discovered. The drug was expensive to make, but the druggist was charging ten times what the drug cost him to produce. He paid $200 for the radium and charged $2,000 for a small dose of the drug. The sick woman's husband, Heinz, went to everyone he knew to borrow the money, but he could only get together about $1,000, which is half of what it cost. He told the druggist that his wife was dying and asked him to sell it cheaper or let him pay later. But the druggist said: "No, I discovered the drug and I'm going to make money from it." So Heinz got desperate and broke into the man's store to steal the drug for his wife. Should Heinz have broken into the laboratory to steal the drug for his wife? Why or why not? (Kohlberg, 1981)

Research Process

① Research Question

At what age can children first realize that other people can believe something different from their own beliefs?

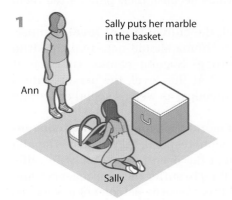

1 Sally puts her marble in the basket.

Ann

Sally

② Method

For the false-belief task, a child between the ages of 3 and 5 sits with an experimenter at a table. The experimenter has cardboard cutouts of a story. In the first cutout, Sally puts her marble in a basket. In the next picture, Sally goes away. In the next scene, Ann takes the marble from the basket and puts it in a box. In the final scene, Sally returns. The researcher asks this critical false-belief question: Where will Sally look for her marble, in the box or the basket?

2 Sally goes away.

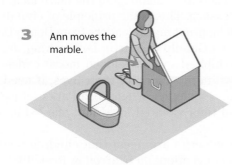

3 Ann moves the marble.

4 Where will Sally look for her marble?

③ Results

A 3-year-old will say that Sally will look in the box, because a 3-year-old cannot distinguish what she or he knows from what Sally knows. Around age 4, however, children can disentangle their own beliefs from other people's beliefs and say, "Sally will look in the basket," because they understand that Sally doesn't know that Ann moved the marble (Gopnik, Meltzoff, & Kuhl, 1999; K. Sullivan, Zaitchik, & Tager-Flusberg, 1994; Wimmer & Perner, 1983).

④ Conclusion

Children learn to untangle their own beliefs from other people's at around age 4.

FIGURE **5.16**

FALSE-BELIEF TASK. Children under 4 will say that Sally will look for the marble in the box, because they saw Ann put it there and can't distinguish between what they know and what Sally knows.

Motive–reasoning		
pre-conventional	To avoid punishment Judgments are based on personal needs	
conventional	Rules are rules and they are not to be broken Judgments are based on needs of society; individual needs serve group needs	
post-conventional	Willing to break law—and suffer the consequences—if it is perceived as unjust or immoral Judgments balance needs of society with personal convictions	

FIGURE 5.17

SUMMARY OF KOHLBERG'S STAGES OF MORAL REASONING. Kohlberg saw a possible progression through three stages of moral reasoning, but not everyone reaches the postconventional stage.

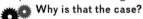 Why is that the case?

preconventional level
The first level in Kohlberg's theory of moral reasoning, focusing on avoiding punishment or maximizing rewards.

conventional level
The second level in Kohlberg's theory of moral reasoning, during which the person values caring, trust, and relationships as well as the social order and lawfulness.

postconventional level
The third level in Kohlberg's theory of moral reasoning, in which the person recognizes universal moral rules that may trump unjust or immoral local rules.

After analyzing the reasoning that people of different ages gave in response to these questions, Kohlberg proposed a three-stage theory of moral reasoning. In Kohlberg's view, moral reasoning moves from being focused on the self to being increasingly focused on others, with a basis in clear personal principles of morality and ethics (see Figure 5.17).

In the first, and least developed, level of moral reasoning, the **preconventional level,** the responses tend to be something like this: "Heinz should not steal the drug because he will get in trouble and go to jail." The reasoning behind the answer has to do with avoiding punishment or maximizing reward. Children obey rules because their parents tell them to comply.

In the second level, the **conventional level,** the person might respond with "Heinz should not steal the drug because stealing is wrong. Society cannot function if people steal all the time." At this level, the person values caring, trust, and relationships, as well as social order and lawfulness.

In the third level of moral reasoning—the **postconventional level**—a person might respond, "Although it is legally wrong, Heinz should steal the drug to save his wife's life. But he also has to be willing to suffer the consequences and go to jail if need be." In this case, the person acknowledges both the norm and the law but argues that there are universal moral rules that may trump unjust or immoral local rules. Therefore, disobeying the more local rule or law may be necessary. This is the principle of civil disobedience embraced by great moral leaders from Henry David Thoreau to Mahatma Gandhi to Martin Luther King, Jr., to Rosa Parks, who exhibited well-developed moral codes for which they were willing to sacrifice their lives, if need be, to set right unjust and immoral laws and societies. When Rosa Parks refused to take a seat in the back of the bus and thus violated local law, she exhibited postconventional moral reasoning.

Research supports Kohlberg's argument that children tend to reason preconventionally and adults conventionally (Carroll & Rest, 1981; Lapsley, 2006). Moreover, research on moral reasoning in different cultures all over the world offers support for the first two stages of Kohlberg's model but challenges his argument for a third. Snarey (1985) reviewed 45 studies on the development of moral reasoning in 27 countries and found universal support for the preconventional and conventional levels of moral reasoning. The postconventional level, however, appears to be limited to Western cultures, which place a strong emphasis on individual values, and postconventional moral reasoning is heavily based in a personal moral code. In contrast, many non-Western cultures emphasize the importance of the group and community, so the highest level of moral reasoning would be likely to involve compassion and caring for others, altruism, and family honor, values that Kohlberg did not measure (Matsumoto & Juang, 2004).

Lawrence Kohlberg

Personality Development during Infancy

After birth, some infants soon settle into a predictable routine. Others do not. Some are generally happy, and others are fussy. Some infants also have lower thresholds for stimulation than others. Based on their classic study of such differences, Alexander Thomas and Stella Chess (1977, 1996) developed an influential model of temperament, with three general categories, that is still widely accepted: the easy child, the difficult child, and the slow-to-warm-up child. The *easy child* is predictable in daily functions, is happy most of the time, and is adaptable. About 40% of children fell into this category. The *difficult child* is unpredictable in daily functions, is unhappy most of the time, and is slow to adapt to new situations. About 10% fell into this category. The *slow-to-warm-up child* is mildly intense in his or her reactions to new situations and mildly irregular in the daily patterns of eating, sleeping, and eliminating. Although his or her first response to new situations might be negative, after repeated exposures, he or she develops an approaching style. About 15% of the children fell into this category. About 35% of the children were not classified by these three dimensions.

Early Socioemotional Development

All mammals need warmth and contact to survive and flourish. Human babies need constant care in order to survive to early childhood. They seem programmed from birth to form close relationships with their primary caregivers. Thanks to some pioneering research that began in the mid-20th century, we know that the quality of those relationships can have lifelong implications.

"During the next stage of my development, Dad, I'll be drawing closer to my mother—I'll get back to you in my teens."

Lee Lorenz/The New Yorker Collection/The Cartoon Bank. Used by permission.

Attachment   Some animals, especially birds, follow and imitate the first large creature they see immediately after birth, a behavior called **imprinting.** The newborn sees this creature as a protector. Usually, this creature also happens to *be* the protector (mom or dad), so it is a good strategy (Lorenz, 1935, 1937). Newborn humans cannot follow around the first large creature they see, so they do not imprint. They *attach* (Kirkpatrick, 2005).

In everyday usage, *attachment* means "connectedness." In human development, **attachment** refers to the strong emotional connection that develops early in life to keep infants close to their caregivers. This relationship shapes the child's social and emotional development and forms the foundation for social relationships later in life.

Psychologist John Bowlby (1969) described the process of emotional attachment between infants and their caregivers and the emotional distress that develops when they are separated. He proposed that the major function of this affection-based bonding system is to protect infants from predation and other threats to survival. In his observations of human infants and primates, Bowlby noted that they both went through a clear sequence of reactions—from protest, to despair, to detachment. Bowlby defined **separation anxiety** as the distress reaction shown by babies (typically at around 9 months of age) when they are separated from their primary caregiver.

On the basis of such observations, Bowlby (1969, 1973, 1980) developed his *attachment theory*, which rests on two fundamental assumptions. First, a responsive and accessible caregiver (usually the mother) creates a secure base for the child, who needs to know that the caregiver is accessible and dependable. With a dependable caregiver, the child can develop confidence and security in exploring

imprinting
The rapid and innate learning of the characteristics of a caregiver very soon after birth.

attachment
The strong emotional connection that develops early in life between infants and their caregivers.

separation anxiety
The distress reaction babies show when they are separated from their primary caregivers (typically shown at around 9 months of age).

the world. The bonding relationship serves the critical function of attaching the caregiver to the infant, thereby making the survival of the infant, and ultimately the species, more likely.

The second assumption of attachment theory is that infants internalize the bonding relationship, which provides a mental model on which they build future friendships and love relationships. Therefore, attachment to a caregiver is the most critical of all relationships. In order for bonding to take place, infants must be more than merely a passive receptor to the caregiver's behavior. It is a bidirectional relationship—the infant and the caregiver respond to each other and influence each other's behavior.

Influenced by Bowlby's work, Mary Ainsworth and her associates (1978) developed a technique for testing Bowlby's assumptions about attachment of infant and caregiver. This procedure, known as the *strange situation*, consists of a 20-minute laboratory session that creates a mildly stressful situation for the baby. The strange situation is designed to see how much the caregiver (usually the mother) is a safe haven when the infant is distressed and a "secure base" from which to explore.

Here is how the strange situation works: After a 1-minute introduction, the mother and her 12-month-old infant are left alone in a playroom. Then a stranger comes into the room, and after a few minutes the stranger begins a brief interaction with the infant. The mother then leaves for two separate 3-minute periods. During the first period, the infant is left alone with the stranger. During the second period, the infant is left completely alone. Then mother and child are reunited. The critical behavior that Ainsworth and colleagues rated was how the distressed infant reacted when the caregiver returned.

From the behavior in this context, Ainsworth et al. (1978) and others described one secure attachment style and three types of insecure attachment. Based on temperamental and contextual factors, babies who are **securely attached** to parents may or may not be distressed on separation. The key issue is that they initiate contact with the parent on return and then can return to play. Securely attached infants are confident in the accessibility and responsiveness of their caregiver, and this security and dependability provide the child with the foundation for play and exploration when the caregiver is absent. About 65% of infants are securely attached.

In all three kinds of insecure attachment, infants lack the ability to engage in effective play and exploration. These three types are insecure-avoidant, insecure-resistant, and insecure-disorganized/disoriented.

Insecure-Avoidant   An insecure-avoidant infant often shows little to no distress in separation episodes, although physiological measures suggest that the infant is indeed under stress. When the mother returns, the infant tends to ignore and avoid her, focusing instead on something else in the room. The infant's avoidance on reunion may reflect the expectation that a bid for more contact would be followed by the parent's rejection. The avoidant classification is most common in Western cultures (15%–20% in the United States and Europe). In cultures such as Africa and Japan, where infant care practices involve almost constant physical contact between mother and infant, the classification is rare (True, Pisani, & Oumar, 2001).

Insecure-Resistant   An insecure-resistant infant cannot be comforted by the mother on reunion and shows difficulty in returning to play. Some babies actively resist contact with the parents at this stage, and others act more passive. The infant's resistance and distress during the reunion may reflect the infant's lack of confidence in being comforted. On average, only about 10%–15% of infants are classified as insecure-resistant (van IJzendoorn & Sagi, 1999).

securely attached
An attachment style characterized by infants who will gradually explore new situations when the caregiver leaves and initiate contact when the caregiver returns after separation.

Challenge Your Assumptions
True or False? All babies are emotionally attached to their caregivers.
False: Only about 65% of infants are securely (emotionally) attached to their primary caregivers.

Insecure-Disorganized/Disoriented These infants show odd, conflicted behaviors in the strange situation. They might approach the mother on re-union, but they do so with their heads averted. Or they might freeze in place for 50 seconds in the mother's presence (Main & Solomon, 1990). Theory and research suggest that these infants are frightened (Main & Hesse, 1990). Kids who have been maltreated are more likely to be insecure-disorganized, and home observations suggest they are afraid of their parents. Not all parents of infants classified as insecure-disorganized/disoriented maltreat their infants (Hesse & Main, 2006). This classification is considered the most insecure, because infants' fear of their attachment figures inhibits the development of a strategy for effective regulation of stress.

The infant-caregiver relationship provides the first context for the development of love in the baby's life. Some research suggests that this initial relationship helps shape adult romantic love relationships because the attachment style from infancy brings something to bear on the ways one connects—or doesn't connect—with a romantic partner (Hazan & Shaver, 1987).

Challenging Assumptions in the Importance of Physical Contact for Well-Being Up until the 1950s, most people—and most psychologists, for that matter—assumed that if children were well fed and well sheltered they would grow and develop normally. Physical touch and contact were considered nice but not necessary for normal, healthy development. As it turns out, this assumption was wrong.

Harry Harlow thought there might be more to infants' desire for contact than a need for nourishment. In his early work, Harlow (1958) noticed that baby monkeys that he had separated from their mothers became very attached to cloth diapers that lined their cages. This strong attachment to cloth made Harlow think that a baby primate needs something soft to cling to. It reminded him of the attachment babies have for their blankets.

To test his hunch that the need for something soft to hold is as fundamental as the need for nutrition, Harlow and his colleagues carried out a series of studies with newborn monkeys, which they separated from their mothers (Arling & Harlow, 1967; Harlow, 1958). They housed them with two types of surrogate mothers constructed of wire and wood (see Figure 5.18). One was composed of just a wire frame with a crude head. The other was a wire frame covered with soft terry cloth. Both "mothers" were heated, and either could be hooked up to a bottle of milk.

In the first study, Harlow removed eight monkeys from their mothers shortly after birth. Cloth and wire mothers were housed in cubicles attached to the infants' cages. By random assignment, half the monkeys received milk from the wire mother; the other half got their milk from the cloth mother. Harlow used the amount of time spent with a surrogate mother as a measure of the affection bond. He found that contact comfort was much more important than the source of food in determining which surrogate mother the monkeys preferred (Harlow, 1958).

Regardless of whether a baby monkey nursed from the cloth mother or the wire mother, it spent most of its time with the cloth one (see Figure 5.19). Monkeys fed by wire surrogates quickly got milk from the wire mom and then ran over to the cloth mom to cuddle. Harlow's findings thus challenged the belief that feeding was the basis for the bond between babies and mothers. He went so far as to say that contact is as essential a function of nursing in humans as is nutrition.

FIGURE **5.18**

THE CLOTH AND WIRE MOTHERS FROM HARLOW'S RESEARCH.

 Which surrogate does the baby spend more time with, and why?

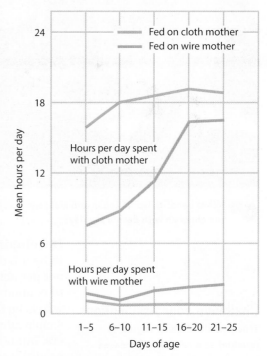

FIGURE **5.19**

TIME MONKEYS SPENT ON CLOTH VERSUS WIRE SURROGATE "MOTHERS." Whether the baby monkeys were fed by the wire mother or the cloth mother, all of them preferred the comfort of the cloth mother. (Harlow, 1958)

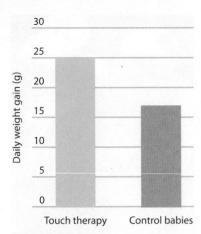

FIGURE **5.20**

WEIGHT GAIN IN PREMATURE INFANTS WHO DID OR DID NOT RECEIVE TOUCH THERAPY. The graph shows the amount of weight gained per day, in grams. Over time, the difference in the weights of the two groups could be expected to increase. Along with the added weight, the massaged babies gained better overall health. (Field et al., 1986)

What benefits would touch and massage therapy provide for children with cerebral palsy?

However, having a cloth surrogate mother was clearly not as good as having a real mother. In follow-up research, Harlow found that monkeys raised without mothers (including some raised with cloth surrogates) were negligent and abusive mothers when they had their own babies. They failed to give their babies proper contact or even to feed them correctly (Arling & Harlow, 1967). One possible conclusion, then, is that they did not know how to behave with their offspring because they hadn't had a live mother themselves, and it would follow that real-life moms are more than a source of physical contact and nutrition. They are role models for future social relationships, especially caregiving.

Because of Harlow's work, physical contact came to be considered central to optimal human development, but not all babies get enough of it. As researcher Tiffany Field noted, preterm human babies who spend weeks or months in special hospital beds, where they are kept warm, protected from infection, and monitored by the latest technology, are rarely touched.

What might be the effects of this deprivation among the neediest babies? To explore this question, Field and her colleagues (1986) tested the impact of touch on tiny premature infants. She randomly assigned 40 preterm infants from a hospital's newborn intensive care unit to either receive touch therapy (experimental group) or not (control group). All of the premature infants lived in isolettes, plastic-covered bassinets designed to prevent infection. The touch therapy involved gently stroking the baby with warmed hands (no gloves) through portholes in the isolette for 15 minutes, three times a day for 10 days. What Field and colleagues found was truly surprising: The regularly touched babies, who had the same diets as those who were not regularly touched, gained significantly more weight and were released from the hospital sooner (see Figure 5.20). Later research showed the same effect in weight gain when mothers touched their preterm infants (Field et al., 2004). Additional research found that touch also leads to reduced stress levels in premature babies and to less diarrhea (Diego et al., 2007; Jump, Fargo, & Akers, 2006).

Touch therapy has also been used to improve motor skills in children with *cerebral palsy*, a movement disorder caused by brain damage at birth (Hernandez-Reif et al., 2005). Moreover, it helps children with autism. A study of Qigong (a Chinese touch therapy) showed improvements in sensory, social, and basic living skills in autistic children (Silva et al., 2007). Finally, massage therapy improves the well-being, motor dexterity, sleeping, and overall health in kids with other disabilities (Barlow et al., 2008). In short, touch is more than just comforting—it can improve physical and mental health.

Developing Relationships and Emotions   It is no doubt frustrating at times to be a baby. Think about it: There are things you need and want, and you are not yet able to ask for them, other than by crying. Yet babies learn other ways to communicate their needs to their caregivers, even before they can talk. One way is by facial expression. At just 7 hours old, newborns can imitate, or *mimic*, simple adult facial expressions (Meltzoff & Moore, 1977, 1983). By imitating others, infants learn to make facial expressions that help them communicate their needs (Iacoboni & Mazziota, 2007). Such infant imitation may be a result of mirror neuron systems in the brain, although the brain mechanisms involved in imitation may extend beyond mirroring (Grossberg & Vladusich, 2010; Lepage & Théoret, 2007).

Babies also seem to know at a very young age what the facial expressions of others mean. Four-month-olds show different patterns of visual attention to angry, fearful, and sad facial expressions in a peek-a-boo game (Montague &

Walker-Andrews, 2001). Moreover, older babies know how to look to their primary caregivers, whom they know they can trust, for information about emotion and situations.

The visual cliff discussed earlier as a way of testing babies' depth perception has also been used to study whether babies look to their caregivers for information about safety (Sorce et al., 1985). If the mother showed fear or anger on her face, the baby did not move over the cliff, but most babies went willingly over the cliff when the mom smiled. What this means is that, by the age of 1, children can make sense of their mothers' emotional facial expressions and use them to know what to do. This ability to make use of social and emotional information from another person, especially a caregiver, is known as **social referencing** (Campos & Stenberg, 1981).

The research on social referencing shows that babies understand the meaning of some facial expressions much earlier than age 1. On the basis of studies measuring visual preference and brain activity, we know that by 7 months babies can discriminate between fearful and happy faces. Babies of this age also understand the emotional meaning of the voice (intonation changes) that tends to go with certain emotional states, such as happy, angry, or sad (T. Grossman, Striano, & Friederici, 2006). Well before 1 year of age, then, babies possess a basic ability to interpret other people's emotions.

Development of Emotions   Babies show emotions very early in life—though not with the subtle variations that adults do. They start with pleasure and pain after birth, and somewhat later they respond to mom's voice or face with a smile. This transition occurs between 2 and 3 months of age (Lavelli & Fogel, 2005). A month later, they laugh in response to playful social interaction.

Signs of anger in facial expression occur as early as 4 months. How do you make young babies angry? One way is to restrain their movement, simply by holding their arms firmly. Between the ages of 4 and 7 months, infants begin to show facial expressions similar to adult expressions of anger when restrained, and the more frustrated they get, the more they show it (Stenberg, Campos, & Emde, 1983).

Other studies tell us that babies may not be able to differentiate their emotions the way adults can (Bridges, 1932). There is evidence that babies use "anger faces" in situations where they might feel fear, such as when they see a noisy toy gorilla head. So it is not clear whether the anger faces at this age are specific to situations that generally provoke anger (Camras et al., 2007; Oster, 2005). With further development and experience, babies refine their emotional expressions.

Learning to regulate and control emotion is not easy for most children. **Emotional competence** is the ability to control emotions and know when it is appropriate to express them (Saarni, 1999; Trentacosta & Izard, 2007). The development of emotional competence starts as early as preschool and continues throughout childhood (Feng et al., 2008; Grolnick, McMenamy, & Kurowski, 2006; Saarni, 1984). Moreover, the better children do in school and the fewer stressful and dysfunctional situations they have at home, the more emotionally skilled and competent they become (Feng et al., 2008; Spinrad et al., 2006).

One aspect of emotional competence is learning to regulate one's emotional behavior. By the age of 9, children realize the impact of their reactions on other people's feelings. Carolyn Saarni (1984) conducted a classic series of studies to uncover how children learn to modify their emotional expressions in the presence of others. She gave first-grade (age 7), third-grade (age 9), and fifth-grade (age 11) children a task to complete and told them that afterward they would get a very desirable toy. The children, however, received a less-than-desirable toy either alone or in the presence of the experimenter. When alone, kids readily showed their disappointment. In the presence of the experimenter, the young

social referencing
The ability to make use of social and emotional information from another person—especially a caregiver—in an uncertain situation.

Connection

One way we learn is by imitating someone else's behavior. This type of learning, seen also in infant mimicry, may be based on mirror neuron systems in the brain.

To learn about these systems, see "The Cells of the Nervous System: Glial Cells and Neurons," Chapter 3, "The Biology of Behavior," p. 79; and "Imitation, Mirror Neurons, and Learning," Chapter 8, "Learning," p. 312.

emotional competence
The ability to control emotions and to know when it is appropriate to express certain emotions.

children (age 7) readily showed their disappointment, but those ages 9 and 11 tried to inhibit facial expressions of negative emotion when receiving an undesirable gift so as not to hurt the experimenter's feelings. Such social smiling comes only with age and maturity (Simonds et al., 2007).

Peer Interaction   As children get older, their social world expands from the intimate environment of the home to include play with other children. Although attachment to the primary caregiver is important for the baby and young child, relations with other children have a big impact after early childhood (J. R. Harris, 1998). Indeed, in early childhood, children do not even interact much with other children, even if other children are playing nearby. Children begin to interact socially during play at about age 3 (Howes & Matheson, 1992).

Most people assume that parents are the biggest influence in a child's life, so they are surprised to learn that, by mid- to late childhood, peers are probably an even bigger influence than parents on a child's development. Why? Peers share equal standing or status in terms of age, gender, skill, or power, so they are important role models. How early does peer influence begin? A study of over 100 British children shows that even 5-year-olds are sensitive to peer criticism. Kids who are more attuned to social and emotional information are more likely to display this sensitivity. Researchers have evaluated children's skills with social and emotional information by giving them tasks such as identifying facial expressions of emotion and determining what a puppet in an acted-out scene or a character in a story might do or feel (Cutting & Dunn, 2002).

In peer interactions, children tend to sort themselves out by gender. First, even when not pressured by adults to do so, children flock to same-sex playmates (Maccoby & Jacklin, 1987). Second, these gender differences in play occur all over the world—in Europe, the United States, Asia, and Africa (Omark, Omark, & Edelman, 1973; Whiting & Edwards, 1988). Eleanor Maccoby (2000) has attributed this same-sex interaction preference to shared preferences for certain types of play. Boys prefer rough-and-tumble play, whereas girls opt for cooperative play (Green & Cillessen, 2008; Maccoby, 2000). Only in adolescence do boys and girls begin to move toward opposite-sex interactions.

Childhood Temperament and Personality Development   What does early childhood temperament predict about adult personality and behavior? One longitudinal study evaluated 1,000 New Zealand children over an 18-year period. The children were assessed on many temperamental, cognitive, medical, and motor dimensions at age 3 and then again about every 2 to 2.5 years until they were 21 years

Are children born with different temperaments and personality, or do they only learn to be different from experience?

old (Caspi, 2000). Ratings by parents of their children at age 3 revealed three basic types of temperament: well-adjusted, undercontrolled, and inhibited.

Eighteen years after the initial assessment, the individuals whose parents had classified them as undercontrolled (impulsive and prone to temper tantrums) at age 3 were impulsive and likely to engage in thrill-seeking behaviors. Compared to well-adjusted kids, this group was also much more likely to be aggressive and hostile, to have more relationship conflict, and to abuse alcohol.

At age 21, the inhibited children were less likely to have social support and were more likely to avoid risk and harm, to be nonassertive and overcontrolled, and to suffer from prolonged depression. They also were somewhat more likely than well-adjusted individuals to attempt suicide or have problems with alcohol. Further, they were about as likely as well-adjusted types (and less likely than the undercontrolled individuals) to have committed a criminal offense. Finally, as adults, inhibited children reported the least amount of social, emotional, and financial support from others. In sum, our temperament at age 3 seems to continue shaping our personalities into adulthood (Kagan, 2003).

A separate study assessed 3- and 4-year-old children for openness to new experiences; that is, they were tested on how curious, exploratory, creative, and imaginative they were. These individuals were assessed again at ages 18 and 23 (Gjerde & Cardilla, 2009). Interestingly, the open and imaginative young boys tended to become self-assured, flexible, and resilient young adults. The results were rather different for the open and imaginative young girls. They tended to become relatively anxious and self-doubting young women. This finding may be explained by socialization differences whereby boys are more encouraged than girls to realize their cognitive potential (Gjerde & Cardilla, 2009). Who we are as young children does foreshadow, sometimes in predictable and other times in unpredictable ways, whom we become as adults.

Quick Quiz 5.2: The Developing Infant and Child

1. In the newborn infant, the sense of _____ is almost fully developed, but the sense of _____ continues to change and improve over the first few years of life.
   a. taste; hearing
   b. vision; taste
   c. vision; hearing
   d. hearing; vision

2. With learning and experience, certain synaptic connections grow stronger, while those that are not strengthened by experience degrade and die off. This process is known as
   a. neural efficiency.
   b. honing.
   c. pruning.
   d. reductionism.

3. People who have had intensive musical training have _____ than nonmusicians.
   a. thicker finger pads
   b. a thicker corpus callosum
   c. a thicker cerebellum
   d. a thicker caudate nucleus

4. Piaget's _____ stage of cognitive development begins when the child can conserve; that is, knows that the amount of a liquid or substance stays the same even when it changes shape.
   a. sensorimotor
   b. abstract-ideational
   c. logical operations
   d. concrete operations

Answers can be found at the end of the chapter.

THE DEVELOPING ADOLESCENT

Adolescence is the transition period between childhood and early adulthood, beginning at about age 11 or 12 and lasting until around age 18. Adolescence is a tumultuous time, made both exciting and difficult by all the changes that have to take place in a relatively short period to turn a girl into a woman and a boy into a man.

adolescence
The transition period between childhood and early adulthood.

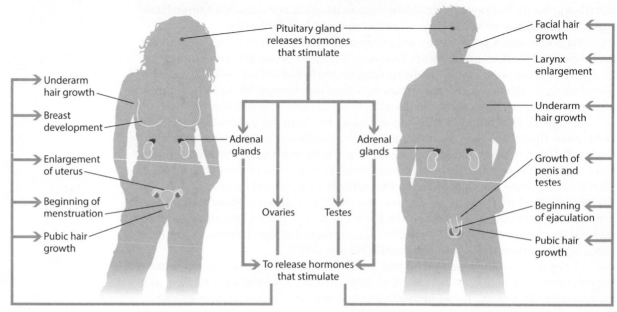

FIGURE **5.21**

PHYSICAL DEVELOPMENT OF MALES AND FEMALES DURING PUBERTY.

Physical Development in Adolescence

puberty
The period when sexual maturation begins; it marks the beginning of adolescence.

menarche
The first menstrual period.

spermarche
The first ejaculation.

Puberty, the period when sexual maturation begins, marks the beginning of adolescence. During puberty, major hormonal changes prepare the body for reproduction and stimulate changes in body size and proportions. On average, girls reach puberty at about age 11 and boys at about age 13. The changes that mark the beginning of puberty stem from the release of sex hormones. First, the pituitary gland sends hormonal signals to the sex glands, telling them to mature. The sex glands, or *gonads,* then release sex hormones (see Figure 5.21). The male gonads are called *testes;* the female gonads are the *ovaries.* The testes release the male sex hormone *testosterone,* which initiates the physical changes we associate with male maturation, such as facial and pubic hair, deepening of the voice, widening of the shoulders, and growth of the penis. The release of the female sex hormone *estradiol* from the ovaries transforms girls into women, with the growth of breasts, the widening of hips, and an increase in body fat.

In girls, breast development can start as early as age 10. The next major change is the onset of menstruation, known as **menarche.** You may be surprised to learn that menstruation is not solely a biological event; indeed, it is also affected by cultural and environmental events. The age of menarche is highly variable, but it often occurs by age 12. In most Western cultures, the age of menarche has dropped from about age 16 during the 1800s to 12 or 13 today. The beginning of menstruation marks the beginning of fertility for a young woman, so this is an important developmental milestone.

In boys, the event that signals readiness to reproduce is **spermarche,** or the first ejaculation. Usually, the first ejaculation is unexpected, and it occurs as a nocturnal emission, or "wet dream." Once a male has ejaculated, technically he can father a child. This presents a primary problem of adolescence: In boys and girls, the body is ready for parenthood far earlier than the mind is.

Cognitive and Brain Development in Adolescence

As the body undergoes dramatic transformation, changes continue to unfold in the brain. During adolescence, children gain the ability to reason about abstract

In the United States, girls start puberty about 2 years earlier than boys. African American girls begin maturing somewhat earlier than European American girls.

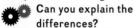 **Can you explain the differences?**

concepts and problems. Recall that Piaget called this stage formal operational, when teens begin to think abstractly and may show the ability to engage in scientific reasoning and hypothesis testing.

Adolescents and even adults do not all develop this reasoning ability to the same degree (Klahr, 2000; Kuhn, Amsel, & O'Loughlin, 1988; Kuhn & Pearsall, 2000; Wilkening & Sodian, 2005). The extent to which they do is related to their ability to think and solve problems systematically, rather than relying on the trial-and-error method that children use. It is also related to the ability to distinguish one's thoughts about how the world works from the evidence for how it really works (Kuhn & Pearsall, 2000). For example, believing that the position of the planets affects human personality does not make it so. Good scientific thinkers realize the world may or may not operate the way they think it does, so they devise step-by-step ways of testing their ideas. This requires the ability to think about alternatives and to question their own thinking.

With adolescence and formal operations, young people begin to ask abstract philosophical, religious, and political questions and form their own beliefs. Moreover, with abstract thinking comes the ability to consider alternatives—not just how things are but how they could be. For instance, science fiction and Internet gaming appeal to adolescents because they involve abstract, imaginative, and alternative forms of thinking.

The cognitive developments of adolescence, such as abstract reasoning and logical thinking, are linked with the dramatic brain development occurring during this period. The frontal lobes are the last areas of the brain to fully develop, and they continue to mature until late adolescence or early adulthood (Fuster, 2002; B. L. Miller & Cummings, 1999; Sowell et al., 2001). They are involved in planning, attention, working memory, abstract thought, and impulse control. The onset of formal operational and scientific thinking occurs after the frontal lobes have developed more fully (Kwon & Lawson, 2000).

It is not so much that the frontal lobes and other brain regions are growing in size but rather that they are growing in neural complexity. Complexity is seen in more myelin and white matter, greater neural coordination or synchrony, and neural pruning. In general, there is a direct relationship between cognitive development and brain development.

A multitude of changes occur in brain development throughout adolescence:

- The brain develops more myelin around the axons, as well as more neural connections (R. D. Fields, 2008; Perrin et al., 2009; Sabbagh, 2006; Sakai, 2005; Shaw et al., 2006). As seen in Figure 5.11, myelination proceeds from the back of the brain to the frontal lobes during the period from childhood to adolescence. The rate and locations of myelination differ between boys and girls (R. D. Fields, 2008; Perrin et al., 2009; Schmithorst, Holland, & Dardzinski, 2008). In girls, this increased white matter organization is in the right hemisphere; in boys, it is in the left hemisphere (Schmithorst et al., 2008). This is one of numerous examples of developmental differences in the brains of boys and girls as they move into the teen years.

- *Neural synchrony,* or the ability of certain types of brain waves to work together to allow for coordinated activity in the brain, also increases throughout adolescence and possibly into early adulthood (Uhlhaas et al., 2009). Abnormal neural synchrony appears to play a role in such disorders as autism and schizophrenia (Uhlhaas & Singer, 2010).

- *Synaptic pruning* reaches its final stages, whereby rarely used synapses are allowed to die off to make the brain more efficient (de Graaf-Peters & Hadders-Algra, 2006; Paus, Keshavan, & Giedd, 2008).

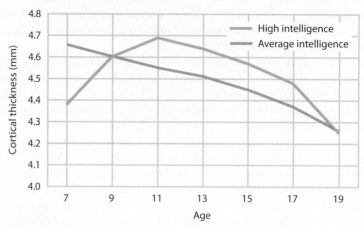

FIGURE **5.22**

THE DEVELOPING BRAIN: CORTICAL THICKNESS AND INTELLIGENCE.

 Can you think of any reasons highly intelligent children at age **7** have a thinner cortex but between the ages of **11** and **17** they have a thicker cortex than average intelligent children?
(Shaw, et. al., 2006)

How the brain develops and, in particular, how the cortex develops affect intelligence. Philip Shaw and colleagues (2006) periodically scanned the brains of more than 300 participants during childhood and adolescence and discovered something surprising. At age 7 the highly intelligent children had thinner frontal cortexes, but by midadolescence their cortexes had become thicker than those of the children with average intelligence. Moreover, by age 19 the thickness of the cortex in the two groups was the same (see Figure 5.22). So the cortex grows thicker into adolescence, and the brains of highly intelligent people are more elastic and trace a different developmental path.

If so much brain growth is occurring, why do teens often seem absent-minded and/or prone to risky and impulsive behavior? Research on other mammals offers some clues to this question. "Teen" mice taught how to learn a maze perform much more slowly than both prepubescent and adult mice. They also have an increased abundance of GABAnergic receptors in the hippocampus at that time, which impairs learning (Shen et al., 2010). Impaired hippocampus functioning, therefore, may be responsible for questionable and risky behavior seen in teen mice and, by extension, teen humans.

In teens, the frontal lobes become overloaded during complex and demanding tasks, whereas the workload is distributed more evenly throughout the brain in adults (Sabbagh, 2006). Moreover, although teenagers have the same basic reasoning skills as adults, the more sophisticated cognitive skills, such as the ability to plan ahead or evaluate the possible consequences of a decision, do not develop until late adolescence or young adulthood (Steinberg, 2010). The tendency of teenagers to engage in impulsive and risky behavior, such as driving at excessive speeds and fighting, can be partly explained by these findings of brain development.

The active development of the teen brain—the growing brain structures, increased myelination, neural synchrony, and synaptic pruning—also helps explain why people are more vulnerable to brain-related dysfunctions and disorders during adolescence (Paus et al., 2008). When so many changes are happening in the brain, it is more vulnerable to toxins and diseases that affect the nervous system.

Social Development in Adolescence

The changes to the brain during adolescence influence social as well as cognitive behavior. Areas of the brain involved in how we interpret other people's faces, our understanding of emotion, and "theory of mind" are still developing into the teen years. These areas include the amygdala, portions of the temporal lobe, and the medial prefrontal cortex (mPFC; Sebastian et al., 2010). For instance, teens use slightly different brain regions to process certain emotions than do adults, indicating that further change occurs during the teen years (Burnett et al., 2008).

Teens are also more sensitive than adults to rejection. In a laboratory task in which a teen is left out of simulated group play (a computer game with unseen partners) and then ostracized for it, the omitted teens showed a much stronger response to rejection than did adults in the same situation. It may be that the sensitivity to rejection in teen years is related to the extended period of development in the prefrontal cortex that occurs over the course of adolescence, but more research is needed to confirm this hypothesis (Sebastian et al., 2010).

With the onset of puberty and adolescence, children begin to focus on the questions of who they are. Just as we try on clothes to see what fits, adolescents try on identities to see what looks good and feels comfortable. One way teens experiment with identity is in how they relate to groups, which groups they identify with, and how they present themselves to others more generally. Group identifications can be very important, long-lasting, and quite distressing to teens if they are challenged (Lemay & Ashmore, 2004). For instance, one of your authors (Erika) ran track and cross-country in high school. Being a runner—an athlete—became an important part of her identity, as did relating to the community of runners at school. This identification lasted well through adulthood. Although identity development occurs across the life span, teens are more self-conscious about the changes associated with them and experience changes more intensely than do children or adults (Steinberg, 2005, 2010).

Puberty brings profound changes not only in the body but also in relationships. Family becomes less central, and peer relationships become the focus of life. Having close, intimate friends during adolescence is associated with many positive social and emotional outcomes, such as self-confidence, better relationships with parents and authority figures, better performance in school, and even better overall adjustment and feelings of self-worth in adulthood (Bagwell, Newcomb, & Bukowski, 1998). In contrast, feeling isolated and lacking close peer relationships during adolescence are associated with poorer performance in school, more conflict with parents and authority figures, and lower self-esteem.

In the teen years, peers start to replace parents as a source of identification (Bukowski & Sippola, 2001; Pugh & Hart, 1999). In the search for who they are, adolescents look to their friends for answers. The values and social rules operating within different peer groups give teens "identity templates," which they use to define themselves (Pugh & Hart, 1999). Moreover, perceived pressure and criticism from others (mother and friends, for instance) foretell whether or not disordered eating might emerge in both male and female teens (Shomaker & Furman, 2009). Reactions from parents and peers also play a role in whether teens end up using alcohol and cigarettes (Kristjansson et al., 2010).

Compared to childhood, however, the most obvious change in adolescent social development is the emergence of sexual interest and sexual relationships. Not only do teens become interested in sexual relationships, but sexual thoughts and feelings also occupy much of their attention and time. The average age for first sexual intercourse for men and women is around 17 years old, although there is quite a bit of variability (Chandra et al., 2005). A sexually mature body combined with a brain that is not fully developed can result in bad judgment, as shown in

Challenge Your Assumptions

True or False? Parents are the main social influence on development through late adolescence.

False: Peers begin to be the primary social influence on teens.

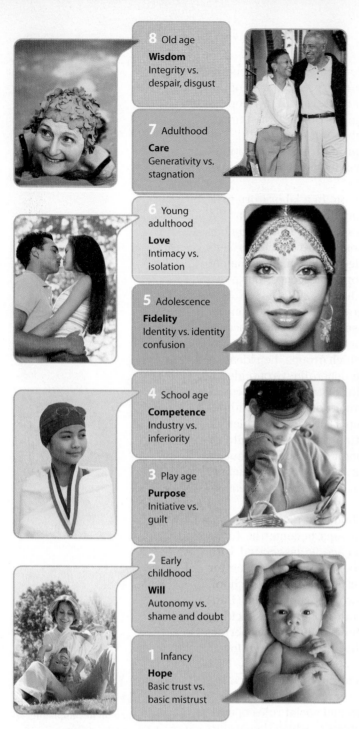

the high rates of unplanned pregnancy and sexually transmitted diseases in teens (CDC, 2005). Sexuality and sexual activity influence how teens think of themselves. Being sexually active increases self-esteem and enhances self-concept in both boys and girls, but it also can lead to an increase in risky behavior (Houlihan et al., 2008).

The teen years are also the time of sexual identity formation. Roughly 88% of teenagers describe themselves as predominantly *heterosexual* (interested only in the opposite sex), while about 1%–2% see themselves as either predominantly *homosexual* (interested only in the same sex) or *bisexual* (interested in both sexes). About 10% of teens say they are confused about their sexual orientation (Remafedi et al., 1992). Another survey showed that about 6% of teens are heterosexual with same-sex attraction/fantasy or behavior (Zhao et al., 2010).

Finally, some adolescents explore their identity through experimenting with drugs and alcohol (S. C. Duncan, Duncan, & Strycker, 2006; Tang & Orwin, 2009). Both parental and peer behavior influence whether someone will start drinking and how his or her drinking behavior develops.

Personality Development in Adolescence Although many aspects of temperament and personality are stable over time, our personalities also grow and change as we age. Erik Erikson (1968) proposed a model of personality development with eight stages, each defined by an identity crisis or conflict (see Figure 5.23). According to Erikson, an identity crisis is an opportunity for adaptive or maladaptive adjustment. Each stage consists of a conflict from which a person may develop a strength or a weakness.

Erikson (1968) saw *identity versus identity confusion* as the conflict during adolescent personality development. Testing, experimenting, and trying on identities are the norm during adolescence. Experimenting allows a person to find out which identities work and which ones don't. The three primary areas of identity formation during adolescence are dating and sexual orientation, religious and political belief systems, and career decisions. The basic strength that develops in adolescence is fidelity, a sense of faith and commitment to an identity.

FIGURE 5.23

ERIKSON'S EIGHT STAGES OF PERSONALITY DEVELOPMENT. Each stage has a core strength (shown in bold type) and a crisis to resolve.

Quick Quiz 5.3: The Developing Adolescent

1. What event marks the beginning of adolescence?
   a. puberty
   b. formal operations
   c. growth of body hair
   d. all of the above

2. In which area of the brain does significant development occur during adolescence?
   a. occipital lobes   c. frontal lobes
   b. hippocampus   d. cerebellum

Answers can be found at the end of the chapter.

Experimenting with different styles of dress appeals to adolescents in the midst of identity formation.

THE DEVELOPING ADULT

As adolescence draws to a close and people enter their 20s, the transition from high school to college or work increases independence. Many changes to behavior occur with the transition from the teens to the 20s, and even across the life span.

Early Adulthood

Major changes in thinking, feeling, and behavior occur during childhood and adolescence, but what happens when you turn 18? Are you suddenly grown-up and "all done"? Not by a long shot. By the time most young people have reached sexual maturity, their lives are still in great flux. Further changes associated with assuming responsibilities for one's own finances, housing, clothing, and career shape the time between adolescence and young adulthood. Although some reliance on parents persists throughout college, when a person reaches adulthood, some threshold has been crossed. This threshold, however, is not defined by landmarks in physical and psychological development, as is the case for childhood and adolescence. Rather, the movement into adulthood entails successful passage through certain life transitions, which end in nearly complete independence from one's parents.

Emerging Adulthood   Arnett (2004) uses the term **emerging adulthood** for the phase between adolescence and young adulthood, which spans ages 18–25. Emerging adulthood is a phase of transition between the teen years and adulthood. Teens rely on their parents for food, clothing, and housing. At about age 18, things change. Young people in their late teens know that soon they will have to assume greater responsibility for keeping themselves alive, and this has broad-reaching implications for behavior and thought.

As young people enter college or the workforce, financial responsibility starts to shift to their shoulders. They continue to try on many behaviors and self-concepts (just as teens do), but this experimentation is tinged by the realization that soon they will have to stabilize a bit and assume more responsibility for their

emerging adulthood
The transitional phase between adolescence and young adulthood; it includes ages 18–25 years.

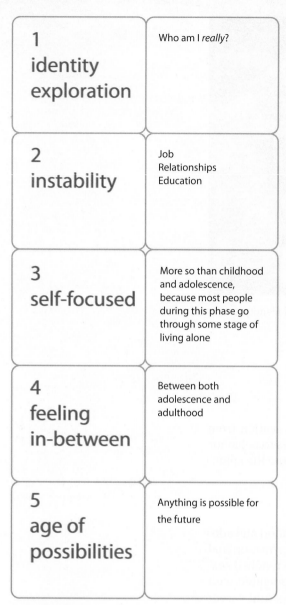

1 identity exploration	Who am I *really*?
2 instability	Job Relationships Education
3 self-focused	More so than childhood and adolescence, because most people during this phase go through some stage of living alone
4 feeling in-between	Between both adolescence and adulthood
5 age of possibilities	Anything is possible for the future

FIGURE 5.24

STATE OF EMERGING ADULTHOOD.

 What factors figure into identity formation of emerging adulthood? (Arnett, 2004)

own livelihoods. Not all young people go to college, of course, but many more do today than did 50 years ago ("Participation in Education," n.d.). Whether or not someone goes to college affects the timing of certain developmental milestones. Women who do not go to college marry and have their first child substantially earlier than those who do (H. S. Klein, 2004).

The key changes during emerging adulthood center on coping with increased responsibility and recognizing the need to make decisions about some of the things one has been exploring (Arnett, 2006). Figure 5.24 shows the key features of emerging adulthood. Although much brain development has happened by the time of emerging adulthood, the brain continues to change and grow. The prefrontal cortex continues to develop and fibers there are increasingly myelinated, which facilitates neural communication. Brain structure changes as well (de Graaf-Peters & Hadders-Algra, 2006). For example, brain areas that organize incoming sensory information and help generate emotional responses change significantly from the early to late teen years (Bennett & Baird, 2006).

An emerging adult necessarily has an emerging identity. Numerous issues figure into identity formation, but we will discuss three: career identity, sexual identity, and ethnic identity.

Career Identity By the time young people are finishing high school, they need to start looking for a job or go to college to train for a career. These choices involve a great deal of soul searching about such questions as how to spend their time, what are their life goals, and what, exactly, might they offer the world (Porfeli & Skorikov, 2010).

Sexual Identity The age of first sexual experience varies by culture, ethnicity, and education, among other factors (Jordahl & Lohman, 2009). In this country, most people become sexually active during adolescence, on average by about age 17 for both men and women (Chandra et al., 2005). Although sexual behavior begins in the teens, issues surrounding psychological sexual maturation and experience occur also in the late teens and extend well into the early 20s. Although young men and women tend to begin sexual activity around the same time, men accumulate sexual encounters more rapidly between the ages of 16 and 26 than do women (Zimmer-Gembeck & Collins, 2008). Adolescents experiment with relationships and partners. Fifty years ago, young people were expected to settle down with a single partner by their early 20s. Today, if you make a commitment to someone you have dated for a while in high school, it is considered a mistake (Arnett, 2004).

Those who readily know they are heterosexual may have a hard enough time developing a sense of sexual identity during adolescence and emerging adulthood, but for those who are either confused about their orientation or identify as lesbian, gay, bisexual, or transgendered (LGBT), it is even harder. The additional pressure from and challenge of dealing with other people's negative attitudes toward their orientation and attempts to fit into a heterosexual identity that is not theirs are linked with depressed mood and even higher incidences of suicide than in heterosexual students (Spencer & Patrick, 2009). These young adults often experience a unique kind of "minority stress" that is different from the pressures experienced by other minorities: There's no guaranteed familial support. Hence, the support from friends becomes even more important.

Ethnic Identity For people of mixed racial heritage, who constitute roughly 2% of the adult U.S. population, and a higher percentage of younger people (U.S. Census Bureau, 2009b), the awareness of one's ethnic identity increases from adolescence to emerging adulthood (French et al., 2006; Syed & Azmitia, 2010). Each parent or grandparent may push for his or her identity to be adopted as the prominent one, and the young person has to decide for him- or herself which one feels right. For example, Rosa is of Chinese and Mexican heritage. She says she feels more Chinese than Mexican, due to her mother's influence (Arnett, 2004).

Biracial people of all ages resist having to identify with one racial group over the other. Doing so can be stressful (Townsend, Markus, & Bergsieker, 2009). Even such mundane tasks as completing simple surveys may force them to choose. Recent versions of the SAT, for example, require students to complete a brief demographic questionnaire on their age, sex, ethnicity, and so on. According to Heidi Durrow (whose mother is Dutch and father is African American), when asked to identify her race, "The satisfactory answer usually isn't: I'm black *and* white. Other people want mixed-race kids to choose who they are" (*Reimagining*, 2010). The same debate followed President Obama—whose father was African and whose mother was European American—throughout the 2008 election and even onto his 2010 census form, where he selected African American as his racial identity. Indeed, biracial children often feel rejected by both groups (Crawford & Alaggia, 2008). Some feel unsupported by parents who do not understand their dilemma.

Gay couples still struggle with even more identity and acceptance issues than heterosexual couples.

Young Adulthood How do you know when you are an adult? At a certain point, some threshold has been crossed, but the criteria for adulthood vary from culture to culture (Cheah & Nelson, 2004). Though some cultures still have rituals of transformation, most modern technological societies rely on the assumption that certain responsibilities occur when the person reaches a certain age. Usually, the transition to **young adulthood** occurs in the 20s, though certain life transitions represent more significant markers than does age (Arnett, 2004; see Figure 5.25). In young adulthood, financial and living arrangements have settled down, and many people marry or form other long-term partnerships (though this, too, is changing). These tasks all push the person to become increasingly engaged with the outside world (Burt & Masten, 2010).

young adulthood
The development stage that usually happens by the mid-20s, when people complete the key developmental tasks of emerging adulthood.

Aberg and colleagues (2009) studied over a million Swedish men who had enlisted for military service at age 18, and they examined data on intelligence, cardiovascular fitness, and muscular strength outcome measures. They found a positive correlation between cardiovascular fitness (but not muscular strength) and better cognitive scores. Further, people whose cardiovascular fitness had improved from 15 to 18 years of age had higher intelligence scores at age 18 years than those whose cardiovascular fitness had declined over that time. What this means is that physical fitness and cognitive functioning are linked in young adulthood. Not only the middle-aged and elderly can benefit cognitively from being physically fit. Young adults can too.

Marriage Over the past 50 years, the average age at which people marry has increased from the

President Barack Obama is the son of an African father and a European American mother. Although he is biracial, he declared himself to be African American on his 2010 census form.

⚙ **What dilemmas do biracial children deal with, and how do they address these issues?**

1 Do you accept responsibility for yourself?

2 Do you make independent decisions about major life events?

3 Are you financially independent?

FIGURE 5.25
ARE YOU AN ADULT?

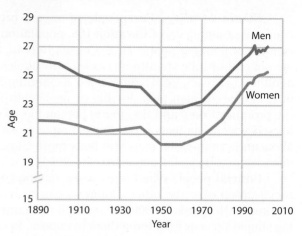

FIGURE 5.26
U.S. MEDIAN AGE AT FIRST MARRIAGE, 1890–2003.
The median age of first marriage has always been above 23 for men and above 21 for women, except in the 1950s, when they were both lower.

What are some of the reasons the median age is now higher than it has been in more than 100 years?

early 20s to the mid- to late 20s for both men and women, though women tend to marry a bit earlier overall (see Figure 5.26; Liu, Elliott, & Umberson, 2009; U.S. Census Bureau, 2009a). Why is marriage being delayed? More people are pursuing higher education, a trend that accounts for the lengthening of young adulthood generally (Arnett, 2004). In addition, more people are living together prior to marriage, though according to survey research, living together before engagement does not predict better marital satisfaction down the line (Rhoades, Stanley, & Markman, 2009).

Parenthood One clear marker of reaching adulthood is having a child, although about 15% of adults never have children, and many people consider themselves to be adults before they become parents (Goodwin, McGill, & Chandra, 2009). The age at which people have their first child has increased steadily over the years, primarily because time spent in college and training means that it takes longer to settle down in industrialized nations (Kokko, Pulkkinen, & Mesiäinen, 2009). As shown in Figure 5.27, there is a direct relationship between education and age of having a first child. Just under 90% of women who drop out of high school have a first child before age 25, whereas less than 25% of women who finish college have a child before age 25 (Martinez, Daniels, & Chandra, 2012).

Personality may also play a role in whether and when people become parents. For instance, shy men become fathers later than men who are not shy. By contrast, shy girls are more conventional and thus even more likely to parent early—less likely to be moving into the world of careers (Caspi, Elder, & Bem, 1988). Both men and women who tend to avoid harm and risk are less likely to have children at all (Jokela et al., 2010).

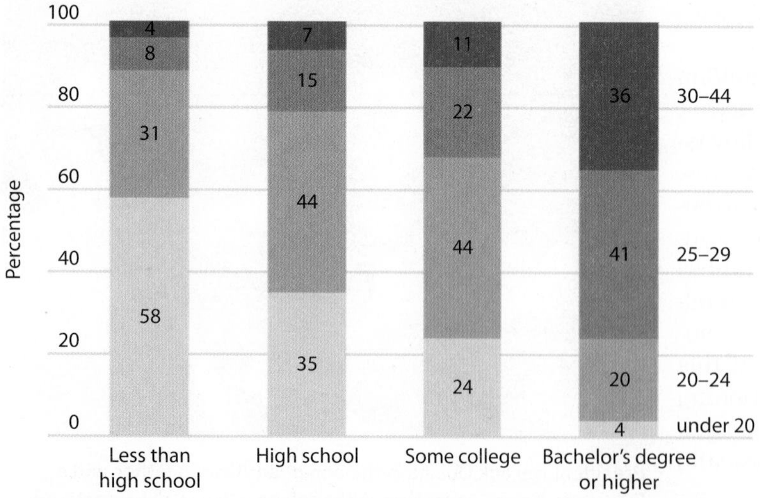

FIGURE 5.27

AGE AT FIRST BIRTH FOR WOMEN AGES 22–44 YEARS, BY EDUCATION: UNITED STATES, 2006–2010. (CDC, 2009).

Early Adult Personality Development Having a solid sense of self and identity is important for early adulthood—the period during one's 20s. In this stage, Erikson believed the primary conflict is between *intimacy and isolation.* Erikson defined **intimacy** as the ability to fuse one's identity with another's without the fear of losing it (Erikson, 1968). If an individual does not develop a relatively secure sense of identity as an adolescent, forming intimate relationships may not be possible during young adulthood. Before they have completely figured out who they are, people may develop very close love relationships and then let the relationship define who they are. Their identity gets lost in the relationship. Then, years later, the relationship may end—because as each person develops his or her own identity, differences surface. The core strength to emerge in young adulthood is *love,* which involves commitment, passion, cooperation, competition, and friendship (Erikson, 1982).

Erik Erikson

Middle Adulthood

After establishing a career and settling down in long-term relationships and, often, having children, one moves into middle adulthood—generally acknowledged to be the ages between 40 and 60 or 65 (Santrock, 2010). Like all developmental stages, middle adulthood has its own unique challenges, two of which involve sensory and physical development.

intimacy
As defined by Erikson, the ability to fuse one's identity with another's without the fear of losing it.

Sensory and Brain Development Many people experience some loss of vision, hearing, or both by middle adulthood. Most people need reading glasses sometime in their 40s, as the lens of the eye loses flexibility (E. B. Goldstein, 2007). For those who already wear glasses or contacts as adults, bifocals may become necessary as they enter their late 40s.

On average, about 10% of adults suffer from normal hearing loss, defined as difficulty in hearing normal conversation, but age, gender, and profession are the three biggest predictors of hearing loss (see Figure 5.28). A recent large-scale study found that as many as 50% of older adults (mean age of 67) experience some degree of hearing loss (Chia et al., 2007). Certain professions are much more prone to suffering hearing loss than others, with farming/agriculture, mining, construction, manufacturing, and certain forms of music being highest on the list (*Work-related hearing loss*, 2001). By age 50, 49% of miners have significant hearing loss, and by age 60 the figure is 70% (*Work-related hearing loss*, 2001). Exposure to loud sounds throughout life, such as rock concerts, heavy machinery, and overuse of headphones, accounts for many hearing problems in people over 40 (Wallhagen et al., 1997). Age-related hearing deficits can stem from problems with the ears, the auditory nerve, or various brain areas and are more common in men than women (J. D. Pearson et al., 1995; Tremblay & Ross, 2007). High-pitched, high-frequency sounds become harder to hear as people get older. Some people report that, as they age, they can hear conversations but cannot always understand them.

Some people also experience a loss of sensitivity to taste and smell, though these changes vary considerably among individuals. Taste buds lose sensitivity, although the ones affected—sweet, salty, bitter, or savory—vary from person to person. These changes do not seem to adversely affect appetite, however (Kremer et al., 2007). As many as half of people over 65 demonstrate significant loss of smell (Doty et al., 1985).

In spite of the potential for sensory losses, the brain remains quite plastic and generative throughout adulthood (Leuner & Gould, 2010). Although the rate of neurogenesis tapers off in middle adulthood compared to young adulthood, in the hippocampus in particular, new neurons still

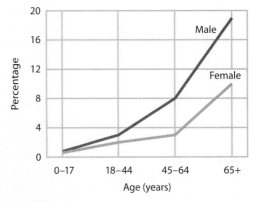

FIGURE **5.28**

PREVALENCE OF HEARING LOSS BY AGE GROUP AND GENDER. From childhood to middle age, men and women are equally likely to suffer hearing loss. After middle age, men far outnumber women in suffering from hearing loss.

individuation
The process of a person's personality becoming whole and full.

generativity
A term Erik Erikson used to describe the process in adulthood of creating new ideas, products, or people.

stagnation
A situation in which an adult becomes more self-focused than oriented toward others and does not contribute in a productive way to society or family.

form. The amount of neurogenesis depends on a number of factors. Opportunities for continued learning throughout life appear to aid neurogenesis, while stress and anxiety hinder it (Leuner & Gould, 2010; Morgenstern, Lombardi, & Schinder, 2008).

Personality Development during Middle Adulthood Carl Jung (1931/1960) argued that in midlife people are confronting the unfulfilled parts of their personality and ideally are developing them as a counterbalance to the other, more fully developed parts of themselves. The process through which someone's personality becomes whole and balanced is what Jung called **individuation.** During middle adulthood a formerly very extroverted and masculine man might become more solitary and less focused on being "macho," but some middle-aged adults cling to their youth, deny their undeveloped selves, and spiral into a crisis of midlife. Jung believed that this midlife crisis is seen in higher divorce rates and more mental breakdowns during midlife than earlier in life.

Erik Erikson proposed that in midlife the crisis we confront is *generativity versus stagnation.* He defined **generativity** as the creation of new ideas, products, or people (Erikson, 1982). Parenting, starting a business, and creating a work of art are different ways of being generative. **Stagnation** occurs when the adult becomes more self-focused than oriented toward others and does not contribute in a productive way to society or family. The core strength of adulthood is *care,* being committed to and caring for the people, ideas, and products one has generated.

A very popular notion of midlife imagines that nearly everyone goes through some kind of "midlife crisis"—quitting their jobs, getting divorced, buying a sports car, contemplating the meaning of life, and becoming painfully aware of the passage of time and impending death. These ideas are, in fact, based on psychological theory, most notably the work of Jung and Erikson. Indeed, many people do experience crises and major life changes during middle adulthood, but the scientific evidence for a crisis being universal or widespread is lacking (Freund & Ritter, 2009). Most people do not change careers or take some other drastic action to change the direction of their lives.

Late Adulthood

The last stage of life begins around age 65 and is labeled "late adulthood." Of the many significant developmental changes occurring during late adulthood, we will focus only on cognition, personality development, and death.

Normal changes in the brain occur with age. Just as body mass gradually decreases with age, so does brain mass (Enzinger et al., 2005). Most normal cognitive decline with aging results in brain changes to the frontal lobes, the part of the brain most involved in working memory, planning, and abstract reasoning (Braver & Barch, 2002; N. Raz, 2000).

The older brain does not change as rapidly as the younger brain, but it remains dynamic (Baltes et al., 2006). New experiences and mastery of new skills continue to give rise to neural branching and growth throughout life (Kemperman, 2006). Learning new skills, such as a new language, a new game, or a new computer activity, can lead to new neural growth (Cotman et al., 2007). Taking up a musical instrument can also stimulate brain growth (Pascual-Leone, 2001; see "Psychology in the Real World" earlier in this chapter).

People often complain about memory problems as they get older, yet cognitive decline in adulthood is a complex topic. Some abilities, such as expertise in a given area, take time to develop and reach a peak in middle adulthood (S. Kim & Hasher, 2005). Verbal memory actually peaks after age 50 (Schaie, 1996). Declines do occur in other kinds of memory, however, especially the kind involved in processing information and maintaining information while making decisions. The rate of decline does not become noticeable until people reach their 60s or 70s. Even then, healthy older people in their 70s who receive training in memory skills show improvements not only in cognitive performance but also in their ability to manage the tasks of daily living, such as shopping, food preparation, financial management, and household tasks (Willis et al., 2006).

In terms of intelligence, we must first distinguish between two distinct kinds—fluid and crystallized. **Fluid intelligence** involves raw mental ability, pattern recognition, and abstract reasoning and is applied to a problem that a person has never confronted before. Problems that require finding relationships, understanding implications, and drawing conclusions all require fluid intelligence. Neither culture nor vocabulary influence fluid intelligence. Knowledge that we have gained from experience and learning, education, and practice, however, is called **crystallized intelligence,** which is influenced by how large your vocabulary is, as well as your knowledge of your culture. Being asked whether Dalmatian is to dog as oriole is to bird is an example of a problem that requires crystallized intelligence.

One of the clearest developmental changes in adult intelligence is the gradual decline in fluid intelligence beginning in middle adulthood, but the strengthening of crystallized intelligence (Schaie, 1996; see Figure 5.29). Only in very late adulthood do we see a leveling off in acquired knowledge and crystallized intelligence. How quickly one processes information, keeping things in mind while solving problems (working memory), and how well one recalls events are key components of fluid intelligence. These skills reach a peak in one's 20s and 30s and then begin to decline (Basak et al., 2008; Hedden & Gabrieli, 2004; Nilsson, 2003; Schaie, 1996).

One way to stave off, or at least reduce, cognitive decline with aging is to exercise (Bherer, Erickson, & Liu-Ambrose, 2013). Older people who had been inactive improved significantly in a wide range of cognitive tasks after aerobic exercise training compared to a control group that did not exercise (Colcombe & Kramer, 2003). Similarly, engaging in meaningful, challenging work can make a huge difference for thinking and the brain.

One cognitive benefit of aging is wisdom, the ability to know what matters, to live well, and to show good judgment (Baltes & Smith, 2008). Wisdom comes with learning from the situations in which we find ourselves. The more we experience, the more we learn about what is important and how to manage our time (Carstensen, 2006). Wisdom also comes from learning not to take things too seriously.

Sometimes more than just normal forgetting occurs with aging. **Dementia** is an unusual degree of loss in cognitive functions and includes memory problems and difficulty in reasoning, solving problems, making decisions, and using language. Age is a risk factor for dementia, but in and of itself, aging does not cause dementia (Fratiglioni, Winblad, & von Strauss, 2007).

Several neurological conditions, including stroke and **Alzheimer's disease,** can lead to dementia in the elderly. It may be impossible to determine which condition is responsible for dementia, because they share symptoms. A *stroke* occurs when a blood vessel that serves the brain is blocked. As a result, the brain tissue served by that vessel does not receive the oxygen and nutrients it needs, and it dies. Multiple strokes are a common source of dementia in the elderly (Schneider et al., 2007). Dead brain tissue after a stroke makes for many little (or sometimes big) cognitive impairments, such as memory loss and confusion.

Alzheimer's disease is a degenerative disease marked by progressive cognitive decline, with symptoms including confusion, memory loss, mood swings,

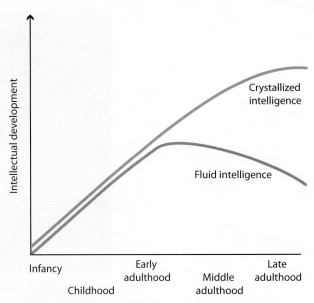

FIGURE 5.29

COGNITIVE DEVELOPMENT OVER THE LIFE SPAN.

 What is crystallized intelligence, and what is fluid intelligence? Why does crystallized intelligence level off at a much later stage than fluid intelligence?

fluid intelligence
Raw mental ability, pattern recognition, and abstract reasoning that can be applied to a problem one has never confronted before.

crystallized intelligence
The kind of knowledge that one gains from experience and learning, education, and practice.

dementia
A loss of mental function, in which many cognitive processes are impaired, such as the ability to remember, reason, solve problems, make decisions, and use language.

Alzheimer's disease
A degenerative disease marked by progressive cognitive decline and characterized by a collection of symptoms, including confusion, memory loss, mood swings, and eventual loss of physical function.

For these aging Japanese baseball players, an active lifestyle has cognitive and social benefits, as well as physical benefits.

- General confusion, disorientation to date, time, or place
- Apathy, irritability, depression, anxiety
- Problems with language, math, abstract thinking, and judgment
- Personality changes with strange quirks or inappropriate behaviors
- Wandering, hiding objects, problems with eating and sleeping
- Late in the disease, paranoia and delusions possible
- Toward the end, total loss of self and inability to control bodily functions

and eventual loss of physical and bodily function (Figure 5.30). Usually affecting older people, Alzheimer's accounts for 60%–70% of the cases of dementia among the elderly (Fratiglioni et al., 2007). *Early-onset Alzheimer's* affects people younger than 65 (Alzheimer's Association, 2008).

Currently, the only way Alzheimer's can be diagnosed definitively is by examining brain tissue after death, although recent progress in brain imaging (such as MRI) may help identify early risk factors (Schmand, Eikelenboom, & van Gool, 2011; Wermke et al., 2008). For the most part, physicians diagnose Alzheimer's by noting a collection of symptoms and structural brain changes (from brain imaging) that they cannot attribute to anything else.

The defining anatomical feature of Alzheimer's is the presence of patches of dead tissue in the brain, especially in the hippocampus and areas of the cortex (Kalat, 2007). As a result, the affected person experiences lapses in memory, confusion, and other cognitive impairments. In addition, low levels of the neurotransmitter acetylcholine inhibit memory formation in people with Alzheimer's (Akaike, 2006). Alzheimer's is progressive, which means that it worsens over time and eventually is fatal. Currently, there is no cure for Alzheimer's, although some drugs do seem to slow the progression of the disease (Hansen et al., 2007). There have been recent advances in developing vaccines that may one day protect people against the disease (Lambracht-Washington & Rosenberg, 2013).

Some evidence suggests that neurogenesis, the growth of new neurons, in the adult brain might offset or even prevent the kind of neural degeneration seen in Alzheimer's and other age-related brain disorders, such as Parkinson's disease (Kaliman et al., 2011;

FIGURE 5.30

TYPICAL SIGNS AND SYMPTOMS OF ALZHEIMER'S DISEASE.
According to the Alzheimer's Association (2013), as many as 5.2 million people in the United States may be living with this fatal disease, most of them over 65.

Petzinger et al., 2013). One of the benefits of aerobic exercise—brisk physical activity that causes the heart and lungs to work harder to meet the body's increased need for oxygen—is that it appears to protect against a decline in higher mental processing and may actually make the brain grow (Bherer et al., 2013; Colcombe et al., 2006; Kaliman et al., 2011; Petzinger et al., 2013). Recent evidence suggests that changes in gene expression (epigenetic influences) may be responsible for the effect that exercise has on neural growth (Kaliman et al., 2011). Environmental enrichment is known to improve memory and learning, improve brain plasticity, and interact with genetic factors to reduce progressive degenerative diseases of the nervous system in rodents (Nithianantharajah & Hannan, 2006). It can also stimulate neurogenesis in humans and help counteract the cognitive effects of neural degeneration (Kempermann, 2006; Steiner, Wolf, & Kempermann, 2006).

What are the benefits of aerobic exercise in preventing mental decline in old age?

Personality Development in Late Adulthood   The final stage of Erikson's theory of personality development is old age, starting around age 60 or 65. The conflict of old age is between *integrity and despair*. Integrity is the feeling of being whole and integrated. It is the sense that all of one's life decisions are coming together. The core strength of old age is *wisdom*. Erikson defined wisdom as being informed and knowledgeable about life and yet having a detachment from it that comes only with old age, when one is no longer in the throes of establishing a family and career.

Death and Dying

Death can be defined in medical terms, though the criteria have changed. Physicians used to pronounce people dead when vital signs, such as heart rate and breathing, ceased. Today medical technology can keep a body alive when the brain is no longer functioning. Brain death occurs when no measurable electrical activity in the brain is evident, but life support equipment may maintain vital signs long after the brain has stopped functioning.

In psychological terms, death is a complex event that marks the end of life. In Western culture, we don't emphasize talking about death. Some Eastern cultures take a different view. In Buddhism, for example, acceptance of death and of the fact that life is not a permanent condition is a touchstone against which life is evaluated. Knowing one has limited time on Earth helps give meaning to daily life (Rinpoche, 1992). Some people with terminal illnesses report that knowing their time is limited helps them find meaning in their lives. Accessing such meaning seems to lessen their despair about dying (McClain, Rosenfeld, & Breitbart, 2003).

People may move through a series of stages in dealing with the end of life. Based on her extensive talks with dying patients, Elizabeth Kübler-Ross (1969) detailed the stages people may move through after learning they are going to die. Initially, they experience denial, a sense of utter disbelief that they are going to die. Next comes anger, in which the dying person feels the injustice of it all. At this stage, the dying person asks, "Why me?" In the bargaining stage, people start negotiating with God or whatever forces of nature they feel may control their fate to try to buy more time. Once the certainty of death sets in, depression may ensue. Finally, there is acceptance of death and the end of life. During this final stage, people often come to terms with their own passing.

Increasingly, people in the United States and other Western countries prepare for death by resolving differences with family and friends and accomplishing their life goals. Some people prepare special rituals or events to mark the final stage of life or to say good-bye to friends and family (Bourgeois & Johnson, 2004). We have only so much control over when we die, but by preparing psychologically for it, not just for ourselves but also for the loved ones who will be left behind, we can bring comfort to many people. Palliative care and hospice are growing branches of medicine that are devoted to end-of-life care (Morrison et al., 2005). The main goal of palliative care is to ease suffering and to make the dying person as comfortable as possible rather than to cure or treat the patient. Similarly, hospice focuses on the overall needs of the patient and family members, such as physical comfort, emotional care, and a dignified death.

Quick Quiz 5.4: The Developing Adult

1. Which of the following enhances neural growth in adulthood?
   a. ginkgo biloba
   b. diet
   c. caffeine
   d. aerobic exercise

2. What is necessary for a definitive diagnosis of Alzheimer's disease?
   a. an fMRI
   b. an autopsy
   c. an EEG
   d. psychological testing

3. As people age and become more aware of their limited time on Earth, they become more _____ about how they expend their resources in personal and emotional relationships.
   a. selective
   b. anxious
   c. regretful
   d. concerned

Answers can be found at the end of the chapter.

Bringing It All Together

Making Connections in Human Development

Technology across the Life Span

Technology is a fact of life in the modern world. From the moment we're born to the moment of our death, technology shapes who we are, how we behave, and with whom we interact. Computers, the Internet, video games, cell phones, social networking sites, and tablets, such as the iPad, pervade daily life. Psychological science has begun to examine how exposure to this much information affects the brains, development, and behavior of people as they move through the major life stages—infancy, childhood, adolescence, and early, middle, and late adulthood.

Infancy and Toddlerhood

It is not much of an exaggeration to say that, even before birth, during birth, and immediately after birth, our development is influenced by technology—for example, the medical technology involved in hospital births. The first postnatal stage of life is infancy and consists of ages 0 to 12 months, followed by toddlerhood, which spans the ages 12 to 36 months.

Cognitive and Brain Development and Technology

If there is one important lesson we have learned from neuroscience over the last 20 years, it is that the brain is incredibly plastic, especially in infancy and early childhood. Early exposure to technology is no different—it changes the brain.

Television, because it is passive (the only action required to use it is viewing), is by far the most popular form of technology used in infancy. Although the American Academy of Pediatrics recommends children ages 0–2 *watch no TV or videos at all*, according to a recent survey, up to 20% of the children ages 0–2 had TVs in their bedrooms, and 63% had watched television on the day before the survey was completed by a parent (see Figure 5.31; Vandewater et al., 2007). Only 4% of infants/toddlers had used a computer (Vandewater et al., 2007). When the question is "Has your child ever watched TV, used a computer, or played video games?" the percentages are a bit

Percentage of children under 2 who have ever...

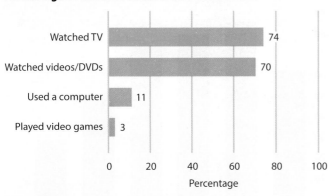

FIGURE **5.31**

RESPONSES TO A SURVEY ABOUT USE OF ELECTRONIC MEDIA BY VERY YOUNG CHILDREN.

higher (Kaiser Family Foundation, 2003). In a meta-analysis of 29 studies, the biggest predictors of screen time in infants and toddlers (under age 3) were race (minority status), positive associations with maternal depression/distress, and child body mass index, yet the gender of the child and the educational status of the mother did not predict infant/toddler screen time (Duch et al., 2013).

Many technological tools have been developed to aid in preschool cognitive development and learning, from Leap-Pad to Baby Einstein. There are even some online programs for teaching infants and toddlers how to use the computer. Data show that early computer use can both help and hinder cognitive development. There is some evidence that infants who learn to use the computer and do tasks other than play games are more likely to be able to read later on than children who use the computer just to play games (Calvert et al., 2005; Castles et al., 2013). Other findings, however, suggest that early media use is associated with having attention deficits later in childhood (Christakis et al., 2004). Recently, Disney has been required to revoke its claims that Baby Einstein is educational, because there are no data indicating it helps infants in any way (Lewin, 2009).

Childhood

Beginning at age 3, language is in full bloom, sentences are spoken, and children are quite mobile and able to get around. Their motor coordination allows them to draw, write, turn a TV on and off, and use a computer.

Cognitive and Brain Development and Technology

Most parents want more than anything for their children to be good learners—to learn to speak well, read, do math, make friends, and in general appreciate their world. The question is how to teach these skills, and for more and more parents the answer involves using some form of technology.

Ever since TV viewing became widespread in the 1950s and 1960s, parents and teachers have worried that watching the "boob tube" would create passive and inactive

children and uncritical learners. Children who watch the most TV tend to do slightly worse at school than children who watch little TV (Potter, 1987; Schmidt & Vandewater, 2008; P. A. Williams et al., 1982), but that is not the full picture. One of the central findings on early TV viewing and learning is that what children watch matters more than how much they watch. If they watch educational programs they tend to do better in school, and if they watch noneducational programs they tend to do worse (Huston et al., 1999; Schmidt & Vandewater, 2008).

Certain kinds of video training may have positive effects on the brains of young children as well. With a simple attention-training computer program, children's brains show more efficient processing in the frontal lobes, where executive planning and attention and focus are most active (Posner & Rothbart, 2007). Moreover, researchers report that video games can enhance cognitive skills such as mental rotation, visual tracking, and even certain kinds of problem solving (De Lisi & Wolford, 2002; Dye & Bavelier, 2004; Holmes, Gathercole, & Dunning, 2009; Schmidt & Vandewater, 2008). One study reported that, in low-income families, children who frequently use the Internet at home had higher scores on standardized tests than did children who used it very infrequently (L. A. Jackson et al., 2006). Similarly, fourth- and fifth-grade urban children who were given laptops at school and who used email frequently had high self-efficacy (confidence in being able to do well) in math and science courses (Shank & Cotten, 2014). In a separate study, after just eleven 30-minute sessions playing *Tetris,* third-grade children improved on tests of mental rotation (De Lisi & Wolford, 2002). Mental rotation tasks require a person to mentally rotate a complex, three-dimensional object to determine which one of three alternatives it is like. It is not clear, however, how or if these improvements on laboratory tasks and games might translate into better academic performance or real-world problem solving.

The news on technology and cognitive development, however, is not all positive. Researchers report that kids who heavily use TV, DVD, social networking, and computers tend to have problems with paying attention and keeping their focus (Schmidt & Vandewater, 2008; Shank & Cotten, 2014). More than 10 hours a week of electronic media use correlates with a lack of physical exercise and poor school performance (Schmidt & Vandewater, 2008; P. A. Williams et al., 1982). Heavy amounts of video gaming—but not TV viewing—were associated with being overweight in children (Vandewater, Shim, & Caplovitz, 2004).

Social-Emotional Development and Technology

Social networking is not very common in children: Because of concerns over safety issues, parents and most sites do not allow children of elementary school age to have accounts. In Australia, however, a recent social networking site has been developed for children ages 6 to 9—it is called SuperClubsPLUS (J. Masters & Barr, 2010). It is an online community for children that allows them to talk to current friends, meet new friends, publish their art or articles, and participate in discussion groups. It is a safe community, because it is monitored by schools, and all material is approved by teachers.

Adolescence

If there is an age group that has been most influenced by technology, it is adolescents. They are even referred to as the Net Generation or Digital Natives. Around 2005, nearly 30% of teens blogged (mostly on MySpace), but by the fall of 2009 nearly three-fourths of teens were using social networking sites such as Facebook (Lenhart et al., 2010). Similarly, mobile device usage (and texting) has risen dramatically just in the last 5 or 6 years. In 2004 only 45% of teens had a cell phone; by 2008 that figure had risen to 71%; and by 2011 it had risen to 77% (Lenhart, 2009, 2012). In 2011 about one in four teens owned a smartphone (Lenhart, 2012). Teen texting increased between 2009 and 2011 from a median of 50 texts a day to 60 a day (Lenhart, 2012). Fourteen- to fifteen-year-old girls send about twice as many texts each day as boys the same age (100 versus 50; Lenhart, 2012).

Cognitive and Brain Development and Technology

Most teens spend 10–15 hours a week on the Internet, gaming, or texting (Lenhart et al., 2010). What effect, then, does this have on their brains and cognitive development? There is not much research on the question of brain activity and computer/media use, but some studies suggest that very distinct brain regions are activated with games containing aggression and violence, though not with other games (Mathiak & Weber, 2006). The anterior cingulate shows the strongest activity when exposed to violence. There is some recent evidence that moderate use of computers for fun and gaming is associated with strong academic performance (grades) but that extensive use is associated with poor academic performance (Bowers & Berland, 2013; Wing, 2008).

How does the widespread "multitasking" in teens affect their attention, learning, or problem solving? Contrary to what many people believe, multitasking comes at a cost. For example, heavy multitaskers are less able to filter out irrelevant information and are more likely to get distracted while working on problem-solving tasks than are light multitaskers (Ophir, Nass, & Wagner, 2009). Similarly, driving while using a hands-free cell phone distracts drivers enough that their reaction time and coordination are on par with someone who is legally drunk (Strayer, Drews, & Couch, 2006). Texting, which requires hand and thumb coordination as well as attention, appears to be even more dangerous while driving (LaPrecious et al., 2009). As novice drivers, teens require more attention to complete the tasks of safely operating and navigating a motor vehicle and are likely at even greater risk.

Social-Emotional Development and Technology

Recall that identity vs. identity confusion is the key conflict during adolescence (Erikson, 1968). More specifically, teens try to figure out who they are and what they like by

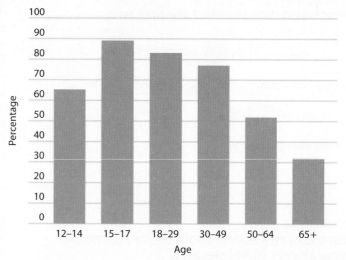

Social network sites include Facebook, Twitter, Pinterest, Instagram, and Tumblr.

FIGURE **5.32**

SOCIAL NETWORK USE IN THE UNITED STATES, 2012. Teens use social networks more than other age groups, but the gap is closing with 30- and 40-year olds (adapted from Duggan & Brenner, 2013; Madden et al., 2013).

exploring different experiences and people to sort out sexuality, careers, and ideology/belief systems. In our electronic world, adolescents use electronic interaction as part of this identity exploration and to connect with others.

Until recently, teens were more likely to use social networking sites to nourish and maintain existing friendships than any other age group, but that has begun to change, with emerging adults having nearly the same amount of users of SNSs as late teens (see Figure 5.32; Duggan & Brenner, 2013; Lenhart et al., 2010; Madden et al., 2013; Subrahmanyam & Greenfield, 2008).

Both good and bad outcomes can and do result from these social networks. Negative outcomes include opening up to sexual predation, bullying, and harassment. Positive outcomes include gaining self-esteem, increasing social circles, and relieving social anxiety. Research conducted in the 1990s reported that, the more time teens spent in online interaction, the lower their degree of social connectedness and well-being (Valkenburg & Peter, 2009). Moreover, teens who form relationships with people they first met over the Internet are more likely to come from families where they have lots of conflict and troubled communication with their parents (Wolak, Mitchell, & Finkelhor, 2002).

Research conducted in the following decade, however, suggests that online communication bolsters and strengthens already existing friendships more than it provides a venue for forming new relationships. Most adolescents use the Internet to talk to friends rather than strangers. Moreover, communicating online with friends increases closeness between friends (Valkenburg & Peter, 2007a).

Just as is true in face-to-face friendships, online relationships can both enhance and lower a person's overall well-being and esteem. Take feedback on your profile as a case in point. When teens receive negative feedback on their online profiles, they experience lower self-esteem, but they get a rush of self-esteem when they receive positive feedback. Such changes in self-esteem in turn affect a person's overall sense of well-being (Valkenburg, Peter, & Schouten, 2006). Interestingly, introverted and socially anxious teens do prefer to disclose personal information more online than offline and seem to use the Internet to compensate for less comfortable face-to-face social skills to form new relationships (Peter, Valkenburg & Schouten, 2005; Pierce, 2009; Valkenburg & Peter, 2009). Extraverted teens, on the other hand, use online communication to enlarge their already large social network—to use the words of one group of researchers, "the rich get richer" (Peter et al., 2005). Teens in particular use the Internet as a means of self-expression and as a way to indicate sexual interest (Subrahmanyam, Greenfield, & Tynes 2004; Subrahmanyam, Šmahel, & Greenfield, 2006).

Easy access to sexual material, sometimes subtle and sometimes very explicit, also allows teens the opportunity to explore their sexuality, by discovering both what they like and what they don't like. Boys tend to enjoy explicit sex sites more than girls do (Cameron et al., 2005). Sexting—sending provocative and sexy images of oneself to a girlfriend or boyfriend—is one high-profile example of teens exploring who they are sexually with the aid of technology. Recent research reported that students—both male and female—with more permissive sexual attitudes are most likely to sext images of themselves (Samimi & Alderson, 2014). Frequently, sending such photos remains a private matter between two individuals, but all too often the person on the receiving end decides to forward these photos to friends, and they become a public matter. Blackmail and harassment are not uncommon in these situations.

Cyberbullying has emerged as a serious pitfall of teen Internet use. **Cyberbullying** is the "willful and repeated harm inflicted through the medium of electronic text" (Patchin & Hinduja, 2006, p. 152). It can be more vicious and aggressive than offline bullying in many cases because of the anonymity of the hurtful language and insults, enabling more uninhibited insults—things someone would rarely say directly to a person's face. The profile of online bullies does not differ much from that of traditional ones, except that they are more depressed than traditional bullies and more females practice online bullying than traditional bullying (Hinduja & Patchin, 2008; Wang, Nansel, & Iannotti, 2011; Ybarra & Mitchell, 2004). Online harassers tend to harass offline too, tend to have poor relationships with their parents, tend to have been heavily disciplined as children, are more likely to abuse drugs, be more depressed, and are not carefully looked after by their parent or guardian (Hinduja & Patchin, 2008;

berbullying
he willful and repeated harm
flicted through the medium
electronic text.

Twyman et al., 2009; Wang et al., 2011; Ybarra & Mitchell, 2004).

Emerging and Early Adulthood

Emerging adulthood covers ages 18 to 25 and early adulthood ages 25 to 40. Today's emerging adults have been dubbed "millennials," and this generation, like others, seems to have its own personality. When a survey asked what makes the generation unique, respondents' top answer was "technology use" ("The Millennials," 2010). To back that up, 75% have profiles on a social networking site, and 83% sleep with their cell phone near or on the bed.

Social-Emotional Development and Technology
Technology is becoming more crucial for young adults who are in the midst of two major life transitions: forming long-term romantic relationships and deciding on and entering a career. Traditional ways of meeting potential life partners have begun to change over the last generation or two. Work, school, family, and friends still are the most common ways in which people meet life partners, with about two-thirds of adults saying that is how they met their partners (Madden & Lenhart, 2006). The Internet, however, is gaining in popularity with each passing year, with roughly 11% of all adults and 18% of the millennial adults saying they used online dating services in 2006 (Madden & Lenhart, 2006). By 2010, emerging adults were the most likely of all age groups to use online dating (Donn & Sherman, 2002; Madden & Lenhart, 2006).

Online relationship seekers have many things in common with traditional date seekers, but they also have a few differences. Online daters place higher value on communication and physical attractiveness than do offline daters (Rosen et al., 2007). How much emotion and self-disclosure an online ad reveals increases the chance of receiving a response (at least in women). For example, ads that used words such as "wonderful" or "excited" had more positive responses than ads that used milder words, such as "fine" or "happy" (Rosen et al., 2007).

Middle Adulthood
Most developmental psychologists place middle adulthood between the ages of 40 and 60 or 65. This age group is also opening up to technology. In 2009 those from 35 to 55 years old were the fastest-growing group on Facebook (J. Smith, 2009).

The literature on the use of social networks by middle-aged adults clearly points to the positive effects of having both face-to-face and electronic networks (N. A. Christakis & Fowler, 2009; Hogeboom et al., 2010; Lubben & Gironda, 1996). The larger one's social support network, the better able one is to cope with stress, depression, and relationship difficulties. Additionally, middle-aged adults who have the largest online social networks also have the largest face-to-face networks (Hogeboom et al., 2010). Perhaps a little later, but like their young adult counterparts, middle-aged adults are turning to the Internet for social networks and dating (Alterovitz & Mendelsohn, 2009; Thayer & Ray, 2006).

Late Adulthood

Today's late adulthood generation did not come of age with computers, cell phones, and the Internet, but they nevertheless have taken up the call of these technologies, even if they are slower to adopt them.

Cognitive and Brain Development and Technology

By age 65, many people notice some degree of cognitive decline, especially in memory and selective attention, planning, and cognitive control. Most of these processes are working memory and executive functioning processes and involve frontal lobe activity (Basak et al., 2008; N. Raz, 2000).

Training programs that stimulate the brain and help it resist or at least slow down normal cognitive decline have become very popular (McArdle & Prindle, 2008; Willis et al., 2006). In one study, 70-year-old participants were randomly assigned to either an experimental condition or a control condition (Basak et al., 2008). The experimental condition consisted of training 70-year-olds for 7 to 8 weeks to learn a video game steeped in strategy and hence requiring the executive functioning skills of planning, reasoning, attention, and working memory. Those in the experimental group improved their cognitive skills: They got faster at playing the game, and their problem solving was more flexible and capable of change; however, the cognitive improvements were specific to the type of training they received (Ball et al., 2002; Basak et al., 2008; McArdle & Prindle, 2008). Nonexperimental longitudinal results confirm the positive effects of computer use on selective attention and memory in the elderly (Siegers, van Boxtel, & Jolles, 2012).

Apparently, video gaming is not the only electronic activity that improves cognitive function in older adults. Internet searching can keep the brain nimble as well. Small and colleagues (2009), for example, measured brain activation (using fMRI) during Internet searching and a text reading task. For experienced "searchers," Internet searching activated more brain areas than simple reading, especially those involved in decision making and reasoning.

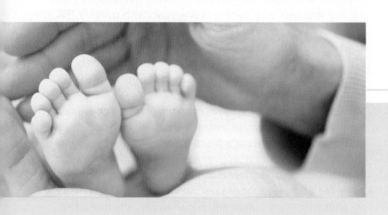

Chapter Review

THE DEVELOPING FETUS

- Life before birth is divided into the germinal, embryonic, and fetal stages.

- *Prenatal programming* refers to a change in developmental trajectory for certain health outcomes that are established in the womb.

- Two common sources of prenatal programming are maternal nutrition and substances known as teratogens, which can harm the developing infant. Mild to profound changes in the brain and body of the fetus can result from diet and chemicals the pregnant mother takes into her body.

THE DEVELOPING INFANT AND CHILD

- The five major senses develop at different rates. Hearing is almost fully developed at birth, but vision is not.

- Learning and experience strengthen certain synaptic connections. Through pruning, synaptic connections that are not reinforced and strengthened by experience degrade and ultimately die off.

- Piaget proposed four major stages of cognitive development: (1) the sensorimotor stage, with object permanence being the major accomplishment; (2) the preoperational stage, when young children begin to think systematically; (3) the concrete operational stage, when school-age children master conservation, the knowledge that the total amount of something stays the same even when its shape or arrangement changes; and (4) the formal operational stage, during which adolescents begin to think logically and abstractly.

- The ability to know and understand what other people are thinking, wanting, or feeling is called theory of mind, typically developed around age 4, when children recognize that other people's beliefs may be different from their own.

- In human development, *attachment* refers to the strong emotional connection that develops early in life to keep infants close to their caregivers. Comfort and touch in infancy are crucial to healthy development.

THE DEVELOPING ADOLESCENT

- For girls, a major change during adolescence is the first menstrual period, known as menarche. For boys, the equivalent change is spermarche, the first ejaculation.

- Brain development continues in adolescence, with the frontal lobes being the last part of the brain to mature.

- Social relationships become paramount in adolescence. Girls tend to have one or two deep friendships and more intimate relationships than boys. Sexual maturity brings sexual behavior, with most adolescents being sexually active by age 18.

THE DEVELOPING ADULT

- Most sensory systems (for example, vision and hearing) gradually decline after middle age.

- Cognitive decline is complex but not inevitable in adults; it mostly begins in the late 60s or early 70s.

- Age is a risk factor for dementia, a loss of mental function in which many cognitive processes, such as the ability to remember, reason, solve problems, make decisions, and use language, are impaired.

- Alzheimer's disease is a degenerative condition marked by progressive cognitive decline, confusion, memory loss, mood swings, as well as eventual loss of physical function.

- Healthy aging is possible through physical exercise and cognitive training.

- One cognitive benefit of aging is wisdom, or the ability to know what matters; to live well; and to show good judgment.

BRINGING IT ALL TOGETHER: MAKING CONNECTIONS IN HUMAN DEVELOPMENT

- Technology affects development from cradle to grave.

- Infants and toddlers are more likely to use TV and video than any other form of technology.

- Educational technologies are widely used at home and school to help children learn to read, learn math, and socialize.

- Adolescents use new forms of technology that affect—both for good and for bad—their cognitive, social-emotional, and physical development.

- Social networking sites help foster friendships and relationships, but they also run the risk of being used for cyberbullying.

- Emerging and young adults use online dating to help them find and maintain close intimate relationships.

- Middle-aged adults are likely to use technology to help them counteract their physical and sensory decline.

- Elderly adults are increasingly turning to computer training to stave off memory and cognitive decline.

Key Terms

adolescence, p. 187
Alzheimer's disease, p. 199
animistic thinking, p. 175
attachment, p. 181
concrete operational stage, p. 177
conservation, p. 176
conventional level, p. 180
crystallized intelligence, p. 199
cyberbullying, p. 205
dementia, p. 199
egocentrism, p. 175
embryo, p. 162

embryonic stage, p. 162
emerging adulthood, p. 193
emotional competence, p. 185
fetal alcohol spectrum disorder (FASD), p. 166
fetal stage, p. 162
fluid intelligence, p. 199
formal operational stage, p. 177
generativity, p. 198
germinal stage, p. 161
human development, p. 160
imprinting, p. 181

individuation, p. 198
intimacy, p. 197
menarche, p. 188
neural migration, p. 162
object permanence, p. 174
personality, p. 166
postconventional level, p. 180
preconventional level, p. 180
prenatal programming, p. 165
preoperational stage, p. 175
pruning, p. 169
puberty, p. 188

securely attached, p. 182
sensorimotor stage, p. 174
separation anxiety, p. 181
social referencing, p. 185
spermarche, p. 188
stagnation, p. 198
temperament, p. 166
teratogens, p. 165
theory of mind, p. 178
young adulthood, p. 195
zone of proximal development, p. 178
zygote, p. 161

Quick Quiz Answers

Quick Quiz 5.1: 1. c 2. b 3. a   **Quick Quiz 5.2:** 1. d 2. c 3. b 4. d   **Quick Quiz 5.3:** 1. d 2. c   **Quick Quiz 5.4:** 1. d 2. b 3. a

6 Consciousness

Chapter Outline

What Is Consciousness?

Two Dimensions of Consciousness: Wakefulness and Awareness

Attention: Focusing Consciousness

Training Consciousness: Meditation

Sleeping and Dreaming

Hypnosis

Altering Consciousness with Drugs

Chapter Review

Challenge Your Assumptions

True or False?

- Driving with a headset is less distracting than driving with a phone in one hand. (see page 219)

- Many people can multitask if they put their minds to it. (see page 220)

- Meditation practice can improve your GRE score. (see page 223)

- You can make up for lost sleep. (see page 229)

- You can't drink yourself to death. (see page 238)

On Super Bowl Sunday, January 30, 1994, your authors' lives changed forever. David, the brother of author Greg Feist, was hit by a car while riding his bicycle home from work. He crashed onto the windshield and then landed on the street. He was not wearing his helmet. Fortunately for David, within just a few minutes, emergency workers whisked him off to one of the top trauma centers in the country. David had suffered a severe traumatic brain injury.

When we arrived at the hospital, David was in a coma. We asked the trauma nurse to explain just how comatose he was. They use a scale, ranging from 3 to 15, to rate the degree of coma and nonresponsiveness. David was a 4. We asked what a 4 meant in practical terms. The nurse picked up the small bottle of saline solution from David's bedside table. "You see this?" she asked. "This is a 3." David was barely alive.

Two weeks after the accident, David opened his eyes, but he was nonresponsive. Five months later, he emerged from his vegetative state and began responding to input from the outside world. Witnessing David's nearly miraculous recovery over the next year not only pushed the limits of our concepts of life and death but also illustrated just how delicate states of consciousness can be.

For a long time, the topic of consciousness—something that occupies the center of our psychological experience—was a neglected area in psychology. Thanks to the cognitive revolution, evolutionary psychology, and neuroscience, which all returned mental phenomena to the forefront of psychological research, the scientific study of consciousness is back. In this chapter, we review what the science of psychology has to say about consciousness.

In particular, we'll explore what consciousness is, examine how we know the contents of our own minds, look at how psychologists have studied the conscious mind, and consider how meditation, sleep, drugs, hypnosis, and mental exercises can modify consciousness. Finally, we'll return to the consciousness-altering effects of brain injury.

WHAT IS CONSCIOUSNESS?

Consider what happens if you walk out of a dark house onto a sunny porch. Many signals assault your brain: The bright light from the sky hits your eyes, which send information to visual processing areas in the thalamus and occipital cortex. The heat from the sun bathes your skin, and temperature sensors there send impulses to the thalamus, somatosensory cortex, and brain stem areas that regulate body temperature. The aroma from the orange blossoms in the yard wafts through your nostrils, quickly moving to the olfactory bulb and emotional centers in the brain, perhaps triggering pleasant memories of the orange trees that grew in front of your grandmother's house. The brain processes these signals instantaneously and simultaneously, and they come together into the experience of right now being on the front porch in the sun. They come together in your consciousness.

In spite of its central role in our experience, consciousness is not easily defined. Most simply, **consciousness** is the awareness of one's surroundings and of what is in one's mind at a given moment. It is our experience of a moment as we move through it, but consciousness also involves the capacity to take in and process information briefly before sending it to specialized areas for further use or storage. Consciousness can change very quickly and dramatically whenever

consciousness
An awareness of one's surroundings and of what's in one's mind at a given moment; it includes aspects of being awake and aware.

new information arrives. Imagine the change in your experience if you step off the porch into a pile of dog droppings.

Consciousness acts as a stage for the "main event" of your brain at a given moment in time. Consider again the example of standing on the front porch with your brain receiving and processing sensory information from all around you. When the connections among the various processing areas of the brain areas become strong enough, a conscious experience occurs (Engel, Debener, & Kranczioch, 2006). The various sensory elements are brought together in what has been called the *global workspace* of consciousness (Baars, 1997; Baars & Franklin, 2003).

Still, much of what we do does not require deliberate, conscious thought. Without thinking about it, we can lift our fingers, choose whom we prefer to talk with, and know how to tie our shoes (Bargh, 1997; Baumeister, Masicampo, & Vohs, 2011). If this is so, why do we need consciousness? Baumeister and his colleagues (2010, 2011)—who reviewed volumes of research in psychology on this question—argue that consciousness is required for any mental processes that involve imagining situations, such as planning future behavior. Also, consciousness is crucial for mental tasks that require working with sequences of information, such as counting, speaking and understanding languages, logical reasoning, and helping people share experiences (Baumeister & Masicampo, 2010; Baumeister et al., 2011).

Many studies have examined the processes of consciousness, including sleeping, dreaming, wakefulness, perception, sensation, responsiveness, and awareness. The subjective aspect of being a conscious human—*what it feels like* to be in love, see red, or have an idea—has eluded science. The focus of this chapter is on psychology's contribution to understanding conscious processes and to developing methods that may bring the subjective aspect of consciousness into clearer view.

TWO DIMENSIONS OF CONSCIOUSNESS: WAKEFULNESS AND AWARENESS

We defined consciousness as the extent to which we are aware of our surroundings and of what's in our minds at a given moment. But consciousness really has two aspects: the degree to which we are awake and the degree to which we are aware. **Wakefulness** refers to alertness, or the extent to which a person is awake or asleep. **Awareness** refers to the monitoring of information from the environment and from one's own thoughts (K. W. Brown & Ryan, 2003). Usually, wakefulness and awareness go hand in hand, but they do not always work together. A person can be awake but not very aware, as is true in vegetative states or extreme drunkenness.

Variations in consciousness can be explained in terms of degrees of wakefulness and awareness (Laureys, 2007). Figure 6.1 shows that each component ranges from low to high and that all states of consciousness exist somewhere in this two-dimensional space. Coma, for example, is one extreme of consciousness and is characterized by very low wakefulness and awareness. The other extreme of consciousness is characterized by high wakefulness and awareness. In contrast, the vegetative state is wakeful but not very aware, as was the case when David opened his eyes but did not respond to the outside world. Let's look at variations in consciousness in more detail, starting with minimal consciousness and moving to moderate and full consciousness.

wakefulness
The degree of alertness reflecting whether a person is awake or asleep.

awareness
The monitoring of information from the environment and from one's own thoughts.

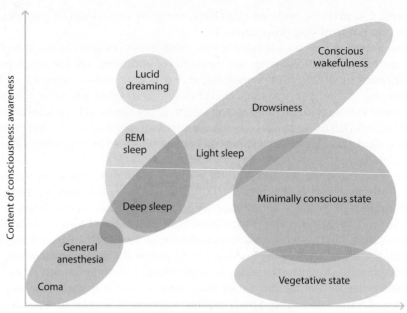

FIGURE **6.1**

TWO DIMENSIONS OF CONSCIOUSNESS. Consciousness exists on a continuum from low to high wakefulness and from little to high awareness.

 Looking at Figure 6.1, what is the difference between a coma and a vegetative state? Between deep sleep and lucid dreaming? Between light sleep and full wakefulness? (Laureys, 2007)

Minimal Consciousness

coma

A state of consciousness in which the eyes are closed and the person is unresponsive and unarousable.

If you have ever fainted, you have experienced a loss of consciousness. **Coma,** in which the eyes are closed and the person is unresponsive, is a much more severe and enduring loss of consciousness than fainting. People cannot be roused from a coma as they can be roused from sleep. Coma generally results from illness or brain injury that damages areas of the brain that control wakefulness—in particular, the reticular formation (Bernat, 2006). In fact, comatose people whose brains show normal sleep patterns are more likely to regain consciousness than are those who do not exhibit these patterns (G.G. Fischer, 2004).

The medical community distinguishes among different degrees of coma with the Glasgow Coma Scale, the instrument used to assess David's level of consciousness (Jain, Dharap, & Gore, 2008; Schutte & Hanks, 2010; Teasdale & Jennett, 1976; see Figure 6.2). The scale uses three factors to classify people on severity of injury: the degree of eye opening, verbal responsiveness, and motor responsiveness. People in the most severe coma have their eyes closed and do

Eye opening	
spontaneous	4
to speech	3
to pain	2
no response	1

Verbal response	
alert and oriented	5
disoriented conversation	4
speaking but nonsensical	3
moans/unintelligible sounds	2
no response	1

Motor response	
follows commands	6
localizes pain	5
withdraws from pain	4
decorticate flexion	3
decerebrate extension	2
no response	1

FIGURE **6.2**

GLASGOW COMA SCALE. This scale is used to classify brain injuries as severe, moderate, or mild. Scores on each of the three sections are summed to provide a total score, which is used to predict chances of recovery in people with traumatic brain injury. (Teasdale & Jennett, 1976)

not respond verbally or motorically. Scores range from 3 to 15 and increase as each component improves. David initially was a 4—a score from which most people do not recover. We are glad to say that he has made a nearly full recovery.

In another form of minimal consciousness, the **vegetative state,** the eyes might be open, but the person is otherwise unresponsive (Owen et al., 2006). The vegetative state has been defined as "wakefulness without awareness" (Bernat, 2006, p. 1181). Physicians used to think that anyone who was vegetative did not receive or in any way respond to stimuli from the environment, primarily because of the lack of a behavioral response. We now know that this is not always the case, thanks to clever studies utilizing measures of brain responsivity.

A highly publicized case study offers insight into the responsiveness of the brain in a vegetative state (Owen et al., 2006). Researchers asked a young woman who was in a vegetative state to imagine a few things, such as walking through her house and playing tennis, while they scanned her brain using fMRI. Surprisingly, her brain showed activation in the same areas as did the brains of people who were conscious and asked to imagine the same things. Not only was this woman responsive while in a vegetative state—she was responding with her brain—but she could also exhibit intentional thought: She followed the researchers' instructions.

This patient may have been in transition from a vegetative state to a *minimally conscious* state, in which the person is barely awake or aware but shows some deliberate movements (Laureys, 2007). People who are minimally conscious show signs of intentional behavior, but they cannot communicate (Laureys, 2007). For example, whereas a vegetative person cannot intentionally track a person with the eyes, a minimally conscious person can.

How to determine a person's degree of awareness remains a complicated medical and ethical issue. Clearly, these recent studies suggest that behavioral nonresponsiveness cannot be the sole determinant of someone's ability to interact with the world, if the brain is responding to input or even complicated instruction. It is a big leap to infer conscious experience from neural firing (Busch, Fründ, & Herrmann, 2009; Overgaard, 2009), but neuroimaging techniques, such as fMRI, might be our best way currently of assessing whether someone who is behaviorally nonresponsive is conscious at all (Owen, 2013).

vegetative state
A state of minimal consciousness, in which the eyes might be open but the person is otherwise unresponsive.

Moderate Consciousness

A great deal of mental activity occurs in the areas between a complete lack of consciousness and full consciousness. Freud used the term *preconscious* to describe material that is potentially accessible but not currently available to awareness (Freud, 1933/1964). An example is the so-called *tip-of-the-tongue phenomenon* (Galin, 1994). We know a person's name, and we know we know it, but we can't come up with it. The experience of knowing that we know a name is conscious, even if we cannot bring the name into awareness. This state can be thought of as *moderate consciousness.*

When we sleep and dream, we are moderately conscious. We may be roused by sounds that are important to us, while ignoring others. But while we sleep there is a perceptual wall in our consciousness that prevents us from perceiving most sensations of the outer world. Psychologists study many other processes that operate at the boundaries of awareness, several of which we discuss in Chapter 7.

Full Consciousness

Even when fully awake we experience fluctuations in consciousness—alertness ebbs and flows. There are periods when we are more alert and present than normal. We may be stimulated and even excited. Or we may become so involved in what we are doing that we lose a sense of time and forget where we are. Some psychologists have called this state *flow* (Csikszentmihalyi, 1990). Flow exists when we thrive in our ability to rise to the occasion of challenging tasks. Think of a sport or craft you really love to do and do well. Think of the times when you were involved in such an activity and everything "clicked" all at once—everything you did was just right. This is the flow state. Our attention is so focused and everything goes so smoothly that an hour may feel like a minute or a minute like an hour. We are so engaged with the experience that time does not matter at all.

mindfulness
A heightened awareness of the present moment, whether of events in one's environment or in one's own mind.

Another state of full consciousness is **mindfulness,** a heightened awareness of the present moment, of events in one's environment and events in one's own mind. When you are talking with a friend, you can be aware of what your friend is saying, how he looks, how his words and tone of voice affect how you feel, and what you are feeling in your own body and mind in response to him (K. W. Brown & Ryan, 2003; Kabat-Zinn, 1990). A more mindful person attends to all of these things; a less mindful person might notice only the friend's words. People vary considerably in how mindful they are, just as they differ in their personalities (Baer et al., 2006; K. W. Brown & Ryan, 2003). People can develop their mindfulness skills using mental training techniques, such as meditation.

Quick Quiz 6.1: Two Dimensions of Consciousness: Wakefulness and Awareness

1. Which brain region plays a key role in maintaining wakefulness?
   a. prefrontal cortex
   b. cerebellum
   c. amygdala
   d. reticular formation

2. _____ is a heightened awareness of the present moment, which can be applied to events in one's environment and events in one's own mind.
   a. Wakefulness
   b. Attention
   c. Mindfulness
   d. Optimism

Answers can be found at the end of the chapter.

ATTENTION: FOCUSING CONSCIOUSNESS

Being conscious—being awake and aware—involves attending to particular parts of our world, so attention is a key aspect of consciousness. It is how we direct the spotlight of awareness.

attention
The limited capacity to process information that is under conscious control.

We can be aware of only a finite amount of material at a time. **Attention** is the limited capacity to process information that is under conscious control (Styles, 2006). When you are in class, it is not possible to type a text message to your friend as well as pay attention to the lecture. If you are texting your thoughts to a friend, you cannot also listen carefully to what the professor is saying. There are several types of attention. We will examine three attentional processes that help determine the contents of consciousness at any given moment: selective attention, sustained attention, and the shifting of attention through multitasking.

Selective Attention

Imagine being in a crowded room where several people are talking, although you want to listen to just one person. You filter out unwanted noise to focus on what you want to hear. If attention is a general process, then focusing conscious attention even more narrowly is **selective attention,** the ability to focus awareness on specific features in the environment while ignoring others. When your professor asks for your "undivided attention," then, she is really interested in getting your selective attention.

selective attention
The ability to focus awareness on specific features in the environment while ignoring others.

The classic scientific evidence for selective attention came from research on a "dichotic listening task" (Broadbent, 1954). In these studies, a participant received one message in one ear and another message in the other ear. Typically, researchers presented several messages to both ears and then told the participant to pay attention to just one ear (the attended ear). They then measured recall for items presented to both ears. Recall was much better for the attended ear. If people were instructed to attend to the left ear message, they showed little to no memory of the message presented to the right (unattended) ear (Broadbent, 1954; Styles, 2006).

In fact, however, if the material presented to the unattended ear is meaningful in some way, it can make its way into consciousness (Treisman, 1964). If you were at a large party, trying to listen to a conversation in spite of a lot of background noise, and someone in another part of the room mentioned your name, you would immediately become aware of the other conversation. Previously, you tuned out the background noise, so that you could follow the first conversation. Now that you have heard your name in that background conversation, however, it becomes figural and you must attend to it. This particular ability to filter out auditory stimuli and then to refocus attention when you hear your name is called the *cocktail party effect* (Moray, 1959; see Figure 6.3).

When we selectively attend, we focus so much on certain things that we are blind to other things. Focusing attention can create gaps in attention and perception. Many magic tricks take advantage of the fact that, with our attention diverted, we can easily be fooled. In one study that clearly demonstrates gaps in attention, researchers showed people a video of two basketball teams, with one team dressed in white T-shirts and the other in black shirts (Simons & Chabris, 1999). They asked participants simply to count the number of times the players

FIGURE **6.3**

THE COCKTAIL PARTY EFFECT. The cocktail party effect is the ability to filter out auditory stimuli and then to refocus attention when you hear your name.

Explain when this effect is most likely to occur.

on the team wearing white T-shirts passed the ball. About half the participants were dumbfounded to learn afterward that they completely missed seeing a person dressed in a gorilla suit walk into the game, pause for a second to beat his chest, and then walk off screen. They were so focused on counting passes made by people wearing white shirts that they ignored everything else. Attending closely to one thing can blind us to other events, even gorillas walking into a basketball game. This phenomenon by which we fail to notice unexpected objects in our surroundings is referred to as *inattentional blindness.*

If we can be inattentive in spite of efforts to attend, does that mean we can prevent the intrusion of unwanted information during concentration? If you are reading an engrossing novel, is it possible to tune out the sounds of your roommate's TV? The *perceptual load model* states that we do not notice potential distracters when a primary task consumes all of our attentional capacity (Lavie et al., 2004). When a primary task is minimally demanding, however, distracters can capture our awareness. In a laboratory experiment on this phenomenon, participants were asked to view a drawing of a cross on a computer screen. The two arms of the cross were different colors, and one arm was subtly shorter than the other.

In the low perceptual load condition, participants had to name the color of the arm. In the high perceptual load condition, participants had to say which arm was longer, a more difficult task. The researchers then introduced an irrelevant stimulus (a square) and looked at which group was more likely to see it.

Those who were less busy—the people in the low perceptual load condition—were more likely to see the square than were those in the high perceptual load condition (Lavie, 2007). Perceptual load theory might explain why it is easier to ignore the TV when you are lost in an engrossing novel than when you are reading a boring chapter in a book. It might also explain why we might miss certain things when our minds are too busy. What could happen if you missed seeing a pedestrian while driving because you were texting? See "Psychology in the Real World" for a discussion of the effects of phone use on attention in drivers.

Conscious attention occurs when neurons from many distinct brain regions work together—a process referred to as *synchronization.* Imaging techniques, such as fMRI, reveal synchronization in brain regions that are equally active. When synchronization occurs, we might have a conscious experience (Kranzioch et al., 2005). Imagine that you see an apple: Before you experience "apple," several areas of your brain are active, such as those responding to the object's shape (round) and color (red) and where the object is in your visual field. The synchrony of cell assemblies may be what binds together these separate experiences (of round and red, etc.) into the experience of an apple. This process harkens back to our earlier discussion of consciousness as a global workspace, and it shows how neuroscience is beginning to address how a moment of conscious experience actually occurs (Engel et al., 2006).

Sustained Attention

Staying focused on a task is difficult, especially if the task both requires a high degree of concentration and can have life-or-death consequences. As we discussed in Chapter 4, air traffic controllers must focus on an airplane on a visual display. To do so, they must coordinate with other airplanes, controllers, and pilots to make sure that each plane lands where it should without crossing the paths of other planes that are landing or taking off. This ability to maintain focused awareness on a target is known as **sustained attention.**

What are the limits of people's abilities to sustain their focused attention on one task? The airlines need to know this, as do many other industries that require careful attention on the part of their employees. Researchers study sustained attention using tasks such as the Continuous Performance Test (CPT). Imagine

sustained attention
The ability to maintain focused awareness on a target or an idea.

For air traffic controllers, the ability to sustain attention for long stretches of time is fundamental to the safety of air travelers. Yet research suggests that most people have difficulty focusing attention on a continuous performance task for more than 15 minutes.

What does this suggest about highly focused occupations, such as air traffic controller?

having to detect the letter *Y* among other, similar letters (such as *X*s) shown very rapidly, one by one, on a computer screen. The CPT requires that the participant maintain attentional focus for an extended period of time. Most people cannot perform well on CPT tasks for more than about 15 minutes, and their accuracy in detecting targets declines considerably after 5 to 7 minutes (Nuechterlein & Parasuraman, 1983; Parasuraman, 1998).

Multitasking: The Implications of Shifting Attention

Sustained attention is compromised during multitasking. We think about multitasking as a modern problem that emerged from our increasingly digital lifestyles, but research on multitasking began in mid-20th century, on industrial psychological research questions on jobs that involved competing demands on one's attention (e.g., pilots, air traffic controllers). Early on, the data indicated that people cannot typically do two things in parallel; rather, they switch between tasks, or leave and return, repeatedly, while trying to keep in mind the previous task before moving to others (Meyer & Kieras, 1997).

The evidence suggests that truly concurrent, or parallel, task performance/engagement rarely occurs (Borst, Taatgen, & van Rijn, 2010). Instead, what we consider to be parallel multitasking really involves fast switching of one's attention from task to task. Switching from task to task necessarily interrupts sustained attention. Also, the person loses time when he or she makes the switch, especially on more complex tasks. That is, if a person switches from simple task to simple task (such as from watching a video to checking a Social Networking Site [SNS]), the amount of lost time is low, but if he or she moves away from a more substantial task (such as writing a paper or reading an article) to an SNS and back, then more time is lost. Switching also compromises memory for the tasks at hand. A study of office workers showed that, once people switched away from their

Psychology in the Real World

Hazards of Using a Mobile Device or Texting While Driving

People generally acknowledge the potential hazards of phone use while driving, yet the practice is widespread. Sixty-nine percent of U.S. adults in 2011 said they had used a cell phone while driving in the last 30 days—more than three times the rate in the United Kingdom and almost twice as many as in Germany (Naumann & Dellinger, 2013). In 2012, nearly half of U.S. high school students admitted to texting while driving, a behavior that is positively correlated with other unsafe driving practices, such as not wearing a seat belt and driving after drinking alcohol (Olsen, Shults, & Eaton, 2013).

Almost a decade of research shows that phone conversations and texting while driving distract the driver, even when the hands are free by diverting attention from the demanding tasks of safely operating and navigating a car (Caird et al., 2008). Think of all the things one has to manage while driving: scanning the road, operating the pedals and gears, watching for other cars and pedestrians, and remembering directions. Texting or talking interferes with the attentional resources and perceptual skills needed for such driving-related tasks.

Many psychological factors predict phone use while driving. In one of the few studies to examine the association, O'Conner and colleagues (2013) found that those who compulsively thought about messages and their phones even when the devices were turned off had had more automobile accidents. Recent research also reveals that the teens who are most likely to use their phones while driving

are those who believe that not doing so would be boring, or those who fear that their peers will think their parents are running their lives or that they will be viewed differently from their friends (Hafetz et al., 2010). Additionally, feeling attached to the phone increases the odds of using it while driving, over and above perceptions of risk (Weller et al., 2013). An fMRI study of people driving in a simulator while using a hands-free device showed that activity in the regions of the brain involved in processing spatial information (the parietal lobe) decreased by 37% when they listened to sentences while driving, whereas activity in the areas associated with language processing increased. Their driving was also worse. This suggests that conversations divert attentional resources from the task of driving (Just, Keller & Cynkar, 2008).

How dangerous is it to text or call while driving? The National Highway Traffic Safety Administration reports that in 2010 nearly 1,000 deaths and more than 24,000 injuries were directly related to cell phone use while driving (National Highway Traffic Safety Administration, 2010). Using a phone while driving is similar to drunk driving in that the drivers follow other cars too closely, show slower braking reactions, and have more accidents (Strayer et al., 2006). In a meta-analysis of 33 studies on over 2,000 participants, cell phone use during driving was found to be just as dangerous in terms of slowing down reaction times, whether the callers were using handheld or hands-free devices (Caird et al., 2008). Strayer and Drews

work to another activity, they forgot what they were doing prior to the distraction (Gonzalez & Mark, 2004). In order to compensate for interrupted work, people tend to work faster. The cost of this sped-up, interrupted work, however, is more stress (Mark, Gudith, & Klocke, 2008).

Multitasking compromises learning. Foerde and colleagues (2006) asked students to perform a weather prediction task. Half were randomly assigned to do the task with distraction (listening to beeps on headphones), half without the distraction. While both groups recalled what they learned with similar accuracy, the distraction group members were less able to extrapolate what they had learned from the task to another weather prediction simulation.

Salvucci and Taatgen (2008) proposed the *threaded cognition* theory of multitasking behavior to explain limitations on concurrent multitasking. According to threaded cognition theory, although we can be involved in more than one task at a time, a particular resource (e.g., a perceptual system, a cognitive system, a motor system) can only be used by one task at a time. For instance, if two tasks require the involvement of your vision (such as monitoring the road while driving and reading a text message), only one of them can progress, and involvement with one task will necessarily interfere with the other. If a resource is needed by more than one task, a bottleneck, or backup, can develop in the attempt to access

FIGURE **6.4**

RESEARCH PARTICIPANT IN A COMPUTERIZED DRIVING SIMULATOR. The simulator provides a 180-degree city street interactive driving display in a realistic car interior. The "driver" is wearing a hands-free cell phone headset.

 Can you pay attention to both driving and your phone conversation at the same time? What does the research say about most people's ability to multitask and split their attention?

(2007a) did several experiments with people in a driving simulator (see Figure 6.4). Some of the participants wore a hands-free headset and engaged in a conversation while doing a driving task; the others had no cell phone and simply drove. In the first study, the researchers inserted into the driving scene several objects that drivers were not told they'd need to attend to and were later tested on recognition of these objects. People talking on a phone saw half as many objects as those not on the phone; they were not fully paying attention to the driving situation.

Another experimental study showed that using the phone, texting, and eating while driving all impaired performance on a driving simulator task, but texting led to significantly slower reaction times than the other distracting activities (Cobb et al., 2010). Compared to a control condition, new drivers, while texting, made substantially more errors in shifting out of their lane and noticing traffic signs in a driving simulator task (Hosking, Young, & Regan, 2006). Even more frightening was that they spent 400% more time with their eyes off the road. Such effects may be particularly problematic for new drivers, who are less experienced, have more accidents, and tend to engage in more distracting activities while driving (Neyens & Boyle, 2007).

Think twice or three times before using a phone or texting while driving. The data are clear—it is dangerous and sometimes fatal.

Challenge Your Assumptions

True or False? Driving with a headset is less distracting than driving with a phone in one hand.

False: Driving hands-free is just as distracting as driving with a handheld phone.

consciousness (Borst et al., 2010). There is also a central control mechanism that may have to decide when to allocate resources, which we might think of as the cook in the kitchen who decides what to do and when to do it (Salvucci & Taatgen, 2008). For instance, if you have to engage in a new task (such as driving to a new location you do not have memorized) you cannot also speak on a cell phone.

Thus, there is bottlenecking with multitasking, a place where tasks compete for access to the workspace of consciousness or where attention is focused at a given point in time. This is a key reason multitasking is much more likely an exercise in rapid switching between tasks rather than actual performance of two at the same time.

There is increasing evidence that SNSs, such as Facebook, are the source of most of college students' multitasking behavior while working (Judd, 2014). Indeed, increases in use of SNS sites in class are associated with decrements in GPA, more so than other technological distractions, such as texting (Junco, 2012). If SNS distractions are a problem for you, apps, programs, and plug-ins are available that will allow you to set a given amount of time in which access to Facebook, Twitter, Reddit, or other SNSs is blocked. The "Psychology in the Real World" feature showcases an extremely dangerous kind of multitasking: texting or using a cell phone while driving.

Due to the overwhelming popularity of portable devices, people are multitasking more than ever. About 40% of people in the United States who own mobile devices, such as a smartphone, use them while watching TV, some engaging with three screens at once (phone, laptop, TV; *40% of Tablet and Smartphone Owners*, 2011). Quite apart from the problems of multitasking, just having a mobile device with you and allowing it to compete for your attention means that it is siphoning off a portion of your already limited conscious resources all the time. Consider these statistics about usage: 67% of cell owners say they check their phones (for messages, etc.) even in the absence of ringing or vibrating; 44% of mobile users have kept their phones near the bed, so that they don't miss any messages (Brenner, 2013).

Some people swear they can do more than one thing at a time, without compromising their performance on either task. Watson and Strayer (2010) conducted a study to see if there really are any "supertaskers" who show no performance decrements in an auditory attentional task in the presence of distractors. All participants were tested in a single-task versus a dual-task condition. A vast majority of people showed significant decrements in attention in the dual task condition, but 2.5% showed no decrement. The authors [Watson & Strayer] conclude that there are a few "supertaskers" out there who have excellent mechanisms of cognitive control, but the vast majority of us cannot do it.

One of your authors, Erika, went without her phone for a couple of days when it was water-damaged and noticed just how often she had the impulse to reach for it and check it. Taking one mobile-free day a week is a useful practice to help remind you of how much your experience is tethered to your mobile device.

Challenge Your Assumptions

True or False? Many people can multitask if they put their minds to it.

False: Multitasking is nearly impossible, and almost no one can attend to two tasks at once.

Quick Quiz 6.2: Attention: Focusing Consciousness

1. What term best describes not perceiving a person in a gorilla suit when asked to count the number of people playing basketball?
   a. inattentional blindness
   b. not paying attention
   c. absent-mindedness
   d. minimally conscious state

2. You are at a loud gathering, talking to a friend. The noise of the chatter is nearly deafening, but all of a sudden you hear your name spoken above the noise. This is known as the
   a. self-recognition effect.
   b. cocktail party effect.
   c. attentional effect.
   d. divided attention effect.

Answers can be found at the end of the chapter.

TRAINING CONSCIOUSNESS: MEDITATION

Connection

Every time you make a memory or learn something new, you change your brain by strengthening synaptic connections or growing new neurons.

See "Synaptic Change during Learning," Chapter 8, "Learning," p. 314.

meditation
A practice that people use to calm the mind, stabilize concentration, focus attention, and enhance awareness of the present moment.

Anytime you read, reason, solve problems, or learn something new, you are sharpening your mental skills. Some age-old techniques, however, are designed specifically to train the conscious mind. **Meditation** refers to a wide variety of practices that people use to calm the mind, stabilize concentration, focus attention, and enhance awareness of the present moment. There are many types of meditation techniques, with different goals. To improve concentration, meditators might spend minutes or even hours sitting still, relaxed yet alert, focusing their attention on the sensations of breathing, noticing how the breath moves into and out of their mouths and noses. In this case, meditators attempt to keep their attention on the breath. If their minds wander, they bring their attention back to the breath. This simple, ancient practice calms the mind and stabilizes attention (Wallace, 2006).

Psychologists and neuroscientists study the effects of such meditative practices on mental processes, emotion, and brain function. This research illustrates the dynamic relationship between mental life and neural structure.

Meditation and Conscious Experience

Many forms of meditation develop mindfulness, a fully conscious state of heightened awareness of the present moment. Unlike concentration techniques, mindfulness meditation encourages attention to the details of momentary experience, such as all the thoughts, feelings, and sensations available at present (Baer et al., 2006). People with high scores on mindfulness questionnaires also score high on measures of well-being and optimism, are more in tune with their emotional states, and are less self-conscious and anxious. In addition, people who practice meditation consistently have higher mindfulness scores than those who do not (K. W. Brown & Ryan, 2003). Mindfulness-based meditation training appears to enhance well-being, reduce stress, decrease depression, improve physical health, and reduce pain (Anderson et al., 2007; R. E. Jung et al., 2010; Kabat-Zinn et al., 1998; Sahdra et al., 2011; J. D. Teasdale et al., 2000; Zeidan et al., 2011).

Meditation can improve attentional skills as well (Jha, Krompinger, & Baime, 2007; Kaul et al., 2010). In the first true experiment on this question, 64 experienced meditators were randomly assigned to a control group or to receive intensive training in concentration meditation (similar to the breathing technique described at the beginning of this section), which they practiced for several hours a day for 3 months. All participants were assessed before, during, and after the 3-month training (MacLean et al., 2010). Specifically, concentration meditation makes people perceive visual objects—lines, at least—with greater sensitivity and helps them attend to such objects longer (which is an increase in sustained attention). These effects are akin to having sharper vision for a longer period of time. The same type of training also improves response inhibition, which is the ability to resist impulsive responding (Sahdra et al., 2011). Shorter-term training in meditation, such as completion of an 8-week training course, also increases vigilance (Lutz et al., 2009) and enhances working memory, or the capacity to keep multiple things in mind while solving problems or making decisions (van Vugt & Jha, 2011). Recent studies show that an 8-week training course in mindfulness meditation can reduce the likelihood of attention shifts among multiple tasks, reduce job stress, and improve memory, potentially counteracting multitasking in stressful work environments (Levy et al., 2012).

Meditation Training and the Brain

Meditation changes brain function and structure. After 8 weeks of mindfulness meditation training, people with no previous meditation experience showed significant increases in EEG activity in the left frontal cortex (an area associated with positive mood) and decreases in negative mood (Davidson et al., 2003). These EEG changes persisted for at least 4 months after training. Another study has linked meditation-related changes in brain activity with quicker performance in an attentional task. Such findings help tell us whether measurable differences in brain activity really mean anything in terms of actual behavior (Lutz et al., 2009).

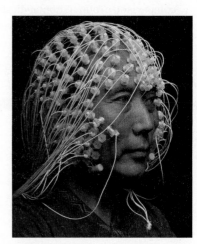

Meditation, an integral part of the Buddhist spiritual practice for thousands of years, develops concentration and mindfulness. Here a Buddhist monk is being outfitted with EEG electrodes for monitoring his brain during meditation.

In another study, MRI scans revealed thicker brain tissue in the areas of the cortex associated with attention, sensitivity to bodily sensations, and the processing of external sensory information in very experienced meditators compared to a group of nonmeditators (Lazar et al., 2005). Those who had meditated the longest showed the greatest cortical thickness in certain areas. The finding has since been replicated in a study of Zen meditators (J. A. Grant et al., 2010). Such correlational findings suggest that meditation can grow the brain, but an experimental design is required to uncover a causal link between meditation training and brain changes. A recent experiment studied people new to meditation. Compared to a control group, novices assigned to an 8-week meditation training program showed increases in growth in brain tissue in the areas relevant to attention and emotion processing, which appeared to be linked with changes in emotional well-being over the 8-week period (Hölzel et al., 2011). For more on whether meditation training can improve memory, see "Research Process" (Figure 6.5).

Connection

What aspects of experimental designs allow for conclusions about cause and effect?

See "Research Methods in Psychology," Chapter 2, "Conducting Research in Psychology," p. 41.

Quick Quiz 6.3: Training Consciousness: Meditation

1. Which of the following does meditation appear to improve?
   a. mindfulness
   b. attention
   c. well-being
   d. all of the above

2. A study of brain images of experienced meditators and a comparison group of nonmeditators found that the experienced meditators' brains showed evidence of

   a. thicker cortex in brain areas associated with attention and sensitivity to sensory information.
   b. more diverse synaptic connections throughout the cerebellum.
   c. cortical thinning throughout motor areas but thickening in frontal areas.
   d. less synaptic death than in nonmeditators.

   Answers can be found at the end of the chapter.

SLEEPING AND DREAMING

Meditation offers specific practices for working with consciousness. Yet consciousness varies constantly on a daily basis without much intervention, by virtue of our degree of wakefulness or our moods. In this section, we discuss two major sources of variation of consciousness: sleeping and dreaming.

Sleeping

A 5-year-old boy once described sleep as "when I go to my bed and I think about nothing." Typically, we think of sleep as a time of rest and relaxation, when we put the day's events out of our minds. Although our conscious experience of sleep may be of nothing, it is, in fact, a very active process. We behave while we sleep—moving, dreaming, sometimes even talking and walking. The sleeping brain is very active, but it is only partially processing information from the outside world.

Sleep has two essential characteristics: It has a perceptual wall between the conscious mind and the outside world, and the sleeping state can be immediately reversed (Dement, 1999). In sleep, awareness of the outside world is greatly diminished, but not completely. The mind is still able to filter relevant from irrelevant stimuli: A baby's cry may awaken a parent, but much louder sounds (such as a TV blaring in the room) may not. Moreover, because sleep is reversible, it is different from coma.

Sleep and Circadian Rhythms Sleep occurs in the context of a daily sleep-wake cycle, which follows a pattern known as a circadian rhythm. **Circadian rhythms** are the variations in physiological processes that cycle within

circadian rhythms
Variations in physiological processes that cycle within approximately a 24-hour period, including the sleep–wake cycle.

Research Process

① Research Question

Can just 2 weeks of mindfulness meditation training improve working memory and Graduate Record Exam (GRE) performance and reduce mind wandering?

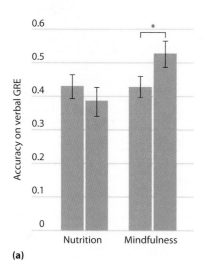

(a)

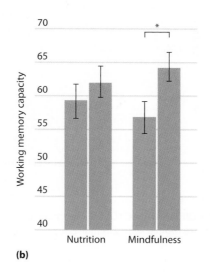

(b)

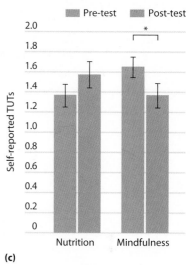

(c)

② Method

Forty-eight undergraduate students (34 females) were randomly assigned to either the experimental (mindfulness training) or the control (nutrition class) condition. One week before and then again 1 week after these courses participants took cognitive tests (working memory and GRE verbal subtest).

The mindfulness training met four times a week for 45 minutes a session and lasted 2 weeks. The mindfulness class focused on posture and breath, allowing the mind to rest instead of suppressing thoughts, lessening distracting thoughts and reframing them as mental projections. A *nutrition class* also met four times a week for 2 weeks and students had to log their daily food intakes (but did not have to make any changes to their diets). *Working memory* was assessed with an operation span task, where participants saw three letters presented one at a time and had to recall those letters in correct order immediately afterwards. Finally, *mind wandering* was assessed by asking participants at unpredictable times during the GRE and working memory tasks how much their attention was focused on the task at hand.

③ Results

GRE, working memory, and mind wandering scores prior to training and the class were the same between the two groups. But after the 2 weeks of training, those in mindfulness meditation course had improved their working memory and the GRE scores and lowered their mind wandering compared to the nutrition class students. Because the groups were the same before but different after the training sessions, the likely cause of the change was the training.

④ Conclusion

Mindfulness training in as little as 2 weeks can have significant impact on improving memory and verbal problem solving while also reducing the mind's tendency to wander between tasks.

Challenge Your Assumptions

True or False? Meditation practice can improve your GRE score.

True: Research has linked meditation-related changes in brain activity with quicker and better performance in attentional tasks.

FIGURE **6.5**

CAN MINDFULNESS MEDITATION TRAINING IMPROVE WORKING MEMORY AND GRE PERFORMANCE? Pre- and post-training scores on working GRE (a), working memory (b), and mind wandering (c) for those in nutrition class (control group) and those in mindfulness training class (experimental group). TUT = task-unrelated thought; mind wandering. Asterisks (*) indicate statistically significant differences between the two groups ($p < .05$). (Mrazek, M. D., Franklin, M. S., Phillips, D. T., Baird, B., & Schooler, J. W. [2013]. Mindfulness training improves memory capacity and GRE performance while reducing mind wandering. *Psychological Science,* online publication at doi: 10.1177/0956797612459659.)

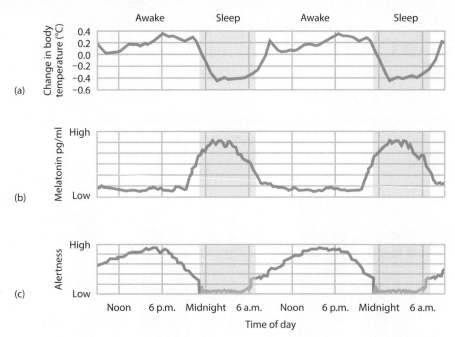

FIGURE **6.6**

HUMAN CIRCADIAN CYCLES. Our body temperature (a), melatonin levels (b), and alertness (c) fluctuate regularly on 24-hour circadian cycles. (Monk, Folkarc, & Wedderburn, 1996.)

approximately a 24-hour period. Many physiological systems, including the sleep–wake cycle, feeding, hormone production, and cellular regeneration, vary on a circadian basis (Refinetti, 2006). In Figure 6.6 we see how three bodily processes—body temperature, the hormone melatonin, and alertness—fluctuate on a circadian cycle. Body temperature, for instance, peaks a few hours before bed and soon after waking up, then drops during sleep. That our bodies go through 24-hour cycles is the reason we are sharper at some times of the day than others and why we experience jet lag. Shortening or lengthening our days by traveling across time zones throws the circadian cycles off, and it takes time for the body to readjust to the new daily cycle.

The body has an internal timekeeper located in the hypothalamus, called the suprachiasmatic nucleus (SCN), which regulates physiological activity on daily cycles (R. Y. Moore & Eichler, 1972; D. Weaver, 1998). When the retina in the eye senses light in the morning, it stimulates the SCN, which in turn signals the nearby *pineal gland* to decrease the amount of melatonin it releases (Itri et al., 2004). *Melatonin* is a hormone that plays a role in relaxation and drowsiness. In the evening, decreased activity in the SCN prompts the secretion of melatonin, which increases relaxation. Because of its role in relaxation, melatonin can be taken as a drug to combat the effects of jet lag. Research suggests that, for some people, it can be effective in reducing the disruptive effects of jet travel, but more so when we travel ahead in time (east) than backward in time (west; Atkinson, Reilly, & Waterhouse, 2007).

The Sleeping Brain   Until the 1950s, people assumed the brain was relatively inactive during sleep, except for dreaming. In the 1950s, Nathaniel Kleitman and Eugene Aserinsky were studying attention in children and noticed that, when children lost attention and fell asleep, their eyes moved rapidly underneath their eyelids (Bulkeley, 1997). Not only were these movements important in sleep, but they occurred in everyone throughout the night. Kleitman and Aserinsky coined the term **rapid eye movements (REM)** to describe their discovery (Dement, 1999). REM revolutionized the study of sleep and dreaming.

rapid eye movements (REM)
Quick movements of the eye that occur during sleep, thought to mark the phases of dreaming.

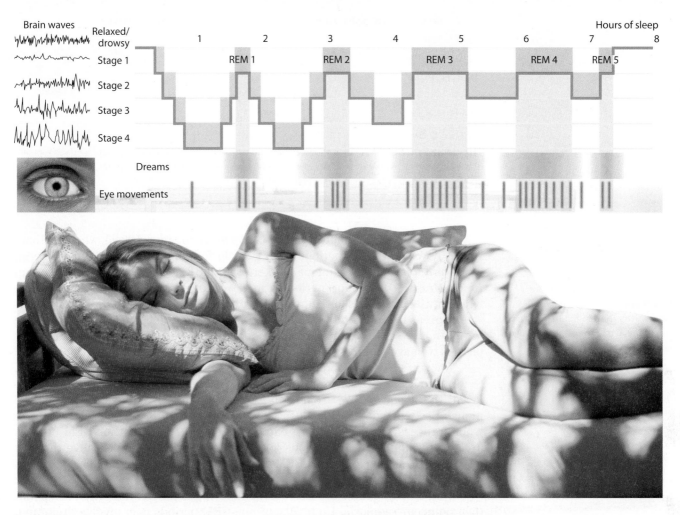

FIGURE **6.7**

TYPES OF BRAIN WAVES AND DIFFERENT STAGES OF CONSCIOUSNESS AND SLEEP.
Each stage of wakefulness and sleep is marked by a unique pattern of brain wave. For the typical 7-hour night of sleep for an adult, there are about five cycles of sleep.

⚙⚙ **What happens to the amount of dreaming as the night progresses?**

The brain, as it turns out, is very active during sleep. With EEG technology, scientists have learned that sleep changes throughout the night, and distinct patterns of brain activity characterize these changes (Bulkeley, 1997; Dement, 1999). Each state of wakefulness and sleep has its own pattern of brain electrical activity. When we are awake, brain activity is characterized by rapid, low-energy waves known as **beta waves.** When we are awake but relaxed and drowsy, our brain activity switches to slower and slightly higher-energy waves known as **alpha waves.**

The second major form of sleep, called **non-REM,** has relatively few eye movements; those that occur are slow rather than fast. There are four stages of non-REM sleep, each marked by unique brain wave patterns (see Figure 6.7). When the sensory curtain drops and we are no longer responsive to the outside world, we enter Stage 1 of sleep, and our brain waves change to **theta waves,** which are slower and lower in energy than alpha waves. The precise moment when we fall asleep is readily apparent on an EEG display—we move from alpha to slower and lower energy theta wave activity (see Figure 6.8). Stage 1 sleep, however, is a light sleep, and not much stimulation is needed to awaken us from it.

beta waves
Rapid, low-energy brain waves that occur when one is awake.

alpha waves
Brain waves that occur when one is relaxed and drowsy; they are slower, higher-energy waves than beta waves.

non-REM
The form of sleep with few eye movements, which are slow rather than fast.

theta waves
Brain waves that occur during Stage 1 sleep; they are slower, lower-energy waves than alpha waves.

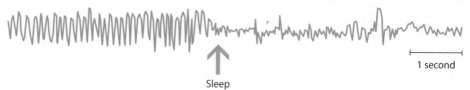

Relaxed-drowsy (alpha waves)   Stage 1 sleep (theta waves)

1 second

Sleep

FIGURE **6.8**

THE ONSET OF SLEEP. An EEG shows the abrupt transition from higher-energy alpha waves typical of the drowsy but awake state to the lower-energy theta waves of Stage 1 sleep. This transition occurs in a period of less than 10 seconds.

delta waves
Brain waves that dominate Stage 3 sleep; they are higher-energy waves than theta waves.

After about 5–7 minutes in Stage 1, we move to Stage 2 sleep, when the theta waves now show short periods of extremely fast and somewhat higher-energy *sleep spindles*. The other unique markers of Stage 2 sleep are sudden, high-energy *K-complexes*. After a short period of time, we move from Stage 2 to Stage 3 sleep, which initially consists of theta waves with some higher-energy **delta waves.** As we progress through Stage 3, more and more delta waves appear, and we have fewer and fewer sleep spindles and K-complexes. When the latter disappear completely, we have entered our deepest stage of sleep, Stage 4.

Shortly after entering Stage 4 sleep, we start going back through Stage 3, Stage 2, and Stage 1. On return to Stage 1, our eyes begin to move rapidly underneath the eyelids. We are now in REM sleep and are actively dreaming. The night's first episode of REM sleep lasts for only about 8–10 minutes before the whole process starts over. With each progressive cycle, the non-REM periods are shorter and the REM periods longer (Dement, 1999). Adults move through about four to six cycles of non-REM and REM sleep every night. Each cycle lasts roughly 90 minutes.

Full-blown dreams are less common during non-REM than REM sleep, but they do occur regularly. Up to 70% of non-REM periods may involve dreaming, but the dreams differ from REM dreams: They tend to be less detailed, less active, and more like regular thinking (Bulkeley, 1997; Foulkes, 1996; Kahan, 2001).

The Development of Sleep over the Life Span   Newborns of many species, especially humans, spend more time in REM sleep than in non-REM sleep. In humans, REM sleep declines rapidly over the life span (see Figure 6.9). Although newborns typically sleep for only a few hours at a time—much to the chagrin of their sleep-deprived parents—they might spend a total of 8 hours in REM sleep and another 8 hours in non-REM sleep *per day.* The percentage of total sleep that is REM stays close to 50% for the first 3 months of life. By 8 months, it has fallen to 33%, and by age 1 it has dropped to about 28%. During adolescence and adulthood, the amount of sleep that involves REM steadily decreases.

The fact that newborns and infants spend so much more time in REM sleep than adults has led some researchers to hypothesize that the main function of REM sleep is to assist in brain growth and development. The amount of REM sleep over the life span does correspond to the degree of brain plasticity and neural growth (Dement, 1999). Our brains are most plastic in infancy and childhood and less so in adulthood—precisely the pattern seen in REM sleep. REM sleep, just like new neural growth, continues throughout our lives—it just decreases with age.

The Function of Sleep   Sleep supports several restorative processes in the CNS: neural growth, metabolic cleanup in the brain, memory consolidation, and protection against cellular damage (Bellesi et al., 2013; Xie et al., 2013; see Figure 6.10). In mice, there are substantial increases in the exchange

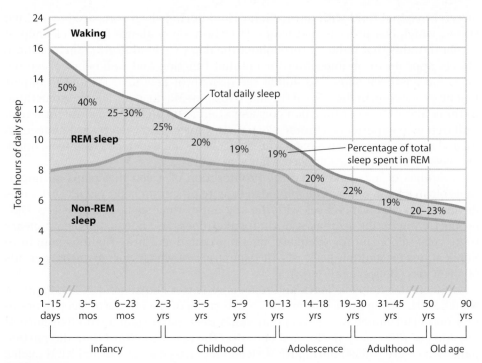

FIGURE **6.9**

SLEEP ACROSS THE LIFE SPAN.

Which groups require more hours of sleep and more time in **REM** sleep? From what you have learned about brain development, why do you think that is the case?

to help with metabolic cleanup in the brain

to restore neural growth

to consolidate memory

to produce enzymes that protect against cellular damage

FIGURE **6.10**

THE FUNCTIONS OF SLEEP. A good night's sleep before an exam may do more for your performance than an all-night cram session.

of cerebrospinal fluid with intracellular fluid during sleep compared to waking states, which is a process that may reflect how sleep allows for the cleanup of cerebral toxins that build up throughout the day (Xie et al., 2013). Each of these effects appears to be important for optimal function and well-being. Sleep deprivation has been shown to inhibit the growth of new neurons and to impair myelin production in the CNS in rodents (Guzman-Marin et al., 2003)—something to think about the next time you consider staying up all night to cram for a test. Children who experience chronic sleep disturbances show decreased connectivity and neuron loss in key memory areas of the brain, which has long-term implications for cognitive development (Jan et al., 2010).

Studies in mice show that the proliferation of a cell that plays an important role in myelin production (oligodendrocyte precursor cells, or OPCs) doubles during sleep, and it increases with the amount of time spent in REM sleep. OPC production actually decreases during wakefulness, so adequate sleep appears to be very important for adequate myelin production. These findings may have implications for multiple sclerosis, the symptoms of which worsen during periods of sleep loss (Bellesi et al., 2013).

Sleep also helps us learn and remember better (Karni et al., 1994; Payne & Nadel, 2004; Stickgold & Walker, 2007). In a study of the effects of sleep deprivation on performance in a perceptual skills task, participants who had normal amounts of REM sleep performed better on the task afterward than did participants who were roused during REM sleep and missed some normal REM cycles (Karni et al., 1994). Neuroimaging studies of people learning to navigate a virtual maze show increases in activation in the hippocampus, the brain structure that is central to memory formation and learning (see Chapters 3, 7, and 8). If people sleep after this training, the same kind of hippocampal activity resurfaces during slow-wave sleep. The more hippocampal activation shown during slow-wave sleep, the better the person performs on the task the next day (Peigneux et al., 2004; Stickgold & Walker, 2007). In short, task learning is replayed in the brain during sleep, and this brain practice helps performance the next day. Napping after learning a task may improve performance as well (Wamsley, Tucker, Payne & Stickgold, 2010).

Apparently, it is not just a matter of total sleep hours but also *when* you sleep that matters. Research shows that what is really important is getting sleep at the right time, or getting nested inside the appropriate circadian cycle (Buxton et al., 2012). You can even get away with less sleep than once thought necessary, as long as it comes at the right time.

Third, sleep fights cell damage. When our bodies use energy through the process of metabolism, some cells are damaged. Specifically, when we metabolize oxygen, by-products of this process known as free radicals damage cells, including brain cells (Harmon, 2006). Sleep aids cell function by triggering the production of enzymes that fight cell damage (Ramanathan et al., 2002). Similarly, sleep slows metabolism itself, thereby slowing the rate of cellular damage (Wouters-Adriaens & Westerterp, 2006).

What seems optimal for health is the right amount of sleep—more is not necessarily better. A recent meta-analysis of 16 prospective studies on sleep and mortality looked at the relationship between the amount of sleep people averaged nightly over their lifetimes and death (from any cause). People who slept between 6 and 8 hours a day lived longer than those who slept much less or more than that amount (Cappuccio et al., 2010).

Sleep Deprivation and Sleep Debt   Not only does sleep facilitate learning and memory but it also is necessary for everyday functioning; however, 40% of adults in the United States suffer from sleep deprivation (Dement, 1999). Are you one of them? You are probably sleep deprived if you need an alarm clock to wake up, if you sleep longer on the weekends than on weekdays, or if you fall asleep during lectures (Maas, 1998).

Recent surveys show that the typical adult gets about 6 hours and 40 minutes of sleep on weekdays and 7 hours and 25 minutes on weekends (National Sleep Foundation, 2008). Sleep expert William Dement (1999) developed the concept of *sleep debt* to represent the amount of sleep our brains owe our bodies. It is like a monetary debt that must be "paid back." Simply put, if you get 2 hours less sleep one night, then you owe your body 2 hours additional sleep the next night (or within a few days). Sleeping longer on weekends is a way to pay back a little bit of the sleep debt accumulated during the week.

Most people don't pay back their sleep debt, so they pay in other ways: daytime drowsiness, the use of stimulants (such as caffeine or nicotine), a lack of focused attention, and impaired learning and memory. The most dangerous payback comes in the form of accidents. A high percentage of automobile, airplane, boating, and job-related accidents are caused by sleep deprivation and sleep debt. As many as 30% of all automobile accidents can be attributed to drowsiness (Dement, 1999). When roughly 40,000 people die every year in this country from automobile accidents, more than 10,000 lives are lost due to sleep deprivation. (See Figure 6.11 for tips on how to get a good night's sleep.)

Not surprisingly, sleep deprivation affects mental health as well. Scores on measures of anxiety, depression, and paranoia increase with sleep loss (Kahn-Greene et al., 2007). In terms of daily sleep variations, the effects might not be immediate, and wear and tear might take a few days to show up. Consider this: Barber and colleagues (2010) asked students to complete a daily sleep log as well as online diaries of psychological symptoms and perceived stress in life over a 5-day period (Monday through Friday). They found that a few days of sleep deficiency early in the week, even when people try to offset this debt with subsequent sleep, can contribute to psychological strain later in the week (Barber et al., 2010). Not all sleep loss can be replenished, and inconsistent sleep patterns can wear us down.

Disorders of Sleep   For most people, sleeping 6 to 8 hours a day is a welcome experience, notwithstanding the occasional nightmare or restless night. For an estimated 20% of the U.S. population, however, nighttime is often fraught with problems (Dement, 1999). Let's consider four disorders of sleep: insomnia, sleepwalking, narcolepsy, and hypersomnia.

Insomnia is defined as taking more than 20 minutes to fall asleep, having trouble staying asleep, and/or not feeling rested after a night's sleep for 2 or more consecutive weeks (Krystal, 2005). Somewhere between 15% and 20% of U.S. adults suffer from insomnia (N. J. Pearson, Johnson, & Nahin, 2006). Some sleep experts consider insomnia more a symptom of other maladies than a disorder in its own right, although there is some debate on this matter (Stepanski, 2006). There are many possible causes of insomnia for instance, restless leg syndrome, erratic hours, medical conditions, psychological disorders (such as depression), and excessive use of alcohol (Dement, 1999; Roehrs, Zorick, & Roth, 2000). Iron deficiency may also cause insomnia. This fact might explain why women, who

tips for better sleep

- Go to bed and get up at the same time each day.
- Avoid caffeine, nicotine, beer, wine and liquor in the 4 to 6 hours before bedtime.
- Don't exercise within 2 hours of bedtime.
- Don't eat large meals within 2 hours of bedtime.
- Don't nap later than 3 p.m.
- Sleep in a dark, quiet room that isn't too hot or cold for you.
- If you can't fall asleep within 20 minutes, get up and do something quiet.
- Wind down in the 30 minutes before bedtime by doing something relaxing.

FIGURE **6.11**

SLEEP BETTER. Everyone has trouble falling asleep occasionally. Following these simple suggestions can help you avoid persistent problems with sleeplessness. (Calamaro, Mason, & Ratcliffe, 2009; Higuchi et al., 2005; National Sleep Foundation, 2008.)

Challenge Your Assumptions

True or False? You can make up for lost sleep.

True. It is possible to make up for lost sleep by getting extra sleep. Most people, however, do not pay back their "sleep debt," and it continues to negatively affect their thinking and behavior.

insomnia

A sleep disorder characterized by difficulty falling and staying asleep, as well as not feeling rested.

are more likely to be iron deficient, show higher rates of insomnia than men (K. A. Lee, 2006; Mizuno et al., 2005).

Drug treatments for insomnia, such as the popular sleep aid Ambien, work by increasing the effects of gamma-aminobutyric acid (GABA), the neurotransmitter that decreases central nervous system activity. In this way, sleep aids produce a general feeling of relaxation. Several nondrug therapies, such as meditation and cognitive-behavioral therapy, help relieve symptoms of insomnia as well (Babson, Feldner, & Badour, 2010; Ong, Shapiro, & Manber, 2008). *Imagery rehearsal,* in which one rewrites out a nightmare and mentally rehearses images from the newly rescripted scenario while awake, is effective in treating nightmare-related insomnia (Wellisch & Cohen, 2011). Another nondrug treatment for insomnia is meditation, which can improve sleep even for people who do not experience insomnia (Kaul et al., 2010).

Sleepwalking occurs when a person gets out of bed during sleep, usually during the first third of the sleep cycle, and engages in activities that normally occur during wakefulness, such as walking, eating, dressing, or bathing. People who sleepwalk are difficult to rouse and do not remember having been up after waking in the morning. Because sleepwalking occurs during non-REM sleep, the sleepwalker is not likely to be acting out a dream. Sleepwalking occurs in about 4%–15% of children and about 1.5%–2.5% of adults (Guilleminault et al., 2005).

The main feature of **narcolepsy,** another sleep disorder, is excessive daytime sleepiness. People with this condition may fall asleep at inopportune times throughout the day, often with little to no warning. They may also experience *cataplexy,* a weakness of facial muscles and the muscles in limbs (Nishino, 2007). The origin of narcolepsy may lie in disrupted nighttime sleep patterns. Narcolepsy is often a function of insomnia; EEG studies reveal that people who suffer from narcolepsy show some abnormality in sleep spindles and disruption of REM sleeping patterns. Narcolepsy appears to have a genetic basis. It is most often treated with amphetamines, which help prevent daytime sleepiness, and antidepressants, which can help with cataplexy. Neither treatment addresses the nighttime sleep disruptions (Nishino, 2007; Tafti, Dauvilliers, & Overeem, 2007).

Hypersomnia exists when a person sleeps more than 10 hours a day for 2 weeks or more. Hypersomnia involves strong urges to nap throughout the day, often at inappropriate times, such as during meals or in the middle of conversations. It can be caused by other sleep disorders, such as apnea, brain injury, or depression. Adolescents who commit suicide are more likely to have suffered from hypersomnia than are those who do not commit suicide (T. Goldstein, Bridge, & Brent, 2008).

Night terrors occur when a person, often a child, speaks incoherently and ultimately awakens suddenly in a terrified state from sleep; night terrors may also involve walking around in one's sleep (Smith, Comella, & Högl, 2008). The individual may scream, bolt upright from bed, and appear very confused and frightened. He or she may wake up sweating and breathing very fast, with dilated pupils. The episodes generally last 10–20 minutes, and then the person returns to a normal sleep. The next morning the individual usually has no recollection of the event. Although night terrors are rare in adults, the adults who do suffer from them tend to exhibit higher levels of depression, anxiety, and obsessive-compulsive traits (Kales et al., 1980). To be clear, night terrors are *not* nightmares, which are typical dreams with a frightening plot. Night terrors do not occur during REM sleep and are not associated with dreams.

Nightmares are frightening or distressing dreams. We all have nightmares from time to time, but some people experience nightmares of such intensity and/or frequency that it can cause insomnia, make their sleep very irregular, or form the basis of serious stress. Nightmares are a huge problem for veterans with post-traumatic stress disorder (PTSD), as well as for people

sleepwalking
A sleep disorder characterized by activities occurring during non-REM sleep that usually occur when one is awake, such as walking and eating.

narcolepsy
A sleep disorder characterized by excessive daytime sleepiness and weakness in facial and limb muscles.

hypersomnia
A sleep disorder characterized by sleeping more than 10 hours a day for 2 weeks or more; it includes an urge to nap during inappropriate times.

night terrors
The state that occurs when a person walks around, speaks incoherently, and ultimately awakens, terrified, from sleep.

Sleepwalking is more common in children than in adults, possibly because it occurs during non-REM sleep, and adults spend less time in non-REM sleep than children do.

dealing with ongoing severe stress or trauma presented by adverse life experiences, such as cancer patients (Berlin, Means, & Edinger, 2010; Wellisch & Cohen, 2011).

Dreaming

Dreaming is one of the most fascinating features of consciousness, but what are dreams exactly? **Dreams** are the succession of images, thoughts, and feelings we experience while asleep. The images are loosely connected by unusual associations and not well recalled afterward. Most of us dream numerous times each night, yet we rarely recall our dreams on waking. When people in sleep labs are awakened, they report dreaming almost always if they were in REM sleep and somewhat regularly if they were in non-REM sleep (Bulkeley, 1997; Dement, 1999).

Do dreams have real meaning, or do they simply reflect the random activity of a complex brain? Psychologists from different perspectives disagree on what dreams are and what they mean.

dreams
Images, thoughts, and feelings experienced during sleep.

Psychoanalytic Theory   In *The Interpretation of Dreams,* Sigmund Freud wrote that dreams are "the royal road to the unconscious" (1900/1953, p. 608). He argued that conflicting impulses, thoughts, feelings, and drives that threaten the waking mind are released as a visual compromise in distorted and disguised form by the sleeping mind. In this view, each dream is an attempt to fulfill unacceptable desires or satisfy unconscious wishes.

According to Freud's theory, dreams operate on two distinct levels of consciousness. The dream that we consciously recall after waking up is only the surface level, which Freud called the **manifest level.** The deeper, unconscious level, where the true meaning of a dream lies, he labeled the **latent level.** In his clinical practice, Freud used psychoanalysis to uncover the latent meaning of his clients' dreams in order to help them resolve the hidden conflicts from which their problems arose.

manifest level
Freud's surface level of dreams, recalled upon waking.

latent level
Freud's deeper, unconscious level of dreams; their meaning is found at this level.

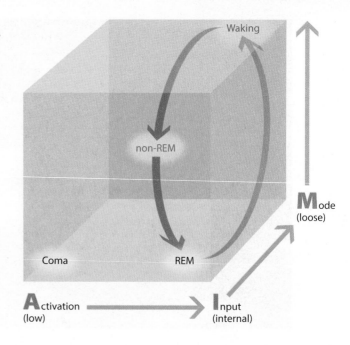

FIGURE **6.12**

HOBSON'S AIM MODEL OF CONSCIOUSNESS. What are the three dimensions of consciousness and their ranges? Each state of consciousness occupies a unique place in this three-dimensional space. Our days normally cycle between waking, non-REM, and REM sleep states of consciousness. (Hobson, 2001)

AIM
Three biologically based dimensions of consciousness—activation, input, and mode.

Biological Theory   One influential biological theory of dreams has been AIM theory, which argues that dreams are devoid of meaning and are a result of random brain activity (Hobson, 2001, 2002). **AIM** stands for three biologically based dimensions of consciousness: **a**ctivation, **i**nput, and **m**ode. *Activation* refers to the amount of neural activation and ranges from low to high activation. *Input* refers to whether stimulation is internal or external. Finally, *mode* refers to the mental state—from logical (wakeful) to loose-illogical (dreaming). These three dimensions (A-I-M) make up a cube, and all states of consciousness occupy a different space in this cube (see Figure 6.12). For example, waking is a highly active, external, and logical mode of consciousness residing in the upper-back-right portion of the cube. Non-REM sleep is moderately active, external, and logical and resides in the middle of the cube. By contrast, REM sleep is highly active, internal, and loose and therefore occupies the lower-front-right portion of the cube.

Cognitive Theory   According to cognitive psychologists, dreams are not that different from everyday thinking. Research shows that some of the standard processes that we use during our waking life, such as imagery, memory, speech, and problem solving, operate in a similar manner during dreaming (Cavallero & Foulkes, 1993; Kahan, 2001). Some people develop an ability to know when they are dreaming (lucid dreaming) and can therefore control the events and outcomes of the dreams (LaBerge, 1985). Others are able to reflect on and evaluate their experiences while dreaming (Kahan, 2001; Kahan & LaBerge, 1994). Also, recall that dreaming occurs during both REM and non-REM periods. Dreaming that occurs during non-REM sleep is closer to waking thought than is REM sleep dreaming—it is less visual, more verbal, and not as loose and unusual in its associations (Dement, 1999; Kahan, 2001).

Combined Theories   Some recent theories promote an integration of cognitive and biological perspectives on dreaming. One such cognitive-biological view suggests that dreams consolidate long-term memories first by strengthening the neural traces of recent events and then by integrating these traces with already stored memories. Dreams also keep existing memories stable, even when new experiences attempt to interfere with older memories (Payne & Nadel, 2004). Particular hormones, such as cortisol, are involved in strengthening these neural connections to consolidate memory. Cortisol levels change throughout sleep stages, with peaks of cortisol matching REM stages of sleep (Payne & Kensinger, 2010; Payne & Nadel, 2004; Weitzman et al., 1971).

Quick Quiz 6.4: Sleeping and Dreaming

1. When a perceptual wall between the conscious mind and the outside world emerges and we are in a state that is immediately reversible, we are
   a. asleep.
   b. unconscious.
   c. vegetative.
   d. minimally conscious.

2. Research shows that sleep functions to
   a. give our cells some energy.
   b. facilitate learning and memory.
   c. facilitate neural growth.
   d. both b and c

3. Dreaming is most active during what kind of sleep?
   a. non-REM
   b. REM

   c. Stage 3
   d. Stage 4

4. In lucid dreaming, people become aware that they are dreaming and can sometimes even control their dreams. Lucid dreaming is most consistent with which theory of dreams?
   a. psychoanalytic
   b. biological
   c. cognitive
   d. none of the above

Answers can be found at the end of the chapter.

HYPNOSIS

Although the Greek word root *hypnos* means "sleep," hypnotized people are very much awake but have little voluntary control over their own behavior. **Hypnosis** is a state of mind that occurs in compliance with instructions and is characterized by focused attention, suggestibility, absorption, lack of voluntary control over behavior, and suspension of critical faculties of mind (Raz & Shapiro, 2002; J. H. Stewart, 2005). People may be more easily hypnotized if they are relaxed, but they can be hypnotized without relaxation (Raz & Shapiro, 2002). Although

hypnosis
A state characterized by focused attention, suggestibility, absorption, lack of voluntary control over behavior, and the suspension of critical faculties; it occurs when instructed by someone trained in hypnosis; and it may be therapeutic.

Hypnosis therapy has helped people quit smoking. This group of smokers is being hypnotized to believe that cigarettes taste like vomit.

about 65% of the population is mildly to moderately responsive to hypnotic suggestion, only about 15% are highly hypnotizable (Hilgard, 1965; Song, 2006). The rest are resistant to hypnosis.

The mention of hypnosis conjures up images of a performer putting audience volunteers into sleeplike trances and then instructing them to behave in ways that are out of character; however, hypnosis is a clinical tool that should not be confused with stage techniques. Numerous studies support the effectiveness of hypnosis for pain relief during childbirth, dental procedures, and surgery. Further, hypnosis may be effective in treating nicotine addiction, nausea and vomiting related to chemotherapy, and anxiety associated with certain medical procedures (Lang et al., 2006; Montgomery, DuHamel, & Redd, 2000; D. R. Patterson, 2004; Stewart, 2005). The therapeutic benefits of hypnosis are not fully understood, but the availability of brain imaging techniques has motivated efforts to document its effectiveness and to learn how it works to reduce pain (Flammer & Bongartz, 2003; Stewart, 2005). We now know that, during hypnosis, cortical areas activated during normal pain situations (during wakefulness) are not activated at all (Vanhaudenhuyse et al., 2009).

It is not easy to offer a general explanation for how hypnosis works, and theorists offer a range of different perspectives. First, some theorists consider hypnosis to be a state in which one part of the brain operates independently. Ernest Hilgard (1977) showed that under hypnosis one aspect of a person's mind can remain aware and open to stimulation from the outside (such as the hypnotist's voice) while other parts are cut off from external input.

A second theory maintains that hypnosis does not alter consciousness, nor do hypnotized individuals give up control of their behavior. Instead, they behave the way they think a hypnotized person would behave. In short, they are role-playing (Orne, 1959). For decades, this was the prevailing scientific view on hypnosis.

Neuroscientific research suggests a different, third, explanation—that hypnosis is not imitation but rather real brain activity. Neuroscientist Amir Raz and his colleagues have studied whether hypnosis might help eliminate the **Stroop effect,** which is a delayed reaction when there is a mismatch between font color and the meaning of the color word (Raz, Fan, & Posner, 2005). The Stroop task tests visual selective attention; it measures how people deal with conflicting verbal and color information. In a typical Stroop test, participants view the names of colors, such as green, red, and blue, printed in different colors and must name the color in which the word is printed. People are slower to identify the color of words that are printed in a different color from the meaning of the word (such as when the word *blue* is printed in yellow ink) than words that are printed in the same color (*blue* printed in blue). The delay in reaction time caused by mismatching color words and the color in which the words are printed is known as the Stroop effect (Stroop, 1935; see Figure 6.13).

Raz and his colleagues (2005) hypnotized 16 people—8 of whom were highly hypnotizable and 8 less hypnotizable. While hypnotized, the participants received instruction on a Stroop test that they would perform a few days later in an fMRI scanner. After the hypnosis session, all the participants received a posthypnotic suggestion, which is a suggestive statement that a particular behavior will occur sometime in the future. Participants were told that during the test they would see gibberish words in different colors and have to push a button corresponding to the actual color of the letters. The words they saw during the test were names of colors.

Highly hypnotizable people who received the "gibberish" suggestion identified the colors faster than the less hypnotizable people who received the same suggestion. Brain scans taken during the Stroop test showed that the highly hypnotizable people had less activity in the areas of the brain that normally process word meaning, so these areas did not interfere with color recognition.

Stroop effect
On a test, a delay in reaction time when the colors of words and their meanings differ.

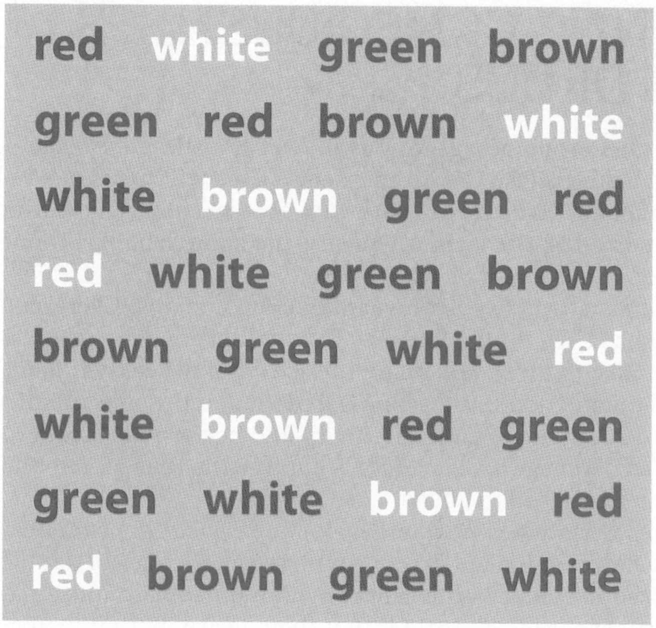

FIGURE **6.13**

THE STROOP EFFECT. Study participants will name the color of the letters more rapidly when their color matches the meaning of the word compared to when there is a mismatch.

Why do you think this is?

The less hypnotizable people were not able to suppress the Stroop effect. In response to the posthypnotic suggestion, the highly hypnotizable people saw real words as gibberish, so they attended only to identifying the color of the letters. These findings support the idea that hypnosis is a real effect in the brain, not just imitation.

Another set of studies addressed the question of whether hypnosis involves role-playing (Derbyshire et al., 2004; Raij et al., 2005). Some participants were administered mild pain, others imagined pain, and a third group experienced hypnotized pain. Hypnotically induced pain activated the same brain circuit as did the real pain. Also, participants reported actually feeling pain for both real and hypnotically induced pain, but not for imagined pain. So both hypnotic pain and real pain activate the same brain regions and produce the same subjective feelings. Imagining pain does not have the same effects. Hypnotic pain, then, is not just an imitation of the real thing. As far as the brain is concerned, it is the same thing.

Quick Quiz 6.5: Hypnosis

1. Scientific research has demonstrated that hypnosis
   a. is a real phenomenon.
   b. is not real but learned.
   c. is only an imagined state of mind.
   d. is something everyone experiences.

2. A groundbreaking area of research has recently demonstrated that, under hypnosis,
   a. hypnotically induced pain creates a subjective experience similar to real pain.

   b. people turn off the areas of the brain that normally process the meaning of words.
   c. hypnotically induced pain activates the same brain circuit as real pain does.
   d. all of the above are correct.

Answers can be found at the end of the chapter.

ALTERING CONSCIOUSNESS WITH DRUGS

Hypnosis creates profound alterations in consciousness for some people. Drugs can change consciousness too. In this section, we will focus on the type of drug known as **psychoactive drugs**, naturally occurring or synthesized substances that, when ingested or otherwise taken into the body, reliably produce qualitative changes in conscious experience.

Psychoactive drug use is universal among humans. Every culture in every recorded age has used mind-altering substances. People use psychoactive drugs for many reasons: to aid in spiritual practice, to improve their health, to explore the self, to regulate mood, to escape boredom and despair, to enhance sensory experience, to stimulate artistic creativity and performance, and to promote social interaction (Weil & Rosen, 1998). Whatever the reason, habitual use of psychoactive drugs can lead to abuse.

Problems arise when people develop a *physical dependence* on a drug to maintain normal function and to cope with the challenges of daily life. For some drugs, repeated use causes tolerance, meaning people require more and more of the drug to get the effect from it that they desire. Withdrawal symptoms are the adverse effects people with physical dependence experience if they stop using a drug. The drugs that lead to physical dependence create the most severe withdrawal symptoms. Alcohol withdrawal for an alcoholic creates many unpleasant side effects, such as delirium tremens (often referred to as the DTs), the symptoms of which may include tremors, insomnia, irritability, seizures, confusion, **hallucinations** (convincing sensory experiences that occur in the absence of an external stimulus), nausea and vomiting, and agitation. In some cases the DTs lead to death.

Psychological dependence occurs when people compulsively use a substance to alleviate boredom, regulate mood, or cope with the challenges of everyday life. People who regularly take sleeping aids to help them fall asleep at night may be unable to sleep without them, even if they are not physically dependent on them. The essence of a compulsive behavior is the inability to control or regulate it. **Addiction** results from the habitual use or physical and psychological dependence on a substance (S. E. Taylor, 2009). People who are addicted continue to use a substance in spite of knowing that it is harmful and often in spite of attempts to quit.

In this section we survey the behavioral, psychological, and neurological effects of the major classes of psychoactive drugs: depressants, stimulants, and hallucinogens (see Figure 6.14). We will consider illegal substances as well as the most commonly used and abused legal ones.

Depressants

Depressants slow down central nervous system activity. Alcohol, sedatives, and opioids (narcotics) are all depressants. In low doses, these drugs generally calm the body and mind. In high doses, they can slow down heart rate and brain activity to dangerously low levels. Alcohol and sedatives increase the activity of GABA, the main inhibitory neurotransmitter in the brain, and decrease the activity of glutamate, the main excitatory neurotransmitter in the brain. If taken during pregnancy, alcohol and sedatives can destroy developing neurons in the fetus's brain, leading to learning disabilities, poor judgment, or mental retardation (Farber & Olney, 2003). Additionally, combining alcohol with sedatives can be lethal. The opioids work differently, as we will see, but they can be equally dangerous. Let's look in more detail at each type of depressant.

psychoactive drugs
Naturally occurring or synthesized substances that, when ingested or otherwise taken into the body, reliably produce qualitative changes in conscious experience.

hallucination
convincing sensory experiences that occur in the absence of an external stimulus

addiction
A condition that results from habitual use or physical and psychological dependence on a substance.

depressants
Substances that decrease or slow down central nervous system activity.

	Drug classification	Short-term effects	Risks
psychoactive drugs	**Depressants** Alcohol	Relaxation, depressed brain activity, slowed behavior, reduced inhibitions	Accidents, brain damage, liver damage, blackouts, birth defects
	Sedatives	Relaxation, sleep	Accidents, slowed heart rate, possible death
	Opioids	Euphoria, pain relief, bodily relaxation	Slowed heart rate and breathing, death
	Stimulants Caffeine	Alertness, nervousness, increased heart rate	Anxiety, insomnia
	Nicotine	Arousal, stimulation, increased heart rate	Cardiovascular disease, lung cancer risk with smoking
	Cocaine	Exhilaration, euphoria, irritability	Insomnia, heart attack, paranoia
	Amphetamines	Increased alertness, excitability, difficulty concentrating	Insomnia, paranoia, accelerated heart rate
	Ecstasy (MDMA)	Mild amphetamine and hallucinogenic effects, high body temperature and dehydration; sense of well-being and social connectedness	Depression, mental deficits, cardiovascular problems
	Hallucinogens Marijuana	Euphoric feelings, relaxation, mild hallucinations, time distortion, attention and memory impairment, fatigue	Memory problems, respiratory illness, immune system impairment
	LSD	Strong hallucinations, distorted time perception, synesthesia	Accidents, insomnia

FIGURE 6.14

COMMON PSYCHOACTIVE DRUGS, THEIR PRIMARY EFFECTS ON CONSCIOUSNESS, AND THEIR RISKS. Only caffeine, nicotine, and marijuana do not carry a risk of overdose, resulting in death.

Alcohol Alcohol is the most widely used depressant. How quickly alcohol is absorbed into the bloodstream depends on a variety of factors, including the amount of food in the stomach and the person's body mass. The amount of alcohol in the bloodstream is the common measure of inebriation known as blood alcohol concentration (BAC). BAC is measured in milligrams of alcohol per 100 milliliters of blood (milligrams %), so a BAC of .10 means that one-tenth of 1 percent, or 1/1,000th, of one's blood content is alcohol. Figure 6.15 shows the amount of alcohol one must consume to reach .08 BAC, which is currently the legal limit for driving in all states in the United States, for various body weights. The figure includes various effects for different BACs.

The more alcohol a person consumes, the more obvious the depressant effects become, sometimes leading to blackouts. These effects are counterintuitive to the loose feeling that many people get in the early stages of drinking alcohol. This apparently stimulating effect occurs because alcohol suppresses the higher social regulatory functions of the cerebral cortex, thereby lowering inhibitions.

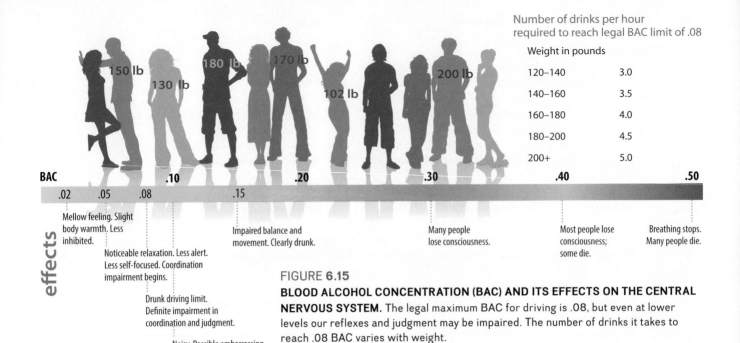

Number of drinks per hour required to reach legal BAC limit of .08	
Weight in pounds	
120–140	3.0
140–160	3.5
160–180	4.0
180–200	4.5
200+	5.0

effects

Mellow feeling. Slight body warmth. Less inhibited.

Noticeable relaxation. Less alert. Less self-focused. Coordination impairment begins.

Drunk driving limit. Definite impairment in coordination and judgment.

Noisy. Possible embarrassing behavior. Mood swings. Reduction in reaction time.

Impaired balance and movement. Clearly drunk.

Many people lose consciousness.

Most people lose consciousness; some die.

Breathing stops. Many people die.

FIGURE 6.15

BLOOD ALCOHOL CONCENTRATION (BAC) AND ITS EFFECTS ON THE CENTRAL NERVOUS SYSTEM. The legal maximum BAC for driving is .08, but even at lower levels our reflexes and judgment may be impaired. The number of drinks it takes to reach .08 BAC varies with weight.

⚙⚙ What other factors besides weight affect how quickly someone passes over the .08 BAC level?

Challenge Your Assumptions

True or False? You can't drink yourself to death.

False: Once blood alcohol exceeds .40, it can be lethal.

Connection

The brain continues to develop throughout adolescence, which makes it quite vulnerable to the effects of drugs and alcohol.

See "The Developing Adolescent," Chapter 5, "Human Development," p. 187.

Alcohol consumption creates numerous health hazards: accidents resulting in injury or death, usually caused by drunk driving; sudden death from binge drinking; blackouts; and increased risk of liver and throat cancers. Liver damage is one of the better-known health effects of drinking alcohol. Over time, heavy drinking, which is defined as more than five drinks per day, leads to fat accumulation and blocks blood flow in the liver. Without an adequate blood supply, liver tissue cannot function properly and dies. Chronic alcoholism causes *cirrhosis*, the accumulation of nonfunctional scar tissue in the liver, an irreversible and eventually fatal condition.

Another powerful example of the interaction between nature and nurture is that heavy drinking over a prolonged period actually shrinks the brain. Brain tissue is lost, creating widespread deficits in cognition and behavior (Mechtcheriakov et al., 2007; Oscar-Berman & Marinkovic, 2003; see Figure 6.16). For example, frontal lobe damage leads to deficits in planning, working memory, and abstract

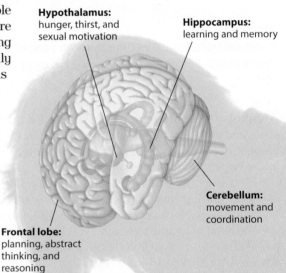

Hypothalamus: hunger, thirst, and sexual motivation

Hippocampus: learning and memory

Cerebellum: movement and coordination

Frontal lobe: planning, abstract thinking, and reasoning

FIGURE 6.16

BRAIN REGIONS MOST AFFECTED BY EXCESSIVE DRINKING. The main regions of the brain most affected by long-term and excessive drinking include the frontal lobes (planning and abstract thinking and reasoning); the hippocampus (learning and memory); the hypothalamus (hunger, thirst, and sexual motivation); and the cerebellum (movement and coordination).

reasoning, whereas damage to the hippocampus leads to deficits in learning and memory. Neurons die from excessive alcohol. When a person is drinking heavily, reductions in both white and gray matter can occur (Sullivan, Harris, & Pfefferbaum, 2010). With abstinence from alcohol, the brain recovers much of its lost volume, especially in the first month of abstinence (Gazdzinski, Durazzo, & Meyerhoff, 2005; Kubota et al., 2001).

Binge drinking is usually defined as at least five drinks in a row for men and four for women (K. M. Jackson, 2008; H. L. Wechsler, Lee, & Kuo, 2002). Some researchers argue, however, that not all binge drinkers are alike and that a distinction should be made between binge drinkers and heavy binge drinkers (seven or more drinks in a row for men and six or more for women; Read et al., 2008). However defined, engaging in frequent episodes of consuming many drinks in a short period of time is an unhealthy pattern of behavior that is becoming increasingly common among college students. About 40% of college students binge drink, and the numbers are rising (National Institute on Alcohol Abuse and Alcoholism, 2005; H. L. Wechsler et al., 2002).

As dangerous and deadly as alcohol can be, mild to moderate alcohol intake, generally defined as no more than two drinks a day, appears to provide protective effects for cardiovascular health. With moderate alcohol use, blood levels rise for the beneficial form of cholesterol (HDL), which has protective effects on the cardiovascular system (King, Mainous, & Geesey, 2008). Although these cardiovascular benefits were initially linked to red wine only, research now shows that many forms of alcohol convey the same advantages (L. M. Hines & Rimm, 2001; Sacco et al., 1999).

Sedatives   Sedatives create a feeling of stupor similar to that of alcohol intoxication. Prescription sedatives, such as barbiturates and benzodiazepines, slow the heart rate, relax skeletal muscles, and tranquilize the mind. Medically, barbiturates are used in anesthesia to calm people down during certain medical procedures and as a temporary sleeping aid. Examples of barbiturates are secobarbital (Seconal), pentobarbital (Nembutal), diazepam (Valium), and chlordiazepoxide (Librium). All these drugs have the potential for both physical and psychological dependence, can be lethal at high doses, and should be used only under strict medical supervision.

Michael Jackson died in June 2009 from a combination of long-term drug abuse and an anesthetic administered illegally by his personal physician.

Opioids   Another class of depressants is the opioids (also called narcotics), a term that applies to all drugs derived from opium or chemicals similar to opium. Such drugs may be derived from natural sources (such as morphine), may be partially synthetic (such as heroin), or may be entirely synthetic (such as codeine). Modern synthetic opioids include oxycodone (Percocet or Percodan), which is prescribed for moderate to severe pain, and hydrocodone (Vicodin), which is prescribed for milder pain.

The effects of specific opioids vary, depending on the form and strength of the substance. Opioids depress central nervous system activity, slowing heart rate, respiration, and digestion and suppressing the cough center. In fact, pharmaceutical companies marketed heroin as a cough suppressant in the early 20th century. Prescription cough medicines today often include codeine, a safer alternative to heroin.

Opioids have been used for centuries as pain relievers. These drugs make use of the body's own naturally occurring opioid systems. Our own bodies produce *endorphins*, opioid-like proteins that bind to opioid receptors in the brain and act as natural painkillers. The stronger opioids—opium, morphine, and heroin—produce feelings of overwhelming bliss, euphoria, and bodily relaxation. The feeling is so good that nothing else matters. As one intravenous heroin user said, "It's so good. Don't even try it once" (Weil & Rosen, 1998).

Generally, opioids (including the newer, widely prescribed synthetic opioids) have a high potential for abuse (Paulozzi, 2006). Contrary to the popular image, not all addicts are junkies on the street. Some people develop an addiction to opioids while being treated for chronic pain (Gallagher & Rosenthal, 2008). Opioids slow the heart and breathing; high doses can kill by stopping the heart and breathing (Hayes, Klein-Schwartz, & Doyon, 2008). For many of these drugs, the amount required to feel an effect may not be that much less than the amount that can be deadly, especially in people who have developed tolerance. Some newer therapeutic opioids, such as buprenorphine, can be taken at higher doses with less risk of overdose (R. E. Johnson, Fudala, & Payne, 2005).

Stimulants

Stimulants activate the nervous system. Although many stimulants are illegal, two of the most widely used psychoactive drugs are the legal stimulants caffeine and nicotine.

Caffeine   If you drink coffee, tea, cocoa, or certain soft drinks (including energy drinks) regularly, you are a stimulant user (see Figure 6.17). Caffeine is the world's most commonly consumed psychoactive drug, ingested by 90% of North American adults on a daily basis (Lovett, 2005). The effects of mild to moderate caffeine intake are increased alertness, increased heart rate, loss of motor coordination, insomnia, and nervousness. Too much caffeine can make people jittery and anxious. Caffeine is also a diuretic, which means it increases urine output.

If regular caffeine users stop consuming caffeine, they can experience withdrawal symptoms, the most common of which is headache. Giving up caffeine can also lead to fatigue and decreased energy, depressed mood, and difficulty concentrating (Juliano & Griffiths, 2004). These withdrawal effects show that caffeine creates physical dependence. To eliminate these negative withdrawal effects, people who want to stop using caffeine should gradually reduce their consumption over time.

Nicotine   The active drug in tobacco, nicotine, is a powerful stimulant. Tobacco is used throughout the world. As of 2008, approximately 21% (45.1 million) of American adults smoked cigarettes regularly (American Heart Association, 2010).

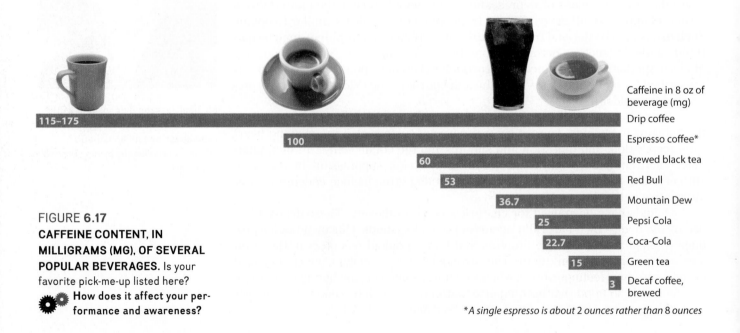

FIGURE 6.17
CAFFEINE CONTENT, IN MILLIGRAMS (MG), OF SEVERAL POPULAR BEVERAGES. Is your favorite pick-me-up listed here? **How does it affect your performance and awareness?**

Caffeine in 8 oz of beverage (mg)

115–175	Drip coffee
100	Espresso coffee*
60	Brewed black tea
53	Red Bull
36.7	Mountain Dew
25	Pepsi Cola
22.7	Coca-Cola
15	Green tea
3	Decaf coffee, brewed

*A single espresso is about 2 ounces rather than 8 ounces

Smoking tobacco puts nicotine into the bloodstream almost immediately; within 8 seconds of inhalation, it reaches the brain. As a stimulant, nicotine increases heart rate and rate of respiration, and it creates a feeling of arousal. Over time, the cardiovascular arousal associated with nicotine use increases the risk of high blood pressure and heart disease. Ironically, many nicotine users report that cigarettes calm them down. This perception may stem from the fact that nicotine relaxes the skeletal muscles even as it arouses the autonomic nervous system.

Nicotine is extremely addictive. It creates high tolerance, physical dependence, and unpleasant withdrawal symptoms. The high that heroin creates is more intense than the feeling of arousal from cigarettes, and the disruption to daily life of the heroin addict is more extreme than that of the smoker, but in terms of how difficult it is to quit, nicotine ranks higher than heroin (Keenan et al., 1994).

There are many known health risks in smoking. Cigarette smoking reduces life expectancy on average by 10 years, increases the risk for lung cancer more than 10-fold, and triples the risk of death from heart disease in both men and women (CDC, 2001; Doll et al., 2004). The U.S. surgeon general has reported that smoking is also conclusively linked to leukemia, cataracts, pneumonia, and cancers of the cervix, kidney, pancreas, and stomach.

Tobacco smoke contains many cancer-causing agents that trigger severe damage to DNA and can inhibit DNA repair in lung cells. Tobacco smoke also contains carbon monoxide, a toxic substance that displaces oxygen in the bloodstream, depriving tissues of needed oxygen. This is one reason smokers often feel out of breath (CDC, 2001; Doll et al., 2004; Z. Feng et al., 2006; Health and Human Services, 2004). Carbon monoxide from smoking also makes people look older than they are, because it reduces the blood supply to skin tissue. Tobacco smoking increases skin wrinkles even in young smokers (Koh et al., 2002).

Cocaine For centuries, South American Indians have chewed the coca leaf for its stimulant and digestion-aiding properties (Weil & Rosen, 1998). The most notable component in the coca plant is cocaine, a psychoactive substance that when isolated from the coca leaf is a much stronger stimulant than chewed coca. When snorted, cocaine increases heart rate and produces a short-lived but intense rush of euphoria. It can also lead to a sense of invulnerability and power. Physiologically, cocaine induces a sense of exhilaration by increasing the availability of the neurotransmitters dopamine and serotonin in synapses (Mateo et al., 2004).

The brevity of the cocaine high helps explain why people abuse it—they keep chasing after a short-lived euphoria with even more cocaine. Some people inject (free-base) cocaine or smoke crack cocaine, a form of cocaine that is sold on the streets in pellets. Along with being extremely addictive, cocaine can cause other health problems, including increased heart rate and irregular heartbeat, increased risk of heart attack, and, occasionally, death (Weil & Rosen, 1998).

Amphetamines Amphetamines are synthetically produced compounds that produce long-lasting excitation of the sympathetic nervous system, the part of the nervous system that keeps us ready for action. There are three main forms, all of which are pills: methamphetamine (meth), dextroamphetamine (Dexedrine), and amphetamine sulfate (Benzedrine, or "speed"). Methamphetamine is highly addictive. The street drug called crystal meth is a crystallized form of methamphetamine that is smoked. Most people who abuse amphetamines get them from health care providers. Common medical uses of amphetamines are to suppress appetite and to treat symptoms of attention deficit hyperactivity disorder.

Amphetamines raise heart rate, increase motivation, and elevate mood. The effects vary with the dosage and manner of use, but other short-term effects may include insomnia, stomach distress, headaches, decreased libido, and difficulty concentrating. Long-term use can lead to severe depression, paranoia, loss of control over one's behavior, and in some cases amphetamine psychosis, a condition marked by hallucinations. Withdrawal from chronic amphetamine use creates unpleasant symptoms, such as fatigue, anxiety and depression, hunger, overeating, and disordered thought and behavior.

Ecstasy The psychoactive drug MDMA (3,4-Methylenedioxymethamphetamine), also known as ecstasy, is chemically similar to both methamphetamine and the active ingredient in psilocybin mushrooms, making the drug both a stimulant and a mild hallucinogen. At moderate to high doses, MDMA produces mild sensory hallucinations as well as physiological arousal. It is sometimes called "the love drug," because it produces feelings of euphoria, warmth, and connectedness with others. Among friends, it dissolves interpersonal barriers and produces feelings of affection and a desire to touch and hug. This effect may be why MDMA became popular in dance clubs, but the greater accessibility of emotions is one reason MDMA has received attention for its therapeutic applications.

New research shows that MDMA can be helpful in the treatment of post-traumatic stress disorder (PTSD), largely because it makes emotions more accessible (Oehen, et al., 2013). PTSD (as we will discuss in Chapter 15) is triggered by a horrifying life event (e.g., experiencing war, witnessing the murder of a loved one, surviving a horrific natural disaster), and those who suffer from it experience anxiety and flashbacks, and they have lost access to their original experience around the trauma, which impedes the treatment of the condition. Further evidence for the effects of MDMA on emotions is research showing that it enhances empathic connection and willingness to help others (Hysek et al., 2013).

The dangers of MDMA include increased risk of depression with repeated use, slower processing times on cognitive tasks, and greater impulsivity (J. H. Halpern et al., 2004). Long-term effects include persistent mental deficits, low mood, and serotonin deficiencies in certain areas of the brain (Thomasius et al., 2006). On the other hand, there may be some therapeutic applications of this drug as well. In a few studies, therapists introduced low doses of MDMA in the treatment of post-traumatic stress disorder, as it appears to help clients tap into hard-to-access emotional experiences (Bouso et al., 2008).

Hallucinogens

The third major class of psychoactive drugs is the hallucinogens. As the name implies, **hallucinogens** create distorted perceptions of reality, ranging from mild to extreme. Sometimes they also alter thought and mood. There are numerous hallucinogens, but we will discuss only marijuana, LSD, and psilocybin.

Marijuana Marijuana comes from the blossoms and leaves of the *Cannabis sativa* plant. People use the hemp fibers for clothing and other practical goods. They use the blossoms to alter consciousness and for medicinal properties. The active ingredient in cannabis is tetrahydrocannibinol (THC), a plant cannabinoid, which affects the brain and body when people eat or smoke it. Marijuana alters mood to create euphoria and changes perception, especially one's perception of time and food. It makes time appear to slow down and makes food more desirable (Crystal, Maxwell, & Hohmann, 2003; Nicoll & Alger, 2004). Marijuana is classified as a hallucinogen, although people rarely

Connection

Our moods are tightly linked to transmitter systems in the brain. Dopamine is released when we feel good, and serotonin affects how sociable and affectionate we feel.

See "Common Neurotransmitters," Chapter 3, "The Biology of Behavior," p. 85.

hallucinogens
Substances that create distorted perceptions of reality, ranging from mild to extreme.

In light of marijuana's known effectiveness in treating certain medical conditions, 20 U.S. states (as of late 2013) have decriminalized marijuana use for medical purposes. California, where Jeff Braun runs a cannabis dispensary, allows patients with a doctor's recommendation to obtain marijuana for personal use.

experience hallucinations when using low or moderate doses. Such experiences occur more readily when people eat it.

Marijuana is not addictive in the physiological sense; it does not lead to physical dependence and withdrawal symptoms the way nicotine and heroin do. In the course of long-term habitual use, however, people develop cravings for marijuana when they are without it, and these cravings have a physiological basis (Wölfling, Flor, & Grüsser, 2008). People can become psychologically dependent on marijuana or use it compulsively.

Many researchers have argued that regular marijuana smoking increases the risk for lung cancer, as marijuana smoke contains many of the same cancer-causing agents as cigarette smoke (Tashkin et al., 2002). One large-scale study, however, found no increased risk for lung cancer among heavy marijuana smokers compared to nonsmokers (Tashkin, 2006). A study in New Zealand, for example, showed a moderate increase in lung cancer in heavy pot smokers under the age of 55 (Aldington et al., 2008). Heavy marijuana smoking increases the likelihood of a variety of respiratory illnesses, can cause immune system impairment, and appears to lead to memory problems (Kanayama et al., 2004; Tashkin et al., 2002). Regular marijuana use is common in adolescents who later develop schizophrenia, which has led some people to suggest a link between marijuana use and schizophrenia in people who might be genetically predisposed to this disorder (Arseneault et al., 2004).

Contrary to U.S. government reports that marijuana has no medical value, marijuana and the **endocannabinoids,** a class of marijuana-like chemicals produced by our own bodies, offer promise for the medical treatment of various physical and even some psychological disorders ("Marijuana Research," 2004; Nicoll & Alger, 2004). Marijuana is known for its effective prevention and treatment of nausea: It has been recommended and prescribed for people who suffer chemotherapy-related nausea or the involuntary weight loss due to AIDS. Research shows that marijuana may help people eat not by increasing appetite but by making food appear more appealing (Nicoll & Alger, 2004). Additionally, marijuana and its derivatives may be helpful for the treatment of pain. Marijuana-activated receptors in brain areas modulate pain and may work more safely and more effectively than opioids (Hohmann et al., 2005). Cannabinoids such as

endocannabinoids
Natural, marijuana-like substances produced by the body.

marijuana and medical cannabis preparations reduce the symptoms of neuropathic pain, one of the most common types of chronic pain (Rahn & Hohmann, 2009), and they show promise in the treatment of migraine headaches. As of late 2013, 20 U.S. states, plus the District of Columbia, had legalized marijuana for medical use (*20 Legal*, 2013). Two states have legalized marijuana completely (Washington and Colorado), and nationally the tide is turning toward more widespread accessibility of this popular drug, which will allow for more research into the pros and cons of using it.

LSD LSD (lysergic acid diethylamide-25), or "acid," is a synthesized form of lysergic acid, which is derived from the grain fungus ergot. People notice dramatic changes in conscious experience when they ingest LSD. These experiences include altered visual perceptions (such as seeing the tracks that your hand makes when you move it through the air or seeing the lines dance about on a page), enhanced color perception, hallucinations, and synesthesia, which is when we "see" sounds or "hear" visual images (see Chapter 4). Neurochemically, LSD appears to work by increasing the levels of the neurotransmitters dopamine and serotonin. Serotonin activity in turn increases the excitatory neurotransmitter glutamate, which may play a role in creating hallucinations (Marek & Aghajanian, 1996; Scruggs, Schmidt, & Deutch, 2003).

The known side effects of LSD include increased body temperature, increased blood pressure, insomnia, and psychosis-like symptoms in some people. Because it can temporarily separate a person from reality, for some people LSD use can lead to panic and negative experiences, known as bad trips. For other people, it can have the opposite effect and lead to very profound, life-altering experiences (Strassman, 1984; Weil & Rosen, 1998).

Psilocybin Psilocybin is the active ingredient of hallucinogenic mushrooms. Experimental studies on the use of psilocybin show that the "trips" can lead to profound spiritual experiences, even in studies where people were "blind" to what they were taking (Griffiths et al., 2006). What is more, the spiritual insights they experienced seemed to be fairly stable, as they endured 14 months following the drug exposure (Griffiths et al., 2008), and mood improvements endured for a similar amount of time (Griffiths et al., 2011). Mood changes from psilocybin seem to be dependent on synapses using serotonin, a neurotransmitter associated with positive moods (Kometer et al., 2012). Psilocybin-related spiritual changes seem to be consistent with changes in personality occasioned by psilocybin experience. Controlled studies of the effects of a single, controlled dose of psilocybin in people who have had no experience with the drug show that the psychedelic experience is so profound that it can change personality, making people score significantly on the basic personality dimension of "openness to experience" from before taking high doses of the drug in just one session (MacLean, Johnson, & Griffiths, 2011). Marijuana, psilocybin, and LSD all appear to help relieve headache pain—in particular, cluster headaches, a type of migraine (McGenney, 2012).

Quick Quiz 6.6: Altering Consciousness with Drugs

1. Even though it can make people feel more aroused in social settings, this popular drug is a depressant.
   a. alcohol
   b. heroin
   c. cocaine
   d. marijuana

2. This stimulant can be as addictive as heroin.
   a. caffeine
   b. ecstasy
   c. nicotine
   d. morphine

Answers can be found at the end of the chapter.

Bringing It All Together

Making Connections in Consciousness

Brain Injury Revisited

Remember David? Today, nearly two decades after his brain injury, David functions pretty well. His most profound deficits are problems with consciousness that affect attention, memory, and learning. By revisiting David's situation and the effects of brain injury on consciousness in general, we can integrate many of the topics addressed in this chapter.

David moved through various stages of conscious awareness in his first year of recovery. He went from comatose to vegetative to responsive in 5 months, but even when he was responding to the outside world, he was minimally conscious. In some cases of brain injury, this is a transitional state to full consciousness; sometimes it is a permanent state. Fortunately, in David's case, minimal consciousness eventually led to full consciousness. His brain gradually became more and more responsive. How does this happen? We do not know for sure. What we do know is that people with damage to lower brain regions that control basic functions, such as sleep-wake cycles, are less likely to regain consciousness than are people with damage to the cerebral cortex (Laureys, 2007). David had cortical damage.

David's consciousness bears permanent scars from his injury. When he is working on a task, David can suddenly become distracted and forget what he is doing. We all experience this kind of distraction from time to time, but for David it can be disabling. He might be emptying the dishwasher and overhear someone saying something about baseball. Hearing the word *baseball,* David might look up and—as a fanatic about baseball statistics—suddenly have some thought about the sport. He will then ask Greg if he knew, say, that Joe DiMaggio had a lifetime fielding percentage of .978. Then he'll head to his room to send an email to his other brother about the same topic. By the time he's finished sending the email, David has forgotten all about emptying the dishwasher.

Such distractibility may be due to problems with selective attention. Indeed, David has a hard time staying on task and filtering out or setting aside information to deal with at a later time. As soon as he heard *baseball,* David thought of Joe DiMaggio and simply had to talk about him. He couldn't set the topic aside briefly. As a result, he lost the ability to continue unloading the dishwasher. People with brain damage, especially to the frontal lobes, have trouble blocking out extraneous information and using selective attention to stay on task

(Ries & Marks, 2005). Some studies show that such individuals perform poorly on the Stroop test, possibly because it takes them longer to process information overall (Mathias & Wheaton, 2007). For David, a related problem is an inability to concentrate on one thing for any extended period of time; he shows deficits in sustained attention. Research confirms that, in general, people with traumatic brain injury have deficits in sustained attention (Mathias & Wheaton, 2007).

Sleeping and dreaming may also change with brain injury. How people sleep while comatose or vegetative may be an important predictor of recovery. People in coma who show more organized EEG patterns during sleep have less disability later and a greater likelihood of survival than those whose brain patterns are less organized while sleeping (Valente et al., 2002). After they have regained consciousness, sleep and wakefulness may be disrupted. David's sleep is not normal. He suffers from hypersomnia, or excessive sleeping. Sometimes he sleeps 14 hours a day; other times he has trouble sleeping at night and naps frequently throughout the day. Insomnia and chronic fatigue are also common in people with traumatic brain injury (Ouellet, Beaulieu-Bonneau, & Morin, 2006; Ouellet & Morin, 2006).

Brain injury can also lead to disruptions in dreaming, probably as a consequence of disordered sleep, though this doesn't seem to be a problem for David. It may depend on the location of the brain injury. Some people who sleep normally following traumatic brain injury nevertheless have problems with dreaming, indicating that different areas of the brain may be responsible for sleeping and dreaming. People with damage to the areas of cortex involved in the integration of sensory information and the limbic system and areas around it or the links between these areas show the greatest dreaming deficits and, in some cases, a total absence of dreaming (Domhoff, 2001; Solms, 2000). Although not dreaming might seem insignificant, many people who experience a total lack of dreaming due to brain injury also lack "initiative, curiosity, and fantasy" in waking life (Domhoff, 2001, p. 16).

Finally, drug use and abuse can occur in people who are coping with the challenges of a brain injury. It is most common among those who experience depression and anxiety (Anson & Ponsford, 2006).

Chapter Review

WHAT IS CONSCIOUSNESS?

- Consciousness is an awareness of one's surroundings and of what's in one's mind at a given moment. It is also the limited portion of the mind of which we are aware at any given moment, sometimes called a global workspace.

TWO DIMENSIONS OF CONSCIOUSNESS: WAKEFULNESS AND AWARENESS

- Consciousness has two aspects: the degree to which we are awake and the degree to which we are aware.

- Three levels of consciousness stem from these two dimensions. First, *minimal consciousness* refers to states when people are barely awake or aware, such as coma and vegetative states. Second, moderate consciousness includes phenomena such as being preconscious, having words on the tip of the tongue, and sleeping and dreaming. Third, full consciousness is a high degree of wakefulness and awareness and ranges from normal waking states to states of flow and mindfulness.

ATTENTION: FOCUSING CONSCIOUSNESS

- Attention is focused awareness.

- Selective attention is the process by which we filter out unwanted stimuli while focusing on other stimuli. It can result in inattentional blindness, the failure to notice the unexpected. Sustained attention is the ability to stay focused on one thing.

TRAINING CONSCIOUSNESS: MEDITATION

- Meditation is a form of mental training that can be used to calm the mind, stabilize concentration, or enhance awareness of the present moment.

- Evidence from brain imaging studies suggests that meditation has lasting effects on mood, concentration, and learning.

SLEEPING AND DREAMING

- Four stages of sleep are characterized by different EEG patterns. We move through Stages 1–4 roughly once every 90 minutes during the night. Rapid eye movement (REM) sleep occurs only during Stage 1 sleep, when most dreaming occurs. Most sleep consists of non-REM sleep.

- Sleep is important for three major restorative processes: neural growth, memory consolidation, and the formation of enzymes that protect against cellular damage.

- Sleep disorders affect about 20% of the U.S. population. Insomnia, sleepwalking, narcolepsy, and hypersomnia are the most common sleep disorders.

- Dreams consist of images, thoughts, and feelings that we experience while we sleep. Freud maintained that dreams are attempts to fulfill unconscious wishes. A biological theory of dreams, AIM, argues that dreaming is the result of moderate levels of brain activation and internal focus, coupled with looseness of thought. The cognitive view argues that dreams do not differ greatly from normal waking forms of thinking, as seen most clearly in lucid dreaming.

HYPNOSIS

- Hypnosis is a state of mind that occurs naturally and is established by compliance with instructions. It is characterized by focused attention, suggestibility, absorption, lack of voluntary control over behavior, and suspension of critical faculties of mind.

- Research not only shows that hypnosis has a real physiological and neurological basis but also points to ways that hypnosis may serve as a model for understanding attention.

ALTERING CONSCIOUSNESS WITH DRUGS

- A psychoactive drug is a naturally occurring or synthesized substance that produces qualitative changes in conscious experience. The three major categories of psychoactive drugs are depressants, stimulants, and hallucinogens.

- Depressants decrease central nervous system activity. Alcohol, sedatives, and opioids are all depressants. Typically, people develop tolerance for these drugs quickly, withdrawal is unpleasant, and the risk of overdose is high.

- Stimulants increase central nervous system activity.

- The most commonly used stimulants are caffeine and nicotine. Cocaine, amphetamines, and ecstasy all have stronger stimulant properties than caffeine and nicotine and carry a high risk of abuse and physical and psychological problems.

- Hallucinogens create altered sensations and perceptions. The two most widely known examples are marijuana and LSD. Heavy marijuana smoking increases the risk of respiratory ailments, impairs immune system functioning, and can lead to memory problems. Marijuana mimics the effects of endocannabinoids, pain-relieving substances produced in the body.

BRINGING IT ALL TOGETHER: MAKING CONNECTIONS IN CONSCIOUSNESS

- Brain injury can affect many different aspects of consciousness, depending on the location and extent of the damage.

- As happened to David, brain damage interferes with selective attention, creating difficulties with staying on task, as well as with sleep and dreaming.

Key Terms

addiction, p. 236
AIM, p. 232
alpha waves, p. 225
attention, p. 214
awareness, p. 211
beta waves, p. 225
circadian rhythms, p. 222
coma, p. 212
consciousness, p. 210
delta waves, p. 226
depressants, p. 236
dreams, p. 231

endocannabinoids, p. 243
hallucinations, p. 236
hallucinogens, p. 242
hypersomnia, p. 230
hypnosis, p. 233
insomnia, p. 229
latent level, p. 231
manifest level, p. 231
meditation, p. 220
mindfulness, p. 214
narcolepsy, p. 230
night terrors, p. 230

non-REM, p. 225
psychoactive drugs, p. 236
rapid eye movements (REM), p. 224
selective attention, p. 215
sleepwalking, p. 230
stimulants, p. 240
Stroop effect, p. 234
sustained attention, p. 216
theta waves, p. 225
vegetative state, p. 213
wakefulness, p. 211

Quick Quiz Answers

Quick Quiz 6.1: 1. d 2. c   **Quick Quiz 6.2:** 1. a 2. b   **Quick Quiz 6.3:** 1. d 2. a   **Quick Quiz 6.4:** 1. a 2. d 3. b 4. c
Quick Quiz 6.5: 1. a 2. d   **Quick Quiz 6.6:** 1. a 2. c

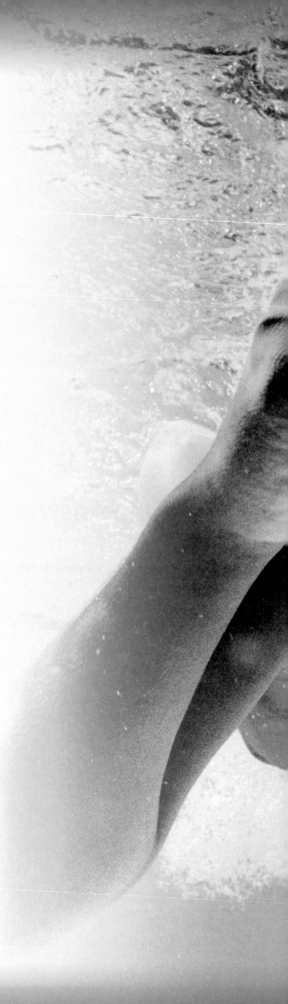

7 Memory

Chapter Outline

Three Types of Memory
The Biological Basis of Memory
Forgetting and Memory Loss
Chapter Review

Challenge Your Assumptions

True or False?

- No one can remember every single day of his or her adult life. (see page 251)

- We can know things we don't remember. (see page 258)

- Drugs can prevent potentially traumatic memories from becoming traumatic. (see page 266)

- Mild electrical stimulation to the brain cannot enhance memory. (see page 269)

- Emotional memories are easier to recall than non-emotional memories. (see page 273)

- Memory of traumatic events cannot be inherited from a previous generation. (see page 274)

- Eyewitness memories are usually accurate. (see page 278)

I magine being able to remember nearly every single day of your life, going back to childhood. Think about that for a second: every single day. All of the good things, the bad things, and even the trivial, everyday things. Most of us are lucky to remember one or two things from a specific time a few months back or perhaps from more than 10 years ago. Very few people, and scientists have only confirmed the existence of about 20 such individuals, can remember some detail of every single day (Elias, 2009). The first known person with this ability, now termed *hyperthymestic syndrome* (*thymesis* means "memory" in Greek), is Jill Price (E. S. Parker, Cahill, & McGaugh, 2006).

Jill Price

Jill's ability extends back to 18 months of age, when she remembers being in her crib (E. S. Parker et al., 2006). Around age 8 Jill began to remember almost every day of her life. By age 14 she could remember *every* day of her life. So if you name any day since 1980, she will have a memory for that day, but the truly remarkable thing is that her memories are instantaneous—she doesn't have to work to recall them. "*November 14, 1981*, a Saturday: My dad's forty-fifth birthday. That night a school group I was joining, the Rasonians, was initiating new members and taking us out in Westwood. *July 18, 1984*, a Wednesday: A quiet summer day. I picked up the book *Helter Skelter* and read it for the second time" (Price, 2008, p. 10). What is equally fascinating about Jill is that her IQ is only average and she is somewhat below average in memorizing lists of words or numbers.

Someone else with an incredible memory is Daniel Tammet, whose abilities have to do with numbers, not personal memories. Tammet memorized 22,514 digits of pi in just 3 weeks. Most people can recall perhaps 7–10 digits of pi without too much trouble (3.14159265. . .), but Daniel carried out this feat to more than 22,500 digits! What makes his accomplishment all the more amazing is that there is no pattern in pi, and he recalled the digits without a single mistake. It took him more than 5 hours to recite the numbers. His "trick" is an uncanny ability to see numbers as shapes and colors. As he described in his memoir, he does not remember numerals but rather a landscape of shapes and colors (Tammet, 2006). In fact, his rendition of how he sees the first 20 digits of pi is presented in Figure 7.1.

Needless to say, Jill's and Daniel's memory abilities are anything but normal or typical. Scans of Jill's brain reveal two unusually large regions associated with kinds of memory, suggesting that her ability is based on the unique size of her brain structures (Elias, 2009). Daniel is on the autism spectrum and suffered a severe epileptic seizure when he was 4 years old, after which his

FIGURE **7.1**

EXTRAORDINARY NUMERIC MEMORY. This is Daniel Tammet's description of how he sees the first 20 digits of pi; he memorized 22,514 digits in just 3 weeks.

abilities with numbers and calculations began. Moreover, because he sees numbers as shapes and colors, he is also a *synesthete,* someone who experiences sensations in one sense when a different sense is stimulated.

However, they both tell us important information about how normal memory works. Jill's memories, for instance, are what psychologists refer to as long-term autobiographical memories, because they involve particular personal episodes or events from her life. These memories are different from the recall of word lists or facts; they involve different parts of the brain. As we will see later in the chapter, Daniel is using a mnemonic device, a method we all use to help us remember a series of things.

What psychological scientists know about memory—both spectacular and mundane—is the topic of this chapter. The following are the three main findings about memory:

1. There are three types of memory (sensory, short-term, and long-term), which last for different amounts of time.

2. Different memory systems involve different areas of the brain.

3. We reconstruct memories from our past experiences, rather than recording accurate images of what has happened.

Challenge Your Assumptions

True or False? No one can remember every single day of his or her adult life.

False: Some people—only about 20 known in the world—have superior autobiographical memory.

Connection

Daniel's form of synesthesia is perhaps the most common form—seeing numbers as colors. Other forms include hearing smells, smelling touch, and tasting shapes. Synesthesia probably occurs because of a cross-wiring of neural connections in the brain.

See "Synesthesia," Chapter 4, "Sensing and Perceiving Our World," p. 151.

THREE TYPES OF MEMORY

Until the 1950s, psychologists thought of memory as one thing. Either people remembered things or they didn't. As we've seen so often throughout this text, a single case in science changed their understanding and made it clear that there are different kinds of memory. The case involved Henry Molaison. When he was 9 years old, Molaison—better known to scientists as H. M.—was hit by a bicyclist (Squire, 2009). He suffered a brain injury, which resulted in severe epileptic seizures. To stop these seizures, doctors removed the hippocampus on both sides of H. M.'s brain, as well as the adjoining brain structures (see Figure 7.2). The seizures stopped, but at quite a cost: H. M. lost the ability to form new memories. He lived forever in the present.

Brenda Milner, the neuropsychologist who examined H. M. regularly for more than 30 years, had to introduce herself each time they met. What makes H. M.'s story even more remarkable is that most of the memories he had formed prior to the surgery, at age 27, remained intact.

Milner's (1962) work with Molaison provided the first documented evidence of distinct kinds of memory in operation. For example, she gave him a standard learning task, in which he had to trace inside the outline of a star while looking at the star in a mirror (see Figure 7.3a). This task is particularly difficult because the mirror image of every movement is reversed. True to Milner's expectations, H. M. had no recollection of doing this task, even though he had been trained on it for days and had even done it up to 10 times in 1 day.

Brenda Milner

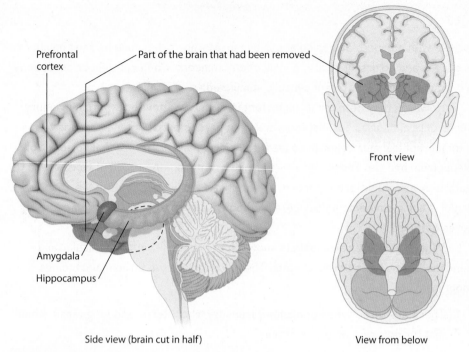

Prefrontal cortex

Part of the brain that had been removed

Front view

Amygdala

Hippocampus

Side view (brain cut in half)

View from below

FIGURE **7.2**

PORTIONS OF H. M.'S BRAIN REMOVED DURING SURGERY. Patient H. M. had most of his hippocampus and the adjacent tissues in the temporal lobe removed from both hemispheres of his brain. (Carey, 2008)

memory
The ability to store and use information; also the store of what has been learned and remembered.

three-stage model of memory
The classification of memories based on duration as sensory, short-term, and long-term.

sensory memory
The part of memory that holds information in its original sensory form for a very brief period of time, usually about half a second or less.

short-term memory
The part of memory that temporarily (2 to 30 seconds) stores a limited amount of information before it is either transferred to long-term storage or forgotten.

long-term memory
The part of memory that has the capacity to store a vast amount of information for as little as 30 seconds and as long as a lifetime.

Each time he did it, H. M. said that it was a completely new task. Yet contrary to what you might expect, some part of his brain knew and remembered the task, because the drawings improved the more often he worked on them (see Figure 7.3b). Although Molaison may have lost the ability to form new memories of his experiences, some type of memory formation must have occurred, or he would not have improved on the task.

How might one explain this contradictory finding? As H. M.'s case illustrates, being unable to consciously recall experiences doesn't mean there is no memory of an event. We are incapable of intentionally bringing into awareness much of what we remember, such as memories that have been put away for some time or memories for how to do things, such as tie one's shoes or ride a bike. Many things we know are outside of conscious awareness. Most generally, **memory** is simply the ability to store and use information. It need not be a conscious recollection.

Some memories last much longer than others. The **three-stage model of memory** classifies three types of memories based on how long the memories last: sensory memory, short-term memory, and long-term memory (R. C. Atkinson & Shiffrin, 1971). **Sensory memory** holds information in its original sensory form for a very brief period of time, usually about half a second or less. **Short-term memory** temporarily stores a limited amount of information before it is either transferred to long-term storage or forgotten. Information stays in short-term memory for 2 to 30 seconds—about long enough to remember a phone number before you dial it. **Long-term memory** has the capacity to store a vast amount of information for as little as 30 seconds and as long as a lifetime. Here reside the memories of your first pet and your knowledge of how to read. As the three-stage

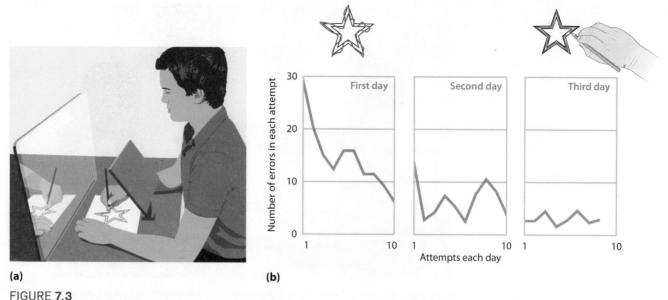

(a)   **(b)**

FIGURE **7.3**

A CASE STUDY OF MEMORY WITHOUT RECOLLECTION. Although H. M.'s memory problems prevented him from recalling ever having completed this star tracing task, some part of his brain clearly did "recall" the task. He got better and better at it over time. (Kandel, 2006. Kandel, Kupferman, & Iverson, 2000)

model suggests, memory formation is an active, dynamic process. Let's look at the stages of memory in more depth.

Sensory Memory

As we interact with the world, our sensory systems are stimulated—we may smell, taste, feel, see, or hear an experience. In fact, two or more sensory systems may contribute information about a single experience, as when we dig into a bag of buttery popcorn while watching a scary movie. In Chapter 4, we saw that sensory neurons respond to sensory stimuli by sending signals to the brain for processing. Sensory memory is made up of the brief traces of a sensation left by the firing of neurons in the brain. These traces last from less than half a second up to 2 or 3 seconds. Sensation is the first step toward the creation of a long-term memory.

Because seeing and hearing are key sources of information for humans, the two kinds of sensory memory that have received the most attention from memory researchers are iconic and echoic memory (Craik, 1979). *Iconic memory* is a brief visual record left on the retina of the eye, whereas *echoic memory* is the short-term retention of sounds. In a simple laboratory demonstration of iconic memory, four digits, such as "5 4 7 1," are flashed on a computer screen for 30 milliseconds. (A millisecond is a thousandth of a second.) Then the screen goes blank. At 30 milliseconds, the information is barely perceived at all. Yet when a blank screen follows the numbers, most people have no trouble recalling them. However, if the same four digits are followed on the screen by "# # # #," people have a lot of trouble recalling any digits and often report that they did not see any digits at all (R. F. Thompson & Madigan, 2005). The presentation of the symbols interferes with the ability to recall the digits. This demonstration suggests that all sensory memory traces are preserved for very short periods of time and are very fragile.

How good are you at remembering names of people after meeting them for the first time? Unless you rehearse them, names often don't make the transition to long-term memory.

Short-Term, or Working, Memory

We often need to stay focused on something temporarily to solve a problem or perform a task, such as getting to a restaurant soon after hearing the directions on the phone. To do so, we put our short-term memory to work. Because short-term memory is a place to temporarily store information we need while working on a problem, psychologists also refer to it as **working memory,** the part of memory required to attend to and solve a problem at hand. When we no longer need the information, we forget it. Although we will use the terms *short-term memory* and *working memory* interchangeably, bear in mind that *short-term memory* emphasizes the duration of this type of memory, whereas the term *working memory* emphasizes its function.

working memory
The part of memory required to attend to and solve a problem at hand; often used interchangeably with *short-term memory.*

Examples of tasks that involve short-term, or working, memory are reading, talking, and listening to someone speak. We use working memory to keep track of what we have just read or what we are about to say, but for only a brief period of time. Working memories can be transferred to long-term memory if they are practiced; otherwise, they are lost.

Short-Term Memory Capacity Most of us hear someone's phone number, repeat it a few times, and then place the call. The number of items that can be held in short-term memory is called short-term memory capacity, and it is limited to about seven items (Feldman-Barrett, Tugade, & Engle, 2004; G. A. Miller, 1956). It is not a coincidence that local phone numbers in this country contain seven digits. The short-term memory capacity of most people is between five and nine units of letters, digits, or chunks of information, but there are substantial individual differences in this capacity. Some people struggle with three or four bits of information, whereas others easily handle 11 or 12 (Baddeley, 2003).

One of the best ways to increase short-term memory capacity is to transform what you want to remember into a smaller set of meaningful units, or chunks, a process known as

chunking (R. F. Thompson & Madigan, 2005). For example, 4155557982 is much more difficult to remember than the chunks of (415) 555-7982. Social Security numbers follow the same idea: 555-66-8888 is easier to remember than 555668888.

How Short-Term Memory Works   One researcher, Alan Baddeley (2003, 2007), has suggested that working memory consists of three distinct processes: *attending* to a stimulus, *storing* information about the stimulus, and *rehearsing* the stored process to help solve a problem. In Baddeley's model, the first process, focusing and switching attention, is carried out by a master attentional control system. This attention system is supported by three temporary storage systems, one for sounds and language (phonological), one for images and spatial relations (visuospatial), and one that provides temporary storage for specific events (a buffer; see Figure 7.4).

The *central executive* decides where to focus attention and selectively hones in on specific aspects of a stimulus. Attention allows us to focus on the task at hand and develop a plan for solving a problem. We are bombarded by dozens of sensations every second. How do we know which are important and deserve our attention and which we can ignore? According to Baddeley's model, children and

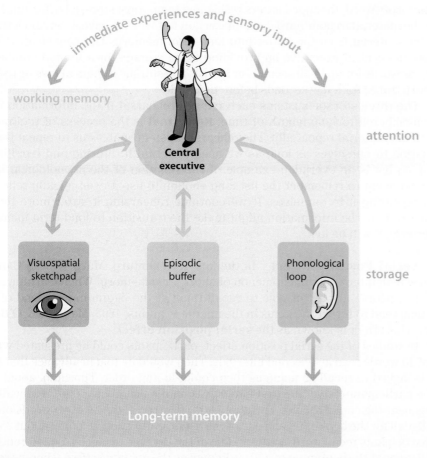

FIGURE **7.4**

BADDELEY'S MODEL OF SHORT-TERM MEMORY. The four components of short-term memory are the central executive, which focuses attention, and three storage systems (visuospatial sketchpad, episodic buffer, and phonological loop). Once our attention is focused on something, we need short-term places to store the relevant information. Images and spatial relations are stored in one storage center; events and experiences in another; and language and sounds in another. (Baddeley, 2003)

people with brain injuries (at least those with frontal lobe damage) have a difficult time screening out irrelevant information, because they lack well-developed or fully functioning central executives.

Once information is taken in and attended to, it is sent to a temporary store: the *visuospatial sketchpad* if it is visual or spatial information, the *episodic buffer* if it is a specific event or experience, or the *phonological loop* if it is sound or linguistic information.

The *visuospatial sketchpad*, as the name implies, briefly provides storage for visual and spatial sensations, such as images, photos, scenes, and three-dimensional objects. Like verbal information stored in the phonological loop, a visual image created on the visuospatial sketchpad lasts only seconds before it fades—unless we attend to it and process it more deeply. Normally, we can hold a small number of images (three or four) in short-term storage. An example is a cognitive map that you visualize while someone is giving you directions to an unfamiliar location. If you are going to find your way there, however, you have to move this map from sensory memory to short-term memory by verbalizing and rehearsing the directions ("left at the stop sign, right at the Quicki-Mart . . ."). Depending on how complex the directions are, you might even move them to long-term memory. The *episodic buffer* is a temporary store for information that will become long-term memories of specific events. You can think of the episodic buffer as being like a buffer in your computer software. When you type something in a word processing program, such as Microsoft Word, the typed letters reside in a temporary store, a buffer, until you save the material to your hard disk, unless you tell Word to save it. Saving it transfers the material from the buffer into long-term memory. The *phonological loop* assists the central executive by providing extra storage for a limited number of digits or words for up to 30 seconds at a time. The storage system allows us to hold memory traces for a few seconds before they fade.

The three storage systems each require rehearsal if the information is to be remembered for any length of time. **Rehearsal** is the process of reciting or practicing material repeatedly. The rehearsal system enables us to repeat the information to ourselves as long as we need to retain it. Storing and recalling a shopping list is an everyday example of the function of the phonological loop. When we want to remember the list long enough to use it, we typically rehearse it by repeating it to ourselves. If we continue rehearsing it, after more than a minute or two, the information might make the transition to long-term memory. Otherwise, it will be lost.

The Serial Position Effect In the late 19th century, Mary Whiton Calkins observed an interesting phenomenon of short-term memory. When learning a list of items, people are better able to recall them at the beginning and end of the list; they tend to forget the items in the middle (Calkins, 1898; Madigan & O'Hara, 1992). This effect is known as the **serial position effect.**

In studies of the serial position effect, participants could be presented with a list of 15 words read at 1-second intervals. They would be told in advance that they will be asked to recall as many as they could, in any order. Typically, about 50% of the participants recall the first two words on the list, about 50%–75% recall the words near the end of the list, and about 90%–95% recall the last two words on the list. Recall for the beginning and end of the list is pretty good, but only about 25% of the participants recall words in the middle of the list. The tendency to preferentially recall items at the beginning of a list is known as the *primacy effect*, whereas recall for items at the end of a list is known as the *recency effect* (see Figure 7.5).

The main explanation offered for the primacy effect is that the items in the beginning of the list are quickly rehearsed and transferred to long-term memory storage, so they are remembered. The items in the middle of the list haven't made that trip to long-term memory yet. The recency effect results from those items at the end still being held in short-term memory. They are therefore accessible. The

rehearsal
The process of repeatedly practicing material, so that it enters long-term memory.

serial position effect
The tendency to have better recall for items in a list according to their position in the list.

items in the middle cannot be rehearsed as more and more items are being added to the list. These new items interfere with the rehearsal of those presented before, which can prevent long-term storage. For instance, if people hear 15 words and are asked to say three digits immediately after the 15th word is read, then words in the 10th through 15th places are no better recalled than words in the 5th through 9th places (about 25% recall). Recall is superior without the interfering task (R. F. Thompson & Madigan, 2005). Recent neuroimaging data support the idea that the serial position effect results from both short-term and long-term memory processes and greater brain activation during early (primary) and late (recency) stages of perceiving stimuli (Azizian & Polich, 2007; Talmi et al., 2005).

Because of the serial position effect, we are more likely to remember the first and last parts of a book, TV program, movie, or commercial than to recall the middle. Writers, directors, and politicians know about this tendency, either consciously or not, and try to place the most important information near the beginning and end of their works.

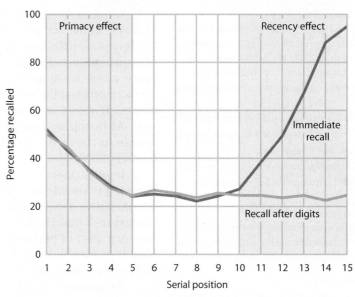

FIGURE 7.5

SERIAL POSITION EFFECTS AND RECALL. People have the best recall of items that are in the beginning of a series (primacy) or at the end of a series (recency). The recency effects go away if people are given a distracting task, such as having to recall digits before recalling the words in a list.

 How might the serial position effect explain our ability to remember some parts of books or movies better than other parts? (R. F. Thompson & Madigan, 2005)

Long-Term Memory

In April 2006, during the centennial of the 1906 San Francisco earthquake, a 109-year-old survivor reported these two memories from that disaster: "I remember the smell of the smoke [from the fires afterward] . . . and the cow running down California Street with its tail in the air" (Nolte & Yollin, 2006). Memories that are 100 years old definitely qualify as long-term memories! Yet according to our definition of long-term memory as "any information that is stored for at least 30 to 40 seconds and up to a lifetime," things that you remember from earlier today—the topic of a psychology lecture, for example—are also in long-term storage. So is information you remember for only a few weeks, such as material for your next midterm exam. Will you remember the material you learned in this course 20 years from now? That depends on a number of factors, but primarily it depends on how often you use or rehearse the information.

Long-term memory is what most people think of when they think of memory. Long-term memory is also the most complex form of memory: There are two distinct types and four distinct stages of processing.

Types of Long-Term Memory People often forget specific things, but they typically do not forget how to tie their shoes, ride a bike, or even add 6 to 12. How is it possible that a person can forget names but almost never forget skills such as simple arithmetic? The short answer is that there is more than one type of memory, and the types operate differently. At the broadest level, there are two types: implicit and explicit memory. How to ride a bike or add is implicit; where you left your car keys is explicit. H. M.'s case, described at the beginning of the chapter, is important partly because it helped psychologists change their long-held perspective on memory by distinguishing between implicit and explicit memory.

Once learned, the skills for riding a bicycle become implicit memories that we recall without effort.

implicit memory
The type of memory made up of knowledge based on previous experience, such as skills we perform automatically once we have mastered them; it resides outside conscious awareness.

Challenge Your Assumptions

True or False? We can know things we don't remember.

True: Many things we know we have no conscious verbal recollection of.

procedural memory
The type of memory made up of implicit knowledge for almost any behavior or physical skill we have learned.

priming
A kind of implicit memory that arises when recall is improved by earlier exposure to the same or similar stimuli.

explicit memory
Knowledge that consists of the conscious recall of facts and events; also known as declarative memory.

semantic memory
The form of memory that recalls facts and general knowledge, such as what we learn in school.

episodic memory
The form of memory that recalls the experiences we have had.

Implicit Memory When we know or remember something but don't consciously know we remember it, we are tapping into **implicit memory,** also known as *nondeclarative memory,* because we cannot directly recall this type of memory. Instead, implicit memory is based on prior experience, and it is the place where we store knowledge of previous experience, such as skills we perform automatically once we have mastered them—how to ride a bicycle, for instance. If asked to describe how we perform these skills, we can't do so very well. Although we can perform many skills automatically, we don't have ready access to the memory of the many steps they require (Kandel, Kupfermann, & Iversen, 2000).

Implicit memory includes procedural memory and priming. **Procedural memory** is knowledge we hold for almost any behavior or physical skill we learn, whether it is how to play golf, ride a bike, drive a car, or tie a shoe. The star-tracing task that H. M. worked on (Figure 7.3a) is another example of procedural memory. Part of his brain remembered the mirror task because his performance improved each time he did it. The part of his brain responsible for conscious recall did not remember the task, however.

Priming is a kind of implicit memory that occurs when recall is improved by prior exposure to the same or similar stimuli. In one laboratory demonstration of priming, people with memory problems (an amnesia group) were compared to individuals without such problems (a comparison group) on a word-learning task.

When asked to recall a list of words they were exposed to, the people in the amnesia group demonstrated much less recall than did the comparison group (see Figure 7.6), but when they were given the first three letters of the words as a prime, or memory aid, the amnesia group performed at least as well as the comparison group (Squire, 1987). What is intriguing about this outcome is that the amnesia group had no conscious recollection of having seen the words before. Like H. M., who was primed by his previous learning of the star-tracing task, people with severe long-term memory problems show a remarkable ability to recall words if they have been primed. Images associated with events such as high school graduation are stored temporarily by the visuospatial sketchpad in short-term memory before making the trip to long-term memory. The emotions that accompany such occasions increase the likelihood that our memories of them will last a lifetime.

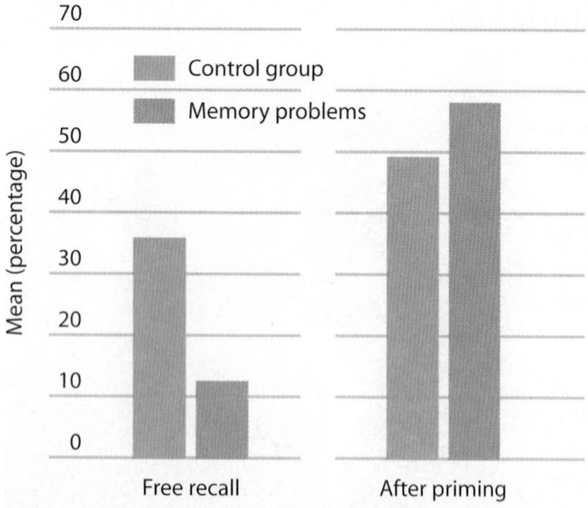

FIGURE 7.6
RECALL OF WORDS WITH AND WITHOUT PRIMING.
What effect does priming have on recall, and does priming affect people with memory problems differently than those with no memory problems? Looking at the figure, what would you conclude? (Squire, 1987)

Explicit Memory **Explicit memory** is the conscious recall of facts and events. Explicit memory is sometimes called *declarative memory,* because it refers to memories that can be deliberately accessed or *declared.* There are two distinct kinds of explicit memory: semantic and episodic (Tulving, 1972, 1985).

Semantic memory is our memory for facts and knowledge, such as what we learn in school. **Episodic memory** is our memory for the experiences we have had. Remembering that Baton Rouge is the capital of Louisiana is an example of semantic memory, whereas remembering your high school graduation is an episodic memory. Episodic memories are more personal and autobiographical than semantic memories.

Stages in Long-Term Memory For sensory input to make the transition from sensory memory to short-term memory and then to long-term memory, it must go through four processing stages: encoding, consolidation, storage, and retrieval. Relatively few experiences survive this process, but those that do can become lifelong memories. These four stages occur for

Images associated with events such as high school graduation are stored temporarily by the visuospatial sketchpad in short-term memory before making the trip to long-term memory. The emotions that accompany such occasions increase the likelihood that our memories of them will last a lifetime.

Associating images with information we want to remember, such as vocabulary words, helps encode the material more deeply. Here, a man is trying to associate an image of a panda with its Chinese character.

implicit and explicit memories alike, but they are more typical of explicit long-term memory, because we more consciously rehearse and retrieve this type of memory.

Encoding **Encoding** is the means by which we attend to, take in, and process new information. This phase is absolutely crucial for storage in long-term memory. Attention drives the encoding process. If we fail to pay attention or try to multitask, an experience is not going to be processed deeply enough to be stored for a long period. In general, we remember visual images more easily than verbal descriptions (Craik, 1979). Why? One explanation is that visual images create a richer and more detailed representation in memory than do words and therefore are more deeply encoded (Craik, 1979).

Psychologists describe two kinds of encoding processes: one that happens with little effort and one that takes significant effort (Hasher & Zacks, 1979). **Automatic processing** happens with little effort or conscious attention to the task. Because these experiences are automatic, our recall of them does not improve much with practice. Furthermore, they are often not processed as deeply and are less likely to be recalled later. For instance, you most likely encoded what you ate for breakfast this morning without trying, but by this evening you may have trouble recalling what you ate hours earlier. Episodic memory involves this kind of automatic processing.

Now think about what you learn in college. You read the text, attend lectures, take notes, and study those notes, usually multiple times. Before an exam, you then go over these materials again and again. Needless to say, this kind of learning takes work. **Effortful processing** occurs when we carefully attend to and put conscious effort into remembering information. Effortful processing is the basis of semantic memory, and it usually involves rehearsal of the information, so that it goes from short-term to long-term memory. Interestingly, advancing age tends to lessen recall for events and experiences that require effortful processing, but not for those that involve automatic processing (Hasher & Zacks, 1979).

To review, memory formation starts with sensory input from the outside world (see Figure 7.7). If we do not pay attention to it, the sensation vanishes and

encoding
The process by which the brain attends to, takes in, and integrates new information; the first stage of long-term memory formation.

Connection

Besides the ability to consciously recall a memory, what other forms of consciousness affect our behavior without our knowing it?

See "Two Dimensions of Consciousness: Wakefulness and Awareness," Chapter 6, "Consciousness," p. 211.

automatic processing
Encoding of information that occurs with little effort or conscious attention to the task.

effortful processing
Encoding of information that occurs with careful attention and conscious effort.

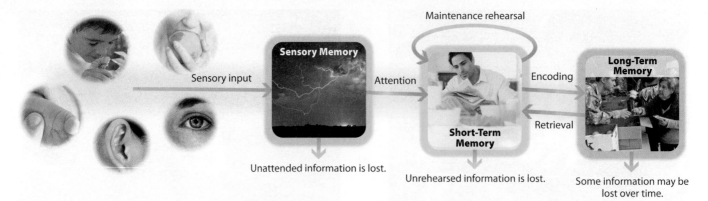

Maintenance rehearsal

Sensory Memory

Sensory input

Attention

Short-Term Memory

Encoding

Retrieval

Long-Term Memory

Unattended information is lost.

Unrehearsed information is lost.

Some information may be lost over time.

FIGURE **7.7**

THREE TYPES OF MEMORY. When our sense organs are stimulated, the nervous system forms a very brief image, or trace, of what we saw, heard, tasted, felt, or smelled (sensory memory). If we don't attend to it, we forget it immediately. If we do pay attention, the information is passed on to short-term memory. Here, if we attend to it only briefly, it will remain in short-term memory as long as we need it, but then it will be forgotten. If we rehearse it over and over, the information is processed more deeply and passed on to long-term memory. If we encode the information deeply, it becomes a long-term memory. Some long-term memories fade or are forgotten over time. (R. C. Atkinson & Shiffrin, 1971)

levels of processing
The concept that, the more deeply people encode information, the better they will recall it.

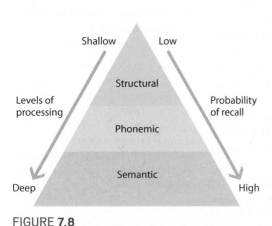

FIGURE **7.8**

LEVELS-OF-PROCESSING MODEL OF MEMORY AND RECALL. The level at which we process information affects the probability of recall. The deeper we process information, the more likely we are to recall it. Structural processing is the shallowest level of processing and the least likely to be recalled. Semantic processing is both the deepest and the most likely to be recalled. (Craik & Lockhart, 1972)

the information is lost. If we pay attention to it, the sensation becomes a short-term memory. Once the sensation enters short-term memory, either it makes the transition to long-term memory within about 30 seconds or it disappears. If we repeat or rehearse the information actively, if we apply some other memory-enhancing technique, or if we experience a strong emotion and the information at the same time, the original sensation becomes a long-term memory.

The connection between encoding and remembering is at the core of the levels-of-processing approach to memory (Craik & Lockhart, 1972). The idea behind **levels of processing** is that, the more deeply people encode information, the better they will recall it. Thomas Hyde and James Jenkins (1973) created a standard procedure for manipulating depth of processing in which they typically presented a list of about 28 words with a 5-second interval between words. To eliminate primacy and recency effects, the researchers ignored participants' recall of the first two and the last two words on the list. Excluding these four words left 24 possible words to be recalled. Participants heard beforehand that they would be given a list of words and should focus on a specific aspect of the words. Participants were not told that they would be asked to recall as many words as possible, so they were somewhat surprised when they were asked to name them.

Based on word-recall studies, researchers have identified three levels of processing: structural, phonemic, and semantic (Craik & Tulving, 1975; Hyde & Jenkins, 1973; see Figure 7.8). *Structural processing* is the shallowest level. When studying structural processing, researchers might have directed participants to focus on the structure of a word by asking questions such as "Is the word in capital letters?" To study *phonemic processing*, or midlevel processing, they asked questions to focus participants' attention on the sound of the word, such as "Does the word rhyme with _____?" *Semantic processing* is the deepest level of processing. Participants in studies of semantic processing were asked to think about the meaning of the words and answer questions such as "Would the word fit the sentence: 'He met a _____ in the street?'"

Results across many studies find the best recall when words are encoded more deeply and worse recall for words that are processed less deeply (Craik & Tulving, 1975; Hyde & Jenkins, 1973; Lockhart & Craik, 1990). Craik and Tulving (1975) conducted 10 experiments in which they manipulated the participants' level of processing with target words (between 48 and 60 words) and found that, the deeper the level of processing became, the better the recall was (see Figure 7.9). The take-away message is that, the more deeply you process material, the better you will remember it. We will come back to this point in our discussion of the role of memory in studying at the end of this chapter.

A common way to encode information deeply is to use mnemonic (pronounced neh'-mon-ik) devices. A **mnemonic device** is a scheme that helps people remember information. Rhyming, chunking, and rehearsal are types of mnemonic devices. Others include imagery and acronyms. Imagery can be used to remember a set of words or a list of objects in a set order. Simply form a mental image of each word or object in a specific place along a route you know very well, such as from your home to your school. Rehearse this a few times. Then when you need to recall the word or object list, take a mental stroll along the familiar path and the visual images of the list should be relatively easy to recall (R. F. Thompson & Madigan, 2005). Remember our discussion of Daniel Tammet at the beginning of the chapter—the young man who could recall pi out to 22,514 digits by seeing the landscape of shapes and colors? These served as mnemonic devices for him.

Acronyms are a type of mnemonic device. We usually create acronyms by combining the first letters of each word or object we need to remember. Acronyms work best when they form a word we can pronounce or some other meaningful unit. For example, the acronym RADAR is easier to remember than "**Ra**dio **D**etection **an**d **R**anging" and "ROY G. BIV" is easier to remember the colors of the rainbow than "red, orange, yellow, green, blue, indigo, and violet."

You might have your own favorite mnemonic devices to help you encode material that you need to know for an exam. If you have never tried this approach to studying, you might be surprised at how much it improves memory.

Consolidation The second stage of long-term memory formation is **consolidation,** the process of establishing, stabilizing, or solidifying a memory (Kandel, 2006; McGaugh, 2000; Moscovitch, 2010). A consolidated memory is resistant to distraction, interference, and decay (Dubai, 2004). As we'll discuss in some detail shortly, new proteins are manufactured in the brain during long-term memory formation, and consolidation provides time for these proteins to develop. Once the proteins needed for consolidation have formed, a memory is beyond the effects of interference and decay.

Sleep plays an important role in memory consolidation. Psychologists have long known that we recall information better after we "sleep on it" than after the same amount of time if we stay awake. Recent findings indicate that not only does sleep stabilize the memory but it also enhances memory and makes it stronger (Walker & Stickgold, 2006; Wamsley, Tucker, Payne, Benavides, et al., 2010). Moreover, sleep deprivation has been shown to have a detrimental effect on memory (Stickgold, 2005). We can conclude, then, that cramming all night before an exam is not the best study strategy. (We'll consider better alternatives in the "Bringing It All Together" section at the end of this chapter.) Research shows that learning over long periods of time and evenly spaced sessions leads to better recall (Kornell & Bjork, 2007; Kornell et al., 2010).

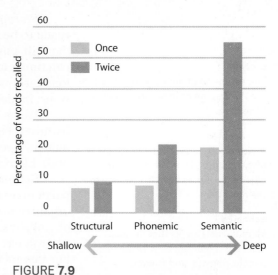

FIGURE **7.9**
RESULTS OF LEVELS OF PROCESSING AND RECALL. These results show that, the more deeply people process information, the better they recall it. If people are presented a word list twice, the effect of depth of processing on recall is even stronger. (Craik & Lockhart, 1975)

mnemonic device
A method, such as a rhyme or an acronym, devised to help people remember information.

consolidation
The process of establishing, stabilizing, or solidifying a memory; the second stage of long-term memory formation.

storage
The retention of memory over time;
the third stage of long-term memory
formation.

hierarchies
A way of organizing related pieces
of information from the most specific feature they have in common to
the most general.

schemas
Mental frameworks that develop
from our experiences with particular
people, objects, and events.

associative network
A chain of associations between
related concepts.

Storage Once memories have been encoded and consolidated, they are ready to be stored. Storing a memory is akin to putting something—say, a birthday gift purchased months ahead of time—away in a special place where you can find it later. **Storage,** the retention of memory over time, is the third stage of long-term memory formation. We organize and store memories in at least three ways: in hierarchies, schemas, and networks.

We use **hierarchies** to organize related information from the most specific feature they have in common to the most general. An example is the hierarchy human (specific), hominid (less specific), primate, mammal, and animal (general). Each step moves to a more general category in the hierarchy.

Schemas are mental frameworks that develop from our experiences with particular objects or events. They act as a filter through which we encode and organize information about our world. Once formed, schemas tell us how people, objects, and events are most likely to look or act. Because schemas help us organize and understand experiences, they can also aid memory and recall. For instance, if your favorite childhood pet was a Chihuahua, your schema of Chihuahuas would be a very positive one that predisposes you to expect other Chihuahuas to act as friendly and fun-loving as yours did. Because you had so many happy experiences with your Chihuahua as a child, when you see one now you are able to most easily remember the enjoyable experiences you had with your own pet. Likewise, you are less likely to remember the negative and aggressive experiences you may have had with your dog, because they do not fit your schema of the happy Chihuahua. For better and for worse, schemas bias our memory and perception.

Hierarchies and concepts bring order and organization to our perceptions and experiences. The psychological process that binds concepts together is *association.* Associations are linked together in networks by their degree of closeness or relatedness (Hopfield, 1982). An **associative network** is a chain of associations between related concepts. Each concept or association in a network is referred to as a *node.* The links between the nodes are associations. When people think of a concept, and its node is activated, they are primed and more likely to make an association to a nearby concept or node (Collins & Loftus, 1975). Figure 7.10 illustrates an associative network for the concept of fire engine. "Fire engine" activates both vehicle and color networks of association, and it may well activate others not shown here (such as emergency).

Neural networks also use associations to explain how memory works. Unlike associative networks, *neural networks* are computer models that imitate the way neurons talk to each other (Chappell & Humphreys, 1994). Neural networks have nodes, too, but their nodes are not single concepts, such as colors or vehicles. Rather, these nodes are information-processing units. Neural networks are analogous to the nervous system, where the nodes in a network are single cells (neurons) that can process

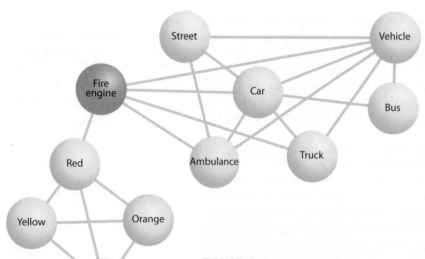

FIGURE **7.10**

AN ASSOCIATIVE NETWORK. Associative networks are chains of association between related concepts or nodes that get activated. The closer concepts are to each other, the more directly related they are and the more likely they are to activate the other node. The network for "fire engine" is a rich associative network of related concepts. (Collins & Loftus, 1975)

information. The more the nodes in a neural network communicate with each other, the stronger the link between nodes. As we will discuss later in this chapter and in the next, repeated connection between neurons leads to stronger connections, as well as stronger memories and learning (Hebb, 1949).

Well-known models of memory storage that integrate associative and neural networks are parallel distributed processing. *Parallel distributed processing (PDP)* models propose that associations involve the simultaneous activity of many nodes (McClelland, 1988; McClelland & Rogers, 2003; McClelland & Rumelhart, 1985). Many nodes can fire at the same time, spreading or distributing activation to other nodes in the network. This spread of activation can serve a priming function, making certain memories more likely than others to be stored. Recent work in neuroscience reveals that such PDP models may do a good job of explaining how neurons and genes work together to store new long-term memories (Mendelsohn, Furman, & Dudai, 2010; Miyashita et al., 2008).

Retrieval The work of encoding, consolidating, and storing memories would be wasted if we could not retrieve information when we needed it, which is the fourth stage of long-term memory. **Retrieval** is the recovery of information stored in memory. It's remembering where you put that birthday gift you bought early—or that you even bought one—when it comes time to present it to your friend. The ease of retrieval and the time frame over which we can recall a particular event or piece of knowledge is determined by the previous stages of memory. How did we encode it? Did we consolidate it? Did we store it where we can access it? Additionally, whenever we retrieve a memory, we need to focus our attention on remembering, which requires working memory. Retrieval, attention, and working memory are related activities.

Implicit memories, such as how to ride a bicycle, are retrieved without conscious effort. Explicit memories are the ones that require conscious effort for retrieval. An example is the date of a friend's birthday—factual information that is encoded and stored for later recall. But factual information is not always properly encoded and stored, and we cannot always retrieve it at will. A common retrieval problem is the inability to remember the name of a person only minutes after meeting her, even if we repeated her name immediately after hearing it. What most likely happens in this situation is that we fail to pay enough attention to the person's name when we first hear it and focus instead on the whole social interaction. Consequently, we do not encode, consolidate, and store the name very deeply. When we try to retrieve it, we cannot. We'll explore retrieval problems in more detail when we talk about forgetting, and later the "Bringing It All Together" section outlines some strategies for improving retrieval.

retrieval
The recovery of information stored in memory; the fourth stage of long-term memory.

Quick Quiz 7.1: Three Types of Memory

1. Suppose you met a person who could remember things that happened well before she had surgery but who was now incapable of forming new long-term memories. What part of her brain was most likely affected by the surgery?
   a. hypothalamus
   c. insula
   b. hippocampus
   d. amygdala

2. The brief traces of a touch or a smell left by the firing of neurons in the brain are examples of
   a. perceptual memory.
   c. implicit memory.
   b. long-term potentiation.
   d. sensory memory.

3. What kind of memory do we use to keep someone's phone number in mind right after we've learned it?
   a. working memory
   c. long-term memory
   b. iconic memory
   d. sensory memory

4. What type of memory allows us to perform skills, such as tying our shoes, automatically once we have mastered them?
   a. explicit memory
   c. procedural memory
   b. declarative memory
   d. echoic memory

5. For sensory input to make the transition from sensory memory to short-term memory to long-term memory, it must go through which four processing stages?
   a. encoding, consolidation, storage, and retrieval
   b. encoding, reconstruction, storage, and retrieval
   c. encoding, consolidation, storage, and remembering
   d. encoding, reconstruction, storage, and remembering

Answers can be found at the end of the chapter.

THE BIOLOGICAL BASIS OF MEMORY

At the beginning of this chapter we introduced H. M., who lost the ability to make new long-term memories after having his hippocampus and nearby brain sections removed. Why was he still able to retrieve memories stored before the surgery? And how was he able to learn the star-tracing task more and more rapidly each time it was presented, even though he didn't remember learning it before?

We can answer these questions only if we understand that memory consists of many different systems, each of which uses distinct regions of the brain (Poldrack & Foerde, 2008; Schacter & Tulving, 1994; Squire, 2009). As noted in the previous section, there are multiple long-term memory systems, and each system involves its own distinct brain regions (Eichenbaum, 2010). One anatomically based model of memory systems proposes three long-term memory systems: procedural-implicit, emotional, and declarative-explicit (see Figure 7.11).

Long-term memories begin with sensations being processed into output from cortical sensory association areas, such as the auditory or visual association areas. Depending on the kind of memory system involved, the output goes to different brain regions. For instance, when we are learning to do things (implicit procedures), output goes mostly to the cerebellum and striatum. When we experience an emotional event, output goes to the amygdala. And when we consciously and explicitly remember personal events (episodes), facts, and information, output goes mostly to the hippocampus. After being processed by the hippocampus, however, the memory is stored back in the cortical association area from where it came.

H. M. had a very difficult time making new long-term explicit memories because of the damage to his hippocampus and surrounding areas. He could learn tasks such as the star-tracing task, however, because his cerebellum and striatum, which are involved in implicitly learning to carry out procedures, were intact.

The overview of sensory, short-term, and long-term memory systems and the brain is this: Sensory memories are processed (encoded) in the various sensory cortexes; short-term memory is processed in the hippocampus and frontal lobes; and long-term memories are stored in different parts of the cortex and subcortex and retrieved with the help of areas associated with the **prefrontal cortex.** The prefrontal cortex is the frontmost region of the frontal lobes. It plays an important part in attention, appropriate social behavior,

prefrontal cortex
The frontmost region of the frontal lobes; it plays an important role in attention, appropriate social behavior, impulse control, and working memory.

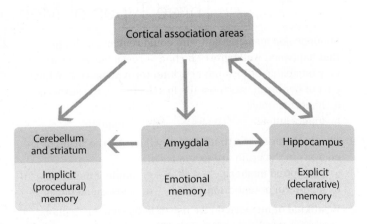

FIGURE **7.11**

THREE LONG-TERM MEMORY SYSTEMS. Memories begin with parallel output from cortical sensory association areas, such as the auditory or visual association areas. Depending on the kind of memory system involved, the output goes to different brain regions. For instance, when we learn to do things (often implicit procedures), output goes mostly to the cerebellum and striatum. When we experience an emotional event, output goes to the amygdala. And when we remember explicit personal events (episodes), facts, and information, output goes mostly to the hippocampus. Those rehearsed and attended-to memories are then returned and stored in the cortical areas from which they came. Think of the hippocampus as being more like a librarian than a library. It processes, organizes, and directs memories and then returns them to the appropriate location in the cortex for long-term storage. (Eichenbaum, 2010)

impulse control, and working memory (Baier et al., 2010). Now that we know something about the three types of memory, we can explore the neuroscience of memory.

The Neural Basis of Memory

In the first half of the 20th century, much of psychology ignored the biological basis of memory and learning, but not all psychologists did. Based on his studies of brain anatomy and behavior, Donald Hebb (1949) developed a theory of how neural connections form and how synaptic connections change with learning and memory. Hebb proposed that, when the synapse of one neuron repeatedly fires and excites another neuron, there is a permanent change in the receiving neuron, the excitatory neuron, or both, which strengthens the synaptic connection. This strengthening process is called **long-term potentiation (LTP;** Whitlock et al., 2006). When synapses fire more readily, learning becomes easier and more efficient.

Hebb further suggested that repeated stimulation of a group of neurons leads to the formation of *cell assemblies,* networks of nerve cells that persist even after stimulation has stopped. The more times synapses in these assemblies fire together, Hebb asserted, the stronger the network becomes, increasing the likelihood that they will fire together again. Simply put, *neurons that fire together, wire together* (see Figure 7.12). Initially, neurons are not connected, but with stimulation, clusters of neurons fire together. If repeated and continued, these clusters form long-term bonds and are consolidated into a memory. What is now referred to as Hebb's law led to another important conclusion from his theory: *Use it or lose it*. If the cell assemblies are not stimulated repeatedly, eventually the synaptic connections weaken and we forget.

No one suspected a link between the hippocampus and memory formation, however, until a student of Hebb's, Brenda Milner, reported clinical observations of Henry Molaison (H. M.). Her observations supported Hebb's theories (Milner, 1962; Milner, Corkin, & Teuber, 1968; Penfield & Milner, 1958). Moving beyond the case study approach of Milner, Eric Kandel and his colleagues were able to conduct systematic research into the biological basis of learning and memory.

Kandel (2001) wanted to study memory and learning in the neurologically simplest animal he knew, the sea slug (*Aplysia*). Sea slugs have far fewer neurons than humans, and their neurons can also be seen with the naked eye. When Kandel's group administered a shock to the tail of the sea slug, it responded with

long-term potentiation (LTP)
The strengthening of a synaptic connection that results when a synapse of one neuron repeatedly fires and excites another neuron.

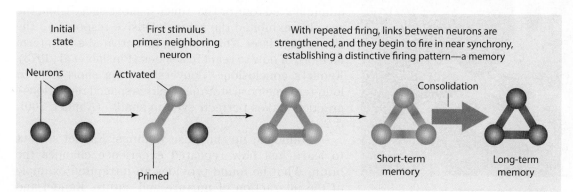

FIGURE **7.12**

NEURAL FORMATION OF NEW MEMORY—LONG-TERM POTENTIATION. (Adapted from Adler, J. [2012, May]. Erasing painful memories. *Scientific American.* Reproduced with permission of Emily Cooper.)

Psychology in the Real World

Manipulating Memory with Drugs and Drinks

We have learned in this chapter how memories are formed from neural connections being strengthened and even from new dendrite and neural growth. The regular and consistent firing of neurons consolidates their connectivity, and memories form from these connections. Cells that fire together, wire together.

As it turns out, there is now both basic and applied research on how and why particular drugs do or do not enhance memory. Memory researchers, including Kandel and his colleagues, have joined the quest for new drugs to enhance not just memory decline but also memory in general. As we saw earlier in the chapter, this research has demonstrated the power of the gene-regulating protein CREB to help form memories (Alberini & Chen, 2012; Stern & Alberini, 2013; Xia et al., 2009; J. C. P. Yin et al., 1995). Indeed, flies bred to have an excess of CREB demonstrated super powers of memory: Instead of needing 10 trials to learn to avoid a scented room, they needed only one trial (J. C. P. Yin et al., 1995). Based on this basic science, others are researching drugs that stimulate the production of CREB and other memory-enhancing

Challenge Your Assumptions

True or False? Drugs can prevent potentially traumatic memories from becoming traumatic.

True: At least in mice, research demonstrates it is possible to administer a drug that interferes with strong negative memory formation. Drugs for humans are still years away from being available.

proteins in the brain (Xia et al., 2009). Clinical trials, however, with humans are still at least a few years away.

A number of memory-oriented biotech companies, however, have started developing memory-enhancing drugs (Mangialasche et al., 2010). These drugs have focused on enhancing memory in general as well as slowing the onset of age-related cognitive decline. The Food and Drug Administration (FDA) has approved two drugs for the treatment of Alzheimer's disease: Aricept and Reminyl. Both of these drugs boost levels of *acetylcholine,* a memory-enhancing neurotransmitter that is deficient in Alzheimer's patients (Birks, 2009; Hansen et al., 2008).

Laboratory research has found drugs that block or dampen the process of memory formation. Why would they want to do that? The most obvious application of this kind of drug is to prevent traumatic experiences—such as abuse, car accidents, or war experiences—from developing into post-traumatic stress disorder (PTSD), a condition in which a person who has experienced an extremely traumatic event, such as being a crime victim or a soldier in battle, relives the event over and over. The way these drugs work is by blocking the protein synthesis that Kandel's lab demonstrated is needed in the formation of long-term memories (J. Adler, 2012; Lauzon et al., 2013; Pittman et al., 2002; Soeter & Kindt, 2010; Yao et al., 2008). Commercial drugs to dampen traumatic memories, however, are still in the developmental stage and are years away from being on the market.

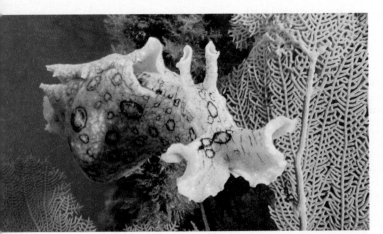

In Kandel's study, the sea slug (*Aplysia*) created a long-term memory of how to react to shock.

Why did Kandel want to use a sea slug to study human memory?

a defensive posture. If the researchers administered the shock only once, the sea slug's defensive response persisted for only about 10 minutes. If the shock was administered four or five times in close succession, the sea slug exhibited the same defensive response to the shock days later. The sea slug had created a long-term memory of how to react to a shock (Pinsker et al., 1973). Kandel's conclusion: "Conversion from short-term to long-term memory storage requires spaced repetition—practice makes perfect, even in snails" (Kandel, 2001, p. 294).

Following up on these findings, Kandel set out to learn just how repeated experience changes the brain. What he found provides an intriguing example of the interaction of nurture and nature. Kandel and his colleagues discovered that repeated stimulation of a neuron actually sends signals to the nucleus of the

Can prescription and nonprescription stimulants and herbal medications enhance memory? There are no doubt bogus and unscientific claims about pills, herbs, and drinks enhancing memory, such as this recent headline from an ad in the *San Francisco Chronicle* (January 13, 2013): "Memory Pill Helps the Brain Like Prescription Glasses Help the Eyes." The ad went on to claim that the pill "helps users match the memory power of others 15 years younger in as little as 30 days!" Contrary to what many college students believe, there is mixed evidence that the nonmedicinal use of stimulants, such as Adderall or Ritalin, improves memory (Ilieva, Boland, & Farah, 2013). The positive effects of these drugs happen only in low doses (Mehta, Sahakian, & Robbins, 2001). Higher doses of prescription stimulants can actually interfere with and block memory formation (Devilbiss & Berridge, 2008). Similarly, caffeine in general and over-the-counter energy drinks (with caffeine and other chemicals, such as taurine) in particular have mixed effects in their capacity to enhance memory (Giles et al., 2012; Howard & Marczinski, 2010). There is nonclinical trial evidence that long-term, regular consumption of foods and drinks rich in a chemical compound known as *flavonoids* can enhance memory and preserve cognitive function in elderly people by protecting neurons, stimulating blood flow, and inducing neurogenesis (J. P. Spencer, 2010). Grapes, blueberries, green tea, and cacao beans (made into chocolate) are rich in flavonoids. The more definitive clinical trial research has yet to be carried out.

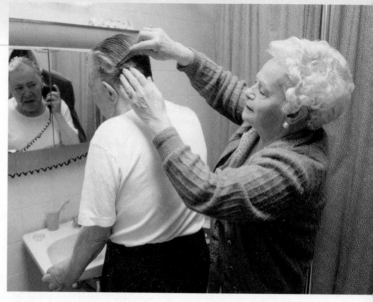

The science of memory has led to some promising treatments for problems with memory, yet not all "memory pills" are equally effective.

Which drugs or drinks are more effective at enhancing memory than others?
Be leery of pills that claim to "increase your mental power." One day, however, Alzheimer's disease and other memory problems may be a thing of the past.

Research on herbal medication and memory enhancement is also mixed. Numerous claims of herbal effects on memory are unsupported, but the most solid evidence suggests that the ground-up leaves of the *ginkgo biloba* tree can be moderately effective in delaying symptoms of mild to moderate Alzheimer's disease (Le Bars et al., 1997). More recent and clinical trial evidence, however, has failed to support these earlier findings (Hirsch, 2013; Vellas et al., 2012).

cell, where its DNA is stored. These signals trigger the production of *CREB*, a protein that switches on the genes responsible for the development of new synapses. Repetition brings about the growth of new synapses, which stabilize a new memory (see Figure 7.13). Both the timing and the frequency of neural firing are crucial in making a memory permanent. By repeatedly pulling away from a shock, the sea slug rehearsed and remembered a defensive behavior. Thus, experience from the outside world (repeated stimulation) changes genes and the way in which they are expressed (Kandel, 2006).

People, too, need to rehearse an idea or a thought many times in order to create a long-term memory. Strong emotions also make memories stick. In the process, our brains literally grow more synapses, thereby strengthening the neural connections—they become different brains. Experience changes the brain, and these changes then change how we respond to our environment. Kandel found the link between behavior and long-term memory that Hebb had speculated about in his model. These findings laid the foundation for developing drugs that help memory and/or delay memory declines in dementia (see "Psychology in the Real World").

Connection

Kandel's findings explain how and why the brains of mice reared in enriched environments are heavier and have more dendrites than the brains of mice reared in impoverished environments.

See "Brain Plasticity and Neurogenesis," Chapter 3, "The Biology of Behavior," p. 100.

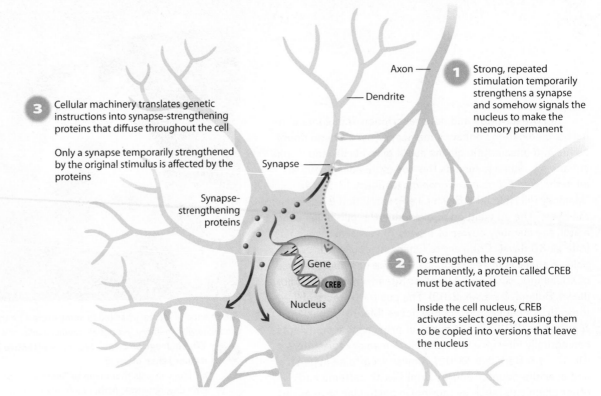

Axon

Dendrite

1 Strong, repeated stimulation temporarily strengthens a synapse and somehow signals the nucleus to make the memory permanent

3 Cellular machinery translates genetic instructions into synapse-strengthening proteins that diffuse throughout the cell

Only a synapse temporarily strengthened by the original stimulus is affected by the proteins

Synapse

Synapse-strengthening proteins

Gene

CREB

Nucleus

2 To strengthen the synapse permanently, a protein called CREB must be activated

Inside the cell nucleus, CREB activates select genes, causing them to be copied into versions that leave the nucleus

FIGURE **7.13**

HOW MEMORIES STICK. When we experience something emotionally important or an experience is repeated over and over, synapses fire repeated neural impulses, as if to say, "This is important; remember this event" (1). These repeated neural firings in turn strengthen the synapse by activating a protein called CREB (2). CREB then turns on certain genes, which set into motion a process that builds other proteins that strengthen the synaptic connection (3). This process makes memories last in our minds, in effect "tattooing" the event in our brains. Thus, the timing and frequency of neural firings are crucial in making a memory permanent—an idea or a thought needs to be rehearsed many times if it is to pass from short-term to long-term memory. (R. D. Fields, 2005)

Challenging Assumptions in Brain Stimulation and Memory

It is perhaps obvious—at least in retrospect—that drugs that alter neural functioning and change gene expression in the brain can enhance or dampen memory formation, but what about electrical charges applied on the outside of the skull? Could they possibly accomplish the same thing? It almost seems like voodoo, magic, or pseudoscience to make such a claim.

There is a growing body of scientific evidence that stimulating the brain with very weak electrical charges can indeed enhance memory and learning. The modern form of this research was so hard to believe to established scientists that it took more than 5 years before a scientific journal accepted the basic finding. The scientist who challenged the field's assumptions, Alberto Priori, put it this way: "People kept telling me it can't be true, it's too easy and simple" (Hurley, 2013, p. 51). Other criticisms were that the charge was too weak to pass through the skull (less than 10 milliamps) or that it was too dangerous. As it turns out, none of the criticisms were true (Hurley, 2013).

Electrical stimulation of the brain in one form or another has been around for more than 250 years. Indeed, Ben Franklin suffered amnesia after

FIGURE **7.14**

TRANSCRANIAL DIRECT CURRENT STIMULATION. A typical transcranial direct current stimulation (tDCS) setup.

 Can very low voltage (less than 10 milliamps) enhance memory formation? How? Growing evidence suggests that it can.

accidently administering an electric shock to his head (Kadosh & Elliot, 2013). Its medical use goes back to the 1740s, and it was used successfully to treat people with depression as early as 1804 (Utz et al., 2010). In the mid-1960s, Albert (1966) was the first to report its positive effect on memory consolidation. It wasn't until the mid- to late 1990s, however, with Priori's work that the modern period of brain stimulation research really took off as a field of research (Priori et al., 1998).

Electrical stimulation of the brain is technically called **transcranial direct current stimulation,** or **tDCS.** The basic idea is straightforward: A very weak voltage (less than 10 one-thousands of an amp or 10 milliamps) is administered via at least two electrodes (at least one positive and at least one negative) placed on the scalp (see Figure 7.14). The technique is both painless and safe (Utz et al, 2010). The research on cognitive enhancement and tDCS has reported that positively charged (anodal) stimulation increases memory in general and that negatively charged (cathodal) stimulation interferes with memory (Brasil-Neto, 2012; Fregni et al., 2005; Utz et al., 2010). More specifically, implicit memory and working memory are enhanced when part of the left prefrontal cortex (PFC) is stimulated (Fregni et al., 2005; Kincses et al., 2004; Utz et al., 2010; see Research Process, Figure 7.15, for more details of the Fregni et al., 2005 study). Research has also shown that transcranial electrical stimulation of the frontal lobe during slow wave sleep improves recall of word pairs (Marshall et al., 2004); and of the temporoparietal lobes improves word recognition memory in Alzheimer's patients (Ferrucci et al., 2008).

The Sensory Cortexes

Our sensory memory system is fairly straightforward. As we saw in Chapter 4, sensory neurons carry information about external stimuli from our sense organs to different parts of the brain. First, the sensation travels to the thalamus, which

transcranial direct current stimulation (tDCS)
Electrical stimulation of the brain.

Challenge Your Assumptions

True or False? Mild electrical stimulation to the brain cannot enhance memory.

False: Various studies support the idea that mild electrical stimulation of the brain can improve memory.

Connection

Why do smells evoke particularly strong and specific memories?

See "Smell (Olfaction)," Chapter 4, "Sensing and Perceiving Our World," p. 148.

Research Process

① Research Question

Does very weak electrical stimulation of the prefrontal cortex (PFC) enhance short-term (working) memory?

② Method

To assess working memory, participants were presented with a letter (A–J) for 30 milliseconds on a computer screen. A new letter was displayed every 2 seconds. The working memory task was to recall whether a letter was the same as one presented three letters previously and hence is dubbed the "three back task."

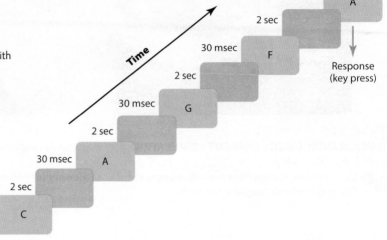

Starting 5 min prior to and continuing during the 5 min duration of the working memory task participants received very weak (<10 milliamp) electrical brain stimulation (tDCS; total time was 10 min). For baseline comparison, participants also underwent the same procedure except with a "sham" stimulation (that is, no stimulation was actually administered). Half of the participants received the active stimulation first and half the sham first and there was a 1-hour "wash out" session in between sessions to erase any effects of the previous session.

③ Results

When the PFC was stimulated total number of letters recalled out of 30 was significantly higher than when during sham stimulation.

④ Conclusion

A brief (10-min) transcranial direct current stimulation (tDCS) of the prefrontal cortex (PFC) does enhance working memory.

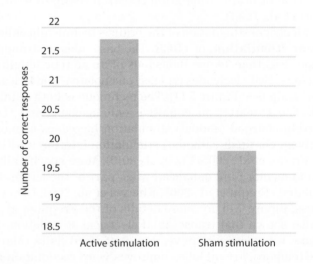

FIGURE **7.15**

ELECTRICAL STIMULATION AND SHORT-TERM MEMORY. In the 2005 study by Fregni and his colleagues, letters are presented for 30 milliseconds (ms), followed by a 2-second orange screen, followed by another 30 ms presentation of a different letter. (Fregni, 2005)

then relays the sensory information to the cerebral cortex for further processing. Three of the five sensory systems have a dedicated sensory cortex for processing sensory stimuli. The visual cortex is located in the occipital lobes, the auditory cortex is in the temporal lobes, and the somatosensory cortex (touch) is in the parietal lobes. Taste and smell do not have their own processing regions, although a particular smell can elicit a very strong and immediate memory, even if it's been decades since you were exposed to that scent.

Pathways of Short-Term Memory in the Hippocampus and Prefrontal Cortex

The prefrontal cortex determines what information in the environment is worthy of our attention. Only then does a sensory memory make its way from the prefrontal cortex to the hippocampus. In other words, the encoding stage of memory formation activates the prefrontal cortex as well as the hippocampus, where the memory is consolidated through rehearsal and repetition (R. D. Fields, 2005; Kandel et al., 2000). The repeated firing of neural impulses necessary to convert a short-term memory into a long-term one occurs mostly in the hippocampus. Memory consolidation in the hippocampus may take hours, days, or sometimes weeks before the memory is transferred back to the cortex for permanent storage. As mentioned earlier, think of the hippocampus as being like a librarian—with aid from the frontal lobes, it processes, organizes, and directs memories and then returns them to the appropriate location in the cortex for long-term storage.

The hippocampus does not do all of the work in working memory, however. Attention and focus require the prefrontal cortex. Remember that key functions of working memory are to focus attention and to plan action. When we speak, read, solve problems, or make some other use of working memory, we rely on the prefrontal cortex to keep the crucial information accessible (Baddeley, 1998; Baier et al., 2010; Kandel, 2006; B. L. Miller & Cummings, 1999; Miyake et al., 2000).

The other main function of working memory is rehearsal. Auditory input is processed and rehearsed via the phonological loop from the prefrontal cortex to the language comprehension center (Wernicke's region) in the rear of the left parietal lobes (Paulesu, Frith, & Frackowiak, 1993; Schacter, 2001). The processing pathway for visual information and the visuospatial sketchpad goes from the prefrontal cortex to the temporal lobes (for spatial information) and then to the occipital lobes (for visual information; Baddeley, 2003). Figure 7.16 highlights the regions of the brain that play a role in short-term (working) memory.

Long-Term Memory Storage in the Cortex

Most memories begin and end in the cortex, but in between, as we have seen, they are processed in the hippocampus, where some are converted to long-term memory. Because long-term memory is the most permanent form of memory, it is also the most complex when it comes to brain activity and location.

We store the different types of long-term memory in different places in the brain. Explicit long-term memories are stored in the cortex, specifically in the area where the original sensation was processed (Ji & Wilson, 2007). Implicit memories are stored in structures in the subcortex, specifically in the striatum (part of the basal ganglia), amygdala, and cerebellum (Kandel, 2006; see Figure 7.17).

When we actively try to recall information, especially words, from long-term memory, we use the prefrontal cortex (Gershberg & Shimamura, 1995; Mangels

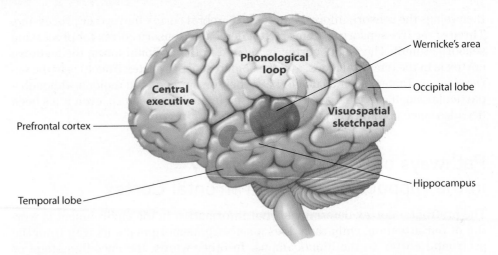

FIGURE **7.16**

BRAIN REGIONS INVOLVED IN WORKING MEMORY. The prefrontal cortex focuses attention on sensory stimuli and holds information long enough for us to solve a problem; then it transfers the information to the hippocampus for memory consolidation. The temporal and occipital lobes, as well as Wernicke's area, are active in the rehearsal of the auditory and visuospatial information needed by working memory.

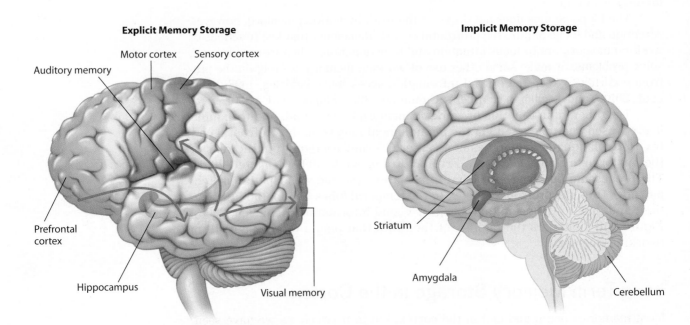

FIGURE **7.17**

BRAIN REGIONS INVOLVED IN LONG-TERM MEMORY. Many different brain areas are involved in memory. The hippocampus is involved in laying down and retrieving memories, particularly personal ones and those related to finding your way about. After being processed in the hippocampus, explicit long-term memories are returned to the cortex for storage in the area where the sensory information was processed originally. Implicit memories are processed and stored in the cortex, the striatum, and the amygdala. (Kandel, 2006)

et al., 1996; R. F. Thompson & Madigan, 2005). Retrieving information requires attention and focus, and hence it involves working memory, which is predominantly an activity of the prefrontal cortex.

Implicit memories are also processed and stored in different parts of the brain. Priming, for example, occurs mostly in the cortex. Procedural memories for skills and habits involve the striatum. The amygdala is crucial for associating particular events with emotional responses, such as happiness or fear. So when we learn to associate a neighbor's house with a mean dog and we become afraid of going there, the amygdala is the part of our brain that is most involved.

Much of what we know in psychology comes from studying questions from different perspectives. Much of what psychologists have learned about memory and the brain has come not from studying normal brains but from studying people who have suffered brain injury. The different functions of the cortex and hippocampus in memory explain why some brain-injured people can remember skills and behaviors but not knowledge, events, and facts. As we have mentioned, memories for behaviors and skills are implicit, and we process them mostly in the subcortex. We process and store explicit memories for events and facts mostly in the cortex. This can occur only if the hippocampus is intact and can pass them on for long-term cortical storage. Even if part of the hippocampus is removed, we cannot easily form new long-term memories.

Damage to the areas of the cortex involved in processing particular kinds of information can lead to deficits in that knowledge system. For instance, damage to the temporal lobe often results in problems with one's sense of direction—that is, spatial problems. In Chapter 6 we introduced David, who suffered a major brain injury when hit by a car. David's injury involved portions of the left temporal lobe of his brain. Since his accident, David can get lost easily in almost any location except his immediate neighborhood, which he sees daily. Even there, he knows that, if he wanders more than a few blocks down the street, he may become disoriented and lose his way.

Thus, specialized knowledge in certain brain regions plays a role in memory for that kind of knowledge, such as spatial skills. This is just one example of the ways in which anatomy and function guide memory. Another example is emotion. The brain regions involved in memory are anatomically linked to those involved in emotion. Not surprisingly, emotion and memory are intimately connected.

Emotion, Memory, and the Brain

Why is it that you can remember in great detail the events of your first date but cannot recall what you ate for breakfast 3 days ago? Generally speaking, emotional memories are easier to recall than are factual ones. Emotions help us encode and retrieve memories. When emotions occur—especially negative ones—attention is focused and details are noted, because emotions usually are connected with events that have important implications for the individual.

As such, these events may be important to recall. From an evolutionary perspective, it makes sense for creatures to have better recall of anything that may have significance for their well-being, as emotional events do.

How does emotion help memory? One way, as we'll see in more detail in the next section, is through biochemical and genetic processes. Emotional events switch on genes that build proteins to strengthen the synaptic connections between neurons. These proteins also stimulate the formation of new synapses and even new neurons (Kandel, 2006). All of these structures make the memory "stick" for a long period of time.

Additionally, emotion helps memory by way of anatomy. Important structures for memory—the amygdala and the hippocampus—are linked to key structures for emotion. These two structures lie next to each other in the brain and are connected

Challenge Your Assumptions
True or False? Emotional memories are easier to recall than non-emotional memories.
True: Strong emotional experiences are often the most remembered experiences.

Challenge Your Assumptions

True or False? Memory of traumatic events cannot be inherited from a previous generation.

False: Conditioned fears are experienced in mice one and two generations removed from the original conditioned fear.

Connection

One of the primary functions of sleep is to consolidate memories and facilitate new neural growth.

See "Sleeping," Chapter 6, "Consciousness," p. 222.

flashbulb memories
Detailed, especially vivid memories of very specific, highly charged events.

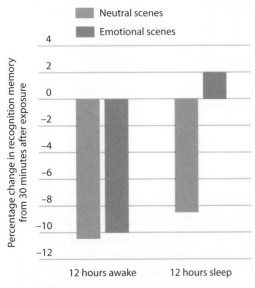

FIGURE **7.18**

WHAT KIND OF INFORMATION HAS IMPROVED RECALL AFTER SLEEP? Only people who get sleep and are exposed to emotional scenes consolidate their memories after a night's sleep. They not only maintain their memories, compared to 30 minutes after initially being exposed to them, but also slightly improve them 12 hours later after sleep. The same emotional scenes, however, are not remembered well if the person stays awake. Moreover, uninteresting or neutral scenes are forgotten both with sleep and staying awake. (Payne & Kensinger, 2010)

by many nerve fibers. Indeed, these two structures become activated simultaneously during emotional experiences (Strange & Dolan, 2006). The amygdala is involved in assigning emotional significance to events and is crucial in encoding information relevant to emotional experiences, especially fear (Dolcos, LeBar, & Cabeza, 2005; Phelps & LeDoux, 2005; Sigurdsson et al., 2007). People remember the visual details of an object better if negative emotions were aroused while viewing it (Kensinger, Garoff-Eaton, & Schacter, 2007). One mechanism through which emotional arousal affects memory formation is the release of norepinephrine (Tully & Bolshakov, 2010). This neurotransmitter makes synaptic connections between neurons more plastic—that is, it changes the structure of the synaptic connections. Neural plasticity in turn is necessary for making the connection between synapses stronger; hence, an event becomes more memorable. Moreover, as unbelievable as it may seem, olfactory memories paired with fear experiences through conditioning—at least in mice—seem to be passed down to the next generations via epigenetic processes (Dias & Ressler, 2013). Second- and third-generation mice have the same fear response to a conditioned smell that their parents and grandparents had. In short, traumatic memories may well be inherited.

In a study on memory, emotion, and sleep, the evidence suggests that sleep helps consolidate memories, especially of emotional experiences (Baran et al., 2012; Payne & Kensinger, 2010). The participants were shown images that were either neutral (such as a yellow car on a city street) or emotional (the same yellow car with a person lying injured after having crashed the car). The researchers then tested the participants' recall of these images soon (30 minutes) after showing them to the participants; the participants recalled about 80% of the neutral images and nearly 90% of the emotional images. Next, the researchers waited 12 hours to retest the participants' memories. In one 12-hour condition, the participants were awake the whole time (during the day, from morning to night); in the second condition, the participants slept for at least 6 hours (from night to the next morning). What the researchers found was quite interesting: Recall declined in three of the four conditions; the exception was recall for the emotional images after sleep (see Figure 7.18). Only when the images were emotionally charged and only after sleep did the participants' recall improve slightly. When the images were neutral or after the participants had stayed awake, their recall declined. Sleep helps consolidate memories, at least if they are emotional memories.

The relationship between emotion and memory is far from perfect. Sometimes emotions distort our memories. As we have just reviewed, emotion enhances memory in many different ways, but the accuracy of these memories is a different story. The details of emotional memories tend to be less accurate than those of non-emotional memories (Phelps & Sharot, 2008). Emotional memories are often held with great confidence, but with blindness to their inaccuracy. In addition, in terms of autobiographical memories, when people look back over their lives they recall the pleasant times rather than the negative ones. So there is a positive bias in autobiographical memory recall. The "good ol' days" are good partly because we remember the good more readily than we remember the bad (Walker, Skowronski, & Thompson, 2003).

No doubt there are certain powerful events you remember vividly. For instance, most people remember exactly what they were doing when two jets flew into the World Trade Center towers on September 11, 2001. Your authors also know exactly what they were doing when they heard John Lennon was killed (Erika was doing her American history homework, in her red chenille bathrobe, when her brother told her of the announcement on *Monday Night Football*).

Such detailed, especially vivid memories of very specific, highly charged events are known as **flashbulb memories,** in reference to how they are experienced and recalled like snapshot pictures (R. Brown & Kulik, 1977). These recollections tend to be highly charged with emotion, which marks them for recall in some way. For years people thought flashbulb memories were more accurate than less emotional memories, but we now know that this is not true. Rather than being accurate representations of specific emotional events, the emotion makes every aspect of the event more susceptible to the reconstructive process of memory formation, bringing irrelevant as well as relevant information into the recollection (Lanciano, Curci, & Semin, 2010). As such, flashbulb memories are really just special cases of emotional memories.

The importance of the amygdala in making emotional events memorable is seen in people with damaged amygdalas. They do not recall emotional events better than non-emotional events (Adolphs et al., 1997). In fact, there is evidence that amygdala damage can impair memories for the overall feeling of an event, but not for details. The details are still there, but the emotional accent is gone (Adolphs, Tranel, & Buchanan, 2005). Moreover, damage to the left amygdala results in deficits in verbal recall of emotional events (Buchanan et al., 2001).

We do not have normal recall of traumatic events—those that are extremely stressful or horrifying. We may recall such events quite vividly or not at all, or we may alternate between recollection and memory loss. But stress may both enhance the encoding of information and impair the retrieval of emotional memories (Buchanan & Tranel, 2008). For example, refugees who have endured extreme emotional stress show impaired recall of specific episodic memories; cancer survivors with PTSD show impaired semantic memory (Moradi et al., 2008). It is possible that the loss of autobiographical memory is a way of regulating or coping with extreme emotional stress.

Not all battle scars are physical. Post-traumatic stress disorder (PTSD), a condition that forces sufferers to relive terrifying events over and over, makes readjusting to civilian life difficult for an increasing number of war veterans. After returning to the United States from Iraq, this soldier was diagnosed with PTSD.

Quick Quiz 7.2: The Biological Basis of Memory

1. When we actively try to recall information, especially words, from long-term memory, we use the
   a. occipital cortex.
   b. prefrontal cortex.
   c. parietal cortex.
   d. parahippocampal gyrus.

2. Rehearsal makes memories stick. So does
   a. drunkenness.
   b. storage.
   c. emotion.
   d. fatigue.

3. Neurons that _____ together, _____ together.
   a. grow; sow
   b. lie; die
   c. synapse; degrade
   d. fire; wire

4. One sea slug had frequent and closely-spaced-in-time puffs of air administered to it. Another had frequent puffs but they were not closely spaced. Yet another slug had one puff administered to it. Which one is most likely to remember this aversive event?
   a. the one with frequent and closely spaced air puffs
   b. the one with frequent but not closely spaced air puffs
   c. the one with one air puff
   d. They all are equally likely to remember the event.

5. CREB is a(n) _____ that switches on genes responsible for the development of new synapses.
   a. amino acid
   b. protein
   c. neurotransmitter
   d. enzyme

6. For which of the following is there at least some scientific evidence that it can enhance memory?
   a. caffeine
   b. ginkgo biloba
   c. drugs that enhance the protein CREB
   d. all of the above

Answers can be found at the end of the chapter.

FORGETTING AND MEMORY LOSS

forgetting
The weakening or loss of memories over time.

So far we have discussed two of the three principles of memory: There are three types of memory, and different types of memory involve different areas of the brain. Here we examine the third principle: Memory and **forgetting** are much more of a subjective and reconstructive process than an objective one. It is all too easy to think of the mind as an objective recorder of events, but human memory is not an objective recorder of experience. In the process of remembering, we select, distort, bias, and forget events (Levy, Kuhl, & Wagner, 2010; Schacter, 2001).

Forms of Forgetting

interference
Disruption of memory that occurs when other information competes with the information we are trying to recall.

retroactive interference
Disruption of memory that occurs when new experiences or information cause people to forget previously learned experiences or information.

proactive interference
Disruption of memory that occurs when previously learned information interferes with the learning of new information.

forgetting curve
A graphic depiction of how recall steadily declines over time.

absent-mindedness
A form of forgetfulness that results from inattention.

One reason we forget is **interference,** which occurs when other information competes with the information we are trying to recall. Interference can happen in one of two ways (Jacoby, Hessels, & Bopp, 2001). First, **retroactive interference** occurs when new experiences or information cause people to forget previously learned experiences or information. Memory's vulnerability to interference from information that follows immediately after an event has profound applications. For example, the recall of a crime by an eyewitness, even if only minutes after the crime (which it usually is not), will be distorted by the events that occur in those few minutes (or hours or days or weeks) after the crime. A second type of interference, **proactive interference,** occurs when previously learned information interferes with the learning of new information. Perhaps the serial position effect occurs because the process of remembering the first words interferes proactively with recall of the middle words.

Research on forgetting began in the 1880s with Herman Ebbinghaus, who found that recall shows a steady decline over time (Erdelyi, 2010). This decline is what is now called Ebbinghaus's **forgetting curve.** A classic demonstration of the forgetting curve comes from the work of Norman Slamecka and Brian McElree (1983). Participants in their research were given a long list of words to learn. Some saw the list once; others saw it three times. Moreover, some were asked to recall the list either immediately or 1, 2, 3, or 4 days later. When Slamecka and McElree plotted the results, they produced the classic forgetting curve. Recall was between 70% and 80% immediately, but it declined steadily for each additional day between learning and recalling the word list (see Figure 7.19). It is noteworthy that seeing the list three times, compared to once, increased recall only a little bit.

Most normal forgetting occurs because we don't pay close attention when we first learn or experience something, so we never encode or consolidate the memory very well. In contrast, **absent-mindedness** is a form of forgetfulness that involves attention as well as memory (Cheyne, Carriere, & Smilek, 2006; Robertson, 2003). For example, Sandra is distraught over not being able to find her keys. After spending 10 minutes looking all over the house in all of the obvious places, she finally goes out the front door to the car, only to discover that the keys are still in the lock to the house. Such experiences happen when we do not pay close attention or we divide our attention among different tasks.

Divided attention is likely to lead to absent-mindedness. Talking on your cell phone while writing an email can only lead to poor encoding of the phone conversation, the email, or both. You are much less likely to remember things if you try to multitask. Paying attention is crucial to long-term recall.

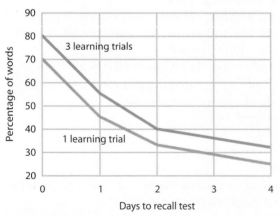

FIGURE **7.19**

THE FORGETTING CURVE. Forgetting happens in a predictable way over time. The forgetting curve shows that, with each passing day, we remember less, though the rate of decline slows. (Slamecka & McElree, 1983)

Absent-mindedness increases with age, but it typically is not a problem until people reach their 70s (Schacter, 2001). Due to the slowing of processing speed and less ability to filter out irrelevant information with age, some degree of dementia or age-related memory decline is common in people in their 60s and 70s (Salthouse, 2000; Van Gerven et al., 2007). As is true with all cognitive capacities, there are vast differences among individuals in memory decline with age. Some people show little decline into their 90s, while others begin to experience it in their 40s.

Education seems to have a positive effect on age-related decline. Schmand and colleagues (1997) discovered that, when trying to recall a list of words 30 minutes after learning them, people in their early to mid-80s with low education recalled less than 50% of the words, whereas those in the same age group with high education recalled about 60% of the words. One of the few cross-cultural studies to compare age-related memory decline found no cultural differences in the effect (Crook et al., 1992). Age-related memory decline, in other words, appears to be universal (Matsumoto & Juang, 2004).

Another form of forgetting is **blocking,** or the inability to retrieve some information that once was stored—say, a person's name or an old phone number (Schacter, 2001). It simply won't resurface, despite our efforts. One example of blocking is the frustrating *tip-of-the-tongue* phenomenon in which we can almost recall something but the memory eludes us. We might even know that the word begins with a particular letter. We say to ourselves, I know it! It's right there. I can even see her face. Her name begins with an *M*. More often than not, it does begin with that letter. **Repression,** in which the retrieval of memories that have been encoded and stored is actively inhibited, is another example of blocking. Memories of a traumatic experience are more likely to be repressed than are other memories. The implication is that, under the right circumstances—during psychotherapy, for instance—the person may suddenly remember the repressed event. We come back to this topic in the next section when we discuss "recovered memories."

A final form of misremembering or forgetting is **suggestibility,** which occurs when memories are implanted in our minds based on leading questions, comments, or suggestions from someone else or some other source. We are most prone to suggestions that are present in the interval between our original experience and the time we are asked to recall it.

Elizabeth Loftus has conducted the most systematic research on two major types of memory distortion: eyewitness testimony and false and recovered memories. Her findings changed our understanding of how memory works. Eyewitness testimony may be the deciding evidence presented at a trial, so the reliability of eyewitnesses' recall is a central concern for judges, lawyers, and jurors. Historically, lawyers and jurors have been prone to believe the testimony of eyewitnesses unless it was contradicted by firm, hard evidence. Loftus and her colleagues, however, were among the first memory researchers to demonstrate that people's memories of events, even under the best of circumstances, are not very accurate and are susceptible to suggestion (E. Loftus, 1996, 2003). In one classic study, Loftus and her colleagues showed participants an event on videotape and then asked them to answer questions, some of which contained misleading suggestions about the event they had just witnessed. A misleading suggestion, for instance, could be about what a person on the tape was wearing. After answering these questions, participants were asked to recall specific details about the event they had seen on videotape. The results showed that participants are likely to incorporate suggestions about the wrong clothing into their memory and even elaborate on them.

Another classic study from Loftus's lab indicates how changing the wording of a question impacts people's recall for events. People will estimate higher speeds of travel when asked "How fast were the cars going when they *smashed*

Connection

Most people think they can multitask well. Research shows otherwise—especially when it comes to talking on the phone while driving.

See "Sustained Attention," Chapter 6, "Consciousness," p. 216.

blocking
The inability to retrieve some information that once was stored.

repression
The unconscious act of keeping threatening thoughts, feelings, or impulses out of consciousness.

suggestibility
A memory problem that occurs when memories are implanted in our minds based on leading questions, comments, or suggestions by someone else or some other source.

into each other?" rather than "How fast were the cars going when they *hit* each other?" (E. Loftus, 2003). With the first question, people also are more likely to report seeing broken glass than with the second question, simply because one word in the question is different. This effect is unconscious: People have no idea and will even deny that they have responded differently to the different wording in the questions.

The most fascinating, if not the most disturbing, example of suggestibility comes from research on false memories and recovered memories. **False memories** are memories for events that never happened but were suggested by someone or something (E. F. Loftus, 1997; Loftus & Pickrell, 1995). With a false memory, an individual develops an actual memory, sometimes very elaborate and detailed, based on false information. Loftus pioneered the technique of suggesting falsely that subjects in her studies experienced some event and then later asking them about their memories of that event. To be sure, a majority of the subjects never recalled anything, but across eight studies, on average 31% of the participants did create false memories (Lindsay et al., 2004). In case you are wondering, people with hyperthymestic memory (superior autobiographical memory)—such as Jill Price, whom we discussed in the opening of the chapter—are not immune to false memories (Patihis et al., 2013).

A **recovered memory** is supposedly from a real event—a memory that was encoded and stored but is not retrieved for a long period of time; the memory is retrieved after a later event brings it suddenly to consciousness. Recovered memories have been blocked or repressed for years. Recent research shows that people who suffered childhood sexual abuse do, in fact, have less specific autobiographical memories than people who did not suffer childhood sexual abuse (Raymaekers et al., 2010). They are not likely to remember specific events on specific days from their childhood. Their memories tend to be general—for example, "when I was about 9, one summer our family took a trip to New York. But I can't recall any specific details of the trip." Interestingly, however, compared to people with recovered memories, those who were abused and had continuous recall of

false memories
Memories for events that never happened but were suggested by someone or something.

Challenge Your Assumptions

True or False? Eyewitness memories are usually accurate.

False: Eyewitness memories, even if they are reported soon after the crime, range from mildly inaccurate to severely inaccurate.

recovered memory
A memory supposedly from a real event; it was encoded and stored but not retrieved for a long period of time, until a later event brings it suddenly to consciousness.

Leading questions might influence how an eyewitness recalls a car accident. Did these cars "hit" each other or "smash" each other?

the event (that is, did not have to recover the memory later) have equally poor specific autobiographical memories (Raymaekers et al., 2010). Traumatic events may alter how people store memories and, as a defense, make them less likely to be specific in their recall.

The topic of recovered memories, however, is controversial. Sometimes they are triggered while a person is under the care of a psychotherapist. Controversy arises when it is not clear whether the psychotherapist has helped a patient recover a memory of an actual event or has unwittingly suggested an event that the client "remembers." If the event involves traumatic experiences, such as physical or sexual abuse, and people's lives are at stake, recovered memory becomes an explosive topic, as it did when the phenomenon first came to light in the early 1990s.

The 1990s saw the peak of the controversy over recovered memories. The so-called memory wars often pitted academic memory researchers against psychotherapists. The debate has died down somewhat, partly because everyone recognizes the truths on both sides: A large segment of the population really does experience abuse in childhood, and unprofessional suggestions by therapists can lead to falsely recovered memories (Ost, 2009).

Memory Loss Caused by Brain Injury and Disease

When people forget due to injury or disease to the brain, the condition is known as **amnesia.** Two types of amnesia associated with organic injury or disease are anterograde amnesia and retrograde amnesia (Collinson, Meyyappan, & Rosenfeld, 2009). **Anterograde amnesia** is the inability to remember events and experiences that occur *after* an injury or the onset of a disease. People with anterograde amnesia fail to make new long-term memories. They recall experiences for only a short period of time, perhaps 10 minutes or less. H. M., whose case we recounted earlier in the chapter, had anterograde amnesia after his hippocampus had been removed. **Retrograde amnesia** is an inability to recall events or experiences that happened *before* the onset of the disease or injury. The memory loss in this type of amnesia might involve only the incident that preceded it or might include years of memories. Accidents almost always result in retrograde amnesia of the event itself. Car accident victims, for instance, will usually say that they do not remember the accident.

David Feist's brain injury (from Chapter 6) resulted in problems with both anterograde and retrograde amnesia. A typical example of David's anterograde amnesia is that, on meeting friends who visit infrequently, David will forget having met them at all and say, "Have I told you about my memory problem?"

An example of the retrograde amnesia that David experiences is that he cannot remember anything that happened in the months before his accident, which includes completing a very difficult bicycle ride, which he would have considered "the memory of a lifetime." His accident erased this event from his long-term memory, likely because the region of his cortex that stored those memories was permanently damaged or destroyed.

A severe form of age-related memory loss occurs in the organic brain disease known as Alzheimer's disease. Although it can affect people in their 40s or 50s, Alzheimer's disease usually strikes people in their 60s, 70s, and 80s (Toyota et al., 2007). It results in progressive memory loss, ending with complete memory loss. For instance, forgetting the death of a spouse is common among people who suffer from moderate to severe forms of Alzheimer's. They may go through the whole grieving process over and over, as if each time someone reminds them that their loved ones are gone they are hearing the news for the first time. In Alzheimer's disease, experiences are lost due to anterograde amnesia, which can be caused by retroactive interference and absent-mindedness.

amnesia
Memory loss due to brain injury or disease.

anterograde amnesia
An inability to remember events and experiences that occur after an injury or the onset of a disease.

retrograde amnesia
An inability to recall events or experiences that happened before the onset of a disease or injury.

Quick Quiz 7.3: Forgetting and Memory Loss

1. Sofia is fluent in Spanish and is now trying to learn French. Much of it comes easy to her, yet she keeps forgetting some French words that are similar to yet different from their Spanish equivalent. The kind of forgetting that Sofia is suffering from is
   a. amnesia.
   b. retroactive interference.
   c. proactive interference.
   d. blocking.

2. The fact that changing the wording of a question impacts people's recall for events illustrates which kind of forgetting?
   a. retroactive interference
   b. traceability
   c. rephrasing
   d. suggestibility

3. Gwendolyn is 29 years old and is now convinced that she was abused as a child. From the time she was 9 until she was 28, however, she had no recollection of the abuse. Gwendolyn has
   a. a false memory.
   b. retrograde amnesia.
   c. proactive interference.
   d. a recovered memory.

4. Jon was in an automobile accident. It has now been a month since his accident, and he has no recollection of the 2 days after the accident. He suffers from
   a. anterograde amnesia.
   b. retrograde amnesia.
   c. post-traumatic amnesia.
   d. selective amnesia.

Answers can be found at the end of the chapter.

Bringing It All Together
Making Connections in Memory
How to Study

One of the most common questions students have while learning about memory in introductory psychology is "How can I use this material to study more efficiently?" This question may come up after the first exam, especially from students who expected an A but got a C. "What did I do wrong? I reread my notes, highlighted the book; how come I didn't do better?" It turns out that the things that worked for you in high school might not work anymore. To master a lot of complex new material, you may have to adopt new study strategies. You can make psychological science work for you by using the years of research about memory to optimize how to learn new material and prepare for exams (Bjork, 2001; Kornell & Bjork, 2007; Kornell et al., 2010).

Consider that anything you hear in lecture or read in the book—after a brief stint in sensory memory—is in that vulnerable place called short-term memory. Your job is to move this information into long-term memory and then to retrieve it for an exam. In particular, the material you learn in any class—new facts, terms, processes, and so on—is semantic memory. Like all long-term memories, how well you remember this material begins with encoding.

1. *Go to class and pay attention.* Attending and paying attention in lecture is the first very important step. If there is something you don't understand when the instructor first mentions it, ask a question about it right away. If you are too shy to do so in class or you can't get a word in edgewise with your instructor, note it in the margin of your notes, so that you can go back to it later. Consider that, if you don't attend to it now, you'll forget it by the end of class. Why?

   The interference of new material presented afterward, the fact that your stomach is growling, and thoughts of getting to your next class in time will make it difficult for you to remember what you wanted to ask. If you don't rehearse or work with the material in some way, it will be gone. By being in class and hearing in more detail what was posted on the lecture outline and what you read in the text, you give yourself another context in which to work with the material: engaging your attention. Avoid creating sources of interference, such as talking with a friend, text messaging, or emailing during lecture. If you start optimizing how you encode material in class, you will be ahead of the game. If you can do this, you are much more likely to store the information in long-term memory and be able to retrieve it easily during the exam. Who knows, some of the information might even stay with you longer than that.

2. *Read the text before class.* To increase the odds of learning and remembering the material for a long

period of time, it is important to read the material in the text, because it helps you establish a network of associations in which to fit the new material, so that when you hear your instructor talk about it you have a place to put the information—you can make the associations. A related encoding tool is connecting the new material you learn to things you have already experienced, so you begin to build more associations.

What else can help at the encoding stage? Many professors post lecture outlines electronically before class, which, like reading the text in advance, gives you the opportunity to begin encoding and storing material from the upcoming lecture before you get there. Reading through both lecture material and text assignments before going to class *primes* you to process the lecture material in a deep and meaningful way.

3. *Study deeply, not shallowly.* In addition to the lecture and book information, you can improve the way you study the material outside of class. What you have learned from levels of processing theory can help you in your approach to studying. According to depth of processing theory and research, the more deeply you process material, the better you will be able to recall it. Rereading notes and highlighting the text are both examples of shallow processing; they involve rote rehearsal. You want to process the material semantically, to work with the meaning of the material, which enhances your depth of processing and memory. Simply reading a definition of a term such as *storage* over and over again is not all that different from repeating a list of nonsense words, but if you attempt to work with the meaning of the material, you will remember it better. Think about it. *Storage* is a word we use a lot, and you only recently saw it related to memory. In everyday speech, it means "to put something away and keep it there," such as storing your memorabilia from high school in the attic of your parents' house. You put your yearbooks, varsity jacket, and track trophies into a box and take them to the attic. You label the box and make a mental note—maybe even a cognitive map—of where you put the box, so that you will be able to retrieve it later. Memory storage is just like this. It is the process of putting something away and leaving it there for future use. If you can elaborate your understanding of concepts such as storage in this way, you don't have to remember their word-for-word definitions, because you understand what they mean. That's good semantic processing. Add a few salient visual images to the mix—maybe an old bicycle and Darth Vader costume in the attic—and your depth of processing increases.

Also, the more different ways you work with material, the better you learn it. Connecting the concept of storage with your own experience—storing your high school things in a box—places *storage* into a semantic network of associations, with meaningful nodes in other networks: high school (friends, sports, classes, graduation), your parents' attic (and all the attic junk you know is up there), and boxes and other forms of storage (file cabinets, closets). By making the material personally relevant, you are adding the element of emotional significance, which strengthens the associations. Moreover, every time you succeed at storing information deeply and permanently in long-term memory, you change your brain. Proteins in your neurons are activating genes that promote the growth of new dendrites and synapses.

Recent research on student study habits shows that spacing out study activities is also important. Students tend to cram right before an exam, thinking that this is the most effective approach to learning. However, spacing things out and covering topics or chapters in separate study sessions, using both studying and self-testing of that material, is much more effective for long-term memory (Kornell & Bjork, 2007; Kornell et al., 2010).

4. *Form a study group.* Another way to increase depth of processing is to form a study group. Getting together with a few other students to review and discuss the material before an exam can be enormously helpful, as long as you prepare beforehand. Meeting with your peers to discuss course material adds new information, fills in gaps, and helps build up new semantic networks, but most importantly it offers a context in which to talk about the material. You might also have a peer who can explain a concept in a way that your instructor did not. Study groups foster discourse, social interaction, and the need to make another person understand you. This requires semantic processing, preparation, and some emotional charge. It is also important to have time between meeting with the study group and taking the test, so that you can go over any lingering questions that may have arisen during study group and consolidate your learning. To be sure that the material you are studying becomes consolidated, or firmly established, make a point of sleeping well after studying.

5. *Devise meaningful mnemonics.* Will you be able to access the information you learned when you need it? What can you do while studying to facilitate retrieval? Reviewing material with a study group is like a practice test, which is a nice evaluation of retrieval ability. Also, using an easy-to-remember mnemonic device during encoding may make it easier to retrieve the information later. If you make a concept personally relevant and integrate it into a semantic network, you can provide yourself with labels or tags as memory prompts. So, for example, to remember the meaning of memory *storage,* you can just think *attic* and you will activate that whole network of associations.

Chapter Review

THREE TYPES OF MEMORY

- Memory systems are classified as sensory, short-term (working), and long-term.

- Sensory memory is the brief trace of a sensory experience that lasts from less than half a second to 2 or 3 seconds. Iconic memory is the trace memory of a visual sensation. Echoic memory is the short-term retention of sounds.

- Short-term memory holds a limited amount of information for about 2 to 30 seconds, or as long as we continue to rehearse it, before we either transfer it to long-term memory or forget it. Baddeley's model of working memory describes how we are able to hold information in short-term memory while solving a problem.

- The serial position effect is a phenomenon of short-term memory whereby we most likely remember information that comes first and last in a series.

- Long-term memory is the repository of any material that we retain for between 30 seconds and a lifetime. It includes implicit memory, in which skills, behaviors, and procedures we don't consciously retrieve are stored, and explicit memories of events and facts stored for conscious recall.

- Long-term memory is divided into four stages: encoding, consolidation, storage, and retrieval.

- Encoding results from automatic processing or from effortful processing, such as rehearsal. The more deeply we encode information, the more likely we are to recall it. Mnemonic devices, such as acronyms, aid the encoding process.

- During consolidation, memory becomes firmly established and resistant to distraction, interference, and decay.

- Storage is the retention of information over time. Information can be stored via hierarchies, schemas, or association networks. According to parallel distributive processing (PDP) models, associations and neural processing result from the synchronized activity of many units or nodes.

- Retrieval is the recall of stored information from long-term memory.

THE BIOLOGICAL BASIS OF MEMORY

- Clusters of neurons that fire together are the biological foundation of memory (long-term potentiation).

- Different memories are processed in different areas of the brain. Sensory memories are processed primarily by their respective sensory cortexes. Short-term memories are processed mostly by the hippocampus and frontal lobes. Long-term memories are stored for the most part in the areas of the cortex where they were processed as sensory memories.

- Repetition and sometimes strong emotion initiate neural activity that converts short-term memories into long-term memories. In long-term memory formation, proteins activate genes, which turn on the production of new dendrites and synapses.

- In short-term memory, existing synapses grow stronger with rehearsal, but no new ones form.

- Certain drugs, drinks and transcranial direct current stimulation can enhance (or block) memory formation.

FORGETTING AND MEMORY LOSS

- One form of forgetting is interference, which can happen in one of two ways. Retroactive interference occurs when new experiences or information cause people to forget previously learned experiences or information. Proactive interference occurs when previously learned information interferes with the learning of new information.

- The two most serious effects of suggestibility are false memories and recovered memories. A false memory is a recollection of an event that never happened, whereas a recovered memory resurfaces after it was completely forgotten.

BRINGING IT ALL TOGETHER: MAKING CONNECTIONS IN MEMORY

- Going to class and paying attention to lectures help you encode lecture material deeply.

- Reading the book before a lecture will help you build a richer network of associations of the lecture material.

- You can process material deeply by rehearsing and spacing out your studying.

- Forming a study group facilitates deeper processing of material, because you have to learn by generating information, not simply reading or hearing it.

Key Terms

absent-mindedness, p. 276
amnesia, p. 279
anterograde amnesia, p. 279
associative network, p. 262
automatic processing, p. 259
blocking, p. 277
chunking, p. 255
consolidation, p. 261
effortful processing, p. 259
encoding, p. 259
episodic memory, p. 258
explicit memory, p. 258
false memories, p. 278

flashbulb memories, p. 274
forgetting, p. 276
forgetting curve, p. 276
hierarchies, p. 262
implicit memory, p. 258
interference, p. 276
levels of processing, p. 260
long-term memory, p. 252
long-term potentiation (LTP), p. 265
memory, p. 252
mnemonic device, p. 261
prefrontal cortex, p. 264

priming, p. 258
proactive interference, p. 276
procedural memory, p. 258
recovered memory, p. 278
rehearsal, p. 256
repression, p. 277
retrieval, p. 263
retroactive interference, p. 276
retrograde amnesia, p. 279

schemas, p. 262
semantic memory, p. 258
sensory memory, p. 252
serial position effect, p. 256
short-term memory, p. 252
storage, p. 262
suggestibility, p. 277
three-stage model of memory, p. 252
transcranial direct current stimulation (tDCS), p. 269
working memory, p. 254

Quick Quiz Answers

Quick Quiz 7.1: 1. b 2. d 3. a 4. c 5. a   **Quick Quiz 7.2:** 1. b 2. c 3. d 4. a 5. b 6. d   **Quick Quiz 7.3:** 1. c 2. d 3. d 4. a

8 Learning

Chapter Outline

Basic Processes of Learning
Conditioning Models of Learning
Social Learning Theory
The Interaction of Nature and Nurture
  in Learning
Chapter Review

Challenge Your Assumptions

True or False?

- Negative reinforcement is the same as punishment. (see page 295)

- Humans and lab rats basically learn in the same way. (see page 301)

- Children are not affected by watching violent cartoons or movies. (see page 309)

- Pulling an all-nighter is not a good way to study for an exam. (see page 315)

W e are constantly responding to events in the world. Some situations produce lasting changes in us, whereas others do not. Consider these ways in which situations might change a person:

- You are in a well-lit room and someone suddenly turns off the lights. At first you cannot see, but gradually, as your pupils dilate to let in more light in the dim surroundings, your eyes adapt to the dark and you can discern some objects you could not see previously.

- When Ellen enters her grandmother's home, there is always a distinct scent of eucalyptus and black pepper. After staying a little while inside the house, however, she no longer notices the smells at all.

- When he was a child, Timothy was regularly bullied by a boy named Ryan. As an adult, whenever he meets a person named Ryan his palms start to sweat and his heart races.

- A young girl sees her mother putting on makeup in a mirror and pursing her lips while applying lipstick. The girl copies her mother's lip movements. Later that afternoon the girl looks in the mirror again, and she purses her lips.

- A father teaches his 5-year-old son how to make a peanut butter sandwich. The next day, the boy successfully makes himself a peanut butter sandwich.

- You visit a new restaurant. The food is delicious and the service is good, so you plan to go again.

Which of these cases do you consider to be examples of learning? *Dark adaptation* is a sensory process, in which the muscles of the iris contract in response to low illumination levels. Eyes can do this automatically, and they will do it in any situation of low illumination without *any* prior experience.

The fact that Ellen could no longer notice the scent of her grandmother's house is an example of *habituation,* the sensory process by which organisms adapt to constant stimulation. The result is a change in response—from smelling odors to not smelling them—that stems from experience. The change is a fairly short-lived one, however. An argument can be made that habituation is not learning, because it can disappear immediately with a slight change in the stimulus. For example, if Ellen just stepped outside for a minute and then went back inside, she would notice the scent again. Still, habituation is often regarded as learning in its simplest form (Carew & Kandel, 1973).

Timothy's fear and anxiety when he meets any Ryan is a form of *learning by association.* Timothy associates *Ryan* with intimidation and violence, and that learned association is long-lasting, thereby affecting his immediate response to all Ryans for several years.

The girl copying her mother's behavior is *mimicry.* The fact that the girl repeated the lip-pursing gesture later that afternoon suggests that she learned to do it by watching and copying her mother. Learning by observation also played a role in the way the boy learned how to make a sandwich from watching his father.

In the restaurant example, our choice of restaurant was rewarded by good service and food, both of which are consequences that increase the likelihood that we will return to the same restaurant in the future.

In this chapter we will explore what learning is. In so doing, we will examine three major theories of learning—classical conditioning, operant conditioning, and social learning theory. We will also explore the role of evolution in learning and how learning both emerges from and changes the brain.

BASIC PROCESSES OF LEARNING

Psychologists define **learning** as an enduring change in behavior that occurs with experience. This definition sounds simple, but there are many forms of learning—from a child developing a preference for certain foods to a student learning a foreign language. As we try things out in the world, changes in sensation, perception, behavior, and brain functions alter who we are, what we know, what we feel, and what we can do. The essence of learning involves acquiring new knowledge, skills, values, or behaviors.

Learning and memory work together. Without them, we could not process, retain, or make use of new information. Learning occurs when information moves from short-term to long-term memory. During this process, new knowledge is stored in networks in the brain. For this reason, we don't have to learn to ride a bicycle every time we want to go for a spin. Once we have mastered the skill, we can retrieve that knowledge from memory and pedal away without thinking about it.

learning
An enduring change in behavior that occurs with experience.

Connection

Right now you are habituated to dozens of stimuli—including the feel of clothing on your skin. Now you are sensitized to it. How so?

See "The Long, Strange Trip from Sensation to Perception," Chapter 4, "Sensing and Perceiving Our World," p. 119.

Association

Association, in which one piece of information from the environment is linked repeatedly with another and the organism begins to connect the two sources of information, is one mechanism that supports learning. Learning by association can be powerful. One of the authors, Erika, gets serious motion sickness on boats, in cars, and sometimes on planes. Several years ago, she tried to join friends on a deep-sea fishing trip. Having taken prescription antinausea medication in preparation for the trip, she was confident she would have a good day. Before leaving the yacht harbor that morning, the folks in the boating party ate some doughnuts. Erika chose her favorite flavor, old-fashioned chocolate. Twenty minutes later, the boat left the harbor. Within 5 minutes, Erika was vomiting, and she was violently ill for the next several hours before the boat turned around. For 10 years thereafter, the mere sight or smell of a chocolate doughnut made Erika nauseated.

Associations form simply as a result of two events occurring together, whether or not the relationship between them makes any sense. In our example, the taste and smell of the doughnut was linked with nausea in Erika's mind, even though motion (not the doughnut) had caused her sickness. Association is at the core of this kind of learning, known as condition taste aversion. By virtue of their connection, one event may come to suggest that the other will occur.

association
The process by which two pieces of information from the environment are repeatedly linked, so that we begin to connect them in our minds.

CONDITIONING MODELS OF LEARNING

Conditioning is a form of associative learning in which a behavior becomes more likely because the organism links that behavior with certain events in its environment. Erika, for example, was *conditioned* to feel nausea to chocolate doughnuts because she associated that food with the growing motion sickness she felt as the boat left the yacht harbor.

Psychologists distinguish between two types of conditioning: classical and operant. Both are forms of associative learning. In classical conditioning, organisms learn from the relations between stimuli. In operant conditioning, organisms learn from the consequences of their behavior. Let's look at these two forms in more detail.

conditioning
A form of association learning in which behaviors are triggered by associations with events in the environment.

Classical Conditioning

classical conditioning
A form of associative learning in which a neutral stimulus becomes associated with a stimulus to which one has an automatic, inborn response.

In **classical conditioning,** learning occurs when a neutral stimulus becomes associated with a stimulus to which the learner has an automatic, inborn response. Exactly how this works will become clearer if we consider the pioneering example of Ivan Pavlov and his dogs.

Pavlov's Dogs   Ivan Pavlov received the Nobel Prize in Medicine in 1904 for his research on saliva and digestion. While he was studying digestion in dogs, Pavlov (1906, 1928) discovered classical conditioning quite accidentally—a famous example of how scientists looking at one thing inadvertently discover another. As often happens, luck, keen observation, and serendipity led to this important scientific discovery.

In order to examine digestive enzymes in the dogs' saliva, Pavlov and his technicians placed tubes in the dogs' mouths to collect their saliva. Then they placed meat powder in their mouths, which naturally produces salivation. After doing this for a while, Pavlov noticed that the dogs began to salivate even before the meat powder was presented. It was as though the sounds of the technician preparing the apparatus signaled to the dogs that meat powder was about to come (Fancher, 1996). Pavlov reasoned that the dogs had formed an association between a stimulus that had no inherent food value (the sound of the apparatus) and one that did (the meat powder). Could he teach a dog to salivate to something else?

He designed a laboratory experiment that mimicked the conditions in which the dogs salivated to sounds made by the technician. Working with various dogs, Pavlov presented a neutral stimulus (a bell sound) just before showing them the meat powder. The dogs had no previous experience with the bell, but they salivated to the meat powder, because dogs always salivate to meat powder, from the first time they smell it. Salivation is a reflex, an automatic response to a particular stimulus (food) that requires no learning.

Pavlov presented the bell along with the meat powder to the dogs over and over again. The dogs salivated. Then he tried presenting the bell alone to see if the dogs might now link the bell with the meat powder in the way the first dogs linked the noise of the apparatus with the meat powder. The dogs salivated to the bell alone. By virtue of the association made during repeated pairings with meat powder, the nonappetizing bell had come to signal "meat powder" to the dogs. The dogs had learned that they would get meat powder after the bell sounded.

Pavlov and his dogs

unconditioned response (UCR)
The natural automatic, inborn reaction to a stimulus.

unconditioned stimulus (UCS)
Environmental input that always produces the same unlearned response.

How Classical Conditioning Works   Pavlov called the kind of learning he'd observed the *conditioning of reflexes;* psychologists now call it *classical conditioning.* He coined the term **unconditioned response (UCR)** to describe an automatic, inborn response to a stimulus. *Unconditioned* simply means "unlearned." In Pavlov's research, salivation was the UCR. Pavlov used the term **unconditioned stimulus (UCS)** to refer to the environmental input (meat powder) that always produced the same unlearned response (salivation). Without learning, the UCS always produces the UCR; in Pavlov's experiment, meat powder—the UCS— always led to salivation—the UCR.

Food makes you salivate, pressure on your eye makes you blink, and a tap just below your kneecap causes your leg to jerk forth. These reflexes are unlearned, fixed responses to specific types of environmental stimuli. Pavlov defined reflexes, such as salivation in response to food, as fixed stimulus-response patterns. Classical conditioning is the modification of these stimulus-response (S-R) relationships with experience. Pavlov presented the neutral stimulus (bell) right before the UCS (meat powder); salivation in the presence of meat powder was the UCR.

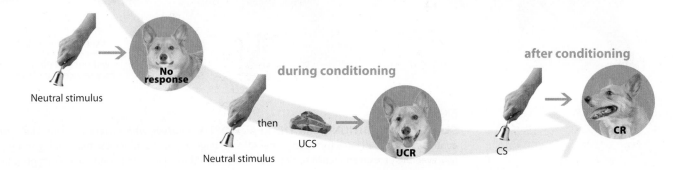

UCS

UCR

FIGURE 8.1

CLASSICAL CONDITIONING. A dog's natural reflex is to salivate to food. The food is an unconditioned stimulus (UCS), and salivation is an unconditioned response (UCR). Before conditioning, a dog will not salivate when a bell rings. During conditioning, the bell is presented right before the food appears. The dog salivates (UCR) because of the food (UCS). After repeatedly hearing the ringing bell right before being presented with the food, the dog will begin to salivate. Now the ringing bell has become a conditioned stimulus (CS), and salivation to the sound of the bell alone has become a conditioned response (CR).

Neutral stimulus

No response

during conditioning

after conditioning

then

Neutral stimulus

UCS

UCR

CS

CR

After repeated pairings of the bell with meat powder and the bell alone led to salivation, the bell became a *conditioned stimulus*. A **conditioned stimulus (CS)** is a previously neutral stimulus that an organism learns to associate with the UCS. If salivation occurred in response to the CS (as it did in Pavlov's experiment), it would then be called a conditioned response. A **conditioned response (CR)** is a behavior that an organism learns to perform when presented with the CS alone. Figure 8.1 shows how classical conditioning works.

Notice that Figure 8.1 shows the neutral stimulus being presented just before the UCS. This process is known as *forward conditioning*. One can also present the neutral stimulus and UCS simultaneously. When the neutral stimulus follows the UCS, a process called *backward conditioning*, conditioning is less successful. An example of backward conditioning would be sounding the bell after presenting the food to Pavlov's dogs.

Based on repeated, painstakingly careful experimentation, Pavlov laid out certain criteria for stimulus-response conditioning to succeed (Pavlov, 1906, 1928). Two of the most fundamental criteria are as follows:

1. Multiple pairings of UCS and neutral stimulus (CS) are necessary for an association to occur and for the CS to produce the conditioned response.

2. The UCS and CS must be paired or presented very close together in time in order for an association to form.

When a behavior has been conditioned to occur in the presence of a given stimulus, it may also increase in the presence of similar stimuli. For instance, for several years, Erika felt nauseated not only to chocolate doughnuts but also to glazed doughnuts. This phenomenon, known as **stimulus generalization,** is the extension of the association between UCS and CS to a broad array of similar stimuli. The opposite of stimulus generalization is **stimulus discrimination,** which occurs when a CR (such as salivation) occurs only to exactly the stimulus to which it was conditioned. If Pavlov's dogs did not salivate to a buzzer but only to a bell, they would discriminate the conditioned stimulus (bell) from other stimuli (buzzers, clicks, and so on).

Can a conditioned response be unlearned? Would you expect Pavlov's dogs to continue salivating indefinitely in response to the bell alone? It turns out that

conditioned stimulus (CS)
A previously neutral input that an organism learns to associated with a UCS.

conditioned response (CR)
A behavior that an organism learns to perform when presented with a CS.

stimulus generalization
Extension of the association between UCS and CS to include a broad array of similar stimuli.

stimulus discrimination
Restriction of a CR (such as salivation) only to exactly the CS to which it was conditioned.

Unconditioned
stimulus:
bee sting
1

Unconditioned
response: pain,
which can lead to fear
2

Conditioned
response:
fear of bees
3

Extinction: repeated
exposure to bees
without getting stung
may reduce fear of bees.
4

FIGURE **8.2**

CLASSICAL CONDITIONING IN THE REAL WORLD. A person who suffered a painful bee sting continues to fear all bees for a long time. After enough exposure to bees without being stung, however, the person can learn to not react with fear. At this point, the conditioned response (fear) is extinguished.

extinction
The weakening and disappearance of a conditioned response in the absence of the pairing of UCS and CS.

spontaneous recovery
The sudden reappearance of an extinguished response.

the dogs gradually stopped salivating to the bell (CS) once they learned that the bell was no longer being accompanied by meat powder (UCS). This weakening and disappearance of a conditioned response is called **extinction,** and it occurs when the UCS is no longer paired with the CS. It can be difficult to extinguish behaviors. Sometimes it takes 100 or more presentations of a CS without the UCS to achieve extinction, and still the behavior might return. Consider the case of a young man who had had a bad experience with a bee sting when he was 4 years old. Thereafter, he had an extreme reaction to the sight of bees. Psychologists can treat this kind of abnormal fear reaction using extinction. Exposing the man repeatedly to bees in situations in which he does not get stung helps him learn that they will not always sting. This experience reduces the extreme fear reaction he has to bees (see Figures 8.2 and 8.3).

The sudden reappearance of an extinguished response is known as **spontaneous recovery** (see Figure 8.3). One example of spontaneous recovery

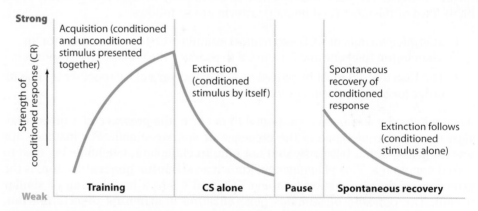

FIGURE **8.3**

ACQUISITION, EXTINCTION, AND SPONTANEOUS RECOVERY IN CLASSICAL CONDITIONING. The graph shows how a conditioned response (CR) gradually becomes stronger during conditioning, weakens when the conditioned stimulus (CS) is no longer paired with the UCS, and disappears (extinction). Following a pause during which the CS is not presented, spontaneous recovery of the CR may occur briefly before it is extinguished again.

comes from a man who was involved in a car accident. His car was sideswiped as he was making a blind turn from a parking lot. After the accident, he would have a panic attack whenever he passed that lot, so he couldn't park there. Several months later the attacks stopped, and he started parking there again. Then, one day as he approached the parking lot, he had an unexpected panic attack. A learned response he thought had been extinguished suddenly came back. Research on spontaneous recovery suggests that extinction never completely eliminates the response, only suppresses it (Moody, Sunsay, & Bouton, 2006). After a response has been extinguished, it is quite common for it to reappear spontaneously if a person returns to the setting where the conditioning originally took place.

Why does classical conditioning—the ability to associate innate stimulus-response patterns with novel stimuli—work? It may be adaptive in an evolutionary sense. We need to be able to associate certain types of stimuli with potential harm and to respond quickly to new stimuli that present threats. For instance, we might not be hardwired to see long, sharp metal objects as dangerous, but once we see that pressing one of them against the skin causes bleeding, then we know it is dangerous. Most animals can learn such things readily, and it helps them survive and reproduce. It is by virtue of experience and association that many objects acquire their meaning for us. That knives are dangerous is something we learn. The fact that classical conditioning is a powerful learning device for nearly all creatures suggests that it has advantages for survival.

The Conditioning of Little Albert   Pavlov's work caught the attention of young psychologists in the United States in the early 20th century. They saw in Pavlov's research the first systematic account of a scientific procedure for studying behavior. One American psychologist, John Watson, felt strongly that classical conditioning could be used to shape human behavior:

> Give me a dozen healthy infants, well-formed, and my own specified world to bring them up in and I'll guarantee to take any one at random and train him to become any type of specialist I might select—doctor, lawyer, artist, merchant-chief, and yes, even beggar-man and thief, regardless of his talents, penchants, tendencies, abilities, vocations, and race of his ancestors. (J. B. Watson, 1925, p. 82)

Watson's complete faith in the ability to mold human behavior seems naïve today, and some would even call it dangerous. Yet Watson and his view of infants as blank slates helped push psychology—which Watson defined as "the study

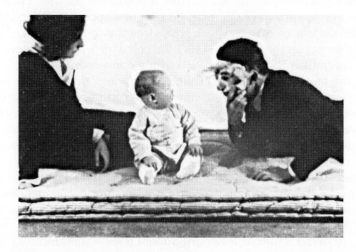

Little Albert with Rosalie Rayner and John B. Watson

of behavior"—forward as a science. To Watson, classical conditioning offered a model for transforming the field.

In a classic study of the power of conditioning techniques, Watson conditioned a baby, known as Little Albert, to fear white rats and other white, fluffy objects. When Watson and his colleague Rosalie Rayner first met Albert, they brought out a white rat and showed it to him. He was curious but not afraid of it. Then Watson and Rayner (1920) paired the presentation of the rat with a very loud noise (the sound of a hammer striking a steel bar right behind Albert's head). Naturally, the loud sound (a UCS) startled Albert (the UCR), and he got very upset.

After repeated pairings of the loud sound with the rat, seeing the rat alone (the CS) upset Albert. On further testing, Albert's fear grew to include an intense emotional response not only to white rats but also to many other white, fluffy items, including John Watson's fake white beard. This is an example of stimulus generalization.

Regrettably, Little Albert did not undergo deconditioning (J. B. Watson & Rayner, 1920). Controversy surrounded this case for years, and it is still not clear what happened to Little Albert. We see in this case that psychology in its infancy lacked clear ethical guidelines for research. Watson's "experiment" raised many ethical issues, particularly about the need to safeguard the rights of individuals who cannot give informed consent to participate in research. Still, Watson is remembered as the father of behaviorism for his role in establishing psychology as the study of behavior. Recently, evidence shared from the autopsy of Little Albert suggests he may have had some brain abnormalities at birth, which would suggest he was not the "normal" infant Watson proclaimed him to be (Fridlund et al., 2012).

Connection

The ethics of human research today would not allow Watson to do his research on Little Albert.

See "Ethical Research with Humans," Chapter 2, "Conducting Research in Psychology," p. 62.

Operant Conditioning

Unlike Little Albert's fear of white rats and other reactions that people can elicit from other people, some behaviors occur spontaneously. In the late 19th century, Edward L. Thorndike (1905) noted that rewarding consequences can make a spontaneous behavior more likely to occur again. He found that a cat would escape from a specially designed cage if left to its own devices for a while, not necessarily because it figured out how to get out but because certain motions were rewarded by the door opening (see Figure 8.4). This reward made it more likely that the specific behavior that led to the door opening would happen again if the cat were again confined in the same cage. In addition, the time it took the cat to escape decreased over time. The plot of the rate at which learning occurs over time is known as a learning curve (see Figure 8.4). In the same way, you might go back to a café you had casually walked into if you found out that it had free wireless Internet service and gave out tasty samples of its pastries. Thorndike labeled this principle the **law of effect,** which states that the consequences of a behavior increase (or decrease) the likelihood that the behavior will be repeated.

Like Thorndike, B. F. Skinner viewed the consequences of an individual's actions as the most important determinants of behavior (Skinner, 1938, 1953). Skinner set out to explain the environmental factors that led Thorndike's cat to learn to open the cage (or you to return to the café). Skinner wanted to know how disorganized, spontaneous behavior becomes organized, and exactly what role the consequences of an action play in the organization of the response. Figure 8.5 shows how consequences may increase behavior.

Skinner (1938) coined the term *operant* to refer to behavior that acts—or operates—on the environment to produce specific consequences. **Operant conditioning** is the process of modifying behavior by manipulating the consequences of that behavior. According to Skinner, a behavior that is rewarded is more likely to occur again. If a hungry animal does something that is followed by the presentation of food, then the animal is more likely to repeat the behavior

law of effect
The consequences of a behavior increase (or decrease) the likelihood that the behavior will be repeated.

operant conditioning
The process of changing behavior by manipulating the consequences of that behavior.

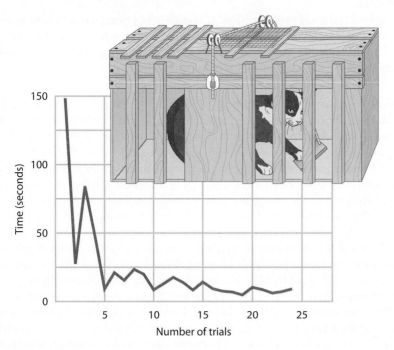

FIGURE **8.4**

THE LEARNING CURVE. Depicted here is the box from which Thorndike's cats learned to escape. Thorndike found that a cat would escape from a specially designed cage if left to its own devices for a while, not necessarily because it figured out how to get out but because certain motions eventually were rewarded by the door's opening. This reward of the opening door made it more likely that the specific behavior that had led to the opening door would happen again if the cat were again confined in the same cage. The graph shows the amount of time it took the cat to escape. Initially, it took more than 2 minutes, but after just a few trials, the cat could consistently escape in about 10 seconds.

FIGURE **8.5**

THREE EXAMPLES OF HOW CONSEQUENCES CAN INCREASE OR REINFORCE BEHAVIOR.

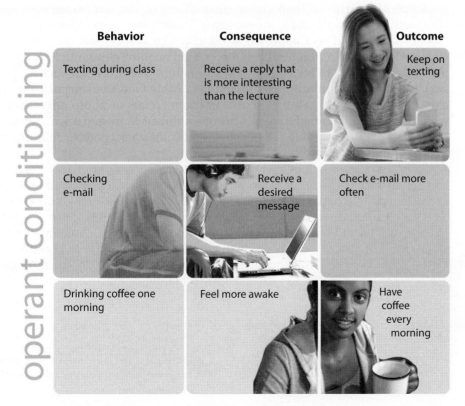

that preceded the food presentation. If a café gives you free wireless access, you might go back. In contrast to classical conditioning, which modifies an involuntary behavior (such as salivation), operant conditioning works when voluntary behavior is made more likely by its consequences.

Reinforcement and Punishment   When the consequences of a behavior increase the likelihood that a behavior will occur again, the behavior is reinforced, or strengthened. A **reinforcer** is any internal or external event that increases a behavior. When a baby sees he can get a big smile from his mother when he smiles at her, he is likely to smile more often (Adamson & Bakeman, 1985). The mother's smile in response to the infant's is a reinforcer that increases the frequency of smiling by the baby, because parental smiles are inherently rewarding to babies. This is a key point. Reinforcers have to be things that the learner wants in order for them to influence the likelihood that a behavior will occur again. For example, you will continue getting paid on a regular basis if you do your job. You want the money, so you keep working hard, but if your employer gave you paper clips for your hard work, you'd probably quit. Similarly, if your credit card company offered iTunes credits for using your card, you might use it more often. This last case shows how corporations apply principles of operant conditioning to make a profit. All of these examples differ from classical conditioning, in which two things become linked because they occur together, whether or not they are inherently rewarding.

With operant conditioning, Skinner developed a programmatic approach to using schedules of reinforcement for modifying behavior. This basic system has been applied widely with much success in education, animal training, and numerous behavioral treatments for everything from weight loss and smoking cessation to the treatment of autism in children.

There are two kinds of reinforcers: primary and secondary. **Primary reinforcers** are not learned. They are innate and often satisfy biological needs. Food, water, sex, and even artificial sweeteners are primary reinforcers (Vaughan, 2009). Many drugs, such as caffeine and nicotine, are primary reinforcers by virtue of their stimulating effects on the central nervous system (Bernardi & Spanagel, 2013). **Secondary (conditioned) reinforcers,** such as money, grades, and peer approval, are learned by association, usually via classical conditioning. A potential reinforcer may acquire pleasant characteristics if it is associated with something that is inherently reinforcing (such as food or sex). Advertisers regularly take advantage of this fact. Consider ads for sports cars. If a sports car is always shown in commercials or photo advertisements with attractive individuals, then it becomes linked in memory with something that is inherently desirable. The car itself becomes a secondary reinforcer due to its association with sex.

Reinforcement can be positive or negative—not in terms of being good or bad, but in terms of whether a stimulus is added to a situation (positive) or taken away (negative). **Positive reinforcement** occurs when the presentation or addition of a stimulus to a situation increases the likelihood of a behavior. Giving extra credit points for turning in homework on time would be positive reinforcement if it led to students submitting their assignments on time. The term **negative reinforcement** refers to the removal of a stimulus to *increase* behavior. Frequently,

reinforcer
An internal or external event that increases the frequency of a behavior.

B. F. Skinner

primary reinforcers
Innate, unlearned reinforcers that satisfy biological needs (such as food, water, or sex).

secondary (conditioned) reinforcers
Reinforcers that are learned by association, usually via classical conditioning (such as money, grades, and peer approval).

positive reinforcement
The presentation or addition of a stimulus after a behavior occurs that increases how often that behavior will occur.

negative reinforcement
The removal of a stimulus after a behavior to increase the frequency of that behavior.

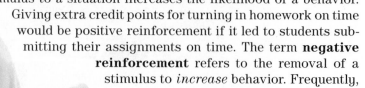

A smile is inherently rewarding for babies.
 How might the principles of operant conditioning explain why the baby would smile at Mommy even more?

the stimulus removed is something unpleasant. As an example, consider the beeper that sounds in your car until you fasten your seat belt. The *removal* of the annoying beeping is negative reinforcement for fastening the seat belt.

Is the distinction between positive and negative reinforcement important? Some behavioral psychologists have argued that it is unnecessary and, at times, difficult to make (Baron & Galizio, 2006; Michael, 1975). Here is an illustration of how this distinction can be confusing. Let's say you drink coffee to wake up. From one perspective, the wakefulness induced by the caffeine is positive reinforcement for drinking coffee, but are you really increasing wakefulness or decreasing fatigue (which would be negative reinforcement for drinking coffee)? Either way, the consequence for behavior is the same—you drink more coffee.

Negative reinforcement is often confused with **punishment,** which is any stimulus that *decreases* the frequency of a behavior. Like reinforcement, punishment can be positive or negative. Remember, however, that punishers *decrease* the frequency of behavior. By definition, negative reinforcers *increase* desired behaviors, so they cannot be punishers.

Typically, when most people think of punishment, they think of **positive punishment,** the addition of a stimulus that decreases behavior. A classic example of a positive punisher is spanking. Spanking a child (adding a stimulus) is positive punishment if it decreases the undesirable behavior. Similarly, if you are fined for parking in the faculty lot and stop parking there, you have received positive punishment. **Negative punishment** decreases behavior by removing a stimulus, usually a desirable stimulus. Revoking a child's TV-watching privileges for repeatedly hitting a sibling is a form of negative punishment if it stops the hitting. Figure 8.6 summarizes positive and negative forms of punishment and reinforcement.

punishment
A stimulus that decreases the frequency of a behavior.

positive punishment
The addition of a stimulus that decreases behavior.

negative punishment
The removal of a stimulus to decrease behavior.

result:	(+) add a stimulus	(−) take away a stimulus
increase in behavior using reinforcement	**Positive reinforcement** You exercise a few times and feel better. **Result:** You exercise more often.	**Negative reinforcement** You buckle your seat belt and the annoying buzzer sound is removed. **Result:** You continue using your seat belt. 
decrease in behavior using punishment	 **Positive punishment** You park in the faculty parking lot. You then receive a fine. **Result:** You stop parking in the faculty lot.	**Negative punishment** You talk back to your mom. She takes away TV and videos for a week. **Result:** You stop talking back to your mom. 

FIGURE 8.6

POSITIVE AND NEGATIVE REINFORCEMENT AND PUNISHMENT IN OPERANT CONDITIONING. It is the actual result, not the intended result, that matters. For example, if an intended punisher does not decrease the behavior, it is not a punishment.

Skinner emphasized that reinforcement is a much more effective way of modifying behavior than is punishment (Skinner, 1953). Specifically, using reinforcement to increase desirable behaviors works better than using punishment in an attempt to decrease undesirable behaviors. Let's say a girl hit her brother because he took away her toy. Instead of punishing the girl for hitting her brother, the parents could reinforce more desirable behaviors for dealing with the stolen toy—the girl could tell her brother that it upset her that he took the toy and suggest that, if he would please give it back, they could share it for a while. When the little girl acted in this preferable way, the parents could commend her, perhaps by giving her special privileges (such as more playtime). This in turn would increase the likelihood that the girl would use something more appropriate than physical retaliation. Punishment, as it focuses on decreasing or eliminating behaviors, doesn't tell kids what they should be doing, only what they shouldn't be doing. Reinforcement offers them an alternative.

How Operant Conditioning Works In classical conditioning, organisms learn about the relationships between stimuli; in operant conditioning, organisms learn from the consequences of their behavior. The basic idea behind operant conditioning is that any behavior that is reinforced becomes strengthened and is more likely to occur in the future. Behaviors are reinforced because they are instrumental in obtaining particular results.

Substance use and abuse can be learned through operant conditioning. When people try a substance such as alcohol or nicotine for the first time and it makes them feel elated (a positive reinforcer) or removes their fears (a negative reinforcer), they will be more likely to use that drug again in the future. The problem with many drugs (especially alcohol and nicotine) is that the body adjusts to their presence, and more and more of the drug is required to get the desired effect. When increasing amounts of the drug are required to obtain reinforcement—to get "high"—then the behavior of taking the drug increases even more. This is one reason drug addictions are so powerful and hard to overcome.

To test his conditioning principles, Skinner created the **Skinner box,** a simple chamber in which a small animal can move around, with a food dispenser and a response lever to trigger food delivery (see Figure 8.7). The Skinner box has been modified in recent years to allow for computer collection of responses, but many laboratories still use chambers very similar to Skinner's original device.

How exactly does someone do operant conditioning? How can you get a rat to press a lever? Rats have no inherent interest in lever pressing. You might give the rat a food pellet for pressing the lever, but how do you get the animal to press the lever in the first place?

Skinner trained a rat to perform a desired behavior (such as lever pressing) by reinforcing behaviors that occurred when the rat came closer and closer to pressing the lever. If you put a rat in a Skinner box, sooner or later—as a function of its random movements—it will come closer to the lever. When it does, you reinforce that behavior by giving it some food.

Eventually, the rat makes an association between getting closer to a particular region of the chamber and food appearing. More specifically, the rat learns that the

Skinner box
A simple chamber used for the operant conditioning of small animals.

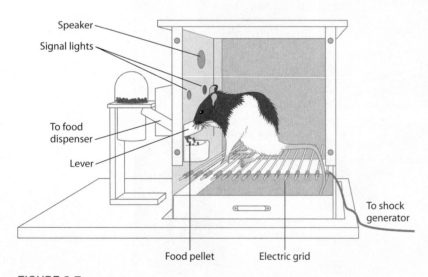

FIGURE **8.7**
THE SKINNER BOX. This modern Skinner box provides a small space in which the rat can move and a lever to press that delivers food as a reinforcer. A small region of the floor can be set up to deliver a shock as a punisher. The rats learn through punishment to avoid that region of the floor.

Through shaping and reinforcement, pigeons can learn to discriminate colors.

appearance of food seems to be contingent on getting over to that region of the chamber. The researcher then increases the requirements for food presentation. Now brushing up against the lever will be reinforced with a food pellet. Finally, the rat has to press the lever to get the food.

Gradually reinforcing behaviors that come closer and closer to the target behavior will eventually produce the target behavior. The reinforcement of successive approximations of a desired behavior is called **shaping.** Shaping behavior is a bit like shaping clay, for the idea really is that an organism can be molded to do things that it typically wouldn't do. Professional trainers rely on shaping to get animals to perform tricks or to be guide dogs to assist people with disabilities.

Does shaping work with humans? Let's say you're trying to teach your friend how to drive a car with a stick shift. The first time he tries, even if he makes a few mistakes and stalls a few times, you might give him lots of encouragement and praise. Later, when you're trying to get him to master changing gears smoothly, you give praise only when each movement is done correctly. You are reinforcing successive approximations of the desired behavior, and as your student gets closer and closer to the desired behavior, the criteria for reinforcement become more stringent. By the 15th attempt, bucking forward a few feet before stalling gets no praise. In fact, there are numerous applications of shaping with humans. Parents use it all the time to help teach their children new tasks (e.g., how to ride a bicycle).

In operant conditioning, extinction occurs when a behavior stops being reinforced. So if a rat presses the lever and repeatedly gets no food, the lever-pressing behavior will decrease and eventually disappear. If you keep leaving phone or text messages for someone you want to ask on a date, but he or she never returns your calls or texts, eventually you will stop trying to contact this person. The calling or texting behavior has been extinguished. Figure 8.8 compares classical and operant conditioning.

Applications of Operant Conditioning Operant conditioning also offers a powerful method for modifying behavior in the treatment of several disorders in humans, such as phobias (severe, specific fears), nicotine addiction, and learning disabilities (Anthonisen et al., 2005; Lamb et al., 2004; Lovaas, 1987). Treatment programs based on operant methods effectively reduce self-harming behaviors in

shaping
The reinforcement of successive approximations of a desired behavior.

	Classical conditioning	Operant conditioning
basic principle	Learning to associate a conditioned stimulus (CS) and a conditioned response (CR).	Reinforcement increases the frequency of a behavior. Punishment decreases the frequency of a behavior.
nature of behavior	The behavior is based on an organism's involuntary behavior: its reflexes. The behavior is elicited by the unconditioned stimulus (UCS) or conditioned stimulus (CS).	The behavior is based on an organism's voluntary action. The consequence of the behavior creates the likelihood of its increasing or decreasing the behavior.
order of events	Before conditioning occurs, a UCS leads to a UCR. After conditioning, a CS leads to a CR.	Reinforcement leads to an increase in behavior. Punishment leads to a decrease in behavior.
example	A bee stings a child (UCS). The child feels pain (UCR) from the sting. The child then develops a strong fear (CR) when the child sees bees (CS).	**Negative reinforcement** Buckling a seat belt removes the annoying buzzer, so you're more likely to buckle the seat belt again. **Negative punishment** A child who misbehaves and loses TV and video for a week is less likely to repeat that behavior again.

FIGURE **8.8**
THE DIFFERENCES BETWEEN CLASSICAL AND OPERANT CONDITIONING.

adults with intellectual deficiencies (Chowdhury & Benson, 2011) and in suicidal teens with borderline personality disorder (Klein & Miller, 2011). Shaping is used to help improve the attention span in people with schizophrenia (Silverstein, Menditto, & Stuve, 2001).

One important application of operant conditioning is in the treatment of autism (Beadle-Brown, Murphy, & Wing, 2006; Lovaas, 1987; Soorya, Carpenter, & Romanczyk, 2011). Applied behavioral analysis (ABA), developed by Ivar Lovaas at UCLA, uses reinforcement to increase the frequency of adaptive behaviors in autistic children and, in some cases, punishment to decrease the likelihood of maladaptive behaviors. The intensive program involves ignoring harmful or undesirable behaviors, such as hand flapping, twirling, or licking of objects, as well as aggressive behaviors. It also involves reinforcing desirable behaviors, such as contact with others and appropriate toy play. Although ABA appears to be quite effective in reducing many harmful and aggressive behaviors in young autistic children and in improving cognitive functions across many age groups, it appears to be a bit less effective in improving the socioemotional deficits of autism (Beadle-Brown et al., 2006; Matson et al., 2012; Virués-Ortega, 2010).

Schedules of Reinforcement   Reinforcers can be arranged (scheduled) to follow behavior under a variety of conditions or rules, called **schedules of reinforcement.** Although a powerful tool in the laboratory, it is sometimes difficult to describe complex human behavior in terms of simple reinforcement schedules. Nonetheless, there are some parallels.

Reinforcers may be presented every time a behavior occurs or only occasionally. **Continuous reinforcement** means rewarding a behavior every time it occurs. Giving a dog a biscuit every time it jumps is continuous reinforcement. **Intermittent reinforcement** does not occur after every response.

Intermittent reinforcement produces a stronger behavioral response than continuous reinforcement does. Why? The explanation has to do with memory and expectation. If an animal gets a food pellet every time it hits a lever, it will remember and expect that food will appear each time it presses the lever, but if it sometimes receives food after one lever press and other times it takes five or 10 presses, the animal will not learn a predictable pattern. It will keep responding as fast as possible in hope that eventually it will receive food, because it is not sure when food will come.

It is well documented that intermittent reinforcement produces stronger responses—in terms of both rate of responding and resistance to extinction—than does continuous reinforcement (Ferster & Skinner, 1957). Think about your own behavior: How often do you check email each day? Maybe you check it several times a day. Some people are essentially "addicted" to email or social network sites, checking them dozens of times a day. This behavior is very easy to explain in terms of operant conditioning. Occasionally, a very important or interesting (reinforcing) email or post arrives, but we don't know when the next one will come (intermittent), so we check and we check, each time hoping for that important message, a behavior shaped by intermittent reinforcement.

Skinner identified four schedules of reinforcement (see Figure 8.9). These schedules can be distinguished on the basis of whether reinforcement occurs after a set number of responses or after a certain amount of time has passed since the last reinforcement.

In a **fixed-ratio (FR) schedule,** reinforcement follows a set number of responses. The pattern becomes predictable, so the response rate is not steady. Typically, there is a pause in response immediately after reinforcement occurs, and then the response rate increases. An FR schedule produces a steep, stepwise pattern of

schedules of reinforcement
Patterns of intermittent reinforcement distinguished by whether reinforcement occurs after a set number of responses or after a certain amount of time has passed since the last reinforcement.

continuous reinforcement
Reinforcement of a behavior every time it occurs.

intermittent reinforcement
Reinforcement of a behavior—but not after every response.

fixed-ratio (FR) schedule
A pattern of intermittent reinforcement in which reinforcement follows a set number of responses.

FIGURE **8.9**

SCHEDULES OF REINFORCEMENT. Workers who are paid for the number of units they produce are reinforced on a fixed-ratio schedule. Winnings from playing slot machines vary in amount and in the interval between payoffs, which reinforce behavior on a variable-ratio schedule. An example of a fixed-interval schedule is not attending lecture after taking an exam. A variable-interval schedule occurs when you continue to text a friend, who doesn't respond, until you get an answer; the number of times you have to text varies over time.

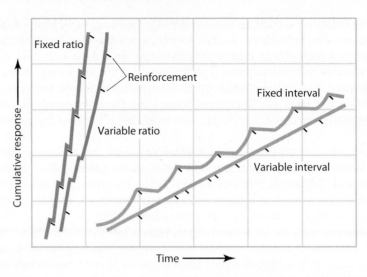

FIGURE 8.10

EFFECTS OF DIFFERENT SCHEDULES OF REINFORCEMENT ON LEARNING. Different schedules of reinforcement lead to different rates of response. Each hash mark indicates when a reinforcer is administered. Ratio schedules of reinforcement result in more of the reinforced behavior being performed over a given amount of time (the two steep slopes) than interval schedules of reinforcement (the two flatter slopes). Also, the fixed-interval schedule leads to the classic "scallop" effect, which indicates that responses decrease immediately after the reinforcer is administered and then increase again as the next reinforcer draws near.

response, as shown in Figure 8.10. One example is a worker being paid by the number of units he or she produces, whether the units are pajama sets or pizzas delivered. A worker whose wages or tips depend on the number he or she produces will work faster, possibly risking injury, to make more money.

A **variable-ratio (VR) schedule,** in which the number of responses needed for reinforcement varies, produces a very steady rate of response, because the individual is not quite sure how many responses are necessary to obtain reinforcement (see Figure 8.10). VR schedules produce reinforcement around a mean number of responses, but the exact ratio differs for each trial. Thus, the mean may be set at 10 responses, but some trials may require 10 responses for reinforcement, some 20, some five, some seven, and so on. A slot machine is an example of a device that delivers reinforcement on a VR schedule. The player cannot know how many pulls of the slot machine arm it will take to win. On one occasion it might take just one pull to win a small jackpot. Other times dozens of quarters might be spent before winning. Casinos make a lot of money capitalizing on the steady rate of response produced by a variable-ratio schedule—gamblers do not.

In a **fixed-interval (FI) schedule,** reinforcement always follows the first response after a set amount of time—say, every 4 seconds. This produces a pattern in which the rate of response immediately following reinforcement is low. The response rate accelerates as the time of reinforcement approaches. A graph of the FI schedule produces a scalloped pattern, as in Figure 8.10. An example of the effects of a fixed-interval schedule is one's studying behavior before and after a test. If tests are given every 4 weeks, students learn that immediately after the test their performance will not be evaluated, so we would expect to see a drop in rate of studying at that time. The same is true of class attendance before and after exams.

In a **variable-interval (VI) schedule,** the first response is reinforced after time periods of different durations have passed. The researcher sets a mean interval length around which the intervals will vary. For example, the mean interval

variable-ratio (VR) schedule
A pattern of intermittent reinforcement in which the number of responses needed for reinforcement changes.

fixed-interval (FI) schedule
A pattern of intermittent reinforcement in which responses are always reinforced after a set period of time has passed.

variable-interval (VI) schedule
A pattern of intermittent reinforcement in which responses are reinforced after time periods of different durations have passed.

may be 5 seconds, but sometimes reinforcement occurs after 10 seconds, sometimes after 1 second, sometimes after 5 seconds, and so on. The variable nature of the interval makes it difficult for the subject to predict when reinforcement will occur. Variable-interval schedules therefore produce a steady, moderate rate of response (see Figure 8.10). Suppose you are trying to reach a good friend on the phone but every time you call you get her voice mail. You can tell she is on the line already, so you keep calling back every few minutes to see if she is off. Her conversation can last only so long. Eventually, she will pick up the phone (your reward), but the wait time is unpredictable. In other words, reinforcement follows a variable-interval schedule.

Challenging Assumptions about Conditioning Models of Learning

Traditional learning theory assumes that the principles of conditioning are universal—classical conditioning and operant conditioning each work pretty much the same way in different species of animals. In fact, Skinner maintained that, given the proper reinforcement, almost any animal could be taught to do almost anything.

Skinner's faith in universal principles of learning was so strong that he was convinced that what he learned about a rat or pigeon in a conditioning chamber was representative of most species' learning in any context. In one sense Skinner was correct. The biochemical processes involved in learning and memory are the same in slugs as in humans (Kandel, 2006). Skinner was also suggesting that we could understand learning by training behavior, not because it is inherently interesting to us or to the animal but rather because trained behavior is easily observed. The specific species or the behavior does not make a difference; however, some of the basic assumptions of conditioning models of learning did not go unchallenged. Three domains of research challenged traditional learning theory:

- Conditioned taste aversion
- Instinctive drift
- Latent learning

Conditioned Taste Aversion   As we discussed, Erika's chocolate doughnut and deep-sea fishing experience led to a case of **conditioned taste aversion,** the learned avoidance of a particular taste when nausea occurs at about the same time as the food (Garcia, Kimeldorf, & Koelling, 1955). Whether or not the food actually causes the sickness, it is experienced that way in future encounters.

Traditional learning theory would explain conditioned taste aversion as a special case of classical conditioning, in which a neutral or even pleasant taste is linked with the unconditioned causes of nausea. This learned association (say, between a doughnut and nausea) is not much different from the one made by Pavlov's dogs (see Figure 8.11). The catch is that classical conditioning requires repeated pairings of the CS and the UCS to create and maintain a conditioned response, but in the case of the chocolate doughnut, the doughnut (the CS) acquired the ability to induce nausea (CR) after a brief pairing with the motion of the boat (UCS), more than 30 minutes after the doughnut was eaten.

The person responsible for discovering and describing this kind of learning was John Garcia. In the 1950s Garcia and his colleagues wondered whether rats in their laboratory had developed a taste aversion for the food and water they had consumed while they received radiation for one of the lab's experiments. He and his colleagues (1955) at the U.S. Naval Laboratory decided to look more closely

conditioned taste aversion
The learned avoidance of a particular taste or food.

John Garcia

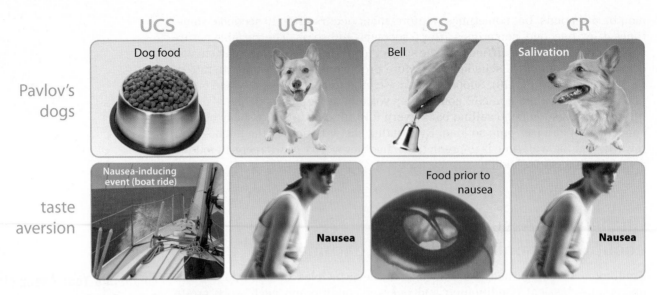

	UCS	UCR	CS	CR
Pavlov's dogs	Dog food		Bell	Salivation
taste aversion	Nausea-inducing event (boat ride)	Nausea	Food prior to nausea	Nausea

FIGURE **8.11**

A CLASSICAL CONDITIONING MODEL OF TASTE AVERSION.

at this phenomenon by conditioning rats to develop an aversion to a taste they liked—saccharin water. They began with the following questions:

1. Could taste aversion to saccharin water occur by pairing the taste with radiation (a UCS for nausea)?

2. How long would the taste aversion last without repeated exposure to radiation (the UCS)?

Garcia's team varied the type of fluid presented during a radiation period (plain water or saccharin water) and the radiation exposure level (none, low, or moderate dose). One control group had access to plain water during a 6-hour period of exposure to radiation (irradiation). Another control group received saccharin water and no radiation. In the experimental conditions, rats received saccharin water during periods of low or moderate irradiation. According to traditional classical conditioning, the UCS and CS must be paired very closely in time—typically, no more than a few seconds apart. However, in some cases, several minutes passed between the time the rats were irradiated (UCS) and the time they drank the fluid (CS).

Following the conditioning period in which the rats were irradiated or not, all the rats were housed in cages with two drinking bottles, one containing plain water and one with saccharin water. At this time, taste aversion was measured, and the dependent variable was how much saccharin water the rats consumed.

There were no changes in the control groups' water preferences, but in the two experimental groups, aversion occurred (see Figure 8.12). Regardless of radiation level, rats that had been drinking saccharin water during irradiation consumed significantly less saccharin water after conditioning. This result answered the first question the researchers had posed: Rats could be conditioned to avoid a taste they previously liked. Also, the drop in intake of saccharin water lasted for at least 30 days. This finding answered the second question about how long such conditioning might last.

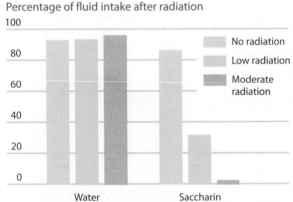

Percentage of fluid intake after radiation

No radiation
Low radiation
Moderate radiation

Fluid during irradiation

FIGURE **8.12**

CONDITIONED TASTE AVERSION. Compared to rats that received no nausea-producing radiation, rats exposed to radiation (UCS) while drinking saccharin water (CS) developed a long-lasting aversion to saccharin water (CR).

Which item in this story is analogous to the chocolate doughnut in Erika's story of conditioned taste aversion? (Garcia et al., 1955)

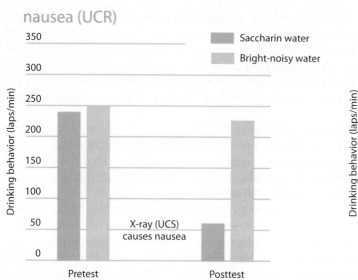
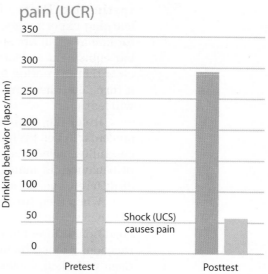

FIGURE **8.13**

LIMITS ON CONDITIONED TASTE AVERSION. Contrary to predictions from traditional learning theory, taste aversion conditioning depends on the stimulus. Conditioned taste aversion occurs only to the kind of stimulus that makes biological sense. For example, nausea produces aversion to taste, but not to noise and light, as shown in the graph on the left. Pain produces aversion to frightening stimuli, such as noise and bright lights, but not to saccharin water, as shown in the graph on the right. (Garcia & Koelling, 1966)

Garcia's subsequent research derailed another assumption of traditional learning theory: that reflexive responses (such as nausea) could be conditioned to any kind of stimulus. Garcia and Koelling (1966) varied the type of aversive stimulus (UCS) to which rats were exposed and the type of neutral stimulus (CS). Nausea (the UCR) was induced by exposure to X-rays, whereas pain (the other UCR) was induced by electrical shocks sent through the floor of the cage. When the rat licked the drinking tube, it received the CS of either saccharin water or "bright-noisy water" (plain water accompanied by a light and a buzzer that went on when the rat touched the drinking tube). The UCS for half the rats was irradiation-induced nausea. The other half received a shock. The irradiated rats avoided the sweet water but not the bright-noisy water (see Figure 8.13), whereas the rats that had received a mildly painful shock avoided the bright-noisy water but not the sweet water. The researchers described the first response as "conditioned nausea" and the second as "conditioned fear."

The key finding here is that, contrary to the predictions of traditional learning theory, an organism cannot be conditioned to respond to just any "neutral" stimulus paired with an unconditioned stimulus. We can learn certain things only under certain conditions. In other words, nausea can be conditioned to a taste but not to a light, because taste is relevant to eating, but light is not.

As another example of how research can radically change what we think we know, Garcia's research on taste aversion undermined two key assumptions of classical conditioning: (1) that conditioning could happen only if an organism were exposed repeatedly within a brief time span to the UCS and CS together, and (2) that organisms could learn to associate any two stimuli. With respect to the first assumption, Garcia showed in other research that the CS and UCS can be separated by as much as 75 minutes and still lead to conditioned taste aversion (Garcia, Ervin, & Koelling, 1966). With respect to the second assumption, the "bright-noisy water" findings showed that only certain stimuli can be conditioned to produce nausea (Garcia & Koelling, 1966). More specifically, you cannot make someone be nauseated by a sound or a sight as easily as by a taste.

Instinctive Drift   Many studies of conditioning used different species in learning experiments. Results from rats were readily assumed to be relevant for humans, but are species really interchangeable? Also, is learning to press a bar equivalent to learning to play the piano? Over many years, it has become clear that the notion of the equivalence of species and tasks is problematic. As it turns out, there are limits to what different species will learn and how they will learn it.

Ironically, this conclusion stemmed from the research of two of Skinner's students, Keller Breland and Marian Breland. Initially, the Brelands (1961) successfully applied traditional operant conditioning principles to shaping all kinds of behaviors in many kinds of animals. In fact, they successfully conditioned 38 different species and more than 6,000 animals.

When they turned their attention to species whose learning behavior had not been studied, however, they began to experience failures. When they tried to condition different animal species to insert poker chips into a vending machine, raccoons rubbed them instead of putting them in the slot machine, pigs rooted them with their snouts, and chickens pecked at them. When describing the raccoons' "problematic behavior," Breland and Breland wrote,

> The rubbing behavior became worse and worse as time went on, in spite of non-reinforcement. . . . These egregious failures came as a rather considerable shock to us, for there was nothing in our background in behaviorism to prepare us for such gross inabilities to predict and control the behavior of animals with which we had been working for years. (Breland & Breland, 1961, p. 683)

Initially, the Brelands considered such behavior misguided and even titled their article "The Misbehavior of Organisms." Once again, new science toppled old assumptions to offer new perspectives. With research, it became clear to the Brelands that these behaviors were not "misbehaviors" but normal expressions of innate instincts. It seems that raccoons naturally wash, pigs root, and chickens peck. Breland and Breland (1961) called this effect **instinctive drift,** which they defined as learned behavior that shifts toward instinctive, unlearned behavior tendencies.

Instinctive drift challenges the behaviorist conviction that learning always results either from associating an event with an unconditioned stimulus or from shaping by reinforcement or punishment. The Brelands' findings imply that there are biological limitations, or constraints, on learning. According to the **biological constraint model** of learning, some behaviors are inherently more likely to be learned than others (Garcia, McGowan, & Green, 1972; Seligman & Hager, 1972). Biology constrains options so that the adaptive ones are more likely to occur than the maladaptive ones.

Constraints on learning have positive evolutionary implications: They guide organisms in a direction that speeds up learning and aids survival or reproductive success. This model explains instinctive drift. Humans are geared toward learning language—one could say we "instinctively drift" toward speaking. It is very easy for us to learn to speak, assuming we are simply exposed to language early in infancy and childhood. Reading, writing, and arithmetic, however, are not so easily learned, which is one reason we need to go to school to learn these skills. We do not need to go to school to learn to speak. School might help with teaching us formal grammar and syntax, but we all use a grammar and kind of syntax.

Instinctive drift and biological constraints provide excellent examples of the limits nature places on nurture. Biology makes it possible for humans, but not chimpanzees, to talk. Experience interacting with the capacity for speech determines not only whether an individual learns to talk but also the language he or she learns. As we have seen, Garcia's groundbreaking research revised traditional thinking about classical conditioning within the limits of biology.

instinctive drift
Learned behavior that shifts toward instinctive, unlearned behavior tendencies.

biological constraint model
A view on learning which proposes that some behaviors are inherently more likely to be learned than others.

Latent Learning   Even before the Brelands studied biological constraints and learning, other psychologists challenged some of the basic assumptions of learning theory. One was Edward Tolman. Like many other learning researchers, Tolman ran rats through mazes. In one key study, hungry rats were randomly assigned to three groups (Tolman & Honzik, 1930). Rats in Group 1 were rewarded with food if they reached the end of a maze. Rats in this group became better and better at maze running, thanks to the reliable reinforcement of a food reward. Rats in Group 2 received no food for their work, and not surprisingly, they never ran the maze very well. They had no reinforcement. These results are what standard behaviorism would predict.

The rats in Group 3, however, received no reinforcement for running the maze—at least not at first. Like Group 2, they did not run the maze very well. But after a set of nonreinforced trials, they started being reinforced with food for their maze running. Suddenly, these rats started running the maze really well. It was as if they had been learning all along. In fact, the Group 3 rats even started performing better than the rats in Group 1.

How might we explain this outcome? Tolman argued that the rats in Group 3 had been learning all along—they just didn't show it before they started being reinforced. **Latent learning** is a type of learning that occurs in the absence of reinforcement and is not demonstrated until later, when reinforcement occurs. Tolman reasoned that these rats had formed internal *cognitive maps*—like pictures in their minds—of the maze from all the practice they had received. When they finally had rewards waiting for them, the rats could use these maps to run the maze more efficiently. It is difficult to know whether the rats really had maps of the maze in their minds. What is clear from these findings is that some learning can occur in the absence of reinforcement. Running the maze, even without rewards, helped the rats in Group 3 run much better when reinforcement was available.

Tolman's important research set the stage for future work on the role of thought in learning, something that Skinner (1990) and other behaviorists deemed irrelevant. Tolman's work also showed that prior experience—whether reinforced or not—aids future learning. Further, it suggested that motivation plays a part in learning. The idea of latent learning implies that learning sometimes stays hidden until the learner is motivated to perform.

latent learning
Learning that occurs in the absence of reinforcement and is not demonstrated until later, when reinforcement occurs.

Connection

People who cannot form new memories nevertheless learn. The body can learn things of which the conscious mind is not aware.

See "Long-Term Memory," Chapter 7, "Memory," p. 257.

Quick Quiz 8.1: Basic Processes and Conditioning Models of Learning

1. Using the definition provided in the text, which is the best example of learning?
   a. A plant moves toward the sun in order to get the best sunlight.
   b. A newborn baby automatically grabs a finger placed in its palm.
   c. A cat perks up its ears and looks toward a sound.
   d. Ten-year-old Jerry can snowboard down the mountain after practicing for a week.

2. Because we always use a can opener when getting their food, cats Scooter and Belle run into the kitchen each time they hear someone open the drawer where the can opener is kept. According to the text, the cats have
   a. remembered what cat food is.
   b. made an association between the drawer opening and being fed.
   c. habituated to noises in the kitchen.
   d. done none of the above.

3. A rat presses a lever, resulting in food delivery. The rat then presses the lever more frequently. This is an example of
   a. punishment.
   b. higher-order conditioning.
   c. reinforcement.
   d. extinction.

4. In a typical classical conditioning experiment, a neutral stimulus is
   a. repeatedly paired with the UCR.
   b. not paired with any other stimulus.
   c. repeatedly paired with the CS.
   d. repeatedly paired with the UCS.

5. A reinforcer is anything that _____; a punisher is anything that _____.
   a. makes a behavior less likely; makes a behavior more likely

b. makes a behavior more likely; makes a behavior less likely
c. is positive; is negative
d. is shaped; is extinguished

6. A slot machine player cannot know how many pulls of the slot machine arm it will take to win. On one occasion it might take just one pull to win a small jackpot. Other times dozens of quarters might be spent before winning. This payout schedule is what kind of schedule of reinforcement?
a. fixed-interval
b. fixed-ratio
c. variable-interval
d. variable-ratio

Answers can be found at the end of the chapter.

SOCIAL LEARNING THEORY

Albert Bandura

enactive learning
Learning by doing.

observational learning
Learning by watching the behavior of others.

We all look to others for clues on how to behave. Think about how you first learned to tie your shoes or even to swim. Did someone just explain the way to do it? Or did you try random motions and then get praise from your teacher every time you did something right? There may have been some random success, but chances are you learned the right movements by copying what your swim teacher or parent did. There is more to learning than associating one thing with another (classical conditioning) or doing something and then being reinforced for it (operant conditioning). Classical and operant conditioning explain many aspects of learning, but they neglect the powerful role of modeling in the learning process. Until the 1940s and 1950s, the two major schools of thought in learning were behaviorist—namely, classical and operant conditioning. Both of these approaches to learning completely ignore the role of thoughts, motives, and social modeling. Albert Bandura was to change this.

Obviously, people learn from their own experience, from their own successes and failures, and from trial and error, but if we had to learn everything that way, not only would the process take much, much longer but it also would require reinventing what others have already learned, over and over again. Learning by observing others is much more efficient. Albert Bandura proposed that we learn both by doing and by observing. Bandura (1986) called learning by doing **enactive learning** and learning by watching the behavior of others **observational learning.**

One of the most influential psychologists of all time, Bandura's path to psychology was an unplanned, fortuitous event. As an undergraduate, he had to take morning classes, because in the afternoon he worked to make ends meet. He drove to school with friends who were pre-med and engineering majors, who had classes even earlier than his. Instead of sitting around waiting for his first class to start, he decided to look for early-morning classes. "One morning, I was wasting time in the library. Someone had forgotten to return a course catalog and I thumbed through it attempting to find a filler course to occupy the early time slot. I noticed a course in psychology that would serve as excellent filler. It sparked my interest and I found a career" (Pajares, 2004).

As a graduate student in the 1940s, Albert Bandura thought the two major conditioning approaches were on to something but that each left out important, commonsense views of how learning happens. In Bandura's words,

> The prevailing analyses of learning focused almost entirely on learning through the effects of one's actions [operant conditioning]. . . . I found this behavioristic theorizing discordant with the obvious social reality that much of what we learn is through the power of social modeling. I could not imagine a culture in which its language, mores, familial customs and practices, occupational competencies, and educational, religious, and political practices were gradually shaped in each new member by rewarding and punishing consequences of their trial-and-error performances. (Bandura, 2006, p. 51)

At the time, only one book, *Social Learning and Imitation* by Neal Miller and John Dollard (1941), had been written on learning that took a social perspective. Bandura was more taken by this approach than by classical or operant conditioning, but he was not completely happy with Miller and Dollard's view of social learning (Bandura, 2006). He believed it was too simplistic, and he soon developed his own views of how observing and imitating others is at the foundation of much of human learning. His dissatisfaction propelled him to develop his own view on social learning, or what he now calls social-cognitive learning.

Bandura's **social learning theory** (1986) goes beyond traditional conditioning approaches to include observation and modeling as major components of learning. **Modeling** is Bandura's term for the process of observing and imitating behaviors performed by others. Modeling is everywhere. Younger children mimic the behavior of their older siblings. We pick up figures of speech and mannerisms from our closest friends. Modeling is more likely to occur in some people than in others, more likely after some behaviors than others, and more likely after some consequences than others.

Modeling is only one aspect of social learning theory. According to Bandura (1986), social learning also works through reinforcement. Remember from operant conditioning that the consequences of our behavior influence whether we repeat those behaviors. People learn best those things they are rewarded for doing, whether the rewards are external (such as praise, money, candy) or internal (such as joy and satisfaction). Bandura noted that reinforcement matters not only for the person carrying out the behavior but also for those who watch. Advertisers make use of this phenomenon all the time. When teenagers see young adults getting a lot of attention and having fun while they are drinking beer, they might be more likely to want to drink beer themselves. People will do things they see others doing, especially if the model's behavior is rewarded.

In the 1960s, Bandura and his colleagues demonstrated the power of observational learning in a series of classic studies—the Bobo doll studies. They came up with clever experiments to show how two key elements of social learning—modeling and reinforcement—affect behavior. The first study focused on the power of observational learning on aggressive behavior (Bandura, Ross, & Ross, 1961). Children observed an adult either being aggressive or not being aggressive with an inflatable doll, called a Bobo doll. Half saw the adult play politely with the Bobo doll. The others saw the adult sock the Bobo doll hard, hit it with a rubber mallet, and kick it around. Afterward, one at a time, the kids entered a room filled with toys (including the ones the model played with) and

social learning theory
A description of the kind of learning that occurs when we model or imitate the behavior of others.

modeling
The imitation of behaviors performed by others.

Children who observed an adult model being aggressive with a Bobo doll (left) in a study by Bandura tended to behave aggressively when given the opportunity to play with the doll (right).
What kind of learning is this? What conditions might increase the likelihood of children modeling this adult behavior?

were allowed free play. Children who had seen the adults act aggressively with the doll were much more likely to be aggressive when they had the chance to play with the Bobo than were those who had seen the adults play pleasantly with the doll. In fact, they adopted many of the same actions the adults had used. Thus, these initial studies demonstrated the power of modeling in the learning of aggression.

Another key study showed how reinforcement works with modeling to lead to learning (Bandura, Ross, & Ross, 1963). Again using an experimental design, this time the researchers introduced another variable: What happened to the models after they had behaved aggressively? The children saw one of four films: one with no models, one with two adult men who interacted in a nonaggressive manner, and two films with adult men who played aggressively with each other, but in one the aggressive man was punished, whereas in the other he was rewarded. The first two films (no model and nonaggressive models) were control conditions, whereas the last two (aggression) were experimental conditions. In the films shown to the experimental groups, one man was aggressive toward the other man. The aggressive man hit the nonaggressive man with a rubber mallet and shot darts at him. He also roughed up the inflatable Bobo doll. A key element of this study is that the films also showed what happened to the aggressive adult after the interaction. There were two possibilities. The aggressive adult was either punished (he lost the conflict and ended up cowering in the corner) or rewarded (he won the conflict and got to play with all the toys) for his aggression. The research design is summarized in Figure 8.14.

After seeing the film, the children had an opportunity to play with the Bobo doll and other toys they had seen in the film. Just as in the previous set of studies, how the kids acted with the doll and other toys was the main dependent

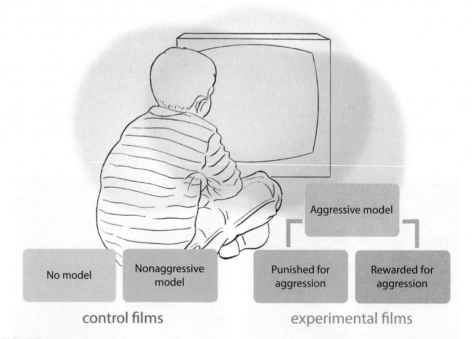

FIGURE **8.14**

EXPERIMENTAL DESIGN FOR BANDURA'S STUDY OF OBSERVATIONAL LEARNING AND AGGRESSION. Children viewed one of four films: one with no model, one with nonaggressive adult models, or one of two with an aggressive adult model, in which the model is either punished for being aggressive or rewarded for it. (Bandura, Ross, & Ross, 1963)

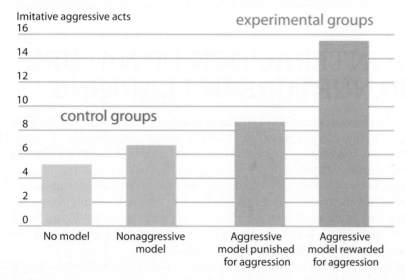

Do you think there is too much violence on TV? Explain.

variable. The primary finding from the previous study was replicated: Those who had viewed aggression were more aggressive with the doll than were those who had not seen aggression (see Figure 8.15), but the consequences for the model also mattered. The children who had seen the aggressive adult rewarded for his aggression were more violent with the toys and Bobo doll than were those who had seen the aggressive adult get punished. Those who had not seen an aggressive model did not show much aggression with the toys, nor did those who had seen the adult punished. These studies show how modeling and reinforcement can work together to influence behavior. Kids are more likely to copy behavior that they see others being rewarded for.

FIGURE 8.15

THE EFFECT OF MODELING AND REWARD ON LEARNED AGGRESSIVE BEHAVIOR. This graph depicts the number of imitative aggressive acts by children who had viewed one of four film conditions. The children who had seen the aggressive adults get rewarded for their aggression showed more aggressive acts, such as hitting the Bobo doll with a hammer or punching it, than did the children in the other three categories. (Bandura, Ross, & Ross, 1963)

The Bobo doll studies were pivotal in showing how children learn aggression and other violent behaviors from viewing aggression in others. The results, of course, have implications for the effect of violence on television, in movies, and in video games on children and teens. Numerous studies have demonstrated that kids behave more violently after exposure to violence in the media (Bushman & Anderson, 2001). Consider this startling example: Two teenage lovers, Ben Darras and Sarah Edmondson, apparently under the influence of drugs and Oliver Stone's movie *Natural Born Killer,* went on a killing spree. Stone's movie had depicted two young lovers on a wild and drug-filled rampage, callously killing and robbing people. After the copycat killers were arrested, they claimed they had also taken drugs and played Stone's movie in a continuous loop all night ("Natural Born Copycats," 2002).

Quick Quiz 8.2: Social Learning Theory

1. Barbara just started a new job, and she watches how her colleagues dress and act. The type of learning Barbara is doing is
   a. observational learning.
   b. enactive learning.
   c. operant conditioning.
   d. reinforcement.

2. The major finding(s) from Bandura's Bobo doll experiments were that
   a. children learn to be aggressive by watching other people be aggressive.
   b. children learn to be aggressive by observing reinforced aggression in others.

   c. children learn to be aggressive only if they see someone of the same sex be aggressive.
   d. Both a and b are correct.

3. Research generally shows that children
   a. are not at all likely to be aggressive after watching aggression on TV or in movies.
   b. are likely to be aggressive after watching aggression on TV or in movies.
   c. are more aggressive after watching aggression on TV or in movies only if they are from impoverished backgrounds.
   d. know the difference between movies and real life and are not influenced by movie violence.

Answers can be found at the end of the chapter.

THE INTERACTION OF NATURE AND NURTURE IN LEARNING

The early behaviorists refused to study anything that could not be directly observed, including mental processes and any potentially relevant biological structures. Watson and Skinner, in particular, took the position that all learning was a function of either stimuli (classical conditioning) or consequences (operant conditioning), both of which come from the outside environment. Although Skinner acknowledged the role of genetics in behavior, he and Watson ignored the role of cognitive and brain processes in learning, because these could not be observed (Skinner, 1938, 1990). Likewise, the behaviorists did not consider any form of instinctive behavior worthy of scientific study.

As we have seen, behaviorism sprang in part from a desire to study behavior in a measurable way. In behaviorism's heyday, there simply was no technology available for observing brain function or measuring its activity. When such technologies began to appear in the 1950s, the behaviorist model was challenged from various angles. Learning, it turns out, is not just an environmental process. It results from the constant interaction of the brain and the environment. A recent study examined whether children ages 7 to 12 with learning disabilities benefited from math tutoring (Ashkenazi et al., 2013). All the students in the study benefited some from tutoring, but not all equally. Those who improved the most had larger hippocampi than those who did not benefit as much. Further, those students who had strong connections between the hippocampus and PFC and basal ganglia benefited the most from tutoring. Biology makes learning possible, and learning changes biology. Extreme forms of behaviorism paint a picture of learning resulting primarily from one's experiences. It is an extreme environmental, or nature-only, view. Few modern behaviorists agree with such a one-sided view. In this section, we look at four learning processes that illustrate the dynamic interplay between nature and nurture in learning: imprinting, imitation, synaptic change, and brain growth with enrichment.

Imprinting

Not all forms of learning depend on reward and reinforcement. A good example is imprinting, the rapid and innate learning of the characteristics of a caregiver within a very short period of time after birth (Lorenz, 1935, 1937). Mammals and birds, which are born helpless, need to form a strong bond to a caregiver almost immediately after birth to avoid getting lost or being killed by a predator. We know this from **ethology,** the scientific study of animal behavior, and especially from the work of Austrian ethologist and winner of the 1973 Nobel Prize in Medicine, Konrad Lorenz, who studied imprinting extensively in birds. He observed that, soon after they hatched, ducklings and goslings (baby geese) learned to follow whatever they saw most, be it a mother duck or goose or, surprisingly, a human. This parent figure tends to be the first moving object the young animal sees within the first few days of life. Usually, this figure is the animal's mother, but it need not be, as Lorenz found out when he became an imprinted parent to a flock of goslings.

ethology
The scientific study of animal behaviors.

Imprinting provides clear evidence of a *sensitivity period* in learning: a period when a particular type of learning occurs very readily if an animal is exposed to a particular stimulus or situation. The brain seems to be primed at a particular time for a particular kind of learning. Once the animal has moved beyond that sensitivity period, it becomes much harder, if not impossible, to learn certain skills or make use of certain kinds of information. Once a "parent" has been imprinted on young ducks or geese, that learning is permanent and cannot be unlearned. Imprinting, in other words, can be learned soon after birth—or not at all. After a certain age, imprinting cannot be learned, unlearned, or relearned—it cannot be modified at all.

Although imprinting does not occur in humans, young babies do develop an important bond with their primary caregivers that serves much the same function (see Chapter 5). Imprinting and sensitivity periods in learning remind us that the mind is not a blank slate, able to learn anything

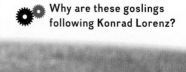
Why are these goslings following Konrad Lorenz?

at any time, given the right reinforcers and stimuli. The brain is structured in such a way that certain kinds of experiences are more or less easily learned at different periods in life; language learning by humans is one example, as discussed in Chapter 9.

Imitation, Mirror Neurons, and Learning

Humans imitate one another. Imitation is fundamental to the way in which human and nonhuman primates learn. As we discussed in the section on social learning theory, classical and operant conditioning do not take into account the powerful role of imitation in the learning process. Infants begin copying the behavior of adults and other children almost immediately. Babies as young as 7 hours old imitate simple adult facial expressions (Meltzoff & Moore, 1977, 1983).

Imitation by infants may be a result of mirror neuron systems (MNS) in the brain (Lepage & Théoret, 2007), although evidence suggests that MNS only becomes functional sometime between 3 and 6 months of life (Turati et al., 2013). As discussed in Chapter 3, humans and other primates have mirror neurons, which respond in much the same way while watching an action as they do while performing an action (Iacoboni & Mazziotta, 2007; Rizzolatti et al., 1996); see the Research Process for this chapter (Figure 8.16). Simply put, for some neurons in the frontal lobe of the cerebral cortex, the experience of watching someone else do something is like doing it yourself. When a monkey observes another monkey or a human grab a peanut, the same neurons fire in the frontal lobe as fire when the observing monkey actually grabs a peanut (Fogassi & Ferrari, 2006). It is likely that mirror neuron systems are involved in imitation and social learning (Filimon et al., 2007; Iacoboni et al., 1999; D. E. Lyons, 2009). Autistic children, who have trouble imitating others' gestures, may have deficits in mirror neuron systems (Bernier & Dawson, 2009; Oberman & Ramachandran, 2007; J. H. G. Williams et al., 2006), though it does not appear to be a general deficit in mirror neurons (Enticott et al., 2013).

Connection

Mirror neurons help explain why even infants imitate adult behavior so easily.

See "Early Socioemotional Development," Chapter 5, "Human Development," p. 181.

Like father, like son. We learn by observing and imitating others.

Research Process

1 Research Question

Rizzolatti and colleagues (1996) were studying neurons involved in hand movements in monkeys, when they made an accidental discovery: The same motor neurons fired when the monkey observed an experimenter grabbing an object as when the monkey made a similar action itself. It made the researchers wonder: Does the brain contain neurons that rehearse motor actions during observational learning?

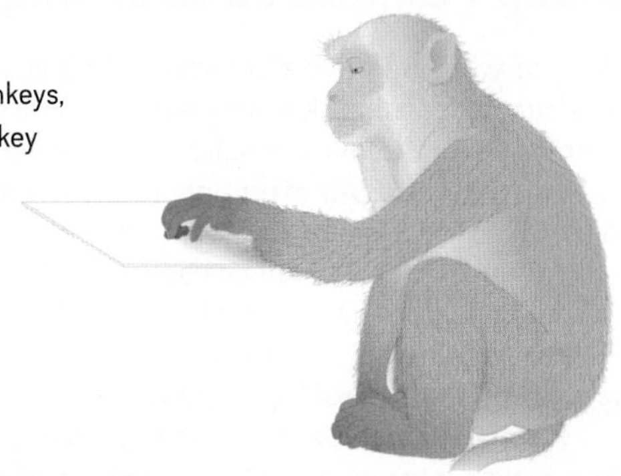

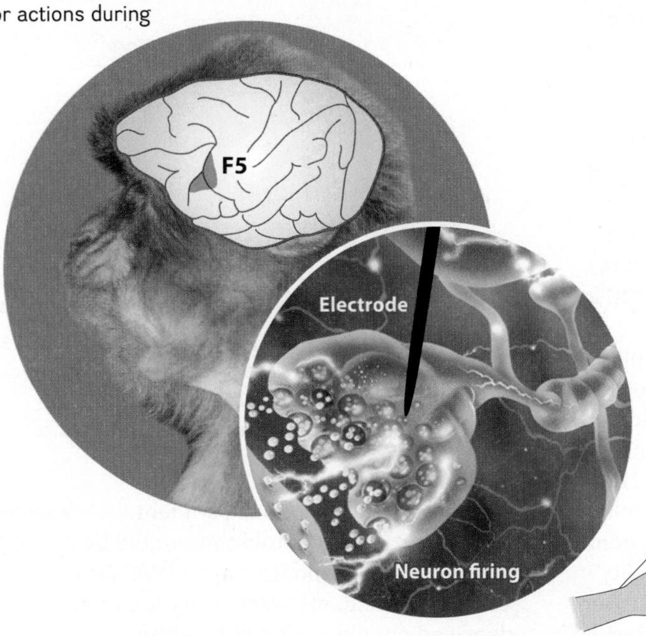

F5

Electrode

Neuron firing

2 Method

In a descriptive study of two monkeys, the researchers monitored activity of individual neurons in the motor cortex. They implanted a wire electrode in the motor cortex (area F5) and measured the firing rate of a single neuron while the monkey either grasped a piece of food itself or saw the experimenter pick it up.

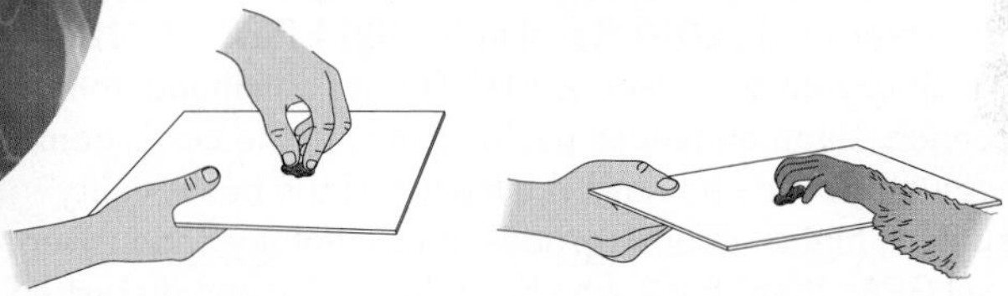

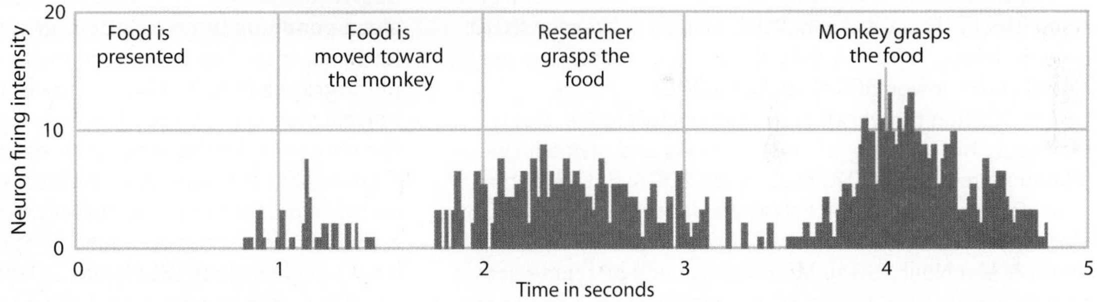

| Food is presented | Food is moved toward the monkey | Researcher grasps the food | Monkey grasps the food |

Neuron firing intensity

Time in seconds

3 Results

The graph shows the results of firing patterns in area F5 when food is presented, when it is moved toward the monkey, when the researcher grasps food, and when the monkey grasps food. The peaks of the graph are taller when the firing rate in area F5 is faster. They are shorter when the firing rate is slower. Notice that there is minimal firing when the monkey simply looks at the food. The firing rates increase during observation of grasping and during grasping itself. More importantly, the pattern of firing is similar when action is observed and when action is made by the monkey itself. Neurons that fire during action and observation of similar actions are called mirror neurons.

4 Conclusion

Mirror neurons support the function of rehearsal during learning. By watching others' actions, we "exercise" the motor regions of the brain involved in making those actions. This, in turn, allows us to perform the same behavior more readily.

FIGURE 8.16

THE DISCOVERY OF MIRROR NEURONS. Mirror neurons in the brain respond in much the same way while watching an action as they do when performing an action. (Rizzolatti, G., Fadiga, L., Gallese, V., & Fogassi, L. (1996). Premotorcortex and the recognition of motor actions. *Cognitive Brain Research*, 3, 131–141.)

Psychology in the Real World

Sleep Facilitates Learning

Much of what we have discussed in this chapter concerns very simple learning that may not sound directly relevant to how you might learn in school. To learn material in a class, you have to pay attention, take in new information, form new associations, and then store the information in a form that you can recall or use later. The processes of consciousness, memory, and learning all come together in classroom learning. Our topic in this section is simple—you need sleep to do all of these things.

Few college students get the sleep required to help their brains learn at an optimal level. It's almost regarded as a rite of passage for college students to "pull all-nighters" before exams and term papers. Sleep deprivation is rampant during the transition from high school to college and among college students (Buboltz et al., 2006; Carskadon & Davis, 1989).

A growing scientific literature shows that sleep plays an important role in learning. Beginning in infancy, better sleep is associated with increases in cognitive functioning—it enhances and consolidates what we learn during the day (Bernier et al., 2010; Karni et al., 1994; Payne & Nadel, 2004; Stickgold & Walker, 2007). During childhood and adolescence, sleep enhances performance in the classroom. College students who have the most and the best-quality sleep have higher course grades in psychology and higher overall GPAs than those who have disruptive and disturbed sleep (Beebe, Rose, & Amin, 2010; Gilbert & Weaver, 2010; Howell, Jahrig, & Powell, 2004). Pulling all-nighters is associated with a lower GPA (Thacher, 2008).

In addition to overall academic performance, sleep facilitates the learning of specific tasks and procedures (Ellenbogen et al., 2007; Gaab et al., 2004; S. C. Mednick et al., 2009; S. C. Mednick, Nakayama, & Stickgold, 2003; McKenna et al., in press; Payne & Kensinger, 2010; C. Smith & MacNeill, 1994). Motor skills such as typing are approximately 20% faster after a night's sleep compared to before sleep (Kuriyama, Stickgold, & Walker, 2004).

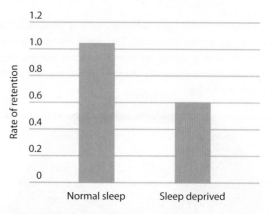

FIGURE 8.17

SLEEP DEPRIVATION AND RECALL OF EMOTIONAL PHOTOGRAPHS AFTER 36 HOURS. Students' recall for visual images is increased by 40% if they sleep normally, compared to students who are sleep-deprived.
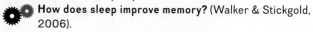 **How does sleep improve memory?** (Walker & Stickgold, 2006).

In another study on recall, students were shown photographs but were not told they would be asked to recall the details of the photographs (Walker & Stickgold, 2006). Participants were assigned to either a sleep-deprived condition (2 nights without sleep) or a normal sleep condition (8 hours). Both groups were unexpectedly (to them) tested on how much they could recall about the photographs they had been shown 36 hours earlier. The normal sleep group recalled 40% more details about the photographs than the sleep-deprived group (see Figure 8.17). It seems that children show greater improvements in performance on certain memory tasks following a night of sleep than do adults; that is, they benefit more from a night's sleep (Stickgold, 2013).

There are several possible means by which sleep facilitates learning, but one of the main mechanisms

Synaptic Change during Learning

If you've ever tried to learn a second language, you know that if you don't use it for a while you forget what you've learned. Similarly, you will probably forget much of the material you learn in this class soon after the exam, even if you learn it well to begin with. Why is that?

In Chapter 7 we saw what Hebb's work on learning and memory revealed about the plasticity of the brain: "Neurons that fire together, wire together" and "use it or lose it." We also discussed Kandel's studies on the sea slug *Aplysia*. Both

involved is the spontaneous replay and consolidation of daily events during sleep. Evidence for this conclusion comes from both animal and human research (Ji & Wilson, 2007; O'Neill et al., 2010; Wilson & McNaughton, 1994). A fascinating example of this finding involves research with rats (Ji & Wilson, 2007). Before running a maze, rats had very thin electrodes painlessly implanted in their hippocampi (learning and memory centers) to measure the activity patterns of specific neurons. When the mice were running the maze, a particular pattern of neural firing was observed. Much to the researchers' surprise, while these rats slept, a *very* similar pattern of brain activity was replayed in the hippocampus and the visual cortex. In other words, while they slept, their brains spontaneously and without effort were rehearsing and consolidating what had been learned during the day. In fact, the phenomenon of "sleeping on" a problem by working it out spontaneously during the night and having a solution suddenly appear in the morning is probably related to the rehearsal and replay of learned experience (Walker & Stickgold, 2006). Dozens of human studies support a strong role for sleep in memory consolidation and learning (Diekelmann, Wilhelm, & Born, 2009), though the effects may vary as a function of age and the nature of the material to be remembered (Wilson et al., 2012).

Even the most basic processes of learning—classical and operant conditioning—are affected by sleep. Even an eyeblink can be conditioned to occur in response to a neutral stimulus (such as a sound). This is textbook classical conditioning. In a study of sleep-deprived and non-sleep-deprived college students, those who missed out on REM sleep showed serious deficits in even this simple kind of conditioning (Ohno et al., 2002). It seems that adequate REM sleep, in particular, is even crucial for basic motor learning (C. T. Smith, Aubrey, & Peters, 2004).

If sleep facilitates learning and memory—and yet college students are notoriously sleep-deprived—then what can you do to help combat this problem without resorting to drugs such as caffeine and other addicting stimulants? To simply implore you to get more sleep is a bit unrealistic and vague, yet it is the single most helpful thing you can do to overcome the sleep-deficit effect on learning. The following are a few specific recommendations on how you can use sleep to improve your school performance.

First, get more sleep the night or two before an exam. Studying for hours and hours all through the night is not very efficient, because what you try to learn has no time to replay and consolidate in your brain. Second, short midday naps enhance learning, alertness, and memory (S. C. Mednick & Ehman, 2006; Waterhouse et al., 2007). If you can steal a 20- to 30-minute nap during the day, this will help with alertness, attention, and memory (not to mention physical performance as well). Finally, if you have trouble getting a good night's sleep, try exercising more. Aerobic exercise provides the best benefits to neural growth, learning, attention, and alertness (Hillman et al., 2008; B. L. Marks et al., 2007; Pereira et al., 2007). Even a brief period of exercise (10 minutes) can temporarily increase alertness, memory, and performance (Horne & Foster, 1995; Sallinen et al., 2008). Regular and longer periods of exercise are associated with both better sleep and better performance in school (S. Brand et al., 2010; LeDuc, Caldwell, & Ruyak, 2000). The connection between exercise and sleep is simple: Students who exercise more tend to sleep longer and have better-quality sleep.

Challenge Your Assumptions

True or False? Pulling an all-nighter is not a good way to study for an exam.

True: Memory is impaired after a night of poor sleep; sleep, especially REM sleep, consolidates and strengthens memories.

areas of research provided experimental evidence of the neural basis of learning and memory (Kandel, 2006; Pinsker et al., 1973). Specifically, certain proteins become activated in short- and long-term memory formation and learning. These proteins change preexisting synaptic connections and cause the growth of new synapses (H. L. Fields, 2005; Kandel, 2001). What this means is that learning *is* the growth of new synapses. Synaptic connections between neurons become stronger and even grow during long-term associative learning. The brain literally grows and changes as we learn. The development and frequent use of new synaptic connections in response to stimulation from the environment strengthen

What effect does regular practice have on synaptic connections?

the associated memories and make learning easier. So having experiences repeated over a short period of time is often essential for moving an experience from short-term to long-term memory—that is, for learning to take place. The saying "practice makes perfect" is quite relevant here. To learn and become proficient at something requires repeating the behavior over and over. Synapses need to grow and strengthen.

However, the same synaptic connections will weaken if they aren't used regularly, resulting in forgetting and the loss of learning. Thus, when we stop using learned information, the synapses that support our knowledge weaken and ultimately degrade—and we forget what we once knew. Practice, use, and rehearsal are important in retaining what we have learned.

If you play a musical instrument, you have experienced this phenomenon directly. The more you practice the scales on your piano or guitar, for example, the more synaptic connections you build and the stronger they become. The scales become easier and easier to play. The sensations and movements associated with the increased experience of playing occupy a greater area of your motor cortex and, in effect, change the mapping of touch information in your brain (Pascual-Leone, 2001). If you stop practicing, those connections weaken, the brain map changes, and the scales are harder to recall the next time you try to play. Sleep also consolidates what we learn during the day (see "Psychology in the Real World").

Experience, Enrichment, and Brain Growth

As we have seen again and again, experience changes the brain. Recall the discussion in Chapter 2 of the classic work demonstrating that rats reared in enriched or normal environments grow more neural connections and learn to run mazes faster than genetically identical rats raised in impoverished environments (E. L. Bennett et al., 1964; Rosenzweig et al., 1962).

Building on this research, later experiments showed that animals do not have to be raised from birth in an enriched environment to benefit. Laboratory mice, for example, can have identical "childhoods" (the first 21 days of their lives) and then be randomly assigned to three different environments: no enrichment, short enrichment (68 days), and long enrichment (6 months). The longer they live in an enriched environment, the more neural growth there is in the hippocampus (Kempermann & Gage, 1999). More importantly, however, simply being in an enriched environment is not even the best way to stimulate the growth of new neurons: Being in an enriched environment that continues to have new and novel forms of stimulation is even better (Kempermann & Gage, 1999). What is more, enrichment can reverse age-related reductions in neural growth (neurogenesis) in rats (Speisman et al., 2013).

In an effort to better understand what aspects of an enriched environment facilitate the growth of new neurons, researchers compared the effects of social interaction, swimming, running, and maze learning on neurogenesis (Pereira et al., 2007; van Praag, Kempermann, & Gage, 1999). Only the running condition led to hippocampal neurogenesis, which is consistent with several studies that show that physical exercise benefits neural growth (Li et al., 2013). Similar enrichment effects on neuron growth occur in other species besides rats, including

Connection

Can experience and learning generate new neurons in an elderly person?

See "The Developing Adult," Chapter 5, "Human Development," p. 193.

birds, primates, and humans (Doetsch & Scharff, 2001; Eriksson et al., 1998; E. Gould et al., 2001; Hillman, Erickson, & Kramer, 2008). In a review of more than 200 studies of both humans and animals, Hötting and Röder (2013) reported that, due to neuroplasticity, physically active people and animals have an increased capacity for learning and other cognitive tasks.

Quick Quiz 8.3: The Interaction of Nature and Nurture in Learning

1. Because Konrad Lorenz was the first and only animal baby geese knew for the first few weeks of their lives, they thought Lorenz was their "mother." This kind of association is known as
   a. reinforcement.
   b. imprinting.
   c. learning.
   d. conditioning.

2. What biological structure(s) or system(s) best explain why we cry along with characters in a sad movie?
   a. mirror neurons
   b. sensory neurons
   c. frontal lobes
   d. hypothalamus

3. Research on learning and the brain has shown that rats raised in impoverished environments
   a. learn just as quickly as rats raised in enriched environments.
   b. have the same number of neurons in the hippocampus as rats raised in enriched environments.
   c. learn more slowly but have the same number of neurons and synaptic connections as rats raised in enriched environments.
   d. learn more slowly and have fewer neurons and synaptic connections than rats raised in enriched environments.

Answers can be found at the end of the chapter.

Bringing It All Together

Making Connections in Learning

Why Do People Smoke?

As you have probably figured out by now, human behavior is complex, so it should be no surprise that any given behavior may be acquired and maintained by means of several types of learning (classical, operant, and/or social), all operating in the context of a human being who has a personality and history. Consider, for example, cigarette smoking (see Figure 8.18). The acquisition of smoking behavior—how people become smokers in the first place—is perhaps best explained by social learning theory (Bandura, 1969, 1986). The sensory qualities of cigarette smoking on first experience are anything but pleasant—coughing, dizziness, and nausea—but most smokers start smoking as teenagers, and most teens start smoking because they seek some of the rewards that appear to come with smoking: coolness, peer acceptance, looking like an adult. (All of these rewards are secondary reinforcers, which acquire their reinforcing characteristics by means of classical and operant conditioning.) Kids see that others who smoke get some of these rewards for smoking. Thus, they might model smoking behavior in order to obtain these rewards themselves. They might view "being seen as cool"—a form of peer acceptance—as desirable, so being seen as cool becomes a reinforcer for

the smoking behaviors of others. "Whenever Mom gets stressed, she smokes a cigarette to relax—maybe that will work for me too" is another example of social learning.

Once someone has become an established smoker, operant conditioning helps maintain smoking behavior. Smoking is bolstered by a number of positive reinforcers: arousal of the sympathetic nervous system (the "rush" of smoking), mild relaxation of the muscles, and, in some cases, increased peer acceptance. Smoking also has a number of negative reinforcers, such as the removal of stress, the removal of social isolation for some smokers, and a reduced appetite. The power of these reinforcers, combined with the physiologically addictive properties of nicotine, makes it very difficult to quit smoking. Moreover, the potential punishers of smoking—a substantially increased risk of lung cancer and heart disease—are threats that are so far off in the future for teens that they tend to ignore them. It is for this reason that some psychologists who are concerned with preventing teen smoking have tried to link smoking with unpleasant images and effects (such as ugliness and social rejection). The hope is that, by using both classical and operant conditioning, they can

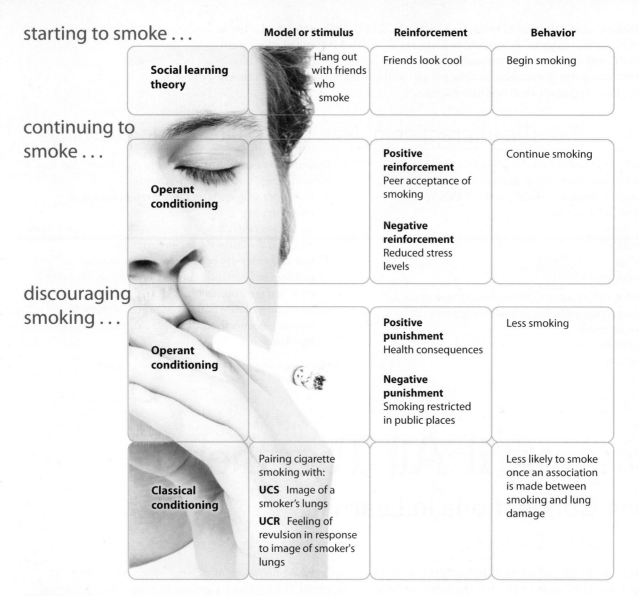

starting to smoke . . .	Model or stimulus	Reinforcement	Behavior
Social learning theory	Hang out with friends who smoke	Friends look cool	Begin smoking
continuing to smoke . . . **Operant conditioning**		**Positive reinforcement** Peer acceptance of smoking **Negative reinforcement** Reduced stress levels	Continue smoking
discouraging smoking . . . **Operant conditioning**		**Positive punishment** Health consequences **Negative punishment** Smoking restricted in public places	Less smoking
Classical conditioning	Pairing cigarette smoking with: **UCS** Image of a smoker's lungs **UCR** Feeling of revulsion in response to image of smoker's lungs		Less likely to smoke once an association is made between smoking and lung damage

FIGURE 8.18

HOW LEARNING THEORIES EXPLAIN SMOKING BEHAVIOR.

How do different theories of learning explain why people start smoking and continue smoking?

make smoking appear less rewarding. In order to discourage smoking, some public health campaigns show pictures of diseased lungs or smokers who look older than they are. It is an effort to teach people to have an unpleasant association with a cigarette and therefore stop smoking.

Like many complex human behaviors, smoking derives from numerous other influences besides conditioning. Gender, personality, and sociocultural characteristics are some of the factors that may interact with conditioning and biology to influence people to start smoking and affect whether they successfully quit.

Although numerous studies have found no evidence for gender differences in the factors related to smoking, one large-scale study found that gender influences susceptibility to smoking, the way people work with their urges to

smoke, and the ability to successfully quit (Ellickson, Tucker, & Klein, 2001). Whether friends smoke plays a stronger role in whether adolescent girls attempt and succeed at quitting smoking than it does in boys. In a study of the effects of smoking abstinence (and therefore nicotine withdrawal) on craving and cognitive performance in male and female adolescent smokers, girls reported greater tobacco cravings and symptoms of nicotine withdrawal than boys, but boys performed worse on two cognitive tasks during nicotine withdrawal (Jacobsen et al., 2005). Taken together, these studies suggest that gender may interact with social and cognitive factors to maintain smoking by influencing whether teens decide to attempt to quit (girls have more social pressures to try to quit) and the extent to which the effects of nicotine withdrawal are debilitating (the adverse effects on performance are worse for boys). These are just some of the factors that may explain why more boys smoke than girls, although the gap is narrowing (L. A. Robinson & Kleseges, 1997).

Other research shows that personality style predicts whether people start smoking and whether they try to stop, introducing yet another variable into this complex behavior. A study of personality and smoking found that people who are more sociable, impulsive, rebellious, hostile, and sensation seeking are more likely to start smoking and less likely to quit successfully than those who do not have these personal characteristics (Lipkus et al., 1994). This finding fits with established theory that extraverts are more likely to be smokers than introverts, because extraverts have a physiological need for stimulation and therefore seek experiences that are physiologically arousing, such as smoking, drinking, and thrill-seeking feats (Eysenck, 1980). Furthermore, a lack of certain cognitive skills, including long-term thinking and planning abilities, in some adolescents may predispose them to smoke. Not having a long-term perspective, they fail to understand the negative effects of smoking on health (Dinn, Aycicegi, & Harris, 2004). This explanation makes sense if we consider the prevalence of health promotion efforts designed to discourage people from smoking. The urges or need for stimulation may combine with cognitive factors and social learning (modeling peer behavior) to make it very difficult for some people to resist smoking.

The presence of models for smoking (such as parents and friends) figures among the environmental factors that influence smoking behavior. A study of more than 6,000 seventh-grade girls and boys reported differences between African Americans and European Americans in their exposure to peer and parent role models for smoking, which may account for discrepancies in smoking rates in these groups (Robinson & Kleseges, 1997). Specifically, the African American children were less likely to smoke than the European American children, and they had fewer family members and friends who smoked. They also believed that smoking was less common than did European American children. These findings indicate that cultural variables (ethnic group), social factors (the availability of role models), and basic principles of learning (observational learning) can all interact to influence whether young people start smoking (Ellickson et al., 2004).

Given the role that reinforcement plays in the acquisition of smoking behavior, it is not surprising that operant conditioning has been used to help people kick the smoking habit. **Behavior modification** techniques, which apply the principles of operant conditioning to changing behavior, have been particularly effective in helping people quit smoking, especially when combined with nicotine replacement therapies (such as gum or the patch), which ease the symptoms of withdrawal. Smokers who participate in such programs are likely to live longer than those who don't (Anthonisen et al., 2005).

behavior modification Principles of operant conditioning used to change behavior.

Chapter Review

BASIC PROCESSES OF LEARNING

- Learning is an enduring change in behavior that results from experience. It involves changes in sensation, perception, behavior, and brain function.

- Learning by association is a simple form of learning that links two pieces of information from the environment with one another because, in our experience, they repeatedly occur together.

CONDITIONING MODELS OF LEARNING

- Classical conditioning centers on stimulus-response (SR) relationships. It involves the modification of reflexes with experience. A conditioned response occurs when a neutral stimulus (such as a bell) elicits what was previously an unconditioned response (such as salivation) to an unconditioned stimulus (such as food) when it is presented alone. After conditioning, the neutral stimulus is called a conditioned stimulus.

- In operant conditioning, the consequences of spontaneous behavior are manipulated in order to elicit the desired behavior. According to Skinner, certain consequences make a behavior more likely to occur again. When the consequences of a behavior increase the likelihood that a behavior will occur again, the behavior has been reinforced. Reinforcement can be positive (something added) or negative (something subtracted).

- In contrast, punishment decreases the likelihood that a behavior will occur again. The stimuli used for reinforcement and punishment are unrelated to the target behavior. Shaping is the reinforcement of successive approximations of a desired behavior.

- Reinforcement may be presented every time a behavior occurs or only occasionally. Intermittent reinforcement, reinforcement that does not occur after every response, produces a stronger behavioral response than does continuous reinforcement. Four schedules of reinforcement dictate how an intermittent reinforcement might be implemented: fixed-ratio, variable-ratio, fixed-interval, and variable-interval.

- Conditioned taste aversion, the learned avoidance of a particular taste or food if sickness occurs at the same time as or shortly after exposure to it, can develop after only one exposure. The time lapse between exposure and sickness may be an hour or more.

- Biological constraints limit the development of a conditioned response to a neutral stimulus that is relevant to the situation. For example, it is easier to make someone nauseated by a taste than by a sound or a sight.

- Biology limits behavioral options in order to make the adaptive ones more likely. The biological constraint model of learning suggests that some behaviors are inherently more likely to be learned than others. Instinctive drift, in which an organism fails to learn the target behavior because it conflicts with a stronger instinctive behavior, is a type of biological constraint.

- Latent learning occurs in the absence of reinforcement and is not demonstrated until later, when reinforcement occurs.

SOCIAL LEARNING THEORY

- Social learning theory takes into account the role of social influence in learning. Imitation, or modeling, plays a key role in how we learn, and it can work with reinforcement to shape behavior. Bandura proposed that reinforcement makes learning more likely not only for the person doing the behavior but also for observers.

- Modeling is the process of observing and imitating behaviors performed by others, particularly behaviors that are rewarded in others.

THE INTERACTION OF NATURE AND NURTURE IN LEARNING

- Examples of the bidirectional relationship between learning and the brain include imprinting, the rapid and innate learning of the characteristics of a caregiver within a very short period of time after birth; sensitivity periods, when the brain is most receptive to learning certain skills; imitation; the growth and strengthening of synaptic connections in response to environmental stimuli; and environmental enrichment.

BRINGING IT ALL TOGETHER: MAKING CONNECTIONS IN LEARNING

- All of the major learning perspectives, as well as other factors, are needed to fully explain behaviors such as smoking.

- Applications derived from models of learning, such as behavior modification, may help people unlearn unwanted or undesirable behaviors, such as smoking.

Key Terms

association, p. 287
behavior modification, p. 319
biological constraint model, p. 304
classical conditioning, p. 288
conditioned response (CR), p. 289
conditioned stimulus (CS), p. 289
conditioned taste aversion, p. 301
conditioning, p. 287
continuous reinforcement, p. 299
enactive learning, p. 306

ethology, p. 311
extinction, p. 290
fixed-interval (FI) schedule, p. 300
fixed-ratio (FR) schedule, p. 299
instinctive drift, p. 304
intermittent reinforcement, p. 299
latent learning, p. 305
law of effect, p. 292
learning, p. 287
modeling, p. 307

negative punishment, p. 295
negative reinforcement, p. 294
observational learning, p. 306
operant conditioning, p. 292
positive punishment, p. 295
positive reinforcement, p. 294
primary reinforcers, p. 294
punishment, p. 295
reinforcer, p. 294
schedules of reinforcement, p. 299

secondary (conditioned)
reinforcers, p. 294
shaping, p. 297
Skinner box, p. 296
social learning theory, p. 307
spontaneous recovery, p. 290

stimulus discrimination, p. 289
stimulus generalization, p. 289
unconditioned response (UCR),
p. 288
unconditioned stimulus (UCS),
p. 288

variable-interval (VI) schedule,
p. 300
variable-ratio (VR) schedule,
p. 300

Quick Quiz Answers

Quick Quiz 8.1: 1. d 2. b 3. c 4. d 5. b 6. d   **Quick Quiz 8.2:** 1. a 2. d 3. b   **Quick Quiz 8.3:** 1. b 2. a 3. d

9 Language and Thought

Chapter Outline

Language
Thinking, Reasoning, and Decision Making
Chapter Review

Challenge Your Assumptions

True or False?

- Learning grammar is easy only for highly educated people. (see page 331)

- Critical thinking involves seeing only the weaknesses and flaws in ideas. (see page 344)

- Humans are generally rational in their decision making. (see page 349)

- Eighteen-year-olds cannot learn to speak a second language without an accent just as easily as a 6-year-old. (see page 352)

- Children raised from infancy with two languages (bilingually) seldom confuse the two languages. (see page 354)

خلائق كما من اخلائقنا واوليائكما
فتح واعادى فتح اي من خلقك ه
والنشر به نقال فتح
الفتح المحكم والفاح للحاكم
ـه بنا ونبر فتحنا بالجو وانت
وفتح البلد كذا ونحو وغير

وهو ان اذا ظفر به فقد
الا تعالى فتح بنا بالجو
ونبر فتحنا بالجو ه
افتح بيننا وبين قومنا بالحق
وللفتح الدين كفروا
بالعذاب بهم لا ذلك
اربها ذلك لينفصل بينا
وللفصل نحو ان يكون
وظهر الحق معناه
ـال النا محالك
ـد والحديث بين
وليس ذلك بالوجه

[الصفحة اليسرى]

ـه له ليغفر لك الله ما تقدم
وذلك آية لا يجوز ان نقول فتح لك ه
دينك وقيل فتح له الحج والاصابة
الى الحق وقيل الفتح البين الهداية الى
والثالث النصر ف
للناس من رحمة لعنى ما خصّ هو به من رزق ف ه
تعالى حتى اذا فتحت ياب
والخامس البعث ف
يا ايها اعناب سبيلاي بعثنا عليهم عذابا
الفتح اى ه
الآخرة اى حتى اذا خلناهم جهنم اذا هم مبلسه
الياس والسادس فتح الباب قال ان ه
والتشديد للتنصيره
مفتوحة في الاكثر وروى لنا ابو احمد
ما لت افح انوا و غلف
عامة الناس وقال انف ه
وغيره من اهل العربية ف
والقليل وفطت بالتشديد لا يكون الا ه
منها كلمته ه والسابع النصر ف

As they awaited the birth of their first child, Mike and Lisa had a decision to make: In what language should they raise their child? Mike was born in Greece but had moved to the United States at age 11, so he was fluent in both Greek and English. Lisa was an American raised in California, but she was also near-native fluent in French and conversationally fluent in Greek. They never questioned wanting their daughter to be bilingual in both Greek and English—partly because they believed her thinking would be more flexible from the different language structures (e.g., verbs are in different places). They weren't even aware of the research that confirms this hunch and shows that being bilingual facilitates cognitive and intellectual development and boasts flexible, creative thinking; it even appears to delay the onset of dementia later in life (Bialystok & Craik, 2010; Bialystok, Craik, & Ryan, 2006). In short, raising their child bilingually made sense for both cultural and cognitive reasons.

Yet how would Lisa and Mike go about raising their daughter, Zoé, to be bilingual? Would one parent speak one language and the other another language? They chose a different route: They decided they would both speak to her only in Greek from day 1. They reasoned that raising Zoé in America guaranteed her ease in picking up English quickly from grandparents, aunts, uncles, cousins, neighbors, and playmates. Indeed, research shows that children pick up a culturally dominant language outside the home very quickly and often prefer it (as it is the language of most of their friends), so Greek would need strong support at home. Mike and Lisa would speak only Greek during Zoé's infancy and early childhood, taking annual trips to Greece to visit family.

Some family friends and relatives wondered whether not teaching Zoé the language of her larger environment (English) would confuse her and put her at a disadvantage. Also, wouldn't she try to speak Greek to people who spoke only English? After all, young children don't even have a concept of "English" or "Greek"—they just speak.

Zoé ended up having little trouble in both languages. She is now 9 years old and has spoken fluent Greek from toddlerhood and by age 5 was fluent in English. Given that English is her second language, it is not unusual for her to become fluent later than English-only speaking children. Most importantly, she intuitively knows who understands which language and never tries to speak Greek to her American relatives or English to her Greek relatives. Interestingly, Zoé had decided by age 4 or so, however, that at home she wanted to speak English, so now the primary language at home is English. She attends a Greek school once a week and takes long visits with family in Greece, which helps maintain her fluency. Whether coincidence or not, she is quite artistic and creative.

Language is so much a part of being human that we forget it is possible to think without words. However, when we dream, visually imagine something, or experience a strong sensation (such as a touch or a smell), our thoughts are not initially word-bound, and surely the thoughts of young babies are not verbal. Still, most of our thoughts are translated into words. Even a smell is quickly labeled as a rose or a cake in the oven and, so, becomes a verbal experience as well as a sensory one. Language and thought develop side by side, with few exceptions. One is not possible without the other, at least in adult humans. Some linguists, in fact, have argued that abstract thought can only have evolved in the context of complex language (Perlovsky & Ilin, 2013).

This chapter introduces the psychology of language and thought, both separately and together. First we look at language by exploring its nature, evolution, and development in humans. Then we turn to current psychological research and theory concerning how we represent our thoughts visually and verbally. We look at how people reason, form judgments, and make decisions. Finally, we bring all these topics together by examining how and when learning a second language changes our brains and affects our ability to reason, solve problems, and think flexibly. We will continue the discussion of thought in Chapter 10, where we discuss intelligence, problem solving, and creativity.

LANGUAGE

If you lived 300,000 years ago, before language was fully developed, how would you think and communicate if everyone you met could only grunt and groan? Much like the other primates on the planet, you would communicate with other humans only about immediate, concrete states. Everything you knew would be experienced directly through smell, taste, hearing, sight, or touch. Your memory would be limited chiefly to events in the recent past; you would have no language with which to process events and store them in long-term memory. Without language, culture and civilization as we now know it could not exist, and your ways of thinking, understanding, and transmitting knowledge would be limited to the here and now.

Bonobos do communicate with one another—not with words but by leaving trail markers on the floor of the tropical forests where they live.

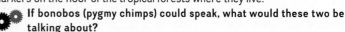 If bonobos (pygmy chimps) could speak, what would these two be talking about?

The Nature of Language

Linguists define **human language** as an open and symbolic communication system that has rules of grammar and allows its users to express abstract and distant ideas (Bickerton, 1995). To be *open* is to have a dynamic system free to change, and to be *symbolic* is to have no real connection between a sound and the meaning or idea associated with it. Sounds are parts of words that symbolize meaning and ideas. Words in turn are put together in ways that follow the rules of syntax and grammar. **Syntax** refers to the rules for arranging words and symbols in sentences (or parts of sentences), whereas **grammar** comprises the entire set of rules for combining symbols and sounds to speak and write a particular language and includes such things in English as subject-verb agreement, plurals, and the use of possessives.

The easiest way to demonstrate the arbitrary nature of the connection between sound and meaning is to point out that we can say exactly the same sentence in almost every language in the world, of which there are nearly 7,000. For example, "I am reading the book" can also be "Ich lese das Buch" in German," "Estoy leyendo el libro" in Spanish, "Je lis le livre" in French, and "Я читаю книгу" in Russian. Each language has its own distinct sounds for saying the same thing. Because this is true, ideas can often be directly translated—more or less—from one language to another, a topic we return to in "Bringing It All Together" at the end of the chapter.

human language
A communication system specific to *Homo sapiens;* it is open and symbolic, has rules of grammar, and allows its users to express abstract and distant ideas.

syntax
The rules for arranging words and symbols to form sentences or parts of sentences in a particular language.

grammar
The entire set of rules for combining symbols and sounds to speak and write a particular language.

Human language is unique because it is the only system capable of transmitting abstract ideas. Although most animals communicate, for the most part they are able to signal to other members of their species only their immediate and concrete states, such as being angry, threatened, hungry, hurt, or eager to reproduce (Deacon, 1997). Humans can discuss not only immediate feelings and needs but also abstract and remote ideas or states of being, such as infinity, God, the afterlife, the universe—or whether Macs are better than PCs.

The Evolution of Language in Humans

As far as we know, earlier species of humans, such as *Homo erectus* and *Homo neanderthalensis*, had, at most, very rudimentary language, called **protolanguage,** or pre-language (Arbib, Liebal, & Pika, 2008; Givón & Malle, 2002; Johansson, 2013). No one knows for sure when fully grammatical language first appeared, but archaeologists and linguists suggest that probably only our species (*Homo sapiens*) has used grammatical and syntactical language. If so, language is less than 150,000 years old.

Because the development of fully grammatical language is such a big and unusual step, scientists think that the evolution of language and evolution of the brain were intertwined. Anthropologists and psychologists suggest that the complexity of the human brain and the human ability to use language co-evolved. As our ancestors moved from protolanguage to grammatical language, they required brains with greater working memory and the ability for abstract thought (Arbib et al., 2008; Deacon, 1997; Dunbar, 2001).

As the human brain, and especially the frontal lobes, grew larger and larger, people became capable of thinking and communicating more and more complex and abstract thoughts. Increases in the size of human social groups may have triggered an increase in brain size as well. The more complex a group is, the greater is its members' need to communicate and cooperate (Dunbar, 2001). The needs for reciprocating and cooperating also played a role in the evolution of human language (Nowak & Sigmund, 2005).

Language Development in Individuals

If you have ever traveled to a country where you don't speak the language, you know that a foreign language can seem like a single, continuous string of sounds. It is hard to know where one word ends and the next one begins, unless you have been hearing and speaking that language since early childhood. As young children develop their understanding of language, they learn that the sounds coming from the mouths of the people around them are meaningful units that form words.

In a child's language development, the ability to understand words develops before the ability to produce words (Fenson et al., 1994). We can easily observe that comprehension comes first, because babies can do many things that are asked of them, such as pointing to their nose, long before they can say the words associated with those actions. Language comprehension, as we saw in Chapter 3, occurs in the left hemisphere of the brain, in the region called Wernicke's area, whereas language production is associated with the left-hemisphere region called Broca's area (see Figure 9.1). The fact that infants understand language before they start speaking suggests that Wernicke's area develops earlier than Broca's area.

protolanguage
Very rudimentary language used by earlier species of *Homo;* also known as pre-language.

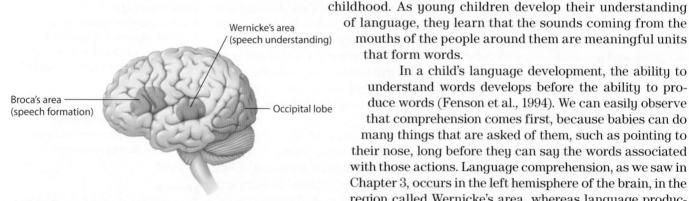

Wernicke's area
(speech understanding)

Broca's area
(speech formation)

Occipital lobe

FIGURE 9.1

WERNICKE'S AND BROCA'S AREAS AND THE OCCIPITAL LOBES. The occipital lobes are home to the visual cortex. As we'll see later, thinking involves both verbal and visual representations.

Stages of Language Development   The first speech sounds humans make consist almost exclusively of vowels, such as "aah, ee, ooh." Most infants begin uttering repeated vowel sounds, called **cooing,** during the first 6 months. Cooing sounds are universal: They vary little from hearing to deaf babies or among babies from all over the world.

Babbling, the infant's experimentation with a complex range of sounds or phonemes, overlaps with cooing, and it starts at around 5 or 6 months of age. Although babbling includes consonants as wells as vowels, the sounds are not yet recognizable as words. At first, babies babble single syllables, such as "buh" and "duh"; later they utter "gibberish," simply a string of single syllables, such as "da, buh, ma, wee."

At first, babbling babies make many more sounds than they hear in their native language, because babies' brains have not yet been fully shaped by their native language. They can also hear more sounds than their parents can (Jusczyk, 1997; Plunkett, 1997). Adults who speak certain Asian languages—which do not distinguish between "r" and "l," for example—do not perceive a difference between these two sounds, but their toddlers do. As children progress through the babbling stage, and with repeated exposure to the subset of sounds in their native language, they "prune" away sounds that are not used in that language and lose the ability to say or perceive nonnative sounds (Goto, 1971; Kuhl, Stevens, & Hayashi, 2006).

At the end of the babbling stage, usually at around 12 months, **one-word utterances** emerge. Now children first speak such classic words as "mama," "dada," "more," and the all-important "no!" One-word utterances are likely descended from protolanguage. Like toddlers, our ancestors probably made up sounds for objects (nouns) and actions (verbs) before they developed more complex sentences (Goldfield, 2000).

Whether a word is at the beginning, middle, or end of a sentence seems to be related to how likely young children are to learn that word. Children tend to acquire words that are spoken at the ends of sentences first. In languages that are structured in the order of subject-verb-object, such as English, children acquire nouns earlier than verbs, because objects are nouns. In languages that are structured subject-object-verb, such as Japanese, children acquire verbs earlier than nouns (Chan, Brandone, & Tardif, 2009; Clancy, 1985; Tardif, Gelman, & Xu, 1999). In English, we say, "Maria read the book," whereas in Japanese people say, "Maria the book read." English-speaking children learn *book* before *read*, whereas Japanese-speaking children learn the Japanese version of *read* before *book*.

This tendency to learn the last word in a sentence first may reflect the memory phenomenon called the *recency effect*, discussed in Chapter 7. Starting around 18 months, children make **two-word utterances,** such as "my ball," "mo wawa" (more water), or "go way" (go away). During this phase of language development, parents often find themselves serving as translators for other people, because their children create unique ways of saying things. For instance, our youngest son, Evan, would say "ba" for any kind of water, because he had learned to say "ba" to mean "bottle of water." He extended "ba" to other types of water, such as a lake, pool, or bathtub, which we easily understood. Our baby-sitters did not, however, so we had to translate "Evanese" for them.

By age 2½ or 3, most children have entered the third phase of language development—the **sentence phase**—in which they begin speaking in fully grammatical sentences. This transition happens so quickly that linguists usually have a tough time studying it. Linguist Steven Pinker uses a boy named Adam as an example. At age 2, Adam

cooing
The first sounds humans make, other than crying, consisting almost exclusively of vowels; it occurs during the first 6 months of life.

babbling
Sounds made as a result of the infant's experimentation with a complex range of phonemes, which include consonants as well as vowels; it starts at around 5–6 months of age.

one-word utterances
Single words, such as "mama," "dada," "more," or "no!"; they occur around 12 months of age.

two-word utterances
Phrases children put together, starting around 18 months, such as "my ball," "mo wawa," or "go way."

sentence phase
The stage at which children begin speaking in fully grammatical sentences, usually age 2½ to 3.

By age 3, children have begun to speak in fully grammatical sentences. Also, their brains are nearly adult size.

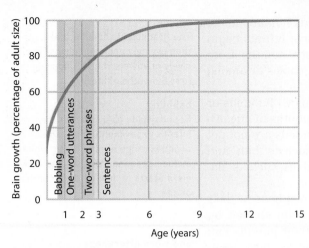

FIGURE 9.2

THE ASSOCIATION BETWEEN BRAIN GROWTH AND LANGUAGE DEVELOPMENT. As a child's brain approaches its final adult size, the onset and rapid development of language match the rapid growth of the brain. At age 1, when the child's brain is less than 50% of its adult size, the infant is babbling and perhaps saying a few words. By age 3, when the brain is 75%–80% of its adult size, the child has progressed to two-word phrases and short sentences. (Sakai, 2005)

would say, "Play checkers. Big drum. I got horn." Less than a year later, at age 3, he would say, "I going come in fourteen minutes. You dress me up like a baby elephant. You know how to put it back together" (Pinker, 1994, pp. 273–274). These sentences may not always be what adults consider grammatically correct, but they are grammatical sentences.

In sum, children go through a very predictable sequence in acquiring language: from cooing to babbling, one-word utterances, two-word utterances, and finally adultlike sentence structure, a stage that is reached around age 3. These stages in speech development map remarkably well onto the growth in the child's overall brain size (see Figure 9.2). There is a steep rise in both brain growth and language between the ages of 1 and 3. The brain of a 3-year-old child has reached about 80% of adult size. At about this age, children can form adultlike sentences.

The Sensitivity Period An important principle of language development is that, if children are not exposed to any human language before a certain age, their language abilities never fully develop (Lenneberg, 1967; Newport, 2003; Uylings, 2006). This sensitivity period, and optimal learning time for language acquisition, begins in the first years of life and ends at about age 12. Severe neglect and lack of exposure to language during this period cause permanent problems in language development. As Uylings (2006) points out, sensitivity periods end after neural pruning and neural wiring have reached their peak, at which point the plasticity of neural connections becomes less flexible.

One of the most dramatic examples of the importance of the sensitivity period in language development is the case of an abused and severely neglected girl, known as "Genie." When she was 2 years old, a family doctor diagnosed Genie as being mildly retarded (Rymer, 1993). Her father, who was mentally unstable, interpreted this to mean that she was severely retarded and needed "protection." He tied her to a chair all day long and caged her in a crib at night. Moreover, he beat her every time she tried to speak and barked at her like a dog. This abuse lasted until Genie was 13½, when her mother finally ran away, taking Genie with her. The local social worker whose help they sought thought Genie was 6 or 7 years old, because she was only 4 feet 6 inches tall and weighed 59 pounds. The social worker arranged for the State of California to take temporary custody of the child. At that time, Genie could speak only a few words, such as "stopit" or "nomore."

At age 17, after 4 years of language training, Genie's language skills were still extremely delayed. She could communicate simple ideas, but her speech was limited mainly to ungrammatical sentences. She said things such as "Spot chew glove" or "Applesauce buy store" (*Transcripts,* 1997). In this sense, her language ability was at the level of a young child's. Her language comprehension, however, was much better than her language production. She understood much of what was said to her. Brain imaging revealed something very unusual about Genie's brain activity while speaking or listening: The activity was located mostly in her right hemisphere (Curtiss, 1977). Recall that language ability is located in the left hemisphere. The case of Genie suggests that left-hemisphere speech development requires stimulation from the environment during a certain sensitivity period if it is to develop properly.

As tragic as Genie's story is, it reveals something very important about language: We need verbal stimulation from others, and we need it while we are young if we are to develop fully and completely the ability to speak. Now in her

50s, Genie lives in supportive foster care. The movie *Mockingbird Don't Sing*, released in 2001, is based on her life.

Because Genie had other cognitive deficits at birth, her case is not a clear test of the sensitivity period hypothesis. Clearer evidence comes from cases of people born deaf who were not spoken to in sign language and did not learn it until later in life. Consistent with the idea of a sensitivity period, deaf people who learn sign language after early childhood never become as proficient as those who learn sign language early in life (DeKeyser & Larson-Hall, 2005).

Theories of Language Acquisition

Unless they suffer from some sort of disease or deficit, all humans learn to speak, including those who were born deaf. Many children who can't hear learn spoken language in order to communicate with hearing individuals, but many rely heavily on sign language as well. Sign language is every bit as complex and communicative as spoken language. This suggests that we have innate, genetically based structures in the brain that enable us to learn language, but the vast differences in how well each of us learns to speak illustrate the importance of environmental stimulation. Different theories of language acquisition emphasize the contributions of nature and nurture to language differently, but they all agree that both are involved.

Sociocultural Theories We learn language from the people around us. We acquire vocabulary by hearing others speak, and we figure out what they mean by the context (Hoff, 2006; Y. Zhang et al., 2008). Children who hear more total and unique words, and more complex sentences, develop their language faster and more richly than those who do not (Gathercole & Hoff, 2007; Hart & Risley, 1992, 1995; Huttenlocher et al., 2002; Pan et al., 2005). In a review of the evidence for how environment shapes and molds language acquisition, Erika Hoff (2006) provides a partial list of the environmental influences on language. They include culture, socioeconomic status, birth order, school, peers, television, and parents. Each of these influences has a rich research history demonstrating how sociocultural forces shape language development, particularly the timing of vocabulary development.

The richness of a child's vocabulary is very much a function of how many words are spoken in the family. Hart and Risely (1992, 1995) examined language development in 42 families with young children from three different economic and educational groups: professional, middle and working class, and unemployed (welfare). Each month for over 2 years (from when the children were 10 months to 3 years of age), the researchers tape-recorded and analyzed in-home verbal interactions.

One major finding was that the children all started to speak around the same time and they developed good structure and use of language. Children, however, from professional families heard an average of 2,153 words per hour, those from middle- and working-class families heard an average of 1,251 words per hour, and those from unemployed (welfare) families heard an average of 616 words per hour. Extending these numbers to total words heard in a year, by age 4 the children from the unemployed families would have heard about 32 million fewer words than the children from professional families.

These differences in amount of words spoken to translated into differences in the child's own vocabulary (see Figure 9.3).

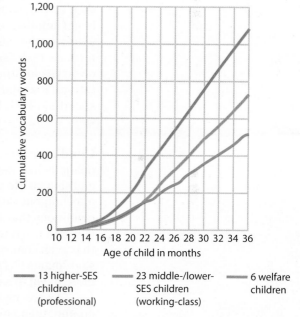

FIGURE 9.3

DEVELOPMENT OF VOCABULARY AS A FUNCTION OF SOCIOECOMIC STATUS OF THE FAMILY. Given the differences between families in the numbers of words spoken to children, it is not surprising that these differences would translate into differences in the children's vocabulary. In this graph we see the development of total vocabulary size over the 2.5-year period in children in three socioeconomic status (SES) groups: professional, middle-/working-class, and unemployed (welfare). By age 3, children from professional families are using more than twice as many different words as children from welfare families. (Hart, Risley, 1995)

By age 3, the average vocabulary of the children from unemployed (welfare) families was around 500 words, whereas for professional families it was around 1,100 words. The children from the professional families also heard more encouragement words than discouragement words than did the children from either the working-/middle-class or welfare-recipient families.

Much of what we learn comes from imitating family members. Recall that imitation is doing exactly what you see someone else do, and with certain behaviors imitation is evident immediately after birth. Newborns as young as 50 minutes old will stick out their tongues or open their mouths when they see an adult do so (Meltzoff & Moore, 1983). At a slightly older age, babies try to imitate the speech sounds they hear (Kuhl & Meltzoff, 1997). Adults in turn do many things to encourage imitation, such as speaking in a higher pitch, raising and lowering the volume of their voice, using simpler sentence structures, emphasizing the here and now, and using emotion to communicate their messages (Fernald & Morikawa, 1993; M. L. Rice, 1989). These changes in adult speech patterns—which appear to be universal—are referred to as **child-directed speech.**

The richness of verbal stimulation from family members affects the timing of a child's vocabulary development (Hoff, 2006). For instance, the children of very verbally responsive mothers reach the 50-word vocabulary milestone a full 5 months earlier than do children of less verbally responsive mothers. More generally, much of the differences in the timing of the child's vocabulary development can be explained by three characteristics of the mother: her socioeconomic status, her vocabulary use, and her personality characteristics.

Although these are mostly social processes we have been discussing, they also demonstrate profound interdependence with brain processes, which is yet another example of the interplay between nature and nurture. Mirror neurons, the clusters of brain cells that fire not only when an individual performs a task (such as sticking out one's tongue) but also when an individual observes another person do the same task, facilitate social learning and imitation (Rizzolatti & Arbib, 1998; Rizzolatti & Craighero, 2004). Many human social skills, including speech, develop because our brains allow and foster such social learning.

Conditioning and Learning Theory   B. F. Skinner (1957) believed that language is like any other behavior: something that exists because it is reinforced and shaped. He proposed that we speak not because we want to convey an idea or a feeling but rather because we have been reinforced for doing so. What are the conditions that bring about or reinforce verbal behavior? According to Skinner, children learn to speak a particular language because, when they say anything that even comes close to a word, the parents smile and say things like "Wow! She said 'mama'!" The parents' reaction has a reinforcing effect, making the child more likely to say that word.

As we just discussed, young children begin language development by cooing, then babbling, then uttering one and two words until they begin to say short phrases and sentences. Skinner explained this progression in terms of shaping, successive approximations, and reinforcement: The first approximation of a complex behavior will be reinforced. When a toddler utters "mama," she gets more of her mother's attention and smiles than she does when she utters "baba." The child learns first that the word *mama* matters and soon thereafter learns what it means. In a short while the child is saying "mama go bye-bye." Each step is subsequently reinforced until the child reaches the final behavior—in this case, speaking in fully grammatical sentences, such as "Mommy is going away."

Nativist Theory   There is little doubt that language development, such as the acquisition of certain words, is shaped partly by parental responses. When a child

child-directed speech
Changes in adult speech patterns—apparently universal—when speaking to young children or infants; characterized by higher pitch, changes in voice volume, use of simpler sentences, emphasis on the here and now, and use of emotion to communicate messages.

correctly names an object for the first time, the parents lavish much praise and encouragement: "Yes, that's right! Spot is a doggy!" However, such reinforcement does not occur as consistently for other aspects of language development, such as syntax and grammar rules. Still, children seem to learn these aspects with little difficulty, and they tend to *overgeneralize* language rules; they may add *ed* to *run* to form the past tense because adding *ed* is the typical way of forming the past tense in English. Instead of saying "Spot ran," then, the child says "Spot runned." Reinforcement cannot explain this formation, because children most likely have never heard "runned" from their parents and, so, have not been reinforced for using it. In other words, it is impossible to learn novel utterances through imitation and reinforcement. One cannot use shaping to teach someone to say something no one has ever said. So Skinner's explanation of language acquisition cannot fully explain how we learn language.

Some linguists contend that we discover language rather than learn it, that language development is "native," or inborn, the main assumption of the **nativist view of language.** In this view, the brain is structured, or "wired," for language learning; as you have learned, Broca's and Wernicke's areas are dedicated to speech production and comprehension, respectively. The linguist Noam Chomsky (1972, 1986) has argued that humans are born with a **language acquisition device (LAD)**—an innate, biologically based capacity to acquire language. Just as birds are biologically built to fly, humans are biologically built to speak. We are not born with a capacity to learn a particular language, such as Chinese or English, but rather we are simply born with a capacity to learn "language." Further, Chomsky (1972, 2000) has suggested that there is essentially a single universal grammar underlying all human languages; each language is simply a specific expression of this universal grammar.

Chomsky argues for a built-in language acquisition device (LAD) partly because of how easily and automatically humans learn to do this very complex and difficult thing: speak in complete and grammatical sentences. It is universal, and it develops intuitively in children in about the same way and at the same time all over the world, regardless of which language they learn. Any child can learn equally easily any language as his or her native language. If you grew up in certain regions of Africa, you would be speaking Swahili; certain parts of Asia, Mandarin; certain parts of Europe, German.

Chomsky also argues that our biologically based language acquisition device must have *principles* of universal grammar that allow a child to learn any native language (Chomsky, 2000; Radford, 1997). Universal grammar follows universal principles. For instance, a universal grammar principle might be "Languages have subjects, objects, and verbs." All languages have these components of speech, but they vary in location in sentences. As we saw earlier in the chapter, English is a subject-verb-object (S-V-O) language, whereas Japanese is a subject-object-verb (S-O-V) language.

Although there are universal principles for language, each language sets limits, or parameters, for what is correct in terms of word orders and other aspects. We learn these parameters as we learn to speak: Verbs go before objects in English but after them in Japanese. Parameters make clear why it is relatively easy for a child to learn a particular language. Once children learn the rules of their language, forming grammatically correct sentences becomes relatively easy because of a built-in language acquisition device (Dunbar, 2001; Pinker, 1994).

Nature, Nurture, and Language Learning   As we have seen, different theorists emphasize different contributions of nature and nurture. Social and learning theorists argue for the importance of social input and stimulation, whereas nativist theorists argue for the importance of brain structures and genetic factors. Both perspectives are needed to fully explain language. Most scholars of language agree that acquiring language involves natural abilities, which are modified by

nativist view of language
The idea that we discover language rather than learn it, that language development is inborn.

language acquisition device (LAD)
An innate, biologically based capacity to acquire language, proposed by Noam Chomsky as part of his nativist view of language.

Noam Chomsky

Connection
One reason newborn infants are capable of imitating behavior immediately after birth is that humans and other animals have mirror neurons.

See "The Cells of the Nervous System: Glial Cells and Neurons," Chapter 3, "The Biology of Behavior," p. 79, and "Imitation, Mirror Neurons, and Learning," Chapter 8, "Learning," p. 312.

Challenge Your Assumptions
True or False? Learning grammar is easy only for highly educated people.
False: Learning the grammar of one's native language is an automatic and relatively effortless skill for humans.

According to Noam Chomsky, regardless of where we are born or what language we are exposed to, we have no trouble learning it.

the language learner's environment (Hoff, 2006; Lidz & Gleitman, 2004; MacWhinney, 1999). The term *innately guided learning* captures the interaction between nature and nurture very well (Elman et al., 1996). We learn to speak, but in doing so we are guided by our innate capacity for language learning. The importance of both nature and nurture is starkly illustrated by the case of Genie: She could speak, and even learned a few words as a child, but her environment was so barren that her language development was severely stunted.

Still, genetic factors and innate structures have a stronger influence on some aspects of language development, whereas environmental conditions have a greater influence on other aspects. For instance, grammar is more innate and genetically influenced than is vocabulary, which is more strongly shaped by input from the environment (Dale et al., 2000; Hoff, 2006). Recall that one common way to determine how much of a trait is due to genetic influence is to compare identical twin pairs to fraternal twin pairs (see Chapter 2). If a trait is strongly genetically influenced, it will show much stronger correlations in identical twins than in fraternal twins, because identical twins are more genetically alike. Dale and colleagues (2000) compared vocabulary and grammar skills in 1,008 identical twin pairs to the same skills in 1,890 fraternal twin pairs; all were about 2 years old. The children's parents assessed their vocabulary and grammar skills by completing questionnaires dealing with the kinds of words and sentences their children could say. Identical twin pairs were more similar in vocabulary and grammar. Figures from the study show that genetics influences about 25% of vocabulary development and about 40% of learning about grammar (Dale et al., 2000).

Moreover, brain systems not only are involved with language development but also change together over time (Szaflarski et al., 2006). Not surprisingly, between the ages of 5 and 11 years, the brain regions associated with language (Broca's area and Wernicke's area; see Figure 9.4) increase in activity during language processing.

Animals of all kinds communicate with members of their own species. Birds sing songs to tell other birds where they are,

Studies of twins, like these fraternal twins, suggest that grammar is influenced more by genetics than by the environment, whereas vocabulary is influenced more by the environment than by genetics.

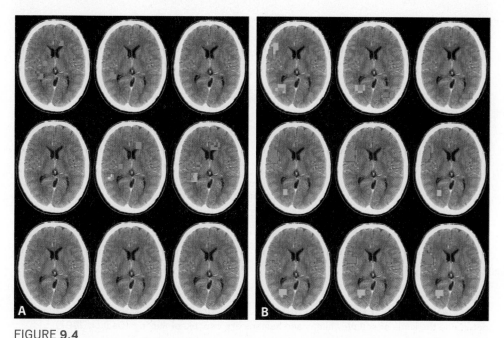

FIGURE **9.4**

DEVELOPMENT OF LANGUAGE REGIONS IN THE BRAIN. Brain regions that decrease in activity from ages 5 to 11 are shown in A, whereas brain regions that gain in activity during language processing are shown in B. The regions that decrease are in the left insula, cingulate gyrus, and thalamus, whereas the regions that increase in activity are the well-known Broca's and Wernicke's regions of the left hemisphere. (Szaflarski et al., 2006)

that they want to mate, or that a predator is nearby; sometimes they sing just for the fun of it (Rothenberg, 2005). Whales sing long, melancholic (to human ears) tones that other whales hear from miles away. Bees dance to tell other bees where nectar can be found. Apes in the wild communicate only what they want other apes to do—not their internal states, feelings, or desires, as humans often do (Tomasello & Hermann, 2010). But do these forms of animal communication represent the ability to use language as humans do?

Can Other Species Learn Human Language?

For centuries it was argued that the capacity for language is what separates humans from other animals. Yet if humans share almost all of their genes with chimps, and humans and apes share a common ancestor from roughly 6 million years ago, an obvious question is, Is it possible for apes to learn human language?

Chimps do not have a vocal apparatus that allows them to speak, so they are physically incapable of making the same range of sounds that humans can (see Figure 9.5). The only way humans can teach apes to communicate is to use a nonvocal sign language, most often American Sign Language (ASL). A number of captive apes have learned ASL to different degrees and have been able to communicate with humans. Allen and Beatrix Gardner, for instance, have compiled more than 400 ASL signs that three chimps named Dar, Tatu, and Moja acquired in the course of extensive training (R. A. Gardner, Gardner, & Van Cantfort, 1989). Their first chimp, Washoe, learned to sign almost 200 distinct words. Another chimp, Sarah, developed a vocabulary of about 100 words (Premack, 1971). Perhaps the most linguistically gifted ape to date is Kanzi, a bonobo chimp (J. Cohen, 2010; Rumbaugh, Beran, & Savage-Rumbaugh, 2003).

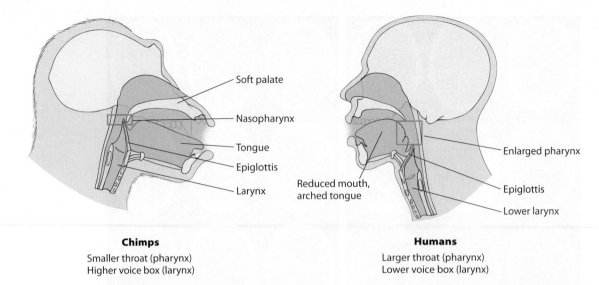

Soft palate

Nasopharynx

Tongue

Epiglottis

Larynx

Enlarged pharynx

Reduced mouth, arched tongue

Epiglottis

Lower larynx

Chimps
Smaller throat (pharynx)
Higher voice box (larynx)

Humans
Larger throat (pharynx)
Lower voice box (larynx)

FIGURE **9.5**

VOCAL ANATOMY OF CHIMPS AND HUMANS. Vocal structures (throat, voice box, tongue) determine the kinds of sounds chimps and humans are capable of making. (Deacon, 1997)

Kanzi was the son of Matata, which had been caught wild in Zaire. When Matata was an adult, linguist Sue Savage-Rumbaugh attempted to teach her sign language, with limited success. Kanzi was present during these training sessions but was not formally taught any signs. Savage-Rumbaugh soon discovered, however, that Kanzi had been paying attention to the signs being taught to his mother. Moreover, he learned more quickly and developed a larger vocabulary than his mother. The research team decided to compare Kanzi's language comprehension

Kanzi, a bonobo that understands at least 3,000 English words, uses symbols to communicate with his teacher, linguist Sue Savage-Rumbaugh.

to that of a 2½-year-old human child, Alia. At the time, Kanzi was 7 years old. Both Kanzi and Alia were given 660 spoken requests to see whether they understood them well enough to carry them out. The requests were things such as "Take the shoe to the bathroom," "Give Karen an apple," and "Put the pine needles in the refrigerator" and reversals such as "Make the doggie bite the snake," then "Make the snake bite the doggie" (Rumbaugh, et al., 2003, p. 411). Alia and Kanzi performed these commands at very similar levels of success—about 70%. Since then, Kanzi, now 27 years old, has learned to comprehend as many as 3,000 English words (Raffaele, 2006).

If apes can learn sign language, do they use it to talk with each other? The answer seems to be sometimes, in some circumstances, and in some species of ape. So what do apes sign to one another about? Fouts and colleagues (1984) analyzed the types of conversations five signing chimpanzees had among themselves. They found that 88% of the conversations were about social interaction, play, and reassurance, whereas the other 12% were about feeding, grooming, cleaning, discipline, and chimps signing, or "talking," to themselves (just as we humans talk to ourselves; Fouts, Fouts, & Schoenfeld, 1984). More incredibly, one chimp, also named Washoe, spontaneously began teaching her adopted son, Loulis, how to sign (Fouts, 1997). Human trainers were careful not to sign around Loulis to ensure that he would learn only from Washoe. After just 8 weeks with Washoe, Loulis regularly signed with humans, and after 18 months he had learned about 20 signs.

However, even the most linguistically talented apes are limited in their language ability compared to humans, although they do appear to have some basic level of meta-cognition, or knowing what they know and do not know (Beran, Smith, & Perdue, 2013). First, the developmental sequence in which they acquire signs is slower than the sequence in which humans do so. A gorilla named Koko acquired signs at about half the speed of very young human children (S. T. Parker & McKinney, 1999), and Loulis learned only about one sign a month during his first 18 months of learning. In addition, apes seldom progress beyond two- or three-word combinations, which means that their highest level of language learning is equivalent to the level achieved by a toddler in terms of vocabulary and sentence structure. Adult apes may have vocabularies of 100 to 300 words, whereas an average high school student knows 60,000 words (Hauser, Chomsky, & Fitch, 2002; S. T. Parker & McKinney, 1999). Finally, nonhuman primates seldom either understand or consistently use correct word order (syntax). For example, one chimp, named Nim Chimsky, after linguist Noam Chomsky, would alternate among "Banana give Nim," "Give Nim banana," and "Banana Nim give" (Terrace, 1987).

Given the successes and limits of language acquisition by apes, the scientific community is split on the question of whether apes really can use language to communicate with humans (J. Cohen, 2010). On the one hand, some researchers emphasize the linguistic abilities of apes. Often they have raised these apes as children of their own and taught them language. Such close relationships can also bias their perceptions, causing them to see things that may or may not be there. On the other hand, others, often linguists with little direct experience with apes, emphasize the linguistic limitations of apes. The main conclusion to draw from these opposing views is that the capacity for learning language in rudimentary form evolved from our early ancestors—ancestors common to both humans and apes (Deacon, 1997).

Language, Culture, and Thought

Does the language we speak cause us to see the world in a particular way? Can people who speak vastly different languages communicate effectively, even in translation? After we learn our native language, can we still learn about concepts that do not exist in our language but only in other languages?

Support for the linguistic determinism hypothesis comes from studies of the Pirahã tribe in Brazil. Think what it would be like to try to understand an idea or a concept for which you had no word.

linguistic determinism hypothesis
The proposition that our language determines our way of thinking and our perceptions of the world; the view taken by Sapir and Whorf.

According to the *Whorf-Sapir hypothesis,* language creates thought as much as thought creates language (Whorf, 1956). Anthropologists Benjamin Whorf and Edward Sapir, the authors of the Whorf-Sapir hypothesis, suggested that language shapes our thoughts and perceptions to such an extent that people who speak languages that lack a common foundation, such as English and Chinese, have difficulty directly communicating and translating their ideas from one language to the other. Taken to its logical conclusion, the Whorf-Sapir view leads to the **linguistic determinism hypothesis,** which states that our language determines our way of thinking and our perceptions of the world. In this view, if there are no words for certain objects or concepts in one's language, it is not possible to think about those objects or concepts.

An example offers support for the linguistic determinism hypothesis. The Pirahã, a very small tribe of only about 200 people living in the Amazon area of Brazil, are challenging some of science's most basic notions of language, numbers, memory, perception, and thought (Everett, 2005). The Pirahã have no words for the numbers higher than 2. As a result, it is nearly impossible for them to learn concepts such as 10. Because of their language, and not because of intelligence, they have difficulty learning simple arithmetic relationships, such as $3 + 1$ (Gordon, 2004).

Linguists studying the Pirahã claim that the Pirahã have no way to include one clause within another and do not construct sentences that start with words such as *when, before,* and *after.* They can construct only independent clauses. For example, they cannot say something like "When I finish eating, I want to speak to you." Instead, they must say two things: "I finish eating. I speak to you" (Bower, 2005). This claim is radical, because it directly challenges the concept of a universal grammar. According to Chomsky, a cornerstone of universal grammar is that all languages embed clauses within clauses. The Pirahã, however, do not construct sentences that start with words such as *when, before,* and *after,* and as a result they are limited to talking about the here and now and only about what is directly observable. Not surprisingly, they lack stories about the ancient past—they have no stories, for instance, of how the world began, and they refer only to known, living relatives.

Nonetheless, the view that language determines our thinking is almost certainly overstated. Most research on the topic shows how language influences rather than determines our thinking (Boroditsky, 2001; Newcombe & Uttal, 2006;

Regier & Kay, 2009; Regier et al., 2010). This position is known as *linguistic relativism.* A good example of linguistic relativism was reported in a study on how language affects color perception (Winawer et al., 2007). Russian has distinct words for lighter blues (*goluboy*) and darker blues (*siniy*). English has only *blue.* When researchers presented 20 different shades of blue to both Russian and English speakers, they discovered that Russian speakers were faster—by milliseconds—at discriminating between these two shades of blue that came from within the same category (either within *goluboy* or within *siniy*) than when they came from different categories of blue; see the Research Process for this chapter (Figure 9.6). For English speakers, however, who have no words for the different categories of blue, the category of blue made no difference. This is a typical finding on how language influences but does not determine thinking and perception.

As these examples illustrate, thought, memory, number, and perception are all tied to language. In fact, language is a close cousin to thought—humans rely on language for organizing, storing, and communicating ideas. Our ability to think, reason, and make decisions often takes verbal form. Let's therefore turn our attention to human thought, reasoning, and decision making.

Quick Quiz 9.1: Language

1. A language's rules for arranging words and symbols in a sentence or parts of a sentence is called
   a. grammar.
   b. lexicon.
   c. syntax.
   d. representation.

2. During which stage of language development do babies make many more sounds than they hear in their native languages?
   a. babbling
   b. cooing
   c. one-word utterances
   d. telegraphic speech

3. According to Skinner, children learn to speak a particular language because

   a. they possess an inherent ability to speak.
   b. they engage in imitation of what they hear.
   c. they have a language acquisition device.
   d. they get reinforcement from their parents for various utterances.

4. Which theory of language argues that, if there are no words for certain objects or concepts in one's language, one is unable to think about those objects or concepts?
   a. nativist theory
   b. theory of innately guided learning
   c. linguistic determinism hypothesis
   d. Skinnerian theory of language

Answers can be found at the end of the chapter.

THINKING, REASONING, AND DECISION MAKING

What does it mean to know something? If our bodies do something automatically, such as breathing or digesting food, can we say that we know how to breathe and digest or that we just do it?

These questions suggest that knowledge is distinct from instinct, and certainly it is. In this section we explore some questions about mental processes, such as how we come to know anything, as well as how we know that we know anything. Psychologists use the word **cognition,** which means "to know," to refer to the mental processes involved in acquiring, processing, and storing knowledge. Recall that cognitive psychology is the science of how people think, learn, remember, and perceive (Sternberg, 2006a). Humans are unique in their ability to represent ideas and think abstract and symbolic thoughts.

cognition
The mental processes involved in acquiring, processing, and storing knowledge.

Research Process

1 Research Question

Is people's ability to discriminate colors altered by language? Unlike English, Russian has two distinct words for lighter blues (*goluboy*) *and darker blues (siniy)*; English does not. Does knowledge of these different color categories affect how quickly a person can discriminate between different shades of blue?

2 Method

Winawer and colleagues (2007) designed a quasi-experiment to measure color discrimination performance in native English and Russian speakers in a simple perceptual task. Twenty color stimuli spanning the Russian *siniy/goluboy* range were used. The participants viewed colors arranged in a triad (*right*). Their task was to indicate as quickly and accurately as possible which of the two bottom color square's was identical to the top square.

The prediction was that for the Russian speakers the time it took them to identify the color as matching the target would depend on whether the color was in the same category or a different one. For English speakers there would be no real difference in reaction times for blues that were in the same or a different Russian color category.

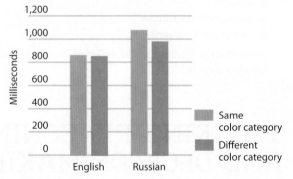

3 Results

Russian speakers were faster at discriminating blues that came from different color categories than at discriminating blues that came from within the same category. For English speakers, response time did not differ for same versus different category of blue, because there is only one category of blue in English.

Mean reaction time to identify color block as different from target

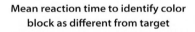

4 Conclusion

Knowledge of words for different categories of blue does affect how quickly people can discriminate between examples of blue. Notice, however, that the English speakers performed very well overall—in fact, they were faster than Russian speakers—but their performance was not affected by the different language categories. Language knowledge can influence thought.

FIGURE **9.6**

LANGUAGE AND COLOR DISCRIMINATION. Words for colors influence our perception of thinking about those colors. (Winawer, J., Witthoft, N., Frank, M. C., Wu, L., Wade, A. R., & Boroditsky, L. [2007]. Russian blues reveal effect of language on color discrimination. *Proceedings of the National Academy of Sciences, 104,* 7780–7785.)

We will consider three fundamental questions about cognition and reasoning:

- How do we represent thoughts in our minds?
- How do we reason about evidence?
- How do we make judgments and decisions?

How Do We Represent Thoughts in Our Minds?

Have you ever wondered, Where exactly in my brain is a thought? Cognitive psychologists and neuroscientists have and have even conducted research to find an answer. Cognitive psychologists, however, frame the question this way: How do we store or represent thoughts in our minds?

Even with the most up-to-date brain imaging technology, we cannot actually see inside the brain as it conjures up an image or comes up with a solution to a problem. Imaging techniques can only measure changes in blood flow, which suggest brain activity. We cannot and probably never will be able to *see* thoughts and ideas, but it is clear that we all have thoughts, memories, and ideas, so the question arises: How do we use our brains to store and maintain these mental processes?

Cognitive psychologists approach this question by proposing that we store and process ideas, knowledge, and memories as *mental representations*. A **mental representation** is a structure in the mind—such as an idea or image—that stands for something else, such as an external object or thing (Thagard, 2005). In general, mental representations are frequently not about things we are currently sensing (seeing, touching, or smelling, for instance) but rather about things we sensed in the past. Mental representations, therefore, allow us to think about and remember things in the past and to imagine things in the future. They also allow us to think about abstract ideas that have no physical existence, such as love, truth, beauty, and justice. For the most part, we represent ideas and thoughts in our minds with images (visually) and with words (verbally).

How does the brain store and maintain mental processes?

Visual Representation   We think in both images and words. The visual system, located mostly in the occipital lobes (see Figure 9.1), is older in evolutionary terms than the verbal system. It also develops before verbal ability (Givón, 2002). Consider how babies respond to picture books before they learn to talk.

Every animal with eyes perceives visual images, but only those animals with significant cortex are better able to keep and store visual sensations in mind after the sensory stimulation stops. Indeed, visual perception occurs while the stimulus is still present, as we learned in Chapter 4. **Visual imagery,** however, consists of visual representations created by the brain after the original stimulus is no longer present (Kosslyn, 2005). The brain is active much the same way during visual imagery as it is during visual perception. Thus, you would have a hard time distinguishing between a brain image of someone actually perceiving something and a brain image of someone imagining seeing the same thing (W. L. Thompson & Kosslyn, 2000).

Being able to imagine things that are not currently being perceived is a very useful and complex skill, although about 2% of the population cannot do it at all (Kosslyn, 2002). People clearly differ in their ability to imagine an event or object in their "mind's eye" (Ganis, Thompson, & Kosslyn, 2009; Kosslyn, Van Kleeck, & Kirby, 1990). If you have the ability to imagine outcomes, you can make them more likely to happen. For instance, if you first form a mental image of an ideal performance, such as hitting a home run or playing a piece of music without errors, you are more likely to perform that activity better (Hale, Seiser, & McGuire, 2005). Neuroscientists have shown that the brain is activated in much the same way while imagining a task as it is while performing that task (Bonnet et al.,

mental representation
A structure in the mind—such as an idea or image—that stands for something else, such as an external object or thing sensed in the past or future, not the present.

visual imagery
A visual representation created by the brain after the original stimulus is no longer present.

Many successful athletes use visual imaging to improve their performance. Visualizing success can help make it happen.

1997). So next time you are getting ready to play a game of tennis or perform a Mozart sonata, imagine doing your best. It can help you succeed.

Visual imagery and visual imagination can also be critical to many creative accomplishments, in both art and science (A. Miller, 1996). Albert Einstein made it quite clear that words were not involved or came after the fact when he was developing his most creative ideas. When describing how he came up with his ideas for the theory of relativity, Einstein said, "These thoughts did not come in any verbal formulation. I rarely think in words at all. A thought comes and I may try to express it in words later" (quoted in Wertheimer, 1959, p. 228). He often visually imagined certain thought experiments, such as riding on a light beam or traveling at the speed of light in an elevator. Other physicists have argued that Einstein's great creativity dried up when he could no longer produce such visual images (Feist, 2006b).

The process of imagining an object rotating in three-dimensional space is known as **mental rotation.** Look at the shapes in Figure 9.7. The pairs are either the same or different, and your task is to decide which is which. If you are like most people, it will take you about 2.5 seconds for each pair to determine whether the two shapes are the same (a and b) or different (c).

Researchers examining gender differences in the performance of mental rotation tasks have reported moderate to large gender effects, with boys and men

mental rotation
The process of imagining an object turning in three-dimensional space.

  (a) 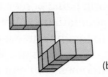 (b) 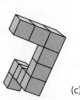 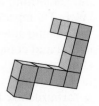 (c)

FIGURE **9.7**

MENTAL ROTATION. In this example, the figures on the right are always rotated 80 degrees compared to the figures on the left. It takes most people about 2.5 seconds to mentally rotate the figures. The pairs in (a) and (b) are the same, whereas the pair in (c) is different. (R. Shepard & Metzler, 1971)

generally doing better than girls and women (Geary & DeSoto, 2001; D. Halpern, 2004; J. S. Hyde, 1990). Cross-cultural research has shown that these effects also appear in China, Ecuador, Ireland, and Japan (Flaherty, 2005; Geary & DeSoto, 2001; Silverman, Choi, & Peters, 2007). It may not only be gender directly that leads to differences in spatial ability but also one's gender role identification. That is, in a meta-analysis of 12 studies, girls and women and boys and men who self-identify as "masculine" have higher spatial ability scores than those who identify as "feminine" (Reilly & Neumann, 2013).

One possible cause of this gender difference in spatial ability appears to be levels of the male sex hormone testosterone (Kimura, 2007). Female rats injected with testosterone during development perform better than noninjected female rats on spatial tasks (maze running; Berenbaum, Korman, & Leveroni, 1995). The relationship in humans, however, among testosterone, gender, and spatial ability is complex and not linear (Ceci & Williams, 2010). In humans, it is females with relatively high levels and males with relatively low levels of testosterone who perform best on spatial tasks. So it is too simple to say that high levels of testosterone alone result in better spatial skills. In humans, this is true only for women. For men, having low levels of testosterone leads to better spatial skills (Ceci & Williams, 2010; Hines et al., 2003).

Verbal Representation   A major function of thought is to organize and classify our perceptions into categories. One way in which humans organize their environment is by naming things and giving them labels. We organize our sensory experience by putting like with like and then distinguishing that group of things from other groups of things.

We do this by first finding similar features and then forming concepts and building categories based on those similarities. The most basic unit of knowledge is a **concept,** which is a mental grouping of objects, events, or people. The concept "fruit" includes yellow, red, blue, orange, and green fruit, as well as large and small fruit, but what an apple and a banana have in common defines the concept "fruit": the edible part of a plant that contains seeds.

Concepts help us organize our perceptions of the world. We can store and process these concepts in at least two ways: in a hierarchy and by parallel distributed processing, which we discussed in Chapter 7. A **concept hierarchy** lets us know that certain concepts are related in a particular way, with some being general and others specific. In so doing, it helps us order and understand our world.

A more complex model of how we store and organize knowledge in the brain is *parallel distributed processing (PDP).* As you'll recall from Chapter 7, the PDP model proposes that associations between concepts activate many networks or nodes at the same time (McClelland, 1988; McClelland & Rogers, 2003; McClelland & Rumelhart, 1985). The nodes are neuronlike and involve patterns of activation over the network. Concepts are activated in the network based on how strongly associated with or connected to each other they are. They are also arranged by similarity as well as hierarchy. For instance, animals such as birds and fish are closer to each other and farther away from plants, such as trees and flowers. The location of a concept is based on its relation to other concepts. In Figure 9.8, "living thing" is the most general conceptual category, of which there are two particular examples, "plants" and "animals." The relationship between nodes takes the form of "CAN," "HAS," or "IS." An animal CAN move, HAS skin, and IS a bird or fish, whereas a plant HAS roots and IS a flower or tree. A fish in turn HAS scales and gills, IS a salmon, and CAN swim. We can use these relationships and networks to reason about things: If a bird can fly and a robin is a bird, then a robin can fly.

A **category** is a concept that organizes other concepts around what they all share in common. For instance, all things that move and eat belong to the

concept
A mental grouping of objects, events, or people.

concept hierarchy
An arrangement of related concepts in a particular way, with some being general and others specific.

category
A concept that organizes other concepts around what they all share in common.

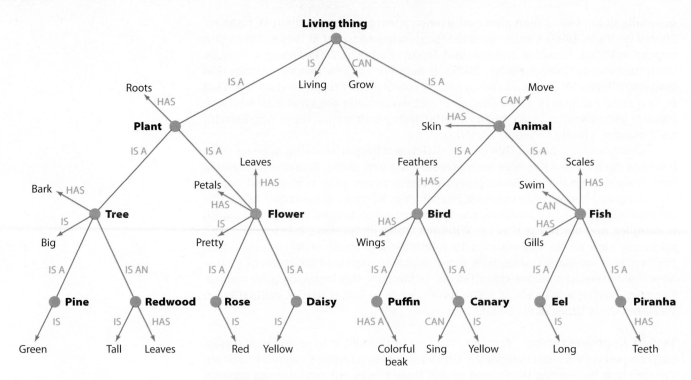

FIGURE **9.8**

A PARALLEL DISTRIBUTED NETWORK OF THE VERBAL CONCEPT "LIVING THING."
Concepts, printed in bold type, are represented by circles, or nodes, and are interconnected.
The properties of concepts are depicted by arrows, which represent statements. Relationships
are shown in CAPS. The concept Flower, for instance, HAS petals and leaves, IS pretty, IS
a plant, and IS a rose or a daisy. The concept Plant is more general than Rose and Daisy.
(McClelland & Rogers, 2003)

prototypes
The best-fitting examples of a
category.

category "animals," whereas all living things that grow out of the earth and do
not eat are in the category "plants." Categories can be either *well defined* (e.g., triangles, cars) or *fuzzy* (e.g., good, consciousness). In addition, some examples of
a category fit that category better than others. "Robin" for example, fits and represents the category "bird" better than does "ostrich," because ostriches cannot
fly, are big, and have long legs. The best-fitting examples of a category are known
as **prototypes** (Rosch, 1973). Thus, a robin is a better prototype for the category
"bird" than an ostrich is.

Now that we have developed concepts and categories to help organize the
mind's representations, how do we use them to make sense of our world and to
reason about them? In the next section we'll consider an answer to this question
as we talk about humans' reasoning ability.

How Do We Reason about Evidence?

reasoning
The process of drawing inferences
or conclusions from principles and
evidence.

Almost anytime we use the word *because*, we are reasoning (for example, "She is
smiling at me because she likes me"). **Reasoning** is the process of drawing inferences or conclusions from principles and evidence (Sternberg, 2006a). Sometimes
reasoning allows us to draw sound or correct conclusions, yet this is not always
the case. Consider the statement "The FBI and CIA are both out to get me because
I always see people looking at me." The conclusion is not a sound one, for it is
based only on the evidence that people are looking at the individual. It's probably
not correct, either.

Cognitive psychologists distinguish between two kinds of reasoning drawn from formal logic: deductive and inductive. **Deductive reasoning** occurs when we reason from general statements of what is known to specific conclusions. The specific conclusion is always correct if the general statement is true—for instance,

> All humans are mortal (premise A).
> Socrates is human (premise B).
> Therefore, Socrates must be mortal (conclusion).

That Socrates is mortal is a logical conclusion that has to be true if the two premises are true. Consider the following:

> All humans are green (premise A).
> Socrates is a human (premise B).
> Therefore, Socrates must be green (false conclusion).

This reasoning obviously leads to a false conclusion, because it is based on false premise A. Even though the structure of the two arguments is exactly the same, one leads to a correct conclusion, but the other does not. When scientists make specific predictions from their general theories, they are engaging in deductive reasoning.

Inductive reasoning draws general conclusions from specific evidence. Such conclusions are less certain than those drawn from deductive reasoning, because many different conclusions might be consistent with a specific fact. With induction, the best we can hope for are highly likely conclusions. An example is "All the peaches I have eaten have been sweet; therefore, all peaches are sweet." All it takes is one unsweet peach to undermine that conclusion. A better inductive conclusion would be that *most* peaches are sweet. When scientists develop theories, they use inductive reasoning, because they offer general statements that explain many specific facts or observations. When we use inductive reasoning, we often use **causal inferences,** judgments about whether one thing causes another thing (Koslowski, 1996): "Every time I get chilled, I catch a cold. So getting chilled must cause colds."

Inductive reasoning and causal inferences are related to a phenomenon seen in most people, including scientists: **confirmation bias,** or the tendency to selectively attend to information that supports one's general beliefs while ignoring information or evidence that contradicts one's beliefs. In the 1960s, Peter Wason conducted classic research to demonstrate the pervasiveness of confirmation bias. Wason (1960) decided to find out whether people propose and test hypotheses systematically and, more to the point, whether they would be more likely to falsify or to confirm their own theories.

Wason gave students the task of determining the hidden rule behind a sequence of three numbers, known as a *triplet*. The students were asked to guess at the rule by writing down triplets that they thought conformed to it and the reason they selected them. They could make as many guesses and explanatory statements as they wished, until they thought they knew the rule. The experimenter, who knew the hidden rule, could answer only "yes" or "no" to the students' guesses and was not allowed to say whether their reasons were correct or incorrect. For instance, if the experimenter gave the students the triplet "2-4-6," the students might guess a triplet of "6-8-10" and state that the hidden rule is "continuous series of even numbers." In this case, the guess is right but the rule is incorrect, so the experimenter would say "yes" to the guess but "no" to the rule. The students would then have to keep proposing triplets to test other reasons until they came up with the specific rule.

Out of frustration, students could throw out a triplet with seemingly no pattern to it, such as "1-10-21." Imagine their surprise when the experimenter said "yes" to that seemingly nonsensical triplet! Yet the triplet "1-10-21" conformed to

deductive reasoning
Reasoning from general statements of what is known to specific conclusions.

inductive reasoning
Reasoning to general conclusions from specific evidence.

causal inferences
Judgments about the causation of one thing by another.

confirmation bias
The tendency to selectively attend to information that supports one's general beliefs while ignoring information or evidence that contradicts one's beliefs.

the rule the experimenter had in mind, because that rule was simply "three numbers that must ascend in order of magnitude." As this experiment shows, people are so inclined to test only ideas that confirm their beliefs that they forget that one of the best ways to test an idea is to try to tear it down or disconfirm it, the foundation of the scientific method. Most people, though, look only for information that confirms what they already believe and seldom look for information that disconfirms what they think.

Critical Thinking

You've probably heard about "critical thinking" quite often. Teachers are always talking about getting their students to think critically. So what exactly is critical thinking?

We can answer this question in part by examining the origin of the word *critical*. It comes from the ancient Greek word *kritikos* and means "to question, to make sense of, and to be able to analyze; or to be skilled at judging" (Chaffee, 1999, p. 32). Educator Paul Chance has provided a more complete definition of **critical thinking:** "The ability to analyze facts, generate and organize ideas, defend opinions, make comparisons, draw inferences, evaluate arguments, and solve problems" (Chance, 1986, p. 6). The core traits of critical thinking are sound analysis, evaluation, and the formation of ideas based on the evidence at hand.

In the late 1980s a group of educators, philosophers, psychologists, and biological and physical scientists organized a conference around the topic of critical thinking in education, and there they arrived at a consensus on what it means to be a good critical thinker. They were nearly unanimous in identifying six activities or qualities that define critical thinking (Facione, 1990).

What a Critical Thinker Does

- Analyze
- Evaluate
- Make inferences
- Interpret
- Explain
- Self-regulate

If you become skilled in these activities, or at least in most of them, you will be able to think critically. In particular, you will be able to counter assertions that have little basis in reality, and you will know the difference between sound and faulty reasoning. For instance, the following argument was made by Charles Johnson, a former president of the International Flat Earth Research Society: "Nobody knows anything about the true shape of the world. The known, inhabited world is flat. Just as a guess, I'd say that the dome of heaven is about 4,000 miles away, and the stars are about as far as San Francisco is from Boston."

Instead of simply saying "That's silly," "That's stupid," or "That's just wrong," a critical thinker would examine the claim by analyzing it, evaluating it, and drawing conclusions based on the facts and evidence at hand. A great deal of evidence directly and clearly contradicts the belief that Earth is flat. Just consider these two pieces of evidence: (1) The top of a ship is the last thing we see as it sails out to sea because it is sailing on a sphere rather than on a flat surface (see Figure 9.9), and (2) images and photographs taken from

critical thinking
The process by which one analyzes, evaluates, and forms ideas.

Challenge Your Assumptions

True or False? Critical thinking involves seeing only the weaknesses and flaws in ideas.

False: Critical thinking involves seeing both strengths and weaknesses in claims and evidence.

FIGURE 9.9

EVIDENCE THAT THE EARTH IS NOT FLAT. The drawing on the left shows how a ship would appear as it came into view if Earth were flat. On the right we see the ship coming into view on a round Earth.

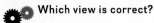 **Which view is correct?**

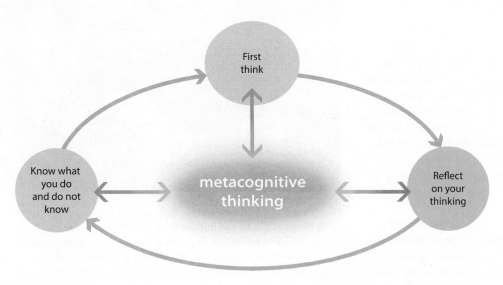

FIGURE 9.10

METACOGNITIVE THINKING. In an era marked by 24/7 information overload, we often leap to overly simplistic or incorrect conclusions based on what we think we "know."

 Can you think of a time when you were surprised by what you didn't know after you felt confident, such as on an exam or some other experience?

spaceships and satellites show Earth as a round sphere with half of it shining in the light of the sun.

Critical thinking and its cousin, scientific thinking, both involve being able to think metacognitively. **Metacognitive thinking** requires the ability first to think and then to reflect on one's own thinking (Feist, 2006b; Kuhn & Pearsall, 2000). People who can think metacognitively are able to question their own thinking (see Figure 9.10). This ability is not universal, however. Without specific training, many people find it difficult to question their own thinking. If one were able to do so as a matter of course, one could more readily dismiss a line of thinking as wrong when it was not supported by evidence. See "Psychology in the Real World" to learn how to develop critical thinking outside the classroom.

metacognitive thinking
The process that includes the ability first to think and then to reflect on one's own thinking.

How Do We Make Judgments and Decisions?

Should you go to class or not? Should you wear a green or brown shirt? Paper or plastic? Can you make it across the street without getting hit by that car? Should you have a glass of water or a soda? We make hundreds of decisions

Psychology in the Real World

Applying Critical Thinking beyond the Classroom

Critical thinking is a necessary skill in almost every walk of life. We can apply it to any domain in which we form beliefs and opinions, such as making political arguments, deciding whether someone has committed a crime, and evaluating the claims of a company advertising a product.

To apply critical thinking skills, we should ask ourselves, What is the evidence for this conclusion, and is it valid? Suppose you are on a jury in a murder trial. The primary evidence on which the case is based is eyewitness testimony: Two people picked out the defendant from a lineup. The prosecutor offers no other concrete evidence, such as DNA findings, fingerprints, bloodstains, or ballistic (bullet) matching. Your job is to decide whether the defendant committed the murder. You will want to draw on your critical thinking skills, because in this situation ignoring evidence and basing judgments on bias can have costly, even deadly, consequences.

Unfortunately, many people, including adults, sometimes lack critical and scientific thinking skills (Ransdell, 2010). Recall that scientific thinking is metacognitive thinking that is used to generate, test, reflect upon, and revise theories. Deanna Kuhn studied the connection between scientific and informal (everyday) reasoning in adults (Kuhn, 1993). She asked 160 people (teenagers and people in their 20s, 40s, and 60s) their theories on three topics: What causes prisoners to return to a life of crime, what causes children to fail in school, and what causes unemployment? After stating their theories, participants were asked for evidence on which they based their ideas. Only 40% of the participants could give actual evidence—information based on actual observations that bear on the theory's correctness. For instance, a man in his 20s who theorized that poor nutrition causes children to fail in school answered the question "What would show that?" with "[They get poor grades because] they are lacking something in their body." He fails to understand what evidence is and how it is different from his beliefs. He simply restates his belief in a different way. When asked to come up with reasons their thinking may be wrong, many actively resisted. As one participant said, "If I knew from the evidence that I'm wrong, I wouldn't say what I am saying." Others were even more stubborn, saying things such as "They'll never prove me wrong." Scientific and critical thinking both require that

President Barack Obama and his chief advisors had to weigh a wide range of issues and options in considering the capture or killing of Osama bin Laden. The mission was very dangerous and the outcome was uncertain. Critical thinking was essential in weighing the possible costs and benefits in taking any action.

we be open to evidence that bears on whether our ideas are correct or not, even if we are not happy with the evidence.

Developing critical thinking has consequences beyond the classroom and even beyond studies in psychology. To summarize,

The ideal critical thinker is habitually inquisitive, well-informed, trustful of reason, open-minded, flexible, fair-minded in evaluation, honest in facing personal biases, prudent in making judgments, willing to reconsider, clear about issues, orderly in assessing complex matters, diligent in seeking relevant information, reasonable in the selection of criteria, focused in inquiry, and persistent in seeking results that are as precise as the subject and the circumstances of inquiry permit. Thus, becoming good critical thinkers means working toward this ideal. It combines developing critical thinking skills with nurturing those dispositions that consistently yield useful insights and that are the basis of a rational and democratic society. (Facione, 1990, p. 2)

every day, and each of those decisions is based on many different assumptions, judgments, and estimates. We also make judgments countless times each day. Every time we say things such as "I decided . . .," "Chances are . . .," "It is unlikely . . .," or "She probably did that because . . .," we are judging how likely something is to happen.

As it turns out, most often we use mental shortcuts to make decisions. These shortcuts, known as **heuristics,** are methods for making complex and uncertain decisions and judgments (Kahneman & Tversky, 1972). Consider the thought processes involved in deciding how to avoid being hit by a car when crossing a busy street. Instead of reasoning out each step systematically, we check oncoming traffic in both directions and quickly judge how fast the cars are moving and how fast we can get across. We base the decision to step off the curb or not on our quick judgment of the pace of the oncoming cars. We usually don't debate with ourselves for very long before making that decision. Heuristics allow us to come to quick and efficient decisions.

We use many types of heuristics. Here we look briefly at the two most common types: the representativeness heuristic and the availability heuristic.

The Representativeness Heuristic We use the **representativeness heuristic** when we estimate the probability of one event based on how typical or representative it is of another event (Tversky & Kahneman, 1974). For example, consider this information about Joe: He is not overweight, wears glasses, and reads poetry. Now we ask you to answer this question: Is Joe more likely to be a truck driver or a professor of English at an Ivy League university? It's simply an *either-or* decision that most people get wrong: Joe is more likely to be a truck driver!

To understand why this is so, we need to be aware of base rates, or how common something is in the population as a whole. The concept of a base rate

Finding one item in a large supermarket is made easier by heuristics. If you're looking for cold juice, you can narrow your search to a few places where cold beverages are stored and ignore all the other aisles. Deciding on a specific juice drink might be harder.

can be applied to people, events, or things. For example, six out of 100,000 people contract brain cancer in a given year; that is the base rate for brain cancer. Taking the four descriptors *truck driver, not overweight, wears glasses,* and *reads poetry*, let's consider the base rates for those segments of the U.S. population. First (assuming that by *truck driver* we mean a semi driver), there are about 3 million truck drivers in the United States (*Trucking Stats and FAQ's,* n.d.). Second, because about two-thirds of the adults in the U.S. population are overweight (see Chapter 11), we can use the figure 67% to determine how many truck drivers are overweight—about 2 million. This leaves 1 million truck drivers who are not overweight. Third, about 50% of adults wear corrective lenses (National Eye Institute, 2002). Fifty percent of 1 million leaves us with 500,000 not-overweight, glasses-wearing truck drivers. Last, it is difficult to estimate how many people read poetry, but even a very conservative figure of 1% of the population leaves us with 5,000 truck drivers who wear glasses, are not overweight, and read poetry. Once we have established that figure, we can simply ask ourselves whether there are more than 5,000 professors of English at the eight Ivy League universities. There are approximately 50 professors of English at each of the eight schools, meaning there are about 400 Ivy League English professors. So, in fact, even though it goes against our prejudices, Joe is more likely to be a truck driver than a professor of English at an Ivy League university. The information (not overweight, glasses, poetry) is so *representative* of an English professor and not a truck driver that we ignored the base-rate differences when we made our initial decision. There are simply many more truck drivers than English professors.

The Availability Heuristic The second major type of heuristic is the **availability heuristic,** which is a strategy we use when we make decisions based on the ease with which estimates come to mind or how available they are to our awareness (Tversky & Kahneman, 1974). One example of the availability heuristic occurs when people are asked whether they are more likely to be killed while flying in an airplane or while driving in a car. Some might answer that they are more likely to be killed in plane crashes, even though statistics show that far more fatalities are caused by auto accidents than by plane crashes. According to the National Safety Council (*The Odds of Dying from . . . ,* 2010), in 2006 the odds of dying in one's lifetime in an automobile accident was 1 in 85, whereas the odds of dying in a plane crash during one's lifetime was 1 in 5,682—a ratio of about 66 to 1. We may want to believe we are safer in cars than airplanes, but remember, "don't believe everything you think."

We may think we have a greater chance of dying in a plane crash because the thought of such a death conjures up dramatic images, referred to as *vividness.* Thoughts of large numbers of people dying violent deaths in plane crashes, therefore, are readily available because they are vivid. Vividness and availability lead us to overestimate how likely certain events are.

Additional research by Kahneman and Tversky (1972) revealed other areas in which people are less than rational in their decision making and judgments. For example, if people were rational they would realize that the odds of two events occurring together can never exceed the odds of either A or B occurring separately. Let's consider a specific example: The odds of your both (A) winning the lottery and (B) getting a promotion on the same day can never be greater than the odds of either one of these events happening alone. Sometimes, though, we get information that can be so

availability heuristic
A device we use to make decisions based on the ease with which estimates come to mind or how available they are to our awareness.

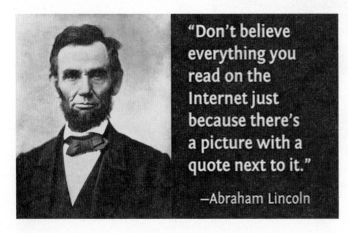
"Don't believe everything you read on the Internet just because there's a picture with a quote next to it."
—Abraham Lincoln

representative of a stereotype that it biases us, and we are likely to forget this simple rule of logic and make an error in judgment. Take the classic example of Linda offered by Tversky and Kahneman (1983, p. 297):

> Linda is 31 years old, single, outspoken, and very bright. She majored in philosophy. As a student, she was deeply concerned with issues of discrimination and social justice, and participated in anti-nuclear demonstrations.

Now you are asked the odds of each of the following: (A) that Linda is active in the feminist movement, (B) that Linda is a bank teller, and (C) that Linda is a bank teller and is active in the feminist movement. It is clear that A is more likely than B, but what about B compared to C? Remember that the combination of two events cannot be more likely than either event separately. Yet because what we are told about Linda is representative of feminists (A) and not of bank tellers (B), we are likely to say what 85% of the participants said—namely, that (C) is more likely than (B). In this case, the representativeness heuristic led to an error known as the **conjunction fallacy,** which occurs when people say that the combination of two events is more likely than either event alone.

These findings and others like them point to the conclusion that people sometimes ignore base rates, sometimes are biased by stereotypes, and sometimes use shortcuts to arrive quickly, but not completely rationally, at their decisions and conclusions. In short, Kahneman and Tversky demonstrated that people bypass fully rational decision making and make use of automatic shortcuts in their reasoning and judgments.

Heuristics and their importance in decision making and judgments are relatively new concepts in psychology. These notions developed from research in the early 1970s by Kahneman and Tversky. How they came up with the idea for carrying out this research provides an interesting glimpse into how psychologists make discoveries by challenging assumptions held by other scientists.

Challenging Assumptions in Human Rationality   Are the mental processes you use to make decisions based on reasonable, rational thought? Are you sure? Most of us like to think we are always reasonable and rational, yet a Nobel Prize was awarded in 2002 for findings showing that people often make decisions, especially economic decisions, that are not rational and reasonable.

For much of the 20th century, cognitive scientists and economists who studied human decision making believed that people generally make rational decisions. Specifically, it was thought that, when given a choice between two or more options, humans will choose the one that is most likely to help them achieve their particular goals—that is, the rational choice. Economists called this *rational choice theory* (Scott, 2000).

As we saw in the case of confirmation bias, not all reasoning is rational. In the 1970s, Tversky and Kahneman began to challenge rational choice theory with their research on human judgment and decision making. Their collaboration began when both were at the Hebrew University in Israel, where Kahneman was teaching a graduate seminar in applied psychology. "In what turned out to be a life-changing event," Kahneman writes, "I asked my younger colleague Amos Tversky to tell the class about what was going on in his field of judgment and decision-making" (Kahneman, 2002). In the seminar, Tversky demonstrated how people make judgments about the probability of events. He combined red and white poker chips in two different bags and in two different ratios as an example. He explained that people are generally rational in their judgments; they take into account differences in base rates. Using his bags of poker chips, he demonstrated that the odds are higher that a red chip will come from a bag with

conjunction fallacy
An error in logic that occurs when people say that the combination of two events is more likely than either event alone.

Challenge Your Assumptions
True or False? Humans are generally rational in their decision making.
False: Research on heuristics shows that people do not always come to rational conclusions and decisions.

Daniel Kahneman

a base rate of 70/30 red to white chips than from a bag with a base rate of 30/70 red to white chips.

Tversky's conclusion that people are rational and make use of base-rate information, however, started a lively debate in the seminar, as Kahneman later described:

> The idea . . . did not seem to fit with the everyday observation of people commonly jumping to conclusions. [Tversky] went in to the seminar believing in his findings that people are relatively rational judges but left with that belief shaken. . . . I do remember that Amos and I decided to meet for lunch to discuss our hunches about the manner in which probabilities are "really" judged. There we exchanged personal accounts of our own recurrent errors of judgment in this domain, and decided to study the statistical intuitions of experts. (Kahneman, 2002)

As Kahneman recently recounted, it was this back and forth in that seminar that led him to realize that he and Tversky were an "exceptional team" (personal communication, October 1, 2010). From there, they went on to do research which demonstrated that people are often less than rational in their decision making. These conclusions changed psychology, economics, and philosophy (e.g., Tversky & Kahneman, 1974).

To some economists and philosophers, Kahneman and Tversky's findings were nothing short of revolutionary, although not everyone appreciated them. A well-known American philosopher told Kahneman, who had started to describe some of his findings at a dinner party, "I am not really interested in the psychology of stupidity," and walked away (Kahneman, 2002).

By the late 1970s Kahneman and Tversky had begun to apply their ideas of decision making to economics (Kahneman & Tversky, 1979). They were particularly intrigued by situations that pitted people's intuitions against their rational choices. They discovered that people often make economic decisions based on intuition rather than rational choice. For example, which of the following would you pick?

a. A coin toss (50-50) chance for $1,000
b. $460 for sure

Most people choose the certain option (certainty effect). But what about the following choices? Which would you choose?

a. A 100% chance of losing $3,000
b. An 80% chance of losing $4,000 and a 20% chance of losing nothing

Now which of the following would you choose?

c. A 100% chance of winning $3,000
d. An 80% chance of winning $4,000 and a 20% chance of winning nothing

Only 20% of the people chose d, whereas 92% of the people chose b (Kahneman & Tversky, 1979). People treat wins and losses differently. People are risk-averse when faced with the prospect of winning and risk-loving when faced with the prospect of losing. Put differently, people are more averse to losing money than they are attracted to winning it. Most people will not choose an option in which they might lose $20 unless they have a chance of gaining at least $40. Notice the asymmetry in this. A $20 loss has to be balanced by a $40 gain, not $20. These results are not what standard (rational) economic theory would predict, but they are what Kahneman and Tversky's "prospect theory" predicted.

Amos Tversky

Many of us are not rational consumers. The fact that we cannot afford to buy three pairs of shoes at a time does not mean that we do not buy them.

Quick Quiz 9.2: Thinking, Reasoning, and Decision Making

1. Structures in the mind—such as an idea or image—that stand for something else, such as an external object or thing, are known as
   a. memories.
   b. mental representations.
   c. mental rotation.
   d. visions.

2. Which of the following would be considered a prototype for fruit?
   a. kiwi
   b. tomato
   c. avocado
   d. apple

3. When we reason from general statements of what is known to specific conclusions, we are engaging in
   a. hypothesis testing.
   b. inductive reasoning.
   c. deductive reasoning.
   d. logic.

4. What distinguishes scientific thinking from nonscientific thinking?
   a. the ability to separate belief from evidence
   b. the ability to reason
   c. concept formation
   d. the use of heuristics

5. _____ are mental shortcuts for making complex and uncertain decisions and judgments.
   a. Categories
   b. Schemas
   c. Calculations
   d. Heuristics

6. Which of the following makes people believe they are more likely to die in a plane crash than a car crash?
   a. the fear schema
   b. the availability heuristic
   c. concept formation
   d. the representativeness heuristic

Answers can be found at the end of the chapter.

Bringing It All Together
Making Connections in Language and Thought

Learning a Second Language

As we saw with Mike, Lisa, and Zoé at the beginning of the chapter, learning multiple languages can be difficult and challenging but it also offers cognitive advantages compared to speaking only one language. Vocabulary tests often reveal higher vocabulary in monolingual children than bilingual children, but the latter have better executive functioning skills than the former (Bialystok et al., 2010; Hoff et al., 2012). Bilingualism offers a perfect topic to bring together research findings on how language and thought are closely connected, because we can address these questions:

1. When are our brains most sensitive to learning a second language, and why can some people speak a second language with no accent from their first language?

2. Is a second language processed differently in the brain than a first language?

3. Do we think and reason differently in different languages?

4. Does learning a second language make us more creative and more able to think about our thinking (metacognitive)?

Sensitivity Periods and Second-Language Acquisition

There is a sensitive period for second-language acquisition: Children learn second languages more quickly than adults do and speak them more fluently (Birdsong, 2006; DeKeyser & Larson-Hall, 2005; K. H. S. Kim et al., 1997; Sakai, 2005; Uylings, 2006). A strong negative correlation exists between the age of learning the second language and the proficiency of speaking that language (DeKeyser & Larson-Hall, 2005). The younger a person is when he or she acquires the second language, the more proficiently the person speaks that language. Starting around age 7, learning a second language starts to become a little more

Challenge Your Assumptions

True or False? Eighteen-year-olds cannot learn to speak a second language without an accent just as easily as a 6-year-old.
True: The window for learning to speak a second language with no trace of one's native language seems to be early to mid-adolescence.

difficult, and proficiency is reduced; and by around early adolescence (ages 13 to 15), the sensitive period for learning to speak a second language without an accent appears to end (Birdsong, 2005; Flege, Munro, & MacKay, 1995a, 1995b; Long, 1990; Jiang et al., 2009; Oyama, 1976; Sakai, 2005). For example, native English speakers evaluated the strength of the accent in English spoken by Italian immigrants to the United States (Oyama, 1976). The length of time the immigrants had been in the United States did not affect the strength or thickness of their accent, but the age at which they had moved to the United States did. If they were 6 when they immigrated and had been in the country for only 2 years, they had much less of an accent than if they were 30 years old when they learned the language but had been in the United States for 10 years. A systematic review of the literature by Long (1990) confirmed this finding from dozens of studies. Thus, as a time for learning to speak a second language without an accent, childhood is better than adolescence and adolescence is better than adulthood. Although the finding is robust that age of second-language acquisition affects the accent level of nonnative speakers, numerous social factors lessen this effect, such as continued education, the amount of second language that is used, and gender (Flege, 1999; Flege et al., 1995a, 1995b; Hakuta, Bialystok, & Wiley, 2003).

Second-Language Learning and the Brain

People who are fluent in two languages apparently are capable of more efficient cognitive processing than those who speak only one. Psychologists examined the ability of speakers of one and two languages to perform cognitive tasks (Bialystok et al., 2006). They found that those who

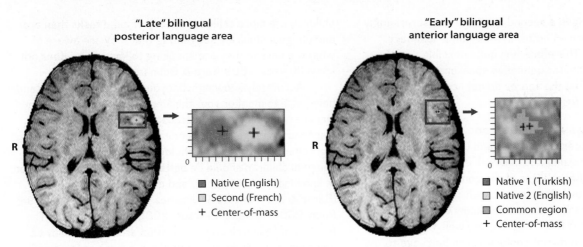

"Late" bilingual
posterior language area

"Early" bilingual
anterior language area

R

■ Native (English)
□ Second (French)
+ Center-of-mass

R

■ Native 1 (Turkish)
□ Native 2 (English)
■ Common region
+ Center-of-mass

FIGURE **9.11**

ACTIVATION IN BROCA'S AREA FOR LATE LEARNERS AND EARLY LEARNERS OF A SECOND LANGUAGE. People who learn a second language later in life (after the age of 16) use different areas of the brain to produce speech in two languages, as shown by the images on the left. People who learn a second language in childhood show activation in overlapping areas of the brain when producing speech in two languages, as shown on the right. In other words, the brain of the early learner responds almost identically when the person is speaking either language. Perhaps the reason that late learners are less fluent is that the brain treats the two languages differently. (K. H. S. Kim et al., 1997)

spoke two languages performed better on the cognitive tasks and continued to do so later in life.

Learning another language may also have a long-term beneficial effect on the brain. When matched for age, gender, and other qualities, elderly speakers of two languages develop dementia more than 4 years later than do elderly speakers of only one language (Bialystok & Craik, 2010). What is most interesting about these results is that they once again support the view that stimulation from the environment—in this case, learning another language—can enrich our brains and enable them to process information more efficiently.

Neuroscientists have begun to demonstrate even more directly the long-lasting effects of learning two languages. First, compared to single-language 6- to 9-month-old infants, bilingual infants of the same age do not discriminate similar sounds; by 10 to 11 months, however, there are no differences between the two groups in their ability to discriminate sounds (Garcia-Sierra et al., 2011). This suggests that the brains of bilingual babies are more responsive to a wide range of sounds, which in turn may explain their greater cognitive flexibility later in life.

Second, compared to single-language speakers, bilingual speakers have a greater density of neurons in the language centers of the brain (Mechelli et al., 2004). Not only that, but neural density is also proportional to the age at which the person learned the second language. The earlier the second language is learned, the greater the neural density (Mechelli et al., 2004). These findings demonstrate yet again how the brain is shaped by experience.

Third, bilingual people exhibit differences in brain activation, depending on when they learned their second

language (K. H. S. Kim et al., 1997). What is most fascinating is that the brains of people who learn a second language early in life are more efficient at language processing and more similar when speaking in both languages than are the brains of people who learn a second language late in life. If someone learns a second language early in life, essentially at the same time they learn their first language, the brain regions that are active during speech (production) overlap almost completely. On the other hand, if a person learns a second language years after learning the first language, the brain regions that are active during speech (production) are next to each other but hardly overlap (see Figure 9.11).

What is equally fascinating is that the same pattern does not hold for comprehension or listening. The brains of both early and late second-language learners show the same areas of activation when the learners are listening to their first and second languages (K. H. S. Kim et al., 1997). Thus, the age at which a person learns a second language is reflected in differences in the brain, but only in areas involved in producing rather than understanding speech.

Reasoning in a Second Language

It is difficult enough to get through a college entrance exam, such as the Scholastic Aptitude Test (SAT), in one's native language. Imagine doing it in a second language in which you are not perfectly fluent. Each year thousands of foreign students seeking admission to American universities undertake this challenge. The SAT includes questions that require deductive reasoning, such as text comprehension. In research that compared students' deductive reasoning in their native language and their deductive reasoning in a second language, not surprisingly the students performed better in their native language (D'Anglejan, 1979). Therefore, it is quite possible that the validity of these tests for nonnative speakers is somewhat questionable and that the scores do not accurately portray the aptitude of the test takers.

Second-Language Acquisition and Metacognition

Remember the concerns that Mike and Lisa's family and friends had about raising Zoé in Greek only and letting others teach her English? One of the concerns was how Zoé would even know when to speak which language with whom. Her American relatives didn't know Greek, and her Greek relatives didn't know English very well. One explanation for why children do not confuse which language to speak to which group of people is "theory of mind," a topic we first introduced in Chapter 5. By about age 4, children understand that other people's thoughts and ideas are different from their own. Research shows that bilingual

children are more skilled in theory of mind tasks than are monolingual children, suggesting that they are aware of what the person they are speaking to knows and does not know (Kovács, 2009; Tare & Gelman, 2010).

Accurately knowing what you do and do not know and being able to monitor your thinking as you work on a problem are two hallmarks of metacognition. Because learning a second language requires one to think about one's thinking, some linguists and psychologists have proposed that bilingual children should be better than monolingual children at knowing what they know and monitoring their thinking (Barac & Bialystok, 2012; Jimenez, Garcia, & Pearson, 1994; Ruan, 2004; Tobias & Everson, 2002; Wenden, 1998). The findings of research on this question are mixed. It may be, however, that metacognitive thinking is more pronounced when one is first learning a second language than later, when one is rather fluent (Tobias & Everson, 2002).

Other studies have also reported at least partial support for the idea that speaking two languages facilitates creative, flexible, and original problem solving (Kovács & Mehler, 2009; Landry, 1973; Lasagabaster, 2000; Ricciardelli, 1992; L. Zhang, 2010). In a quantitative review (meta-analysis) of a large body of research, Ricciardelli reported that 20 out of 24 published studies had found that bilingual students scored higher on creativity tasks than did monolingual students. Flexible and creative thinking thus is closely aligned with metacognitive thinking (Sternberg, 2004).

Challenge Your Assumptions

True or False? Children raised from infancy with two languages (bilingually) seldom confuse the two languages.

True: Probably because they are sensitive to what other people know and don't know, bilingual children seldom mix up languages or speak the wrong language to someone.

Chapter Review

LANGUAGE

- Human language is an open, symbolic communication system that follows rules of syntax and grammar.

- Individuals develop language in a four-stage sequence, beginning with cooing and babbling in infancy. At about 12 months of age, toddlers start making their first one-word utterances. At around 18 months, babies progress to two-word utterances. By age 2½ to 3, most children enter the short-sentence phase. Continued language development requires stimulation from other people during a sensitive period between about the first 6 years of life and age 12.

- There are three major theories of language. Social-cultural theories propose that we learn vocabulary by hearing others speak and figure out what they mean by the context. Conditioning and learning theories argue that language is like any other learned behavior, something that occurs because it is reinforced and shaped. Nativist theories argue that humans possess a language acquisition device (LAD), an innate, biologically based capacity to acquire language that comes with a general and universal grammar.

THINKING, REASONING, AND DECISION MAKING

- Cognitive psychology is the scientific study of how people think, learn, remember, and perceive.

- We use visual and verbal representations in our minds as mental structures or processes for an image or idea. Concepts and categories are mental representations we use to organize our world. Prototypes are the best-fitting examples of a category.

- We use reasoning to draw inferences, or conclusions, from principles and evidence. In deductive reasoning, we start with a general statement of what is known and draw specific conclusions from it. We use inductive reasoning to draw general conclusions from specific evidence. These conclusions are less certain, because many different conclusions might be consistent with a specific fact.

- Confirmation bias is the tendency to selectively attend to information that confirms one's general beliefs while ignoring information or evidence that contradicts one's beliefs.

- Critical thinking uses sound reasoning when analyzing facts, generating and organizing ideas, defending opinions, making comparisons, drawing inferences, evaluating arguments, and solving problems.

- Scientific thinking is metacognitive thinking used to generate, test, reflect upon, and revise theories.

- Heuristics are shortcuts we use in making judgments. We use the representativeness heuristic when we estimate the probability of one event based on how typical it is of another event. We use the availability heuristic to make estimates based on the ease with which we can bring an event or object to mind.

BRINGING IT ALL TOGETHER: MAKING CONNECTIONS IN LANGUAGE AND THOUGHT

- Children who learn a second language early, during a sensitive period that ends around age 15, speak it more fluently, without an accent, and with greater proficiency than do older children or adults.

- Bilingualism appears to enhance cognitive processing and is associated with a lower rate of dementia in the elderly.

- People who learn a second language in childhood process both languages in roughly the same area of the brain, whereas in later learners, processing of the two languages occurs in two scarcely overlapping areas.

- At least initially, learning a second language may enhance metacognition, the knowledge of what we know and don't know, and foster flexible thinking and creative problem solving.

Key Terms

availability heuristic, p. 348
babbling, p. 327
category, p. 341
causal inferences, p. 343
child-directed speech, p. 330
cognition, p. 337
concept, p. 341
concept hierarchy, p. 341
confirmation bias, p. 343
conjunction fallacy, p. 349
cooing, p. 327

critical thinking, p. 344
deductive reasoning, p. 343
grammar, p. 325
heuristics, p. 347
human language, p. 325
inductive reasoning, p. 343
language acquisition device (LAD), p. 331
linguistic determinism hypothesis, p. 336
mental representation, p. 339
mental rotation, p. 340

metacognitive thinking, p. 345
nativist view of language, p. 331
one-word utterances, p. 327
protolanguage, p. 326
prototypes, p. 342
reasoning, p. 342
representativeness heuristic, p. 347
sentence phase, p. 327
syntax, p. 325
two-word utterances, p. 327
visual imagery, p. 339

Quick Quiz Answers

Quick Quiz 9.1: 1. c 2. a 3. d 4. c   **Quick Quiz 9.2:** 1. b 2. d 3. c 4. a 5. d 6. b

10 Intelligence, Problem Solving, and Creativity

Chapter Outline

Intelligence
Problem Solving
Creativity
Chapter Review

Challenge Your Assumptions

True or False?

- Intelligence is a single, general capacity.
  (see page 359)

- People with high IQs have larger brains.
  (see page 371)

- As people get older, genetics plays a stronger
  and stronger role in how intelligent they are.
  (see page 375)

- If a person has original thoughts or behavior,
  he or she is creative. (see page 384)

- People with very high IQs are geniuses.
  (see page 391)

Bob, a sixth-grader, was petrified by the woman who was about to administer an IQ test. "As she distributed the test booklets, I could feel my insides chill" (Sternberg, 1988, p. ix). Sure enough, as Bob attempted to solve the problems, his fears and anxieties got the best of him. He could hardly concentrate and couldn't finish. "I knew I had bombed. . . . There are those who think they fail but really succeed, and there are those who really fail. Unfortunately, I was among the latter" (p. ix). Then to add to the humiliation, Bob was sent to retake the test with fifth-graders; however, his fears of taking the test with his peers went away completely, and this time he did very well on the IQ test.

As a child, Scott had an auditory processing disability that made processing words in real time difficult. This made school and learning a challenge. "When I performed poorly on an IQ test, I had to repeat third grade. I remember thinking to myself: *Gosh, I must be really behind if they don't think I'm ready to handle fourth grade*" (S. B. Kaufman, 2013, p. ii, emphasis in the original). Scott was placed in special education classes, where the expectations for learning and success were very low. He felt quite ungifted growing up.

Finally, what do Tom Cruise, Thomas Edison, Bob Weir, Alexander Graham Bell, Albert Einstein, Robin Williams, Cher, Leonardo da Vinci, Henry Ford, John Lennon, Stephen Spielberg, and Whoopi Goldberg all have in common? They are (were) all dyslexic; they had a reading/learning disability (*Famous People*, 2013).

Bob (Robert Sternberg) went on to attend Yale as an undergraduate; he earned a PhD from Stanford and became a world famous professor of psychology, with expertise in intelligence and creativity. As we see later in the chapter, Sternberg has been one of the main voices challenging traditional conceptualizations of intelligence. Scott (S. B. Kaufman) earned a PhD from Yale (and was a student of Sternberg's). Using his personal experiences and his research on the topic, he authored a best-selling book entitled *Ungifted: Intelligence Redefined*. To be sure, the list of incredibly talented and creative people with learning disabilities is vast.

As these cases show, conventional intelligence may be inadequate to explain greatness, and they raise questions about what intelligence is and how it relates to genius and creativity. Are we born smart, or does this capacity grow with training? Is intelligence a single, general skill or many different skills? Psychologists agree that there are capacities that shape how smart people are, and these constitute the three central topics of this chapter: intelligence, problem solving, and creativity. In this chapter, we will discuss what intelligence is and how it is measured, we will look at a practical ability called *problem solving*, and then we will examine the process of solving problems in unique ways known as *creativity*. Throughout, we aim to show how these topics overlap considerably yet also reveal distinct capabilities of the human mind.

INTELLIGENCE

Many people consider intelligence the primary trait that sets humans apart from other animals, but what is intelligence? Is it the same as being generally smart, or is it more complex? Is it a single ability or many different abilities? Intelligence can be defined in a number of ways, and even the experts cannot agree on a definition. Over the years, groups of intelligence experts have convened for

Question	Theory	Summary
How intelligent are you?	Spearman's general intelligence (g)	Intelligence is a single, general capacity.
How are you intelligent?	Thurstone's multiple factors	Intelligence consists of 7 primary mental abilities, including spatial ability, memory, perceptual speed, and word fluency.
How are you intelligent?	Cattell–Horn–Carroll (CHC) hierarchical intelligence	Intelligence can be broken down into 3 levels of ability: general, broad, and narrow.
How are you intelligent?	Sternberg's triarchic theory	Intelligence is made up of 3 abilities (analytical, creative, and practical) necessary for success.
How are you intelligent?	Gardner's multiple intelligences	Intelligence includes at least 8 distinct capacities, including musical intelligence, interpersonal intelligence, and bodily-kinesthetic intelligence.

FIGURE **10.1**

THEORIES OF INTELLIGENCE. There are two principal views of intelligence. One considers intelligence as a single, measurable ability. The other looks at intelligence as comprising several distinct abilities.

the purpose of defining intelligence (Neisser et al., 1996; Snyderman & Rothman, 1987; Sternberg & Detterman, 1986).

Defining Intelligence

Intelligence may be our inherent potential for learning, how fast we are able to learn, or the body of knowledge we possess. It may also include the ability to do things in ways that other people have never tried. The definition of intelligence that we will use encompasses all these qualities. According to the experts, **intelligence** is a set of cognitive skills that includes abstract thinking, reasoning, problem solving, and the ability to acquire knowledge. Other, less-agreed-on qualities of intelligence include mathematical ability, general knowledge, and creativity (see Figure 10.1).

intelligence
A set of cognitive skills that include abstract thinking, reasoning, problem solving, and the ability to acquire knowledge.

Theories of Intelligence

Theories of intelligence started sprouting up in the early 1900s, soon after the first modern intelligence tests appeared. Two distinct views dominate our understanding of intelligence. One view says that intelligence is a single, general ability; the other says that intelligence consists of multiple abilities.

Traditional Models of Intelligence: Intelligence as a Single, General Ability Charles Spearman (1904, 1923) developed the first theory of intelligence and proposed that it is best thought of as a single, general capacity, or ability. Spearman came to this conclusion after research consistently showed that specific dimensions, or factors, of intelligence—namely, spatial, verbal, perceptual, and quantitative factors—correlated strongly with one another, suggesting that they were all measuring pretty much the same thing. People who achieve high scores on the verbal section of an intelligence test are also likely to have high scores on the spatial, perceptual, and quantitative sections.

Challenge Your Assumptions
True or False? Intelligence is a single, general capacity.
Neither True nor False: Some psychologists and educators argue that intelligence is one general, intercorrelated skill, whereas others argue it is many distinct, relatively uncorrelated abilities.

g-factor theory
Spearman's theory that intelligence is a single, general (g) factor made up of specific components.

multiple-factor theory of intelligence
The idea that intelligence consists of distinct dimensions and is not just a single factor.

Spearman's theory is now known as a **g-factor theory** of intelligence, because it describes intelligence as a single, *general* factor made up of specific components. This theory influenced intelligence test construction for most of the 20th century. Most intelligence tests determine a person's overall intelligence score by his or her scores on specific subtests. G-factor theory implies that this single number accurately reflects a person's intelligence—the higher, the better. A person who scores 115 on an intelligence test is generally more intelligent than a person who scores 100, a perspective illustrated by the question, *How* intelligent are you? (see Figure 10.1).

Challenging Assumptions of Traditional Views of Intelligence: Intelligence as Multiple Abilities   Critics of the g-factor theory insisted that test scores by themselves ignore important aspects of intelligence that the traditional tests don't measure. This view, the **multiple-factor theory of intelligence,** holds that the different aspects of intelligence are distinct enough that multiple abilities must be considered, not just one. This perspective is illustrated by the question, *How* are you intelligent? (see Figure 10.1).

One of the first people to "break intelligence in two" was Raymond Cattell, with his notion of *fluid* and *crystallized intelligence* (Horn & Cattell, 1966), terms introduced in Chapter 5, "Human Development." Recall that fluid intelligence involves raw mental ability, pattern recognition, and abstract reasoning and is applied to a problem that you have never confronted before. Fluid intelligence is not influenced by culture or the size of your vocabulary. Instead, it simply involves how fast you learn new things. So some children just learn to read, write, and do math more quickly and easily than others. One commonly used measure of fluid intelligence is *Raven's Progressive Matrices Test* (see Figure 10.2). Matrix reasoning is fluid intelligence, because it does not depend on acquired knowledge and involves the ability to find patterns.

By contrast, crystallized intelligence involves using skills, experience, and knowledge to solve problems. This form of intelligence stems from the size of your vocabulary, as well as your knowledge of your culture. For example, understanding the meaning of a written paragraph requires crystallized intelligence, because it requires you to use your experience and knowledge to solve the problem. Vocabulary tests are also measures of crystallized intelligence.

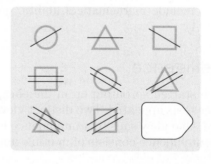

FIGURE 10.2

AN EXAMPLE FROM RAVEN'S PROGRESSIVE MATRICES TEST. This sample problem requires fluid intelligence. It is nonverbal and requires pattern recognition, not prior acquired knowledge. For this reason, this test is often considered a "culture-free" test of intelligence.

 Can you figure out which of the numbered bottom figures would be next in the series of nine? (Simulated items similar to those in the Raven's Progressive Matrices. Copyright © 1998 by NCS Pearson, Inc. Reproduced with permission. All rights reserved. "Raven's Progressive Matrices" is a trademark, in the US and/or other countries, of Pearson Education, Inc. or its affiliates.)

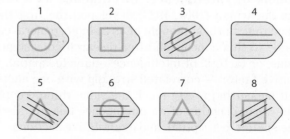

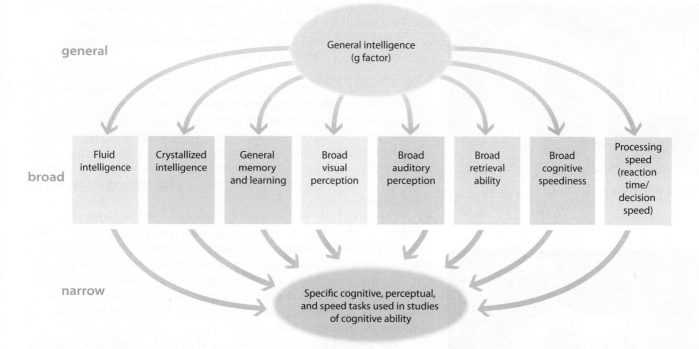

general

General intelligence
(g factor)

broad

| Fluid intelligence | Crystallized intelligence | General memory and learning | Broad visual perception | Broad auditory perception | Broad retrieval ability | Broad cognitive speediness | Processing speed (reaction time/ decision speed) |

narrow

Specific cognitive, perceptual, and speed tasks used in studies of cognitive ability

FIGURE 10.3

THE CATTELL-HORN-CARROLL (CHC) MODEL OF INTELLIGENCE. This hierarchical model integrates the concept of a general intelligence with several, broadly defined abilities, including fluid and crystallized intelligence. The broad categories consist of more specific abilities, such as speed of reasoning (fluid intelligence) and language comprehension (crystallized intelligence). (Carroll, 1993)

John Carroll (1993) further subdivided intelligence when he reviewed and integrated more than 450 sets of intelligence data published from the 1930s to the mid-1980s and concluded that the Cattell-Horn model of fluid and crystallized intelligence best fit the existing evidence. Carroll extended the model, however, arguing that intelligence actually consists of three levels, arranged in a hierarchy. At the top is **general intelligence,** at the middle is **broad intelligence,** and at the bottom is **narrow intelligence.** General intelligence is very similar to Spearman's concept of "g." Broad intelligence consists of abilities such as crystallized and fluid intelligence, as well as memory, learning, and processing speed. Narrow intelligence consists of nearly 70 distinct abilities, such as speed of reasoning and general sequential reasoning for fluid intelligence and reading, spelling, and language comprehension for crystallized intelligence (see Figure 10.3). Because this model includes Cattell and Horn's crystallized and fluid intelligence, it has become known as the Cattell-Horn-Carroll (CHC) model of intelligence.

Robert Sternberg and Howard Gardner, however, proposed theories of intelligence that challenged traditional models. We first encountered Sternberg in the beginning of the chapter as the test-anxious boy who "flunked" an IQ test. He took this failure, however, as a spark for his interest in intelligence and challenged the traditional intelligence model as one general ability:

> Almost all my ideas for research have emerged from areas in which I have weaknesses. I became interested in psychology because, as a child, I performed poorly on group intelligence tests. I have continued my study of intelligence even until the present day, still trying to figure out what went wrong when I took those tests. (I like to attribute my poor scores to test anxiety, although that may be a

general intelligence
One of Carroll's three levels of intelligence; very similar to Spearman's concept of "g."

broad intelligence
One of Carroll's three levels of intelligence, including abilities such as crystallized and fluid intelligence, as well as memory, learning, and processing speed.

narrow intelligence
One of Carroll's three levels of intelligence, including many distinct abilities.

Connection

As we go from young adulthood to middle adulthood, our experience-based (crystallized) intelligence continues to improve. Abstract and culture-free (fluid) intelligence, however, peaks during our 20s.

See "The Developing Adult," Chapter 5, "Human Development," p. 193.

Robert Sternberg

How do athletes use practical intelligence to solve problems on the court or field?

successful intelligence
According to Sternberg, an integrated set of abilities needed to attain success in life.

triarchic theory of intelligence
Sternberg's three-part model of intelligence, including analytic, creative, and practical intelligence.

rationalization.) . . . So I recommend to you that, if you are bad at something, you use that as a basis to get new ideas about what you can study in psychology! (Personal communication, May 30, 2010)

In fact, Sternberg has spent a career focusing not simply on intelligence but on **successful intelligence,** which he defines as an integrated set of information-processing and cognitive abilities needed for life success (Sternberg, 2005, p. 104). Three interrelated but distinct abilities make up successful intelligence: analytic, creative, and practical intelligence (Sternberg, 1985, 2006b). Sternberg's three-part theory is known as the **triarchic theory of intelligence.**

The first type of intelligence, *analytic intelligence,* involves judging, evaluating, or comparing and contrasting information (Sternberg, 1998). Analytic intelligence resembles the kind of academic intelligence that leads to high scores on tests of intelligence. For example, an analytic problem might require a person to decipher the meaning of an uncommon word from its context in a sentence, or it might ask the person to determine the next number in a series of numbers (Sternberg, 2003).

The second form of intelligence is *creative intelligence,* which involves coming up with fresh and useful ideas for solving problems. For example, a person might be given a number of cartoon images and then be asked to come up with a caption for each one (Sternberg, 2006b). Traditional measures of intelligence do not measure creative intelligence well.

The third processing skill, *practical intelligence,* is the ability to solve problems of everyday life efficiently. Practical intelligence plays a role in knowing how to do one's job well and requires knowledge and skills that one learns "on the street" rather than in the classroom. A practical intelligence problem might ask people to come up with three solutions to an everyday problem they are currently experiencing in their lives, such as how to live on a fixed income (Sternberg, 2003).

Howard Gardner (1983, 1993), another scholar of the multifaceted view of intelligence, argues that intelligence consists of at least eight distinct capacities: linguistic, mathematical-logical, musical, bodily-kinesthetic, spatial, intrapersonal, interpersonal, and naturalistic. *Naturalistic intelligence,* for instance, is the ability to recognize, classify, and understand the plants and animals in one's environment. In cultures that have formal science, highly skilled people in this domain of intelligence are likely to become biologists, botanists, and animal scientists or veterinarians. In cultures without formal science, they are the most talented hunters, gatherers, and farmers. *Interpersonal intelligence* is the ability to perceive and understand other people's intentions, emotions, motives, and behaviors and is very closely related to what other psychologists refer to as "emotional intelligence." Interpersonally intelligent people therefore work well and know how to get along with others. See Figure 10.4 for a complete listing, with definitions, of Gardner's eight intelligences.

Scholars are strongly divided, however, over Gardner's theory. Those who have the most problems with it tend to be psychologists, because they see little value in calling skills such as music, movement, and social skills "intelligence" and argue that Gardner has not provided tests of these intelligences. Moreover, there have been few direct empirical tests on Gardner's theory, and therefore some argue that his ideas are more theoretical than empirical. For some psychologists and many educators, however, Gardner's ideas address two facts: (1) Different students learn in different ways, and (2) some students who have

Intelligence	Definition	Representative Professions
linguistic	Ability to learn, understand, and use both spoken and written language	Poets, writers, lawyers, politicians
logical-mathematical	Ability to analyze information and problems logically and to perform mathematical operations	Scientists, engineers, accountants
musical	Ability in performing, composing, or appreciating musical patterns	Musicians, dancers, song-writers
bodily-kinesthetic	Ability to use one's body or parts of it to solve problems or create products	Athletes, dancers, mechanics, craftspeople
spatial	Ability to think about and solve problems in three-dimensional space	Navigators, pilots, architects, sculptors
interpersonal	Ability to understand and be aware of other people's intentions, motivations, thoughts, and desires; also the ability to work well with and get along with others	Psychologists, social workers, teachers, politicians
intrapersonal	Ability to be aware of, understand, and regulate one's own behavior, thoughts, feelings, and motivations	Psychologists, monks, priests
naturalistic	Ability to recognize, classify, and understand the plants and animals in one's environment	Naturalists, biologists, botanists, veterinarians, hunters, farmers

FIGURE **10.4**

GARDNER'S MULTIPLE INTELLIGENCES. The far-right column lists professions that are well served by each ability.

demonstrated ability in some areas fail academic subjects and do poorly on traditional intelligence tests (Kornhaber, Fierros, & Veenema, 2004). They may even drop out of school.

How should teachers nurture and teach these failing students—all students—given the fact that there are different styles of learning? Entire schools have been designed to enhance the "intelligences" of students. We describe a few of these programs in "Psychology in the Real World."

Measuring Intelligence

Like various theories of intelligence, tests of intelligence (commonly called IQ tests) are controversial. They raise questions such as these: How does someone interpret a person's score on an intelligence test? Where does a person stand compared to everyone else? How do we know that a given test is any good at all? The numerous attempts to answer these questions over the years have been based on the way intelligence was understood at the time the tests were devised.

Howard Gardner

Psychology in the Real World

Bringing Multiple Intelligences to School

The chief motivation behind bringing multiple intelligences (MI) to the school setting is to avoid some of the limitations of traditional testing and teaching that discourage students who do not do well. Gardner (1999) realized that testing in the usual sense would have to be abandoned and classrooms would have to be arranged and equipped with materials that stimulate and foster each of the forms of intelligence. Under this model, classrooms may be arranged with areas meant for dance, exercise, and construction. The materials may include board games, art and music materials, nature specimens (e.g., a fish tank), and natural objects.

An educational principle based on MI theory is that children should have some freedom to choose activities on their own. If they ignore certain kinds of activities, their teachers provide encouragement and "bridges" for them to try the neglected activities. If students are reluctant to tell stories, a teacher might encourage them to build a diorama (a three-dimensional model). The teacher might then ask the students to tell a story about what is happening to the people and animals in the diorama.

More than 40 schools in the United States have been designed to put into practice the development of all Gardner's forms of intelligence (Armstrong, 2009; Kornhaber et al., 2004; Kunkel, 2009). One example is the Key Learning Community in Indianapolis, Indiana. It opened in 1987 as a public elementary and middle school. Assessment takes place at the end of the school year, when each student presents a project based on any or all of the intelligences on which he or she has focused during the year. Students often present their project as a performance, such as a play, a poetry reading, or an artistic interpretation. They may also write papers on what they have learned. Each presentation is videotaped and put into the student's portfolio, which serves as a record of the student's cognitive and emotional development. Students in these schools still must take the local school district's standardized tests, and when they do, they perform at least as well as students from other schools (*Key Learning Community*, n.d.; Kornhaber et al., 2004). Moreover, most of the schools adopting this model have reported that the MI approach helped decrease disciplinary problems and increase parent participation. Finally, the performance of students with learning disabilities improved markedly when they attended MI schools.

In short, the MI schools teach to different learning styles and to their students' different intellectual talents. For some students, at least, this alternative fosters academic achievement that might not occur in a traditional setting.

Evaluating the effectiveness of programs like the Key Learning Community is difficult in a culture dominated by test scores as the main criterion of success (Kunkel, 2009). This is especially true because MI-based programs emphasize community service, the completion of projects, and apprenticeships. In a recent survey of Key students (among a community with a 73% poverty rate, which works against successfully completing school in traditional school settings), the results showed that 88% of Key students graduate and 91% go on to further education or training after high school (Kunkel, 2009).

Should naturalistic intelligence be nurtured in the same way as mathematical skills, verbal ability, and at least five other kinds of intelligence?

Traditional Measures of Intelligence   Intelligence tests were among the first psychological tests. The French scholar Alfred Binet deserves the most credit for developing the first true test of intelligence. In the early 1900s, the government hired Binet to identify students who would benefit most from special instruction techniques. For this purpose, Binet and a colleague, Theodore Simon, developed a test containing 30 problems of increasing difficulty. Their idea that the ability to solve increasingly difficult problems depends on age became widely influential and has since become known as **mental age,** the equivalent chronological age a child has reached based on his or her performance on an intelligence test. Children are given a mental age not according to how old they are in years but rather according to the level or age group at which they can solve problems. Mental age is a norm, or average, because it is based on what most children at a particular age level can do.

A few years after Binet developed the concept of mental age, a German psychologist, William Stern, introduced the *intelligence ratio,* in which mental age (MA) is divided by chronological age (CA) and multiplied by 100 to determine an intelligence score. The ratio of mental age over chronological age is commonly known as a person's *intelligence quotient,* or *IQ.* If a child had a mental age of 10 and was 10 years old, she had an IQ of 100 (10/10 × 100). But if she had a mental age of 12 and was only 10 years old, she had an IQ of 120; if she had a mental age of 8 and was 10 years old, her IQ was 80. This ratio was very useful in the early years of IQ testing with children, but it is no longer used. Today IQ scores are based on how well a child does on tests relative to norms or standards established by testing children of the same age.

About 10 years after Binet published his first test, Lewis Terman, an American psychologist, translated the test for American students. Because Terman taught at Stanford University, he named the test the *Stanford-Binet test.* The most significant changes Terman made were to establish national norms and to adopt and apply the ratio score of MA/CA to a widely used IQ test.

In the 1930s, David Wechsler created new intelligence tests to measure adult intelligence. Wechsler's test became known as the *Wechsler Adult Intelligence Scale,* or *WAIS* (Wechsler, 1944, 1958). Later he developed a test for children, the *Wechsler Intelligence Scale for Children* (*WISC*). At present, these two tests are the ones most frequently administered in the United States (Wasserman & Tulsky, 2005). To sample the kinds of problems included on one of these IQ tests, see Figure 10.5. The current versions of both the Stanford-Binet and the WAIS are based on modern theories about intelligence.

Modern Measures of Intelligence   For 50 years, IQ tests were based on the assumption that intelligence is a single quality. The developers of both the Stanford-Binet and the Wechsler tests failed to take into account Jean Piaget's work on cognitive development and newer findings from neuroscience. As discussed in Chapter 5, Piaget found that the cognitive abilities of young children are fundamentally different from those of adolescents and that cognitive development occurs in stages rather than gradually over time. Adolescents can reason abstractly, for example, but young children cannot; however, IQ tests continued to give very similar problems to young children, teenagers, and adults, changing only the level of difficulty. Moreover, until the 1980s, IQ test developers ignored advances in neuroscience (A. S. Kaufman, 1979). In the late 20th century, a new approach to intelligence testing incorporated Piaget's ideas, findings from neuroscience, and learning style differences.

As advances in neuroscience led to greater understanding of how the brain solves problems, psychologists became increasingly aware of the limits of existing IQ tests. By the late 1970s, alternatives to the two dominant IQ tests (Stanford-Binet and Wechsler) began to be published. One of the best known of these alternatives, developed by Nadeen and Alan Kaufman, is

mental age
The equivalent chronological age a child has reached based on his or her performance on an IQ test.

Alan and Nadeen Kaufman

Similarities

An individual must think logically and abstractly to answer a number of questions about how things might be similar.

Example: "In what ways are boats and trains the same?"

Comprehension

This subscale is designed to measure an individual's judgment and common sense.

Example: "Why do individuals buy automobile insurance?"

Picture Arrangement

A series of pictures out of sequence is shown to an individual, who is asked to place them in their proper order to tell an appropriate story. This subscale evaluates how individuals integrate information to make it logical and meaningful.

Example: "The pictures below need to be placed in an appropriate order to tell a story."

Block Design

An individual must assemble a set of multicolored blocks to match designs that the examiner shows. Visual-motor coordination, perceptual organization, and the ability to visualize spatially are assessed.

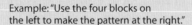

Example: "Use the four blocks on the left to make the pattern at the right."

FIGURE 10.5

IQ TEST PROBLEMS SIMILAR TO THOSE ON THE WECHSLER ADULT INTELLIGENCE SCALE (WAIS). The WAIS and the Wechsler Intelligence Scale for Children are the most widely administered intelligence tests in the United States. (Simulated items similar to those found on the Wechsler Adult Intelligence Scale–Revised [WAIS-R]. Copyright © 1981, 1955 by NCS Pearson, Inc. Reproduced with permission. All rights reserved. "Wechsler Adult Intelligence Scale" and "WAIS" are trademarks, in the US and/or other countries, of Pearson Education, Inc. or its affiliates.)

the *Kaufman-Assessment Battery for Children,* or *K-ABC* (A. S. Kaufman & Kaufman, 1983). The K-ABC differed from the Stanford-Binet and Wechsler tests in four ways. First, it was the first IQ test to be guided by theories of intelligence, in particular Cattell and Horn's concepts of fluid and crystallized intelligence and Piaget's theory of cognitive development. Second, influenced by Piaget, the Kaufmans included fundamentally different kinds of problems for children of different ages, as well as problems at varied levels of difficulty. Third, unlike older tests, the K-ABC measured several distinct aspects of intelligence. Finally, influenced by neuroscience and information processing theory, the K-ABC assessed different types of learning styles. In this sense, the K-ABC was the first of many intelligence tests informed by contemporary ideas about how the brain works and develops (A. D. Kaufman & Kaufman, 1983).

Tests may still produce an overall IQ score, but now they also yield scores on as many as seven dimensions of intelligence. Influenced by the CHC model, the newest versions of both the WAIS (WAIS-IV) and the WISC (WISC-IV) include scores on four dimensions: verbal comprehension, perceptual reasoning, working memory, and processing speed (T. P. Hogan, 2007). Working memory, which holds information in mind for a short period, so that it can be used to solve a problem at hand, is one dimension that was missing before 1985. For examples of working memory tasks included in the Wechsler scales, see Figure 10.6.

Connection

Working memory is another term for *short-term memory.* In general, people can retain only about seven bits of information in short-term memory.

See "Short-Term, or Working, Memory," Chapter 7, "Memory," p. 257.

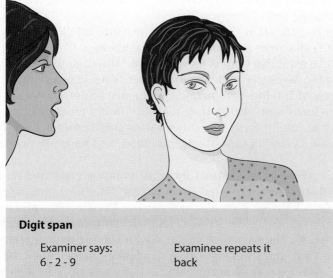

Digit span

Examiner says:
6 - 2 - 9

Examinee repeats it back

Examiner says:
7 - 4 - 6 - 1 - 4 - 8 - 3 - 9

Examinee repeats it back

Letter-number sequencing

Examiner says:
L - 7 - C - 3

Examinee has to repeat the sequence with numbers in ascending order and then letters in alphabetical order
3 - 7 - C - L

FIGURE **10.6**

SIMULATED EXAMPLES OF WORKING MEMORY TASKS ON THE WECHSLER SCALES OF INTELLIGENCE. The latest version of the WISC and the WAIS also assess verbal comprehension, perceptual reasoning, and processing speed. (Simulated items similar to those in Wechsler Intelligence Scale for Children–Fourth Edition [WISC-IV]. Copyright © 2003 by NCS Pearson, Inc. Reproduced with permission. All rights reserved. "Wechsler Intelligence Scale for Children" and "WISC" are trademarks, in the US and/or other countries, of Pearson Education, Inc. or its affiliates.)

Also influenced by the CHC model, the fifth edition of the Stanford-Binet test assesses five factors of general intelligence, each with verbal and nonverbal dimensions (Roid & Pomplun, 2005). In addition to assessing fluid and crystallized intelligence, the newest version of the Stanford-Binet assesses quantitative reasoning, visual-spatial processing, and working memory.

In sum, current intelligence tests reflect contemporary thinking about intelligence as a general quality with many dimensions. Since the development of the CHC model and publication of the first version of the K-ABC, all other major IQ tests have followed suit and developed more theory-driven and complex tests of at least five aspects of intelligence rather than just two or three.

Reliability and Validity of IQ Tests   Tests are meaningful only if they are both reliable and valid. **Reliability** refers to the consistency of results. If a test is reliable, a person who takes the same test on two different occasions will obtain very similar scores on both occasions. Reliability over time is referred to as **test-retest reliability.** IQ tests tend to be extremely reliable over time. A second form of reliability exists when questions on a given subtest tend to correlate very highly with other items on the subtest, meaning that the test's **internal reliability** is very high. Overall, test makers have done a good job of creating reliable IQ tests (Gregory, 2007).

Validity requires that the tests really measure intelligence, not something else, and that test scores predict real-world outcomes. The validity of a test is more difficult to establish than is its reliability. Although there is a great deal of evidence that the Wechsler and Stanford-Binet tests, among others, do provide valid measures of intelligence, many intelligence experts—notably, Sternberg and Gardner—have argued that they measure only verbal, spatial, and mathematical forms of intelligence. The other forms that Gardner identified—social, emotional, musical, bodily-kinesthetic, practical, and naturalistic—are not measured at all.

There are at least two distinct forms of validity: construct and predictive. **Construct validity** refers to what we have just discussed: that a test measures the concept, or *construct,* it claims to measure. **Predictive validity** addresses the question of whether the construct is related positively to real-world outcomes, such as school achievement or job success. IQ tests do predict certain real-world outcomes, the first and foremost being academic performance. IQ scores predict students' grades, school performance, and class rank in high school quite well. That is, after all, what they were meant to predict. For example, preschool scores on two IQ tests taken by children in the Head Start Program accurately predicted the children's academic achievement scores from kindergarten to sixth grade (Lamp & Krohn, 2001). Moreover, scores from the WAIS predict both one's academic class rank in high school and one's college GPA (Gregory, 2007). Even though IQ can predict the kind of job you may get and how much money you may earn, it cannot predict how happy and satisfied you will be with your life or how well you will do in your job (Gow et al., 2005).

Are IQ Tests Biased?   Given the differences among groups in average IQ scores, it is tempting to conclude that IQ tests are biased and unfair (Ford, 2008). Yet group differences on tests in and of themselves do not necessarily mean the tests are biased, but it may mean they are unfair. Whether a test is biased or unfair or both involves two separate, though related, issues.

Let's first be clear about what each term means and then examine the evidence for each. The general public attaches a different meaning to *bias* than scientists do. The general public may use the term *bias* to refer to the notion that group differences in IQ scores are caused by different cultural and educational environments, not by real differences in intelligence. This view is known as **cultural test bias** (C. R. Reynolds, 2000). Given how complex and

reliability
The consistency of a measurement, such as an intelligence test.

test-retest reliability
The consistency of scores on a test over time.

internal reliability
A characteristic of intelligence test in which questions on a given subtest tend to correlate very highly with other items on the subtest.

validity
The degree to which a test accurately measures what it purports to measure, such as intelligence, and not something else, and the degree to which it predicts real-world outcomes.

construct validity
The degree to which a test measures the concept it claims to measure, such as intelligence.

predictive validity
The degree to which intelligence test scores are positively related to real-world outcomes, such as school achievement or job success, and thus have predictive value.

cultural test bias
The notion that group differences in IQ scores are caused by different cultural and educational backgrounds, not by real differences in intelligence.

Are IQ tests unfair to a particular group of individuals?

controversial the causes of intelligence are, there is quite a bit of disagreement in the general population about what causes group differences on IQ test scores. Even when different groups agree that IQ testing has cultural bias, the underlying causes are still disputed (see "Race-Ethnicity and Intelligence" later in this chapter).

When scientists speak of **test bias** in an IQ test, however, they refer to whether a test predicts outcomes equally well for different groups. A test is biased if it is a more valid measure for one group than for another. If an IQ test predicts academic achievement better for Hispanics than for Asians, it is biased. Researchers have found, however, very little evidence for the existence of this kind of bias in IQ tests (R. T. Brown, Reynolds, & Whitaker, 1999; Hunter & Schmidt, 2000; C. R. Reynolds, 2000). Intelligence tests are developed using norms that reflect the makeup of the general population. Just because different groups score differently on a given test does not automatically mean that it is biased. If the test is equally valid for different groups and they still score differently on it, the test is not biased. It may be unfair, but it's not biased.

Test fairness, on the other hand, reflects values, philosophical differences, and the ways in which test results are applied (Gregory, 2007). Test results, especially IQ test results, are meant to be applied—often by people in education, the military, and business. Problems arise when people use IQ test results unfairly to deny certain groups access to universities or jobs. Test fairness, in this sense, concerns the application of the test results rather than the test itself. An unbiased test result could be applied unfairly.

test bias
A characteristic of a test that produces different outcomes for different groups.

test fairness
A judgment about how test results are applied to different groups based on values and philosophical inclinations.

Extremes of Intelligence

Intelligence varies in a predictable way, which is most easily seen in the frequency of different IQ scores in the population. When one plots the scores on a graph, one sees a very clear bell curve, with most people falling in the middle and a few people at the high and low ends of the curve. This shape is referred to as a *bell curve* because it is shaped like a bell. In the bell curve for IQ scores in Figure 10.7, we can see that 68% of test-takers will score between 85 and 115 and almost all—99.7%—will score between 55 and 145. It is at the two ends of

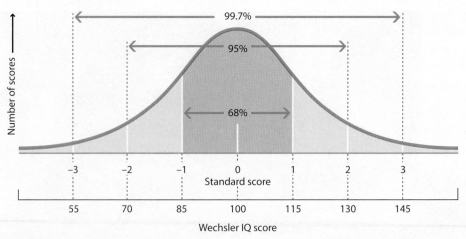

FIGURE **10.7**

NORMAL DISTRIBUTION OF IQ TEST SCORES (BELL CURVE). The vast majority of people (95%) achieve scores between 70 and 130 on the Wechsler IQ scales. The norm is 100. The higher the standard score is, whether positive or negative, the further away the scores are from the norm. Only a small percentage is found at the extremes.

intellectual disability
Significant limitations in intellectual functioning as well as in everyday adaptive behavior, which start before age 18.

adaptive behavior
Adjustment to and coping with everyday life.

the curve, or distribution, that we find "extremes of intelligence"—specifically, intellectual disability and giftedness.

Intellectual Disability   To meet the criteria for **intellectual disability** (formerly known as mental retardation), an individual must show significant limitations in intellectual functioning as well as in everyday adaptive behavior, and these deficits must start before age 18 (American Psychiatric Association [APA], 2013). Historically, intellectual disability was defined and diagnosed solely on the basis of IQ, with 70 being the most common cutoff score.

There are four levels of intellectual disability, depending on how adaptive the behavior or thinking is: mild, moderate, severe, and profound. A general starting point for mild intellectual disability begins with having an IQ of no more than 70 or 75. More recently, however, a different criterion, adaptive behavior, has become the predominant diagnostic standard for intellectual disability (APA, 2013). **Adaptive behavior** is defined as how well a person adjusts to and copes with everyday life (T. P. Hogan, 2007). For example, how well can the person feed or dress himself or herself? Does the individual have the ability to tell time, make change, or read simple words? At a more complex level, one might ask whether he or she can take a bus or follow the news on TV. Most current diagnoses of intellectual disability emphasize adaptive functioning over IQ scores. They therefore measure a person's everyday abilities more than his or her academic performance.

The origins of intellectual disability vary and are many, but there are at least three main causes:

- Chromosomal-genetic abnormalities (e.g., Down syndrome and Fragile X syndrome)
- Prenatal abnormalities (e.g., fetal alcohol syndrome)
- Environmental deprivation

Down syndrome
A chromosomal disorder characterized by mild to profound intellectual disability.

In about 50% of cases, the cause of intellectual disability is *organic*, meaning that it is genetic or the result of brain damage. **Down syndrome,** a disorder that results from a condition known as trisomy-21, in which a person has three rather than two number 21 chromosomes, is an example of a chromosomal cause. The genetic cause of Down syndrome is not fully known, but it is related to maternal age. Children born to older women are more likely to develop trisomy-21 and Down syndrome ("What Causes Down Syndrome?" 2011). Fragile X syndrome is a disorder on the X chromosome, resulting in the abnormal development of a gene involved in neural development. People with Fragile X syndrome often have stunted cognitive development and social interactions.

As we first discussed in Chapter 6, fetal alcohol syndrome is a prenatal cause of intellectual disability, and it occurs when the mother drinks while pregnant (Streissguth et al., 1989). If the pregnant mother is also exposed to other chemicals—for example, lead, manganese, or mercury—that affect brain development or is physically abused, the risk of intellectual disability also increases (Dietrich et al., 1991; S. Jacobson & Jacobson, 2000; Mash & Wolf, 2010).

Finally, environmental deprivation, such as neglect and poor nutrition, is to blame for some cases of intellectual disability. Sometimes called *familial-cultural retardation*, this type is more prevalent among people of low socioeconomic status, tends to occur in more than one family member, and tends to be mild (Kerig & Wenar, 2006; Mash & Wolf, 2010).

Like this happy couple, many people with Down syndrome have full, productive lives in spite of their intellectual limitations.

Giftedness Giftedness lies at the high end of the intelligence spectrum. Starting in about the third grade in the United States, students who do very well in school and well on standardized tests of intelligence are sometimes placed in "gifted" programs. In most schools, children are admitted to such a program if they score 130–140 or above on a standardized IQ test, such as the WISC or Stanford-Binet.

The brains of highly intelligent people have a surprising and unique characteristic. There is a positive relationship (a correlation between .30 and .40, on average) between brain size and intelligence, meaning that highly intelligent people actually have more brain volume than less intelligent people (McDaniel, 2005; G. F. Miller & Penke, 2007; Ziegler et al., 2013). This relationship seems to be strongest in the areas of the brain associated with working memory, executive functioning, and attention (Frangou, Chitins, & Williams, 2004).

Prodigies A **prodigy** is a young person who is extremely gifted and precocious in one area, such as math, music, art, or chess, and is at least average in intelligence (Feldman, 2004). Most often, prodigies are under the age of 20. Sometimes they possess extreme talent in more than one domain, such as math and language. Probably the world's most famous child prodigy was Wolfgang Amadeus Mozart, who was playing keyboard by age 3 and composing symphonies by age 8. Although they are relatively rare, some people display extreme early talent in visual arts. Akiane Kramarik is an example. She was sketching incredibly lifelike drawings by age 4 and producing world-class paintings by age 9. She loves drawing and painting so much that she wakes each morning at 4 a.m. to express herself on canvas (Kramarik, 2006). What makes Kramarik even more unusual is that she is also an accomplished and published poet. In short, she is both visually and verbally gifted.

In addition to documenting individual cases of intellectual prodigies, researchers have conducted large-scale studies of mathematical prodigies. The best known of these is the Study for Mathematically Precocious Youth (SMPY;

Challenge Your Assumptions
True or False? People with high IQs have larger brains.
True: Brain volume, especially in the regions of the brain that control working memory and executive function, is increased in people with high IQ compared to those with average IQ.

prodigy
A young person who is extremely gifted and precocious in one area and at least average in intelligence.

Akiane Kramarik is a gifted young artist who has been painting and drawing since she was a small child. With her parents' encouragement, she has developed her natural creative abilities to an extraordinary level. She also writes poetry.

Stanley, 1996). Begun in 1971, the SMPY is a 50-year longitudinal study of extremely talented people, especially in math. To qualify for the SMPY, students had to score 700 on the SAT-Quantitative and 630 or higher on the SAT-Verbal *before* their 13th birthday. Only about 1 in 10,000 test-takers achieves a score of 700 or above (Lubinski et al., 2006). Students in the latter group go on to have very successful careers. Follow-up research 25–35 years later showed that many of them attended top universities at both the undergraduate and graduate levels and then went on to become successful scientists, mathematicians, engineers, and doctors (Lubinski & Benbow, 2006; Wai, Lubinski, & Benbow, 2009).

Savants   Since at least the 1700s, there have been reports of people with **savant syndrome,** a very rare condition characterized by serious mental handicaps and isolated areas of ability or remarkable giftedness (Treffert, 2006). Savants (the word *savant* comes from the French word for "knowing") have low overall intelligence, typically with an IQ below 70, and an incredible ability for calculating numbers, recalling events, playing music, or drawing. Many of these individuals cannot speak at all or speak poorly.

Although it is difficult to know for sure, by some estimates, there are only about 100 savants in the world today, about 50% of whom suffer from autistic spectrum disorder and the other 50% from some other kind of psychological disorder, such as brain injury, epilepsy, or intellectual disability (Treffert, 2006). Savant syndrome occurs most often in five major areas of talent: music (usually piano), art, math, calendar calculations, and spatial/mechanical skills (Treffert, 2006). A relatively common form is seen in individuals who can immediately calculate the day of the week on which a particular date in history fell. For example, if asked to name the day of the week for June 15, 1899, they would correctly answer "Thursday." Others with savant syndrome can take apart clocks, toys, bicycles, and other machines and rebuild them with expert precision.

savant syndrome
A very rare condition in which people with serious mental handicaps also show isolated areas of ability or brilliance.

In Chapter 7, we met Daniel Tammet, whose uncanny memory skills enable him to recall pi to 22,514 digits and calculate complex mathematical problems almost instantaneously. Tammet has savant syndrome as well as high-functioning autism and synesthesia, which, as you might recall from Chapter 4, occurs when a person experiences sensations in one sense when a different sense is stimulated. In Tammet's case, he sees each number as a distinct color and shape, and this is the secret behind his uncanny memory for numbers and calculations. For example, he finds the 762nd to 769th digits (a series of six 9s) of pi to be a beautiful "deep, thick rim of dark blue light" (Tammet, 2006, p. 179). Recent research points to superior math ability among children with high-functioning autism compared to typically developing children (Iuculano et al., 2014).

Another person with savant syndrome was Kim Peek. Although Peek was most famous as the inspiration for the movie *Rain Man*, his abilities went much further than the movie suggests. He was one of the world's only true speed-readers—he could read a page in about 3 seconds and retain essentially every word. Incredibly, Peek memorized about 9,000 books after reading them only *once*. He immediately provided biographical information about any of the U.S. presidents; could tell you the zip code of any city or borough in the United States; and could identify who composed almost any piece of classical music, stating where it was composed and when it was first performed. Like some other savants, he also could tell you more or less instantly the day of the week on which any date in history fell.

Given his phenomenal abilities, it is easy to forget that Peek was unable to do many basic things—such as dress himself. Indeed, his tested IQ was 73, which is in the range for people with severe autism. Socially, he was very awkward, and he liked to repeat certain phrases, saying over and over again how great was the person he had just met. He also did not understand metaphors such as "get a hold of yourself." Instead, he interpreted everything literally. His adaptive functioning skills were poor, and his father had to take care of him on a daily basis. A scan of his brain revealed that Peek, like some other savants, had no corpus callosum and very little cerebellum (Treffert & Christensen, 2005). The absence of a corpus callosum means that information processed in one of the brain's hemispheres cannot be communicated to the other hemisphere.

Connection

Daniel Tammet uses mnemonic devices, a memory tool, to help him remember the value of pi. He retraces the shapes, colors, and textures in his head and then just reads the number. How do mnemonic devices aid memory?

See "Long-Term Memory," Chapter 7, "Memory," p. 257.

The Nature and Nurture of Human Intelligence

If you want to start an argument, all you need to do is take a strong stance on one of the following positions: (1) A person's intelligence is determined almost completely by genetics, or (2) a person's intelligence is determined almost completely by the environment in which he or she is raised. Most people realize that intelligence results from a combination of "being born that way" and "being brought up that way" by our family and teachers. What is most remarkable is the complexity of the interaction between these two forces.

One way we see the interaction between environment and biological forces is in how the brain responds differently to different kinds of problems, intelligence problems among them. The region most often involved in various IQ tasks is the prefrontal cortex (Colom et al., 2009; DeYoung et al., 2009; Duncan et al., 2000; Haier et al., 2004; R. E. Jung & Haier, 2007). When a person is working on verbal tasks, only the left prefrontal region of the brain is activated. When an individual is working on spatial tasks, however, the prefrontal cortexes of both the left and the right hemispheres, as well as the occipital cortex, are activated (see Figure 10.8; Duncan et al., 2000; Haier et al., 2004; R. E. Jung & Haier, 2007). Moreover, the frontal lobe is more involved when an individual is performing fluid intelligence tasks, such as pattern recognition, than when the person is

Spatial Task

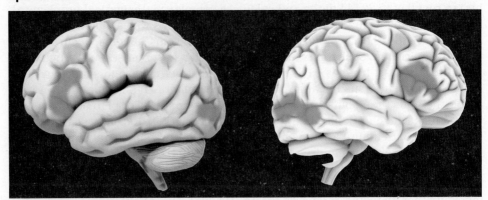

Left Hemisphere   Right Hemisphere

Verbal Task

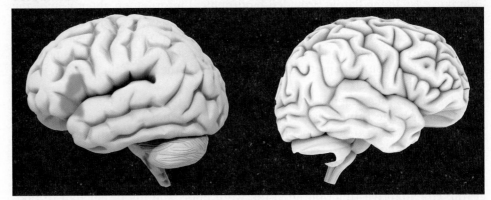

Left Hemisphere   Right Hemisphere

FIGURE **10.8**

BRAIN ACTIVATION WHILE WORKING ON IQ PROBLEMS. The red areas show activation during two different IQ tasks, a verbal task and a spatial task. The spatial task activates the frontal lobe in both the right and left hemispheres, whereas the verbal task activates only the left frontal lobe region (Broca's area). (Duncan et al., 2000)

performing tasks that involve crystallized intelligence and learned experiences (Gray & Thompson, 2004).

Furthermore, twin-adoption and family studies demonstrate the interconnectedness of nature and nurture in intelligence. As we saw in Chapter 3, these kinds of studies allow researchers to hold one factor constant while varying the other one. The more genetically related people are, the more similar they are in IQ, even if reared apart (see Figure 10.9). Identical twins reared apart are more similar in their levels of intelligence than are fraternal twins reared together. Similarly, dozens of studies have shown that adopted children's overall intelligence is more similar to that of their biological parents than to that of their adoptive parents (Munsinger, 1975). Yet adoption—hence, the environment—can also enhance a child's IQ (van IJzendoorn & Juffer, 2005). Compared to orphans not adopted, adopted children tend to have higher IQs. In sum, genetic factors ("nature," or heritability) account for about 50% of the variability in intelligence among individuals; environment ("nurture") accounts for about 40%; the remaining 10% is, as yet, unexplained (Grigorenko, 2000; Lynn, 2006; Plomin & Petrill, 1997).

One fascinating set of findings concerns the fact that from infancy to adolescence the environment has progressively less of an influence on

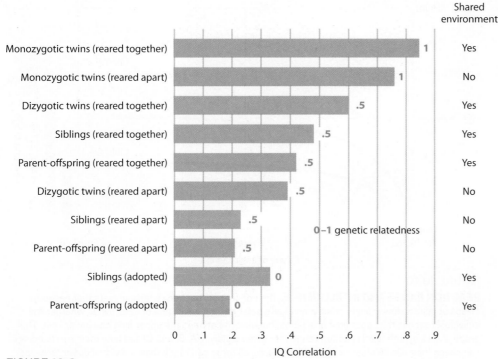

FIGURE 10.9

GENETIC AND ENVIRONMENTAL EFFECTS ON IQ. The numbers in orange represent genetic relatedness. Genetic relatedness of 1 means 100% genetic similarity; .5 means 50% genetic similarity; and 0 means no genetic similarity. Monozygotic twins are identical twins. Dizygotic twins are fraternal twins. (Adapted from Grigorenko, 2000; Plomin & Petrill, 1997)

intelligence (Bartels et al., 2002; Bouchard & McGue, 1981; Brant et al., 2009; Tucker-Drob et al., 2011). Children above the median (50th percentile) on IQ, however, have a longer period of being influenced by the environment (sensitivity period) than those below the median (Brant et al., 2013). That is, high-IQ children show a pattern of neuroplasticity that is more childlike (i.e., more "plastic"), because they have neural networks that are shaped longer by the environment.

The concept of reaction range provides further evidence for the interaction of biology and environment in determining a person's intelligence. A **reaction range** is a genetically determined range within which a given trait, such as intelligence, may fall; that trait's exact value, however, depends on the quality of the individual's environment (Gottlieb, 1991; Scarr, 1981; Turkheimer & Gottesman, 1991; R. A. Weinberg, 1989). For most people in most environments, the reaction range for IQ is about 25 points—meaning that a given person may end up scoring anywhere in a 25-point range on an IQ test, depending on the kind of environment in which he or she was raised (R. A. Weinberg, 1989). Being raised in an enriched environment means someone is likely to obtain an IQ score near the upper limit of his or her reaction range; being raised in an impoverished environment means one is likely to obtain a score near the lower limit; and being raised in a normal environment means one is likely to obtain a score in the middle of his or her reaction range (see Figure 10.10). The important point here is that genes do not determine behavior but rather establish the range of possible behaviors.

Environment, however, is a complex thing. Only part of the environmental influence on intelligence comes from being in the same household and sharing experiences. The other part comes from experiences that family members

Challenge Your Assumptions
True or False? As people get older, genetics plays a stronger and stronger role in how intelligent they are.
True: Heritability, or genetic influence, increases its influence with age from infancy to adolescence.

reaction range
For a given trait, such as IQ, the genetically determined range of responses by an individual to his or her environment.

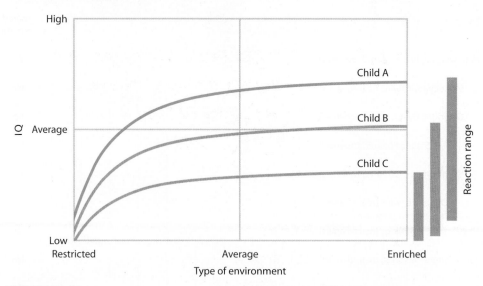

FIGURE **10.10**

REACTION RANGE AND INTELLIGENCE. The concept of reaction range suggests that heredity places upper and lower limits on an individual's potential, but environment determines whether the individual reaches the upper limit or a point somewhere between the upper limit and lower limit. This graph shows hypothetical reaction ranges for three children (A, B, and C) and how their surroundings can shape their IQs. With enriched environments, all three can reach their individual upper limits, as shown on the right side of the graph.

 What does this graph tell you about the effect of a restricted environment on intelligence? (Seifert, Hoffnung, & Hoffnung, 2000)

do not share—each person's unique environmental experiences. One such experience is the prenatal environment and what happens to the fetus during pregnancy. Toxins ingested by the mother, either intentionally or unintentionally, may influence the child's intelligence. Alcohol, drugs, and viral infections in a pregnant woman can seriously lower her child's overall intelligence (Dietrich et al., 1991; S. Jacobson & Jacobson, 2000; Ruff, 1999; Steinhausen & Spohr, 1998; Streissguth et al., 1989).

Other aspects of intelligence stem from the joint influence of nature and nurture factors. One such example is birth weight. For many years, researchers and physicians have known that insufficient birth weight—a sign of severe prenatal malnutrition—creates a high risk for cognitive impairment (and thus impaired intelligence) later in life. Only recently, however, has anyone examined whether birth weight matters for children born at a normal weight. Broekman and colleagues (2009) obtained birth weight, head measurement, and length information on over 1,500 children born in Singapore. All infants were born in the normal healthy weight/size range. After the children had reached age 7, the researchers conducted yearly intelligence testing on them. Longer birth length, higher birth weight, and larger head circumference within the normal birth size range (neither undernourished nor obese) are associated with higher IQ scores later in childhood; the bigger children had higher IQs. Why might this be? Certain prenatal factors affecting fetal growth, such as maternal stress, also influence cognitive development. When a pregnant woman is under severe stress, her stress hormones might affect the growth of new neurons in the baby's brain (Oitzl et al., 2010).

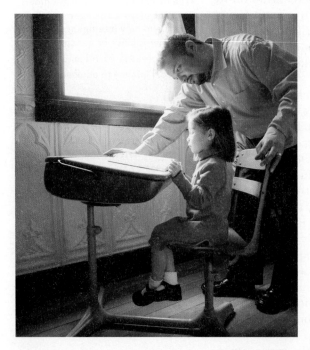

Reading to children regularly from the time they are very young as part of an enriched environment may enhance their IQ.

Group Differences in Intelligence Scores

Given the importance of intelligence to success in life, the question of whether there are group differences in intelligence is bound to stir up controversy (Fancher, 1985). Research on this topic has political and social implications, and from time to time scientists who have studied group differences in intelligence have been harassed or threatened. If there are differences in intelligence between racial-ethnic groups or genders, what should we do as a society to compensate for those differences to level the playing field? Can that even be done?

Race-Ethnicity and Intelligence   In the 1960s and 1970s, Arthur Jensen received death threats for publishing research that not only reported differences in IQ among racial-ethnic groups but also argued that, because IQ is under genetic influence, racial-ethnic differences in IQ must be at least partly genetic in origin (Jensen, 1969). It was another highly controversial book, published in the mid-1990s, that most recently ignited an academic, political, and cultural firestorm over intelligence. The book was called simply *The Bell Curve*, but its subtitle hinted at the more controversial contents: *Intelligence and Class Structure in American Life*. The authors, Richard Herrnstein and Charles Murray (1994), summarized the results of a study on racial-ethnic group differences, social class, and intelligence among 12,000 individuals. They concluded what many others had before and since: First, racial-ethnic groups vary on IQ scores; second, differences in IQ contribute, to a large extent, to differences in education and income (Gottfredson, 1997). Their conclusion suggested that group differences in IQ, and hence in education and income, can be explained in part by genetics.

After *The Bell Curve*, when all of the smoke cleared and tempers settled down, there was still no widely accepted and agreed-on explanation for racial-ethnic differences on IQ scores. There are a few schools of thought on the causes (in addition to the one that attributes the difference in part to genetics). Some experts maintain that racial-ethnic differences in IQ result from biases in IQ tests that favor people from certain cultural backgrounds over others (D. Ford, 2008; C. R. Reynolds, 2000). Others have argued that differences in IQ scores based on race-ethnicity are meaningless, because race is mostly a social construct with little scientific support or biological foundation (Sternberg, Grigorenko, & Kidd, 2005). These psychologists also point out that heritability findings apply only within the group of people studied, not between groups. So it is a misinterpretation of heritability to argue that group differences are due to genetics, even if IQ is heritable (Sternberg et al., 2005).

The conclusion that genetics influences intelligence is often interpreted—or misinterpreted—as implying that IQ levels are determined at birth or conception. If this were so, then trying to change IQ levels with intervention programs such as Head Start would likely be unsuccessful (Herrnstein & Murray, 1994). Such a conclusion is faulty for two reasons. First, genes interact with environmental forces, and therefore environment can shape gene expression. We saw this in Chapter 3 with the concept of epigenesis. Similarly, the concept of a reaction range makes clear the connection between genes and the environment. Second, interventions have succeeded in changing IQ levels. Children raised under conditions of severe neglect and abuse who were adopted within the first few years of life showed tremendous growth in brain size and gains in IQ scores. Those adopted later in life or not adopted at all did not show increases in IQ scores (B. D. Perry, 2002). Moreover, one longitudinal study randomly assigned infants either to an early educational intervention program or to a control group. All children were from socially disadvantaged households. The intervention program lasted until age 5 and focused on language, social, emotional, and cognitive stimulation. The children from both groups were studied again at ages 12, 15, and 21. The findings were clear: During adolescence and early adulthood, those who had been in the intervention program had higher IQ scores, performed better in school, and obtained higher-paying jobs than those in the control condition

Men and women may have their differences, but intelligence isn't one of them.

(F. A. Campbell & Ramey, 1995; F. A. Campbell et al., 2002). In short, both genetic and environmental forces play important roles in determining IQ scores.

Gender and Intelligence Larry Hedges and Amy Nowell (1995) reviewed six nationally representative sets of IQ scores. Each set ranged from 12,000 to 73,000 participants altogether. They concluded that there are relatively few differences between the sexes in cognitive ability; men and women are equally intelligent. Indeed, most research on overall intelligence and gender has reported no difference between men and women on average.

There is one area of variability in intelligence among men and women, illustrated in Figure 10.11. Men are more likely than women to score at either end of the range, especially in some areas, and more frequently score at the high or low end of the scale on tests of science, math, spatial reasoning, and social studies (Ceci & Williams, 2007; Gallagher & Kaufman, 2005). Some recent evidence suggests that self-identifying as masculine—for both men and women—is associated with increased spatial skills (Reilly & Neumann, 2013). Women, however, consistently tend to do better than men in writing, reading comprehension, perceptual speed, and associative memory (Deary et al., 2003; Hedges & Nowell, 1995; Maccoby & Jacklin, 1974).

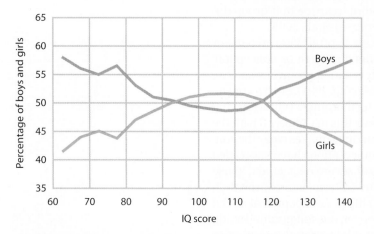

FIGURE **10.11**

GENDER VARIABILITY IN INTELLIGENCE. Results from more than 80,000 Scottish children found that mean IQ scores were nearly identical. Mean IQ was 100.5 for boys and 100.6 for girls. Boys were much more likely to be at the two extreme ends of intelligence, however. They made up 58% of the scores at 60 and 140, whereas girls made up only about 42% of those scores. (Deary et al., 2003)

Non-Western Views of Intelligence

Ask people in the United States or Europe what it means to be intelligent. Then ask people in Kenya, China, Malaysia, and Bolivia. No doubt you will get very different answers. Western cultures emphasize verbal and cognitive skills first, whereas many African cultures see social skills, such as being socially responsible, cooperative, and active in family and social life, to be crucial aspects of intelligence (Ruzgis &

Grigorenko, 1994; Serpell, 1982). Asian cultures have traditionally emphasized humility, awareness, doing the right thing, and mindfulness as important qualities of intelligence (Sternberg, 2000). Doing well in school and being quick to learn are not universally acknowledged to be essential qualities of intelligence. Sternberg and his colleagues have examined practical intelligence in cultures where academic intelligence is not valued as highly as it is in Western cultures. They have found that children in Kenya and Tanzania may not do well at solving "bookish" analytic problems but do very well at solving everyday, practical problems (Sternberg, 1998).

Problems that require intelligence are just one kind of problem we face. Problem solving—our next topic—pervades almost everything we do, from our choice of a major in college to our choice of friends, where we live, how we vote, and so on.

Quick Quiz 10.1: Intelligence

1. Which of the following skills is NOT part of the definition of intelligence?
   a. abstract reasoning
   b. problem solving
   c. knowledge acquisition
   d. remote associations

2. Historically, a child's IQ was calculated by dividing _____ by chronological age and multiplying by _____.
   a. perceptual skill; 100
   b. mental age; 50
   c. perceptual skill; 50
   d. mental age; 100

3. The Kaufmans changed the field of intelligence testing by developing an IQ test that
   a. could be universally applied.
   b. was grounded in psychological theory and knowledge of the brain.

   c. was reliable and valid.
   d. was culture-free and fair.

4. _____ involves raw mental ability, pattern recognition, and abstract reasoning and is applied to a problem that a person has never confronted before.
   a. Crystallized intelligence
   b. Narrow intelligence
   c. Fluid intelligence
   d. General intelligence

5. Someone who is good at detecting whether a person is lying has high
   a. interpersonal intelligence.
   b. naturalistic intelligence.
   c. practical intelligence.
   d. creative intelligence.

Answers can be found at the end of the chapter.

PROBLEM SOLVING

None of us go through a day without having to solve a problem, because every time we face a task that we do not know how to carry out, we are confronted with a problem (Simon, 1978). On any given day, you may have to budget your time so that you can study for your test and go to a party with friends or figure out the most efficient route to drive to a place you have never visited.

Psychologists have examined how people go about solving problems, often by presenting research participants with problems and studying how they solve them. Take a few minutes to work on each of the following problems. Some are easy but others not so easy, but give them a try. We will return to each problem later in the section.

- How would you solve the problem of rising world temperatures?
- Pretend you have three jars (A, B, and C), each containing a set amount of water. Add or subtract the given amounts in each jar to come up with a set final amount. For instance, Jar A holds 21 units of water, Jar B 127 units, and Jar C 3 units. Using any of the jars, discard or add water as needed to end up with 100 units of water. Figure 10.12 shows some variations you can try.

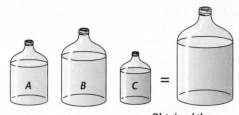

Problem	Jar A	Jar B	Jar C	Obtained the amount
1	21	127	3	100
2	14	163	25	99
3	18	43	10	5
4	9	42	6	21
5	20	59	4	31
6	23	49	3	20
7	15	39	3	18

FIGURE **10.12**

WATER JAR PROBLEMS AND MENTAL SET. The task is to use any combination of Jars A, B, and C, subtracting or adding jars of "water" to obtain the desired amount. (Luchins & Luchins, 1970)

FIGURE **10.13**

TWO-STRING PROBLEM. How do you connect two strings if you can't reach the second one without dropping the first one? (The answer appears at the end of the chapter.)

- Figure 10.13 is a picture of a person in a room with two strings hanging from the ceiling. Also in the room are a pole, clamp, extension cord, table, chair, and a pair of pliers. The task is to tie the two pieces of string together. The strings, however, are too short for the person to hold onto one and grab the other. How would you go about tying the strings together?

- In Figure 10.14a, how would you mount the candle on the wall without having it drip wax on the floor?

- Look at the nine dots in Figure 10.14b. Connect all the dots using only four straight lines without lifting up your pen or pencil from the paper once you've started.

- In Figure 10.14c, arrange six matchsticks of equal length to make four equilateral triangles, the sides of which are one matchstick long.

Types of Problems

convergent thinking problems
Problems that have known solutions and require analytical thinking and the use of learned strategies and knowledge to come up with the correct answer.

Convergent thinking problems have known solutions, which can be reached by narrowing down a set of possible answers. Intelligence tests and college entrance exams include convergent problems. Figuring out how to operate a new coffeemaker is a convergent problem. There is one right way to brew coffee with a given machine. Convergent problems require analytic thinking and crystallized intelligence—the problem solver has to analyze the problem and then apply learned strategies and knowledge to come up with the answer.

Some problems, however, may not have a known solution. Consider the question posed earlier: How would you solve the problem of rising world temperatures? There are many possible solutions to such problems, some of which work

The Candle Problem
How would you mount a candle on a wall so that it won't drip wax on a table or a floor while it is burning?

(a)

The Nine-Dot Problem
Take out a piece of paper and copy the arrangement of dots shown below. Without lifting your pencil, connect the dots using only four straight lines.

(b)

The Six-Matchstick Problem
Arrange six matchsticks of equal length to make four equilateral triangles, the sides of which are one matchstick long.

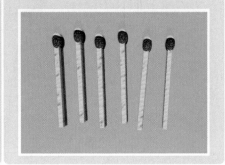

(c)

FIGURE **10.14**

PROBLEM SOLVING. (a) How would you mount the candle on the wall without having it drip wax on the floor while it is burning? (b) Connect all nine dots with four straight lines—without lifting your pencil. (c) Arrange six matchsticks of equal length to make four equilateral triangles, the sides of which are one matchstick long. (The answers to [b] and [c] appear at the end of the chapter).

better than others. These kinds of problems are known as **divergent thinking problems.** To solve them, we must break away from our normal problem-solving strategies and make unusual associations to arrive at novel ways of thinking about a problem. Imagine that your new dormmate snores so loudly you can't sleep. How would you solve this problem? Divergence may lead to redefining the problem in a way that makes finding a solution more likely. These kinds of problems require fluid and creative intelligence.

divergent thinking problems
Problems that have no known solutions and require novel solutions.

Solution Strategies

Psychologists describe three kinds of strategies people use to solve different kinds of problems: algorithms, insight, and thinking outside the box. When you were solving the water jug problems in Figure 10.12, did you realize that the last two could be solved much more easily than the first five? If you are like about 75% of the population, you continued to use the solution pattern you may have discovered in solving the first few problems. **Algorithms** are step-by-step formulas or procedures for solving problems. In this case, the algorithm is "Jar B - Jar A - Jar C (twice)."

algorithm
A step-by-step procedure or formula for solving a problem.

Not all solutions involve algorithms. Some occur with a flash of insight. One of the best-known examples of insight occurred in ancient Greece, when the philosopher-scientist Archimedes solved the problem of how to determine whether a crown contained anything besides gold. The solution came to him in a flash when he saw the water level rise as he entered the public baths. Because gold is heavier than other metals, it will displace more water, so by seeing how much water it displaced, Archimedes would be able to determine whether the crown was pure gold without melting it down. The insight excited him so much that, without pausing to dress, he ran out of the baths, yelling, "*Eureka!*" (Greek for "I have found it!"). In honor of Archimedes, these kinds of sudden solutions are referred to as either **Eureka insights** or **insight solutions.**

A modern version of a "Eureka solution" happened to George de Mestral, a Swiss engineer (Stephens, 2007). de Mestral often went on hikes in the Alps with his dog. When they returned home, he noticed that his clothes and his dog's fur had caught thistle burrs, which he found on close inspection to have hooks

Eureka insight (insight solution)
A sudden solution that comes to mind in a flash.

"Never, ever, think outside the box."

on the ends. The dog's fur and his clothes contained loops that snagged the plants. In a flash, de Mestral realized that a fastener could be made to connect to loops. The best part about the hook-and-loop system was that it was easily reversible and could be fastened over and over again. de Mestral invented Velcro, now a common fastener of such things as shoe straps, backpacks, and clothing.

One solution to the two-string problem in Figure 10.13 often comes as a Eureka insight (Maier, 1931). With or without a hint of the string swaying, you might have suddenly realized that the pliers or any other heavy object could be used as a weight (after you had cut the string a bit so it could swing). You could tie it to the shorter string, then swing into motion. As you stood holding the other string, the weighted string would swing over; you could grab it and tie the two together.

The third problem-solving strategy is turning a problem around and thinking about it from a different perspective. If you have ever heard the phrase "thinking outside the box," you now know where it comes from—the nine-dot problem (Figure 10.14b). **Thinking outside the box** requires you to break free of self-imposed conceptual constraints and think about a problem differently in order to solve it. If you came up with a solution, it required that you go outside the self-imposed "box" that the nine dots create in your mind. There is no such box in reality, but you perceive one. Once you think outside the box, a couple of solutions may come to you rather easily (see the end of the chapter for the solution). Creative thinkers regularly think flexibly and differently about problems by challenging their own assumptions (Feist, 1999).

Obstacles to Solutions

The difficulties people encounter in solving the nine-dot problem also point to some of the common obstacles we face in solving all kinds of problems. One of the biggest blocks to solving a problem is cognitive **fixation,** or the inability to break out of a particular mind-set in order to think about a problem from a fresh perspective. Fixation prevents many people from seeing possible solutions to the match problem (Figure 10.14c). It is difficult, for example, to see that you must think in three dimensions in order to solve the match-triangle problem (see end of chapter for solution in three dimensions). This solution may not be obvious because people become fixated on a self-imposed mental set in which "I have to solve this problem in two dimensions." Note that the instructions do not require this—people unconsciously impose such rules themselves.

Solutions themselves can sometimes be an obstacle: For the jar problem, the algorithm used to solve it also creates a **mental set,** which is a tendency to continue to use problem-solving strategies that have worked in the past, even if better solutions are available (Luchins & Luchins, 1970). This mental set probably made you miss the easier solutions to Problems 6 and 7 in Figure 10.12: Jar A − Jar C and Jar A + Jar C, respectively. Luchins and Luchins (1970) found that, if Problems 1 to 5 were not given first, 100% of adults saw the direct solution. In contrast, if they first received Problems 1 to 5 and had to develop an algorithm, only 24% found the more direct solutions to Problems 6 and 7. Education and training also create mental sets. When we learn solution strategies in school and in the workplace, we learn how to solve problems. Sometimes these solutions are algorithms and sometimes insights, but strategies can blind us to more novel, efficient, and even creative solutions. It becomes hard to step back and see problems from a fresh perspective.

thinking outside the box
An approach to problem solving that requires breaking free of self-imposed conceptual constraints and thinking about a problem differently in order to solve it.

fixation
The inability to break out of a particular mind-set in order to think about a problem from a fresh perspective.

mental set
A tendency to continue to use problem-solving strategies that have worked in the past, even if better solutions are available.

Another obstacle to successful problem solving is our tendency to be blind to unusual uses of common, everyday things or procedures: This is known as **functional fixedness** (Duncker, 1945). A good example of functional fixedness occurs when people try to solve the two-string problem. People are used to thinking of pliers as tools for holding or gripping something so that it can be turned, twisted, or cut, but a pair of pliers can also be used as a weight at the end of a string to cause it to swing like a pendulum. Figuring out a new way to use pliers is an example of thinking outside the box to find a creative solution to a problem. As mentioned earlier, creative thinkers often think differently about how to solve a problem.

functional fixedness
A mind-set in which one is blind to unusual uses of common, everyday things or procedures.

Quick Quiz 10.2: Problem Solving

1. What kind of problems require you to narrow down the range of possible solutions to arrive at the correct answer?
   a. simple problems
   b. convergent thinking problems
   c. algorithms
   d. divergent thinking problems

2. A child discovers that 2×2 is the same as $2 + 2$. He therefore wrongly concludes that 3×3 is the same as $3 + 3$. What tendency is affecting this child's problem-solving strategies?
   a. mental set
   b. divergent thinking

   c. test bias
   d. response bias

3. An inability to break out of a particular frame of mind in order to think about a problem from a fresh perspective is known as
   a. perpetuation.
   b. mental set.
   c. fixation.
   d. functional fixedness.

Answers can be found at the end of the chapter.

CREATIVITY

What was it about Leonardo da Vinci that made him so versatile as an artist and inventor? What was going on in the mind of Isaac Newton when he realized the significance of an apple falling from a tree? Why are some people able to paint magnificent landscapes, while others can hardly draw a straight line? The answer is that these individuals are more creative than the average person.

The ability to think or act creatively is highly prized in our society (Feist, 1999; Sawyer, 2006; Simonton, 1999). All of society's advances—artistic, musical, industrial, governmental, legal, and scientific—happen because a person or group of people come up with a creative idea. Creative thinking is related to, yet distinct from, both intelligence and problem solving.

What Is Creativity?

Read the following two paragraphs, written by different people, and think about what each one means and whether they are equally "creative":

> They're all so different Boylan talking about the shape of my foot he noticed at once even before he was introduced when I was in the DBC with Poldy laughing and trying to listen I was waggling my foot we both ordered 2 teas and plain bread and butter I saw him looking with his two old maids of sisters when I stood up and asked the girl where it was what do I care with it dropping out of me and that black closed breeches he made me buy takes you half an hour to let down wetting all myself always with some brand new fad every other week. . . .

This creation in which we live began with the Dominant Nature as an Identification Body of a completed evolutionary Strong Material creation in a Major Body Resistance Force. And is fulfilling the Nature Identification in a like Weaker Material Identification creation in which Two Major Bodies have already fulfilled radio body balances, and embodying a Third Material Identification Embodiment of both.

Challenge Your Assumptions

True or False? If a person has original thoughts or behavior, he or she is creative.

False: Originality by itself is not enough to determine that a person's thoughts or behavior is creative; the thoughts or behavior must also be meaningful and useful (to someone).

creativity
Thinking or behavior that is both novel and meaningful.

The first paragraph is an excerpt from James Joyce's great novel *Ulysses*. The second paragraph was written by a person who has schizophrenia and is an example of what is called *word salad*, a collection of words that are mixed up in sentences with no real meaning (R. White, 1964). These two paragraphs demonstrate an essential point about what creativity is and what it is not. It is not simply original thinking, for the paragraphs are equally original. They are both unusual, and both give voice to sentences that probably had not been uttered or written before these writers penned them. For something to be deemed creative, however, it not only has to be original but also must be useful or adaptive and solve a problem. Joyce's paragraph does that because it's part of solving the problem of telling a story. The second paragraph is not creative, because it is not useful or meaningful to someone and it does not solve a problem.

Creativity, then, is thought or behavior that is both novel (original) and meaningful (Amabile, 1996; Beghetto & Kaufman, 2007; Feist, 1999; MacKinnon, 1970; Plucker, Beghetto, & Dow, 2004). The meaningful criterion requires that someone at some time sees value and usefulness in the creative accomplishment. Truly creative works are often appreciated in the creator's lifetime, but not always. For instance, Vincent van Gogh sold very few of his paintings while alive, but his creative genius is now fully appreciated by novices and experts alike, and his paintings are worth millions.

Stages of Creative Problem Solving

Creative problem solving is a process with distinct stages. Long ago, Graham Wallas (1926) identified four stages of creative problem solving: preparation, incubation, insight, and elaboration-verification. The first stage, *preparation*, involves discovering and defining the problem and then attempting to solve it. This leads to the second stage, *incubation*, or putting the problem aside for a while and working on something else. The third stage, *insight*, is a Eureka moment when the solution comes immediately to mind. The fourth, and final, stage of creative problem solving is *elaboration-verification*. The solution, even if it has the feel of certainty, still needs to be confirmed. How it is confirmed depends on what kind of task is involved. The verification process is different for everyday problems and for problems in art, literature, music, science, technology, invention, or philosophy.

WHERE EARL GETS HIS IDEAS

Creativity and the Brain

Imagine what was going on in Newton's brain when he "discovered" gravity or in Einstein's when he came up with the theory of relativity. Of course, we'll never know what was going on in the minds of these geniuses from the past, but neuroscientists are beginning to uncover what happens in the brain when a typical person has a

Can you think of other creative geniuses who changed society in some important way?

Marie
Curie

Leonardo
da Vinci

Virginia
Woolf

Vincent
van Gogh

Albert
Einstein

Eureka insight or when creative people solve problems compared to less creative people (R. E. Jung et al., 2010; R. E. Jung et al., 2013). The research has revealed three consistent findings: Creative insight increases frontal lobe activity, insights occur in the right hemisphere rather than the left, and creative people solving creative problems show more balanced activity between their right and left frontal lobes.

Creative Insight Results in Increased Frontal Lobe Activity   The frontal lobes are active in abstract reasoning, planning, focused working memory, and the integration of sensory input. Creativity involves integrating ideas in novel and valuable ways. It is not surprising, therefore, that modern neuroscience supports the conclusion that creative problem solving and insights involve frontal lobe activity (Carlsson, Wendt, & Risberg, 2000; Chow & Cummings, 1999; Feist, 2004; Folley & Park, 2005; Mell, Howard, & Miller, 2003; Takeuchi et al., 2010). Recent research examined whether greater neural connection in the frontal lobe is associated with greater levels of creativity. Takeuchi and colleagues (2010) measured creativity and neural connectivity in 55 college students. The creativity tasks involved generating unique ideas for how to use everyday objects. For example, students were asked such questions as, Other than reading, how can we use newspapers? Neural connectivity was measured with an MRI technique that assesses the volume of neurons in a given region in the brain. The greater the neural volume, the greater the connectivity. Takeuchi and colleagues found a direct and positive relationship between the students' creativity scores and their neural connectivity, especially in the frontal lobe. Greater connectivity suggests more myelinated neurons and hence more efficient communication between the neurons. Recall from Chapter 3 that axons are often covered with myelin, which facilitates neural transmission. It may be that more creative people have both more connections between neurons and more myelin. Further research, however, is needed to confirm this idea.

Creative Insight and the Right Hemisphere   One kind of problem that has been used in creativity/brain research is a *remote association* word problem (Mednick & Mednick, 1967). Remote association problems display three words at one time to the participant, who must then come up with a single word that could be used with all three of the words. The single word could be added to each of the words to create a compound word, or it could modify one of the displayed words in some way. This requires the participant to form a nonobvious, or "remote," association in order to solve the problem. If the three words were *French, shoe,*

Research Process

1 Research Question

Is the brain activity of creative people different from the brain activity of less creative people while solving problems?

2 Method

Carlsson and colleagues (2000) selected participants who during earlier testing scored either high or low on creativity problems. They were grouped as "highly creative" or "less creative" based on these earlier results. Participants in these two groups were each given a noncreative task and a creative task to complete while in a brain scanner. Brain activity was measured by cerebral blood flow to compare the two conditions. Blood flow increases to brain areas that are active. The creative task consisted of having participants list as many possible uses of an everyday object (a brick) as they could think of. A noncreative task consisted of a simple request to count numbers aloud, starting with 1.

3 Results

Results showed more left than right frontal lobe activity in the less creative participants. Highly creative participants, however, showed a balance in right and left frontal lobe activity. Orange regions in the figure show areas of increased activity while solving creative problems compared to noncreative problems. Green regions show areas of decreased activity. The more creative participants (on the left) use both left and right hemispheres in the frontal region while working on creative problems, whereas the less creative participants (on the right) showed increased activity only in their frontal lobe.

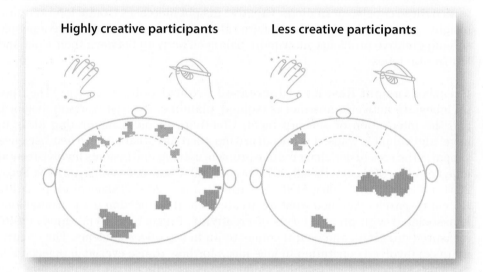

Highly creative participants | Less creative participants

4 Conclusion

Creative people make more balanced use of the parts of the brain involved in focused attention, abstract reasoning, and planning while solving problems than do less creative people. This finding may appear to contradict what we just said about the importance of the right hemisphere in creative problem solving, but it does not. The right hemisphere findings are from noncreative participants who are coming up with insight solutions. The balanced hemisphere result comes from comparing creative to less creative people. In both cases, right hemisphere activity is more pronounced in creative people than in less creative people.

FIGURE **10.15**

BALANCED BRAIN ACTIVITY IN CREATIVE PEOPLE. ("On the Neurobiology of Creativity: Differences in Frontal Activity between High and Low Creative Subjects," by I. Carlsson, P. Wendt, and J. Risberg, 2000, *Neuropsychologia*, 38, 873–885.)

and *car,* what one word could you think of that could be used with the other three? What if the three words were *pine, crab,* and *sauce*? (The answers appear at the end of the chapter.) Interestingly, people often solve these kinds of problems with Eureka insights.

In one set of studies, researchers presented remote association tests to either the right or left visual fields of participants. These participants were not selected for high or low levels of creativity. The researchers presented the information to the individual visual fields because they wanted to control which hemisphere of the brain processed the information. Recall from Chapter 3 that information presented to the left visual field is processed in the brain's right hemisphere and information presented to the right visual field is processed in the brain's left hemisphere. When the problem was presented in the left visual field and processed in the right hemisphere, insight into the problems occurred much more frequently than when the problem was presented to the right visual field and processed in the left hemisphere (Beeman & Bowden, 2000; Bowden & Jung-Beeman, 2003). Moreover, when researchers took brain images using fMRI and EEG while people were solving insight problems, they found that sudden insights consistently activated the right hemisphere more than the left (Bowden et al., 2005). Similarly, patients with damage to the frontal region of their right hemisphere are less able to solve problems requiring insight than people without damage to their right hemisphere (L. A. Miller & Tippett, 1996).

Creativity and Balanced Activity between the Hemispheres The third consistent finding from the neuroscience of creativity is that, when solving problems, creative people have more balanced brain activity between the hemispheres than less creative people (Takeuchi et al., 2010). In particular, while solving problems, they show equally active areas in their right and left frontal lobes, which translates into a widening rather than a narrowing of attention and a greater flexibility in moving from one way of thinking to another (Carlsson et al., 2000; Goel & Vartanian, 2005); see the Research Process for this chapter (Figure 10.15). Widening one's attention and being able to shift ways of thinking easily and flexibly are hallmarks of creative thinking (Feist, 2004; Martindale, 1999).

Cognitive Processes in Creative Thinking

Creative thinking entails unique cognitive processes (Lee & Therriault, 2011). Psychologists who study the cognitive aspects of creative thought have focused on visual thinking, fluency, flexibility, and originality. Visual imagery occurs when we see a solution in our "mind's eye." Many scientists, artists, and writers solve problems by using creative mental images (A. Miller, 1996). Einstein, for example, often visualized a situation, such as riding in an elevator traveling at the speed of light. Imagining such a scenario and then thinking about what would happen to a light beam he emitted led to his discovery of the theory of relativity.

Cognitive psychologists have developed clever experiments to test people's ability to come up with creative mental images. They display images of letters or geometric shapes and ask participants to combine some of them in a creative way (Finke, Ward, & Smith, 1992). Figure 10.16a contains a set of such objects. Three of these images are chosen at random during each trial, and the participant's task is to assemble them in such a way as to create a recognizable shape or pattern. Various solutions are presented in Figure 10.16b.

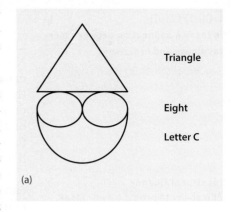

(a)

Triangle

Eight

Letter C

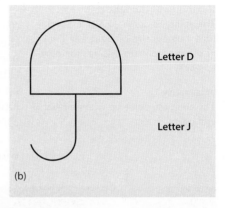

(b)

Letter D

Letter J

FIGURE **10.16**

CREATIVE PROBLEM SOLVING USING MENTAL IMAGERY.

(a) Three stimulus shapes at a time are presented to a person, whose task it is to combine them in any way to produce a single image or object. (b) These are some of the solutions created using the shapes in (a). (Finke et al., 1992)

Connection

Is there a connection between mental illness and creativity?

See "Bringing It All Together," Chapter 15, "Psychological Disorders," p. 583.

ideational fluency
The ability to produce many ideas.

flexibility of thought
The ability to come up with many different categories of ideas and think of other responses besides the obvious one.

originality
The ability to come up with unusual and novel ideas.

The ability to produce many ideas is central to creative thought. This ability is termed **ideational fluency** (Guilford, 1967). Highly creative people usually come up with more ideas for a given problem than less creative people do. Not all the ideas will be equally useful, but having a large number of ideas increases the chance that any one of them will be a useful or adaptive solution to the problem at hand. J. P. Guilford developed the *Alternate Uses* test to measure creativity. In this test, participants are given a common object, such as a brick or a pencil, and are asked to write down all the possible uses they can think of for the object within a limited amount of time. An ideationally fluent person can list many alternate uses for the object within a short period.

The ability to produce many ideas does not by itself guarantee that one can break out of one's mental set and think of unusual uses. A creative person can also come up with many different categories of ideas and think of other responses besides the obvious one. This ability is called **flexibility of thought** (Guilford, 1967). In the Alternate Uses test, flexibility of thought is gauged by the number of categories of response a person offers. If all the answers for the uses of a brick involve building something, the person is not displaying flexible thinking but remaining within one, rather obvious category. In contrast, coming up with uses that involve building, painting, writing, weights, step stools, and ballasts means a person is a flexible thinker, because those uses cut across many different categories.

The third cognitive process involved in creative thought is **originality,** which means thinking of unusual and novel ideas. In the Alternate Uses test, the test-taker's originality is scored by comparing his or her responses to a set of norms developed from the answers given by thousands of respondents who have already taken the test. A person's answer is scored as original if it is rare or uncommon compared to the norms. Again using the brick as an example, a higher originality score is given to "step stool" than to "paperweight," because there are fewer instances of "step stool" in the norms. In this sense, an original response is the same as an infrequent response, but originality in itself is not enough to explain creative thought. Creative thinking occurs when a person combines all three cognitive processes at once—fluency, flexibility, and originality.

The Creative Personality

We have seen how creative people differ from others by their brain activity and cognitive style. What about their personalities? Do creative people tend to have unique personalities? If so, what personality characteristics tend to be found in highly creative people? The best way to answer these questions is by looking at what all the published studies on the topic say—that is, by conducting a meta-analysis.

Feist (1998) conducted such a meta-analysis by locating all the published studies that reported the personality qualities of artists and scientists (see also Batey & Furnham, 2008). Twenty-six studies on almost 5,000 participants had reported the personality traits of scientists compared to norms; 29 studies on almost 4,400 participants had reported the personality traits of artists compared to norms. Creative artists and scientists do share some common personality traits (see Figure 10.17). One of

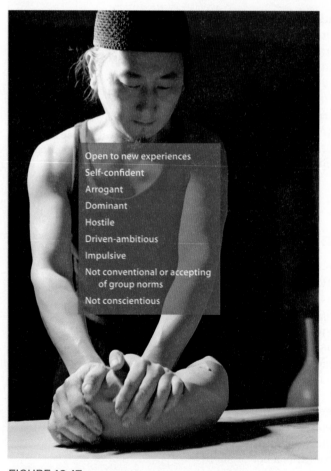

Open to new experiences
Self-confident
Arrogant
Dominant
Hostile
Driven-ambitious
Impulsive
Not conventional or accepting of group norms
Not conscientious

FIGURE 10.17

PERSONALITY TRAITS SHARED BY CREATIVE ARTISTS AND SCIENTISTS.

the most pronounced personality traits of creative artists and scientists, is openness to experience, which is the tendency to enjoy and seek out new experiences, new foods, new places, and new ideas. Highly creative people have this quality, which is not surprising, given that creativity involves novel thoughts and behavior (Batey, Furnham, & Safiullina, 2010; Furnham & Bachtiar, 2008; Greengross, Martin, & Miller, 2012; Hughes, Furnham, & Batey, 2013; Prahbu, Sutton, & Sauser, 2008). Also, they are unconventional and tend to have a firm belief that they possess a better way of doing things. In some, this comes off as self-confidence and in others as arrogance (Feist, 1993). Despite the similarities, artists are more emotionally sensitive and unstable than scientists (Feist, 1998; Ludwig, 1995).

Quick Quiz 10.3: Creativity

1. Creative thinking or behavior is both novel and
   a. interesting.
   b. artistic.
   c. meaningful.
   d. unusual.

2. The four stages of creative problem solving are preparation, incubation, insight, and
   a. elaboration-verification.
   b. validation.
   c. discrimination.
   d. resolution.

3. When compared to less creative people, creative people show what pattern of brain activity while solving problems?
   a. asymmetry between the hemispheres
   b. balance between the hemispheres
   c. parietal lobe activation
   d. occipital lobe activation

4. What is measured by the task in which participants are asked to think of as many different uses for a brick as they can?
   a. originality
   b. flexibility of thought
   c. functional fixedness
   d. both a and b

Answers can be found at the end of the chapter.

Bringing It All Together

Making Connections in Intelligence, Problem Solving, and Creativity

Genius, Intelligence, and Creativity

For many people, finding out that someone has an extremely high IQ (140 and above) is enough to call him or her a "genius," but are all very smart people necessarily geniuses? Moreover, does having an extremely high IQ mean the person will be creative? These are fascinating and important questions and they beg two other questions:

1. What is genius?
2. Is intelligence necessary and sufficient for creativity?

What Is Genius?

What makes someone a genius? Is superior intelligence enough? Consider Marilyn vos Savant. Most people have not heard of her, although she writes a weekly nationally syndicated column for *Parade* magazine. She has the world's highest recorded IQ ever—an off-the-chart 228—yet she has not created master works of note. Genius is not, as some

have claimed, simply being smart or having a very high IQ (Simonton, 1999). Having an IQ of 130 or 140, which puts someone in the top 1% or higher of the population, does not guarantee producing creative works of lasting influence.

Something other than intelligence must go into the making of a genius. **Genius** is high intelligence combined with creative accomplishments that have a tremendous impact on a given field (Simonton, 1999). The paintings, plays, buildings, novels, and scientific discoveries of geniuses change their respective fields. Literature was never the same after Shakespeare or Virginia Woolf. Physics has not been the same since Newton, Einstein, and Marie Curie. Art has not been the same since van Gogh and Picasso. Music has not

genius
High intelligence combined with creative accomplishments that have a tremendous impact on a given field.

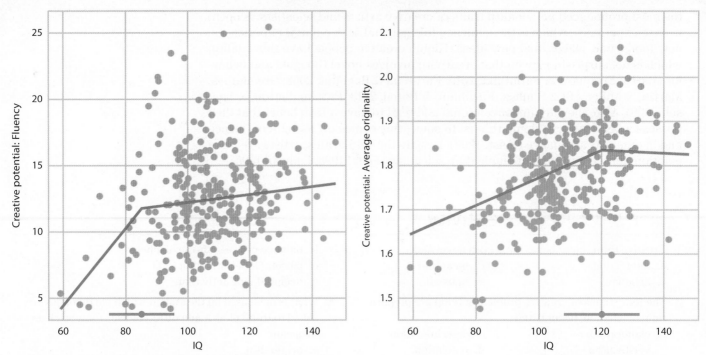

(a) An IQ of 85 is the breakpoint, or threshold, for the relationship between IQ and fluency/number of ideas (creative potential).

(b) An IQ of 120 is the breakpoint for the relationship between IQ and originality of ideas (creative potential).

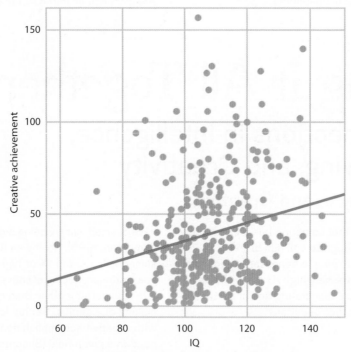

(c) There is no threshold for the relationship between IQ and creative achievement.

FIGURE 10.18

IQ THRESHOLDS FOR CREATIVE POTENTIAL (FLUENCY AND ORIGINALITY) AND CREATIVE ACHIEVEMENT. In these scatterplots, each dot represents a person's IQ score and his or her score on a different measure of creativity. The line through the dots represents the slope of the relationship. A diagonal line is a significant relationship, but a flat line is no relationship. The sharp change in direction of the line is the threshold, or breakpoint. (Jauk et al., 2013)

What does the threshold, or breakpoint, tell you about whether IQ is a necessary and sufficient condition for different forms of creative potential and creative achievement?

been the same since Bach and Beethoven. If people's accomplishments change their field, other people appreciate their importance sooner or later. Having a major impact on a field and being appreciated for the accomplishments is what distinguishes genius from geniuslike IQ. For every Shakespeare, Beethoven, Leonardo, and Einstein, there are many more people with equally high intelligence who make no significant contributions to society. Moreover, there have been people of truly monumental creative accomplishment whose intelligence was only somewhat above average. Charles Darwin, was—by his own admission—of only modestly high intelligence (Simonton, 1999), but his accomplishments have had as much impact on science and culture as those of just about any other person. By this standard, he was a genius.

Is Intelligence Necessary and Sufficient for Creativity?

Genius, by definition, and creativity are closely related, but what about intelligence and creativity? Does being really smart make a person more creative? The relationship between intelligence and creativity is not a simple one. Starting in the 1950s and 1960s, creativity researchers concluded there was a threshold on intelligence, below which the relationship with creativity was positive, above which there was no relationship (Guilford, 1967). A threshold is the point at which the relationship goes from being significant to not significant, which was argued to be an IQ of 120. Creativity and intelligence were positively

related below an IQ of 120 but unrelated above this threshold. This would imply that intelligence is a necessary condition, but not a sufficient one, for creativity.

More recent investigations, however, have shown a more complex relationship between intelligence and creativity (Jauk et al., 2013; Joy, 2012; R. E. Jung et al., 2009; Karwowski & Gralewski, 2013; J. C. Kaufman & Plucker, 2011; H. K. Kim, 2005; Nusbaum & Silvia, 2011; Preckel, Holling, & Wiese, 2006). For example, Jauk and colleagues (2013) report different thresholds for different aspects of creative potential (doing well on tests of creativity). If number of ideas (fluency) is the measure of creative potential, the threshold is only an IQ of 85; however, if originality of ideas is the measure of potential, then support for the threshold of 120 is reported (see Figures 10.18a and 10.18b). In other words, high intelligence predicts original ideas more than just quantity or number of ideas. Moreover, when the measure of creativity is achievement (actually producing creative works in art, music, or science), there is no threshold (see Figure 10.18c). Intelligence is positively related to creativity—meaning that, the more intelligent people are, the more likely they are to produce creative works.

Challenge Your Assumptions

True or False? People with very high IQs are geniuses.
False: IQ alone does not determine genius; genius requires creative accomplishments that change some aspect of society.

Chapter Review

INTELLIGENCE

- Intelligence is a set of cognitive skills that includes abstract thinking, reasoning, problem solving, and the ability to acquire knowledge.

- There are two major theories of the nature of intelligence. The single-factor, or general-factor, theory argues that intelligence at its core is one, overall ability. The other theory, the multifactor theory, says that intelligence consists of multiple abilities.

- Some of the factors of intelligence in the multifactor theory are crystallized and fluid intelligence, as well as analytic, practical, musical, and bodily-kinesthetic intelligence.

- Measures of intelligence, including the Stanford-Binet test and the Wechsler Adult Scale of Intelligence (WAIS), tend to be reliable and predictive of certain outcomes (school achievement), but not others (happiness or satisfaction with one's job).

- Intelligence ranges widely on a continuum from very low to very high. On the extremely low end is intellectual disability and on the extremely high end is giftedness.

- Group differences in IQ exist for race and gender, yet there is much debate concerning the possible explanations for these differences.

PROBLEM SOLVING

- Two distinct kinds of problem exist. Convergent thinking problems have known solutions, which can be reached by narrowing down a set of possible answers. Divergent thinking problems have no known solution; they require us to break away from our normal problem-solving strategies and make unusual associations to arrive at novel ways of thinking about a problem.

- People use different kinds of strategies to solve problems. Algorithms are formulas that guarantee correct solutions to particular problems. Thinking outside the box requires one to break free of self-imposed conceptual constraints and think about a problem differently in order to solve it. Eureka insights involve a sudden understanding of a solution.

- Obstacles to solutions include fixation, or an inability to break out of a particular mind-set in order to think about a problem from a fresh perspective; mental set, the tendency to continue to use problem-solving strategies that have worked in the past; and functional fixedness, the tendency to be blind to unusual uses of common, everyday things or procedures.

CREATIVITY

- Creativity is thought or behavior that is both novel and meaningful or adaptive.

- Genius is closely related to creativity in that it combines high intelligence with achievements that change entire fields (art, music, science, technology, business).

- Researchers have uncovered three principles of creative thinking and the brain: Creative insight increases frontal lobe activity; insights occur in the right hemisphere rather than the left; and creative people solving creative problems show more balanced activity between their right and left frontal lobes. Cognitive processes commonly associated with creative thinking are visual imagery, flexibility (coming up with many different categories of ideas), ideational fluency (the ability to produce many ideas), and originality (thinking of novel solutions).

- Creative people tend to have open, self-confident, arrogant, and unconventional personalities.

BRINGING IT ALL TOGETHER: MAKING CONNECTIONS IN INTELLIGENCE, PROBLEM SOLVING, AND CREATIVITY

- Intelligence, genius, and creativity are related but distinct concepts. Intelligence appears to be necessary but not sufficient for both genius and creativity.

Key Terms

adaptive behavior, p. 370
algorithm, p. 381
broad intelligence, p. 361
construct validity, p. 368
convergent thinking problems, p. 380
creativity, p. 384
cultural test bias, p. 368
divergent thinking problems, p. 381
Down syndrome, p. 370

Eureka insight (insight solution), p. 381
fixation, p. 382
flexibility of thought, p. 388
functional fixedness, p. 383
general intelligence, p. 361
genius, p. 389
g-factor theory, p. 360
ideational fluency, p. 388
internal reliability, p. 368
intellectual disability, p. 370

intelligence, p. 359
mental age, p. 365
mental set, p. 382
multiple-factor theory of intelligence, p. 360
narrow intelligence, p. 361
originality, p. 388
predictive validity, p. 368
prodigy, p. 371
reaction range, p. 375
reliability, p. 368

savant syndrome, p. 372
successful intelligence, p. 362
test bias, p. 369
test fairness, p. 369
test-retest reliability, p. 368
thinking outside the box, p. 382
triarchic theory of intelligence, p. 362
validity, p. 368

Quick Quiz Answers

Quick Quiz 10.1: 1. d 2. d 3. b 4. c 5. a **Quick Quiz 10.2:** 1. b 2. a 3. c **Quick Quiz 10.3:** 1. c 2. a 3. b 4. d

The solution to the first remote association on p. 385 is "horn," and the second on p. 387 is "apple."

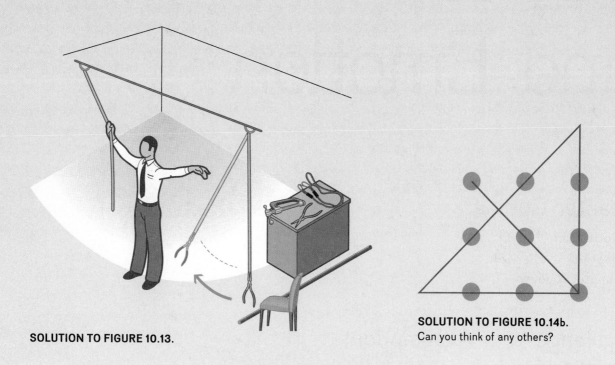

SOLUTION TO FIGURE 10.13.

SOLUTION TO FIGURE 10.14b.
Can you think of any others?

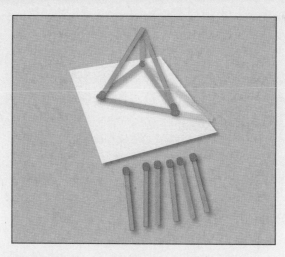

SOLUTION TO FIGURE 10.14c.

11 Motivation and Emotion

Chapter Outline

Motivation

Emotion

Chapter Review

Challenge Your Assumptions

True or False?

- Craving sweet, fatty, and salty foods is a socially and culturally determined preference. (see page 402)

- Eating smaller and more frequent meals can help you lose weight. (see page 404)

- Getting enough sleep can help you lose weight. (see page 405)

- Women are just as likely as men to engage in casual sex. (see page 409)

- Many species of animals engage in homosexual behavior. (see page 411)

- People in different cultures express emotion differently on their faces. (see page 427)

- More money leads to greater happiness. (see page 437)

Beck Weathers was finally doing what he long dreamed of doing: climb Mt. Everest. Being a pathologist, Weathers had already accomplished a lot in his 49 years, but he also struggled with bouts of depression and found challenging exercises to be effective ways of coping with his depression (Weathers, 2000).

All went well for the 2 months Weathers and his team spent on Mt. Everest to adjust to the altitude and conditions until they finally decided conditions were right to attempt to summit the 29,029-foot (8,848-meter) peak: Weathers had to stop slightly below the 28,000-foot mark. Completely exhausted, depleted of oxygen, and literally blinded by the conditions, Weathers could not continue and promised his guide, Rob Hall, he would wait for his return from summiting with another client.

Not knowing that his guide and the other client would wind up in trouble, Weathers waited hours. He refused offers by two groups to help him back down because of his promise to Hall. After hours of waiting alone, Beck finally joined a few others going down the mountain, but it was too late. They got caught in a fierce storm that came out of nowhere and had to spend the night in nearly 100 mph winds and temperatures of 30 below zero Fahrenheit.

The next morning Anatoli Boukreev, a Russian guide, came upon Beck's five-person group. The storm was still blasting at full force, so Boukreev could not guide more than one or two at a time down to the 26,000-foot Camp Four. Even though he believed that the remaining two people, one of whom was Weathers, were dead or better left for dead, he did send another rescue team up. When the rescuers got to the duo lying in the snow, they both were still breathing but close to death. It would be dangerous to try to take them down the mountain, so they were left for dead—again. Word got back to camp, and a phone call was made to his wife in Dallas, informing her of Beck's death.

Weathers remained in the subzero temperatures and snow for more than 12 hours, and "[t]hen . . . for some unknowable reason a light went on in the reptilian core of Beck's inanimate brain and he floated back to consciousness" (Krakauer, 1996, p. 264). When he first woke up in the snow, Weathers thought he was in a dream. He was no longer cold, and he was motivated to survive: "I was overwhelmed by an enormous, encompassing sense of melancholy. That I would not say good-bye to my family, that I would never again say 'I love you' to my wife, that I would never again hold my children, was just not acceptable. 'Keep moving' I said to myself again and again" (Weathers, 2000, Chapter 6, para. 28).

He fell many times on his way down to camp. After finding his way back to Camp Four, using wind direction as his only guide, and getting into a sleeping bag, the people there were still convinced that he would be dead by morning and was left alone to die—yet again! Only Jon Krakauer, best-selling author of *Into Thin Air*, decided to check on Weathers as others prepared to leave the camp the next day and "was shocked to discover that Beck was still alive" (Krakauer, 1996, p. 267).

After another day of horrifically difficult climbing, being guided footstep by footstep, Weathers finally made it to a lower camp at around 20,000 feet, but how was he going to make it off the mountain? The answer was one, beyond-belief act of heroism: the highest helicopter rescue ever performed by Madan Khatri Chhetri. At that elevation, helicopters can't get enough lift. The pilot risked his own life, but he succeeded, and Beck Weathers survived beyond all expectation and reason.

Weathers's survival is not only one of miraculous drive and motivation but also one of how emotion can often fuel motivation. The thought of never seeing his wife and children again gave Weathers the strength and perseverance to make it back down to camp. Although he was left for dead three times and ended up losing both hands and his nose to frostbite, Weathers survived and became a better husband and father (Weathers, 2000). Motivation and emotion are important forces of survival, and in this chapter we explore how these two forces shape human thought and behavior.

MOTIVATION

Consider what the following situations have in common:

A baby seeking a nipple
A girl studying for a math exam
A homeless person searching for food in a garbage can
A scientist conducting research
A couple having sex
A man climbing Mt. Everest

These are all examples of motivated behaviors. Babies seek the nipple because they need contact and nutrition; a girl might study for a test because she finds the material fascinating. There might be various reasons for a behavior, but each involves **motivation**, the urge to move toward one's goals, an energetic push toward accomplishing tasks, such as getting dinner, getting rich, and getting lucky.

Needs, drives, and incentives all contribute to motivation. **Needs** are states of cellular or bodily deficiency that compel drives. These are what your body seeks. Examples are your needs for water, food, and oxygen. **Drives** occur when our bodies are deficient in some need. If we are extremely thirsty, we are driven to drink. All our physiological needs have drive components. Figure 11.1 shows the drive components associated with various physiological and psychological needs. Motivated behaviors, therefore, result from needs and drives.

If drives push us into action, then incentives pull us into action. An **incentive** is any external object or event that motivates behavior. In general, drives come from the body, whereas incentives come from the environment. Financial independence, a gold medal at the Olympics, and academic success are all possible incentives behind training or studying.

Models of Motivation

Psychologists propose many models, or explanations, for motivation. Some focus more on internal drives, some more on external incentives, and others on both.

The Drive Reduction Model   When our physiological systems are out of balance or depleted, we are driven to reduce this depleted state (Hull, 1943; McKinley et al., 2004; Weisinger et al., 1993). Recall that a drive is the perceived internal state of tension that arises when our bodies are lacking in some basic physiological capacity, such as food or water. Central to drive reduction is the idea of

motivation
The urge to move toward one's goals, to accomplish tasks.

needs
Inherently biological states of deficiency (cellular or bodily) that compel drives.

drives
The perceived states of tension that occur when our bodies are deficient in some need, creating an urge to relieve the tension.

incentive
Any external object or event that motivates behavior.

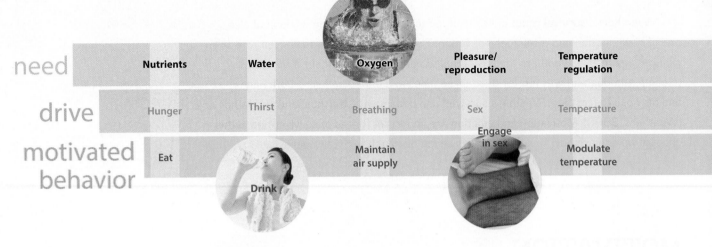

need	Nutrients	Water	Oxygen	Pleasure/ reproduction	Temperature regulation
drive	Hunger	Thirst	Breathing	Sex	Temperature
motivated behavior	Eat	Drink	Maintain air supply	Engage in sex	Modulate temperature

FIGURE 11.1

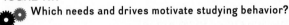 Which needs and drives motivate studying behavior?

homeostasis
The process by which all organisms work to maintain physiological equilibrium, or balance, around an optimal set point.

set point
The ideal fixed setting of a particular physiological system, such as internal body temperature.

maintaining physiological balance, or **homeostasis** (Cannon, 1929). All organisms are motivated to maintain physiological equilibrium around an optimal **set point,** the ideal, fixed setting of a particular physiological system. Set points are important mechanisms that allow homeostasis to work. We have set points for hunger, thirst, respiration, and many other drives. For example, if we get too cold, we shiver to warm up. The normal human body temperature of 98.6°F is like setting your thermostat to 68°F to warm your home (see Figure 11.2). When the temperature in the room has fallen more than a degree or two lower than the set point, the thermostat switches on the heater. Once the temperature has been brought back within the ideal set-point range, the thermostat turns off. In short, set points guide us to a "happy medium" in our needs. We automatically seek states that are "just right."

For homeostasis to work, our bodies must have sensors that detect their current states and any changes that cause them to deviate from the set point. Most of these sensory detectors are mechanisms in the brain. If our bodily states move too far from the set point, these mechanisms motivate us to take action—to raid the refrigerator, for example—to reduce our state of discomfort. Certain brain mechanisms evaluate the options and decide what to do to meet a biological need based on the information the brain is getting from our organs and tissues.

The Optimal Arousal Model When do we operate at our best? Can we be too wound up to perform well?

FIGURE 11.2

MODELS OF HOMEOSTASIS. Detectors in the brain stabilize the body's physiological state by comparing the current state (for example, blood sugar level, body fluids, body temperature) to a set point. If the body is far from the set point, the organism is motivated to correct the imbalance (for example, by seeking food or putting on a sweater). Sensory feedback to the brain tells it when the set point has been achieved, and the brain then tells the body to stop correcting. This feedback system keeps the body's physiological systems at their ideal set point. (Berridge, 2004)

Current state
Sensory detector (thermostat)
Compare to set point (temperature setting on the thermostat)
• If near goal, do nothing
• If far from goal, do something
Raise state
Lower state
Too low (cold)
Too high (hot)
Correct state (heater)
Correct state (air conditioner)

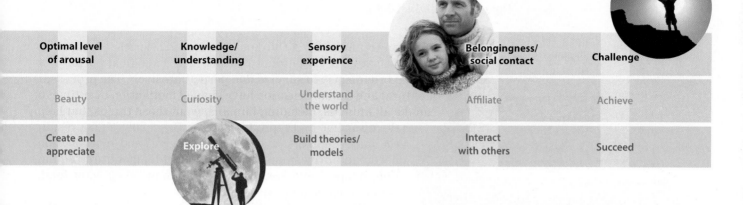

Optimal level of arousal	Knowledge/ understanding	Sensory experience	Belongingness/ social contact	Challenge
Beauty	Curiosity	Understand the world	Affiliate	Achieve
Create and appreciate	Explore	Build theories/ models	Interact with others	Succeed

The "optimal level of arousal" is another model that focuses on internal drive states; it is based on research by Yerkes and Dodson (1908). It proposes that we function best when we are moderately aroused, or energized. Both low and high arousal/energy levels lead to poor performance (Yerkes & Dodson, 1908). The finding is so common that it is now referred to as the **Yerkes-Dodson law** (see Figure 11.3).

   The optimal arousal model of motivation argues that humans are motivated to be in situations that are neither too stimulating nor not stimulating enough. Support for the optimal arousal model comes from sensory deprivation research. It involves having a person lie down on a bed or in a sensory deprivation (salt-water) tank. Classic research from the 1950s demonstrated that people could not remain in sensory deprivation for more than 2 to 3 days, even if they were paid double their daily wage for each day they remained in the tank (Bexton, Heron, & Scott, 1954). After long periods of sensory deprivation, people begin to hallucinate, their cognitive ability and concentration suffer, and they develop childish emotional responses. Sensory deprivation in rats shrinks the brain regions most involved in the senses that have been deprived, another example of the plasticity of the brain (Cheetham et al., 2007; Finnerty, Roberts, & Connors, 1999).

   In the 1990s, Mihaly Csikszentmihalyi introduced the concept of *flow* to describe how people perform best and are most creative when they are optimally challenged relative to their abilities (Csikszentmihalyi, 1990, 1996). Others have applied a similar model to explain learning and motivation (Day, 1982). According to this school of thought, needs such as curiosity, learning, interest, beauty-aesthetics,

Yerkes-Dodson law
The principle that moderate levels of arousal lead to optimal performance.

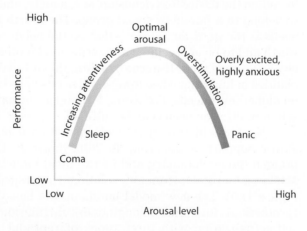

FIGURE **11.3**

YERKES-DODSON LAW. The Yerkes-Dodson law states that performance is best when we are optimally aroused; to be optimally aroused is to be moderately aroused. Performance is worst when we are either not very aroused (asleep or not paying attention) or overly aroused (highly excited or anxious). (B. D. Smith, 1998)

competence, challenge, flow states, and optimal experiences are motivated by the desire to be optimally aroused (Berlyne, 1960; Csikszentmihalyi, 1990; Deci & Ryan, 1985; Silvia, 2006).

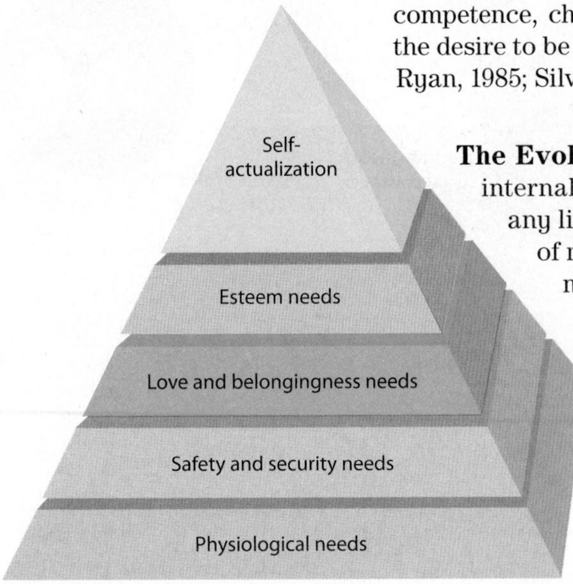

FIGURE 11.4

MASLOW'S HIERARCHY OF NEEDS.

Is it possible to satisfy needs of personal development, such as self-actualization, when physiological needs, such as hunger, are not met? Why or why not?

self-actualization
The inherent drive to realize one's full potential.

The Evolutionary Model A third model of motivation that focuses on internal drive states is evolutionary theory. The biological purpose of any living organism is to survive and perpetuate itself. The processes of natural and sexual selection have shaped motivation over time to make all animals, including humans, want those things that help them survive and reproduce (D. M. Buss, 2003). As a result, the major motives involve basic survival and reproduction needs and drives: hunger, thirst, body-temperature regulation, oxygen, and sex. Our bodies "know" they want food, water, oxygen, and—after adolescence—sex.

Desires, wants, and needs have been shaped over the course of human evolution to guide behavior either toward adaptive or away from maladaptive actions (D. M. Buss, 2003; G. F. Miller, 2000). In most cases, we are unaware that our behavior is related to these drives. We tend to do something because it is pleasing and we stop doing something to remove ourselves from some undesirable state.

The Hierarchical Model Another model of motivation, which combines drives and incentives, is Abraham Maslow's hierarchy of needs (Maslow, 1970). The essence of Maslow's hierarchy is simple: Needs range from the most basic physiological necessities to the highest, most psychological needs for growth and fulfillment (see Figure 11.4). At the lowest level of the hierarchy are *physiological needs*, such as the needs for food, water, oxygen, and adequate body temperature. At the next level are *safety needs*, which include physical security, stability, dependency, protection, and freedom from threats, such as war, assault, and terrorism. We need to be fed and out of danger's way before we can pay attention to higher-level needs.

The third level in the hierarchy consists of the *love and belongingness needs,* including the desire for friendship, sex, a mate, and children, as well as the desire to belong to a family or social group. The fourth level in Maslow's hierarchy of needs is the *need for esteem*—that is, the need to appreciate oneself and one's worth and to be appreciated and respected by others. The top level in the hierarchy is the need for **self-actualization,** the full realization of one's potentials and abilities in life. Only when lower-level needs have been satisfied can people focus on higher-level needs. For example, hunger and safety needs must be met before self-actualization needs can be fulfilled.

Maslow's hierarchy, as well known as it is, has had relatively little scientific support or updating. In 2010, however, Doug Kenrick and colleagues bridged the evolutionary and hierarchical models of motivation by modifying Maslow's hierarchy from an evolutionary perspective (Kenrick et al., 2010; see Figure 11.5). The new model builds on the basic needs—physiological, safety (protection), love and belongingness (affiliation), and esteem—and replaces self-actualization with three types of reproductive goals: acquiring a mate, retaining a mate, and parenting. In addition, in the new model, the levels overlap rather than replace earlier needs, clarifying that they do not go away but can be activated whenever needed.

We have two very basic drive states: hunger and sex. Hunger is the drive behind survival, and sex is the drive behind reproduction.

Hunger: Survival of the Individual

All animals need to replenish the energy continuously being used by their bodies. The rate at which we consume energy is known as *metabolism*. When our energy has been depleted, hunger drives us to replenish it by eating. Hunger is not just an internal biological process, however. It is the product of biological processes interacting with external, environmental ones.

The Biology of When We Eat Internal signals control the desire to eat or stop eating. From a drive-reduction perspective, being hungry depends not only on how much food we have consumed recently but also on how much energy is available for organ function. Hunger has four biological components: the stomach, the blood, the brain, and hormones and neurochemicals.

When we get hungry, our stomach starts to growl from gastric secretions the brain activates when we think of, see, or smell food. Hunger can also cause the stomach to contract when the stomach and small intestine have been relatively empty for about 2 hours. Although stomach contractions correspond with hunger pangs, they do not cause hunger. You might be surprised to learn that people who have their stomachs removed for medical reasons still feel hunger, as do rats whose nerves between the stomach and the brain have been cut (T. S. Brown & Wallace, 1980; Cannon & Washburn, 1912). Thus, the stomach does not act by itself to produce feelings of hunger; other biological systems are also involved.

One of these other signals comes from blood sugar. **Glucose,** a simple sugar in the blood that provides energy for cells throughout the body, including the brain, is the most important source of energy for the body. Although fat and protein provide their own forms of energy, some organs, including the brain, can use only glucose. Our blood sugar level drops when we don't eat for long periods, and the hypothalamus, which monitors glucose levels, will trigger the drive to obtain food.

As with almost all behavior, many regions of the brain are involved in eating. The hypothalamus regulates all basic physiological needs and acts as hunger's sensory detector. The body signals the hypothalamus about the nutritional needs of the cells. Various parts of the hypothalamus in turn send signals to different brain regions to either start or stop eating (Berthoud, 2002; Stellar, 1954).

Hormones and neurochemicals also play a role in hunger. Some of these substances stimulate appetite; others suppress it (Rowland, Li, & Morien, 1996; Simpson & Bloom, 2010; G. Williams et al., 2004). Two of the numerous hormones that stimulate appetite are neuropeptide Y (NPY) and ghrelin (G. Williams et al., 2004). When an animal is hungry or underfed, NPY is released in the hypothalamus to stimulate appetite. Ghrelin stimulates the release of dopamine (the feel-good neurotransmitter) and sends hunger signals to the brain, thereby stimulating hunger (Simpson & Bloom, 2010). Ghrelin levels rise when we are hungry and fall drastically after we eat. Endocannabinoids are naturally occurring neurochemicals that can also increase appetite. Blocking receptor sites for endocannabinoids leads to a decrease in eating and to weight loss (Kirkham, 2005; Nicoll & Alger, 2004).

Among the hormones that suppress appetite are insulin and leptin (Simpson & Bloom, 2010; G. Williams et al., 2004). One of the most important hormonal effects on hunger comes from insulin, which is produced by the pancreas. Rising glucose levels stimulate insulin production; insulin in turn transports

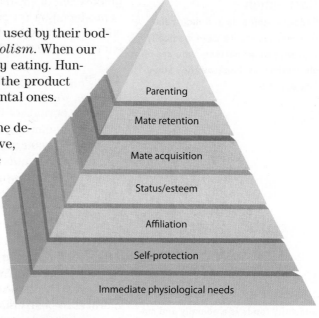

FIGURE **11.5**

EVOLUTIONARY UPDATE TO MASLOW'S HIERARCHY OF NEEDS. An evolutionary revision of Maslow's hierarchy of needs replaces self-actualization at the highest level with three levels of reproductive needs, in the order of their developmental appearance (acquiring a mate, retaining a mate, and parenting). Another change is that the new model conceptualizes the stages as overlapping, rather than replacing, previous stages.

glucose
A simple sugar that provides energy for cells throughout the body, including the brain.

Connection

Endocannabinoids and their relative, marijuana, are used medically to treat cancer patients who are on chemotherapy, because they stimulate appetite.

See "Hallucinogens," Chapter 6, "Consciousness," p. 242.

Challenge Your Assumptions

True or False? Craving sweet, fatty, and salty foods is a socially and culturally determined preference.

False: The fact that we crave basic foodstuffs is very much a product of evolution.

Actress Jennifer Lawrence is clear about liking her body and not wanting to be hungry to make other people happy: "You look how you look, you have to be comfortable. What are you going to do? Be hungry every single day to make other people happy? That's just dumb."

glucose out of the blood and into the cells. As a result, hunger decreases. Leptin is produced by fat cells and inhibits neurons in the hypothalamus that contain NPY (appetite stimulant), thereby signaling the body that it has had enough to eat (Friedman & Halaas, 1998).

The Psychology of What We Eat   What we eat is shaped by both nature and nurture. We crave foods that are essential to our bodies but that were scarce during early periods of human evolution, but we also learn to like and crave particular foods common in our culture.

Food preferences are very much shaped by evolutionary forces. Without realizing it, most humans crave the basic nutrients that our bodies require and that were scarce during ancestral times: sugar, salt, and fat. The fast-food industry capitalizes on this fact by creating foods that are rich in these substances (Moss, 2013). Companies conduct research to determine precisely the optimal levels of flavors that people crave—the so-called bliss point. Sweets and fats are no longer scarce in industrialized society, and their easy access and overconsumption contribute to increasing problems of obesity.

Our choice of what we eat is also driven by culture. That some people eat cows and others worms is, for the most part, culturally determined. Different cultures expose children to different flavors. Different cultures expose children to unique flavor combinations or shape food preferences while people are young. For instance, people in very cold climates commonly eat raw animal fat: Icelanders eat raw whale blubber pickled in whey; the Inuit eat raw seal fat. In contrast, cow brains and tongue are commonly eaten in Mexico. Exposure does not immediately lead to preference, however (Pliner, 1982; Rozin, 1996). It often takes multiple exposures before children will come to like a food that they initially disliked (Birch & Fisher, 1996; Birch & Marlin, 1982). The more often people eat certain foods, the more they like them. Once people develop a preference for a kind of food, they are motivated and even driven to eat that kind of food. If you develop a strong liking for Mexican food, but then spend a year studying in Europe or Asia, where there is little Mexican food, you will probably be driven to seek out any kind of burrito.

The Motive to Be Thin and the Tendency toward Obesity   Fat provides a way of storing energy for future use. In our evolutionary past, this was important in case food became scarce, but in modern, industrialized societies with abundant food, fat is a liability.

Because our lifestyle generally is sedentary compared with earlier times, we need less food to be healthy. Our ideas about beauty have also been transformed as a result of having more food available than we need. Thinness has come to define attractiveness, and being thin has become a cultural obsession. For example, 61% of high school girls in the United States are trying to lose weight (Daee et al., 2002). Among U.S. adults, 73% of women and 55% of men wish to weigh less (Yaemsiri, Slining, & Agarwal, 2011). The obsession with thinness sometimes leads to the development of eating disorders. At the same time, obesity rates have increased dramatically over the last 50 years.

How do we define obesity? Any definition of being overweight must consider both height and weight. Therefore, in evaluating an individual's weight, the U.S. government and medical doctors use body mass index (BMI), which is determined by dividing weight by height squared to yield a weight-to-height ratio (see Figure 11.6). The ideal BMI is between 19 and 24, with 25 to 29 considered overweight and 30 or above considered obese. According to the Centers for Disease Control and Prevention (CDC), in 2008, more than one-third of adult Americans were obese, one-third were overweight, and less than one-third were of ideal weight (Flegal et al., 2010). Moreover, rates of obesity have climbed rapidly over the last 20 years—from 12% in 1991, to 18% in 1998, to 34% in 2008 (Flegal et al.,

		Normal						Overweight						Obese						
BMI	**19**	**20**	**21**	**22**	**23**	**24**	**25**	**26**	**27**	**28**	**29**	**30**	**31**	**32**	**33**	**34**	**35**	**36**	**37**	**38**	**39**
Height (inches)																					
58	91	96	100	105	110	115	119	124	129	134	138	143	148	153	158	162	167	172	177	181	186
59	94	99	104	109	114	119	124	128	133	138	143	148	153	158	163	168	173	178	183	188	193
60	97	102	107	112	118	123	128	133	138	143	148	153	158	163	168	174	179	184	189	194	199
61	100	106	111	116	122	127	132	137	143	148	153	158	164	169	174	180	185	190	195	201	206
62	104	109	115	120	126	131	136	142	147	153	158	164	169	175	180	186	191	196	202	207	213
63	107	113	118	124	130	135	141	146	152	158	163	169	175	180	186	191	197	203	208	214	220
64	110	116	122	128	134	140	145	151	157	163	169	174	180	186	192	197	204	209	215	221	227
65	114	120	126	132	138	144	150	156	162	168	174	180	186	192	198	204	210	216	222	228	234
66	118	124	130	136	142	148	155	161	167	173	179	186	192	198	204	210	216	223	229	235	241
67	121	127	134	140	146	153	159	166	172	178	185	191	198	204	211	217	223	230	236	242	249
68	125	131	138	144	151	158	164	171	177	184	190	197	203	210	216	223	230	236	243	249	256
69	128	135	142	149	155	162	169	176	182	189	196	203	209	216	223	230	236	243	250	257	263
70	132	139	146	153	160	167	174	181	188	195	202	209	216	222	229	235	243	250	257	264	271
71	136	143	150	157	165	172	179	186	193	200	208	215	222	229	236	243	250	257	265	272	279
72	140	147	154	162	169	177	184	191	199	206	213	221	228	235	242	250	258	265	272	279	287
73	144	151	159	166	174	182	189	197	204	212	219	227	235	242	250	257	265	272	280	288	295
74	148	155	163	171	179	186	194	202	210	218	225	233	241	249	256	264	272	280	287	295	303
75	152	160	168	176	184	192	200	208	216	224	232	240	248	256	264	272	279	287	295	303	311
76	156	154	172	180	189	197	205	213	221	230	238	246	254	263	271	279	287	295	304	312	320

FIGURE **11.6**

BODY MASS INDEX (BMI).

 Do you consider yourself to be normal, overweight, or obese? BMI provides a good, initial indicator of whether your estimate is on target. To determine your body mass index, find your height in the left column and go across to your body weight. Then, at the top of the chart, locate the BMI for your height and weight. Because BMI does not take muscle mass into account, it is best to also include waist circumference in determining the health risk of one's weight.

2010; Mokdad et al., 1999). To be sure, BMI alone is not a complete measure of fitness, because it does not take muscle mass into account. A better all-around index, therefore, takes waist circumference into account as well as BMI. For men, the at-risk waist circumference is 40 inches or more; for women, it is 35 inches or more (*Assessing your weight,* n.d.).

People who are overweight tend to misperceive their body image as lighter than it really is. In a recent study of more than 3,500 young Mexican adults (ages 18–20), most of the normal-weight people (79%) accurately perceived their weight as normal by BMI standards. The obese people (BMI $\geq$ 30), however, greatly underestimated their weight: Only 9.5% accurately classified themselves as obese (Andrade et al., 2012). Similar misperceptions of body image in overweight Canadian children and adolescents have been reported (Maximova et al., 2008).

Weight gain is subject to environmental influence, but biological factors also play a role. Genes appear to be responsible for about 70% of adult weight (Allison et al., 1994; Hamer & Copeland, 1998). One study found that adults who had been adopted as children were much closer in weight to their biological parents than to their adoptive parents (Maes, Neale, & Eaves, 1997). In addition, in some obese people the gene that produces the hormone leptin, which normally suppresses appetite, has suffered a mutation and therefore does not function properly (Hamer & Copeland, 1998).

Genes also control the number of fat cells a person has, which has been set by childhood and adolescence and does not change much after that (Spalding et al., 2008). Each year about 10% of our fat cells die, but they are replaced by roughly the same number of new ones (Spalding et al., 2008). Dieting does not change this. When people diet, they are not decreasing the number of fats cells they have but rather how much fat each cell stores. The stable number of adult fat cells may explain why it is so hard to keep off weight that has been lost.

Common Myths about Dieting: Challenging Assumptions about Diet
There are some widely held beliefs about weight loss that have little or no empirical or scientific support. We review two here. First, the most pervasive and misleading myths involve fats and carbohydrates. The thinking is that low-fat and low-carb diets are good and high-fat and high-carb diets are bad, but it's not that simple (Ebbeling et al., 2007; B. V. Howard et al., 2006). There are different kinds of fats and carbohydrates; some are good and healthy, while others are not. Saturated fats, found in red meats, are less healthy and lead to greater weight gain than unsaturated fats, such as those found in avocado or olive oil. Likewise, carbohydrates can be simple or complex, with high-fiber foods being high in complex carbs and sugars being high in simple carbs. A more sound approach to losing weight and having a healthful diet is to aim for a low-glycemic (blood sugar level) diet, defined as approximately 40% carbohydrate, 40% fat, and 20% protein (Ebbeling et al., 2007). A low-fat diet by comparison consists of approximately 20% fat.

In general, it is healthier and easier to lose weight when diets are relatively low glycemic (e.g., fruits, vegetables, grains, and beans), which means avoiding high-glycemic foods, such as white bread, pasta, rice, baked goods, and low-fiber cereals.[1] Low-glycemic foods are digested more slowly than high-glycemic foods and hence a person feels full longer and eats less. Research is clear that high-glycemic diets are risk factors for coronary heart disease and adult-onset diabetes (Dong et al., 2012; Salmerón et al., 1997).

The second idea worth challenging about eating is that having smaller but more frequent meals (say, five or six) a day is one way to lose weight. The scientific evidence for this is mixed at best and seems contradictory (Cameron, Cyr, & Doucet, 2010; Parks & McCrory, 2005). Eating smaller, more frequent meals does not lead to weight loss.

Why Dieting Does Not Work—and What Does   For everyone who has tried to lose weight by dieting, we have bad news for you: Dieting generally does not work—not in the long-term, at least. Traci Mann and colleagues (2007) conducted a meta-analysis of 31 high-quality published studies on long-term weight loss from dieting and reported that diets work only for a minority of the population. Even worse, the dieters in the studies would have been better off if they had never dieted at all. Their weight would have been the same, but their bodies would not have gone through the stressful yo-yoing in weight. Losing and regaining weight is associated with heart disease, stroke, diabetes, and altered immune function.

People typically lose about 5 to 10 pounds within the first 6 months they start dieting (Mann et al., 2007). Within 2 to 5 years, however, the vast majority has not only gained all of the weight back but also weigh more than when they started dieting. In one study of more than 19,000 older men over a 4-year period, the single best predictor of weight gain was whether or not the men had lost weight on a diet soon before the study began.

Challenge Your Assumptions
True or False? Eating smaller and more frequent meals can help you lose weight.
False: The evidence suggests that small, frequent meals do not lead to weight loss.

Traci Mann

[1] The glycemic index places foods on a scale from 0 to 100, with 100 being highest in glycemia. Foods in the 70 to 100 range are considered high glycemic; 56 to 69 are considered moderate; and 55 or below are considered low glycemic. If you are interested in seeing the glycemic index score for 100 common foods, go to http://www.health.harvard.edu/newsweek/Glycemic_index_and_glycemic_load_for_100_foods.htm.

Health and social scientists have accumulated a fairly clear body of evidence for the kinds of lifestyle changes that are needed for losing weight and keeping it off for more than a year (Centers for Disease Control and Prevention, 2009; Chaput & Tremblay, 2012; N. A. Christakis & Fowler, 2009; Culvers, 2010; J. Murray, 2009):

- Eat slowly—it takes 20 minutes after eating before your brain knows you are full.
- Write down what you eat for at least 1 month.
- Monitor your weight regularly (at least a few times a month).
- Choose low-fat and/or whole-grain foods (a low-glycemic diet) as snacks.
- Eat what you want but in moderation.
- Stop eating when you feel full.
- Drink lots of water, which, among other things, fills your stomach and decreases a tendency to overeat.
- Ensure at least moderate physical activity each day totaling approximately 30 minutes (could be as short as three 10-minute sessions).
- Get support from your friends and family.
- Get good sleep.

The last two points deserve elaboration. Recent research confirms the remarkable power of our social groups to affect our overall health and lifestyle habits, including weight loss and weight gain (N. A. Christakis & Fowler, 2009; R. Wing & Jeffery, 1999). For example, a study by Wing and Jeffery (1999) reported that only 23% of those who enrolled alone in a weight-loss program kept the weight off 10 months after treatment compared to 66% of those who enrolled with friends and received social support training (see Figure 11.7). On average, those who were recruited with friends lost 33% more weight than those who were recruited alone. Note, however, that this outcome is relatively brief—only 10 months—so we don't know what percentage of any group kept the weight off for 2 or more years.

Second, a surprising finding on weight loss concerns its connection with adequate sleep. People who do not get enough sleep have more trouble losing weight than those who get adequate sleep (Chaput & Tremblay, 2012; Chaput, Després, & Tremblay, 2007). There are two reasons for this. First, sleep deprivation seems to change brain signals, making food more appealing (and hence the person eats more). Second, sleep deprivation decreases the activity of the appetite-suppressing hormone leptin, leading to a sense of never being full. This is yet another reason to get a good night's sleep!

Eating Disorders Some people develop such concern about their bodies and how much they weigh that they develop an eating disorder. Although we discuss psychological disorders more fully in Chapter 15, we briefly introduce the concept here. For any behavior to be disordered, it must be dysfunctional, disturbing, distressing, and deviant (American Psychiatric Association, 2013). Dysfunction is interference with everyday functioning, as well as disruption of one's personal and professional life. *Disturbing* and *distressing* imply that the behavior is not wanted and causes stress for either the person suffering from it or the individual's family, friends, and social contacts. *Deviant* implies that these are not common, everyday behaviors but relatively rare in the population.

Eating disorders meet the criteria for a psychological disorder. The two primary types of eating disorders are anorexia nervosa and bulimia nervosa. **Anorexia nervosa** involves an extreme fear about being overweight that leads to a severe restriction of food intake (American Psychiatric Association, 2013). This

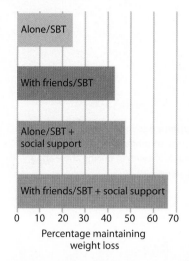

FIGURE 11.7
PERCENTAGE OF PARTICIPANTS WHO MAINTAINED THEIR WEIGHT LOSS IN FULL 10 MONTHS AFTER TREATMENT. SBT = standard behavioral treatment; alone = recruited alone. (Wing & Jeffery, 1999, p. 37)

Challenge Your Assumptions
True or False? Getting enough sleep can help you lose weight.
True: People who get 7 to 8 hours of sleep on a regular basis lose weight more easily than those who get only 5 to 6 hours of sleep.

anorexia nervosa
An extreme fear about being overweight that leads to a severe restriction of food intake.

caloric restriction typically does not allow a person to maintain at least 85% of the low end of his or her ideal weight—that is, a BMI about 16 or less. At its core, anorexia involves an extremely distorted body image, with the person believing he or she is too heavy regardless of how thin he or she really is. BMIs in the range of 15 or less can lead to death, and about 4% of those who suffer from anorexia will die from the disorder (Crow et al., 2009).

The second well-known eating disorder is bulimia nervosa. A person suffering from **bulimia nervosa** is prone to binge eating and feeling a lack of control during the eating session. Binge eating involves eating much more food at one time than the average person would, such as having a half gallon of ice cream as a late-night snack. A person with bulimia regularly engages in self-induced vomiting, the use of laxatives or diuretics, strict dieting or fasting, or vigorous exercise in order to prevent weight gain.

The causes of anorexia and bulimia are unknown, although a number of factors appear to put people at risk for this disorder, such as reactivity to stress, genetics, epigenetics, and personality. In short, they result from both nature and nurture. Women are much more likely than men to develop anorexia or bulimia (Nolen-Hoeksema, 2007). Women with eating disorders show higher physiological reactivity to stress.

A growing body of literature has examined the genetic and epigenetic basis of eating disorders (Bulik et al., 2006; Scherag, Hebebrand, & Hinney, 2010; Thornton, Mazzeo, & Bulik, 2011). For example, in a review of many twin and twin-adoption studies, Thornton and colleagues reported heritability coefficients that averaged around 60%, suggesting that genes explain about 60% of the variance in eating disorders. Moreover, people who had demonstrated a proneness to anxiety, depression, and low self-esteem (as measured by the trait of neuroticism) later were more likely to develop anorexia. Other studies report that many personality traits distinguish

bulimia nervosa
Prone to binge eating and feeling a lack of control during the eating session.

Amy Winehouse before and after the onset of anorexia nervosa.

anorexics. In addition to being higher in neuroticism, anorexics are also more conscientious, more introverted, and less open to new situations than are nonanorexics (Bollen & Wojciechowski, 2004). Recent questionnaire data suggest that both men and women with eating disorders seek approval from others and are more likely to have insecure attachments to their caregivers (Abbate-Daga et al., 2010).

Sex: Survival of the Species

Without food, we would starve to death. Without sex, individuals would not die but, if everyone went without sex, our species would die. At the species level, we have sex to propagate the species. As individuals, we have sex because it is enjoyable.

Human Sexual Response Like many basic questions, "What is sex?" is more complex than it would appear. We define **sexual behavior** as actions that produce arousal and increase the likelihood of orgasm.

Masters and Johnson (1966) were the first scientists to study the human sexual response systematically and directly. One of their major findings was that men and women go through four phases of sexual arousal—excitement, plateau, orgasm, and resolution—but they do so somewhat differently (see Figure 11.8). The major signs of the initial excitement phase are vaginal lubrication in females and erection in males. In the plateau phase, excitement level remains high but is preorgasmic. In men, the plateau phase might be rather short, but orgasm almost always follows. In women, the plateau phase often lasts longer than in men but is not necessarily followed by orgasm. Some women stay in the plateau phase for a while, then pass to the resolution phase without achieving orgasm. These women also have a gradual resolution phase. An even more striking gender difference is the ability of women to have multiple orgasms. Men always have a refractory period immediately following orgasm in which erection is lost and orgasm is not possible.

Updated models of female sexual arousal suggest that the initial sexual response in women involves more psychological processes than simply desire and

sexual behavior
Actions that produce arousal and increase the likelihood of orgasm.

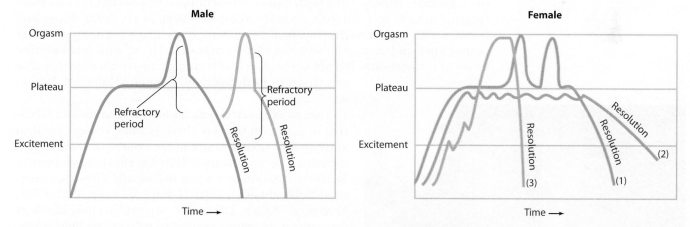

FIGURE 11.8

THE SEXUAL RESPONSE CYCLE IN MEN AND WOMEN. The four phases are excitement, plateau, orgasm, and resolution. Women are more varied in their sexual response than men. There are at least three distinct types of response in women. In (1), we see a response pattern much like men's, except that there is a possibility of multiple orgasm. In (2), we see a woman who gets aroused and stays at the plateau level, never reaching orgasm. In (3), we see a pattern in which the woman gets aroused and excited, skips the plateau phase, and has a quick resolution phase. In men, there is only one pattern, though a second orgasm can occur after a refractory period. (Passer & Smith, 1998)

arousal (Basson, 2000). Desire and arousal do not happen spontaneously in many women, who often require the right balance of thoughts and feelings dealing with intimacy, closeness, trust, and lack of fear and anxiety. These thoughts and feelings play off and feed arousal, which in turn leads to deeper feelings of intimacy and closeness. Arousal continues to increase and may or may not lead to orgasm, but arousal and excitement are important and meaningful even without orgasm (Basson, 2000).

The Biology of Sexual Behavior This newer model of sexual response matches well with brain imaging research on sexual arousal and orgasm. Many of the brain regions involved in emotion, which we will discuss shortly, are also involved in the stages of sexual arousal prior to orgasm. As is true of many physiological drives, such as hunger, the hypothalamus plays a crucial role in sexual behavior (Dominguez & Hull, 2005; M. Hines, 2010). In humans, lesions in the back portion of the hypothalamus lead to a decrease in sexual behavior, whereas electrical stimulation of the same region leads to an increase in sexual behavior, especially in males (Dominguez & Hull, 2005). In addition, the part of the hypothalamus involved in sexual behavior is larger in men than in women (Allen & Gorski, 2007).

Brain activity changes during orgasm—surprisingly, certain brain regions actually shut down. Gert Holstege and colleagues from the Netherlands took brain images of women while they were having an orgasm (being manually stimulated by their partners) and while they were faking it (Georgiadis et al., 2006). Achieving a real orgasm always involved deactivation of the brain regions associated with fear and anxiety in the amygdala and hippocampus, as well as parts of the cortex involved in consciousness. During faked orgasms, however, these brain regions remained activated. For men, brain deactivation occurred only in the left amygdala during orgasm (Holstege et al., 2003).

Testosterone, the major male sex hormone, controls sex drive in both men and women (N. M. Morris et al., 1987; Persky et al., 1978). The role of testosterone in the female sex drive was discovered accidentally when women whose adrenal glands had been removed lost their sex drive (Waxenberg, Drellich, & Sutherland, 1959). The adrenal glands produce testosterone. Moreover, younger women have both higher levels of male sex hormones and more frequent sexual activity than do older women (Persky et al., 1982). Males and females with high baseline levels of testosterone are more sexually active at earlier ages and engage in sex more frequently than those with low baseline levels of testosterone. It's not surprising that testosterone treatments increase sex drive in both men and women (Bolour & Braunstein, 2005).

In most species, females are not continually receptive to males. In women, there is some regular cyclical activity and sexual desire in the course of their 28-day menstrual cycle. Female-initiated sexual behavior peaks around ovulation and again before and after menstruation (Bullivant et al., 2004; C. Ford & Beach, 1951; Udry, Morris, & Waller, 1973). The strongest cyclical effect for women, however, occurs in relation to their fantasies involving men other than their regular sex partner (D. M. Buss, 2003), which increases in frequency and intensity as women approach ovulation (Bullivant et al., 2004). Such an increase in sex drive makes sense from an evolutionary and biological perspective, because a woman is most likely to become pregnant during ovulation. This is a case in which biological motives drive behavior.

Testosterone, the primary male sex hormone, also controls women's sex drive.

Culture and Sexual Behavior What is acceptable and normal sexual behavior varies from culture to culture. Perspectives on this basic human experience are many and varied. In a classic study of sexual behavior and culture, Clellan Ford and Frank Beach (1951) studied attitudes toward sex before and after marriage in 190 cultures. They identified three kinds of societies in terms of sexual attitudes: Restrictive societies restrict sex before and outside of marriage; semirestrictive societies place formal prohibitions on pre- and extramarital sex that are not strictly enforced; and permissive societies place few restrictions on sex. Thirty years later, Broude and Greene (1980) conducted a similar study of 141 non-Western cultures and found that, for women, premarital sex was mildly to moderately disapproved of in 30% of the societies and strongly disapproved of in 26%. Extramarital sex was common among men in 69% of the cultures and among women in 57% of the cultures.

Gender and the Drive for Casual Sex The belief that men are more promiscuous than women is widespread, but is it true? In a word, yes. Research consistently shows that men are more willing to engage in and are more interested in casual sex (see, for example, M. J. Bailey, Kirk et al., 2000; D. M. Buss, 2003; R. D. Clark & Hatfield, 1989; Maticka-Tyndale, Harold, & Opperman, 2003; Schmitt, 2003). For instance, in a meta-analysis of 177 studies of gender and sexual attitudes and behavior published between 1966 and 1990, Oliver and Hyde (1993) reported that men, on average, have much more positive attitudes toward casual sex and are slightly more likely to approve of premarital or extramarital sex. A follow-up meta-analysis of research published between 1993 and 2007 found similar but somewhat smaller gender differences in casual sex (Petersen & Hyde, 2010).

Schmitt (2003) collected data from more than 16,000 men and women in 52 nations and 6 continents and found universal support for men preferring more variety and greater number of sexual partners than women in both the short-term and long-term. The result of men compared to women having more variety of sexual partners seems to hold in the elderly as well (Waite et al., 2009).

Russell Clark III and Elaine Hatfield (1989, 2003) conducted a classic study on the question of gender differences and casual sex. Research assistants approached strangers of the opposite sex and asked them whether they would be willing to go on a date, come over to their place, or go to bed with them. As you can see in the Research Process for this chapter (Figure 11.9), the results were striking. Three-quarters of the men said they were willing to have sex with a stranger of the opposite sex, but not one woman was willing to do so!

Parental investment theory offers an explanation for the gender difference in attitude toward casual sex. If pregnancy results, the cost of having sex is quite different for men and women (Trivers, 1972). Biologically, the only assured contribution from men to parenthood is the act of sex itself. If a woman becomes pregnant, however, her contribution includes 9 months of carrying the fetus, a good portion of which might involve pregnancy sickness; the painful labor and delivery; and approximately 18 years of caring for the child. Therefore, women would be less motivated to have sex with little emotional commitment—a single sexual encounter could have consequences that endure a lifetime.

Sexual Orientation What drives most people to be attracted predominantly to the opposite sex, yet a significant minority to be attracted to the same sex? **Sexual orientation** is the disposition to be attracted to the opposite sex (heterosexual), the same sex (homosexual), or both sexes (bisexual). Historically, sexual orientation was thought of as an either-or proposition: A person was either heterosexual or homosexual. In the 1940s, Alfred Kinsey proposed a radically new view of sexual orientation: It exists on a continuum from exclusively

Challenge Your Assumptions
True or False? Women are just as likely as men to engage in casual sex.

False: Women are, in fact, less willing to engage in casual sex with a stranger than are men. Can you think of other reasons that might be?

sexual orientation
The disposition to be attracted to the opposite sex (heterosexual), the same sex (homosexual), or both sexes (bisexual).

Research Process

1 Research Question

Are there differences between men and women in their interest in casual sex? The researchers hypothesized that men are more eager for casual sex than are women.

2 Method

Clark and Hatfield (1989) developed a brief survey to address the research question. Research assistants who were college students approached students of the opposite sex. After a brief introduction, the research assistant would ask each student one of these questions: "Would you go out with me tonight?" "Would you come over to my apartment tonight?" or "Would you go to bed with me tonight?"

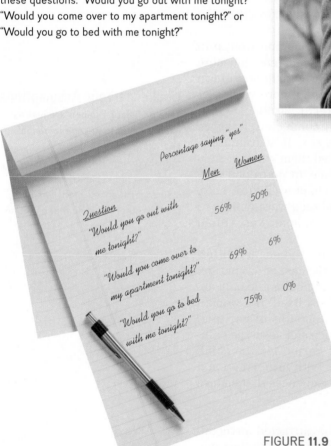

	Percentage saying "yes"	
Question	Men	Women
"Would you go out with me tonight?"	56%	50%
"Would you come over to my apartment tonight?"	69%	6%
"Would you go to bed with me tonight?"	75%	0%

3 Results

This table gives responses to the various questions, by gender.

4 Conclusion

Men and women were equally likely to agree to go on a date with someone they didn't really know. As the proposal became increasingly intimate, however, women backed off. Consistent with the hypothesis, men were much more likely than women to agree to have sex. This finding would be predicted by parental investment theory, which states that the cost of having sex is quite different for men and women.

FIGURE **11.9**

GENDER AND CASUAL SEX. A simple survey revealed gender differences in the interest in casual sex.

 Do more men or women agree to casual sex with an opposite-sex stranger? Why do you think that is the case? Source: "Gender Differences in Willingness to Engage in Casual Sex," by R. D. Clark III and E. Hatfield, 1989, *Journal of Psychology and Human Sexuality, 2,* 39–55.

heterosexual to exclusively homosexual (Kinsey, Pomeroy, & Martin, 1948; Savin-Williams & Vrangalova, 2013; Sell, 1997). After interviewing thousands of individuals, Kinsey and his colleagues realized that sexual orientation was not either-or and devised a 7-point scale from 0 to 6, with 0 being exclusively heterosexual. Current research generally supports this more continual notion of sexual orientation (Chandra et al., 2011; Savin-Williams & Vrangalova, 2013). There is growing evidence for the distinct category of "mostly heterosexual," a strong but not exclusive leaning toward opposite sex partners (Chandra et al., 2011; Savin-Williams & Vrangalova, 2013).

Approximately 90% of U.S. men and women identify as exclusively heterosexual (Chandra et al., 2011). Between 1% and 5% of the adult male population and 1% and 3.5% of the adult female population classify themselves as predominantly homosexual (Chandra et al., 2011; LeVay & Hamer, 1994; Tarmann, 2002). For men, sexual orientation tends to be either-or, producing a dip between 2 and 4 on Kinsey's 7-point scale (the bisexual range). For women, however, there is a more gradual decrease from exclusively heterosexual to exclusively homosexual, with more women identifying themselves as mostly heterosexual or bisexual (Chandra et al., 2009; Diamond, 2008; Hamer & Copeland, 1998; Rahman, 2005; Savin-Williams et al., 2013). With the recognition of a range of orientation, attitudes toward same-sex relationships and marriage are changing rapidly over much of the industrialized world, with same-sex marriage becoming legal in 16 countries in 2013 ("Gay Marriage," 2013).

Naturalistic observations of animals suggest that same-sex pairings may be much more common than previously thought. Same-sex sexual behavior is seen in numerous species, including beetles, penguins, and snakes (N. W. Bailey & Zuk, 2009). In the Laysan albatross, for example, a high proportion (more than 30%) of pair-bonded birds are females, which care for eggs and raise young together (Young, Zaun, & VanderWerf, 2008). Scientists still cannot explain the prevalence of same-sex sexual or matelike behavior across different species, because the framework for understanding sexual behavior relies on sex being an adaptation to support perpetuating the species.

Many people wonder what causes a person to be sexually attracted to someone of the opposite sex or the same sex. The age-old nature-nurture question inevitably arises: Is sexual orientation more a result of biology or of upbringing and environment? Both are involved in sexual orientation, and in complex ways (M. J. Bailey, Dunne, & Martin, 2000). There is evidence that our first biological environment—the womb—exerts a long-term effect on our sexual orientation. Research has revealed that, to some extent, individuals exposed to relatively high levels of testosterone in the womb are more likely to be attracted to women, whereas those exposed to relatively low levels of testosterone are more likely to be attracted to men (K. M. Cohen, 2002; Ellis & Ames, 1987; Hines, 2010; Rahman, 2005). Moreover, girls who were exposed to high levels of testosterone in the womb are more likely to be masculinized physically and behaviorally and tend to be somewhat more attracted to women than are girls who were not (Hines, 2010; Meyer-Bahlburg et al., 2008).

Sexual orientation is influenced by both nature and nurture.

The hypothalamus also seems to be involved in sexual orientation, which is not surprising, given its key role in sexual behavior (Hines, 2010). Intrigued by research showing that a small region in the hypothalamus involved in sexual behavior is about twice as large in men's brains as in women's, Simon LeVay (1991) decided to examine this structure in the brains of gay and straight men, and he found that this region was substantially smaller in gay men than in straight men—about the size of women's. As this is a correlational study, we cannot know exactly what this means—whether the small size of this brain region causes homosexuality or whether homosexual behavior shapes this region of the brain. This is yet another example of the mutual interaction of biology and behavior.

Some studies point to other brain differences between homosexual and heterosexual men. A brain imaging study of men showed that a region of the corpus callosum (the band of myelinated neurons that communicates between the cerebral hemispheres) is thicker in homosexual than in heterosexual men (Witelson et al., 2008). Another study indicates that different neural circuits are activated in homosexual versus heterosexual men while watching erotic films (Hu et al., 2008). These findings are all quite new, and it is not known whether they hold for women, but they do point to a biological basis for sexual orientation.

Genetic research suggests that sexual orientation is partly under genetic influence, at least in men. Studies of twins indicate that genetics plays a bigger role in determining sexual orientation in men than in women. For women, environmental factors seem to have a strong influence on sexual orientation. Female twins raised in the same household are much more likely to have the

same sexual orientation than are female twins raised in different households, regardless of whether they are identical or fraternal twins. For males, the degree of genetic relationship seems to matter most in twin sexual orientation (M. J. Bailey et al., 2000; Demir & Dickson, 2005; Hamer & Copeland, 1998; J. S. Hyde, 2005; Rahman, 2005). Recently, some biologists have argued that epigenetic influences during fetal development, more than genetic influences, play a role in the development of sexual orientation (Rice, Friberg, & Gavrilets, 2012). Genes being turned off by epigenetic markers may be affecting the development of sexual orientation.

Scholars have also proposed a number of social-environmental theories to explain the origins of sexual orientation. These theories argue that sexual orientation is a social construction (Bell, Weinberg, & Hammersmith, 1981; Van Wyk & Geist, 1984). Some social-environmental theories of sexual orientation have argued, for example, that child play, early peer relations, differences in how parents treat boys and girls, and gender identity are important factors in the development of sexual orientation, both heterosexual and homosexual. Many studies report that engaging in play more typical of the opposite sex early in childhood predicts a homosexual orientation later in life, in both men and women (M. J. Bailey & Zucker, 1995; K. M. Cohen, 2002). These environmental theories are quite consistent with biological ones. Biology could start the development of sexual orientation, which in turn would be strengthened or discouraged by environmental factors. The two sets of explanations work best in cooperation.

The Needs to Belong and to Excel

As we saw in Maslow's hierarchy of needs, human needs extend beyond the physiological needs of hunger and sex. The need for social contact and belonging—what psychologists call affiliation—and the need to excel and compete with others—what psychologists call achievement—are universal.

The Need to Belong: Affiliation   As we discuss in more detail in Chapter 14, "Social Behavior," humans are inherently social and affiliative creatures. Just think about how important it has been throughout your life—elementary school, middle school, high school, and now college—to have friends and to be accepted, even before there were Facebook friends and Instagram and Twitter followers. We depend on other people our entire lives, especially at life's beginning and end. It is not surprising, therefore, that our need to belong and to be accepted by others is one of the strongest of all human needs (A. Adler, 1956; Baumeister & Leary, 1995; H. A. Murray, 1938/1962). Particular parts of our brains are dedicated to and are activated uniquely by affiliation needs (C. DeWall et al., 2012; N. Eisenberger et al., 2003; Quirin et al., 2013). Further, some psychologists argue that one's self-esteem, or sense of worth, is directly a function of being accepted or rejected by other people (Leary, 2007). Being accepted by others increases our self-esteem, whereas being rejected lowers it.

No doubt one reason that social networks sites became instantly popular the world over was they tapped in to our need to connect and to belong (C. Lee & Chiou, 2013). If social networks are forms of belonging and connection, and belonging increases self-esteem, then it stands to reason that the use of social network sites (SNSs), such as Facebook, can increase self-esteem and well being—and it does (J. Kim & Lee, 2011; Nadkarni & Hofmann, 2012; Yu et al., 2010). Research also reveals that SNS use is associated with number of friends (both in person and online), a need to be liked by many people (popularity), extraversion, and a lack of social loneliness (Nadkarni & Hofmann, 2012; Ryan & Xenos, 2011; Utz, Tanis, & Vermeulen, 2012).

What does your social network look like?

One of your authors (Greg)—inspired by his 15-year-old son Jerry's desire to climb a mountain—at the 14,179-foot peak of Mt. Shasta in July 2013. After waking up at 12:45 a.m. and leaving basecamp at 9,900 feet at 2:15 a.m., Greg and Jerry reached the peak by 9:45 a.m. Drive, motivation, and perseverance, in addition to training and preparation (and good luck with weather), are a must in order to pull off such a physical and mental challenge.

achievement motivation
A desire to do things well and overcome obstacles.

The opposite of being accepted is being rejected, which can be one of the more painful experiences in life. A lack of belongingness leads to both physical and psychological problems, ranging from having more health problems to being more likely to commit suicide (Baumeister & Leary, 1995; Nadkarni & Hofmann, 2012). Moreover, being rejected or being bullied makes people more prone to anger and aggression toward others (Leary, Twenge, & Quinlivan, 2006). Many explosive, violent episodes are preceded by a person's being fired from work or being rejected by peers, a lover, or a spouse (K. D. Williams & Zudro, 2001). For example, many of the high-profile school shootings over the last 12 years, such as Columbine, Virginia Tech, and Sandy Hook, were carried out by boys and men who were teased, bullied, or rejected by their peers (Leary et al., 2003).

The Need to Excel: Achievement Some people, such as successful athletes, businesspeople, and politicians, have a tremendous need to excel and to be the best at what they do, but in truth, almost everyone strives to overcome shortcomings and imperfections (A. Adler, 1956). In the process, some people compete fiercely with other people, whereas others compete more with themselves.

The motivation to succeed raises the question of how to define achievement. David McClelland and his colleague John Atkinson emphasized that **achievement motivation** is a desire to do things well and overcome difficulties and obstacles (D. C. McClelland, 1985). However, those obstacles can be measured only in terms of one's goals. When David Feist (whom you met in Chapter 6) was coming out of his vegetative state following his bicycle accident, lifting a finger was a tremendous achievement, yet for a highly driven, accomplished, and motivated athlete, a silver medal at the Olympics might be a crushing defeat.

Atkinson (1964) argued that the tendency to achieve success is a function of three things: motivation to succeed, the expectation of success, and the incentive value of the success (see also D. C. McClelland, 1985). Let's apply Atkinson's model to your motivation to obtain a good grade in this introductory psychology course. Your *motivation to succeed* is the extent to which you want to be successful, which differs for everyone. For some students, an *A−* might be disappointing, whereas for others, a *B+* might be a great accomplishment.

Expectation of success is an individual's evaluation of the likelihood of succeeding at a task. Your evaluation of your performance in this course consists of two beliefs: whether you have the ability to do well and what the actual outcome is likely to be. These two beliefs may not match. For instance, some students may see themselves as quite capable of doing well, but because of some missed classes, they may not obtain a high grade for the course.

Incentive value stems from two factors. First, success at the task has to be important to you. Second, the more difficult the task and the lower the odds of succeeding at it, the more meaningful and satisfying it'll be if you do succeed. The incentive value for doing well in introductory psychology differs, depending on what a good grade in the course means to you. If you are a psychology major and if your GPA plays an important role in your class standing or your scholarship, then your introductory psychology grade might have a higher incentive value than it would if you were a physics major taking the course to satisfy a general education requirement. Succeeding at something that is considered very difficult means more to most people than succeeding at something they consider easy, but the degree of difficulty may not provide much useful feedback about abilities.

Motivation in the Workplace

What keeps someone motivated to do well in a job? Industrial/organizational (I/O) psychologists study motivation and behavior in work contexts (Aamodt, 2010). Consider an I/O question very important to businesses: What motivates employees to work at their best?

Three Models of Employee Motivation   What would you prefer most in your job—money or interesting, enjoyable work? The most sensible answer is probably "both." In fact, "interesting work," "good wages," and "job security" have been the top priorities among employees in surveys from the 1940s onward (Wiley, 1997).

From a behavioral perspective, the bottom line for business is productivity. Historically, many businesses and companies have operated using principles of operant conditioning to motivate workers to perform well—that is, good behavior is rewarded by pay increases, promotions, and incentives. More recently, however, some companies have questioned whether money and reward are really the best motivators and instead have emphasized supportive and pleasant work environments, autonomy, enjoyment, and challenge in their workers. There are at least three competing models of how to best motivate workers and make them more productive:

- Extrinsic motivation
- Intrinsic motivation
- Organizational support for the well-being of employees

Extrinsic Motivation   Some models, influenced by Skinner's discoveries of the power of reinforcement to shape behavior, argue that reward, money, and feedback are all important as powerful shapers of workplace behavior (Aamodt, 2010; R. Eisenberger & Cameron, 1996). Known as **extrinsic motivation,** this motivation comes from outside the person and usually involves rewards and praises. Extrinsic motivators are used to get people to do things they themselves wouldn't normally do or perhaps don't like doing, as when children get an allowance for cleaning their rooms and doing the dishes.

Psychological research offers much support for the power of reward and extrinsic motivation on behavior (Bandura, 1997; R. Eisenberger, Rhoades, & Cameron, 1999; Gneezy, Meier, & Rey-Biel, 2011; Harackiewicz & Sansone, 1991; Skinner, 1971). Reward not only can increase a particular behavior but also can increase performance and feelings of competency. When rewards are connected directly to performance, workers will be more motivated to do a job well than when they simply receive positive feedback without a reward (Harackiewicz & Sansone, 1991).

However, extrinsic motivation has its drawbacks (D'Ausilio, 2008; Gneezy et al., 2011); it requires the reward to be constant. If the reward goes away, the motivation to continue goes away and the worker stops doing the rewarded behavior. Similarly, if the reward stays the same and doesn't increase, motivation will drop. The bar must constantly be raised, and pay must continue increasing. In addition, reward has a way of narrowing focus, so it works for simple tasks, but narrow focus hinders creative thinking and the expanded focus required to

extrinsic motivation
Motivation that comes from outside the person and usually involves rewards and praises.

motivation in the
workplace

Extrinsic
motivation

Intrinsic
motivation

Perceived support by supervisors
and organizations

What kind of motivation do you think is most effective in the workplace: extrinsic or intrinsic? Explain.

intrinsic motivation
Motivation that comes from within a person and includes the elements of challenge, enjoyment, mastery, and autonomy.

solve difficult problems. Finally, reward can sometimes remove a person's own desire to perform a task out of pure enjoyment. If people perceive that they are being controlled by others, then their own intrinsic interest in doing the task dwindles, because reward and evaluation by other people undercut one's own pleasure in doing a task. For example, if you enjoyed reading in middle school and then your parents started paying you for every 25 pages you read, you might start reading for money rather than for pleasure. In this case, your intrinsic enjoyment of reading would have been destroyed by external reward.

Intrinsic Motivation   The rock musician Tom Petty recently summed up the second model of work motivation very well: "I think any time you're making a living at what you love to do, you're blessed. That's what I try to instill in my kids. Go after what you really love and find a way to make that work for you, and then you'll be a happy person" (Fong-Torres, 2010). **Intrinsic motivation** happens when you want to do something simply because you enjoy doing it. This type of motivation has four components (Amabile & Khaire, 2008; Amabile et al., 1994; Deci & Ryan, 1985; Miao, Lund, & Evan et al., 2009):

- *Challenge:* How much do you enjoy the thrill and excitement of new challenges?
- *Enjoyment:* How much pleasure do you receive from the process of doing the task?
- *Mastery:* Do you gain a sense of accomplishment and pride in doing a difficult task?
- *Autonomy and self-determination:* Do you believe that you are free to determine much of what you do and how you do it?

Teresa Amabile and her colleagues argue that intrinsic motivators help employees work creatively and productively (Amabile & Khaire, 2008; Amabile & Kramer, 2007). They present evidence that the companies that most successfully motivate their employees and inspire their creativity are those that

- don't have executives who think they are the only source of good ideas but rather elicit and champion ideas from anyone in the company, as long as they are good, creative ideas;
- open the organization to a diverse number of perspectives, based on ethnicity, gender, age, and experience;
- have managers or executives who know when to put controls on the creative process (commercialization phase) and when not to (idea generation phase); and
- create positive emotions in workers, such as satisfaction, pride, and elation, because positive emotion is likely to make workers more creative, productive, and committed to the company.

Intrinsic motivation is not a static attribute. It changes as life circumstances change. We see this with the various components of intrinsic motivation (Miao et al., 2009). For example, the need for challenge rises for employees in their 20s to 30s but then drops as they move toward late middle age and the end of their careers. However, enjoyment, which is the emotional component of intrinsic motivation, drops only a little over the course of one's career.

FIGURE **11.10**

MODEL LINKING ORGANIZATIONAL SUPPORT TO COMMITMENT TO STAY WITH A COMPANY. (Adapted from D. G. Allen et al., 2003)

Perceived Support by Supervisors and Organizations How much employees believe that the organization appreciates and supports their contributions and well-being, known as **perceived organizational support,** plays a big role in keeping them motivated and committed to working at that company (D. G. Allen, Shore, & Griffeth, 2003; R. Eisenberger et al., 2002; Kottke & Sharafinski, 1988; Shore & Wayne, 1993; Yoon & Thye, 2000). Few things can be more deflating than working hard at something and then having it taken for granted or not appreciated by the people whose opinions matter most to you. Eder and R. Eisenberger (2008) reported research that supports the idea that, when employees work at companies that care about their well-being, they are happier at their jobs, experience less stress, and are more motivated to stay at their jobs. In addition, they are less likely to miss workdays, be late for work, or take long lunch breaks.

In another study, Allen, Shore, and Griffeth (2003) predicted that perceived organizational support would be positively related to both how committed employees were to their company and how satisfied with their jobs they would be. Two samples were studied: first, 264 salespeople at a large department store in the southeastern United States and, second, 442 insurance agents at a large national insurance company. Allen and colleagues found that perceptions of fairness and opportunity affect perceptions of organizational support, which affect the likelihood of commitment to a company (see Figure 11.10).

perceived organizational support Employees' beliefs about how much the organization appreciates and supports their contributions and well-being.

Quick Quiz 11.1: Motivation

1. Which model of motivation can be compared to the thermostat in your house?
   a. evolutionary
   b. drive-reduction
   c. optimal arousal
   d. hierarchical

2. In addition to blood sugar (glucose) and the hypothalamus, and as discussed in this chapter, what is another important biological system involved in regulating hunger?
   a. adrenaline
   b. the liver
   c. hormones
   d. protein

3. Most research on weight loss has reported that
   a. losing weight is very difficult for most people.
   b. losing weight is relatively easy initially, but keeping it off is very difficult.
   c. keeping weight off is relatively easy for most people.
   d. losing weight is relatively easy and so is keeping it off.

4. Which of the following statements is FALSE?
   a. Testosterone is both a cause and an effect of sexual behavior.
   b. Testosterone is associated with sex drive in both men and women.
   c. Testosterone is associated with sex drive in men only.
   d. Men and women have different sexual response cycles.

Answers can be found at the end of the chapter.

EMOTION

Emotions are also powerful motivators of human behavior, though they differ from basic drives, such as hunger, thirst, and sex, in several ways. First, drives are linked to very specific needs or triggers, whereas emotions are not (Tomkins, 1962, 1981). Hunger comes from a need for food, thirst from a need for water, physical desire from a need for sex. Happiness, in contrast, occurs in response to an infinite variety of triggers, such as smelling a rose, visiting a friend, reading a good story, or watching a sunset. Second, emotions can override biological drives (Tomkins, 1962). Sexual desire is a powerful motivator, but it can be derailed by emotion. Recall that sexual orgasm cannot occur unless the areas of the brain involved in fear and anxiety are shut down (Georgiadis et al., 2006). The emotion of disgust can easily override the fundamental drive of hunger. Why? Disgust is important for survival. It arises when we come across something that is potentially toxic or harmful and capitalizes on our inborn aversion to contamination (Oaten, Stevenson, & Case, 2009; Rozin & Fallon, 1987). It is preferable for spoiled food to seem unappetizing, because it decreases our chances of ingesting harmful bacteria, molds, or parasites. Simply put, emotions can turn off the drives of hunger, thirst, and sex (Neuberg, Kenrick, & Schaller, 2011; Oaten et al., 2009).

Some emotions, like disgust and fear, are very primitive, survival-oriented responses to certain kinds of situations that are present in many species in the animal kingdom (Ekman, 1992). Others, like embarrassment and shame, require a sense of right and wrong and, so, may be present only in humans (Tangney, Stuewig, & Mashek, 2007).

What Are Emotions?

Emotions are brief, acute changes in conscious experience and physiology that occur in response to a meaningful situation in a person's environment. They emerge from our interactions with the world and are triggered by situations that are relevant to our personal goals, physical safety, or well-being. Because emotions stem from situations that are important to us, they reveal much about what makes us tick.

Types of Affect Psychologists use the term *affect* to refer to a variety of emotional phenomena, including emotions, moods, and affective traits. Emotions make us pay attention, forcing us to set priorities and deal with life-relevant situations (Ekman, 1992; R. S. Lazarus, 1991; Levenson, 1994). They occupy the foreground of our consciousness, often dominating our awareness. In fact, emotions can impact memory, perception, attention, and decision making (J. D. Cohen, 2005; Phelps, 2006).

Moods are transient changes in affect that fluctuate throughout the day or over several days. We experience moods both physiologically and psychologically, and they tend to last longer than most emotions (Davidson, 1994; Ekman, 1984; Hedges, Jandorf, & Stone, 1985). Moods make certain emotions more likely to occur than others. An irritable mood, for instance, makes people more easily angered than usual. If you are irritated, a slight inconvenience that normally would not bother you, such as having to wait in a slow line at the supermarket, might cause you to speak rudely to the clerk.

Some emotional qualities are longer-lasting, however. **Affective traits** are enduring aspects of our personalities that set the threshold for the occurrence of particular emotional states, such as hostility (which potentiates anger) or anxiety (which potentiates fear; Ekman, 1984; R. S. Lazarus, 1991; Rosenberg, 1998). People who have the affective trait of hostility aren't always

emotions
Brief, acute changes in conscious experience and physiology that occur in response to a personally meaningful situation.

Connection

Emotional events are remembered better than nonemotional events, almost as if they were seared into our brains.

See "Emotion, Memory, and the Brain," Chapter 7, "Memory," p. 273.

moods
Affective states that operate in the background of consciousness and tend to last longer than most emotions.

affective traits
Stable predispositions toward certain types of emotional responses.

Judging from her expression, what do you think this woman is feeling?

angry, but they have hair triggers. If they get cut off in traffic, they are more likely to shout an obscenity at the other driver. For several minutes or likely even longer, hostile people will continue focusing on the event—how they were wronged—making for repeated and/or prolonged experiences of anger (Ekman, 2003).

Basic Emotions   Although humans experience an infinite variety of emotional states, a small set of emotions appears to be common to all humans and, thus, may be a product of our evolutionary past (Ekman, 1992). These **basic emotions**—anger, disgust, fear, happiness, sadness, and surprise (see Figure 11.11)—are fundamental states that play a role in essential life tasks, such as protecting oneself and loved ones from harm (fear), progressing toward the realization of a goal (happiness), or experiencing irrevocable loss (sadness; Ekman, 1992; P. J. Lang & Bradley, 2010; Oatley & Johnson-Laird, 2011). The basic emotions are not single states; rather, they are categories or groups of related emotions, what Ekman (1992) describes as emotion families. For instance, the fear family, which includes anxiety, trepidation, and nervousness, may arise in response to a threat to physical safety. The happiness family includes joy, contentment, elation, amusement, and exhilaration, among others.

Emotions as Evolutionary Adaptations   Why do we have emotions? From an evolutionary perspective, emotions are adaptations to particular problems in our ancestral past and so contributed to survival and reproductive success (Tooby & Cosmides, 1990). According to one evolutionary view, emotions bring our physiological systems together to help us deal efficiently with critical situations (Levenson, 1988; Mauss et al., 2005; Rosenberg & Ekman, 1994). When danger approaches, the heart pumps blood to the skeletal muscles to enable quick

basic emotions
A set of emotions that are common to all humans; they include anger, disgust, fear, happiness, sadness, and surprise.

Basic emotions	Self-conscious emotions
Anger	Embarrassment
Disgust	Guilt
Fear	Humiliation
Happiness	Pride
Sadness	Shame
Surprise	

FIGURE **11.11**
BASIC AND SELF-CONSCIOUS EMOTIONS.
(Ekman, 1992; Tracy et al., 2007)

movement in case escape is necessary, the respiratory system works harder to bring in more oxygen, and the brain prioritizes attention, so that we can figure out what we need to do to protect ourselves. This view of emotions as organized responses best illustrates the adaptive value of negative emotions, such as anger and fear, which enable people to respond efficiently to a significant challenge or obstacle.

What about happiness or other emotions that are not responses to obstacles or threats? Positive emotions, such as contentment, happiness, love, and amusement, solve different kinds of adaptive problems. According to the **broaden-and-build model,** positive emotions widen our cognitive perspective, making our thinking more expansive and enabling the acquisition of new skills (Fredrickson, 1998, 2001). Negative emotions promote a narrow, vigilant way of looking at the world (Derryberry & Tucker, 1994). Play, for example, especially the rough-and-tumble play of animals and young children, is a kind of fun that helps develop physical and strategic skills, which may be useful for hunting, escaping, or defensive fighting.

Several studies suggest that positive emotions broaden one's attentional focus (Fredrickson & Branigan, 2005). When in positive moods, people perform poorly on tasks of selective attention that require a narrow focus but better on tasks that require a broader attentional focus (Rowe, Hirsch, & Anderson, 2007). Also, when people show authentic smiles of enjoyment, attention is broadened (K. J. Johnson, Waugh, & Fredrickson, 2010). A broadening of thinking induced by positive emotional states may also underlie the effects of positive emotion on creative thinking (Fredrickson, 1998). In a standard creative thinking task in which people were instructed to think of as many uses as they could for a brick, people in a positive mood thought of more uses (and more novel uses) than those experiencing negative emotions (Isen, Daubman, & Nowicki, 1987; Rowe et al., 2007). In a perceptual task, positive emotions also enhance attention to visual information in the outer edges of a visual display, compared to the center (Wadlinger & Isaacowitz, 2006).

Clearly, numerous findings imply that positive emotions enable people to take more information from any given visual scene, but there is very little research on how this works. Recent studies point to basic differences in how people process visual stimuli when in positive versus neutral states, not all of which are improvements, adding a more nuanced understanding to how positive emotions influence attention. Vanlessen and colleagues (2013) assigned participants to a positive or neutral mood induction, gave them various visual-processing tasks, and measured event-related potentials (ERPs, electrical signals from the scalp) throughout testing. The results suggested that positive emotions impaired performance in early processing of visual information by releasing the inhibitory effects of the prefrontal cortex on attention. The net effect might be a looser, broader focus on visual input, but more data are needed. Indeed, positive emotions do tend to lead to more global versus specific information processing, but this effect depends on motivational factors (Gable & Harmon-Jones, 2008, 2010).

Self-Conscious Emotions   The pride a child feels at learning how to ride a bike and the shame of being caught in a lie are examples of **self-conscious emotions,** which occur as a function of how well we live up to our expectations, the expectations of others, or the rules set by society (Tracy et al., 2007; Tangney et al., 2007; see Figure 11.11). These emotions, which include shame, guilt, humiliation, embarrassment, and pride, require a sense of self and the ability to reflect on one's own actions. Let's look at pride and embarrassment in detail.

Pride has a recognizable expression, which involves body movements, a smile, the head tilted upward, and a slightly expanded chest (see Figure 11.12).

broaden-and-build model
Fredrickson's model for positive emotions, which posits that they widen our cognitive perspective and help us acquire useful life skills.

self-conscious emotions
Types of emotion that require a sense of self and the ability to reflect on actions; they occur as a function of meeting expectations (or not) by society's rules.

FIGURE **11.12**

THE EXPRESSION OF PRIDE. Jamaican sprinter Usain Bolt shows the typical pride display after winning the gold medal in the 100-meter sprint. This display is innate; even blind people who have never seen it make the same pose after a victory.

This behavior is recognized as pride by children and adults in America and by people in a preliterate, socially isolated tribe in West Africa (Tracy & Robins, 2008). These cross-cultural recognition data from very diverse groups suggest that this pride expression may be common across the globe, but more data are needed. People show elements of this behavior when in situations that produce pride, such as winning medals at the Olympics (Tracy & Matsumoto, 2008). Pride is an emotion that is associated with superiority over others and higher social status—even in cultures that do not value social status differences (Tracy et al., 2013).

We all know what it feels like to be embarrassed. You are admiring yourself in the mirror when you realize your roommate has walked in and caught you preening. Embarrassment involves an unintentional revelation about yourself to someone else. Being embarrassed makes you feel self-conscious, as if you have violated some social rule. People often get giggly when embarrassed and act as if they want to make amends for some sort of social transgression (Keltner, 1995; Tangney et al., 2007). Keltner (1995) describes the facial expression of embarrassment, which he argues appeases and placates those who have seen one's mistake. The embarrassment expression involves a sequence of facial and gestural actions, each of which may correspond to some sort of social function (see Figure 11.13).

In another study, Feinberg, Willer, and Keltner (2012) asked people to imagine themselves in various embarrassing situations (such as asking a woman with a protruding stomach if she is pregnant and finding out she is not!) and to recall an embarrassing experience by spending 4 minutes telling this story aloud to a video camera. Analyses of the videotaped behavior, questionnaire data, and performance on game tasks revealed that the people who expressed more embarrassment were more concerned about others in social situations and more generous in their offerings of money to others (Feinberg et al., 2012). These findings suggest that embarrassing experiences, though often uncomfortable, may provide an important prosocial function.

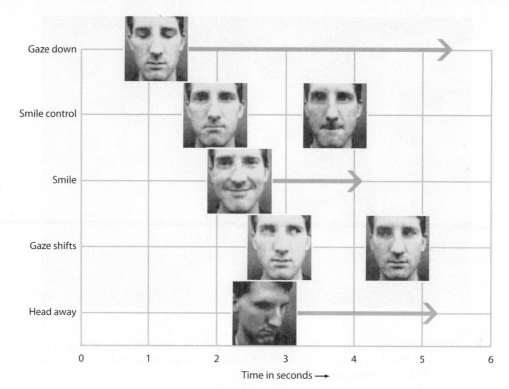

FIGURE 11.13

TYPICAL FACIAL EXPRESSIONS OF EMBARRASSMENT. The display of embarrassment involves a sequence of actions, each of which might serve a social function. First there is a smile, which may reflect amusement at one's own transgression. Then the eyes gaze away, as if to indicate a desire to escape the awkward situation. Smile control is an attempt to dampen the amusement, as well as looking downward and turning the head away. (Keltner, 1995)

Gaze down
Smile control
Smile
Gaze shifts
Head away

Time in seconds →

Emotion as a Process

Imagine you are hiking in the mountains and a cougar crosses your path. Your heart starts racing, your breathing speeds up, and you start sweating. You want to get away as fast as possible, but you are not sure if you should run or freeze. Very likely, your face looks like the one shown in Figure 11.14. You are frightened. Fear provides one example of how emotions quickly change our experience, physiology, and behavior. For decades psychologists debated which of these three aspects best defined what an emotion is. Most researchers today agree that emotions are characterized by all of these components, which unfold in time. The *emotion process* (see Figure 11.15) shows us how the components of emotion emerge (J. J. Gross, 2002; R. S. Lazarus, 1991; Levenson, 1994).

Emotions emerge in response to situations we encounter in the world or in our thoughts, called *antecedent events*. Not everyone responds to the same situation in the same way. An individual evaluates the antecedent event to determine whether it is potentially harmful or beneficial as per such criteria as safety or personal goals (R. S. Lazarus, 1991). Depending on the results of that appraisal, he or she may experience an emotional response.

The emotional response in turn produces changes in physiology, behavior, expression, and felt experience. The direction of the arrows moving from left to right in Figure 11.15 is only part of the story. As the reverse-curved arrow suggests, the process can move in the other direction as well. That is, the activation of facial and physiological responses might enhance the emotion, becoming yet another kind of input for a new emotional experience. Levenson (2003) points out that, in addition to the antecedent events that are external to us, there may be internal inputs into the emotion process, inputs provided by facial and physiological changes. Once we generate emotions, we sometimes attempt to modify them, regulate them, or make them go away, which in turn involves new appraisals and new responses. To some extent, then, the emotion process moves in a loop rather than in a single direction.

FIGURE 11.14

Most people would be likely to recognize this facial expression as fear.

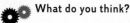 **What do you think?**

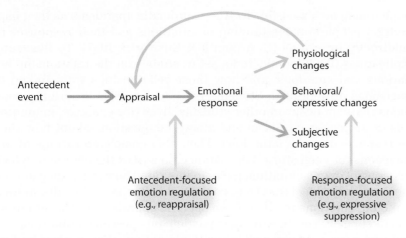

FIGURE 11.15

THE EMOTION PROCESS. Emotions start with an event that is appraised as relevant to one's goals. If the event is deemed relevant, an emotional response begins, which consists of physiological changes, behavioral and expressive changes, and subjective changes in feelings. Changes in the body's physiology, behavior, and subjective feelings then feed back to the appraisal process and become inputs for experiencing new emotions. Attempts to regulate (modify, change, or suppress) emotion can occur early or late in the emotion process.

Appraisal in the Emotion Process Whether an event or a situation leads to an emotion depends on how the person appraises it. **Appraisal** is the evaluation of a situation with respect to how relevant it is to one's own welfare (R. S. Lazarus, 1991). Appraisal need not be a conscious, deliberate thought process. Most of the time it probably occurs automatically, outside of awareness, and it may occur in an instant (Barrett, Ochsner, & Gross, 2007).

Appraisal drives the process by which emotions are elicited (Roseman, 1984; Scherer, Dan, & Flykt, 2006). It explains why the level of happiness expressed by Olympic athletes can be greater for winners of bronze medals (third place) than for winners of silver medal (second place; Medvec, Madey, & Gilovich, 1995). Bronze medalists can easily imagine an alternative outcome: They may not have even placed. Compared to that outcome, third is great. Silver medalists, on the other hand, can easily imagine having won first place! Compared to that outcome, second might be felt as disappointing.

Examples of appraisal dimensions include control (how much control you feel you have in a situation), agency (whether you or someone else made something happen), pleasantness, and fairness (Ellsworth & Scherer, 2003). The type of appraisal that occurs determines the type of the emotion generated. Fear, for instance, arises in situations of uncertainty and over which we feel we have little control (Arnold, 1960; Ellsworth & Scherer, 2003; R. S. Lazarus, 1991).

appraisal
The evaluation of a situation with respect to how relevant it is to one's own welfare; it drives the process by which emotions are elicited.

What frightens you? Many people are afraid of potentially threatening situations over which they have little control.

Although it may be impossible to study automatic appraisals as they happen, research on people's understanding of situations and their responses to them can indirectly inform us (C. A. Smith & Ellsworth, 1987). To illustrate, Tong and colleagues (2009) conducted a set of studies on the relationship between situations and emotions, and how those relationships were linked to certain dimensions of appraisal. Students read brief stories describing common situations that can occur in other students' lives (for example, managing the demands of an important class) and answered questions about how they would have responded to the situations. They also completed ratings of appraisal dimensions for each story. For instance, to assess the degree to which someone felt control over a situation, participants rated how much they agreed with comments such as "I feel that I can control what happens." Results showed that, as predicted, emotions resulted from specific appraisals of the situation. Sadness was likely in stories in which the participants perceived that they had little control and were not responsible for the situation (that is, they had no agency).

Regulation of Emotion   People can intentionally or unintentionally change their emotions or the extent to which they experience certain emotions. The term **emotion regulation** refers to the cognitive and behavioral efforts people use to modify their emotions. Figure 11.15 shows how attempts to regulate emotions may occur at the beginning or end of the emotion process (J. J. Gross, 1998; J. J. Gross, Richards, & John, 2006). An example of emotion regulation that can occur early in the emotion process is **reappraisal,** in which people reevaluate their views of an event so that a different emotion results. Rather than seeing your next midterm as an opportunity for failure, an outlook that might create fear or anxiety, you might reappraise the exam as a challenging opportunity to prove how much you have learned, an outlook that can lead to eager anticipation.

Another kind of emotion regulation operates when people want to make an unpleasant feeling go away. An example of this kind of strategy is **expressive suppression,** the deliberate attempt to inhibit the outward display of an emotion (J. J. Gross et al., 2006). In order to avoid a confrontation, you might literally bite your lip rather than tell your roommates that they are slobs for letting the dishes pile up. Instructing people to suppress their negative emotions can decrease the experience of negative emotion, but it increases activation of the sympathetic nervous system and sustains the emotional response (J. J. Gross & Levenson, 1997).

The Emotional Response   Whether processed consciously or automatically, emotional responses emerge from events appraised as relevant to one's safety or personal goals. As shown in Figure 11.15, the **emotional response** includes physiological, behavioral/expressive, and subjective changes.

Physiological Changes in Emotion   Emotions produce physiological changes, such as increases in heart rate and respiration rate. The physiological system responsible for changes during an emotional response is the autonomic nervous system (ANS), which governs structures and processes over which we have little conscious control, such as changes in heart rate and blood pressure and the release of hormones. The ANS plays a crucial role in emotional response because it activates other systems that are needed for action, including the circulatory and respiratory systems.

Once elicited, emotions engage the ANS almost immediately. For emotions that are concerned with survival and protection from harm, such as fear, the sympathetic branch of the ANS is activated. Sympathetic activity mobilizes body resources into an organized response to a real or imagined environmental

emotion regulation
The cognitive and behavioral efforts people make to modify their emotions.

reappraisal
An emotion regulation strategy in which one reevaluates an event so that a different emotion results.

expressive suppression
A response-focused strategy for regulating emotion that involves a deliberate attempt to inhibit the outward manifestation of an emotion.

emotional response
The physiological, behavioral/expressive, and subjective changes that occur when emotions are generated.

threat. The heart pumps blood rapidly to the muscles; oxygen intake in the lungs increases; and processes that are not immediately necessary for action, such as digestion, shut down, so that energy is conserved for more urgent body functions.

The patterns of ANS activity can vary, depending on the emotion elicited. Anger increases heart rate more than fear does; disgust slows the heart (Ekman, Levenson, & Friesen, 1983; Levenson, Ekman, & Friesen, 1990). Such autonomic nervous system changes appear to be common to people all over the world (Levenson et al., 1992; Tsai, Levenson, & Carstensen, 2000; Tsai et al., 2002). Cross-cultural data on the physiology of emotion support the view of emotions as evolutionarily old, as does evidence of emotion in nonhuman primates, other mammals, birds, and even fish (Paul, Harding, & Mendl, 2005).

Positive emotions engage the parasympathetic branch of the ANS, purportedly returning the body to a more relaxed, responsive state (Levenson, 2003). For example, Fredrickson and Levenson (1998) showed participants a fear-eliciting film and followed it with clips known to elicit sadness, amusement, contentment, or no emotions at all. They measured cardiovascular activity while the participants viewed the films and again afterward. Cardiovascular activation elicited by the negative film returned to baseline levels more quickly in people who saw a pleasant film (amusement or contentment) after the fear film than it did in those who saw films leading to sad or nonemotional conditions. This ability of positive emotions to "undo" the effects of negative emotional arousal by helping return the body to a state of relaxation may result from parasympathetic nervous system activation.

Behavioral-Expressive Changes in Emotion Emotions create expressive changes in the face and voice, as well as behavioral tendencies toward particular types of action (Frijda, 1986). People show their emotions—knowingly or not— through both verbal and nonverbal means, such as changes in facial behavior and vocal intonation. Although researchers have studied both facial and vocal expressions of emotion, the most extensive body of research has focused on facial expressions.

Facial Expression of Emotion Humans are predisposed to respond to faces. Newborn babies mimic the facial expressions of adults. At 5 months they can discriminate between different types of facial expressions of emotion; and by 1 year of age they rely on the faces of their caregivers to convey important information about how they might act (Meltzoff & Moore, 1977; Schwartz, Izard, & Ansul, 1985; Sorce et al., 1985). There are specialized neurons in the brain for responding to faces, and certain brain areas are specialized for particular facial expressions, such as fear (Adolphs et al., 1994, 2005; Kanwisher, 2000).

Much of what we know about facial expression of emotion was originally based on studies of people's ability to recognize emotion in the human face. Charles Darwin was the first modern thinker to formally propose that facial expressions reveal different emotions and offer a theory for the evolution of emotional expression in *The Expression of the Emotions in Man and Animals* (Darwin, 1872/1998). Darwin described in detail how people and animals display emotions through their faces and bodies.

It was not until the 1960s, however, that psychologists began conducting the research that directly addressed Darwin's claims. In his early studies of people's judgments of emotion in the human face, Silvan Tomkins showed participants numerous photographs of European Americans posing different emotions and asked them to decide which emotion may have been felt. Researchers obtained pretty strong evidence of agreement on the emotional meaning of those facial expressions, with roughly 70% or more of the

Is Leonardo da Vinci's **Mona Lisa** smiling out of pleasure or merely posing a smile in her portrait?

Do facial expressions of emotion have the same meaning in different cultural groups? What do you think this child is feeling?

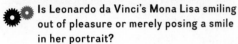

universal
Common to all human beings and seen in cultures all over the world.

respondents providing the same answer for each photo. Most people recognize facial expression similar to that in Figure 11.14 as fear. Similarly, when Ekman and Friesen showed Tomkins's pictures to people in the United States, Japan, Argentina, and Chile, there was a high degree of consensus on the emotional meanings of a core set of facial expressions (Ekman & Friesen, 1969). At about the same time, Carroll Izard's (1969) study and results also supported the high level of consensus on the meaning of facial expressions of emotion across numerous cultural groups. These studies and others backed Darwin's (1872/1998) assertion that the facial expressions of certain "basic" emotions, such as anger, disgust, fear, happiness, sadness, and surprise, are **universal,** or common to all human beings.

One problem with these early studies on emotion recognition, however, is that all the participants lived in literate, industrialized cultures. Maybe the findings of cross-cultural consistency in facial expression recognition reflected the spread of the popular media rather than the existence of a universal human skill. People in Japan and the United States might have agreed on the emotional meaning of certain expressions because they had seen portrayals of actors in movies. The only way to resolve this question was to collect data from preliterate people who were isolated from industrialized society, which is what Ekman did by studying an isolated, preliterate group: the Fore tribe from Papua New Guinea.

Ekman and his colleagues showed pictures of facial expressions of emotion—similar to those that had been used in other studies—to find out which emotions, if any, the Fore tribe members saw (Ekman, Sorenson, & Friesen, 1969). But how could he gather such data from a culture without a written language? After experimenting fairly unsuccessfully with a few different approaches, he settled on a technique that had been used with children, who also do not have a written language. The method involved presenting stories about emotional situations to New Guineans and showing them a set of three photographed faces per story. Examples of the stories are "He [she] is angry and about to fight" (which should lead participants to pick an "angry" face) or "She [he]

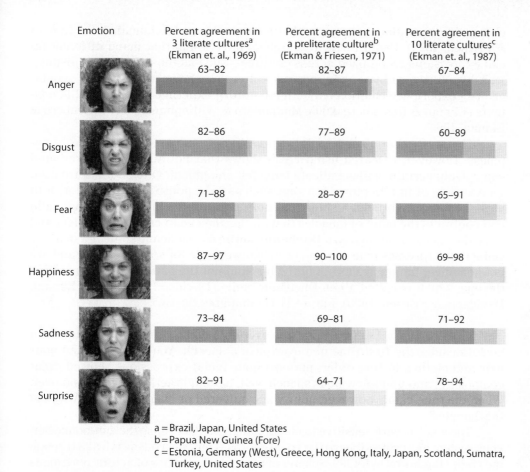

Emotion	Percent agreement in 3 literate cultures[a] (Ekman et. al., 1969)	Percent agreement in a preliterate culture[b] (Ekman & Friesen, 1971)	Percent agreement in 10 literate cultures[c] (Ekman et. al., 1987)
Anger	63–82	82–87	67–84
Disgust	82–86	77–89	60–89
Fear	71–88	28–87	65–91
Happiness	87–97	90–100	69–98
Sadness	73–84	69–81	71–92
Surprise	82–91	64–71	78–94

a = Brazil, Japan, United States
b = Papua New Guinea (Fore)
c = Estonia, Germany (West), Greece, Hong Kong, Italy, Japan, Scotland, Sumatra, Turkey, United States

FIGURE **11.16**

CONSISTENCY IN EXPRESSIONS OF BASIC EMOTION ACROSS LITERATE AND PRELITERATE CULTURES.

is looking at something that smells bad" (for disgust). Then the experimenter asked the listeners which of the three faces matched the story. With this method, the degree of consensus was much higher.

Both children and adult New Guineans consistently discriminated the "correct" face from other faces; that is, they consistently matched a given story with the face that would have been predicted, and the results matched the data from studies of people in literate cultures (Ekman & Friesen, 1971). Results showed that the range of agreement was relatively high for five of the six basic emotions (Ekman & Friesen, 1971; Ekman et al., 1969). Follow-up research conducted 20 years later showed similar high-level agreement across 10 literate cultures (Ekman et al., 1987). For summaries of facial recognition data across several cross-cultural studies, see Figure 11.16.

Universality does not require 100% consistency in people's recognition of emotion. Culture, gender, personality, and other contextual factors can influence how we interpret other people's facial expressions (Haidt & Keltner, 1999). In spite of the factors that pull for differences, there is a remarkable consistency in the human understanding of a core set of basic emotions.

Numerous studies that measure facial behavior from video show that many of the same expressions (and variations) recognized cross-culturally also occur in spontaneous behavior (Ekman & Rosenberg, 2005). The **Facial Action Coding System (FACS)** is a widely used method by which coders describe the

Challenge Your Assumptions

True or False? People in different cultures express emotion differently on their faces.

False: There is widespread universality in how basic emotions get expressed on the human face.

Facial Action Coding System (FACS)
A widely used method for measuring all the observable muscular movements that are possible in the human face.

observable muscular movements that are possible in the human face (Ekman & Friesen, 1978). Using FACS, researchers have found that many different facial expressions recognized across cultures—such as those for anger, disgust, fear, happiness, sadness, and surprise—are also shown when people spontaneously experience emotions in both laboratory experiments and real-life contexts (Ekman & Rosenberg, 2005; Matsumoto & Willingham, 2006; Rosenberg & Ekman, 1994).

The most recognizable facial expression of emotion is the smile of happiness. However, research using FACS shows that not all smiles are created equal. Only certain smiles indicate truly felt enjoyment. Other smiles are used for a variety of interpersonal reasons, such as to be polite in conversation or to mask negative emotions. A smile that both pulls up the lip corners diagonally and contracts the band of muscles that circles the eye to create crow's feet and raise the cheeks is known as a **Duchenne smile.** A Duchenne smile is a genuine smile that expresses true enjoyment. When we smile for social reasons and are not genuinely happy, we use only the lips and not the band of muscles around the eye, which is called a non-Duchenne smile (Davidson et al., 1990; Ekman, Davidson, & Friesen, 1990). Figure 11.17 compares the two.

Vocal Expression of Emotion   Have you ever noticed how your voice can betray you? Consider the first time you ever gave a speech. You may have had your hair and clothes in fine order; perhaps your facial expressions showed great composure; and you knew your speech well, having practiced it over and over. When the time came, however, your voice quivered or even squeaked! Why did this happen?

The voice is very sensitive to emotional arousal, because the autonomic nervous system has projections to the vocal chords. Thus, nervousness leaks through the voice (Bachorowski, 1999; Scherer et al., 1991). In studies of actors' portrayals of emotions through spoken nonsense sentences, certain emotions (anger, fear, joy) were associated with higher pitch and volume, while sadness was associated with lower pitch and volume (Scherer et al., 1991).

We have discussed how people can recognize emotion from the face, but can you tell what someone is feeling simply by hearing vocal changes? Even though cross-cultural research reveals cultural variability, vocal emotion recognition appears to be a basic human social skill (Scherer, Banse, & Wallbott, 2001). Research suggests that people do a fairly good job of recognizing emotion from the voice alone. When asked to provide what they think are vocalizations for each of 22 different recorded emotional states, people can guess which emotion the speaker is trying to convey (Simon-Thomas et al., 2009).

There may be differences among positive emotion vocalizations (Simon-Thomas et al., 2009). For instance, laughter is a well-known vocal expression of emotion. Studies of people watching funny films show that there are several different types of laughs (Bachorowski, Smoski, & Owren, 2001). Some people grunt or snort, while others open their mouths with a big guffaw. Voiced laughs—those that involve vibration of the vocal fold and typically involve expelling air out of the mouth—generate more positive ratings when evaluated on such features as likeability, sexiness, and friendliness (Bachorowski & Owren, 2001). Simply put, voiced laughs make people happy.

Vocal and facial response systems can work together in emotion expression. The same vocalization can sound different depending on the speaker's facial expression. This happens because lip movements affect vocal characteristics. You can actually hear a smile or a frown, as people can reliably distinguish between laughs made with these various expressions on the face (Bachorowski, 1999).

Duchenne smile
A smile that expresses true enjoyment, involving both the muscles that pull up the lip corners diagonally and those that contract the band of muscles encircling the eye.

FIGURE **11.17**

A DUCHENNE SMILE VERSUS A NON-DUCHENNE SMILE. Both photos depict a smile of the same intensity, but they differ in the involvement of the muscles around the eyes.

Which one is a Duchenne, or true enjoyment, smile?

Subjective Experience of Emotion The third component of the emotional response is referred to as the **subjective experience of emotion,** which refers to the quality of our conscious experience during an emotional response. When people talk about how an emotion *feels,* they are referring to subjective experience. Each emotion creates a unique feeling: Anger feels different from sadness, which feels different from happiness. The subjective aspect of emotion draws on bodily changes, as well as effects on cognition, for emotions can activate associations with images and memories of significant events.

subjective experience of emotion The changes in the quality of conscious experience that occur during emotional responses.

What produces subjective feelings of emotion? For centuries theorists have argued over this question. Perhaps the most influential theory was proposed by William James (1884) and Carl Lange (1885/1992). The **James-Lange theory of emotion** says that our perception of the physiological changes that accompany emotions creates the subjective emotional experience. Without the perception of bodily changes, they argued, there is no emotional experience. Moreover, the changes that accompany different emotional states are unique. We experience fear as feeling different from sadness because we perceive different body changes for each emotion—in short, "I am trembling, and therefore I am afraid; or I feel a lump in my throat, and therefore I am sad."

James-Lange theory of emotion The idea that it is the perception of the physiological changes that accompany emotions that produces the subjective emotional experience.

The James-Lange theory is not without its critics, most notable among them Walter Cannon (1927), who argued that feedback from bodily organs is not specific enough to account for the varieties of emotional experience. Still, several lines of evidence support the James-Lange view that sensory feedback from physiologically activated body systems plays a role in emotional experience. When people in many cultures are asked to identify the body sensations associated with emotions, they differentiate among several emotional states. For instance, "stomach sensations" are associated most strongly with disgust, and sadness with a lump in the throat (Breugelmans et al., 2005; see Figure 11.18).

Research on facial feedback also supports the idea that feedback from body sensations creates emotional experience. The **facial feedback hypothesis** posits that sensory feedback from the facial musculature during expression affects emotional experience (Tomkins, 1962). Sensory neurons from the face do innervate key emotion areas of the brain, especially the amygdala (Hennenlotter et al., 2009). In fact, research suggests that our facial expressions enhance our emotional feelings. People report feeling a particular emotion when they pose on their faces the muscular movements of that emotion expression (Strack, Martin,

facial feedback hypothesis Sensory feedback from the facial musculature during expression affects emotional experience.

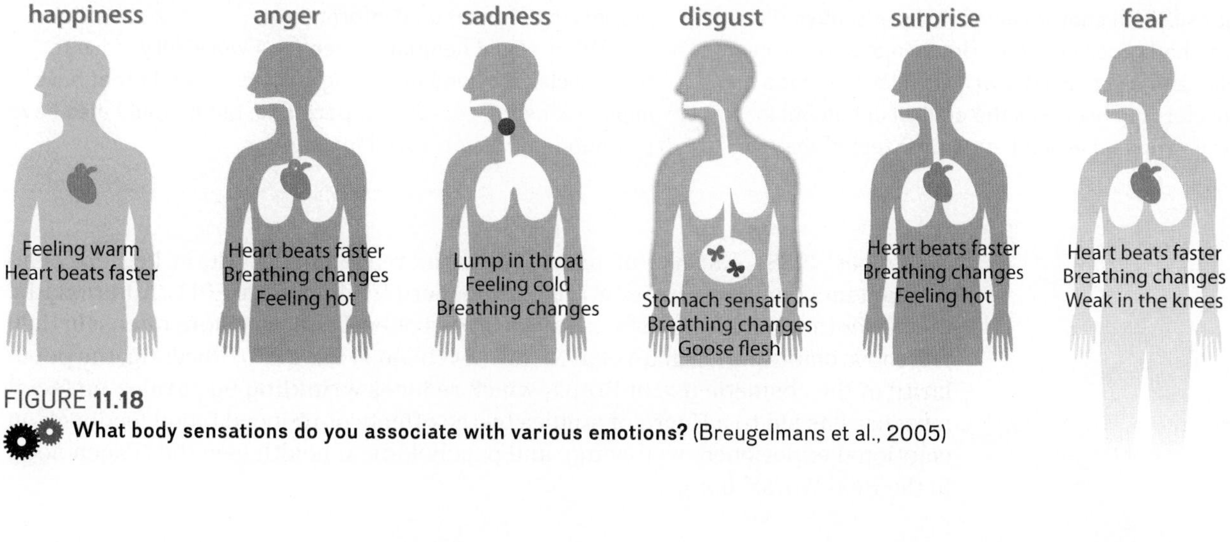
happiness
Feeling warm
Heart beats faster
anger
Heart beats faster
Breathing changes
Feeling hot
sadness
Lump in throat
Feeling cold
Breathing changes
disgust
Stomach sensations
Breathing changes
Goose flesh
surprise
Heart beats faster
Breathing changes
Feeling hot
fear
Heart beats faster
Breathing changes
Weak in the knees

FIGURE **11.18**
What body sensations do you associate with various emotions? (Breugelmans et al., 2005)

Psychology in the Real World

Botox and Emotion

Botox is the trade name of a preparation of a potentially lethal neurotoxin called *botulism toxin,* a protein produced by a bacterium found in spoiled and improperly canned foods (Allergan, Inc., 2013; Rossetto et al., 2013). Botulism toxin causes muscular paralysis by blocking the release of acetylcholine at neuromuscular synapses, which can be fatal if the involuntary muscles of breathing are affected (Rossetto et al., 2013).

How did the voluntary injection of a poison become the most popular cosmetic procedure in the general population (Lorenc et al., 2013)? In 1989, Clark and Berris documented the usefulness of micro-doses of botulism toxin as a treatment for people who had developed facial asymmetries due to partial paralysis from stroke or other health problems. They also noticed a diminution of wrinkles in the paralyzed areas, and the cosmetic applications became obvious. Botox reduces wrinkles by paralyzing facial muscles by relaxing muscular contractions underlying facial creases. As a result, the area looks smoother and younger. The effects wear off after about 6 months or so, at which time many people get new injections. Botox is commonly injected into the area between the eyebrows where short, vertical wrinkles, often referred to as "glabellar frown lines," appear. Under normal conditions, the muscles (most notably, the *corrugator* muscles) underlying these wrinkles pull the eyebrows together and down. These actions occur in the expression of many negative emotions, including anger, sadness, and fear.

What are the consequences of these muscles not working for months at a time? As we know from research on the facial feedback hypothesis, sensory feedback from the facial muscles enhances emotional experience (Dimberg & Söderkvist, 2011). Paralyzing facial muscles would impair facial feedback and possibly diminish emotional experience. Initial studies found that Botox does reduce negative emotional experience (Alam et al., 2008). For example, Davis and colleagues (2010) showed emotionally evocative films to people who had received either Botox injections or injections with Restalyne, a cosmetic wrinkle filler that does not paralyze muscles (the filler was the control condition) in the glabellar region and around the crow's feet of the eyes

(an area that can be involved in smiles of enjoyment; Ekman et al., 1990). Although both groups experienced emotions, Botox (but not Restalyne) reduced the intensity of *both* positive and negative emotion. The effects of Botox on the glabellar area have been found to be useful in the treatment of depression in clinical trials (Wollmer et al., 2012), but the effects of crow's feet injections on positive emotion suggest we should be careful about where Botox is used.

Botox-induced paralysis of facial muscles not only affects the facial expressions and experience of emotion, it can also affect one's ability to read emotions in others. Injection with Botox impairs people's ability to read others' facial expressions of emotions, most likely by impairing facial mimicry (Neal & Chartrand, 2011). Mimicry occurs when people imitate the behavior of others without realizing it. Facial mimicry, probably by means of facial feedback, contributes to our ability to recognize emotional expressions in others and plays an important role in the development of empathy (Chartrand & Dalton, 2009). By extension, we can see how long-term Botox use might impair socioemotional capacities.

The absence of facial movement in the processing of emotional information seems to extend beyond our ability to recognize other people's facial expressions—it may play an important role in how we process emotional information of all types. Havas and colleagues (2010) asked women before and after they received Botox injections to read happy, sad, and angry sentences. After each sentence, the participant was asked to respond to a simple yes/no comprehension question, which could be answered with a single keystroke. The researchers were interested in how long it took the participants to make the keystroke. Reaction times were significantly longer after Botox injections, which suggests that the inhibition of facial feedback from Botox impairs the processing of emotional information.

What would happen if injections were very close to the muscles involved in smiling? Not only would that have implications for personal experience, but it would also have profound effects on social interaction.

& Stepper, 1988). Ratings of pleasantness increase when certain key emotion-relevant facial muscles are contracted (Dimberg & Söderkvist, 2011). Additionally, the better that people pose facial expressions of emotion, the more intensely they feel those emotions (Ekman et al., 1983; Levenson et al., 1990). Recently, the popularity of the cosmetic use of Botox, which reduces wrinkling by paralyzing facial muscles, has led to a flurry of studies on the effects of reduced facial feedback on emotional experience, well-being, and psychological health (see the "Psychology in the Real World" box).

Emotion and the Brain

So far we have examined the emotion process in detail, from the eliciting event to the appraisal mechanisms that bring forth the emotional response to the resulting changes in physiology, expression, and experience. Missing from this picture is the brain, which participates in every aspect of the emotion process.

Affective neuroscience, the field devoted to studying the brain's role in emotion, is rapidly growing. Most current evidence tells us that emotional information is processed in brain circuits that involve several brain structures, and emotion processing is highly interlinked with cognitive processing (Pessoa, 2008). Although there is no main emotion center in the brain, we can identify some key areas for emotion processing, including the amygdala and the prefrontal cortex (see Figure 11.19).

Anatomically, the amygdala has connections with many important brain regions, including structures that appear to be involved in emotion and memory: the hypothalamus, which controls the ANS; the hippocampus, which plays a crucial role in memory; the thalamus, which receives information from the sense organs; and the cerebral cortex. The amygdala appears to contribute to appraisal of the emotional significance of stimuli, with a specialized function for noticing fear-relevant information (Johansen et al., 2011; Öhman, 2002; Phelps & LeDoux, 2005).

Much of the research on the amygdala has centered on its pivotal role in quick appraisals during threatening or fear-inducing situations (LeDoux, 1996, 2000). Along these lines, Joseph LeDoux and his colleagues have used classical conditioning of fear in rats as a model for studying emotion in the human brain (Johansen et al., 2011; Wilensky et al., 2006). In their experiment, a rat is exposed to a tone, which is emotionally neutral at first. Then the tone is repeatedly paired with an aversive stimulus, an electric shock (the unconditioned stimulus, or UCS). After repeated pairings with the shock, the tone itself becomes a fear-eliciting stimulus (the conditioned stimulus, or CS). When the researchers examined the circuitry of fear conditioning in the rat brain, they found that the side and middle of the amygdala are most active in learning to be afraid of the tone (Johansen et al., 2011; Wilensky et al., 2006).

There is evidence of the amygdala's role in fear in humans as well (Johansen et al., 2011; Mühlberger et al., 2011). People with damaged amygdalae do not show normal physiological reactions under fear conditioning. They tend to trust faces that most people find to be untrustworthy and have trouble recognizing facial expressions of fear, especially in the eyes (Adolphs et al., 1994, 2005; Adolphs, Tranel, & Damasio, 1998; Phelps & LeDoux, 2005). Brain imaging studies of people with intact brains reveal increased amygdala activation when they are exposed to fear faces, and an inactive amygdala when they view other facial expressions of emotion (Breiter et al., 1996). Whereas certain regions of the amygdala are more involved in fear, other regions are more involved in anger and rage (Panksepp, 2000). Tumors of the amygdala have been found in violent criminals, such as in Charles Whitman, who climbed the tower at the University of Texas in 1966 and, in a 90-minute shooting spree, killed 19 people and wounded 38 (*Charles J. Whitman Catastrophe*, 1966, cited in Joseph, n.d.).

The case of Phineas Gage, the 19th-century railroad worker who survived a severe injury to his prefrontal cortex (see Chapter 3), provided early evidence of the importance of the prefrontal cortex in emotion and personality. Gage's prefrontal cortex injury transformed him from a relatively mild-mannered man into an impatient, easily enraged individual. More recently, studies show that the prefrontal cortex is one of the more active regions of the brain in the

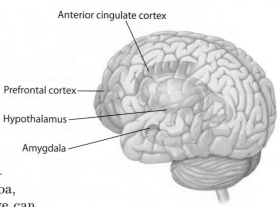

Anterior cingulate cortex

Prefrontal cortex

Hypothalamus

Amygdala

FIGURE 11.19

THE FOUR MAIN REGIONS OF THE EMOTIONAL BRAIN. No single area of the brain is responsible for emotion, but the amygdala, prefrontal cortex, anterior cingulate cortex, and hypothalamus play key roles in the way we experience emotion and remember emotional experiences.

experience of emotions. Damage to the left prefrontal cortex results in depression (P. L. Morris et al., 1996; Sackeim et al., 1982). According to EEG studies that measure cortical activity, clinically depressed people show less activity in the left prefrontal cortex than do nondepressed people (Davidson, 2001; Herrington et al., 2010).

Due to its involvement in planning, impulse control, and working memory, the prefrontal cortex plays a role in the appraisal and reappraisal of emotion (Etkin, Egner, & Kalish, 2011; B. L. Miller & Cummings, 1999; Miyake et al., 2000). Kevin Ochsner and his colleagues (2002) reported that the amygdala is more involved in determining whether a situation merits an emotional response at all, whereas the prefrontal cortex may be more involved in determining options for response, regulation, or reappraisal. Given that there are neural connections between the prefrontal cortex and the amygdala, this finding and others like it may indicate that certain regions of the prefrontal cortex influence the emotional responses produced by the amygdala (Davidson, 2004; Pessoa, 2008; Pessoa, Padmala, & Morland, 2005). Increasing evidence suggests that the medial prefrontal cortex is crucially involved in evaluating the personal relevance of events (Abraham, 2013), which is, in essence, appraisal.

Other regions of the brain are involved in emotions as well (Dalgleish, 2004). A meta-analysis of more than 55 brain imaging studies reports that the anterior cingulate cortex (ACC) is active when people either recall or imagine emotional experiences (Phan et al., 2002; also see Figure 11.19). New evidence points to the ACC being closely linked to the appraisal and expression of emotion (Etkin et al., 2011). The ACC is also the brain region that is active in both physical pain and the pain of rejection or exclusion (N. Eisenberger et al., 2003; Etkin et al., 2011).

What happens in the brain when we experience positive emotions? Several studies suggest that the left prefrontal cortex is more involved in positive emotions than the right (Davidson, 2004; Davidson et al., 1990; Mühlberger et al., 2011). These regions are primarily involved in emotions that have approach components (emotions that impel the organism to move toward something or someone), which includes the negative emotion of anger as well as positive emotions (Harmon-Jones, 2003). The hypothalamus also appears to be a pleasure or reward center, because animals will forgo food and drink to receive stimulation there (Olds & Milner, 1954). Similarly, humans report feeling pleasure when this region is stimulated (Heath, 1975).

The neuropeptide oxytocin is well known for its role in lactation and bonding in mammals, especially females (A. Campbell, 2008). We now know that it plays a broad role in positive emotional states, especially those involving affiliation or connection with others (H. Lee et al., 2009). When adults are given doses of oxytocin, both males and females are more likely to want to be around other people (A. Campbell, 2008), to help others (Ebstein et al., 2010), to cooperate with others (Declerck, Boone, & Kiyonari, 2010), and to show greater generosity toward others (Zak, Stanton, & Ahmadi, 2007). Also, oxytocin makes people better at recognizing facial expressions of happiness, especially subtle ones (which are harder to read), but not the other emotions. It's as if oxytocin enhances responsiveness to positive emotional states, especially when the information is subtle (Marsh, Yu, Pine, & Blair, 2010).

Finally, the insula is the brain structure most involved in interoception, or the perception of

Connection

The prefrontal cortex plays a key role in working memory by evaluating sensory information and designating it for storage or disposal.

See "Pathways of Short-Term Memory in the Hippocampus and Prefrontal Cortex," Chapter 7, "Memory," p. 271.

What happens when we experience positive emotions?

sensations arising within the body. In fMRI studies, the insula is active during the experience of pain and empathy for another's pain (Singer et al., 2004). This brain structure also appears to play an important role in disgust, which is an emotion associated with a high degree of internal bodily sensations. Visualizing disgusting scenes leads to activation of the insula as well as the ACC (Schienle, Shäfer, & Vaitl, 2008). Insular activity is reduced when women attempt to regulate their disgust with reappraisal (Giuliani, Drabant, & Gross, 2010; Goldin et al., 2008). Certain areas of the insula are so specific to disgust that they show activation to facial expressions of disgust but not to those of distaste (von dem Hagen et al., 2009).

How Culture Impacts Emotion Expression

The research on facial expression recognition from New Guinea led to an integration of the two competing perspectives, culture differences and universality. Soon after returning from New Guinea, Ekman (1972) proposed the **neurocultural theory of emotion** to account for the fact that certain aspects of emotion, such as the facial expressions and physiological changes of basic emotions, are similar in all humans, whereas other aspects, such as how people appraise situations and regulate their emotion expressions in front of others, vary from one culture to another.

Anthropologists have offered numerous examples of cultural variability in emotion expression—such as the case of Samurai women who smiled broadly after learning that their husbands or sons had died in battle (Ekman, 1973). Such examples suggest that facial expressions of happiness and sadness are not universal. How can the findings on the universality of facial expressions jibe with the fact that there are cultural differences in emotions? Ekman and Friesen (Ekman, 1972; Friesen, 1972) proposed the concept of display rules to address this dilemma. **Display rules** are learned norms or rules, often taught very early, about when it is appropriate to show certain expressions of emotion and to whom one should show them (Ekman, 1972).

neurocultural theory of emotion
Elkman's explanation that some aspects of emotion, such as facial expressions and physiological changes associated with emotion, are universal and others, such as emotion regulation, are culturally derived.

display rules
Learned norms or rules, often taught very early, about when it is appropriate to express certain emotions and to whom one should show them.

Culture affects emotion expression in many ways. *Schadenfreude* is a German expression that combines the words for "harm or injury" (*schaden*) and "joy" (*freude*) and is used to describe the times when people gain pleasure or joy from other people's misfortune or injury, such as when a rival gets hurt or when someone we don't like is humiliated. It is even seen in slapstick comedy.

As it turns out, Samurai women were expected to be proud of a son or husband who had been killed in battle, and the society required them to display joy at the news. In the United States we expect winners not to boast, losers not to mope, and men not to cry in public (although this last norm is changing).

The first empirical support for display rules came from a study comparing disgust expressions in American and Japanese students (Ekman, 1972; Friesen, 1972). Both groups viewed a film showing a very graphic medical procedure, but in two different conditions: in the presence of an authority figure and alone. When alone, both groups felt perfectly comfortable expressing the obvious response—disgust. When in the presence of an authority figure, the Japanese students did not show disgust, and they masked their responses with non-Duchenne (fake) smiles. American students, however, showed about the same level of disgust in both conditions. The expressive differences between groups emerged in a situation in which the cultures had very different norms about expression, but not in the solo viewing condition. More recent research on display rules and expression supports and extends these original findings (Matsumoto, Yoo & Fontaine, 2008). There are notable variations in the intensity of facial expressions of emotion across cultures, even across smaller groups, such as European Americans (Tsai & Chentsova-Dutton, 2003). Overwhelmingly, people across many cultures show remarkably similar emotion displays in highly emotional situations—in the Olympics, for example (Matsumoto & Willingham, 2006).

Darwin (1872/1998) asserted that facial expressions evolved due to their functional role in survival, which if true would speak to why some expressions may be universal. For instance, the expression of fear, with its raised brows and widely opened eyes, increased the scope of vision for someone looking for options for escape. Recent research shows that people posing fear faces actually see better in tests of peripheral vision and quickness of eye movements. These appearance changes may actually reveal the function of the fear face hypothesized by Darwin—to enable people to respond more quickly to danger (Susskind et al., 2008).

There seem to be some universals in vocalizations of emotion as well. Motherese, the sing-songy manner with which mothers speak to their babies, shows remarkable consistency worldwide and may be a unique adaptation particularly suited to infant perception (Fernald, 1992). Nonverbal vocalizations of emotion, such as grunts, retching noises, and laughs, also seem to be recognized cross-culturally (Sauter et al., 2010). In a study using methods very similar to those Ekman used with a preliterate New Guinea culture to classify facial expressions, Sauter and colleagues (2010) asked Namibians to match voices with the emotion stories that may have elicited them. Namibians and native English speakers made remarkably similar judgments, despite being from widely separate cultures.

In sum, when and how we express emotion on our face is determined both by innate, biologically determined factors and by culturally learned influences, such as display rules, that may vary from one culture to another. The evidence strongly suggests that all humans share a core set of basic facial expressions of emotion.

Gender and Emotion

If cultural factors can influence emotion expression, what about gender, which is both culturally and biologically driven? People all around the world think women are more emotional than men (Fischer & Manstead, 2000), but what do the data say? An overwhelming amount of data speak to no sex differences in emotion, but a few areas stand out as potential areas of difference: the verbal description of emotion, facial expression, and brain physiology.

Women talk more about emotions than men do. In a study of older married couples discussing an area of conflict in their marriage, the women were more likely to use words expressing distress and anger, whereas the men were more likely to withdraw from conflict (Levenson, Carstensen, & Gottman, 1994). Women are more likely to describe their reactions to a particular experience with more refinement than men, using phrases such as "I felt angry and upset" rather than the more general phrase "I felt bad" (Barrett et al., 2000).

Women outperform men in accurately recognizing facial expressions of emotion, especially more subtle emotion expressions (Hall & Matsumoto, 2004; Hoffmann et al., 2010; Merten, 2005). This benefit may extend beyond face recognition. Collignon and colleagues (2010) compared men's and women's processing of emotional information about fear and disgust from several channels: the face alone, the voice alone, and both together. Women outperformed men in the recognition of emotion across all three modes of presentation, but this is emotion recognition. What about actual emotional behavior when one is experiencing emotions? In general, women smile more often than men (LaFrance, Hecht, & Paluk, 2003). Otherwise, there is very little evidence of consistent sex differences in the facial expression of emotion (J. J. Gross & John, 1998).

Women tend to talk about emotions more than men do, but there is little difference in the facial expressions of men and women during emotional experiences.

A few studies have noted sex differences in how the brain processes emotions. Exposure to pictures of animal or human attacks provokes greater amygdala activation in men than in women, which suggests a greater tendency toward aggressive action in men (Schienle et al., 2008). Also, during efforts to regulate emotion by cognitive reappraisal, men and women show different patterns of brain activation, which suggests that men and women may use different brain areas to modulate their emotional responses (Domes et al., 2010). A recent meta-analysis of many different studies reported that women in general show greater left amygdala activation to fear and negative affect, whereas men show greater left amygdala activity to positive emotion (J. S. Stevens & Hamann, 2012). Further research is needed, however, to fully appreciate the meaning of these differences. Generally, the similarities between the sexes in terms of emotion and the brain outweigh the differences (T. D. Wagner & Ochsner, 2005).

Emotional Intelligence

Culture and gender can shape emotional behavior, but there are individual differences in the way people use and regulate their emotions. Varying emotional skills suggest the existence of an underlying emotional intelligence that varies among people, as with IQ.

In the mid-1990s Daniel Goleman published the book *Emotional Intelligence*, which popularized the idea that emotional skills are crucial in determining how well one does in life—both professionally and personally. Goleman (1995) drew heavily on research by Peter Salovey and John Mayer, who had introduced the concept of emotional intelligence in 1990 (Salovey & Mayer, 1990). **Emotional intelligence** is the ability to recognize emotions in oneself and others, empathic understanding, and the skills for regulating emotions in oneself and others, which may be at least as important to one's success in life as academic achievement.

A natural application of this work is in the field of education. Researchers have taught schoolchildren strategies for regulating emotion in order to reduce

emotional intelligence
The ability to recognize emotions in oneself and others, empathic understanding, and the skills for regulating emotions in oneself and others.

maladaptive behavior and improve academic performance; these strategies are referred to as *socioemotional learning,* or SEL (Conduct Problems Prevention Research Group, 1999a, 1999b; Kam, Greenberg, & Kusché, 2004). Typically, IQ is seen as the best predictor of school performance. We now know that training in emotional skills not only improves emotional behavior and functioning but also enhances cognitive performance as well as school performance (M. J. Hogan et al., 2010).

One groundbreaking SEL program is PATHS (Providing Alternative Thinking Strategies), developed by Mark Greenberg and Carol Kusché (M. T. Greenberg & Kusché, 1998; Kusché & Greenberg, 1994). The PATHS program gives teachers a detailed curriculum for improving children's emotional awareness and regulation skills and for enhancing their social competence. Research in which classrooms were randomly assigned to receive the PATHS curriculum or not (thereby continuing as usual) shows that PATHS leads to improvements in social and emotional skills in high-risk children, a reduction of aggressive behaviors in both normal and special-needs children, fewer depressive symptoms in special-needs kids, and improvements in classroom functioning (Conduct Problems Prevention Research Group, 1999a, 1999b; Kam et al., 2004). Other prevention programs, such as Head Start, have also applied the theory and methods of emotion research to decrease behavior problems in schools, and initial results are promising (Izard et al., 2004).

More than a decade after the implementation of major SEL programs, it is possible to see how the development of socioemotional learning might be linked to academic success. A large-scale meta-analysis of more than 500 studies shows that SEL programs significantly improve children's academic performance (Durlak et al., 2007). Specifically, children who participate in these programs have better attendance and exhibit less disruptive classroom behavior; they like school more and have higher GPAs.

Emotional intelligence may be an enduring characteristic or skill—like other forms of intelligence. Several questionnaires are designed to measure emotional intelligence, much as intelligence tests have traditionally been used to measure IQ. Two such instruments are the EQ-I (Bar-On, 2004) and the Mayer-Salovey-Caruso Emotional Intelligence Test, or MSCEIT (J. D. Mayer et al., 2003). With such tools, researchers can look at the relationship between emotional intelligence scores and other academic and nonacademic variables. Such trait measures of emotional intelligence correlate with higher GPA in adolescent boys and girls (M. J. Hogan et al., 2010), less job burnout in teachers (Platsidou, 2010), better coping with stress (Mikolajczak & Luminet, 2008), and improvements in mental and physical health (Schutte et al., 2007).

Quick Quiz 11.2: Emotion

1. The fact that sexual orgasm cannot occur unless the areas of the brain involved in fear and anxiety are shut down illustrates what basic feature of emotions versus drives?
   a. Drives have supremacy over emotions.
   b. Emotions can override biological drives.
   c. Emotions and drives serve similar masters.
   d. Drives must be resolved before emotions can motivate behavior.

2. Which of the following is NOT a self-conscious emotion?
   a. pride
   b. embarrassment
   c. hostility
   d. shame

3. According to the view of emotions as a process, _____ drive(s) the process by which emotions are elicited.
   a. emotional responses
   b. expressive changes
   c. physiological changes
   d. appraisal

4. Which of the following is NOT a basic emotion?
   a. fear
   b. happiness
   c. disgust
   d. shame

5. The social norm set forth by our culture, which says that winners should not gloat, is an example of a(n)
   a. display rule.
   b. human universal.
   c. affective trail.
   d. antecedent event.

6. The _____ appears to play a very important role in appraisal of the emotional significance of stimuli, with a specialized function of noticing fear-relevant information.
   a. amygdala
   b. hypothalamus
   c. prefrontal cortex
   d. insula

7. Which kind of emotion phrases are women more apt to use than men?
   a. more general comments, such as "I feel bad"
   b. more specific comments, such as "I am upset and angry"
   c. more affective imagery, such as "my fear is blue and cold"
   d. phrases such as "I will blow my top!"

Answers can be found at the end of the chapter.

Bringing It All Together
Making Connections in Motivation and Emotion
Living a Satisfied and Well-Lived Life

Emotion and motivation go together. Both are activated when issues of well-being, survival, and appetite are involved (Lang & Bradley, 2010). We are motivated and driven to keep doing things that are beneficial to our well-being. When we achieve important goals that we were driven to work on, we feel happy and/or proud. Likewise, if we fail, we experience sadness, anger, anxiety, or depression.

What do we want out of life? For many of us the answer is happiness and a good life. Two topics that integrate much of what we have discussed on motivation and emotion are living a satisfied life and living a flourishing life (eudemonia).

Motivation, Emotion, and a Satisfied Life
The word *happiness* often refers to a brief emotion, but it can also refer to **life satisfaction,** our overall evaluation of our own lives and how we are doing (Diener et al., 1999). Psychologists consider life satisfaction to be a subset of **subjective well-being,** which also includes satisfaction in domains such as career, family, finances, and social networks. Maslow's hierarchical model of motivation offers a useful framework for a discussion of motivation and happiness, since both basic and higher-level needs contribute to life satisfaction.

Basic Needs and Happiness
It is a well-known adage that money cannot buy happiness, but basic needs must be met for a person to be relatively satisfied with life. Accordingly, industrialized countries have higher levels of well-being than nonindustrialized countries, because those in industrialized nations are more likely to have food and shelter (see Figure 11.20). In modern society, we require money to buy food, clothes, and shelter.

At a national level, in the early stages of a country's development, increased income makes people happier with their lives. After a relatively modest level of increased income, however, money makes little difference and may even be a hindrance to happiness. In general, the higher a country's gross national product (GNP), the higher its well-being, but there are many exceptions, especially in Latin America. Countries such as Mexico and Colombia are just as happy as countries such as Denmark, Iceland, and Switzerland, in spite of having only half their per-person GNP. Moreover, when absolute income rose in the United States from the late 1940s to the late 1990s, well-being and life satisfaction stayed constant (Diener & Seligman, 2004).

At the individual level, there is a modest and complex relationship between income and overall life satisfaction as well. Having more money does make people slightly happier,

life satisfaction
Our overall evaluation of our lives; an aspect of subjective well-being.

subjective well-being
A state consisting of life satisfaction, domain satisfactions, and positive and negative affect.

Challenge Your Assumptions
True or False? More money leads to greater happiness.
Somewhat True, Somewhat False: Modest gains in income lead to higher levels of happiness; after that, there is no increase.

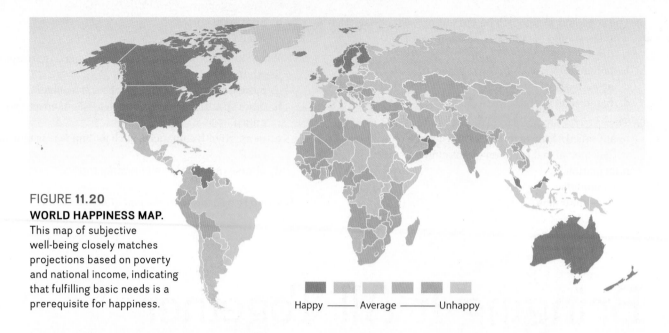

FIGURE **11.20**

WORLD HAPPINESS MAP.
This map of subjective well-being closely matches projections based on poverty and national income, indicating that fulfilling basic needs is a prerequisite for happiness.

Happy ——— Average ——— Unhappy

but this is true only for those driven by money (Diener et al., 1999; Nickerson et al., 2003). The relationship between spending money and being happy depends on whom you are spending. In an experiment, people assigned randomly to spend money on others were happier than those who spent it on themselves (Dunn, Aknin, & Norton, 2008).

Diet and weight also relate to overall happiness in various ways. First, having a healthy diet is associated with high life satisfaction (Due et al., 1991; Valois et al., 2003). On the other hand, being overweight—having a body mass index higher than 25—is associated with low life satisfaction (Ball, Crawford, & Kenardy, 2004; Nieman et al., 2000; Sarlio-Lähteenkorva, 2001; Zullig, Pun, & Huebner, 2007). Second, long-term weight loss, which less than 10% of dieters are able to maintain, is related to increases in life satisfaction (Korkeila et al., 1998; Valois et al., 2003). Obese people who have had gastric bypass surgery experience enhanced well-being after their procedure (Bocchieri Riccardi, 2007).

Having a satisfying sex life can be a source of overall happiness and well-being. A worldwide survey of more than 27,000 men and women from 29 countries found a positive relationship between how happy people were in their lives in general and how happy they were in their sexual lives (Laumann et al., 2006). Subjective well-being and sexual satisfaction were highest in European and Western cultures (e.g., Germany, Austria, Spain, Canada, and the United States).

Higher Needs and Happiness

Once a person or a country crosses the $12,000 per-person-per-year GNP, close relationships matter most for overall levels of happiness (Headey, 2008). This would explain why people from Denmark are consistently the happiest people on the planet. The Danish are more interested in fostering healthy relationships than in increasing their personal wealth or climbing the career ladder (Christensen, Herskind, & Vaupel, 2006).

Bruce Headey (2008) reported in a 20-year longitudinal study that people who value noncompetitive goals, such as spending time with a spouse, children, and friends, tend to become happier and more satisfied with life over time. However, people who most value competitive achievement goals, such as career advancement and material gains, actually decrease in happiness over time. When the main goal is monetary or career-advancing, all that people have to look forward to after they achieve their goals is more competition—not a recipe for happiness and well-being.

Another higher-level need is the cognitive need to explore and understand the world. People who are curious and challenge themselves tend to be happier than people who would rather stick with what they know (Diener et al., 1999; M. Gallagher & Lopez, 2007; Headey, 2008). This finding is consistent with the broaden-and-build model of positive emotion we discussed earlier, which assumes that positive emotional states lead to expansive thoughts and behavior. The connection between openness to novel experiences and life satisfaction is also consistent with the optimal arousal theories of motivation, which assert that people seek out challenging and moderately arousing situations for optimal performance.

Motivation, Emotion, and the Well-Lived Life

Being happy and satisfied with one's life is obviously important, but so is a well-lived, meaningful, and fully functioning life. What role do motivation and emotion play in living the well-lived life?

The Well-Lived Life and Intrinsic Motivation

Recall the distinction between intrinsic and extrinsic motivation: Intrinsic motivation involves doing activities because we enjoy the process of doing them and they are

"I've got the bowl, the bone, the big yard. I know I should be happy."
© 1992 Mike Twohy/The New Yorker Collection/cartoonbank.com

ends in themselves, whereas extrinsic motivation involves doing activities because they bring us external reward and recognition and are a means to an end.

Living the well-lived life is most often driven by intrinsic goals and motives of doing activities that we find inherently enjoyable (Ryan, Huta, & Deci, 2008). People who flourish are those who exhibit high levels of well-being while showing few signs of mental illness (Keyes & Lopez, 2002). Although living a well-lived life and flourishing involve positive emotions, they are more about how we live and what we do rather than simply feeling good.

People who live a well-lived life are also characterized by finding meaning in life. As is true of Maslow's self-actualizing people, they often are driven by a sense of purpose beyond their own personal lives. They find meaning in their lives in general and even in negative and tragic experiences, which tend to be associated with life satisfaction and happiness (L. A. King & Hicks, 2012). Historically, the search for meaning has been associated with spirituality, which also appears to play a role in people's search for a lasting sense of well-being (Argyle, 2001; Holder, Coleman, & Wallace, 2010).

The Well-Lived Life, Affiliation, and Positive Emotions

The need for human contact and relationship is deep-seated in human evolution. As we saw with the concept of attachment (Chapter 5), all mammals—especially humans—require others during early stages of life for their very survival. The social needs for relatedness and affiliation are general conditions of being human, but people who flourish and have a well-lived life experience these even more strongly than most (Ryan et al., 2008). As a result of this greater sense of connection to others, these individuals often experience a deep sense of empathy with and compassion for others (Ryan et al., 2008).

Flourishers—as people who live life well are called—are also more likely to experience more positive emotional states, and they report more frequency of feeling satisfied, having a life with direction, and contributing to society (Catalino & Fredrickson, 2011; Fredrickson & Losada, 2005; Keyes, 2002). Catalino and Fredrickson (2011) found that when flourishers experience pleasant everyday events they get a bigger "boost" from positive emotions than nonflourishers do; that is, they feel better about these experiences. Similarly, Fredrickson and Losada (2005) reported that those who are flourishing have more than a 3 to 1 ratio of positive to negative emotional experiences.

Chapter Review

MOTIVATION

- The psychology of motivation addresses the question of why people do what they do.

- Motivation encompasses needs, drives, and motivated behavior. A motive is anything that energizes or directs behavior.

- Needs are states of cellular or bodily deficiency that compel drives, such as the need for water, food, and oxygen. Drives are the perceived states of tension that occur when our bodies are deficient in some need—such as thirst, hunger, or breathing.

- Maslow organized the forces that drive human behavior into a hierarchy, in which lower-level biological needs are subordinate to higher-level needs.

- Hunger is a basic drive that ensures that we take in sufficient nutrition to survive.

- Internal signals of hunger include sensations of the stomach and blood glucose levels, both of which are coordinated by sensors in the brain; external signals for hunger include the sight and smell of food, as well as culturally influenced preferences.

- Eating disorders are complex and dangerous outcomes of a culture obsessed with thinness. At the same time, rates of obesity have increased dramatically over the last 50 years in the United States.

- Like all human motives, sexual desire results from a complex interplay of both biological and social forces.

- The hypothalamus plays an important role in sexual arousal.

- Hormones, especially testosterone, regulate sexual drive.

- Research on gender differences and casual sex tends to find that males are more likely than females to engage in casual sex.

- Sexual orientation is a motive that involves both biological and social influences.

- The need to belong and to connect with others is one of the strongest and most basic of human needs and is behind the popularity of social networking.

- One's tendency to achieve success is a function of three things: motivation to succeed, expectation of success, and the incentive value of the success.

- Motivation to work comes in three kinds: extrinsic motivators (rewards, money, and positive feedback), intrinsic motivators (pleasure, joy, challenge, and autonomy), and organizational support (belief that the company cares about you and your well-being).

EMOTION

- Unlike the longer-lasting moods and affective traits, emotions are acute, multifaceted responses to important events in our environment.

- Emotion can best be understood as a process that unfolds over time, beginning with exposure to an antecedent event, then appraisal.

- Appraisal determines whether an emotion occurs.

- Emotional responses include changes in behavior/expression, physiology, and subjective experience.

- Emotion regulation is an umbrella term for anything we do to try to change or otherwise manipulate the emotions we experience.

- From an evolutionary perspective, emotions organize bodily systems for a quick and efficient response to an important environmental event. This model applies best to negative emotions. Positive emotions, according to the broaden-and-build model, expand our thinking and help us develop knowledge and skills.

- The facial expressions of a set of basic emotions—anger, disgust, fear, happiness, sadness, and surprise—are recognized universally and appear to have evolutionary significance.

- Self-conscious emotions are a function of how well we live up to our expectations, the expectations of others, or the rules set by society. They require a sense of self and the ability to reflect on one's own actions. Shame, guilt, humiliation, embarrassment, and pride are examples of self-conscious emotions.

- Display rules show how cultural factors can lead to differences in the expression of emotion. Cultural variability is less apparent in the physiological changes associated with emotions.

- Physiological changes of negative emotions tend to be associated with higher arousal and activation of the sympathetic branch of the autonomic nervous system. Many physiological changes of positive emotions engage the parasympathetic nervous system to relax the body.

- Scientists are not sure what produces the subjective experience of emotion. The James-Lange theory holds that the perception of bodily changes plays an important role in an emotional experience.

- The brain is involved in every aspect of the emotion process, from appraisal to regulation. Although many brain structures appear to be crucial to emotions, the amygdala and the prefrontal cortex are major players.

- Men and women differ in how they talk about their emotional experiences, and women tend to smile more than men. The sexes, however, are much more similar than different in their emotionality.

- Emotional intelligence is the ability to recognize emotions in oneself and others, the development of empathic understanding, and the skills for regulating emotions in oneself and others; it may be at least as important to one's success in life as academic achievement.

BRINGING IT ALL TOGETHER: MAKING CONNECTIONS IN MOTIVATION AND EMOTION

- Happiness, life satisfaction, and subjective well-being are not directly related to income.

- People who flourish and live the well-lived life are driven more by intrinsic pleasure, find more meaning in both positive and negative events, and are more likely to experience positive emotion than are those who are not flourishing.

Key Terms

achievement motivation, p. 414

affective traits, p. 418

anorexia nervosa, p. 405

appraisal, p. 423

basic emotions, p. 419

broaden-and-build model, p. 420

bulimia nervosa, p. 406

display rules, p. 433

drives, p. 397

Duchenne smile, p. 428

emotion regulation, p. 424

emotional intelligence, p. 435

emotional response, p. 424

emotions, p. 418

expressive suppression, p. 424

extrinsic motivation, p. 415

Facial Action Coding System (FACS), p. 427

facial feedback hypothesis, p. 429

glucose, p. 401

homeostasis, p. 398

incentive, p. 397

intrinsic motivation, p. 416

James-Lange theory of emotion, p. 429

life satisfaction, p. 437

moods, p. 418

motivation, p. 397

needs, p. 397

neurocultural theory of emotion, p. 433

perceived organizational support, p. 417

reappraisal, p. 424

self-actualization, p. 400

self-conscious emotions, p. 420

set point, p. 398

sexual behavior, p. 407

sexual orientation, p. 409

subjective experience of emotion, p. 429

subjective well-being, p. 437

universal, p. 426

Yerkes-Dodson law, p. 399

Quick Quiz Answers

Quick Quiz 11.1: 1. b 2. c 3. b 4. c   **Quick Quiz 11.2:** 1. b 2. c 3. d 4. d 5. a 6. a 7. b

12 Stress and Health

Chapter Outline

Stress
Coping
How Stress and Coping Affect Health
Chapter Review

Challenge Your Assumptions

True or False?

- There is a gene for stress. (see page 452)

- Stress makes your hair suddenly turn gray. (see page 458)

- People who are Type A are really anxious and high-strung. (see page 465)

- Exercise can turn fat into muscle after one workout. (see page 469)

- Stress is always bad for your health. (see page 472)

It seems that every semester when final exams roll around *something* happens to Dora's health. One year she had a huge canker sore under her tongue and could hardly talk for a few days. Another time she had horrific headaches. Both problems occurred shortly after the most intense studying period of the semester, making it hard for her to concentrate on her exams, and sometimes ruining the beginning of her break.

Kyle has herpes, a virus that often remains dormant in the body but occasionally causes very painful and itchy sores. His outbreaks always seem to occur when he's been stressed out. Moreover, the more he worries about the possibility of an outbreak, the more likely he is to get one.

Estelle, 52, takes care of her 75-year-old mother, who has advanced Alzheimer's disease. It is exhausting work, because her mother is losing the ability to perform many daily tasks (such as preparing food or bathing), and it is made worse because her mother's emotions have become very unpredictable. Confused from the disease, she yells at Estelle frequently and blames her daughter for her problems. Estelle has a hard time coping with this stress and finds herself drinking vodka for relief, far more often than she knows she should.

As a new recruit in the military, George was exhausted from the daily physical challenges and sleep deprivation (less than 5 hours a night) that were part of the rigorous, challenging, and stressful summer cadet training program. George, however, had always been driven and disciplined and stuck to his goals and interests. He was determined to make it through training, even though a relatively large number of recruits did not. He not only finished, he thrived and was one of the highest ranked trainees at graduation.

Each of these real-life cases highlights a kind of life stress and shows how stress might affect health. What causes stress, and what effects does stress have on us? Why do some people manage to see a situation as challenging rather than burdensome, whereas others don't? Can stress really make us sick?

In this chapter we examine the psychological and physiological nature of stress and the related topic of coping. We then survey some major topics in the field of health psychology, a discipline that emerged from an interest in the effects of stress on physical health. We will highlight how stress emerges from and modifies mental and physical processes, how differences in people's ability to deal with life's challenges influence the functioning of their bodies, as well as how these bodily responses can affect how people think and feel. Few other topics in psychology illustrate as clearly the interdependence of nature and nurture.

STRESS

The term *stress* can refer to a wide variety of phenomena. We speak of having a stressful life when the pressures of daily life interfere with our ability to maintain a sense of well-being. Sometimes people talk about "feeling stressed," as if stress were an emotional state, one that involved anxiety and exhaustion. Some people are "stressed" by minor events such as a parking ticket or a missed train, whereas others seem to sail through life amid a great number of demands—work, family, school—all the while maintaining a sense of well-being and balance.

Driving, particularly in high-traffic urban areas, can elicit a stress response.

What physiological changes might we expect to see in this woman right now?

Stress occurs when a situation overwhelms a person's perceived ability to meet the demands of that situation. As with emotions, we evaluate our experiences of stressful situations and attempt to cope with the challenges they pose. Suppose you are doing poorly in a class, and you have the final exam in one week. At first, you may feel stressed, but then you realize that, with more review of the material, study group meetings, and more sleep, you could do better. You resolve to make these changes to improve your chances for a good final exam grade. As a result, the feeling of stress may decrease.

Stress as Stimulus or Response

Stress has different meanings in different contexts. We often think of stress as something that happens *to* us, as situations that push us to the limit or threaten our safety or well-being. Or stress can be the relentless onslaught of difficulties, such as being late on a term paper, the car breaking down, realizing there is no money in the bank, and then getting into an argument with a roommate all in one week. We call these events that push us to the limit or exceed our ability to manage the situation at hand **stressors.** The focus on the situations that cause stress is known as the *stimulus view of stress.*

In contrast, stress can be internal to us; we can think of it as the feeling we experience when events are too much to handle. The *response view of stress* focuses on the physiological changes that occur when someone encounters an excessively challenging situation. Later in the chapter, we explore Hans Selye's view of stress as a physiological response.

Clearly, stress is much more than being in certain challenging situations, and it is much more than physiological responses. Stress emerges from people's interpretations of the relevance of certain stressors to their lives and their ability to deal with them. This *relational view of stress* defines stress as a particular relationship between people and the situations in which they find themselves.

We will look briefly at the view of stress as a stimulus, which has dominated psychological research for many years. Then we will explore the relational

stress
A response elicited when a situation overwhelms a person's perceived ability to meet the demands of the situation.

stressors
Events that trigger a stress response.

Life Event	Value
Death of spouse	100
Divorce	73
Marital separation	65
Jail term	63
Death of close family member	63
Change in financial state	38
Death of a close friend	37
Change to a different line of work	36
Foreclosure of mortgage	30
Change in responsibilities at work	29
Change in sleeping habits	16
Change in eating habits	15
Vacation	13
Christmas	12
Minor legal violations	11

FIGURE **12.1**

SOCIAL READJUSTMENT RATING SCALE.
Developed by Holmes and Rahe (1967), this
scale quantifies stress in terms of major life
changes. The higher the value, the greater the
stress associated with the event.

view, before turning to the research on stress as a physiological response,
which sets a foundation for our understanding of how stress can affect
health.

Stress as a Stimulus Some events demand an overwhelming
amount of our energy and time. Any number of things can be stressors:
unpleasant situations, such as divorce, financial troubles, or illness, or
pleasant situations, such as a wedding or the birth of a child. Psychologists measure stress as a stimulus by quantifying the number of stressors a person experiences during a given period. Two major categories
of stressors are major life events and daily hassles.

Any situation that creates a major upheaval in a person's life might
lead to stress. Indeed, one approach to measuring stress as a stimulus
focuses on major life events. In the late 1960s, Thomas Holmes and
Richard Rahe developed the Social Readjustment Rating Scale (SRRS),
an instrument to quantify stress in terms of major life changes. This
scale, shown in Figure 12.1, consists of a list of events that might be
considered life changing; each is assigned a corresponding life change
value. After a person has responded to the questions on the scale, a
researcher can calculate the total amount of stress the respondent is
experiencing by adding up relative stress values, which were derived
from previous research, known as Life Change Units (Holmes & Rahe,
1967).

The SRRS is easy to administer and score, but it has some drawbacks. First, it ignores the fact that people view similar events differently. While some people might find marriage more stressful than a
major work change, for others it may be vice versa (Scully, Tosi, & Banning, 2000). Second, by measuring stress in terms of life events, the SRRS fails to
consider differences in people's emotional responses to stressors. Nevertheless,
the SRRS is still widely used in research on stress and health, and it relates to
measures of mental and physical health (N. H. Gottlieb & Green, 1984).

Sometimes little things really bother us. The accumulation of minor
irritations—traffic, too much homework, relationship troubles—might wear us
down, both mentally and physically. The Hassles and Uplifts Scale measures the
frequency and intensity of minor irritations (hassles) and the positive events of
daily life that may counteract their damaging effects (Kanner et al., 1981). A number of studies report positive correlations between the frequency of daily hassles
and self-reported health symptoms (DeLongis, Folkman, & Lazarus, 1988; Feist
et al., 1995; Kohn, Lafreniere, & Gurevich, 1991). Some data indicate that hassles
are more strongly related to health outcomes than are major life events (Kohn
et al., 1991; Weinberger, Hiner, & Tierney, 1987).

A major limitation to measuring both major life events and hassles is that
not all people view situations in the same way. A poorly prepared student might
dread an exam, but a student who has studied thoroughly might welcome it as
a challenge. This example points to the ways in which people differ in their responses to situations. Using this logic, Lazarus and Folkman (1984) argued that,
because people do not view similar situations in the same way, it is misleading to
examine stress solely in terms of the situations that may call it forth. We have to
look at the person in relation to the situation.

Relationship between Person and Situation As we saw with emotion,
when we first encounter a situation in our environment, we quickly appraise what
it means for us. Lazarus and Folkman (1984) talk about two kinds of appraisal.
Primary appraisal is an assessment of what a situation means to us. The outcome of this appraisal determines whether an emotional response might occur.
If we view the event as personally irrelevant, we feel no emotion. If we view it as

primary appraisal
Quick assessment of the meaning of
a given environmental event for an
individual.

1 antecedent event

2 appraisal

Beneficial to me ⟶ Positive emotion

Threatening to me

3
Negative emotion ⟶ **stress**

Not relevant to me ⟶ No emotion

TSUNAMI HAZARD ZONE
IN CASE OF EARTHQUAKE, GO
TO HIGH GROUND OR INLAND

FIGURE 12.2

THE EMOTION/STRESS PROCESS. When events are appraised as threatening, negative emotions occur.

According to this model, under what conditions does stress occur?

personally relevant, the event may be either contrary to or consistent with our goals or welfare. If we appraise it as contrary to our well-being, we feel a negative emotion, which might cause stress. If we appraise it as consistent with our well-being, we feel a positive emotion. Figure 12.2 depicts the process by which different appraisals lead to different emotional outcomes. Even though both pleasant and unpleasant *events* might lead to stress, stress emerges from negative emotional responses to events that we cannot get under control. Any kind of event—pleasant or unpleasant—might lead to such emotional reactions. For example, a wedding is a pleasant event that can be stressful.

Emotional events may escalate into stress when we cannot deal with the demands that the event entails. According to Lazarus and Folkman, we assess the resources available to cope with stress in a process called **secondary appraisal.** When we find ourselves in a stressful situation, we try to figure out what to do about that situation, how to resolve it, or how to make the unpleasant feeling it creates go away.

The Physiology of Stress

When we experience situations as stressful, physiological changes occur in our bodies. Most notably, the autonomic nervous system (ANS), the endocrine system, and the brain interact to create a range of changes in bodily systems.

The ANS, as discussed in Chapter 3, consists of all the neurons that serve the organs and the glands. Because it is linked to the body systems that support

Connection

Like stress, emotions are generated by our appraisals of events in our lives. How we evaluate the meaning of certain situations—whether a smile from a stranger or an upcoming exam—determines whether we feel threatened or joyful in response to that situation.

See "Emotion as a Process," Chapter 11, "Motivation and Emotion," p. 422.

secondary appraisal
Self-assessment of the resources available to cope with stress.

Physiological changes that enable us to respond quickly during an emergency can take a toll on our bodies if stress persists.

action, the ANS plays a crucial role in the stress response. These systems include the circulatory system, to pump blood to large muscle groups during times of emergency, and the respiratory system, to provide the oxygen required so that those muscles can function.

The second major system involved in stress is the endocrine system, which consists of the major hormone-releasing glands. The term **neuroendocrine system** refers to the hormonal systems involved in emotions and stress. The interactions among various organs, glands, and nervous system chemicals lay the groundwork for the dynamic interplay between psychological experience and physiological functioning.

The hypothalamus, the pituitary gland, and the adrenal glands are key structures in the neuroendocrine regulation of stress responses. The hypothalamus links the nervous system to parts of the endocrine system relevant to emotions: Hypothalamic neurons release chemicals that stimulate the release of hormones from the pituitary gland, which sits just beneath it and is connected to brain stem structures that control the ANS. The pituitary releases hormones that play a key role in the stress response. The adrenal glands, which sit atop the kidneys, release several stress-related hormones: the catecholamines, which control ANS activation, and the **glucocorticoids,** which maintain the activation of physiological systems during emergencies.

Once activated, the hypothalamus initiates a series of endocrine events that profoundly affect the body. Two major neuroendocrine pathways are activated: the adrenal-medullary system and the hypothalamus-pituitary-adrenal axis (see Figure 12.3). First in line is the **adrenal-medullary system,** in which the hypothalamus sends instructions to the brain stem to activate sympathetic neurons. Then sympathetic neurons tell the adrenal gland to release the important catecholamine norepinephrine. Norepinephrine activates the sympathetic response, increasing heart rate, rate of respiration, and blood pressure to make the body ready for action.

The sympathetic response evolved because rapid mobilization of the body's resources in emergency situations had clear survival and reproductive benefits. In cases of stress, however, this activation is prolonged. Moreover, if we live with prolonged stress-inducing situations, our bodies remain in "emergency

neuroendocrine system
The hormonal systems involved in emotion and stress.

glucocorticoids
Hormones responsible for maintaining the activation of physiological systems during emergencies.

adrenal-medullary system
A major neuroendocrine pathway stimulated during stress, in which the hypothalamus activates the sympathetic nervous system.

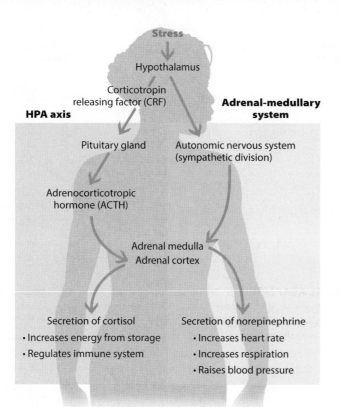

FIGURE **12.3**

THE HPA AXIS AND THE ADRENAL-MEDULLARY SYSTEM. During emotional arousal and stress, the hypothalamus activates the neuroendocrine system to prepare the body's response. The hypothalamus releases CRF, which stimulates the pituitary to release ACTH. ACTH then stimulates the cortex of the adrenal gland to release the "stress hormone" cortisol.

mode" for long periods of time. Thus, a response that is adaptive in the short term can take a toll on the body in the long term, leading, for example, to sustained increases in blood pressure and heart rate. Think about how you feel when something startles you: Your heart races; you start breathing heavily; you're in a state of high alert. Now imagine what it would be like to remain in that condition for several days.

The other major neuroendocrine pathway in stress responses is the **hypothalamic-pituitary-adrenal (HPA) axis.** Recall that the hypothalamus releases substances, called releasing factors, that tell the pituitary when to release various hormones. During emotional arousal and stress, the hypothalamus releases a substance called corticotropin-releasing factor (CRF), which stimulates the pituitary to release adrenocorticotropic hormone (ACTH). ACTH then stimulates the cortex of the adrenal gland to release cortisol, the major glucocorticoid produced in humans, which is commonly known as the "stress hormone." When the level of cortisol in the blood adequately meets the body's metabolic needs, the hypothalamus stops releasing CRF, thereby reducing the release of cortisol. This kind of negative feedback occurs throughout the neuroendocrine system.

Cortisol has many important functions. It plays a role in the breakdown of complex molecules into simpler ones to release energy and, so, plays an important role in ensuring that more glucose is available for fuel in the bloodstream (Rose, Vegiopoulos, & Herzig, 2010). Cortisol also regulates the immune system, by reducing the number of immune cells in the bloodstream. In so doing, chronically elevated cortisol may impact the immune system's ability to protect the body against infection (Lovell & Wetherell, 2011).

hypothalamic-pituitary-adrenal (HPA) axis
A major neuroendocrine pathway relevant to the stress response involving the hypothalamus, pituitary gland, and the adrenal cortex.

Connection
The sympathetic branch of the ANS activates the body; the parasympathetic branch calms the body. Both play a role in how the body responds to and recovers from stress.

See "The Nervous System," Chapter 3, "The Biology of Behavior," p. 78, and "Emotion as a Process," Chapter 11, "Motivation and Emotion," p. 422.

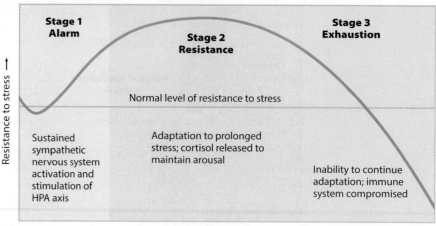

FIGURE 12.4

SELYE'S GENERAL ADAPTATION SYNDROME (GAS). In the alarm stage, the body's resources are mobilized in response to a stressor. Resistance occurs when the body can no longer sustain the emergency response and the organism must find other ways to ward off the threat. If the threat persists, eventually the body's resources become depleted, physical exhaustion occurs, and illness becomes much more likely.

general adaptation syndrome (GAS)
As defined by Hans Selye, a generalized, nonspecific set of changes in the body that occur during extreme stress.

alarm stage
The phase of the general adaptation syndrome in which all of the body's resources respond to a perceived threat.

resistance stage
In the general adaptation syndrome, the body's extended effort to deal with a threat.

exhaustion stage
The phase of the general adaptation syndrome when all the body's resources for fighting a threat have been depleted and illness is more likely.

The General Adaptation Syndrome (GAS) In 1946, Austrian physiologist Hans Selye proposed a three-stage model to describe the changes in physiology that occur during exposure to severe stressors. Selye believed that attempts to adapt to overwhelming stressors cause the body to wear down and eventually get sick. With homeostasis as his starting point, Selye viewed the changes the body goes through when confronted with extreme situational demands as manifestations of adaptation to stress. He exposed animals to stressors, such as extreme temperature change, severe electrical shock, radiation, or heavy exercise (Selye, 1976).

Selye proposed that all stress causes a generalized, nonspecific set of changes in the body—no matter what the type of elicitor. He measured hormones, metabolism, organ function, and other variables and observed a consistent pattern of responses regardless of the stressor. Selye (1946) coined the term **general adaptation syndrome (GAS)** to describe this general pattern of responses to prolonged exposure to stress.

The GAS consists of three stages: alarm, resistance, and exhaustion (see Figure 12.4). Upon exposure to a stressor, an animal enters a state of physiological shock, called the **alarm stage,** which is the body's emergency response to a threat. The alarm stage mobilizes the body's resources to act via the effects of adrenal-medullary activation of the sympathetic nervous system. During this stage the HPA axis is active as well, and the sustained release of cortisol from the adrenal glands may move from being helpful (by making more fuel available) to being harmful in the long run (by suppressing certain aspects of immune function).

Animals, however, cannot persist in the alarm stage for long. With continued exposure to the stressor, they will either die or find other ways of coping with the enduring threat. When they develop other ways to cope, they enter the second stage of adaptation, the **resistance stage.** Resistance implies that the organism tries to manage the threat. This extended effort, however, takes its toll physically and psychologically by diverting resources from the maintenance of normal bodily functions. With repeated exposure to a stressor, animals enter the **exhaustion stage.** At this stage, their resources for fighting off threats have been depleted, and illness becomes much more likely. Have you ever come down with a cold or other illness a week or so after final exams? You get the idea.

Selye's model laid the groundwork for research on the physiology of stress, but soon it became clear that his GAS model did not fit all stress responses. First, Selye studied extreme physical stressors, such as nearly freezing an animal to death or repeatedly exposing it to severe electrical shock, and subjected animals to these stressors for prolonged periods. Questions arose as to whether the bodily changes that occurred in response to such severe demands in animals provided a good model for enduring the stress of, say, divorce or financial troubles in humans. Second, some researchers questioned the idea that a syndrome of body responses to stress occurred regardless of the type of stressor.

In the 1970s, research challenged Selye's assumption that the stress response is a general one. Mason (1971, 1975) showed that an animal's response to a stressor differed depending on its psychological state. If the animal could anticipate a stressor, it showed a less severe physiological response than an animal that could not anticipate a stressor (Mason, 1971). Further, research conducted during the 1980s showed that different emotions produce different patterns of ANS activation, casting further doubt on Selye's idea of a generalized physiological response to any environmental demand (Ekman, Levenson, & Friesen, 1983).

How We Adapt to Stress Most accounts of the physiology of stress (such as Selye's) think of stress as a deviation from balance. Recovery from stress occurs when all systems return to normal. This view stems from the notion of homeostasis—the idea that, unless we are being provoked by something, we are humming along at an even-keeled *baseline* state, and we return to the same state after the stress. Moreover, homeostasis implies that just one system in the body struggles to return to baseline at a time (*homeo-* means "same"). Suppose you were walking in a desert: The homeostasis view says that you would sweat to cool your body to return to an ideal temperature. If you think about it for a minute, you'll realize that this is not ideal. If your body did this, you would become dehydrated (Sapolsky, 1998). Thus, a new concept was needed to explain the more complex and dynamic changes that occur when the body is stressed.

Some researchers offer an alternative explanation to how we adapt to stress. Rather than a state of balance, they say, our normal state is one of actively responding to the world around us. This more dynamic, responsive "resting" state is known as **allostasis,** which means that the body achieves stability through change (Karatsoreos & McEwen, 2011; Schulkin, 2005; Sterling & Eyer, 1988). *Allo* means "different" or "changing." Thinking of the baseline state as one of dynamic responsiveness makes it easier to understand the effects of stress on the body (Juster, McEwen, & Lupien, 2010). Back to the example of walking in the desert: The concept of allostasis emphasizes that your body would respond in many ways, not simply by sweating. Your kidneys would start producing less; mucous membranes in your eyes and skin would dry out; even your veins and arteries would constrict to maintain blood pressure with a smaller volume of blood. The concept of allostasis makes clear that our bodies can respond adaptively to challenge for only a short period of time. If we are pushed too long, the body's active attempts to adapt are sustained, and we are taxed. The body starts to wear down, as the *allostatic load*—the amount of wear and tear on the system to which the body must adapt—becomes too much to bear. This is how stress causes illness.

allostasis
The process by which the body achieves stability through physiological change.

Stress and the Brain So far we have emphasized how stress affects a wide array of physiological responses, most of which involve systems outside the central nervous system. What about the brain? We tend to think of stress as being

Connection
Do you think an ethics review board would allow Selye to conduct his research on extreme stressors in animals today? Why or why not?

See "Ethical Research with Animals," Chapter 2, "Conducting Research in Psychology," p. 64.

caused by processes within the brain, for it is our interpretations of the events in the world that trigger emotions, but the physiological activation triggered by stress also affects the brain. Cortisol has a profound effect on the hippocampus, a brain structure that plays a pivotal role in memory; the hippocampus contains one of the greatest concentrations of cortisol receptors in the brain (McEwen, De Kloet, & Rostene, 1986). Unfortunately, stress-related cortisol release causes hippocampal dendrites to shrink, which can interfere with several types of memory. Chronic stress reduces neurogenesis in the hippocampus, and it may inhibit the synaptic plasticity in the hippocampus and neocortex, impacting learning and memory formation (Anacker et al., 2013; Artola, 2008; Wang et al., 2008). Animal research shows that excessive stress in a pregnant mother can affect the development of several brain areas—including the amygdala, hippocampus, hypothalamus, and corpus callosum—in her offspring (Charil et al., 2010).

Severely adverse experiences early in life—what we would consider serious stressors—can affect the amount of cortisol receptors in the hippocampus (McGowan, 2012). They also show increased susceptibility to chronic diseases of aging (G. E. Miller et al., 2009).

Coping plays a big role in the duration of stress responses and whether they develop sufficiently to become harmful to the brain and body. In monkeys, more effective coping with stress increases neurogenesis in the hippocampus, which offers the hopeful suggestion that the adverse effects of stress on the brain may be reversible (Lyons et al., 2010). In a fascinating study of rats, researchers found that increased experience with sex—even chronic exposure to sex—also increases neurogenesis in the hippocampus (Leuner, Glasper, & Gould, 2010)!

Stress and Genes   No single "stress gene" dictates how the body responds to stress in the way a cancer gene might turn cancer cells on and off. Instead, several complex processes involving stress, genes, and endocrines regulate the relationship between stress and disease (Cole, 2009, 2010). From this complex area of research, we can distill out a few key points. First, the effects of chronic social isolation on illness appear to be regulated by genetic factors (Cole 2010; Cole et al., 2007). Also, those genes associated with the human stress response seem critical to certain chronic diseases (Capri et al., 2006). Finally, genes appear to play a role in the relationship between the stress of social isolation and diseases that involve inflammatory processes, such as heart disease and cancer (Cole et al., 2010; Khatami, 2009; Miller et al., 2009).

Challenge Your Assumptions

True or False? There is a gene for stress.

False: There is no single gene for stress (or any psychological trait).

Connections

The hippocampus, located deep inside the brain, is critical for memory formation.

See "Overview of Brain Regions," Chapter 3, "The Biology of Behavior," p. 92, and "Pathways of Short-Term Memory in the Hippocampus and Prefrontal Cortex," Chapter 7, "Memory," p. 271.

Quick Quiz 12.1: Stress

1. According to the definition provided in the text, which of the following is the best example of stress?
   a. Maria is studying for one exam.
   b. Maria is studying for three exams on the same day, but she has a handle on all three.
   c. Maria is studying for two exams on the same day and feels unprepared for both of them.
   d. Maria is angry with her boyfriend.

2. This view of stress focuses on the physiological changes that occur when someone encounters an excessively challenging situation.
   a. stimulus
   b. response
   c. relational
   d. situational

3. The model of adaptation that says there is stability through change is the
   a. functional view.
   b. physiological view.
   c. homeostatic view.
   d. allostatic view.

4. Which part of the nervous system becomes most involved when we are feeling stressed?
   a. hypothalamic-pituitary-adrenal (HPA) axis
   b. temporal lobes
   c. hippocampus
   d. frontal lobes

Answers can be found at the end of the chapter.

COPING

Generally, **coping** refers to anything people do to deal with or manage stress or emotions. When we walk away from someone who is making us angry or complain about our boss to a friend, we are coping with stresses in our lives. In this section we explore various ways people cope with stress.

coping
The act of dealing with stress or emotions.

Coping Strategies

People don't like feeling bad, so they try to get out of situations that create unpleasantness or look for ways to change their negative feelings. Psychologists Richard Lazarus and Susan Folkman (1984) differentiated between these two types of coping strategies, labeling them *problem-focused* and *emotion-focused* coping. The strategy of social support combines problem-focused and emotion-focused coping strategies. Figure 12.5 provides an overview of these three coping strategies.

Problem-Focused Coping **Problem-focused coping** strategies aim to change the situation that is creating stress. If your roommate plays a stereo loudly while you are sleeping, you might choose to discuss it with her, buy earplugs, or cut the speaker wires. Each of these choices is a form of problem-focused coping; each is geared toward changing the situation that created the stress. Examples of problem-focused coping strategies include devising a plan to solve the problem, seeking social support as a way to gather information,

problem-focused coping
A way of dealing with stress that aims to change the situation that is creating stress.

Strategy	Example
problem-focused strategy Solve the problem Seek social support Take assertive action	Roommate's stereo too loud: Focus on how to make it quiet. An assertive act might be to cut the stereo speaker wires.
emotion-focused strategy Reappraise Distancing Use escape-avoidance Seek social support Exercise self-control Emotional disclosure Accept responsibility	Breakup with a partner: Focus on how to feel better. An escape-avoidance act may be to take a vacation to get away from the former partner. Write about it to unburden emotions.
social support strategy Combines problem-focused and emotion-focused strategies Develop social connectedness Seek advice from or talk with friends and loved ones	Support groups: Giving and showing support to other people may increase longevity.

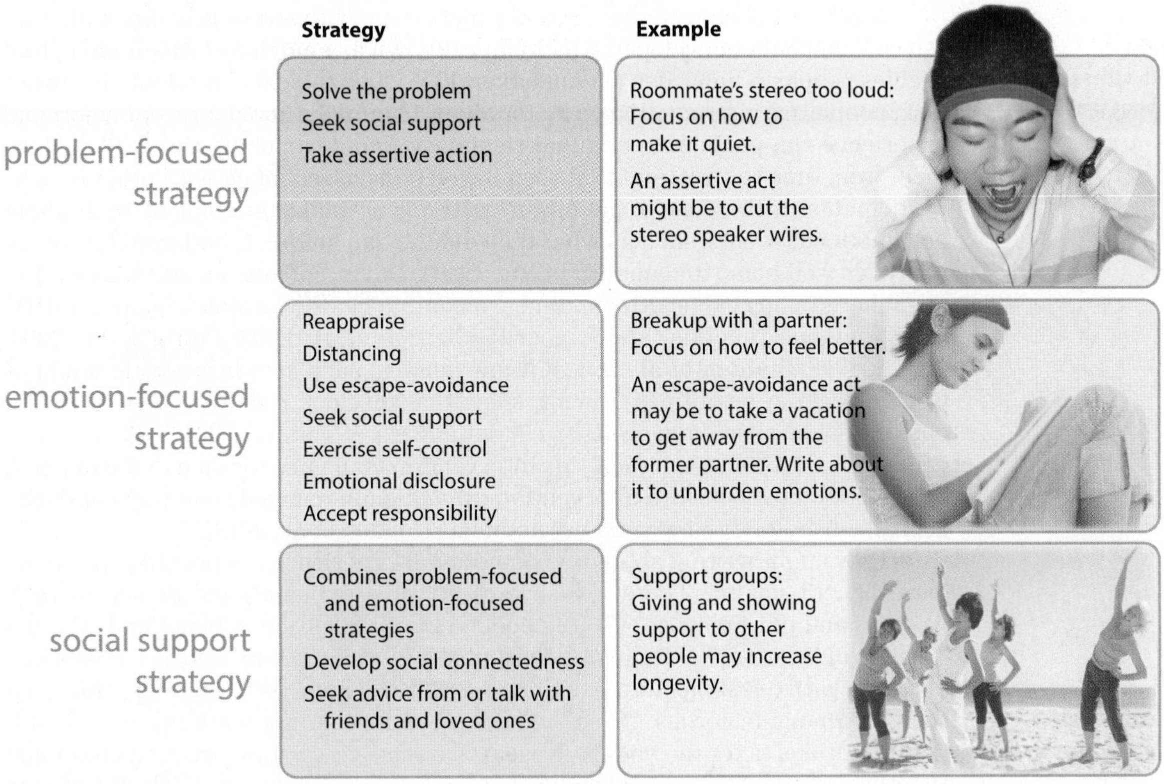

FIGURE **12.5**
COPING STRATEGIES. We tend to apply problem-focused coping strategies to change a stressful situation and emotion-focused coping strategies in situations we feel we cannot control.

and taking assertive action. Problem-focused coping focuses attention on the stress-provoking situation, and we are most likely to use it when we think we can change the situation.

Emotion-Focused Coping In contrast, **emotion-focused coping** aims to regulate the experience of distress. Lazarus and Folkman describe several forms of emotion-focused coping, including *reappraisal*, the reevaluation of a situation in light of new information or additional thought; *distancing*, or attempting to separate oneself from an emotional experience; *escape-avoidance*, wishful thinking or doing something to get one's mind off the situation (such as going to the movies); *seeking social support* by talking with friends for purposes of emotional support; *self-control*, or trying to regulate one's feelings or actions regarding the problem; and *accepting responsibility*, acknowledging one's role in the stress-eliciting situation (Lazarus & Folkman, 1984).

When a situation is beyond one's control, certain types of emotion-focused coping—especially reappraisal—can be helpful in regulating the emotional aspects of stress, but other kinds of emotion-focused coping can be problematic. A study of people coping with the loss of a partner to AIDS found that engaging in reappraisal correlated with increases in positive mood (Moskowitz et al., 1996). Cognitive coping strategies such as reappraisal seem more effective in reducing depression and anxiety in men with HIV than do social support and substance use (Kraaj et al., 2008).

Willful suppression of upsetting emotions, which is a form of self-control, can lead to chronic physiological arousal and is associated with poor psychological adjustment (J. J. Gross & Levenson, 1993; J. J. Gross, Richards, & John, 2006). Moreover, some strategies that we use to reduce the experience of distress, such as drinking, smoking, and other forms of drug use, may be maladaptive (Hien & Miele, 2003).

It is widely believed that a good way to cope with stress is to "let it all out." James Pennebaker developed a technique, known as **emotional disclosure,** that enables people to unburden (Pennebaker, 1995). In a typical emotional disclosure task, people are instructed to write for about 15 minutes about a recent emotional experience—in particular, one that they have found troubling, that still bothers them from time to time, and that they haven't discussed much with other people. Participants in the control condition write for a similar amount of time about nonemotional events, such as what they did the day before. Emotional disclosure improves well-being and quality of life (Craft, Davis, & Paulson, 2012), as well as a number of physical health outcomes, including health variables related to HIV/AIDS, immune function, and cancer (O'Cleirigh et al., 2008; Petrie et al., 2004; Smyth, 1998; Stanton et al., 2002). A few studies, such as a large-scale study of women seeking fertility treatment, show that disclosure did not benefit health outcomes, however (Panagopoulou, Montgomery, & Tarlatzis, 2010). There is evidence that the effectiveness of this intervention may vary for men and women. A brief emotional disclosure intervention dramatically reduced symptoms of PTSD, depression, and HIV in women but not men (Ironson et al., 2013).

How might writing about one's emotional experiences, especially traumatic ones, benefit health? There are several possible explanations. People in both Western and non-Western cultures believe that confession is beneficial. For the Ndembu of West Africa, for instance, public confession allows for the transformation of negative feelings into positive ones in the community, thereby promoting social harmony (Georges, 1995). It is also thought that *not* working through difficult emotions taxes the body, as research on the association between emotional suppression and ANS arousal suggests (J. J. Gross & Levenson, 1993). When confession or disclosure occurs, then, one should observe a decrease in sympathetic nervous system activation or a return to a more relaxed state. In fact, numerous laboratory studies have found that just talking about a traumatic event creates noticeable reductions in autonomic measures such as blood pressure and sweating (Pennebaker, 1995). Writing about positive experiences also benefits mental and physical health, presumably by other mechanisms, such as helping the person maintain a broader focus on life (Burton & King, 2009).

Social Support   Social support is a coping strategy that combines problem- and emotion-focused coping. Our friends and loved ones provide advice, give hugs, or simply listen when we are under stress. Social support not only is one of the most frequently used ways of coping but also can benefit physical health. The *direct effects hypothesis* states that social support is beneficial to mental and physical health whether or not the person is under stress. Sheldon Cohen (2004) has pointed out that being part of a social network guarantees the availability of certain resources. Our social networks may offer guidelines for health-related behaviors, help us regulate our emotions, and give us a sense of identity. We may learn from friends that running or jogging can help us feel better when we're stressed. Examples of social connectedness include being married, belonging to social groups such as churches or clubs, and having many friends. Friends provide an outlet for sharing emotional distress, offering comfort as well as advice.

Alternatively, social support may buffer the impact of stress under certain conditions, such as a highly stressful life. This is known as the *buffering hypothesis*. One influential study found that regular participation in a support group in which members discussed their emotional difficulties improved well-being and extended survival in women with advanced breast cancer (Spiegel et al., 1989), though this finding has not replicated consistently (Edelman et al., 1999; Edmonds, Lockwood, & Cunningham, 1999; P. J. Goodwin, 2004; P. J. Goodwin et al., 2001).

How well a person is integrated into a *social network* influences health. A social network is simply a cluster of related people, such as family members, spouses, friends, coworkers, or neighbors. This web of friends and acquaintances is related to but not the same as an electronic social network, such as the kind you might have on Facebook. When people are well integrated into a social network, social support can buffer the effects of stress by providing interpersonal resources for emotional support and problem solving (S. Cohen & Wills, 1985). The health benefits of social connectedness include longer life and reduced susceptibility to colds (Berkman & Glass, 2000; S. Cohen et al., 2003). A recent study that followed more than 12,000 people over 32 years examined the role of social networks in quitting smoking (Christakis & Fowler, 2008). Social networks influenced the likelihood that a person would stop smoking, but not all social connections had the same effect. If a spouse stopped smoking, the chance the other spouse would also stop went up by 67%; if a friend stopped smoking, the chance another friend stopped went up by 36%; and if a coworker stopped smoking, the chance another worker stopped went up by 34%. So the effect of the other person's behavior on any given person depended to some extent on how close they were to each other.

Social networks may be harmful to health as well. In a study of 12,000 people, researchers looked at the influence of obesity in the same social network. The risk of obesity spread among people who were socially connected. If a person became obese (with a body mass index, or BMI, greater than 30), his or her friends, family members, spouse, or neighbors were more likely to become obese. As was true with smoking, however, not all social connections had the same effect. For instance, if a person's friend became obese over a given period of time, that person's chance of becoming obese increased 57%; if a sibling became obese, the chance increased 40%; and if a spouse became obese, the chance increased 37% (Christakis & Fowler, 2007). Moreover, gender mattered. Individuals of the same gender in a social network influenced same-sexed individuals more than

Connection

Emotion regulation is another term for the strategies we use to alter our emotional state and is similar to *emotion-focused coping*. Both terms refer to efforts to change the way we feel.

See "Emotion as a Process," Chapter 11, "Motivation and Emotion," p. 422.

opposite-sexed individuals. In another study, infectious diseases (such as the flu) spread more rapidly among connected individuals than they did among randomly studied groups of people (Christakis & Fowler, 2010). This undesirable aspect of social networks, however, might help in the detection and prevention of further outbreaks.

Social resources clearly play a role in health-related behavior and how we manage stress, but so do our own personal resources. Life is not just a course in stress management but rather a daily journey through a series of joys as well as challenges.

The Positive Psychology of Coping

Traditionally, research on stress and coping has focused on how people respond to threatening situations and manage the distress associated with them. For years, however, some psychologists have argued that it is an oversimplification to assume that stress involves only negative emotions and their management (Folkman & Moskowitz, 2000; Lazarus, Kanner, & Folkman, 1980; Seligman & Csikszentmihalyi, 2000). This section discusses various ways in which positive psychological states have been studied in relation to stress and coping.

Positive Traits, Positive Emotions   Some people approach the world in a positive way, and as a result their experience of distress is reduced compared to that of others. *Optimists* tend to emphasize the positive, see the glass as "half full" rather than as "half empty," and believe that things will turn out well (Carver, Scheier, & Segerstrom, 2010). *Pessimists*, by contrast, emphasize the negative; for them, the glass is always half empty and the future uncertain. Optimists are less likely to feel helpless or depressed, adjust better to negative life events, and show better general mental health than do pessimists (Chang, 1998; N. Smith, Young, & Lee, 2004). Optimism may also benefit physical health (Kubzansky et al., 2001). By seeing the world positively, optimists may appraise events in such a way that negative emotions are less likely and positive emotions more likely. They may be more likely to see potentially stressful situations as challenges rather than threats. Research shows that, the more optimistic a person is, the less likely it is that he or she will die from cardiovascular disease (Giltay et al., 2004). Furthermore, changes in optimism are related to changes in positive emotion that predict immune function (Segerstrom & Sephton, 2010). Surprisingly, believing that you have some control over situations in life, especially traumatic situations, can improve your psychological health (Taylor, 1989). Health psychologist Shelley Taylor has studied various groups of people suffering from chronic, debilitating, and often fatal diseases such as breast cancer, heart disease, and HIV/AIDS. She has found that people who believe they have some control over their illness—in spite of medical evidence to the contrary—are actually happier and less stressed than less optimistic people with the same diseases (Hegelson & Taylor, 1993; G. M. Reed et al., 1994; Taylor, 1989). As it turns out, these perceptions of control provide the greatest benefits in situations that are severe or uncontrollable (Taylor et al., 2000).

Positive emotions may facilitate recovery from the physiological effects of negative emotions. One study of men infected with HIV found slower disease progression in those who were happier (Moskowitz, 2003). Fredrickson and Levenson (1998) showed participants a fear-eliciting film; followed it with a sad, pleasant, or neutral film; and measured cardiovascular activity throughout the film-viewing and post-film-viewing period. Cardiovascular activation elicited by the fear film returned to baseline levels more quickly in people who saw the pleasant film after the fear film, but not in people experiencing the sad or neutral condition. Thus, positive emotions may help the body return to a state of calmness. In fact, research is pointing to a number of potentially beneficial effects of positive emotion on the body—such as lowering blood pressure and regulating cortisol—that we are just beginning to understand (Dockray & Steptoe, 2010).

Tugade and Fredrickson (2004) looked at how resilience affected people's ability to recover from stress. *Resilience* is a personality trait that means being more flexible and able to bounce back from difficult situations. Resilient people experience quicker recovery from stress-induced cardiovascular arousal, in part because they are more likely to find some positive meaning in a difficult situation (Folkman, 1997; Tugade & Fredrickson, 2004).

Recently, the concept of *grit* has received attention in psychology and the popular press. Grit is related to resilience, but is not identical with it (Duckworth et al., 2007). The two major components of grit are having a resilient response to adverse situations and a stick-to-it-ness or perservering in one's passions and interests over long periods of time (Duckworth & Quinn, 2009). Grit is not only whether one can bounce back from failure but also how much one sticks to tasks over long periods of time. Having the same interest for years and being a hardworker are examples of being gritty. Research has demonstrated that being "gritty" predicts who does well in school, who stays with rigorous military training, and who does well in spelling bees over and above intelligence, personality, or talent (Duckworth et al., 2007; Maddi et al., 2012).

Finding Meaning Perhaps the key to psychological health is to be open enough to notice the other things going on in life, even in the midst of tragedy. Positive psychological traits and states do play a big role in whether people are able to find meaning in stressful and tragic events (Folkman, 1997; Folkman & Moskowitz, 2000; Park & Folkman, 1997; Tugade & Fredrickson, 2004). People with terminal illnesses who notice beauty amidst their pain and find opportunities for positive experiences are happier than those who don't, and they may even live longer (Folkman, 1997; Moskowitz, 2003). Resilient people who managed to experience positive moods amidst their despair in the wake of the September 11, 2001, terrorist attacks were more likely to thrive and less likely to fall into depression than those who were less resilient (Fredrickson et al., 2003). A fascinating set of studies by Elissa Epel and her colleagues reveals some of the connections between biology and environment that play a role in people's responses to stress and their effects on health. In "Psychology in the Real World," we describe how Epel and her colleagues (2004; T. L. Jacobs et al., 2010) demonstrated that stress affects aging at the cellular level.

Quick Quiz 12.2: Coping

1. You buy earplugs, so that you can sleep when your roommate plays loud music at 1:00 a.m. You have used what kind of coping?
   a. problem-focused
   b. emotion-focused
   c. stimulus-focused
   d. meaning-focused

2. Research has found that having a well-connected social network of friends, family, neighbors, and coworkers is _____ for health outcomes.
   a. never beneficial
   b. sometimes beneficial
   c. sometimes beneficial and sometimes harmful
   d. always beneficial

3. "Seeing the glass as half full," or being optimistic, is likely to have what kind of effect on a person's response to stress and illness?
   a. no real effect
   b. a negative effect
   c. a positive effect
   d. the same effect as being pessimistic would

4. Who would be most likely to bounce back quickly from a very stressful experience?
   a. a pessimist
   b. a young person
   c. someone who holds in his or her feelings and pretends the event did not happen
   d. a resilient person

Answers can be found at the end of the chapter.

Psychology in the Real World

Does Stress Cause Aging?

Stress often makes people look worn out. As mentioned earlier, this is one of Selye's main ideas: Physiologically, long-term stress wears down the body, making a person more vulnerable to illness ("the exhaustion stage"). People often refer to the stresses of life as wearing them out or causing gray hairs. Is there any evidence, however, that this everyday logic has any basis in the physiology of aging? Can stress actually make you age more quickly?

Contrary to common wisdom, there is little evidence that stress or trauma can suddenly turn a person's hair gray overnight. Most scientific and medical evidence points to purely genetic explanations for hair graying (Nishimura, Granter, & Fisher, 2005; Tobin, 2004). A certain kind of stress does seem to cause gray hair: cellular stress that occurs with aging and toxins from the environment (Nishimura et al., 2005).

Over the last decade, however, mounting evidence has accumulated that stress is related to and even causes aging (Lin, Epel, & Blackburn, 2012; Tomiyama et al., 2012). In an innovative study of the physiological effects of stress, psychologist Elissa Epel and her colleagues (2004) examined indicators of cellular aging in healthy women who were biological mothers of either normal or chronically ill children. The mothers reported on the amount of stress they perceived in their daily lives, using a standard questionnaire.

The researchers derived indicators of cellular aging from tests on blood samples collected from each woman. In particular, they examined the telomeres of chromosomes in the DNA of certain white blood cells. *Telomeres* are part of the chromosome involved in replication during the process of cell division. With age, telomeres shorten; moreover, the activity of **telomerase,** an enzyme that adds DNA sequences to telomeres, decreases with age. Both of these variables are good measures of aging.

telomerase
An enzyme that adds DNA sequences to telomeres.

Epel and her colleagues measured stress not in terms of life conditions per se but in terms of the duration of stress a woman *perceived* in her life; the results showed that, the more stress a woman perceived, the shorter the telomeres

Ask any mother of young children how she feels. Chances are, she'll tell you she's exhausted. Long-term stress that is perceived as severe can speed up the process of cellular aging.

and the lower the level of telomerase activity in her blood, conditions that imply older cells. In practical terms, these women's cells were "the equivalent of 9–17 additional years" older than those of women who perceived less stress (Epel et al., 2004, p. 17314). A different analysis of the same sample found a positive relationship between measures of cellular aging and the stress-relevant hormones norepinephrine and cortisol (Epel et al., 2006). Even though we do not yet know how cellular aging translates into body age and health changes, this research provides a fascinating example of how stress can wear down the body, another example of nature and nurture working together.

If stress can accelerate cellular aging, can engaging in practices that reduce stress or promote well-being enhance cellular health? A recent study of the psychological and physiological effects of intensive meditation training addressed this question. Positive psychological changes that occur during meditation training are associated with higher activity of telomerase (T. L. Jacobs et al., 2010). Specifically, increases in self-reported purpose in life and perceived control predicted greater telomerase activity. This is the first study to link positive changes in psychological status with changes in telomerase.

Challenge Your Assumptions

True or False? Stress makes your hair suddenly turn gray.

False: Most research suggests that psychological stress plays little to no role in premature graying of hair.

HOW STRESS AND COPING AFFECT HEALTH

Our discussion so far has implied that stress increases a person's susceptibility to disease. This idea is one of the oldest expressions of the interplay between nature and nurture, and it forms the central tenet of **psychosomatic theory.** Even though people tend to use the term *psychosomatic* to refer to an illness that is "all in the head" or, by implication, "made up," this is a misconception of the theory. Rather, *psychosomatics* deal with how emotional factors can increase the likelihood of certain disorders occurring or worsening. Even the well-known link between stress and ulcers is not a matter of simple causality. Stress increases the likelihood of ulcers by changing the chemical balance in the gut, but certain preconditions must be met for that internal environment to produce ulcers (Yoemans, 2011).

The field of health psychology grew out of psychosomatic medicine. **Health psychology** is the study of psychological factors related to health and illness. It includes disease onset, prevention, treatment, and rehabilitation and involves clinical practice as well as research. Research in health psychology ranges from studies of how psychological variables enhance health or increase susceptibility to disease to the role of social factors in doctor-patient communication. Two models can explain the relationship between stress and illness; both illustrate the dynamic interplay among environmental situations, people's interpretations of them, and changes in body functioning. The **physiological reactivity model** examines how the sustained physiological activation associated with the stress response can affect body systems in such a way as to increase the likelihood that illness or disease will occur. As such, this model is rooted in psychosomatic medicine. By contrast, the **health behavior approach** focuses on the behaviors in which people engage, such as diet, exercise, or substance abuse, which may make them more susceptible to illness or may enhance health. These explanations are not mutually exclusive. For example, a person might experience sustained blood pressure elevation due to stress and drink heavily during a time of intense stress, both of which would affect the person's health.

psychosomatic theory
The idea that emotional factors can lead to the occurrence or worsening of illness.

health psychology
The study of the role psychological factors play in regard to health and illness.

physiological reactivity model
An explanation for the causal role of stress-related bodily changes in illness.

health behavior approach
An explanation for illness or health that focuses on the role of behaviors such as diet, exercise, or substance abuse.

Eating in response to stress may make us feel good temporarily, but it may also make us more susceptible to certain diseases.

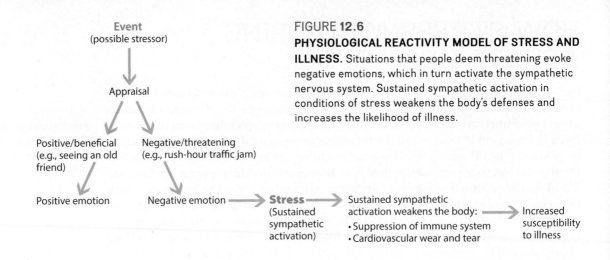

Event
(possible stressor)

↓

Appraisal

↙   ↘

Positive/beneficial   Negative/threatening
(e.g., seeing an old   (e.g., rush-hour traffic jam)
friend)

↓   ↓

Positive emotion   Negative emotion → **Stress** → Sustained sympathetic → Increased
                                              (Sustained   activation weakens the body: susceptibility
                                              sympathetic   • Suppression of immune system   to illness
                                              activation)   • Cardiovascular wear and tear

FIGURE 12.6

PHYSIOLOGICAL REACTIVITY MODEL OF STRESS AND ILLNESS. Situations that people deem threatening evoke negative emotions, which in turn activate the sympathetic nervous system. Sustained sympathetic activation in conditions of stress weakens the body's defenses and increases the likelihood of illness.

Figure 12.6 depicts the physiological reactivity model. (We discuss the health behavior approach later in the chapter.) You will notice similarities between this and the emotion/stress process diagram in Figure 12.2: Each begins with the elicitation of negative emotion and stress. In the physiological reactivity model, however, the activation of the sympathetic nervous system persists and creates sustained physiological arousal (recall Selye's exhaustion stage). A wide array of body systems may be affected by sustained stress, but a few key systems have been the focus of much research.

The physiological reactivity model starts with sustained physiological arousal. Earlier we said that the sympathetic branch of the autonomic nervous system activates organ systems to enable an animal to respond to emergency situations. The effects of sympathetic arousal on the heart and lungs (increasing pumping and oxygen intake) help the animal act quickly and thus survive. From an evolutionary perspective, these effects were advantageous because of their ability to enable a quick and efficient response; however, the same type of emotional response occurs in daily life, in most cases without an outlet for action, as when you are stuck in traffic or annoyed with a coworker. Thus, the activation persists for hours or days, or it is elicited repeatedly in similar situations over many years. Under such conditions, you can become ill as a result of the recurring arousal produced by stress-related body changes (Sapolsky, 1998).

The **cardiovascular system,** which consists of the heart and all the blood vessels of the body, is especially susceptible to the effects of sustained arousal. During activation of the sympathetic nervous system, heart rate and blood pressure increase. In sustained physiological activation, heart rate and blood pressure remain elevated or are activated repeatedly over extended periods. Frequent blood pressure elevations can damage arteries by reducing their elasticity and increasing the likelihood of fatty buildup. These processes set the stage for heart disease.

The immune system suffers from the effects of sustained arousal, and impaired immune function increases susceptibility to disease. How does this work? Sustained activation of the HPA axis leads to sustained release of cortisol, which inhibits the production of certain immune cells. In the short term, the suppression of immune cell production makes sense, because in an emergency immune cells might not be immediately necessary. Over the long term, however, immune suppression makes a person more susceptible to certain diseases.

Challenging Assumptions in How the Nervous and Immune Systems Are Linked With the general adaptation syndrome, Hans Selye provided a framework for thinking about how stress might make the body vulnerable to

cardiovascular system
The heart, the blood, and all the blood vessels.

disease, and he implied that this vulnerability might be due to the effects of stress on the immune system. No one knew whether psychological factors could affect the immune system until some groundbreaking research of the 1970s.

The job of the immune system is to defend the body against foreign substances. Before the 1970s, the prevailing view was that the immune system operated independently of the central nervous system, which implied that the immune system was invulnerable to thoughts, feelings, and stress. As far as anyone knew at the time, there were no anatomical or chemical connections between immune system structures and any aspect of the nervous system that would allow them to communicate. Even though most physicians believed that stress made people sick, or at least sicker, they did not consider it physiologically possible for psychological conditions to have any effect on the immune system; however, that was about to be challenged.

Robert Ader was replicating some classic experiments on conditioned taste aversion. Recall from Chapter 8 that conditioned taste aversion is a form of classical conditioning in which a neutral taste, after repeated pairing with a substance that induces nausea and vomiting, will come to produce those characteristics when it is presented alone. In the early research, saccharin water was paired with radiation, which causes nausea (Garcia, Kimeldorf, & Koelling, 1955). In his work, Ader paired a chemical that induces nausea with saccharin water to create taste aversion to the saccharin water. Some rats were exposed to a lot of saccharin water even after they had learned to associate it with nausea, and something else unusual was happening to those rats—they were dying! Why?

Ader remembered that the toxin he was using to induce nausea also happened to be an immunosuppressant, something that suppresses immune system function. Perhaps, he reasoned, in addition to learning to avoid saccharin water, the rats were acquiring conditioned immunosuppression from the repeated pairing of the saccharin solution with the immunosuppressant, but how could rats *learn* immunosuppression?

To suggest any connection between psychological processes and immune system functioning ran counter to the view in medicine that the immune system operates independently of the central nervous system (Boorboor, 2002). Nevertheless, Ader and his colleague, Nicholas Cohen, ran a series of experiments to determine whether immunosuppression could be classically conditioned in rats (Ader & Cohen, 1975). They conditioned nausea in an experimental group by pairing saccharin water with injections of the immunosuppressant. They also created two control groups: a group that was injected with a placebo around the time they drank saccharin water (which served as a control for the stress-inducing effects of injection in the absence of conditioning) and a group that received the immunosuppressant and plain water (a nonconditioning control group).

Ader and Cohen then tested whether the immune system was, in fact, suppressed in rats with immunosuppressant-induced conditioned taste aversion. They reintroduced the conditioned stimulus, in this case saccharin, and then introduced an **antigen,** a substance foreign to the body. The blood of rats that had been conditioned to avoid saccharin via the immunosuppressant showed much weaker antibody responses to the antigen than did rats injected with the placebo. By demonstrating that one could classically condition the suppression of an antibody response to an antigen, Ader and Cohen had shown that there must be connections between the CNS and the immune system.

The Birth of Psychoneuroimmunology

Not long after Ader and Cohen published their results on conditioned immunosuppression, some important findings in biomedical science increased the credibility of their results. In the late 1970s and early 1980s, scientists discovered that

antigen
Any foreign substance that triggers an immune response.

Connection

Conditioned taste aversion is a type of learning similar to what happened when Pavlov's dogs learned to salivate to the sound of a bell (classical conditioning).

See "Classical Conditioning," Chapter 8, "Learning," p. 288.

A newborn's immune system is still developing. Antibodies present in the mother's breast milk protect the baby from infection until the infant's own immune system has matured.

the ANS is linked to immune system structures such as the thymus gland and that immune cells have receptors for and can produce certain stress hormones (E. M. Smith & Blalock, 1988). There was now solid behavioral and biological evidence for what Selye and others had believed all along—that psychological processes and immune processes interact. The field of **psychoneuroimmunology (PNI),** the science of how psychological factors relate to immune changes, was born.

Today, the field of PNI examines the relationships among the brain, thought, feeling, endocrine changes, and immune system functioning. As a discipline, PNI is concerned with any kind of connection between psychological processes and the immune system. For instance, there are chemical linkages between psychological processes and immune system changes. Chemicals involved in the stress response, such as cortisol and norepinephrine, influence the number of immune cells produced in the body. This is a means by which stress can affect the immune system.

Furthermore, connections between the central nervous system and immune system are bidirectional. Just as stress can change immune function, certain immune changes (such as the release of chemicals called *cytokines,* which regulate immune response) can feed back and influence brain areas involved in mood regulation (A. H. Miller, Capuron, & Raison, 2005; Nishida et al., 2002).

Overview of the Immune System   The human immune system defends the body against invasion by disease, inspects the body for cells that may take on dangerous mutations, and performs basic housekeeping functions, such as cleaning up cellular debris after an injury. There are two basic lines of defense: natural immunity and acquired immunity. **Natural immunity** consists of a number of inborn processes that help remove foreign substances from the body. These responses typically are very quick, and they provide the first line of defense upon exposure to antigens. Forms of natural immunity include phagocytosis and inflammation. *Phagocytosis* is a process by which a white blood cell engulfs a substance (usually an antigen or another cell) and digests it or moves it to a place where it will be destroyed. *Inflammation* is a process by which tissues are restored following injury. After you cut your finger, for example, blood vessels at the injured area contract and dilate to increase blood flow to the area, creating warmth and redness. The damaged cells release enzymes to destroy invading microorganisms.

The immune system comprises several kinds of white blood cells, including those responsible for phagocytosis. Other white blood cells, called *lymphocytes,* control acquired immunity. **Acquired immunity** involves a number of endocrine and cellular processes that recognize specific antigens and then reproduce specialized cells or circulating proteins to fight those antigens. Acquired immunity is so called because it involves experience—an effective immune response occurs only after prior exposure to a particular antigen. Every cold we get leads to an acquired immune response. As a result, we are less likely to get sick if we encounter that particular virus again. Acquired immune responses take longer to initiate than natural immune responses, because the former involve recognition

psychoneuroimmunology (PNI)
The science of how psychological factors can relate to changes in the immune system.

natural immunity
The form of immunity that is the first response to antigens.

acquired immunity
Immunity provided by antibodies produced in the body in response to specific antigens.

processes and the duplication of cells. On subsequent exposure to a specific antigen, however, acquired immune responses can be rapid and efficient. Vaccines, for example, provide a safe initial exposure and an acquired immune response that protects us against disease.

Acquired immunity involves two classes of lymphocytes, called B and T lymphocytes. In response to specific antigens, *B lymphocytes* release antibodies into the bloodstream. Antibodies destroy antigens directly. The *T lymphocytes*, or "T cells," fight antigens not by releasing antibodies but by means of cellular processes, collectively known as **cellular immunity**.

cellular immunity
The immune response that occurs when T lymphocytes (T cells) fight antigens.

Research on Stress, Immune Function, and Health   The physiological reactivity model predicts that the physiological effects of stress, when sustained over time, will eventually weaken the immune system. Theorists have extended the model a step further, reasoning that *immunosuppression* increases susceptibility to disease by reducing the body's ability to fight invading bacteria or viruses or its ability to fight off potentially cancerous cells, or both. This is why psychologists, in collaboration with medical researchers, began conducting studies of stress and immune function (e.g., S. Cohen et al., 2012). The basic idea is simple: If researchers can show that stress affects immune variables, it should follow that such immune system changes would leave the organism more susceptible to disease. In reality, many studies link stress with changes in immune system measures, but very few have shown that these changes affect susceptibility to disease.

Results from animal research show that a variety of chronic stressors can weaken responses to antigens, reduce the numbers of certain immune cells, and impair immune cell functions such as responses to vaccines (Glaser & Kiecolt-Glaser, 2005). Some of the stressors tested in animal studies are maternal separation, inescapable shock, abrupt temperature change, and loud noise. In research with humans, one obviously cannot abuse people, but occasionally researchers have manipulated stress by randomly assigning people to participate in a stressful task, such as public speaking, or an emotion-evoking task, such as writing about a traumatic event (Pennebaker, Kiecolt-Glaser, & Glaser, 1988). The more common approach in human research, however, is to rely on naturally occurring stressors, such as final exams, sleep deprivation, loud noise, abuse, poverty, bereavement, divorce, and caring for an Alzheimer's or AIDS patient. These studies use various measures of immunity as dependent variables: numbers of certain lymphocytes, tests of how effectively certain lymphocytes function either in a test tube or in a living person, the toxicity of tumor-fighting cells called *natural killer cells*, and the quantities of chemicals that regulate lymphocytes.

Although the major finding in studies of humans is that stressors are associated with changes in various kinds of immune function, it is often difficult to know whether the observed immune changes have meaningful effects on health. A few studies address this concern by including measures of illness that are controlled by immune mechanisms. In a study of people caring for Alzheimer's patients, the caregivers and a matched comparison group (all volunteers for the study) received small puncture wounds. They then returned to the laboratory for wound healing assessments and blood tests to measure immune variables. Compared to the comparison group, the caregivers exhibited substantially slower healing of puncture wounds and reductions in the chemicals involved in healing (Kiecolt-Glaser et al., 1995).

Studies that have examined long-term, chronic abuse, neglect, and poverty on children's health and well-being report rather profound emotional, psychological, and epigenetic effects on risk for disease and suicide later in life (Labonte et al., 2012; Miller et al., 2009). Labonte and colleagues (2012) studied the brains of people who had committed suicide, some of whom were abused as children (they also studied the brains of controls who had died by means other than suicide). Relative to controls and nonabused suicides, abused suicides had epigenetic changes in gene expression involved in HPA activity consistent with abnormally elevated stress response. As we discussed earlier, the HPA axis is crucial to immune function and a balanced release of hormones in response to stress. Childhood poverty, too, can be a chronic stressor, programming the body to have a long-term elevated stress response (for example, increased cortisol response), leaving people more vulnerable to chronic illness and disease in their 40s and 50s (Miller & Chen, 2013; Miller et al., 2009).

What about stress and the common cold, an infectious illness mediated by the immune system? Sheldon Cohen and his colleagues (S. Cohen, Tyrrell, & Smith, 1993; S. Cohen et al., 2003; S. Cohen et al., 2012) have studied the interplay of stress and social connectedness in people's susceptibility to the common cold. Susceptibility is the key issue here, as exposure to the cold virus does not guarantee that a person will get sick. You and your roommate might both spend time with a friend who is sick, but only one of you might catch the cold. In these studies, Cohen and his colleagues exposed people to a virus; measured perceived stress in some participants as well as external stressors and social networks; and clinically verified whether or not people got sick. They used a clever means by which to measure how sick people were, such as weighing tissues to approximate how much mucus they produced! As it turns out, the perception of stress—rather than the number of stressors to which people had been exposed—predicted whether people developed a cold (S. Cohen et al., 1993). Further, having more meaningful social interactions in one's daily life reduces susceptibility to colds (S. Cohen et al., 2003). Perceiving oneself as lower in socioeconomic status also predicts susceptibility to the common cold in people exposed to the virus, independent of one's actual socioeconomic status (S. Cohen et al., 2008).

The relationship between stress and illness, then, is not driven by the situation as much as by how the individual evaluates that situation. In terms of susceptibility to the common cold, *perceived* stress matters more than actual exposure to stressors; *perceived* low socioeconomic status matters more than actual socioeconomic status. These results remind us of the importance of examining stress not just as a stimulus (number of stressors) but also in terms of how people respond to the stressors and cope with possible stress (transactional view). As discussed earlier, social support and connectedness might buffer the effects of stress by providing interpersonal resources for emotional support and problem solving (S. Cohen & Wills, 1985).

Is time urgency the component of the Type A Behavior Pattern that predicts heart disease?

Psychological Risk Factors for Heart Disease

Heart disease is the number one killer of both men and women in the United States (American Heart Association, 2005; Lethbridge-Cejku & Vickerie, 2005). We saw earlier that the physiological changes associated with negative emotions and stress affect the cardiovascular system. Research has identified a number of psychological risk factors for heart disease, including hostility, anger, and depression.

Type A and Anger For centuries scientists have argued that personality and emotion play a role in the development of heart disease, but research on this topic did not begin until the middle of the 20th century. It began in the waiting room of cardiologist Meyer Friedman's office in San Francisco. A janitor pointed out to Friedman that the upholstery on the chairs in his waiting room was wearing out much more quickly than that on chairs in other waiting rooms. He wondered whether Friedman's patients fidgeted a lot. Friedman said that he had noticed that many of his patients were tense and impatient. Friedman and his colleague Ray Rosenman decided to study the effects of such an emotional style on a person's risk of developing heart disease. They described a set of psychological characteristics they believed put people at risk for heart disease: impatience, competitiveness, hostility, and time urgency. They named it the **Type A Behavior Pattern (TABP)** and explained that this pattern emerges when under conditions of challenge or stress. That is, Type A people are not always impatient and hostile, but when they find themselves in high-pressure situations they exhibit this pattern of behavior.

Friedman and Rosenman hypothesized that people who exhibit the TABP *under provocation* are at greater risk for heart disease than those who do not. After developing an interview to measure Type A behavior, they tracked 3,000 healthy white men for 8 years. They found that Type A behavior predicted the incidence of coronary heart disease, over and above such traditional risk factors as blood pressure, cholesterol, and age (Rosenman et al., 1964). This finding shocked the medical world—no one had anticipated that something psychological could affect heart disease! Other major studies replicated the finding that the presence of Type A behavior predicted the incidence of heart disease and extended it to women (French-Belgian Collaborative Group, 1982; Haynes et al., 1978).

Twenty-two years later, Rosenman and Friedman conducted a follow-up study on their original participants (Rosenman et al., 1975). Surprisingly, Type A behavior did *not* predict death from heart disease in this group. Then another major study of men and women produced null findings as well (Shekelle et al., 1985). Could it really be that Type A behavior did not affect the incidence of heart disease after all?

Remembering that Type A is a collection of various characteristics, Matthews and her colleagues (1977) decided to take a closer look at the follow-up interviews from Friedman and Rosenman's original sample. She reasoned that maybe certain aspects of Type A were still relevant to coronary health, even if the overall pattern did not predict death. Matthews studied how each component of the Type A pattern (hostility, time urgency, competitiveness, and impatience) related to coronary outcomes. As it turned out, *hostility* was the only component that predicted death from heart disease at a 22-year follow-up. As a result of Matthews's findings, the measurement of global Type A has been abandoned, for the most part, in favor of more specific measures of hostility.

Suddenly, the focus changed to the study of hostility and cardiovascular health. In subsequent research, specific measures of hostility again positively correlated with the degree of arterial blockage and other cardiovascular conditions much more so than general Type A behavior did (Suarez, Bates, & Harralson, 1998; Suarez et al., 1993; Suarez & Williams, 1989; R. B. Williams et al., 1980).

How might having a hostile personality put someone at greater risk for heart disease? Hostility is an affective trait, which some emotion theorists say sets a threshold for the likelihood of particular emotional responses (Ekman, 1984; Rosenberg, 1998). By this logic, hostile people would have a lower threshold for the elicitation of anger. To link hostility and anger to heart disease, we need to look at a special version of the physiological reactivity model known as the cardiovascular reactivity model (see Figure 12.7). In the **cardiovascular reactivity (CVR) model,** hostility can increase the likelihood of heart disease through at least two causal routes. On one route, hostility makes the elicitation of

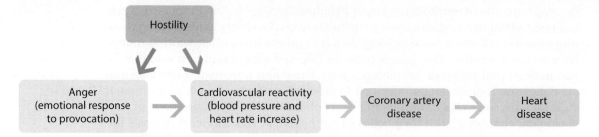

FIGURE **12.7**

CARDIOVASCULAR REACTIVITY MODEL OF STRESS AND ILLNESS. This version of the physiological reactivity model links hostility and anger to heart disease. Repeated cardiovascular reactivity leads to coronary artery disease and heart disease.

anger more likely and more frequent (this route starts with the red arrow in Figure 12.7). Frequent episodes of anger lead to frequent cardiovascular reactivity. Over time, repeated cardiovascular reactivity sets the stage for the development of coronary artery disease. As coronary artery disease develops, the narrowed arteries deprive the heart of the blood it needs to function properly; thus, progressive coronary artery disease can lead to coronary heart disease. The yellow arrows in the diagram designate the transition between repeated cardiovascular reactivity and coronary artery disease and the later development of coronary heart disease. The second route, indicated by the blue arrow in Figure 12.7, is a direct path from hostility to how much cardiovascular reactivity certain people experience, without the need for anger.

In support of the first route, research shows that anger does affect cardiovascular outcomes. For instance, anger can lead to heightened and prolonged blood pressure reactivity (Schuler & O'Brien, 1997; Siegman et al., 1992). In coronary patients, the risk of heart attack increases significantly during the hour following an outburst of anger (Moller et al., 1999). A study of coronary patients undergoing the Type A Structured Interview found that episodes of insufficient blood supply to the muscle of the heart were more likely to occur when those patients displayed facial expressions of anger (Rosenberg et al., 2001).

Depression   A hostile disposition is not the only trait relevant to cardiac health. Depression, a mood disorder involving sadness and lethargy, is also associated with increased severity of symptoms and increased risk of death from coronary heart disease (Geerlings et al., 2002; Glassman & Shapiro, 1998). Large-scale meta-analyses report that, for people with coronary heart disease, being clinically depressed significantly increases the risk of death from the disease (Barth, Schumacher, & Hermann-Lingen, 2004; Tully & Cosh, 2013). Also, the chemicals involved in inflammation that present a risk for coronary heart disease are present at higher levels in people who are depressed than in others (Barth et al., 2004; Empana et al., 2005). Studies such as these make it hard to know which comes first—the heart disease or the depression. A recent large-scale prospective study, however, showed that depression scores predicted death from cardiovascular disease and overall mortality (Nabi et al., 2010).

Research on Health-Relevant Behavior

Earlier we mentioned another pathway to illness called the *health behavior approach*. People engage in behaviors that either increase risk for disease or help prevent disease. Some health behaviors are conscious lifestyle choices, such as how and what to eat or whether or not to exercise. Others may begin as conscious choices but over time become habits with serious health implications, such as smoking, drinking alcohol, and taking other drugs. Sometimes, when stressed, people may turn to tobacco, alcohol, or food to calm themselves down or cheer themselves up. This is emotion-focused coping. Long-term use of some of these substances can create health problems and may increase the likelihood of major, sometimes fatal, illnesses.

Smoking   Many smokers say they have a cigarette when they are stressed because it calms them down. However, nicotine, the drug component of cigarette smoke, is a stimulant. Nicotine activates the sympathetic nervous system, increasing heart rate and blood pressure, but relaxes the skeletal muscles, which is probably why some people find it calming. They use nicotine for emotion regulation, but cigarette smoking is harmful to health in many ways. According to the U.S. Department of Health and Human Services (USDHHS; 2006), it is the single most preventable cause of death in the United States. Cigarette smoking reduces life expectancy by an average of 10 years, increases one's risk for lung cancer more than 10-fold, and triples the risk of death from heart disease in both men and women (Centers for Disease Control and Prevention [CDC], 2001; Doll et al., 2004). Smoking also increases the risk of many other cancers, stroke, lung disease, emphysema, and male impotence (USDHHS, 2006). The increased risk of mortality associated with smoking is found in several cultures (Jacobs et al., 1999). Although the rates of smoking in the United States have dropped considerably in recent years, still about 20% of the U.S. population smokes cigarettes. With over 1,000 people a day under the age of 18 in the United States taking up smoking, this is a major health problem (USDHHS, 2006).

We are exposed to *secondhand smoke* by being near someone who is smoking. Analyses of the composition of the smoke burned from the end of a cigarette indicate that it is high in carcinogens (sometimes higher than the smoke inhaled by the smoker) and is a health threat to those who inhale it passively. In fact, a person who breathes secondhand smoke regularly is at increased risk of all the same health problems that the smoker is (USDHHS, 2006).

Drinking Alcohol   Some people drink alcohol to calm down or loosen up. Alcohol is a depressant, which means it slows down central nervous system functions. Alcohol can cause liver damage, and severe alcoholism can lead to a serious liver condition known as cirrhosis (Baan et al., 2007; Schiff, 1997). Heavy alcohol consumption also increases the likelihood of liver cancer and cancers of the digestive tract, not to mention an increased risk for accidents due to alcohol's effect on motor and cognitive performance. Not all the news regarding alcohol is bad, however. Considerable data indicate that regular but moderate alcohol consumption (one to two drinks), especially with food, may reduce the risk of coronary heart disease, the number one killer in the developed world (Guiraud et al., 2008; Renaud & de Lorgeril, 1992).

Diet and Eating   Eating well promotes health. Eating saturated fats, such as those found in meats and dairy products, increases risk for heart disease, while eating other essential fats, such as those found in certain kinds of fish and nuts, may have protective effects (Schaefer, Gleason, & Dansinger, 2005). The consumption of high-fiber, less-fatty foods, such as whole grains and plenty of leafy green vegetables, may help protect against cancers of the colon and rectum, although the data are somewhat inconclusive (Cummings et al., 1992). It is well known that excessive weight gain is risky. Obesity increases a person's risk for heart disease, high blood pressure, adult-onset diabetes, and certain cancers (McTiernan, 2005). Increasingly, we can see how diet, exercise, and lifestyle interact in ways that can profoundly impact health (Powell et al., 2010).

A healthy diet rich in fruits, vegetables, and whole grains and low in fat may protect against heart disease and certain cancers and prevent conditions associated with obesity, such as adult-onset diabetes.

Eating and Stress   Some people eat to cope with stress. In fact, sugary foods in particular help some people feel better and calm down, which makes it likely they will continue to do such eating. Research now supports the connection between eating and stress reduction: Stress increases eating and in turn eating reduces stress reactivity in the HPA axis (Dallman, Pecoraro, & la Fleur, 2005). When a person eats in response to stress, stress-related physiological activity decreases and reward pathways in the brain are stimulated. These areas release endorphins, which make people feel better. Thus, people eat under stress because they get a "good feeling" reward—like a drug high—from the brain (Adam & Epel, 2007). The relationship between stress and eating might vary across individuals, however. Sproesser and colleagues (2014) found that people who eat more under stress eat less when relieved of that stress, while people who eat less under stress might be more likely to eat more when the stress subsides.

Stress-induced eating, however, is risky, as it increases fat in the abdominal area (compared to other places), which is a predictor of heart disease in men and women (Epel et al., 2000; Rexrode, Buring, & Manson, 2001; Rexrode et al., 1998). This is especially true if the stress-induced eating includes sugary junk foods (Kuo et al., 2007).

Exercise   Besides not smoking, one of the best things you can do for your health is to exercise regularly, which reduces the risk of heart disease, stroke, and certain types of cancer (Noda et al., 2005; Thune & Furberg, 2001). Exercise helps keep diabetes under control and slows the rate of bone loss in older women (Cussler et al., 2005). Data show that moderate exercise, even as little as walking 20–25 minutes a day three or four times per week, can extend life by 3 to 4 years (Franco et al., 2005). In addition, exercise offers a healthy way to regulate mood, as it reduces anxiety and depression (Barbour, Edenfield, & Blumenthal, 2007; Binder et al., 2004).

One of the best ways to affect your metabolism, and as a result change your weight, is by exercising regularly. Did you know that introducing just a brief (10 minutes or so) exercise regimen can make a difference in your metabolism? Such metabolic changes can change your genes (Lewis et al., 2010). This lends credibility to the idea that you can change your set point with exercise and thereby eat less.

It's obvious that exercise improves fitness. Regular exercise helps prevent heart disease, reduces the risk of Type II diabetes, offsets certain cancers, and improves mood (Alex et al., 2013; Crouch, Wilson, & Newbury, 2011; Teo et al., 2013). In addition to the cardiovascular benefits, exercise can reduce fat cells and support the cellular processes that grow muscle (Barrés et al., 2012; Ronn et al., 2013). In a study by Ronn and colleagues (2013), researchers took a variety of fitness and health measures from 23 healthy but inactive men, who later underwent a 6-month exercise intervention program, after which they were measured again. The men were more fit and lost weight after the training, but what was most interesting was how epigenetic differences in genes that played a role in fat storage lowered the risk for Type II diabetes and obesity.

Researchers looked at whether a single exercise session could change the genetics of muscle cells of otherwise sedentary people (Barrés et al., 2012). They obtained small tissue samples from participants both before and after a single 400-calorie burning exercise cycle session. Some were instructed to exercise vigorously, while others were instructed to pedal more gently. They found changes in the DNA methylation of muscle cells after only one workout and these changes were most pronounced among the participants who rode most vigorously.

Exercise also helps your brain. One correlational study found that the most physically fit third- and fifth-grade children also performed the highest on standardized math and reading tests (Hillman, Erickson, & Kramer, 2008). Also, exercise promotes the growth of new neurons (neurogenesis) in the hippocampus, the area of the brain most involved in learning and memory (Pereira et al., 2007). Compared to mice that did not exercise, mice that exercised showed increased activity in their hippocampi after exercising for 2 weeks. They also developed new neurons in the same region of the hippocampus. Increased activity was directly related to neural growth. In fact, similar treadmill studies in rats show that exercise can offset age-related memory loss due to a reduction in neurogenesis in the hippocampus (S.-E. Kim et al., 2010) and may decrease depressive-like behavior in chronically stressed rats (Marais, Stein, & Daniels, 2009). Similar effects have been found with humans as well; see the Research Process for this chapter (Figure 12.8). Being physically fit appears to make the brain fit, and it may offset age-related cognitive decline in the elderly (Bherer, Erickson, & Liu-Ambrose, 2013; Kirk-Sanchez & McGough, 2013; Valenzuela et al., 2012).

Nakajima and colleagues (2010) reported that chronic moderate exercise counteracts the typical age-related decline in methylation (a form of epigenetic change in gene expression, mentioned in Chapter 3) in the *ASC* gene, a gene involved in immune function. Such exercise in 65-year-olds returns their *ASC* function to the age of typical 35-year-olds. This is one mechanism to explain some of the health benefits of exercise.

Although most people realize that exercise has numerous health benefits, many of which receive a great deal of popular press, people are still slow to change their behavior. Human behavior is notoriously difficult to change. Still, it can be done, often by offering reward or incentive for making changes. Jackson and colleagues (T. Jackson, Gao, & Chen, 2014) studied 26 lean and overweight Chinese women, who viewed images of active (running, dancing, playing tennis, and so on) versus sedentary people (lounging, sitting at a desk), interspersed with images of nature landscapes (as controls), all while in the fMRI scanner. The women were asked to imagine themselves doing these various behaviors. Compared to the leaner women, the overweight women showed brain activation patterns suggesting negative emotional associations with the idea of exercising. Specifically, overweight women showed less activation in brain reward centers and more activation in areas associated with negative emotional processing. Taken together with other findings that overweight people show evidence of

Challenge Your Assumptions

True or False? Exercise can turn fat into muscle after one workout.

True: Just one session of exercise can turn on genetic processes that convert fat cells to muscle cells.

Research Process

① Research Question

Will exercise increase brain activity and stimulate neural growth in humans?

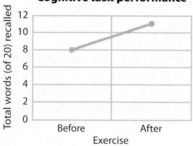

② Method

Having found that exercise was correlated with neural growth in the hippocampus of mice, Pereira and colleagues (2007) conducted a study to look for the same effects in humans. They recruited 11 adults (ages 21–45) with below-average cardiovascular fitness to take part in an exercise program four times a week for 12 weeks. Each session lasted about 1 hour and consisted of a combination of stretching, aerobic training, and cooling down. Brain images were made before and after the training with MRI to measure changes in blood volume, an indirect measure of neural growth.

The hippocampus is the brain region most involved in learning and memory, so participants' memories were tested before and after the program with a list of 20 words read by the experimenter, to find out whether there was any change in memory capacity. Participants were distracted with another word list and were then asked to recall as many words from the original list as they could.

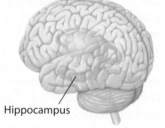

Hippocampus

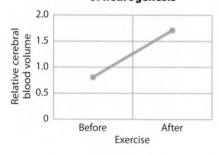

Brain activity (blood volume) in the hippocampus—an indirect measure of neurogenesis

Relative cerebral blood volume

Before / After — Exercise

Cognitive task performance

Total words (of 20) recalled

Before / After — Exercise

③ Results

MRIs performed before and after the exercise program revealed that cerebral blood flow increased after the program. In addition, participants improved their performance on a cognitive test after 12 weeks of exercise.

④ Conclusion

After exercising regularly, people who had been out of shape showed improvement in memory. This improvement is correlated with—and perhaps a consequence of—new neural growth in the region of the brain most involved in learning and memory, the hippocampus. Although we cannot conclude from the correlations revealed by this study that physical exercise causes improvements in memory, these findings suggest that exercise not only makes the body more fit, but it also makes the brain more fit.

FIGURE **12.8**

EFFECTS OF EXERCISE ON THE BRAIN. Physical exercise is as good for the brain as it is for the body. ("An In Vivo Correlate of Exercise-Induced Neurogenesis in the Adult Dentate Gyrus," by A. C. Pereira, D. E. Huddleston, A. M. Brickman, A. A. Sosunov, R. Hen, G. M. McKhann . . . S. A. Small, 2007, *Proceedings of the National Academy of Sciences, 104*, 5638–5643.)

brain-related *positive* activation in response to images of food and eating, this finding builds our understanding of the brain processes involved in struggles with weight.

Meditation for Stress Reduction and Health We have already discussed how positive emotions can reduce the physiological activation caused by negative emotions and how higher positive affect may help people with diseases like AIDS live longer (Moskowitz, 2003). Given the harmful effects of stress, strategies designed to reduce stress can benefit both mental and physical health. One such strategy is meditation.

Mindfulness meditation involves both paying attention to the present moment and being aware that everything that may arise in one's mind, be it a thought, an emotion, or a sensation, will eventually fade away. The meditator is trained to note experiences as they occur, without clinging to or ascribing value to them. These skills allow one to keep thoughts and emotions in perspective and help prevent an unhealthy obsession with negative emotions (Kabat-Zinn, 1990).

Researchers have applied mindfulness meditation training to stress reduction, pain relief, and the treatment of physical disorders. Kabat-Zinn and his colleagues have developed and studied the effectiveness of a program called Mindfulness-Based Stress Reduction (MBSR) for treating a variety of physical and psychological conditions. MBSR training reduces self-reported pain and pain-related behaviors in people suffering from chronic pain (Kabat-Zinn, Lipworth, & Burney, 1985). Also, MBSR training leads to significant and substantial reductions in anxiety, depression, and fear in people who have various types of anxiety disorder (Kabat-Zinn et al., 1992).

Mindfulness training helps other health conditions as well, especially those that may worsen with stress. Consider psoriasis, an annoying and often painful rash that can be exacerbated by stress (Chapman & Moynihan, 2009). Mindfulness training improves the rate of skin healing in people with psoriasis (Kabat-Zinn et al., 1998). Mindfulness meditation techniques appear to be effective in reducing the stress-related immune changes underlying skin outbreaks. Such meditation training appears to help in treating eating disorders, recovering from substance abuse, and enhancing the quality of life in people with multiple sclerosis (P. Grossman et al., 2010; Liehr et al., 2010; Masuda & Wendell, 2010).

How might meditation improve health?

Connection

Mindfulness meditation can improve well-being, cognition, and brain function.

See "Training Consciousness: Meditation," Chapter 6, "Consciousness," p. 220.

Quick Quiz 12.3: How Stress and Coping Affect Health

1. If a psychologist studies how diet and sleep affect overall health, which view would best match her research?
   a. physiological reactivity
   b. general adaptation syndrome
   c. health behavior approach
   d. homeostasis view

2. Martin is very prone to anger, impatient, and competitive; he is always in a hurry and feeling rushed. Martin probably suffers from
   a. Type A Behavior Pattern.
   b. Type B Behavior Pattern.
   c. hostility.
   d. high drive disorder.

3. Which personality trait is most strongly related to the development of heart disease?
   a. anxiety
   b. hostility
   c. depression
   d. introversion

4. Exercise helps
   a. decrease stress.
   b. improve cardiovascular health.
   c. stimulate neural growth.
   d. all of the above.

Answers can be found at the end of the chapter.

Bringing It All Together

Making Connections in Stress and Health

Good Stress, Bad Stress, and the Power of Belief

Throughout this chapter we have advocated the view that stress is generally bad for your health. We have discussed evidence that stress increases susceptibility to infection, cardiovascular disease, certain cancers, chronic inflammation, and cellular aging. As we have seen, however, the connection between stress and illness in the published literature is far from perfect.

Two recent areas of research challenge the assumption that stress is always bad for you. One area suggests that certain short-term (acute) stress responses might actually be good for our health. The other area shows how our ways of thinking can modify whether we are vulnerable to stress and, subsequently, whether we get sick. Both areas suggest that our notions of the stress and illness relationship have been oversimplified, the discussion of which allows for the integration of many of the important concepts in this chapter.

Challenge Your Assumptions

True or False? Stress is always bad for your health.

False: Not all stress is the same. Acute (short-lived) stress is, in fact, good for your health.

Acute versus Chronic Stress

Short-term (acute) stress is good for your health, but what precisely constitutes *acute* stress and how do we distinguish it from chronic stress? How brief is brief? A leading researcher in this area, Firdhaus Dhabhar (2009) suggests that acute stress is stress that lasts minutes to hours (such as anxiety in the preparation for a final exam), whereas chronic stress lasts months to years (such as having to stay in an abusive relationship).

An increasingly large body of research shows that acute stress may not be harmful to health at all; it might actually be beneficial. Recall Hans Selye's work on the GAS, which argued that, in the short term, stress is an adaptive response by our bodies to deal with emergency. In this new area of work, we are seeing that responding to some challenges with stress may confer benefits to health—more so than not responding at all! How could that be?

Recent research shows that acute stress may actually promote healing (Dhabhar, 2013). The GAS predicts that in the alarm stage the body mobilizes to deal with a challenge or threat. Heart rate and respiration increase as an initial response to an emergency (fight or flight) to enable the person to respond quickly (run away from danger, for example).

So, too, might an initial immune response mobilize cells to fight antigens (foreign substances) that might enter the body when there is a cut. Most of the research on the benefits of acute stress looked at nonspecific immunity, such as initial skin response to infection, something that has important implications for wound healing (Dhabhar, 2013).

In one key study, mice were randomly assigned to a stress or nonstress condition (being constrained in a plastic tube), then received repeated UV radiation, which can initiate squamous cell carcinoma, a type of skin cancer (Dhabhar, 2009). Researchers repeated this stressor several times during the middle of a 10-week irradiation period and measured whether tumors occurred, what their sizes were, the cell composition of the tumors, and many blood measures. Compared to no-stress controls, the short-term stress group showed fewer tumors, more immune cells, and better immune cell function.

We see these nonstress benefits on a practical level, as well. One groundbreaking study of people undergoing knee surgery showed that the patients who exhibited stress-related immune cell activation had better knee mobility than those who did not (Rosenberger et al., 2009). In other words, mild stress helped them heal faster.

Perceptions of Stress

The second way in which we might question whether stress is always bad for health involves the way thoughts and beliefs can change the effects of stress on health. We have discussed concepts in this chapter that point to how the "goodness" or "badness" of stress depends on whether you perceive or believe that something (a stressor) is overwhelming or not. The question, therefore, is, If you change your mind about stress, can you change how your body responds to it?

Stress in many ways is more subjective than objective—the same experiences will be considered stressful or not by different people. Earlier in the chapter, we questioned the value of viewing "stress" simply in terms of the stimulus that we encounter (e.g., work, marriage, illness, exams) or the response (physiological activation, immune changes). You might also recall the role of appraisal in determining whether a given situation is stressful or not, and the key role of appraisal in that process. Once we have appraised something as threatening and too much to handle and the stress response ensues, how we cope with the stress matters. Coping strategies, such as reappraisal of the situation, can turn something from a stressor into a nonstressor. In this way, not all stress is equal, and certainly not all stress is illness producing.

Reframing situations is not the only way that one might use thoughts to offset the harmful effects of stress. What we believe might do this as well. The belief that stress makes you sick has become almost accepted as a truism in our society, even though—as we have already discussed—the data show that the relationship is not particularly strong and not really clear. Keller and colleagues (2012) examined *beliefs* about whether stress makes you sick might actually make you sick. The study made use of a household survey conducted by the National Center for Health (NCHS; 2000) on almost 30,000 people in the United States who were asked numerous questions about stress: how much stress they experienced over the past year; how much distress they had in their lives; whether they had done anything to reduce the amount of stress in life; what their health behaviors were; and most importantly how much has stress affected their health (a lot, some, hardly, or none). The major dependent, or outcome, variable of interest was whether the respondent had died from *any* cause in the 8-year period following the survey. Death information was obtained from the National Death Index (NDI).

As predicted, those with the highest stress were most likely to die 8 years later. What is most surprising, however, was that it was *not* how much "stress" they had in life but whether they believed stress could make them sick (Keller et al., 2012). Specifically, those who reported the most stress *and* believed stress could make them sick were the most likely to be dead after 8 years! This is alarming but also hopeful, as it shows that we *can* change our beliefs, and therefore our longevity.

We have long known that changing beliefs is a huge aspect of trying to change behavior. Interventions aimed at changing people's beliefs about health have shown mixed effectiveness in changing behavior, mainly because it is very difficult to change beliefs. Consider the number of programs designed to educate people about safe sex and not using drugs—many never have an impact on behavior, because beliefs are so strongly held (Mantler, 2013). Still, some programs aimed at changing one's belief about health-related behaviors have an impact on health outcomes, such as prenatal smoke exposure in pregnant women (Kazemi, Ehsanpour, & Nekoei-Zahraei, 2012) and colon cancer screening (Rawl et al., 2012). Beliefs and perceptions can be powerful tools in coping with stress and turning bad stress into good stress.

Chapter Review

STRESS

- Stress results when we appraise the demands of a situation as exceeding our ability to cope with or manage those demands. Researchers often define stress in terms of events or our physiological responses to certain events.

- Primary appraisal is the initial evaluation of how threatening a situation is. Secondary appraisal involves evaluation of resources to manage the stressful situation or the feelings it generates.

- Most stress-related physiological changes are observed in the autonomic nervous system (ANS), especially the sympathetic branch.

- The adrenal-medullary system controls the release of catecholamines, chemicals that activate heart rate, respiration, and other responses that prepare the organism to deal with emergency situations.

- The hypothalamic-pituitary-adrenal (HPA) axis releases the hormone cortisol, which frees up glucose as a source of energy.

- The stress response is beneficial in short-term, emergency situations but not over the long term. When sustained over time, the stress response can weaken the body.

- Hans Selye proposed a three-stage model, the general adaptation syndrome (GAS), to describe how the body reacts and adapts to chronic, extreme stress. In the alarm stage, the body is in emergency mode and all body systems are activated for quick response. In the resistance stage, the body gradually adjusts to the high level of stress created by the demands of its environment. In the exhaustion stage the body is unable to sustain the response and becomes more susceptible to illness.

- Mason and others argued that Selye had overlooked the fact that people respond to different situations with different emotions and made a case for greater specificity in the stress response. Research shows that different emotions are indeed associated with different patterns of ANS response.

COPING

- Some strategies for coping are problem-focused, in that they address how to remedy or change the situation that called forth the stress response. Others are emotion-focused, aimed at reducing the emotional distress or unpleasant experience created by a stressful situation.

- Social support can profoundly improve mental and physical health. Social networks influence health behavior, both positively and negatively.

- Some people are more likely than others to believe that they have control over situations, and this belief may make them healthier.

- Some people experience positive affect even in dramatically stressful situations. Positive affect, in turn, may facilitate recovery from the negative emotional arousal of stress.

HOW STRESS AND COPING AFFECT HEALTH

- There are two major approaches to studying how stress leads to illness: the physiological reactivity model and the health behavior model.

- The physiological reactivity model examines how the psychological effects of sustained stress make illness more likely.

- Psychoneuroimmunology (PNI) encompasses research on any type of connection between the CNS and the immune system.

- The work of Ader and Cohen on classically conditioned immunosuppression showed a relationship between psychological processes and changes in immune function.

- The immune system defends the body against disease. Immunity consists of natural and acquired aspects. When antigens are present, lymphocytes either release antibodies into the blood or bind directly with the antigen to disable it.

- Numerous studies have demonstrated the effects of stress on regulation of the immune system. The most convincing argument for a meaningful stress-immune connection comes from studies that measure the experience of stress, immune measures, and related illness outcomes.

- The Type A Behavior Pattern, a way of responding to demanding situations with hostility, time urgency, and competitiveness, can predict the later development of heart disease. The hostility component of the Type A pattern best predicts coronary heart disease.

- The cardiovascular reactivity model offers a perspective for understanding how hostility might increase risk for heart disease. Hostility increases the likelihood and frequency of the physiological effects of anger, which over time increases the likelihood of hardened arteries and, eventually, coronary heart disease.

- People engage in behaviors that enhance health as well as those that make them more susceptible to illness. Behaviors such as smoking and drinking alcohol increase risk for major illness such as heart disease, cancer, and liver disease. Eating in response to stress also imposes risks.

- Healthy diet and exercise can extend life and enhance brain function.

BRINGING IT ALL TOGETHER: MAKING CONNECTIONS IN STRESS AND HEALTH

- Stress is not inherently good or bad. Different kinds of stress and different perceptions of stress have different effects on our bodies and minds. Acute stress can be beneficial, whereas chronic stress can be harmful.

- Perceiving stress as harmful to us increases its harmful effects on us.

Key Terms

acquired immunity, p. 462
adrenal-medullary system, p. 448

alarm stage, p. 450
allostasis, p. 451
antigen, p. 461

cardiovascular reactivity (CVR) model, p. 465
cardiovascular system, p. 460

cellular immunity, p. 463

coping, p. 453

emotional disclosure, p. 454

emotion-focused coping, p. 454

exhaustion stage, p. 450

general adaptation syndrome (GAS), p. 450

glucocorticoids, p. 448

health behavior approach, p. 459

hypothalamic-pituitary-adrenal (HPA) axis, p. 449

natural immunity, p. 462

neuroendocrine system, p. 448

physiological reactivity model, p. 459

primary appraisal, p. 446

problem-focused coping, p. 453

psychoneuroimmunology (PNI), p. 462

psychosomatic theory, p. 459

resistance stage, p. 450

secondary appraisal, p. 447

stress, p. 445

stressors, p. 445

telomerase, p. 458

Type A Behavior Pattern (TABP), p. 465

Quick Quiz Answers

Quick Quiz 12.1: 1. c 2. b 3. d 4. a   **Quick Quiz 12.2:** 1. a 2. c 3. c 4. d   **Quick Quiz 12.3:** 1. c 2. a 3. b 4. d

13 Personality: The Uniqueness of the Individual

Chapter Outline

Defining Personality
The Nature and Nurture of Personality
How Do Theorists Explain Personality?
How Is Personality Measured?
Chapter Review

Challenge Your Assumptions

True or False?

- Your personality is determined mostly by your family environment. (see page 482)

- Many different kinds of animals have personality in the sense that humans do. (see page 486)

- Freud's ideas are interesting historically, but have no scientific support. (see page 490)

- Facebook "likes" reliably predict your personality traits. (see page 502)

- Your personality predicts future success in your career better than letters of recommendation, educational credentials, or interviews. (see page 504)

- People can usually change their personalities if they try. (see page 506)

J erry and Evan are brothers—Jerry is 16, and Evan is 12. They have similar yet distinct personalities. Both are curious, intelligent, socially skilled, full of energy, and active. Jerry, the older of the two, is quiet much of the time (except around his best friends) and is prone to being mildly anxious, especially around spiders. He would not go up and talk to a stranger if his life depended on it. Jerry loves sports and is physically very active, having ridden multiple 75-mile bike rides and climbed a 14,000-foot mountain (Mt. Shasta) before his 16th birthday.

Evan, by contrast, is very expressive, artistic, dramatic, energetic, aggressive, and fearless. He loves breaking rules just for the fun of it and, without a shred of shyness, will ask a stranger a question or strike up a conversation. Moreover, he can easily tell you what he is thinking and feeling and describe the details of why something bothers him. All you get from Jerry is an "I don't know" or "Nothing" when he's asked what's bothering him or "good" and "fine" when he's asked how he liked something. Often during play, even if alone, Evan will pose intense anger and scowl at pretend enemies. Evan is not interested in sports, but he can and does spend hours upon hours making and editing videos.

We, your authors, know these two boys very well: They are our children (we are married, in case you forgot)! Although we highlight them here, Jerry and Evan could be any pair of brothers. This kind of contrast is more the rule than the exception among siblings. If you have brothers or sisters, this description, at least in outline form, probably rings true. How is it that two people— reared in similar environments by the same parents—can have such different personalities?

To answer this question, we must address what personality is, examine classic and current research on the nature and nurture of personality, review the major theoretical explanations for what personality is and how it develops, and describe how personality is measured. Last, we connect many of these topics by reviewing the issue of personality change.

DEFINING PERSONALITY

When psychologists use the term personality, they are referring to the unique and relatively enduring set of behaviors, feelings, thoughts, and motives that characterize an individual (J. Feist, Feist, & Roberts, 2013; B. Roberts & Mroczek, 2008). The definition of *personality* includes two key components. First, personality is what distinguishes us from one another and makes us unique. Second, personality is relatively enduring, or consistent. Let's consider these key components in more detail.

The first major component of personality involves the uniqueness of an individual's thoughts, feelings, and behavior. Different people will respond to almost every situation in different ways. Consider what happens when one driver cuts in front of another. Some people react to such an incident with "road rage," while others take it in stride. A characteristic of personality—hostility—may determine whether someone responds with road rage or not. Personality, therefore, is about uniqueness, or *individual differences*. The concept of personality would not exist if everyone acted and thought alike. Research supports the strength of individual differences: Even when a strong authority figure creates extreme pressure to obey, not everyone will do so (Milgram, 1963). Personality psychology is concerned with the different ways people act in the same situation.

A second part of the definition of personality is its relatively enduring consistency: both across different situations and over time. *Consistency across situations* refers to the notion that a person behaves the same way in different situations and carries who he or she is into almost every situation. Consistency over time, in contrast, is the extent to which a person behaves the same way throughout the life span.

Bringing these two components of personality together, we label a person as "friendly" only if we observe her behaving in a friendly manner in situations in which most others might not act friendly and she does so consistently over time and in many different situations. A friendly person might behave in a friendly manner at a party, while having coffee with friends, or when meeting someone for the first time. We would say that this person's friendly behavior is unique and consistent.

Friendliness is a personality **trait,** or a disposition to behave consistently in a particular way. Although traits make up a large part of an individual's personality, they are not quite synonymous with it. *Personality* is the broader term, because it comprises traits but also motives, thoughts, self-concept, and feelings.

One important principle of personality traits is that they, like intelligence, are normally distributed in the population. Recall from Chapter 10 (Figure 10.7) that a normal distribution exists when a graph of all the scores is symmetrical and bell-shaped. A few people exist at both the extreme low and extreme high ends of the distribution, but most people are average. Consider the traits of anxiety (neuroticism), warmth, and extraversion. A few people, for instance, are barely anxious, and a few are extremely anxious, but most people are somewhere in the middle (see Figure 13.1). The same is true for extraversion, warmth, and any other personality trait.

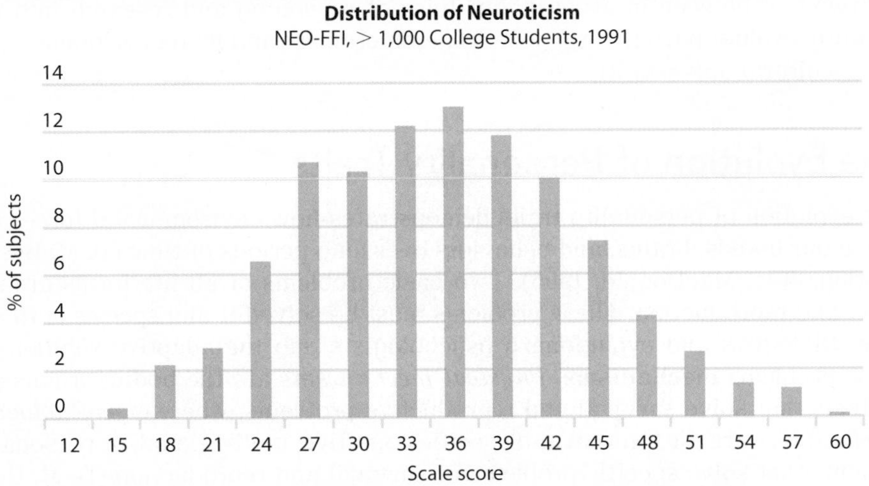

trait
A disposition to behave consistently in a particular way.

Distribution of Neuroticism
NEO-FFI, > 1,000 College Students, 1991

FIGURE **13.1**

DISTRIBUTION OF NEUROTICISM IN THE POPULATION. When we measure personality traits, such as how prone to anxiety and negative emotion people are, and then plot the number of people at all scores from low to high, we end up with a normal—or bell-shaped—distribution. Most people score in the middle, with a few on the extremes. (Source: https://bspace.berkeley.edu/access/content/group/0f4d90d8-c107-467d-000e-28cb28b3815b/Lecture%20Supplements/stats_meths/images/neuroticism.gif)

Where might you be on the distribution?

behavioral thresholds
The points at which a person moves from not having a particular response to having one.

Another important principle of traits is that they are directly connected to behavior. They lower **behavioral thresholds,** or the points at which you move from not having a particular response to having one (Allport, 1937; Feist & Barron, 2003; Rosenberg, 1998). A low threshold means you are very likely to behave in a particular way, whereas a high threshold means you are not. For instance, Carlos is shy, which means he has a low threshold for feeling awkward. If he were introduced to a group of strangers, he would likely feel uncomfortable. In the same situation, however, Karen, who is outgoing, would probably feel comfortable, because she has a much higher threshold for social awkwardness. Their optimal levels of arousal—or thresholds—are different. In short, traits lower behavioral thresholds and are directly connected to behavior.

Quick Quiz 13.1: Defining Personality

1. Two characteristics of personality are
   a. uniqueness and instability in behavior.
   b. uniqueness and consistency in behavior.
   c. consistency in behavior and identity formation.
   d. uniqueness and change in behavior.

2. A statistical property of most personality traits is that they are
   a. unreliably measured.
   b. randomly distributed.
   c. normally distributed.
   d. skewed distributions.

Answers can be found at the end of the chapter.

THE NATURE AND NURTURE OF PERSONALITY

The forces of both nature and nurture shape personality. The interaction between the two can be seen in at least four lines of reasoning and research into personality: evolutionary theory, genetics, temperament and fetal development, and cross-cultural universality.

The Evolution of Personality Traits

The evolution of personality traits demonstrates how environmental forces can shape our bodies, brains, and behaviors over long periods of time (D. M. Buss & Hawley, 2011; MacDonald, 1995). Two basic problems of all life forms are survival and reproduction. These problems must be solved if any species is to survive. Biologists and evolutionary psychologists dub the adaptive solutions to these problems **mechanisms.** *Physical mechanisms* are the bodily organs and systems that solve survival and reproductive problems, whereas *psychological mechanisms* are the internal and specific cognitive, motivational, or personality systems that solve specific problems of survival and reproduction (D. M. Buss, 1991, 2011).

In many animals, but especially humans, personality traits are one form of psychological mechanism that evolved to solve problems of adaptation (D. M. Buss, 2009, 2011; D. M. Buss & Greiling, 1999; Buss & Hawley, 2011; R. A. Duckworth, 2010; MacDonald, 1995; McCrae & Costa, 1999). Personality traits are strategies for solving reproductive and survival problems (D. M. Buss, 1991, 2011). MacDonald (1995) refers to personality differences as "viable alternative strategies for maximizing fitness" (sexual and survival). For example, the

mechanisms
Adaptive solutions to problems of survival and reproduction.

tendency to be sensitive to threats may well have been adaptive in dangerous environments like those in which our ancestors lived. Heightened anxiety would provide a signal of danger and threat; its absence would quickly lead to extinction of the species. Consider a hunter on the savannah. He hears the growl of a large animal and becomes fearful. If he does not feel anxious, he might not hide, and that would have dire consequences for his safety and his likelihood of catching dinner. By the same token, the other extreme—hypersensitivity to threats—would be debilitating and disruptive to everyday functioning. If the same man who became fearful at hearing the growl of a large animal also became fearful with every rustling of leaves or every sound of the wind, he would have a hard time functioning in everyday life. Having some degree of fearfulness is adaptive, and people with that quality were more likely to survive, reproduce, and pass on that disposition.

To be sure, there are both costs and benefits to each personality dimension (Nettle, 2006, 2011). Benefits to anxiety are being sensitive to danger or threats, but at a cost of increased difficulty in relationships. Similarly, benefits to extraversion, for example, are an increase in status and sexual relationships, but the costs include an increase of having accidents, disease, or social conflict.

Naturally selected traits are favored if they increase one's chances of survival and reproductive success, whereas sexually selected traits make one more attractive to the opposite sex. A study of over 400 individuals, many of whom were creative artists and poets, revealed a positive correlation between creativity and sexual success. More creative people were also more sexually active (Nettle & Clegg, 2005). The researchers argue that their findings support the theory, first proposed by Darwin and more recently by Geoffrey Miller (2000), that human creative ability is a sexually selected trait, because it is a quality that increases one's attractiveness to members of the opposite sex.

Genetics and Personality

Recall from Chapter 3 that complex traits are almost never the result of a single gene and that our genome is the starting point, not the end point, for how our genes are expressed (our phenotype). There is no "smart" gene, "shy" gene, or "aggressive" gene. We discuss these two themes in detail later in this section, but first let's look at how *behavioral geneticists* study the relationship between genes and personality.

When studying behavioral genetics, researchers use two major methods to examine the relationship among genetics, behavior, and personality. With the first method, the **quantitative trait loci (QTL) approach,** they look for the location of specific bits of DNA on genes that might be associated with particular behaviors. In this sense, it is a search for "genetic markers" of behavior. The traits are quantitative, because they are markers for behaviors that are expressed on a broad continuum, from very little to very much. Anxiety is a quantitative trait, because some people are not at all anxious, most people are average, and a few are very anxious. The QTL method uncovers the location on particular genes that is associated with high or low levels of a trait.

QTL research points to genetic markers for several basic personality traits, such as novelty or thrill seeking, impulsivity, and neuroticism/anxiety (Benjamin et al., 1996; Hamer & Copeland, 1998; Lesch et al., 1996; Plomin & Caspi, 1999; Retz et al., 2010; Rutter, 2006). Consider the case of thrill seeking, a trait that entails risk taking. People with this trait may seek out highly exciting activities, such as bungee jumping, mountain climbing, or scuba diving. Thrill-seeking activities create a "rush" of excitement—a positive feeling that may be related to the release of dopamine, a neurotransmitter associated with physiological arousal. Given the possible connection between dopamine and thrill seeking,

quantitative trait loci (QTL) approach
A technique in behavioral genetics that looks for the location on genes that might be associated with particular behaviors.

one theory suggests that people who are deficient in dopamine tend to seek out exciting situations as a way of increasing their dopamine release and making up for deficient levels of dopamine.

In the mid-1990s, researchers presented the first genetic evidence to support this theory. The gene *DRD4* is involved in dopamine production in the limbic system, and the longer the gene sequence, the less efficient dopamine production is. In other words, long versions of the *DRD4* gene are associated with less efficient dopamine production. If the theory is correct, people who seek out thrills should have the longer form of this gene, and that is exactly what the research has shown (Ebstein et al., 1996; Hamer & Copeland, 1998). An exciting aspect of this finding is that it was the first to demonstrate a specific genetic influence on a normal (nonpathological) personality trait.

As discussed more fully in Chapter 3, the second method for examining the effect that genetics plays in behavior and personality is the study of twins, both identical and fraternal, who have been raised together or apart. Twin studies have found that most basic personality traits have heritability estimates of between 40% and 60%. In other words, an individual's genetic makeup goes about halfway toward explaining his or her basic traits. For instance, the trait of extraversion, or outgoingness, often correlates around .50 for identical twins and around .24 for fraternal twins, which leads to a heritability estimate of 48% (see Figure 13.2). Likewise, between 50% and 55% of the differences in neuroticism and conscientiousness are due to genetics, and about 40% of differences in openness and agreeableness are due to genetics (Bouchard & Loehlin, 2001; Caspi, Roberts, & Shiner, 2003; Krueger & Johnson, 2008; Loehlin et al., 1998; Plomin & Caspi, 1999; Tellegen et al., 1988).

Such a figure leaves roughly 50% of the differences in personality to be explained by three nongenetic sources: shared environment, unshared environment, and error. Even the environment is not just one thing but needs to be broken into multiple parts. Shared environment consists of living conditions that siblings have in common, such as parents or household, whereas unshared

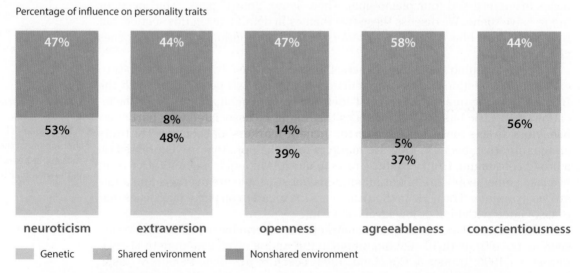

Percentage of influence on personality traits

neuroticism	extraversion	openness	agreeableness	conscientiousness
47%	44%	47%	58%	44%
53%	8% / 48%	14% / 39%	5% / 37%	56%

☐ Genetic   ☐ Shared environment   ☐ Nonshared environment

FIGURE **13.2**

NATURE AND NURTURE OF PERSONALITY: HERITABILITY OF FIVE TRAITS. Twin studies indicate that heredity (genetics) accounts for 50%–60% of most traits, slightly less for agreeableness and openness. What's surprising is that the influence of the shared environment (home and family) on these traits is small, compared with the influence of the nonshared environment. (Plomin & Caspi, 1999)

environment consists of things like birth order, different friends, different teachers, and different social groups. Surprisingly, research indicates that the "unshared" environment—differences in birth order or peer groups or even changes in parenting style and attitudes over time—seems to matter most (see Figure 13.2; Arseneault et al., 2003; Bouchard & Loehlin, 2001; Krueger & Johnson, 2008; Plomin & Caspi, 1999; Rutter, 2006). Personality is influenced by our environment, but surprisingly more by the experiences we do *not* share with our family members, such as peer group influences.

Temperament and the Fetal Environment

Recall from Chapter 5 that temperament is the biologically based disposition to behave in certain ways, which lays the foundation for later personality traits. Evidence suggests that temperament and personality differences are manifest even before birth. Apparently, fetal activity and heart rate can reveal something about temperament differences over the first year of life. In particular, a high heart rate at 36 weeks' gestation (nearly full term) foreshadowed less predictable eating and sleeping habits 3 and 6 months after birth and less emotionality at 6 months after birth. Having high activity levels at 36 weeks' gestation predicted being slow to adapt to new people or situations and having more irregular eating and sleeping habits at 3 and 6 months, as well as being more difficult or fussy at 6 months (DiPietro, 2012; DiPietro et al., 1996).

The prenatal environment may play an important role in shaping personality. One outcome of the prenatal environment is birth weight, with low birth weight being associated with a poor prenatal environment. Recent evidence reports that birth weight is positively correlated with many important outcomes, such as brain volume (Walhovd et al., 2012), and negatively correlated with cautiousness, shyness, and risk aversion later in life—meaning low birth weight babies are more cautious, shy, and risk averse (Waxman et al., 2013).

Another outcome of prenatal environment is differences in serotonin production. These differences play a critical role in brain and neural development, which in turn affect personality development (Oberlander, 2012). Abnormal serotonin function is also involved in the stress response, which is linked with the development of anxiety and depression later in life (McEwen, 2005; Oberlander, 2012). In fact, the amount of stress the mother experiences during pregnancy may alter the infant's own stress response. Infants born to mothers who experienced an unusual amount of stress during pregnancy tend to have impaired stress function; higher baseline levels of stress hormones; and a faster, stronger, and more pronounced physiological response to stress, all of which persist into childhood (Barbazanges et al., 1996; A. S. Clark & Schneider, 1997; F. Rice, Jones, & Thapar, 2007).

Personality and Culture: Universality and Differences

Additional evidence that both nature and nurture shape personality comes from cross-cultural research on personality traits. If personality dispositions are part of our biology, we would expect the same personality dimensions or traits to appear in cultures all over the world. Environment and culture, however, might modify temperament and make certain traits more likely in some societies than in others. There is evidence for both of these perspectives.

Researchers have investigated the personality traits of extraversion, neuroticism, agreeableness, openness to experience, conscientiousness, and psychoticism (Carlo et al., 2014). Research confirms the existence of these personality traits

Connection

Many people think a single gene affects behavior—that we have a gene for "aggression," for example. Any given behavior or personality trait, however, is never the result of a single gene but rather of many genes.

See "Genes and Behavior," Chapter 3, "The Biology of Behavior," p. 73.

Connection

Are some babies and toddlers temperamentally fussy and more difficult to care for than others? As we explain in the chapter on human development, with very little influence from the environment, some newborns are fussy and unpredictable, and they get upset in new situations, whereas others are generally happy, predictable, and curious in new situations.

See "The Developing Infant and Child," Chapter 5, "Human Development," p. 167.

not only in Western cultures (the United States, the United Kingdom, Germany, Australia, Iceland, Spain, Portugal) but also in Asian (China, Japan, South Korea), African (Zimbabwe), Middle Eastern (Iran, Israel), and Pacific Rim (Malaysia and the Philippines) cultures (Benet-Martinez & Oishi, 2008; McCrae, 2002; McCrae & Allik, 2002; McCrae & Costa, 1997). One study of more than 880,000 people from 62 countries on every continent reported universal changes in personality (Bleidorn et al., 2013). From early to mid-adulthood, people become less anxious and extraverted and more open, agreeable, and conscientious. There were, however, also some cultural differences in these changes (Bleidorn et al., 2013). Similarly, one measure of five major dimensions of personality, the NEO-Personality Inventory (PI), has been translated into more than 40 languages, and the same five personality dimensions have emerged in every one (Rolland, 2002). People from vastly different cultural backgrounds exhibit these traits—evidence of their universal and biological basis.

However, people in different cultures differ on certain dimensions of personality (Güngör et al., 2013; McCrae et al., 2010). Once again, it is useful to appreciate behavior and personality from multiple perspectives (Bleidorn et al., 2013). In particular, people in Asian cultures exhibit qualities that fit a dimension of "interpersonal relatedness" that is rarely seen in Western cultures. Interpersonal relatedness includes such behaviors and attitudes as a respectful, obedient demeanor toward others, a belief in saving "face" (allowing a "losing" party to suffer a loss and yet maintain esteem and reputation), and an emphasis on harmonious relationships. This dimension of personality reflects how people in Asian cultures tend to be more concerned about the impact of their behavior on their family, friends, and social groups (known as *collectivism*), whereas people in Western cultures are more concerned with how their behavior will affect their personal goals (known as *individualism*; Cross & Markus, 1999; Hofstede, 2001). Thus, an Asian employee who is offered a promotion that would require relocating to another city may be concerned primarily with how the move would affect

In Japan and other Asian cultures, respect for others and an emphasis on harmonious interpersonal relationships take precedence over individual concerns. Interpersonal relatedness as a dimension of personality is rare in the West.

his family. On the other hand, the primary consideration of a Western employee might be how the move would increase her chances of someday becoming an executive in a major corporation.

Challenging Assumptions in Animal Personality

A few years ago, your authors adopted two 7-month-old kittens: "Scooter" (a male) and his sister, "Belle." Now 4 years old, these two cats could hardly be more different in terms of their behavior. Scooter is curious and sociable. He explored every inch of his new home on the first day and forces himself into every one of our activities—eating, watching TV, working at the computer, and sleeping. Not once has he been afraid of any situation. He approaches everything with glee and wonder. Belle, however, has been anxious and shy from the beginning. It took her about 3 days to come out of hiding and become comfortable with her new home. She plays, but not so much with strangers, which we were for the first few days.

Belle and Scooter—the authors' cats

To pet owners the question of animal personality seems to have an obvious answer: Of course animals have distinct personalities. Just look at Scooter and Belle. To psychologists the question might seem to be stretching the definition of personality too far. If we claim that animals have personality, might we simply be projecting human qualities onto them, what scientists term *anthropomorphizing*? Most people who have owned more than one cat or dog can identify differences in the personalities of their pets. Some pets are calm, while others are excitable; some are friendly and readily approach strangers, whereas others are more reserved and wary. Even if we can see evidence of personality in animals such as dogs and cats, can we see it in other animals? Do mice have personality? Birds? Reptiles? Fish? Worms?

Until the 1990s, most psychologists would have argued that the term *personality* made sense only as applied to humans. From the 1990s on, however, a solid body of evidence began to challenge the assumption that personality differences are mostly limited to humans (Cote et al., 2014; Dingemanse et al., 2002; Gosling & John, 1999; Morton et al., 2013; J. Uher, 2008; Zimmer, 2005). Gosling and Oliver John (1999) conducted a meta-analysis of 19 studies across 12 nonhuman species. They found evidence for at least 14 nonhuman species with personality traits that can be categorized along the same dimensions as human personality. The summary of these findings is presented in Figure 13.3. Keep in mind that the labels from the Big Five are general labels, and the specific ones used in these studies vary somewhat. For instance, neuroticism is sometimes called emotional stability, excitability, fearfulness, emotional reactivity, fear-avoidance, or emotionality. Agreeableness is sometimes labeled aggression, hostility, understanding, opportunistic, sociability, affection, or fighting-timidity. In addition, dominance-submission is a trait that is often seen and measured in nonhuman animals, but it does not fit into any of the Big Five categories. These ratings of animal personality were made by one of two behavioral observation techniques: either by animal trainers who had extensive knowledge of the individual animals or by trained observers with no history with the animals but who were trained until they could reliably evaluate the dimensions in question.

It may not surprise you that primates and other mammals tend to share the largest number of personality traits with humans (Morton et al., 2013; T. A. Weinstein, Capitanio, & Gosling, 2008). Chimpanzees, our closest relative, however, share with humans a distinct "conscientiousness" dimension. Such a finding suggests that conscientiousness—which involves impulse control and therefore requires highly developed brain regions capable of controlling impulses—is the most recently evolved personality trait. Thus, with the exception of chimps and

	Neuroticism	Extraversion	Agreeableness	Openness	Conscientiousness
chimpanzee	✔	✔	✔		✔
horse[a]	✔	✔	✔		✔
rhesus monkey	✔	✔	✔		
gorilla	✔	✔	✔		
dog	✔	✔	✔	✔[b]	
cat	✔	✔	✔	✔[b]	
hyena	✔		✔		
pig		✔	✔		
vervet monkey		✔	✔		
donkey		✔	✔		
rat	✔		✔		
guppy	✔	✔			
octopus	✔	✔			
chickadee[c]					

[a] Based on Morris, Gale, and Duffy (2002).
[b] Competence/learning is a mixture of openness and conscientiousness.
[c] Based on Dingemanse et al. (2002).

FIGURE **13.3**

PERSONALITY DIMENSIONS ACROSS SPECIES. Ratings by trainers who know the animals or by trained observers produced these results, which suggest that animals do have personalities and that they share some traits with humans. Note that domestic dogs and cats have a "competence" or "learning" dimension that is a mixture of openness and conscientiousness. Where no check mark appears, there is no evidence for that trait in that species. (Gosling & John, 1999)

horses, animals other than humans do not possess the required brain structures to control impulse and to organize and plan their activities in advance. Even with chimps, the conscientiousness dimension was somewhat narrowly defined as being methodical, lacking attention, and being goal directed (Freeman et al., 2013). Two very interesting recent findings are that horses high in neuroticism and low in extraversion are most susceptible to pain (Ijichi, Collins, & Elwood, 2013) and that chimps high in openness, dominance, and being methodical spent the longest time working on foraging puzzles that involved finding food (Hopper et al., 2013).

What challenged people's assumptions the most, however, was research reporting that wild birds, fish, and even octopuses possess humanlike personality traits. For instance, in a study of a European bird resembling a chickadee, when researchers placed a foreign object, such as a battery or a Pink Panther doll, into the cage, some birds were consistently curious and explored the novel object, while others consistently withdrew and avoided the object (Zimmer, 2005; Dingemanse et al., 2002). The researchers called these differences in birds "bold" and "shy." These differences are much like those psychologists observe when they place an infant in a room with a stranger. Approach-boldness and shyness-avoidance are also dimensions of human temperament.

Challenge Your Assumptions
True or False? Many different kinds of animals have personality in the sense that humans do.
True: Primates, in particular, but most mammals and even nonmammals share personality traits with humans.

1. The genetic marker for thrill seeking involves genetic differences in which neurotransmitter?
   a. dopamine
   b. acetylcholine
   c. serotonin
   d. norepinephrine

2. Researchers obtain estimates of how heritable personality traits are by
   a. studying biochemical markers of personality.
   b. analyzing DNA in rats reared together.
   c. documenting family histories.
   d. studying twins.

3. People in Asian cultures exhibit qualities that suggest a personality dimension of _____ that is rarely seen in Western cultures.
   a. anxiety
   b. interpersonal relatedness
   c. separation distress
   d. agreeableness

4. Which of the human Big Five personality characteristics appears only in humans, chimpanzees, and horses?
   a. openness
   b. extraversion
   c. conscientiousness
   d. agreeableness

Answers can be found at the end of the chapter.

HOW DO THEORISTS EXPLAIN PERSONALITY?

Some people are calm and relaxed, but others are regularly nervous and anxious; some are warm and friendly, whereas others are hostile and aggressive. How do we explain such differences in personality style? Let's take a look at the answers theorists have provided. The major explanations can be grouped into five distinct theoretical camps: psychoanalysis, humanism, social–cognitive learning, trait theory, and biological theory. As you will see, each offers a different perspective on the phenomenon of personality.

Psychoanalytic Theories

Psychoanalytic theories are all based on or are variations of Freud's seminal ideas.

Sigmund Freud   Undoubtedly the most famous of all psychologists is Sigmund Freud (1856–1939). Freud not only proposed an overarching theory of personality and psychotherapy but also founded the movement known as psychoanalysis and, in the process of doing so, essentially invented the field of psychotherapy.

As mentioned in Chapter 1, the starting point for Freud's theory of psychoanalysis is the idea that the unconscious is the most powerful force in personality. More generally, Freud described three layers of consciousness: unconscious, preconscious, and conscious. The conscious layer is what we are aware of at any given moment in time, whereas the preconscious is just below the surface of awareness. It is not currently conscious but can become so relatively easily. Because the conscious and preconscious layers are less important in Freud's theory, we will focus instead on the unconscious.

According to Freud, the **unconscious** contains all the drives, urges, or instincts that are outside awareness but nonetheless motivate most of our speech, thoughts, feelings, or actions. Before Freud, most people assumed that what we consciously think, feel, and believe is a relatively accurate and important source of information for explaining our behavior and personality.

unconscious
One of Freud's three levels of consciousness; it contains all the drives, urges, or instincts that are outside awareness but nonetheless motivate most of our speech, thoughts, feelings, or actions.

Theories of personality, like all scientific theories, are based on theorists' observations and are used to generate research hypotheses.

What observations about personality does this photograph bring to mind?

Connection

Cognitive psychologists refer to mental processes that occur outside awareness as "implicit" or "automatic." Much of what we learn and remember is implicit.

See "Long-Term Memory Storage in the Cortex," Chapter 7, "Memory," p. 271, and "Basic Processes of Learning," Chapter 8, "Learning," p. 287.

id
One of Freud's provinces of the mind; the seat of impulse and desire; the part of our personality that we do not yet own; it owns or controls us.

ego
One of Freud's provinces of the mind; a sense of self; the only part of the mind that is in direct contact with the outside world; it operates on the "reality principle."

superego
One of Freud's provinces of the mind; the part of the self that monitors or controls behavior; it "stands over us" and evaluates our actions in terms of right and wrong; hence, our conscience.

Freud believed that much of what we do and the reasons we do it are hidden from our awareness and revealed to us only in distorted forms, such as slips of the tongue and dreams (S. Freud, 1900/1953, 1901/1960). The technique of free association, whereby people are encouraged to speak about anything on their minds without censoring their thoughts, also provides access to the unconscious (see Chapter 16 for a discussion of free association). He developed an elaborate system for interpreting the meaning of dreams, because they were the best way to understand a person's unconscious.

Freud also developed the notion that the human mind has three distinct "provinces," or regions, involved in the control and regulation of impulses. The first province—developed in infancy—is the **id,** the seat of impulse and desire. The id is the part of our personality that owns or controls us. Its sole function is to seek pleasure; it is therefore founded in the "pleasure principle" and operates on the "do it" principle. By the end of the first year of life, a sense of self, or **ego,** has begun to emerge. It is the only part of the mind that is in direct contact with the outside world, and it operates on the "reality principle." If the id wants pleasure, the ego makes a realistic attempt to obtain it. The last part of the mind to develop, around age 2 or 3, is the **superego,** the part of the self that monitors and controls behavior. The superego "stands over us" and evaluates our actions in terms of right and wrong; hence, it is our conscience. It operates on the "moralistic principle," is the control center of the personality, and frequently applies the brakes to the impulses of the id.

In a healthy person, the ego mediates this conflict between impulse and control. Freud believed that some people are mostly id-driven, whereas others are mostly superego-driven. People who are overly impulsive and pleasure seeking have an uncontrolled id. People who are overly controlling and repress their impulses have an exaggerated superego. The healthiest person is one in whom the ego is most developed and can control, in a realistic and healthy way, the conflict between impulse and control (see Figure 13.4).

Another of Freud's major contributions to psychology is the concept of psychological **defense mechanisms** (S. Freud, 1926/1959). Although Freud first described these mechanisms, his daughter, Anna, developed them further (A. Freud, 1946). Just as the physical body has the immune system to protect it from foreign substances, the mind also protects itself from harmful, threatening, and anxiety-provoking thoughts, feelings, or impulses. All defense mechanisms share two qualities: (1) They operate unconsciously, and (2) they deny and distort reality in some way.

The most basic of all defense mechanisms is repression; it underlies all the other defense mechanisms. Repression is the unconscious act of keeping threatening or disturbing thoughts, feelings, or impulses out of consciousness. The impulses that are most likely to be repressed are sexual and aggressive impulses, because these are inherently the most threatening. Although repression may keep these impulses and thoughts out of awareness, they may be expressed in disguised or distorted form. In fact, they often reveal themselves through dreams, slips of the tongue, or neurotic behavior.

Reaction formation occurs when an unpleasant idea, feeling, or impulse is turned into its opposite. This often results in exaggerated or compulsive feelings and behavior (S. Freud, 1926/1959). A woman may resent and even hate her mother, but because these feelings are not acceptable to her or to society, she turns them into showy, exaggerated love. Homophobia is another example: Hatred and aggression toward homosexuals might well be a reaction against fear of one's own latent homosexual impulses.

In **projection,** people deny and repress their own particular ideas, feelings, or impulses and project them onto others. For example, a man may desire a married woman, but instead of recognizing his feelings, he projects his desire onto the woman and believes that she is seducing him. Another defense is **sublimation,** which involves expressing a socially unacceptable impulse in a socially acceptable and even desirable way. Freud believed that most creative achievements are motivated by sublimated impulses, usually sexual or aggressive. That is, unfulfilled sexual desire or aggressive impulses drive much creative output. Thus, for example, a man who is hopelessly in love with an unattainable woman may engage in sublimation, channeling his feelings into writing a novel whose main characters closely resemble him and the woman he desires.

Freud is one of the most complex figures in the history of psychology. His theories have had a significant and lasting influence on Western thought. Large segments of 20th-century art and literature were directly or indirectly influenced by Freud's views of human nature, from James Joyce's use of stream of consciousness to Salvador Dalí's surrealistic paintings (Adams & Szaluta, 1996; Brivic, 1980; Kimball, 2003). Over the last generation, however, many research-oriented psychologists have dismissed Freud as a pseudoscientist, because he did not support his ideas with research that could be replicated. His status as a scientist is questionable, but his insights as a clinician still have scientific merit. In the late 1990s, a group of neuroscientists began to argue that the latest evidence from neuroscience confirms certain of Freud's ideas. According to Antonio Damasio, a well-known contemporary neuroscientist, "we can say that Freud's insights on the nature of consciousness are consonant with the most advanced contemporary neuroscience views" (quoted in Solms & Turnbull, 2002, p. 93).

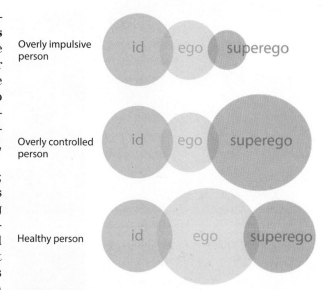

FIGURE **13.4**

THE RELATIVE INFLUENCES OF ID, EGO, AND SUPEREGO IN THREE TYPES OF PEOPLE. Freud argued that the relative sizes and strengths of the id, ego, and superego (as symbolized by the size of the circles) contributed to whether a person is overly impulsive, neurotically repressed and overcontrolled, or psychologically balanced and healthy. (J. Feist, Feist, & Roberts, 2013)

defense mechanisms
Unconscious strategies the mind uses to protect itself from anxiety by denying and distorting reality in some way.

reaction formation
A defense mechanism that occurs when an unpleasant idea, feeling, or impulse is turned into its opposite.

projection
A defense mechanism in which people deny particular ideas, feelings, or impulses and project them onto others.

sublimation
A defense mechanism that involves expressing a socially unacceptable impulse in a socially acceptable way.

To honor Freud's contributions to psychology, his last home, in London, has been preserved as a museum. His patients would lie on this couch during treatment sessions.

Challenge Your Assumptions

True or False? Freud's ideas are interesting historically, but have no scientific support.

True and False: Some parts of Freud's ideas are supported by modern science (the power of the unconscious and the lasting impact of childhood experiences), but others are not (sexual stages).

striving for superiority
According to Adler, the major drive behind all behavior, whereby humans naturally strive to overcome their inherent inferiorities or deficiencies, both physical and psychological.

inferiority complex
An unhealthy need to dominate or upstage others as a way of compensating for feelings of deficiency.

Others argue that Freud's ideas about the power of the unconscious, the conflicting nature of motives, and the importance of early childhood experience on adult personality have had a lasting impact and have survived empirical testing (Weston, 1998).

For all of Freud's genius, however, he became dogmatic about his ideas after he had published them. Any followers who seriously challenged them might have been ejected from Freud's inner circle or official society. Some of these followers went on to develop their own theories of psychoanalysis. Among them were Alfred Adler, Carl Jung, and Karen Horney.

Alfred Adler The first to break away from Freud, Alfred Adler (1870–1937) saw himself as Freud's colleague rather than follower. When he disagreed with Freud on the major motives underlying behavior, he had to resign from the presidency of Freud's Vienna Psychoanalytic Society. Adler's first major assumption was that humans naturally strive to overcome their inherent inferiorities or deficiencies, both physical and psychological. This **striving for superiority,** not sex or aggression, is the major drive behind all behavior (A. Adler, 1956). Adler introduced the term *compensation* to explain how this process unfolds. All people, he pointed out, begin life as young, immature, and helpless. As they grow, they strive toward growth and completion. In the process, they attempt to compensate for their feelings of weakness or inferiority. Although all people do this to some extent, some develop an unhealthy need to dominate or upstage others as a way of compensating for feelings of inferiority—that is, they develop an **inferiority complex.**

Another key idea in Adler's theory of individual psychology is the importance of birth order in influencing personality (A. Adler, 1931). Adler noticed consistent differences in the personalities of first-born, middle-born, and last-born individuals. First-born children tend to have strong feelings of superiority and power. After all, by definition, first-born children are older and more mature than their siblings. First-borns can be nurturing of others, but they are sometimes highly critical and have a strong need to be right. Second children tend to be motivated and cooperative, but they can become overly competitive. Youngest children can be realistically ambitious but also pampered and dependent on others. Finally, only children can be socially mature, but they sometimes lack social interest and have exaggerated feelings of superiority.

Carl Jung   Though younger, Carl Jung (1875–1961) became more widely known than Adler. Jung's signature idea was that the unconscious has two distinct forms: personal and collective (Jung, 1964). The **personal unconscious** consists of all our repressed and hidden thoughts, feelings, and motives. This is similar to Freud's notion of the unconscious. Jung also believed, however, that there is a second kind of unconscious, one that belongs not to the individual but to the species. He called it the **collective unconscious,** and it consists of the shared experiences of our ancestors—God, mother, life, death, water, earth, aggression, survival— that have been transmitted from generation to generation. Jung decided that there must be some kind of collective unconsciousness that would explain the many instances in which dreams, religions, legends, and myths share the same content, even though the people who created them have never directly or even indirectly communicated with one another. The idea of a collective unconscious came naturally to Jung, because he was extraordinarily well versed in world mythology, world religion, and archeology. However, he was less well versed in biological theory or genetics; thus, his understanding of the mechanisms involved was inconsistent and, at times, based on faulty assumptions, such as experiences being inherited from generation to generation.

The collective unconscious is made up of **archetypes:** ancient or archaic images that result from common ancestral experiences. Their content is made manifest most often in our dreams but also in fantasies, hallucinations, myths, and religious themes. Jung postulated many archetypes, including the shadow, anima, and animus. The **shadow** is the dark and morally objectionable part of ourselves. We all have impulses that are dark and disturbing; in fact, most often we project evil and darkness onto our enemies and deny that we ourselves are evil or capable of it. Shadow figures are found everywhere in politics, literature,

personal unconscious
According to Jung, a form of consciousness that consists of all our repressed and hidden thoughts, feelings, and motives.

collective unconscious
According to Jung, a form of consciousness that consists of the shared experiences of our ancestors—God, mother, life, death, water, earth, aggression, survival— that have been passed down from generation to generation.

archetypes
Ancient or archaic images that result from common ancestral experiences.

shadow
According to Jung, the dark and morally objectionable part of ourselves.

Darth Vader, the villain from the movie *Star Wars*, epitomizes Jung's shadow archetype of the dark, morally repugnant side of human nature.

and art, not to mention movies: Darth Vader of *Star Wars* clearly personifies the shadow figure.

The **anima** is the female part of the male personality, and the **animus** is the male part of the female personality. All people possess characteristics and traits—not to mention hormones—that are typical of both genders, but men tend to deny and repress their feminine side, or anima. Women likewise tend to deny or repress their masculine side, or animus. Full personality development requires acknowledging and being receptive to these unconscious or less well-developed sides of one's personality.

Karen Horney   One of the first major female voices in the psychoanalytic movement was that of Karen Horney (pronounced "horn-eye"; 1885–1952). Compared to Freud, Horney focused more on the social and cultural forces behind neurosis and the neurotic personality, and indeed her approach is labeled "psychoanalytic social theory." The essence of Horney's theory is that neurosis stems from basic hostility and basic anxiety. *Basic hostility* is anger or rage that originates in childhood and stems from fear of being neglected or rejected by one's parents. Because hostility toward one's parents is so threatening, it is often turned inward and converted into *basic anxiety,* which Horney defined as "a feeling of being isolated and helpless in a world conceived as potentially hostile" (1950, p. 18).

Although basic anxiety in itself is not neurotic—it can give rise to normal behaviors—in some people it can result in neurotic behaviors. Horney argued that all people defend themselves against basic anxiety (isolation and helplessness) by developing particular needs or trends (see Figure 13.5). If these needs

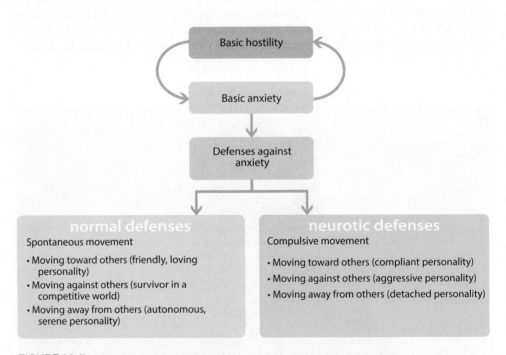

FIGURE 13.5

INTERACTION AMONG HOSTILITY, ANXIETY, AND DEFENSES IN HORNEY'S THEORY.
Hostility and anxiety mutually influence one another, and the person then defends him- or herself by developing either normal or neurotic defenses. Horney maintained that we all may develop defenses, but in neurotic individuals, these needs become compulsive.

 Can you think of someone you know who uses these defenses normally and someone else who uses them neurotically?

---

anima
According to Jung, the female part of the male personality.

animus
According to Jung, the male part of the female personality.

become compulsive and the person is unable to switch from one need to another as the situation demands, that person is neurotic. The three neurotic trends or needs are

1. *Moving toward others* (the compliant personality)
2. *Moving against others* (the aggressive personality)
3. *Moving away from others* (the detached personality)

Neurotically moving toward others involves consistently needing or clinging to other people, belittling oneself, getting people to feel sorry for "poor little me," and almost completely repressing feelings of anger and hostility. Neurotically moving against others involves puffing oneself up in an obvious and public manner, "chest-beating," competing against others at almost everything, and being prone to hostility and anger. Finally, neurotically moving away from others involves developing a detached and "cool" demeanor—not responding emotionally, not caring, and being "above it all." One way to avoid feeling isolated and helpless is not to feel anything. Whenever someone tries to get close to a detached person and open up to him or her, the detached person withdraws and closes up. Detached individuals are unwilling to make commitments, especially to long-term relationships (Horney, 1945).

Neuropsychoanalysis One of the major criticisms of Freudian theory has been its lack of empirical or scientific foundation. Critics claimed that it was more "armchair speculation" than scientifically testable hypotheses (Crews, 1998). Although there is some validity to some of these criticisms, it is also true that certain Freudian assumptions—that unconscious motives affect our thinking and reasoning, and that dreams are mostly about repressed ideas—have received recent scientific support (Westen et al., 2006).

In fact, **neuropsychoanalysis,** a scientific movement that started in the late 1990s, combined Freudian ideas with neuroscientific methods (Wright & Panksepp, 2012). By combining the subjective insights into the mind made by Freud with the objective insights of the mind gained by neuroscience, neuropsychoanalysts are closing the divide that existed between Freud's ideas and science. Neuropsychoanalysts argue that at least seven core assumptions made by Freud have received recent scientific support (Solms, 2004; Westen, Gabbard, & Ortigo, 2008; Westen et al., 2006):

neuropsychoanalysis
A new scientific movement started in the late 1990s that combined Freudian ideas with neuroscientific methods.

- The importance of early childhood experience on later personality development
- Unconscious motivation
- Repression and defense mechanisms
- The pleasure principle
- Primitive drives
- Dreams as wish fulfillment
- Thinking and perception being guided by unconscious motives and emotions

A recent study from a Freudian perspective examined the ways unconscious feelings and motives affect how people judge presidential candidates (Westen et al., 2006). The researchers found that people tended to gloss over contradictions made by their preferred candidate; they didn't see them as real contradictions. They did, however, latch on to the contradictions of their nonpreferred candidate. Such a result is quite consistent with the Freudian notion of repression, where people ignore or deny threatening ideas. In addition, neuroimaging results of the study showed that motivated reasoning involves different brain regions than nonmotivated reasoning. Motivated reasoning is reasoning that is influenced by our wishes and desires. To be more exact, both forms of reasoning involve the prefrontal cortex, but different regions. In addition, motivated reasoning activated regions of the brain involved in emotional responses (anterior cingulate cortex and the insula), whereas nonmotivated reasoning did not.

Humanistic–Positive Psychological Theories

A second major perspective explaining personality comes from a *humanistic approach*, which is optimistic about human nature, believing that humans are naturally interested in realizing their full potential. Humanists argue that psychology needs to study humans at their best as well as at their worst. As Abraham Maslow wrote (1968, p. 5), "Freud supplied us with the sick half of psychology, and we must now fill it with the healthy half." The term *humanism* is not commonly used today, mostly because many adherents of this approach did not conduct empirical research, yet the movement has been rekindled since the late 1990s under a new label: *positive psychology*. Positive psychology embraces and generates empirical research, but its fundamental ideas come from two major thinkers in the humanistic tradition: Abraham Maslow and Carl Rogers (Seligman & Csikszentmihalyi, 2000).

Abraham Maslow We discussed one of Abraham Maslow's (1908–1970) major ideas in Chapter 11: his hierarchy of needs. An important concept that followed from his theory of needs was that of self-actualization, which stood at the top of the hierarchy. This term refers to people's inherent drive to realize their full potential (an idea that was influenced by Adler's notion of striving for superiority; Maslow, 1970). Very few people attain this highest level of the hierarchy of needs, because very few are "fully human," or living life at its fullest and achieving their full potential.

Based on an examination of historical figures whom he considered self-actualizing, Maslow identified a set of characteristics that he believed to be more common in self-actualizing individuals than in other people (Maslow, 1970). He listed 15 characteristics, five of which we summarize here:

1. *Spontaneity, simplicity, naturalness:* Self-actualizing people sometimes can appear quite childlike in their ability to be spontaneous and straightforward; they do not pretend to be what they are not.

2. *Problem-centered (have a "calling"):* Self-actualizing people often experience moments of profound personal importance or personal meaning (what Maslow called "peak experiences"), and these experiences shape the rest of their lives. A sense of what they were meant to do with their lives is suddenly revealed to them, and they devote the rest of their lives to it. These individuals are focused and secure in who they are and what matters most to them—and often their concerns have great philosophical, spiritual, political, artistic, or scientific meaning.

3. *Creativity (self-actualizing rather than specialized):* Problems confront us dozens, if not hundreds, of times each day. Self-actualizing people are able to readily solve problems with originality and novelty. By *creativity,* Maslow does not mean creativity as expressed in art or science (specialized creativity) but rather the kind of creativity that can be found in everyday life (self-actualizing creativity). Practical, everyday creativity is more important than professional achievement, although self-actualized people may be creative in their work as well.

4. *Deep interpersonal relations:* Self-actualizing individuals are likely to have few but profound relationships. They do not call 10 or 15 people their

"best friends" or even "friends" but instead may have close relationships with only one or two people. These relationships, however, are intensely intimate; they share deep thoughts and feelings about themselves, each other, and the world.

5. *Resistance to enculturation:* Self-actualizing people are less likely than most people to be influenced by the ideas and attitudes of others. Their ideas are solidly their own; because they have a clear sense of direction in life, they don't look to others for guidance on what to think or how to behave.

Carl Rogers   Another key figure in the humanistic–positive psychology tradition was the psychotherapist Carl Rogers (1902–1987). Rogers developed a unique form of psychotherapy based on the assumption that people naturally strive toward growth and fulfillment and need unconditional positive regard for that to happen (Rogers, 1980). **Unconditional positive regard** is the ability to respect and appreciate another person unconditionally—that is, regardless of the person's behavior. This may sound easy, but, in fact, it is very difficult. Even if someone violates our basic assumptions of what it means to be a good, decent, and moral person, we still appreciate, respect, and even love him or her as a person. It requires that we separate person from behavior, which can be difficult even for parents and their children. To love people only when they do things that we want and like is to love them conditionally.

In contrast to Maslow, Rogers had a specific, measurable way of defining the self-actualizing tendency and psychological adjustment. To Rogers, all of us have two distinct ways of seeing and evaluating ourselves: as we really are and as we ideally would like to be. The first he called the real self and the second the ideal self (Rogers, 1959). Rogers then defined psychological adjustment as congruence between the real and ideal selves.

In the late 1990s a modern offshoot to humanism began under the name *positive psychology* (Seligman & Csikszentmihalyi, 2000). The core idea behind positive psychology is a focus on positive states and experiences, such as hope, optimism, wisdom, creativity, spirituality, and positive emotions (for example, happiness). In contrast to the humanistic psychologists, however, positive psychologists are more likely to base their ideas in research than in speculation, clinical practice, and observation.

Connection

A truly starving person is not concerned with art and beauty. Maslow's hierarchy of needs describes how the basic needs (such as hunger, thirst) must be satisfied before one can pursue the higher needs, such as self-actualization.

See "Models of Motivation," Chapter 11, "Motivation and Emotion," p. 397.

unconditional positive regard Acceptance of another person regardless of his or her behavior.

Carl Rogers (second from right) leads a group therapy session. His client-centered therapy approach is discussed in Chapter 16.

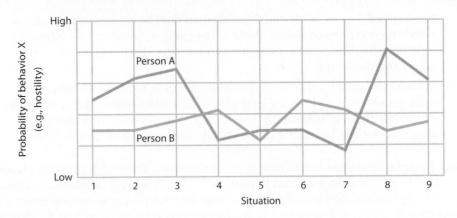

FIGURE **13.6**

HYPOTHETICAL PERSON-SITUATION BEHAVIOR INTERACTION.

 Looking at the graph, what conclusion would you draw about which person is more hostile overall, Person A or Person B? People respond to different situations differently, producing unique personality-situation profiles. Here, Person A is more hostile than Person B in the first three situations. They are roughly the same in the middle four situations. So saying that Person A is more hostile than Person B would be misleading and simplistic. It depends on the situation. (Mischel & Shoda, 1995)

Social–Cognitive Learning Theories

A third major category of personality theory is based on the social–cognitive learning perspective, exemplified by the research and writings of Walter Mischel. As we have seen, personality traits produce consistent behavior over time and across situations. A hostile person may be less hostile in one situation (for example, being run into by a child) than in another (for example, being cut off in traffic). Compared to a nonhostile person, he or she is likely to be more hostile in many—but not all—situations. Mischel says that people are not consistent across all situations (Mischel, 2009; Mischel & Shoda, 1995, 1999), because it would be pathological not to change one's behavior when the situation changes. The qualities a person brings to each situation interact with the situation to make the behavior change when the situation changes. Figure 13.6 illustrates how people and situations interact according to Mischel's theory. The figure presents the probabilities of two individuals (A and B) acting in a hostile manner across nine different situations. As you can see, Person A is more likely to be hostile in six of the nine situations, so we would label this person "hostile." Notice two things: (1) There are a few situations in which Person B is more hostile, and (2) Person B is more stable and consistent across all nine situations, whereas Person A is sometimes very hostile but at other times not hostile at all. This hypothetical situation demonstrates how the person, situation, and behavior interact.

Trait Theories

A fourth general perspective that explains personality is the trait approach, which assumes that traits, or dispositions, are the major force behind personality, but which traits are most important? Between the 1930s and the 1980s, dozens of different measures of personality were developed, but almost none of them measured the same personality traits. Some psychologists argued for the central importance of hostility, authoritarianism, introversion, intelligence, repression, and impulsivity, while others cited psychopathic deviance, tolerance, or psychological insight. Until personality psychologists could reach a consensus on a set of traits that make up personality across cultures, no progress could be made in the study of personality, for it would mean different things to different people.

As far back as the 1930s, Gordon Allport (1897–1967) tried to figure out how many personality traits existed (Allport & Odbert, 1936). He began with the idea that language would be a good place to start looking. He argued quite simply that, if a word exists for a trait, it must be important. He approached the problem by taking an English dictionary and combing through it page by page and counting each time a term described a person. After going through and counting all the personally descriptive words, he came away with nearly 18,000 words in English. A few problems arose, however. First, some of these terms—such as *sad, angry, bored,* or *annoyed*—described temporary states. Others were personal evaluations (*wonderful, unhelpful*) or descriptions of physical traits (*tall, heavy*). Finally, others were essentially synonyms, such as *friendly* and *nice*. When he fixed these problems, he still ended up with more than 4,000 English words that were personally descriptive. He went on to argue, however, that most individuals could typically be described with only about 10 or so central traits.

By the 1980s, personality researchers had amassed evidence for the existence of five universal and widely agreed-upon dimensions of personality (Costa & McCrae, 1992; Digman, 1990; John & Srivastava, 1999). This perspective is known as the **Big Five** or **five-factor model;** the five dimensions are openness to experience, conscientiousness, extraversion, agreeableness, and neuroticism (see Figure 13.7). An easy way to remember these is to use the acronym O-C-E-A-N or C-A-N-O-E.

The Big Five dimensions are more of a taxonomy, or categorization scheme, than a theory. They describe but do not explain personality. In the 1990s, Robert McCrae (1949) and Paul Costa (1942) proposed a theory around the Big Five personality dimensions. The two primary components of their theory are basic tendencies and characteristic adaptations (McCrae & Costa, 1996, 1999, 2008). The Big Five personality dimensions, along with our talents, aptitudes, and cognitive abilities, are referred to as **basic tendencies,** and they have their origin

Big Five (five-factor model)
A theory of personality that includes the following five dimensions: openness to experience, conscientiousness, extraversion, agreeableness, and neuroticism (OCEAN).

basic tendencies
The essence of personality: the Big Five personality dimensions, as well as talents, aptitudes, and cognitive abilities.

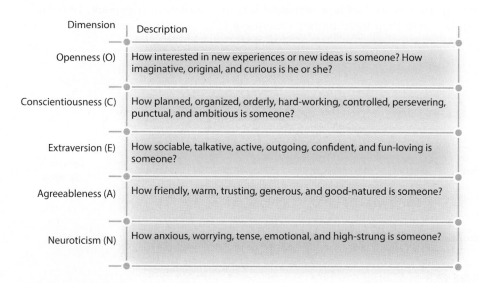

Dimension	Description
Openness (O)	How interested in new experiences or new ideas is someone? How imaginative, original, and curious is he or she?
Conscientiousness (C)	How planned, organized, orderly, hard-working, controlled, persevering, punctual, and ambitious is someone?
Extraversion (E)	How sociable, talkative, active, outgoing, confident, and fun-loving is someone?
Agreeableness (A)	How friendly, warm, trusting, generous, and good-natured is someone?
Neuroticism (N)	How anxious, worrying, tense, emotional, and high-strung is someone?

FIGURE **13.7**
BIG FIVE DIMENSIONS OF PERSONALITY. The acronym OCEAN (or CANOE) will help you remember the five dimensions.

in biological forces. McCrae and Costa take a clear but somewhat controversial stance in arguing that these basic tendencies are due solely to internal or biological factors such as genes, hormones, and brain structures.

Biological Theories

The fifth way of explaining personality theoretically, biological theory, does provide explanations for McCrae and Costa's scheme. The biological theories of personality assume that differences in personality are partly based in differences in structures and systems in the central nervous system, such as genetics, hormones, and neurotransmitters (Eysenck, 1990; Gray, 1970, 1987). Among the most important of these theories for personality is the one proposed by Hans Eysenck (1916–1997), who argued for the fundamental importance of biology in shaping personality. Eysenck (1947, 1982, 1990) proposed three, rather than five, fundamental dimensions of personality. Two are included in the Big Five, neuroticism and extraversion. The third, *psychoticism*, is a combination of the three other traits from the Big Five of openness, conscientiousness, and agreeableness. Psychoticism consists of traits such as "aggressive," "cold," "antisocial," "impulsive," "egocentric," "nonconforming," and "creative." All three personality dimensions are hierarchical; that is, neuroticism, extraversion, and psychoticism each comprise more specific traits, which in turn comprise even more specific traits (see Figure 13.8).

Eysenck developed a model in which differences in personality are caused by the combined influences of genes, neurochemistry, and certain characteristics of the central nervous system (Eysenck, 1997). The main idea behind Eysenck's model is that differences in individuals' genomes (DNA) create a different level of arousal and sensitivity to stimulation. These differences in genetics and levels of arousal and sensitivity lead to differences in the three primary dimensions of personality: psychoticism, extraversion, and neuroticism (P-E-N). Personality differences in dimensions in turn lead to differences in learning, conditioning, perception, and memory. These cognitive-perceptual-learning differences lead to differences in social behaviors such as sociability, criminality, sexual behavior, and creativity.

Evidence supports the connection between central nervous system arousal and personality traits, especially extraversion-introversion. Specifically, differences in cortical arousal and sensory thresholds lead to differences in extraversion-introversion. **Cortical arousal** refers to how active the brain is at a resting state as well as how sensitive it is to stimulation (Eysenck, 1997; Gale, 1983). Because they have higher baseline levels of cortical arousal, introverts

cortical arousal
The brain's level of activity at a resting state and its sensitivity to stimulation

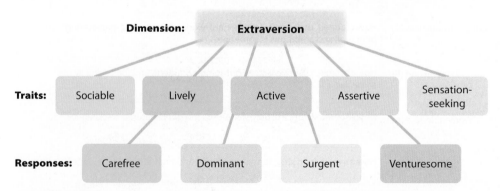

FIGURE **13.8**

EYSENCK'S HIERARCHY OF PERSONALITY TRAITS FOR EXTRAVERSION. For each of the three dimensions of personality, Eysenck developed a hierarchy of related traits and behavioral responses. (Eysenck, 1990)

require a lower stimulus level to arouse them and reach their "comfort zone" than do extraverts. Eysenck argued that lower thresholds to arousal imply greater sensitivity to stimuli. Stimulation, whether it is a new place or new people, can easily become overwhelming for an introvert. Therefore, introverts consistently shy away from or withdraw from stimulating environments. By the same token, extraverts, with low cortical arousal and high thresholds of arousal, seek out and enjoy highly stimulating experiences (Eysenck, 1990, 1997). Introversion or inhibition can thus be seen as a way of coping with an inherently aroused and sensitive central nervous system.

A number of different approaches to understanding personality have been proposed by different theorists. The primary assumptions and key ideas of each of the five approaches are presented in Figure 13.9.

	Assumptions	Theorist	Key ideas
Psychoanalytic	Our personality resides in the unconscious and early childhood experiences lay the foundation for adult personality.	Freud	Unconscious, Preconscious, Conscious Id, Ego, Superego
		Adler	Striving for superiority Compensation Inferiority complex Birth order
		Jung	Personal unconscious, Collective unconscious Archetypes: shadow, anima, animus
		Horney	Basic hostility, basic anxiety, defenses against anxiety
Humanistic–Positive	We have a natural interest in becoming the best person possible.	Maslow	Strive to become the best possible person Self-actualization
		Rogers	Strive toward growth and fulfillment through unconditional positive regard Real self, Ideal self
Social–Cognitive	A person's behavior changes in different situations.	Mischel	Behavior results from the interaction of the cognitive and emotional qualities of the person and the particular situation he or she is in.
Traits	Traits are the major force behind personality.	McCrae/Costa	**O**penness to experience **C**onscientiousness **E**xtraversion **A**greeableness **N**euroticism Five-Factor Model includes: Basic tendencies—biologically based Characteristic adaptations—culturally based
Biological	We have a biological foundation for our personality traits.	Allport	Personality is a product of both heredity and environment.
		Eysenck	**P**sychoticism **E**xtraversion **N**euroticism Differences in genetics, neurochemistry, and CNS cause personality differences.

FIGURE **13.9**
SUMMARY OF FIVE APPROACHES TO PERSONALITY.

Quick Quiz 13.3: How Do Theorists Explain Personality?

1. Hatred and aggression toward homosexuals as a reaction to fear of one's own homosexual impulses is an example of which Freudian defense mechanism?
   a. reaction formation
   b. psychosexual stages
   c. repression
   d. projection

2. According to Jung, the collective unconscious is made up of ancient or archaic images that result from common ancestral experiences called
   a. core-relational themes.
   b. the animus.
   c. the inferiority complex.
   d. archetypes.

3. The key assumption of humanistic theorists, such as Maslow and Rogers, is that people
   a. are driven by unconscious motives.
   b. strive toward growth and fulfillment.
   c. learn from observing others.
   d. none of the above.

4. The Big Five dimensions of personality are openness to experience, conscientiousness, extraversion, _____, and _____.
   a. depression; neuroticism
   b. agreeableness; neuroticism
   c. agreeableness; introversion
   d. anxiousness; introversion

Answers can be found at the end of the chapter.

HOW IS PERSONALITY MEASURED?

Defining and explaining personality are of prime importance, but you can define and explain only what you can measure. So how do psychologists measure and study personality? Four distinct methods are most common: behavioral observation, interviewing, projective tests, and questionnaires.

Behavioral Observation

The most direct and objective method for gathering personality data is to observe behavior and simply count specific behaviors that are associated with particular traits, such as aggression, hostility, friendliness, anxiety, or conscientiousness. However, collecting valid data is more difficult than it might seem. For instance, choosing to rate the fairly straightforward example of "aggression" raises many questions. What specific behaviors will count as aggression? Hitting? Insulting? Sarcasm? How does a researcher quantify each behavior—on a continuum from none to a great deal, or simply on the basis of whether it is present or not? Over what time period will the behavior be observed? Where will the behavior take place: in a real-world setting or in a laboratory? Who will rate the behavior? How do we know that different observers will view a given behavior in the same way?

These questions address the issue of measurement in general and reliability in particular. If two or more raters are to accurately rate and agree upon their ratings, there must be **inter-rater reliability.** The researchers must first establish an exact definition of the trait they wish to measure, identify the behaviors that make up that trait, and practice rating it against experienced, expert, and reliable raters. The new raters are deemed "reliable" if their ratings compare well with established norms or expert ratings, usually with a correlation of .80 or higher.

When children or others, such as animals, who cannot evaluate or report on their own personalities are being assessed, behavioral observations are required. The advantages of behavioral observations are that they do not depend on people's view of themselves, as self-report measurements do, and they are direct and relatively objective.

Despite these strengths, behavioral observations are costly and time-consuming. Moreover, not all personality traits can be observed by other people.

inter-rater reliability
A measure of how much agreement there is in ratings when using two or more raters or coders to rate personality or behavior in other people.

Anxiety and depression, for instance, although they can be expressed through behavior, are often experienced internally and subjectively—external observations can't tell the whole story. For these kinds of personality traits, a person's own reporting—a self-report—is more reliable. Self-reports can be obtained in three ways: interviewing, projective tests, and questionnaires.

Interviewing

Sitting down with another person face-to-face is probably the most natural and comfortable of all personality assessment techniques. Interviewing is an ideal way to gather important information about a person's life. From the participant's perspective, interviewing is usually more engaging and pleasant than completing a questionnaire. The clear advantage for participants is the open-ended nature of the interview, in which they can say anything they wish in response to a question. Of course, this is also a drawback of interviewing. What does a response mean? How are responses scored and by whom? What criteria are used? These issues are similar to those associated with behavioral ratings, but with interviews the "behavior" is a verbal response to a question that must be coded reliably and accurately. Thus, the ease of interviews from the participant's perspective is offset by the difficulty of scoring responses reliably.

Projective Tests

Projective tests present an ambiguous stimulus or situation to participants and ask them to give their interpretation of or tell a story about what they see. These techniques are based on the assumption, stemming from psychoanalysis, that unconscious wishes, thoughts, and motives will be "projected" onto the task. By interpreting an entire series of such answers, a psychologist can identify consistent unconscious themes. One of the most widely used projective tests is the Rorschach Inkblot Test.

In the **Rorschach Inkblot Test,** a series of ambiguous inkblots are presented one at a time, and the participant is asked to say what he or she sees in each one (see Figure 13.10). The responses are recorded and then coded by a trained coder (most often a psychologist or psychotherapist) as to how much human and nonhuman "movement," color, form, and shading the participant sees in each card (Exner, 1974; Masling & Borenstein, 2005). Not only is the test used to measure unconscious motives, but its supporters also claim that responses can help them diagnose various psychological disorders, such as depression, suicidal thoughts, pedophilia, post-traumatic stress disorder, or anxiety disorders (Guarnaccia et al., 2001; Nash et al., 1993; Ryan, Baerwald, & McGlone, 2008; Sloan, Arsenault, & Hilsenroth, 2002; Xiang, Shen, & Li, 2009).

Personality Questionnaires

Because of the expense and time that behavioral ratings and interviews require, along with the relative unreliability of projective tests, the most common way of measuring personality is asking participants to summarize their own behavioral tendencies by means of questionnaires. **Personality questionnaires** consist of individual statements, or items;

projective tests
Personality assessment in which participants are presented with a vague stimulus or situation and asked to interpret it or tell a story about what they see.

Rorschach Inkblot Test
A projective test in which the participant is asked to respond to a series of ambiguous inkblots.

personality questionnaires
Self-report instruments on which respondents indicate the extent to which they agree or disagree with a series of statements as they apply to their personalities.

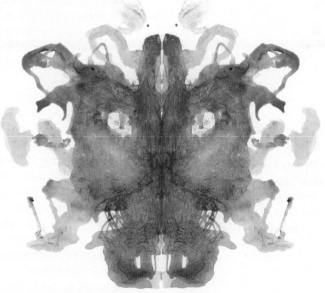

FIGURE **13.10**

AN INKBLOT SIMILAR TO THOSE FOUND ON A RORSCHACH INKBLOT CARD. In the Rorschach Inkblot Test, a person is asked to interpret the inkblot however he or she wishes. After the participant has interpreted a dozen or more cards, psychologists can form ideas about what kinds of thoughts, feelings, and motives are consistently being "projected."

respondents indicate the extent to which they agree or disagree with each statement as it applies to their personalities. Responses are usually arranged on a *Likert scale,* which attaches numbers to descriptive responses, such as 1, "completely disagree"; 3, "neither agree nor disagree"; and 5, "completely agree."

Questionnaires are developed with years of validation using either the rational or the empirical method. The **rational, or face valid, method** involves using reason or theory to come up with a question. If we wanted to develop a new measure of anxiety, we could include an item like "I feel anxious much of the time." This is a "face valid" item, because what it measures (anxiety) is clear and can be taken at face value. A frequently used personality questionnaire that uses the face valid method is the NEO-PI (Costa & McCrae, 1992). The problem with such questionnaires, however, is that because the questions are transparent, participants might give socially desirable or false answers rather than honest ones. For example, for the item "I am anxious much of the time," someone might not want to admit to frequently feeling anxious and hence might not answer honestly.

The **empirical method** focuses instead on whether responses to various items differentiate between the groups it should (Gough & Bradley, 1996). If preliminary studies show that the statement "I prefer baths to showers" is answered a certain way by anxious people and a different way by nonanxious people (thereby discriminating between these two groups), it is used in a measure of anxiety. This method requires an outside criterion of who is anxious or not, such as a therapist's evaluation of the anxiety levels, to relate to such items. If the evidence shows that it does distinguish the two groups, then it is used in the questionnaire.

Two of the most widely used personality questionnaires were developed using the empirical method: the Minnesota Multiphasic Personality Inventory (MMPI) and the California Personality Inventory (CPI). The *MMPI* is used by psychotherapists to assess the degree and kind of a person's psychiatric personality traits, such as depression, paranoia, or psychopathic deviance (antisocial personality; Tellegen et al., 2003). The *CPI,* however, is a measure of nonpathological, or normal, personality traits such as sociability, responsibility, dominance, or self-control (Gough & Bradley, 1996). Both the MMPI and the CPI consist of questions that target groups answer differently from the general population. In "Psychology in the Real World," we describe how personality predicts college major, career interest, and job performance.

Social Network Measurement of Personality

As we have been discussing throughout the text, social networks such as Facebook, Twitter, and Instagram have changed how we communicate and interact, but did you know that how you use them reflects on who you are and what kind of personality you have? Psychologists are not yet able to use your SNS footprint and behavior to measure your personality, but they are getting close (Ortigosa, Carro, & Quiroga, 2014). The content of a personal website, musical preferences, and online profiles and the number and density of SNS friends predict personality traits (Kosinski, Stillwell, & Graepel, 2013; Kosinski et al., 2013; Marcus, Machilek, & Schütz, 2006; Ortigosa et al., 2013; Özgüven & Mucan, 2013; Rentfrow & Gosling, 2003). Perhaps the most fascinating result is that what you "like" on Facebook strongly predicts your personality, as well as your intelligence, race, age, sexual orientation, and political affiliation (Kosinski et al., 2013). Analyzing the Facebook "likes" of 58,000 people, Kosinski, Stillwell, and Graepel (2013) found that liking "The Colbert Report" puts a person in the 87th percentile on openness but only the 23rd percentile on extraversion (see Figure 13.11). Liking "Mitt Romney," however, puts a person in the 93rd percentile on conscientiousness and 85th on emotional stability (the opposite of neuroticism).

rational (face valid) method
A method for developing questionnaire items that involves using reason or theory to come up with a question.

empirical method
A method for developing questionnaire items that focuses on including questions that characterize the group the questionnaire is intended to distinguish.

Challenge Your Assumptions
True or False? Facebook "likes" reliably predict your personality traits.
True: What we "like" on Facebook has been used to accurately predict our personality traits.

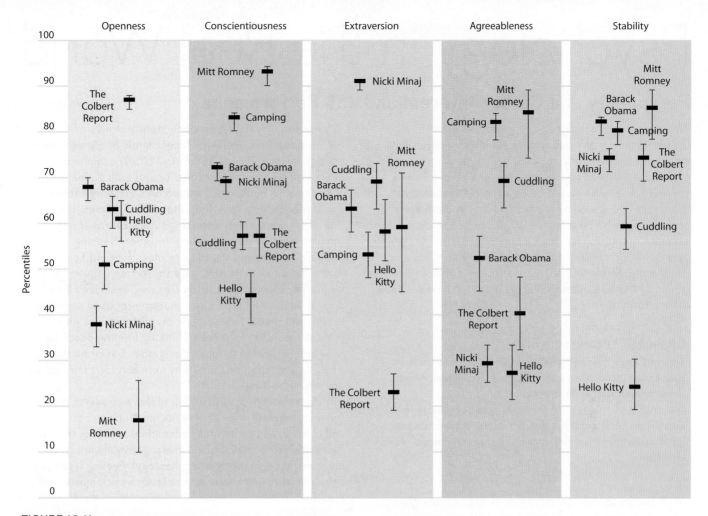

FIGURE 13.11

SELECTIVE FACEBOOK "LIKES" AND ONE'S SCORES (PERCENTILES) ON THE BIG FIVE DIMENSIONS OF PERSONALITY. People who "like" *The Colbert Report* are in the 87th percentile on openness to experience but only in the 23rd percentile on extraversion. (Adapted from Kosinski, Stillwell, & Graepel [2013]; reprinted with Permission, *Proceedings of the National Academy of Sciences*)

Quick Quiz 13.4: How Is Personality Measured?

1. The most objective method for gathering information about personality traits is to
   a. observe behavior.
   b. conduct interviews.
   c. administer questionnaires.
   d. do genetic testing.

2. The Rorschach Inkblot Test is an example of which type of personality measurement?
   a. structure interview
   b. questionnaire

   c. projective test
   d. standardized test

3. Scales that use response categories ranging from 1 to 5 (with labels ranging from 1 for "completely agree" to 5 for "completely disagree") are called
   a. ratio scales.
   b. Likert scales.
   c. face valid.
   d. dichotomous.

Answers can be found at the end of the chapter.

Psychology in the Real World

Personality and Career Interest and Job Performance

Would you want a surgeon operating on you who is known for being anxious and nervous? How about having a police officer in your hometown who is violent and aggressive? Would you want to buy something from a shy and socially awkward salesperson? Personality is important when it comes to jobs. Would you believe that personality tests do a better job of predicting your future success in your career than interviews, school credentials, or letters of recommendation? They do (Charmorro-Premuzic & Steinmetz, 2013). Conscientiousness is generally the best personality predictor of how well you will perform in your job.

Challenge Your Assumptions

True or False? Your personality predicts future success in your career better than letters of recommendation, educational credentials, or interviews.

True: Although they are not as widely used, personality tests do a better job of predicting future success at jobs than traditional application materials such as educational credentials or interviews.

If you go to your university or college career guidance counselor, he or she will very likely use personality tests in advising you in your career choices (Costa, 1996; Mount et al., 2005). Governments and organizations also rely on them to select the right people for particular jobs (Carless, 1999; De Fruyt & Murvielde, 1999). Indeed, Hammer and Macdaid (1992) provide a list of occupations most and least similar to one's personality. Among other things, personality traits predict the majors and careers we select, what kinds of employers select us, how people perform at jobs, and how likely they are to leave them once they get them.

Personality and Career and College Major Interest

The first stage of job selection—for college students, at least—is picking a major. You may not be surprised to learn that different personality types are attracted to and interested in different kinds of majors. College majors are generally classified using three career codes, with the first one being primary (Emery, 2006). For example, psychology is SIE (Social-Investigative-Enterprising), economics is IAS (Investigative-Artistic-Social), and biology is IRE (Investigative-Realistic-Enterprising).

Personality research consistently shows that different personalities prefer different kinds of careers and college majors. Pulver and Kelly (2008) examined the association between personality and college major using a measure of personality based on Carl Jung's theory, the Myers-Briggs Type Indicator (MBTI; Myers, 1962). The MBTI consists of opposing types: Extraversion-Introversion, Thinking-Feeling, Intuition-Sensing, and Judging-Perceiving. People are classified either as an extravert or an introvert, as a thinker or a feeler, and so on. For example, Intuition-Sensing describes how people prefer to take in information—focused on what is real and actual (sensing) or on patterns and meanings in data (intuiting), whereas Thinking-Feeling describes how people prefer to make decisions—based on logical analysis (thinking) or guided by concern for their impact on others (feeling).

Pulver and Kelly (2008) found that extraverts preferred social and enterprising majors (such as psychology, social work, and elementary education), whereas thinking types preferred realistic and investigative majors (such as mechanical engineering or archeology). Feeling types preferred artistic and social majors (such as art, music, and theater).

Similarly, Larson and colleagues (2010) examined whether personality scores reliably differentiated majors in 368 undergraduate students, but they used a different measure of personality. In this study, students completed the Multidimensional Personality Questionnaire (MPQ; Tellegen, 2000), a self-reported measure of personality that is scored on 11 primary personality traits, including social closeness, aggression (low agreeableness), harm-avoidance, and absorption.

Results showed that education majors scored higher than engineering majors on social closeness, whereas business majors scored significantly lower on agreeableness than humanities and architecture/design majors. In addition, architecture/design majors were more absorbed than business majors. Elementary education majors scored highest on harm-avoidance (avoiding situations where one can get hurt) and social closeness out of the nine majors. Similar research reported that harm-avoidance is negatively related to realistic interests and specifically interests in mechanical activities (Staggs, Larson, & Borgen, 2007). In other words, mechanical and athletic majors are not as likely as other majors to be afraid or driven to avoid harmful situations.

Personality-Environment Fit and Job Performance

Because so much research shows certain personalities matching certain majors and jobs, researchers have proposed a theory of fit between personality and job. Holland calls this idea "congruence," stating that "people find environments reinforcing and satisfying when environmental patterns resemble their personality patterns" (Holland, 1985, p. 53). I/O psychologists also refer to this notion of congruence as "person-organization fit," or how well matched the person is to his or her work environment (Kristof-Brown, Zimmerman, & Johnson, 2005). Numerous large-scale meta-analyses of over a thousand studies show that fit between personality and job does matter (Assouline & Meier, 1987; Kristof-Brown et al., 2005; Verquer, Beehr, & Wagner, 2003). The better the fit, the more satisfied people are with their jobs, the less likely they are to leave their jobs, and the more successful they will be.

Measures of fit and congruence allow employers not only to use personality measures to recruit/hire workers who best fit the job but also to weed out people who might behave counterproductively. A *counterproductive work behavior* can be defined as anything done by the employee that is intentionally negative for the organization (MacLane & Walmsley, 2010). Such behavior might include such major infractions as betraying company secrets or employee theft, but it may also involve minor transgressions, such as working nonproductively (spending too much time on Facebook or other Internet sites, for example).

What sort of personal characteristics have been linked with counterproductive workplace behavior? Of the traditional Big Five traits, people who are more conscientious, agreeable, and emotionally stable are less likely to engage in behaviors that harm their companies (Berry, Ones, & Sackett, 2007). In another study, a cluster of personality scales from the widely used California Psychological Inventory was able to reliably predict police officers who consistently used excessive force and provided drugs to inmates (Hargrave & Hiatt, 1989). More specifically, the problematic officers scored unusually low on the CPI's Self-control, Socialization, and Responsibility scales.

Government and business organizations sometimes use measures of personality in screening job applicants.
What kind of person do you think would make an effective police officer?

Personality and Switching Jobs

Personality traits also predict how long people stay in or switch their jobs. Two of the Big Five dimensions—openness to experience and agreeableness—appear to be most predictive of leaving jobs early in one's career. Recall that people with high openness to experience prefer new experiences over routine ones and that people high in agreeableness are warm, caring, and friendly. Researchers have reported that people high in openness and low in agreeableness are most likely to switch jobs and/or companies (Vinson, Connelly, & Ones, 2007; Wille, De Fruyt, & Feys, 2010).

In sum, people who are matched to their jobs make better, happier, more productive employees. Personality has wide-ranging influence over the kinds of careers we are interested in, how well various careers fit who we are, how long we stay, and how well we do in particular careers.

Bringing It All Together

Making Connections in Personality

Does Personality Change over Time?

Personality is at the center of who we are. Recall our definition of personality as the unique and enduring manner in which a person thinks, feels, and behaves. Although it shows considerable stability over our lifetime, it also changes and develops between our infant and adult years. Personality consistency and change illustrate many of the principles discussed in this chapter. All definitions, theories, and measures of personality confront the question of consistency and change of personality.

Personality Consistency

In many ways, it is more difficult to change our personalities than we think. Much of who we are remains rather stable and consistent over our lifetimes. When we talk about personality consistency, however, we mean relative consistency. In fact, that is one of the lessons learned from Walter Mischel's work on how qualities and traits interact with specific situations to bring about different behavior across different situations (Kammrath, Mendoza-Denton, & Mischel, 2005; Mischel, 2009; Mischel & Shoda, 1999). No one is consistent all of the time or in all situations. Consistency is a matter of degree.

Longitudinal studies, those that examine the same people over a period of time, reveal high levels of stability of personality traits. Early in their collaboration, Costa and McCrae (1976) conducted a longitudinal study of personality, expecting to find that personality traits change over time. To their surprise, they found a high degree of stability over a 10-year period. Another set of longitudinal studies revealed very small changes in neuroticism, extraversion, and openness over a period of 6 to 9 years (Costa et al., 2000; McCrae & Costa, 2003).

Challenge Your Assumptions

True or False? People can usually change their personalities if they try.

False: Personality traits are quite stable in adulthood, although there is also some change in early adulthood.

Most parents or observers of infants and toddlers are quick to project subtle signs of their children's interest or talent into the future, but do our personalities and traits at age 3 portend future outcomes such as employment, mental illness, criminal behavior, and quality of interpersonal relationships? Jack and Jeanne Block conducted some of the first long-term studies of human temperament and personality. They conducted interviews, behavioral observations, and personality questionnaires and found that children who were impulsive, aggressive, and tended to cry at age 3 were most likely to use drugs during adolescence (Block, Block, & Keyes, 1988). Similarly, temperament ratings were made on nearly one thousand 3-year-olds, who were then followed up through their teens, 20s, and 30s. Being undercontrolled and impulsive at age 3 predicted adult alcoholism, drug abuse, and gambling problems (Caspi, 2000; Slutske et al., 2012).

Research from behavior genetics has demonstrated that personality stability between adolescence and adulthood is largely due to genetic factors (Blonigen et al., 2006; Gillespie et al., 2003; Krueger & Johnson, 2008; Takahashi et al., 2007). More specifically, genetics contributes to the personality consistency we see from adolescence to adulthood, whereas environmental factors contribute to both stability and change in personality traits (Takahashi et al., 2007).

Personality Change

We all like to think we can change—that we have the power to change our destructive habits and become a better person. Can we? Research does support some degree of personality change as we move from adolescence through adulthood and as we adapt to changes in life circumstances.

Typical Personality Change across the Life Span

Recent research confirms that some degree of change in personality occurs normally from adolescence to adulthood and into old age (Allemand, Zimprich, & Hendriks, 2008; Josefsson et al., 2013; Letzring, Edmonds, & Hampson, 2014; Lodi-Smith et al., 2009; Roberts & Mroczek, 2008). The most impressive evidence comes from a meta-analysis of 92 studies that assessed personality change in over 50,000 individuals on the Big Five dimensions of personality (Roberts, Walton, & Viechtbauer, 2006). In general, people become steadily more agreeable and conscientious from adolescence to late adulthood (see Figure 13.12) and tend to become more assertive or dominant and emotionally stable from adolescence to middle adulthood and then level off on these personality dimensions. Finally, people generally become more sociable (social vitality) and open to new experiences from

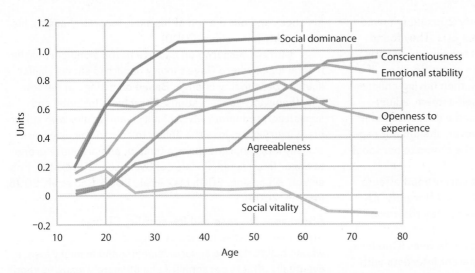

FIGURE **13.12**

PERSONALITY CHANGE FROM ADOLESCENCE TO LATE ADULTHOOD. This graph shows the results of a meta-analysis of personality change on the Big Five dimensions across 92 studies and involving more than 50,000 individuals. The scale of change is measured in standardized units. 0 units means no change. Emotional stability is the opposite end of neuroticism. (Roberts, Walton, & Viechtbauer, 2006)

Connection

Children who are rated by their parents as being undercontrolled at age 3 are more likely than other children to have drinking problems, to get in trouble with the law, and even to attempt suicide by age 21.

See "The Developing Infant and Child," Chapter 5, "Human Development," p. 167.

adolescence to early adulthood. These traits level off in adulthood and then decline in older adulthood. The same pattern of change is seen in cross-sectional research that examines personality differences in different age groups at the same time (Allemand et al., 2008). Together, these results make clear that personality is not set in plaster once we reach adulthood.

Personality Change after Changes in Life Circumstances

Not only does personality show some degree of change during normal life-span development but it also is open to change when we experience big changes in our lives, such as living abroad, becoming a parent, suffering a brain injury, or developing Alzheimer's disease.

Living Abroad and Personality Change

Living in a foreign country for a short or long period of time is becoming more common, especially with the popularity of study abroad programs. This raises two questions related to personality: Are those who decide to study abroad different in personality than those

who don't, and what effect does living abroad have on one's personality? Sojourners (those who travel and live abroad) compared to nonsojourners have baseline personalities (before the travel) that are mostly more open and extraverted (Camperio-Ciana et al., 2007; Jokela, 2009; Zimmerman & Neyer, 2013). Being open to experience and being outgoing, sociable, and thrill seeking are qualities that predict who will select the travelling experience.

The answer to the question of whether living abroad changes personality is "yes it does." The personality traits that most consistently change after life abroad are an increase in agreeableness and a decrease in neuroticism; that is, an increase in emotional stability. (Zimmerman & Neyer, 2013). Living abroad seems to make people more agreeable and friendly in their interaction with others and less anxious, sad, and depressed. Although more cognitive than personality traits, critical and creative thinking also seem to increase in those who live abroad (C. Lee, Therriault, & Linderholm, 2012; Savicki et al., 2004). Moreover, personality change seems to happen mostly by people acculturating to the new culture and taking on traits of the new culture (Güngör et al., 2013).

Parenting and Personality Change

Few events change a person as much as becoming the primary caregiver for a totally helpless infant. How does such a major transition affect one's personality? The answer seems to be that it depends on many factors. Paris and Helson (2002) conducted a longitudinal study of female college seniors in their early 20s and followed them until they reached their 50s and 60s. They found that becoming a mother affected personality differently, depending on the woman's evaluation of motherhood. If a woman liked being a full-time mother, then having children led to an increase in her flexibility, self-esteem, adjustment, resourcefulness, and control and a decrease in her dependence and fearfulness. If, however, she did not especially enjoy being a full-time mother, the opposite personality changes were observed.

Other researchers report that parenthood affects the personalities of mothers and fathers differently. Although self-concept in general seems to stay the same for both mothers and fathers, self-esteem goes down and irritability goes up in mothers but not in fathers (Onodera, 2003). Similarly, the gender of the parent interacts with the temperament of the child. Compared to having a child with an "easy temperament," having one with a "difficult temperament" is more likely to increase the father's but not the mother's anxiety (Sirignono & Lachman, 1985). The biggest personality change seems to come from increases in a personal sense of control and mastery if parents have an "easy" child and decreases on these dimensions if they have a "difficult" child (Sirignono & Lachman, 1985). Having a child who is difficult undermines the belief that parents can truly control the life and behavior of their children.

Although not quite parenting, mentoring children by college students can also lead to change in personality. In a study of more than 100 college students who mentored aggressive, at-risk children for three semesters, researchers reported decreases in the mentors' levels of openness, conscientiousness, extraversion, and agreeableness (Faith et al., 2011).

Brain Injury and Personality Change

Do you remember Phineas Gage from Chapter 3? He was the railroad foreman who had a tamping iron shoot through his cheek and out the top of his skull, forever changing his personality (Macmillan, 2000).

Current research on damage to the same part of the frontal lobes where Gage's injury occurred shows similar kinds of personality change. Based on ratings of personality (behavioral observations, Rorschach Inkblots, and semistructured interviews), children and adults who suffer brain injury often lose the ability to control impulses, are socially inappropriate, have a temper, and are more prone to anger (Mathiesen, Förster, & Svendsen, 2004; Max, Robertson, & Lansing, 2001; Max et al., 2006; Rao et al., 2008; Romain, 2008).

Alzheimer's Disease and Personality Change

Alzheimer's disease is a major degenerative brain disease whose hallmarks are severe dementia and memory loss. It eventually affects personality and ultimately leads to death (Azadfar et al., 2014). Using the NEO-PI as a measure of the Big Five personality dimensions, various studies have shown that neuroticism increases and openness and conscientiousness decrease after the onset of Alzheimer's disease (Chatterjee et al., 1992; L. Clark et al., 2000; Strauss, Pasupathi, & Chatterjee, 1993). Two studies have also reported a decrease in extraversion (Strauss et al., 1993; R. Williams, Briggs, & Coleman, 1995), and at least one study, described in the Research Process for this chapter (see Figure 13.13), has reported a decrease in agreeableness (Chatterjee et al., 1992). Most studies, however, report no change on the agreeableness dimension. Research using other measures of personality have reported that Alzheimer's patients became less kind, generous, enthusiastic, and self-reliant and more irritable and out-of-touch (S. Petry et al., 1989; Talassi et al., 2007). Some research has reported that personality change can even precede the onset of the disease (Balsis, Carpenter, & Storandt, 2005). In other words, there is a biological basis for our personalities. Changes in the brain are often accompanied by personality changes.

Research Process

1 Research Questions

Does Alzheimer's disease change an individual's personality? Do different observers agree on the nature of personality change after a person develops Alzheimer's disease?

Jack and Lucy before Alzheimer's diagnosis

2 Method

Eleven elderly men and 11 elderly women (mean age = 72) who met the criteria for Alzheimer's disease, based on cognitive testing and brain images, participated in this correlational study by Strauss and colleagues (1993). The primary caregiver (most often a spouse) and a secondary good friend or family member each rated the patient's personality using the NEO-PI. The NEO-PI measures the Big Five personality dimensions of neuroticism, extraversion, openness, agreeableness, and conscientiousness. Raters were asked to remember when the symptoms of Alzheimer's first started and then pick a period of a few years prior to that and rate the person's personality at that time. Approximately 2 to 3 months later, each rater was asked to evaluate the patient's personality again, but this time as he or she was then—after the onset of Alzheimer's.

Lucy after diagnosis

Personality rating by Jack and his daughter

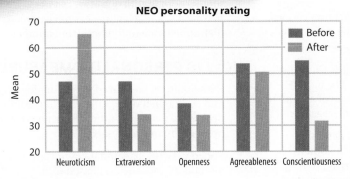

NEO personality rating

3 Results

Personality ratings of the person showed changes in three of the Big Five dimensions of personality after the onset of Alzheimer's disease. People were rated higher in neuroticism (anxiety) and lower in extraversion, openness, and conscientiousness. Agreeableness did not change. Independent ratings by secondary raters matched those of the primary raters and showed the same pattern.

4 Conclusion

Primary and secondary raters agreed that after the onset of Alzheimer's disease people became more anxious, less extraverted, less open, and less conscientious. Other studies have replicated these general findings (Clark et al., 2000; Williams, Briggs, & Coleman, 1995). Alzheimer's changes personality in predictable ways.

FIGURE **13.13**

PERSONALITY CHANGE AFTER ALZHEIMER'S DISEASE. Source: "Concordance between Observers in Descriptions of Personality Change in Alzheimer's Disease," by M. E. Strauss, M. Pasupathi, & A. Chatterjee, 1993, *Psychology & Aging, 8*, 475–480.

Chapter Review

DEFINING PERSONALITY

- Personality is the essence of who we are—both our uniqueness and our consistency. Personality traits function to change behavioral thresholds and make certain behaviors more likely and others less likely.

THE NATURE AND NURTURE OF PERSONALITY

- Personality is an expression of both nature and nurture. Personality traits have evolved through natural and sexual selection, in which genetic and environmental forces work in tandem in shaping an individual's personality.

- Studies of infant temperament offer further support for a biological basis for adult personality. Infants make their way into the world with different and unique ways of behaving. Children may be temperamentally easy, difficult, or slow to warm up.

HOW DO THEORISTS EXPLAIN PERSONALITY?

- Theories of personality organize and explain observations, as well as stimulate testable hypotheses. Five perspectives explain personality differences and development.

- The first perspective, Freud's psychoanalytic theory, assumes distinct levels of consciousness. The most important of these is the unconscious, the level at which most thoughts, feelings, motives, and images reside.

- Freud developed the idea of psychological defense mechanisms, which defend us against psychological threats by unconsciously denying or distorting reality. Repression, for example, is the unconscious process of keeping disturbing thoughts, feelings, or impulses out of consciousness.

- Three followers of Freud broke their ties with him to establish their own views. Alfred Adler argued that striving for superiority is the primary motive underlying almost all behavior. Carl Jung introduced the idea of the personal unconscious and the collective unconscious. Karen Horney developed a psychoanalytic social theory

centered on three neurotic trends: moving toward others, moving against others, and moving away from others.

- Contemporary research in neuroscience is beginning to provide empirical support for some of Freud's theories.

- The second perspective, humanistic theory, emphasizes psychological growth and health. Abraham Maslow developed a detailed concept of self-actualization; that is, the inherent tendency to strive to realize one's full potential. Carl Rogers developed the concept of unconditional positive regard to help people achieve self-fulfillment.

- The third perspective, the social–cognitive learning theory of Walter Mischel, is based on the belief that consistent personality characteristics interact with the environment to produce a person's unique behaviors.

- Trait theory, the fourth perspective, argues for a universal and stable personality structure that consists of five dimensions of personality: openness, conscientiousness, extraversion, agreeableness, and neuroticism (O-C-E-A-N). These traits are normally distributed in the population, with most people falling somewhere between the two extremes on each trait.

- The fifth perspective includes biological theories such as those of Hans Eysenck. Eysenck argued for three fundamental dimensions of personality: psychoticism, extraversion, and neuroticism (P-E-N). Eysenck's theory holds that differences in individuals' cortical arousal and sensitivity threshold lead to differences in introversion and extraversion.

- Confirming the importance of the biological basis of personality, personality psychologists and animal behaviorists have begun to explore the nature of animal personality. They have found not only that other primates and mammals exhibit many consistent and unique personality qualities but also that birds, fish, octopuses, and even insects have personality traits that distinguish one individual from another.

HOW IS PERSONALITY MEASURED?

- Personality is measured in four major ways: observing and coding behavior; interviewing; administering projective tests; and administering structured personality questionnaires.

- Social network use and behavior is a new and upcoming method for measuring personality.

BRINGING IT ALL TOGETHER: MAKING CONNECTIONS IN PERSONALITY

- Most of the major topics in this chapter can be connected by highlighting research demonstrating the stability and change in personality over time. Genetic forces contribute to personality stability, whereas environmental factors contribute to both stability and change.

Key Terms

anima, p. 492
animus, p. 492
archetypes, p. 491
basic tendencies, p. 497
behavioral thresholds, p. 480
Big Five (five-factor model), p. 497
collective unconscious, p. 491
cortical arousal, p. 498
defense mechanisms, p. 489
ego, p. 488
empirical method, p. 502

id, p. 488
inferiority complex, p. 490
inter-rater reliability, p. 500
mechanisms, p. 480
neuropsychoanalysis, p. 493
personal unconscious, p. 491
personality questionnaires, p. 501
projection, p. 489
projective tests, p. 501
quantitative trait loci (QTL) approach, p. 481

rational (face valid) method, p. 502
reaction formation, p. 489
Rorschach Inkblot Test, p. 501
shadow, p. 491
striving for superiority, p. 490
sublimation, p. 489
superego, p. 488
trait, p. 479
unconditional positive regard, p. 495
unconscious, p. 487

Quick Quiz Answers

Quick Quiz 13.1: 1. b 2. c   **Quick Quiz 13.2:** 1. a 2. d 3. b 4. c   **Quick Quiz 13.3:** 1. a 2. d 3. b 4. b
Quick Quiz 13.4: 1. a 2. c 3. b

14 Social Behavior

Chapter Outline

Group Living and Social Influence
Social Perception
Attitudes and Behavior
Social Relations
Chapter Review

Challenge Your Assumptions

True or False?

- Being left out really hurts. (see page 514)

- I know whether I am prejudiced or not.
  (see page 529)

- People will sometimes risk their lives to help
  others. (see page 538)

- Attractive faces are anything but average.
  (see page 542)

Thalia and her closest friend from high school, Deidre, chose to go to the same university. They roomed with other people, but they still saw each other frequently. Although their friendship felt a bit different, Thalia understood that they had different classes and some new friends. For years, Deidre had invited her to the family cabin to go skiing each winter, and Thalia took it for granted that she'd be going, even though she was always formally asked. When winter rolled around that freshman year, Thalia asked Deidre when they'd be heading to the snow. Deidre said softly, "I invited my new roommate this year." Thalia—stunned—felt like she'd been kicked in the stomach.

Being rejected hurts. In fact, social exclusion creates physical pain. In one study on the neural basis for social pain, participants were taken into a lab with an fMRI scanner and were told they would be involved in an electronic ball tossing game called "Cyberball" (Eisenberger, Lieberman, & Williams, 2003; Masten et al., 2009). Once inside the scanner, they could see, on a screen, a Cyberball game that was apparently in progress between two other research participants in scanners in different rooms. Unknown to the participants, there were no other people playing the game. After watching the "others" play for a few throws, the participants joined in. For a while, the three players continued playing Cyberball together. After seven throws, the other players stopped throwing the ball to the participants and resumed their game. In effect, the participants was left out, as Thalia had been. Participants reported being upset about their exclusion. What's more, the fMRI scans showed activation of brain circuitry involved in physical pain, especially those areas that are involved with how unpleasant pain feels. This kind of *social pain* can be relieved by painkillers like Tylenol (DeWall et al., 2010) and may affect endocrine systems that support social connection (Maner et al., 2010). People who are more sensitive to physical pain are more sensitive to the pain of rejection, and these differences may have a genetic basis (Eisenberger et al., 2006; Way, Taylor, & Eisenberger, 2009). Further, people who trust their interaction partners and have higher self-esteem are less likely to experience social pain when excluded (Yanagisawa, et al., 2011).

Challenge Your Assumptions

True or False? Being left out really hurts.

True: When we are excluded, it causes the experience of pain and activates similar brain circuitry as does physical pain.

Why does it hurt to be excluded? Like other social animals, humans form important bonds with other members of our species. We depend on other people to raise us and to cooperate with us in the presence of threats (Neuberg & Cottrell, 2006). As a result, the ways in which we relate to others play a huge role in our lives, and the need to belong is ingrained in our biology (Way et al., 2009). In this chapter, we will discuss why belonging to a group matters to us, as well as other key aspects of social behavior, such as how the presence of other people influences our behavior, how we perceive our social world, how we form attitudes, and how we make friends. These topics are the focus of social psychology, which studies the effects of the real or imagined presence of others on people's thoughts, feelings, and actions. The research in social psychology repeatedly reflects an important theme of this book, that no one perspective tells us everything there is to know about something. What is particularly interesting in social psychology is just how often our perspective on things is influenced in dramatic or subtle ways by others—often without our even being aware of it.

GROUP LIVING AND SOCIAL INFLUENCE

The social nature of human beings stems from the importance of group living in our evolutionary history. We are not solitary animals. Group living offered many advantages in human evolution, such as increased safety in the presence of danger, cooperation with others to complete challenging tasks (such as hunting), and child rearing (Brewer & Caporael, 2006; Melis & Semmann, 2010). This heritage explains why people work to preserve group membership and why they modify their behavior when in the presence of others. In this section we examine how the presence of other people affects performance and one's willingness to go along with the group. As we will see, social factors can push people to do things they might not otherwise do.

You may have noticed that sometimes you perform a task better with others around and sometimes you do worse. Such effects are seen in animals as diverse as humans, chimps, birds, and even cockroaches (Gates & Allee, 1933; Klopfer, 1958). The effect of having others present can depend on the situation or task at hand, how easy or difficult the task is, and how excited you are. **Social facilitation** occurs when the presence of others improves our performance. Over a century ago, Norman Triplett (1898) noticed that he bicycled faster when he rode with others. In a laboratory test of the idea that the presence of others improves performance, Triplett asked children to wind a fishing reel as fast as they could. He tested them alone and among other kids doing the same thing. Sure enough, they wound faster when other kids were present—they showed social facilitation, which usually occurs for tasks we find easy, we know well, or we can perform well (Zajonc, 1965).

Social loafing is the opposite; it occurs when the presence of others causes individuals to relax their standards (Harkins, 1987). If you are singing in a choir and there are dozens of other voices supporting yours, you are less likely to sing your heart out. You alone are not responsible for the sound, so the diffusion of responsibility alters your behavior (you loaf). If you are singing a solo, you might belt it out—because all the responsibility rests on your shoulders.

Conformity

Social facilitation is a subtle way in which the presence of others changes our actions. More direct social factors also pressure us to act in certain ways. Society imposes rules about acceptable behavior, called **social norms.** Examples of social norms include "Boys don't cry," "Don't pick your nose in public," and "Don't be a sore loser." Norms vary by culture, too. Burping at the dinner table is considered rude in the United States, but in some parts of East Asia, belching is seen as a compliment to the chef.

Most of the time we conform to the social norms of our culture. **Conformity** occurs when people adjust their behavior to what others are doing or adhere to cultural norms. The reasons for conformity vary, depending on the situation. **Informational social influence** occurs when people conform to the behavior of others because they view them as a source of knowledge about what they are supposed to do. Consider the incoming freshmen who look to other students for information about where to hang out, how to behave in class, and the like. Informational social influence is most pronounced in ambiguous or novel situations. We rely on it all the time, especially as children.

Normative social influence is the type of conformity that occurs when people go along with the behavior of others in order to be accepted by the group. A classic example is peer pressure, in which people engage in certain

Connection

Our level of arousal also affects our performance, according to the Yerkes-Dodson law. People perform better on an exam if they are slightly anxious than they would if they were either totally relaxed or very anxious.

See "Models of Motivation," Chapter 11, "Motivation and Emotion," p. 397.

social facilitation
When the presence of others improves one's performance.

social loafing
The phenomenon in which the presence of others causes one to relax one's standards and slack off.

social norms
Rules about acceptable behavior imposed by the cultural context in which one lives.

conformity
The tendency of people to adjust their behavior to what others are doing or to adhere to the norms of their culture.

informational social influence
Conformity to the behavior of others because one views them as a source of knowledge about what one is supposed to do.

normative social influence
Conformity to the behavior of others in order to be accepted by them.

In nomadic cultures, such as Mongolia, extended family groups have traditionally stayed together, sharing food, shelter, livestock, child rearing, and all other aspects of daily life. **How might communal living in isolated surroundings affect an individual's behavior?**

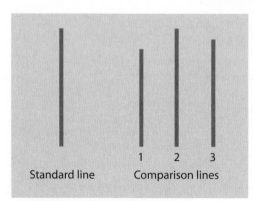

FIGURE **14.1**

STIMULUS LINES PRESENTED TO PARTICIPANTS IN THE ASCH CONFORMITY STUDIES. Each participant was asked to say which of the comparison lines (1, 2, or 3) matched the length of the standard line. The answers were always clear-cut; in this case, the answer is "2." The conformity manipulation involved the confederates in the group giving an obviously wrong answer (such as "1") and then seeing how the participant answered. (Passer & Smith, 2008)

behaviors, such as drinking or trying drugs, so that they will be accepted by a particular social group. This phenomenon is widespread. Look at yourself and your peers. Do you wear the same kinds of clothes? How many of you have similar hairstyles? Consider a more subtle example of normative social influence. You emerge from the theater after going to a movie with friends, not sure whether you liked the movie or not, although everyone else in the group loved the film and is talking about it. By the end of the evening you may also be talking about what a great film it was and may have actually convinced yourself that you loved it. We are not always aware of how other people shape our behavior and beliefs.

One of the classic studies of social psychology, conducted by Solomon Asch in 1951, demonstrates the power of normative social influence. Asch devoted his career to understanding situations in which perception is not a direct function of the physical properties of stimuli. For example, he found that our perceptions of the angle of a line can be biased by the frame around it (Witkin & Asch, 1948). Asch wondered whether the social world might also shape our perceptions. If pressured by the opinions of others, would people say they saw something that clearly wasn't there? Asch didn't think they would, but he was wrong.

Asch assembled several groups of six or seven people in the lab and told them he was researching visual acuity. He was really interested in conformity but didn't tell his participants what he was really researching, in case the information influenced their behavior. Asch then showed the participants two cards—one with a standard line, the other displaying three lines of varying length. The participant's job was to pick the one line out of the three that matched the standard line. As you can see in Figure 14.1, the task was easy. This comparison process was repeated 18 times and, on each occasion, participants gave their answers out loud.

The one real participant didn't know that the other so-called participants were *confederates*, people who actually worked for the experimenter. The one real participant was always seated in the last chair and heard the judgments of all of the other group members before making a choice. On the first six trials everyone gave the obvious and correct answer. Starting on the seventh trial, however, the confederates started giving wrong answers. On the first of the rigged trials, the first confederate would glance at the cards and confidently say, "The answer is line 1," even when it clearly was not correct. The next confederate would nod in agreement and say, "Yes, it is line 1." After five or six people in a row gave the wrong answers—remember, this is a *very* easy task—it was the real participant's turn. Participants faced a choice: Agree with everyone else's clearly erroneous judgments or give the answer that they personally thought was correct.

While none of the participants agreed with the group all of the time, 76% of them went along with the group at least once when a group answer was clearly wrong. On average, participants answered incorrectly 37% of the time. Yet when left alone to do the task, participants made errors less than 1% of the time.

How does the design of this study make it a test of normative rather than informational social influence? Judging the lengths of the lines was really easy—there was no need for participants to look to others for information about the right answer. When participants worked alone, they rarely made errors; however, in the situation just described, after all the confederates had given the same wrong answer, many participants conformed by also giving the clearly wrong answer.

Indeed, sometimes people go to great lengths to do what the group is doing, when it does not make sense, especially when groups are engaged in decision making. This phenomenon, called **groupthink**, occurs when the thinking of the group takes over, so much so that group members forgo logic or critical analysis in the service of reaching a decision (Janis, 1983). Juries that are hard-pressed to reach a verdict sometimes engage in groupthink, as do governments under pressure. According to the Senate Intelligence Committee's report on intelligence failures leading up to the 2003 invasion of Iraq, the erroneous CIA assertion that Iraq possessed weapons of mass destruction—the primary justification for the invasion—was based on groupthink by an administration invested in finding a reason to attack Iraq (U.S. Senate, 2004).

Culture affects conformity as well. In collectivist cultures, groups matter more than the individual, so any group-preserving behavior (such as conformity) would be valued and encouraged. In Japan, the company that one works for is elevated to the status of family. An employee is expected to make personal sacrifices for the company to preserve group unity (A. S. Miller & Kanazawa, 2000). Cross-cultural replications of the Asch experiments reveal that people in collectivist cultures like Japan are more likely to conform than are people in individualistic cultures like the United States (Bond & Smith, 1996).

Neuroscience research sheds light on the brain mechanisms involved in conformity. When people are made aware that their beliefs differ from those of most other people in a group, a brain region active when we make an error becomes active (Klucharev et al., 2009). In other words, the brain acts as though we've made a mistake when we deviate from the group opinion.

groupthink
A situation in which the thinking of the group takes over, so much so that group members forgo logic or critical analysis in the service of reaching a decision.

Connection

In an individualistic culture, behavior is determined more by personal goals than by group goals, whereas in a collectivist culture, behavior is determined more by shared goals.

See "Personality and Culture: Universality and Differences," Chapter 13, "Personality: The Uniqueness of the Individual," p. 483.

Minority Social Influence

At times a single individual or small number of individuals can influence an entire group. In social psychology, a single person or small group within a larger group is called a *minority*, while the larger group is referred to as the *majority*. Just as the majority pushes for group unity, the minority can push for independence and uniqueness. After all, if people always conformed, how would change occur

(Moscovici, 1985)? In order to change the majority view, however, the minority must present a consistent, unwavering message.

Most often, minority opinion shifts majority opinion by means of informational social influence. If a group encounters a situation in which the members are unsure of what to do and a minority carefully presents a well-thought-out position to the majority, then the majority might accept it. This is how juries can change course. Juries must provide unanimous decisions, and sometimes only one voice disagrees with the majority. If that minority of one offers a logical argument for the dissenting opinion, the majority view might be changed.

Obedience

obedience
A type of conformity in which a person yields to the will of another person.

Another kind of conformity, called **obedience,** occurs when people yield to the social pressure of an authority figure. Social psychological research on obedience emerged in response to real-life concerns in the aftermath of World War II. The horrific events of the Holocaust raised troubling questions: How could an entire nation endorse the extermination of millions of people? Were *all* Germans evil? Adolf Hitler did not act alone—a supporting cast of thousands was necessary to annihilate so many people. Former Nazi officers who testified in war trials after the war said they were "following orders." The same rationale was offered in 2004 by U.S. soldiers who humiliated and tortured Iraqi prisoners at Abu Ghraib.

Will people do horrible things if an authority figure orders them to do so? One psychologist spurred into action by the Nazi atrocities was Stanley Milgram. A Jew whose family had left Europe before Hitler's rise to power, Milgram spent much of his early academic life trying to make sense of the Holocaust (Blass, 2004). With the support of his graduate advisor, Solomon Asch, Milgram decided to investigate whether people would conform even when their actions could harm others.

Stanley Milgram

Milgram recruited people from the community to participate in an experiment at Yale University. A participant arrived at the lab and sat down next to another supposed participant, who was a confederate. The experimenter, who looked very official in a white lab coat, told both individuals that they would be participating in a study on the effects of mild punishment on memory. He then assigned them to be either a teacher or a learner by asking them to pull a note that said either "teacher" or "learner" from a bowl. The drawing was rigged, however, so that the real participant always landed the "teacher" role and the confederate got the "learner" role. Then the experimenter showed both the teacher and the learner to the room where the learner would sit. The learner's task involved learning and repeating lists of words. The learner was told that every time he made an error he would receive a mild electric shock, delivered by the teacher. With each mistake the shocks would increase in intensity. Both teacher and learner saw the chair where the learner would sit, which had restraints to make sure the electrodes had a good contact when he received the shock. The teacher then received a sample shock of very low voltage to get a sense of what the learner would experience. In actuality, this was the only real shock administered during the entire experiment.

Then they went to the teacher's room. The teacher sat at a table behind a panel of switches. Under each switch was a label indicating voltage level, which ranged, in 15-volt increments, from 15 volts ("mild shock") all the way up to 450 (labeled "XXX"), with 315 volts designated as "Danger: Severe shock" (see Figure 14.2a). The teacher was reminded that if the learner made mistakes, he or she would have to deliver a shock and with each mistake would have to increase the level.

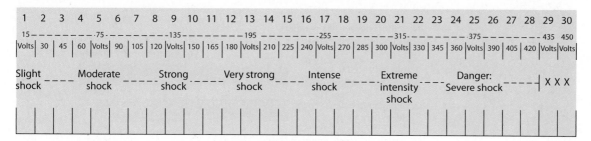

(a) Control panel seen by the "teacher"

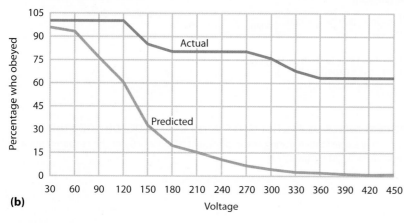

(b)

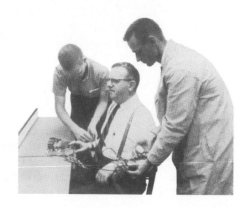

(c)

FIGURE 14.2

MILGRAM'S STUDY OF OBEDIENCE. (a) This is the control panel seen by the "teacher." (b) Experts consulted by Milgram prior to the study predicted that, at higher voltages, participants would refuse to administer further shocks to the "learner." As the graph shows, the experts were wrong. At the highest voltages, when the experimenter told them the experiment must continue in spite of the "learner's" protests, 60% of the "teachers" continued to administer "shocks." (c) The "learner" is strapped in for Milgram's study. (Milgram, 1974)

The experiment began uneventfully. Then the learner made occasional mistakes. At lower levels of shock, the learner gave no real response to the pretend shocks. As the teacher moved up the shock scale and the learner supposedly made more errors, the teacher and experimenter could hear a yelp of pain come from the learner with each shock. (In fact, the learner played a prerecorded tape of his responses to the shock.) At this point, many teachers asked the experimenter if they should go on, and he would say, "The experiment requires that you go on."

Before beginning the experiments, Milgram polled experts to see how many "teachers" they thought would go along with the experimenter's demands to administer high levels of shock. One group of experts, psychiatrists, predicted that only about 30% would administer shocks as high as 150 volts, less than 4% would go to the 300-volt level, and only 1 person in 1,000 would go all the way to 450 volts. How far do *you* think most people would go in administering shocks?

The results differed drastically from these predictions. As shown in Figure 14.2b, at 150 volts, the point at which the learner yelled, "Get me out of here! My heart's starting to bother me! I refuse to go on! Let me out!" there was a drop in obedience—from 100% to about 83%. Some participants stopped, but many, although visibly uncomfortable, continued with the experiment. What is alarming is how many people went all the way up to the end of the shock scale, despite the yells and protests (and eventual silence) of the learner. Twenty-six

Connection

Do you think participants were treated ethically in the Milgram study? What are the obligations of researchers to ensure the ethical treatment of participants in research?

See "Research Ethics," Chapter 2, "Conducting Research in Psychology," p. 62.

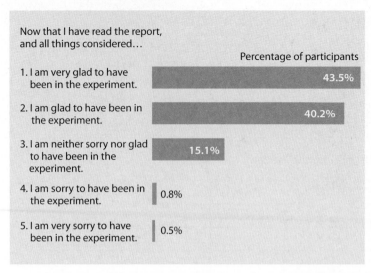

Now that I have read the report, and all things considered...

Percentage of participants

1. I am very glad to have been in the experiment. 43.5%

2. I am glad to have been in the experiment. 40.2%

3. I am neither sorry nor glad to have been in the experiment. 15.1%

4. I am sorry to have been in the experiment. 0.8%

5. I am very sorry to have been in the experiment. 0.5%

FIGURE **14.3**

QUESTIONNAIRE RESPONSES OF PARTICIPANTS IN MILGRAM'S OBEDIENCE STUDY.
Despite the distress they experienced during the experiment, the majority of the respondents did not regret their involvement. (Milgram, 1974)

of the 40 participants in the original experiment (65%) went all the way to 450 volts (Milgram, 1963, 1974). Men and women were equally likely to reach the 450-volt level.

Milgram's experiments show that reasonable people may do things that seem cruel and unusual in the presence of powerful social influence. Several "teachers" did protest and yet went on when the experimenter urged them to continue. When asked, "Who is going to take responsibility if that guy gets hurt?" the experimenter would say, "I have full responsibility, please continue." Somehow, the belief that someone else (the authority figure) was responsible for their actions alleviated feelings of guilt or concern in some of the participants. This is akin to former Nazi officers saying, "I was just following orders," but who really has the final responsibility?

Because participants clearly experienced mental anguish while taking part in the study, it sparked a fierce debate about ethics in research. Milgram contacted his participants later and asked whether they regretted having participated. Less than 2% did (see Figure 14.3).

You might think that you would never administer those shocks or that people today would know better. Not so. In 2006, social psychologist Jerry Burger conducted a modified version of Milgram's original study with college students. An important change from the original study was that, when the participants began to protest, they were told to continue rather than told that they *had* to continue. Also, once participants passed the 150-volt range, the experiment stopped. By making these changes, the researchers were able to obtain permission from the American Psychological Association to conduct the experiment, which otherwise would not meet current standards for the ethical treatment of human participants. As in Milgram's experiment, Burger reported that two-thirds of the participants obeyed the authority figure and continued to administer shocks after the "learner" began protesting. Milgram's controversial study continues to inspire investigation and reinterpretation, including studies that suggest that people are more likely to follow authority not just for situational reasons but because they think the authority knew the right thing to do (Haslam & Reicher, 2012).

1. Sometimes people perform better—for example, ride a bike faster—when they are in groups than when alone. Social psychologists call this
   a. the Yerkes-Dodson principle.
   b. social loafing.
   c. social facilitation.
   d. conformity.

2. People who are of a minority opinion in a group are most likely to change the opinion of the majority by
   a. getting them to conform to group pressure.
   b. using reason and logic.
   c. trying to shame them.
   d. presenting a well-formed persuasive argument.

3. When put in a situation where an individual has to say something about the length of a line that goes against what everyone else in the group has said, most people
   a. eventually conform at least once and go along with the group.

b. always conform and go along with the group.
c. never conform and go along with the group.
d. pretend not to be paying attention.

4. In Milgram's study on obedience, under pressure from an authority figure, approximately what percentage of the participants gave the maximum punishment of 450 volts to the learner's incorrect answers?
   a. 25%
   b. 50%
   c. 65%
   d. 90%

Answers can be found at the end of the chapter.

SOCIAL PERCEPTION

Social processes not only influence our behavior but also guide our perceptions of the behavior of others. For example, we wonder why people do what they do. *Why does Maria wear those clothes?* We wonder whether we can believe what people say. *Is he lying to me?* We form impressions and attitudes about other people. *Ashan is smart.* These are all matters of *social perception*, the way in which we make sense of our social world.

Attribution

We often wonder why people do the things they do (Kelley & Michela, 1980), and we try to explain their actions. **Attributions** are the inferences we make about the causes of other people's behavior.

Social psychologist Fritz Heider (1958) made an important distinction between two types of attributions. Internal, or *dispositional, attributions* ascribe other people's behavior to something within them, such as their personalities, motives, or attitudes. Let's say that Chris flunked a test. A dispositional attribution would be "Chris flunked the test because he is too lazy to study." The person making this attribution assumed that Chris's flunking is a result of something about him, but it is also possible that Chris's failing grade resulted from some external factor. Perhaps the test was too hard. People make external, or *situational, attributions* when they think that something outside the person, such as the nature of the situation, is the cause of his or her behavior. If Jake says that Chris failed because the exam was too hard, Jake has made a situational attribution for Chris's grade.

We tend to evaluate our own behavior in different ways depending on whether we have succeeded or failed. For instance, it is likely that Chris would attribute his failure on a test to something about the situation—say, the test was too hard or the professor unfair—rather than to his own abilities. If Chris had aced the test, however, it is likely he'd attribute his success to his own skills.

attributions
Inferences made about the causes of other people's behavior.

Meeting potential mates in a group of singles might make some people seem shy.
Would you make the fundamental attribution error in a situation like this and assume that shyness is a personality trait?

self-serving bias
The tendency to make situational attributions for our failures but dispositional attributions for our successes.

fundamental attribution error
The tendency to explain others' behavior in dispositional rather than situational terms.

Making situational attributions for our failures but dispositional attributions for our successes is known as a **self-serving bias.**

People tend to explain other people's behavior in terms of dispositional attributions rather than situational ones, a bias in judgment known as the **fundamental attribution error** (Ross, 1977). This is not to say that dispositions don't matter but rather that, when making attributions of other people's behavior, we tend to think that dispositional characteristics matter the most. People living in Asian cultures, such as India and Japan, are much less likely to make the fundamental attribution error than are European Americans (Choi, Nisbett, & Norenzayan, 1999). This seems to be due to a cultural tendency for Asians to explain behaviors—even things as extreme as murder—in situational terms (M. W. Morris & Peng, 1994; Norenzayan & Nisbett, 2000).

Detecting Deception

Connection

Cultural differences in big-picture versus detailed processing are seen in performance on visual perception tasks, too.

See "Perceiving Visual Stimuli," Chapter 4, "Sensing and Perceiving Our World," p. 130.

One way that we try to figure out others is by judging whether or not they are being truthful. Most people think that they know when people lie to them. According to the research, however, most of us are not effective lie detectors. Most people perform no better than the accuracy rate of chance guessing in detecting deception from people's behavior (Ekman & O'Sullivan, 1991).

Why are we unsuccessful at catching liars? Most of us rely on misleading cues. We put too much weight on what people are saying, overinterpret ambiguous nonverbal cues (thinking any sign of nervousness means a person is lying), ignore relevant nonverbal information, and get fooled by signs of warmth and competence (Ekman & O'Sullivan, 1991). If people learn to focus instead on inconsistent behaviors (shaking the head while saying yes) and signs of emotion that don't match what people are saying, then they become better "lie detectors." There are no foolproof ways of detecting deception, however.

The best lie detectors attend to nonverbal information more than verbal information (Frank & Ekman, 1997). In a study of experts who should be good at catching liars, such as U.S. Secret Service agents, FBI agents, CIA agents, police, judges, and psychiatrists, only the Secret Service agents performed significantly better than if they had been guessing (Ekman & O'Sullivan, 1991). Psychologists with a special interest in deception have also been shown to do much better than others in detecting deceit (Ekman, O'Sullivan, & Frank, 1999).

Work on deception attracts much public interest. In 2009, Fox premiered the TV drama *Lie to Me*, based on the deception research of Paul Ekman. The protagonist, the fictitious Cal Lightman, and his colleagues read facial expressions and other nonverbal behaviors to determine whether people are lying in this crime-oriented drama. The science in the show was vetted by experts on deception and facial expression (Paul Ekman and Erika Rosenberg).

Schemas

Whether we are trying to determine if people are lying or simply trying to make sense of simple actions, our own ideas of how the world works influence our perceptions of it. People develop models, or *schemas*, of the social world, which function as lenses through which we filter our perceptions. We first discussed schemas in Chapter 7 and defined them broadly as ways of knowing that we develop from our experiences with particular objects or events. In the area of social perception, schemas are ways of knowing that affect how we view our social world.

We rely on schemas when forming impressions of other people, especially when we encounter ambiguous information. Imagine you are invited to dinner and notice that one of the guests has slurred speech and walks shakily across the room. You assume—reasonably—that she is drunk. Later you learn that she has Parkinson's disease, a neurological condition that affects motor coordination. Slurred speech and shaky walking are common symptoms of this disorder. You assumed that the woman was drunk because the schema of drunkenness was much more *accessible* to you than that of Parkinson's disease.

Stereotypes

Schemas of how people are likely to behave based simply on the groups to which they belong are known as **stereotypes.** When we resort to stereotypes, we form conclusions about people before we even interact with them just because they are of a certain race-ethnicity or live in a certain place. As a result, we end up judging people not by their actions but by our notions of how they might act.

stereotypes
Schemas of how people are likely to behave based simply on groups to which they belong.

What stereotypes do these images bring to mind?

People resort to stereotypes because they allow for quick—but often inaccurate—impressions, especially if we do not know someone very well. The human mind has a tendency to categorize and understand all members of a group in terms of characteristics that are typical of the group (Rosch, 1975). So if we meet someone new and learn that he or she belongs to a particular (racial-ethnic, social, political, or religious) group, we rely on what we think we know about that group to anticipate how this new person might behave. fMRI scans show that, when people avoid thinking in this stereotyped way, the prefrontal cortex—an area involved in inhibiting inappropriate responses—is activated (De Neys, Vartanian, & Goel, 2008). This suggests that, when you rely on stereotypes, you are not thinking carefully.

Take a look at a few of the common stereotypes that exist in U.S. culture:

Jocks are dumb.
Jews are cheap.
Middle Eastern men with beards might be terrorists.

Connection

Another name for mental shortcuts we use in decision making is *heuristics*. Heuristics can be adaptive but also can lead to flawed thinking.

See "How Do We Make Judgments and Decisions?" Chapter 9, "Language and Thought," p. 345.

With stereotypes, we have formed conclusions about people even before we interact with them. Stereotypes may originate in something that is factual but that does not characterize a whole group. The terrorists involved in the September 11, 2001, attacks in the United States, for example, were Middle Eastern men, many of whom had beards—but not all Middle Eastern men with beards are terrorists. Most serial killers in the United States have been young white men. Does that mean all young white men are serial killers (Apsche, 1993)?

During his 2008 run for the presidency, Barack Obama faced numerous stereotypes associated with his name (which has Muslim roots), his mixed race-ethnicity, and his education. People who did not know much about him were more likely to believe rumors that he was a Muslim (although he is not). The implication that he was a Muslim activated the terrorist stereotype we just discussed. Some rivals stereotyped Obama as an elitist, because he had gone to Harvard Law School. They tried to link him with stereotypical notions that well-educated people are out of touch with average people, even though he had grown up in a low-income household and right out of college had worked with the poor and unemployed in Chicago.

Exclusion and Inclusion

As a result of having evolved for group living, we tend to judge others and ourselves. These judgments may stem from defending ourselves against other groups and competing with them for limited resources (Neuberg & Cottrell, 2006). That is, the machinery exists for using cognitive and emotional processes to separate "us" from "them." Perceiving others as different from us has several consequences:

1. We sometimes evaluate and treat people differently because of the group they belong to.

2. Our actions are based on in-group/out-group distinctions ("us" versus "them").

3. It hurts to be excluded from our group.

When we show positive feelings toward people in our own group and negative feelings toward those in other groups, we are displaying **in-group/out-group bias.** Think back to the rivalry between your high school and its crosstown rival. Everyone who went to your school was part of your in-group, and you identified with all of them and felt pride belonging to that group. Everyone who went to the other school was part of the out-group, and you felt competitive whenever the two

in-group/out-group bias
The tendency to show positive feelings toward people who belong to the same group as we do, and negative feelings toward those in other groups.

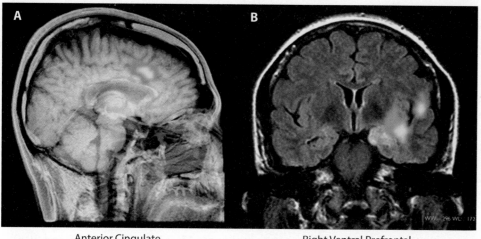

Anterior Cingulate
x = −8

Right Ventral Prefrontal
y = 28

FIGURE **14.4**

BRAIN REGIONS ACTIVATED BY SOCIAL PAIN. Exclusion from an electronic ball-tossing game increased blood flow to the same areas of the brain activated by physical pain. The increase in activity in the anterior cingulate cortex (A) and in the right front section of the prefrontal cortex (B) shows up in these fMRI images as patches of orange and yellow. (Eisenberger et al., 2003)

schools interacted. Moreover, you likely made many distinctions between students and groups at your school but categorized everyone who went to the other school into one group: "them." The tendency to see all members of an out-group as the same is known as **out-group homogeneity.**

One result of the human tendency to include and exclude others is that sometimes we get left out. As illustrated by the scenario that opens this chapter, rejection hurts. One possible reason it hurts to be left out is that social connections are as important to us as our physical safety—so important that the brain's physical pain circuits also evolved to signal when we have been excluded from the group (see Figure 14.4; Eisenberger et al., 2003; MacDonald, Kingsbury, & Shaw, 2005; MacDonald & Leary, 2005; Masten et al., 2009). An interesting corollary of the pain finding is that, when people read friendly messages from those people with whom they feel socially connected, they feel physically warm and show brain activation patterns that correspond to the areas active during actual physical warmth (Inagaki & Eisenberger, 2013). Thus, there appears to be mapping of physical and social pain in our lived experience of others.

In modern life, we separate physical from social needs, but in early human evolution, these two needs were often intertwined. To be included in a social group meant you were fed, you were secure, and you could reproduce. Being excluded threatened not only survival but also the chance to reproduce (MacDonald et al., 2005). The need for connection runs so deep down the phylogenetic tree that you find it in social insects. When raised without social contact, cockroaches show behavioral deficiencies, including poor mating skills, reduced willingness to interact with others, and impaired foraging (Lihoreau, Brepson, & Rivault, 2009).

Humans also form social groups through social networks, which are webs of people who share common interests, professions, or familial relations (Christakis & Fowler, 2009). Both real-life and electronic social networks play an important role in social life. See "Psychology in the Real World."

out-group homogeneity
The tendency to see all members of an out-group as the same.

Psychology in the Real World

The Social Psychology of Social Networks

Social networks form among people who share interests. You might be in one network as a function of your school, another by virtue of familial relationships, and yet another because of your musical taste. Networks are defined by associations among people that branch and spread beyond those people one knows directly (Christakis & Fowler, 2009).

Everything from physical health habits to moods can spread in a social network—often unbeknownst to all involved. By *spread* we mean that these behaviors are more common among members of a network than among people who are not in the same network. Eating behavior, drinking habits, smoking, loneliness, happiness, and cooperative behavior all spread in this way (Cacioppo, Fowler, & Christakis, 2009; Christakis & Fowler, 2007, 2008; Fowler & Christakis, 2008, 2010; Rosenquist et al., 2010).

Nicholas Christakis and James Fowler (2009), pioneers in research on social networks, report that attitudes, behaviors, and habits move through social networks via the *three degrees rule*. For instance, your behavior (say, your food preferences) can affect your friends (one degree) and their friends (two degrees) and their friends' friends (three degrees). So we are influenced by and influence our friends within three degrees of separation, but not much beyond that (Christakis & Fowler, 2009).

How does something like smoking behavior spread in a network? Social psychological processes such as conformity and peer influence play a role; that is, you might be more likely to smoke if the people you know smoke and it is regarded as "OK" to smoke in your social circles. Mimicry, or the process by which we mirror the actions of others, may be one means by which our emotional behavior can impact another person. In such cases, however, the behavior gets distorted as it moves outward toward others, much as a message gets modified when it is passed among many people (Christakis & Fowler, 2009).

Real-life social networks have existed for ages, but social networking sites (SNSs)—electronic forums for interaction with friends and acquaintances—are relatively new. Although in their infancy, SNSs such as Facebook, Instagram, and Twitter are now a major means of social interaction among people ages 15–25. Between 2005 and 2010, there was a major shift from e-mail as the major form of Internet use to SNSs such as Facebook (Judd & Kennedy, 2010). By January 2011, Facebook alone had more than half a billion users worldwide ("The Many Facets," 2011), although there is evidence that Facebook use is declining, just as MySpace did in the early 2010s (Cannarella & Spechler, 2014). Even though SNSs are electronic, they influence real-world social connections (Christakis & Fowler, 2009). For instance, SNS use contributes to perceptions of quality of social interaction and supports socialization (Yu et al., 2010) and increases the likelihood of being exposed to differing political views regardless of one's political affiliation (Y. Kim, 2011).

Still, these two types of networks might work quite differently. Given how Facebook is arranged, ideas and preferences ("likes") instantly spread much more rapidly than they would in a real-world social network. It is possible that the three degrees rule may not apply to SNSs or that the limits of influence may be wider. Also, surveys of Facebook use show that people of all ages share much more private information publicly than they realize (Brandtzæg, Lüders, & Skjetne, 2010). People readily disclose drug and alcohol use more freely on SNSs than they might in real-world public settings (Moran, Snelson, & Elison-Bowers, 2010).

Prejudice and Discrimination

We have discussed many processes that affect group behavior and how we view others. Unfortunately, as people try to make sense of each other and rely on schemas to decide who is similar or who is different, they sometimes use stereotypes to unfairly categorize others, which can fuel prejudice and discrimination.

A **prejudice** is a biased attitude toward a group of people or an individual member of a group based on unfair generalizations about what members of that group are like (Allport, 1954). Prejudicial thinking often stems from stereotypes rather than from careful observation of people's behavior. Prejudices are generally negative and often based on insufficient information. Prejudices based on race-ethnicity are called *racism;* those based on sex are called *sexism.* If

prejudice
A biased attitude toward a group of people or an individual member of a group based on unfair generalizations about what members of that group are like.

 How did social networks, such as Facebook and Twitter, play a key role in the revolutions in the Middle East and North Africa in the spring of 2011?

Indeed, certain people are more likely to make optimal use of privacy features than others—women more than men and younger people more often than older people (Litt, 2013).

Not everyone is equally interested in using SNSs, and people use them differently. Some users post frequently, while some prefer to read others' postings only. Not surprisingly, a number of personality factors relate to Facebook use, as we discussed in Chapter 13. People who score higher on measures of conscientiousness have more friends; those who score higher on openness to experience are more expressive in their personal profiles; and those who score high on introversion have smaller social networks than extraverts (Amichai-Hamburger & Vinitzky, 2010). People who score either low or high on neuroticism share more information than people with moderate levels of neuroticism.

Although Facebook and Twitter are international, people in Asia use Asian SNSs more often: QQ in China, Cyworld in Korea, and Mixi in Japan (Y. G. Ji et al., 2010). In spite of many similarities between cultures in how people use SNSs, there are some differences in how they use SNSs

to obtain what is known as *social capital*. Social capital is the value, or payoff (socially, professionally), one gains by connecting with others. Korean and Chinese users rely more on searching and friending functions to build bridges with others, while American users use direct communication (such as wall postings) to foster more intimate relationships with online friends in their networks (Y. G. Ji et al., 2010).

Payoff for SNS use takes many forms. Many people use SNSs to get reinforcement for their views or images—in Facebook terms, one way to measure that is by means of receiving "likes" for one's postings. In fact, the number of "likes" received shapes future posting behavior. A large-scale survey indicated that people who get reinforced by "likes" for disclosing personal information online (such as posting pictures, relationship status, whereabouts of social activities) are more likely to disclose even more in the future (Trepte & Reinecke, 2013). Also, we tend to "like" the posts of people who "like" our posts. Although many use SNSs primarily for enjoyment, some of the biggest factors that determine usage involve the behavior of our "friends." Facebook use is affected by how many of one's peers are using it, as well as perceptions of reciprocity in liking behavior (e.g., if you "like" their stuff, they will "like" yours; Lin & Lu, 2011). Here we see the power of social influence on SNS behavior.

Both real and virtual social networks spread information to large numbers of people in a short period of time—often to powerful effect. In February 2011, the people of Egypt protested the authoritarian government of Hosni Mubarak. Within a matter of days, early reports and images of police violence against peaceful protestors had spread to millions of young Egyptians via Twitter and Facebook. This, along with other information, incited a successful revolution, which ultimately led to Mubarak's resignation.

a business executive does not seriously consider a highly qualified female applicant for a high-level management job because he is convinced that women are not capable of leading a company, his thinking is prejudicial. More precisely, he is sexist. Not offering her an interview—even if she is the best-qualified applicant in the pool—is discrimination. **Discrimination** is the preferential treatment of certain people that is usually driven by prejudicial attitudes. Discrimination can also result from institutionalized rules, such as the requirement that flight attendants cannot be excessively overweight.

Prejudicial attitudes are learned early in life; and even if they are formally abandoned later in life, these reactions can become quite automatic (Banaji & Greenwald, 1995). Consider the case of Edith, a 21-year-old European American college student who is politically liberal and an activist for progressive causes. However, when Edith walks to her car at night, if an African American man is on the other side of the street, she becomes nervous

discrimination
The preferential treatment of certain people, usually driven by prejudicial attitudes.

without knowing why. She is not a racist! Why does this happen? Prejudices can operate outside conscious awareness, and they sometimes stand in stark contrast to one's conscious beliefs (Devine, 1989). Even a person who works hard at being fair may have a hard time overcoming biases that are automatic and deeply learned. There may also be an evolutionary basis for our automatic responses: The mechanism of recognizing group members may have evolved to preserve group harmony, cohesion, and close alliances (Melis & Semmann, 2010; Neuberg & Cottrell, 2006).

Challenging Assumptions in Social Behavior

Mahzarin Banaji

Prejudice operates both inside and outside a person's awareness. As in Edith's case, much racial-ethnic bias is unconscious and in conflict with consciously held views. Two social psychologists, Mahzarin Banaji and Anthony Greenwald, suspected there was a disconnect between people's conscious and unconscious views of prejudice and developed a way of measuring what they called *implicit bias.*

Social psychologists distinguish between *explicit* and *implicit* prejudice. Explicit ideas are plainly stated. Implicit views are indirect, perhaps unconscious. An explicit reference to a desire to have sex with someone is "I want to go to bed with you." An implicit reference is "Why don't you come by my place and watch a movie with me?" Measuring implicit knowledge and beliefs presents a challenge.

Banaji and Greenwald had become interested in implicit social thought and attitudes but were unhappy about the lack of scientific measures of them (Greenwald & Banaji, 1995). Greenwald and his colleagues had developed a computer program that measured implicit cognitive attitudes toward flowers and insects.

There were four steps to the program. First, participants had to press a computer keyboard letter with their left hand for flowers and a different key with their right hand for insects. Second, they had to do the same for pleasant words (left hand) and unpleasant words (right hand). Third, flowers and pleasant words were combined (left hand), and insects and unpleasant words were combined (right hand). When Greenwald did this, he found these three tasks very easy and did them very quickly. Things changed when he got to the fourth and final condition. Now flowers, which used to be left hand, and insects, which used to be right hand, were switched, but the pleasant and unpleasant words stayed on the same side. In other words, flowers were now paired with unpleasant words and insects with pleasant words. Greenwald was much slower at making these associations. He thought he could get better with practice but, to his surprise, he couldn't. There was no way to change the implicit association. He quickly realized this might be the measure of implicit social attitudes they were seeking (Greenwald, 2009).

Anthony Greenwald

When Banaji took the same test, her results looked about the same as Greenwald's. Banaji and Greenwald, though concerned about what their scores might reveal about their own latent attitudes, knew they were on to something. They dubbed the new test the *Implicit Associations Test (IAT).*

Most famously, Greenwald and Banaji applied the IAT to concepts of race and ethnicity. Faster response times on the test indicate that people more readily associate two concepts; slower response times indicate a less automatic association. European Americans tend to respond more slowly to pairings of "Black" (words or faces) with positive words than they do to pairings of "Black" with negative words (Dasgupta et al., 2000; Greenwald, McGhee, & Schwartz, 1998). This holds even for people whose questionnaire responses indicate that they do not hold racist attitudes. Interestingly, African Americans respond more slowly to pairings of "White American" with positive words than they do to pairings of "White American" with negative words. Banaji and Greenwald (1995) have also reported evidence of implicit gender bias using the IAT; female and male college students more readily associated "fame" with male names than with female names.

In the roughly 20 years since the IAT's publication, more than 600 published research papers, in areas ranging from marketing to neuroscience, have used the IAT technique. IAT scores predict suicidal tendencies, consumer preferences, political preferences, sexual orientation, symptoms of post-traumatic stress disorder, and drug and alcohol use (Anselmi et al., 2013; Greenwald et al., 2009; Lindgren et al., 2013; Nock et al., 2010). Indeed, the IAT is an excellent teaching tool for anyone confronting his or her own implicit prejudice. Results from the test can be used to reduce prejudice and sensitize individuals and groups to the fact that these prejudices operate in subtle yet powerful ways. In 1998 Banaji, Greenwald, and Nosek established a nonprofit organization (Project Implicit) to help people apply the IAT technique. Banaji lives by her own advice. She was so dismayed by her own performance on race- and gender-based IATs—in spite of being a minority woman herself—that she changed her behavior. In addition to the nonprofit work, she does little things to help undo her deeply held biases, such as displaying pictures of prominent Black men and women from history in her office.

Challenge Your Assumptions
True or False? I know whether I am prejudiced or not.

False: In spite of our best intentions or conscious beliefs, deeply held biases are often implicit, or outside our conscious awareness.

Quick Quiz 14.2: Social Perception

1. Our tendency to conclude that Alex must have an aggressive personality because we see him hit Bobby once on the playground is an example of
   a. a stereotype.
   b. a prejudice.
   c. deception.
   d. the fundamental attribution error.

2. "College professors are absent-minded" is an example of
   a. an attitude.
   b. an attribution.
   c. a stereotype.
   d. a prejudice.

3. Out-group homogeneity is the tendency to
   a. see people outside our group as looking or acting alike.
   b. see people inside our group as looking or acting alike.
   c. believe people outside our group think the same way we do.
   d. believe people inside our group think the same way we do.

4. Brandon believes women are not very good at math. However, as a computer scientist, he has always been able to treat women the same way he treats men at work. Which of the following statements is true?
   a. Brandon is prejudiced against women.
   b. Brandon's behavior is an example of discrimination.
   c. Brandon's beliefs are based on stereotypes.
   d. Both a and c are true.

5. Measuring how long it takes a person to pair positive or negative terms with particular ethnic groups is used in social psychology as a measure of
   a. explicit racism.
   b. implicit racism.
   c. stereotypes.
   d. reaction time.

Answers can be found at the end of the chapter.

ATTITUDES AND BEHAVIOR

People use the word *attitude* frequently, but what does it mean? Social psychologists define **attitudes** as a person's favorable or unfavorable feelings, beliefs, or actions toward an object, an idea, or a person (Olson & Zanna, 1993). Thus, attitudes have affective, cognitive, and behavioral components. The *affective* component includes the feelings or emotions associated with the belief; the *cognitive* component consists of the rational thoughts and beliefs that make up the attitude; and the *behavioral* component includes the motive to act in a particular

attitudes
An individual's favorable or unfavorable beliefs, feelings, or actions toward an object, an idea, or a person.

way toward the person or object of the attitude. Consider Elizabeth, who is a huge Giants fan. She loves the team (affective), knows all about each starting player (cognitive), and has bought season tickets to their home games (behavioral).

Attitudes differ by how heavily each component is weighted. Some attitudes are more cognitive, such as your beliefs about the best way to slice a mango. Others may be more affective, such as your attitude about the death penalty. Our attitudes and beliefs stem from our history as a species as well as our history as individuals.

The Nature and Nurture of Attitudes

Some of our most basic attitudes may be instinctive, while others are learned. Certain negative attitudes and emotional responses, such as fear of snakes or the nearly universal human revulsion for bodily waste and decaying matter, may be so important for human survival that they are part of our genetic heritage (D. M. Buss, 1999). Evolutionary pressures to preserve group membership favor in-group bias (fear of those who are different). Because humans evolved in small social groups in threatening environments, it made sense for people to trust those who were most like them. In addition, the tendency to automatically make quick good-bad and like-dislike assessments is a fundamental cognitive process with clear evolutionary benefits: It helps people make quick decisions in life-threatening situations (Cunningham & Zelazo, 2006; Neuberg & Cottrell, 2006).

On the other hand, many of our attitudes come from experience. In some cases, we learn attitudes through both direct and indirect instruction by others. We may adopt the musical preferences of our friends. Sometimes we like ideas or objects simply because they are familiar. *Mere exposure*, or direct experience with an object, an idea, or a person, increases our overall preference for it (Zajonc, 1968). The things that we come to like from exposure can be trivial, such as abstract symbols, or very meaningful, such as human faces. For example, Zajonc (1968) showed people nonsense words 5, 10, or 25 times; the more often they saw a word, the more they reported liking it.

Attitude Change

Are people willing to switch attitudes based on evidence or a persuasive argument? What role do personality and persuasion play in our willingness to change attitudes? These are just some of the questions asked by social psychologists interested in attitude change. We examine two major reasons for changes in attitude: cognitive dissonance and persuasion.

cognitive dissonance
The feeling of discomfort caused by information that is different from a person's conception of himself or herself as a reasonable and sensible person.

Cognitive Dissonance The theory of cognitive dissonance offers one explanation for why and how we change our attitudes. **Cognitive dissonance** is the feeling of discomfort caused by information that is at odds with one's conception of oneself as a reasonable and sensible person (Festinger, 1957). Because we don't like feeling uncomfortable, we are motivated to try to reduce the discomfort. Three options are available for decreasing the discomfort created by dissonance:

1. We can change our behavior to make it consistent with dissonant cognition.
2. We can attempt to justify our behavior by changing one of the cognitions to make it more consistent with our behavior.
3. We can add new cognitions that are consistent with the behavior and that therefore support it.

When people experience cognitive dissonance, they go to extreme lengths to reduce it. In this way, they reduce their discomfort and maintain self-esteem.

change behavior		Quit smoking.
justify smoking by changing cognitions associated with it		"Smoking is not that harmful." "Results of research on smoking and cancer are not as conclusive as people think they are."
change cognitions so as to justify smoking		"It makes me feel good, so it's worth it, whatever the risk."

FIGURE **14.5**

COGNITIVE DISSONANCE AND SMOKING. People smoke even though they know it's unhealthy. To reduce their cognitive dissonance, smokers might try one of these approaches, including quitting.

People end up rationalizing or justifying their not-so-adaptive behavior in order to reduce cognitive dissonance.

Smoking offers a classic example of an irrational behavior in which many people engage. Smoking can cause lung cancer, emphysema, and heart disease. Still, many people continue to smoke. True, they are addicted. Cognitively, however, smokers must manage the conflict between their notion of themselves as rational beings and the fact that they engage in a very risky habit. To reduce the unpleasant feeling these dissonant thoughts and behaviors create, people who smoke may behave in one of the three ways just listed, as seen in Figure 14.5. People will work hard to rationally defend behaviors or strongly held positions in order to reduce the dissonance—the uncomfortable feeling—produced by opposing arguments.

Making use of the tendency toward dissonance around high-risk behaviors, such as smoking, is one approach to treating them. Simmons and colleagues (2013) created a web-based program in which smokers watched a video of health information about the dangers of smoking (or a control video about nutrition). Then they were asked to make a video about themselves for the purpose of "promoting a healthy lifestyle," which would be shown to peers, in which they were asked to mention their smoking as well as other aspects of their lives. This potentially created dissonance, given the antismoking video they had just viewed. Consistent with the idea that people will change behavior or attitudes to reduce dissonance, the smokers with the most dissonant situation (those who viewed the video about the health effects of smoking) had significantly higher scores on a "motivation to quit" questionnaire than those in the control condition (Simmons et al., 2013).

persuasion
The act of attempting to change the opinions, beliefs, or choices of others by explanation or argument.

Persuasion Persuasion changes attitude as well. **Persuasion** is an attempt by a person or group to change our opinions, beliefs, or choices by explaining or arguing their position. Persuasion is all around us all the time; friends, family, teachers, politicians, salespeople, and advertisers often want to change our minds about something. The success of persuasion depends on three things: who the persuader is (source), the method used to convey the message, and who the receiver (audience) is (Lippa, 1994).

First, how trustworthy, prestigious, and likeable is the source of the message? The more prestigious and trustworthy the persuader, the more likely he or she is to succeed in persuading us. If the persuader is also attractive and familiar, so much the better. This is why people want to buy pain relievers promoted in commercials by famous TV doctors rather than unknown figures. The perceived credibility of the character enhances the credibility of the product.

Second, what methods of persuasion are used? Politicians often rely on fear to convince us to support their policies or candidacy. An example is the so-called Willie Horton ad that was shown during the 1988 U.S. presidential campaign. When Democratic presidential candidate Michael Dukakis was governor of Massachusetts, he supported a weekend release program for prisoners. One of the prisoners, Willie Horton, committed armed robbery and rape during such a weekend. A group supporting the Republican candidate, George H. W. Bush, ran a TV ad showing prisoners walking out of a prison yard with a voice-over about Horton. It ran regularly on stations across the country. It played on people's fears of dangerous criminals, and it linked that fear with Dukakis. That commercial is thought to have played a major role in Dukakis's loss to Bush.

Fear campaigns work only if they actually create fear in the audience (Witte & Allen, 2000). Most ads meant to scare us don't scare us enough to change our behavior. Simply citing statistics about the health risks of smoking is not very effective at getting people to change their behavior. People rarely believe that they will suffer the negative consequences implied by the ads.

Last, who is the targeted audience or receiver of the message? People are not equally malleable in their opinions or behavior. The more people know about a topic and the firmer their prior opinions are, the less likely they are to change their attitudes (Eagly & Chaiken, 1998). Political campaigners know this well. Candidates often focus their efforts—especially near election day—on swing states that either have voted inconsistently in the past or have a mix of party preferences. In regions that have voted Republican for years, say, campaigning by Democratic candidates may be a waste of time.

Quick Quiz 14.3: Attitudes and Behavior

1. Janice is a college student who is active in politics. She considers voting to be very important for everyone, especially young people. So she volunteers 5 hours a week to staff a table at the student union, encouraging students to register to vote, for any political party. Her stance toward voting is best described as a(n)
   a. belief.
   b. attitude.
   c. attribution.
   d. bias.

2. Levon considers himself to be a healthy person. He eats a healthy diet and exercises 4 days a week, yet he is a smoker. His attitude toward smoking before he became a smoker was very negative. Now that he is a smoker,

however, his attitude is not so negative. The change in his attitude is best explained by
   a. attribution.
   b. persuasion.
   c. mere exposure.
   d. cognitive dissonance.

3. Social psychologists have demonstrated that three things matter most in whether an argument will persuade other people or not. The three things are
   a. source, method, and audience.
   b. source, believability, and audience.
   c. logic, believability, and audience.
   d. pressure to conform, source, and authority.

Answers can be found at the end of the chapter.

SOCIAL RELATIONS

We constantly interact with other people. Sometimes these interactions lead to special connections with others that grow into friendship or even love. Other times we clash and find ourselves in conflict with others. In this section we discuss three kinds of social interaction: aggression, helping, and attraction.

The Nature and Nurture of Aggression

Aggression is part of life. All animals compete with others, both within and outside their species, for survival. Almost every animal can be aggressive, and many animals kill others in order to survive. Humans are unique in that they often engage in aggression and violent behavior even when their survival is not at issue. **Aggression** refers to violent behavior that is intended to cause psychological or physical harm, or both, to another being. By definition, aggression is deliberate. A dentist who performs a root canal may hurt a patient, but we hardly would call that behavior aggressive. Aggression is often provoked by anger, but not always.

When aggression stems from feelings of anger, it is called *hostile aggression*. When aggression is a means to achieve some goal, it is called *instrumental aggression*. The hostile type of aggression is easy to understand. While you are driving, someone cuts you off on the road. You honk and, in response, the other driver makes an obscene hand gesture toward you. The hand gesture is an aggressive action.

An example of instrumental aggression occurs in football when a defensive lineman smashes down a ball carrier to prevent the opponent from scoring. The goal is to prevent scoring by the other team, not to hurt the ball carrier. In this case, the aggressive action is considered to be justified by its instrumental goal.

Where does aggression come from, and why are people aggressive? Some people are more prone to violence than others. An individual's genetic disposition may play a role, but genes by themselves are seldom enough to cause violent behavior (Miczek et al., 2007). Caspi and colleagues (2002) found that, when genetic factors combine with an abusive and neglectful environment, the likelihood of committing violence increases dramatically.

Moreover, research on murderers points to a cluster of traits shared by most of these individuals: being male, growing up in an abusive and neglectful household, having at least one psychological disorder, and having experienced some kind of injury to the head or brain (Pincus, 1999, 2001; Strueber, Lueck, & Roth, 2006–2007; Yang et al., 2010). Having only one of these traits is not enough—all must be present for a person to become antisocial and prone to violence. In other words, the person's disposition interacts with certain environmental influences to make aggressive behavior more likely.

Several brain areas are involved in aggression, including the hypothalamus, the amygdala, and the prefrontal cortex (Pincus, 1999). More specifically, the part of the prefrontal cortex responsible for impulse control often is functionally impaired in aggressive and violent people (Grafman et al., 1996). Amygdala damage is found frequently in murderers (DeLisi, Umphress, & Vaughn, 2009). Similarly, as a result of head injuries, psychopathology, or abuse, murderers may have moderate to severe problems with frontal lobe functioning, which involves impulse control, emotional intelligence, working memory, and attention (Strueber et al., 2006–2007) or reductions in the size of the hippocampus (Yang et al., 2010). Living in a constant state of fear can lead to neural systems being primed for unusually high levels of anxiety, impulsive behavior, and vigilance or a constant state of alertness (Bishop, 2007). These are all conditions that may bring about violent behaviors.

Connection

How does hostility differ from anger? Hostility is a personality characteristic that sets the threshold for the emotion of anger.

See "What Are Emotions?" in Chapter 11, "Motivation and Emotion," p. 418.

aggression
Violent behavior that is intended to cause psychological or physical harm, or both, to another being.

In addition to these brain structures, two hormones are consistently related to high levels of aggression: testosterone and serotonin. A number of lines of evidence point to testosterone's role. As the male sex hormone, it may be responsible for boys being more aggressive than girls at most ages (Maccoby & Jacklin, 1974). In adults, the great majority of people arrested for criminal offenses are men (Strueber et al., 2006–2007). Relatively high levels of testosterone, whether in men or women, correlate positively with a propensity toward violence. Among both male and female prisoners, naturally occurring testosterone levels are higher in criminals convicted of violent crimes than in those convicted of nonviolent crimes (Dabbs, Carr, & Frady, 1995; Dabbs & Hargrove, 1997). In an experimental study, giving testosterone reduced performance on an empathy task in women (University of Cambridge, 2011). Serotonin has a broad range of effects on behavior, one of which is keeping anger and anxiety in check. Research shows that low levels of serotonin make aggression more likely in humans and animals (Moffitt et al., 1998; Raleigh et al., 1991).

Does violence in video games and other visual media increase the likelihood of aggressive behavior?

Social Influences on Aggression Situations that prevent us from reaching our goals are likely to make us aggressive. Moreover, the closer we are to our goal when we become frustrated, the more aggressive our response. A classic study by Harris (1974) demonstrated this effect. Confederates of the researchers cut in front of people in lines for movies or crowded restaurants. Sometimes they cut in front of the second person in line; other times they cut in front of someone farther back in line. The response of the person standing behind the intruder was much more aggressive when the confederate cut in front of the person second in line—closest to the goal.

Similarly, situations that lead to anger stimulate aggression, especially hostile aggression. Threats to our safety or the safety of our families fall into this category. Aggressive responses may be motivated by anger and/or fear. Road rage is a good example of such a situation, and aggressive driving is most likely to happen when people are angry (Nesbit, Conger, & Conger, 2007).

Observing aggressive people and the consequences of their actions can make us more aggressive. This is the fundamental idea behind Albert Bandura's *social learning theory*. Bandura's research demonstrated repeatedly that, if children see adults punching an inflatable Bobo doll, they will do it, too, especially if they see the adult being rewarded for the aggressive behavior.

How does the Bobo doll research apply to real-life aggression? According to longitudinal studies of men and women, the more violence people watch on TV when they are children, the more violent behavior they will exhibit as adults (Huesmann, Moise-Titus, & Podolski, 2003). This correlational result does not prove that TV is the cause of the aggressive behavior; however, more controlled experiments also suggest that watching TV violence leads to aggressive behavior in children. Liebert and Baron (1972) showed a violent TV program to a group of children. The control group saw an exciting but nonviolent sporting event that had the same running time as the violent program. Children were randomly assigned to the two groups. After viewing one of the programs, each child was allowed to play in another room with a group of children. Those who had watched the violent program were far more aggressive in their play than those who saw the nonviolent show.

Until recently, the evidence was overwhelming that exposure to violent programs or video games increased aggression in kids (Bushman & Anderson, 2001; Kirsh, 2006). Results from a recent meta-analysis suggest, however, that the effects of watching violence on aggressive behavior have been exaggerated.

It seems many of the studies fail to consider how other factors (such as sex, personality, and family violence) may also play a role in aggressive behavior (Ferguson & Kilburn, 2009). There is clearly a relationship between viewing violence and aggression, but the size of the effects is a matter of great debate (C. A. Anderson et al., 2010; Ferguson & Kilburn, 2010).

Whether or not viewing violence increases aggressive behavior, repeatedly seeing or participating in violent action in a virtual world may make young people less sensitive to violence. In one study, researchers randomly assigned more than 250 male and female college students to play either a violent or a nonviolent video game for 20 minutes (Carnagey, Anderson, & Bushman, 2007). Then they measured the participants' physiological responses to films of real-life violence, such as courtroom outbursts, police confrontations, shootings, and prison fights. The students who played the violent video games showed less physiological arousal (as measured by heart rate and sweating) while watching films of real people being stabbed and shot than did the students who had played the nonviolent games. In a similar study, young men with a history of playing video games showed reduced brain activation to real-life violence, and this reduced brain activation correlated with aggression in a behavioral task (Bartholow, Bushman, & Sestir, 2006). Such nonreaction to violence is disturbing.

Connection

Social learning theory offers an explanation of modeling, the kind of learning in which we imitate the behavior of others.

See "Social Learning Theory," Chapter 8, "Learning," p. 306.

Prosocial Behavior

Just as people can harm others through aggression, sometimes people can be extraordinarily kind to others. **Prosocial behavior** benefits others. In this section we will explore social processes that benefit others: altruism and empathy.

prosocial behavior
Action that is beneficial to others.

Sometimes humans do extraordinary things for others at great cost to themselves. Consider the case of Wesley Autrey. One morning in January 2007, Autrey and his two daughters were waiting for the subway in New York City. Suddenly, a teenager standing nearby began convulsing and collapsed on the platform. Among the dozens of people there, only Autrey and a few others stopped to help the young man. They thought they had stabilized him, but the young man got up, tottered, and fell onto the tracks. The headlights of an oncoming train appeared, and in an instant Autrey jumped onto the tracks to help the young man. When Autrey realized that he could not pull the teen off the tracks before the train hit them, he lay on top of him and pressed him down firmly in a bear hug. The train went over both men without touching them.

Autrey heard the screams of onlookers. "We're okay down here," he yelled, "but I've got two daughters up there. Let them know their father's okay." He heard cries of wonder and applause (Buckley, 2007). When interviewed later, Autrey said he had done nothing heroic. He had simply decided to help someone in need. "I didn't want the man's body to get run over," he said. "Plus, I was with my daughters and I didn't want them to see that" (CBS News, 2007).

Would you jump in front of an oncoming train to help a complete stranger? How many people do you think would? What makes people help other people? Most evidence, both from real life and from laboratory studies, indicates that most people would not help a stranger, especially if many others were present but doing nothing. Social psychologists have studied various factors that influence whether people will help others.

The Bystander Effect Late one night, Kitty Genovese walked from her parked car to her apartment building in New York City after coming home from her job as a bar manager. As she approached the building, a man accosted her and stabbed her in the back. She screamed, "Oh my God, he stabbed me! Help me!" Fearing that her cries for help would be heeded, her attacker ran away. Lights went on in the apartment building, and a few people looked out, but no

In 1964, Kitty Genovese was attacked and killed while residents of her Queens neighborhood, shown in this photo taken after the murder, ignored her screams.

 How does the research on the bystander effect explain why no one came to her aid?

bystander effect
A phenomenon in which the greater the number of bystanders who witness an emergency the less likely any one of them is to help.

altruism
Selfless attitudes and behavior toward others.

one called the police or went to help her. The man returned and renewed his attack. Genovese's screams were heard by numerous people, but still no one went to help. The 28-year-old Genovese died from her wounds before someone summoned the police.

How could so many people ignore the screams of a young woman being brutally attacked? What kind of attribution—either dispositional or situational—best explains this behavior? The Kitty Genovese case received tons of publicity, and it spurred a great deal of research in social psychology. John Darley and Bibb Latané (1968) used science to understand why no one came to Genovese's rescue. They did an experiment in which research participants heard another participant choking over an intercom (what they actually heard was an audiotape). The researchers led some of the participants to believe that they were the only ones hearing the person choking, while others thought many participants were hearing it. Of the participants who thought they alone were hearing the choking man, 85% tried to help. Of those who thought many other people were also hearing the man choking, only 62% tried to help. Here's the bottom line: The more people who witness an emergency, the less likely any one of them will help. Latané and Darley called this phenomenon the **bystander effect.**

One explanation of the bystander effect involves *diffusion of responsibility;* that is, when there are many people around, an individual's responsibility to act seems decreased. It makes sense when you think about it. When you alone witness an emergency, you know that you are the only source of aid. If several people are present, however, you might not regard it as your responsibility to help the person in need. Someone else might take care of it. Indeed, this is probably why no one helped poor Kitty Genovese. A lot of people were around, so everyone assumed "somebody else must have called the police."

Several factors influence whether or not someone will intervene in an emergency. One is whether people actually notice the event. When people are in a hurry, they are less likely to notice an emergency (Darley & Batson, 1973). Moreover, when many people are present and doing nothing, a person is less likely to interpret an event as an emergency. This is an example of informational social influence, because in this ambiguous situation people look to others for clues as to what should be done. If everyone else is doing nothing, then maybe there's no emergency after all.

Even if we notice an event and interpret it as an emergency, we must decide that it is our responsibility to do something. In addition to a diffusion of responsibility, people often do a cost-benefit analysis to determine whether helping is worth the cost. Sometimes it is dangerous to be helpful. If you get to this step and decide it is worth helping, you still might not know how to help. If you witness someone having a heart attack and want to help, you might not know CPR. Even if you've passed all the previous hurdles, you may not be able to help after all, but you can still call 911.

Altruism   The term **altruism** refers to a selfless concern for and giving of aid to others. Because altruists often expose themselves to greater danger than those who selfishly protect themselves, helping poses risks to personal survival. For this reason, altruism makes no sense from an evolutionary perspective (Dawkins, 1989). So why do humans and other animals sometimes engage in altruistic behavior?

From an evolutionary point of view, true altruism has no clear survival advantage. **How can we explain altruistic behavior?**

Evolutionary theory offers two explanations for altruistic behavior: kin selection and reciprocal altruism. **Kin selection** is the evolutionary mechanism that prompts individuals to help their close relatives, or kin, so that they will survive to reproduce and pass on related genes to their offspring (Hamilton, 1964). For instance, a dominant macaque monkey will share food with a subordinate monkey only if the two are close relatives (Belisle & Chapais, 2001; Furuichi, 1983). Individuals who help close relatives may be risking their lives, but they are also increasing the chances that, if they do not survive, at least some of their genes will survive in their relatives.

Kin selection is more common in social animals, such as bees. Greenberg (1979) bred bees to have varied degrees of genetic relatedness and then released them near a nest watched by guard bees. Because the nest was crowded, not every bee could get in. Guard bees more often let in the closely related bees than the distantly related bees. There is evidence for kin selection in humans, too. Burnstein and colleagues (Burnstein, Crandall, & Kitayama, 1994) asked people to specify whom they would be most likely to help in life-and-death situations and in non-life-and-death situations. People reported they would be more likely to help a relative in life-and-death situations. In fact, when people are rescuing others from a burning building, they are much more likely to look for relatives first (Sime, 1983).

Another evolutionary explanation for altruistic behavior is **reciprocal altruism,** helping others in the hope that they will help you in the future (Trivers, 1971, 1985). It is easier for humans to survive when group members cooperate, and reciprocal altruism promotes such cooperation. You might help another member of your group if you believe that you might benefit in some way as a result. From an evolutionary perspective, reciprocal altruism should be most common in species that are social, for only animals that live in groups have opportunities to benefit from reciprocal helping.

Some people have argued that these evolutionary mechanisms do not adequately explain all altruistic behavior. After all, what about Wesley Autrey? Some social psychologists argue that in our relations with others we try to maximize our gains and minimize our losses (Thibaut & Kelley, 1959). This is the essence of **social exchange theory,** a nonevolutionary explanation of altruistic behavior that says we help others because such behavior can be rewarding, but we will help only if the rewards will outweigh the costs. How can helping be rewarding? For one thing, helping someone in need relieves our own distress at witnessing

kin selection
The evolutionary favoring of genes that prompts individuals to help their relatives, or kin.

reciprocal altruism
The act of helping others in the hope that they will help us in the future.

social exchange theory
The idea that we help others when we decide that the benefits to ourselves are likely to outweigh the costs.

Challenge Your Assumptions
**True or False? People will some-
times risk their lives to help others.**

True: People will sometimes put
themselves at great risk to help others, without giving their own safety
a second thought. These are rare
acts of heroism, but they happen and
are difficult to explain by current
theories of altruistic behavior.

suffering. Also, helping someone is an investment in the future, because it is possible that they will help us when we need help. In this sense, social exchange is
essentially the same as reciprocal altruism.

According to social exchange theory, truly selfless altruism does not exist.
What about Wesley Autrey? Were his actions representative of selfless altruism?
He did say that he didn't want his daughters to see the man die. Perhaps by helping, Autrey was protecting the psychological well-being of his kids (which is kin
selection after all). Human and nonhuman primates may have both selfish and
nonselfish motives for the helping (de Waal & Suchak, 2010). An example of a selfish motive would be helping a suffering person to ease the guilt of not helping. In
nonselfish helping, the helper derives no personal benefit.

Whatever the cause of altruistic behavior, psychological science is uncovering more and more evidence of the benefits of being kind and lending a hand. First,
helping feels good, better than indulging ourselves, whether we are talking about
sacrifices we make in our most intimate relationships (Kogan et al., 2010) or giving
gifts or resources to strangers (Dunn, Aknin, & Norton, 2008). In fact, the joy of
giving is seen even in toddlers (Aknin, Hamlin, & Dunn, 2012). A large-scale interview and questionnaire study showed that helping behavior may be beneficial for
health—it may help buffer against the effects of stress (Poulin et al., 2013). Specifically, the researchers found an overall connection between stress and mortality in
the 5-year period following the study—the more stress, the more likely to be dead
5 years after the study started—with a crucial exception. If people reported that
they regularly lent a hand to others, this stress-mortality link was broken.

There are other benefits to being kind. When given the opportunity to think
of others—to be generous, as it were—people are more likely to change behavior
if they see that the behavior change is for the general good. In one clever but very
simple study, Grant and Hoffman (2011) conducted a study on whether such an
approach might help medical professionals increase hand washing (one of the
major factors in preventing the spread of disease in health care settings). In one
bathroom, they put a sign encouraging all employees to wash their hands, as it
would help them (the employees themselves) not get sick. In another bathroom,
they printed a similar sign, but this one said it would help them prevent others
from getting sick. They only changed one word in the sign to change this meaning. They then kept track of how much soap was used in each bathroom, as a
measure of hand washing. Surprisingly, more soap was used in the bathroom in
which the sign emphasized the effects of hand washing behavior on the health of
others, which indicates that concern for others provided a greater motivation for
behavior change.

empathy
The ability to share the feelings
of others and understand their
situations.

empathy-altruism hypothesis
The idea that people help others
selflessly only when they feel
empathy for them.

Empathy   C. Daniel Batson (1991) has proposed that true selfless helping occurs only when there is empathy. **Empathy** can be defined as sharing feeling and
understanding about another person's situation. According to Batson's **empathy-
altruism hypothesis,** people will offer selfless help only when they truly empathize with the victim. Consider the following example: A professor is talking with
a student in his office. While pleading with the professor to postpone an upcoming test, the student begins to cry. Reacting to the student's distress, the professor
becomes upset as well. The professor decides to help the student by postponing
the test. Batson and his colleagues believe that two different motivations may
underlie the professor's behavior.

The first motivation Batson calls the *egoistic motivation.* The professor may
help the student in order to relieve the professor's own distress. This is not true
altruism and would fit with social exchange theory, in which the reward is the
reduction of distress. A second motivation, *empathic motivation,* holds that the
professor's behavior may spring from an altruistic desire to reduce the distress of
the person in need. Unlike the egoistic helper, the empathic helper serves another
with the primary goal of helping the student through the crisis.

In order to understand the brain mechanisms of empathy, Singer and colleagues examined brain activation during a person's real pain experience and when witnessing the pain of a loved one (Singer et al., 2004). They created an experiment to study the response to a loved one's pain in the confines of an fMRI scanner. Singer obtained measures of functional brain activity in the female partner of a couple while the woman herself received a painful stimulus to her hand and then while she witnessed her male partner receiving the same painful stimulus; see the Research Process for this chapter (Figure 14.6). The actual pain stimulus, which was a mild electric shock delivered by an electrode attached to the hand, activated a well-known pain circuit in the brain, involving the somatosensory cortex, insula, anterior cingulate cortex (ACC), thalamus, and cerebellum. When her partner was experiencing pain, only those structures in the pain circuit that are triggered by the emotional aspect of pain showed activation, most notably the front region of the insula and the ACC. So when a partner experiences pain, people truly do feel it *with* their loved ones. Increasing evidence across various studies now supports the idea that the insula and anterior cingulate are key neural structures involved in empathy (Berhardt & Singer, 2012).

Psychological science has recently turned to understanding other prosocial states underlying prosocial behavior; foremost among them is compassion. **Compassion** is a state of relationship in which one feels kindness toward another who is suffering and one feels motivated to help relieve that suffering. Compassion may motivate helping behavior. Currently, there are several training programs designed to help people develop their compassion, many of them coming from major universities, such as Stanford (see http://ccare.stanford.edu/) and Emory (http://tibet.emory.edu/cbct/). These programs draw on meditation practices from Buddhism that are designed to develop compassion, but they are accessible to people from any religious background (or no religion). Such compassion training programs appear to increase positive affect and self-reported compassion, support helping behavior, and promote beneficial physiological changes (Condon et al., 2013; Fredrickson et al., 2008; Jazaieri et al., 2012, 2013; Pace et al., 2009; Weng et al., 2013).

compassion
A state of relationship in which one feels kindness toward another who is suffering and one feels motivated to help relieve that suffering.

Liking, Attraction, and Love

What makes one person want to be with another? Is this process different for friends and lovers? What is love, anyway? In this section we will see how psychologists tackle a few questions of the human heart. Let's first examine how we come to like and be attracted to other people, and then we'll take a look at love.

Familiarity, Similarity, and Attraction As we have seen throughout this chapter, research in social psychology shows that merely being exposed to an object, an idea, or a person causes you to like it more (Zajonc, 1968). The more often we see a face, the more we like it.

People with similar ideas, values, and interests are more likely to like one another and share satisfying, long-lasting relationships (Keller, Thiessen, & Young, 1996). For example, researchers randomly assigned male college students to be roommates in a certain dorm at the beginning of the year. Roommates who became real friends had common backgrounds, similar majors, and similar political viewpoints (Newcomb, 1961). People report that they like and want to help others who have similar personalities, attitudes, or beliefs (Wakimoto & Fujihara, 2004; Westmaas & Silver, 2006). Finally, people also tend to be attracted to and partner with people of a level of attractiveness similar to themselves—a phenomenon known as *assortative mating* (D. M. Buss, 2004). There is a moderately strong correlation between the personality of one's ideal

Research Process

1 Research Question

If empathy really is feeling what another person is feeling, are pain circuits in the brain activated similarly when someone feels pain and when empathizing with a loved one's pain?

2 Method

In a quasi-experimental study, Tania Singer and colleagues (2004) used fMRI to measure brain activation in women when they received a mild shock to the hand and while they witnessed their partner receiving the same painful stimulus.

The partner sat next to the fMRI scanner. The woman and her partner placed their right hands on a tilted board, which allowed the woman to see her and her partner's right hand with the help of a mirror. On a large screen the woman saw visual cues that indicated whether she or her partner would get low pain or high pain. When administered, the shock lasted for 2 seconds.

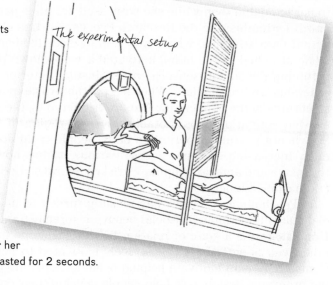

The experimental setup

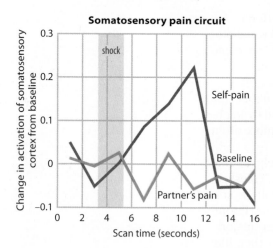

Emotional pain circuit

Change in ACC activation from baseline

shock

Partner's pain

Baseline

Self-pain

Scan time (seconds)

Somatosensory pain circuit

Change in activation of somatosensory cortex from baseline

shock

Self-pain

Baseline

Partner's pain

Scan time (seconds)

3 Results

A mild shock was administered 3.5 seconds after the scan began, lasting for 2 seconds. The scans showed that self-pain activated all the structures in the pain circuit, while the partner's pain (the empathic pain condition) mainly activated the structures typically involved only in the emotional aspect of pain (anterior cingulate cortex, or ACC, and the insula). The graphs show brain activation for the women as a change from a baseline (pain-free) state.

▽ The similarity in patterns of activation in the ACC across these two conditions suggests that the women empathized with—that is, *felt*—their partner's pain.

△ The difference in patterns of activation in the somatosensory cortex suggests that the women did not experience the same sensory aspects of pain when their partners received the shock as when they received the shock themselves.

Pain circuits in the brain

Anterior cingulate cortex (ACC)

Somatosensory cortex

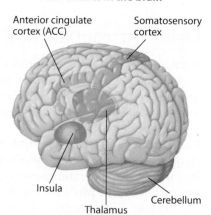

Insula

Thalamus

Cerebellum

4 Conclusion

Experienced pain activates all pain networks in the brain (emotional and sensory), but empathic pain activates only the emotional pain network. When a loved one experiences pain, people truly do feel their loved one's pain, but that feeling may be more emotional than sensory.

FIGURE **14.6**

FEELING ANOTHER'S PAIN. Empathy for a loved one's pain involves brain circuitry that is activated by real pain. Source: "Empathy for Pain Involves the Affective but Not Sensory Components of Pain," by T. Singer, B. Seymour, J. O. O'Doherty, H. Kaube, R. J. Dolan, & C. D. Frith, 2004, *Science, 303,* 1157–1162.

partner and one's own personality; married couples also often have strongly correlated ages, levels of intelligence, and imaginativeness (Botwin, Buss, & Shackelford, 1997; M. C. Keller et al., 1996).

Physical and Chemical Attractiveness   Humans worldwide value physical attractiveness in partners (D. M. Buss, 1999; Etcoff, 1999; G. F. Miller, 2000), but what, exactly, is considered to be attractive? In research on attractiveness, people rate average and symmetrical faces as more attractive than less average and less symmetrical faces. *Average*, in this case, does not mean "common." Rather, *average* means that the size, location, and shape of each feature of the face—nose, eyes, mouth, cheekbones—are mathematically average in the population. They are neither too big nor too small, neither too far apart nor too close together. Look at the faces in Figure 14.7. These faces were produced by computer technology that morphed images of several real faces together. The more faces averaged, the higher the attractiveness ratings. People rated the 8-face composite as more attractive than the 4-face composite; the 16-face composite as more attractive than the 8; and the 32-face composite as more attractive than the 16 (Langlois & Roggman, 1990; Langlois, Roggman, & Musselman, 1994). Although standards for beauty vary by culture, average faces are rated as most attractive all over the world (Langlois & Roggman, 1990). Furthermore, infants as young as 6 or 9 months of age also tend to prefer average faces over others,

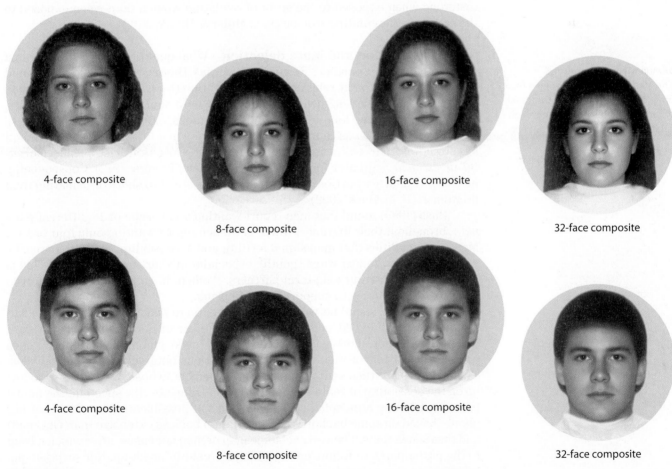

4-face composite

8-face composite

16-face composite

32-face composite

4-face composite

8-face composite

16-face composite

32-face composite

FIGURE **14.7**

RATING PHYSICAL ATTRACTIVENESS. The more faces that are morphed into one image, the more they move toward having average features. As they become more average in features, the faces are perceived as increasing in attractiveness.

Challenge Your Assumptions

True or False? Attractive faces are anything but average.

False: Probably for evolutionary reasons regarding fitness, people the world over tend to find faces that mathematically average the features of many faces the most attractive.

sexual strategies theory
The idea that men and women face different problems when they seek out mates, so they often approach relationships in very different ways.

although they are too young for other people to have had much influence over their face preferences (Hoss & Langlois, 2003).

Averaged faces tend to be more symmetrical, and people seem to prefer symmetry when they rate faces for attractiveness (Etcoff, 1999). Moreover, symmetry is a rough indicator of genetic fitness; that is, symmetrical faces and bodies are signs of fewer genetic mutations (G. F. Miller, 2000).

Scent plays a role in attraction, but we are not talking about perfumes. Pheromones—scents produced by animals that have an effect on other members of the same species—are well-established modes of social communication among many animal species. They are full of sexual and organizational messages, but whether they operate or even exist in humans has been a matter of debate (Brennan, 2010).

Apparently, scent matters in humans as well, but not in the way you would think. In a clever experiment, researchers instructed men and women to wear a clean T-shirt to bed for two nights (Thornhill et al., 2003). The shirt had no perfumes and was not washed with deodorant soaps. The T-shirts were returned to the lab and sealed in zippered bags. An independent group of students rated the attractiveness of pictures of the people who had worn the shirts. Another group of students smelled and rated the T-shirts on attractiveness of odor. Men preferred the scent of women in their fertile phase; fertile women preferred the scent of men who were most symmetrical.

In a similar study in which men smelled women's shirts, researchers measured men's testosterone levels in response to the smells. Men released more testosterone when exposed to the scent of ovulating women than when exposed to the scent of nonovulating women (S. L. Miller & Maner, 2010).

Sexual Attraction and Mate Selection What qualities do you look for in a prospective sexual partner? **Sexual strategies theory** suggests that men and women often approach relationships differently (D. M. Buss & Schmitt, 1993). In virtually all societies, men and women use both short-term matings (affairs, one-night stands) and long-term matings (marriages, extended companionships). Both are effective ways to increase one's reproductive fitness, but each strategy has strengths and weaknesses. Sex differences in attraction arise because *parental investment* is greater for women than for men (Trivers, 1972). Consequently, men devote a larger portion of their total mating effort to short-term mating than do women (D. M. Buss, 1999).

Buss (1999) found that men report wanting an average of 18 different partners throughout their lifetimes, whereas women report wanting only four or five. Men value qualities that may signal fertility and accessibility (e.g., large breasts, wide hips compared to waist, youth), especially in short-term partners. This is less true in evaluating long-term partners. Women, in contrast, value men who can provide resources to support their offspring.

These days, social network sites have begun to play a major role in the dating game. Sites like OkCupid and Tinder make use of people's reliance on their mobile devices and shortened attention spans to make matches. OkCupid matches people on the basis of their responses to questions obtained ahead of time. Possible matches are then sent via email to the member, whose option it is to follow up on the possibility of real-life contact. Tinder translates the speed-dating model to the mobile app atmosphere. The user looks at possible matches on his or her phone (based on some background information but less extensive than OkCupid) and then sends texts. Then an exchange may or may not ensue, after which it is up to the participants to follow up regarding a "real-life" meet-up. Not surprisingly, behavior on these dating sites is often governed by personality, socioeconomical factors, and race, just as is face-to-face interaction. A detailed analysis of over 125,000 OkCupid users revealed that, although people freely interact with members of various races, there is a pattern to use. People are much less likely to cross racial lines when initiating a contact than when responding to one, though experience with interracial communication increases the likelihood of such behavior in the future (K. Lewis, 2013).

Mate selection factors might drive sexual partnerships, but these evolutionary pressures operate outside conscious awareness. Once people mate, it is the love that may develop between two people that keeps them together, but what is love?

Love   As a concept, love is not easy to define. It takes many different forms and means different things to different people at different times in their lives.

Types of Love   Humans love in many different ways. We love our parents, lovers, friends, brothers and sisters, children, dogs, lattes, and music. How do we account for the variations? One well-known theory is Robert Sternberg's **triangular theory of love** (Sternberg, 1986). Sternberg proposed that three components—intimacy, passion, and commitment, in various combinations—can explain all the forms of human love (see Figure 14.8). *Intimacy* refers to close, connected, and bonded feelings in loving relationships. *Passion* refers to the drives that lead to romance, physical attraction, and sexual consummation, accompanied by physiological changes and arousal. *Commitment* refers to both the decision to love someone—or not—and the decision to commit to love for the long term.

These three components are present in different amounts for different kinds of love. *Companionate love* exists when intimacy and commitment are high and passion is low. In *passionate love*, intimacy and passion are high and commitment is low. *Lust* is characterized by a lot of passion but no intimacy or commitment. In contrast, arranged marriages are all about commitment, at least in the beginning, with no intimacy or passion.

Love as Attachment   Love is also closely connected to a well-known psychological phenomenon: attachment. An important concept in human development, attachment is an affection-based bond between infants and their primary caregivers that protects infants from threats to their survival (Bowlby, 1969). Attachment researchers distinguish among secure, avoidant, and anxious/ambivalent attachment styles (Ainsworth et al., 1978).

The attachment system established when we are infants forms a template for our adult relationships with others, including our intimate partners, according to Cynthia Hazan and Phillip Shaver (1987). Hazan and Shaver argued that the infant-caregiver attachment system underlies the important dynamics and individual differences in adult romantic relationships. By categorizing people's infant-caregiver attachment style based on an adult attachment interview, they found that securely attached adults report that they easily get close to others, readily trust others, and have more satisfying romantic relationships. Anxious/ambivalent adults tend to have less satisfying relationships, are more preoccupied with them, and fear that their partners do not want the intimacy they desire. Avoidant adults are uncomfortable being close to others and have less satisfying relationships (Hazan & Shaver, 1987).

As you can see, we have a partial understanding of how liking, attraction, and love work, but psychological science has yet to explain how these elements come together. Evolutionary psychology offers one integrative framework. In this view, for example, liking and loving both evolved to help ensure survival of the species.

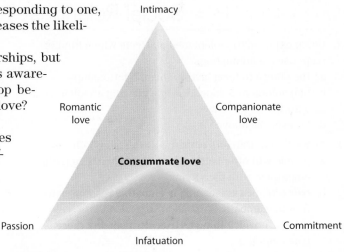

FIGURE **14.8**

STERNBERG'S TRIANGULAR THEORY OF LOVE. In Sternberg's model, all types of love are made up of three components: intimacy, passion, and commitment. Each type of love consists of a different balance of the three components. When all three exist in equal proportions, consummate love exists. (Sternberg, 1986)

triangular theory of love
Sternberg's idea that three components (intimacy, passion, and commitment, in various combinations) can explain all the forms of human love.

Connection

Men are more likely than women to be interested in casual sex.

See "Sex: Survival of the Species," Chapter 11, "Motivation and Emotion," p. 407, for an evolutionary explanation.

Connection

Attachment is a bidirectional relationship requiring the active participation of infants and caregivers.

See "Early Socioemotional Development," Chapter 5, "Human Development," p. 181.

1. Being exposed to violent media affects which kind of responses in young boys?
   a. the ability to form lasting social relationships
   b. physiological responses while viewing a violent film
   c. a and b
   d. none of the above

2. According to Batson's empathy-altruism hypothesis,
   a. people will offer selfless help only when they truly empathize with the victim.
   b. true altruism exists only in empathic responses to family members.
   c. there is no such thing as true altruism, but there is true empathy.
   d. empathy and altruism are linked only in cases of heroic rescues.

3. What kind of faces do people tend to find more attractive?
   a. faces that have unique features rarely seen in the common population
   b. faces that are arithmetically average
   c. faces in which the eyebrow-to-nose ratio is less than 1
   d. none of the above

4. Adults who tend to have less satisfying relationships, are more preoccupied with them, and fear that their partners do not want the intimacy they desire can be categorized as having what type of attachment style?
   a. securely attached
   b. suppressively attached
   c. avoidant
   d. anxious/ambivalent

Answers can be found at the end of the chapter.

Bringing It All Together
Making Connections in Social Behavior
Analysis of the Jonestown Cult

The tragic mass suicide of hundreds of members of the People's Temple in Jonestown, Guyana, illustrates many of the social-psychological concepts discussed in this chapter. In late November 1978, under the direction of the Reverend Jim Jones, members of this group fed a poison-laced drink to their children and then drank it themselves. More than 900 adults and children died; most were found lying together, arm in arm.

Most of the members of the People's Temple went willingly to their deaths. Why? After years of indoctrination and isolation from mainstream society, they had been led into complete commitment to Jones and the People's Temple. People's Temple had all the hallmarks of a cult.

cult
An extremist group led by a charismatic, totalitarian leader in which coercive methods are used to prevent members from leaving the group.

A **cult** is an extremist group led by a charismatic, totalitarian leader in which coercive methods are used to prevent members from leaving the group.

If we apply social-psychological theory to an analysis of these events, they become more comprehensible, because we can see that the members of the People's Temple were not very different from us. Four principles of social psychology—persuasion, conformity, obedience, and cognitive dissonance—can shed light on the tragedy of Jonestown (Osherow, 1999).

Jim Jones and the People's Temple
Jim Jones founded the People's Temple in Indiana in 1958, preaching a message of brotherhood, racial integration, and freedom from poverty. His group helped feed and employ the poor. Jones presented a public image of a beloved leader who promoted a vision of racial harmony.

Jim Jones

Throughout the 1960s, the group grew in size and popularity, but rumors surfaced that Jones used coercive methods to keep people from leaving the People's Temple. In the mid-1970s, after a great deal of bad publicity, Jones and his followers moved to a jungle outpost he called Jonestown, in Guyana, South America. In 1978, U.S. Congressman Leo Ryan heard reports that the People's Temple was holding members against their will, and he led a delegation of government officials, reporters, and concerned relatives to Jonestown to talk with residents about how they liked living there. Two families secretly informed Ryan that they wanted out. As Ryan's party and these two "defector" families tried to board their plane for the United States, Temple gunmen ambushed and killed five people, including Congressman Ryan. This ambush precipitated the mass suicide, an act that Jones and his followers had rehearsed many times. It was their final act of rebellion against the system that they believed forced them into exile.

The Role of Persuasion

Jones was a charismatic figure. He sought out people who needed to hear his message: the urban poor, minorities, the elderly, ex-addicts, and convicts. Potential members of the People's Temple first encountered an almost idyllic scene in which blacks and whites lived, worked, and worshiped together in total harmony. Guests were greeted warmly and invited to share a meal. Jones also gave them miracles. He cured diseases; he made predictions that came true with uncanny frequency. Members were motivated to believe in Jones; they appreciated the racial harmony, sense of purpose, and relief from feelings of worthlessness that the People's Temple provided.

Jones carefully managed his public image. He used letter writing and the political clout of hundreds of cult members to praise him and impress the politicians and reporters who supported the People's Temple, as well as to criticize and intimidate its opponents. Most important, Jones limited the information available to members.

The Role of Conformity and Obedience

Conformity played a role in the People's Temple from the outset. Even getting into the group was not easy. People underwent a strict initiation process, which actually drew members more firmly into the group. As they became increasingly involved in the People's Temple, they committed themselves more strongly to the group, because they were required to donate their property and 25% of their income to the church. Before they entered the meeting room for each service, they wrote self-incriminating letters, which were turned over to the church. If anyone objected, the refusal was interpreted as a "lack of faith" in Jones. All of these rules made the group more important than the individuals, making conformity to the group all the more likely.

As he gradually increased his demands, Jones also exposed cult members to the concept of a "final ritual," mass suicide. Rehearsals of this ritual tested followers

and their faith in Jones. In essence, Jones was making use of what social psychologists call the *foot-in-the-door* technique by getting people to agree to a moderate request (i.e., rehearsal). Once cult members had agreed to engage in frequent rehearsals of mass suicide, it became easier for them to go through with the real thing.

The suicides at Jonestown can be viewed as the product of obedience—people complying with the orders of a leader and reacting to the threat of force. In the People's Temple, whatever Jim Jones commanded, the members did. Jones was a forceful authority. By the early 1970s, the members of the People's Temple lived in constant fear of severe punishment—brutal beatings coupled with public humiliation—for committing trivial or even inadvertent offenses. Milgram's experiments show us that the power of authority need not be so explicitly threatening to create compliance with demands. Nor does the consensus of the group need to be coercive, as Asch's experiments on conformity indicate. However, Jones's power was both threatening and coercive.

Jones used threats to impose the discipline and devotion he demanded, and he took steps to eliminate any behavior that might encourage resistance among his followers. As Solomon Asch found in his experiments on conformity, if just one confederate expresses an opinion different from that of the majority, the rate of conformity drastically declines. This is minority social influence. In the People's Temple, Jones tolerated no dissent, made sure that members had no allegiance more powerful than their loyalty to him, and tried to make the alternative of leaving the church unthinkable. Anyone who dared to dissent was terrorized as a traitor, thereby squelching the possibility of minority social influence.

These are some of the victims of the mass suicide at Jonestown, Guyana, in 1978. People's Temple leader Jim Jones used his status as an authority figure to persuade, intimidate, and indoctrinate his followers over several years, apparently convincing them that death was the only alternative to being captured and separated from the group.

How did Jones do this? He used informers who reported indiscretions, split families to prevent allegiances, and forced parents to give over their children to the Temple. He thereby created conditions in which kin selection could not promote helping between members. Similarly, Jones worked to dissolve marital bonds by forcing couples into extramarital relations (sometimes with Jones himself). "Families are part of the enemy system," Jones said, because they weakened the individual's dedication to the cause. Not surprisingly, it was very hard to leave the cult. Not being able to defect or escape from the group, people had little choice but to conform.

The Role of Cognitive Dissonance

Cognitive dissonance helps explain why cult members believed Jones to the end and why so few defected. People did not become cult members all at once. Rather, the process of justifying their choice and becoming committed to Jones unfolded slowly over the course of weeks and months, sometimes years. Jones knew what he was doing.

Starting the process with harsh acts of initiation is a perfect way to get people to rationalize their otherwise embarrassing behavior. If people don't see the group they are about to join very positively, how can they possibly justify going through such humiliation in order to get in?

Even so, how could members not seek to escape and accept killing themselves and their children so easily? These acts were the product of a situation that made dissent impossible and faith in Jones and the Temple absolute. Once they were isolated from the rest of the world at Jonestown, escape was impossible. When escape is impossible, people rationalize their predicament. The members of the People's Temple reduced their cognitive dissonance by changing their attitude to conform with their behavior. In this case, they told themselves that Jones was great and his message was wonderful. When the time to commit suicide finally arrived, most of the members clearly drank the juice quite willingly and by their own choice, so strong was their belief in Jones and his message.

Chapter Review

GROUP LIVING AND SOCIAL INFLUENCE

- Social psychology is the study of the effects of the real or imagined presence of others on people's thoughts, feelings, and actions.

- We act differently when other people are present than we do when we are alone. Sometimes our performance is improved when we are with other people; sometimes it is hindered. In addition, people adjust their behavior in order to conform to what others are doing or to adhere to the rules of their culture.

- An individual can change the majority opinion of a group, but doing so takes perseverance and consistency.

- Obedience to authority can and has led to numerous instances of people doing things they otherwise would not, from soldiers in Nazi Germany and Abu Ghraib prison in Iraq to participants in Milgram's studies.

SOCIAL PERCEPTION

- We are constantly drawing conclusions about why people do what they do; that is, we make attributions. Sometimes we say that internal qualities of the person were the cause of a behavior. Other times we see outside forces in the environment as the cause of a person's behavior.

- When forming opinions about others, we use schemas about individuals based on what they are like or are likely to do based simply on the group they belong to. Opinions formed this way are stereotypes. Similarly, a prejudice is an attitude toward a group of people or an individual member of a group based on unfair generalizations about that group. Finally, discrimination is preferential treatment of certain people that is driven by prejudicial attitudes.

- Applying stereotypes, prejudices, and discrimination to people based on their racial-ethnic group affiliations is racism. Racism operates both inside (explicitly) and outside (implicitly) our awareness.

ATTITUDES AND BEHAVIOR

- Psychologists define attitudes as a person's favorable or unfavorable beliefs, feelings, or actions toward an object, an idea, or a person. People's attitudes and behaviors do not always match and are often resistant to change.

- One explanation for why and how people change their attitudes is cognitive dissonance, which is the feeling of discomfort caused by information that differs from one's conception of oneself as a reasonable and sensible person.

- Persuasion is another way in which attitudes can be changed.

SOCIAL RELATIONS

- People hurt other people, help other people, and are attracted to and love other people.

- *Aggression* refers to violent behaviors that are intended to cause psychological and/or physical harm to another being. Aggression stems from a complex interplay of genetic and social forces.

- The more people who witness an accident or a crime, the more likely it is that no one will call for help or intervene. This phenomenon is the bystander effect.

- People also act in prosocial ways to help others in need. In life-and-death situations, kin selection explains why people are most willing to help those who are most closely related to them.

- Relationships that are bound by similarities in personality, attitude, intelligence, and attractiveness tend to last the longest.

- People all over the world rate as most attractive those faces that possess average and symmetrical features. Sexual strategies theory suggests that men and women face different problems when they seek out mates, so they often approach relationships in very different ways.

- Sternberg's triangular theory of love states that all of the different forms of love each consist of different amounts of the three components: intimacy, passion, and commitment. Romantic love, for example, exists when intimacy and passion are present but commitment is absent.

BRINGING IT ALL TOGETHER: MAKING CONNECTIONS IN SOCIAL BEHAVIOR

- The People's Temple was a cult, which is an extremist group led by a charismatic, totalitarian leader who uses coercive methods to prevent members from leaving the group.

- The methods Jim Jones used to ensure his followers' obedience and conformity included persuasion, rigid discipline and punishment of dissent, isolation, separation from family, and forced marital infidelity. Cult members resolved cognitive dissonance brought on by their situation through rationalization, telling themselves that Jones was a great leader with a wonderful message.

Key Terms

aggression, p. 533
altruism, p. 536
attitudes, p. 529
attributions, p. 521
bystander effect, p. 536
cognitive dissonance, p. 530
compassion, p. 539
conformity, p. 515
cult, p. 544
discrimination, p. 527
empathy, p. 538

empathy-altruism hypothesis, p. 538
fundamental attribution error, p. 522
groupthink, p. 517
informational social influence, p. 515
in-group/out-group bias, p. 524
kin selection, p. 537
normative social influence, p. 515

obedience, p. 518
out-group homogeneity, p. 525
persuasion, p. 532
prejudice, p. 526
prosocial behavior, p. 535
reciprocal altruism, p. 537
self-serving bias, p. 522
sexual strategies theory, p. 542

social exchange theory, p. 537
social facilitation, p. 515
social loafing, p. 515
social norms, p. 515
stereotypes, p. 523
triangular theory of love, p. 543

Quick Quiz Answers

Quick Quiz 14.1: 1. c 2. d 3. a 4. c   **Quick Quiz 14.2:** 1. d 2. c 3. a 4. d 5. b   **Quick Quiz 14.3:** 1. b 2. d 3. a
Quick Quiz 14.4: 1. b 2. a 3. b 4. d

15 Psychological Disorders

Chapter Outline

Defining Psychological Disorders
Neurodevelopmental Disorders
Schizophrenia
Depressive Disorders
Bipolar Disorder
Anxiety Disorders
Obsessive-Compulsive Disorder
Post-Traumatic Stress Disorder
Dissociative Disorders
Somatic Symptom Disorders
Personality Disorders
Chapter Review

Challenge Your Assumptions

True or False?

- Most people who suffer from mental illness are dangerous. (see page 552)
- Mental disorders are relatively rare, and most families are free of mental disorders. (see page 553)
- Schizophrenia is a disorder of split personalities. (see page 558)
- Extreme stress can make you depressed. (see page 565)
- All the great artists in history can be viewed as psychologically disturbed. (see page 583)

Langley and Homer Collyer were brothers who lived in a large three-story house in New York City (Frost & Steketee, 2010). In March 1947, police were called because a neighbor reported that one of the brothers had died in the house. The police, however, could not enter through the front door or any other doors or windows on the first floor. All entrances were blocked with household items and appliances—newspapers, boxes, pianos, and car parts, to name but a few examples. When the fire department finally gained entrance on the second and third floors, what they found (after workers spent a total of 3 weeks cleaning out the house) was astonishing: a car, a horse-drawn carriage, 14 grand pianos, a rusted bicycle, even a two-headed fetus. All in all, more than 170 tons (340,000 pounds) of stuff were removed from the house. The entire house was filled from floor to ceiling, and the only way to move around was through tunnels. As it turned out, the booby-trapped boxes the brothers had set up to prevent anyone from coming in had apparently caused Langley's death. Homer, however, was blind and relied on Langley to feed him; and so when Langley died, Homer gradually starved to death. The Collyer brothers were among the first widely publicized compulsive hoarders—people who collect stuff to the point that it interferes with everyday functioning.

Ted Bundy was a handsome, well-educated, and charming man, who also happened to be one of the worst serial killers in U.S. history—murdering between 20 and 100 women, though most likely about 35 (Keppel, 2005; K. M. Sullivan, 2009). Between 1974 and 1978, he charmed young female students between the ages of 15 and 25 with a story of being hurt and needing help to carry his books. Once they were in his car, he would often batter them with a baseball bat or crowbar and sometimes have sex with the body.

Vincent van Gogh and Paul Gauguin—the artists—had an intense argument on December 23, 1888, a Sunday evening in the middle of winter. Over what they argued, we do not know. What we do know is how it ended: van Gogh, in a fit of rage, took a razor and cut off the lower portion of his left ear. He then wrapped the earlobe in a newspaper and gave it to a prostitute named Rachel, telling her to "keep this object carefully" (Runyan, 1981).

That the Collyer brothers, Bundy, and van Gogh each had some kind of disordered behavior is apparent. What is not so easy to agree on, however, is how to define psychological disorder in general and how to specify the concrete criteria for particular disorders. Clearly, these three examples are extreme cases, but behavior varies along a continuum from more to less disordered. In this chapter, we describe many psychological disorders and explain some of what is known about how they develop. As we discuss the causes of these disorders, we will focus on explanations that intertwine the biological with the environmental (Kendler, 2005; Moffitt, Caspi, & Rutter, 2005; Uher & McGuffin, 2010). We will begin by considering what it means for behavior to be disordered and how disorders are diagnosed. At the end of the chapter we will explore the topic of creativity and psychological disorders and consider whether artists are more likely than the general population to suffer from a psychological disorder.

DEFINING PSYCHOLOGICAL DISORDERS

Creative artists such as Vincent van Gogh are different from most people. So, too, are spelling bee champs, Olympic athletes, and class valedictorians, yet *different* does not mean *disordered*. Does a young child who has more than 5,000 baseball cards and can tell you something about every one of them suffer from a psychological disorder? What about people who wash their hands for 45 minutes 10 times a day? How do psychologists distinguish behavior that is simply different from behavior that is disordered?

Human behavior is complex and highly variable. Certain ways of behaving in the world are shown by more of the population on a regular basis and seem to be well adapted for functioning well in certain environments. These might be behaviors we call *normal*. Less common ways of behaving might be revealed through exceptional talent or might not be well suited for the environment. We might consider these less common behaviors disordered, because they do not function well in the world. It is with this context in mind that we use the term *psychological disorders*.

Over time, understanding of and explanations for psychological disorders have gone through many significant changes. As discussed in Chapter 1, the medical model became the prevalent explanation for psychological disorders beginning in the 19th century and has lasted until now. The primary assumption of the medical model is that mental, like physical, illnesses are best diagnosed and treated as medical illnesses. Psychiatry is a branch of medicine, so it is not a coincidence that terms such as *illness*, *diagnosis*, and *therapy* or *treatment* are used in the context of psychological disorders. Borrowing from medicine, in their attempt to understand and treat psychological disorders, psychologists and psychiatrists aim to group them into a smaller set of categories. The classification and diagnosis of psychological disorders is fraught with ambiguity and disagreement. The first attempt to do so in the United States began with the government census of 1840 and simply had one category: "idiocy/insanity" (S. Greenberg, Shuman, & Meyer 2004). The first official attempt at diagnosing mental disorders in the United States came in 1952 with the publication of the *Diagnostic and Statistical Manual (DSM)*. It was not until the third edition in 1980 that diagnoses became grounded in scientific evidence and clinical observations rather than theory. Currently in its fifth edition, the *DSM-5* has continued the tradition of defining disorders based on a combination of scientific evidence and clinical observations (American Psychiatric Association [APA], 2013).

How do psychologists define *mental disorder?* Following a long-standing tradition, the *DSM-5* defines a mental disorder as a **syndrome**—a set of related conditions—of clinically significant disturbances of thoughts, feelings, or behaviors. More specifically, they argue for the "4 Ds" of determining whether something is a mental disorder (APA, 2013). There has to be

>*disturbance* of thought, emotion, or behavior,
>*dysfunction* of biological or developmental processes,
>*distress or disability* in everyday life (especially relationships or work), and
>*deviant* thought, emotion, or behavior, but only if also dysfunctional; deviance alone is not enough.

Let's look at each of these a little more closely. Psychological disorders are distinguished by their clinically significant *disturbance* of psychological processes of thought, emotion, and behavior. Mental disorders are

Is the act of cutting one's ear off—as van Gogh did after a violent disagreement with friend and fellow painter Paul Gauguin—necessarily a sign of psychological disorder?

Connection

Early conceptualizations of mental illness blamed demons and spirits. The modern medical model originated in the 1800s in Europe.

See "A Brief History of the Practice of Clinical Psychology" Chapter 1, "Introduction to Psychology," p. 11.

syndrome
A set of related conditions.

Do you think this person has a psychological disorder?
Recall that a behavior must be deviant, distressing to the individual, and dysfunctional to be classified as disordered.

Challenge Your Assumptions

True or False? Most people who suffer from mental illness are dangerous.

False: Most people who suffer from mental illness are not dangerous to others or even themselves.

Connection

Eating disorders and their symptoms are discussed more fully in "Eating Disorders," Chapter 11, "Motivation and Emotion," p. 405.

distinguished from physical disorders that affect physiological and bodily structures and processes. *Dysfunctional* behavior interferes with everyday functioning, such as participating in everyday social relationships, holding a regular job, or being productive, and occasionally it can be a risk to oneself or others. *Distressing* behavior leads to discomfort, pain, or anguish, either in the person directly or in others, especially family members. The distressing element is one reason we say a person is "suffering" from a disorder. *Deviant* literally means "different from the norm," or different from what most people do. It is important to point out, as the *DSM-5* does, that deviant behavior can be classified as disordered only if it is also dysfunctional. Albert Einstein was deviant in his intelligence and creativity, but he was not suffering from a psychological disorder. Behaviors that possess only one or even two of these "4 Ds" are not typically classified as disordered. Finally, if a behavior is culturally accepted it cannot be a disorder, such as hallucinations of shamans in some preliterate cultures.

Most people suffering from psychological disorders do not pose a risk to others, but some do. For instance, people who are sexually attracted to children (pedophiles) and individuals with violent impulse disorder could be a very real danger to others. Others may pose a risk to themselves; for example, people with severe depression are at heightened risk of attempting suicide (APA, 2013).

The *DSM-5* derives from an American perspective of psychological illness. More than previous editions, the *DSM-5* tries to expand beyond the U.S. perspective by aiming to be consistent with international standards for disorder classification and discussing the prevalence rates of certain disorders in different countries. Some disorders are found only in certain cultures. For instance, in some Southeast Asian cultures, certain men suffer from *koro*, the debilitating belief that one's genitals are retracting into one's body. In parts of the Middle East, some people suffer from *zar*—the belief that they are possessed by spirits—and run around in fits of laughter, shouting, and singing (Watters, 2010).

Additionally, some disorders spread from culture to culture (Watters, 2010). For example, in China, anorexia nervosa has been extremely rare; when it was described, the fear of being fat was not a symptom. Sufferers most frequently complained of having bloated stomachs. However, a single widely publicized case of anorexia in 1994 that led to the death of a Hong Kong teenager suddenly made anorexia a much more commonly reported disorder—rates of the disorder had increased dramatically by the late 1990s. Moreover, because the journalists in Hong Kong who were covering the story tended to use the American *DSM* to describe the disorder, with the increase in prevalence also came a change in symptoms. After the publicity surrounding this case, more and more Chinese people with anorexia began to complain mostly of their fear of being fat, not of bloated stomachs. In short, their disorder became more Americanized.

There has always been debate about the best way to approach categorizing psychological disorders. Critics have argued since the 1990s about the somewhat arbitrary designations of the *DSM*, and indeed the *DSM-5* has been met with controversy. Some critics claim the approach of classifying disorders on the basis of shared symptoms, which has long been the *DSM* approach, has resulted in too many categories and may be antiquated (Tavris, 2013). Others have recently argued that the *DSM* ignores biology and that diseases should be classified by shared biological underpinnings (Jabr, 2013). Recent evidence from more than 60,000 people worldwide suggests that five major psychiatric disorders (autism spectrum disorder, attention deficit hyperactivity disorder, bipolar disorder, depression, and schizophrenia) actually have a common genetic cause (Cross-Disorder Group of the Psychiatric Genomics Consortium, 2013). Moreover, recent evidence suggests—as with intelligence—that one general dimension or factor underlies all of the major psychological disorders (Caspi et al., 2014). Such findings imply that mental disorders are not as distinct and different as the *DSM-5* categories would imply.

How common are mental disorders? The answer is that they are surprisingly common (see Figure 15.1). In a given year, 26% of the U.S. population suffers from a diagnosable disorder. Even though these are non-normative patterns of behavior, they are not rare. Over the course of an entire lifetime, almost half (46%) of the adults in the United States will suffer from at least one psychological disorder. Similar percentages have been reported in New Zealand and Spain (Moffitt et al., 2010; Serrano-Blanco et al., 2010). In the United States, more than half of those 46% will suffer from two or more disorders (Kessler et al., 2005). The existence of two or more disorders at the same time is called **comorbidity.** Some recent research suggests that fear-based disorders (phobias and panic disorder) may often develop first and predict the onset of other disorders later in life (Kessler et al., 2012).

The *DSM-5* describes 21 major categories of disorder, covering more than 350 distinct disorders. Figure 15.2 lists the major ones. In this chapter, we examine 10 of the 21 major disorders:

neurodevelopmental disorders
schizophrenia

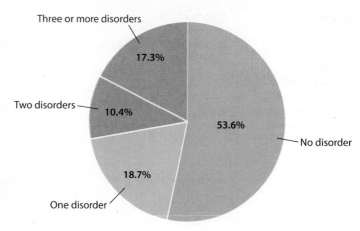

FIGURE **15.1**

PERCENTAGE OF AMERICAN ADULTS WHO WILL EXPERIENCE A PSYCHOLOGICAL DISORDER AT SOME POINT DURING THEIR LIVES. Of the 46% of the population who will suffer a psychological disorder during their lifetime, more than half will suffer from at least two different disorders. (Kessler et al., 2005)

Challenge Your Assumptions

True or False? Mental disorders are relatively rare, and most families are free of mental disorders.
False: Almost half of adults will suffer from a diagnosable mental illness of some kind during their lifetime.

Connection

Dementia and Alzheimer's disease are neurocognitive disorders related to age. Other disorders, such as sleep disorders, can occur at any time in a person's life.

See "Late Adulthood," Chapter 5, "Human Development," p. 198, and "Disorders of Sleep," Chapter 6, "Consciousness," p. 229.

comorbidity
The occurrence of two or more psychological disorders at the same time.

FIGURE **15.2**
**MAJOR
PSYCHOLOGICAL
DISORDERS.**
Although *DSM-5*
describes more
than 350 disorders,
these are the most
common. (APA,
2013)

Disorder	Description
Disorders usually first diagnosed in infancy, childhood, or adolescence	Attention deficit hyperactivity disorder; autistic spectrum disorders; learning disorders; conduct and oppositional disorder; separation anxiety disorder; and feeding, tic, and elimination disorders.
Anxiety disorders	Characterized by motor tension, hyperactivity, and apprehensive expectation/thoughts. Include generalized anxiety disorder, panic disorder, phobic disorder, and post-traumatic stress disorder.
Somatic symptom disorders	Occur when psychological symptoms take a physical form even though no physical causes can be found. Include hypochondriasis and conversion disorder.
Factitious disorders	Characterized by the individual's deliberate fabrication of a medical or mental disorder to gain medical attention.
Dissociative disorders	Involve a sudden loss of memory or change of identity.
Delirium, dementia, amnestic, and other cognitive disorders	Disorders involving problems in consciousness and cognition, such as substance-induced delirium or dementia related to Alzheimer's disease.
Mood disorders	Characterized by a primary disturbance in mood; include depressive disorders and bipolar disorder (sometimes called manic depression).
Schizophrenia and other psychotic disorders	Characterized by distorted thoughts and perceptions, odd communication, inappropriate emotion, and other unusual behaviors.
Substance-related disorders	Characterized by abuse or dependence on drugs, such as alcohol, cocaine, and hallucinogens.
Sexual and gender-identity disorders	Consist of three main types of disorders: gender-identity disorders (person is not comfortable with identity as a female or male), paraphilias (person has a preference for unusual sexual acts to stimulate sexual arousal), and sexual dysfunctions (impairments in sexual functioning).
Eating disorders	Include anorexia nervosa and bulimia nervosa (see Chapter 11).
Sleep disorders	Consist of primary sleep disorders, such as insomnia and narcolepsy, and sleep disorders due to a general medical condition, such as sleep apnea (see Chapter 6).
Impulse-control disorders not elsewhere classified	Include kleptomania, pyromania, and compulsive gambling.
Adjustment disorders	Characterized by distressing emotional or behavioral symptoms in response to an identifiable stressor.
Intellectual disability	Low intellectual functioning and an inability to adapt to everyday life (see Chapter 10).
Personality disorders	Develop when personality traits become inflexible and maladaptive.
Other conditions that may be a focus of clinical attention	Include relational problems (with a partner, sibling, and so on), problems related to abuse or neglect (physical abuse of a child, for example), or additional conditions (such as bereavement, academic problems, and religious or spiritual problems).

depressive disorders
bipolar disorders
anxiety disorders
obsessive-compulsive disorder
post-traumatic stress disorder
dissociative disorders
somatic symptom disorders
personality disorders

NEURODEVELOPMENTAL DISORDERS

Although most clinical diagnoses are reserved for adults (older than 18), a number of disorders are prominent in childhood. The *DSM-5* refers to these as *neuro-developmental disorders*, which include intellectual disabilities (formerly mental retardation) and learning disabilities. We discuss two of them: attention deficit hyperactivity disorder (ADHD) and autism spectrum disorder. See Figure 15.3 for an overview of these two disorders.

Subtypes of Neurodevelopmental Disorders

Jade seldom can work more than a few minutes on any task, whether it is doing homework, reading, or even watching television. At school, she is constantly fidgeting in her chair and blurts out whatever she is thinking. Jade's teacher regularly must ask her to be quiet and stop disrupting others. Her homework is full of careless mistakes, even though she usually knows the answers. With these symptoms, psychologists would probably diagnose Jade as suffering from **attention deficit hyperactivity disorder (ADHD).** To receive the diagnosis of ADHD, the child must have displayed these symptoms before age 12. Between

attention deficit hyperactivity disorder (ADHD)
A childhood disorder characterized by inability to focus attention for more than a few minutes, to remain still and quiet, and to do careful work.

Disorder	Major symptoms	Behaviors
Attention deficit hyperactivity disorder (ADHD)	Inattention	Often fails to give close attention to details or makes careless mistakes, cannot sustain attention, does not listen when spoken to, does not follow through on instructions
	Hyperactivity	Fidgets with hands or feet, leaves seat in classroom when sitting is expected, inappropriate and excessive running or climbing, talks excessively
	Impulsivity	Blurts out answers before question is complete, cannot wait turn, often intrudes or interrupts others
Autism spectrum disorder	Impaired social interaction	Has impaired eye-to-eye gaze and facial expressions, fails to develop peer relationships, lacks sharing interests
	Impaired communication	Has impaired or severely delayed speech; language use is stereotypic or repetitive
	Repetitive and stereotypic behaviors	Shows preoccupation and repetitive interests or behaviors (such as finger or hand flapping), inflexible routines or rituals

FIGURE **15.3**
SYMPTOMS AND BEHAVIORS OF TWO CHILDHOOD DISORDERS. (APA, 2013)

5% and 10% of American school-age children, 8% of children in the United Kingdom, and 3%–5% of children worldwide meet the diagnostic criteria of ADHD (Alloway, Elliott, & Holmes, 2010; Kessler et al., 2005). Boys are more likely to be diagnosed with ADHD than girls by a ratio of about 2 to 1 (APA, 2013). ADHD begins in childhood but, for about 30%, the symptoms continue into adulthood (Barbaresi et al., 2013).

Let's consider Antoine, who until age 1 behaved in ways that seemed "normal." At the end of that year, however, subtle signs indicated that his development wasn't typical: He didn't babble or point to objects, he made very little eye contact, and he was hardly speaking at 18 months. When he did speak he often simply repeated what someone else had said, and later he would say "you" when he meant "I." Moreover, he regularly flapped his hands. Finally, he became very interested in the details and sensory experience of objects. He often would smell and taste toys. Psychologists would diagnose Antoine with **autism spectrum disorder** (**ASD,** formerly known as autism, from *autos,* meaning "self"). Autism spectrum disorder is characterized by severe language and social impairment combined with repetitive habits and inward-focused behaviors.

Evidence suggests that people with autism spectrum disorder are extremely sensitive to sensory stimulation and have trouble integrating multiple sources of sensory information, such as sight, sound, and touch (Iarocci & McDonald, 2006; Reynolds & Lane, 2008). Children with ASD also are more interested in inanimate objects than in people and social activities, and have difficulty with joint attention (Baron-Cohen et al., 2001). **Joint attention** is the ability to make eye contact with others and to look in the same direction as someone else. For example, if a mother points at something she is interested in, a child with ASD is less likely to look in the same direction. Researchers who were not aware of diagnoses and who closely examined eye contact made by children on their first-birthday home videos were able to correctly classify children as having autism spectrum disorder 77% of the time (Osterling & Dawson, 1994). Historically, approximately 5 to 6 children in 1,000 in the United States met the criteria for ASD, but current estimates say that up to 1% of the U.S. population meets the criteria for ASD (APA, 2013). Rates also have increased in other countries, such as Israel (Davidovitch et al., 2013) and India (Mamidala et al., 2013). Some researchers believe the disorder may be overdiagnosed; however, the evidence suggests the rise is mostly due to increased awareness.

Autism encompasses a range of disorders, ranging from severe disability to high functioning. On the high-functioning end of the spectrum, children have impaired social interest and skills and restricted interests, but they may be quite advanced in their speech and have above-average intelligence (APA, 2013). For instance, children on the high-functioning end of the spectrum may engage adults in long-winded and "professorial" discussions on one, rather narrow topic. Because Hans Asperger (1991/1944) first described this type of high-functioning autistic behavior, it became known as Asperger syndrome. The *DSM-5* eliminated Asperger syndrome as a separate diagnostic category, although many people previously diagnosed as such still identify with the term and may call themselves "Aspies."

Causes of Neurodevelopmental Disorders

Neurodevelopmental disorders sometimes stem from genetic factors that may remain latent unless triggered by an environmental condition (Howe, 2010; Larsson, Larsson, & Lichtenstein, 2004). For ADHD, one of the environmental factors is whether the mother smokes while pregnant. However, smoking during pregnancy leads to conduct and impulse problems only if the child has one

autism spectrum disorder (ASD)
A childhood disorder characterized by severe language and social impairment along with repetitive habits and inward-focused behaviors.

joint attention
The ability to make eye contact with others and to look in the same direction as someone else.

People at the high-functioning end of autism spectrum disorder may have independent, productive lives in spite of their social impairments and narrow interests. One such individual is Temple Grandin, who earned a PhD in animal science and became a professor at Colorado State University. A leading animal rights advocate, Grandin has designed humane facilities for livestock and has written and spoken extensively about animal rights.

form of a dopamine gene but not another (Kahn et al., 2003). Neither prenatal smoke exposure alone nor the dopamine genotype alone is significantly associated with increased behavior disorders. One environmental factor, long suspected by many parents to cause ADHD, is excessive sugar consumption (Bussing et al., 2007). Controlled clinical studies, however, do not support a relationship between the amount of sugar consumed and hyperactivity, and this conclusion has held in other countries (Y. Kim & Chang, 2011; Whalen & Henker, 1998).

Brain activity in general is less pronounced in people with ADHD than in those without it (Zametkin et al., 1990; Zang et al., 2005). An understimulated brain explains the "paradoxical" effects of giving children with ADHD a stimulant to calm them down. The stimulant elevates their abnormally low nervous system activity, and they require less stimulation and activity from the outside.

Head size is a marker of possible autism spectrum disorder. Often the brain is smaller than normal at birth but grows much faster during the first few years of life than the brains of nonautistic children (Courchesne, Campbell, & Solso, 2010). The brain of a 5-year-old with ASD is the same size as that of a typical 13-year-old (Blakeslee, 2005). Although we do not yet know which genes are involved, this abnormal rate of brain growth is almost certainly due to genetic influences. In addition, the frontal lobes, where much processing of social information occurs, are less well connected in children with ASD than in nonautistic children (Belmonte et al., 2004). Finally, recent evidence shows that the amygdala in children with ASD is 13% larger than in children without the disorder (Bachevalier, 2011; Mosconi et al., 2009).

A promising theory about the origins of autism spectrum disorder is based on the mirror neurons (Ramachandran & Oberman, 2006). As we saw in earlier chapters, mirror neurons fire both when a person performs a particular behavior (such as reaching for an object) and when he or she simply watches someone else performing the same behavior. Mirror neurons are thought to be involved in many, if not most, social behaviors, such as observational learning, imitation, and even language learning. Because children with ASD are deficient in these skills, neuroscientists have predicted that mirror neurons malfunction in ASD children; research results show that this is indeed the case (Ramachandran & Oberman, 2006). People at the high-functioning end of autism spectrum disorder may have independent, productive lives in spite of their social impairments and narrow interests. One such individual is Temple Grandin, who earned a PhD in animal science and became a professor at Colorado State University. A leading animal rights advocate, Grandin has designed humane facilities for livestock and has written and spoken extensively about animal rights.

Quick Quiz 15.1: Neurodevelopmental Disorders

1. Jolo is a 5-year-old boy who does not speak, waves his arms around a lot, does not make eye contact, and does not seem to connect with other kids or adults. Jolo may have which disorder?
   a. autistic spectrum disorder
   b. ADHD
   c. childhood depression
   d. theory of mind

2. Kelly fidgets a lot, blurts out what she is thinking, and makes many careless mistakes in her homework, even when she knows the answers. Kelly most likely would be diagnosed with which childhood disorder?
   a. low IQ
   b. autistic spectrum disorder
   c. anxiety disorder
   d. ADHD

Answers can be found at the end of the chapter.

SCHIZOPHRENIA

Challenge Your Assumptions

True or False? Schizophrenia is a disorder of split personalities.

False: Schizophrenia and split personality (multiple personality, now known as dissociative disorder) are very different disorders.

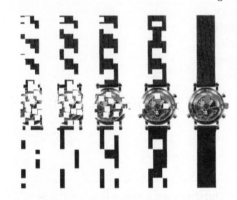

FIGURE **15.4**

INABILITY TO PERCEIVE FRAGMENTS IN SCHIZOPHRENIA. Perceiving fragments as parts of a whole can be difficult for people with schizophrenia. When normal subjects view fractured images like these in sequence, they identify the object quickly, but individuals with schizophrenia often cannot make that leap swiftly. (Javitt & Coyle, 2004)

Some disorders result primarily from disturbances of thought and perception; as a group, these are known as the **psychotic disorders.** They are characterized by an inability to distinguish real from imagined perceptions. One very serious psychotic disorder is **schizophrenia,** which involves profound disturbances in thought and emotion—in particular, impairments in perception, such as hallucinations. Emil Kraepelin, who coined the term *schizophrenia* (literally "split mind") in the 1890s, viewed the disorder as a split from reality, not a split attitude or split personality, as is sometimes mistakenly assumed. According to the National Institute of Mental Health (NIMH, 2007), approximately 1% of the American population is afflicted with this disorder at any given time, making schizophrenia much less common than depression. Genetically, however, if a first-degree relative (a biological parent, sibling, or child) has the disorder, the odds of a person having the disorder rise to 10% (NIMH, 2007).

Major Symptoms of Schizophrenia

For a diagnosis of schizophrenia, at least two of the following symptoms must persist for 1 month. Moreover, at least one of these symptoms must come from the first three (delusions, hallucinations, or disorganized speech; APA, 2013):

- Delusions
- Hallucinations
- Disorganized speech
- Grossly disorganized behavior or catatonic behavior (immobile and unresponsive, though awake)
- Negative symptoms (such as not speaking or being unable to experience emotion)

The symptoms of schizophrenia fall into three major categories: positive, negative, and cognitive. Note that "positive" and "negative" in this context do not mean "good" and "bad" but rather the "presence" and "absence" of behaviors. The bizarre perceptual experiences associated with schizophrenia are known as **positive symptoms.** These include hallucinations, delusional thinking, and disorganized thought and speech. Typically, perception is poorly integrated as well. Look, for instance, at the pictures of watches in Figure 15.4. People with schizophrenia have trouble putting the fragmented image together and perceiving it as a watch.

Hallucinations are convincing sensory experiences that occur in the absence of an external stimulus. Auditory hallucinations are the most common type of hallucination in schizophrenia, typically taking the form of hearing voices inside one's head in the absence of external auditory stimulation. The following account from a person with schizophrenia describes an auditory hallucination:

> Recently my mind has played tricks on me, creating The People inside my head who sometimes come out to haunt me and torment me. They surround me in rooms, hide behind trees and under the snow outside. They taunt me and scream at me and devise plans to break my spirit. The voices come and go, but The People are always there, always real. ("I Feel I Am Trapped," 1986)

People with schizophrenia experience such voices as real and are convinced that someone is living inside their heads. This is a defining feature of psychosis (Nolen-Hoeksema, 2007). Similar to but distinct from hallucinations, **delusions** are false beliefs, often exaggerated claims, that a person holds in spite of evidence to the contrary, such as the idea that one is Jesus Christ.

Other patients experience less flamboyant, but no less disabling, symptoms that are characterized by an absence of what would be considered appropriate behavior. These **negative symptoms** include nonresponsiveness, emotional flatness, immobility or the striking of strange poses (catatonia), reduction of speaking, and inability to complete tasks. Traditionally, negative symptoms have been harder to diagnose and treat than positive symptoms.

People with schizophrenia show **cognitive symptoms,** including problems with working memory, attention, verbal and visual learning and memory, reasoning and problem solving, speed of processing, and disordered speech (Barch, 2005). For example, the speech of a person with schizophrenia often follows grammatical rules, but the content makes little sense. Such utterances are referred to as **word salad.** Similarly, patients sometimes make up new words. In the following example, a woman who believed she was the only female professor at the "University of Smithsonian" (no such place) in England uses new words to produce a word salad.

> I am here from a foreign university . . . and you have to have a "plausity" of all acts of amendment to go through for the children's code . . . and it is no mental disturbance or "putenance." . . . It is an "amorition" law. . . . It is like their "privatilinia" and the children have to have this "accentuative" law so they don't go into the "mortite" law of the church. (Vetter, 1968, p. 306)

Nature and Nurture Explanations of Schizophrenia

Schizophrenia offers a perfect, though tragic, illustration of the dynamic interplay between biology and experience in the development of a psychological disorder. Historically, this explanation has been called the **diathesis-stress model.** *Diathesis* is the Greek word for "predisposition," so the diathesis-stress view is that biological predispositions plus stress or abusive environments together produce psychological disorders. Some researchers describe the diathesis-stress interaction between biological dispositions and environmental forces as a two-stage model (Kandel, 2000a; Lewis & Levitt, 2002). Stage one is the biological-genetic foundation, or disposition, and stage two is an environmental event that occurs at some point after conception, such as maternal infection, chronic stress, or certain drug use (such as marijuana or amphetamines) at particular critical points in development (Fergusson, Horwood, & Ridder, 2005).

Although genetic factors play an important role in the development of schizophrenia, they do not make it inevitable. The heritability rates are 70%–85%, suggesting that the disorder is due largely to genetic influences (Cardno & Gottesman, 2000; Gebicke-Haerter, 2012; Harrison & Owen, 2003; Kandel, 2000a; Lewis & Levitt, 2002; Vyas et al., 2010). Scientists have identified as many as 19 genes that contribute to schizophrenia, but the mechanisms they regulate have only recently been understood by neuroscientists (Harrison & Owen, 2003; Harrison & Weinberger, 2005; Mei & Xiong, 2008; Stefansson et al., 2009). The fact that one identical twin can develop schizophrenia, whereas the other genetically identical twin may not develop it, indicates that genes alone do not cause schizophrenia. Instead, genes can be epigenetically turned on or off by environmental experiences during brain development to produce the disorder (Gebicke-Haerter, 2012; A. W. Grossman et al., 2003; Moffitt et al., 2005; Petronis, 2004). Recent research has reported up to 100 genes related

delusions
One of the symptoms of schizophrenia: false beliefs or exaggerations held despite evidence to the contrary, such as the idea that one is a famous person.

negative symptoms
Symptoms that include nonresponsiveness, immobility, emotional flatness, problems with speech, and inability to complete tasks.

cognitive symptoms (of schizophrenia)
Problems with working memory, attention, verbal and visual learning and memory, reasoning and problem solving, processing, and speech.

word salad
The speech of people with schizophrenia, which may follow grammatical rules but be nonsensical in terms of content.

diathesis–stress model
Explanation for the origin of psychological disorders as a combination of biological predispositions (diathesis) plus stress or an abusive environment.

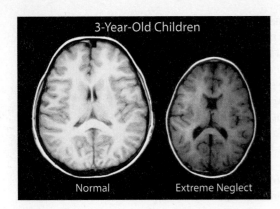

3-Year-Old Children

Normal | Extreme Neglect

FIGURE 15.5

EFFECT OF EXTREME NEGLECT ON BRAIN DEVELOPMENT. These MRI images show the brain of a typically developing 3-year-old child who has had a normal amount of cognitive, social, and linguistic stimulation (left) and that of a 3-year-old child who was deprived of regular social, linguistic, tactile, or cognitive stimulation (right). Growth is clearly stunted in the child who suffered from extreme neglect. Additionally, the dark, butterfly-shaped structures (ventricles) are much larger in the child who suffered from extreme neglect. Enlarged ventricles are common in people with schizophrenia. (Perry, 2002)

to schizophrenia with epigenetic tags (methyl-groups; Gebicke-Haerter, 2012).

The more abuse and neglect (adverse experiences) children experience in their early home lives, the more likely they are to suffer from schizophrenia later (Edwards et al., 2003; Whitfield et al., 2005). Adverse experiences in the form of abuse and neglect often happen during the critical periods of brain growth and development (see Figure 15.5; Perry, 2002). In the child who suffered extreme neglect, notice the much smaller overall brain size as well as the enlarged ventricles (butterfly shapes) in the middle of the brain. These features are two of the major brain abnormalities characteristic of schizophrenia. One of the oldest findings on the brain and schizophrenia is the tendency of people with schizophrenia to have enlarged ventricles (the fluid-filled spaces in the brain; Lieberman et al., 2001).

Although we may not yet know their causes or how exactly they interact with environmental forces, certain biological and brain abnormalities are hallmarks of schizophrenia. In this section, we will consider some of the better-known ones: maternal infection, dysfunctional prefrontal and hippocampus activity, enlarged ventricles, an excess of dopamine activity in the basal ganglia, and a deficiency in the neurotransmitter glutamate.

Maternal Infections and Schizophrenia As first discussed in Chapter 3, during fetal development, neural growth can occur at a rate of 250,000 new neurons per minute and peak at approximately *3 million* per minute (Purves & Lichtman, 1985)! Consequently, what happens to both the mother and the fetus is crucial; any kind of disease or toxic substance experienced by the mother may dramatically affect neural growth in the fetus. If a woman contracts an infection during pregnancy, the risk of the child's developing schizophrenia later in life increases dramatically (Boska, 2008; A. S. Brown, 2006; Koenig, 2006; J. Moreno et al., 2011). Prenatal exposure to infections and diseases such as influenza, rubella, toxoplasmosis, and herpes has been linked to increased risk of schizophrenia (A. S. Brown, 2006; Buka et al., 2001) and deficits in brain development (J. Moreno et al., 2011; Short et al., 2010). The effect appears not to exist, however, during the first and second trimesters of pregnancy (months 1–6; Selten et al., 2010).

Schizophrenia and the Brain Abnormal brain development before birth may be responsible for many of the brain dysfunctions that are characteristic of schizophrenia (Lewis & Levitt, 2002). One mechanism by which maternal infections, for instance, may increase the risk of schizophrenia is by affecting the path neurons take when they migrate during fetal brain growth (Kandel, 2000a; Koenig, 2006). One of the most widely recognized brain abnormalities is a dysfunctional prefrontal cortex and its working memory; in people with schizophrenia, there is evidence of both reduced and excessive activity in that area (Andreasen et al., 1997; Barch, 2005; Goldman-Rakic, 1999; D. R. Weinberger et al., 2001; Vyas et al., 2010). Moreover, the genes in the prefrontal cortex that regulate how synapses function are dysfunctional in people with schizophrenia compared to those without the disease (Mirnics et al., 2000). Often the hippocampus is smaller in people with schizophrenia compared to those without the disorder (Barch, 2005; Harrison, 2004). See Figure 15.6 for an overview of these and other areas of the brain affected by schizophrenia.

Brain problems in schizophrenia may not be simply a function of abnormalities in certain structures but may also stem from problems in the communications

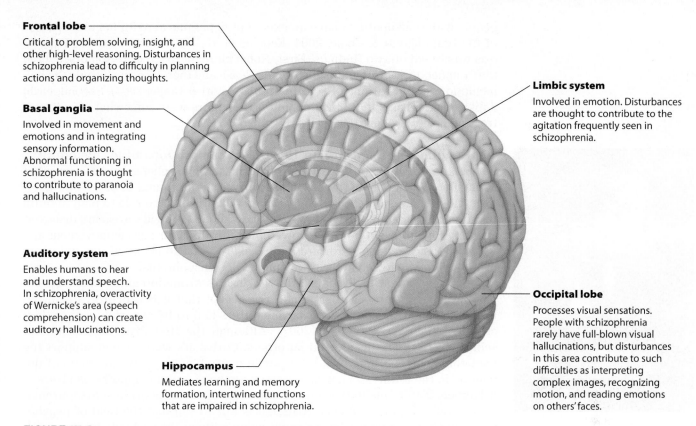

Frontal lobe

Critical to problem solving, insight, and other high-level reasoning. Disturbances in schizophrenia lead to difficulty in planning actions and organizing thoughts.

Basal ganglia

Involved in movement and emotions and in integrating sensory information. Abnormal functioning in schizophrenia is thought to contribute to paranoia and hallucinations.

Auditory system

Enables humans to hear and understand speech. In schizophrenia, overactivity of Wernicke's area (speech comprehension) can create auditory hallucinations.

Hippocampus

Mediates learning and memory formation, intertwined functions that are impaired in schizophrenia.

Limbic system

Involved in emotion. Disturbances are thought to contribute to the agitation frequently seen in schizophrenia.

Occipital lobe

Processes visual sensations. People with schizophrenia rarely have full-blown visual hallucinations, but disturbances in this area contribute to such difficulties as interpreting complex images, recognizing motion, and reading emotions on others' faces.

FIGURE **15.6**

AREAS OF THE BRAIN IMPAIRED BY SCHIZOPHRENIA. The structures highlighted here do not function normally in people with schizophrenia. Limbic system structures not shown here are the hypothalamus, amygdala, and cingulate gyrus. (Javitt & Coyle, 2004)

among groups of neurons. In people without schizophrenia, neural networks are efficiently clustered in close groups and move in and out of orderly and chaotic patterns of firing (Bassett et al., 2008). This process is essential for learning and memory. In people with schizophrenia, however, these networks are less clustered, less efficient, and more disorderly, especially in the frontal lobes (Bassett et al., 2008).

An obvious positive symptom of schizophrenia is hallucinations. What is going on in the brain during a hallucination? Brain imaging studies show that hallucinations activate the brain in ways similar, but not identical, to real external stimulation (Shergill et al., 2000; Shergill et al., 2003; Silbersweig et al., 1995). For example, activity in the auditory cortex of the temporal lobe and the visual cortex of the occipital lobe during visual and auditory hallucinations shows striking similarities to the kind of brain activity that occurs when visual and auditory stimuli are present. The part of the brain involved in interpreting and comprehending speech (Wernicke's area of the left hemisphere) is also activated during hallucinations (Stephane, Barton, & Boutros, 2001). Also noteworthy, however, is the lack of activity in the frontal lobes during the hallucination, which suggests that the person is unable to monitor and determine the source of the images or sounds (Shergill et al., 2003).

Neurochemistry of Schizophrenia For decades, the prevailing view on the neurochemistry of schizophrenia was the *dopamine hypothesis*, which states that

Connection

During fetal development, the brain is extremely vulnerable to many different kinds of toxins.

See "Nature and Nurture Influences on Fetal Development," Chapter 5, "Human Development," p. 165.

people with schizophrenia have an excess of dopamine activity in certain areas of the brain (Javitt & Coyle, 2004; Kegeles et al., 2010). The dopamine hypothesis was based on two findings. First, Nobel laureate Arvid Carlsson discovered that amphetamines stimulate dopamine release and therefore may mimic the hallucinations and delusions of schizophrenia (Javitt & Coyle, 2004). Second, early antipsychotic drugs that block dopamine receptors were somewhat effective at treating positive symptoms.

Challenging Assumptions in the Discovery of Dopamine   Before 1952, no one knew that dopamine is a neurotransmitter. The belief at the time was that dopamine was merely a precursor of epinephrine (Yeragani et al., 2010). Moreover, most scientists were convinced that dopamine had no role to play in brain function (Carlsson, 1987). We now know, partly due to Arvid Carlsson's discoveries, that dopamine not only is involved in controlling our muscle movement and with the basic feelings of reward and pleasure but also is one of the main neurotransmitters involved in the development of schizophrenia.

Arvid Carlsson

However, nearly 10 years after Carlsson's groundbreaking work on dopamine, many neuroscientists could not accept that it is a neurotransmitter, because they still believed neurotransmitters had to be electrical rather than chemical (Iversen & Iversen, 2007). Although the first drug treatments for schizophrenia were discovered by others, Carlsson's work helped support the view that schizophrenia is at least partly caused by excessive amounts of dopamine in the brain—a view now known as the dopamine hypothesis (Iversen & Iversen, 2007). Due to the central role that dopamine plays in schizophrenia, Parkinson's disease, and even ADHD, it is fair to say that the field of psychopharmacology would not be the same today without the early pioneering work of Arvid Carlsson.

There are, however, some problems with the dopamine hypothesis and schizophrenia. As we discuss in more detail in the next chapter, dopamine-specific medications (major tranquilizers) effectively treat only positive symptoms and even then are not entirely effective. In addition, only a minority of the people who receive the traditional drug treatment find it effective in managing their symptoms (Javitt & Coyle, 2004). When researchers became aware that another set of recreational drugs led to schizophrenia-like symptoms that did not directly involve dopamine, they turned their attention to these drugs. These drugs, PCP ("angel dust") and ketamine (an animal anesthetic, used recreationally as "Vit K" or "Special K"), do not affect dopamine production; instead, they impair the functioning of a different neurotransmitter, glutamate, and one of its receptors, NMDA. Glutamate is a major excitatory neurotransmitter that regulates the release of dopamine. PCP and ketamine block the action of glutamate, thus producing the same kinds of disturbances seen in schizophrenia (Harrison & Owen, 2003; Moghaddam, 2003). Glutamate deficiencies, then, may also explain many of the symptoms of schizophrenia (Javitt & Coyle, 2004). A gene related to glutamate plays a role in prefrontal cortex functioning in schizophrenics, which further supports a role for glutamate in the disorder (Fallgatter et al., 2010).

These findings stimulated researchers to explore the role of glutamate in schizophrenia more fully. Not only is it crucial in learning, memory, neural processing, and brain development, but it also amplifies certain neural signals, making some stimuli more important than others (Goff & Coyle, 2001; Javitt & Coyle, 2004; Mayer, 2004). This process is crucial to selective attention; that is, focusing attention on some items of information while ignoring others. Thus, dysfunction in glutamate action would explain why people with schizophrenia have trouble with selective attention, cognitive control, and working memory.

1. Which of the following is a negative symptom of schizophrenia?
   a. hallucinations
   b. delusions of grandeur
   c. catatonia
   d. fatigue

2. The heritability rate for schizophrenia is roughly
   a. 100%.
   b. 60%.
   c. 80%.
   d. 25%.

3. Low levels of which neurotransmitter might explain why people with schizophrenia have trouble with selective attention, cognitive control, and working memory?
   a. acetylcholine
   b. glutamate
   c. norepinephrine
   d. GABA

Answers can be found at the end of the chapter.

DEPRESSIVE DISORDERS

If schizophrenia and other psychotic disorders are expressions of thought and perceptual disturbances, then bipolar disorder and depression are expressions of disturbance in mood and emotion. The depressive disorders, bipolar disorders, and anxiety disorder are marked especially by disturbances in emotional behavior that prevent people from functioning effectively in everyday life.

We all feel blue from time to time. Feeling sad after being rejected by a lover or failing an exam presents a normal response to life challenges, as does getting into a funk after a series of hard breaks. Yet being unable to leave your bed for days or failing to eat from a profound sense of despair or disinterest in doing anything—often without direct provocation—is something different altogether, and it may reflect an underlying disorder in psychological health.

According to the *DSM-5*, there are several forms of **depressive disorder.** What most people refer to as "depression" is formally called **major depressive disorder,** a chronic condition characterized by enduring changes in mood, motivation, and sense of self-worth. According to *DSM-5*, to be diagnosed with major depressive disorder, one must have at least five of nine symptoms associated with major depression, which must continue for at least 2 consecutive weeks (APA, 2013):

1. Depressed (sad, listless) mood that stays low all day for several days
2. Reduced interest or pleasure in doing anything
3. Significant change in body weight (indicating dieting or overeating)
4. Sleep disturbances
5. Sluggishness or restlessness
6. Daily fatigue or loss of energy
7. Daily feelings of worthlessness, self-reproach, or excessive guilt
8. Lack of ability to concentrate or think clearly
9. Recurrent thoughts of death or suicidal ideation

Most importantly, symptoms must significantly impact daily functioning, in terms of both social and work-related contexts, and they must be a source of distress, in order to be the basis for a diagnosis of major depressive disorder. Overall, approximately 7% of the American population has major depressive disorder, but the occurrence varies depending on age and sex. The disorder is three times more likely in 18- to 29-year-olds than in 60+-year-olds. Females experience depression up to three times more often than males (teen and up; APA, 2013).

depressive disorder
The highest-order category of the depressive disorders; it subsumes all forms of depression, including major depressive disorder and persistent depressive disorder.

major depressive disorder
A mood disorder characterized by pervasive low mood, lack of motivation, low energy, and feelings of worthlessness and guilt that last for at least 2 consecutive weeks.

persistent depressive disorder (PDD)
A form of depression that is milder in intensity but longer in duration than major depressive disorder.

Other forms of depressive disorder have milder symptoms but last longer. One of these milder forms is **persistent depressive disorder** (**PDD,** previously called *dysthymia*). Most of the symptoms are the same as in a major depressive disorder, but they are less intense in PDD, though the depressive mood lasts most of the day and most of the time for at least 2 years.

Depression manifests itself differently in different people, but only rarely is it only about feeling blue. Although sadness is the emotion most associated with depression, many find the lack of interest in or ability to *feel* anything (positive or negative) to be the most disabling aspect of living with depression. The Pulitzer Prize-winning novelist William Styron, who went through a major depressive episode in his 60s, offered a poignant account of the experience in his book *Darkness Visible*. For Styron, as for many seriously depressed people, the feelings of despair reached a point at which ending his life seemed to be the only guaranteed source of relief:

> I had not as yet chosen the mode of my departure, but I knew that that step would come next, and soon, as inescapable as nightfall. . . . Late one bitterly cold night, when I knew that I could not possibly get myself through the following day, I sat in the living room of the house bundled up against the chill. . . . I had forced myself to watch the tape of a movie. . . . At one point in the film . . . came a contralto voice, a sudden soaring passage from the Brahms *Alto Rhapsody*.
>
> This sound, which like all music—indeed, like all pleasure— I had been numbly unresponsive to for months, pierced my heart like a dagger, and in a flood of swift recollection I thought of all the joys the house had known; the children who had rushed through its rooms, the festivals, the love and work, the honestly earned slumber, the voices and the nimble commotion. . . . All this I realized was more than I could ever abandon. . . . I drew upon some last gleam of sanity to perceive the terrifying dimensions of the mortal predicament I had fallen into. I woke up my wife and soon telephone calls were made. The next day I was admitted to the hospital. (1990, pp. 63–67)

What factors and symptoms are needed before everyday blues turn into a diagnosis of major depressive disorder?

The kind of unbearable hopelessness we see in Styron's comments may be one reason that people with depression are at a higher risk of committing suicide than others. Indeed, suicide is a major risk for people with depression, and suicidal thinking is included as a symptom of depression (APA, 2013; Hawton et al., 2013).

Nature and Nurture Explanations of Depression

Depression is sometimes caused by a stressful or traumatic life event, such as physical or sexual abuse, but not always. For some people, depression just comes on, like using a switch to turn on a light. To the extent that this is true, the reason some people, but not others, develop depression stems from a combination of neurochemistry and life circumstance—the diathesis-stress model again (Bukh et al., 2009).

Abusive and extremely stressful environments increase one's risk for depression later in life. Researchers studying adverse experiences found that people who reported the most adverse childhood experiences were more likely to be depressed than people who reported no adverse childhood experiences (Anda et al., 2006; Pietrek et al., 2013; Wang et al., 2010). Indeed, the role of stress in the development of depression is not trivial (Wang et al., 2010; A. A. Weinstein et al., 2010). In animals, experimental-induced stress kills neurons in the hippocampus, which can lead to symptoms of depression (B. L. Jacobs, 2004; B. L. Jacobs, van Praag, & Gage, 2000; Kendler, Karkowski, & Prescott, 1999). In humans, stressful events, especially social rejection, start a host of biological reactions, including activating the hypothalamic-pituitary-adrenal (HPA) system, which increases the likelihood of developing depression (Slavich et al., 2010). Indeed, recent evidence suggests that stress is associated with accelerated aging of cells, which in turn is associated with depression (Simon et al., 2006; Wolkowitz et al., 2010). Medications that make more serotonin available in the brain stimulate neural growth, which lessens the symptoms of depression (Malberg et al., 2000; Papakostos et al., 2008). This may be an important avenue for treatment, given that depression is associated with decreased brain density, which may reflect stress-related neuronal death (Lai, 2013).

The physiological effects of depression may be observable even at the sub-cellular level. The mitochondria are structures inside cells (in this case, inside neurons) that play a key role in cell metabolism. Several studies point to mitochondrial dysfunction in specific brain tissues linked with the occurrence of depression, but it is not clear if this is a cause or an effect of the disease (Tobe, 2013).

Stressful environments, however, appear to interact with particular biological dispositions and personality traits to produce depression, especially in people who have experienced stress, trauma, and abuse (Clark, 2005; Hankin, 2010; Krueger, 1999; Slavich et al., 2010; Uher & McGuffin, 2010). People who are deficient in the neurotransmitters serotonin and neuropeptide Y (NPY) are most susceptible to depression after experiencing extremely stressful situations (Lowry et al., 2008; Morales-Medina, Dumont, & Quirion, 2010; Risch et al., 2009). For example, a meta-analysis of 34 studies found support for an interaction between differences in serotonin genes, adverse experiences, and the development of depression (Uher & McGuffin, 2010). One of the 34 studies in this meta-analysis provides a nice example of the research into the nature-nurture origins of depression; see the "Research Process" for more details (Figure 15.7). Also, the personality traits of anxiety, neuroticism, and negative emotionality, for instance, are most associated with vulnerability to depression.

Stressful life events, such as the death of a loved one, can trigger a major depressive episode in people who have a genetic predisposition for depression.

Challenge Your Assumptions

True or False? Extreme stress can make you depressed.

True: Stress can cause depression and even premature aging of cells.

Research Process

① Research Question

How do genetic and environmental differences interact to affect the development of depression?

② Method

Avshalom Caspi and colleagues followed a group of nearly 1,000 people from age 3 until age 26 (Caspi, Sugden, et al., 2003). The investigators measured life events experienced by the participants at different ages. They obtained data on the presence of long and short forms of the serotonin gene in the participants' genotypes. One form (allele) comes from each parent.

③ Results

They found that people who had inherited two short forms (s/s) of the serotonin gene were more likely to exhibit depressive symptoms following stressful life events than were those who had inherited the long form (l/l). For example, in the graph shown here, we see that if people experience a few major stressful events (no more than two), their risk of having a major depressive episode does not increase, regardless of which form of the serotonin gene they carry. But if they experience three or four stressful events, the likelihood that they will have a major depressive episode nearly doubles or triples in those with the short form compared to those with the long form.

④ Conclusion

Depression is most likely in individuals who carry the short form of the gene *and* experience many severe life stressors. Neither condition by itself is likely to lead to depression.

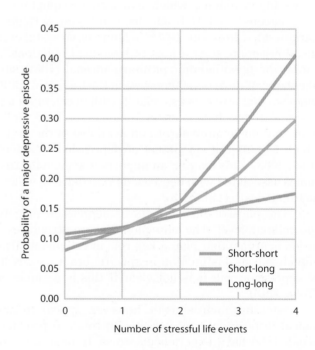

FIGURE **15.7**

GENE-ENVIRONMENT INTERACTION IN THE DEVELOPMENT OF DEPRESSION. Individuals with at least one short allele of the serotonin gene are more likely to experience depression than those with two long alleles. Those with two short forms of the gene are most vulnerable to depression if they experience at least three stressful life events. ("Influence of Life Stress on Depression: Moderation by a Polymorphism in the 5-HTT Gene," by A. Caspi, K. Sugden, T. E. Moffitt, A. Taylor, I. W. Craig, H. Harrington, . . . Poulton, R., 2003, *Science, 301,* 386–389.)

BIPOLAR DISORDER

People who suffer from **bipolar disorder** experience severe mood fluctuations, cycling between very low (major depressive) and very high (manic or hypomanic) episodes. (At one time, this disorder was called manic depression.) **Manic episodes** typically involve increased energy, sleeplessness, euphoria, irritability, delusions of grandeur, increased sex drive, and "racing" thoughts that last *at least 1 week*. **Hypomanic episodes** are nearly the same symptoms but shorter in duration—they last *at least 4 days* (APA, 2013). A useful mnemonic for remembering the symptoms of mania is D-I-G-F-A-S-T (Carlat, 1998):

D = Distractibility
I = Indiscretion
G = Grandiosity
F = Flight of ideas
A = Activity increased
S = Sleep (decreased need for)
T = Talkativeness

The *DSM-5* distinguishes between two kinds of bipolar disorder, depending on the severity of the mania (APA, 2013). Bipolar I is more severe because it involves meeting the criteria for mania (at least 7 days), whereas bipolar II is less severe because it involves meeting the criteria for hypomania (at least 4 days). Recall that *hypo* means "below," so hypomania is not as severe as mania. Thus, the degree of depression is the same in bipolar I and II, but the mania is less severe in bipolar II than in I.

People with either form of bipolar disorder often find the initial onset of the manic phase pleasant, especially compared to the dullness and despair of the depressive phase. Unfortunately, the symptoms quickly become quite unpleasant and frightening. The manic upswing spirals out of control, often leading to frenetic activity, excessive energy, and grandiose thinking, in which sufferers think they have relationships with important people or expertise in areas where they have none. Indiscretion occurs when a person says things that are somewhat inappropriate or gets involved in promiscuous sexual relationships. Figure 15.8 lists the characteristics and symptoms of depression and bipolar disorder.

Virginia Woolf, the groundbreaking early-20th-century novelist, suffered from bipolar disorder. She dealt with bouts of severe depression and frenetic

bipolar disorder
A mood disorder characterized by substantial mood fluctuations, cycling between very low (depressive) and very high (manic) moods.

manic episodes
One mood cycle in bipolar disorder, typically involving increased energy, sleeplessness, euphoria, irritability, delusions of grandeur, increased sex drive, and "racing" thoughts that last at least 1 week.

hypomanic episodes
Consists of same symptoms as manic episodes (e.g., increased energy, sleeplessness, euphoria, irritability, delusions of grandeur, increased sex drive, and "racing" thoughts) but are shorter in duration.

	Major symptoms	**Behaviors**
major depressive disorder	Low mood, lack of motivation, low energy, feelings of worthlessness and guilt that last for at least two weeks	Change in eating behavior, intense anxiety or sadness, feeling of being disconnected, and/or inability to take pleasure in enjoyable experiences
bipolar disorder	Extreme swings in mood between depressive and manic episodes	Manic episodes characterized by distractibility, increased activity, euphoria, grandiosity, decreased need for sleep, talkativeness, flight of ideas, and indiscretion

FIGURE 15.8

MAJOR SYMPTOMS AND BEHAVIORS OF DEPRESSIVE DISORDERS AND BIPOLAR DISORDER. (APA, 2013)

mania, which ultimately led to her suicide in 1941. Virginia's husband, the writer Leonard Woolf, offered revealing descriptions of her condition while manic:

> She talked almost without stopping for two or three days, paying no attention to anyone in the room or anything said to her. For about a day when she was coherent, the sentences meant something, though it was nearly all wildly insane. Then gradually it became completely incoherent, a mere jumble of dissociated words. (quoted in Jamison, 1993, p. 29)

cyclothymia
A relatively mild but longer-lasting form of bipolar disorder.

In an even milder but longer-lasting form of bipolar disorder called **cyclothymia,** both the manic and the depressive episodes are less severe than they are in bipolar II disorder—that is, the hypomanic and depressive symptoms never reach the criteria for hypomania and major depression.

Causes of Bipolar Disorder

What causes bipolar disorder? As is true for other psychological disorders, multiple biological and environmental factors appear to interact in ways scientists are only now beginning to understand. The dynamic relationship between the environment and the brain in bipolar disorder may be seen as early as prenatal development. Fetuses exposed to large amounts of alcohol may suffer permanent effects, including increased risks for bipolar disorder as well as depression, schizophrenia, alcoholism, intellectual disability and drug abuse (Famy, Streissguth, & Unis, 1998; O'Conner & Paley, 2006).

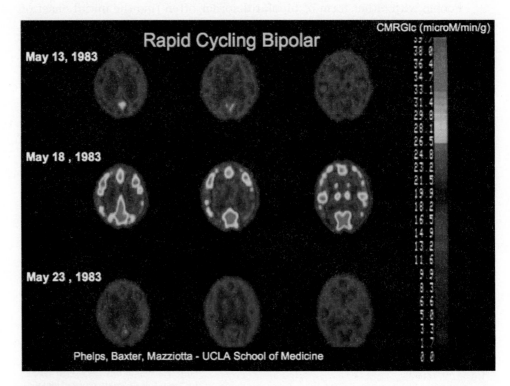

FIGURE **15.9**

THE BIPOLAR BRAIN. PET scan images show the brain of someone with bipolar disorder over the course of 10 days. Blue and green indicate low levels of brain activity, and red and yellow indicate high levels of brain activity. The top and bottom images show the low activity of depression, whereas the middle images show an increased level of brain activity during mania. Note how quickly this person cycled in and then out of the manic phase (10 days).

The genetics of bipolar disorder are complex. Many variations of genes appear to play a role in the development of the disorder, the specifics of which are only beginning to be understood (Comer, 2007; Luykx et al., 2010; Shastry, 2005). Twin studies also point to a role for genetics in bipolar disorder. If one identical twin develops bipolar disorder, there is a 40%–70% chance that the other twin will also develop the disorder (Müller-Oerlinghausen, Berghöfer, & Bauer, 2002; Shastry, 2005). Even if the chance is 70% that both twins will have the disorder, life events, such as stress and trauma, also play a role in the development of bipolar disorder (Müller-Oerlinghausen et al., 2002; Shastry, 2005).

Abnormalities in the brains of people who suffer from bipolar disorder may be a cause or a result of the biochemical, genetic, and environmental elements that contribute to the disorder. The prefrontal cortex, amygdala, hippocampus, and basal ganglia all may play a role (Müller-Oerlinghausen et al., 2002; Shastry, 2005). Overactivity in many of these regions is evident in the PET scan images displayed in Figure 15.9, showing up as red areas compared to the blue regions that indicate depressed mood. There may also be problems in the connectivity among the key regions involved in emotional processing, such as the prefrontal cortex and amygdala (Chepenik et al., 2010).

Neurochemistry is also important in bipolar disorder. In both the manic and depressed phases, serotonin levels are low, but low serotonin may be coupled with high levels of norepinephrine in the manic phase and with low levels in the depressed phase (Comer, 2007; Müller-Oerlinghausen et al., 2002). In addition, thyroid hormones, which control metabolism, are sometimes present in either abnormally high or low levels in people with bipolar disorder (M. Bauer & Whybrow, 2001; Müller-Oerlinghausen et al., 2002).

Quick Quiz 15.3: Depressive Disorders and Bipolar Disorder

1. Latresha is not hungry, is extremely tired, and doesn't feel like doing much of anything. She often feels that life is just hopeless. These symptoms have been going on for 2 months now. She probably is suffering from which mood disorder?
   a. generalized anxiety disorder
   b. bipolar disorder
   c. major depressive disorder
   d. obsessive-compulsive disorder

2. David went home for Christmas break and found that his mother, who was usually depressed, had just purchased dozens of birdhouses from a local gift store. She'd had each custom-wrapped and was planning to give them to all the extended members of the family and all her neighbors, whom she claimed to love like family. She had

spent thousands of dollars. What might be going on with David's mom?
   a. She had won the lottery.
   b. She has bipolar disorder.
   c. She has an overactive hypothalamus.
   d. She is just depressed.

3. Which neurotransmitter is reduced in both the manic and the depressive phases of bipolar disorder?
   a. acetylcholine
   b. dopamine
   c. norepinephrine
   d. serotonin

Answers can be found at the end of the chapter.

ANXIETY DISORDERS

Fear and anxiety are normal reactions to danger or future threat. These emotions create bodily changes—such as increases in heart rate—that support useful responses to danger. For some, however, fear and anxiety can get out of hand, occurring repeatedly in response to imagined threat and sometimes persisting for days. For about 26% of the U.S. population, though, anxious states can interfere with everyday functioning (Kessler et al., 2012). In this section we discuss five of the more common forms of anxiety disorders (see Figure 15.10).

Disorder	Major symptoms	Behaviors
Generalized anxiety disorder (GAD)	Pervasive/excessive anxiety lasting at least 6 months	Inability to relax
Panic disorder	Persistent worry about having a panic attack	*Panic attack:* Heart palpitations, trembling, dizziness, intense dread, and fear of dying *Panic disorder:* Prone to panic attacks, concerned about having a panic attack and about embarrassment of having a panic attack
Agoraphobia	Fear of not being able to escape or of help not being available if panic attack should occur in public place	Unwilling to leave home so as to avoid panic attacks
Social phobia	Persistent fear of humiliation in the presence of others	Highly anxious, extremely self-conscious about appearance or behavior or both, possibly housebound
Specific phobias	Undue anxiety response to particular objects or situations	Intense fear or panic when confronted with particular situations or objects or even when thinking about them

FIGURE 15.10

MAJOR SYMPTOMS AND CRITERIA OF SPECIFIC ANXIETY DISORDERS. (APA, 2013)

What overarching symptom do all of these disorders share?

Generalized Anxiety Disorder

generalized anxiety disorder (GAD)
A state of pervasive and excessive anxiety lasting at least 6 months.

Generalized anxiety disorder (GAD) is a common anxiety disorder, characterized by a pervasive, excessive, hard-to-control state of anxiety or worry that lasts at least 6 months (APA, 2013). People with GAD may also have trouble with sleep, body restlessness or agitation, difficulty concentrating, or muscle tension. Adults must exhibit at least three of the preceding symptoms to receive a diagnosis of GAD (APA, 2013). GAD affects between 3% and 9% of the U.S. population, although females are twice as likely as males to have GAD (APA, 2013). It is also more common in the United States in people of European descent than in those of non-European descent.

Unlike those suffering from other anxiety disorders, people with GAD often have been anxious throughout their lives and cannot recall when they began to feel that way (Barlow, 2004). In everyday language, we might call such people "worrywarts"—those who worry about anything and everything, often out of proportion to the actual threat. The writer, director, and actor Woody Allen has made a career out of his pervasive tendency to worry. Allen says he uses filmmaking and writing as a creative distraction from his pervasive anxiety (Briggs, 2005). The constant anxiety of GAD can be debilitating, however, preventing many people who suffer from it from being able to work at all.

Panic Disorder

panic attacks
Brief episodes of anxiety associated with a perception of threat and occurring because of fear of danger, an inability to escape, embarrassment, or specific objects.

The core of panic disorder is the panic attack. **Panic attacks** involve sudden changes in body and mind, characterized by an overwhelming sense of impending doom, heart palpitations, trembling, sweating, shortness of breath, dizziness, intense dread, nausea, and even a fear of dying. Such attacks are associated with perceptions of threat and can occur for a number of reasons: fear of danger, an inability to escape, fear of embarrassment, or fear of a specific category of objects. Panic attacks usually last about 10 minutes but sometimes come and go over a period of an hour or more. Due to their physiological effects, people undergoing a panic attack may believe they are having a heart attack or are "going crazy."

Panic disorder is defined by frequent panic attacks and pervasive and persistent fear, worry, embarrassment, and concern about having future panic attacks (APA, 2013). The preoccupation with and anxiety over having another attack create an anxious mood, which then increases the likelihood of more worrisome thoughts and, ironically, another attack. Thus, panic disorder creates a positive feedback cycle, wherein anxiety about future attacks hijacks the body's emergency response system and catapults it out of control. To receive a diagnosis of panic disorder, a panic attack must be followed by at least a month of persistent worry over future attacks, along with the development of potentially maladaptive behaviors to avoid attacks (e.g., avoidance of putting oneself in unfamiliar situations).

People who have only occasional panic attacks without intense anxiety or fear about the possibility of future panic attacks do not qualify for the diagnosis of panic disorder. Although about 10% of the U.S. population has experienced a panic attack in the past 12 months (B. F. Grant et al., 2006), only about 2%–3% of the population has panic disorder (APA, 2013). In the United States, panic disorder is more common in women than men and less common in older adults. Overall, in Asian, African, and Latin American countries, the rates are very low—less than 1%—and the specific concerns or persistent worries appear to vary by culture (APA, 2013).

panic disorder
An anxiety disorder characterized by panic attacks and persistent anxiety about having more attacks.

Social Phobia (Social Anxiety Disorder)

A **phobia** is a persistent and unreasonable fear of a particular object, situation, or activity (APA, 2013). Some people suffer extreme anxiety when they have to interact with other people, viewing each interaction as a possible opportunity to be scrutinized by others. **Social phobia,** or **social anxiety disorder,** is marked by a pronounced fear of humiliation or embarrassment in the presence of others or severe self-consciousness about one's appearance, behavior, or both. Consider the case of Sarah, who hates going to the grocery store: She would not dare ask anyone working there how to find an item, out of fear that she might look stupid for not being able to find it herself. She doesn't want anyone to know she is anxious about being in the store. She is concerned that her voice might quiver when forced to say the obligatory "hello" to the cashier. This would make her seem really foolish, and everybody would stare at her foolishness.

phobia
An anxiety disorder: an ongoing and irrational fear of a particular object, situation, or activity.

social phobia (social anxiety disorder)
An anxiety disorder: fear of humiliation in the presence of others, characterized by intense self-consciousness about one's appearance, behavior, or both.

Fear like Sarah's can be paralyzing, making it very difficult to go out into public situations, even though in most cases the person recognizes that these fears are irrational. Unfortunately, the high degree of anxious arousal produced by social phobia may lead the person to act very nervously and thus, in a self-fulfilling way, exhibit behaviors that do attract other people's attention.

Agoraphobia

Agoraphobia is the most severe of all phobias (Bouton, Mineka, & Barlow, 2001). Contrary to popular

People with social phobia are extremely self-conscious and fearful of embarrassing themselves in front of others.

agoraphobia
An anxiety disorder involving fear of being in places from which escape might be difficult or in which help might not be available, should a panic attack occur.

belief, the primary "fear" in agoraphobia is not of being out in public. Formally, **agoraphobia** is intense anxiety, fear, and panic about being in places from which escape might be difficult or in which help might not be available, should a panic attack occur, such as in open spaces, in a public market, in line somewhere, outside of the home alone, or in enclosed spaces (e.g., movie theaters; APA, 2013). This fear of being unable to escape keeps people at home, where they feel safe. Panic attacks are associated with agoraphobia in about one-third of all cases.

Specific Phobias

Only a few of us enjoy spiders, snakes, or heights, but most of us feel only mild levels of anxiety about such objects or experiences. Some of us, however, go beyond mild levels of fear. In the United States, up to 9% of the population has a *specific phobia* for a particular object or situation, such as spiders (arachnophobia), heights, flying, enclosed spaces (claustrophobia), doctors and dentists, or snakes (APA, 2013). Specific phobias are marked by an intense and immediate fear, even panic, when confronted with very particular situations or objects; even thinking about those situations or objects may set off the fear reaction. People with specific phobias are not generally anxious people, but they will do almost anything to avoid coming in contact with the feared object or experiencing the feared event or object. Megan Fox, Britney Spears, and Jennifer Aniston all fear flying. Aniston, for instance, feels compelled to perform the same ritual each time she boards a plane ("Jennifer Aniston Talks," 2009), a "good luck" superstition in the face of her fear:

Actress Jennifer Aniston has spoken publicly about her fear of flying and the ritual she performs before each flight.

> If I walk onto an airplane, I always have to go on with my right foot first and tap the outside of the plane. I have always done it. For luck. Someone told me to do it and I don't remember when that was. But it's kind of stuck.

Nature and Nurture Explanations of Anxiety Disorders

How do anxiety disorders develop? Like all animals, humans have evolved fear mechanisms to determine whether a situation is safe and whether we need to try to fight or flee (LeDoux, 2000). Additionally, as is true for most complex traits, some people are more genetically disposed to anxiety than others. Anxiety disorders—and most other psychological disorders—result from the interplay between biological and environmental factors. Instead of offering either biological or social theories of disorders, we present integrated nature-nurture (diathesis-stress) explanations.

Three biological factors that make people vulnerable to anxiety disorders are deficiencies in the neurotransmitter GABA, their genetic heritage, and their personalities. Researchers have discovered that people who are prone to anxiety are deficient in receptors for GABA, a major inhibitory neurotransmitter (Charney, 2004; Nikolaus et al., 2010). Deficiencies in GABA lead to excessive activation in certain brain regions, especially the limbic structures associated with fear. Moreover, the fact that major medications for treating anxiety disorders work on GABA receptors is further evidence for GABA's role in anxiety. Genetic heritability estimates for generalized anxiety, panic disorder, and agoraphobia range from 30%–40% (Hettema, Neale, & Kendler, 2001; Maron, Hettema, & Shlik, 2010).

As for personality, people who are high in neuroticism—prone to worry, anxiety, and nervousness—are more likely to develop anxiety disorders (Eysenck, 1982; Hamer & Copeland, 1998). Degree of extraversion may play a role in some anxiety disorders as well. For instance, in panic disorder, people who are more introverted are more likely than those who are extraverted to avoid putting themselves in public situations (Rosellini et al., 2010).

An ambitious study that is changing the way psychologists view the interaction between biology and environment in the development of psychological disorders, including anxiety disorders, is the Adverse Childhood Experiences (ACE) study. For the ACE study, more than 17,000 participants have been interviewed about eight "adverse childhood experiences," including abuse, domestic violence, and serious household dysfunction (meaning that someone in the household abused drugs, had a psychological disorder, or committed criminal acts). Researchers correlated the adverse childhood experiences with health and mental health outcomes in adulthood.

The results were dramatic. The more adverse childhood experience participants reported, the worse the psychological outcomes. For example, someone who reported four or more adverse childhood experiences was two and a half times as likely to suffer from anxiety disorder as someone who reported no adverse childhood experiences (Anda et al., 2006). Perry (2002) found that when children were removed from neglectful home environments at age 1 or 2 and placed in caring foster homes, the size of their brains increased dramatically. If they were removed from the neglectful environment after age 4, however, there was little increase in brain size (circumference). If they were removed after age 5, there was almost no increase (see Figure 15.11).

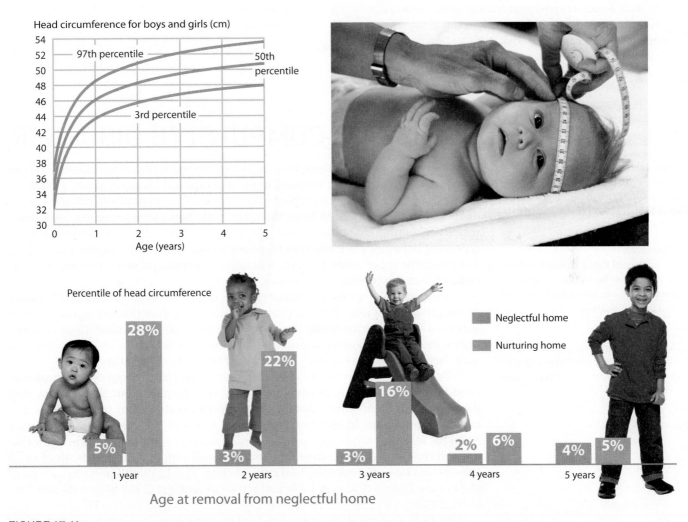

FIGURE **15.11**

EFFECTS OF NEGLECT AND REMOVAL FROM NEGLECTFUL ENVIRONMENTS ON CHILDREN'S BRAIN SIZE. Percentile of head circumference means the percentage of people in the population who have heads that are a particular size or smaller. Thus, 30th percentile means that only 30% of people have that size or smaller. The younger the child is when he or she is removed from a neglectful home, the larger the brain/head size is after 1 year in a nurturing foster home. (Perry, 2002)

Generally, for a child's brain size to be anywhere near normal, the child needs regular environmental stimulation by about age 4.

In summary, people who have the bad luck of having a genetic predisposition to anxiety, low levels of GABA, or the personality trait of neuroticism *along with* the experience of chronic stress or abuse are most likely to develop anxiety disorders. Those who have the biological predispositions *or* experience abuse are next most likely to develop these disorders, whereas those who have *neither* biological vulnerability nor chronically stressful experiences are least likely to develop these disorders.

Quick Quiz 15.4: Anxiety Disorders

1. The occurrence of two or more disorders at the same time is known as
   a. bipolar disorder.
   b. comorbidity.
   c. dipolarity.
   d. syndrome.

2. Maya is so preoccupied with fears of embarrassing or humiliating herself in public that she avoids going shopping or out for walks in town. What disorder best describes this set of symptoms?
   a. generalized anxiety disorder
   b. specific phobia

   c. panic disorder
   d. social phobia

3. People who are prone to anxiety are deficient in receptors for _____, a major inhibitory neurotransmitter.
   a. GABA
   b. glutamate
   c. serotonin
   d. dopamine

Answers can be found at the end of the chapter.

OBSESSIVE-COMPULSIVE DISORDER

obsessive-compulsive disorder (OCD)
An anxiety disorder in which obsessive thoughts lead to compulsive behaviors.

obsession
An unwanted thought, word, phrase, or image that persistently and repeatedly comes into a person's mind and causes distress.

compulsion
A repetitive behavior performed in response to uncontrollable urges or according to a ritualistic set of rules.

Obsessive-compulsive disorder (OCD) is a disorder that is manifested in both thought and behavior. An **obsession** is an unwanted thought, word, phrase, or image that persistently and repeatedly comes into a person's mind and causes distress. People with OCD have thoughts that they cannot dismiss, especially negative thoughts that most people can disregard (APA, 2013). A **compulsion** is a repetitive behavior performed in response to uncontrollable urges or according to a ritualistic set of rules. In short, obsessions are thought disturbances, whereas compulsions are repetitive behaviors.

Obsessive-compulsive disorder most often involves cleaning, checking, or counting behaviors that interfere with everyday functioning. A man who is obsessed with security might check that the front door is locked 15 or 20 times before being able to drive away; a woman who is obsessed with germs might wash her hands dozens or even hundreds of times throughout the day.

People who suffer from OCD often know that their thoughts are irrational, or at least that their compulsive behaviors are excessive, but they cannot stop themselves. In some cases, compulsive behaviors stem from superstitions. For example, a man might feel the need to tap the wall 65 times before leaving a room for fear that not doing so will mean that his parents will die. He knows rationally that there is no connection between wall tapping and the death of one's parents, but he performs the ritual nevertheless. The 12-month prevalence rate of OCD in the United States is 1.2%, and internationally it is between 1.1% and 1.8% (APA, 2013).

In OCD, too many thoughts are held in awareness, too much importance is ascribed to all thoughts (rational or irrational), and thinking about one's thoughts is excessive (Janeck et al., 2003). Research on cognitive performance in people with OCD reveals a preoccupation with conscious thinking; it is hard for people with this disorder to keep certain ideas or information out of their awareness.

Causes of Obsessive-Compulsive Disorder

Some scientists argue that the brain circuit that connects the caudate, the anterior cingulate cortex (ACC), and the limbic structures (such as the amygdala and hypothalamus) is working overtime in OCD (Aouizerate et al., 2004; J. M. Schwartz, 1999a, 1999b). The overactive ACC creates a perpetual feeling that something is wrong, which the limbic system structures translate into anxiety. In turn, anxiety stimulates more intrusive thoughts, which sometimes become compulsive actions. These actions occur as behavioral responses aimed at reducing the tensions or anxiety generated by the situation (from the caudate nucleus). Relief may be experienced, but only briefly, before the anxiety returns. The cycle goes on endlessly, due to the hyperactivity of the brain circuit—which is stuck in the "on" position. So this circuit involving the ACC, caudate nucleus, and limbic structures supports the obsessive thinking and compulsive responding (K. D. Fitzgerald et al., 2005; Guehl et al., 2008).

QUICK QUIZ 15.5: Obsessive-Compulsive Disorder

1. Rebecca has to count to seven chews every time she eats. If she is interrupted or loses count, she has to start all over again. This is an example of a(n)
   a. compulsion.
   b. obsession.
   c. anxiety.
   d. panic attack.

2. Joshua is constantly worried about getting sick from the germs everywhere he goes. He can't help but think about the germs, the germs, the germs. This is an example of a(n)
   a. compulsion.
   b. obsession.
   c. anxiety.
   d. panic attack.

Answers can be found at the end of the chapter.

POST-TRAUMATIC STRESS DISORDER

Post-traumatic stress disorder (PTSD) is one of the trauma- and stressor-related disorders and involves a set of intrusive and persistent cognitive, emotional, and physiological symptoms triggered by exposure to a catastrophic or horrifying event—such as experiences of war, attempted murder, rape, natural disasters, the sudden death of a loved one, or physical or sexual abuse. In order to receive a diagnosis of PTSD, one must have directly experienced a traumatic event or witnessed such an event occurring to others, learned of a violent or accidental extreme trauma (e.g., death or sexual violence) occurring to a loved one, and/or repeatedly been exposed to or reminded of the details of such an event (APA, 2013). People suffering from PTSD experience a number of intrusive symptoms that last for at least 1 month. These may include recurring intrusive thoughts, feelings, or memories of the traumatic event, either while awake or dreaming, as well as *flashbacks*, vivid reactions in which the person feels as if he or she were experiencing the traumatic event all over again. There may be avoidance of situations or stimuli that might trigger the recollection of the event, as well as a number of persistent cognitive symptoms, such as a distorted view of oneself and self-blame associated with the trauma, as well as persistent emotional and physiological reactivity. For instance, people with PTSD are easily startled, may have hair-trigger tempers, and may be reckless or self-destructive.

War veterans are at increased risk not only for PTSD but also for depression, drug abuse, and suicide after returning home. The depth of despair in war-induced

Post-traumatic stress disorder (PTSD)
A type of trauma- and stressor-related disorder that involves intrusive and persistent cognitive, emotional, and physiological symptoms triggered by catastrophic or horrifying events.

PTSD is seen in the following suicide note from an Iraq war veteran who took his own life in June 2013: "All day, every day a screaming agony in every nerve ending in my body. It is nothing short of torture. My mind is a wasteland, filled with visions of incredible horror, unceasing depression, and crippling anxiety" (Cook, 2013). Upwards of 24% of the veterans from Iraq have developed PTSD (Renshaw, 2011; Roehr, 2007; Tanielian & Jaycox, 2008). In fact, the hypothalamic-pituitary axis, a major neuroendocrine system of the stress response (see Chapter 12), may be dysfunctional in war veterans with PTSD (Golier, Caramanica & Yehuda, 2012).

People of all ages can experience post-traumatic stress symptoms, including children who have experienced a serious trauma, such as extreme physical or sexual abuse (APA, 2013; Nixon et al., 2010). Compared to healthy controls, children with post-traumatic stress symptoms show reduced brain activity in the hippocampus while performing a verbal memory task (Carrion et al., 2010). The hippocampus plays a central role in learning and memory, so these results suggest that post-traumatic stress interferes with learning.

DISSOCIATIVE DISORDERS

dissociative disorders
Psychological disorders characterized by extreme splits or gaps in memory, identity, or consciousness.

Daydreaming and being caught up in a great novel or movie are common, everyday experiences in which we may lose our sense of time, space, and ourselves. **Dissociative disorders** magnify this effect: They produce extreme disruptions or gaps in memory, identity, or consciousness. These disorders lack a clear physical cause, such as brain injury, and often stem from extreme stress, trauma, or abusive experiences, especially during childhood. Although dissociative disorders are often associated with trauma, the *DSM-5* places them in their own category. We focus on the most dramatic dissociative disorder: dissociative identity disorder.

Dissociative Identity Disorder

dissociative identity disorder (DID)
A dissociative disorder in which a person develops at least two distinct personalities, each with its own memories, thoughts, behaviors, and emotions. Some psychiatrists question the legitimacy of the disorder.

People with **dissociative identity disorder (DID)** develop at least two distinct personalities, each with a unique set of memories, behaviors, thoughts, and emotions. Consider the case of Eric, 29, who was found wandering around a shopping mall in Daytona Beach, Florida:

> Eric began talking to doctors in two voices: the infantile rhythms of "young Eric," a dim and frightened child, and the measured tones of "older Eric," who told a tale of terror and child abuse. According to "older Eric," after his immigrant German parents died, a harsh stepfather and his mistress took Eric from his native South Carolina to a drug dealer's hideout in a Florida swamp. Eric said he was raped by several gang members and watched his stepfather murder two men. (quoted in Comer, 2007, p. 208)

Eric had 27 distinct personalities, 3 of whom were female. Among these personalities were Dwight, a middle-aged and quiet man; Michael, an arrogant jock; Phillip, an argumentative lawyer; and Jeffrey, a blind, mute, and rather hysterical man.

Eric is a classic example of what used to be called "multiple personality disorder" but is now referred to as dissociative identity disorder. The symptoms of dissociative identity disorder include two or more distinct personality states, amnesia, and self-destructive behaviors. People with dissociative identity disorder may not remember anything about an experience or a particular period of their life and may cut themselves. Up to 70% have attempted suicide. Also somewhat common are fugue states, in which people do not recall anything about how they got to where they are. For instance, they might end up at a beach or nightclub or at home but have no memory of how they came to be there.

Although it may not be diagnosed until adolescence, DID often develops in childhood but may develop at any period of life (APA, 2013; Comer, 2007). Although the sample size was relatively small, one study found that only about 1.5% of people had the disorder during the last 12-month period prior to the survey (APA, 2013). A history of sexual or physical abuse is very common. In another study, more than 90% of people with DID reported being either sexually or physically abused (Ellason, Ross, & Fuchs, 1996).

However, the diagnosis of DID is somewhat controversial, with some psychiatrists claiming the diagnosis is not real but rather is produced unintentionally by therapists themselves (Putnam & McHugh, 2005). Further, there is a lack of solid research on the causes of the disorder. According to a recent review of a decade's worth of published cases of DID, the causes are still not well understood and are controversial, and actual occurrence rates are hard to identify (Boysen & VanBergen, 2013; Brand, Loewenstein & Speigel, 2013).

Causes of Dissociative Disorders

People who suffer from dissociative disorders have one characteristic in common: They lived through a highly traumatic experience. Many suffered sexual or physical abuse or survived a terrible accident or natural disaster in which a loved one was killed. Most explanations of dissociative disorders view them as a coping strategy gone awry (Putnam, 2006). The experience was so traumatic that the individual disconnects or dissociates the self from the event as a way of having it happen not to "him" or "her" but rather to "someone else." However, not everyone who experiences traumatic events develops a dissociative disorder. Also, some researchers and clinicians argue that DID results from a complex interaction of social-cognitive factors, including problems with attention and memory, disruptions in the sleep-wake cycle, and exposure to trauma or intense stress (Lynn et al., 2012). Other theorists argue that particular personality traits, such as susceptibility to hypnotism, make some people more likely to develop dissociative disorders (Kihlstrom, 2005).

SOMATIC SYMPTOM DISORDERS

Some disorders take bodily or physical form and mimic physical diseases. The general term for these disorders is **somatic symptom disorders.** As you may recall from our discussion of the neuron, *soma* means "body"; hence, the term *somatic* means "bodily." An older term for bodily disorders—hypochondriasis—has now been divided into two related but distinct disorders: somatic symptom disorder and illness anxiety disorder.

somatic symptom disorder
A psychological disorder in which a person complains of multiple physical disorders that cause disruption and that persist for at least 6 months.

Somatic symptom disorder occurs when a person complains of multiple physical disorders that cause distress and disruption of the person's life and that persist for at least 6 months. This disorder has the following two main criteria (APA, 2013):

- One or more distressing somatic symptoms that disrupt daily life
- Excessive thoughts, feelings, or behaviors related to bodily symptoms

Somatic symptom disorder occurs in 5%–7% of the U.S. adult population (APA, 2013).

Some people have just the fear of the somatic symptoms and therefore would be diagnosed with **illness anxiety disorder,** DSM5 says illness preoccupation must be present for at least 6 months. A person with this disorder will also frequently and excessively check for the symptoms.

illness anxiety disorder
Fear of somatic symptoms but without any somatic symptoms.

With the Internet and easy access to medical information, more and more people are self-diagnosing without evidence of real symptoms and without professional evaluations. People who self-diagnose primarily from information found on the Internet are informally referred to as *cyberchondriacs* (R. W. White & Horvitz, 2009).

Quick Quiz 15.6: PTSD, Dissociative Disorders, and Somatic Symptom Disorders

1. What is one of the most serious and common mental disorders suffered by war veterans?
   a. dissociative disorder
   b. somatic symptom disorder
   c. post-traumatic stress disorder
   d. schizophrenia
2. _____ produce extreme splits or gaps in memory, identity, or consciousness.
   a. Dissociative disorders
   b. Bipolar disorders
   c. Mood disorders
   d. Cognitive disorders

3. The primary difference between somatic symptom disorder and illness anxiety disorder is
   a. illness anxiety disorder does not have somatic symptoms.
   b. illness anxiety disorder has only somatic symptoms.
   c. only somatic symptom disorder involves persistent concern about bodily symptoms.
   d. only somatic symptom disorder involves anxiety.

Answers can be found at the end of the chapter.

PERSONALITY DISORDERS

personality disorders
Patterns of cognition, emotion, and behavior that develop in late childhood or adolescence and are maladaptive and inflexible; more consistent than clinical disorders.

As we saw in Chapter 13, personality consists of an individual's unique, long-term behavior patterns. **Personality disorders** are maladaptive and inflexible patterns of cognition, emotion, and behavior that generally develop in late childhood or adolescence and continue into adulthood. There are three distinct clusters of personality disorders: odd-eccentric, dramatic-emotional, and anxious-fearful (see Figure 15.12). Almost 15% of the general adult population (older than 18) and 20% of the young adult population (ages 18–25) suffer from some form of personality disorder (APA, 2013; Blanco et al., 2008; Lenzenweger et al., 2007).

Odd-Eccentric Personality Disorders

schizoid personality disorder
An odd-eccentric personality disorder characterized by a desire to avoid close relationships as well as by emotional aloofness, reclusivity, and a lack of humor.

schizotypal personality disorder
An odd-eccentric personality disorder characterized by a desire to live in an isolated and asocial life but also by the presence of odd thoughts, perceptual distortions, and beliefs.

paranoid personality disorder
An odd-eccentric personality disorder characterized by extreme suspicions and mistrust of others in unwarranted and maladaptive ways.

The three major odd-eccentric personality disorders are schizoid, schizotypal, and paranoid (APA, 2013). People with **schizoid personality disorder** do not want close relationships; are emotionally aloof, reclusive, and humorless; and want to live solitary lives. They always choose solitary activities; have little to no interest in sex; lack any close friends; and appear indifferent to praise or criticism from others. Similarly, a person with **schizotypal personality disorder** is isolated and asocial but in addition has very odd thoughts, perceptual distortions, and beliefs. For instance, people with schizotypal personality disorder may believe that stories on TV or in the newspaper were written directly about them. Moreover, the person dresses, acts, and appears in peculiar or eccentric ways.

People with **paranoid personality disorder** are extremely suspicious and mistrustful of other people, in ways that are both unwarranted and not adaptive. They may often test the loyalty of their friends and lovers because they believe others are trying to harm them. They may be regularly suspicious of their spouses' faithfulness even if there is no evidence they have been unfaithful. If someone does slight or insult them, they often hold a grudge for an unusually long time. For example, if someone with paranoid personality disorder discovers

Cluster	Major symptoms	Personality disorders
Odd-eccentric	Lack of interest in social relationships, inappropriate or flat emotion, thought, and coldness	Schizoid
	Isolated, odd, and bizarre thoughts and beliefs	Schizotypal
	Extreme, unwarranted, and maladaptive suspicion	Paranoid
Dramatic-emotional	Wild, exaggerated behaviors, extreme need for attention, suicidal, seductive, unstable relationships, shifting moods	Histrionic
	Shifting moods, dramatic, impulsive, self-injury (e.g., cutting)	Borderline
	Grandiose thoughts and sense of one's importance, exploitative, arrogant, lack of concern for others	Narcissistic
	Impulsive, violent, deceptive, and criminal behavior; no respect for social norms, ruthless	Antisocial
Anxious-fearful	Anxious and worrying, sense of inadequacy, fear of being criticized, nervousness, avoids social interaction	Avoidant
	Pervasive selflessness, need to be cared for, fear of rejection, total dependence on and submission to others	Dependent
	Extreme perfectionism and anxiety over minor disruption of routine, very rigid activities and relationships, pervades most aspects of everyday life	Obsessive-compulsive

FIGURE **15.12**

THREE CLUSTERS OF PERSONALITY DISORDERS AND THEIR MAJOR SYMPTOMS.
(APA, 2013)

that a colleague has just been promoted to a position she had wanted, she might conclude that the boss does not appreciate her and is actively trying to sabotage her career. When she sees coworkers talking later that day, she might assume that they are talking about her in a disparaging manner.

Dramatic-Emotional Personality Disorders

Another class of personality disorder involves dramatic and emotional disorders, of which there are four (APA, 2013). People with **histrionic personality disorder** want very much to be the center of attention and often behave in very dramatic, seductive, flamboyant, and exaggerated ways. They can also be very emotional, intense, self-centered, and shallow in their emotions and relationships. Those with **borderline personality disorder** have out-of-control emotions, are very afraid of being abandoned by others, and vacillate between idealizing and despising those who are close to them. They are more likely than most to hurt themselves (cutting, burning, or attempting suicide) or suffer from eating disorders or substance abuse. Individuals with **narcissistic personality disorder** have an extremely positive and arrogant self-image, and most of their time and attention are self-focused. They have an exaggerated sense of self-importance and are grandiose. As a result, they often make unrealistic and unreasonable demands of others and ignore others' needs or wishes. They may be quite successful and climb the career ladder very quickly, but their narcissism often isolates them from others.

To many, the most captivating of all personality disorders is antisocial personality. Formerly known as "sociopathic" or "psychopathic" personality, **antisocial personality disorder** is marked by extremely impulsive, deceptive, violent, ruthless, and callous behaviors. People with antisocial personality

histrionic personality disorder
A dramatic-emotional personality disorder characterized by the desire to be the center of attention and by dramatic, seductive, flamboyant, and exaggerated behaviors.

borderline personality disorder
A dramatic-emotional personality disorder characterized by out-of-control emotions, fear of being abandoned by others, and vacillation between idealizing and despising people who are close to the person with the disorder.

narcissistic personality disorder
A dramatic-emotional personality disorder characterized by having an extremely positive and arrogant self-image and being extraordinarily self-centered; other symptoms are an exaggerated sense of self-importance and grandiosity.

antisocial personality disorder
A dramatic-emotional personality disorder characterized by extremely impulsive, ruthless, and callous behaviors; a serious and potentially dangerous disorder.

disorder are most likely to engage in criminal, deceptive, and violent behaviors. Although only about 3% of the population has this disorder, between 45% and 75% of male prison inmates are diagnosed with it (Fazel & Danesh, 2002; Hare, 1993). Only about 20% of female prisoners are diagnosed with antisocial personality disorder (Fazel & Danesh, 2002). Do not confuse *antisocial* with *asocial*. Antisocial personality is a serious and potentially dangerous disorder, whereas being asocial simply means being shy and not enjoying social situations. Indeed, the case of serial killer Ted Bundy, with whom we opened the chapter, is an extreme example of someone suffering from antisocial personality disorder.

Anxious-Fearful Personality Disorders

The third cluster of personality disorders consists of the avoidant, dependent, and obsessive-compulsive personality disorders. Each of these is characterized by persistent high levels of anxiety, nervousness, and fear.

People with **avoidant personality disorder** are so afraid of being criticized that they avoid interacting with others and become socially isolated. They often feel inadequate and have low self-esteem; therefore, they tend to choose professions that allow them to be alone. People with **dependent personality disorder** fear rejection and have a strong need to be cared for. They feel safe only in dependent relationships with others; ironically, however, they tend to drive others away because they are so clingy and demanding. People with **obsessive-compulsive personality disorder (OCPD)** are very rigid in their habits, extremely perfectionistic in how things have to be done, and frequently very rigid list makers and rule followers. This personality disorder is similar to the clinical disorder with the same name but is more general and does not have true obsessions and compulsions. Also, people with OCD know they have a problem, whereas people with OCPD are convinced their way is the right and only way things can be done. In short, OCD is usually focused only on cleanliness or checking, whereas obsessive-compulsive personality disorder is focused on all aspects of a person's life, as illustrated in the following case study of a 32-year-old accountant:

> For many years he has maintained an almost inviolate schedule. On weekdays he arises at 6:47, has two eggs soft-boiled for 2 minutes, 45 seconds, and is at his desk at 8:15. Lunch is at 12:00, dinner at 6:00, bedtime at 11:00. He has separate Saturday and Sunday schedules, the latter characterized by a methodical and thorough trip through the *New York Times*. Any change in schedule causes him to feel varying degrees of anxiety, annoyance, and a sense that he is doing something wrong and wasting his time. . . . [His] major problems are with women and follow the same repetitive pattern. At first, things go well. Soon, however, he begins to resent the intrusion upon his schedule a woman inevitably causes. This is most strongly illustrated in the bedtime arrangements. He must spray his sinuses, take two aspirin, straighten the apartment, do 35 sit-ups and read two pages of the dictionary.
> (Spitzer and colleagues, quoted in Nolen-Hoeksema, 2007, pp. 451–452)

Nature and Nurture Explanations of Personality Disorders

Research on murderers has identified a cluster of traits possessed by most of these violent criminals: being male, coming from abusive and neglectful households, having at least one psychological disorder (often antisocial personality disorder), and having suffered some kind of injury to the head or brain (Pincus, 1999, 2001; Strueber, Lueck, & Roth, 2006–2007). The frontal lobes and amygdala

avoidant personality disorder
An anxious-fearful personality disorder characterized by extreme fear of being criticized, low self-esteem, and avoidance of social interaction.

dependent personality disorder
An anxious-fearful personality disorder characterized by fear of being rejected and a strong need to be cared for.

obsessive-compulsive personality disorder (OCPD)
An anxious-fearful personality disorder characterized by rigid habits and extreme perfectionism; more general than obsessive-compulsive disorder.

In the film *Monster*, Charlize Theron portrayed Aileen Wuornos, a prostitute who confessed to killing several men. Abandoned by her parents in childhood, Wuornos later ran away from her grandparents' home and turned to prostitution to support herself. At one of her trials, a psychiatrist testified that she was mentally ill with borderline personality disorder. Nevertheless, she was convicted of murder and later executed.

of many violent criminals are unusually disordered in size, activity, and function (Raine, 2013; Yang et al., 2009). Just being abused, having a psychological disorder, or suffering a brain injury is not enough. To become antisocial and violent, a person usually has to experience all of these conditions.

Moreover, as a result of suffering head injuries, living in a constant state of fear and abuse, or both, murderers almost always have moderate to severe problems of impulse control, social intelligence, working memory, and attention (Strueber et al., 2006–2007). Recall the principle of neuroplasticity from Chapter 3. Research on brain development suggests that living under a constant threat of abuse and stress changes the neural connectivity in the brain, making it less likely to develop many complex synaptic connections, especially in the frontal lobes. Being in a constant state of fear often leads to neural systems that are primed for unusually high levels of anxiety, impulsive behavior, and a state of constant alertness. These are all conditions that might lead to violent or criminal behaviors. Finally, genetics interacts with abusive experience to create personality disorders. Different forms of one particular gene, for instance, when coupled with being abused as a child, make violent and antisocial behavior in adulthood more likely (Caspi et al., 2002).

Connection

Neuroplasticity occurs when neurons and hence brain structure and function change as a result of input from the environment.

See "Brain Plasticity and Neurogenesis," Chapter 3, "The Biology of Behavior," p. 100.

Connection

How does our first environment—the womb—shape the expression of our genes?

See "Epigenetics: How the Environment Changes Gene Expression," Chapter 3, "The Biology of Behavior," p. 76.

Quick Quiz 15.7: Personality Disorders

1. People with _____ personality disorder are so afraid of being criticized that they stay away from others and become socially isolated.
   a. borderline
   b. avoidant
   c. dependent
   d. psychopathic

2. Individuals with which kind of personality disorder are most likely to commit crimes and end up in jail?
   a. asocial
   b. narcissistic
   c. antisocial
   d. avoidant

Answers can be found at the end of the chapter.

Psychology in the Real World

Can Internet Use Become an Addiction?

In March 2010, police discovered that a couple in South Korea had starved their 3-month-old daughter due to neglect caused by their constant preoccupation with the online multiplayer fantasy game *Prius Online*. The tragic irony is that in the parents' version of *Prius Online*, they were raising a virtual baby (Greenemeier, 2013)!

As this case demonstrates, some people just can't stay offline. For many people, this in itself may not be a serious problem. In some cases, however, people are online all day; they check their Facebook or Twitter feeds dozens or even hundreds of times a day, and they cannot continue their work or activities around the home without logging on. For them, Internet use has become so intrusive that it adversely affects their professional and personal lives in the real world.

As with all disorders, something becomes a problem once it causes clinically significant disruptions of everyday life. For the first time, the *DSM-5* includes a category called Internet gaming disorder, but due to insufficient and inconclusive evidence it is classified as a "Condition for Further Study." Any five of nine criteria must be present during a 12-month period for a diagnosis to be made:

1. Preoccupation with Internet games (not Internet gambling)
2. Withdrawal symptoms when games are taken away (e.g., irritability, sadness, anxiety)
3. Tolerance—that is, more and more time is needed to be satisfied
4. Unsuccessful attempts to stop or control one's habit
5. Loss of interest in previous hobbies and entertainment
6. Continued excessive use despite knowing of their psychological problems
7. Deceives family, friends, and therapists about how much one plays games
8. Use of Internet games to cope or escape from a negative mood
9. Jeopardized or loss of a significant relationship, job, or educational/career opportunity due to Internet gaming activity

Some of these criteria are, in fact, signs of addiction—namely, tolerance, mood regulation, and disruption of relationships, job, or school. Moreover, researchers have suggested that some people do experience behavioral withdrawal symptoms, such as emotions of irritation and anger, when the computer or smartphone is not available (Block, 2008). The Chinese government has labeled compulsive and disruptive Internet use "an addiction" (APA, 2013).

Although there are more than 250 publications on gaming or Internet use disorder, and some evidence does suggest it may be addictive, mental health professionals do not completely agree on whether excessive and dysfunctional Internet use is an addiction, a compulsion, or an impulse disorder (Petry & O'Brien, 2013).

In a review of the research from the United States, between 9.8% and 15.2% of high school and college students met the criteria for Internet dependency (M. Moreno et al., 2011). Averages from studies across Europe and Asia report that 12% excessively play computer games, 10% abuse them, and 3% are dependent upon them. In China, prevalence rates for Internet disorder range from 8%–13.5%, with males outnumbering females about two to one (Wu et al., 2013). For Massively Multiplayer Online Role-Playing Games (MMORPGs), the rates of dysfunctional use were even higher, with 18% experiencing academic, health, or relationship problems (and 8% saying they spend more than 40 hours a week playing video games).

Worldwide, more people than ever before are relying on their mobile devices for texting, using social network sites, and perusing the Internet. Some psychologists describe *mobile addiction* as the excessive, impulsive checking and use of a mobile device (e.g., smartphone), especially in potentially dangerous or illegal contexts, such as while driving (Salehan & Negahban, 2013).

Whether these forms of technology dependency meet the criteria for mental disorders remains to be seen, but we know that overuse of such devices may have deleterious effects, such as impaired cognition and task performance while multitasking (Borst, Taatgen, & Van Rijn, 2010). As more and more of us engage our time in such multitasking, we are likely to feel the effects of such chronic distraction on a social level.

Bringing It All Together

Making Connections in Psychological Disorders

Creativity and Mental Health

For thousands of years, people have associated "madness" with "genius." Many of the world's most creative people have been touched by more than their fair share of mental instability, if not outright "madness." Perhaps, some have argued, that is just the price of greatness (Ludwig, 1995). Amadeus Mozart, Ludwig von Beethoven, Robert Schumann, Vincent van Gogh, Virginia Woolf, Ernest Hemingway, William Styron, Jackson Pollock, Howard Hughes, Sylvia Plath, Salvador Dalí, and the Nobel Prize-winning mathematician John F. Nash, Jr., are just some of the creative geniuses who have suffered from a psychological disorder. So many creative individuals have experienced some psychological condition that many people think creativity and disorders of the mind are connected. The term *mad genius* reflects this belief. To be clear, however, suffering from psychological disorders is not necessary to be creative. There are, however—at least in art, literature, poetry, and music—higher rates of disorders than in the general population (Ludwig, 1995; Post, 1994).

Challenge Your Assumptions

True or False? All the great artists in history can be viewed as psychologically disturbed.

False: Creative artists are at higher risk for mental illness over the course of their lifetimes, but there are many exceptions to the rule. There is no causal connection between the two.

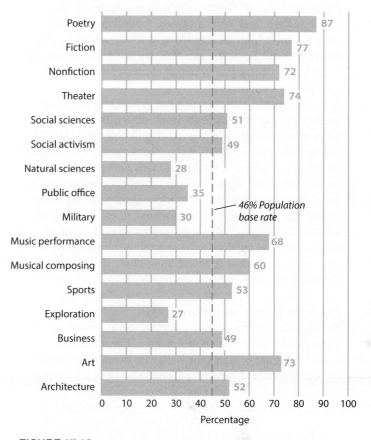

FIGURE **15.13**

LIFETIME RATES OF PSYCHOLOGICAL DISORDERS IN FAMOUS PEOPLE IN 16 PROFESSIONS. (Adapted from Ludwig, 1995)

Exploring the connection between psychological disorders and creativity offers an opportunity to look again at the topics discussed in this chapter. We address two questions: (1) What is the evidence that creative people suffer from psychological disorders at a higher rate than the rest of the population? (2) Which disorders are more likely to be linked with creativity?

Evidence for a Relationship between Creativity and Psychological Disorders

To help us answer the first question, we can look at an impressive study of creativity and psychological disorder conducted by Arnold Ludwig. In a biographical study of 1,005 eminent people in 18 professions, Ludwig (1995) examined the lifetime rates of psychological disorder across the professions and over lifetimes. Lifetime rate is the likelihood that a person will suffer a disorder at some point in his or her lifetime. Lifetime rates for any psychiatric illness are remarkably high for people in the arts: 87% of poets, 77% of fiction writers, 74% of actors, 73% of visual artists, 72% of nonfiction writers, 68% of musical performers, and 60% of musical composers (see Figure 15.13). Compare these figures with the 46% lifetime rate in the general population for any disorder (Kessler et al., 2005). The data from this large-scale study clearly indicate a higher prevalence of disorder in creative artists than in the general population.

Which Disorders Affect Creative Individuals?

Not all disorders are associated with creative ability. There is evidence, however, for a connection between creativity and many of the disorders discussed in this chapter.

Autism Spectrum Disorder and Creativity

Some people with Autism spectrum disorder are extremely gifted in one domain, such as music or math, a phenomenon known as savant syndrome (see Chapter 10). Most autistic savants do not produce great works of original genius, because their amazing feats of calculation and recall are not original. However, some savants produce truly creative works of art, usually math analyses, musical compositions, drawings, or paintings (M. Fitzgerald, 2004). One of the 20th century's greatest mathematicians, Srinivasa Ramanujan, showed clear signs of childhood autism (Fitzgerald, 2004). Composer Wolfgang Amadeus Mozart also may have been such a savant. A contemporary creative savant is Matt Savage (born in 1992), who was diagnosed with autism at the age of 3. He is a professional jazz musician and composer who had recorded three albums by the time he was 14.

Asperger syndrome, or what is now known as high-functioning autism, has been associated with creative ability in science, math, and engineering (E. J. Austin, 2005; Baron-Cohen et al., 2001). Baron-Cohen and his colleagues report that engineers, mathematicians, and physical scientists score much higher than nonscientists on measures of high-functioning autism or Asperger syndrome and score higher than social scientists on a nonclinical measure of autism. Children with Asperger are more than twice as likely as normal children to have a father or grandfather who was an engineer (Baron-Cohen et al., 1997; Baron-Cohen et al., 1998; Baron-Cohen et al., 2001).

Psychotic Symptoms and Creativity

Having unusual thoughts is common to both creative people and those with schizophrenia. For instance, much of the art of Salvador Dalí, who claimed to be psychotic, consists of bizarre, dreamlike images bordering on the kinds of delusions experienced by people with schizophrenia. John F. Nash, Jr., the mathematician made famous by the book and movie *A Beautiful Mind*, is a creative person who also has schizophrenia (Nasar, 1998). He is creative despite, rather than because of, the psychotic episodes he has experienced; all of his creative work preceded his schizophrenic symptoms and stopped after they began.

It is the milder psychotic symptoms, however, that are most strongly associated with creativity (Fink et al., 2012; Kinney et al., 2000–2001; Nettle & Clegg, 2005; Schuldberg, 2000–2001). Each of the following groups of people manifest unusual thought processes that are milder than those of schizophrenia: first-degree relatives of individuals with schizophrenia, people with schizotypal personality disorder, and those who score high on the normal personality dimension of psychoticism (see Chapter 13). These people are more likely to have unusual thought processes that develop into creative achievements that other people recognize to be significant (Burch et al., 2006; Fisher et al., 2004). Having a lot of ideas come to mind quickly can lead to many unusual associations that may be creative, but they may also be so unusual as to be similar to the bizarre associations seen in people with schizophrenia (Carson, Peterson, & Higgins, 2003; Eysenck, 1995; Fink et al., 2012). Recent evidence has uncovered variations in a gene (*neuregulin 1*) that appears to connect psychosis and creativity; it may partially explain why a maladaptive trait such as schizophrenia would continue in the gene pool (Keri, 2009; Venkatasubramanian & Kalmady, 2010).

Depression and Creativity

Emotional distress is a familiar companion to creative people. Many highly creative people have suffered from major depression (Ludwig, 1995). Across the 16 professions identified in Figure 15.13, the lifetime rate of just depression

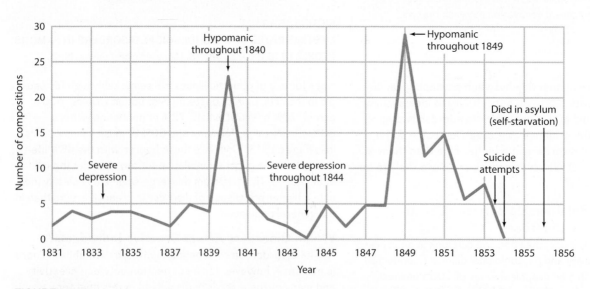

FIGURE 15.14

BIPOLAR DISORDER AND CREATIVITY IN THE WORK OF ROBERT SCHUMANN. The composer's creative output coincided directly with the highs and lows of his disorder. His most productive years (1840 and 1849) were marked by his most hypomanic periods. (Adapted from Slater & Meyer, 1959)

was 30%, with poets (77%), fiction writers (59%), and visual artists (50%) having the highest rates. In addition, poets are 20 times more likely to commit suicide, a key indicator for depression, than most people (Ludwig, 1995). One recent study, in fact, found that social rejection combined with a biological disposition toward depression enhanced participants' artistic creativity (Akinola & Mendes, 2008). In less creative populations, there is often only a weak relationship between depression and creativity (Silvia & Kimbrel, 2010).

Connection

Creative thinking requires novelty and connections among ideas.

See "What Is Creativity?" in Chapter 10, "Intelligence, Problem Solving, and Creativity," p. 383.

Although highly creative artists and writers may have a higher rate of depression than the general population, depressive episodes themselves do not generate much creative output. Recall that a complete lack of motivation is a common symptom of depression, so lower productivity would follow. Still, the experiences one has while depressed might inspire and motivate the creation of works of art as a way of understanding it.

Bipolar Disorder and Creativity

For more than three decades, studies of the relationship between psychological disorders and creativity have devoted more attention to bipolar illness than to any other condition (Andreasen & Glick, 1988; Bowden, 1994; Fodor & Laird, 2004; Jamison, 1993; Ludwig, 1995). Actors (17%), poets (13%), architects (13%), and nonfiction writers (11%) all exceed a 10% lifetime rate of bipolar disorder—10 times the rate in the general population (Ludwig, 1995).

There is a positive relationship between bipolar disorder and creative thought. For instance, some studies show that highly creative people are more likely than noncreative people to have bipolar disorder (Andreasen, 1987, 2006; Jamison, 1993; Jamison et al., 1980; R. L. Richards, 1994). Others report the other side of the coin: People with bipolar disorder are likely to be more creative than those without this condition (Fodor & Laird, 2004; R. L. Richards, 1994; R. L. Richards & Kinney, 1990). Indeed, many creative individuals throughout history have been bipolar (Jamison, 1993).

The manic phase is more likely than the depressive phase to generate creative behavior (Andreasen & Glick, 1988; Jamison et al., 1980). For example, Robert Schumann's creative output spiked with his manic episodes (see Figure 15.14). Few artists and writers are creative during their depressed phases; rather, they are creatively inspired during the milder form of mania, the hypomanic phase.

Chapter Review

DEFINING PSYCHOLOGICAL DISORDERS

- Psychologists agree on four general criteria for a psychological disorder: disruptive, distressing, dysfunctional, and deviant (but only if also dysfunctional).

- A major tool for diagnosing disorders is the *Diagnostic and Statistical Manual (DSM-5)*.

NEURODEVELOPMENTAL DISORDERS

- The most common disorders to affect children are attention deficit hyperactivity disorder (ADHD) and autism spectrum disorder.

- ADHD consists of severe inattention, hyperactivity, and impulsivity.

- Children with autism spectrum disorder (ASD) show very inward-focused behaviors, with severe language and social impairment combined with repetitive habits and behaviors. They also have serious deficits in understanding other people's thoughts, feelings, and intentions.

SCHIZOPHRENIA

- Schizophrenia is a psychotic disorder of profound disturbances in thought, perception, and emotion.

- Positive symptoms of schizophrenia include hallucinations, delusional thinking, and disorganized thought and speech.

- Negative symptoms of schizophrenia include nonresponsiveness, flattened affect, immobility or strange poses, reduction of speaking, and inability to complete tasks.

- Cognitive symptoms of schizophrenia include disordered thinking, including impaired attention and profound difficulty in monitoring conflicting sources of information.

DEPRESSIVE DISORDERS

- People with major depressive disorder experience a pervasive low mood, lack of motivation, low energy, and feelings of worthlessness and guilt.

BIPOLAR DISORDER

- Bipolar disorder involves substantial mood fluctuation between depressive and manic episodes, with bipolar I being more severe and longer-lasting than bipolar II.

ANXIETY DISORDERS

- Anxiety disorders occur when fears and worrying are out of proportion to the situation and interfere with everyday functioning.

- Generalized anxiety disorder, a pervasive state of anxiety lasting at least 6 months, consists of excessive worrying about relatively minor events of daily life.

- Panic disorder is extreme anxiety about having a panic attack.

- Social phobia (social anxiety disorder), a pronounced fear of humiliation in the presence of others, is marked by severe self-consciousness about appearance, behavior, or both.

- Specific phobias involve an intense fear when confronted with particular situations or objects, such as spiders or heights.

OBSESSIVE-COMPULSIVE DISORDER

- Obsessive-compulsive disorder is a disorder of thought (obsession) and behavior (compulsion).

- Obsessions are anxiety-producing thoughts that can preoccupy a person throughout the day and are beyond the person's control.

- Compulsions are repetitive behaviors, which are often rituals that people have developed to control the anxiety created by the obsessions.

POST-TRAUMATIC STRESS DISORDER

- PTSD involves a set of intrusive and persistent cognitive, emotional, and physiological symptoms triggered by exposure to a catastrophic or horrifying event—such as experiences of war, attempted murder, rape, natural disasters, sudden death of a loved one, or physical or sexual abuse.

DISSOCIATIVE DISORDERS

- Dissociative disorders entail the loss of a sense of time and space but also involve extreme gaps in memories, identity, or consciousness.

- People with dissociative identity disorder (DID) develop at least two distinct personalities, each of whom has a unique set of memories, behaviors, thoughts, and emotions. Some experts have reservations about classifying DID as a disorder.

SOMATIC SYMPTOM DISORDERS

- Somatic symptom disorder occurs when a person complains of one or more distressing somatic symptoms that disrupt daily life coupled with excessive thoughts, feelings or behaviors related to the bodily symptoms.

- Illness anxiety disorder is diagnosed in the absence of somatic symptoms and when the person nevertheless has a preoccupation with and extreme anxiety about acquiring a serious illness.

PERSONALITY DISORDERS

- Personality disorders differ from clinical disorders in being generally a more consistent part of a person's personality than the clinical disorders (e.g., schizophrenia, depression, and bipolar disorder).

- The schizoid personality is very emotionally cold, reclusive, humorless, or uninteresting; someone with schizotypal personality disorder expresses very odd thoughts and behavior, is socially isolated, and has a restricted range of emotions.

- Paranoid personality disorder is marked by extreme suspiciousness and mistrust of other people, in ways that are both unwarranted and not adaptive.

- Those with borderline personality disorder suffer from out-of-control emotions, are very afraid of being abandoned by others, and vacillate between idealizing those close to them and despising them.

- People with dependent personality disorder fear rejection and have such a strong need to be cared for that they form very clingy relationships with others.

- Antisocial personality disorder is marked by extremely impulsive, deceptive, violent, and ruthless behaviors.

BRINGING IT ALL TOGETHER: MAKING CONNECTIONS IN PSYCHOLOGICAL DISORDERS

- Creativity and psychological disorders are related, especially in the arts. Disorders such as depression, bipolar disorder, anxiety disorders, substance abuse, and suicide occur at higher rates in creative artists than in members of other professions and in the general population.

Key Terms

agoraphobia, p. 572

antisocial personality disorder, p. 579

attention deficit hyperactivity disorder (ADHD), p. 555

autism spectrum disorder (ASD), p. 556

avoidant personality disorder, p. 580

bipolar disorder, p. 567

borderline personality disorder, p. 579

cognitive symptoms (of schizophrenia), p. 559

comorbidity, p. 553

compulsion, p. 574

cyclothymia, p. 568

delusions, p. 559

dependent personality disorder, p. 580

depressive disorder, p. 563

diathesis-stress model, p. 559

dissociative disorders, p. 576

dissociative identity disorder (DID), p. 576

generalized anxiety disorder (GAD), p. 570

hallucinations, p. 558

histrionic personality disorder, p. 579

hypomanic episodes, p. 567

illness anxiety disorder, p. 577

joint attention, p. 556

major depressive disorder, p. 563

manic episodes, p. 567

narcissistic personality disorder, p. 579

negative symptoms (of schizophrenia), p. 559

obsession, p. 574

obsessive-compulsive disorder (OCD), p. 574

obsessive-compulsive personality disorder (OCPD), p. 580

panic attacks, p. 570

panic disorder, p. 571

paranoid personality disorder, p. 578

persistent depressive disorder (PDD), p. 564

personality disorders, p. 578

phobia, p. 571

positive symptoms (of schizophrenia), p. 558

post-traumatic stress disorder (PTSD), p. 575

psychotic disorders, p. 558

schizoid personality disorder, p. 578

schizophrenia, p. 558

schizotypal personality disorder, p. 578

social phobia (social anxiety disorder), p. 571

somatic symptom disorders, p. 577

syndrome, p. 551

word salad, p. 559

Quick Quiz Answers

Quick Quiz 15.1: 1. a 2. d   **Quick Quiz 15.2:** 1. c 2. c 3. b   **Quick Quiz 15.3:** 1. c 2. b 3. d   **Quick Quiz 15.4:** 1. b 2. d 3. a

Quick Quiz 15.5: 1. a 2. b   **Quick Quiz 15.6:** 1. c 2. a 3. a   **Quick Quiz 15.7:** 1. a 2. c

16 Treatment of Psychological Disorders

Chapter Outline

Biomedical Treatments for Psychological Disorders
Psychological Treatments for Psychological Disorders
Technology-Based Treatments for Psychological Disorders
Combined Approaches
Emerging Therapies
Preventing Disorders
Chapter Review

Challenge Your Assumptions

True or False?

- Shock therapy is never effective and is no longer used. (see page 596)

- Direct stimulation of neurons by electrical impulse is science fiction and is not used in treatment today. (see page 596)

- People can learn to not be afraid of flying. (see page 603)

- Talk therapy might make people feel better, but it does not change the brain. (see page 607)

589

Sometime in the year 2000, Deanna's world began to shut down. For no apparent reason, she fell into a severe and enduring depression: She felt no sense of emotional connection to anyone, utter despair, and ultimately an enduring emotional numbness. Deanna said it felt as if all the color had drained out of her life (Dobbs, 2006b). She tried everything, including psychotherapy, a vast array of medications, electroconvulsive therapy—nothing helped end her misery in any lasting way. She often thought about suicide.

Then Deanna volunteered for an innovative and risky experimental treatment under the leadership of psychiatrist Helen Mayberg. Mayberg implanted an electrode deep in Deanna's brain to stimulate areas thought to be involved in the neurocircuitry of depression. Immediately after the electrode was activated, the colors seeped back into her life. How could deep brain stimulation turn off depression like a switch? Was this momentary relief or a permanent cure?

In this chapter we discuss not only Mayberg's innovative discovery of brain stimulation for the treatment of severe depression but also more mainstream therapies, such as how restructuring thoughts can alleviate depression, panic disorder, and specific phobias. Moreover, we examine the various drug treatments for psychological disorders, describe their features, and look at how well they work, as well as consider less traditional approaches that make use of integrative therapies, meditation, or even virtual reality. The multitude of approaches reflects the ongoing challenge of treating psychological disorders.

Nowhere is the complex interaction between biology and the environment on more profound display than in the development and treatment of psychological disorders. Although we begin by discussing biomedical treatments and psychological treatments separately for clarity, bear in mind that both categories of treatment work together in modifying the brain, thought, feeling, and behavior.

The biomedical approaches comprise drugs, surgical treatments, and electric and magnetic treatments. The psychological therapies include psychoanalytic, humanistic, cognitive, and behavior therapies. The technology-based therapies make use of computer- or Internet-based treatments. The combined therapies either use drugs and psychotherapies together or might combine less traditional approaches, such as meditation, with more traditional techniques. Let's first consider the biomedical treatments, starting with the most widely used: drug therapies.

BIOMEDICAL TREATMENTS FOR PSYCHOLOGICAL DISORDERS

As mentioned in the opening of the chapter, mental health professionals rely on four major forms of treatment to help alleviate the symptoms of—and sometimes to cure—psychological disorders: biomedical, psychological, technology-based, and combined therapies (see Figure 16.1). While most mental health professionals rely on all four, each practitioner works from a perspective based on training, personal interest, and experience. In other words, the same disorder can be treated in different ways depending on the clinician. People seeking treatment should keep in mind these differences in perspective when selecting someone to help, because different clinician backgrounds don't always lead to the same clinical outcome (see "Psychology in the Real World," p. 614).

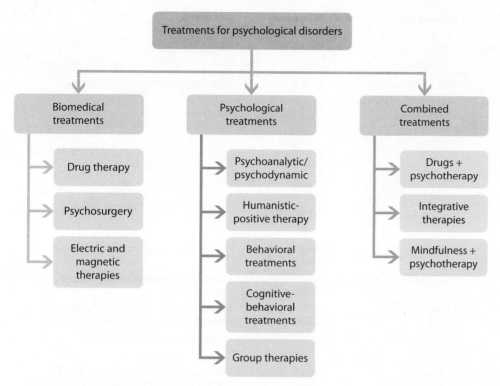

FIGURE **16.1**

SOME MAJOR APPROACHES TO THE TREATMENT OF PSYCHOLOGICAL DISORDERS.

Drug Therapies

Numerous pharmaceutical drugs are available for the treatment of psychological disorders. Drugs can be used to treat, but usually not cure, everything from mild anxiety to schizophrenia.

Drug Treatments for Schizophrenia Today, drug therapies are typically the first choice for schizophrenia. Prior to the 1950s, there were no drugs to treat the disorder. In 1952, the French physician Henri Laborit discovered that a class of drugs, the **phenothiazines,** helped diminish hallucinations, confusion, agitation, and paranoia in people with schizophrenia. He made this discovery by accident, after looking for a way to reduce the shock that sometimes occurs after major surgery (shock results when the body does not receive enough blood, and tissues are therefore deprived of oxygen; "Drug for Treating Schizophrenia," 1998).

Phenothiazines block dopamine receptors in the brain. As discussed in Chapter 15, the prevailing view for decades was that schizophrenia resulted from an excess of dopamine in the brain—a view dubbed the *dopamine hypothesis.* Although the dopamine hypothesis has come into question, the major drugs for schizophrenia are still those that reduce the availability of dopamine in the brain (Javitt & Coyle, 2004).

The best-known phenothiazine is chlorpromazine (marketed as Thorazine in the United States). Another drug, haloperidol (Haldol), discovered at about the same time, showed similar effects on schizophrenic symptoms. The phenothiazines and haloperidol are known as **traditional antipsychotics,** because they were the first medications used to manage psychotic symptoms. Unfortunately, they have many unpleasant side effects, including fatigue, visual impairments, and a condition called **tardive dyskinesia,** which consists of repetitive, involuntary movements of the jaw, tongue, face, and mouth (such as grimacing and lip smacking) and body

phenothiazines
Drugs used to treat schizophrenia; they help diminish hallucinations, confusion, agitation, and paranoia but also have adverse side effects.

traditional antipsychotics
Historically, the first medications used to manage psychotic symptoms.

tardive dyskinesia
Repetitive, involuntary movements of the jaw, tongue, face, and mouth and body tremors resulting from the extended use of traditional antipsychotic drugs.

Connection

Do you need a caffeinated beverage to get you going in the morning— and more throughout the day to stay alert? People who require more and more caffeine or other drugs, including prescription drugs, have developed a drug tolerance.

See "Altering Consciousness with Drugs," Chapter 6, "Consciousness," p. 236.

Disorder	Class of drug treatment	Drug name	Side effects
Schizophrenia	Chlorpromazine	Thorazine	Fatigue, visual impairment, tardive dyskinesia
	Haloperidol	Haldol	Fatigue, visual impairment, tardive dyskinesia
	Clozapine	Clozaril	Weight gain, increased risk of diabetes, reduction of white blood cells
	Risperidone	Risperdal	Weight gain, increased risk of diabetes, reduction of white blood cells
Anxiety	SSRIs	Paxil, Prozac Zoloft, Celexa	Agitation, insomnia, nausea, difficulty achieving orgasm; rare cases of increased risk for suicide
	Benzodiazepines	Valium Librium	Can be addictive
	Barbiturates	Pentobarbital	Slows breathing and heart rate; can lead to overdose
Depression	MAO inhibitors	Nardil Parnate	Dangerous increases in blood pressure
	Tricyclic antidepressants	Elavil Anafranil	Dry mouth, weight gain, irritability, confusion, constipation
	SSRIs	Paxil, Prozac Zoloft, Celexa	Agitation, insomnia, nausea, difficulty achieving orgasm; rare cases of increased risk for suicide
	Bupropione	Wellbutrin	Weight loss, dry mouth, headaches
Bipolar disorder	Lithium	Lithobid	Diarrhea, nausea, tremors, kidney failure, cognitive effects, adverse cardiac effects

FIGURE 16.2

SUMMARY OF DRUGS USED TO TREAT PSYCHOLOGICAL DISORDERS. Most of the major psychological disorders can be treated with some form of medication, to varying degrees of effectiveness and with various side effects.

atypical antipsychotics
New antipsychotic drugs, which do not create tardive dyskinesia.

Connection

Schizophrenia and other disorders can be caused in part by genes that are expressed only under specific environmental circumstances.

See "Nature and Nurture Explanations of Schizophrenia," Chapter 15, "Psychological Disorders," p. 559.

monoamine oxidase (MAO) inhibitors
A class of drugs used to treat depression; they slow the breakdown of monoamine neurotransmitters in the brain.

tremors. Tardive dyskinesia is particularly problematic, as the effects often continue for months after the drugs have been discontinued (Trugman, 1998).

Some newer antipsychotic drugs, called **atypical antipsychotics,** do not have these side effects and are considered by many physicians as the first line of treatment for schizophrenia. Clozapine (Clozaril), olanzapine (Zyprexa), and risperidone (Risperdal) are examples of atypical antipsychotics. These drugs preferentially block a different type of dopamine receptor than the traditional antipsychotics do, which makes them less likely to create tardive dyskinesia (Potkin et al., 2003). However, atypical antipsychotics also affect the activity of other neurotransmitters in the brain. In rare cases, an excess of serotonin occurs, which can lead to tremors, diarrhea, delirium, neuromuscular rigidity, and high body temperature (Dvir & Smallwood, 2008). Unfortunately, even these medications can produce some unpleasant or dangerous side effects, such as major weight gain, increased risk of diabetes, a reduction in the number of certain white blood cells, and rarely a particular kind of cancer (Javitt & Coyle, 2004; Lieberman et al., 2005; A. S. Young et al., 2010). Figure 16.2 summarizes some major disorders, their primary drug therapies, and the side effects of each medication.

Drug Treatments for Depressive and Anxiety Disorders Six major categories of drugs are used to treat mood and anxiety disorders: monoamine oxidase (MAO) inhibitors, tricyclic antidepressants, selective serotonin reuptake inhibitors (SSRIs), benzodiazepines, barbiturates, and lithium.

The **monoamine oxidase (MAO) inhibitors** were among the first pharmaceuticals used to treat depression (Burgess, 2009). These drugs reduce the action of the enzyme monoamine oxidase, which breaks down monoamine neurotransmitters (including norepinephrine, epinephrine, dopamine, and serotonin) in the brain. By inhibiting the action of this enzyme, MAO inhibitors allow more of these neurotransmitters to stay active in the synapse for a longer time, which presumably improves mood. Brand names include Marplan, Nardil, and Parnate. Unfortunately, MAO inhibitors interact with many foods and common over-the-counter drugs, such as antihistamines, to produce undesirable, even dangerous, side effects—such as life-threatening increases in blood pressure. Therefore, they are not often prescribed for depression (Fiedorowicz & Swartz, 2004; Yamada & Yasuhara, 2004). A transdermal patch, which allows administration of an MAO inhibitor without its having to enter the digestive tract, may provide some of the benefits of these drugs without the risks caused by their interactions with foods (Pae et al., 2007).

Tricyclic antidepressants, such as imipramine and amitriptyline, marketed under the trade names Elavil and Anafranil, are still popular for treating depression. They are also used in chronic pain management, as treatment for attention deficit hyperactivity disorder (ADHD), and as a treatment for bedwetting. These drugs appear to work by blocking the reuptake of serotonin and norepinephrine almost equally, so that more of these neurotransmitters are available in the brain. However, the tricyclics produce unpleasant side effects, such as dry mouth, weight gain, irritability, confusion, and constipation (Zeino, Sisson, & Bjarnason, 2010).

tricyclic antidepressants
Drugs used for treating depression as well as chronic pain and ADHD.

Many of the unpleasant side effects of the tricyclic antidepressants come from their effects on norepinephrine. People with depression have serotonin deficiencies (Delgado et al., 1994; Drevets et al., 1999). Therefore, the development of drugs that target only serotonin offered hope for treatment with fewer side effects. One class of drugs brought to the market in the 1990s, the **selective serotonin reuptake inhibitors (SSRIs),** make more serotonin available in the synapse. Prozac (fluoxetine), Zoloft (sertraline), Paxil (paroxetine), and Celexa (citalopram) are some of the more widely used SSRIs and are among the most widely prescribed psychotherapeutic drugs in the United States.

selective serotonin reuptake inhibitors (SSRIs)
Drugs prescribed primarily for depression and some anxiety disorders; they work by making more serotonin available in the synapse.

Here is how SSRIs work: Serotonin, like all neurotransmitters, is released from the presynaptic neuron into the synapse. It then binds with serotonin-specific receptor sites on the postsynaptic neuron to stimulate the firing of that neuron. Normally, neurotransmitters that do not bind with the postsynaptic neuron either are taken back up into the presynaptic neuron (the reuptake process) or are destroyed by enzymes in the synapse. The SSRIs inhibit the reuptake process, thereby allowing more serotonin to bind with the postsynaptic neuron (Murphy, 2010; see Figure 16.3).

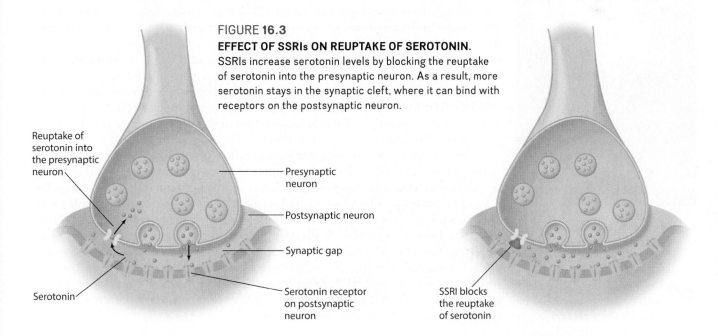

FIGURE **16.3**

EFFECT OF SSRIs ON REUPTAKE OF SEROTONIN.
SSRIs increase serotonin levels by blocking the reuptake of serotonin into the presynaptic neuron. As a result, more serotonin stays in the synaptic cleft, where it can bind with receptors on the postsynaptic neuron.

Reuptake of serotonin into the presynaptic neuron

Presynaptic neuron

Postsynaptic neuron

Synaptic gap

Serotonin

Serotonin receptor on postsynaptic neuron

SSRI blocks the reuptake of serotonin

Connection

Deficiencies in either the amount or the utilization of serotonin in certain parts of the brain are often found in people with depression.

See "Nature and Nurture Explanations of Depression," Chapter 15, "Psychological Disorders," p. 565.

benzodiazepines
A class of anxiety-reducing drugs that can be addictive but are less dangerous than barbiturates.

barbiturates
A class of anxiety-reducing sedatives that can be addictive and carry a risk of overdose.

lithium
A salt that is prescribed for its ability to stabilize the mania associated with bipolar disorder.

Actor Robert Downey, Jr., has struggled with symptoms of bipolar disorder and drug abuse for a number of years.

Can you think of pros and cons to taking medications to treat bipolar disorder?

By allowing more serotonin to be used, the SSRIs alleviate some of the symptoms of depression. Serotonin-only drugs do not produce the undesirable side effects that the tricyclics, which affect both serotonin and norepinephrine activity, may produce (Cipriani et al., 2010).

As mentioned previously, SSRI medications create far fewer unpleasant side effects than do tricyclic antidepressants. For this reason they have become popular, even among people who are not particularly ill but want to feel happier. Although these drugs are prescribed primarily for depression, they are also used to treat certain anxiety disorders, especially OCD, as well as disorders of impulse control, such as compulsive gambling (Vaswani, Linda, & Ramesh, 2003). SSRIs, however, can have some side effects, such as agitation, insomnia, nausea, and difficulty in achieving orgasm. This last side effect has led some physicians to prescribe SSRIs to treat premature ejaculation (Waldinger et al., 2004). Another highly publicized but infrequent side effect of SSRI is an increased likelihood of suicide attempt compared to other treatments for depression (Fergusson et al., 2005). The recently publicized cases of teens on SSRIs committing suicide often neglect to report that adolescents are usually in severely depressed states when they are prescribed SSRIs and are therefore more likely to attempt or to commit suicide, no matter the prescription (Wessely & Kerwin, 2004). Widespread antidepressant use may be associated with a decrease in suicide rates worldwide, but the nature of that relationship is a matter of debate (Isacsson et al., 2010).

Two major classes of drugs, the **benzodiazepines** (Valium, Librium) and the **barbiturates,** are prescribed for anxiety. Both have calming effects and can be addictive, but barbiturates have the higher risk of overdose. People with anxiety disorders often take SSRIs as well. We will discuss the drug treatment of anxiety disorders in more detail later in this chapter's "Bringing It All Together" section.

The treatment of bipolar disorder presents many challenges, as the manic episodes have to be regulated, the depressive episodes prevented, and the shifts from one type of episode to the other controlled. Because no one drug can manage all these effects, treatment often consists of a combination of drug therapies. **Lithium** has long been prescribed for its ability to stabilize the mania associated with bipolar disorder. We do not know how lithium works, although it appears to influence many neurotransmitter systems in the brain, including glutamate, the major excitatory neurotransmitter in the brain, which appears to play a substantial role in schizophrenia (Chuang, 2004; Jope, 1999). Taking lithium can be unpleasant and dangerous, because it can cause diarrhea, nausea, tremors, cognitive problems, kidney failure, brain damage, and even adverse cardiac effects (Aichorn et al., 2006). Also, because the amount of lithium required for effective treatment is not very different from the amount that can cause harm, it is difficult to determine the effective dosage. In addition, some people develop tolerance to lithium after years of treatment, making the drug less effective (R. M. Post et al., 1998). For these reasons, physicians need to monitor their patients' lithium levels carefully by regularly testing their blood.

Due to toxicity concerns, physicians often favor other drugs to treat the mania phase, including drugs prescribed to prevent convulsions, either alone or in combination with lithium. Currently, the most commonly used drugs for managing mania are the atypical antipsychotics, such as olanzapine (trade name Zyprexa) and valproate (marketed as Depakote or Depacon; Jarema, 2007; Malhi, Adams, & Berk, 2010). These drugs are showing effectiveness in the United States as well as in other countries, such as Russia and South Korea (Kuliko & Komarov, 2013; López-Muñoz et al., 2013). The use of atypical antipsychotics in treating mood disorders in general (e.g., for anxiety, bipolar disorder, and depression) is increasing, partly because the dosage required to be effective is rather low and therefore has fewer side effects (Blier, 2005).

Psychosurgery

Recall from Chapter 1 the evidence from very early human history of attempts to cure insanity by trephining, which is drilling a hole in the skull to allow evil spirits to escape. Although current psychological disorders are not usually treated by surgical means, early-20th-century physicians experimented with surgery to disrupt the transmission of brain signals in people suffering from psychosis. In a procedure known as **prefrontal lobotomy,** they severed connections between the prefrontal cortex and the lower portion of the brain. Because the prefrontal cortex is involved in thinking (and, we now know, is crucial for working memory and planned action) and the lower areas are more concerned with emotion, they believed the surgery would modify behavior and possibly disengage the disruptive thought patterns involved in hallucinations and confused thinking. Typically, however, prefrontal lobotomies produced profound personality changes, often leaving the patient listless or subject to seizures; some patients were even reduced to a vegetative state (Mashour, Walker, & Martuza, 2005).

Rosemary Kennedy, younger sister to John F. Kennedy, underwent a lobotomy when she was 23 years old to treat her erratic, often violent mood swings. Instead of producing the desired calming effect, the lobotomy left Rosemary mentally incapacitated. She would stare blankly at walls for hours on end and lost the ability to speak coherently (Lerner, 1996).

After the introduction of the traditional antipsychotic medications, lobotomy fell out of favor. Moreover, the practice was widely regarded as cruel and inhumane. Today a very few, highly constrained forms of brain surgery are occasionally performed, but only as a last resort after other forms of treatment have been unsuccessful (Mashour et al., 2005).

prefrontal lobotomy
A form of psychosurgery in which the connections between the prefrontal cortex and the lower portion of the brain are severed; it is no longer in use.

electroconvulsive therapy (ECT)
The treatment of last resort for severe depression that involves passing an electrical current through a person's brain in order to induce a seizure.

Electric and Magnetic Therapies

Although brain surgery for psychological disorders is rare, there are other ways to stimulate or decrease brain activation. Bizarre as it seems, electrical current can be used to help ease the suffering caused by certain psychological disorders. The application of electrical current as a medical practice goes back centuries: Apparently, the ancient Romans used electric fish to treat headaches (Abrams, 1997). As we saw in the chapter opening, one of the more innovative applications of electrical stimulation may well hold the key to unlocking the mystery of depression.

Electroconvulsive Therapy The notion of "shock therapy" conjures up images of barbaric torture of psychiatric patients, yet electroconvulsive therapy is still used and can be effective for severe cases of depression in people who have not responded to other therapies (Fink, 2006). **Electroconvulsive therapy (ECT)** involves passing an electrical current through a person's brain in order to induce a seizure. The origins of ECT stem from the observation that people who have seizures become calm afterwards (Abrams, 1997). Physicians thought that ECT could be an effective treatment for schizophrenia, because the induced seizures would calm the patient. Research eventually demonstrated, however, that ECT did not treat the symptoms of schizophrenia effectively at all, and it disappeared as a

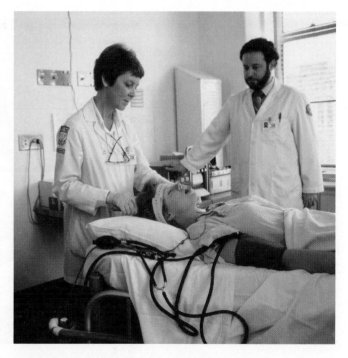

Challenging the assumptions of earlier generations of psychiatrists, more current therapists discovered that ECT is an effective treatment for depression but not schizophrenia.

repetitive transcranial magnetic stimulation (TMS)
A treatment for severe depression involving exposure of specific brain structures to bursts of high-intensity magnetic fields instead of electricity.

viable therapy for years. It resurfaced later as a treatment for people with severe cases of depression.

Today, ECT is administered by connecting electrodes to the patient's head and passing an electrical current (ranging from 60 to 140 volts) through the brain for one-third to one-half second. The voltage is not lethal, because it is administered only to the head—indeed, the same voltage to the chest would be lethal. The treatment is called electro*convulsive* because the procedure produces a brief seizure, including bodily convulsions. To minimize the convulsions, patients are given an anesthetic and a muscle relaxant prior to ECT. Standard ECT treatment involves up to 12 sessions over the course of several weeks. Some people report immediate relief of their depressive symptoms after treatment, although scientists do not fully understand how ECT works to relieve them (Nolen-Hoeksema, 2007). The downside to ECT is that it creates some permanent memory loss and other types of cognitive damage, because it actually destroys some brain tissue. Using ECT on one side of the brain rather than both appears to reduce the risk of memory loss (Squire, 1977).

Repetitive Transcranial Magnetic Stimulation The idea of somehow stimulating or manipulating brain activity with an external application of energy has enduring appeal. Some practitioners have tried to find a way to do this without creating more harm. ECT was a good idea in some respects, but as just mentioned, it leaves people with memory damage and other negative effects. In **repetitive transcranial magnetic stimulation (TMS),** physicians expose particular brain structures to bursts of high-intensity magnetic fields instead of electricity. Like ECT, repetitive transcranial magnetic stimulation is usually reserved for people with severe depression who have not responded well to other forms of therapy. Although some people experience relief from this therapy, it is not yet clear how much magnetic stimulation is optimal and for what length of time (P. B. Fitzgerald et al., 2006; Turner-Shea, Bruno, & Pridmore, 2006). TMS has also shown preliminary success in treating the negative symptoms of schizophrenia (Brunelin et al., 2010).

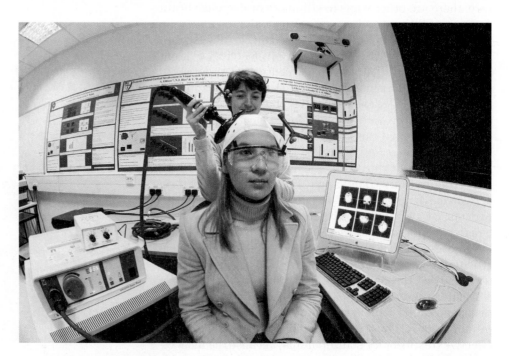

Repetitive transcranial magnetic stimulation exposes specific areas of the brain to bursts of high-intensity magnetic fields and may be used to treat people with severe depression when other options have failed.

Deep Brain Stimulation One of the most promising and exciting new treatments for various psychological disorders involves deep brain stimulation, which entails implanting electrodes into the brain to allow for electrical stimulation of specific brain regions and clusters of neurons. The technique first received attention as a treatment for Parkinson's disease, but as we will discuss in more detail in the next section, it soon showed promise for people with severe depression (Drevets et al., 1997; Mayberg, 2003; Shestyuk et al., 2005). Stimulating certain areas of the brain involved in emotion and reward in people with severe depression leads to substantial improvements in their moods.

Deep brain stimulation more recently has shown promise in treating other psychological disorders as well, such as anorexia (Lipsman et al., 2013) and Alzheimer's disease. For instance, by stimulating the regions of the hippocampus involved in memory formation, deep brain stimulation has helped slow down dementia (Laxton & Lozano, 2012; Lyketsos et al., 2012; G. S. Smith et al., 2012).

Helen Mayberg

Challenging Assumptions in the Treatment of Severe Depression

In her quest to understand the brain circuitry of depression, psychiatrist and neurologist Helen Mayberg was the first to discover what appears to be a neural switch that activates depression. The path that led Mayberg to discover how a brain region called Brodmann's Area 25 (we'll call it Area 25) may control depression is an interesting story of how scientific discovery depends on challenging assumptions, luck, tenacity, creativity, vision, and hard work.

No one had ever thought about applying deep brain stimulation to depressed brain regions. In a stroke of creative insight, Mayberg did. She tried it with 12 patients whose severe depression had failed to respond to anything else. She and her colleagues implanted electrodes in Area 25 and delivered voltage to that area from an external stimulator. For 11 of the patients, the depression ceased almost immediately (Mayberg et al., 2005). Shortly after activation of the electrodes, these patients said that they felt "sudden calmness or lightness," "disappearance of the void," or "connectedness."

Mayberg and her colleagues had stumbled on a surprising phenomenon: Area 25 was actually *hyperactive* in these depressed patients! Rather than discounting this unexpected finding, Mayberg tested it further. She found the same pattern of overactivation in Area 25 in depressed people with Alzheimer's, epilepsy, and Huntington's disease (Mayberg, 1997). Perhaps it played a role in depression more generally.

Finding overactivation in any brain area of depressed people challenged researchers' and clinicians' assumptions, since many had found that depression was related to underactivity rather than overactivity of certain cortical areas (Shestyuk et al., 2005). Specifically, Mayberg found overactivity in Area 25 located in the cingulate region of the prefrontal cortex and surrounded by the limbic system and its emotional and memory centers of the brain (see Figure 16.4). Mayberg reasoned that if Area 25 plays a key role in sustaining depressive thinking, one should see a reduction in activity in this area after successful treatment for the disorder. This, in fact, is what she and her colleagues found (Goldapple et al., 2004; Kennedy et al., 2001). Mayberg also found activity in Area 25 when otherwise healthy people recalled sad memories (Mayberg et al., 1999).

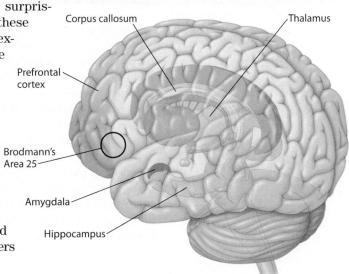

FIGURE **16.4**

BRODMANN'S AREA 25, THE PREFRONTAL CORTEX, AND THE LIMBIC SYSTEM. Brodmann's Area 25 is located in the cingulate region of the prefrontal cortex, where it is surrounded by the corpus callosum and structures of the limbic system (amygdala, hippocampus, thalamus). The limbic system is important in regulating emotion and motivation.

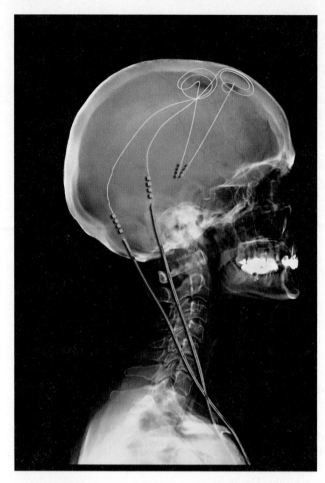

FIGURE 16.5

DEEP BRAIN ELECTRODES AND STIMULATOR FOR STIMULATION OF AREA 25 IN DEPRESSED PATIENTS. A pacemaker implanted in the person's chest sends electrical impulses to electrodes projecting down into Area 25 of the frontal cortex.

Figure 16.5 illustrates the location of the implanted electrodes and the wearable pacemaker for stimulating them. Note that the treatment involves brain stimulation in the operating room as well as a method for stimulating the implants in daily life. Patients wear an external pacemaker that controls the delivery of electrical stimulation to Area 25.

In the following passage, Mayberg describes what happened when the stimulator was turned on to activate the electrode just implanted in Area 25 in the brain of Deanna, the woman described in the chapter opening. What follows is Mayberg's account of what Deanna said when, unbeknownst to Deanna, the surgical team had turned on the stimulator:

> "So we turn it on," Mayberg told me later, "and all of a sudden she says to me, 'It's very strange,' she says, 'I know you've been with me in the operating room this whole time. I know you care about me. But it's not that. I don't know what you just did. But I'm looking at you, and it's like I just feel suddenly more connected to you.'"
>
> Mayberg, stunned, signaled with her hand to the others, out of Deanna's view, to turn the stimulator off. "And they turn it off," Mayberg said, "and she goes: 'God, it's just so odd. You just went away again. I guess it wasn't really anything.'
>
> "It was subtle like a brick," Mayberg told me. "There's no reason for her to say that. Zero. And all through those tapes I have of her, every time she's in the clinic beforehand, she always talks about this disconnect, this closeness and sense of affiliation she misses, that was so agonizingly painful for her to lose. And there it was. It was back in an instant." (Dobbs, 2006a)

Although most people who have had the procedure experience dramatic improvements or complete elimination of their depression, a few do not. Large-scale clinical trials are under way in which Mayberg and others are studying the effects of the stimulation of Area 25 on larger groups of people with treatment-resistant depression. Initial findings suggest that deep brain stimulation offers relief for the symptoms of severe depression without impairing cognitive function, and the effects have lasted up to 1 year (Bewernick et al., 2012; Lozano, Mayberg, & Kennedy, 2012; Mayberg, 2009; Rizvi et al., 2009; Schlaepfer et al., 2013). Moreover, follow-up research has expanded our understanding of the brain regions involved in treating depression with deep brain stimulation. For example, Schlaepfer (2013) has reported evidence that brain regions other than Area 25 involved in treating depression with deep brain stimulation include the medial forebrain bundle and the nucleus accumbens—regions intimately connected to reward and pleasure.

Effectiveness of Biomedical Treatments

Therapies are only as good as they are effective. At the end of each specific form of therapy, we evaluate the current evidence for how effective this type of therapy is.

The SSRIs and tricyclics show comparable effectiveness in the treatment of depression (Kendrick et al., 2006). Both do a reasonable job of regulating depression and are preferable to the MAO inhibitors, given the undesirable, possibly dangerous side effects of the latter. Of the various classes of antidepressants, the SSRIs have the fewest adverse side effects, and people seem to tolerate them better for long-term use (Nemeroff, 2007). Still, these drugs can take up to 4 weeks to have an effect. Presumably, this is how long it takes synapses to produce enough new receptor sites to make use of the increased amounts of serotonin made available by SSRIs.

Recent studies, however, suggest that some of the more popular drugs for depression might not be as effective as was once thought. A study by Turner and colleagues (2008) suggests that the medical journals were biased in their publications of findings on the effectiveness of antidepressants. Nearly one-third of all FDA studies—most of which reported negative results on antidepressants—were not published. As a result, for over a decade the impression of the effectiveness of these medications was overestimated (94% versus the more modest and more representative 51%). According to a large-scale meta-analysis, most widely used prescription antidepressants may be no better than placebos for people with mild to moderate depression. For those with severe depression, they are beneficial when compared to placebos (Fournier et al., 2010). The SSRI fluoxetine (Prozac) actually can harm certain kinds of neural growth and block synapse formation (Xu et al., 2010). A large, randomized trial in Romania compared the effectiveness and cost-effectiveness of drug treatment with Prozac and two kinds of psychotherapy (cognitive therapy and rational emotive therapy). They measured depression scores before, twice during, and 6 months after a 14-week treatment course. The psychological therapies were more effective than Prozac, as well as more cost-effective. It is not clear whether the same results would hold in the United States (Sava et al., 2009). Given that over 20% of the U.S. population takes these drugs, some researchers have challenged the assumption that the SSRIs are effective or that their effect comes through their increase in serotonin reception (G. Greenberg, 2013; I. Kirsch et al., 2002).

Lithium is still widely used for the treatment of mania. Lithium does appear to have long-term effectiveness in treating bipolar disorder (Berghöfer et al., 2008). The evidence, however, for lithium's effectiveness in treating "acute" phases of mania is weak in spite of its regular use for this purpose in the United States (C. Reed et al., 2009). Lithium does not appear to be superior to anticonvulsant or antipsychotic medications, or both, in regulating manic episodes. Moreover, these other medications have fewer toxic side effects. Some research indicates that lithium may be most effective in preventing relapse and suicide in people with bipolar disorder, but many providers are not aware of this benefit (Carney & Goodwin, 2005).

The treatment of schizophrenia still presents a huge problem for mental health professionals. Both traditional and atypical antipsychotic drugs work best on the positive symptoms of schizophrenia, such as hallucinations and delusions, but are generally less effective on the negative symptoms, such as flattened affect, as well as on the cognitive confusion that is characteristic of the disorder (Javitt & Coyle, 2004). One atypical antipsychotic, clozapine (Clorazil), does appear to be somewhat effective in treating the negative symptoms, but it also has a potentially serious side effect: diabetes (Javitt & Coyle, 2004). One of the major problems in treating schizophrenia, however, is persuading patients to continue taking the medication. Because of the unpleasant and often dangerous side effects of these drugs, patients often stop taking them. Up to 74% of people using traditional and atypical antipsychotics discontinue treatment (Lieberman et al., 2005; McEvoy et al., 2006). Recent evidence that glutamate may drive the neurotransmitter system in schizophrenia offers hope for the development of more effective, less aversive drug therapies for the disorder (Patil et al., 2007).

ECT is regarded as a treatment of last resort for severely depressed people who have not responded to any other therapy. Although many patients report immediate relief with ECT treatment, its benefits usually last only as long as the treatments are maintained. Also, ECT can have severe side effects, including memory loss and confusion. ECT treatment to one hemisphere of the brain appears to work better than treatment to both hemispheres and creates fewer cognitive side effects (Sackheim et al., 1993). A controlled trial found that ECT and pharmacological therapy for depression were about equally effective in preventing relapse in people with major depressive disorder, but each form of treatment helped only about half the people studied (Kellner et al., 2006).

Quick Quiz 16.1: Biomedical Treatments for Psychological Disorders

1. The antidepressant medications known as the SSRIs work by
   a. inhibiting monoamine oxidase.
   b. decreasing serotonin levels by inhibiting the reuptake of serotonin into the presynaptic neuron.
   c. increasing serotonin levels by inhibiting the reuptake of serotonin into the presynaptic neuron.
   d. reducing the activity of the neurotransmitter glutamate.

2. Your Aunt Julia has been in treatment for years for schizophrenia. She often has jerky spastic movements, which she tells you are from her medication, not the disorder itself. What side effect is she experiencing?
   a. intolerance
   b. reactive dysphoria
   c. tardive dyskinesia
   d. insomnia

3. Electroconvulsive therapy (ECT) is still in limited use for people with which disorder?
   a. schizophrenia
   b. obsessive-compulsive disorder

   c. generalized anxiety disorder
   d. major depressive disorder

4. Helen Mayberg was surprised to find that brain images of Area 25 showed _____ in people with severe depression and helped devise a way to treat them with deep brain stimulation.
   a. reduced activity
   b. overactivity
   c. tumors
   d. reduced blood flow

5. Both traditional and atypical antipsychotic drugs work best on the _____ symptoms of schizophrenia, but they are generally less effective on the _____ symptoms.
   a. negative; positive
   b. positive; negative
   c. cognitive; emotional
   d. emotional; cognitive

Answers can be found at the end of the chapter.

PSYCHOLOGICAL TREATMENTS FOR PSYCHOLOGICAL DISORDERS

psychotherapy
The use of psychological techniques to modify maladaptive behaviors or thought patterns, or both, and to help patients develop insight into their own behavior.

A number of psychological therapies have developed alongside the various medications and biologically based techniques for treating psychological disorders. **Psychotherapy** is the use of psychological techniques to modify maladaptive behaviors or thought patterns, or both, and to help patients develop insight into their own behavior. In psychotherapy a therapist and a client work together, or a therapist works with a group of people.

People may engage in psychotherapy for self-development as well as for the treatment of psychological disorders. The types of psychotherapeutic approaches in treating disorders are outlined in Figure 16.1: psychoanalytic therapy, humanistic/positive therapy, behavior therapies, cognitive treatments, cognitive-behavioral treatments, and group therapy. Each type of psychotherapy has its own explanation of what causes different disorders as well as how they should be treated.

Psychoanalytic Therapy

psychoanalytic therapy
Therapy aimed at uncovering the unconscious motives that underlie psychological problems.

The oldest and most direct lineage to Freudian therapy is known as *psychoanalytic therapy*. Based on Sigmund Freud's own practices, **psychoanalytic therapy** is the original form of "talk therapy" and is oriented toward major personality change with a focus on uncovering unconscious motives, especially through dream interpretation. It tends to require meeting three to five times a week. Currently classical, or Freudian, psychoanalysis is relatively rare. Freudian psychoanalysis, so innovative in its day, is today influential in how it inspires various perspectives in talk therapy, many of which have taken off in very different directions from where Freud started.

Sigmund Freud argued that "dreams are the royal road to the unconscious" (Freud, 1900/1953, p. 608). Freud's two major techniques for interpreting dreams in order to uncover their unconscious content were free association and symbols. In **free association,** the client recounts a dream and then tries to take one image or idea and say whatever comes to mind, regardless of how threatening, disgusting, or troubling it may be. After this has been done with the first image, the process is repeated until the client has made associations with all the recalled dream images. Ideally, somewhere in the chain of free associations is a connection that unlocks the key to the dream. The second technique for interpreting dreams is through *symbols;* that is, dream images are thought of as representing, or being symbolic of, something else. Classic examples of symbols are a snake symbolizing a penis and a cave representing a vagina. If the techniques just described are successful, the patient becomes aware of the disturbing thoughts in his or her unconscious, and the problematic symptoms decrease.

In the process of **transference,** the client unconsciously reacts to someone in a current relationship as though that person were someone from the client's past. While the client is in therapy, that someone is the therapist, but it can be anyone in the person's present life circumstances. For example, a woman whose father was verbally abusive to her might find herself shirking her job responsibilities because she experiences extreme fear when her older male supervisor at work speaks with even a slightly raised voice. The supervisor thinks this is an overreaction, but he does not realize that the woman's response stems from her relating to him as if he were her father. If these reactions occur during a therapy session, as they often do, the therapist can use the transference to help the client understand how her behavior and emotions in current relationships are influenced by her relationship with her father. By working through the unconsciously transferred feelings in the therapeutic setting, a client might be freed from their powerful grip in other settings.

Like transference, defense mechanisms are also central to psychodynamic theory and therapy. Freud and his daughter Anna (who was also a noted psychoanalyst) described many different defense mechanisms, all of which operate unconsciously and involve defending against anxiety and threats to the ego. The most basic one is repression, which involves forcing threatening feelings, ideas, or motives into the unconscious. In psychodynamic therapy, dream interpretation and transference are used to uncover repressed defenses and unconscious wishes.

Some or all of these techniques may lead the client to **catharsis,** the process of releasing intense, often unconscious, emotions in a therapeutic setting.

Humanistic/Positive Therapy

Humanistic/positive therapies seek to help the client reach his or her greatest potential. This field originated as *humanistic psychology,* with work of Carl Rogers (1951), who developed **client-centered therapy.** Client-centered therapy holds that people have mental health problems because there is a gap between who they are and who they would ideally like to be. The therapist must show the client unconditional positive regard—that is, genuine acceptance and empathy for the client, regardless of what he or she has said or done. The goal is to create an atmosphere in which clients can communicate their feelings with certainty

free association
A psychotherapeutic technique in which the client takes one image or idea from a dream and says whatever comes to mind, regardless of how threatening, disgusting, or troubling it may be.

transference
The process in psychotherapy in which the client reacts to a person in a present relationship as though that person were someone from the client's past.

catharsis
The process of releasing intense, often unconscious, emotions in a therapeutic setting.

client-centered therapy
A form of humanistic therapy in which the therapist shows unconditional positive regard for the client.

Carl Rogers (far right) leads a group therapy session.

that they are being understood rather than judged. If this unconditional positive regard is effective, the client will develop a strong sense of self-worth and the confidence to strive for self-fulfillment.

More recently, positive psychology has developed its own form of psychotherapy, generally referred to as *positive psychotherapy* (Rashid, 2008; Seligman, Rashid, & Parks, 2006). This therapy focuses explicitly on increasing a person's happiness, well-being, and positive emotions. Depression, for example, is treated not only by reducing helplessness, sense of worthlessness, and negative emotions but also by actively trying to create a greater sense of well-being and a sense of gratitude. Gratitude training, for instance, involves daily exercises in noticing and finding things in life for which one is grateful and thankful. People who regularly acknowledge what they have to be thankful for have a higher sense of well-being and happiness (Emmons & McCullough, 2003).

Behavior Therapies

In **behavior therapies,** therapists apply the principles of classical and operant conditioning to treat psychological disorders. They focus on changing behavior rather than thoughts, feelings, or motives. The idea is to help clients eliminate undesirable behaviors and increase the frequency of desirable ones.

Behavioral therapists employ the basic principles of operant conditioning through the use of **token economies** to treat maladaptive behaviors. This technique is based on a simple principle: Desirable behaviors are reinforced with a token, such as a small chip or fake coin, which the client can then exchange for privileges. Parents can use this approach with their children—if their room is messy and they clean it, they get a token. The kids can turn in five tokens for candy or a toy. The more this happens, the more likely they are to clean their rooms, or so the logic goes.

In the realm of mental health, the technique was used with some success in the 1950s and 1960s to reduce undesirable psychotic behaviors in patients in mental institutions (Nolen-Hoeksema, 2007). Recent uses include the treatment of substance abuse by people with schizophrenia. Each time the patients did not use drugs, they were rewarded with small amounts of money. Coupled with problem-solving and social-skills training, this token system helped control substance abuse in hospitalized patients with schizophrenia, who are generally very

behavior therapies
Therapies that apply the principles of classical and operant conditioning in the treatment of psychological disorders.

token economies
A behavioral technique in which desirable behaviors are reinforced with a token, such as a small chip or fake coin, which can be exchanged for privileges.

Connection

Principles of classical and operant conditioning, including the powerful effect of reinforcement on learning, are the foundation of many behavior therapies.

See "Conditioning Models of Learning," Chapter 8, "Learning," p. 287.

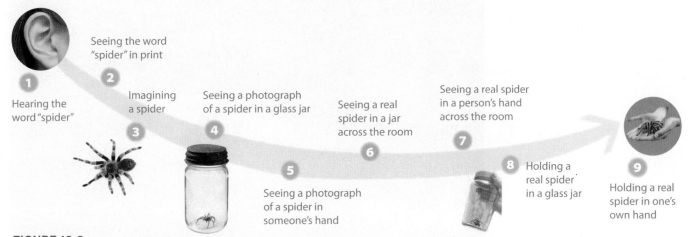

FIGURE 16.6

HIERARCHY OF EXPOSURE TO SPIDERS (THE PHOBIC OBJECT) IN A PATIENT WITH ARACHNOPHOBIA.

hard to treat (Bellack et al., 2006). Also, the use of token economies may encourage socially appropriate behaviors and enhance life skills in children with autism spectrum disorder (Matson & Boisjoli, 2009).

Systematic desensitization is a widely used application of behavior therapy that is especially effective for treating simple phobias (Tyron, 2005). Systematic desensitization pairs relaxation with gradual exposure to a phobic object. First, the therapist generates a hierarchy of increasing contact with the feared object, ranging from mild to extreme. Figure 16.6 shows a possible hierarchy for a person with arachnophobia (a fear of spiders). In addition to increasing exposure, the therapist helps the client learn relaxation techniques that he or she can use when experiencing anxiety, especially anxiety related to the phobic object. The therapist works to help the client relax and then exposes the client to the phobic stimulus at gradually increasing levels of intensity. The idea to pair two incompatible body responses, relaxation and anxiety, is a clever one. People cannot be both relaxed and anxious at the same time. It works! Systematic desensitization often successfully treats phobias and some other anxiety disorders (Tyron, 2005).

Systematic desensitization involves three levels of exposure to a phobic object: imagined, virtual, and real. In imagined exposure, people simply imagine contact with the phobic object. The next level is virtual reality exposure. At this stage, the individual may be shown photographs or exposed to a virtual reality computer simulation. For instance, one type of virtual reality software allows clients to simulate flying during treatment for flying phobia, as depicted in Figure 16.7 (Wiederhold & Wiederhold, 2005). The most realistic level of exposure is in vivo exposure, in which the client makes real-life contact with the phobic object.

Implosion therapy, or **flooding,** is a form of in vivo exposure in which the client experiences extreme exposure to the phobic object, as when someone who is arachnophobic is asked to hold three hairy tarantulas at once. Flooding, in this sense, is very different from systematic desensitization. Flooding involves heavy exposure to the feared object, whereas systematic desensitization involves gradually making the person less sensitive to the feared object, one step at a time.

Cognitive and Cognitive-Behavioral Treatments

Any type of psychotherapy that works to restructure irrational thought patterns is known as **cognitive therapy.** Typically, in cognitive therapy the therapist helps the client identify irrational thought patterns and then challenges these thoughts.

systematic desensitization
A behavior therapy technique, often used for phobias, in which the therapist pairs relaxation with gradual exposure to a phobic object, generating a hierarchy of increasing contact with the feared object.

Challenge Your Assumptions
True or False? People can learn to not be afraid of flying.
True: Behavior therapy can teach people to not be afraid of flying.

flooding
A form of in vivo exposure in which the client experiences extreme exposure to the phobic object.

cognitive therapy
Any type of psychotherapy that works to restructure irrational thought patterns.

FIGURE **16.7**

SYSTEMATIC DESENSITIZATION IN THE TREATMENT OF FLYING PHOBIA. Because it is impractical and expensive to do therapy while on an airplane, simulating flying in a virtual reality format is an effective and cost-efficient way of systematically desensitizing people who are afraid of flying.

Cognitive therapy (CT) is structured and problem-oriented, with the primary goal of fixing erroneous thought patterns, as we will illustrate with an example shortly. It is also time-limited and involves a collaborative effort by the therapist and the client. In using cognitive therapy, the therapist relies on what is known as the Socratic method: The therapist poses questions that help the client recognize erroneous logic that may support problematic thinking (Beck & Emery, 1985).

Let's consider the real-life case of Carlos, a 39-year-old man suffering from major depressive disorder. Carlos had tried several medications for his depression and had undergone one voluntary hospitalization, without satisfactory effects. His general practitioner, Dr. Hsu, recommended him for cognitive therapy. Many therapists believe that depressed people perceive events in such a way that they see only potentially adverse outcomes. Cognitive therapy for depression aims to point out the negative bias in such depressive thinking. Consider the following exchange between Carlos and his therapist, Dr. Walden (Gorenstein & Comer, 2002, pp. 54–55):

> **DR. WALDEN:** You say you are a "basket case" and can barely function. What leads you to those conclusions?
>
> **CARLOS:** Well, I've been hospitalized. That's how bad it's been. I just can't believe it.
>
> **DR. WALDEN:** . . . Tell me again what led to the hospitalization.
>
> **CARLOS:** I sort of panicked when the medicine didn't help, and I stopped going to work or anything else. Dr. Hsu figured that as long as I wasn't working, I might as well go into the hospital where I could try different drugs without having to manage all the side effects on my own. I also was pretty miserable at the time. I told Dr. Hsu my family might be better off without me.
>
> **DR. WALDEN:** Do you think they would be better off?
>
> **CARLOS:** I don't know. I'm not doing them much good.
>
> **DR. WALDEN:** What would life be like for them without you?

Cognitive-behavioral therapy focuses on changing a client's way of thinking in order to avoid irrational thoughts. Asking the client to break down problems into steps that can be tackled one at a time illustrates this approach.

CARLOS: It would be terrible for them. I suppose saying they'd be better off without me is going too far. As bad off as I am, I'm still able to do a few things.

DR. WALDEN: What are you able to do?

CARLOS: Well, I'm not in the hospital anymore. And I don't think I will be back either. . . . I mainly went in because I thought I could get better treatment or whatever. But it didn't pan out, so what would be the point of going back in?

DR. WALDEN: So the fact that you were in the hospital isn't really a sign that you are now or were ever a "basket case," which I take to mean someone who is completely helpless and cannot function.

Notice how Dr. Walden helps Carlos use his own logic to point out errors in the thinking that supports his notion of being worthless. For instance, Dr. Walden helps Carlos see that in spite of being hospitalized for depression, he was neither useless to his family nor totally unable to do things. Carlos came to realize that he really wasn't a "basket case" after all (Gorenstein & Comer, 2002).

Often therapists integrate cognitive techniques for restructuring irrational thoughts with behavioral techniques to shape desirable behaviors in what is known as **cognitive-behavioral therapy (CBT).** As the name implies, the focus of CBT is to change both thoughts and behavior. CBT entails restructuring thoughts, loosening the client's belief in irrational thoughts that may perpetuate the disorder, and offering incentives for acquiring more adaptive thought and behavior patterns. Cognitive-behavioral therapy is a short-term psychological treatment that has been successfully applied to disorders as varied as depression, phobias, post-traumatic stress disorder (PTSD), obsessive-compulsive disorder, eating disorders, and substance abuse. Think of CBT as a tool for teaching skills that curtail *depressogenic thinking,* or thinking that tends to help generate depressed moods. CBT has revolutionized the treatment of many psychological disorders.

CBT helps clients change the way they evaluate potential emotional threats. To do this, CBT encourages reappraisal, which entails reexamining a situation that was previously seen as stressful. For example, people who are depressed often hold the depressogenic thought that they can't do anything because all tasks seem insurmountable. Through problem solving, clients can learn to adopt a new outlook. For depressed people who think they cannot do anything, the approach would be to list the various steps in a given task and then work on each step until the task is completed. Not only will the client successfully accomplish the task but that accomplishment may also have the further benefit of improving mood. Research on the cognitive processes involved in CBT in relation to treatment effectiveness shows that people who engage in more problem solving during CBT reap more benefits (Chen, Jordan, & Thompson, 2006).

cognitive-behavioral therapy (CBT)
An approach to treating psychological disorders that combines techniques for restructuring irrational thoughts with operant and classical conditioning techniques to shape desirable behaviors.

Group Therapy

In **group therapy,** several people who share a common problem all meet regularly with a therapist to help themselves and one another; the therapist acts as a facilitator. Group therapy often follows a structured process, with clear treatment goals such as learning to overcome social anxiety disorder. The group serves as both a source of support and an aid to the therapeutic process by allowing several people with a common problem to listen to, discuss with, and critique one another. The interactions among participants becomes as much a part of the treatment as people's individual comments. These relationships become real-life contexts in which the various issues play out in front of the group. The presence of other people with the same problem also helps remove feelings of isolation.

group therapy
A therapeutic setting in which several people who share a common problem all meet regularly with a therapist to help themselves and one another.

support groups
Meetings of people who share a common situation, be it a disorder, a disease, or an ill family member.

Groups can offer less structured therapeutic contexts as well. **Support groups** are meetings of people who share a common situation, be it a disorder, a disease, or an ill family member. They meet regularly to share experiences, usually without programmatic treatment goals. They usually have a facilitator, a regular meeting time, and an open format. Support groups offer a sense of community, a forum for information exchange, and a place to share feelings for people who may have felt isolated by their situation. Support groups are widely available for people with all types of psychological disorders, as well as those living with chronic illnesses, such as diabetes or cancer.

Groups can be categorized in terms of their focus, such as eating disorders, substance abuse, OCD, or bereavement, and may be time-limited or ongoing. Time-limited groups run for a set number of sessions, tend to follow a program of treatment, and usually do not add members after the first few meetings. Ongoing groups, in contrast, welcome new members as they appear. Alcoholics Anonymous (AA) and other substance abuse groups that follow AA's 12-step approach are examples of ongoing groups. Also in this category are "life support groups," in which people who are coping with, say, a spouse with a brain tumor or a son with major depressive disorder can meet and share their feelings about what they are going through.

Psychological treatments have been used not only to alleviate psychological disorders but also to help prevent the development of such disorders. Given the difficulties in treating many psychological disorders and the costs to individuals and society of the large numbers of people suffering from such conditions, prevention programs are an increasing area of effort in psychology and medicine (see the "Preventing Disorders" section later in this chapter). Figure 16.8

Therapy	Cause of problem	Goal of therapy	Techniques
Psychodynamic	Disorders are symptoms of unconscious and repressed thoughts, feelings, and motives.	Work to uncover repressed and unconscious thoughts, feelings, and motives (defense mechanisms).	Dream interpretation, free association, transference Catharsis
Humanistic	Conditions are blocking personal growth.	Create conditions for optimal growth.	Unconditional positive regard, empathic listening
Behavior	Maladaptive behavior has been reinforced and rewarded.	Change reinforcers and rewards to change maladaptive behavior.	Classical and operant conditioning; token economies; systematic desensitization
Cognitive	Irrational thoughts lead to disordered behaviors.	Change emotions/irrational thoughts.	Critical questioning (Socratic method)
Cognitive–behavioral	Maladaptive behaviors have been reinforced and irrational thoughts have developed.	Change thoughts and behavior.	Restructure thoughts and offer incentives for acquiring more adaptive thoughts and behaviors; reappraisal
Group	Being isolated and unsupported makes disorders worse.	Facilitate support groups and sense of community so person realizes he or she is not alone.	Support groups; 12-step programs

FIGURE **16.8**

CAUSES, GOALS, AND TECHNIQUES OF PSYCHOLOGICAL THERAPIES. Each major psychological perspective has its own theory of what causes psychological disorders, as well as distinct goals and techniques of treatment.

summarizes the psychotherapies discussed in this section and lists what each therapy addresses as the causes of a disorder, as well as the therapy's treatment goals and techniques.

Effectiveness of Psychological Treatments

An increasingly prevalent view is that therapists need to make treatment choices based on the empirical evidence of their efficacy—that is, they need to be **evidence-based therapies** (APA Presidential Task Force, 2006). However, very little research has addressed the issue of which psychotherapies work best for various disorders. Decades ago, a review of the literature on the effectiveness of various types of psychotherapies showed that people who received any kind of therapy were better off on a number of outcomes relevant to mental status than were most people who did not receive therapy (M. Smith & Glass, 1977). The study revealed no significant differences between behavior therapies and psychodynamic ones. Current meta-analyses of the effectiveness of psychotherapy continue to show that most forms of therapy are effective and few significant differences exist in effectiveness among general psychotherapy, cognitive-behavioral therapy, and psychodynamic therapy (Shedler, 2010). This conclusion is sometimes referred to as the **dodo bird verdict,** after the dodo bird in *Alice in Wonderland* (Luborsky, Singer, & Luborsky, 1975). The dodo bird proclaims, "Everybody has won, and must have prizes." The idea is that psychotherapy tends to work, but which kind of therapy one has appears not to matter too much.

However, this assessment does not mean there are no differences in effectiveness. In some cases, the usefulness of psychotherapy depends on the nature of the disorder being treated and the state of the patient's mental health. Some conditions are more responsive to psychological intervention than others. Personality disorders are best helped with psychodynamic psychotherapy (Shedler, 2010), phobias with behavior therapy (Tyron, 2005), and schizophrenia with drug therapy (Javitt & Coyle, 2004). For instance, people with schizophrenia experience such disordered thinking that it may be very difficult to teach them to work with their feelings and thoughts in order to change their behavior. That said, long-term group therapy appears to improve the basic life skills of people with schizophrenia (Sigman & Hassan, 2006).

People experiencing depressive disorders are much more responsive to psychological approaches than are people suffering from schizophrenic disorders, but the approach needs to be matched up carefully with the disorder. Systematic desensitization, for example, is quite effective for treating a simple phobia but is inappropriate for treating depression. Length of treatment matters as well. As therapy continues, effectiveness declines (K. I. Howard et al., 1986; Kopta, 2003). Perhaps the potency of a psychological treatment begins to wear out after a certain point, or maybe only the harder-to-treat cases stay in therapy longer (Barkham et al., 2006).

Cognitive therapy and cognitive-behavioral therapy have shown perhaps the greatest effectiveness of any form of psychotherapy for treating various psychological disorders, but they are especially effective for certain cases of depression and anxiety disorders (Kehle, 2008; Tolin, 2010; Venning et al., 2009). Recent data suggest that cognitive therapy is as effective as antidepressants in treating severe depression (Hollon et al., 2005). In one study, depicted in the Research Process for this chapter (Figure 16.9), experimental groups of individuals diagnosed with depression received either cognitive therapy or drug therapy, while a control group was treated with a placebo. Cognitive therapy was as effective as drug therapy in treating depression, with fewer risks (DeRubeis et al., 2005). In the treatment of obsessive-compulsive disorder, CBT slows metabolism in the caudate nucleus, an area of the brain that is overactive in people suffering from this disorder (Linden, 2006). In short, psychotherapy can change the brain.

evidence-based therapies
Treatment choices based on empirical evidence that they produce the desired outcome.

dodo bird verdict
The finding that most forms of therapy are effective and few significant differences exist in effectiveness among standard therapies.

Challenge Your Assumptions
True or False? Talk therapy might make people feel better, but it does not change the brain.
False: Psychotherapy can and does change the brain.

Research Process

 Research Question

Is cognitive therapy as effective as the more expensive anti-depressant medication in treating people with depression?

 Method

Two hundred forty patients with moderate to serious depression participated in a 16-week experimental study. Half of them were randomly assigned to the anti-depressant medication condition, and the other half were randomly assigned to either the cognitive therapy or placebo pill condition. The medication group received Paxil (paroxetine) for 16 weeks and no psychotherapy. The cognitive therapy group received individualized cognitive psychotherapy on a regular basis for 16 weeks. Those in the placebo pill condition received the placebo for 8 weeks and Paxil for the final 8 weeks.

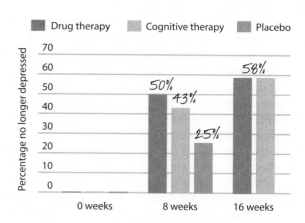

Depression scores were measured twice a week for all 16 weeks using a standard depression questionnaire, the Hamilton Depression Rating Scale. A score of 12 and above is representative of depression. Participants had to have initial scores of 20 or higher to be included in the study.

 Results

The criterion for the absence of depression was a score lower than 12 on the Hamilton Depression Rating Scale. After 8 weeks, 50% of the medication group, 43% of the cognitive therapy group, and 25% of the placebo group were no longer depressed, as the graph shows. After 16 weeks, 58% of both the medication and cognitive therapy groups were no longer depressed.

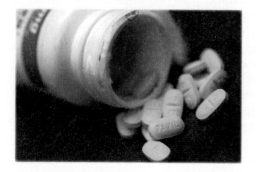

Conclusion

After 16 weeks of treatment, cognitive therapy and drug therapy were equally effective in treating depression, and both were superior to a placebo condition.

FIGURE 16.9

COMPARING COGNITIVE THERAPY AND DRUG THERAPY IN THE TREATMENT OF DEPRESSION. Is cognitive therapy as effective as medications in the treatment of major depression? In practice, cognitive therapy and drug therapy are often combined effectively to treat depression. ("Cognitive Therapy vs Medications in the Treatment of Moderate to Severe Depression," by R. J. DeRubeis, S. Hollon, J. Amsterdam, R. Shelton, P. Young, R. Salomon, . . . R. Gallop, 2005, *Archives of General Psychiatry, 62,* 409–416.)

Behavioral treatments such as systematic desensitization are very effective in treating certain anxiety disorders, especially simple phobias, including performance anxiety and public speaking (Lazarus & Abramovitz, 2004; Tyron, 2005). In vivo exposure appears to offer the most effective treatment of simple phobias, such as snake phobia, but people are more likely to drop out of such therapies than are those undergoing other forms of systematic desensitization (J. Buchanan & Houlihan, 2008; Choy, Fyer, & Lipsitz, 2007).

Quick Quiz 16.2: Psychological Treatments for Psychological Disorders

1. José's therapist asks to hear about José's week. José tells him about some difficulty he is having with his wife and how he feels worthless in his marriage. The therapist expresses his empathy and understanding. He tells José he knows what it's like to feel worthless and how uncomfortable that feeling is. What therapeutic approach is José's therapist taking?
   a. humanistic/positive
   b. cognitive-behavioral
   c. cognitive
   d. psychodynamic

2. Which of the following methods is widely used for the effective treatment of simple phobias?
   a. flooding (implosion therapy)
   b. token economies
   c. client-centered therapy
   d. systematic desensitization

3. Often therapists integrate cognitive techniques for restructuring irrational thoughts with behavioral techniques to shape desirable behaviors in what is known as cognitive
   a. behavioral therapy.
   b. humanistic therapy.
   c. psychodynamic therapy.
   d. behavior modification.

4. What is the safest and best form of treatment for depression?
   a. Paxil
   b. prevention
   c. group therapy
   d. cognitive therapy

Answers can be found at the end of the chapter.

TECHNOLOGY-BASED TREATMENTS FOR PSYCHOLOGICAL DISORDERS

A number of new therapies make use of technology or the Internet to complement current therapies or make psychotherapeutic techniques available to people who might otherwise not have access to therapy or seek it out. These are the **technology-based therapies.**

In **virtual reality therapies,** virtual (digital simulation) environments create therapeutic situations that might be hard to create otherwise. For instance, virtual reality therapy has been used for the treatment of phobias, such as a fear of flying (as we saw in the section on desensitization), or the treatment of PTSD by re-creating a traumatic situation (McLay et al., 2010, 2012; Ready et al., 2010; Riva, 2009). Both of these situations would be either costly or nearly impossible to replicate in real-life therapy (Cukor et al., 2009). Recent research shows virtual reality therapy to also be an effective treatment for social phobia (P. L. Anderson et al., 2013).

The Internet can be used as an online therapeutic environment as well. The virtual world known as Second Life provides a place for people to meet, interact, and develop a social milieu. This online program, which has been downloaded by 15 million users around the world, is a virtual environment where people interact with others in real time. It is mostly used recreationally but increasingly commercially and therapeutically as well (Lisetti et al., 2009). Therapeutically, the participants are patients and therapists, each of whom has an avatar (hence

technology-based therapies
Therapies that make use of technology or the Internet to complement current therapies or make psychotherapeutic techniques available to more people.

virtual reality therapies
Therapies that use virtual (digital simulation) environments to create therapeutic situations that would be hard to create otherwise.

the name *avatar therapy*). Both people can talk through a headset to give their avatars a voice, or they can chat by text written on screen. Each participant can walk, fly, travel to different locations, and manipulate his or her own facial expressions and body language. As with other online games, participants encounter other avatars and interact with them.

Effectiveness of Technology-Based Therapy

James Herbert at Drexel University is studying the effectiveness of Second Life treatment for social phobia (social anxiety disorder). His group offers CBT in Second Life, in 12 weekly sessions. Through avatars, a client meets with a therapist in a private, secure virtual room. Clients learn new techniques and get opportunities to practice. Second Life offers people with social anxiety—who avoid therapy that requires them to get out of the house and go to a new environment—a "safe" form of psychotherapy, because they are not directly observed or exposed to ridicule and embarrassing situations. Research on the effectiveness of Second Life is still ongoing (Gorrindo & Groves, 2009; Ku et al., 2005; Yuen et al., 2009). Drawbacks to technology-based therapy, however, include its difficulty in ensuring confidentiality and in intervening if patients become an immediate danger to themselves or others.

Other digital therapeutic techniques make direct use of the Internet for both access to materials and the creation of online environments in which treatment can occur. Titov and colleagues (2010), for example, administered treatment programs (e.g., CBT) online to people with a variety of anxiety disorders. Evidence indicates that electronic distribution can work effectively for certain anxiety symptoms, including measures of panic disorder (Wims et al., 2010).

COMBINED APPROACHES

Some approaches combine different types of psychotherapy or combine nontraditional practices with traditional approaches. Sometimes the optimal treatment for a psychological disorder may be to combine drugs with psychotherapy. We will look at several combined approaches: drugs and psychotherapy, integrative therapy, and mindfulness training and psychotherapy.

Drugs and Psychotherapy

Given the dynamic interplay between biological and psychological influences in many psychological disorders, combined treatments might work better than either alone (Ganasen, Ipser, & Stein, 2010). The drugs can modify some of the debilitating effects of a disorder enough that patients can function sufficiently well to learn techniques that might help in changing their problematic thinking and behavior. This approach works best for depressive and anxiety disorders, in which thinking is not severely impaired. A combined therapy to manage depression might employ drugs to help manage the depressive state along with CBT to help clients recognize and control the thought patterns that may push them into depressive states (Cuijpers et al., 2010; J. D. Teasdale et al., 2000).

Integrative Therapy

Some therapists take an *eclectic* approach to psychotherapy, which means they draw on numerous techniques in their work with clients. These clinicians are typically trained in many methods and use those that seem most appropriate, given the situation, without loyalty to any particular orientation or treatment. This approach is known as **integrative therapy** (Norcross, Bike, & Evans, 2009; Prochaska & Norcross, 2007). For a client showing symptoms of simple phobia and suffering from depression, behavioral therapy may be best for treating the phobia while cognitive techniques may work better for the depression. Problems of self-esteem might best be treated with a humanistic approach.

The vast majority of clinical psychologists practicing in the United States say they take an integrative-eclectic approach to treating disorders (Norcross, Bike, & Evans, 2009; Norcross, Karpiak, & Lister, 2005). These practitioners share the experience that no one therapeutic approach is effective for all psychological disorders.

Prolonged exposure therapy is an integrative treatment program for people who have post-traumatic stress disorder (PTSD; Foa et al., 2005; Powers et al., 2010). It combines CBT with the imagined exposure form of systematic desensitization and relaxation. For clients with PTSD, this involves a course of individual therapy in which clients directly process traumatic events and thus reduce trauma-induced psychological disturbances. Thus, a person with combat-related PTSD might revisit traumatic war scenes (such as the death of a compatriot) in her mind and engage in cognitive approaches with the therapist to reduce irrational thinking about her role in that event (e.g., she could not have saved him). This technique has been used effectively for the treatment of combat- and rape-related PTSD (Cahill et al., 2006; Foa et al., 1999, 2005; Nacash et al., 2007; Powers et al., 2010). Sometimes drugs prescribed for anxiety disorders are used in combination with prolonged exposure therapy to treat PTSD (Rothbaum et al., 2006).

integrative therapy
An eclectic approach in which a therapist draws on different treatment approaches and uses those that seem most appropriate for the situation.

Mindfulness Training and Psychotherapy

Some newer therapies integrate the nontraditional practice of mindfulness meditation with psychotherapeutic techniques to treat psychological disorders (Chiesa, Brambilla, & Serretti, 2010; N. Farb et al., 2010). In mindfulness meditation, the meditator is trained to calm the body and the mind and to notice the thoughts or feelings that might draw his or her attention, without getting pulled around by them and without clinging to them. These skills help people keep thoughts or emotions in perspective. We will explore two combined approaches in this vein: mindfulness-based cognitive therapy and dialectical behavior therapy.

John Teasdale and his colleagues pioneered the applications of mindfulness meditation to the treatment of major depressive disorder (Segal, Williams, & Teasdale, 2002; Teasdale et al., 2000). Their approach combines elements of CBT with mindfulness meditation to create a treatment known as **mindfulness-based cognitive therapy (MBCT).** Both mindfulness meditation and cognitive therapy involve restructuring one's thoughts. Standard cognitive therapy helps depressed people recognize their depressogenic thought patterns and has been very effective in reducing relapse when administered during depressive episodes. Mindfulness meditation develops skills for approaching thoughts nonjudgmentally and enhances people's ability to realize that they are neither bound by their thoughts nor defined by them. To the extent that depression stems from recursive "negative" thought patterns in which the person becomes caught in a feedback loop that is reinforced by repeated episodes of depression, mindfulness meditation might help the patient break out of these loops (Farb et al., 2010; J. D. Teasdale et al., 1995).

Connection

Mindfulness meditation practices help people become aware of everything that occurs in the mind and recognize it for what it is: a thought, an emotion, or a sensation that will arise and dissipate.

See "Meditation and Conscious Experience," Chapter 6, "Consciousness," p. 221.

mindfulness-based cognitive therapy (MBCT)
An approach that combines elements of CBT with mindfulness meditation to help people with depression learn to recognize and restructure negative thought patterns.

Meditation-based therapies have been used with some success in the treatment of both positive and negative symptoms of schizophrenia. A general goal in mindfulness meditation is for a person to gain perspective on his or her own thoughts and feelings and, ultimately, change the person's relationships with them. The most common treatment for the positive symptoms of schizophrenia is to try to reduce hallucinations (usually voices) by the use of tranquilizers that ultimately sedate the mind. The downside of such treatment is cognitive dulling—lots of unpleasant side effects. As a result, many people choose not to take their drugs.

But what if people with schizophrenia could learn to live more easily with these symptoms and not be defined and utterly controlled by them? A new approach in the treatment of schizophrenic symptoms focuses on changing the relationship with the voices rather than trying to make them go away. Mindfulness training for schizophrenia takes this novel approach.

A regular regimen of several brief sessions of mindfulness meditation may help people with schizophrenia keep their "voices," or auditory hallucinations, in perspective and not believe them to be real. Initial controlled and case studies indicate that people with schizophrenia experience less distress and improved functioning after such training (Chadwick et al., 2009; K. N. Taylor, Harper, & Chadwick, 2009). Another type of meditation, loving-kindness meditation, which helps cultivate a sense of caring for self and others, may offer promise in the treatment of the negative symptoms of schizophrenia (D. P. Johnson et al., 2011).

Another combined treatment involving mindfulness is **dialectical behavior therapy (DBT),** a program developed for the treatment of borderline personality disorder (Linehan, 1993). DBT integrates elements of CBT with exercises aimed at developing mindfulness without meditation. The training, which involves individual as well as group therapy, is designed to help clients develop a nonjudgmental attitude toward their emotions and to accept their current behavior. These skills and attitudes form the cornerstone of personality change, enabling clients to learn how to regulate their own emotions (Linehan et al., 1991).

Effectiveness of Combined Approaches

In spite of the logic for combining drugs with cognitive-behavioral therapy for both the treatment and the prevention of depression (Nolen-Hoeksema, 2007), few studies have systematically examined the relative benefits of drugs, psychotherapy, and the combination of the two. However, a 14-month study of mental health in more than 500 children examined the relative effectiveness of medication, behavior therapy, and the combination of the two approaches in treating a variety of disorders (J. H. Edwards, 2002). For ADHD, the combination of drugs and behavior therapy was superior to behavioral intervention and better than medication alone for most outcome measures (J. H. Edwards, 2002). Other research has reported that combining psychosocial intervention with atypical antipsychotic medication effectively reduces relapse rates and increases general functioning in those suffering from schizophrenia for up to 12 months after treatment (B. Kim et al., 2008).

Clinical research shows that prolonged exposure therapy (an integrative CBT approach) is effective, substantially reducing the symptoms of PTSD over extended periods of up to 18 months after treatment is complete (Foa et al., 1999). Although it has still not been widely adopted by clinicians, prolonged exposure therapy shows substantial benefits compared to no therapy, supportive counseling, and other procedures designed to reduce stress (Cahill et al., 2006).

The advantage of mindfulness-based cognitive therapy compared with standard cognitive therapy is that it works when the person is in a nondepressive state, so it might help prevent relapse. Breakthrough initial work on MBCT showed that it can prevent relapse in people who have had at least three previous depressive episodes. Participants who had recently completed successful drug therapy for their most recent bout of depression were randomly assigned to participate in MBCT or to continue with the treatment they otherwise would have received (treatment as usual), which included seeking help from other sources, such as family or a doctor (Segal, Williams, & Teasdale, 2002). Figure 16.10 shows that those who practiced MBCT relapsed into depression only about half as often as those who received treatment as usual (J. D. Teasdale et al., 2000). More recently, MBCT was shown to be effective in preventing depressive relapse regardless of the number of previous depressive episodes (Geschwind et al., 2012), and in reducing experiences of anxiety and stress in nonclinical samples (Kaviani, Javaheri, & Hatami, 2011). By restructuring thoughts, MBCT actually restructures synaptic connections involved in learning, memory, and emotion—another example of how experience can restructure the brain.

Borderline personality disorder has long been considered nearly untreatable, but dialectical behavior therapy became the first treatment effective in reducing the symptoms (Soler et al., 2009). DBT reduces self-inflicted harmful behaviors, lowers scores on depression questionnaires, decreases dysfunctional patterns associated with substance abuse, and increases the likelihood of staying in treatment (Koerner & Linehan, 2000; Kröger et al., 2006; Linehan, Heard, & Armstrong, 1993). Most important, DBT reduces the risk of suicide attempts—the most disastrous risk associated with borderline personality disorder—much more than does nonbehavioral psychotherapy (Linehan et al., 2006). Not only is DBT effective in treating borderline personality disorder, but it has also been adapted to treat eating disorders, conduct disorders, and domestic violence (Kristeller, Baer, & Quillian-Wolever, 2006; Nelson-Gray et al., 2006; Rathus, Cavuoto, & Passarelli, 2006). In a recent study of a group of people with a variety of diagnoses, participation in a weekly DBT course led to reductions in self-reported anxiety and depression and offered participants an increased sense of hope (Ritschel, Cheavens, & Nelson, 2012).

For all of the variety of treatments available, one of the most challenging aspects of psychological interventions is finding a therapist. Psychology in the Real World, offers practical information on how to choose a therapist.

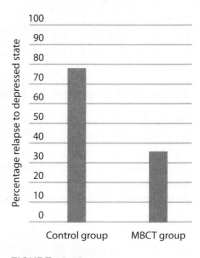

FIGURE **16.10**

EFFECTIVENESS OF MINDFULNESS-BASED COGNITIVE THERAPY (MBCT) FOR DEPRESSION. When people with depression were treated with mindfulness-based cognitive therapy, they were much less likely to experience a relapse compared to a comparison group of people with depression who received treatment as usual. (J. D. Teasdale et al., 2000)

Quick Quiz 16.3: Combined Approaches

1. Dr. Chisholm believes that different disorders require different techniques and strategies for treatment. She is most likely a practitioner of
   a. psychoanalysis.
   b. positive psychotherapy.
   c. mindfulness meditation.
   d. integrative therapy.

2. Combining drugs with psychotherapy works well for which of the following disorders?
   a. mood disorders
   b. anxiety disorders

   c. both a and b
   d. neither a nor b

3. Dialectical behavior therapy (DBT) is a combined treatment program developed for the treatment of
   a. schizophrenia.
   b. borderline personality disorder.
   c. bipolar disorder.
   d. panic disorder.

Answers can be found at the end of the chapter.

Psychology in the Real World

How to Choose a Therapist

Nearly 50% of the adult population at some point in their lives will suffer from a psychological disorder, whether it is phobia, depression, anxiety, schizophrenia, or something else (Kessler et al., 2005). However, only a subset of those who need therapy seek it out or receive it (*Mental health,* 2001). Why? One reason has to do with the stigma of "seeing a shrink"—many people do not want their friends, family, or coworkers and bosses to know they are seeing a therapist. There is a stigma attached to the need for mental health treatment (*Mental health,* 2001). Moreover, people often think they have friends and family who can help them so they don't need a therapist. In fact, therapists are trained professionals who have more knowledge, understanding, and training to deal with a whole range of mental health concerns than family and friends. These two forms of help, of course, are not mutually exclusive and should both be sought in unison.

Indeed, research on the effectiveness of treatment shows consistently that treatment is better than no treatment. Suppose that you or a friend or family member is showing signs of difficulty coping or adjusting and would like to find a good therapist. How would you go about doing that?

First, you need to understand the different types of therapists and what they can and cannot do. As briefly described in Chapter 1, most therapists fall into the following five groups:

- *Psychiatrists* are medical doctors who specialize in psychiatry. They are typically the only therapists who can prescribe medications. They often treat the most severe psychological disorders.

- *Clinical psychologists* are trained to help people with moderate to severe psychological disorders that interfere with everyday functioning. They assess, diagnose, and treat people with disorders. They are often trained in PhD (doctorate of philosophy) programs but also in PsyD programs (doctorate of psychology). Clinical psychologists often focus on past experiences as the causes of current problems.

- *Counselors* work in social settings and help people adjust to normal work- and family-related difficulties. They focus on the present rather than the past. Counselors are often trained in education departments and receive either a doctorate of education (EdD) or a master's degree in counseling.

- *Social workers* have a master's degree in social work (MSW) and are trained in clinical practice. Once they pass the licensing exam, they are licensed clinical social workers (LCSWs).

- *Marriage and family therapists (MFTs)* are people who receive a master's degree in clinical psychology; they have many hours of supervised training and pass the licensing exam. As the name implies, MFTs specialize

EMERGING THERAPIES

There are exciting new therapies on the horizon, but they are not yet fully developed and tested for widespread application. In this section, we briefly highlight a few of the more interesting new developments that appear to offer great promise for future treatment.

One new possible treatment involves using light to stimulate neural activity in certain brain regions—a technique generally known as **optogenetics,** a combination of light (hence the *opto* prefix) stimulation and genetics to manipulate the activity of individual neurons (Deisseroth, 2010). Optogenetics was chosen as "Breakthrough of the Decade" by *Science* magazine in 2010. The technique has been used in various mental health–related applications, such as treating OCD and chemical dependency. In one recent study, researchers used light to stimulate neurons in the orbitofrontal region of the brain in mice and were able to decrease compulsive behaviors (Burguière et al., 2013). In another study using mice, researchers stimulated the neurons in the reward center of the brain (the nucleus accumbens) that are activated by cocaine and,

optogenetics
A treatment that uses a combination of light stimulation and genetics to manipulate the activity of individual neurons.

in helping couples and families deal with conflict or difficulties.

A therapist's experience is important (Saisan, Smith, & Segal, 2010). You should look for someone who is trained and has experience in the area in which you are having difficulty. For instance, if you are experiencing obsessive-compulsive disorder, your therapist should have experience helping people with this disorder.

Note that these specialists are not qualified to practice therapy just because they have earned their primary degree (e.g., MD, PhD, PsyD, MSW). They must also undergo up to 1,500 hours of supervised training and pass a licensing exam before they can practice therapy. Therefore, at a minimum you want to make sure the therapist you are considering is licensed and in good standing. Each state has a regulatory board that can tell you whether complaints have been filed against a therapist. Some regulatory websites are dedicated to particular kinds of therapists, such as MFTs (see, for example, http://www.amftrb.org/).

In finding a therapist, trusting your gut feeling is important. Relationships with therapists, after all, *are* relationships. Some work and some do not. You have to feel comfortable with and trust your therapist. You should feel comfortable setting up a trial period of perhaps five or six sessions and then determining whether you want to continue. All good therapists will respect your decision to go elsewhere if therapy is not working for you and won't try to make you feel guilty or convince you to stay. If they do, that is a red flag (Saisan et al., 2010).

The approach and orientation of the therapist may matter to you. Some approaches are very short-term and targeted, and others are very long-term and general. You have to decide which is right for you. Two of the more common approaches are cognitive-behavioral therapy (CBT) and psychoanalytic/psychodynamic therapy. Most therapists will take an eclectic or integrative approach, even if they were trained in a particular orientation. Even those trained in a particular orientation, such as psychodynamic or cognitive-behavioral, may use techniques from different orientations if they feel that those will work best for a particular person.

Finally, once you make all of these decisions, you still need to find a therapist who fits your needs. The most common resources for assisting in finding a therapist are your family doctor, your family and friends, lists of providers recommended by your insurance plan, and mental health associations. So ask a doctor or a friend when you are beginning to search for a therapist. Get advice from multiple sources and see whether there is any overlap. Once you have a recommendation, it is wise to speak with the therapist on the phone to get a sense of your comfort level with this person, or try an initial session. You should not feel obligated to continue with someone if you feel the connection is not right.

when silenced, greatly decreased the appetite for cocaine (Witten et al., 2010). Optogenetics may offer such precise access to specific areas of the brain that it may allow for carefully targeted stimulation-based treatments (some variation on deep brain stimulation), possibly replacing drug therapies that offer much less precise control of mood and behavior (Touriño, Eban-Rothschild, & de Lecea, 2013).

Another potentially exciting future therapy is the regulation of specific genes involved in various mental disorders. A steady stream of recent research has confirmed the role of one particular gene (*neuregulin 1*) in the development of schizophrenia (Law et al., 2006; Mei & Xiong 2008; Yin et al., 2013). Although still in early stages in animals, therapies based on this understanding may be quite beneficial in controlling some of the major symptoms of schizophrenia (Mei & Xiong, 2008; D.-M. Yin et al., 2013).

Some promising new areas of treatment make use of accidental findings of treatments used for other purposes. Consider the case of Botox, which is used for cosmetic purposes. Botox treatment for wrinkles involves injection of a very small amount of botulism toxin (a naturally occurring paralytic agent)

Believe it or not, optogenetics carefully controls electrical impulses to the brain that activate specific neurons. This technique offers promise for the treatment of psychological disorders in humans, such as compulsive disorders.

into the facial muscles underlying common wrinkle areas (such as the area between the eyebrows), causing paralysis and relaxing nearby wrinkles. Once the Botox is injected, people frown less. As discussed in Chapter 11, there is fairly strong evidence for facial feedback contributing to the experience of emotion, so if you reduce muscle feedback from the face, you reduce the emotional experience (Dimberg & Söderkvist, 2011). A handful of studies have shown that after Botox injections to the glabellar region, people feel less depressed (Davis et al., 2010), because feedback to the brain from the facial muscles involved in certain negative emotions is reduced. There is even evidence for significant improvements in mood for people who have major depressive disorder (Wollmer et al., 2012). Botox may offer an easy new treatment for certain types of depression, but further research is needed to test the long-term effectiveness of this treatment. Botox treatment is not without drawbacks, however, as it can reduce one's ability to read other people's facial expressions, which is likely due to reduced facial mimicry during social interaction (Neal & Chartrand, 2011).

Quick Quiz 16.4: Emerging Therapies

1. Optogenetics has shown promise in the treatment of which of the following disorders?
   a. depression
   b. schizophrenia
   c. obsessive-compulsive disorder
   d. all of the above

Answers can be found at the end of the chapter.

2. How does Botox work to improve mood?
   a. by stimulating the brain centers involved in emotion and reward
   b. by paralyzing the facial muscles involved in negative emotions
   c. both a and b
   d. neither a nor b

PREVENTING DISORDERS

The best and safest form of treatment for psychological disorders is prevention. *Prevention* focuses on identifying risk factors for disorders, targeting at-risk populations, and offering training programs that decrease the likelihood of disorders occurring. Many prevention efforts are under way in this country, but most focus on depression, the number one mental health concern in the United States (Kessler et al., 2005).

Just as a healthy diet and an exercise program can help prevent heart disease, prevention programs train people to behave in ways that help stave off depression and other psychological disorders. Preventing depression in at-risk groups, for instance, has decreased the onset of depression by as much as 25% (Beekman et al., 2010). This rate compares well to the success rate for those who receive therapy. Many prevention programs focus on children, because interventions earlier in life increase the likelihood of making a difference. A recent meta-analysis of more than 30 intervention programs for depression in teens found that shorter interventions and those that involve homework are the most effective (Stice et al., 2009).

Teen depression is a growing problem and the major cause of suicide in young people (Wessely & Kerwin, 2004). In a large-scale study of the risk factors for adolescent depression, Van Voorhees and colleagues (2008) conducted face-to-face interviews of teens in grades 7–12 in the home, obtained parent surveys, and measured depressive symptoms using a questionnaire. They found that several characteristics put teens at risk for a depressive episode: being female, being of a nonwhite race-ethnicity, having low-income status, being in poor health, and experiencing parental conflict. Teens who felt a connection among family members, warmth from their parents, and peer acceptance; who did better in school; and who participated in religious activities were less likely to have a depressive episode (Van Voorhees et al., 2008). Research on elementary school children reports similar findings (Dallaire et al., 2008).

In addition to poverty and unemployment, psychosocial factors—especially life stress and a pessimistic outlook on life—increase the risk of depression (Southwick, Vythilingam, & Charney, 2005). For this reason, some intervention programs for teens focus on teaching them skills for dealing with stress, including developing a more optimistic outlook. One after-school program for teens at risk of developing depression is based on CBT. The participants have already experienced mild to moderate symptoms of the disorder; therefore, this program involves retraining in ways of thinking about adversity in life. Clarke and colleagues (1995) reported that compared to those who did not receive the training, those who participated were significantly less likely to become clinically depressed 18 months later.

Another program, the Penn Resiliency Program (PRP), is designed to prevent depression and other psychological disorders by teaching resilience and skills for coping with stress, problem solving (flexibility in the face of adverse or challenging circumstances), and cognitive restructuring (learning to change one's perspective on events). In a meta-analysis of 17 interventions on nearly 2,500 teenagers, Brunwasser and colleagues found that PRP participants had reported fewer depressive symptoms at postintervention and both follow-up assessments compared with youths receiving no intervention (Brunwasser, Gillham, & Kim, 2009). More specifically, in a large-scale study

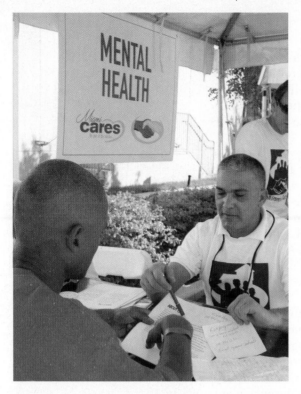

of 697 middle school children, the PRP was administered in weekly 90-minute sessions over a 12-week period (Gillham et al., 2007). PRP significantly reduced depressive symptoms at follow-up compared to a control group and to another intervention, which was not aimed at resiliency, in two of the three schools.

In a similar prevention program, students were assigned to a control group or to an 8-week training program, which consisted of a weekly, 90-minute workshop based on PRP. The group in the training program reported significantly fewer symptoms of anxiety and depression and significantly greater well-being. Although there were no differences between the groups on depressive episodes 6 months later, the students in the training program had increased their ability to achieve an optimistic outlook (Seligman, Schulman, & Tryon, 2007). This is a crucial skill, because depressive thinking is characterized by a tendency to see the negative in any situation. For example, if a glass is filled halfway, someone who is thinking negatively sees the glass as half empty. Helping people look at things differently—in this case, seeing the glass as half full—should help prevent a relapse into depression (J. D. Teasdale et al., 2000). Thus, positive outlooks ingrained early in life ought to help prevent a lifetime of depression.

Some people resist seeking mental health treatment. **Can you think of reasons it is important to offer public education of mental health?**

Bringing It All Together

Making Connections in the Treatment of Psychological Disorders

Approaches to the Treatment of OCD and Anxiety Disorders

Obsessive-compulsive disorder and anxiety disorders are diverse groups of conditions. Although they share the core symptoms of fear and anxiety, the *DSM-5* treats them as separate categories. Because they are so diverse, mental health practitioners use a wide variety of treatment strategies to help people with these disorders. Due to their varied symptoms and treatments, these disorders offer a useful context in which to illustrate the application of the treatments discussed in this chapter.

Drug Therapies

Drug therapies play a major role in the management and treatment of obsessive-compulsive disorder and anxiety disorders. The main categories of medication used for treatment are the antidepressants and the antianxiety drugs.

Antidepressants

Many doctors prescribe SSRIs for the treatment of OCD, anxiety disorders, social phobia, post-traumatic stress disorder (PTSD), and panic disorder. People who take SSRIs for these disorders report that these medications help them disengage from the repetitive cycle of anxiety-provoking thoughts that otherwise would snowball into anxiety. As a result, the SSRIs may help change patterns of thinking when combined with the thought restructuring of CBT and may allow OCD patients to apply cognitive techniques to learn how to think differently. Recent findings that people with OCD who take SSRIs often relapse suggest that combining these drugs with psychological treatments might be more effective than the drugs alone (Catapano et al., 2006). The SSRIs are also considered the first line of treatment for generalized anxiety disorder (Baldwin & Polkinghorn, 2005).

Other antidepressants are prescribed for OCD and anxiety disorders, but much less often. Most tricyclic antidepressants apparently do not work for people with OCD, for example, but do work for certain anxiety disorders. One tricyclic, clomipramine (CMI), however, is most effective on norepinephrine synapses and actually reduces the symptoms of OCD. Because tricyclics have numerous side effects, medical professionals tend to prescribe SSRIs instead (Bleier, Habib, & Flament, 2006).

Antianxiety Medications

Drugs that soothe the agitation of anxiety are used to treat anxiety disorders, especially for people who suffer from panic attacks. Occasionally, physicians prescribe beta-blockers—drugs that block the action of neurotransmitters such as norepinephrine—to quickly calm the aroused sympathetic nervous system. One such drug is propanolol, which is often used to treat high blood pressure and other cardiovascular conditions. These medications calm the physiological symptoms of anxiety by bringing down heart rate, blood pressure, and breathing rate. The benzodiazepines (for example, Valium) also calm the physiological arousal caused by anxiety and are widely prescribed for social phobia, panic disorder, and generalized anxiety disorder. They can also treat or prevent panic attacks in high-anxiety situations, but they are best used only occasionally. When regular users discontinue benzodiazepine use, they experience withdrawal symptoms, such as insomnia, tremors, increased anxiety, tachycardia (rapid heartbeat), and sweating. Newer antianxiety medications, such as buspirone (used for generalized anxiety disorder), are less likely to create withdrawal symptoms, but they require longer, continuous usage to be effective. The newer selective norepinephrine reuptake inhibitors, as well as SSRIs, are also used in the treatment of anxiety disorders (Dell'Osso et al., 2009).

Psychotherapeutic Treatments

As we have seen, cognitive-behavioral therapy helps people with anxiety disorders identify irrational thoughts and undo thinking patterns that support fear; it also helps them modify their responses to anxiety-provoking situations. CBT effectively treats specific phobias and social phobia in children as well as adults (Hirshfeld-Becker et al., 2010). According to a recent meta-analysis, CBT appears to be superior to other psychotherapeutic approaches in treating anxiety disorders overall (Tolin, 2010).

Group CBT therapy is particularly effective in treating social phobia (Hofman et al., 2006; Tolin, 2010). Such contexts usually involve weekly meetings for about 12 weeks, as well as homework assignments each week. In addition to the normal benefits of CBT for reducing anxious thoughts and behaviors, the social factors involved in a group play a key role in the therapy's effectiveness. Because all the participants have gone through similar situations and can share their experiences, this support helps prevent feelings of isolation and helplessness. Also, group members provide examples of success. If someone in a social phobia group has managed to go to a deli, order a sandwich, and pay the cashier and it went well, this provides an example that simple social transactions really can be done. Other group members might be inspired to try it themselves. Avatar therapy, with virtual reality group CBT, is now being used to treat social phobia as well (Riva, 2009).

Traditional psychodynamic therapies viewed anxiety as the main symptom of what was then commonly called neurosis. Neuroses, according to Freud, most often stemmed from repressed thoughts, feelings, and impulses that usually originated in childhood experiences. Therefore, the main approach of psychodynamic therapies is to uncover the unconscious thoughts, feelings, and impulses that lead to symptoms. Most commonly, this is achieved through dream interpretation, free association, the uncovering of defense mechanisms, and catharsis. Symptom relief requires insight, and insight requires the emotional release of repressed feelings.

We have already discussed the use of systematic desensitization for the treatment of specific phobias. This process couples relaxation training with gradual exposure to the feared object and is very effective for the treatment of specific phobias, such as fears of animals, flying, and heights (Aitken & Benson, 1984; Wiederhold & Wiederhold, 2005).

Combined and Integrative Therapies and Anxiety

Sometimes medication can help people get "over the hump" of crippling symptoms, so that a nondrug therapy has a chance to work. Such is the case with the combination of either antidepressants or antianxiety medications and CBT or systematic desensitization. Often the course of medication treatment is short-term, until the psychotherapeutic training begins to take effect. Alternatively, the medication may be decreased slowly during the course of psychological treatment.

Combining drug therapy and psychotherapy offers hope for treating anxiety disorders, particularly OCD. For example, in a review of the literature on children and teens who suffer from obsessive-compulsive disorder, Kaiser and Bouvard (2009) found that combining drug therapy with CBT was almost always as effective and sometimes more effective than either one alone. Although combined therapies are recommended, a review of the treatment efficacy of combined therapies versus single therapy for anxiety disorders yielded little consistent evidence that combined therapy works better (Black, 2006). In fact, in some cases, drug mechanisms may inhibit the thought processes necessary to make a cognitive or behavior therapy work, as may be the case with combined drug-exposure therapy for anxiety disorders (Otto, McHugh, & Kantak, 2010).

There is evidence that integrative psychotherapeutic approaches offer potential relief from a range of anxiety disorders. As already noted, OCD may be treated with mindfulness meditation practices and cognitive therapy. Mindfulness-based cognitive therapy shows promise in the treatment of generalized anxiety disorder (S. Evans et al., 2008). Also, dialectical behavior therapy (DBT), which was developed to treat borderline personality disorder, has been used effectively to treat post-traumatic stress disorder (Wagner & Linehan, 2006).

Chapter Review

BIOMEDICAL TREATMENTS FOR PSYCHOLOGICAL DISORDERS

- Both biomedical and psychological approaches are used to treat psychological disorders. Drugs are the most commonly used biomedical treatment.

- Many different drugs are used to treat depression. The older antidepressants include the monoamine oxidase (MAO) inhibitors and the tricyclic antidepressants. The selective serotonin reuptake inhibitors (SSRIs) reduce the reuptake of serotonin at the synapse and create far fewer unpleasant side effects than the older antidepressants.

- Helen Mayberg discovered what may be a neural switch for depression, known as Area 25. Deep brain stimulation of Area 25 can provide sudden relief from depression in people who have failed to respond to any other treatment.

- The SSRIs and tricyclics are equally effective in the treatment of depression. The SSRIs have the fewest adverse side effects and seem to be tolerated better for long-term use.

- Lithium is prescribed to stabilize the mania associated with bipolar disorder. Due to the toxicity of lithium, medical professionals often prescribe other drugs to regulate manic episodes.

- The evidence for lithium's effectiveness in treating bipolar disorder is weak, in spite of its regular use for this purpose in the United States. It does not appear to be superior to less toxic anticonvulsants or antipsychotics in regulating manic episodes.

- Drug therapies for schizophrenia include the traditional antipsychotics, which are rarely prescribed these days due to their adverse side effects, and the atypical antipsychotics. The atypical antipsychotics do not lead to tardive dyskinesia, and they are somewhat better at treating negative symptoms.

- Both traditional and atypical antipsychotic drugs work best on the positive symptoms of schizophrenia. Certain atypical antipsychotic drugs may relieve the negative symptoms.

- Psychosurgery is brain surgery performed to treat psychological disorders. Prefrontal lobotomy was once used to reduce psychotic behavior, but it is now considered an outdated and cruel procedure.

- Electroconvulsive therapy (ECT) involves passing electrical current through the brain to induce a seizure. Because ECT can lead to memory loss, the only currently acceptable clinical application of ECT is for cases of severe depression that fail to respond to any other treatment.

- Although many patients report immediate relief with ECT, usually it is effective only as long as treatments are maintained. Also, the adverse effects of ECT on memory can be fairly severe.

PSYCHOLOGICAL TREATMENTS FOR PSYCHOLOGICAL DISORDERS

- Psychotherapy is the use of psychological techniques to modify maladaptive behaviors or thought patterns, or both, and to develop insight into the client's behavior.

- Psychodynamic therapies aim to uncover unconscious conflicts, motives, or other underlying psychological difficulties. Psychodynamic therapists use several techniques, such as free association, to access the unconscious.

- Humanistic/positive therapies, such as client-centered therapy, help clients realize their full potential. Therapists create an atmosphere in which clients can communicate their feelings with the certainty that they are being understood rather than judged.

- Behavior therapies apply the principles of conditioning to the treatment of disorders. Systematic desensitization, a widely used behavioral method, pairs relaxation with gradual exposure to a phobic object.

- Cognitive therapies work to restructure irrational thought patterns. Often therapists combine cognitive techniques for changing irrational thoughts with behavioral techniques to shape desirable behaviors in what is known as cognitive-behavioral therapy (CBT). CBT is a short-term psychological treatment that has been successfully applied to many disorders.

- Psychotherapy is more effective for certain disorders than for others. CBT may be the most effective form of psychotherapy, especially for certain cases of depression and anxiety disorders.

TECHNOLOGY-BASED TREATMENTS FOR PSYCHOLOGICAL DISORDERS

- A number of newer therapies make use of technology or the Internet to complement current therapies or to make psychotherapeutic techniques available to people who might otherwise not have access to them or seek them out.

- Virtual reality therapies, a subset of which is known as "avatar therapy," use virtual environments (digital simulations) that create therapeutic situations that might be hard to create otherwise.

COMBINED APPROACHES

- Combined treatments are increasingly common in practice. These include methods that combine drugs with psychotherapy and those that combine various forms of psychotherapy with each other. Mindfulness practices have also been added to traditional treatments.

- Many treatments, including CBT, are administered as group therapy. Group contexts serve as both a source of support and an aid to the therapeutic process, allowing several people with similar problems to listen, discuss, and criticize one another.

- In some cases, the most effective treatments for many psychological disorders integrate one form of treatment with another.

EMERGING THERAPIES

- Some therapies, such as optogenetics, gene manipulation, and even Botox, are "not yet ready for prime time" but show promise for the future.

PREVENTING DISORDERS

- Prevention focuses on identifying the risk factors for disorders, targeting at-risk populations, and offering training programs that decrease the likelihood of disorders occurring.

- Many prevention efforts are under way in this country, but most focus on the prevention of depression, the number one mental health concern in the United States.

BRINGING IT ALL TOGETHER: MAKING CONNECTIONS IN THE TREATMENT OF PSYCHOLOGICAL DISORDERS

- Both drug therapy and psychotherapy together are often used to treat obsessive-compulsive disorder (OCD) and anxiety disorder.

Key Terms

atypical antipsychotics, p. 592
barbiturates, p. 594
behavior therapies, p. 602
benzodiazepines, p. 594
catharsis, p. 601
client-centered therapy, p. 601
cognitive-behavioral therapy (CBT), p. 605
cognitive therapy, p. 603
dialectical behavior therapy (DBT), p. 612
dodo bird verdict, p. 607
electroconvulsive therapy (ECT), p. 595

evidence-based therapies, p. 607
flooding, p. 603
free association, p. 601
group therapy, p. 605
integrative therapy, p. 611
lithium, p. 594
mindfulness-based cognitive therapy (MBCT), p. 611
monoamine oxidase (MAO) inhibitors, p. 592
optogenetics, p. 614
phenothiazines, p. 591
prefrontal lobotomy, p. 595
psychoanalytic therapy, p. 600

psychotherapy, p. 600
repetitive transcranial magnetic stimulation, p. 596
selective serotonin reuptake inhibitors (SSRIs), p. 593
support groups, p. 606
systematic desensitization, p. 603
tardive dyskinesia, p. 591
technology-based therapies, p. 609
token economies, p. 602
traditional antipsychotics, p. 591
transference, p. 601
tricyclic antidepressants, p. 593
virtual reality therapies, p. 609

Quick Quiz Answers

Quick Quiz 16.1: 1. b 2. c 3. d 4. b 5. b   **Quick Quiz 16.2:** 1. a 2. d 3. a 4. b   **Quick Quiz 16.3:** 1. d 2. c 3. b
Quick Quiz 16.4: 1. c 2. b

Glossary

absent-mindedness a form of forgetfulness that results from inattention.

absolute threshold the lowest intensity level of a stimulus a person can detect half of the time.

accommodation the process by which the muscles control the shape of the lens to adjust to viewing objects at different distances.

acetylcholine (ACh) a neurotransmitter that controls muscle movement and plays a role in mental processes such as learning, memory, attention, sleeping, and dreaming.

achievement motivation a desire to do things well and overcome obstacles.

acquired immunity immunity provided by antibodies produced in the body in response to specific antigens.

action potential the impulse of positive charge that runs down an axon.

adaptations inherited solutions to ancestral problems that have been selected for because they contribute in some way to reproductive success.

adaptive behavior adjustment to and coping with everyday life.

addiction a condition that results from habitual use or physical and psychological dependence on a substance.

adolescence the transition period between childhood and adulthood.

adrenal glands endocrine structures that release hormones important in regulating the stress response and emotions.

adrenal-medullary system a major neuro-endocrine pathway stimulated during stress, in which the hypothalamus activates the sympathetic nervous system.

affective traits stable predispositions toward certain types of emotional responses.

afterimages visual images that remain after removal of or looking away from the stimulus.

aggression violent behavior that is intended to cause psychological or physical harm, or both, to another being.

agoraphobia an anxiety disorder involving fear of being in places from which escape might be difficult or in which help might not be available, should a panic attack occur.

AIM three biologically based dimensions of consciousness—activation, input, and mode.

alarm stage the phase of the general adaptation syndrome in which all of the body's resources respond to a perceived threat.

algorithm a step-by-step procedure or formula for solving a problem.

alleles different forms of a gene.

all-or-none principle the idea that, once the threshold has been crossed, either an action potential fires or it does not.

allostasis the process by which the body achieves stability through physiological change.

alpha waves the pattern of brain activity when one is relaxed and drowsy; slower, higher-energy waves than beta waves.

altruism selfless attitudes and behavior toward others.

Alzheimer's disease a degenerative disease marked by progressive cognitive decline and characterized by a collection of symptoms, including confusion, memory loss, mood swings, and eventual loss of physical function.

amnesia memory loss due to brain injury or disease.

amygdala a small, almond-shaped structure located directly in front of the hippocampus; has connections with many important brain regions and is important for processing emotional information, especially that related to fear.

anima according to Jung, the female part of the male personality.

animistic thinking a belief that inanimate objects are alive.

animus according to Jung, the male part of the female personality.

anorexia nervosa an eating disorder in which people cannot maintain 85% of their ideal body weight for their height, have an intense fear of eating, and have a distorted body image.

anterograde amnesia the inability to remember events and experiences that occur after an injury or the onset of a disease.

antigen any foreign substance that triggers an immune response.

antisocial personality disorder dramatic-emotional personality disorder characterized by extremely impulsive, deceptive, violent, ruthless, and callous behaviors; a serious and potentially dangerous disorder.

aphasia a deficit in the ability to speak or comprehend language.

appraisal the evaluation of a situation with respect to how relevant it is to one's own welfare; drives the process by which emotions are elicited.

arborization the growth and formation of new dendrites.

archetypes ancient or archaic images that result from common ancestral experiences.

association a process by which two pieces of information from the environment are repeatedly linked, so that we begin to connect them in our minds.

associative network a chain of associations between related concepts.

asylums facilities for treating the mentally ill in Europe during the Middle Ages and into the 19th century.

attachment the strong emotional connection that develops early in life between infants and their caregivers.

attention the limited capacity to process information that is under conscious control.

attention deficit hyperactivity disorder (ADHD) a childhood disorder characterized by inability to focus attention for more than a few minutes, to remain still and quiet, to do careful work.

attitudes an individual's favorable or unfavorable beliefs, feelings, or actions toward an object, an idea, or a person.

attributions inferences made about the causes of other people's behavior.

atypical antipsychotics newer antipsychotic drugs, which do not create tardive dyskinesia.

auditory nerve the nerve that receives action potentials from the hair cells and transmits auditory information to the brain.

autism spectrum disorder (ASD) a childhood disorder characterized by severe language and social impairment along with repetitive habits and inward-focused behaviors.

automatic processing encoding of information that occurs with little effort or conscious attention to the task.

autonomic nervous system (ANS) all the nerves of the peripheral nervous system that serve involuntary systems of the body, such as the internal organs and glands.

availability heuristic a device we use to make decisions based on the ease with which estimates come to mind or how available they are to our awareness.

avoidant personality disorder an anxious-fearful personality disorder characterized by extreme fear of being criticized, low self-esteem, and avoidance of social interaction.

awareness monitoring of information from the environment and from one's own thoughts.

axon a long projection that extends from a neuron's soma; it transmits electrical impulses toward the adjacent neuron and stimulates the release of neurotransmitters.

babbling sounds made as a result of the infant's experimentation with a complex range of phonemes, which include consonants as well as vowels; starts around 5–6 months of age.

barbiturates a class of anxiety-reducing sedatives that can be addictive and carry a risk of overdose.

basal ganglia a collection of structures surrounding the thalamus; involved in voluntary motor control.

basic emotions the set of emotions that are common to all humans; includes anger, disgust, fear, happiness, sadness, and surprise.

basic tendencies the essence of personality: the Big Five personality dimensions, as well as talents, aptitudes, and cognitive abilities.

basilar membrane a membrane that runs through the cochlea; contains the hair cells.

behavior modification the principles of operant conditioning used to change behavior.

behavior therapies therapies that apply the principles of classical and operant conditioning in the treatment of psychological disorders.

behavioral genetics the scientific study of the role of heredity in behavior.

behavioral measures measures based on systematic observation of people's actions either in their normal environment or in a laboratory setting.

behavioral neuroscience the study of the links among brain, mind, and behavior.

behavioral thresholds the points at which a person moves from not having a particular response to having one.

behaviorism a school of psychology which proposed that psychology can be a true science only if it examines observable behavior, not ideas, thoughts, feelings, or motives.

benzodiazepines a class of anxiety-reducing drugs that can be addictive but are less dangerous than barbiturates.

beta waves the pattern of brain activity when one is awake; rapid, low-energy waves.

Big Five (five-factor model) a theory of personality that includes the following five dimensions: openness to experience, conscientiousness, extraversion, agreeableness, and neuroticism (OCEAN).

binocular depth cues aids to depth perception that rely on input from both eyes.

biological constraint model a view on learning which proposes that some behaviors are inherently more likely to be learned than others.

biological psychology the study of the relationship between bodily systems and chemicals and how they influence behavior and thought.

bipolar disorder a mood disorder characterized by substantial mood fluctuations, cycling between very low (depressive) and very high (manic) moods.

blocking the inability to retrieve some information that once was stored.

bodily senses the senses based in the skin, the body, or any membrane surfaces.

borderline personality disorder a dramatic-emotional personality disorder characterized by out-of-control emotions, fear of being abandoned by others, and vacillation between idealizing and despising people who are close to the person with the disorder.

bottom-up processing the idea that perception is a process of building a perceptual experience from smaller pieces.

broad intelligence one of Carroll's three levels of intelligence; includes abilities such as crystallized and fluid intelligence, memory, learning, and processing speed.

broaden-and-build model Fredrickson's model for positive emotions, which posits that they widen our cognitive perspective and help us acquire useful life skills.

Broca's area the area in the left frontal lobe responsible for the ability to produce speech.

bulimia nervosa an eating disorder characterized by binge eating and a perceived lack of control during the eating session.

bystander effect a phenomenon in which the greater the number of bystanders who witness an emergency, the less likely any one of them is to help.

cardiovascular reactivity (CVR) model the hypothesis that hostility can increase the likelihood of heart disease through at least two different causal routes.

cardiovascular system the heart, the blood, and all the blood vessels.

case study a study design in which a psychologist, often a therapist, observes one person over a long period of time.

catecholamines chemicals released from the adrenal glands that function as hormones and as neurotransmitters to control ANS activation.

category a concept that organizes other concepts around what they all share in common.

catharsis the process of releasing intense, often unconscious emotions in a therapeutic setting.

causal inferences judgments about causation of one thing by another.

cellular immunity the immune response that occurs when T lymphocytes (T cells) fight antigens.

central nervous system (CNS) the part of the nervous system that comprises the brain and spinal cord.

cerebellum a hindbrain structure involved in body movement, balance, coordination, fine-tuning motor skills, and cognitive activities such as learning and language.

cerebral cortex the thin outer layer of the cerebrum, in which much of human thought, planning, perception, and consciousness takes place.

cerebrum each of the large halves of the brain; covered with convolutions, or folds.

child-directed speech changes in adult speech patterns—apparently universal—when speaking to young children or infants; characterized by higher pitch, changes in voice volume, use of simpler sentences, emphasis on the here and now, and use of emotion to communicate messages.

chromosome a coiled-up thread of DNA.

chunking breaking down a list of items to be remembered into a smaller set of meaningful units.

cingulate gyrus a beltlike structure in the middle of the brain; plays an important role in attention and cognitive control.

circadian rhythms the variations in physiological processes that cycle within approximately a 24-hour period, including the sleep-wake cycle.

classical conditioning a form of associative learning in which a neutral stimulus becomes associated with a stimulus to which one has an automatic, inborn response.

client-centered therapy a form of humanistic therapy in which the therapist shows unconditional positive regard for the patient.

clinical psychology the treatment of mental, emotional, and behavioral disorders and the promotion of psychological health.

cochlea a bony tube of the inner ear, which is curled like a snail's shell and filled with fluid.

cognition mental processes involved in acquiring, processing, and storing knowledge.

cognitive-behavioral therapy (CBT) an approach to treating psychological disorders that combines techniques for restructuring irrational thoughts with operant and classical conditioning techniques to shape desirable behaviors.

cognitive dissonance the feeling of discomfort caused by information that is different from a person's conception of himself or herself as a reasonable and sensible person.

cognitive psychology the study of how people perceive, remember, think, speak, and solve problems.

cognitive symptoms (of schizophrenia) problems with working memory, attention, verbal and visual learning and memory, reasoning and problem solving, processing, and speech.

cognitive therapy any type of psychotherapy that works to restructure irrational thought patterns.

collective unconscious according to Jung, the form of consciousness that consists of the shared experiences of our ancestors—God, mother, life, death, water, earth, aggression, survival—that have been passed down from generation to generation.

coma a state of consciousness in which the eyes are closed and the person is unresponsive and unarousable.

comorbidity the occurrence of two or more psychological disorders at the same time.

compassion a state of relationship in which one feels kindness toward another who is suffering and one feels motivated to help relieve that suffering.

compulsion a repetitive behavior performed in response to uncontrollable urges or according to a ritualistic set of rules.

concept a mental grouping of objects, events, or people.

concept hierarchy an arrangement of related concepts in a particular way, with some being general and others specific.

concrete operational stage Piaget's third stage of cognitive development, which spans ages 6–11, during which the child can perform mental operations—such as reversing—on real objects or events.

conditioned response (CR) a behavior that an organism learns to perform when presented with the CS.

conditioned stimulus (CS) a previously neutral input that an organism learns to associate with the UCS.

conditioned taste aversion the learned avoidance of a particular taste or food.

conditioning a form of associative learning in which behaviors are triggered by associations with events in the environment.

cones photoreceptors that are responsible for color vision and are most functional in conditions of bright light.

confirmation bias the tendency to selectively attend to information that supports one's general beliefs while ignoring information or evidence that contradicts one's beliefs.

conformity the tendency of people to adjust their behavior to what others are doing or to adhere to the norms of their culture.

confounding variable the variable whose influence on the dependent variable cannot be separated from the independent variable being examined.

conjunction fallacy an error in logic that occurs when people say the combination of two events is more likely than either event alone.

consciousness an awareness of one's surroundings and of what's in one's mind at a given moment; includes aspects of being awake and aware.

conservation recognition that when some properties (such as shape) of an object change, other properties (such as volume) remain constant.

consolidation the process of establishing, stabilizing, or solidifying a memory; the second stage of long-term memory formation.

construct validity the degree to which a test measures the concept it claims to measure, such as intelligence.

continuity the Gestalt law that says we see points or lines in such a way that they follow a continuous path.

continuous reinforcement reinforcement of a behavior every time it occurs.

control group a group of research participants who are treated in exactly the same manner as the experimental group, except that they do not receive the independent variable, or treatment.

conventional level the second level in Kohlberg's theory of moral reasoning, during which the person values caring, trust, and relationships as well as the social order and lawfulness.

convergent thinking problems problems that have known solutions and require analytic thinking and the use of learned strategies and knowledge to come up with the correct answer.

cooing the first sounds humans make other than crying, consisting almost exclusively of vowels; occurs during the first 6 months of life.

coping the act of dealing with stress or emotions.

cornea the clear, hard covering that protects the lens of the eye.

corpus callosum nerve fibers that connect the two hemispheres of the brain.

correlation coefficients statistics that range from −1.0 to +1.0 and assess the strength and direction of association between two variables.

correlational designs studies that measure two or more variables and their relationship to one another; not designed to show causation.

cortical arousal the brain's level of activity at a resting state and its sensitivity to stimulation.

cortisol a stress hormone produced by the body to ensure that the body gets enough fuel during emotional arousal and stress.

creativity thinking and/or behavior that is both novel—original and useful—and adaptive.

critical thinking a process by which one analyzes, evaluates, and forms ideas.

crystallized intelligence the kind of knowledge that one gains from experience and learning, education, and practice.

cult an extremist group led by a charismatic, totalitarian leader in which coercive methods are used to prevent members from leaving the group.

cultural test bias the notion that group differences in IQ scores are caused by different cultural and educational backgrounds, not by real differences in intelligence.

cyberbullying the willful and repeated harm inflicted through the medium of electronic text.

cyclothymia a relatively mild form of bipolar disorder.

dark adaptation the process of adjustment to seeing in the dark.

debriefing the explanation of the purposes of a study following data collection.

deductive reasoning reasoning from general statements of what is known to specific conclusions.

defense mechanisms unconscious strategies the mind uses to protect itself from anxiety by denying and distorting reality in some way.

delta waves type of brain activity that dominates Stage 3 sleep; higher energy than theta waves.

delusions one of the symptoms of schizophrenia: false beliefs or exaggerations held despite evidence to the contrary, such as the idea that one is a famous person.

dementia a loss of mental function, in which many cognitive processes are impaired, such as the ability to remember, reason, solve problems, make decisions, and use language.

dendrites fingerlike projections from a neuron's soma that receive incoming messages from other neurons.

dependent personality disorder an anxious-fearful personality disorder characterized by fear of being rejected and a strong need to be cared for.

dependent variable in an experiment, the outcome or response to the experimental manipulation.

depressants substances that decrease or slow down central nervous system activity.

depressive disorder the highest order category of the depressive disorders and subsumes all forms of depression, including major depressive disorder and persistent depressive disorder.

depth perception the ability to see things in three dimensions and to discriminate what is near from what is far.

descriptive designs study designs in which the researcher defines a problem and variable of interest but makes no prediction and does not control or manipulate anything.

descriptive statistics measures used to describe and summarize research.

developmental psychology the study of how thought and behavior change and remain stable across the life span.

dialectical behavior therapy (DBT) treatment that integrates elements of CBT with exercises aimed at developing mindfulness without meditation and is used to treat borderline personality disorders.

diathesis-stress biological predispositions plus stress or abusive environments together produce psychological disorders.

diathesis-stress model an explanation for the origin of psychological disorders as a combination of biological predispositions (diathesis) plus stress or an abusive environment.

difference threshold the smallest amount of change between two stimuli that a person can detect half of the time.

discrimination the preferential treatment of certain people, usually driven by prejudicial attitudes.

display rules learned norms or rules, often taught very early, about when it is appropriate to express certain emotions and to whom one should show them.

dissociative disorders psychological disorders characterized by extreme splits or gaps in memory, identity, or consciousness.

dissociative identity disorder (DID) a dissociative disorder in which a person develops at least two distinct personalities, each with its own memories, thoughts, behaviors, and emotions; some psychiatrists question the legitimacy of the disorder.

divergent thinking problems problems that have no known solutions and require novel solutions.

DNA (deoxyribonucleic acid) a large molecule that contains genes.

dodo bird verdict the finding that most forms of therapy are effective and few significant differences exist in effectiveness among standard therapies.

dominant alleles alleles that show their effect even if there is only one allele for that trait in the pair.

dopamine a neurotransmitter released in response to behaviors that feel good or are rewarding to the person or animal; also involved in voluntary motor control.

double-blind studies studies in which neither the participants nor the researchers administering the treatment know who has been assigned to the experimental or control group.

Down syndrome a chromosomal disorder characterized by mild to profound intellectual disability.

dreams images, thoughts, and feelings experienced during sleep.

drives the perceived states of tension that occur when our bodies are deficient in some need, creating an urge to relieve the tension.

Duchenne smile a smile that expresses true enjoyment, involving both the muscles that pull up the lip corners diagonally and those that contract the band of muscles encircling the eye.

educational psychology the study of how students learn, the effectiveness of particular teaching techniques, the social psychology of schools, and the psychology of teaching.

effect size a measure of the strength of the relationship between two variables or the extent of an experimental effect.

effortful processing encoding of information that occurs with careful attention and conscious effort.

ego one of Freud's provinces of the mind; a sense of self; the only part of the mind that is in direct contact with the outside world; operates on the "reality principle."

egocentrism viewing the world from one's own perspective and not being capable of seeing things from another person's perspective.

electroconvulsive therapy (ECT) the treatment of last resort for severe depression that involves passing an electrical current through a person's brain in order to induce a seizure.

electroencephalography (EEG) a method for measuring brain activity in which the electrical activity of the brain is recorded from electrodes placed on a person's scalp.

embryo a developing organism from 2 weeks until about 8 weeks after conception.

embryonic stage the second prenatal stage, from 2 weeks to 8 weeks after conception, when all of the major organs form.

emerging adulthood the transitional phase between adolescence and young adulthood; includes ages 18–25 years.

emotion-focused coping a way of dealing with stress that aims to regulate the experience of distress.

emotion regulation the cognitive and behavioral efforts people make to modify their emotions.

emotional competence the ability to control emotions and know when it is appropriate to express certain emotions.

emotional disclosure a way of coping with stress through writing or talking about the situation.

emotional intelligence the ability to recognize emotions in oneself and others, empathic understanding, and skills for regulating emotions in oneself and others.

emotional response the physiological, behavioral/expressive, and subjective changes that occur when emotions are generated.

emotions brief, acute changes in conscious experience and physiology that occur in response to a personally meaningful situation.

empathy the ability to share the feelings of others and understand their situations.

empathy-altruism hypothesis the idea that people help others selflessly only when they feel empathy for them.

empirical method a method for developing questionnaire items that focuses on including questions that characterize the group the questionnaire is intended to distinguish.

empiricism the view that all knowledge and thoughts come from experience.

enactive learning learning by doing.

encoding the process by which the brain attends to, takes in, and integrates new information; the first stage of long-term memory formation.

endocannabinoids natural, marijuana-like substances produced by the body.

endocrine system the system of glands that secrete and regulate hormones in the body.

enzymatic degradation a way of removing excess neurotransmitter from the synapse in which enzymes specific for that neurotransmitter bind with the neurotransmitter and destroy it.

epigenetics the study of changes in the way genes are turned on or off without a change in the sequence of DNA.

epinephrine also known as adrenaline, a neurotransmitter that arouses bodily systems (such as increasing heart rate).

episodic memory the form of memory that recalls the experiences we have had.

ethics the rules governing the conduct of a person or group in general or in a specific situation—or more simply, standards of right and wrong.

ethology the scientific study of animal behavior.

Eureka insight (insight solution) a sudden solution that comes to mind in a flash.

event-related potential (ERP) a technique that extracts electrical activity from raw EEG data to measure cognitive processes.

evidence-based therapies treatment choices based on empirical evidence that they produce the desired outcome.

evolution the change over time in the frequency with which specific genes occur within a breeding species.

evolutionary psychology the branch of psychology that studies human behavior by asking what adaptive problems it may have solved for our early ancestors.

exhaustion stage the phase of the general adaptation syndrome when all resources for fighting the threat have been depleted and illness is more likely.

experiment a research design that includes independent and dependent variables and random assignment of participants to control and experimental groups or conditions.

experimental group a group consisting of those participants who will receive the treatment or whatever is predicted to change behavior.

experimenter expectancy effects a result that occurs when the behavior of the participants is influenced by the experimenter's knowledge of who is in the control group and who is in the experimental group.

explicit memory knowledge that consists of the conscious recall of facts and events; also known as declarative memory.

expressive suppression a response-focused strategy for regulating emotion that involves the deliberate attempt to inhibit the outward manifestation of an emotion.

extinction the weakening and disappearance of a conditioned response in the absence of reinforcement.

extrinsic motivation motivation that comes from outside the person and usually involves rewards and praises.

Facial Action Coding System (FACS) a widely used method for measuring all observable muscular movements that are possible in the human face.

facial feedback hypothesis sensory feedback from the facial musculature during expression affects emotional experience.

false memories memories for events that never happened but were suggested by someone or something.

feature detectors neurons in the visual cortex that analyze the retinal image and respond to specific aspects of shapes, such as angles and movements.

fetal alcohol spectrum disorder (FASD) a consequence of prenatal alcohol exposure that causes multiple problems, notably brain damage.

fetal stage the third prenatal stage, which begins with the formation of bone cells 8 weeks after conception and ends at birth.

fixation the inability to break out of a particular mind-set in order to think about a problem from a fresh perspective.

fixed interval (FI) schedule a pattern of intermittent reinforcement in which responses are always reinforced after a set period of time has passed.

fixed ratio (FR) schedule a pattern of intermittent reinforcement in which reinforcement follows a set number of responses.

flashbulb memories detailed, especially vivid memories of very specific, highly charged events.

flexibility of thought the ability to come up with many different categories of ideas and think of other responses besides the obvious one.

flooding form of in vivo exposure in which the client experiences extreme exposure to the phobic object.

fluid intelligence raw mental ability, pattern recognition, and abstract reasoning that can be applied to a problem one has never confronted before.

forensic psychology the field that blends psychology, law, and criminal justice.

forgetting the weakening or loss of memories over time.

forgetting curve a graphic depiction of how recall steadily declines over time.

formal operational stage Piaget's final stage of cognitive development, from age 11 or 12 on through adulthood, when formal logic is possible.

fovea a spot on the back of the retina that contains the highest concentration of cones in the retina; place of clearest vision.

fraternal twins twins that develop from two different eggs fertilized by two different sperm.

free association a psychotherapeutic technique in which the client takes one image or idea from a dream and says whatever comes to mind, regardless of how threatening, disgusting, or troubling it may be.

frequency the number of times a particular score occurs in a set of data.

functional fixedness a mind-set in which one is blind to unusual uses of common, everyday things or procedures.

functional MRI (fMRI) a brain imaging technique that uses magnetic fields to produce detailed images of activity in areas of the brain and other soft tissues.

functionalism the 19th-century school of psychology that argued it was better to look at why the mind works the way it does than to describe its parts.

fundamental attribution error the tendency to explain others' behavior in dispositional rather than situational terms.

GABA (gamma-aminobutyric acid) a major inhibitory neurotransmitter in the brain that tells postsynaptic neurons *not* to fire; it slows CNS activity and is necessary to regulate and control neural activity.

gate control theory of pain the idea that the spinal cord regulates the experience of pain by either opening or closing neural channels, called *gates*, that transmit pain sensations to the brain.

gene-by-environment interaction research a method of studying heritability by comparing genetic markers; allows researchers to assess how genetic differences interact with the environment to produce certain behaviors in some people but not in others.

general adaptation syndrome (GAS) as defined by Hans Selye, a generalized, nonspecific set of changes in the body that occur during extreme stress.

general intelligence one of Carroll's three levels of intelligence; very similar to Spearman's concept of "g."

generalized anxiety disorder (GAD) a state of pervasive and excessive anxiety lasting at least 6 months.

generativity a term Erik Erikson used to describe the process in adulthood of creating new ideas, products, or people.

genes small segments of DNA that contain information for producing proteins.

genius high intelligence combined with creative accomplishments that have a tremendous impact on a given field.

genome all the genetic information in DNA.

genotype the entire genetic makeup of an organism.

germinal stage the first prenatal stage of development, which begins at conception and lasts 2 weeks.

Gestalt psychology a theory of psychology that maintains that we perceive things as wholes rather than as a compilation of parts.

g-factor theory Spearman's theory that intelligence is a single general (g) factor made up of specific components.

glial cells central nervous system cells that provide structural support, promote efficient communication between neurons, and serve as scavengers, removing cellular debris.

glucocorticoids hormones responsible for maintaining the activation of physiological systems during emergencies.

glucose a simple sugar that provides energy for cells throughout the body, including the brain.

glutamate a major excitatory neurotransmitter in the brain that increases the likelihood that a postsynaptic neuron will fire; important in learning, memory, neural processing, and brain development.

graded potentials small changes in membrane potential that by themselves are insufficient to trigger an action potential.

grammar the entire set of rules for combining symbols and sounds to speak and write a particular language.

group therapy a therapeutic setting in which several people who share a common problem all meet regularly with a therapist to help themselves and one another.

groupthink a situation in which the thinking of the group takes over, so much so that group members forgo logic or critical analysis in the service of reaching a decision.

hair cells inner ear sensory receptors for sound that transduce sound vibrations into neural impulses.

hallucinations convincing sensory experiences that occur in the absence of an external stimulus.

hallucinogens substances that create distorted perceptions of reality ranging from mild to extreme.

health behavior approach an explanation for illness or health that focuses on the role of behaviors such as diet, exercise, or substance abuse.

health psychology the study of the role psychological factors play in regard to health and illness.

heritability the extent to which a characteristic is influenced by genetics.

heuristics mental shortcuts; methods for making complex and uncertain decisions and judgments.

hierarchies ways of organizing related pieces of information from the most specific feature they have in common to the most general.

hippocampus a limbic structure that wraps itself around the thalamus; plays a vital role in learning and memory.

histrionic personality disorder a dramatic-emotional personality disorder characterized by the desire to be the center of attention and by dramatic, seductive, flamboyant, and exaggerated behaviors.

homeostasis the process by which all organisms work to maintain physiological equilibrium, or balance around an optimal set point.

hormones chemicals, secreted by glands, that travel in the bloodstream and carry messages to tissues and organs all over the body.

human development the study of change and continuity in the individual across the life span.

human language a communication system specific to *Homo sapiens;* it is open and symbolic, has rules of grammar, and allows its users to express abstract and distant ideas.

humanistic psychology a theory of psychology that focuses on personal growth and meaning as a way of reaching one's highest potential.

hypersomnia a sleep difficulty characterized by sleeping more than 10 hours a day for 2 weeks or more; includes an urge to nap during inappropriate times.

hypnosis a state characterized by focused attention, suggestibility, absorption, lack of voluntary control over behavior, and suspension of critical faculties; occurs when instructed by someone trained in hypnosis; may be therapeutic.

hypomanic episodes symptoms of mania (e.g., increased energy, euphoria, racing thoughts) but that are less severe.

hypothalamic-pituitary-adrenal (HPA) axis a major neuroendocrine pathway relevant to the stress response involving the hypothalamus, pituitary gland, and adrenal cortex.

hypothalamus a limbic structure; the master regulator of almost all major drives and motives we have, such as hunger, thirst, temperature, and sexual behavior; also controls the pituitary gland.

hypothesis a specific, informed, and testable prediction of the outcome of a particular set of conditions in a research design.

id one of Freud's provinces of the mind; the seat of impulse and desire; the part of our personality that we do not yet own; it owns or controls us.

ideational fluency the ability to produce many ideas.

identical twins twins that develop from a single fertilized egg that splits into two independent cells.

illness anxiety disorder preoccupation with and anxiety about acquiring a serious illness for at least 6 months.

implicit memory a kind of memory made up of knowledge based on previous experience, such as skills that we perform automatically once we have mastered them; resides outside conscious awareness.

imprinting the rapid and innate learning of the characteristics of a caregiver very soon after birth.

incentive any external object or event that motivates behavior.

independent variable a property that is manipulated by the experimenter under controlled conditions to determine whether it causes the predicted outcome of an experiment.

individuation the process of a person's personality becoming whole and full.

inductive reasoning reasoning to general conclusions from specific evidence.

industrial/organizational (I/O) psychology the application of psychological concepts and questions to work settings.

inferential statistics analyses of data that allow us to test hypotheses and make an inference as to how likely a sample score is to occur in a population.

inferiority complex an unhealthy need to dominate or upstage others as a way of compensating for feelings of deficiency.

informational social influence conformity to the behavior of others because one views them as a source of knowledge about what one is supposed to do.

in-group/out-group bias a tendency to show positive feelings toward people who belong to the same group as we do, and negative feelings toward those in other groups.

insomnia a sleep difficulty characterized by difficulty falling and staying asleep, as well as not feeling rested.

instinctive drift learned behavior that shifts toward instinctive, unlearned behavior tendencies.

institutional review boards (IRBs) organizations that evaluate research proposals to make sure research involving humans does not cause undue harm or distress.

insula a small structure inside the cerebrum that plays an important role in the perception of bodily sensations, emotional states, empathy, and addictive behavior.

integrative therapy an eclectic approach in which the therapist draws on different treatment approaches and uses those that seem most appropriate for the situation.

intellectual disability significant limitations in intellectual functioning as well as in everyday adaptive behavior, which start before age 18.

intelligence a set of cognitive skills that includes abstract thinking, reasoning, problem solving, and the ability to acquire knowledge.

interference disruption of memory because other information competes with the information we are trying to recall.

intermittent reinforcement reinforcement of a behavior—but not after every response.

internal reliability a characteristic of an intelligence test in which questions on a given subtest tend to correlate very highly with other items on the subtest.

interneurons neurons that communicate only with other neurons.

inter-rater reliability a measure of how much agreement there is in ratings when using two or more raters or coders to rate personality or other behaviors.

intimacy as defined by Erikson, the ability to fuse one's identity with another's without the fear of losing it.

intrinsic motivation motivation that comes from within a person and includes the elements of challenge, enjoyment, mastery, and autonomy.

introspection the main method of investigation for structuralists; it involves looking into one's own mind for information about the nature of conscious experience.

ions chemically charged particles that predominate in bodily fluids; found both inside and outside cells.

iris the muscle that forms the colored part of the eye; it adjusts the pupil to regulate the amount of light that enters the eye.

James-Lange theory of emotion the idea that it is the perception of the physiological changes that accompany emotions that produces the subjective emotional experience.

joint attention the ability to make eye contact with others and to look in the same direction that someone else is looking.

kin selection the evolutionary favoring of genes that prompt individuals to help their relatives, or kin.

language acquisition device (LAD) an innate, biologically based capacity to acquire language, proposed by Noam Chomsky as part of his nativist view of language.

latent learning learning that occurs in the absence of reinforcement and is not demonstrated until later, when reinforcement occurs.

latent level Freud's deeper, unconscious level of dreams; their meaning is found at this level.

law of closure the tendency to perceive a whole object in the absence of complete information.

law of effect the consequences of a behavior increase (or decrease) the likelihood that the behavior will be repeated.

learning enduring changes in behavior that occur with experience.

learning curve the rate at which learning occurs over time.

lens the structure that sits behind the pupil; it bends the light rays that enter the eye to focus images on the retina.

levels of processing the concept that the more deeply people encode information, the better they will recall it.

life satisfaction the overall evaluation we make of our lives and an aspect of subjective well-being.

linguistic determinism hypothesis the proposition that our language determines our way of thinking and our perceptions of the world; the view taken by Sapir and Whorf.

lithium a salt that is prescribed for its ability to stabilize the mania associated with bipolar disorder.

long-term potentiation (LTP) the strengthening of a synaptic connection that results when a synapse of one neuron repeatedly fires and excites another neuron.

long-term memory the part of memory that has the capacity to store a vast amount of information for as little as 30 seconds and as long as a lifetime.

long-term potentiation the strengthening of a synaptic connection that results when synapse of one neuron repeatedly fires and excites another neuron.

magnetic resonance imaging (MRI) a brain imaging technique that uses magnetic fields to produce detailed images of the structure of the brain and other soft tissues.

major depressive disorder a mood disorder characterized by pervasive low mood, lack of motivation, low energy, and feelings of worthlessness and guilt that last for at least 2 consecutive weeks.

manic episodes one mood cycle in bipolar disorder, typically involving increased energy, sleeplessness, euphoria, irritability, delusions of grandeur, increased sex drive, and "racing" thoughts that last at least 1 week.

manifest level Freud's surface level of dreams, recalled upon waking.

mean the arithmetic average of a series of numbers.

measures the tools and techniques used to assess thought or behavior.

mechanisms adaptive solutions to problems of survival and reproduction.

mechanoreceptors receptor cells in the skin that are sensitive to different tactile qualities, such as shape, grooves, vibrations, and movements.

median the score that separates the lower half of scores from the upper half.

meditation practices that people use to calm the mind, stabilize concentration, focus attention, and enhance awareness of the present moment.

medulla a hindbrain structure that extends directly from the spinal cord; regulates breathing, heart rate, and blood pressure.

memory the ability to store and use information; also the store of what has been learned and remembered.

menarche the first menstrual period.

mental age the equivalent chronological age a child has reached based on his or her performance on an IQ test.

mental representation a structure in the mind—such as an idea or image—that stands for something else, such as an external object or thing sensed in the past or future, not the present.

mental rotation the process of imagining an object turning in three-dimensional space.

mental set a tendency to continue to use problem-solving strategies that have worked in the past, even if better solutions are available.

meta-analysis a research technique for combining all research results on one question and drawing a conclusion.

metacognitive thinking the process that includes the ability first to think and then to reflect on one's own thinking.

mindfulness a heightened awareness of the present moment, whether of events in one's environment or in one's own mind.

mindfulness-based cognitive therapy (MBCT) an approach that combines elements of CBT with mindfulness meditation to help people with depression learn to recognize and restructure negative thought patterns.

mirror neurons nerve cells that are active when we observe others performing an action as well as when we are performing the same action.

mnemonic device a method devised to help us remember information, such as a rhyme or an acronym.

mode a statistic that represents the most commonly occurring score or value.

modeling the imitation of behaviors performed by others.

monoamine oxidase (MAO) inhibitors a class of drugs used to treat depression; they slow the breakdown of monoamine neurotransmitters in the brain.

monocular depth cues aids to depth perception that do not require two eyes.

monogenic the hereditary passing on of traits determined by a single gene.

moods affective states that operate in the background of consciousness and tend to last longer than most emotions.

moral treatment a 19th-century approach to treating the mentally ill with dignity in a caring environment.

motivation the urge to move toward one's goals; to accomplish tasks.

motor neurons nerve cells that carry commands for movement from the brain to the muscles of the body.

multiple-factor theory of intelligence the idea that intelligence consists of distinct dimensions and is not just a single factor.

mutation a random change in genetic sequence.

myelin sheath the fatty substance wrapped around some axons, which insulates the axon, making the nerve impulse travel more efficiently.

narcissistic personality disorder a dramatic-emotional personality disorder characterized by having an extremely positive and arrogant self-image and being extraordinarily self-centered; other symptoms are an exaggerated sense of self-importance and grandiosity.

narcolepsy a sleep disorder characterized by excessive daytime sleepiness and weakness in facial and limb muscles.

narrow intelligence one of Carroll's three levels of intelligence; includes many distinct abilities.

nativist view of language the idea that we discover language rather than learn it, that language development is inborn.

natural immunity the form of immunity that is the first response to antigens.

natural selection a feedback process whereby nature favors one design over another because it has an impact on reproduction.

naturalistic observation a study in which the researcher unobtrusively observes and records behavior in the real world.

nature through nurture the position that the environment constantly interacts with biology to shape who we are and what we do.

needs inherently biological states of deficiency (cellular or bodily) that compel drives.

negative punishment the removal of a stimulus to decrease behavior.

negative reinforcement the removal of a stimulus after a behavior to increase the frequency of that behavior.

negative symptoms (of schizophrenia) symptoms that include nonresponsiveness, emotional flatness, immobility, catatonia, problems with speech, and inability to complete tasks.

neural migration the movement of neurons from one part of the fetal brain to their more permanent destination; occurs during months 3–5 of the fetal stage.

neurocultural theory of emotion Ekman's explanation that some aspects of emotion, such as facial expressions and physiological changes associated with emotion, are universal and others, such as emotion regulation, are culturally derived.

neuroendocrine system the hormonal systems involved in emotions and stress.

neurogenesis the development of new neurons.

neurons the cells that process and transmit information in the nervous system.

neuroplasticity the brain's ability to adopt new functions, reorganize itself, or make new neural connections throughout life, as a function of experience.

neuropsychoanalysis the scientific movement, started in the late 1990s, that combined Freudian ideas with neuroscientific methods.

neurotransmitters chemicals that transmit information between neurons.

night terrors a state that occurs when a person walks around, speaks incoherently, and ultimately awakens, terrified, from sleep.

non-REM the form of sleep with few eye movements, which are slow rather than fast.

norepinephrine a neurotransmitter that activates the sympathetic response to stress, increasing heart rate, rate of respiration, and blood pressure in support of rapid action.

normal distribution a bell curve; a plot of how frequent data are that is perfectly symmetrical, with most scores clustering in the middle and only a few scores at the extremes.

normative social influence conformity to the behavior of others in order to be accepted by them.

obedience a type of conformity in which a person yields to the will of another person.

object permanence the ability to realize that objects still exist when they are not being sensed.

observational learning learning by watching the behavior of others.

obsession an unwanted thought, word, phrase, or image that persistently and repeatedly comes into a person's mind and causes distress.

obsessive-compulsive disorder (OCD) an anxiety disorder in which obsessive thoughts lead to compulsive behaviors.

obsessive-compulsive personality disorder (OCPD) an anxious-fearful personality disorder characterized by rigid habits and extreme perfectionism; more general than obsessive-compulsive disorder.

olfactory bulb a forebrain structure that sends information either directly to the smell-processing areas in the cortex or indirectly to the cortex by way of the thalamus.

olfactory sensory neurons the sensory receptors for smell that reside high up inside the nose.

one-word utterances single words, such as "mama," "dada," "more," or "no!"; occur around 12 months of age.

operant conditioning the process of changing behavior by manipulating the consequences of that behavior.

opponent-process theory the theory that color vision results from cones linked together in three pairs of opposing colors, so that activation of one member of the pair inhibits activity in the other.

optic chiasm the point at which strands of the optic nerve from half of each eye cross over to the opposite side of the brain.

optic nerve the structure composed of the axons of ganglion cells from the retina that carry visual information from the eye to the brain.

optogenetics a treatment that uses a combination of light stimulation and genetics to manipulate the activity of individual neurons.

originality the ability to come up with unusual and novel ideas.

out-group homogeneity the tendency to see all members of an out-group as the same.

pain a complex emotional and sensory experience associated with actual or potential tissue damage.

panic attacks an anxiety disorder; associated with perceptions of threat and occurring because of fear of danger, inability to escape, embarrassment, or specific objects, for example.

panic disorder an anxiety disorder characterized by panic attacks and persistent anxiety about having more attacks.

papillae textured structures on the surface of the tongue; contain thousands of taste buds.

paranoid personality disorder an odd-eccentric personality disorder characterized by extreme suspicions and mistrust of others in unwarranted and maladaptive ways.

parasympathetic nervous system the branch of the autonomic nervous system that usually relaxes or returns the body to a less active, restful state.

perceived organizational support employees' beliefs about how much the organization appreciates and supports their contributions and well-being.

perception a psychological process: the act of organizing and interpreting sensory experience.

perceptual constancy the ability of the brain to preserve perception of objects in spite of changes in retinal image when an object changes in position or distance from the viewer.

perceptual set the effect of frame of mind on perception; a tendency to perceive stimuli in a certain manner.

peripheral nervous system the part of the nervous system that comprises all the nerve cells in the body outside the central nervous system.

persistent depressive disorder (PDD) previously known as *dysthymia* and involves same symptoms as major depression but at less severe levels.

personal unconscious according to Jung, the form of consciousness that consists of all our repressed and hidden thoughts, feelings, and motives.

personality the unique and relatively enduring set of behaviors, feelings, thoughts, and motives that characterize an individual.

personality disorders patterns of cognition, emotion, and behavior that develop in late childhood or adolescence and are maladaptive and inflexible; they are more stable than clinical disorders.

personality psychology the study of what makes people unique and the consistencies in people's behavior across time and situations.

personality questionnaires self-report instruments on which respondents indicate the extent to which they agree or disagree with a series of statements as they apply to their personality.

persuasion the act of attempting to change the opinions, beliefs, or choices of others by explanation or argument.

phenothiazines drugs used to treat schizophrenia; help diminish hallucinations, confusion, agitation, and paranoia but also have adverse side effects.

phenotype an organism's observed characteristics.

phobia an anxiety disorder: an ongoing and irrational fear of a particular object, situation, or activity.

photoreceptors cells in the retina (called rods and cones) that convert light energy into nerve energy.

physiological measures measures of bodily responses, such as blood pressure or heart rate, used to determine changes in psychological state.

physiological reactivity model an explanation for the causal role of stress-related bodily changes in illness.

pituitary gland the master endocrine gland of the body; controls the release of hormones from glands throughout the body.

placebo a substance or treatment that appears identical to the actual treatment but lacks the active substance.

polygenic the process by which many genes interact to create a single characteristic.

pons a hindbrain structure that serves as a bridge between lower brain regions and higher midbrain and forebrain activity.

population the entire group a researcher is interested in—for example, all humans, all adolescents, all boys, all girls, all college students.

positive psychology a scientific approach to studying, understanding, and promoting healthy and positive psychological functioning.

positive punishment the addition of a stimulus that decreases behavior.

positive reinforcement the presentation or addition of a stimulus after a behavior occurs that increases how often that behavior will occur.

positive symptoms (of schizophrenia) the perceptual experiences associated with schizophrenia, including hallucinations, delusional thinking, and disorganized thought and speech.

positron emission tomography (PET) a brain imaging technique that measures blood flow to active areas in the brain.

postconventional level the third level in Kohlberg's theory of moral reasoning, in which the person recognizes universal moral rules that may trump unjust or immoral local rules.

post-traumatic stress disorder (PTSD) a type of trauma- and stressor-related disorder that involves intrusive and persistent cognitive, emotional, and physiological symptoms triggered by catastrophic or horrifying events.

preconventional level the first level in Kohlberg's theory of moral reasoning, focusing on avoiding punishment or maximizing rewards.

predictive validity the degree to which intelligence test scores are positively related to real-world outcomes, such as school achievement or job success, and thus have predictive value.

prefrontal cortex the frontmost region of the frontal lobes; plays an important role in attention, appropriate social behavior, impulse control, and working memory.

prefrontal lobotomy a form of psychosurgery in which the connections between the prefrontal cortex and the lower portion of the brain are severed; no longer in use.

prejudice a biased attitude toward a group of people or an individual member of a group based on unfair generalizations about what members of that group are like.

prenatal programming the process by which events in the womb alter the development of physical and psychological health.

preoperational stage The second major stage of cognitive development (ages 2–5), which begins with the emergence of symbolic thought.

primary appraisal a quick assessment of the meaning of a given environmental event for the individual.

primary reinforcers innate, unlearned reinforcers that satisfy biological needs (such as food, water, or sex).

priming a kind of implicit memory that arises when recall is improved by earlier exposure to the same or similar stimuli.

proactive interference disruption of memory because previously learned information interferes with the learning of new information.

problem-focused coping a way of dealing with stress that aims to change the situation that is creating stress.

procedural memory a kind of memory made up of implicit knowledge for almost any behavior or physical skill we have learned.

prodigy a young person who is extremely gifted and precocious in one area and at least average in intelligence.

projection a defense mechanism in which people deny particular ideas, feelings, or impulses and project them onto others.

projective tests personality assessments in which the participant is presented with a vague stimulus or situation and asked to interpret it or tell a story about what he or she sees.

prosocial behavior action that is beneficial to others.

protolanguage very rudimentary language; also known as pre-language; used by earlier species of *Homo*.

prototypes the best-fitting examples of a category.

proximity a Gestalt law that says we tend to group objects together that are near one another.

pruning the degradation of synapses and dying off of neurons that are not strengthened by experience.

pseudoscience claims presented as scientific that are not supported by evidence obtained with the scientific method.

psychoactive drugs naturally occurring or synthesized substances that, when ingested or otherwise taken into the body, reliably produce qualitative changes in conscious experience.

psychoanalysis a clinically based approach to understanding and treating psychological disorders; assumes that the unconscious mind is the most powerful force behind thought and behavior.

psychoanalytic therapy based on Freud's ideas, a therapeutic approach oriented toward major personality change with a focus on uncovering unconscious motives, especially through dream interpretation.

psychology the scientific study of thought and behavior.

psychoneuroimmunology (PNI) the science of how psychological factors relate to changes in the immune system.

psychophysics the study of how people psychologically perceive physical stimuli such as light, sound waves, and touch.

psychosomatic theory the idea that emotional factors can lead to the occurrence or worsening of illness.

psychotherapy the use of psychological techniques to modify maladaptive behaviors or thought patterns, or both, and to help patients develop insight into their own behavior.

psychotic disorders psychological disorders of thought and perception, characterized by inability to distinguish between real and imagined perceptions.

puberty the period when sexual maturation begins; it marks the beginning of adolescence.

punishment a stimulus that decreases the frequency of a behavior.

pupil the opening in the iris through which light enters the eye.

quantitative trait loci (QTL) approach a technique in behavioral genetics that looks for the location on genes that might be associated with particular behaviors.

quasi-experimental design a research method similar to an experimental design except that it makes use of naturally occurring groups rather than randomly assigning subjects to groups.

random assignment the method used to assign participants to different research conditions, so that all participants have the same chance of being in any specific group.

rapid eye movements (REM) quick movements of the eye that occur during sleep, thought to mark phases of dreaming.

rational (face valid) method a method for developing questionnaire items that involves using reason or theory to come up with a question.

reaction formation a defense mechanism that occurs when an unpleasant idea, feeling, or impulse is turned into its opposite.

reaction range for a given trait, such as IQ, the genetically determined range of responses by an individual to his or her environment.

reappraisal an emotion regulation strategy in which one reevaluates an event, so that a different emotion results.

reasoning the process of drawing inferences or conclusions from principles and evidence.

recessive alleles alleles that show their effects only when both alleles are the same.

reciprocal altruism the act of helping others in the hope that they will help us in the future.

recovered memory a memory from a real event that was encoded, stored, but not retrieved for a long period of time until some later event brings it suddenly to consciousness.

reflexes inborn and involuntary behaviors—such as coughing, swallowing, sneezing, or vomiting—that are elicited by very specific stimuli.

refractory period the span of time, after an action potential has been generated, when the neuron is returning to its resting state and the neuron cannot generate an action potential.

rehearsal the process of repeatedly practicing material, so that it enters long-term memory.

reinforcer an internal or external event that increases the frequency of a behavior.

reliability the consistency of a measurement, such as an intelligence test.

repetitive transcranial magnetic stimulation (TMS) a treatment for severe depression involving exposure of specific brain structures to bursts of high-intensity magnetic fields instead of electricity.

replication the repetition of a study to confirm the results; essential to the scientific process.

representative sample a research sample that accurately reflects the population of people one is studying.

representativeness heuristic a strategy we use to estimate the probability of one event based on how typical it is of another event.

repression the unconscious act of keeping threatening thoughts, feelings, or impulses out of consciousness.

research designs plans of action for how to conduct a scientific study.

resistance stage in the general adaptation syndrome, extended effort by the body to deal with a threat.

resting potential the difference in electrical charge between the inside and outside of the axon when the neuron is at rest.

reticular formation a network of nerve fibers that runs up through both the hindbrain and the midbrain; it is crucial to waking up and falling asleep.

retina the thin layer of nerve tissue that lines the back of the eye.

retrieval the recovery of information stored in memory; the fourth stage of long-term memory.

retroactive interference disruption of memory because new experiences or information causes people to forget previously learned experiences or information.

retrograde amnesia an inability to recall events or experiences that happened before the onset of a disease or injury.

reuptake a way of removing excess neurotransmitter from the synapse, in which excess neurotransmitter is returned to the sending, or presynaptic, neuron for storage in vesicles and future use.

rods photoreceptors that function in low illumination and play a key role in night vision; responsive to dark and light contrast.

Rorschach Inkblot Test a projective test in which the participant is asked to respond to a series of ambiguous inkblots.

samples subsets of the population studied in a research project.

savant syndrome a very rare condition in which people with serious mental handicaps also show isolated areas of ability or brilliance.

schedules of reinforcement patterns of intermittent reinforcement distinguished by whether reinforcement occurs after a set number of responses or after a certain amount of time has passed since the last reinforcement.

schemas mental frameworks that develop from our experiences with particular people, objects, or events.

schizoid personality disorder an odd-eccentric personality disorder characterized by a desire to avoid close relationships as well as by emotional aloofness, reclusivity, and a lack of humor.

schizophrenia a psychotic disorder characterized by significant disturbances in thought and emotion, specifically problems with perception, including hallucinations.

schizotypal personality disorder an odd-eccentric personality disorder characterized by a desire to live an isolated and asocial life, but also by the presence of odd thoughts and beliefs.

scientific method the procedures by which scientists conduct research, consisting of five basic processes: observation, prediction, testing, interpretation, and communication.

scientific thinking a process using the cognitive skills required to generate, test, and revise theories.

secondary appraisal self-assessment of the resources available to cope with stress.

secondary (conditioned) reinforcers reinforcers that are learned by association, usually via classical conditioning (such as money, grades, and peer approval).

securely attached an attachment style characterized by infants who will gradually explore new situations when the caregiver leaves and initiate contact when the caregiver returns after separation.

selective attention the ability to focus awareness on specific features in the environment while ignoring others.

selective serotonin reuptake inhibitors (SSRIs) drugs prescribed primarily for depression and some anxiety disorders that work by making more serotonin available in the synapse.

self-actualization the inherent drive to realize one's full potential.

self-conscious emotions types of emotion that require a sense of self and the ability to reflect on actions; they occur as a function of meeting expectations (or not) and abiding (or not) by society's rules.

self-fulfilling prophecy a statement that affects events to cause the prediction to become true.

self-reports written or oral accounts of a person's thoughts, feelings, or actions.

self-serving bias the tendency to make situational attributions for our failures but dispositional attributions for our successes.

semantic memory a form of memory that recalls facts and general knowledge, such as what we learn in school.

semicircular canals a structure of the inner ear involved in maintaining balance.

sensation a physical process: the stimulation of our sense organs by features of the outer world.

sensorimotor stage Piaget's first stage of cognitive development (ages 0–2), when infants learn about the world by using their senses and by moving their bodies.

sensory adaptation the process by which our sensitivity diminishes when an object constantly stimulates our senses.

sensory memory the part of memory that holds information in its original sensory form for a very brief period of time, usually about half a second or less.

sensory neurons nerve cells that receive incoming sensory information from the sense organs (eye, ear, skin, tongue, nose).

sentence phase the stage when children begin speaking in fully grammatical sentences; usually age 2½ to 3.

separation anxiety the distress reaction shown by babies when they are separated from their primary caregiver (typically shown at around 9 months of age).

serial-position effect the tendency to have better recall for items in a list according to their position in the list.

serotonin a neurotransmitter with wide-ranging effects; involved in dreaming and in controlling emotional states, especially anger, anxiety, and depression.

set point the ideal fixed setting of a particular physiological system, such as internal body temperature.

sexual behavior actions that produce arousal and increase the likelihood of orgasm.

sexual orientation the disposition to be attracted to either the opposite sex (heterosexual), the same sex (homosexual), or both sexes (bisexual).

sexual strategies theory the idea that men and women face different problems when they seek out mates, so they often approach relationships in very different ways.

shadow according to Jung, the dark and morally objectionable part of ourselves.

shamans medicine men or women who treat people with mental problems by driving out their demons with elaborate rituals, such as exorcisms, incantations, and prayers.

shaping the reinforcement of successive approximations of a desired behavior.

short-term memory the part of memory that temporarily (for 2 to 30 seconds) stores a limited amount of information before it is either transferred to long-term storage or forgotten.

signal detection theory the viewpoint that both stimulus intensity and decision-making processes are involved in the detection of a stimulus.

similarity a Gestalt law that says we tend to group like objects together in visual perception.

single-blind studies studies in which participants do not know the experimental condition (group) to which they have been assigned.

Skinner box a simple chamber in which a small animal can move around, with a food dispenser and a response lever to trigger food delivery.

sleepwalking a sleep difficulty characterized by activities occurring during non-REM sleep that usually occur when one is awake, such as walking and eating.

social desirability bias the tendency toward favorable self-presentation that could lead to inaccurate self-reports.

social exchange theory the idea that we help others when we understand that the benefits to ourselves are likely to outweigh the costs.

social facilitation a phenomenon in which the presence of others improves one's performance.

social learning theory a description of the kind of learning that occurs when we model the behavior of others.

social loafing a phenomenon in which the presence of others causes one to relax one's standards and slack off.

social norms rules about acceptable behavior imposed by the cultural context in which one lives.

social phobia (social anxiety disorder) an anxiety disorder: fear of humiliation in the presence of others, characterized by intense self-consciousness about appearance or behavior or both.

social psychology the study of how living among others influences thought, feeling, and behavior.

social referencing the ability to make use of social and emotional information from another person—especially a caregiver—in an uncertain situation.

softwiring in contrast to hardwiring, biological systems—genes, brain structures, brain cells—are inherited but open to modification from the environment.

soma the cell body of the neuron.

somatic nervous system nerve cells of the peripheral nervous system that transmit sensory information to the central nervous system (CNS) and those that transmit information from the CNS to the skeletal muscles.

somatic symptom disorder a psychological disorder in which a person complains of multiple physical disorders that cause disruption and that persist for at least 6 months.

spermarche the first ejaculation.

spontaneous recovery the sudden reappearance of an extinguished response.

sports psychology the study of psychological factors in sports and exercise.

stagnation a situation in which an adult becomes more self-focused than oriented toward others and does not contribute in a productive way to society or family.

standard deviation a statistical measure of how much scores in a sample vary around the mean.

statistics the collection, analysis, interpretation, and presentation of numerical data.

stereotypes schemas of how people are likely to behave based simply on groups to which they belong.

stimulants substances that activate the nervous system.

stimulus discrimination the restriction of a CR (such as salivation) to only the exact CS to which it was conditioned.

stimulus generalization extension of the association between UCS and CS to include a broad array of similar stimuli.

storage the retention of memory over time; the third stage of long-term memory formation.

stress a response elicited when a situation overwhelms a person's perceived ability to meet the demands of the situation.

stressors events that trigger a stress response.

striving for superiority according to Adler, the major drive behind all behavior, whereby humans naturally strive to overcome their inherent inferiorities or deficiencies, both physical and psychological.

Stroop effect a delay in reaction time when the colors of words on a test and their meaning differ.

structuralism the 19th-century school of psychology that argued that breaking down experience into its elemental parts offers the best way to understand thought and behavior.

subjective experience of emotion the changes in the quality of our conscious experience that occur during emotional responses.

subjective well-being the state that consists of life satisfaction, domain satisfactions, and positive and negative affect.

sublimation a defense mechanism that involves expressing a socially unacceptable impulse in a socially acceptable way.

successful intelligence according to Sternberg, an integrated set of abilities needed to attain success in life.

suggestibility a problem with memory that occurs when memories are implanted in our minds based on leading questions, comments, or suggestions by someone else or some other source.

superego one of Freud's provinces of the mind; the part of the self that monitors and controls behavior; "stands over us" and evaluates actions in terms of right and wrong; our conscience.

support groups meetings of people who share a common situation, be it a disorder, a disease, or coping with an ill family member.

sustained attention the ability to maintain focused awareness on a target or an idea.

sympathetic nervous system the branch of the autonomic nervous system that activates bodily systems in times of emergency.

synapse the junction between an axon and the adjacent neuron, where information is transmitted from one neuron to another.

synaptic vesicles tiny sacs in the terminal buttons that contain neurotransmitters.

synaptogenesis the formation of entirely new synapses or connections with other neurons.

syndrome a group, or cluster of related symptoms that are characteristic of a disorder.

synesthesia an unusual sensory experience in which a person experiences sensations in one sense when a different sense is stimulated.

syntax the rules for arranging words and symbols to form sentences or parts of sentences in a particular language.

systematic desensitization a behavioral therapy technique, often used for phobias, in which the therapist pairs relaxation with gradual exposure to a phobic object, generating a hierarchy of increasing contact with the feared object.

tardive dyskinesia repetitive, involuntary movements of jaw, tongue, face, and mouth resulting from the extended use of traditional antipsychotic drugs.

taste buds structures inside the papillae of the tongue that contain the taste receptor cells.

taste receptor cells sensory receptors for taste that reside in the taste buds.

technology-based therapies therapies that make use of technology or the Internet to complement current therapies or to make psychotherapeutic techniques available to more people.

telomerase an enzyme that adds DNA sequences to telomeres.

temperament the biologically based tendency to behave in particular ways from very early in life.

teratogens substances that can disrupt normal prenatal development and cause lifelong deficits.

terminal button a little knob at the end of the axon that contains tiny sacs of neurotransmitters.

test bias a characteristic of a test that produces different outcomes for different groups.

test fairness a judgment about how test results are applied to different groups based on values and philosophical inclinations.

test-retest reliability the consistency of scores on a test over time.

thalamus a forebrain structure that receives information from the senses and relays it to the cerebral cortex for processing.

theory a set of related assumptions from which scientists can make testable predictions.

theory of mind ideas and knowledge about how other people's minds work.

theta waves a pattern of brain activity during Stage 1 sleep; slower, lower-energy waves than alpha waves.

thinking outside the box an approach to problem solving that requires breaking free of self-imposed conceptual constraints and thinking about a problem differently in order to solve it.

three-stage model of memory the classification of memories based on duration as sensory, short-term, and long-term.

token economies a behavioral technique in which desirable behaviors are reinforced with a token, such as a small chip or fake coin, which can be exchanged for privileges.

top-down processing perception of the whole based on our experience and expectations, which guide our perception of smaller, elemental features of a stimulus.

traditional antipsychotics historically, the first medications used to manage psychotic symptoms.

trait a disposition to behave consistently in a particular way.

transcranial direct current stimulation (tDCS) electrical stimulation of the brain.

transduction the conversion of physical into neural information.

transference the process in psychotherapy in which the client reacts to a person in a present relationship as though that person were someone from the client's past.

triangular theory of love Sternberg's idea that three components (intimacy, passion, and commitment), in various combinations, can explain all the forms of human love.

triarchic theory of intelligence Sternberg's three-part model of intelligence, including analytic, creative, and practical intelligence.

trichromatic color theory the theory that all color that we experience results from a mixing of three colors of light (red, green, and blue).

tricyclic antidepressants drugs used for treating depression as well as chronic pain and ADHD.

t-test a statistic that compares two means to see whether they could come from the same population.

twin-adoption studies research into hereditary influence on twins, both identical and fraternal, who were raised apart (adopted) and who were raised together.

two-word utterances phrases children put together, starting around 18 months, such as "my ball," "mo wawa," or "go way."

tympanic membrane the eardrum.

Type A Behavior Pattern (TABP) a way of responding to challenge or stress, characterized by hostility, impatience, competitiveness, and time urgency.

unconditional positive regard the acceptance of another person regardless of his or her behavior.

unconditioned response (UCR) the natural, automatic, inborn reaction to a stimulus.

unconditioned stimulus (UCS) the environmental input that always produces the same unlearned response.

unconscious one of Freud's three levels of consciousness; it contains all the drives, urges, or instincts that are outside awareness but nonetheless motivate most of our speech, thoughts, feelings, or actions.

universal common to all human beings and seen in cultures all over the world.

validity the degree to which a test accurately measures what it purports to measure, such as intelligence, and not something else, and the degree to which it predicts real-world outcomes.

variable a characteristic that changes, or "varies," such as age, gender, weight, intelligence, anxiety, and extraversion.

variable-interval (VI) schedule a pattern of intermittent reinforcement in which responses are reinforced after time periods of different duration have passed.

variable-ratio (VR) schedule a pattern of intermittent reinforcement in which the number of responses needed for reinforcement changes.

vegetative state a state of minimal consciousness in which the eyes might be open, but the person is otherwise unresponsive.

virtual reality therapies therapies that use virtual (digital simulation) environments to create therapeutic situations that would be hard to create otherwise.

visual acuity the ability to see clearly.

visual imagery visual representations created by the brain after the original stimulus is no longer present.

wakefulness the degree of alertness reflecting whether a person is awake or asleep.

Weber's law the finding that the size of a just noticeable difference is a constant fraction of the intensity of the stimulus.

Wernicke's area the area deep in the left temporal lobe responsible for the ability to speak in meaningful sentences and to comprehend the meaning of speech.

word salad the speech of people with schizophrenia, which may follow grammatical rules but be nonsensical in terms of content.

working memory the part of memory required to attend to and solve a problem at hand; also known as short-term memory.

Yerkes-Dodson law the principle that moderate levels of arousal lead to optimal performance.

young adulthood the development stage that usually happens by the mid-20s, when people complete the key developmental tasks of emerging adulthood.

zone of proximal development the distance between what a child can learn alone and what that child can learn assisted by someone else, usually an adult.

zygote the single cell that results when a sperm fertilizes an egg.

References

Aamodt, M. G. (2010). *Industrial/organizational psychology: An applied approach* (6th ed.). Belmont, CA: Wadsworth.

Abbate-Daga, G., Gramaglia, C., Amianto, F., Marzola, E., & Fassino, S. (2010). Attachment insecurity, personality, and body dissatisfaction in eating disorders. *Journal of Nervous and Mental Disease, 198,* 520–524.

Aberg, M. A. I., Pedersen, N. L., Torén K., Svartengrenf, M., Backstrand, B., Johnsson, T., . . . Kuhn, H. G. (2009). Cardiovascular fitness is associated with cognition in young adulthood. *Proceedings of the National Academy of Sciences, 106,* 20906–20911. doi: 10.1073/pnas.0905307106.

Abraham, A. (2013). The world according to me: Personal relevance and the medial prefrontal cortex. *Frontiers in Human Neuroscience, 7,* 341. doi: 10.3389/fnhum.2013.00341.

Abrams, R. (1997). *Electroconvulsive therapy* (3rd ed.). New York, NY: Oxford University Press.

Ackerman, D. (1990). *A natural history of the senses.* New York, NY: Vintage Books.

Adam, T. C., & Epel, E. S. (2007). Stress, eating and the reward system. *Physiology & Behavior, 91,* 449–458.

Adams, L., & Szaluta, J. (1996). *Psychoanalysis and the humanities.* Philadelphia, PA: Brunner/Mazel.

Adamson, L., & Bakeman, R. (1985). Affect and attention: Infants observed with mothers and peers. *Child Development, 56,* 582–593.

Ader, R., & Cohen, N. (1975). Behaviorally conditioned immunosuppression. *Psychosomatic Medicine, 37,* 333–340.

Adler, A. (1931). *What life should mean to you.* New York, NY: Capricorn Books.

Adler, A. (1956). *The individual psychology of Alfred Adler: A systematic presentation in selections from his writings* (H. L. Ansbacher & R. R. Ansbacher, Eds.). New York, NY: Norton.

Adler, J. (Ed.). (2004). *Forensic psychology: Concepts, debates and practice.* Cullupton, England: Willan.

Adler, J. (2012). Erasing painful memories. *Scientific American, 306,* 56–61.

Adolphs, R., Cahill, L., Schul, R., & Babinsky, R. (1997) Impaired declarative memory for emotional material following bilateral amygdala damage in humans. *Learning and Memory, 4,* 291–300.

Adolphs, R., Gosselin, F., Buchanan, T. W., Tranel, D., Schyns, P., & Damasio, A. R. (2005). A mechanism for impaired fear recognition after amygdala damage. *Nature, 433,* 68–72.

Adolphs, R., Tranel, D., & Buchanan, T. W. (2005). Amygdala damage impairs emotional memory for gist but not details of complex stimuli. *Nature Neuroscience, 8,* 512–518.

Adolphs, R., Tranel, D., & Damasio, A. R. (1998, June 4). The human amygdala in social judgment. *Nature, 393,* 470–474.

Adolphs, R., Tranel, D., Damasio, H., & Damasio, A. R. (1994, December 15). Impaired recognition of emotion in facial expressions following bilateral damage to the human amygdala. *Nature, 372,* 669–672.

Aichorn, W., Huber, R., Stuppaeck, C., & Whitworth, A. B. (2006). Cardiomyopathy after long-term treatment with lithium—more than a coincidence? *Journal of Psychopharmacology, 20,* 589–591.

Ainsworth, M. D. S., Blehar, M. C., Waters, E., & Wall, S. (1978). *Patterns of attachment: A psychological study of the Strange Situation.* Hillsdale, NJ: Erlbaum.

Aitken, J. R., & Benson, J. W. (1984). The use of relaxation/desensitization in treating anxiety associated with flying. *Aviation Space and Environmental Medicine, 55,* 196–199.

Akaike, A. (2006). Preclinical evidence of neuroprotection by cholinesterase inhibitors. *Alzheimer Disease and Associated Disorders, 20*(Suppl. 1), S8–S11.

Akinola, M., & Mendes, W. B. (2008). The dark side of creativity: Biological vulnerability and negative emotions lead to greater artistic creativity. *Personality and Social Psychological Bulletin, 34,* 1677–1686.

Aknin, L. B., Hamlin, J. K., & Dunn, E. W. (2012). Giving leads to happiness in young children. *PLoS ONE, 7,* e39211. doi: 10.1371/journal.pone.0039211.

Alam, M., Barrett, K. C., Hodapp, R. M., & Arndt, K. A. (2008). Botulinum toxin and the facial feedback hypothesis: Can looking better make you feel happier? *Journal of the American Academy of Dermatology, 58,* 1061–1072.

Al-Atiyyat, N. M. H. (2009). Cultural diversity and cancer pain. *Journal of Hospice & Palliative Nursing, 11,* 154–164.

Alberini, C. M., & Chen, D. Y. (2012). Memory enhancement: Consolidation, reconsolidation and insulin-like growth factor 2. *Trends in Neurosciences, 35,* 274–283. doi: 10.1016/j.tins.2011.12.007.

Albert, D. J. (1966). The effects of polarizing currents on the consolidation of learning. *Neuropsychologia, 4,* 65–77.

Aldington, S., Harwood, M., Cox, B., Weatherall, M., . . . Beasley, R. (2008). Cannabis use and risk of lung cancer: A case-control study. *European Respiratory Journal, 31,* 280–286.

Alex, C., Lindgren, M., Shapiro, P. A., McKinley, P. S., Brondolo, E. N., Myers, M. M., . . . Sloan, R. P. (2013). Aerobic exercise and strength training effects on cardiovascular sympathetic function in healthy adults: A randomized controlled trial. *Psychosomatic Medicine, 75*(4), 375–381.

Allemand, M., Zimprich, D., & Hendriks, A. A. J. (2008). Age differences in five personality domains across the life span. *Developmental Psychology, 44,* 758–770.

Allen, D. G., Shore, L. M., & Griffeth, R. W. (2003). The role of perceived organizational support and supportive human resource practices in the turnover process. *Journal of Management, 29,* 99–118.

Allen, L., & Gorski, R. (2007). *Sex differences in the bed nucleus of the stria terminalis of the human brain* [e-book]. Cambridge, MA: MIT Press.

Allergan, Inc. (2013). MEDICATION GUIDE BOTOX® Cosmetic (onabotulinumtoxinA) for injection.

Allison, D. B., Heshka, S., Neale, M. C., Lykken, D. T., & Heymsfield, S. B. (1994). A genetic analysis of relative weight among 4,020 twin pairs, with an emphasis on sex effects. *Health Psychology, 13,* 362–365.

Alloway, T., Elliott, J., & Holmes, J. (2010). The prevalence of ADHD-like symptoms in a community sample. *Journal of Attention Disorders, 14,* 52–56. doi: 10.1177/1087054709356197.

Allport, G. W. (1937). *Personality: A psychological interpretation.* New York, NY: Holt, Rinehart & Winston.

Allport, G. W. (1954). *The nature of prejudice.* Cambridge, MA: Addison-Wesley.

Allport, G. W., & Odbert, H. W. (1936). Trait-names: A psycho-lexical study. *Psychological Monographs, 47,* 1–171.

Alt, K. W., Jeunesse, C., Buritrago-Tellez, C. H., Wächter, R., Boes, E., & Pichler, S. L. (1997, May 22). Evidence for stone-age cranial surgery. *Nature, 387*, 360.

Alterovitz, S., & Mendelsohn, G. A. (2009). Partner preferences across the life span: Online dating by older adults. *Psychology and Aging, 24*, 513–517. doi: 10.1037/a0015897.

Altman, J., & Das, G. D. (1966). Autoradiographic and histological studies of postnatal neurogenesis. I. A longitudinal investigation of the kinetics, migration and transformation of cells incorporating tritiated thymidine in neonate rats, with special reference to postnatal neurogenesis in some brain regions. *Journal of Comparative Neurology, 126*, 337–389.

Alzheimer's Association. (2008). *What is Alzheimer's?* Retrieved March 10, 2008, from http://www.alz.org/alzheimers_disease_what_is_alzheimers.asp#plaques

Alzheimer's Association. (2013). *Alzheimer's disease facts and figures, 9*(2). Retrieved January 7, 2014, from http://www.alz.org/downloads/facts_figures_2013.pdf

Amabile, T. M. (1996). *Creativity in context.* Boulder, CO: Westview.

Amabile, T. M., Hill, K. G., Hennessey, B. A., & Tighe, E. M. (1994). The Work Preference Inventory—Assessing intrinsic and extrinsic motivational orientations. *Journal of Personality and Social Psychology, 66*, 950–967.

Amabile, T. M., & Khaire, M. (2008, October). Creativity and the role of the leader. *Harvard Business Review*, 1–11.

Amabile, T. M., & Kramer, S. J. (2007, May). Inner work life: Understanding the subtext of business performance. *Harvard Business Review*, 1–13.

Amaral, D. (2000). The anatomical organization of the central nervous system. In E. R. Kandel, J. H. Schwartz, & T. M. Jessell (Eds.), *Principles of neural science* (4th ed., pp. 317–336). New York, NY: McGraw-Hill.

Amedi, A., Merabet, L. B., Bermpohl, F., & Pascual-Leone, A. (2005). The occipital cortex in the blind. *Current Directions in Psychological Science, 14*, 306–311.

American Heart Association. (2005). *Heart disease and stroke statistics—2005 update.* Dallas, TX: Author.

American Psychiatric Association (APA). (2013). *Diagnostic and statistical manual of mental disorders* (5th ed.). Washington, DC: Author.

Amichai-Hamburger, Y., & Vinitzky, G. (2010). Social network use and personality. *Computers in Human Behavior, 26*, 1289–1295.

Anacker, C., Cattaneo, A., Musaelyan, K., Zunszain, P. A., Horowitz, M., Molteni, R., . . . Pariante, C. M. (2013). Role for the kinase SGK1 in stress, depression, and glucocorticoid effects on hippocampal neurogenesis. *Proceedings of the National Academy of Sciences, 110*, 8708–8713.

Anda, R. F., Felitti, V. J., Bremner, J. D., Walker, J. D., Whitfield, C., Perry, B. D., . . . Giles, W. H. (2006). The enduring effects of abuse and related adverse experiences in childhood: A convergence of evidence from neurobiology and epidemiology. *European Archives of Psychiatry and Clinical Neuroscience, 256*, 174–186.

Anderson, C. A., Shibuya, A., Ihori, N., Swing, E. L., Bushman, B. J., Sakamoto, A., . . . Saleem, M. (2010). Violent video game effects on aggression, empathy, and prosocial behavior in Eastern and Western countries. *Psychological Bulletin, 136*, 151–173.

Anderson, N. D., Lau, M. A., Segal, Z. V., & Bishop, S. R. (2007). Mindfulness-based stress reduction and attentional control. *Clinical Psychology and Psychotherapy, 14*, 449–463.

Anderson, P. L., Price, M., Edwards, S. M., Obassaju, M. A., Schmerts, S. K., Zimand, E., & Calamaras, M. R. (2013). Virtual reality exposure therapy for social anxiety disorder: A randomized controlled trial. *Journal of Consulting and Clinical Psychology*. doi: 10.1037/a0033559.

Andrade, F. C. D, Raffaelli, M., Teran-Garcia, M., Jerman, J. A., Garcia, C. A., & Up Amigos 2009 Study Group. (2012). Weight status misperception among Mexican young adults. *Body Image, 9*, 184–188.

Andreasen, N. C. (1987). Creativity and psychological disorder: Prevalence rates in writers and their first-degree relatives. *American Journal of Psychiatry, 144*, 1288–1292.

Andreasen, N. C. (2006). *The creative brain.* New York, NY: Penguin.

Andreasen, N. C., & Glick, I. D. (1988). Bipolar affective disorder and creativity: Implications and clinical management. *Comprehensive Psychiatry, 29*, 207–216.

Andreasen, N. C., O'Leary, D. S., Flaum, M., Nopoulos, P., Watkins, G. L., Ponto, L. L. B., . . . (1997). Hypofrontality in schizophrenia: Distributed dysfunctional circuits in neuroleptic-naïve patients. *The Lancet, 349*, 1730–1734.

Anselmi, P., Vianello, M., Voci, A., & Robusto, E. (2013). Implicit sexual attitude of heterosexual, gay and bisexual individuals: Disentangling the contribution of specific associations to the overall measure. *PLoS ONE 8*: e78990. doi:10.1371/journal.pone.0078990.

Anson, K., & Ponsford, J. (2006). Coping and emotional adjustment following traumatic brain injury. *Journal of Head Trauma Rehabilitation, 21*, 248–259.

Anthonisen, N. R., Skeans, M. A., Wise, R. A., Manfreda, J., Kanner, R. E., & Connett, J. E. (Lung Health Study Research Group). (2005). The effects of a smoking cessation intervention on 14.5-year mortality: A randomized clinical trial. *Annals of Internal Medicine, 142*, 233–239.

Aouizerate, B., Guehl, D., Cuny, E., Rougier, A., Bioulac, B., Tignol, J., & Burbaud, P. (2004). Pathophysiology of obsessive-compulsive disorder: A necessary link between phenomenology, neuropsychology, imagery and physiology. *Progress in Neurobiology, 72*, 195–221.

APA Presidential Task Force on Evidence-Based Practice, US. (2006). Evidence-based practice in psychology. *American Psychologist, 61*, 271–285.

Apsche, J. (1993). *Probing the mind of a serial killer.* Morrisville, PA: International Information Associates.

Arbib, M., Liebal, K., & Pika, S. (2008). Primate vocalization, gesture, and the evolution of human language. *Current Anthropology, 49*, 1053–1063. doi: 10.1086/593015.

Argyle, M. (2001). *The psychology of happiness* (2nd ed.). New York, NY: Routledge.

Arling, G. L., & Harlow, H. F. (1967). Effects of social deprivation on maternal behavior of rhesus monkeys. *Journal of Comparative and Physiological Psychology, 64*, 371–377.

Armstrong, T. (2009). *Multiple intelligences in the classroom* (3rd ed.). Alexandria, VA: ASCD.

Arnett, J. J. (2004). *Emerging adulthood: The winding road from the late teens to the twenties.* New York, NY: Oxford University Press.

Arnett, J. J. (2006). Emerging adulthood: Understanding the new way of coming of age. In J. J. Arnett and J. L. Tanner (Eds.), *Emerging adults in America: Coming of age in the 21st century* (pp. 3–19). Washington, DC: American Psychological Association.

Arnold, M. B. (1960). *Emotion and personality: Vol. 1. Psychological aspects.* New York, NY: Columbia University Press.

Arseneault, L., Cannon, M., Witton, J., & Murray, R. M. (2004). Causal association between cannabis and psychosis: Examination of the evidence. *British Journal of Psychiatry, 184*, 110–117.

Arseneault, L., Moffitt, T. E., Caspi, A., Taylor, A., Rijsdijik, F., Jaffee, S. R., . . . Measelle, J. (2003). Strong genetic effects on cross-situational antisocial behaviour among 5-year-old children according to mothers, teachers, examiner-observers, and twins' self-reports. *Journal of Child Psychology and Psychiatry, 44*, 832–848.

Artola, A. (2008). Diabetes-, stress- and ageing-related changes in synaptic plasticity in hippocampus and neocortex—The same metaplastic process? *European Journal of Pharmacology, 585,* 153–162.

Asch, S. E. (1951). Effects of group pressure on the modification and distortion of judgments. In H. Guetzkow (Ed.), *Groups, leadership and men.* Pittsburgh, PA: Carnegie Press.

Asch, S. E. (1952). *Social psychology.* New York, NY: Prentice-Hall.

Ashkenazi, S., Black, J. M., Abrams, D. A., Hoeft, F., & Menon, V. (2013). Neurobiological underpinnings of math and reading learning disabilities. *Journal of Learning Disabilities, 46,* 549–569. doi: 10.1177/0022219413483174.

Asperger, H. (1991). "Autistic psychopathy" in childhood (U. Frith, Trans.). In U. Frith (Ed.), *Autism and Asperger syndrome* (pp. 37–62). New York, NY: Cambridge University Press. (Original work published 1944)

Asperger's disorder. (n.d.). Retrieved from http://www.dsm5.org/ProposedRevisions/Pages/proposedrevision.aspx?rid=97#

Assessing your weight and health risk. (n.d.). Retrieved January 12, 2014, from http://www.nhlbi.nih.gov/health/public/hear/obesity/lose_wt.risk.htm

Assouline, M., & Meir, E. I. (1987). Meta-analysis of the relationship between congruence and well-being measures. *Journal of Vocational Behavior, 31,* 319–332.

Atkinson, G., Reilly, T., & Waterhouse, J. (2007). Chronobiological aspects of the sleep-wake cycle and thermoregulation. *Physiology & Behavior, 90*(2), 189.

Atkinson, J. W. (1964). *An introduction to motivation.* New York, NY: Van Nostrand.

Atkinson, R. C., & Shiffrin, R. M. (1971). The control of short-term memory. *Scientific American, 225,* 82–90.

Austin, E. J. (2005). Personality correlates of the broader autism phenotype as assessed by the Autism Spectrum Quotient (AQ). *Personality and Individual Differences, 38,* 451–460.

Austin, M., Hadzi-Pavlovic, D., Leader, L., Saint, K., & Parker, G. (2004). Maternal trait anxiety, depression, and life-event stress in pregnancy: Relationships with infant temperament. *Early Human Development, 81,* 183–190.

Azadfar, P., Akbari, L., Sheibani-Nia, S., Noroozian, M., Assarzadegan, F., & Houshmand, M. (2014). Analysis of APP gene in early onset Alzheimer's disease patients. *Neurobiology of Aging, 35*(3). doi: 10.1016/j.neurobiolaging.2013.10.062.

Azizian, A., & Polich, J. (2007). Evidence for attentional gradient in the serial position memory curve from event-related potentials. *Journal of Cognitive Neuroscience, 19,* 2071–2081.

Baan, R., Straif, K., Grosse, Y., Secretan, B., El Ghissassi, F., Boucard, V. . . . Cogliano, B. (2007). Carcinogenicity of alcoholic beverages. *The Lancet Oncology, 8,* 292–293.

Baars, B. J. (1997). In the theatre of consciousness: Global workspace theory, a rigorous scientific theory of consciousness. *Journal of Consciousness Studies, 4,* 292–309.

Baars, B. J., & Franklin, S. (2003). How conscious experience and working memory interact. *TRENDS in Cognitive Sciences, 7,* 166–172.

Babson, K. A., Feldner, M. T., & Badour, C. L. (2010). Cognitive behavioral therapy for sleep disorders. *Psychiatric Clinics of North America, 33,* 629–640.

Bachevalier, J. (2011). The amygdala in autism spectrum disorders. In E. Hollander, A. Kolevzon, & J. T. Coyle (Eds.), *Textbook of autism spectrum disorders* (pp. 363–374). Arlington, VA: American Psychiatric Publishing.

Bachorowski, J. (1999). Vocal expression and perception of emotion. *Current Directions in Psychological Science, 8,* 53–57.

Bachorowski, J., & Owren, M. J. (2001). Not all laughs are alike: Voiced but not unvoiced laughter readily elicits positive affect. *Psychological Science, 12,* 252–257.

Bachorowski, J., Smoski, M. J., & Owren, M. J. (2001). The acoustic features of human laughter. *Journal of the Acoustical Society of America, 110,* 1581–1597.

Baddeley, A. D. (1998). The central executive: A concept and some misconceptions. *Journal of the International Neuropsychological Society, 4,* 523–526.

Baddeley, A. D. (2003). Working memory: Looking back and looking forward. *Nature Reviews Neuroscience, 4,* 829–839.

Baddeley, A. D. (2007). *Working memory, thought, and action.* New York, NY: Oxford University Press.

Baer, R. A., Smith, G. T., Hopkins, J., Krietemeyer, J., & Toney, L. (2006). Using self-report assessment methods to explore facets of mindfulness. *Assessment, 13,* 27–45.

Bagwell, C. L., Newcomb, A. F., & Bukowski, W. M. (1998). Preadolescent friendship and rejection as predictors of adult adjustment. *Child Development, 69,* 140–153.

Baier, B., Karnath, H., Dieterich, M., Birklein, F., Heinze, C., & Müller, N. G. (2010). Keeping memory clear and stable—The contribution of human basal ganglia and prefrontal cortex to working memory. *Journal of Neuroscience, 30,* 9788–9792. doi: 10.1523/JNEUROSCI.1513–10.2010.

Bailey, M. J., Dunne, M. P., & Martin, N. G. (2000). Genetic and environment effects on sexual orientation and its correlates in an Australian twin sample. *Journal of Personality and Social Psychology, 78,* 524–536.

Bailey, M. J., Kirk, K. M., Zhu, G., Dunne, M. P., & Martin, N. G. (2000). Do individual differences in sociosexuality represent genetic or environmentally contingent strategies? Evidence from the Australian twin registry. *Journal of Personality and Social Psychology, 78,* 537–545.

Bailey, M. J., & Zucker, K. J. (1995). Childhood sex-typed behavior and sexual orientation: A conceptual analysis and quantitative review. *Developmental Psychology, 31,* 43–55.

Bailey, N. W., & Zuk, M. (2009). Same-sex sexual behavior and evolution. *Trends in Ecology & Evolution, 24,* 439–446.

Baillargeon, R., & DeVos, J. (1991). Object permanence in young infants: Further evidence. *Child Development, 62,* 1227–1246.

Baird, J. C., Wagner, M., & Fuld, K. (1990). A simple but powerful theory of the moon illusion. *Journal of Experimental Psychology: Human Perception and Performance, 16,* 675–677.

Baldwin, D. S., & Polkinghorn, C. (2005). Evidence-based pharmacotherapy of generalized anxiety disorder. *International Journal of Neuropsychopharmacology, 8,* 293–302.

Ball, K., Berch, D. B., Helmers, K. F., Jobe, J. B., Leveck, M. D., Marsiske, M., . . . Willis, S. (2002). Effects of cognitive training interventions with older adults: A randomized control trial. *Journal of the American Medical Association, 288,* 2271–2281.

Ball, K., Crawford, D., & Kenardy, J. (2004). Longitudinal relationships among overweight, life satisfaction, and aspirations in young women. *Obesity Research, 12,* 1019–1030.

Ballanyi, K., Panaitescu, B., & Ruangkittisakul, A. (2010). Control of breathing by "Nerve Glue." *Science Signaling, 3*(147), pe41. doi: 10.1126/scisignal.3147pe41.

Balsis, S., Carpenter, B., & Storandt, M. (2005). Personality change precedes clinical diagnosis of dementia of the Alzheimer type. *The Journals of Gerontology: Series B: Psychological Sciences and Social Sciences, 60B,* P98–P101.

Baltes, P. B., Reuter-Lorenz, P. A., & Rösler, F. (Eds.). (2006). *Lifespan development and the brain: The perspective of biocultural co-constructivism.* New York, NY: Cambridge University Press.

Baltes, P. B., & Smith, J. (2008). The fascination of wisdom: Its nature, ontogeny, and function. *Perspectives on Psychological Science, 3,* 56–64.

Banaji, M. R. (2007). Unraveling beliefs. Retrieved from http://www.edge.org/q2007/q07_13.html

Banaji, M. R., & Greenwald, A. G. (1995). Implicit gender stereotyping in judgments of fame. *Journal of Personality and Social Psychology, 68,* 181–198.

Bandura, A. (1969). *Principles of behavior modification.* New York, NY: Holt, Rinehart & Winston.

Bandura, A. (1986). *Social foundations of thought and action: A social cognitive theory.* Englewood Cliffs, NJ: Prentice-Hall.

Bandura, A. (1997). *Self-efficacy: The exercise of control.* New York, NY: Freeman.

Bandura, A. (2006). Autobiography. In M. G. Lindzey & W. M. Runyan (Eds.), *A history of psychology in autobiography* (Vol. 9, pp. 43–75). Washington, DC: American Psychological Association.

Bandura, A., Ross, D., & Ross, S. A. (1961). Transmission of aggression through imitation of aggressive models. *Journal of Abnormal and Social Psychology, 63,* 575–582.

Bandura, A., Ross, D., & Ross, S. A. (1963). Vicarious reinforcement and imitative learning. *Journal of Abnormal and Social Psychology, 67,* 601–608.

Banks, M. S., & Salapatek, P. (1983). Infant visual perception. In P. H. Mussen (Ed.), *Handbook of child psychology* (4th ed., Vol. 2). New York, NY: Wiley.

Bar-On, R. (2004). The Bar-On Emotional Quotient Inventory (EQ-i): Rationale, description, and summary. In G. Geher (Ed.), *Measuring emotional intelligence: Common ground and controversy* (pp. 111–142). Hauppauge, NY: Nova Science.

Barac, R., & Bialystok, E. (2012). Bilingual effects on cognitive and linguistic development: Role of language, cultural background, and education. *Child Development, 83*(2), 413–422.

Baran, B., Pace-Schott, E. F., Ericson, C., & Spencer, R. M. C. (2012). Processing of emotional reactivity and emotional memory over sleep. *Journal of Neuroscience, 32,* 1035–1042. doi: 10.1523/JNEUROSCI.2532-11.2012.

Barbaresi, W. J., Colligan, R. C., Weaver, A. L., Voigt, R. G., Killian, J. M., & Katusic, S. K. (2013, March 4). Mortality, ADHD, and psychosocial adversity in adults with childhood ADHD: A prospective study. *Pediatrics.* doi: 10.1542/peds.2012-2354.

Barbazanges, A., Piazza, P. V., Le Moal, M., & Maccari, S. (1996). Maternal glucocorticoid secretion mediates long-term effects of prenatal stress. *Journal of Neuroscience, 16,* 3943–3949.

Barber, L. K., Munz, D. C., Bagsby, P. G., & Powell, E. D. (2010). Sleep consistency and sufficiency: Are both necessary for less psychological strain? *Stress and Health, 26,* 186–193.

Barbour, K. A., Edenfield, T. M., & Blumenthal, J. A. (2007). Exercise as a treatment for depression and other psychiatric disorders. *Journal of Cardiopulmonary Rehabilitation and Prevention, 27,* 359–367.

Barch, D. M. (2005). The cognitive neuroscience of schizophrenia. *Annual Review of Clinical Psychology, 1,* 321–353.

Bargh, J. A. (1997). The automaticity of everyday life. In R. S. Wyer, Jr. (Ed.), *The automaticity of everyday life: Advances in social cognition* (pp. 1–61). Mahwah, NJ: Erlbaum.

Barkham, M., Connell, J., Stiles, W. B., Miles, J. N. V., Margison, F., Evans, C., & Mellor-Clark, J. (2006). Dose-effect relations and responsive regulation of treatment duration: The good enough level. *Journal of Consulting and Clinical Psychology, 74,* 160–167.

Barlow, D. H. (2004). Psychological treatments. *American Psychologist, 59,* 869–878.

Barlow, J. H., Powell, L. A., Gilchrist, M., & Fotiadou, M. (2008). The effectiveness of the Training and Support Program for parents of children with disabilities: A randomized controlled trial. *Journal of Psychosomatic Research, 64,* 55–62.

Baron, A., & Galizio, M. (2006). The distinction between positive and negative reinforcement: Use with care. *Behavior Analyst, 296,* 141–151.

Baron-Cohen, S., Bolton, P., Wheelwright, S., Scahill, V., Short, L., Mead, G., & Smith, A. (1998). Autism occurs more often in families of physicists, engineers, and mathematicians. *Autism, 2,* 296–301.

Baron-Cohen, S., Wheelwright, S., Skinner, R., Martin, J., & Clubley, E. (2001). The Autism-Spectrum Quotient (AQ): Evidence from Asperger syndrome/high-functioning autism, males and females, scientists and mathematicians. *Journal of Autism & Developmental Disorders, 31,* 5–17.

Baron-Cohen, S., Wheelwright, S., Stott, C., Bolton, P., & Goodyer, I. (1997). Is there a link between engineering and autism? *Autism, 1,* 101–109.

Barr, C. L., Kroft, J., Feng, Y., Wigg, K., Roberts, W., Malone, M., . . . Kennedy, J. L. (2002). The norepinephrine transporter gene and attention-deficit hyperactivity disorder. *American Journal of Medical Genetics, 114,* 255–259.

Barrés, R., Yan, J., Egan, B., Treebak, J. T., Rasmussen, M., Fritz, T., Caidahl, K., Krook, A., O'Gorman, D. J., & Zierath, J. R. (2012). Acute exercise remodels promoter methylation in human skeletal muscle. *Cell Metabolism, 15,* 405–411. doi: 10.1016/j.cmet.2012.01.001.

Barrett, L. F., Lane, R. D., Sechrest, L., & Schwartz, G. E. (2000). Sex differences in emotional awareness. *Personality and Social Psychology Bulletin, 26,* 1027–1035.

Barrett, L. F., Ochsner, K. N., & Gross, J. J. (2007). On the automaticity of emotion. In J. Bargh (Ed.), *Social psychology and the unconscious: The automaticity of higher mental processes* (pp. 173–217). New York, NY: Psychology Press.

Bartels, M., Rietveld, M. J., van Baal, G. C., & Boomsma, D. I. (2002). Genetic and environmental influences on the development of intelligence. *Behavior Genetics, 32,* 237–249.

Barth, J., Schumacher, M., & Herrmann-Lingen, C. (2004). Depression as a risk factor for mortality in patients with coronary heart disease: A meta-analysis. *Psychosomatic Medicine, 66,* 802–813.

Bartholow, B. D., Bushman, B. J., & Sestir, M. A. (2006). Chronic violent video game exposure and desensitization to violence: Behavioral and event-related brain potential data. *Journal of Experimental Social Psychology, 42,* 532–539.

Basak, C., Boot, W. R., Voss, M. W., & Kramer, A. F. (2008). Can training in a real-time strategy video game attenuate cognitive decline in older adults? *Psychology and Aging, 23,* 765–777.

Basbaum A. L., & Jessell, T. M. (2000). The perception of pain. In E. R. Kandel, J. H. Schwartz, & T. M. Jessell (Eds.), *Principles of neural science* (4th ed., pp. 472–491). New York, NY: McGraw-Hill.

Bassett, E. B., Verchinski, B. A., Mattay, V. S., Weinberger, D. R., & Meyer-Lindenberg, A. (2008). Hierarchical organization of human cortical networks in health and schizophrenia. *Journal of Neuroscience, 28,* 9239–9248.

Basson, R. (2000). The female sexual response: A different model. *Journal of Sex & Marital Therapy, 26,* 51–65.

Batey, M., & Furnham, A. (2008). Creativity, intelligence, and personality: A critical review of the scattered literature. *Genetic, Social, and General Psychology Monographs, 132,* 355–429.

Batey, M., Furnham, A., & Safiullina, X. (2010). Intelligence, general knowledge and personality as predictors of creativity. *Learning and Individual Differences, 20*(5), 532–535. doi: 10.1016/j.lindif.2010.04.008.

Batson, C. D. (1991). *The altruism question: Toward a social psychological answer.* Hillsdale, NJ: Erlbaum.

Batson, C. D., Fultz, J., & Schoenrade, P. A. (1987). Distress and empathy: Two qualitatively distinct vicarious emotions with different motivational consequences. *Journal of Personality, 55,* 19–39.

Bauer, F., Korpert, K., Neuberger, M., Raber, A., & Schwetz, F. (1991). Risk factors for hearing loss at different frequencies in a population of 47388 noise-exposed workers. *Journal of Acoustic Society of America, 6,* 3086–3098.

Bauer, M., & Whybrow, P. C. (2001). Thyroid hormone, neural tissue and mood modulation. *World Journal of Biological Psychiatry, 2,* 57–67.

Baumeister, R. F., & Leary, M. (1995). The need to belong: Desire for interpersonal attachments as a fundamental human motivation. *Psychological Bulletin, 117,* 497–529.

Baumeister, R. F., & Masicampo, E. J. (2010). Conscious thought is for facilitating social and cultural interactions: How mental simulations serve the animal-culture interface. *Psychological Review, 117,* 945–971.

Baumeister, R. F., Masicampo, E. J., & Vohs, K. D. (2011). Do conscious thoughts cause behavior? *Annual Review of Psychology, 62,* 331–361.

Baumrind, D. (1964). Some thoughts on ethics of research: After reading Milgram's "Behavioral study of obedience." *American Psychologist, 19,* 421–423.

Bavelier, D., Tomann, A., Hutton, C., Mitchell, T., Corina, D., Liu, G., . . . (2000). Visual attention to the periphery is enhanced in congenitally deaf individuals. *Journal of Neuroscience, 20,* 1–6.

Beadle-Brown, J., Murphy, G., & Wing, L. (2006). The Camberwell cohort 25 years on: Characteristics and changes in skills over time. *Journal of Applied Research in Intellectual Disabilities, 19,* 317–329.

Beauchamp, G. K., & Mennella, J. A. (2009). Early flavor learning and its impact on later feeding behavior. *Journal of Pediatric Gastroenterology & Nutrition, 48,* S25–S30. doi: 10.1097/MPG.0b013e31819774a5.

Beck, A. T., & Emery, G. (1985). *Anxiety disorders and phobias.* New York, NY: Basic Books.

Beebe, D. W., Rose, D., & Amin, R. (2010). Attention, learning, and arousal of experimentally sleep-restricted adolescents in a simulated classroom. *Journal of Adolescent Health, 47,* 523–525. doi: 10.1016/j.jadohealth.2010.03.005.

Beekman, A. T. F., Smit, F., Stek, M. L., Reynolds, C. F., & Cuijpers, P. C. (2010). Preventing depression in high-risk groups. *Current Opinion in Psychiatry, 23,* 8–11.

Beeman, M. J., & Bowden, E. M. (2000). The right hemisphere maintains solution-related activation for yet-to-be solved insight problems. *Memory & Cognition, 28,* 1231–1241.

Beever, T. G., & Chiarello, R. J. (2009). Cerebral dominance in musicians and non-musicians. *Science, 185,* 537–539.

Beghetto, R. A., & Kaufman, J. C. (2007). Toward a broader conception of creativity: A case for mini-c creativity. *Psychology of Aesthetics, Creativity, and the Arts, 1,* 73–79.

Begley, S. (2007). *Train your mind, change your brain.* New York, NY: Ballantine Books.

Belisle, P., & Chapais, B. (2001). Tolerated co-feeding in relation to degree of kinship in Japanese macaques. *Behaviour, 138,* 487–509.

Bell, A. P., Weinberg, M. S., & Hammersmith, S. K. (1981). *Sexual preference: Its development in men and women.* Bloomington: Indiana University Press.

Bellack, A. S., Bennett, M. E., Gearon, J. S., Brown, C. H., & Yang, Y. (2006). A randomized clinical trial of a new behavioral treatment for drug abuse in people with severe and persistent mental illness. *Archives of General Psychiatry, 63,* 426–432.

Bellesi, M., Pfister-Genskow, M., Maret, S., Keles, S., Tononi, G., & Cirelli, C. (2013). Effects of sleep and wake on oligodendrocytes and their precursors. *Journal of Neuroscience, 33,* 14288–14300. doi: http://dx.doi.org/10.1523/JNEUROSCI.5102-12.2013.

Belmonte, M. K., Allen, G., Beckel-Mitchener, A., Boulanger, L. M., Carper, R. A., & Webb, S. J. (2004). Autism and abnormal development of brain connectivity. *Journal of Neuroscience, 24,* 9228–9231.

Bem, D. J., & Horonton, C. (1994). Does psi exist? Replicable evidence for an anomalous process of information transfer. *Psychological Bulletin, 115,* 4–18.

Benet-Martinez, V., & Oishi, S. (2008). Culture and personality. In O. P. John, R. W. Robins, & L. A. Pervin (Eds.), *Handbook of personality: Theory and research* (pp. 542–567). New York, NY: Guilford Press.

Benjamin, J., Li, L., Patterson, C., Greenburg, B. D., Murphy, D. L., & Hamer, D. H. (1996). Population and familial association between the D4 dopamine receptor gene and measures of novelty seeking. *Nature Genetics, 12,* 81–84.

Benjamin, L. T., Jr. (2007). *A brief history of modern psychology.* Malden, MA: Blackwell.

Benner, E. J., Luciano, D., Jo, R., Abdi, K., Paez-Gonzalez, P., Sheng, H., . . . Kuo, C. T. (2013). Protective astrogenesis from the SVZ niche after injury is controlled by Notch modulator Thbs4. *Nature, 497,* 369–374. doi: 10.1038/nature12069.

Bennett, C. M., & Baird, A. A. (2006). Anatomical changes in the emerging adult brain: A voxel-based morphometry study. *Human Brain Mapping, 27,* 766–777.

Bennett, E. L., Diamond, M. C., Krech, D., & Rosenzweig, M. R. (1964). Chemical and anatomical plasticity of brain. *Science, 146,* 610–619.

Bennett, P. J., Sekuler, R., & Sekuler, A. B. (2007). The effects of aging on motion detection and direction identification. *Vision Research, 47,* 799–809.

Beran, M. J., Smith, J. D., & Perdue, B. M. (2013). Language-trained chimpanzees (*Pan troglodytes*) name what they have seen but look first at what they have not seen. *Psychological Science Online First.* doi: 10.1177/0956797612458936.

Berenbaum, S. A., Korman, K., & Leveroni, C. (1995). Early hormones and sex differences in cognitive abilities. *Learning and Individual Differences, 7,* 303–321.

Berghöfer, A., Alda, M., Adli, M., Baethge, C., Bauer, M., Bschor, T., . . . Pfennig, A. (2008). Long-term effectiveness of lithium in bipolar disorder: A multicenter investigation of patients with typical and atypical features. *Journal of Clinical Psychiatry, 69,* 1860–1868. doi: 10.4088/JCP.v69n1203.

Berhardt, B. C., & Singer, T. (2012). The neural basis of empathy. *Annual Review of Neuroscience, 35,* 1–23. doi: 10.1146/annurev-neuro-062111-150536.

Berkman, L. F., & Glass, T. (2000). Social integration, social networks, social support and health. In L. F. Berkman & I. Kawachi (Eds.), *Social epidemiology* (pp. 137–173). New York, NY: Oxford University Press.

Berlin, K. L., Means, M. K., & Edinger, J. D. (2011). Nightmare reduction in a Vietnam veteran using imagery rehearsal therapy. *Journal of Clinical Sleep Medicine, 6,* 487–488.

Berlyne, D. (1960). *Conflict, arousal, and curiosity.* New York, NY: McGraw-Hill.

Berna, C., Leknes, S., Holmes, E. A., Edwards, R. R., Goodwin, G., & Tracey, I. (2010). Induction of depressed mood disrupts emotion regulation neurocircuitry and enhances pain unpleasantness. *Biological Psychiatry, 67,* 1083–1090.

Bernardi, R. E., & Spanagel, R. (2013). The clock δ 19 mutation in mice fails to alter the primary and secondary reinforcing properties of nicotine. *Drug and Alcohol Dependence,* doi: http://dx.doi.org/10.1016/j.drugalcdep.2013.08.024.

Bernat, J. (2006). Chronic disorders of consciousness. *The Lancet, 367,* 1181–1192.

Bernier, A., Carlson, S. M., Bordeleau, S., & Carrier, J. (2010). Relations between physiological and cognitive regulatory systems: Infant sleep regulation and subsequent executive functioning. *Child Development, 81,* 1739–1752. doi: 10.1111/j.1467-8624.2010.01507.x.

Bernier, R., & Dawson, G. (2009). The role of mirror neuron dysfunction in autism. In J. A. Pineda (Ed.), *Mirror neuron systems: The role of mirroring processes in social cognition* (pp. 261–286). Totowa, NJ: Humana Press.

Berridge, K. C. (2004). Motivation concepts in behavioral neuroscience. *Physiology and Behavior, 81,* 179–209.

Berry, C. M., Ones, D. S., & Sackett, P. R. (2007). Interpersonal deviance, organizational deviance, and their common correlates: A review and meta-analysis. *Journal of Applied Psychology, 92,* 410–424.

Berthoud, H. R. (2002). Multiple neural systems controlling food intake and body weight. *Neuroscience and Biobehavioral Reviews, 26,* 393–428.

Bewernick, B. H., Kayser, S., Sturm, V., & Schlaepfer, T. E. (2012). Long-term effects of nucleus accumbens deep brain stimulation in treatment-resistant depression: Evidence for sustained efficacy. *Neuropsychopharmacology, 37*(9), 1975–1985.

Bexton, W. H., Heron, W., & Scott, T. H. (1954). Effects of decreased variation in the sensory environment. *Canadian Journal of Psychology, 8,* 70–76.

Bherer, L., Erickson, K. I., & Liu-Ambrose, T. (2013). A review of the effects of physical activity and exercise on cognitive and brain functions in older adults. *Journal of Aging Research.* doi: 10.1155/2013/657508.

Bialystok, E., Barac, R., Blaye, A., & Poulin-Dubois, D. (2010). Word mapping and executive functioning in young monolingual and bilingual children. *Journal of Cognition and Development, 11*(4), 485–508. doi: 10.1080/15248372.2010.516420.

Bialystok, E., & Craik, F. I. M. (2010). Cognitive and linguistic processing in the bilingual mind. *Current Directions in Psychological Science, 19,* 19–23.

Bialystok, E., Craik, F. I. M., & Ryan, J. (2006). Executive control in a modified antisaccade task: Effects of aging and bilingualism. *Journal of Experimental Psychology: Learning, Memory, & Cognition, 32,* 1341–1354.

Bickerton, D. (1995). *Language and human behavior.* Seattle: University of Washington Press.

Binder, E., Droste, S. K., Ohl, F., & Reul, J. M. (2004). Regular voluntary exercise reduces anxiety-related behavior and impulsiveness in mice. *Behavioural Brain Research, 155,* 197–206.

Biography, Esref Armagan. (n.d.). Retrieved October 23, 2007, from http://www.esrefarmagan.com/bio.html

Birch, L. L., & Fisher, J. A. (1996). The role of experience in the development of children's eating behavior. In E. D. Capaldi (Ed.), *Why we eat what we eat: The psychology of eating* (pp. 113–141). Washington, DC: American Psychological Association.

Birch, L. L., & Marlin, D. W. (1982). I don't like it; I never tried it: Effects of exposure on two-year-old children's food preferences. *Appetite, 3,* 353–360.

Birdsong, D. (2005). Interpreting age effects in second language acquisition. In J. F. Kroll & A. M. B. de Groot (Eds.), *Handbook of bilingualism: Psycholinguistic approaches* (pp. 109–127). New York, NY: Oxford University Press.

Birdsong, D. (2006). Age and second language acquisition and processing: A selective overview. *Language Learning, 56,* 9–49.

Birks, J. (2009). Cholinesterase inhibitors for Alzheimer's disease (review). *Cochrine Library, 1,* CD005593.

Bishop, S. J. (2007). Neurocognitive mechanisms of anxiety: An integrative account. *Trends in Cognitive Sciences, 11,* 307–316.

Bjork, R. A. (2001, March). How to succeed in college: Learn how to learn. *American Psychological Society Observer, 14,* 3, 9.

Black, D. W. (2006). Efficacy of combined pharmacotherapy and psychotherapy versus monotherapy in the treatment of anxiety disorders. *CNS Spectrums, 11,* 29–33.

Blais, A., Gidengil, E., Fourneir, P., Nevitte, N., Everit, J., & Kim, J. (2010). Political judgments, perceptions of facts, and partisan effects. *Electoral Studies, 29,* 1–12.

Blakeslee, S. (2005, February 8). Focus narrows in search for autism's cause. *The New York Times.* Retrieved from http://www.nytimes.com

Blakeslee, S., & Blakeslee, M. (2007). *The body has a mind of its own.* New York, NY: Random House.

Blanco, C., Okuda, M., Wright, C., Hasin, D., Grant, B., Liu, S., & Olfson, M. (2008). Mental health of college students and their non-college-attending peers: Results from the National Epidemiologic Study on Alcohol and Related Conditions. *Archives of General Psychiatry, 65,* 1429–1437. doi: 10.1001/archpsyc.65.12.1429.

Blass, T. (2004). *The man who shocked the world: The life and legacy of Stanley Milgram.* New York, NY: Basic Books.

Bleidorn, W., Klimstra, T. A., Denissen, J. A., Rentfrow, P. J., Potter, J., & Gosling, S. D. (2013). Personality maturation around the world: A cross-cultural examination of social-investment theory. *Psychological Science, 24*(12), 2530–2540. doi: 10.1177/0956797613498396.

Bleier, P., Habib, R., & Flament, M. F. (2006). Pharmacotherapies in the management of obsessive-compulsive disorder. *Canadian Journal of Psychiatry, 51,* 417–430.

Blier, P. (2005). Atypical antipsychotics for mood and anxiety disorders: Safe and effective adjuncts? *Review of Psychiatry and Neuroscience, 30,* 232–233.

Block, J., Block, J. H., & Keyes, S. (1988). Longitudinally foretelling drug usage in adolescence: Early childhood personality and environmental precursors. *Child Development, 59,* 336–355.

Block, J. J. (2008). Issues for *DSM-V:* Internet addiction. *American Journal of Psychiatry, 165,* 306–307.

Blonigen, D. M., Hicks, B. M., Krueger, R. F., Patrick, C. J., & Iacono, W. G. (2006). Continuity and change in psychopathic traits as measured via normal-range personality: A longitudinal-biometric study. *Journal of Abnormal Psychology, 115,* 85–95.

Bocchieri Riccardi, L. (2007). Psychological well-being and relationship changes in women after gastric bypass surgery. *Dissertation Abstracts International: Section B: The Sciences and Engineering, 67*(7-B), 4091.

Boettger, M. K., Grossman, D., & Bär, K.-J. (2013). Thresholds and perception of cold pain, heat pain, and the thermal grill illusion in patients with major depressive disorder. *Psychosomatic Medicine, 75,* 281–287. doi: 10.1097/PSY.ob013e3182881a9c.

Bollen, E., & Wojciechowski, F. L. (2004). Anorexia nervosa subtypes and the Big Five personality factors. *European Eating Disorders Review, 12,* 117–121.

Bolour, S., & Braunstein, G. (2005). Testosterone therapy in women: A review. *International Journal of Impotence Research, 17,* 399–408.

Bond, R., & Smith, P. B. (1996). Culture and conformity: A meta-analysis of studies using Asch's (1952b, 1956) line judgment task. *Psychological Bulletin, 119,* 111–137.

Bonnet, M., Decety, J., Jeannerod, M., & Requin, J. (1997). Mental simulation of an action modulates the excitability of spinal reflex pathways in man. *Cognitive Brain Research, 5,* 221–228.

Boorboor, S. (2002). Integrating the incompatible: The rise of the incorporated immune system. [University of Rochester] *Journal of Undergraduate Research, 1,* 10–26.

Boroditsky, L. (2001). Does language shape thought? Mandarin and English speakers' conceptions of time. *Cognitive Psychology, 43,* 1–22. doi: 10.1006/cogp.2001.0748.

Borst, J. P., Taatgen, N. A., & van Rijn, H. (2010). The problem state: A cognitive bottleneck in multitasking. *Journal of Experimental Psychology. Learning, Memory, and Cognition, 36*(2), 363–382. doi: 10.1037/a0018106.

Boska, P. (2008). Maternal infection during pregnancy and schizophrenia. *Journal of Psychiatry and Neuroscience, 33,* 183–185.

Botvinick, M. M., Cohen, J. D., & Carter, C. S. (2004). Conflict monitoring and anterior cingulate cortex: An update. *Trends in Cognitive Sciences, 8,* 539–546.

Botwin, M., Buss, D. M., & Shackelford, T. K. (1997). Personality and mate preferences: Five factors in mate selection and marital satisfaction. *Journal of Personality and Social Psychology, 65*, 107–136.

Bouchard, T. J., Jr., & Loehlin, J. C. (2001). Genes, evolution, and personality. *Behavioral Genetics, 31*, 243–273.

Bouchard, T. J., Jr., & McGue, M. (1981). Familial studies of intelligence: A review. *Science, 212*, 1055–1059.

Bourgeois, S., & Johnson, A. (2004). Preparing for dying: Meaningful practices in palliative care. *Omega: Journal of Death and Dying, 49*, 99–107.

Bouso, J. C., Doblin, R., Farré, M., Alcázar, M. A., & Gómez-Jarabo, G. (2008). MDMA-assisted psychotherapy using low doses in a small sample of women with chronic posttraumatic stress disorder. *Journal of Psychoactive Drugs, 40*, 225–236.

Bouton, M. E., Mineka, S., & Barlow, D. H. (2001). A modern learning theory perspective on the etiology of panic disorder. *Psychological Review, 108*, 4–32.

Bowden, C. L. (1994). Bipolar disorder and creativity. In M. P. Shaw & M. A. Runco (Eds.), *Creativity and affect* (pp. 73–86). Norwood, NJ: Ablex.

Bowden, E. M., & Jung-Beeman, M. (2003). Aha! Insight experience correlates with solution activation in the right hemisphere. *Psychonomic Bulletin & Review, 10*, 730–737.

Bowden, E. M., Jung-Beeman, M., Fleck, J., & Kounios, J. (2005). New approaches to demystifying insight. *Trends in Cognitive Sciences, 9*, 322–328.

Bower, B. (2005, December 10). The Piraha challenge: An Amazonian tribe takes grammar to a strange place. *Science News, 168*(24). Retrieved from http://www.sciencenews.org

Bowers, A. J., & Berland, M. (2013). Does recreational computer use affect high school achievement? *Educational Technology Research and Development, 61*(1), 51–69. doi: 10.1007/s11423-012-9274-1.

Bowlby, J. (1969). *Attachment and loss: Vol. 1. Attachment.* New York, NY: Basic Books.

Bowlby, J. (1973). *Attachment and loss: Vol. 2. Separation, anxiety, and anger.* New York, NY: Basic Books.

Bowlby, J. (1980). *Attachment and loss: Vol. 3. Loss, sadness, and depression.* New York, NY: Basic Books.

Bowman, L. L., Levine, L. E., Waite, B. M., & Gendron, M. (2010). Can students really multitask? An experimental study of instant messaging while reading. *Computers and Education, 54*, 927–931.

Boyack, K. W., Klavans, R., & Börner, K. (2005). Mapping the backbone of science. *Scientometrics, 64*, 351–374.

Boyd, D. (2007). Why youth (heart) social network sites: The role of networked publics in teenage social life. In D. Buckingham (Ed.), *MacArthur Foundation Series on Digital Learning—Youth, Identity, and Digital Media Volume* (pp. 1–26). Cambridge, MA: MIT Press.

Boysen, G. A., & VanBergen, A. (2013). A review of published research on adult dissociative identity disorder: 2000–2010. *Journal of Nervous and Mental Diseases, 201*, 5–11.

Bradberry, C. W. (2007). Cocaine sensitization and dopamine mediation of cue effects in rodents, monkeys, and humans: Areas of agreement, disagreement, and implications for addiction. *Psychopharmacology, 191*, 705–717.

Bradley, R. M. (1972). Development of the taste bud and gustatory papillae in human fetuses. In J. F. Bosma (Ed.), *The third symposium on oral sensation and perception: The mouth of the infant.* Springfield, IL: Thomas.

Brain, M. (2003). How 3-D glasses work. Retrieved from http://science.howstuffworks.com/3-d-glasses2.htm

Brand, B. L., Loewenstein, R. J., & Speigel, D. (2013). Patients with DID are found and researched more widely than Boysen and VanBergen recognized. *Journal of Nervous and Mental Disease, 201*, 440.

Brand, G., & Millot, J.-L. (2001). Sex differences in human olfaction: Between evidence and enigma. *Quarterly Journal of Experimental Psychology B: Comparative and Physiological Psychology, 54B*, 259–270.

Brand, S., Gerber, M., Beck, J., Hatzinger, M., Pühse, W., & Holsboer-Trachsler, M. (2010). High exercise levels are related to favorable sleep patterns and psychological functioning in adolescents: A comparison of athletes and controls. *Journal of Adolescent Health, 46*, 133–141.

Brant, A. M., Haberstick, B. C., Corley, R. P., Wadsworth, S. J., DeFries, J. C., & Hewitt, J. K. (2009). The developmental etiology of high IQ. *Behavioral Genetics, 39*, 393–405. doi: 10.1007/s10519-009-9268-x.

Brant, A. M., Munakata, Y., Boomsma, D. I., DeFries, J. C., Haworth, C. A., Keller, M. C., . . . Hewitt, J. K. (2013). The nature and nurture of high IQ: An extended sensitive period for intellectual development. *Psychological Science, 24*(8), 1487–1495.

Brandtzæg, P. B., Lüders, M., & Skjetne, J. H. (2010). Too many Facebook "friends"? Content sharing and sociability versus the need for privacy in social network sites. *International Journal of Human-Computer Interaction, 26*, 1006–1030.

Brasil-Neto, J. P. (2012). Learning, memory, and transcranial direct current stimulation. *Frontiers in Psychiatry, 3*, 1–4. doi: 10.3389/fpsyt.2012.00080.

Braver, T. S., & Barch, D. M. (2002). A theory of cognitive control, aging, cognition, and neuromodulation. *Neuroscience and Biobehavioral Reviews, 26*, 809–817.

Breiter, H. C., Etcoff, N. L., Whalen, P. J., Kennedy, W. A., Rauch, S. L., Buckner, R. L., . . . Rosen, B. R. (1996). Response and habituation of the human amygdala during visual processing of facial expressions. *Neuron, 17*, 875–887.

Breland, K., & Breland, M. (1961). The misbehavior of organisms. *American Psychologist, 16*, 681–684.

Brennan, P. A. (2010). On the scent of sexual attraction. *BMC Biology, 8*, 71–74.

Brenner, J. (2013, September 18). Pew Internet: Mobile. Pew Internet and American Life Project. Retrieved November 18, 2013, from http://pewinternet.org/Commentary/2012/February/Pew-Internet-Mobile.aspx

Breugelmans, S. M., Poortinga, Y. H., Ambadar, Z., Setiadi, B., Vaca, J. B., Widiyanto, B., . . . (2005). Body sensations associated with emotions in Rarámuri Indians, rural Javanese, and three student samples. *Emotion, 5*, 166–174.

Brewer, M. B., & Caporael, L. R. (2006). An evolutionary perspective on social identity: Revisiting groups. In M. Schaller, D. T. Kenrick, & J. A. Simpson (Eds.), *Evolution and social psychology* (pp. 143–161). New York, NY: Psychology Press.

Bridges, K. (1932). Emotional development in infancy. *Child Development, 3*, 324–341.

Briggs, C. (2005). Allen uses films to avoid anxiety. *BBC News-Online.* Retrieved July 3, 2008, from http://news.bbc.co.uk/2/hi/entertainment/4539493.stm

Brivic, S. (1980). *Joyce between Freud and Jung.* Port Washington, NY: Kennikat Press.

Broadbent, D. E. (1954). The role of auditory localization in attention and memory span. *Journal of Experimental Psychology, 44*, 51–55.

Broekman, B. F. P., Chan, Y.-H., Chong, Y.-S., Quek, S.-C., Fung, D., Low, Y.-L. . . . Saw, S.-M. (2009). The influence of birth size on intelligence in healthy children. *Pediatrics, 123*, e1011–e1016.

Broude, G., & Greene, S. (1980). Cross-cultural codes on 20 sexual attitudes and practices. In H. Barry & A. Schlegel (Eds.), *Cross-cultural samples and codes* (pp. 313– 333). Pittsburgh, PA: University of Pittsburgh Press.

Brown, A. S. (2006). Prenatal infection as a risk factor for schizophrenia. *Schizophrenia Bulletin, 32*, 200–202.

Brown, K. W., & Ryan, R. M. (2003). The benefits of being present: Mindfulness and its role in psychoogical well-being. *Journal of Personality and Social Psychology, 84,* 822–848.

Brown, R., & Kulik, J. (1977). Flashbulb memories. *Cognition, 5,* 73–99.

Brown, R. T., Reynolds, C. R., & Whitaker, J. S. (1999). Bias in mental testing since Jensen's "Bias in Mental Testing." *School Psychology Quarterly, 14,* 208–238.

Brown, T. S., & Wallace, P. (1980). *Physiological psychology.* New York, NY: Academic Press.

Brown/grizzly bear facts. (n.d.). Retrieved November 5, 2007, from http://www.bear.org/Grizzly/Grizzly_Brown_Bear_Facts.html

Bruder, C. E. G., Piotrowski, A., Gijsbers, A., Andersson, A., Erickson, S., de Stahl, T.D. . . . Dumanski, J. P. (2008). Phenotypically concordant and discordant monozygotic twins display differ DNA copy-number-variation profiles. *American Journal of Human Genetics, 82,* 763–771. doi: 10.1016/j.ajhg.2007.12.011.

Brunelin, J., Poulet, E., Bor, J., Rivet, A., Eche, J., d'Amato, T., & Saoud, M. (2010). Transcranial magnetic stimulation (rTMS) and negative symptoms of schizophrenia. *Annales Médico-Psychologiques, 168,* 422–427.

Bruner, J. S., & Minturn, A. L. (1955). Perceptual identification and perceptual organization. *Journal of General Psychology, 53,* 21–28.

Brunetti, M., Babiloni, C., Ferretti, A., Del Gratta, C., Merla, A., Olivetti, M., . . . Romani, G. L. (2008). Hypothalamus, sexual arousal and psychosexual identity in human males: A functional magnetic resonance imaging study. *European Journal of Neuroscience, 27,* 2922–2927.

Brunwasser, S. M., Gillham, J. E., & Kim, E. S. (2009). A meta-analytic review of Penn Resiliency Program's effect on depressive symptoms. *Journal of Consulting and Clinical Psychology, 77,* 1042–1054.

Bryans, W. A. (1959). Mitotic activity in the brain of the adult white rat. *Anatomical Record, 133,* 65–71.

Buboltz, W. C., Loveland, J., Jenkins, S. M., Brown, F., Soper, B., & Hodges, J. (2006). College student sleep: Relationship to health and academic performance. In M. V. Landow (Ed.), *College students: Mental health and coping strategies* (pp. 1–39). Hauppauge, NY: Nova Science.

Buchanan, J., & Houlihan, D. (2008). The use of in vivo desensitization for the treatment of a specific phobia of earthworms. *Clinical Case Studies, 7,* 12–24. doi: 10.1177/1534650107300863.

Buchanan, T. W., Denburg, N. L., Tranel, D., & Adolphs, R. (2001). Verbal and nonverbal emotional memory following unilateral amygdala damage. *Learning & Memory, 8,* 326–335. doi: 10.1101/lm.40101.

Buchanan, T. W., & Tranel, D. (2008). Stress and emotional memory retrieval: Effects of sex and cortisol response. *Neurobiology of Learning and Memory, 89,* 134–141.

Buck, L. B. (2000). Smell and taste: The chemical senses. In E. R. Kandel, J. H. Schwartz, & T. M. Jessell (Eds.), *Principles of neural science* (4th ed., pp. 625–647). New York, NY: McGraw-Hill.

Buckley, C. (2007, January 3). Man is rescued by stranger on subway tracks. *The New York Times.* Retrieved from http://www.nytimes.com

Buka, S. L., Tsuang, M. T., Torrey, E. F., Klebanoff, M. A., Bernstein, D., & Yolken, R. H. (2001). Maternal infections and subsequent psychosis among offspring. *Archives of General Psychiatry, 58,* 1032–1037.

Bukh, J., Bock, C., Vinberg, M., Werge, T., Gether, U., & Kessing, L. (2009). Interaction between genetic polymorphisms and stressful life events in first episode depression. *Journal of Affective Disorders, 119*(1–3), 107–115. doi: 10.1016/j.jad.2009.02.023.

Bukowski, W. M., & Sippola, L. K. (2001). Groups, individuals, and victimization: A view of the peer system. In J. Juvonen & S. Graham (Eds.), *Peer harassment in school: The plight of the vulnerable and victimized* (pp. 355–377). New York: Guilford.

Bulik, C. M., Sullivan, P. F., Tozzi, F., Furberg, H., Lichtenstein, P., & Pedersen, N. L. (2006). Prevalence, heritability, and prospective risk factors for anorexia nervosa. *Archives of General Psychiatry, 63,* 305–312.

Bulkeley, K. (1997). *An introduction to the psychology of dreaming.* Westport, CT: Praeger.

Bullivant, S. B., Sellergren, S. A., Stern, K., Spencer, N. A., Jacob, S., Mennella, J. A., & McClintock, M. K. (2004). Women's sexual experience during the menstrual cycle: Identification of the sexual phase by noninvasive measurement of luteinizing hormone. *Journal of Sex Research, 41,* 82–93.

Burch, G., Pavelis, C., Hemsley, D. R., & Corr, P. J. (2006). Schizotypy and creativity in visual artists. *British Journal of Psychology, 97,* 177–190.

Burd, L., Roberts, D., Olson, M., & Odendaal, H. (2007). Ethanol and the placenta: A review. *Journal of Maternal-Fetal and Neonatal Medicine, 20,* 361–375.

Burgess, W. (2009). *The depression answer book.* Naperville, IL: Sourcebooks.

Burguière, E., Monteiro, P., Feng, G., & Graybiel, A. M. (2013). Optogenetic stimulation of lateral orbitofronto-striatal pathway suppresses compulsive behaviors. *Science, 340,* 1243–1246. doi: 10.1126/science.1232380.

Burnett, G. B., Moll, J., Frith, C., & Blakemore, S.-J. (2008). Development during adolescence of the neural processing of social emotion. *Journal of Cognitive Neuroscience 21,* 1736–1750.

Burnstein, E., Crandall, C., & Kitayama, S. (1994). Some neo-Darwinian decision rules for altruism: Weighing cues for inclusive fitness as a function of the biological importance of the decision. *Journal of Personality and Social Psychology, 67,* 773–789.

Burt, K. B., & Masten, A. S. (2010). Development in the transition to adulthood: Vulnerabilities and opportunities. In J. E. Grant & M. N. Potenza (Eds.), *Young adult mental health* (pp. 5–18). New York, NY: Oxford University Press.

Burton, C. M., & King, L. A. (2009). The health benefits of writing about positive experiences: The role of broadened cognition. *Psychology & Health, 24,* 867–879.

Busch, N., Fründ, I., & Herrmann, C. (2009). Electrophysiological evidence for different types of change detection and change blindness. *Journal of Cognitive Neuroscience, 22,* 1852–1869.

Bushman, B. J., & Anderson, C. A. (2001). Media violence and the American public: Scientific facts versus media misinformation. *American Psychologist, 56,* 477–489.

Buss, A. H., & Plomin, R. (1984). *Temperament: Early personality traits.* Hillsdale, NJ: Erlbaum.

Buss, D. M. (1999). *Evolutionary psychology: The new science of the mind.* New York, NY: Allyn & Bacon.

Buss, D. M. (2003). *The evolution of desire: Strategies of human mating* (Rev. ed.). New York, NY: Basic Books.

Buss, D. M. (2004). Sex differences in human mate preferences. In H. T. Reis & C. E. Rusbult (Eds.), *Close relationships: Key readings* (pp. 135–151). Philadelphia: Taylor & Francis.

Buss, D. M. (2008). Human nature and individual differences: Evolution of human personality. In O. P. John, R. W. Robins, & L. A. Pervin (Eds.), *Handbook of personality: Theory and research* (pp. 29–60). New York, NY: Guilford Press.

Buss, D. M. (2011). Personality and the adaptive landscape: The role of individual differences in creating and solving social adaptive problems. In D. M. Buss & P. Hawley (Eds.), *The evolution of personality and individual differences* (pp. 29–57). New York, NY: Oxford University Press.

Buss, D. M., & Greiling, H. (1999). Adaptive individual differences. *Journal of Personality, 67,* 209–243.

Buss, D. M., & Hawley, P. H. (Eds.). (2011). *The evolution of personality and individual differences.* New York, NY: Oxford University Press.

Buss, D. M., & Schmitt, D. P. (1993). Sexual strategies theory: An evolutionary perspective on human mating. *Psychological Review, 100*, 204–232.

Bussing, R., Gary, F. A., Mills, T. L., & Wilson Garvan, C. (2007). Cultural variations in parental health beliefs, knowledge, and information sources related to attention-deficit/hyperactivity disorder. *Journal of Family Issues, 28*, 291–318. doi: 10.1177/0192513X06296117.

Buxton, O. M., Cain, S. W., O'Connor, S. P., Porter, J. H., Duffy, J. F., Wang, W., Czeisler, C. A., & Shea, S. A. (2012). Adverse metabolic consequences in humans of prolonged sleep restriction combined with circadian disruption. *Science Translational Medicine, 4*, 129ra43. doi: 10.1126/scitranslmed.3003200.

Cacioppo, J. T., Fowler, J. H., & Christakis, N. A. (2009). Alone in the crowd: The structure and spread of loneliness in a large social network. *Journal of Personality and Social Psychology, 97*, 977–991.

Cahill, S. P., Foa, E. B., Hembree, E. A., Marshall, R. D., & Nacash, N. (2006). Dissemination of exposure therapy in the treatment of posttraumatic stress disorder. *Journal of Traumatic Stress, 19*, 597–610.

Caird, J. K., Willness, C. R., Steel, P., & Scialfa, C. (2008). A meta-analysis of the effects of cell phones on driver performance. *Accident Analysis and Prevention, 40*, 1282–1293.

Calamaro, C. J., Mason, A. T., & Ratcliffe, S. J. (2009). Adolescents living the 24/7 lifestyle: Effects of caffeine and technology on sleep duration and daytime functioning. *Pediatrics 123*(6), 1005–1010.

Calkins, M. W. (1898). Short studies in memory and in association from the Wellesley College Psychological Laboratory. I.: A study of immediate and delayed recall of the concrete and of the verbal. *Psychological Review, 5*, 451–456.

Calvert, S. L., Rideout, V. J., Woolard, J. L., Barr, R. F., & Strouse, G. A. (2005). Age, ethnicity, and socioeconomic patterns in early computer use. *American Behavioral Scientist, 48*, 590–607.

Cameron, J. D., Cyr, M., & Doucet, E. (2010). Increased meal frequency does not promote greater weight loss in subjects who were prescribed an 8-week equi-energetic energy restricted diet. *British Journal of Nutrition, 103*, 1098–1101. doi: 10.1017/S0007114509992984.

Cameron, K., Salazar, L., Bernhardt, J., Burgess-Whitman, N., Wingood, G., & DiClemente, R. (2005). Adolescents' experience with sex on the web: Results from online focus groups. *Journal of Adolescence, 28*(4), 535–540. doi: 10.1016/j.adolescence.2004.10.006.

Campbell, A. (2008). Attachment, aggression and affiliation: The role of oxytocin in female social behavior. *Biological Psychology, 77*, 1–10.

Campbell, F. A., & Ramey, C. T. (1995). Cognitive and school outcomes for high-risk African-American students at middle adolescence: Positive effects of early intervention. *American Educational Research Journal, 32*, 743–772.

Campbell, F. A., Ramey, C. T., Pungello, E. P., Sparling, J., & Miller-Johnson, S. (2002). Early childhood education: Young adult outcomes from the Abecedarian Project. *Applied Developmental Science, 6*, 42–57.

Campos, J. J., & Stenberg, C. (1981). Perception, appraisal, and emotion: The onset of social referencing. In M. E. Lamb & L. R. Sherrod (Eds.), *Infant social cognition: Empirical and theoretical considerations* (pp. 273–314). Hillsdale, NJ: Erlbaum.

Camras, L. A., Oster, H., Bakeman, R., Meng, Z., Ujiie, T., & Campos, J. J. (2007). Do infants show distinct negative facial expressions for fear and anger? Emotional expression in 11-month-old European American, Chinese, and Japanese infants. *Infancy, 11*, 131–155.

Cannarella, J., & Spechler, J. A. (2014). Epidemiological modeling of online social network dynamics. *Unpublished manuscript*. Department of Mechanical and Aerospace Engineering, Princeton University, Princeton, NJ. Retrieved January 22, 2014, from http://arxiv.org/pdf/1401.4208v1.pdf

Cannon, W. B. (1927). The James-Lange theory of emotion: A critical examination and an alternative theory. *American Journal of Psychology, 39*, 10–124.

Cannon, W. B. (1929). *Bodily changes in pain, hunger, fear, and rage: An account of recent researches into the function of emotional excitement*. New York, NY: Appleton.

Cannon, W. B. (1939). *The wisdom of the body*. New York, NY: Norton.

Cannon, W. B., & Washburn, A. L. (1912). An explanation of hunger. *American Journal of Physiology, 29*, 441–454.

Canter, R. R., & Hirsch, J. (1955). An experimental comparison of several psychological scales of weight. *American Journal of Psychology, 68*, 645–649.

Cappuccio, F. P., D'Elia, L., Strazzullo, P., & Miller, M. A. (2010). Sleep duration and all-cause mortality: A systematic review and meta-analysis of prospective studies. *Sleep, 33*, 585–592.

Capri, M., Salvioli, T., Sevini, F., Valensin, S., Celani, L., Monti, D., . . . Franceschi, C. (2006). The genetics of human longevity. *Annals of the New York Academy of Sciences, 1067*, 252–263.

Cardno, A. G., & Gottesman, I. I. (2000). Twin studies of schizophrenia: From bow-and-arrow concordances to Star Wars Mx and functional genomics [Review]. *American Journal of Medical Genetics, 97*, 12–17.

Carew, T. J., & Kandel, E. R. (1973). Acquisition and retention of long-term habituation in *Aplysia:* Correlation of behavioral and cellular processes. *Science, 182*, 1158–1160.

Carey, B. (2008, December 4). H. M., an unforgettable amnesiac, dies at 82. *The New York Times.* Retrieved from http://www.nytimes.com

Carlat, D. J. (1998). The psychiatric review of symptoms: A screening tool for family physicians. *American Family Physician, 58*, 1617–1624.

Carless, S. A. (1999). Career assessment: Holland's vocational interests, personality characteristics, and abilities. *Journal of Career Assessment, 7*, 125–144.

Carlo, G., Knight, G. P., Roesch, S. C., Opal, D., & Davis, A. (2014). Personality across cultures: A critical analysis of Big Five research and current directions. In F. L. Leong, L. Comas-Díaz, G. C. Nagayama Hall, V. C. McLoyd, & J. E. Trimble (Eds.), *APA handbook of multicultural psychology, Vol. 1: Theory and research* (pp. 285–298). Washington, DC: American Psychological Association. doi: 10.1037/14189-015.

Carlsson, A. (1987). Perspectives on the discovery of central monoaminergic neurotransmission. *Annual Review of Neuroscience, 10*, 19–40.

Carlsson, A. (1993). Thirty years of dopamine research. *Advances in Neurology, 60*, 1–10.

Carlsson, A. (2000). Nobel Prize autobiography. Retrieved from http://nobelprize.org/nobel_prizes/medicine/laureates/2000/carlsson-autobio.html

Carlsson, I. (2002). Anxiety and flexibility of defense related to high or low creativity. *Creativity Research Journal, 14*, 341–349.

Carlsson, I., Wendt, P., & Risberg, J. (2000). On the neurobiology of creativity: Differences in frontal activity between high and low creative subjects. *Neuropsychologia, 38*, 873–885.

Carnagey, N. L., Anderson, C. A., & Bushman, B. J. (2007). The effect of video game violence on physiological desensitization to real-life violence. *Journal of Experimental Social Psychology, 43*, 489–496.

Carney, S. M., & Goodwin, G. M. (2005). Lithium—A continuing story in the treatment of bipolar disorder. *Acta Psychiatrica Scandinavica, 111*(Suppl. 426), 7–12.

Carrion, V. G., Hass, B. W., Garrett, A., Song, S., & Rice, A. L. (2010). Reduced hippocampal activity in youth with post-traumatic stress symptoms: An fMRI study. *Journal of Pediatric Psychology, 35*, 559–569.

Carroll, J. B. (1993). *Human cognitive abilities.* New York, NY: Cambridge University Press.

Carroll, J. L., & Rest, J. (1981, December). Development in moral judgment as indicated by rejection of lower-stage statements. *Journal of Research in Personality, 15*(4), 538–544.

Carskadon, M. A., & Davis, S. S. (1989). Sleep-wake patterns in the high-school-to-college transition: Preliminary data. *Sleep Research, 18*, 113.

Carson, S. H., Peterson, J. B., & Higgins, D. M. (2003). Decreased latent inhibition is associated with increased creative achievement in high-functioning individuals. *Journal of Personality and Social Psychology, 85*, 499–506.

Carstensen, L. L. (2006). The influence of a sense of time on human development. *Science, 312*, 1913–1915.

Carstensen, L. L., Fung, H. H., & Charles, S. T. (2003). Socioemotional selectivity theory and the regulation of emotion in the second half of life. *Motivation and Emotion, 27*, 103–123.

Carter, C. S., Mintun, M., Nichols, T. N., & Cohen, J. D. (1997). Anterior cingulate gyrus dysfunction and selective attention deficits in schizophrenia: [15O] H2O PET study during single-trial Stroop task performance. *American Journal of Psychiatry, 154*, 1670–1675.

Caruso, E. M., Mead, N. L., & Balcetis, E. (2009). Political partisanship influences perception of biracial candidates' skin tone. *Proceedings of the National Academy of Sciences, 106*, 20168–20173.

Carver, C. S., Scheier, M. F., & Segerstrom, S. C. (2010). Optimism. *Clinical Psychology Review, 30*, 879–889.

Casey, B. J., Davidson, M., & Rosen, B. (2002). Functional magnetic imaging: Basic principles of and application to developmental science. *Developmental Science, 5*, 301–309.

Caspi, A. (2000). The child is father of the man: Personality continuities from childhood to adulthood. *Journal of Personality and Social Psychology, 78*, 158–172.

Caspi, A., Elder, G. H., & Bem, D. H. (1988). Moving away from the world: Life-course patterns of shy children. *Developmental Psychology, 24*, 824–831.

Caspi, A., Houts, R. M., Belsky, D. W., Goldman-Mellor, S. J., Harrington, H., Israel, S. . . . Moffitt, T. E. (2014). The p-factor: One general psychopathology factor in the structure of psychiatric disorders? *Clinical Psychological Science, 2*, 119–137. doi: 10.1177/2167702613497473.

Caspi, A., McClay, J., Moffitt, T. E., Mill, J., Martin, J., Craig, I. W., . . . (2002). Role of genotype in the cycle of violence in maltreated children. *Science, 297*, 851–853.

Caspi, A., Roberts, B. W., & Shiner, R. L. (2003). Personality development: Stability and change. *Annual Review of Psychology, 56*, 453–484.

Caspi, A., Sugden, K., Moffitt, T. E., Taylor, A., Craig, I. W., Harrington, H., . . . Poulton, R. (2003). Influence of life stress on depression: Moderation by a polymorphism in the 5-HTT gene. *Science, 301*, 386–389.

Cassidy, T. (2006). *Birth: The surprising history of how we are born.* New York: Atlantic Monthly Press.

Castelli, D. M., Hillman, C. H., Buck, S. M., & Erwin, H. (2007). Physical fitness and academic achievement in third- and fifth-grade students. *Journal of Sport & Exercise Psychology, 29*, 239–252.

Castles, A., McLean, G. M. T., Bavin, E., Bretherton, L., Carlin, J., Prior, M., . . . Reilly, S. (2013). Computer use and letter knowledge in pre-school children: A population-based study. *Journal of Paediatrics and Child Health, 49*, 193–198. doi: 10.1111/jpc.12126.

Catalino, L. I., & Fredrickson, B. L. (2011). A Tuesday in the life of a flourisher: The role of positive emotional reactivity in optimal mental health. *Emotion, 11*, 938–950.

Catapano, F., Perris, F., Masella, M., Rossano, F., Cigliano, M., Magliano, L., . . . Maj, M. (2006). Obsessive-compulsive disorder: A 3-year prospective follow-up study of patients treated with serotonin reuptake inhibitors. *Journal of Psychiatric Research, 40*, 502–510.

Cavallero, C., & Foulkes, D. (Eds.). (1993). *Dreaming as cognition.* New York, NY: Harvester-Wheatsheaf.

CBS News. (2007, January 3). Bystander pulls off daring subway rescue. Retrieved from http://www.cbsnews.com/stories/2007/01/03/national/main2324961.shtml?source=search_story

Ceci, S. J., & Williams, W. M. (2007). *Why aren't more women in science? Top researchers debate the evidence.* Washington, DC: American Psychological Association.

Ceci, S. J., & Williams, W. M. (2010). *The mathematics of sex: How biology and society conspire to limit talented women and girls.* New York, NY: Oxford University Press.

Centers for Disease Control and Prevention (CDC). (2001). *Cigarette-smoking related mortality.* Retrieved March 26, 2007, from http://www.cdc.gov/tobacco/research_data/health_consequences/mortali.htm

Centers for Disease Control and Prevention (CDC). (2005). *Sexual behavior and selected health measures: Men and women 15–44 years of age, United States, 2002.* Retrieved March 12, 2008, from http://www.cdc.gov/nchs/data/ad/ad362.pdf

Centers for Disease Control and Prevention (CDC). (2007, August 8). *Smoking during pregnancy.* Retrieved February 23, 2008, from http://www.cdc.gov/tobacco/health_effects/pregnancy.htm

Centers for Disease Control and Prevention. (2009). Healthy eating for a healthy weight. Retrieved from http://www.cdc.gov/healthyweight/healthy_eating/index.html

Chadwick, P., Hughes, S., Russell, D., Russell, I., & Dagnan, D. (2009). Mindfulness groups for distressing voices and paranoia: A replication and randomized feasibility trial. *Behavioral and Cognitive Psychotherapy, 37*, 403–412.

Chaffee, J. (1999). *The thinker's guide to college success* (2nd ed.). Boston, MA: Houghton Mifflin.

Chan, C., Brandone, A., & Tardif, T. (2009). Culture, context, or behavioral control?: English- and Mandarin-speaking mothers' use of nouns and verbs in joint book reading. *Journal of Cross-Cultural Psychology, 40*, 584–602. doi: 10.1177/0022022109335184.

Chance, P. (1986). *Thinking in the classroom: A survey of programs.* New York, NY: Teachers College, Columbia University.

Chandra, A., Martinez, G. M., Mosher, W. D., Abma, J. C., & Jones, J. (2005). Fertility, family planning, and reproductive health of U.S. women: Data from the 2002 National Survey of Family Growth. National Center for Health Statistics. *Vital Health Statistics, 23*, 1–160.

Chandra, A., Mosher, W. D., Copen, C., & Slonean, C. (2011). Sexual behavior, sexual attraction, and sexual identity in the United States: Data from 2006–2008 National Survey of Family Growth. *National Health Statistics Reports, 36*, 1–36, National Center for Health Statistics. Retrieved September 5, 2013, from http://ns1.isminc.com/documents/research/general/TeenSexualBehavior.pdf

Chandra, P. S., Satyanarayana, V. A., Satishchandra, P., Satish, K. S., & Kumar, M. (2009). Do men and women with HIV differ in their quality of life? A study from South India. *AIDS and Behavior, 13*(1), 110–117.

Chang, E. C. (1998). Dispositional optimism and primary and secondary appraisal of a stressor: Controlling for confounding influences and relations to coping and psychological and physical adjustment. *Journal of Personality and Social Psychology, 74*, 1109–1120.

Chapman, B. P., & Moynihan, J. (2009). The brain-skin connection: Role of psychosocial factors and neuropeptides in psoriasis.

Expert Review of Clinical Immunology, 5, 623–627.

Chappell, M., & Humphreys, M. S. (1994). An auto-associative neural network for sparse representations: Analysis and application to models of recognition and cued recall. *Psychological Review, 101,* 103–128.

Chaput, J. P., Després, J. P., & Tremblay, A. (2007). Short sleep duration is associated with reduced leptin levels and increased adiposity: Results from the Québec Family Study. *Obesity, 15,* 253–261.

Chaput, J. P., & Tremblay, A. (2012). Adequate sleep to improve the treatment of obesity. *Canadian Medical Association Journal, 184,* 1975–1976.

Charil, A., Laplante, D. P., Vaillancourt, C., & King, S. (2010). Prenatal stress and brain development. *Brain Research Reviews, 65,* 56–79.

Charmorro-Premuzic, T., & Steinmetz, C. (2013). The perfect hire. *Scientific American Mind, 24,* 43–47.

Charney, D. S. (2004). Psychological mechanisms of resilience and vulnerability: Implications for successful adaptation to extreme stress. *American Journal of Psychiatry, 161,* 195–216.

Chaudhari, N., & Roper, S.D. (2010). The cell biology of taste. *Journal of Cell Biology, 190,* 285–296.

Chartrand, T. L., & Dalton, A. N. (2009). Mimicry: Its ubiquity, importance, and functionality. In T. L. Chartrand & A. N. Dalton (Eds.). *Oxford handbook of human action* (pp. 458–483). New York, NY: Oxford University Press.

Chatterjee, A., Strauss, M. E., Smyth, K. A., & Whitehouse, P. J. (1992). Personality changes in Alzheimer's disease. *Archives of Neurology, 49,* 486–491.

Cheah, C. S. L., & Nelson, L. (2004). The role of acculturation in the emerging adulthood of aboriginal college students. *International Journal of Behavioral Development, 28,* 494–507.

Chechik, G., Meilijson, I., & Ruppin, E. (1999). Neuronal regulation: A mechanism for synaptic pruning during brain maturation. *Neural Computation, 11,* 2151–2170.

Cheetham, C. E. J., Hammond, M. S. L., Edwards, C. J., & Finnerty, G. T. (2007). Sensory experience alters cortical connectivity and synaptic function site specifically. *Journal of Neuroscience, 27,* 3456–3465.

Chen, S. Y., Jordan, C., & Thompson, S. (2006). The effect of cognitive behavioral therapy (CBT) on depression: The role of problem-solving appraisal. *Research on Social Work Practice, 16,* 500–510.

Chepenik, L. G., Raffo, M., Hampson, M., Lacadie, C., Wang, F., Jones, M. M., . . . Blumberg, H. P. (2010). Functional connectivity between ventral prefrontal cortex and amygdala at low frequency in the resting state in bipolar disorder. *Psychiatry Research: Neuroimaging, 182,* 207–210.

Chess, S., & Thomas, A. (1996). *Temperament: Theory and research.* New York, NY: Brunner/Mazel.

Cheyne, J., Carriere, J., & Smilek, D. (2006). Absent-mindedness: Lapses of conscious awareness and everyday cognitive failures. *Consciousness and Cognition: An International Journal, 15,* 578–592. doi: 10.1016/j.concog.2005.11.009.

Chia, E., Wang, J. J., Rochtchina, E., Cumming, R. R., Newall, P., & Mitchell, P. (2007). Hearing impairment and health-related quality of life: The Blue Mountains Hearing Study. *Ear & Hearing, 28,* 187–195.

Chiesa, A., Brambilla, P., & Serretti, A. (2010). Functional neural correlates of mindfulness meditations in comparison with psychotherapy, pharmacotherapy and placebo effect. Is there a link? *Acta Neuropsychiatrica, 22,* 104–117. doi: 10.1111/j.1601-5215.2010.00460.x.

Choi, I., Nisbett, R. E., & Norenzayan, A. (1999). Causal attribution across cultures: Variation and universality. *Psychological Bulletin, 125,* 47–65.

Chomsky, N. (1972). *Language and mind* (2nd ed.). New York, NY: Harcourt Brace Jovanovich.

Chomsky, N. (1986). *Knowledge of language: Its nature, origins, and use.* New York, NY: Praeger.

Chomsky, N. (2000). *New horizons in the study of language and the mind.* Cambridge, England: Cambridge University Press.

Chow, T. W., & Cummings, J. L. (1999). Frontal-subcortical circuits. In B. L. Miller & J. L. Cummings (Eds.), *The human frontal lobes: Functions and disorders* (pp. 3–26). New York, NY: Guilford Press.

Chowdhury, M., & Benson, B. A. (2011). Use of differential reinforcement to reduce behavior problems in adults with intellectual disabilities: A methodological review. *Research in Developmental Disabilities, 324(2),* 383–394.

Choy, Y., Fyer, A. J., & Lipsitz, J. D. (2007). Treatment of specific phobia in adults. *Clinical Psychology Review, 27(3),* 266–286. Advance online publication. doi: 10.1016/j.cpr.2006.10.002.

Christakis, D., Zimmerman, F., DiGiuseppe, D., & McCarty, C. (2004). Early television exposure and subsequent attentional problems in children. *Pediatrics, 113,* 708–713.

Christakis, N. A., & Fowler, J. H. (2007). The spread of obesity in a large social network over 32 years. *New England Journal of Medicine, 357,* 370–379.

Christakis, N. A., & Fowler, J. H. (2008). The collective dynamics of smoking in a large social network. *New England Journal of Medicine, 358,* 2249–2258.

Christakis, N. A., & Fowler, J. H. (2009). *Connected: The surprising power of our social networks and how they shape our lives.* New York, NY: Little, Brown.

Christakis, N. A., & Fowler, J. H. (2010). Social network sensors for early detection of contagious outbreaks. *PLoS ONE, 5(1–8),* e12948. doi: 10.1371/journal.pone.0012948.

Christensen, K., Herskind, A. M., & Vaupel, J. W. (2006). Why Danes are smug: Comparative study of life satisfaction in the European Union. *British Medical Journal, 333,* 1289–1291.

Chuang, D. M. (2004). Lithium protection from glutamate excitotoxicity: Therapeutic implications. *Clinical Neuroscience Research, 4,* 243–252.

Cicchetti, D. (2001). How a child builds a brain. In W. W. Hartup & R. A. Weinberg (Eds.), *Child psychology in retrospect and prospect.* Mahwah, NJ: Erlbaum.

Cipriani, A., La Ferla, T., Furukawa, T. A., Signoretti, A., Nakagawa, A., Churchill, R., . . . Barbui, C. (2010). Sertraline versus other antidepressive agents for depression [Review]. *Cochrane Database of Systematic Reviews,* Issue 4.

Clancy, P. M. (1985). The acquisition of Japanese. In D. Slobin (Ed.), *The cross-linguistic study of language acquisition: Vol. 1. The data.* Hillsdale, NJ: Erlbaum.

Clark, A. S., & Schneider, M. L. (1997). Effects of prenatal stress on behavior in adolescent rhesus monkey. *Annals of the New York Academy of Sciences, 807,* 490–491.

Clark, L., Bosworth, H., Welsh-Bohmer, K., Dawson, D., & Siegler, I. (2000). Relation between informant-rated personality and clinician-rated depression in patients with memory disorders. *Neuropsychiatry, Neuropsychology, & Behavioral Neurology, 13,* 39–47.

Clark, L. A. (2005). Temperament as a unifying basis for personality and psychopathology. *Journal of Abnormal Psychology, 114,* 505–521.

Clark, R. D., III, & Hatfield, E. (1989). Gender differences in willingness to engage in casual sex. *Journal of Psychology and Human Sexuality, 2,* 39–55.

Clark, R. D., III, & Hatfield, E. (2003). Love in the afternoon. *Psychological Inquiry, 14,* 227–231.

Clark, R. P., & Berris, C. E. (1989). Botulinum toxin: A treatment for facial asymmetry caused by facial nerve paralysis. *Plastic and Reconstructive Surgery, 84,* 353–355. doi: 10.1097/01.prs.0000205566.47797.8d.

Clark, W. R., & Grunstein, M. (2000). *Are we hardwired? The role of genes in human behavior.* New York, NY: Oxford University Press.

Clarke, G. N., Hawkins, W., Murphy, M., Sheeber, L. B., Lewinsohn, P. M., & Seeley, J. R. (1995). Targeted prevention of unipolar depressive disorder in an at-risk sample of high school adolescents: A randomized trial of group cognitive intervention. *Journal of the American Academy of Child & Adolescent Psychiatry, 34,* 312–321.

Cobb, J. M., Fluster, Z., Leder, G., Seaver, A., Hendrick, J. L., & Hokanson, J. F. (2010). Information processing demands while texting on a simulated driving task. *Journal of Sport & Exercise Psychology, 32,* S72.

Coe, C. L., & Lubach, G. R. (2008). Fetal programming: Prenatal origins of health and illness. *Current Directions in Psychological Science, 17,* 36–41.

Cohen, J. (2010, April 2). Boxed about the ears, ape language research still standing. *Science, 328,* 38–39.

Cohen, J. D. (2005). The vulcanization of the human brain. *Journal of Economic Perspectives, 19,* 3–24.

Cohen, K. M. (2002). Relationships among childhood sex-atypical behavior, spatial ability, handedness, and sexual orientation in men. *Archives of Sexual Behavior, 31,* 129–143.

Cohen, S. (2004). Social relationships and health. *American Psychologist, 59,* 676–684.

Cohen, S., Alper, C. M., Doyle, W. J., Adler, N., Treanor, J. J., & Turner, R. B. (2008). Objective and subjective socioeconomic status and susceptibility to the common cold. *Health Psychology, 27,* 268–274.

Cohen, S., Doyle, W. J., Turner, R. B., Alper, C. M., & Skoner, D. P. (2003). Sociability and susceptibility to the common cold. *Psychological Science, 14,* 389–395.

Cohen, S., Janicki-Deverts, D., Doyle, W. J., Miller, G. E., Frank, E., Rabin, B. S., & Turner, R. S. (2012). Chronic stress, glucocorticoid receptor resistance, inflammation, and disease risk. *Proceedings of the National Academy of Sciences (PNAS), 109,* 5995–5999. doi: 10.1073/pnas.1118355109.

Cohen, S., Tyrrell, D. A. J., & Smith, A. P. (1993). Negative life events, perceived stress, negative affect, and susceptibility to the common cold. *Journal of Personality and Social Psychology, 64,* 131–140.

Cohen, S., & Wills, T. A. (1985). Stress, social support, and the buffering hypothesis. *Psychological Bulletin, 98,* 310–357.

Colcombe, S. J., Erickson, K. I., Scalf, P. E., Kim, J. S., Praskash, R., McAuley, E., . . . Kramer, A. F. (2006). Aerobic exercise training increases brain volume in aging humans. *Journal of Gerontology, 61,* 1166–1170.

Colcombe, S. J., & Kramer, A. F. (2003). Fitness effects on the cognitive function of older adults: A meta-analytic study. *Psychological Science, 14,* 125–130.

Cole, S. W. (2009). Social regulation of human gene expression. *Current Directions in Psychological Science, 18,* 132–137.

Cole, S. W. (2010). Elevating the perspective on human stress genomics. *Psychoneuroendocrinology, 35,* 955–962.

Cole, S. W., Arevaloa, J. M. G., Takahashia, R., Sloan, E. K., Lutgendorf, S. K., Sood, A. K., . . . Seeman, T. E. (2010). Computational identification of gene–social environment interaction at the human IL6 locus. *Proceedings of the National Academy of Sciences, 107,* 5681–5686.

Cole, S. W., Hawkley, L. C., Arevalo, J. M., Sung, C. Y., Rose, R. M., & Cacioppo, J. T. (2007). Social regulation of gene expression in human leukocytes. *Genome Biology, 8,* R189.1–R189.13.

Collignon, O., Girard, S., Gosselin, F., Saint-Amour, D., Lepore, F., & Lassonde, M. (2010). Women process multisensory emotion expressions more efficiently than men. *Neuropsychologia, 48,* 220–225.

Collins, A., & Loftus, E. F. (1975). A spreading activation theory of semantic processing. *Psychological Review, 82,* 407–428.

Collinson, S. L., Meyyappan, A., & Rosenfeld, J. V. (2009). Injury and recovery: Severe traumatic brain injury. *Brain Injury, 23,* 71–76. doi: 10.1080/02699050802649647.

Colom, R., Haier, R., Head, K., Álvarez-Linera, J., Quiroga, M., Shih, P., & Jung, R. E. (2009). Gray matter correlates of fluid, crystallized, and spatial intelligence: Testing the P-FIT model. *Intelligence, 37*(2), 124–135.

Comer, R. J. (2007). *Abnormal psychology* (6th ed.). New York, NY: Worth.

Comery, T. A., Stamoudis, C. X., Irwin, S. A., & Greenough, W. T. (1996). Increased density of multiple-head dendritic spines on medium-sized spiny neurons of the striatum in rats reared in a complex environment. *Neurobiology of Learning and Memory, 66,* 93–96.

Conduct Problems Prevention Research Group. (1999a). Initial impact of the Fast Track prevention trial for conduct problems: I. The high-risk sample. *Journal of Consulting and Clinical Psychology, 67,* 631–647.

Conduct Problems Prevention Research Group. (1999b). Initial impact of the Fast Track prevention trial for conduct problems: II. Classroom effects. *Journal of Consulting and Clinical Psychology, 67,* 648–657.

Conel, J. L. (1939). *The cortex of the newborn.* Cambridge, MA: Harvard University Press.

Cook, C. C. (2013, July 6). Soldier's suicide note goes viral; family demands better for veterans. *CNN News,* retrieved July 6, 2013, fromt http://www.cnn.com/2013/07/06/us/soldier-suicide-note/index.html?hpt=hp_t2

Costa, P. T. (1996). Work and personality: Use of the NEO–PI–R in industrial/organizational psychology. *Applied Psychology: An International Review, 45,* 225–241.

Costa, P. T., Herbst, J. H., McCrae, R. R., & Siegler, I. C. (2000). Personality at midlife: Stability, intrinsic maturation, and response to life events. *Assessment, 7,* 365–378.

Costa, P. T., & McCrae, R. R. (1980). Influences of extraversion and neuroticism on subjective well-being. *Journal of Personality and Social Psychology, 38,* 668–678.

Costa, P. T., & McCrae, R. R. (1992). *NEO PI-R professional manual.* Odessa, FL: Psychological Assessment Resources.

Cote, J., Clobert, J., Brodin, T., Fogarty, S., & Sih, A. (2014). Personality traits and spatial ecology in nonhuman animals. In P. J. Rentfrow (Ed.), *Geographical psychology: Exploring the interaction of environment and behavior* (pp. 89–112). Washington, DC: American Psychological Association. doi: 10.1037/14272-006.

Cotman, C. W., Berchtold, N. C., & Christie, L. A. (2007). Exercise builds brain health: Key roles of growth factor cascades and inflammation. *Trends in Neurosciences, 30,* 464–472.

Couch, D., & Liamputtong, P. (2008). Online dating and mating: The use of Internet to meet sexual partners. *Qualitative Health Research, 18,* 268–279.

Courchesne, E., Campbell, K., & Solso, S. (2010). Brain growth across the life span in autism: Age-specific changes in anatomical pathology. *Brain Research.* doi: 10.1016/j.brainres.2010.09.101.

Craft, M. A., Davis, G. C., & Paulson, R. M. (2012). Expressive writing in early breast cancer survivors. *Journal of Advanced Nursing, 69,* 305–315. doi: 10.1111/j.1365-2648.2012.06008.x

Craik, F. I. M. (1979). The structure and organization of memory. *Annual Review of Psychology, 30,* 63–102.

Craik, F. I. M., & Lockhart, R. S. (1972). Levels of processing: A framework for memory research. *Journal of Verbal Learning and Verbal Behavior, 11,* 671–684.

Craik, F. I. M., & Tulving, E. (1975). Depth of processing and the retention of words in episodic memory. *Journal of Experimental Psychology: General, 104,* 268–294.

Crain, S., Crain, M. A., & Crain, S. M. (2013). Emotional and physical distress relief using a novel endorphinergic formulation. *Journal of Behavioral and Brain Science, 3,* 441–453.

Crawford, S. E., & Alaggia, R. (2008). The best of both worlds? Family influences on mixed race youth identity development. *Qualitative Social Work, 7,* 81–98.

Crews, F. (1998). *Unauthorized Freud: Doubters confront a legend.* New York, NY: Viking.

Crook, T. H., Youngjohn, J. R., Larrabee, G. J., & Salama, M. (1992). Aging and everyday memory: A cross-cultural study. *Neuropsychology, 6,* 123–136.

Cross, S. E., & Markus, H. (1999). The cultural constitution of personality. In L. A. Pervin & O. P. John (Eds.), *Handbook of personality theory and research* (pp. 378–396). New York, NY: Guilford Press.

Cross-Disorder Group of the Psychiatric Genomics Consortium. (2013, April 20–26). Identification of risk loci with shared effects on five major psychiatric disorders: A genome-wide analysis. *The Lancet, 381,* 1371–1379, http://dx.doi.org/10.1016/S0140-6736(12)62129-1. Retrieved from http://www.sciencedirect.com/science/article/pii/S0140673612621291

Crouch, R., Wilson, A., & Newbury, J. (2011). A systematic review of the effectiveness of primary health education or intervention programs in improving rural women's knowledge of heart disease risk factors and changing lifestyle behaviours. *International Journal of Evidence-Based Healthcare, 9*(3), 236–245.

Crow, S. J., Peterson, C. B., Swanson, S. A., Raymond, N. C., Specker, S., Eckert, E. D., & Mitchell, J. E. (2009). Increased mortality in bulimia nervosa and other eating disorders. *American Journal of Psychiatry, 166,* 1342–1346.

Crump, T. (2001). *A brief history of science.* New York, NY: Carroll & Graf.

Crystal, J. D., Maxwell, K. W., & Hohmann, A. G. (2003). Cannabinoid modulation of sensitivity to time. *Behavioural Brain Research, 144,* 57–66.

Csikszentmihalyi, M. (1990). *Flow: The psychology of optimal experience.* New York, NY: HarperPerennial.

Csikszentmihalyi, M. (1996). *Creativity: Flow and the psychology of discovery and invention.* New York, NY: HarperCollins.

Cuijpers, P., van Straten, A., Hollon, S., & Andersson, G. (2010). The contribution of active medication to combined treatments of psychotherapy and pharmacotherapy for adult depression: A meta-analysis. *Acta Psychiatrica Scandinavica, 121,* 415–423. doi: 10.1111/j.1600-0447.2009.01513.x.

Cukor, J., Spitalnick, J., Difede, J., Rizzo, A., & Rothbaum, B. O. (2009). Emerging treatments for PTSD. *Clinical Psychology Review, 29,* 715–726.

Culvers, J. (2010, April 17). 7 Tips for improving the effectiveness of your diet. Retrieved from http://ezinearticles.com/?7-Tips-For-Improving-the-Effectiveness-of-Your-Diet&id=4128679

Cummings, J. H., Bingham, S. A., Heaton, K. W., & Eastwood, M. A. (1992). Fecal weight, colon cancer risk, and dietary intake of nonstarch polysaccharides (dietary fiber). *Gastroenterology, 103,* 1783–1789.

Cummings, W. C., & Thompson, P. O. (1971). Underwater sounds from the blue whale, *Balenoptera musculus. Journal of the American Acoustical Society, 50,* 1193. doi: 10.1121/1.1912752.

Cunningham, W. A., & Zelazo, P. D. (2006). Attitudes and evaluations: A social cognitive neuroscience perspective. *Trends in Cognitive Sciences, 11,* 97–104.

Curley, J. P., Jensen, C. L, Mashoodh, R., & Champagne, F. A. (2011). Social influences on neurobiology and behavior: Epigenetic effect during development. *Psychoneuroendocrinology.* doi: 10.1016/j.psyneuen.2010.06.005.

Curtiss, S. (1977). *Genie: A psycholinguistic study of a modern-day wild child.* New York, NY: Academic Press.

Cusack, C. L., Swahari, V., Hampton, H. W., Ramsey, J., & Deshmukh, M. (2013). Distinct pathways mediate axon degeneration during apoptosis and axon-specific pruning. *Nature Communications, 4,* 2013/05/21/online VL-4 SP-1876PB at http://dx.doi.org/10.1038/ncomms2910 L3-0.1038/ncomms2910

Cussler, E. C., Going, S. B., Houtkooper, L. B., Stanford, V. A., Blew, R. M., Flint-Wagner, H. G., . . . Lohman, T. G. (2005). Exercise frequency and calcium intake predict 4-year bone changes in postmenopausal women. *Osteoporosis International, 16,* 2129–2141.

Cutting, A. L., & Dunn, J. (2002). The cost of understanding other people: Social cognition predicts young children's sensitivity to criticism. *Journal of Child Psychology and Psychiatry, 43,* 849–860.

Cytowic, R. E. (1989). *Synaesthesia: A union of the senses.* New York, NY: Springer-Verlag.

Czech, C., & Adessi, C. (2004). Disease modifying therapeutic strategies in Alzheimer's disease targeting the amyloid cascade. *Current Neuropharmacology, 2,* 295–307.

D'Anglejan, A. (1979). Solving problems in deductive reasoning: Three experimental studies of adult second language learners. *Working Papers on Bilingualism, No. 17.*

D'Ausilio, R. (2008, September 10). What motivates your employees? Intrinsic vs. extrinsic rewards. Retrieved from http://www.tmcnet.com/channels/performance-management/articles/39417-what-motivates-employees-intrinsic-vs-extrinsic-rewards.htm

Dabbs, J. M., Jr., Carr, T. S., & Frady, R. L. (1995). Testosterone, crime, and misbehavior among 692 male prison inmates. *Personality and Individual Differences, 18,* 627–633.

Dabbs, J. M., Jr., & Hargrove, M. F. (1997). Age, testosterone, and behavior among female prison inmates. *Psychosomatic Medicine, 59,* 477–480.

Daee, A., Robinson, P., Lawson, M., Turpin, J. A., Gregory, B., & Tobias, J. D. (2002). Psychologic and physiologic effects of dieting in adolescents. *Southern Medical Journal, 95,* 1032–1041.

Dale, P. S., Dionne, G., Eley, T. C., & Plomin, R. (2000). Lexical and grammatical development: A behavioural genetic perspective. *Journal of Child Language, 27,* 619–642.

Dalgleish, T. (2004). The emotional brain. *Nature Reviews Neuroscience, 5,* 583–589.

Dallaire, D. H., Cole, D. A., Smith, T. M., Ciesla, J. A., LaGrange, B., Jacquez, F. M., . . . Folmer, A. S. (2008). Predicting children's depressive symptoms from community and individual risk factors. *Journal of Youth and Adolescence, 37,* 830–846.

Dallman, M. F., Pecoraro, N. C., & la Fleur, S. E. (2005). Chronic stress and comfort foods: Self-medication and abdominal obesity. *Brain, Behavior, and Immunity, 19,* 275–280.

Damasio, A. R. (2000). *The feeling of what happens: Body and emotion in the making of consciousness.* Chicago, IL: Harcourt.

Danhauer, J. L., Johnson, C. E., Byrd, A., DeGood, L., Meuel, C., Pecile, A., & Koch, L. L. (2009). Survey of college students on iPod use and hearing health. *Journal of the American Academy of Audiology, 20,* 5–27.

Darley, J. M., & Batson, C. D. (1973). "From Jerusalem to Jericho": A study of situational and dispositional variables in helping behavior. *Journal of Personality and Social Psychology, 27,* 100–108.

Darley, J. M., & Latané, B. (1968). Bystander intervention in emergencies: Diffusion of responsibility. *Journal of Personality and Social Psychology, 8,* 377–383.

Darwin, C. (1998). *The expression of the emotions in man and animals.* New York, NY: Oxford University Press. (Original work published 1872)

Dasgupta, N., McGhee, D. E., Greenwald, A. G., & Banaji, M. R. (2000). Automatic preference for white Americans: Eliminating the familiarity explanation. *Journal of Experimental Social Psychology, 36,* 316–328.

Davidovitch, M., Hemo, B., Manning-Courtney, P., & Fombonne, E. (2013). Prevalence and incidence of autism spectrum disorder in an Israeli population. *Journal of Autism and Developmental Disorders, 43,* 785–793.

Davidson, R. J. (1994). On emotion, mood, and related affective constructs. In P. Ekman & R. J. Davidson (Eds.), *The nature of emotion: Fundamental questions* (pp. 51–55). New York, NY: Oxford University Press.

Davidson, R. J. (2001). Toward a biology of personality and emotion. *Annals of the New York Academy of Sciences, 935,* 191–207.

Davidson, R. J. (2004). What does the prefrontal cortex "do" in affect?: Perspectives on frontal EEG asymmetry research. *Biological Psychology, 67,* 219–233.

Davidson, R. J., Ekman, P., Saron, C., Senulis, J., & Friesen, W. V. (1990). Approach-withdrawal and cerebral asymmetry: Emotional expression and brain physiology I. *Journal of Personality and Social Psychology, 58,* 330–341.

Davidson, R. J., Kabat-Zinn, J., Schumacher, J., Rosenkranz, M., Muller, D., Santorelli, S. F., . . . Sheridan, J. F. (2003). Alterations in brain and immune function produced by mindfulness meditation. *Psychosomatic Medicine, 65,* 564–570.

Davis, J. I., Senghas, A., Brandt, F., & Ochsner, K. N. (2010). The effects of BOTOX injections on emotional experience. *Emotion, 10*(3), 433–40. doi: 10.1037/a0018690.

Dawkins, R. (1989). *The selfish gene* (new ed.). New York, NY: Oxford University Press.

Day, H. I. (1982). Curiosity and the interested explorer. *Performance and Instruction, 21,* 19–22.

De Fruyt, F., & Murvielde, I. (1999). RAISEC types and Big Five traits as predictors of employment status and nature of employment. *Personnel Psychology, 52,* 701–727.

de Graaf-Peters, V. B., & Hadders-Algra, M. (2006). Ontogeny of the human central nervous system: What is happening when? *Early Human Development, 82,* 257–266.

De Lisi, R., & Wolford, J. L. (2002). Improving children's mental rotation accuracy with computer game playing. *Journal of Genetic Psychology, 163,* 272–282.

De Neys, W., Vartanian, O., & Goel, V. (2008). Smarter than we think: When our brains detect that we are biased. *Psychological Science, 19,* 483–489.

de Waal, F. B. M., & Suchak, M. (2010). Prosocial primates: Selfish and unselfish motivations. *Philosophical Transactions of the Royal Society of London B, 365,* 2711–2722.

de Win, M. M. L., Reneman, L., Reitsma, J. B., den Heeten, G. J., Booij, J., & van den Brink, W. (2004). Mood disorders and serotonin transporter density in ecstasy users—The influence of long-term abstention, dose, and gender. *Psychopharmacology, 173,* 376–382.

Deacon, T. (1997). *Symbolic species: Co-evolution of language and the brain.* New York, NY: Norton.

Deary, I. J., Graham, T., Wilson, V., Starr, J. M., & Whalley, L. J. (2003). Population sex differences in IQ at age 11: The Scottish mental survey 1932. *Intelligence, 31,* 533–542.

Debes, R. (2010). Which empathy? Limitations in the mirrored "understanding" of emotion. *Synthese, 175,* 219–239.

DeCasper, A. J., & Fifer, W. (1980). Of human bonding: Newborns prefer their mothers' voices. *Science, 208,* 1174–1176.

DeCasper, A. J., & Spence, M. J. (1986). Pre-natal maternal speech influences newborns' perception of speech sounds. *Infant Behavior & Development, 9,* 133–150.

Deci, E. L., & Ryan, R. M. (1985). *Intrinsic motivation and self-determination in human behavior.* New York, NY: Plenum.

Declerck, C. H., Boone, C., & Kiyonari, T. (2010). Oxytocin and cooperation under conditions of uncertainty: The modulating role of incentives and social information. *Hormones and Behavior, 57,* 368–374.

Deisseroth, K. (2010). Optogenetics. *Nature Methods, 8,* 26–29. doi: 10.1038/nmeth.f.324.

DeKeyser, R., & Larson-Hall, J. (2005). What does the critical period really mean? In J. F. Kroll & A. M. B. DeGroot (Eds.), *Handbook of bilingualism: Psycholinguistic approaches* (pp. 88–108). New York, NY: Oxford University Press.

Delgado, P. L., Price, L. H., Miller, H. L., Salomon, R. M., Aghajanian, G. K., Heninger, G. R., & Charney, D. S. (1994). Serotonin and the neurobiology of depression—Effects of tryptophan depletion in drug-free depressed patients. *Archives of General Psychiatry, 51,* 865–874.

DeLisi, M., Umphress, Z. R., & Vaughn, M. G. (2009). The criminology of the amygdala. *Criminal Justice and Behavior, 36,* 1241–1252.

Dell'Osso, B., Buoli, M., Baldwin, D. S., & Altamura, A. C. (2009). Serotonin norepinephrine reuptake inhibitors (SNRIs) in anxiety disorders: A comprehensive review of their clinical efficacy. *Human Psychopharmacology: Clinical & Experimental, 25,* 17–29.

DeLongis, A., Folkman, S., & Lazarus, R. S. (1988). The impact of daily stress on health and mood: Psychological and social resources as mediators. *Journal of Personality and Social Psychology, 54,* 486–495.

Dement, W. (1999). *The promise of sleep.* New York, NY: Delacorte Press.

Demir, E., & Dickson, B. J. (2005). *fruitless* splicing specifies male courtship behavior in *Drosophila. Cell, 121,* 785–794.

Deoni, S. C. L., Dean, D. C., III, Piryatinsky, I., O'Muircheartaigh, J., Waskiewicz, N., Lehman, K., Han, M., & Dirks, H. (2013). Breastfeeding and early white matter development: A cross-sectional study. *NeuroImage, 82,* 77–86, dx.doi: 10.1016/j.neuroimage.2013.05.090.

Derbyshire, S. W. G., Whalley, M. G., Stenger, A., & Oakley, D. A. (2004). Cerebral activation during hypnotically induced and imagined pain. *NeuroImage, 23,* 392–401.

Derry, G. (1999). *What science is and how it works.* Princeton, NJ: Princeton University Press.

Derryberry, D., & Tucker, D. M. (1994). Motivating the focus of attention. In P. M. Niedenthal & S. Kitayama (Eds.), *The heart's eye: Emotional influences in perception and attention* (pp. 167–196). San Diego, CA: Academic Press.

DeRubeis, R. J., Hollon, S., Amsterdam, J., Shelton, R., Young, P., Salomon, R., . . . Gallop, R. (2005). Cognitive therapy vs medications in the treatment of moderate to severe depression. *Archives of General Psychiatry, 62*(4), 409–416.

Devilbiss, D. M., & Berridge, C. W. (2008). Cognition-enhancing doses of methylphenidate preferentially increase prefrontal cortex neuronal responsivity. *Biological Psychiatry, 64,* 626–635.

Devine, P. (1989). Stereotypes and prejudice: Their automatic and controlled components. *Journal of Personality and Social Psychology, 56,* 5–18.

DeWall, C., Masten, C. L., Powell, C., Combs, D., Schurtz, D. R., & Eisenberger, N. I. (2012). Do neural responses to rejection depend on attachment style? An fMRI study. *Social Cognitive and Affective Neuroscience, 7*(2), 184–192. doi: 10.1093/scan/nsq107.

DeWall, C. N., MacDonald, G., Webster, G. D., Masten, C. L., Baumeister, R. F., Powell, C., . . . Eisenberger, N. I. (2010). Acetaminophen reduces social pain: Behavioral and neural evidence. *Psychological Science, 21,* 931–937.

DeYoung, C., Shamosh, N., Green, A., Braver, T., & Gray, J. (2009). Intellect as distinct from openness: Differences revealed by fMRI of working memory. *Journal of Personality and Social Psychology, 97,* 883–892.

Dhabhar, F. S. (2009). Enhancing versus suppressive effects of stress on immune function: Implications for immuno-protection and immunopathology. *Neuroimmunomodulation, 16,* 300–317.

Dhabhar, F. S. (2013). Psychological stress and immunoprotection versus immunopathology in the skin. *Clinics in Dermatology,*

31, 18–30. Retrieved from http://dx.doi.org/10.1016/j.clindermatol.2011.11.003

Diamond, L. M. (2008). Female bisexuality from adolescence to adulthood: Results from a 10-year longitudinal study. *Developmental Psychology, 44*, 5–14.

Dias, R. G., & Ressler, K. J. (2013). Parental olfactory experience influences behavior and neural structure in subsequent generations. *Nature Neuroscience.* doi: 10.1038/nn.3594. Advanced online publication retrieved December 24, 2013, from http://www.fpamed.com/wp-content/uploads/2013/12/olefactory-gene.pdf

Dickens, C., McGowan, L., & Dale, S. (2003). Impact of depression on experimental pain perception: A systematic review of the literature with meta-analysis. *Psychosomatic Medicine, 65*, 369–375. doi: PSY.0000041622.69462.96.

Diego, M., Field, T., Hernandez-Reif, M., Deeds, O., Ascencio, A., & Begert, G. (2007). Preterm infant massage elicits consistent increases in vagal activity and gastric motility that are associated with greater weight gain. *Acta Paediatrica, 96*, 1588–1591.

Diekelmann, S., Wilhelm, I., & Born, J. (2009). The whats and whens of sleep-dependent memory consolidation. *Sleep Medicine Reviews, 13*, 309–321.

Diener, E., & Seligman, M. E. P. (2004). Beyond money toward an economy of well-being. *Psychological Science, 5*, 1–31.

Diener, E., Suh, E. M., Lucas, R. E., & Smith, H. L. (1999). Subjective well-being: Three decades of progress. *Psychological Bulletin, 125*, 276–302.

Dietrich, K., Succop, P., Berger, O., & Hammond, P. (1991). Lead exposure and the cognitive development of urban preschool children: The Cincinnati Lead Study cohort at age 4 years. *Neurotoxicology and Teratology, 13*(2), 203–211.

Digman, J. M. (1990). Personality structure: Emergence of the Five-Factor Model. *Annual Review in Psychology, 41*, 417–440.

Dimberg, U., & Söderkvist, S. (2011). The voluntary facial action technique: A method to test the facial feedback hypothesis. *Journal of Nonverbal Behavior, 35*, 17–33.

Dingemanse, N. J., Both, C., Drent, P. J., Van Oers, K., & Van Noordwijk, A. J. (2002). Repeatability and heritability of exploratory behaviour in great tits from the wild. *Animal Behaviour, 64*, 929–938.

Dinn, W. M., Aycicegi, A., & Harris, C. L. (2004). Cigarette smoking in a student sample: Neurocognitive and clinical correlates. *Addictive Behaviors, 29*, 107–126.

DiPietro, J. A. (2012). Maternal stress in pregnancy: Considerations for fetal development. *Journal of Adolescent Health, 51*(Suppl. 2), S3–S8. doi: 10.1016/j.jadohealth.2012.04.008.

DiPietro, J. A., Hodgson, D. M., Costigan, K. A., & Johnson, T. R. B. (1996). Fetal antecedents of infant temperament. *Child Development, 67*, 2568–2583.

Distracted driving. (2013, May 23). Retrieved October 17, 2013, from http://www.cdc.gov/motorvehiclesafety/distracted_driving/

Dobbs, D. (2006a, April 2). A depression switch? *New York Times Magazine.* Retrieved from http://www.nytimes.com

Dobbs, D. (2006b, July 30). Turning off depression. *Scientific American Mind, 17*, 26–31.

Dockray, S., & Steptoe, A. (2010). Positive affect and psychobiological processes. *Neuroscience and Biobehavioral Reviews, 35*, 69–75.

Doetsch, F., & Scharff, C. (2001). Challenges for brain repair: Insights from adult neurogenesis in birds and mammals. *Brain, Behavior & Evolution, 58*, 306–322.

Dolcos, F., LaBar, K. S., & Cabeza, R. (2005). Remembering one year later: Role of the amygdala and the temporal lobe memory system in retrieving emotional memories. *Proceedings of the National Academy of Sciences, 102*, 2626–2631.

Dolinoy, D., & Jirtle, R. L. (2008). Environmental epigenomics in human health and disease. *Environmental and Molecular Mutagenesis, 49*, 4–8.

Doll, R., Peto, R., Boreham, J., & Sutherland, I. (2004). Mortality in relation to smoking: 50 years' observations on male British doctors. *British Medical Journal, 328*, 1519–1528.

Domes, G., Schulze, L., Böttger, M., Grossmann, A., . . . Herpertz, S. C. (2010). The neural correlates of sex differences in emotional reactivity and emotion regulation. *Human Brain Mapping, 31*, 758–769.

Domhoff, G. W. (2001). A new neurocognitive theory of dreams. *Dreaming, 11*, 13–33.

Dominguez, J. M., & Hull, E. M. (2005). Dopamine, the medial preoptic area, and male sexual behavior. *Physiology & Behavior, 86*, 356–368.

Dong, J. Y., Zhang, Y.-H., Wang, P., & Qin, L.-Q. (2012). Meta-analysis of dietary glycemic load and glycemic index in relation to risk of coronary heart disease. *American Journal of Cardiology, 109*, 1608–1613.

Donn, J. E., & Sherman, R. C. (2002). Attitudes and practices regarding the formation of romantic relationships on the Internet. *CyberPsychology & Behavior, 5*, 107–122.

Doty, R. L., Applebaum, S., Zusho, H., & Settle, R. G. (1985). Sex differences in odor identification ability: A cross-cultural analysis. *Neuropsychologia, 23*, 667–672.

Doud, A. J., Lucas, J. P., Pisansky, M. T., & He, B. (2011). Continuous three-dimensional control of a virtual helicopter using a motor imagery based brain-computer interface. *PLoS ONE 6*(10), e26322. doi: 10.1371/journal.pone.0026322.

Drevets, W. C., Frank, E., Price, J. C., Kupfer, D. J., Holt, D., Greer, P. J., . . . Mathis, C. (1999). PET imaging of serotonin 1A receptor binding in depression. *Biological Psychiatry, 46*, 1375–1387.

Drevets, W. C., Price, J. L., Simpson, J. R., Todd, R. D., Reich, T., Vannier, M., & Raichle, M. (1997). Subgenual prefrontal cortex abnormalities in mood disorders. *Nature, 386*, 824–827.

Drug for treating schizophrenia identified. (1998). Retrieved from http://www.pbs.org/wgbh/aso/databank/entries/dh52dr.html

Dubai, Y. (2004). The neurobiology of consolidations, or, How stable is the engram? *Annual Review of Psychology, 55*, 51–86.

Duch, H., Fisher, E. M., Ensari, I., & Harrington, A. (2013). Screen time use in children under 3 years old: A systematic review of correlates. *International Journal of Behavioral Nutrition and Physical Activity, 10*, 102. Retrieved November 12, 2013, from http://www.ijbnpa.org/content/10/1/102

Duckworth, A., & Quinn, P. D. (2009). Development and validation of the Short Grit Scale (GRIT–S). *Journal of Personality Assessment, 91*(2), 166–174.

Duckworth, A. L., Peterson, C., Matthews, M. D., & Kelly, D. R. (2007). Grit: Perseverance and passion for long-term goals. *Journal of Personality and Social Psychology, 92*(6), 1087–1101. doi: 10.1037/0022-3514.92.6.1087.

Duckworth, R. A. (2010). Evolution of personality: Developmental constraints on behavioral flexibility. *The Auk, 127*(4), 752–758.

Due, P., Holstein, B. E., Ito, H., & Groth, M. V. (1991). Diet and health behavior in Danish children aged 11–15 years. *Tandlaegernes Tidsskr, 6*(8), 232–237.

Duggan, M., & Brenner, J. (2013, February 14). The demographics of social media users—2012. Retrieved November 16, 2013, from http://pewinternet.org/~/media/Files/Reports/2013/PIP_SocialMediaUsers.pdf

Dunbar, R. I. M. (1996). *Grooming, gossip and the evolution of language.* London, England: Faber & Faber.

Dunbar, R. I. M. (2001). Brains on two legs: Group size and the evolution of intelligence. In F. B. M. deWaal (Ed.), *Tree of origin: What primate behavior can tell us about human social evolution* (pp. 173–191). Cambridge, MA: Harvard University Press.

Duncan, J., Seitz, R. J., Koldny, J., Bor, D., Herzog, H., Ahmed, A., . . . Emslie, H.

(2000, July 21). A neural basis for general intelligence. *Science, 289*, 457–460.

Duncan, S. C., Duncan, T. E., & Strycker, L. A. (2006). Alcohol use from ages 9 to 16: A cohort-sequential latent growth model. *Drug and Alcohol Dependence, 81*, 71–81.

Duncker, K. (1945). On problem-solving. *Psychological Monographs, 58*, ix. (Whole No. 270).

Dunn, E. W., Aknin, L. B., & Norton, M. I. (2008). Spending money on others promotes happiness. *Science, 319*, 1687–1688.

Durlak, J. A., Taylor, R. D., Kawashima, K., Pachan, M. K., DuPre, E. P., Celio, C. I., . . . Weissberg, R. P. (2007). Effects of positive youth development programs on school, family, and community systems. *American Journal of Community Psychology, 39*, 269–286.

Dvir, Y., & Smallwood, P. (2008). Serotonin syndrome: A complex but easily avoidable condition. *General Hospital Psychiatry, 30*, 284–287.

Dye, M. W. G., & Bavelier, D. (2004). Playing video games enhances visual attention in children. *Journal of Vision, 4*, 40A.

Eagly, A. H., & Chaiken, S. (1998). Attitude structure and function. In D. T. Gilbert, S. T. Fiske, & G. Lindzey (Eds.), *The handbook of social psychology* (4th ed., Vol. 1, pp. 269–322). New York, NY: McGraw-Hill.

Ebbeling, C. B., Leidig, M. M., Feldman, H. A., Lovesky, M. M., & Ludwig, D. S. (2007). Effects of a low-glycemic load vs. low-fat diet in obese young adults: A randomized trial. *Journal of the American Medical Association, 297*(19), 2092–2102. doi: 10.1001/jama.297.19.2092.

Ebstein, R. P. (2006). The molecular genetic architecture of human personality: Beyond self-report questionnaires. *Molecular Psychiatry, 11*, 427–445.

Ebstein, R. P., Israel, S., Chew, S. H., Zhong, S., & Knafo, A. (2010). Genetics of human social behavior. *Neuron, 65*, 831–844.

Ebstein, R. P., Novick, O., Umansky, R., Priel, B., Osher, Y., Blaine, D., . . . Belmaker, R. H. (1996). Dopamine D4 receptor D4DR exon III polymorphism associated with the human personality trait of novelty seeking. *Nature Genetics, 12*, 78–80.

Edelman, S., Lemon, J., Bell, D. R., & Kidman, A. D. (1999). Effects of group CBT on the survival time of patients with metastatic breast cancer. *Psychooncology, 8*, 474–481.

Eder, P., & Eisenberger, R. (2008). Perceived organizational support: Reducing the negative influence of coworker withdrawal behavior. *Journal of Management, 34*, 55–68.

Edmonds, C. V., Lockwood, G. A., & Cunningham, A. J. (1999). Psychological response to long-term therapy: A randomized

trial with metastatic breast cancer patients. *Psychooncology, 8*, 74–91.

Edwards, J. H. (2002). Evidenced-based treatment for child ADHD: "Real-world" practice implications. *Journal of Mental Health Counseling, 24*, 126–139.

Edwards, V. J., Holden, G. W., Felitti, V. J., & Anda, R. F. (2003). Relationship between multiple forms of childhood maltreatment and adult mental health in community respondents: Results from the adverse childhood experiences study. *American Journal of Psychiatry, 160*, 1453–1460.

Eichenbaum, H. (2010). Memory systems. *WIREs Cognitive Science, 1*, 478–490.

Eisenberger, N. I., Jarcho, J. M., Lieberman, M. D., & Naliboff, B. D. (2006). An experimental study of shared sensitivity to physical pain and social rejection. *Pain, 126*, 132–138.

Eisenberger, N. J. (2013). The pain of social disconnection: Examining the shared neural underpinnings of physical and social pain. *Nature Reviews Neuroscience*, advance online publication at doi: 10.1038/nrn3231.

Eisenberger, R., & Cameron, J. (1996). Detrimental effects of reward: Reality or myth? *American Psychologist, 51*, 1153–1166.

Eisenberger, R., Rhoades, L., & Cameron, J. (1999). Does pay for performance increase or decrease perceived self-determination and intrinsic motivation? *Journal of Personality and Social Psychology, 77*, 1026–1040.

Eisenberger, R., & Shanock, L. (2003). Rewards, intrinsic motivation and creativity: A case study of methodological and conceptual isolation. *Creativity Research Journal, 15*, 121–130.

Eisenberger, R., Stinglhamber, F., Vandenberghe, C., Sucharski, I., & Rhoades, L. (2002). Perceived supervisor support: Contributions to perceived organizational support and employee retention. *Journal of Applied Psychology, 87*, 565–573.

Ekman, P. (1972). Universals and cultural differences in facial expressions of emotion. In J. Cole (Ed.), *Nebraska Symposium on Motivation 1971, Vol. 19* (pp. 207–283). Lincoln: University of Nebraska Press.

Ekman, P. (1973). Cross-cultural studies of facial expression. In *Darwin and facial expression: A century of research in review* (pp. 169–222). New York, NY: Academic Press.

Ekman, P. (1984). Expression and the nature of emotion. In K. R. Scherer & P. Ekman (Eds.), *Approaches to emotion* (pp. 319–343). Hillsdale, NJ: Erlbaum.

Ekman, P. (1992). An argument for basic emotions. *Cognition & Emotion, 6*, 169–200.

Ekman, P. (2003). *Emotions revealed.* New York, NY: Holt.

Ekman, P., Davidson, R. J., & Friesen, W. V. (1990). The Duchenne smile: Emotional expression and brain physiology II. *Journal of Personality and Social Psychology, 58*, 342–353.

Ekman, P., & Friesen, W. V. (1969). The repertoire of nonverbal behavior—Categories, origins, usage, and coding. *Semiotica, 1*, 49–98.

Ekman, P., & Friesen, W. V. (1971). Constants across cultures in the face and emotion. *Journal of Personality and Social Psychology, 17*, 124–129.

Ekman, P., & Friesen, W. V. (1978). *The Facial Action Coding System.* Palo Alto, CA: Consulting Psychologists Press.

Ekman, P., Friesen, W. V., & Hager, J. (2002). *The Facial Action Coding System* (2nd ed.). Salt Lake City, UT: Research Nexus.

Ekman, P., Friesen, W. V., O'Sullivan, M., Chan, A., Diacoyanni-Tarlatzis, I., Heider, K. . . . (1987). Universals and cultural differences in the judgments of facial expressions of emotion. *Journal of Personality and Social Psychology, 53*, 712–717.

Ekman, P., Levenson, R. W., & Friesen, W. V. (1983). Autonomic nervous system activity distinguishes among emotions. *Science, 221*, 1208–1210.

Ekman, P., & O'Sullivan, M. (1991). Who can catch a liar? *American Psychologist, 46*, 913–920.

Ekman, P., O'Sullivan, M., & Frank, M. G. (1999). A few can catch a liar. *Psychological Science, 10*, 263–266.

Ekman, P., & Rosenberg, E. L. (Eds.). (2005). *What the face reveals: Basic and applied studies of spontaneous facial expression using the Facial Action Coding System (FACS)* (2nd ed.). New York, NY: Oxford University Press.

Ekman, P., Sorenson, E. R., & Friesen, W. V. (1969). Pan-cultural elements in facial displays of emotion. *Science, 164*, 86–88.

Elbert, T., Pantev, C., Wienbruch, C., Rockstroh, B., & Taub, E. (1995). Increased cortical representation of the fingers of the left hand in string players. *Science, 270*, 305–307.

Elias, M. (2009, January 28). MRIs reveal possible source of woman's super-memory. *USA Today.* Retrieved from http://www.usatoday.com

Ellason, J. W., Ross, C. A., & Fuchs, D. L. (1996). Lifetime Axis I and Axis II comorbidity and childhood trauma history in dissociative identity disorder. *Psychiatry, 59*, 255–266.

Ellenbogen, J. M., Hu, P. T., Payne, J. D., Titone, D., & Walker, M. P. (2007). Human relational memory requires time and sleep. *Proceedings of the National Academy of Sciences, 104,* 7723–7728.

Ellickson, P. L., Orlando, M., Tucker, J. S., & Klein, D. J. (2004). From adolescence to young adulthood: Racial/ethnic disparities in smoking. *American Journal of Public Health, 94,* 293–299.

Ellickson, P. L., Tucker, J. S., & Klein, D. J. (2001). Sex differences in predictors of adolescent smoking cessation. *Health Psychology, 20,* 186–195.

Ellis, E., & Ames, M. A. (1987). Neurohormonal functioning and sexual orientation: A theory of heterosexuality-homosexuality. *Psychological Bulletin, 101,* 233–258.

Ellsworth, P. C., & Scherer, K. R. (2003). Appraisal processes in emotion. In R. J. Davidson, K. R. Scherer, & H. Goldsmith (Eds.), *Handbook of affective sciences* (pp. 572–595). New York, NY: Oxford University Press.

Elman, J. L., Bates, E. A., Johnson, M. H., Karmiloff-Smith, A., Parisi, D., & Plunkett, K. (1996). *Rethinking innateness: A connectionist perspective on development.* Cambridge, MA: MIT Press.

Elms, A. (1993). *Uncovering lives: The uneasy alliance between biography and psychology.* New York, NY: Oxford University Press.

Emery, R. A. (2006). Holland codes, careers, and college majors. Retrieved from http://www.hollandcodes.com/support-files/su-careers-majors-and-model.pdf

Emmons, R. A., & McCullough, M. E. (2003). Counting blessings versus burdens: An experimental investigation of gratitude and subjective well-being in daily life. *Journal of Personality and Social Psychology, 84,* 377–389. doi: 10.1037/0022-3514.84.2.377.

Empana, J. P., Sykes, D. H., Luc, G., Juhan-Vague, I., Arveiler, D., Ferrieres, J., . . . Ducimetiere, P. (2005). Contributions of depressive mood and circulating inflammatory markers to coronary heart disease in healthy European men: The Prospective Epidemiological Study of Myocardial Infarction (PRIME). *Circulation, 111,* 2299–2305.

Engel, A. K., Debener, S., & Kranczioch, C. (2006, August). Coming to attention. *Scientific American Mind, 17,* 46–53.

Enticott, P., Kennedy, H. A., Rinehart, N. J., Bradshaw, J., Tonge, B. J., Daskalakis, Z. J., & Fitzgerald, P. B. (2013). Interpersonal motor resonance in autism spectrum disorder: Evidence against a global mirror system deficit. *Frontiers in Human Neuroscience, 7,* 23. doi: 10.3389/fnhum.2013.00218.

Enzinger, C., Fazekas, F., Matthews, P. M., Ropele, S., Schmidt, H., Smith, S., & Schmidt, R. (2005). Risk factors for progression of brain atrophy in aging: Six-year follow-up of normal subjects. *Neurology, 64,* 1704–1711.

Epel, E. S., Blackburn, E. H., Lin, J., Dhabhar, F. S., Adler, N. E., & Morrow, J. D. (2004). Accelerated telomere shortening in response to life stress. *Proceedings of the National Academy of Sciences, 101,* 17312–17315.

Epel, E. S., Lin, J., Wilhelm, F. H., Wolkowitz, O. M., Cawthon, R., Adler, N. E., . . . Blackburn, E. H. (2006). Cell aging in relation to stress arousal and cardiovascular disease risk factors. *Psychoneuroendocrinology, 31,* 277–287.

Epel, E. S., McEwen, B., Seeman, T., Matthews, K., Castellazzo, G., Brownell, K. D., . . . Ickovics, J. R. (2000). Stress and body shape: Stress-induced cortisol secretion is consistently greater among women with central fat. *Psychosomatic Medicine, 62,* 623–632.

Erdelyi, M. (2010). The ups and downs of memory. *American Psychologist, 65,* 623–633. doi: 10.1037/a0020440.

Erikson, E. H. (1963). *Childhood and society.* New York, NY: Norton.

Erikson, E. H. (1968). *Identity: Youth and crisis.* New York, NY: Norton.

Erikson, E. H. (1982). *The life-cycle completed: A review.* New York, NY: Norton.

Eriksson, P. S., Perfilieva, E., Bjork-Eriksson, T., Alborn, A. M., Nordborg, C., Peterson, D. A., & Gage, F. H. (1998). Neurogenesis in the adult human hippocampus. *Nature Medicine, 4,* 1313–1317.

Eroglu, C., & Barres, B. A. (2010, November 11). Regulation of synaptic connectivity by glia. *Nature, 468,* 223–231.

Etcoff, N. (1999). *Survival of the prettiest.* New York, NY: Anchor Books.

Etkin, A., Egner, T., & Kalish, R. (2011). Emotional processing in anterior cingulate and medial prefrontal cortex. *Trends in Cognitive Science, 15,* 85–93.

Evans, L. M., Akiskal, H. S., Greenwood, T. A., Nievergelt, C. M., Keck, P. E., McElroy, S. L., . . . Kelso, J. R. (2007). Suggestive linkage of a chromosomal locus on 18p11 to cyclothymic temperament in bipolar disorder families. *American Journal of Medical Genetics, 147B,* 326–332.

Evans, S., Ferrando, S., Findler, M., Stowell, C., Smart, C., & Haglin, D. (2008). Mindfulness-based cognitive therapy for generalized anxiety disorder. *Journal of Anxiety Disorders, 22,* 716–721.

Everett, D. L. (2005). Cultural constraints on grammar and cognition in Piraha: Another look at the design features of human language. *Current Anthropology, 46,* 621–646.

Exaptations. (2006). Retrieved November 28, 2007, from http://evolution.berkeley.edu/evosite/evo101/IIIE5cExaptations.shtml

Exner, J. E., Jr. (1974). *The Rorschach: A comprehensive system.* New York, NY: Wiley.

Extraordinary people—The boy who sees without eyes. (2007, May 7). [Video file]. From the 2003 television series *Extraordinary People.* Retrieved from http://www.youtube.com/watch?v=qLziFMF4DHA

Eysenck, H. J. (1947). *Dimensions of personality.* London, England: Routledge & Kegan Paul.

Eysenck, H. J. (1980). *The causes and effects of smoking.* London, England: Temple Smith.

Eysenck, H. J. (1982). *Personality, genetics, and behavior: Selected papers.* New York, NY: Praeger.

Eysenck, H. J. (1990). Biological dimensions of personality. In L. A. Pervin (Ed.), *Handbook of personality: Theory and research* (pp. 244–276). New York, NY: Guilford Press.

Eysenck, H. J. (1995). *Genius: The natural history of creativity.* Cambridge, England: Cambridge University Press.

Eysenck, H. J. (1997). Personality and experimental psychology: The unification of psychology and the possibility of a paradigm. *Journal of Personality and Social Psychology, 73,* 1224–1237.

Facione, P. A. (1990). *Critical thinking: A statement of expert consensus for purposes of educational assessment and instruction—The Delphi report.* Millbrae: California Academic Press.

Fallgatter, A. J., Ehlis, A.-C., Herrmann, M. J., Hohoff, C., Reif, A., Freitag, C. M., & Deckert, J. (2010). DTNBP1 (dysbindin) gene variants modulate prefrontal brain function in schizophrenic patients—Support for the glutamate hypothesis of schizophrenias. *Genes, Brain and Behavior, 9,* 489–497.

Faith, M. A., Fiala, S. E., Cavell, T. A., & Hughes, J. N. (2011). Mentoring highly aggressive children: Pre–post changes in mentors' attitudes, personality, and attachment tendencies. *Journal of Primary Prevention, 32*(5–6), 253–270. doi: 10.1007/s10935-011-0254-8.

Famous people with the gift of dyslexia. (2013, April 2). Retrieved January 7, 2014, from Davis Dyslexia Association International, Dyslexia the Gift web site: http://www.dyslexia.com/famous.htm

Famy, C., Streissguth, A. P., & Unis, A. S. (1998). Psychological disorder in adults with fetal alcohol syndrome or fetal alcohol effects. *Journal of Pediatric Psychology, 155,* 552–554.

Fancher, R. E. (1985). *The intelligence men: Makers of the IQ controversy.* New York, NY: Norton.

Fancher, R. E. (1996). *Pioneers of psychology* (3rd ed.). New York, NY: Norton.

Fantz, R. L. (1963). Pattern vision in new-born infants. *Science, 140,* 296–297.

Farb, N., Anderson, A., Mayberg, H., Bean, J., McKeon, D., & Segal, Z. (2010). Minding one's emotions: Mindfulness training alters the neural expression of sadness. *Emotion, 10,* 25–33. doi: 10.1037/a0017151.

Farber, N. B., & Olney, J. W. (2003). Drugs of abuse that cause developing neurons to commit suicide. *Developmental Brain Research, 147,* 37–45.

Fazel, S., & Danesh, J. (2002). Serious mental disorder in 23,000 prisoners: A systematic review of 62 surveys. *The Lancet, 359,* 545–550.

Feinberg, M., Willer, R., & Keltner, D. (2012). Flustered and faithful: Embarrassment as a signal of prosociality. *Journal of Personality and Social Psychology, 102,* 81–97. doi: 10.1037/a0025403.

Feist, G. J. (1993). A structural model of scientific eminence. *Psychological Science, 4,* 366–371.

Feist, G. J. (1998). A meta-analysis of the impact of personality on scientific and artistic creativity. *Personality and Social Psychological Review, 2,* 290–309.

Feist, G. J. (1999). Personality in scientific and artistic creativity. In R. J. Sternberg (Ed.), *Handbook of human creativity* (pp. 273–296). Cambridge, England: Cambridge University Press.

Feist, G. J. (2004). Creativity and the frontal lobes. *Bulletin of Psychology and the Arts, 5,* 21–28.

Feist, G. J. (2006). *The psychology of science and the origins of the scientific mind.* New Haven, CT: Yale University Press.

Feist, G. J., & Barron, F. X. (2003). Predicting creativity from early to late adulthood: Intellect, potential and personality. *Journal of Research in Personality, 37,* 62–88.

Feist, G. J., Bodner, T. E., Jacobs, J. F., Miles, M., & Tan, V. (1995). Integrating top-down and bottom-up structural models of subjective well-being: A longitudinal investigation. *Journal of Personality and Social Psychology, 68,* 138–150.

Feist, J., Feist, G. J., & Roberts, T. A. (2013). *Theories of personality* (8th ed.). New York, NY: McGraw-Hill.

Feldman, D. H. (2004). Child prodigies: A distinctive form of giftedness. In R. J. Sternberg (Ed.), *Definition and conceptions of giftedness* (pp. 133–144). Thousand Oaks, CA: Corwin Press.

Feldman-Barrett, L., Tugade, M. M., & Engle, R. W. (2004). Individual differences in working memory capacity and dual-process theories of mind. *Psychological Bulletin, 130,* 553–573.

Feng, X., Shaw, D. S., Kovacs, M., Lane, T., O'Rourke, F. E., & Alarcon, J. H. (2008). Emotion regulation in preschoolers: The roles of behavioral inhibition, maternal affective behavior, and maternal depression. *Journal of Child Psychology and Psychiatry, 49,* 132–141.

Feng, Z., Hu, W., Hu, Y., & Teng, M. (2006). Acrolein is a major cigarette-related lung cancer agent: Preferential binding at *p53* mutational hotspots and inhibition of DNA repair. *Proceedings of the National Academy of Sciences, 103,* 15404–15409.

Fenson, L., Dale, P., Reznick, J. S., Bates, E., Thal, D. J., & Pethick, S. (1994). Variability in early communicative development. *Monographs of the Society for Research in Child Development, 59* (5, Serial No. 242).

Ferguson, C. J., & Kilburn, J. (2009). The public health risks of media violence: A meta-analytic review. *Journal of Pediatrics, 154,* 759–763.

Ferguson, C. J., & Kilburn, J. (2010). Much ado about nothing: The misestimation and overinterpretation of violent video game effects in Eastern and Western nations: Comment on Anderson et al. (2010). *Psychological Bulletin, 136,* 174–178.

Fergusson, D., Doucette, S., Glass, K. C., Shapiro, S., Healy, D., Hebert, P., . . . (2005). Association between suicide attempts and selective serotonin reuptake inhibitors: Systematic review of randomized controlled trials. *British Medical Journal, 330,* 396–402.

Fergusson, L., Horwood, J., & Ridder, E. M. (2005). Tests of causal linkages between cannabis use and psychotic symptoms. *Addiction, 100,* 354–366.

Fernald, A. (1992). Human maternal vocalizations to infants as biologically relevant signals: An evolutionary perspective. In J. Barkow, L. Cosmides, & J. Toody (Eds.), *The adapted mind: Evolutionary psychology and the generation of culture* (pp. 391–428). New York, NY: Oxford University Press.

Fernald, A., & Morikawa, H. (1993). Common themes and cultural variations in Japanese and American mothers' speech to infants. *Child Development, 64,* 637–656.

Ferrucci, R., Mamell, F., Guidi, I., Mrakic-Sposta, I., Vergari, M., Marceglia, S. . . . Priori, A. (2008). Transcranial direct current stimulation improves recognition memory in Alzheimer disease. *Neurology, 71,* 493–498.

Ferster, C. B., & Skinner, B. F. (1957). *Schedules of reinforcement.* Englewood Cliffs, NJ: Prentice-Hall.

Festinger, L. (1957). *A theory of cognitive dissonance.* Stanford, CA: Stanford University.

Fetz, E. E. (2007). Volitional control of neural activity: Implications for brain-computer interfaces. *Journal of Physiology, 579,* 571–579.

Fiedorowicz, J., & Swartz, K. (2004). The role of monoamine oxidase inhibitors in current psychiatric practice. *Journal of Psychiatric Practice, 10,* 239–248.

Field, T. M., Hernandez-Reif, M., Diego, M., Feijo, L., Vera, Y., & Gil, K. (2004). Massage therapy by parents improves early growth and development. *Infant Behavior and Development, 27,* 435–442.

Field, T. M., Schanberg, S. M., Scafidi, F., Bauer, C. R., Vega-Lahr, N., Garcia, R., . . . Kuhn, C. M. (1986). Tactile/kinesthetic stimulation effects on preterm neonates. *Pediatrics, 77,* 654–658.

Fields, H. L. (2005). *Pain: Mechanisms and management.* New York, NY: McGraw-Hill.

Fields, H. L. (2009, September/October). The psychology of pain. *Scientific American Mind,* 42–49.

Fields, R. D. (2005). Making memories stick. *Scientific American, 292,* 75–81.

Fields, R. D. (2008). White matter matters. *Scientific American, 298,* 54–61.

Filimon, F., Nelson, J. D., Hagler, D. J., & Sereno, M. I. (2007). Human cortical representations for reaching: Mirror neurons for execution, observation, and imagery. *NeuroImage, 37,* 1315–1328.

Finger, S. (1994). *Origins of neuroscience: A history of explorations into brain function.* New York, NY: Oxford University Press.

Fink, A., Slamar-Halbedl, M., Unterrainer, H. F., & Weiss, E. M. (2012). Creativity: Genius, madness, or a combination of both? *Psychology of Aesthetics, Creativity, and the Arts, 6,* 11–18. doi: 10.1037/a0024874.

Fink, M. (2006). ECT in therapy-resistant mania: Does it have a place? *Bipolar Disorders, 8,* 307–309.

Finke, R. A., Ward, T. B., & Smith, S. M. (1992). *Creative cognition: Theory, research and applications.* Cambridge, MA: MIT Press.

Finnerty, G. T., Roberts, L. S. E., & Connors, B. W. (1999). Sensory experience modifies the short-term dynamics of neocortical synapses. *Nature, 400,* 367–371.

Fischer, A. H., & Manstead, A. S. R. (2000). Gender differences in emotion across cultures. In A. H. Fischer (Ed.), *Emotion and gender: Social psychological perspectives* (pp. 91–97). London, England: Cambridge University Press.

Fischer, G. G. (2004). Should I order an EEG? An overview of electroencephalography in the hospital setting at Gundersen Lutheran Medical Center. *Gundersen Lutheran Medical Journal, 3,* 26–29.

Fisher, J. E., Mohanty, A., Herrington, J. D., Koven, N. S., Miller, G. A., & Heller, W. (2004). Neuropsychological evidence for dimensional schizotypy: Implications for creativity and psychopathology. *Journal of Research in Personality, 38,* 24–31.

Fitzgerald, K. D., Welsh, R. C., Gehrig, W. J., Abelson, J. L., Himle, J. A., Liberzon, I., & Taylor, S. F. (2005). Error-related hyperactivity of the anterior cingulate cortex in obsessive-compulsive disorder. *Biological Psychiatry, 57,* 287–294.

Fitzgerald, M. (2004). *Autism and creativity.* Hove, England: Brunner-Routledge.

Fitzgerald, P. B., Benitez, J., de Castella, A. R., Daskalakis, Z. J., & Kulkarni, J. (2006). Naturalistic study of the use of transcranial magnetic stimulation in the treatment of depressive relapse. *Australian and New Zealand Journal of Psychiatry, 40,* 764–768.

Flaherty, M. (2005). Gender differences in mental rotation ability in three cultures: Ireland, Ecuador and Japan. *Psychologia: An International Journal of Psychology in the Orient, 48,* 31–38.

Flammer, E., & Bongartz, W. (2003). On the efficacy of hypnosis: A meta-analytic study. *Contemporary Hypnosis, 20,* 179–197.

Flegal, K. M., Carroll, M. D., Ogden, C. L., & Curtain, L. R. (2010). Prevalence and trends in obesity among US adults, 1999–2008. *Journal of the American Medical Association, 303,* 235–241.

Flege, J. E. (1999). Age of learning and second language speech. In D. Birdsong (Ed.), *Second language acquisition and the critical period hypothesis* (pp. 101–131). Mahwah, NJ: Erlbaum.

Flege, J. E., Munro, M. J., & MacKay, I. R. A. (1995a). Effects of age of second-language learning on the production of English consonants. *Speech Communication, 16,* 1–26.

Flege, J. E., Munro, M. J., & MacKay, I. R. A. (1995b). Factors affecting strength of perceived foreign accent in a second language. *Journal of the Acoustical Society of America, 97,* 2540–2551.

Fleischer, J., Breer, H., & Strotmann, J. (2009). Mammalian olfactory receptors. *Frontiers in Cellular Neuroscience, 3,* 1–10.

Foa, E. B., Dancu, C. V., Hembree, E. A., Jaycox, L. H., Meadows, E. A., & Street, G. P. (1999). A comparison of exposure therapy, stress inoculation training, and their combination for reducing posttraumatic stress disorder in female assault victims. *Journal of Consulting and Clinical Psychology, 67,* 194–200.

Foa, E. B., Hembree, E. A., Cahill, S. P., Rauch, S. A., Riggs, D. S., Feeny, N. C., & Yadin, E. (2005). Randomized trial of prolonged exposure for PTSD with and without cognitive restructuring: Outcome at academic and community clinics. *Journal of Consulting and Clinical Psychology, 73,* 953–964.

Fodor, E. M., & Laird, B. A. (2004). Therapeutic intervention, bipolar inclination, and literary creativity. *Creativity Research Journal, 16,* 149–161.

Foerde, K., Knowlton, B., & Poldrack, R. (2006). Modulation of competing memory systems by distraction. *Proceedings of the National Academy of Sciences, 103,* 11778–11783.

Fogassi, L., & Ferrari, P. F. (2006). Mirror neurons and the evolution of embodied language. *Current Directions in Psychological Science, 16,* 136–141.

Folkman, S. (1997). Positive psychological states and coping with severe stress. *Social Science and Medicine, 45,* 1207–1221.

Folkman, S., & Moskowitz, J. T. (2000). Positive affect and the other side of coping. *American Psychologist, 55,* 647–654.

Folley, B. S., & Park, S. (2005). Verbal creativity and schizotypal personality in relation to prefrontal hemispheric laterality: A behavioral and near-infrared optical imaging study. *Schizophrenia Research, 80,* 271–282.

Fong-Torres, B. (2010, April 25). Tom Petty: "Go after what you love." An interview. *Parade Magazine.*

Fonteille, V., & Stoléru, S. (2011). The cerebral correlates of sexual desire: Functional neuroimaging approach, *Sexologies, 20,* 142–148. Retrieved from http://dx.doi.org/10.1016/j.sexol.2010.03.011

Ford, C., & Beach, F. (1951). *Patterns of sexual behavior.* New York, NY: Harper & Row.

Ford, D. (2008). Intelligence testing and cultural diversity: The need for alternative instruments, policies, and procedures. In J. L. VanTessa-Baska (Ed.), *Alternative assessments with gifted and talented students* (pp. 107–128). Waco, TX: Prufrock Press.

Forgeard, M., Winner. E., Norton, A., & Schlaug, G. (2008). Practicing a musical instrument in childhood is associated with enhanced verbal ability and nonverbal reasoning. *PLoS One, 3,* e3566.

Foulkes, D. (1996). Dream research: 1953–1993. *Sleep: Journal of Sleep Research & Sleep Medicine, 19,* 609–624.

Fournier, J. C., DeRubeis, R. J., Hollon, S. D., Dimidjian, S., Amsterdam, J. D., Shelton, R. C., & Fawcett, I. (2010). Antidepressant drug effects and depression severity: Patient-level meta-analysis. *Journal of the American Medical Association, 303,* 47–53.

Fouts, R. S. (1997). *Next of kin: My conversations with chimpanzees.* New York, NY: Avon.

Fouts, R. S., Fouts, D. H., & Schoenfeld, D. (1984). Sign language conversational interaction between chimpanzees. *Sign Language Studies, 42,* 1–12.

Fowler, J. H., & Christakis, N. A. (2008). The dynamic spread of happiness in a large social network. *British Medical Journal, 337,* a2338.

Fowler, J. H., & Christakis, N. A. (2010). Cooperative behavior cascades in human social networks. *Proceedings of the National Academy of Sciences, 107,* 5334–5338.

Fraga, M. F., Ballestar, E., Paz, M. F., Ropero, S., Setien, F. Ballestar, M. L., . . . Esteller, M. (2005). Epigenetic differences arise during the lifetime of monozygotic twins. *Proceedings of the National Academy of Sciences, 102,* 10604–10609. doi: 10.1073/pnas.0500398102.

Franco, O. H., de Laet, C., Peeters, A., Jonker, J., Mackenbach, J., & Nusselder, W. (2005). Effects of physical activity on life expectancy with cardiovascular disease. *Archives of Internal Medicine, 165,* 2355–2360.

Frangou, S., Chitins, X., & Williams, S. C. R. (2004). Mapping IQ and gray matter density in healthy young people. *NeuroImage, 23,* 800–805. doi: 10.1016/j.neuroimage.2004.05.027.

Frank, M. G., & Ekman, P. (1997). The ability to detect deceit generalizes across different types of high stakes lies. *Journal of Personality and Social Psychology, 72,* 1429–1439.

Fratiglioni, L., Winblad, B., & von Strauss, E. (2007). Prevention of Alzheimer's disease and dementia. Major findings from the Kungsholmen Project. *Physiology & Behavior, 92,* 98–104.

Fredrickson, B. L. (1998). What good are positive emotions? *Review of General Psychology, 2,* 300–319.

Fredrickson, B. L. (2001). The role of positive emotions in positive psychology: The broaden-and-build theory of positive emotions. *American Psychologist, 56,* 218–226.

Fredrickson, B. L., & Branigan, C. (2005). Positive emotions broaden the scope of attention and thought-action repertoires. *Cognition & Emotion, 19,* 313–332.

Fredrickson, B. L., & Joiner, T. (2002). Positive emotions trigger upward spirals toward emotional well-being. *Psychological Science, 13,* 172–175.

Fredrickson, B. L., & Levenson, R. W. (1998). Positive emotions speed recovery from the cardiovascular sequelae of negative emotions. *Cognition & Emotion, 12,* 191–220.

Fredrickson, B. L., & Losada, M. F. (2005). Positive affect and the complex dynamics of human flourishing. *American Psychologist, 60*(7), 678–686. doi: 10.1037/0003-066X.60.7.678.

Fredrickson, B. L., Tugade, M. M., Waugh, C. E., & Larkin, G. R. (2003). What good are positive emotions in crises? A prospective study of resilience and emotions following the terrorist attacks on the United States on September 11th, 2001. *Journal of Personality and Social Psychology, 84,* 365–376.

Freeman, H., Brosnan, S., Hopper, L., Lambeth, S., Schapiro, S., & Gosling, S. (2013). Developing a comprehensive and comparative questionnaire for measuring personality in chimpanzees using a simultaneous top-down/bottom-up design. *American Journal of Primatology 75,* 1042–1053.

Fregni, F., Boggio, P. S., Nitsche, M., Bermpohl, F., Antal, A., Feredoes, E., . . . Pascual-Leone, A. (2005). Anodal transcranial direct current stimulation of the prefrontal motor cortex enhances working memory. *Brain Research, 166,* 23–30. doi: 10.1007/s00221-005-2334-6.

French, S. E., Seidman, E., Allen, L., & Aber, J. L. (2006). The development of ethnic identity during adolescence. *Developmental Psychology, 42,* 1–10.

French-Belgian Collaborative Group. (1982). Ischemic heart disease and psychological patterns: Prevalence and incidence studies in Belgium and France. *Advances in Cardiology, 29,* 25–31.

Freud, A. (1946). *The ego and the mechanisms of defense.* New York, NY: International Universities Press.

Freud, S. (1953). *The interpretation of dreams.* In J. Strachey (Ed. & Trans.), *The standard edition of the complete works of Sigmund Freud* (Vols. 4 & 5). London, England: Hogarth Press. (Original work published 1900)

Freud, S. (1959). *Inhibitions, symptoms, and anxiety.* In J. Strachey (Ed. & Trans.), *Standard edition of the complete works of Sigmund Freud* (Vol. 20). London, England: Hogarth Press. (Original work published 1926)

Freud, S. (1960). *Psychopathology of everyday life.* In J. Strachey (Ed. & Trans.), *Standard edition of the complete works of Sigmund Freud* (Vol. 6). London, England: Hogarth Press. (Original work published 1901)

Freud, S. (1964). *New introductory lectures on psychoanalysis.* In J. Strachey (Ed. & Trans.), *The standard edition of the complete works of Sigmund Freud* (Vol. 22). London, England: Hogarth Press. (Original work published 1933)

Freund, A., & Ritter, J. (2009). Midlife crisis: A debate. *Gerontology, 55,* 582–591. doi: 10.1159/000227322.

Fridlund, A. J., Beck, H. P., Goldie, W. D., & Irons, G. (2012). Little Albert: A neurologically impaired child. *History of Psychology. 15,* 302–327. doi: 10.1037/a0026720.

Friedman, J. M., & Halaas, J. L. (1998). Leptin and the regulation of body weight in mammals. *Nature, 395,* 763–770. doi: 10.1038/27376.

Friesen, W. V. (1972). *Cultural differences in facial expressions in a social situation: An experimental test of the concept of display rules.* Unpublished doctoral dissertation, University of California, San Francisco.

Frijda, N. H. (1986). *The emotions.* Cambridge, England: Cambridge University Press.

Frith, U., & Frith, C. (2010). The social brain: Allowing humans to boldly go where no other species has been. *Philosophical Translations of the Royal Society B: Biological Sciences, 365,* 165–176.

Frokjaer, V. B., Vinberg, M., Erritzoe, D., Svarer, C., Baare, W., Budtz-Joergensen, E., . . . Knudsen, G. M. (2009). High familial risk for mood disorder is associated with low dorsolateral prefrontal cortex serotonin transporter binding. *NeuroImage, 46,* 360–366.

Frost, R. O., & Steketee, G. (2010). *Stuff: Compulsive hoarding and the meaning of things.* Boston, MA: Houghton Mifflin.

Fruntes, V., & Limosin, F. (2008). Schizophrenia and viral infection during neurodevelopment: A pathogenesis model? *Medical Science Monitor, 14,* RA71–RA77.

Fuller, J. L., & Thompson, W. R. (1960). *Behavior genetics.* New York, NY: Wiley.

Furnham, A., & Bachtiar, V. (2008). Personality and intelligence as predictors of creativity. *Personality and Individual Differences, 45,* 613–617.

Furuichi, T. (1983). Interindividual distance and influence of dominance on feeding in a natural Japanese macaque troop. *Primates, 24,* 445–455.

Furumoto, L. (1981). Mary Whiton Calkins (1863–1930). *Psychology of Women Quarterly, 5,* 55–68. doi: 10.1111/j.1471-6402.1981.tb01033.x.

Fuster, J. M. (1999). Cognitive functions of the frontal lobes. In B. L. Miller & J. L. Cummings (Eds.), *The human frontal lobes: Functions and disorders* (pp. 187–195). New York, NY: Guilford Press.

Fuster, J. M. (2002). Frontal lobe and cognitive development. *Journal of Neurocytology, 31,* 373–385.

Gaab, N., Paetzold, M., Becker, M., Walker, M. P., & Schlaug, G. (2004). The influence of sleep on auditory learning—A behavioral study. *NeuroReport, 15,* 731–734.

Gable, P. A., & Harmon-Jones, E. (2008). Approach-motivated positive affect reduces breadth of attention. *Psychological Science, 19,* 476–482. doi: 10.1111/j.1467-9280.2008.02112.x.

Gable, P. A., & Harmon-Jones, E. (2010). The blues broaden, but the nasty narrows: Attentional consequences of negative affects low and high in motivational intensity. *Psychological Science, 21,* 211–215. doi: 10.1177/0956797609359622.

Gage, F. H. (2002). Neurogenesis in the adult brain. *Journal of Neuroscience, 22,* 612–613.

Gage, F. H., Kemperman, G., & Song, H. (Eds.). (2008). *Adult neurogenesis.* Cold Spring Harbor, NY: Cold Spring Harbor Laboratory Press.

Galanter, E. (1962). Contemporary psychophysics. In R. Brown (Ed.), *New directions in psychology* (pp. 87–157). New York, NY: Holt, Rinehart & Winston.

Gale, A. (1983). Electroencephalographic studies of extraversion-introversion: A case study in the psychophysiology of individual differences. *Personality and Individual Differences, 4,* 371–380.

Galin, D. (1994). The structure of awareness: Contemporary applications of William James' forgotten concept of "The Fringe." *Journal of Mind and Behavior, 15,* 375–402.

Gallagher, A. M., & Kaufman, J. C. (2005). *Gender differences in mathematics: An integrative psychological approach.* New York, NY: Cambridge University Press.

Gallagher, M., & Lopez, S. (2007). Curiosity and well-being. *Journal of Positive Psychology, 2*(4), 236–248.

Gallagher, R. M., & Rosenthal, L. J. (2008). Chronic pain and opiates: Balancing pain control and risks in long-term opioid treatment. *Archives of Physical Medicine and Rehabilitation, 89*(Suppl. 1), S77–S82.

Ganasen, K., Ipser, J., & Stein, D. (2010). Augmentation of cognitive behavioral therapy with pharmacotherapy. *Psychiatric Clinics of North America, 33,* 687–699. doi: 10.1016/j.psc.2010.04.008.

Ganis, G., Thompson, W., & Kosslyn, S. (2009). Visual mental imagery: More than "seeing with the mind's eye." In J. R. Brockmole (Ed.), *The visual world in memory* (pp. 215–249). New York, NY: Psychology Press.

Garcia, J., Ervin, F. R., & Koelling, R. (1966). Learning with a prolonged delay of reinforcement. *Psychonomic Science, 5,* 121–122.

Garcia, J., Kimeldorf, D. J., & Koelling, R. A. (1955). A conditioned aversion towards saccharin resulting from exposure to gamma radiation. *Science, 122,* 157–159.

Garcia, J., & Koelling, R. A. (1966). The relation of cue to consequence in avoidance learning. *Psychonomic Science, 4,* 123–124.

Garcia, J., McGowan, B. K., & Green, K. F. (1972). Biological constraints on conditioning. In A. H. Black & W. F. Prokasy (Eds.), *Classical conditioning II: Current research and theory* (pp. 3–27). New York, NY: Appleton-Century-Crofts.

Garcia-Bailo, B., Toguri, C., Eny, K. M., & El-Sohemy, A. (2009). Genetic variation in taste and its influence on food selection. *OMICS: A Journal of Integrative Biology, 13,* 69–80.

Garcia-Sierra, A., Rivera-Gaxiola, M. Percaccio, C. R., Conboy, B. T., Romo, H., Klarman, L., Ortiz, S., & Kuhl, P. (2011). Bilingual language learning: An ERP study relating early brain responses to speech, language input, and later word production. *Journal of Phonetics, 39,* 546–557. doi: 10.1016/j.wocn.2011.07.002.

Gardner, H. (1980). *Artful scribbles: The significance of children's drawings.* New York, NY: Basic Books.

Gardner, H. (1983). *Frames of mind: The theory of multiple intelligences.* New York, NY: Basic Books.

Gardner, H. (1987). *The mind's new science: A history of the cognitive revolution.* New York, NY: Basic Books.

Gardner, H. (1993). *Frames of mind: The theory of multiple intelligences* (2nd ed.). New York, NY: Basic Books.

Gardner, H. (1999). *Intelligence reframed: Multiple intelligences for the 21st century.* New York, NY: Basic Books.

Gardner, R. A., Gardner, B. T., & Van Cantfort, T. E. (Eds.). (1989). *Teaching sign language to chimpanzees.* Albany, NY: SUNY Press.

Garrett, R. K., & Danziger, J. N. (2008). IM = Interruption management? Instant messaging and disruption in the workplace. *Journal of Computer-Mediated Communication, 13,* 23–42.

Gates, M. F., & Allee, W. C. (1933). Conditioned behavior of isolated and grouped cockroaches on a simple maze. *Journal of Comparative Psychology, 15,* 331–358.

Gathercole, V. C. M., & Hoff, E. (2007). Input and the acquisition of language: Three questions. In E. Hoff & M. Shatz (Eds.), *The handbook of language development* (pp. 107–127). Oxford, England: Blackwell.

Gay marriage around the world. (2013, July 16). Pew Research Religion and Public Life Report. Retrieved September 5, 2013, from http://www.pewforum.org/2013/07/16/gay-marriage-around-the-world-2013/#allow

Gazdzinski, S., Durazzo, T. C., & Meyerhoff, D. J. (2005). Temporal dynamics and determinants of whole brain tissue volume changes during recovery from alcohol dependence. *Drug and Alcohol Dependence, 78,* 263–273.

Geary, D., & DeSoto, M. C. (2001). Sex differences in spatial abilities among adults in the United States and China. *Evolution and Cognition, 7,* 172–177.

Gebicke-Haerter, P. J. (2012). Epigenetics of schizophrenia. *Pharmacopsychiatry, 45*(Suppl. 1), S42–S48.

Geerlings, S. W., Beekman, A., Deeg, D., Twisk, J., & van Tilburg, W. (2002). Duration and severity of depression predict mortality in older adults in the community. *Psychological Medicine, 32,* 609–618.

Georges, E. (1995). A cultural and historical perspective on confession. In J. W. Pennebaker (Ed.), *Emotion, disclosure, and health* (pp. 11–22). Washington, DC: American Psychological Association.

Georgiadis, J. R., Kortekaas, R., Kuipers, R., Nieuwenburg, A., Pruim, J., Simone Reinders, A. A. T., & Holstege, G. (2006). Regional cerebral blood flow changes associated with clitorally induced orgasm in healthy women. *European Journal of Neuroscience, 24,* 3305–3316.

Gershberg, F. B., & Shimamura, A. P. (1995). The role of the frontal lobes in the use of organizational strategies in free recall. *Neuropsychologia, 13,* 1305–1333.

Geschwind, N., Peeters, F., Huibers, M., van Os, J., & Wichers, M. (2012). Efficacy of mindfulness-based cognitive therapy in relation to prior history of depression: Randomised controlled trial. *British Journal of Psychiatry, 201,* 320–325. doi: 10.1192/bjp.bp.111.104851.

Gibson, E., & Walk, R. (1960). The visual cliff. *Scientific American, 202,* 64–71.

Gibson, J. J. (1950). *The perception of the visual world.* Boston, MA: Houghton Mifflin.

Gibson, J. J. (1966). *The senses considered as perceptual systems.* Boston, MA: Houghton Miffin.

Giedd, J. N., Blumenthal, J., Jeffries, N. O., Castellanos, F. X., Liu, H., Zijdenbos, A., Paus, T., Evans, A. C., & Rapoport, J. L. (1999). Brain development during childhood and adolescence: A longitudinal MRI study. *Nature Neuroscience 2,* 861–863.

Gilbert, S. P., & Weaver, C. C. (2010). Sleep quality and academic performance in university students: A wake-up call for college psychologists. *Journal of College Student Psychotherapy, 24,* 295–306. doi: 10.1080/ 87568225.2010.509245.

Giles, G. E., Mahoney, C. R., Brunye, T. T., Gardony, A. L., Taylor, H. A., & Kanarek, R. B. (2012). Differential cognitive effects of energy drink ingredients: Caffeine, taurine, and glucose. *Pharmacology, Biochemistry, and Behavior, 102,* 569–577.

Gillespie, N. A., Cloninger, C. R., Heath, A. C., & Martin, N. G. (2003). The genetic and environmental relationship between Cloninger's dimensions of temperament and character. *Personality and Individual Differences, 35,* 1931–1946.

Gillham, J. E., Reivich, K. J., Freres, D. R., Chaplin, T. M., Shatté, A. J., Samuels, B., . . . Martin, E. P. (2007). School-based prevention of depressive symptoms: A randomized controlled study of the effectiveness and specificity of the Penn Resiliency Program. *Journal of Consulting and Clinical Psychology, 75,* 9–19.

Giltay, E. J., Geleijnse, J. M., Zitman, F. G., Hoekstra, T., &. Schouten, E.G. (2004). Dispositional optimism and all-cause and cardiovascular mortality in a prospective cohort of elderly Dutch men and women. *Archives of General Psychiatry, 61,* 1126–1135.

Giuliani, N. R., Drabant, E. M., & Gross, J. J. (2010). Anterior cingulate cortex volume and emotion regulation: Is bigger better? *Biological Psychology, 86,* 379–382.

Givón, T. (2002). The visual information-processing system as an evolutionary precursor of human language. In T. Givón & B. F. Malle (Eds.), *The evolution of language out of pre-language* (pp. 3–50). Amsterdam, Netherlands: John Benjamins.

Givón, T., & Malle, B. F. (Eds.). (2002). *The evolution of language out of pre-language.* Amsterdam, Netherlands: John Benjamins.

Gjerde, P. F., & Cardilla, K. (2009). Developmental implications of openness to experience in preschool children: Gender differences in young adulthood. *Developmental Psychology, 45,* 1455–1464.

Glaser, R., & Kiecolt-Glaser, J. K. (2005). Stress-induced immune dysfunction: Implications for health. *Nature Reviews Immunology, 4,* 243–251.

Glasper, E. R., Leuner, B., & Gould, E. (2008). Adult neurogenesis finds its niche. *Nature Neuroscience, 11,* 708–731.

Glassman, A., & Shapiro, P. (1998). Depression and the course of coronary artery disease. *American Journal of Psychiatry, 155,* 4–11.

Gluckman, P. D., & Hanson, M. A. (2008). Developmental and epigenetic pathways to obesity: An evolutionary-developmental perspective.*International Journal of Obesity, 32,* S62–S71. doi: 10.1038/ijo.2008.240.

Gneezy, U., Meier, S., & Rey-Biel, P. (2011). When and why incentives (don't) work to modify behavior. *Journal of Economic Perspectives, 25,* 1–21.

Goel, V., & Vartanian, O. (2005). Dissociating the roles of right ventral lateral and dorsal lateral prefrontal cortex in generation and maintenance of hypotheses in set-shift problems. *Cerebral Cortex, 15,* 1170–1177.

Goff, D. C., & Coyle, J. T. (2001). The merging role of glutamate in the pathophysiology and treatment of schizophrenia. *American Journal of Psychiatry, 158,* 1367–1377.

Goldapple, K., Segal, Z., Garson, C., Lau, M., Bieling, P., Kennedy, S., & Mayberg, H. (2004). Modulation of cortical-limbic pathways in major depression. *Archives of General Psychiatry, 61,* 34–41.

Goldfield, B. A. (2000). Nouns before verbs in comprehension vs. production: The view from pragmatics. *Journal of Child Language, 27,* 501–520.

Goldin, P., McRae, K., Ramel, W., & Gross, J. J. (2008). The neural bases of emotion regulation: Reappraisal and suppression of negative emotion. *Biological Psychiatry, 63,* 577–586.

Goldman-Rakic, P. S. (1999). The physiological approach: Functional architecture of working memory and disordered cognition in schizophrenia. *Biological Psychiatry, 46,* 650–661.

Goldsmith, T. H. (2006). What birds see. *Scientific American, 295,* 69–75.

Goldstein, E. B. (2007). *Sensation and perception* (7th ed.). Belmont, CA: Thomson-Wadsworth.

Goldstein, T., Bridge, J., & Brent, D. (2008). Sleep disturbance preceding completed suicide in adolescents. *Journal of Consulting and Clinical Psychology, 76*(1), 84–91.

Goleman, D. P. (1995). *Emotional intelligence: Why it can matter more than IQ for character, health and lifelong achievement.* New York, NY: Bantam Books.

Golier, J. A., Caramanica, K., & Yehuda, R. (2012). Neuroendocrine response to CRF stimulation in veterans with and without PTSD in consideration of war zone era. *Psychoneuroendocrinology, 37,* 350–357. doi: 10.1016/j.psyneuen.2011.07.004.

Gonzalez, V., & Mark, G. (2004). "Constant, constant, multi-tasking craziness": Managing multiple working spheres. *Proceedings of ACM CHI'04,* 113–120.

Goodwin, P., McGill, B., & Chandra A. (2009). *Who marries and when? Age at first marriage in the United States, 2002.* NCHS data brief No. 19. Hyattsville, MD: National Center for Health Statistics.

Goodwin, P. J. (2004). Support groups in breast cancer: When a negative result is positive. *Journal of Clinical Oncology, 22,* 4244–4246.

Goodwin, P. J., Leszcz, M., Ennis, M., Koopmans, J., Vincent, L., Guther, H., . . . Hunter, J. (2001). The effect of group psychosocial support on survival in metastatic breast cancer. *New England Journal of Medicine, 345,* 1719–1726.

Gopnik, A. (2009). *The philosophical baby.* New York, NY: Farrar, Straus & Giroux.

Gopnik, A., Meltzoff, A. N., & Kuhl, P. K. (1999). *The scientist in the crib: Minds, brains, and how children learn.* New York, NY: Morrow.

Gordon, P. (2004). Numerical cognition without words: Evidence from Amazonia. *Science, 306,* 496–499.

Gorenstein, E. E., & Comer, R. J. (2002). *Case studies in abnormal psychology.* New York, NY: Worth.

Gorrindo, T., & Groves, J. E. (2009). Computer simulation and virtual reality in the diagnosis and treatment of psychiatric disorders. *Academic Psychiatry, 33,* 413–417.

Gosling, S. D., & John, O. P. (1999). Personality dimensions in non-human animals: A cross-species review. *Current Directions in Psychological Science, 8,* 69–75.

Goto, H. (1971). Auditory perception by normal Japanese adults of the sounds "l" and "r." *Neuropsychologia, 9,* 317–323.

Gottfredson, L. (1997). Mainstream science on intelligence: An editorial with 52 signatories, history, and bibliography. *Intelligence, 24,* 13–23.

Gottlieb, N. H., & Green, L. W. (1984). Life events, social network, life-style, and health: An analysis of the 1979 National Survey of Personal Health Practices and Consequences. *Health Education Quarterly, 11,* 91–105.

Gottlieb, G. (1991). Experiential canalization of behavioral development: Theory. *Developmental Psychology, 27*(1), 4–13. doi: 10.1037/0012-1649.27.1.4.

Gottschalk, S. (2010). The presentation of avatars in Second Life: Self and interaction in social virtual spaces. *Symbolic Interaction, 33,* 501–525.

Gough, H. G., & Bradley, P. (1996). *California psychological inventory manual* (3rd ed.). Palo Alto, CA: Consulting Psychologists Press.

Gould, E., Vail, N., Wagers, M., & Gross, C. G. (2001). Adult-generated hippocampal and neocortical neurons in macaques have a transient existence. *Proceedings of the National Academy of Sciences, 98,* 10910–10917.

Gould, S. J., & Vrba, E. S. (1982). Exaptation: A missing term in the science of form. *Paleobiology, 8,* 4–15.

Gow, A., Whiteman, M., Pattie, A., Whalley, L., Starr, J., & Deary, I. (2005). Lifetime intellectual function and satisfaction with life in old age: Longitudinal cohort study. *British Medical Journal, 331*(7509), 141–142. doi: 10.1136/bmj.38531.675660.F7.

Graff, J., & Mansury, I. M. (2008). Epigenetic codes in cognition and behavior. *Behavioural Brain Research, 192,* 70–87.

Grafman, J., Schwab, K., Warden, D., Pridgeon, A., Brown, H. R., & Salazar, A. M. (1996). Frontal lobe injuries, violence, and aggression: A report of a Vietnam head injury study. *Neurology, 46,* 1231–1238.

Graham, S., & Lowery, B. S. (2004). Priming unconscious racial stereotypes about adolescent offenders. *Law and Human Behavior, 28,* 483–504.

Grant, B. F., Hasin, D. S., Stinson, F. S., Dawson, D. A., Goldstein, R. B., Smith, S., . . . Saha, T. D. (2006). The epidemiology of *DSM-IV-TR* panic disorder and agoraphobia in the United States: Results from the National Epidemiologic Survey on Alcohol and Related Conditions. *Journal of Clinical Psychiatry, 67,* 363–374.

Grant, J. A., Courtemanche, J., Duerden, E. G., Duncan, G. H., & Rainville, P. (2010). Cortical thickness and pain sensitivity in Zen meditators. *Emotion, 10,* 43–53.

Grant, A. M., & Hoffman, D. A. (2011). It's not all about me: Motivating hand hygiene among health care professionals by focusing on patients. *Psychological Science 22,* 1494–1499. doi: 10.1177/0956797611419172.

Gray, J. A. (1970). The psychophysiological basis of introversion-extraversion. *Behaviour Research and Therapy, 8,* 249–266.

Gray, J. A. (1987). Perspectives on anxiety and impulsivity: A commentary. *Journal of Research in Personality, 21,* 493–509.

Gray, J. L., & Thompson, P. (2004). Neurobiology of intelligence: Science and ethics. *Nature Reviews: Neuroscience, 5,* 471–482.

Green, D., & Swets, J. (1974). *Signal detection theory and psychophysics.* Melbourne, FL: Krieger.

Green, V. A., & Cillessen, A. H. N. (2008). Achievement versus maintenance of control in six-year-old children's interactions with peers: An observational study. *Educational Psychology, 28,* 161–180.

Greenberg, G. (2013, September 3). The psychiatric drug crisis. *The New Yorker.* Retrieved September 15, 2013, from http://www.newyorker.com/online/blogs/elements/2013/09/psychiatry-prozac-ssri-mental-health-theory-discredited.html?utm_source=ny&utm_campaign=generalsocial&utm_medium=facebook&mobify=0

Greenberg, L. (1979). Genetic component of bee odor in kin recognition. *Science, 206,* 1095–1097.

Greenberg, M. T., & Kusché, C. A. (1998). *Promoting alternative thinking strategies.* Boulder: University of Colorado, Institute of Behavioral Sciences.

Greenberg, S., Shuman, D. W., & Meyer, R. G. (2004). Unmasking forensic diagnosis. *International Journal of Law and Psychiatry, 27,* 1–15. doi: 10.1016/j.ijlp.2004.01.001. PMID 15019764.

Greenemeier, L. (2013, June). Real world. *Scientific American, 308,* 24.

Greengross, G., Martin, R. A., & Miller, G. (2012). Personality traits, intelligence, humor styles, and humor production ability of professional stand-up comedians compared to college students. *Psychology of Aesthetics, Creativity, and the Arts, 6*, 74–82. doi: 10.1037/a0025774.

Greenough, W. T., Volkmar, F. R., & Juraska, J. M. (1973). Effects of rearing complexity on dendritic branching in frontolateral and temporal cortex of the rat. *Experimental Neurology, 41*, 371–378.

Greenwald, A. G. (2009, March). Interview by ScienceWatch [Web]. Retrieved from http://sciencewatch.com/inter/aut/2009/09-mar/09marGreen/

Greenwald, A. G., & Banaji, M. R. (1995). Implicit social cognition: Attitudes, self-esteem, and stereotypes. *Psychological Review, 102*, 4–27.

Greenwald, A. G., McGhee, D. E., & Schwartz, J. L. K. (1998). Measuring individual differences in implicit cognition: The implicit association test. *Journal of Personality and Social Psychology, 74*, 1464–1480.

Greenwald, A. G., Poehlman, T., Uhlmann, E., & Banaji, M. R. (2009). Understanding and using the Implicit Association Test: III. Meta-analysis of predictive validity. *Journal of Personality and Social Psychology, 97*, 17–41. doi: 10.1037/a0015575.

Gregory, R. J. (2007). *Psychological testing* (5th ed.). New York, NY: Allyn & Bacon.

Griffiths, R. R., Johnson, M. W., Richards, W. A., Richards, B. D., McCann, U., & Jesse, R. (2011). Psilocybin occasioned mystical-type experiences: Immediate and persisting dose-related effects. *Psychopharmacology, 218*(4), 649–665.

Griffiths, R. R., Richards, W. A., Johnson, M. W., McCann, U. D., & Jesse, R. (2008). Mystical-type experiences occasioned by psilocybin mediate the attribution of personal meaning and spiritual significance 14 months later. *Psychopharmacology, 22*, 621–632.

Griffiths, R. R., Richards, W. A., McCann, U., & Jesse, R. (2006). Psilocybin can occasion mystical-type experiences having substantial and sustained personal meaning and spiritual significance. *Psychopharmacology, 187*, 268–283.

Grigorenko, E. (2000). Heritability and intelligence. In R. J. Sternberg (Ed.), *Handbook of intelligence* (pp. 53–91). New York, NY: Cambridge University Press.

Grolnick, W. S., McMenamy, J. M., & Kurowski, C. O. (2006). Emotional self-regulation in infancy and toddlerhood. In L. Balter & C. S. Tamis-LeMonda (Eds.), *Child psychology: A handbook of contemporary issues* (2nd ed., pp. 3–25). New York, NY: Psychology Press.

Groome, L., Mooney, D., Holland, S., Smith, Y., Atterbury, J., & Dykman, R. (2000). Temporal pattern and spectral complexity as stimulus parameters for eliciting a cardiac orienting reflex in human fetuses. *Perception and Psychophysics, 62*(2), 313–320.

Gross, C. G. (2000). Neurogenesis in the adult brain: Death of a dogma. *Nature Reviews Neuroscience, 1*, 67–73.

Gross, J. J. (1998). The emerging field of emotion regulation: An integrative review. *Review of General Psychology, 2*, 271–299.

Gross, J. J. (2002). Emotion regulation: Affective, cognitive, and social consequences. *Psychophysiology, 39*, 281–291. doi: 10.1017/S0048577201393198.

Gross, J. J., & John, O. (1998). Mapping the domain of expressivity: Multimethod evidence for a hierarchical model. *Journal of Personality and Social Psychology, 74*, 170–191.

Gross, J. J., & Levenson, R. W. (1993). Emotional suppression—Physiology, self-report, and expressive behavior. *Journal of Personality and Social Psychology, 64*, 970–986.

Gross, J. J., & Levenson, R. W. (1997). Hiding feelings: The acute effects of inhibiting positive and negative emotions. *Journal of Abnormal Psychology, 106*, 95–103.

Gross, J. J., Richards, J. M., & John, O. P. (2006). Emotion regulation in everyday life. In D. K. Snyder, J. A. Simpson, & J. N. Hughes (Eds.), *Emotion regulation in families: Pathways to dysfunction and health* (pp. 13–35). Washington, DC: American Psychological Association.

Grossberg, S., & Vladusich, T. (2010). How do children learn to follow gaze, share joint attention, imitate their teachers, and use tools during social interactions? *Neural Networks, 23*, 940–965.

Grossman, A. W., Churchill, J. D., McKinney, B. C., Kodish, I. M., Otte, S. L., & Greenough, W. T. (2003). Experience effects on brain development: Possible contributions to psychopathology. *Journal of Child Psychology and Psychiatry, 44*, 33–63.

Grossman, P., Kappos, L., Gensicke, H., D'Souza, M., Mohr, D. C., Penner, I. K., & Steiner, C. (2010). MS quality of life, depression, and fatigue improve after mindfulness training. *Neurology, 75*, 1141–1149.

Grossman, T., Striano, T., & Friederici, A. D. (2006). Crossmodal integration of emotional information from face and voice in the infant brain. *Developmental Science, 9*, 309–315.

Guarnaccia, V., Dill, C. A., Sabatino, S., & Southwick, S. (2001). Scoring accuracy using the comprehensive system for the Rorschach. *Journal of Personality Assessment, 77*, 464–474.

Guarraci, F. A., & Benson, A. (2005). "Coffee, tea and me": Moderate doses of caffeine affect sexual behavior in female rats. *Pharmacology, Biochemistry and Behavior, 82*, 522–530.

Guehl, D., Benazzouz, A., Aouizerate, B., Cuny, E., Rotgé, J.-Y., Rougier, A., . . . (2008). Neuronal correlates of obsessions in the caudate nucleus. *Biological Psychiatry, 63*, 557–562.

Guénard, F., Deshaies, Y., Cianflone, K., Kral, J. G., Marceau, P., & Vohl, M. (2013). Differential methylation in glucoregulatory genes of offspring born before vs. after maternal gastrointestinal bypass surgery. *Proceedings of the National Academy of Sciences*; published ahead of print, May 28, 2013. doi: 10.1073/pnas.1216959110.

Guilford, J. P. (1967). *The nature of human intelligence.* New York, NY: McGraw-Hill.

Guillem, K., & Peoples, L. (2010). Progressive and lasting amplification of accumbal nicotine-seeking neural signals. *Journal of Neuroscience, 30*, 276–286.

Guilleminault, C., Kirisoglu, C., Bao, G., Arias, V., Chan, A., & Li, K. K. (2005). Adult chronic sleepwalking and its treatment based on polysomnography. *Brain, 128*, 1062–1069.

Guiraud, A., deLorgeril, M., Zeghichi, S., Laporte, F., Salen, P., Saks, V., . . . (2008). Interactions of ethanol drinking with n-3 fatty acids in rats: Potential consequences for the cardiovascular system. *British Journal of Nutrition*, 1–8. Advance online publication. Retrieved July 10, 2008. doi: 10.1017/S0007114508981472.

Gunderson, E., Moline, J., & Catalano, P. (1997). Risks of developing noise-induced hearing loss in employees of urban music clubs. *American Journal of Industrial Medicine, 31*, 75–79.

Güngör, D., Bornstein, M. H., DeLeersnyder, J., Cote, L., Ceulemans, E., & Mesquita, B. (2013). Acculturation of personality: A three-culture study of Japanese, Japanese Americans, and European Americans. *Journal of Cross-Cultural Psychology, 44*, 701–718. doi: 10.1177/0022022112470749.

Gupta, S., Agarwal, A., Banerjee, J., & Alvarez, J. G. (2007). The role of oxidative stress in spontaneous abortion and recurrent pregnancy loss: A systematic review. *Obstetrical, Gynecological Survey, 62*, 335–347.

Gutteling, B. M., de Weerth, C., Willemsen-Swinkels, S. H. N., Huizink, A. C., Mulder, E. J. H., Visser, G. H. A., & Buitelaar, J. K. (2005). The effects of prenatal stress on temperament and problem behavior of 27-month-old toddlers. *European Child and Adolescent Psychiatry, 14*, 41–51.

Guzman-Marin, R., Suntsova, N., Methippara, M., Greiffenstein, R., Szymusiak, R., & McGinty, D. (2003). Sleep deprivation suppresses neurogenesis in the adult hippocampus of rats. *European Journal of Neuroscience, 22*, 2111–2116.

Hafetz, J. S., Jacobsohn, L. S., García-España, J., Curry, A. E., & Winston, F. K. (2010). Adolescent drivers' perceptions of the advantages and disadvantages of abstention from in-vehicle cell phone use. *Accident Analysis and Prevention, 42*(6), 1570–1576. doi: 10.1016/j.aap.2010.03.015.

Haider, B., Duque, A., Hasenstaub, A. R., & McCormick, D. A. (2006). Neocortical network activity *in vivo* is generated through a dynamic balance of excitation and inhibition. *Journal of Neuroscience, 26*, 4535–4545.

Haidt, J., & Keltner, D. (1999): Culture and facial expression: Open-ended methods find more expressions and a gradient of recognition. *Cognition & Emotion, 13*, 225–266.

Haier, R. J., Jung, R. E., Yeo, R. A., Head, K., & Alkire, M. T. (2004). Structural brain variation and general intelligence. *Neuro-Image, 23*, 425–433.

Hakuta, K., Bialystok, E., & Wiley, E. (2003). Critical evidence: A test of the critical-period hypothesis for second-language acquisition. *Psychological Science, 14*, 31–38.

Hale, B., Seiser, L., & McGuire, E. J. (2005). Mental imagery. In J. Taylor & J. Wilson (Eds.), *Applying sport psychology: Four perspectives* (pp. 117–135). Champaign, IL: Human Kinetics.

Hall, J. A., & Matsumoto, D. (2004). Gender difference in the judgment of multiple emotions from facial expression. *Emotion, 4*, 201–206.

Halpern, D. (2004). A cognitive-process taxonomy for sex differences in cognitive abilities. *Current Directions in Psychological Science, 13*, 135–139.

Halpern, J. H., Pope, H. G., Sherwood, A. R., Barry, S., Hudson, J. I., & Yurgelun-Todd, D. (2004). Residual neuropsychological effects of illicit 3,4-methylenedioxymethamphet-amine (MDMA) in individuals with minimal exposure to other drugs. *Drug and Alcohol Dependence, 75*, 135–147.

Hamann, S., Herman, R. A., Nolan, C. L., & Wallen, K. (2004). Men and women differ in amygdala response to visual sexual stimuli. *Nature Neuroscience, 7*, 411–416.

Hamer, D., & Copeland, P. (1998). *Living with our genes.* New York, NY: Anchor Books.

Hamilton, W. D. (1964). The genetical evolution of social behaviour I and II. *Journal of Theoretical Biology, 7*, 1–16, 17–52.

Hammer, A. L., & Macdaid, G. P. (1992). *Career report manual.* Palo Alto, CA: Consulting Psychologists Press.

Han, J. (2004). Acupuncture and endorphins. *Neuroscience Letters, 361*, 258–261.

Haney, C., Banks, W. C., & Zimbardo, P. G. (1973). Interpersonal dynamics in a simulated prison. *International Journal of Criminology and Penology, 1*, 69–97.

Hankin, B. L. (2010). Personality and depressive symptoms: Stress generation and cognitive vulnerabilities to depression in a prospective daily diary study. *Journal of Clinical and Social Psychology, 29*, 369–401.

Hannigan, T. P. (1995). Body odor: The international student and cross-cultural communication. *Culture & Psychology, 1*, 497–503.

Hansen, R., Gartlehner, G., Webb, A. P., Morgan, L. C., Moore, C. G., & Jonas, D. E. (2008). Efficacy and safety of donepezil, galantamine, and rivastigmine for the treatment of Alzheimer's disease: A systematic review and meta-analysis. *Journal of Clinical Interventions in Aging, 3*, 211–225.

Hansen, R. A., Gartiehner, G., Lohr, K. N., & Daufer, D. (2007). Functional outcomes of drug treatment in Alzheimer's disease: A systematic review and meta-analysis. *Drugs & Aging, 24*(2), 155–167.

Harackiewicz, J. M., & Sansone, C. (1991). Goals and intrinsic motivation: You can get there from here. In M. L. Maehr & P. R. Pintrich (Eds.), *Advances in motivation and achievement: Goals and self-regulatory processes* (Vol. 7, pp. 21–49). Greenwich, CT: JAI Press.

Hare, R. D. (1993). *Without conscience: The disturbing world of the psychopaths among us.* New York, NY: Pocket Books.

Hargittai, E. (2008). Whose space? Differences among users and non-users of social network sites. *Journal of Computer-Mediated Communication, 13*, 276–297.

Hargrave, G. E., & Hiatt, D. (1989). Use of the California Psychological Inventory in law enforcement officer selection. *Journal of Personality Assessment, 53*, 267–277.

Hargrove, L.J., Simon, A.M., Lipschutz, R., Finucane, S.B., & Kuiken, T.A., (2013). Non-weight-bearing neural control of a powered transfemoral prothesis. *Journal of NeuroEngineering and Rehabilitation, 10*, 62, http://www.jneuroengrehab.com/content/10/1/62.

Hargrove, L. J., Simon, A. M., Young, A. J., Lipschutz, R. D., Finucane, S. B., . . . Kuiken, T. A. (2013). Robotic leg control with EMG decoding in an amputee with nerve transfers. *New England Journal of Medicine, 369*, 1237–1242. Retrieved from http://dx.doi.org/10.1056/NEJMoa1300126

Harkins, S. G. (1987). Social loafing and social facilitation. *Journal of Experimental Social Psychology, 23*, 1–18.

Harlow, H. (1958). The nature of love. *American Psychologist, 13*, 573–685.

Harmon, D. (2006). Free-radical theory of aging: An update. *Annals of the New York Academy of Sciences, 1067*, 10–21.

Harmon-Jones, E. (2003). Clarifying the emotive functions of asymmetrical frontal cortical activity. *Psychophysiology, 40*, 838–848.

Harris, J. R. (1998). *The nurture assumption: Why children turn out the way they do.* New York, NY: Free Press.

Harris, M. B. (1974). Mediators between frustration and aggression in a field experiment. *Journal of Experimental Social Psychology, 10*, 561–571.

Harris, S., Kaplan, J. T., Curiel, A., Bookheimer, S. Y., Iacoboni, M., & Cohen, M. S. (2009). The neural correlates of religious and nonreligious belief. *PLoS One, 4*, e0007272. doi: 10.1371/journal.pone.0007272.

Harris, S., Sheth, S. A., & Cohen, M. S. (2008). Functional neuroimaging of belief, disbelief, and uncertainty. *Annuals of Neurology, 63*, 141–147.

Harris Interactive. (2008). Cell phone usage continues to increase. Retrieved October 18, 2013, from http://www.harrisinteractive.com/vault/Harris-Interactive-Poll-Research-Cell-Phone-Usage-Continues-to-Increase-2008-04.pdf

Harrison, P. J. (2004). The hippocampus in schizophrenia: A review of the neuropathological evidence and its pathophysiological implications. *Psychopharmacology, 174*, 151–162.

Harrison, P. J., & Owen, M. (2003). Genes for schizophrenia? Recent findings and their pathophysiological implications. *The Lancet, 361*, 417–419.

Harrison, P. J., & Weinberger, D. R. (2005). Schizophrenia genes, gene expression, and neuropathology: On the matter of their convergence. *Molecular Psychiatry, 10*, 40–68.

Hart, B., & Risley, T. R. (1992). American parenting of language-learning children: Persisting differences in family-child interactions observed in natural home environments. *Developmental Psychology, 28*(6), 1096–1105. doi: 10.1037/0012-1649.28.6.1096.

Hart, B., & Risley, T. R. (1995). *Meaningful differences in the everyday experience of young American children.* Baltimore, MD: Paul H. Brooks.

Hasher, L., & Zacks, R. T. (1979). Automatic and effortful processes in memory. *Journal of Experimental Psychology: General, 108*, 356–388.

Hauser, M. D., Chomsky, N., & Fitch, W. T. (2002). The faculty of language: What is it, who has it, and how did it evolve? *Science, 298*, 1569–1579.

Haslam, S. A., & Reicher, S. D. (2012) Contesting the "nature" of conformity: What Milgram and Zimbardo's studies really show. *PLoS Biol 10*: e1001426. DOI:10.1371/journal.pbio.1001426.

Havas, D. A., Glenberg, A. M., Gutowski, K. A., Lucarelli, M. J., & Davidson, R. J. (2010). Cosmetic use of botulinum toxin-A affects processing of emotional language. *Psychological Science, 21*, 895–900.

Hawton, K., Comabella, C., Haw, C., & Saunders, K. (2013). Risk factors for suicide in individuals with depression: A systematic review. *Journal of Affective Disorders, 147*, 17–28.

Hayes, B. D., Klein-Schwartz, W., & Doyon, S. (2008). Toxicity of buprenorphine overdoses in children. *Pediatrics, 121*, 782–786.

Haynes, S. G., Levine, S., Scotch, N., Feinleib, M., & Kannel, W. B. (1978). The relationship of psychosocial factors to coronary heart disease in the Framingham Study. I. Methods and risk factors. *American Journal of Epidemiology, 107*, 362–383.

Hazan, C., & Shaver, P. (1987). Romantic love conceptualized as an attachment process. *Journal of Personality and Social Psychology, 52*, 511–524.

Headey, B. (2008). Life goals matter to happiness: A revision of set-point theory. *Social Indicators Research, 86*, 213–231.

Health and Human Services. (2004). *New surgeon general's report expands the list of diseases caused by smoking.* Retrieved August 19, 2008, from http://www.hhs.gov/news/press/2004pres/20040527a.html

Heath, R. G. (1975). Brain function and behavior. *Journal of Nervous and Mental Disease, 160*, 159–175.

Hebb, D. O. (1949). *The organization of behavior: A neuropsychological theory.* New York, NY: Wiley.

Hedden, T., & Gabrieli, J. D. E. (2004). Insights into the ageing mind: A view from cognitive neuroscience. *Nature Reviews Neuroscience, 5*, 87–96.

Hedges, L., & Nowell, A. (1995). Sex differences in mental test scores, variability, and numbers of high-scoring individuals. *Science, 269*, 41–45.

Hedges, S. M., Jandorf, L., & Stone, A. A. (1985). Meaning of daily mood assessments. *Journal of Personality and Social Psychology, 48*, 428–434.

Hegelson, V. S., & Taylor, S. E. (1993). Social comparisons and adjustment among cardiac patients. *Journal of Applied Social Psychology, 23*, 1171–1195.

Heider, F. (1958). *The psychology of interpersonal relations.* New York, NY: Wiley.

Helmholtz, Hermann von (1860). The Young-Helmholtz theory of color vision. Reprinted in Dennis, Wayne (Ed), (1948). *Readings in the history of psychology. Century psychology series,* (pp. 199–205). East Norwalk, CT, US: Appleton-Century-Crofts.

Hennenlotter, A., Dresel, C., Castrop, F., Ceballos Baumann, A. O., Wohlschläger, A. M., & Haslinger, B. (2009). The link between facial feedback and neural activity within central circuitries of emotion—New insights from *Botulinum* toxin–induced denervation of frown muscles. *Cerebral Cortex, 19*, 537–542.

Herbert, A., & Rich, A. (1999). RNA processing in evolution: The logic of soft-wired genomes. *Annals of the New York Academy of Sciences, 870*, 119–132.

Herdener, M., Esposito, F., di Salle, F., Boller, C., Hilti, C. C., Habermeyer, B., . . . Cattapan-Ludewig, K. (2010). Musical training induces functional plasticity in human hippocampus. *Journal of Neuroscience, 30*(4), 1377–1384. doi: 10.1523/JNEUROSCI.4513-09.2010.

Hering, E. (1878). *Zur Lehre vom Lichtsinn.* Vienna, Austria: Gerold.

Hernandez-Reif, M., Field, T., Largie, S., Diego, M., Manigat, N., Seoanes, J., & Bornstein, J. (2005). Cerebral palsy symptoms in children decreased following massage therapy. *Early Child Development and Care, 175*, 445–456.

Herrington, J. D., Heller, W., Mohanty, A., Engels, A. S, Banich, M. T., Webb, A. G., & Miller, G. A. (2010). Localization of asymmetric brain function in emotion and depression. *Psychophysiology, 47*, 442–454.

Herrnstein, R. J., & Murray, C. (1994). *The bell-curve: Intelligence and class structure in American life.* New York, NY: Free Press.

Herz, R. (2004). A naturalistic analysis of autobiographical memories triggered by olfactory visual and auditory stimuli. *Chemical Senses, 29*, 217–224.

Hesse, E., & Main, M. (2006). Frightened, threatening, and dissociative parental behavior in low-risk samples: Description, discussion, and interpretations. *Development and Psychopathology, 18*, 309–343.

Hettema, J. M., Neale, M. C., & Kendler, K. S. (2001). A review and meta-analysis of the genetic epidemiology of anxiety disorders. *American Journal of Psychiatry, 158*, 1568–1578.

Hien, D. A., & Miele, G. M. (2003). Emotion-focused coping as a mediator of maternal cocaine abuse and antisocial behavior. *Psychology of Addictive Behaviors, 17*, 49–55.

Higuchi, S., Motohashi, Y., Liu, Y., & Maeda, A. (2005). Effects of playing a computer game using a bright display on presleep psychological variables, sleep latency, slow wave sleep, and REM sleep. *Journal of Sleep Research, 14*, 267–273.

Hilgard, E. (1965). *Hypnotic susceptibility.* New York, NY: Harcourt, Brace, & World.

Hilgard, E. (1977). *Divided consciousness: Multiple controls in human thought and action.* New York, NY: Wiley.

Hillman, C. H., Buck, S. M., Themanson, J. R., Pontifex, M. B., & Castelli, D. M. (2009). Aerobic fitness and cognitive development: Event-related brain potential and task performance indices of executive control in preadolescent children. *Developmental Psychology, 45*, 114–129.

Hillman, C. H., Erickson, K. I., & Kramer, A. F. (2008). Be smart, exercise your heart: Exercise effects on brain and cognition. *Nature Reviews Neuroscience, 9*, 58–65.

Hinduja, S., & Patchin, J. W. (2008). Cyberbullying: An exploratory analysis of factors related to offending and victimization. *Deviant Behavior, 29*, 129–156.

Hines, L. M., & Rimm, E. B. (2001). Moderate alcohol consumption and coronary heart disease: A review. *Postgraduate Medical Journal, 77*, 747–752.

Hines, M. (2010). Sex-related variation in human behavior and the brain. *Trends in Cognitive Sciences, 14*(10), 448–456. doi: 10.1016/j.tics.2010.07.005.

Hines, M., Fane, B., Pasterski, V., Matthews, G., Conway, G., & Brook, C. (2003). Spatial abilities following prenatal androgen abnormality: Targeting and mental rotations performance in individuals with congenital adrenal hyperplasia. *Psychoneuroendocrinology, 28*, 1010–1026. doi: 10.1016/S0306-4530(02)00121-X.

Hirsch, C. (2013). Ginkgo biloba extract did not reduce risk for Alzheimer disease in elderly patients with memory complaints. *Annals of Internal Medicine, 158* (2), JC7–JC7.

Hirshfeld-Becker, D. R., Masek, B., Henin, A., Blakely, L. R., Pollock-Wurman, R. A., McQuade, J., . . . Biederman, J. (2010). Cognitive behavioral therapy for 4- to 7-year-old children with anxiety disorders: A randomized clinical trial. *Journal of Consulting and Clinical Psychology, 78*, 498–510.

Ho, Y.-C, Cheung, M.-C, & Chan, A. S. (2003). Music training improves verbal but not visual memory: Cross-sectional and longitudinal explorations in children. *Neuropsychology, 17*, 439–450.

Hobson, J. A. (2001). *The dream drugstore: Chemically altered states of consciousness.* Cambridge, MA: MIT Press.

Hobson, J. A. (2002). *Dreaming: An introduction to the science of sleep.* New York, NY: Oxford University Press.

Hochberg, L.R., Bacher, D., Jarosiewicz, B., Masse, N.Y., Simeral, J.D., Vogel, J. . . . Donoghue, J.P. (2012). Reach and grasp by people with tetraplegia using a neurally controlled robotic arm. *Nature, 485*, 372–375. doi: 10.1038/nature11076.

Hodgetts, W., Szarko, R., & Rieger, J. (2009). What is the influence of background noise and exercise on the listening levels of iPod users? *International Journal of Audiology*, *48*, 825–832.

Hoff, E. (2006). How social contexts support and shape language development. *Developmental Review*, *26*, 55–88.

Hoff, E., Core, C., Place, S., Rumiche, R., Senor, M., & Parra, M. (2012). Dual language exposure and early bilingual development. *Journal of Child Language*, *39*, 1–27. doi: 10.1017/S0305000910000759.

Hoffmann, H., Kessler, H., Eppel, T., Rukavina, S., & Traue, H. C. (2010). Expression intensity, gender and facial emotion recognition: Women recognize only subtle facial emotions better than men. *Acta Psychologica*, *135*, 278–283.

Hofman, S. G., Schulz, S. M., Meuret, A. F., Moscovitch, D. A., & Suvak, M. (2006). Sudden gains during therapy of social phobia. *Journal of Consulting and Clinical Psychology*, *74*, 687–697.

Hofstede, G. (2001). *Culture's consequences: Comparing values, behaviors, institutions, and organizations across nations* (2nd ed.). Thousand Oaks, CA: Sage.

Hogan, M. J., Parker, J. D. A., Wiener, J., Watters, C., Wood, L. M., & Oke, A. (2010). Academic success in adolescence: Relationships among verbal IQ, social support and emotional intelligence. *Australian Journal of Psychology*, *62*, 30–41.

Hogan, T. P. (2007). *Psychological testing: A practical introduction* (2nd ed.). New York, NY: John Wiley.

Hogeboom, D. L., McDermott, R. J., Perrin, K. M., Osman, H., & Bell-Ellison, B. A. (2010). Internet use and social networking among middle aged and older adults. *Educational Gerontology*, *36*(2), 93–111. doi: 10.1080/03601270903058507.

Hohmann, A. G., Suplita, R. L., Bolton, N. M., Neely, M. H., Fegley, D., Mangieri, R., . . . Piomelli, D. (2005). An endocannabinoid mechanism for stress-induced analgesia. *Nature*, *435*, 1108–1112.

Holden, C. (1980). Identical twins reared apart. *Science*, *207*, 1323–1328.

Holder, M., Coleman, B., & Wallace, J. (2010). Spirituality, religiousness, and happiness in children aged 8–12 years. *Journal of Happiness Studies*, *11*, 131–150.

Holland, J. L. (1985). *Making vocational choices: A theory of vocational personalities and work environments*. Englewood Cliffs, NJ: Prentice Hall.

Hollon, S. D., DeRubeis, R. J., Shelton, R. C., Amsterdam, J. D., Salomon, R. M., O'Reardon, J. P., . . . Gallop, R. (2005). Prevention of relapse following cognitive therapy vs. medications in moderate to severe depression. *Archives of General Psychiatry*, *62*, 417–422.

Holmes, J., Gathercole, S. E., & Dunning, D. L. (2009). Adaptive training leads to sustained enhancement of poor working memory in children. *Developmental Science*, *12*, F9–F15.

Holmes, T. H., & Rahe, R. H. (1967). The social readjustment rating scale. *Journal of Psychosomatic Research*, *11*, 211–218.

Holstege, G., Georgiadis, J., Paans, A., Meiners, L., van der Graaf, F., & Reinders, A. (2003). Brain activation during human male ejaculation. *Journal of Neuroscience*, *23* (27), 9185–9193.

Hölzel, B. K., Carmody, J., Vangel, M., Congleton, C., Yerramsetti, S. M., Gard, T., & Lazar, S. (2011). Mindfulness practice leads to increases in regional brain gray matter density. *Psychiatry Research: Neuroimaging*, *191*, 36–43. doi: 10.1016/j.pscychresns.2010.08.006.

Hopfield, J. J. (1982). Neural networks and physical systems with emergent collective computational abilities. *Proceedings of the National Academy of Sciences*, *79*, 2554–2558.

Hopper, L., Price, S., Freeman, H., Lambeth, S., Schapiro, S., & Kendal, R. (2013). Influence of personality, age, sex, and estrous state on chimpanzee problem-solving success. *Animal Cognition*. doi: 10.1007/s10071-013-0715-y.

Hopson, J. L. (1998, September/October). Fetal psychology. *Psychology Today*, *31*, 44. Retrieved from http://www.leaderu.com/orgs/tul/psychtoday9809.html

Horn, J. L., & Cattell, R. B. (1966). Refinement and test of the theory of fluid and crystallized general intelligences. *Journal of Educational Psychology*, *57*, 253–270.

Horne, J. A., & Foster, S. C. (1995). Can exercise overcome sleepiness? *Sleep Research*, *24A*, 437.

Horney, K. (1945). *Our inner conflicts: A constructive theory of neurosis*. New York, NY: Norton.

Horney, K. (1950). *Neurosis and human growth: The struggle toward self-realization*. New York, NY: Norton.

Hosking, S., Young, K., & Regan, M. (2006). The effects of text messaging on young novice driver performance: Monash University Accident Research Centre, Report No. 246. Retrieved from http://www.monash.edu.au/muarc/reports/muarc246.pdf

Hoss, R. A., & Langlois, J. H. (2003). Infants prefer attractive faces. In O. Pascalis & A. Slater (Eds.), *The development of face processing in infancy and early childhood: Current perspectives* (pp. 27–38). New York, NY: Nova Science.

Hötting, K., & Röder, B. (2013). Beneficial effects of physical exercise on neuroplasticity and cognition. *Neuroscience and Biobehavioral Reviews*, *37*(9 Pt B), 2243–2257.

Houlihan, A. E., Gibbons, F. X., Gerrard, M., Yeh, H., & Reimer, R. A. (2008). The impact of early sexual onset on the self-concept and subsequent risky behavior of African American adolescents. *Journal of Early Adolescence*, *28*, 70–91.

Howard, B. V., Manson, J. E., Stefanick, M. L., Beresford, S. A., Frank, G., Jones, B., . . . Prentice, R. (2006). Low-fat dietary pattern and weight change over 7 years: The Women's Health Initiative Dietary Modification Trial. *Journal of the American Medical Association*, *295*, 39–49.

Howard, K. I., Kopta, S. M., Krause, M. S., & Orlinsky, D. E. (1986). The dose-effect relationship in psychotherapy. *American Psychologist*, *41*, 159–164.

Howard, M. A., & Marczinski, C. A. (2010). Acute effects of a glucose energy drink on behavioral control. *Experimental Clinical Psychopharmacology*, *18*, 553–561.

Howe, D. (2010). ADHD and its comorbidity: An example of gene-environment interaction and its implications for child and family social work. *Child & Family Social Work*, *15*, 265–275. doi: 10.1111/j.1365-2206.2009.00666.x.

Howell, A. J., Jahrig, J. C., & Powell, R. A. (2004). Sleep quality, sleep propensity and academic performance. *Perceptual and Motor Skills*, *99*, 525–535. doi: 10.2466/PMS.99.5.525-535.

Howes, C., & Matheson, C. C. (1992). Sequences in the development of competent play with peers: Social and social pretend play. *Developmental Psychology*, *28*, 961–974.

Hu, S.-H., Wei, N., Wang, Q.-D., Yan, L.-Q., Wei, E.-Q., Zhang, M.-M., . . . Xu, Y. (2008). Patterns of brain activation during visually evoked sexual arousal differ between homosexual and heterosexual men. *American Journal of Neuroradiology*, *29*, 1890–1896.

Hua, K., Oishi, K., Zhang, J., Wakana, S., Yoshioka, T., Zhang, W., . . . Mori, S. (2009). Mapping of functional areas in the human cortex based on connectivity through association fibers. *Cerebral Cortex*, *19*, 1889–1895.

Huang, A.L., Chen, X., Hoon, M.A., Chandrashekar, J., Guo, W., Tranker, D., . . . Zucker, C.S. (2006). The cells and logic for mammalian sour taste detection. *Nature*, *442*, 934–938. doi: 10.1038/nature05084.

Huang, H., Coleman, S., Bridge, J. A., Yonkers, K., & Katon, W. (2013). A meta-analysis of the relationship between antidepressant use in pregnancy and the risk of preterm birth and low birth weight. *General Hospital Psychiatry*, published online at prepublication at http://dx.doi.org/10.1016/j.genhosppsych.2013.08.002

Hubbard, E. M., & Ramachandran, V. S. (2005). Neurocognitive mechanisms of synesthesia. *Neuron, 48,* 509–520.

Hubel, D., & Wiesel, T. (1962). Receptive fields, binocular interaction and functional architecture in the cat's visual cortex. *Journal of Physiology of London, 160,* 106–154.

Hubel, D., & Wiesel, T. (1979). Brain mechanisms of vision. *Scientific American, 241,* 130–144.

Hudson, W. (1960). Pictorial depth perception in subcultural groups in Africa. *Journal of Social Psychology, 52,* 183–208.

Huesmann, L. R., Moise-Titus, J., & Podolski, C. (2003). Longitudinal relations between children's exposure to TV violence and their aggressive and violent behavior in young adulthood: 1977–1992. *Developmental Psychology, 39,* 201–221.

Huff, D. (1954). *How to lie with statistics.* New York, NY: Norton.

Hughes, D. J., Furnham, A., & Batey, M. (2013). The structure and personality predictors of self-rated creativity. *Thinking Skills and Creativity, 9,* 76–84. doi: 10.1016/j.tsc.2012.10.001.

Hull, C. L. (1943). *Principles of behavior: An introduction to behavior theory.* New York, NY: Appleton-Century.

Hunter, J. E., & Schmidt, F. L. (2000). Racial and gender bias in ability and achievement tests: Resolving the apparent paradox. *Psychology, Public Policy and Law, 6,* 151–158.

Hurley, D. (2013, November 3). Jumper cables for the mind. *The New York Times Magazine,* 50–53.

Hurvich, L.M. (1981). *Color vision.* Sunderland, MA: Sinauer Associates, Inc.

Huston, A. C., Wright, J. C., Marquis J., & Green S. B. (1999). How young children spend their time: Television and other activities. *Developmental Psychology, 35,* 912–925.

Hutchinson, S., Lee, L. H., Gaab, N., & Schlaug, G. (2003). Cerebellar volume of musicians. *Cerebral Cortex, 13,* 943–949.

Huttenlocher, J., Vasilyeva, M., Cymerman, E., & Levine, S. (2002). Language input at home and at school: Relation to child syntax. *Cognitive Psychology, 45,* 337–374.

Hyde, J. S. (1990). Meta-analysis and the psychology of gender differences. *Signs: Journal of Women in Culture & Society, 16,* 53–73.

Hyde, J. S. (2005). The genetics of sexual orientation. In J. S. Hyde (Ed.), *Biological substrates of human sexuality* (pp. 9–20). Washington, DC: American Psychological Association.

Hyde, K. L., Lerch, J., Norton, A., Forgeard, M., Winner, E., Evans, A. C., & Schlaug, G. (2009). Musical training shapes structural brain development. *Journal of Neuroscience, 29,* 3019–3025.

Hyde, T. S., & Jenkins, J. J. (1973). Recall for words as a function of semantic, graphic, and syntactic orienting tasks. *Journal of Verbal Learning and Verbal Behavior, 12,* 471–480.

Hyman, S. E. (2005). Neurotransmitters. *Current Biology, 15,* R154–R158.

Hysek, C. M., Schmid, Y., Simmler, L., Domes, G., Heinrichs, M., Eisenegger, C., . . . Liechti, M. E. (2013). MDMA enhances emotional empathy and prosocial behavior. *Social Cognitive and Affective Neuroscience,* first published online October 4, 2013. doi: 10.1093/scan/nst161.

I feel I am trapped inside my head, banging against its walls, trying desperately to escape. (1986, March 18). *The New York Times.* Retrieved from http://www.nytimes.com

Iacoboni, M., & Mazziotta, J. C. (2007). Mirror neuron system: Basic findings and clinical applications. *Annals of Neurology, 62,* 213–218.

Iacoboni, M., Woods R. P., Brass, M., Bekkering, H., Mazziotta, J. C., & Rizzolatti, G. (1999). Cortical mechanisms of human imitation. *Science, 286,* 2526–2528.

Iarocci, G., & McDonald, J. (2006). Sensory integration and the perceptual experience of persons with autism. *Journal of Autism and Developmental Disorders, 36,* 77–90.

Ijichi, C., Collins, L. M., & Elwood, R. W. (2013). Pain expression is linked to personality in horses. *Applied Animal Behaviour Science.* doi: 10.1016/j.applanim.2013.12.007.

Ilieva, I., Boland, J., & Farah, M. J. (2013). Objective and subjective cognitive enhancing effects of mixed amphetamine salts in healthy people. *Neuropharmacology, 64,* 496–505. doi: 10.1016/j.neuropharm.2012.07.021.

Inagaki, T. K., & and Eisenberger, N. I. (2013). Shared neural mechanisms underlying social warmth and physical warmth. *Psychological Science. XX,* 1–9. online ahead of print, published on September 18, 2013 as DOI: 10.1177/0956797613492773.

Ironson, G., O'Cleirigh, C., Leserman, J., Stuetzle, R., Fordiani, J., Fletcher, M., & Schneiderman, N. (2013). Gender-specific effects of an augmented written emotional disclosure intervention on posttraumatic, depressive, and HIV-disease-related outcomes: A randomized, controlled trial. *Journal of Consulting and Clinical Psychology, 81,* 284–298. doi: http://dx.doi.org/10.1037/a0030814.

Isacsson, G., Rich, C., Jureidini, J., & Raven, M. (2010). The increased use of antidepressants has contributed to the world-wide reduction in suicide rates. *British Journal of Psychiatry, 196,* 429–433.

Isen, A. M., Daubman, K. A., & Nowicki, G. P. (1987). Positive affect facilitates creative problem solving. *Journal of Personality and Social Psychology, 52,* 1122–1131.

Itri, J., Michel, S., Waschek, J., & Colwell, C. (2004). Circadian rhythm in inhibitory synaptic transmission in the mouse suprachiasmatic nucleus. *Journal of Neurophysiology, 92*(1), 311–319.

Iuculano, T., Rosenberg-Lee, M., Supekar, K., Lynch, C. J., Khouzam, A., Phillips, J., Uddin, L. Q., & Menon, V. (2014). Brain organization underlying superior mathematical abilities in children with autism. *Biological Psychiatry, 75,* 223–230. doi: 10.1016.j.biopsych.2013.06.018.

Iversen, S. D., & Iversen, L. L. (2007). Dopamine: 50 years in perspective. *Trends in Neurosciences, 30,* 188–193.

Izard, C. E. (1969). The emotions and emotion constructs in personality and culture research. In R. B. Cattell (Ed.), *Handbook of modern personality theory.* Chicago, IL: Aldine Press.

Izard, C. E., Trentacosta, C. J., King, K. A., & Mostow, A. J. (2004). An emotion-based prevention program for Head Start children. *Early Education & Development, 15,* 407–422.

Jablensky, A., & Woodbury, M. A. (1995). Dementia praecox and manic-depressive insanity in 1908: A Grade of Membership analysis of the Kraepelinian dichotomy. *European Archives of Psychiatry and Clinical Neuroscience, 245,* 202–209.

Jabr, F. (2013, April 30). New DSM-5 ignores biology of mental Illness. *Scientific American.* Retrieved from http://www.scientificamerican.com/article.cfm?id=new-dsm5-ignores-biology-mental-illness

Jackson, K. M. (2008). Heavy episodic drinking: Determining the predictive utility of five or more drinks. *Psychology of Addictive Behaviors, 22,* 68–77.

Jackson, L. A., von Eye, A., Biocca, F. A., Barbatsis, G., Zhao, Y., & Fitzgerald, H. E. (2006). Does home Internet use influence the academic performance of low-income children? *Developmental Psychology, 42,* 429–435.

Jackson, T., Gao, X., & Chen, H. (2014). Differences in neural activation to depictions of physical exercise and sedentary activity: An fMRI study of overweight and lean Chinese women. *International Journal of Obesity,* advance online publication.

Jacobs, B. L. (2004). Depression: The brain finally gets into the act. *Current Directions in Psychological Science, 13,* 103–106.

Jacobs, B. L., van Praag, H., & Gage, F. H. (2000). Adult brain neurogenesis and psychiatry: A novel theory of depression. *Molecular Psychiatry, 5*, 262–269.

Jacobs, D. R., Jr., Adachi, H., Mulder, I., Kromhout, D., Menotti, A., Nissinen, A., & Blackburn, H. (1999). Cigarette smoking and mortality risk: Twenty-five-year follow-up of the Seven Countries Study. *Archives of Internal Medicine, 159*, 733–740.

Jacobs, G. H., & Nathans, J. (2009). The evolution of primate color vision. *Scientific American, 300*, 56–63.

Jacobs, T. L., Epel, E. S., Lin, J., Blackburn, E. H., Wolkowitz, O. M., Bridwell, D. A., . . . Saron, C. D. (2010). Intensive meditation training, immune cell telomerase activity, and psychological mediators. *Psychoneuroendocrinology.* Published online ahead of print. doi: 10.1016/j.psyneuen.2010.09.010.

Jacobsen, L. K., Krystal, J. H., Mencl, E., Westerveld, M., Frost, S. J., & Pugh, K. R. (2005). Effects of smoking and smoking abstinence on cognition in adolescent tobacco smokers. *Biological Psychiatry, 57*, 56–66.

Jacobson, S., & Jacobson, J. (2000). *Teratogenic insult and neurobehavioral function in infancy and childhood.* Mahwah, NJ: Erlbaum.

Jacoby, L. L., Hessels, S., & Bopp, K. (2001). Proactive and retroactive effects in memory performance: Dissociating recollection and accessibility bias. In H. Roediger, J. S. Nairne, I. Neath, & A. M. Suprenant (Eds.), *The nature of remembering: Essays in honor of Robert G. Crowder* (pp. 35–54). Washington, DC: American Psychological Association.

Jain, S., Dharap, S. B., & Gore, M. A. (2008). Early prediction of outcome in very severe closed head injury. *Injury: International Journal of the Care of the Injured, 39*, 598–603.

James, W. (1884). What is an emotion? *Mind, 9*, 188–205.

Jamison, K. R. (1993). *Touched with fire: Manic-depressive illness and the artistic temperament.* New York, NY: Free Press.

Jamison, K. R., Gerner, R. H., Hammen, C., & Padesky, C. (1980). Clouds and silver linings: Positive experiences associated with primary affective disorders. *American Journal of Psychiatry, 137*, 198–202.

Jan, J. E., Reiter, R. J., Bax, M. C. O., Ribary, U., Freeman, R. D., & Wasdell, M. B. (2010). Long-term sleep disturbances in children: A cause of neuronal loss. *European Journal of Pediatric Neurology, 14*, 380–390.

Janeck, A. S., Calamari, J. E., Riemann, B. C., & Heffelfinger, S. K. (2003). Too much thinking about thinking? Metacognitive differences in obsessive-compulsive disorder. *Journal of Anxiety Disorders, 17*, 181–195.

Janis, I. L. (1983). *Groupthink* (2nd ed., rev.). Boston, MA: Houghton Mifflin.

Jarema, M. (2007). Atypical antipsychotics in the treatment of mood disorders. *Current Opinion in Psychiatry, 21*, 23–29.

Jauk, E., Benedek, M., Dunst, B., & Neubauer, A. C. (2013). The relationship between intelligence and creativity: New support for the threshold hypothesis by means of empirical breakpoint detection. *Intelligence, 41*(4), 212–221. doi: 10.1016/j.intell.2013.03.003.

Javitt, D. C., & Coyle, J. T. (2004). Decoding schizophrenia. *Scientific American, 290*, 48–55.

Jazaieri, H., Jinpa, T., McGonigal, K., Rosenberg, E. L., Finkelstein, J., Simon-Thomas, E., . . . Goldin, P. (2012). Enhancing compassion: A randomized controlled trial of a compassion cultivation training program. *Journal of Happiness Studies.* doi: 10.1007/s10902-012-9373-z.

Jazaieri, H., McGonigal, K., Jinpa, T., Doty, J. R., Gross, J. J., & Goldin, P. (2013). A randomized controlled trial of compassion cultivation training: Effects on mindfulness, affect, and emotion regulation. *Motivation & Emotion.* Published online ahead of print. doi: 10.1007/s11031-013-9368-z.

Jeannerod, M. (1995). Mental imagery in the motor context. *Neuropsychologia, 33*, 1419–1432.

Jenkins, W. M., Merzenich, M. M., Ochs, M. T., Allard, T., & Guic-Roble, E. (1990). Functional reorganization of primary somatosensory cortex in adult owl monkeys after behaviorally controlled tactile stimulation. *Journal of Neurophysiology, 63*, 82–104.

Jennifer Aniston talks about her flying ritual. (2009). Retrieved from http://www.imnotobsessed.com/2009/09/30/jennifer-aniston-talks-about-her-flying-ritual

Jensen, A. R. (1969). How much can we boost IQ and scholastic achievement? *Harvard Educational Review, 39*, 1–23.

Jerison, H. J. (2000). The evolution of intelligence. In R. J. Sternberg (Ed.), *The handbook of intelligence* (pp. 216–244). New York, NY: Cambridge University Press.

Jha, A. P., Krompinger, J., & Baime, M. J. (2007). Mindfulness training modifies subsystems of attention. *Cognitive, Affective, & Behavioral Neuroscience, 7*, 109–119.

Ji, D., & Wilson, M. A. (2007). Coordinated memory replay in the visual cortex and hippocampus during sleep. *Nature Neuroscience, 10*, 100–107.

Ji, Y. G., Hwangbo, H., Yi, J. S., Rau, P. L. P., Fang, X., & Ling, C. (2010). The influence of cultural differences on the use of social network services and the formation of social capital. *International Journal of Human-Computer Interaction, 26*, 1100–1121.

Jiang, M., Green, R. J., Henley, T. B., & Masten, W. G. (2009). Acculturation in relation to the acquisition of a second language. *Journal of Multilingual and Multicultural Development, 30*(6), 481–492.

Jimenez, R. T., Garcia, G. E., & Pearson, P. D. (1994). *The metacognitive strategies of Latina/o students who read Spanish and English.* Center for the Study of Reading, Technical Report No. 601. Urbana-Champaign, IL: College of Education.

Johansen, J. P., Cain, C. K., Ostroff, L. E., & LeDoux, J. E. (2011). Molecular mechanisms of fear learning and memory. *Cell, 147*, 509–524.

Johansson, S. (2013). The talking Neanderthals: What do fossils, genetics, and archeology say? *Biolinguistics, 7*, 35–74.

John, O. P., & Srivastava, S. (1999). The Big Five trait taxonomy: History, measurement, and theoretical perspectives. In L. A. Pervin & O. P. John (Eds.), *Handbook of personality theory and research* (pp. 102–138). New York, NY: Guilford Press.

Johnson, D. P., Penn, D. L., Fredrickson, B. L., Kring, A. M., Meyer, P. S. Catalino, L. I., & Brantley, M. (2011). A pilot study of loving-kindness meditation for the negative symptoms of schizophrenia, *Schizophrenia Research, 129*, 137–140. doi: 10.1016/j.schres.2011.02.015.

Johnson, K. J., Waugh, C. E., & Fredrickson, B. L. (2010). Smile to see the forest: Facially expressed positive emotions broaden cognition. *Cognition & Emotion, 24*, 299–321. doi: 10.1080/02699930903384667.

Johnson, R. E., Fudala, P. J., & Payne, R. (2005). Buprenorphine: Considerations for pain management. *Journal of Pain and Symptom Management, 29*, 297–326.

Johnston, J. C., & McClelland, J. L. (1974). Perception of letters in words: Seek not and ye shall find. *Science, 184*, 1192–1994.

Jokela, M. (2009). Personality predicts migration within and between U.S. States. *Journal of Research in Personality, 43*, 79–83. doi: 10.1016/j.jrp.2008.09.005.

Jokela, M., Hintsa, T., Hintsanen, M., & Keltikangas-Jarvinen, L. (2010). Adult temperament and childbearing over the life course. *European Journal of Personality, 24*, 151–166.

Jones, D. K., Knösche, T. R., & Turner, R. (2012). White matter integrity, fiber count, and other fallacies: The do's and don'ts of diffusion MRI. *NeuroImage, 73*, 239–254. doi: /10.1016/j.neuroimage.2012.06.08.

Jope, R. S. (1999). Anti-bipolar therapy: Mechanism of action of lithium. *Molecular Psychiatry, 4*, 117–128.

Jordahl, T., & Lohman, B. J. (2009). A bioecological analysis of risk and protective factors associated with early sexual intercourse of young adolescents. *Children and Youth Services Review, 31,* 1272–1282.

Joseph, R. (n.d.). Charles Whitman: The amygdala and mass murder. Retrieved from http://BrainMind.com/Case5.html

Josefsson, K., Jokela, M., Cloninger, C., Hintsanen, M., Salo, J., Hintsa, T., . . . Keltikangas-Järvinen, L. (2013). Maturity and change in personality: Developmental trends of temperament and character in adulthood. *Development and Psychopathology, 25*(3), 713–727. doi: 10.1017/S0954579413000126.

Joy, S. P. (2012). Origins of originality: Innovation motivation and intelligence in poetry and comics. *Empirical Studies of the Arts, 30*(2), 195–213. doi: 10.2190/EM.30.2.f.

Judd, T. (2014). Making sense of multitasking: The role of Facebook. *Computers & Education, 70,* 194–202. Retrieved from http://dx.doi.org/10.1016/j.compedu.2013.08.013

Judd, T., & Kennedy, G. (2010). A five-year study of on-campus Internet use by undergraduate biomedical students. *Computers & Education, 55,* 1564–1571.

Juliano, L. M., & Griffiths, R. R. (2004). A critical review of caffeine withdrawal: Empirical validation of symptoms and signs, incidence, severity, and associated features. *Psychopharmacology, 176,* 1–29.

Jump, V. K., Fargo, J. D., & Akers, J. F. (2006). Impact of massage therapy on health outcomes among orphaned infants in Ecuador: Results of a randomized clinical trial. *Family & Community Health, 29,* 314–319.

Junco, R. (2012). In-class multitasking and academic performance. *Computers in Human Behavior, 28,* 2236–2243. Retrieved from http://dx.doi.org/10.1016/j.chb.2012.06.031

Jung, C. G. (1931/1960). The stages of life. In H. Read, M. Fordham, & G. Adler (Eds.) & R. F. C. Hull (Trans.), *The collected works of C. G. Jung* (Vol. 8). New York, NY: Pantheon.

Jung, C. G. (1964). The role of the unconscious. In *Collected works* (Vol. 10, Trans. R. F. C. Hull). New York, NY: Bollingen Foundation. (Originally published 1918)

Jung, C. G. (1960). The stages of life. In H. Read, M. Fordham, & G. Adler (Eds.) & R. F. C. Hull (Trans.), *The collected works of C. G. Jung* (Vol. 8). New York, NY: Pantheon. (Originally published 1931)

Jung, R. E., Gasparovic, C., Chavez, R. S., Flores, R. A., Smith, S. M., Caprihan, A., & Yeo, R. A. (2009). Biochemical support for the "threshold" theory of creativity: A magnetic resonance spectroscopy study. *Journal of Neuroscience, 29,* 5319–5325.

Jung, R. E., & Haier, R. J. (2007). The parieto-frontal integration theory (P-FIT) of intelligence: Converging neuroimaging evidence. *Behavioral and Brain Sciences, 30,* 135–187.

Jung, R. E., Mead, B. S., Carrasco, J., & Flores, R. A. (2013). The structure of creative cognition in the human brain. *Frontiers in Human Neuroscience, 7,* 1–13. doi: 10.3389/fnhum.2013.00330.

Jung, R. E., Segal, J. M., Bockholt, H. J., Flores, R. A., Smith, S. M., Chavez, R. S., & Haier, R. J. (2010). Neuroanatomy of creativity. *Human Brain Mapping, 31,* 398–409.

Jung, Y.-H., Kang, D.-H., Jang, J. H., Park, H. Y., Byun, M. S., Kwon, S. J., . . . Kwon, J. S. (2010). The effects of mind-body training on stress reduction, positive affect, and plasma catecholamines. *Neuroscience Letters, 479,* 138–142.

Jusczyk, P. W. (1997). *The discovery of spoken language.* Cambridge, MA: MIT Press.

Jussim, L., & Harber, K. D. (2005). Teacher expectations and self-fulfilling prophecies: Knowns and unknowns, resolved and unresolved controversies. *Personality and Social Psychology Review, 9,* 131–155.

Just, M. A., Keller, T. A., & Cynkar, J. (2008). A decrease in brain activation associated with driving when listening to someone speak. *Brain Research, 1205,* 70–80.

Juster, R.-P., McEwen, B. S., & Lupien, S. J. (2010). Allostatic load biomarkers of chronic stress and impact on health and cognition. *Neuroscience and Biobehavioral Reviews, 35,* 2–16.

Kabat-Zinn, J. (1990). *Full catastrophe living.* New York, NY: Delta.

Kabat-Zinn, J., Lipworth, L., & Burney, R. (1985). The clinical use of mindfulness meditation for the self-regulation of chronic pain. *Journal of Behavioral Medicine, 8,* 163–190.

Kabat-Zinn, J., Massion, A. O., Kristeller, J., Peterson, L. G., Fletcher, K. E., Pbert, L., . . . Santorelli, S. F. (1992). Effectiveness of a meditation-based stress reduction program in the treatment of anxiety disorders. *American Journal of Psychiatry, 149,* 936–943.

Kabat-Zinn, J., Wheeler, E., Light, T., Skillings, A., Scharf, M. J., Cropley, T. G., . . . Bernhard, J. D. (1998). Influence of a mindfulness meditation-based stress reduction intervention on rates of clearing in patients with moderate to severe psoriasis undergoing phototherapy (UVB) and photochemotherapy (PUVA). *Psychosomatic Medicine, 60,* 625–632.

Kadosh, R. C., & Elliot, P. (2013). Brain stimulation has a long history. *Nature, 500,* 529.

Kagan, J. (2003). Biology, context, and developmental inquiry. *Annual Review of Psychology, 54,* 1–23.

Kahan, T. L. (2001). Consciousness in dreaming. A metacognitive approach. In T. Bulkeley (Ed.), *Dreams: A reader on religious, cultural, and psychological dimensions of dreaming* (pp. 333–360). New York, NY: Palgrave Macmillan.

Kahan, T. L., & LaBerge, S. (1994). Lucid dreaming as metacognitions: Implications for cognitive science. *Consciousness and Cognition, 3,* 246–264.

Kahn, R. S., Khoury, J., Nichols, W. C., & Lanphear, B. P. (2003). Role of dopamine transporter genotype and maternal prenatal smoking in childhood hyperactive-impulsive, inattentive, and oppositional behaviors. *Journal of Pediatrics, 143,* 104–110.

Kahneman, D. (2002). Autobiography—Nobel Prize for 2002 in Economics. Retrieved from http://nobelprize.org/nobel_prizes/economics/laureates/2002/kahneman.html

Kahneman, D., & Tversky, A. (1972). Subjective probability: A judgment of representativeness. *Cognitive Psychology, 3,* 430–454.

Kahneman, D., & Tversky, A. (1979). Prospect theory: An analysis of decision under risk. *Econometrica, 47,* 263–292.

Kahn-Greene, E. T., Killgore, D. B., Kamimori, G. H., Balkin, T. J., & Killgore, W. D. S. (2007). The effects of sleep deprivation on symptoms of psychopathology in healthy adults. *Sleep Medicine, 8,* 215–221.

Kaiser, B., & Bouvard, M. (2009). Obsessive-compulsive disorder in children and adolescents: Efficacy of combined treatment. *Clinical Neuropsychiatry: Journal of Treatment Evaluation, 6,* 94–100.

Kaiser Family Foundation. (2003). *Zero to six: Media use in the lives of infants, toddlers, and preschoolers.* Menlo Park, CA: Author.

Kalat, J. W. (2007). *Biological psychology* (9th ed). Belmont, CA: Wadsworth.

Kales, A., Kales, J. D., Soldatos, C. R., Caldwell, A. B., Charney, D. S., & Martin, E. D. (1980). Nightmares: Clinical characteristics and personality patterns. *American Journal of Psychiatry, 137,* 1197–1201.

Kaliman, P., Parrizas, M., Lalanza, J. F., Camins, A., Escoriheula, R. M., & Pallas, M. (2011). Neurophysiological and epigenetic effects of physical exercise on the aging process. *Ageing Research Reviews, 10,* 475–486. doi: 10.1016/j.arr.2011.05.002.

Kam, C. M., Greenberg, M. T., & Kusché, C. A. (2004). Sustained effects of the PATHS curriculum on the social and psychological adjustment of children in special education. *Journal of Emotional and Behavioral Disorders, 12,* 66–78.

Kaminsky, Z., Petronis, A., Wang, S.-C., Levine, B., Ghaffar, O., Floden, D., & Feinstein, A. (2008). Epigenetics of personality traits: An illustrative study of identical twins discordant for risk-taking behavior. *Twin Research and Human Genetics, 11,* 1–11.

Kammrath, L. K., Mendoza-Denton, R., & Mischel, W. (2005). Incorporating *if . . . then . . .* personality signatures in person perception: Beyond the person-situation dichotomy. *Journal of Personality and Social Psychology, 88*, 605–618.

Kanarek, R. B. (1994). Does sucrose or aspartame cause hyperactivity in children? *Nutrition Reviews, 52*, 173–175.

Kanayama, G., Rogowska, J., Pope, H. G., Gruber, S. A., & Yurgelun-Todd, D. A. (2004). Spatial working memory in heavy cannabis users: A functional magnetic resonance imaging study. *Psychopharmacology, 176*, 239–247.

Kandel, E. R. (2000a). Disorders of thought and volition: Schizophrenia. In E. R. Kandel, J. H. Schwartz, & T. M. Jessell (Eds.), *Principles of neural science* (4th ed., pp. 1188–1208). New York, NY: McGraw-Hill.

Kandel, E. R. (2000b). Nerve cells and behavior. In E. R. Kandel, J. M. Schwartz, & T. M. Jessell (Eds.), *Principles of neural science* (4th ed., pp. 19–35). New York, NY: McGraw-Hill.

Kandel, E. R. (2001). The molecular biology of memory storage: A dialogue between genes and synapses. *Science, 294*, 1030–1038.

Kandel, E. R. (2006). *In search of memory: The emergence of a new science of mind.* New York, NY: Norton.

Kandel, E. R., Kupferman, I., & Iversen, S. (2000). Learning and memory. In E. R. Kandel, J. H. Schwartz, & T. M. Jessell (Eds.), *Principles of neural science* (4th ed., pp. 1227–1246). New York, NY: McGraw-Hill.

Kanner, A. D., Coyne, J. C., Schaefer, C., & Lazarus, R. S. (1981). Comparison of two modes of stress measurement: Daily hassles and uplifts versus major life events. *Journal of Behavioral Medicine, 4*, 1–39.

Kanwisher, N. (2000). Domain specificity in face perception. *Nature Neuroscience, 3*, 759.

Karama, S., Lecours, A. R., Leroux, J.-M., Bourgouin, P., Beaudoin, G., Joubert, S., . . . Beauregard, M. (2002). Areas of brain activation in males and females during viewing of erotic film excerpts. *Human Brain Mapping, 16*, 1–13.

Karatsoreos, I. A., & McEwen, B. S. (2011). Psychobiological allostasis: Resistance, resilience and vulnerability. *Trends in Cognitive Sciences, 15*, 576–584, ISSN 1364-6613. Retrieved from http://dx.doi.org/10.1016/j.tics.2011.10.005

Karni, A., Tanne, D., Rubenstein, B. S., Askenasy, J. J. M., & Sagi, D. (1994). Dependence on REM sleep of overnight improvement of a perceptual skill. *Science, 265*, 679–682.

Karwowski, M., & Gralewski, J. (2013). Threshold hypothesis: Fact or artifact? *Thinking Skills and Creativity, 8*, 25–33. doi: 10.1016/j.tsc.2012.05.003.

Kaufman, A. S. (1979). *Intelligent testing with the WISC-R.* New York, NY: Wiley.

Kaufman, A. S., & Kaufman, N. L. (1983). *K-ABC interpretive manual.* Circle Pines, MN: American Guidance Service. (2nd ed., 2004, KABC-II).

Kaufman, J. C., & Plucker, J. A. (2011). Intelligence and creativity. In R. J. Sternberg, & S. B. Kaufman (Eds.), *The Cambridge handbook of intelligence* (pp. 771–783). Cambridge: Cambridge University Press.

Kaufman, S. B. (2013). *Ungifted: Intelligence redefined.* New York, NY: Basic Books.

Kaul, P., Passafiume, J., Sargent, R. C., & O'Hara, B. F. (2010). Meditation acutely improves psychomotor vigilance, and may decrease sleep need. *Behavioral and Brain Functions, 6*, ArtID47. doi: 10.1186/1744-9081-6-47.

Kaviani, H., Javaheri, F., & Hatami, N. (2011). Mindfulness-based cognitive therapy (MBCT) reduces depression and anxiety induced by real stressful setting in non-clinical population. *International Journal of Psychology and Psychology Therapy, 11*, 285–296.

Kawamura, Y., & Kare, M. R. (1987). *Umami: A basic taste.* New York, NY: Marcel Dekker.

Kay, L. M., & Sherman, S. M. (2007). An argument for an olfactory thalamus. *Trends in Neurosciences, 30*, 47–53.

Kazemi, A., Ehsanpour, S., & Nekoei-Zahraei, N. S. (2012). A randomized trial to promote health belief and to reduce environmental tobacco smoke exposure in pregnant women. *Health Education Research, 27*, 151–159. doi: 10.1093/her/cyr102.

Keeler, R. F. (1983). Naturally occurring teratogens from plants. In R. F. Keeler & A. T. Tu (Eds.), *Handbook of natural toxins: Vol. 1. Plant and fungal toxins* (pp. 161–191). New York, NY: Marcel Dekker.

Keenan, R. M., Jenkins, A. J., Cone, E. J., & Henningfield, J. E. (1994). Smoked and IV nicotine, cocaine and heroin have similar abuse liability. *Journal of Addictive Diseases, 13*, 259–269.

Kegeles, L. S., Abi-Dargham, A., Frankle, W. G., Gil, R., Cooper, T. B., Slifstein, M., . . . Laruelle, M. (2010). Increased synaptic dopamine function in associative regions of the striatum in schizophrenia. *Archives in General Psychiatry, 67*, 231–239.

Kehle, S. (2008). The effectiveness of cognitive behavioral therapy for generalized anxiety disorder in a frontline service setting. *Cognitive Behaviour Therapy, 37*, 1–7. doi: 10.1080/16506070802190262.

Keller, A., Litzelman, K., Wisk, L. E., Maddox, T., Cheng, E. R., Creswell, P. D., & Witt, P. (2012). Does the perception that stress affects health matter? The association with health and mortality. *Health Psychology, 31*, 677. doi: 10.1037/a0026743.

Keller, M. C., Thiessen, D., & Young, R. K. (1996). Mate assortment in dating and married couples. *Personality and Individual Differences, 21*, 217–221.

Kelley, H. H., & Michela, J. L. (1980). Attribution theory and research. *Annual Review of Psychology, 31*, 457–501.

Kellman, P. J., & Arterberry, M. E. (2006). Infant visual perception. In D. Kuhn & R. Siegler (Eds.), *Handbook of child psychology: Vol. 2. Cognition, perception, and language* (6th ed., 109–160). Hoboken, NJ: Wiley.

Kellner, C. H., Knapp, R. G., Petrides, G., Rummans, T. A., Husain, M. M., Rasmussen, K., . . . Fink, M. (2006). Continuation electro-convulsive therapy vs. pharmacotherapy for relapse prevention in major depression. *Archives of General Psychiatry, 63*, 1337–1344.

Keltner, D. (1995). Signs of appeasement: Evidence of distinct displays of embarrassment, amusement, and shame. *Journal of Personality and Social Psychology, 68*, 441–454.

Kempermann, G. (2006). Adult neurogenesis. In P. B. Baltes, P. A. Reuter-Lorenz, & F. Rösler (Eds.), *Lifespan development and the brain: The perspective of biocultural co-constructivism* (pp. 82–107). New York, NY: Cambridge University Press.

Kempermann, G., & Gage, F. H. (1999). Experience-dependent regulation of adult hippocampal neurogenesis: Effects of long-term stimulation and stimulus withdrawal. *Hippocampus, 9*, 321–332.

Kendler, K. S. (2005). "A gene for . . .": The nature of gene action in psychiatric disorders. *American Journal of Psychiatry, 162*, 1243–1252.

Kendler, K. S., Karkowski, L. M., & Prescott, C. A. (1999). Causal relationship between stressful life events and the onset of major depression. *American Journal of Psychiatry, 156*, 837–841.

Kendler, K. S., Kuhn, J. W., Vittum, J., Prescott, C. A., & Riley, B. (2005). The interaction of stressful life events and a serotonin transporter polymorphism in the prediction of episodes of major depression. *Archives of General Psychiatry, 62*, 529–535.

Kendrick, T., Peveler, R., Logworth, L., Baldwin, D., Moore, M., Chatwin, J., . . . Thompson, C. (2006). Cost-effectiveness and cost-utility of tricyclic antidepressants, selective serotonin reuptake inhibitors and lofepramine: Randomized controlled trial. *British Journal of Psychiatry, 188*, 337–345.

Kennedy, J. M., & Juricevic, I. (2006). Blind man draws using diminution in three dimensions. *Psychonomic Bulletin & Review, 13*, 506–509.

Kennedy, S. H., Evans, K. R., Krüger, S., Mayberg, H. S., Meyer, J. H., McCann, S., . . . Vaccarino, F. J. (2001). Changes in regional brain glucose metabolism measured with positron emission tomography after paroxetine treatment of major depression. *American Journal of Psychiatry, 158*, 899–905.

Kenrick, D. T., Griskevicius, V., Neuberg, S. L., & Schaller, M. (2010). Renovating the pyramid of needs: Contemporary extensions built upon ancient foundations. *Perspective on Psychological Science, 5*, 292–314. doi: 10.1177/1745691610369469.

Kensinger, E. A., Garoff-Eaton, R. J., & Schacter, D. L. (2007). How negative emotion enhances the visual specificity of a memory. *Journal of Cognitive Neuroscience, 19*, 1872–1887.

Keppel, R. (2005). *The riverman: Ted Bundy and I hunt for the Green River killer.* New York, NY: Pocket Books.

Keri, S. (2009). Genes for psychosis and creativity: A promoter polymorphism of the *neuregulin 1* gene is related to creativity in people with high intellectual achievement. *Psychological Science, 20*, 1070–1073. doi: 10.1111/j.1467-9280.2009.02398.x.

Kerig, P., & Wenar, C. (2006). *Developmental psychology: From infancy through adolescence* (5th ed.). New York, NY: McGraw-Hill.

Kessler, R. C., Avenevoli, S., McLaughlin, K. A., Greif Green, J., Lakoma, M. D., Pine, D. S., . . . Reis Merikangas, K. (2012). Lifetime comorbidity of DSMIV disorders in the US National Comorbidity Survey Replication Adolescent Supplement (NCSA). *Psychological Medicine, 42*, 1997–2010. doi: 10.1017/S0033291712000025.

Kessler, R. C., Berglund, P., Demler, O., Jin, R., Merikangas, K. R., & Walters, E. E. (2005). Lifetime prevalence and age-of-onset distributions of *DSM-IV* disorders in the National Comorbidity Survey replication. *Archives of General Psychiatry, 62*, 593–602.

Key Learning Community. (n.d.). Retrieved July 13, 2007, from http://www.ncrel.org/sdrs/areas/issues/methods/assment/as7key.htm

Keyes, C. L. M. (2002). The mental health continuum: From languishing to flourishing in life. *Journal of Health and Social Behavior, 43*, 207–222.

Keyes, C. L. M., & Lopez, S. J. (2002). Toward a science of mental health: Positive directions in diagnosis and interventions. In C. R. Snyder & S. J. Lopez (Eds.), *Handbook of positive psychology* (pp. 45–59). Oxford, England: Oxford University Press.

Khandaker, G. M., Dibben, G. R. M., & Jones, P. B. (2012). Prenatal maternal influenza and schizophrenia in offspring: What does this tell us about fetal programming of chronic disease? *Journal of Pediatric Infectious Diseases, 7*, 61–68. doi: 10.3233/JPI-120346.

Khatami, M. (2009). Inflammation, aging, and cancer: Tumoricidal versus tumorigenesis of immunity. *Cell Biochemitry Biophysiology, 55*, 55–79.

Kiecolt-Glaser, J. K., Marucha, P. T., Malarkey, W. B., Mercado, A. M., & Glaser, R. (1995). Slowing of wound healing by psychological stress. *The Lancet, 346*, 1194–1196.

Kihlstrom, J. F. (2005). Dissociative disorders. *Annual Review of Clinical Psychology, 1*, 227–253.

Kim, B., Lee, S., Choi, T., Suh, S., Kim, Y., Yook, K., & Lee, E. H. (2008). Effectiveness of a combined therapy of long-acting injectable risperidone and psychosocial intervention for relapse prevention in patients with schizophrenia. *Clinical Psychopharmacology and Neuroscience, 6*, 31–37.

Kim, H. K. (2005). Can only intelligent people be creative? A meta-analysis. *Journal of Secondary Gifted Education, 16*, 57–66.

Kim, J., & Lee, J. E. (2011). The Facebook paths to happiness: Effects of the number of Facebook friends and self-presentation on subjective well-being. *Cyberpsychology, Behavior and Social Networking, 6*, 359–364.

Kim, K. H. S., Relkin, N. R., Lee, K. M., & Hirsch, J. (1997). Distinct cortical areas associated with native and second languages. *Nature, 388*, 171–174.

Kim, S., & Hasher, L. (2005). The attraction effect in decision making: Superior performance by older adults. *Quarterly Journal of Experimental Psychology, 58A*, 120–133.

Kim, S.-E., Ko, I.-G., Kim, B.-K., Shin, M.-S., Cho, S., Kim, C.-J., . . . Jee, Y.-S. (2010). Treadmill exercise prevents aging-induced failure of memory through an increase in neurogenesis and suppression of apoptosis in rat hippocampus. *Experimental Gerontology, 45*, 357–365.

Kim, Y. (2011). The contribution of social network sites to exposure to political difference: The relationships among SNSs, online political messaging, and exposure to cross-cutting perspectives. *Computers in Human Behavior, 27*, 971–977. http://dx.doi.org/10.1016/j.chb.2010.12.001.

Kim, Y., & Chang, H. (2011). Correlation between attention deficit hyperactivity disorder and sugar consumption, quality of diet, and dietary behavior in school children. *Nutrition Research and Practice, 5*, 236–245. doi: 10.4162/nrp.2011.5.3.236.

Kimball, J. (2003). *Joyce and the early Freudians.* Gainesville: University Press of Florida.

Kimura, D. (2007). "Underrepresentation" or misinterpretation? In S. J. Ceci & W. M. Williams (Eds.), *Why aren't more women in science?: Top researchers debate the evidence* (pp. 39–46). Washington, DC: American Psychological Association.

Kincses, T. Z., Antal, A., Nitsche, M. A., Bartfai, O., & Paulus, W. (2004). Facilitation of probabilistic classification learning by transcranial direct current stimulation of the prefrontal cortex in the human. *Neuropsychologia, 42*(1), 113–117.

King, D. E., Mainous, A. G., III, & Geesey, M. E. (2008). Adopting moderate alcohol consumption in middle age: Subsequent cardiovascular events. *American Journal of Medicine, 121*, 201–206.

King, L. A., & Hicks, J. A. (2012). Positive affect and meaning in life: The intersection of hedonism and eudaimonia. In P. P. Wong (Ed.), *The human quest for meaning: Theories, research, and applications* (2nd ed., pp. 125–141). New York, NY: Routledge/Taylor & Francis Group.

Kinney, D. K., Richards, R., Lowing, P. A., LeBlanc, D., Zimbalist, M. E., & Harlan, P. (2000–2001). Creativity in offspring of schizophrenic and control parents: An adoption study. *Creativity Research Journal, 13*, 17–26.

Kinsey, A. C., Pomeroy, W. B., & Martin, C. E. (1948). *Sexual behavior in the human male.* Philadelphia, PA: Saunders.

Kinsey, A. C., Pomeroy, W. B., Martin, C. E., & Gebhard, P. H. (1953). *Sexual behavior in the human female.* Philadelphia, PA: Saunders.

Kirkham, T. C. (2005). Endocannabinoids in the regulation of appetite and body weight. *Behavioral Pharmacology, 16*, 297–313.

Kirkpatrick, L. A. (2005). *Attachment, evolution, and the psychology of religion.* New York, NY: Guilford Press.

Kirk-Sanchez, N. J., & McGough, E. L. (2013). Physical exercise and cognitive performance in the elderly: Current perspectives. *Clinical Interventions in Aging, 9*, 51–62. Retrieved from http://dx.doi.org/10.2147/CIA.S39506

Kirsch, I., Moore, T. J., Scoboria, A., & Nicholls, S. S. (2002). The emperor's new drugs: An analysis of antidepressant medication data submitted to the U.S. Food and Drug Administration. *Prevention & Treatment, 5*, ArtID23. Retrieved from http://www.journals.apa.org/prevention/volume5/pre0050023a.html

Kirsh, S. J. (2006). Cartoon violence and aggression in youth. *Aggression and Violent Behavior, 11*, 547–557.

Kisilevsky, B. S., Muir, D. W., & Low, J. A. (1992). Maturation of human fetal responses to vibroacoustic stimulation. *Child Development, 63,* 1497–1508.

Klahr, D. (2000). *Exploring science: The cognition and development of discovery processes.* Cambridge, MA: MIT Press.

Klein, D. A., & Miller, A. L. (2011). Dialectical behavior therapy for suicidal adolescents with borderline personality disorder. *Child and Adolescent Psychiatric Clinics of North America, 20*(2), 205–216.

Klein, H. S. (2004). *A population history of the United States.* New York, NY: Cambridge University Press.

Klein, R. G. (1999). *The human career: Human biological and cultural origins* (2nd ed.). Chicago, IL: University of Chicago Press.

Kloosterman, K. (2009, August 13). *Teaching the blind to see through sound.* Retrieved from http://www.israel21c.org/

Klopfer, P. H. (1958). Influence of social interaction on learning rates in birds. *Science, 128,* 903.

Klucharev, V., Hytonen, K., Rijpkema, M., Smidts, A., & Fernandez, G. (2009). Reinforcement learning signal predicts social conformity. *Neuron, 61,* 140–151.

Klüver, H., & Bucy, P. (1939). Preliminary analysis of functioning of the temporal lobes in monkeys. *Archives of Neurology and Psychiatry, 42,* 979–1000.

Knox, R. (2007, April 26). *Kids' use of earbuds worries hearing experts.* Retrieved from http://www.npr.org/templates/story/story.php?storyId=9797364

Kobayashi, M., Saito, S., Kobayakawa, T., Deguchi, Y., & Costanzo, R. M. (2006). Cross-cultural comparison of data using the odor stick identification test for Japanese (OSIT-J). *Chemical Senses, 31,* 335–342.

Koenig, J. I. (2006). Schizophrenia: A unique translational opportunity in behavioral neuroendocrinology. *Hormones and Behavior, 50,* 602–611.

Koerner, K., & Linehan, M. M. (2000). Research on dialectical behavior therapy for patients with borderline personality disorder. *Psychiatric Clinics of North America, 23,* 151–167.

Kogan, A., Impett, E. A., Oveis, C., Hui, B., Gordon, A. M., & Keltner, D. (2010). When giving feels good: The intrinsic benefits of sacrifice in romantic relationships for the communally motivated. *Psychological Science, 21,* 1918–1924. doi: 10.1177/0956797610388815.

Koh, J. S., Kang, H., Choi, S. W., & Kim, H. O. (2002). Cigarette smoking associated with premature facial wrinkling: Image analysis of facial skin replicas. *International Journal of Dermatology, 41,* 21–27.

Kohlberg, L. (1981). *Essays on moral development: Vol. I. The philosophy of moral development.* New York, NY: Harper & Row.

Kohn, P. M., Lafreniere, K., & Gurevich, M. (1991). Hassles, health, and personality. *Journal of Personality and Social Psychology, 61,* 478–482.

Kokko, K., Pulkkinen, L., & Mesiäinen, P. (2009). Timing of parenthood in relation to other life transitions and adult social functioning. *International Journal of Behavioral Development, 33,* 356–365.

Kometer, M., Schmidt, A., Bachmann, R., Studerus, E., Seifritz, E., & Vollenweider, F. X. (2012). Psilocybin biases facial recognition, goal-directed behavior, and mood state toward positive relative to negative emotions through different serotonergic subreceptors. *Biological Psychiatry, 72*(11), 898–906. doi: 10.1016/j.biopsych.2012.04.005.

Kopell, B. H., Rezai, A. R., Chang, J. W., & Vitek, J. L. (2006). Anatomy and physiology of the basal ganglia: Implications for deep brain stimulation for Parkinson's disease. *Movement Disorders, 21,* S238–S246.

Kopta, S. M. (2003). The dose-effect relationship in psychotherapy: A defining achievement for Dr. Kenneth Howard. *Journal of Clinical Psychology, 59,* 727–733.

Korkeila, M., Kaprio, J., Rissanen, A., Koshenvuo, M., & Sorensen, T. L. (1998). Predictors of major weight gain in adult Finns: Stress, life satisfaction and personality traits. *International Journal of Obesity Related Metabolic Disorders, 22*(10), 949–957.

Kornell, N., & Bjork, R. A. (2007). The promise and perils of self-regulated study. *Psychonomic Bulletin & Review, 14,* 219–224.

Kornell, N., Castel, A., Eich, T., & Bjork, R. (2010). Spacing as the friend of both memory and induction in young and older adults. *Psychology and Aging, 25,* 498–503. doi: 10.1037/a0017807.

Kornhaber, M. L., Fierros, E., & Veenema, S. (2004). *Multiple intelligences: Best ideas from research and practice.* Boston, MA: Pearson.

Kosinski, M., Bachrach, Y., Kohli, P., Stillwell, D., & Graepel, T. (2013). Manifestations of user personality in website choice and behaviour on online social networks. *Machine Learning.* doi: 10.1007/s10994-013-5415-y.

Kosinski, M., Stillwell, D., & Graepel, T. (2013). Private traits and attributes are predictable from digital records of human behavior. *Proceedings of the National Academy of Sciences of the United States of America, 110*(15), 5802–5805. doi: 10.1073/pnas.1218772110.

Koslowski, B. (1996). *Theory and evidence: The development of scientific reasoning.* Cambridge, MA: MIT Press.

Kosslyn, S. M. (2002, July 15). What shape are a German shepherd's ears?: A talk with Stephen Kosslyn. *Edge.* Retrieved from http://www.edge.org/3rd_culture/kosslyn/kosslyn_index.html

Kosslyn, S. M. (2005). Mental images and the brain. *Cognitive Neuropsychology, 22,* 333–347.

Kosslyn, S. M., Van Kleeck, M. H., & Kirby, K. N. (1990). A neurologically plausible model of individual differences in visual mental imagery. In P. J. Hampson, D. F. Marks, & J. T. E. Richardson (Eds.), *Imagery: Current developments* (pp. 39–77). Florence, KY: Taylor & Frances/Routledge.

Kottke, J. L., & Sharafinski, C. E. (1988). Measuring perceived supervisory and organizational support. *Educational and Psychological Measurement, 48,* 1075–1079.

Kovács, A. M. (2009). Early bilingualism enhances mechanisms of false-belief reasoning. *Developmental Science, 12,* 48–54.

Kovács, A. M., & Mehler, J. (2009). Flexible learning of multiple speech structures in bilingual infants. *Science, 325,* 611–612. doi: 10.1126/science.1173947.

Kounios, J., Frymiare, J. L., Bowden, E. M., Fleck, J. I., Subramaniam, K., Parrish, T. B., & Jung-Beeman, M. (2006). The prepared mind: Neural activity prior to problem presentation predicts subsequent solution by sudden insight. *Psychological Science, 17,* 882–890.

Kraaj, V., van der Veek, S. M. C., Garnefski, N., Schroevers, M., Witlox, R., & Maes, S. (2008). Coping, goal adjustment, and psychological well-being in HIV-infected men who have sex with men. *AIDS Patient Care and STDs, 22,* 395–402.

Krakauer, J. (1996). *Into thin air.* New York, NY: Anchor Books.

Kral, J. G., Biron, S., Simard, S., Hould, F.-S., & Lebel, S. (2006). Large maternal weight loss from obesity surgery prevents transmission of obesity to children who were followed for 2 to 18 years. *Pediatrics, 118,* e1644–e1649.

Kramarik, A. (2006). *Akiane: Her life, her art, her poetry.* Nashville, TN: W Publishing Group.

Kranczioch, C., Debener, S., Schwarzbach, J., Goebel, R., & Engel, A. K. (2005). Neural correlates of conscious perception in the attentional blink. *NeuroImage, 24,* 704–714.

Kremer, S., Bult, J. H., Mojet, J., & Kroeze, J. H. (2007). Food perception with age and its relationship to pleasantness. *Chemical Senses, 32,* 591–602.

Kristeller, J. L., Baer, R. A., & Quillian-Wolever, R. (2006). Mindfulness-based approaches to eating disorders. In R. A. Baer (Ed.), *Mindfulness-based treatment approaches: Clinician's guide to evidence base and applications* (pp. 75–91). San Diego, CA: Elsevier Academic Press.

Kristjansson, A. L., Sigfusdottir, I. D., James, J. E., Allegrante, J. P., & Helgason, A. R. (2010). Perceived parental reactions and peer respect as predictors of adolescent cigarette smoking and alcohol use. *Addictive Behaviors, 35,* 256–259.

Kristof-Brown, A. L., Zimmerman, R. D., & Johnson, E. C. (2005). Consequences of individuals' fit at work: A meta-analysis of person-job, person-organization, person-group, and person-supervisor fit. *Personnel Psychology, 58,* 281–342.

Kroeber, A. L. (1948). *Anthropology.* New York, NY: Harcourt Brace Jovanovich.

Kröger, C., Schweiger, U., Sipos, V., Arnold, R., Kahl, K. G., Schunert, T., . . . Reinecker, H. (2006). Effectiveness of dialectical behavior therapy for borderline personality disorder in an inpatient setting. *Behaviour Research and Therapy, 44,* 1211–1217.

Krueger, R. F. (1999). Personality traits in late adolescence predict mental disorders in early adulthood: A prospective-epidemiological study. *Journal of Personality, 67,* 39–65.

Krueger, R. F., & Johnson, W. (2008). Behavioral genetics and personality: A new look at the integration of nature and nurture. In O. P. John, R. W. Robins, & L. A. Pervin (Eds.), *Handbook of personality: Theory and research* (pp. 287–310). New York, NY: Guilford Press.

Krummel, D., Seligson F., & Guthrie, H. (1996). Hyperactivity: Is candy causal? *Critical Review of Food Science and Nutrition, 36,* 31–47.

Krystal, A. D. (2005). The effect of insomnia definitions, terminology, and classifications on clinical practice. *Journal of American Geriatrics Society, 53,* S255–S263.

Ku, J., Kim, J., Jang, H., Park, S., Kim, S., Kim, C., . . . Kim, S. I. (2005). Relationship between social response to virtual avatar and symptom severity of patients with schizophrenia. *Annual Review of Cyber-Therapy and Telemedicine, 3,* 3143–3149.

Kübler-Ross, E. (1969). *On death and dying.* New York, NY: Macmillan.

Kubota, M., Nakazaki, S., Hirai, S., Saeki, N., Yamaura, A., & Kusaka, T. (2001). Alcohol consumption and frontal lobe shrinkage: Study of 1432 non-alcoholic subjects. *Journal of Neurology, Neurosurgery, and Psychiatry, 71,* 104–106.

Kubzansky, L. D., Sparrow, D., Vokonas, P., & Kawachi, I. (2001). Is the glass half empty or half full? A prospective study of optimism and coronary heart disease in the Normative Aging Study. *Psychosomatic Medicine, 63,* 910–916.

Kuhl, P. K., & Meltzoff, A. N. (1997). Evolution, nativism, and learning in the development of language and speech. In M. Gopnik (Ed.), *The inheritance and innateness of grammars* (pp. 7–44). New York, NY: Oxford University Press.

Kuhl, P. K., Stevens, E., & Hayashi, A. (2006). Infants show a facilitation effect for native language phonetic perception between 6 and 12 months. *Developmental Science, 9,* F13–F21.

Kuhn, D. (1993). Connecting scientific and informal reasoning. *Merrill-Palmer Quarterly, 39,* 74–103.

Kuhn, D., Amsel, E., & O'Loughlin, M. (1988). *The development of scientific thinking skills.* Orlando, FL: Academic Press.

Kuhn, D., & Pearsall, S. (2000). Developmental origins of scientific thinking. *Journal of cognition and development, 1,* 113–129.

Kulikov, A., & Komarov, I. (2013). Cost-effectiveness of atypical antipsychotics as treatment for patients with bipolar disorder (episodes of mania): A comparison between quetiapine, aripiprazole, olanzapine, risperidone and ziprasidone in the Russian health care. *Value in Health, 16,* A61–A62. doi: 10.1016/j.jval.2013.03.1583.

Kunkel, C. (2009). Schooling built on multiple intelligences. *School Administrator, 66,* 24–25.

Kuo, L. E., Kitlinska, J. B., Tilan, J. U., Li, L., Baker, S. B., Johnson, M. D., . . . Zukowska, Z. (2007). Neuropeptide Y acts directly in the periphery on fat tissue and mediates stress-induced obesity and metabolic syndrome. *Nature Medicine, 13,* 803–811.

Kupferman, I., Kandel, E. R., & Iverson, S. (2000). Motivational and addictive states. In E. R. Kandel, J. H. Schwartz, & T. M. Jessell (Eds.), *Principles of neural science* (4th ed., pp. 998–1013). New York, NY: McGraw-Hill.

Kuriyama, K., Stickgold, R., & Walker, M. P. (2004). Sleep-dependent learning and motor skill complexity. *Learning & Memory, 11,* 705–713.

Kurson, R. (2007). *Crashing through: The true story of risk, adventure and the man who dared to see.* New York, NY: Random House.

Kusché, C. A., & Greenberg, M. T. (1994). *The PATHS Curriculum.* Seattle, WA: Developmental Research and Programs.

Kwon, Y., & Lawson, A. E. (2000). Linking brain growth with the development of scientific reasoning ability and conceptual change during adolescence. *Journal of Research in Science Teaching, 37,* 44–62.

La Precious, H., Ware, C., Mason, J., McGuire, E., Lewis, D. W., Pagano, L., &

Alley, W. (2009, May 2). *The distracted teen-age driver.* Paper presented at Pediatric Academic Societies Annual Meeting, Baltimore, MD.

LaBerge, S. (1985). *Lucid dreaming.* Los Angeles, CA: Tarcher.

Labonte, B., Yerko, V., Gross, J., Mechawar, N., Meany, M. J., Szyf, M., & Ruecki, G. (2012). Differential glucocorticoid receptor exon 1_B, 1_C, and 1_H expression and methylation in suicide completers with a history of childhood abuse. *Biological Psychiatry, 72,* 41–48.

LaFrance, M., Hecht, M. A., & Paluk, B. L. (2003). The contingent smile: A meta-analysis of sex differences in smiling. *Psychological Bulletin, 129,* 305–334.

Lagopoulos, J. (2007). Functional MRI: An overview. *Acta Neuropsychiatrica, 19,* 64–65.

Lai, C. (2013). Gray matter volume in major depressive disorder: A meta-analysis of voxel-based morphometry studies. *Psychiatry Research: Neuroimaging, 211,* 37–46. doi: 10.1016/j.pscychresns.2012.06.006.

Lamb, R. J., Morral, A. R., Kirby, K. C., Iguchi, M. Y., & Galbicka, G. (2004). Shaping smoking cessation using percentile schedules. *Drug and Alcohol Dependence, 76,* 247–259.

Lambracht-Washington, D., & Rosenberg, R. N. (2013). Advances in the development of vaccines for Alzheimer's disease. *Discovery Medicine, 15,* 319–325.

Lamp, R., & Krohn, E. (2001). A longitudinal predictive validity investigation of the SB:FE and K-ABC with at-risk children. *Journal of Psychoeducational Assessment, 19,* 334–349.

Lanciano, T., Curci, A., & Semin, G. R. (2010). The emotional and reconstructive determinants of emotional memories: An experimental approach to flashbulb memory investigation. *Memory, 18,* 473–485.

Landry, R. G. (1973). The relationship of second language learning and verbal creativity. *Modern Language Journal, 57,* 110–113.

Lang, E., Berbaum, K., Faintuch, S., Hatsiopoulou, O., Halsey, N., Li, X., Berbaum, M., . . . Baum, J. (2006). Adjunctive self-hypnotic relaxation for outpatient medical procedures: A prospective randomized trial with women undergoing large core breast biopsy. *Pain, 126,* 155–164.

Lang, P. J., & Bradley, M. M. (2010). Emotion and the motivational brain. *Biological Psychology, 84,* 437–450.

Lange, C. (1992). *The emotions* (I. A. Haupt, Trans.). Baltimore, MD: Williams & Wilkins. (Original work published 1885)

Lange, P. G. (2008). Publicly private and privately public: Social networking on YouTube.

Journal of Computer-Mediated Communication, 13, 361–380.

Langlois, J. H., & Roggman, L. A. (1990). Attractive faces are only average. *Psychological Science, 1,* 115–121.

Langlois, J. H., Roggman, L. A., & Musselman, L. (1994). What is average and what is not average about attractive faces? *Psychological Science, 5,* 214–220.

Lapsley, D. K. (2006). Moral stage theory. In M. Killen & J. G. Smetana (Eds.), *Handbook of moral development* (pp. 37–66). Mahwah, NJ: Erlbaum.

Larson, L., Wu, T., Bailey, D., Gasser, C., Bonitz, V., & Borgen, F. (2010). The role of personality in the selection of a major: With and without vocational self-efficacy and interests. *Journal of Vocational Behavior, 76,* 211–222.

Larsson, J., Larsson, H., & Lichtenstein, P. (2004). Genetic and environmental contributions to stability and change of ADHD symptoms between 8 and 13 years of age: A longitudinal twin study. *Journal of American Academy of Child and Adolescent Psychiatry, 43,* 1267–1275.

Lasagabaster, D. (2000). The effects of three bilingual education models on linguistic creativity. *International Review of Applied Linguistics in Language Teaching, 38,* 213–228.

Laschet, J., Kurcewicz, I., Minier, F., Trottier, S., Khallou-Laschet, J., Louvel, J., . . . Pumain, R. (2007). Dysfunction of GABA-sub(A) receptor glycolysis-dependent modulation in human partial epilepsy. *Proceedings of the National Academy of Sciences, 104*(9), 3472–3477. doi: 10.1073/pnas.0606451104.

Laumann, E., Paik, A., Glasser, D., Kang, J., Wang, T., Levinson, B., . . . Gingell, C. (2006). A cross-national study of subjective sexual well-being among older women and men: Findings from the global study of sexual attitudes and behaviors. *Archives of Sexual Behavior, 35*(2), 145–161. doi: 10.1007/s10508-005-9005-3.

Laureys, S. (2007). Eyes open, brain shut. *Scientific American, 296,* 84–89.

Lauzon, N. M., Bechard, M., Ahmad, T., & Laviolette, S. R. (2013). Supra-normal stimulation of dopamine D$_1$ receptors in the prelimbic cortex blocks behavioral expression of both aversive and rewarding associative memories through a cyclic-AMP-dependent signaling pathway. *Neuropharmacology, 67,* 104–114. doi: 10.1016/j.neuropharm.2012.10.029.

Lavelli, M., & Fogel, A. (2005). Developmental changes in the relationship between the infant's attention and emotion during early face-to-face communication: The 2-month transition. *Developmental Psychology, 41,* 265–280.

Lavie, N. (2007). The role of perceptual load in visual awareness. *Brain Research, 1080,* 91–100.

Lavie, N., Hirst, A., De Fockert, J. W., & Viding, E. (2004). Load theory of selective attention and cognitive control. *Journal of Experimental Psychology: General, 133,* 339–354.

Law, A. J., Lipska, B. K., Weickert, C. S., Hyde, T. M., Straub, R. E., Hahimoto, R., . . . Weinberger, D. R. (2006). Neuregulin 1 transcripts are differentially expressed in schizophrenia and regulated by 5′ SNPs associated with the disease. *Proceedings of the National Academy of Sciences USA, 103,* 6747–6752.

Lawless, H. T., Schlake, S., Smythe, J., Lim, J., Yang, H., Chapman, K., & Bolton, B. (2004). Metallic taste and retronasal smell. *Chemical Senses, 29,* 25–33. doi: 10.1093/chemse/bjh003.

Laxton, A. W., & Lozano, A. M. (2012). Deep brain stimulation for the treatment of Alzheimer disease and dementia. *World Neurosurgery,* S28.e1–S28.e8. doi: 10.1016/j.wneu.2012.06.028.

Lazar, S. W., Kerr, C., Wasserman, R. H., Gray, J. R., Greve, D., Treadway, M. T., . . . Fischl, B. (2005). Meditation experience is associated with increased cortical thickness. *NeuroReport, 216,* 1893–1897.

Lazarus, A. A., & Abramovitz, A. (2004). A multimodal behavioral approach to performance anxiety. *Journal of Clinical Psychology, 60,* 831–840.

Lazarus, R. S. (1991). *Emotion and adaptation.* New York, NY: Oxford University Press.

Lazarus, R. S., & Folkman, S. (1984). *Stress, appraisal, and coping.* New York, NY: Springer.

Lazarus, R. S., Kanner, A. A., & Folkman, S. (1980). Emotions: A cognitive-phenomenological analysis. In R. Plutchik & H. Kellerman (Eds.), *Emotion: Theory, research, and experience: Vol. 1. Theories of emotion* (pp. 189–217). New York, NY: Academic Press.

Leary, M. R. (2007). Motivational and emotional aspects of the self. *Annual Review of Psychology, 58,* 317–344.

Leary, M. R., Kowalski, R. M., Smith, L., & Phillips, S. (2003). Teasing, rejection, and violence: Case studies of the school shootings. *Aggressive Behavior, 29,* 202–214.

Leary, M. R., Twenge, J. M., & Quinlivan, E. (2006). Interpersonal rejection as a determinant of anger and aggression. *Personality and Social Psychology Review, 10,* 111–132.

Le Bars, P. L., Katz, M. M., Berman, N., Itil, T. M., Freedman, A. M., &

Schatzberg, A. F. (1997). A placebo-controlled, double-blind, randomized trial of an extract of ginkgo biloba for dementia. *Journal of the American Medical Association, 278,* 1327–1332.

LeDoux, J. (1996). *The emotional brain: The mysterious underpinnings of emotional life.* New York, NY: Simon & Schuster.

LeDoux, J. (2000). Emotion circuits in the brain. *Annual Review of Neuroscience, 23,* 155–184.

LeDoux, J. (2003). *Synaptic self.* New York, NY: Penguin.

LeDuc, P. A., Caldwell, J. A., & Ruyak, P. S. (2000). The effects of exercise as a countermeasure for fatigue in sleep-deprived aviators. *Military Psychology, 12,* 249–266.

Lee, C., & Chiou, W. (2013). Keep logging in! Experimental evidence showing the relation of affiliation needs to the idea of online social networking. *Cyberpsychology, Behavior, and Social Networking, 16*(6), 419–422.

Lee, C., Therriault, D., & Linderholm, T. (2012). On the cognitive benefits of cultural experience: Exploring the relationship between studying abroad and creative thinking. *Applied Cognitive Psychology, 26*(5), 768–778.

Lee, C. S., & Therriault, D. J. (2011). The cognitive underpinnings of creative thought: A latent variable analysis exploring the roles of intelligence and working memory in three creative thinking processes. *Intelligence, 41,* 306–320. doi: 10.106/j.intell2013.04.008.

Lee, H., Macbeth, A. H., Pagani, J. H., & Young, S. W. (2009). Oxytocin: The great facilitator of life. *Progress in Neurobiology, 88,* 127–151.

Lee, K. A. (2006). Sleep dysfunction in women and its management. *Current Treatment Options in Neurology, 8,* 376–386.

Lemay, E. P., Jr., & Ashmore, R. D. (2004). Reactions to perceived categorization by others during the transition to college: Internalization and self-verification processes. *Group Processes & Intergroup Relations, 7,* 173–187.

Lenhart, A. (2009). *Teens and mobile phones over the past five years: Pew Internet looks back.* Washington, DC: Pew Internet & American Life Project. Retrieved from http://www.pewinternet.org/Reports/2009/14--Teens-and-Mobile-Phones-Data-Memo.aspx

Lenhart, A. (2012, March 19). *Teens, smartphones, and texting.* Retrieved November 12, 2013, from http://pewinternet.org/Reports/2012/Teens-and-smartphones.aspx

Lenhart, A., Purcell, K., Smith, A., & Zickuhr, K. (2010). *Social media and young adults: Social media and mobile Internet use among teens and young adults.* Washington, DC: Pew Internet & American Life Project. Retrieved from http://pewinternet.org/

Reports/2010/Social-Media-and-Young-Adults. aspx

Lenneberg, E. (1967). *The biological foundations of language.* New York, NY: Wiley.

Lennie, P. (2000). Colorvision. In E. R. Kandel, J. H. Schwartz, & T. M. Jessell (Eds.), *Principles of neural science* (4th ed., pp. 572–589). New York, NY: McGraw-Hill.

Lenzenweger, M. F., Lane, M. C., Loranger, A. W., & Kessler, R. C. (2007). *DSM-IV* personality disorders in the National Comorbidity Survey Replication. *Biological Psychiatry, 15,* 553–564.

Lepage, J.-F., & Théoret, H. (2007). The mirror neuron system: Grasping others' actions from birth? *Developmental Science, 10,* 513–523.

Lerner, L. (1996). *The Kennedy women: The saga of an American family.* New York, NY: Random House.

Lesch, K. P., Bengel, D., Heils, A., Sabol, S. Z., Greenburg, B. D., Petri, S., . . . Murphy, D. L. (1996). Association of anxiety-related traits with a polymorphism in the serotonin transporter gene regulatory region. *Science, 274,* 1527–1531. doi: 10.1126/science.274.5292.1527.

Lethbridge-Cejku, M., & Vickerie, J. (2005). Summary health statistics for U.S. adults: National Health Interview Survey, 2003. National Center for Health Statistics, *Vital Health Statistics, 10.*

Letzring, T. D., Edmonds, G. W., & Hampson, S. E. (2014). Personality change at mid-life is associated with changes in self-rated health: Evidence from the Hawaii personality and health cohort. *Personality and Individual Differences, 58,* 60–64. doi: 10.1016/j.paid.2013.10.002.

Leuner, B., Glasper, E. R., & Gould, E. (2010). Sexual experience promotes adult neurogenesis in the hippocampus despite an initial elevation in stress hormones. *PLoS ONE, 5,* 1–8. doi: 10.1371/journal.pone.0011597.

Leuner, B., & Gould, E. (2010). Structural plasticity and hippocampal function. *Annual Review of Psychology, 61,* 111–140.

LeVay, S. (1991). A difference in hypothalamic structure between heterosexual and homosexual men. *Science, 253,* 1034–1037.

LeVay, S., & Hamer, D. (1994). Evidence for a biological influence in male homosexuality. *Scientific American, 270,* 44–49.

Levenson, R. W. (1988). Emotion and the autonomic nervous system: A prospectus for research on autonomic specificity. In H. Wagner (Ed.), *Social psychophysiology and emotion: Theory and clinical applications* (pp. 17–42). London, England: Wiley.

Levenson, R. W. (1994). Human emotion: A functional view. In P. Ekman & R. J. Davidson (Eds.), *The nature of emotion* (pp. 123–126). New York, NY: Oxford University Press.

Levenson, R. W. (2003). Blood, sweat, and fears: The autonomic architecture of emotion. *Annals of the New York Academy of Sciences, 1000,* 348–366.

Levenson, R. W., Carstensen, L. L., & Gottman, J. M. (1994). The influence of age and gender on affect, physiology, and their interactions: A study of long-term marriages. *Journal of Personality and Social Psychology, 67,* 56–68.

Levenson, R. W., Ekman, P., & Friesen, W. V. (1990). Voluntary facial action generates emotion-specific autonomic nervous system activity. *Psychophysiology, 27,* 363–384.

Levenson, R. W., Ekman, P., Heider, K., & Friesen, W. V. (1992). Emotion and autonomic nervous system activity in the Minangkabau of West Sumatra. *Journal of Personality and Social Psychology, 62,* 972–988.

Levy, B., Kuhl, B., & Wagner, A. (2010). The functional neuroimaging of forgetting. In S. Della Sala (Ed.), *Forgetting* (pp. 135–163). New York, NY: Psychology Press.

Levy, D. M., Wobbrock, J. O., Kaszniak, A.W., & Ostergren, M. (2012). The effects of mindfulness meditation training on multitasking in a high-stress information environment. *Proceedings of Graphics Interface (GI '12), Toronto, Ontario, May 28–30, 2012,* 45–52.

Lewin, T. (2009, October 23). No Einstein in your crib? Get a refund. *New York Times online.* Retrieved from http://www.nytimes.com

Lewis, D., & Levitt, P. (2002). Schizophrenia as a disorder of neurodevelopment. *Annual Review of Neuroscience, 25,* 409–432. doi: 10.1146/annurev.neuro.25.11270.142754.

Lewis, G. D., Farrell, L., Wood, M. J., Martinovic, M., Arany, Z., Rowe, G. C., . . . Gerszten, R. E. (2010). Metabolic signatures of exercise in human plasma. *Science Translational Medicine, 2,* 33ra37.

Lewis, K. (2013). The limits of racial prejudice. *Proceedings of the National Academy of the Sciences, 110,* 18814–18819. doi: 10.1073/pnas.1308501110.

Li, H., Liang, A., Guan, F., Fan, R., Chi, L., & Yang, B. (2013). Regular treadmill running improves spatial learning and memory performance in young mice through increased hippocampal neurogenesis and decreased stress. *Brain Research, 1531,* 1–8. Retrieved from http://dx.doi.org/10.1016/j.brainres.2013.07.041

Lidz, J., & Gleitman, L. R. (2004). Argument structure and the child's contribution to language learning. *Trends in Cognitive Sciences, 8,* 157–161.

Lieberman, J. A., Chakos, M., Wu, H., Alvir, J., Hoffman, E., Robinson, D., & Bilder, R. (2001). Longitudinal study of brain morphology in first episodes of schizophrenia. *Biological Psychiatry, 49,* 487–499.

Lieberman, J. A., Stroup, T. S., McEvoy, J. P., Swartz, M. S., Rosenheck, R. A., Perkins, D. O., . . . Hsiao, J. K. (2005). Effectiveness of anti-psychotic drugs in patients with chronic schizophrenia. *New England Journal of Medicine, 353,* 1209–1223.

Liebert, R. M., & Baron, R. A. (1972). Some immediate effects of televised violence on children's behavior. *Developmental Psychology, 6,* 469–475.

Liehr, P., Marcus, M. T., Carroll, D., Granmayeh, L. K., Cron, S. G., & Pennebaker, J. W. (2010). Linguistic analysis to assess the effect of a mindfulness intervention on self-change for adults in substance use recovery. *Substance Abuse, 31,* 79–85.

Lihoreau, M., Brepson, L., & Rivault, C. (2009). The weight of the clan: Even in insects, social isolation can induce a behavioural syndrome. *Behavioural Processes, 82,* 81–84.

Lin, J., Epel, E., & Blackburn, E. (2012). Telomeres and lifestyle factors: Roles in cellular aging. *Mutation Research, 730,* 85–89. doi: 10.1016/j.mrfmmm.2011.08.003.

Lin, K., & Lu, H. (2011). Why people use social networking sites: An empirical study integrating network externalities and motivation theory. *Computers in Human Behavior, 27,* 1152–1161.

Linden, D. E. J. (2006). How psychotherapy changes the brain—The contribution of functional neuroimaging. *Molecular Psychiatry, 11,* 528–538.

Lindgren, K. P., Kaysen, D., Werntz, A. J., Gasser, M. L., & Teachman, B. A. (2013). Wounds that can't be seen: Implicit trauma associations predict posttraumatic stress disorder symptoms. *Journal of Behavior Therapy and Experimental Psychiatry, 44,* 368–375. http://dx.doi.org/10.1016/j.jbtep.2013.03.003.

Lindsay, D. S., Hagen, L., Read, J. D., Wade, K. A., & Garry, M. (2004). True photographs and false memories. *Psychological Science, 15,* 149–154.

Linehan, M. M. (1993). *Skills training manual of treating borderline personality disorder.* New York, NY: Guilford Press.

Linehan, M. M., Armstrong, H. E., Suarez, A., Allmon, D., & Heard, H. L. (1991). Cognitive-behavioral treatment of chronically parasuicidal borderline patients. *Archives of General Psychiatry, 48,* 1060–1064.

Linehan, M. M., Comtois, K. A., Murray, A. M., Brown, M. Z., Gallop, R. J., Heard, H. L., . . . Lindenboim, N. (2006). Two-year randomized controlled trial and follow-up of dialectical behavior therapy vs. therapy by experts for suicidal behaviors and borderline personality disorder. *Archives of General Psychiatry, 63,* 757–766.

Linehan, M. M., Heard, H. L., & Armstrong, H. E. (1993). Naturalistic follow-up of a behavioral treatment for chronically parasuicidal borderline patients. *Archives of General Psychiatry, 50,* 971–974.

Lipkus, I. M., Barefoot, J. C., Williams, R. B., & Siegler, I. C. (1994). Personality measures as predictors of smoking initiation and cessation in the UNC alumni heart study. *Health Psychology, 13,* 149–155.

Lippa, R. (1994). *Introduction to social psychology.* Pacific Grove, CA: Brooks/Cole.

Lipsman, N., Woodside, D. B., Giacobbe, P., Hamani, C., Carter, J. C., Norwood, S. J., Sutandar, K., Staab, R., Elias, G., Lyman, C. H., Smith, G. S., & Lozano, A. M. (2013). Subcallosal cingulate deep brain stimulation for treatment-refractory anorexia nervosa: A phase 1 pilot trial. *The Lancet, 381,*1361–1370.

Lisetti, C., Pozzo, E., Lucas, M., Hernandez, F., Selverman, W., Kurtines, B., & Pasztor, A. (2009). Second Life, bio-sensors, and exposure therapy for anxiety disorders. *Annual Review of CyberTherapy and Telemedicine, 7,* 19–21.

Liu, H., Elliott, S., & Umberson, D. (2009). Marriage in young adulthood. In J. E. Grant & M. N. Potenza (Eds.), *Young adult mental health* (pp. 169–280). New York, NY: Oxford University Press.

Litt, E., (2013). Understanding social network site users' privacy tool use. *Computers in Human Behavior, 29,* 1649–1656. http://dx.doi.org/10.1016/j.chb.2013.01.049.

Locke, J. (1959). *An essay concerning human understanding: Vol. 1.* New York, NY: Dover. (Original work published 1690)

Lockhart, R. S., & Craik, F. I. M. (1990). Levels of processing: A retrospective commentary on a framework for memory research. *Canadian Journal of Psychology, 44,* 77–112.

Lodi-Smith, J., Geise, A., Roberts, B., & Robins, R. (2009). Narrating personality change. *Journal of Personality and Social Psychology, 96,* 679–689.

Loehlin, J. C., McCrae, R. R., Costa, P. T., & John, O. P. (1998). Heritabilities of common and measure specific components of the Big Five personality factors. *Journal of Research in Personality, 32,* 431–453.

Loeser, J. D., & Melzack, R. (1999). Pain: An overview. *The Lancet, 353,* 1607–1609.

Loftus, E. (1996). *Eyewitness testimony.* Cambridge, MA: Harvard University Press.

Loftus, E. (2003). Make-believe memories. *American Psychologist, 58,* 864–873.

Loftus, E. F. (1997). Creating false memories. *Scientific American, 277,* 70–75.

Loftus, E. F., & Pickrell, J. E. (1995). The formation of false memories. *Psychiatric Annuals, 25,* 720–725.

Logothetis, N. K., Pauls, J., Augath, M., Trinath, T., & Oeltermann, A. (2001). Neurophysiological investigation of the basis of the fMRI signal. *Nature, 412,* 150–157.

Long, M. (1990). Maturational constraints on language development. *Studies in Second Language Acquisition, 12,* 251–285.

López-Muñoz, F., Shen, W. W., Pae, C., Moreno, R., Rubio, G., Molina, J. D., Noriega, C., Pérez-Nieto, M. A., Huelves, L., & Álamo, C. (2013). Trends in scientific literature on atypical antipsychotics in South Korea: A bibliometric study. *Psychiatry Investigation, 10,* 8–16. doi: 10.4306/pi.2013.10.1.8.

Lorenc, Z. P., Kenkel, J. M. Fagien, S., Hirmand, H., Nestor, M. S., Sclafani, A. P., Sykes, J. M., & Waldorf, H. A. (2013). A review of OnabotulinumtoxinA (Botox). *Aesthetic Surgery Journal, 33,* 9S–12S, doi: 10.1177/1090820X12474629.

Lorenz, K. (1935). Der Kumpan in der Umwelt des Vogels. *Journal of Ornithology, 83,* 137–215.

Lorenz, K. (1937). The companion in the bird's world. *Auk, 54,* 245–273.

Lovaas, O. I. (1987). Behavioral treatment and normal educational and intellectual functioning in young autistic children. *Journal of Consulting and Clinical Psychology, 55,* 3–9.

Lovell, B., & Wetherell, M. A. (2011). The cost of caregiving: Endocrine and immune implications in elderly and non elderly caregivers. *Neuroscience & Biobehavioral Reviews, 35,* 1342–1352.

Lovett, R. (2005, September 24). Coffee: The demon drink? *New Scientist.* Retrieved online on March 14, 2014 at http://www.newscientist.com/article/mg18725181.700-coffee-the-demon-drink.html

Lowry, C. A., Hale, M. W, Evans, A. K., Keerkens, J., Staub, D. R., Gasser, P. J., & Shekhar, A. (2008). Serotonergic systems, anxiety, and affective disorder focus on the dorsomedial part of the dorsal raphe nucleus. *Annals of the New York Academy of Sciences, 1148,* 86–94.

Lozano, A. M., Mayberg, H. S., & Kennedy, S. H. (2012). Response-deep brain stimulation and depression. *Journal of Neurosurgery, 116*(2), 313.

Lubben, J., & Gironda, M. (1996). Assessing social support networks among older people in the United States. In H. Litwin (Ed.), *The social networks of older people: A cross-national analysis.* London, England: Praeger.

Lubinski, D., & Benbow, C. P. (2006). Study of mathematically precocious youth after 35 years: Uncovering antecedents for the development of math-science expertise.

Perspectives on Psychological Science, 1, 316–345.

Lubinski, D., Benbow, C. P., Webb, R. M., & Bleske-Rechek, A. (2006). Tracking exceptional human capital over two decades. *Psychological Science, 17,* 194–199.

Luborsky, L., Singer, B., & Luborsky, L. (1975). Comparative studies of psychotherapy. *Archives of General Psychiatry, 32,* 995–1008.

Luchins, A. S., & Luchins, E. H. (1970). *Wertheimer's seminars revisited: Problem solving and thinking.* Albany, NY: SUNY Press.

Ludwig, A. M. (1995). *The price of greatness.* New York, NY: Guilford Press.

Lutman, M. E., & Spencer, H. S. (1991). Occupational noise and demographic factors in hearing. *Acta Otolaryngologica, Suppl. 476,* 74–84.

Lutz, A., Slagter, H. A., Rawlings, N. B., Francis, A. D., Greischar, L. L., & Davidson, R. J. (2009). Mental training enhances attentional stability: Neural and behavioral evidence. *Journal of Neuroscience, 29,* 13418–13427.

Luykx, J. J., Boks, M. P. M., Terwindt, A. P. R., Bakker, S., Kahn, R. S., & Ophoff, R. A. (2010). The involvement of GSK3β in bipolar disorder: Integrating evidence from multiple types of genetic studies. *European Neuropsychopharmacology, 20,* 357–368.

Lyketsos, C. G., Targum, S. D., Pendergrass, J. C., & Lozano, A. M. (2012). Deep brain stimulation: A novel strategy for treating Alzheimer's disease. *Innovations in Clinical Neuroscience, 9*(11–12), 10.

Lynn, R. (2006). *Race differences in intelligence: An evolutionary analysis.* Augusta, GA: National Summit.

Lynn, S. J., Lilienfeld, S. O., Merckelbach, H., Giesbrecht, T., & van der Kloet, D. (2012). Dissociation and dissociative disorders: Challenging conventional wisdom. *Current Directions in Psychological Science, 21,* 48–53. doi: 10.1177/0963721411429457.

Lyons, D. E. (2009). The rational continuum of human imitation. In J. A. Pineda (Ed.), *Mirror neuron systems: The role of mirroring processes in social cognition* (pp. 77–103). Totowa, NJ: Humana Press.

Lyons, D. M., Buckmaster, P. S., Lee, A. G., Wu, C., Mitra, R., Duffey, L. M., . . . Schatzberg, A. F. (2010). Stress coping stimulates hippocampal neurogenesis in adult monkeys. *Proceedings of the National Academy of Sciences, 107,* 14823–14827.

Ma, X., Hou, X., Edgecombe, G. D., & Strausfeld, N. J. (2012). Complex brain and optic lobes in an early Cambrian arthropod. *Nature, 490*(7419), 258–261. doi:10.1038/nature11495.

Maas, J. (1998). *Power sleep*. New York, NY: Villard.

Macaskill, M. (2008, February 10). Blind taught to "see" like a bat. *The Sunday Times*. Retrieved from http://www.timesonline.co.uk

Maccoby, E. E. (2000). Perspectives on gender development. *International Journal of Behavioral Development, 24*, 398–406.

Maccoby, E. E., & Jacklin, C. N. (1974). *The psychology of sex differences*. Stanford, CA: Stanford University Press.

Maccoby, E. E., & Jacklin, C. N. (1987). Gender segregation in childhood. In H. Reese (Ed.), *Advances in child behavior and development*. New York, NY: Academic Press.

MacDonald, G., Kingsbury, R., & Shaw, S. (2005). *Adding insult to injury: Social pain theory and response to social exclusion*. New York, NY: Psychology Press.

MacDonald, G., & Leary, M. R. (2005). Why does social exclusion hurt? The relationship between social and physical pain. *Psychological Bulletin, 131*, 202–223.

MacKinnon, D. W. (1970). Creativity: A multi-faceted phenomenon. In J. Roslansky (Ed.), *Creativity* (pp. 19–32). Amsterdam, Netherlands: North-Holland.

MacLane, C. N., & Walmsley, P. T. (2010). Reducing counterproductive work behavior through employee selection. *Human Resource Management Review, 20*, 62–72.

MacLean, K. A., Ferrer, E., Aichele, S., Bridwell, D. A., King, B. G., Jacobs, T. L., . . . Saron, C. D. (2010). Intensive meditation training leads to improvements in perceptual discrimination and sustained attention. *Psychological Science, 21*, 829–839.

MacLean, K. A., Johnson, M. W., & Griffiths, R. R. (2011). Mystical experiences occasioned by the hallucinogen psilocybin lead to increases in the personality domain of openness. *Journal of Psychopharmacology, 255*, 1453–1461. doi: 10.1177/0269881111420188.

Macmillan, M. (2000). *An odd kind of fame: Stories of Phineas Gage*. Cambridge, MA: MIT Press.

MacWhinney, B. (1999). *The emergence of language*. Mahwah, NJ: Erlbaum.

Madden, M., & Lenhart, A. (2006). *Online dating*. Washington, DC: Pew Internet & American Life Project. Retrieved from http://www.pewtrusts.org/uploadedFiles/wwwpewtrustsorg/Reports/Society_and_the_Internet/PIP_Online_Dating_0306.pdf

Madden, M., Lenhart, A., Cortesi, S., Gasser, U., Duggan, M., Smith, A., & Beaton, M. (2013, May 21). *Teens, social media, and privacy*. Retrieved November 16, 2013, from http://www.pewinternet.org/Reports/2013/Teens-Social-Media-And-Privacy/Main-Report/Part-1.aspx

Maddi, S. R., Matthews, M. D., Kelly, D. R., Villarreal, B., & White, M. (2012). The role of hardiness and grit in predicting performance and retention of USMA cadets. *Military Psychology, 24*(1), 19–28. doi: 10.1080/08995605.2012.639672.

Madigan, S., & O'Hara, R. (1992). Short-term memory at the turn of the century: Mary Whiton Calkins's memory research. *American Psychologist, 47*, 170–174.

Maes, H. M. M., Neale, M. C., & Eaves, L. J. (1997). Genetic and environmental factors in relative body weight and human adiposity. *Behavior Genetics, 27*, 325–351.

Maestripieri, D., Higley, J. D., Lindell, S. G., Newman, T. K., McCormack, K. M., & Sanchez, M. M. (2006). Early maternal rejection affects the development of monoaminergic systems and adult abusive parenting in rhesus macaques (*Macaca mulatto*). *Behavioral Neuroscience, 120*, 1017–1024.

Maguire, E. A., Woollett, K., & Spiers, H. J. (2006). London taxi drivers and bus drivers: A structural MRI and neuropsychological analysis. *Hippocampus, 16*, 1091–1101.

Maier, N. R. F. (1931). Reasoning in humans: II. The solution of a problem and its appearance. *Journal of Comparative and Physiological Psychology, 12*, 181–194.

Main, M., & Hesse, E. (1990). Lack of resolution of mourning in adulthood and its relationship to infant disorganization: Some speculations regarding causal mechanisms. In M. Greenberg, D. Cicchetti, & E. M. Cummings (Eds.), *Attachment in the preschool years* (pp. 161–184). Chicago, IL: University of Chicago Press.

Main, M., & Solomon, J. (1990). Procedures for identifying infants as disorganized/disoriented during the Ainsworth Strange Situation. In M. Greenberg, D. Cicchetti, & E. M. Cummings (Eds.), *Attachment in the preschool years* (pp. 121–160). Chicago, IL: University of Chicago Press.

Mainieri, A. G., Heim, S., Straube, B., Binkofski, F., & Kircher, T. (2013). Differential role of the mentalizing and the mirror neuron system in the imitation of communicative gestures, *NeuroImage, 81*, 294–305. Retrieved from http://dx.doi.org/10.1016/j.neuroimage.2013.05.021

Malberg, J. E., Eisch, A. J., Nestler, E. J., & Duman, R. S. (2000). Chronic antidepressant treatment increases neurogenesis in adult rat hippocampus. *Journal of Neuroscience, 20*, 9104–9110.

Malhi, G. S., Adams, D., & Berk, M. (2010). The pharmacological treatment of bipolar disorder in primary care. *Medical Journal of Australia, 193*, S24–S30.

Mamidala, M. P., Polinedi, A., Kumar, P., Rajesh, N., Vallamkonda, O. R., Udani, V., Singhal, N., & Rajesh, V. (2013). Prenatal, perinatal and neonatal risk factors of autism spectrum disorder: A comprehensive epidemiological assessment from India. *Research in Developmental Disabilities, 34*, 3004–3013. doi: 10.1016/j.bbr.2011.03.031.

Maner, J. K., Miller, S. L., Schmidt, N. B., & Eckel, L. A. (2010). The endocrinology of exclusion: Rejection elicits motivationally tuned changes in progesterone. *Psychological Science, 21*, 581–588.

Mangels, J. A., Gershberg, F. B., Shimamura, A. P., & Knight, R. T. (1996). Impaired retrieval from remote memory in patients with frontal lobe damage. *Neuropsychology, 10*, 32–41.

Mangialasche, F., Solomon, A., Winblad, B., Mecocci, P., & Kivipelto, M. (2010). Alzheimer's disease: Clinical trials and drug development. *Lancet Neurology, 9*, 702–716.

Mann, T., Tomiyama, A. J., Westling, E., Lew, A.-M., Samuels, B., & Chatman, J. (2007). Medicare's search for effective obesity treatments: Diets are not the answer. *American Psychologist, 62*, 220–233.

Mantler, T. (2013). A systematic review of smoking youths' perceptions of addiction and health risks associated with smoking: Utilizing the framework of the health belief model. *Addiction Research & Theory, 21*, 306–317. Retrieved from http://search.proquest.com/docview/1411060670?accountid=14505

The many facets of Facebook. (2011, January 1). *San Francisco Chronicle*, D-1.

Marais, L., Stein, D. J., & Daniels, W. M. U. (2009). Exercise increases BDNF levels in the striatum and decreases depressive-like behavior in chronically stressed rats. *Metabolic Brain Disease, 24*, 587–597.

Marcus, B., Machilek, F., & Schütz, A. (2006). Personality in cyberspace: Personal web sites as media for personality expressions and impressions. *Journal of Personality and Social Psychology, 90*, 1014–1031.

Marek, G. J., & Aghajanian, G. K. (1996). LSD and the phenethylamine hallucinogen DOI are potent partial agonists at 5-HT2A receptors on interneurons in the rat piriform cortex. *Journal of Pharmacology and Experimental Therapeutics, 278*, 1373–1382.

Marijuana research. (2004, December 8). [Editorial]. *Scientific American, 291*, 8.

Marin, O. (2012). Interneuron dysfunction in psychiatric disorders. *Nature Reviews Neuroscience, 13*, 107–120. doi: 10.1038/nrn3155.

Mark, G., Gudith, D., & Klocke, U. (2008). The cost of interrupted work: More speed and stress. *CHI '08: Proceeding of the twenty-sixth annual SIGCHI conference on human factors in computing systems*. New York, NY: ACM.

Marks, B. L., Madden, D. J., Burcur, B., Provenzale, J. M., White, L. E., Cabeza, R., & Huettel, S. A. (2007). Role of aerobic fitness and aging in cerebral white matter integrity. *Annals of the New York Academy of Sciences, 1097,* 171–174.

Marks, R. (2006). *The superlative, sensitive shark.* Retrieved from http://www.pbs.org/kqed/oceanadventures/episodes/sharks/indepth-senses.html

Markus, H., & Kitayama, S. (1991). Culture and the self: Implications for cognition, emotion, and motivation. *Psychological Review, 98,* 224–253.

Maron, E., Hettema, J. M., & Shlik, J. (2010). Advances in molecular genetics of panic disorder. *Molecular Psychiatry, 15,* 681–701.

Marsh, A. A., Yu, H. H., Pine, D. S., & Blair, R. J. R. (2010). Oxytocin improves specific recognition of positive facial expressions. *Psychopharmacology, 209,* 225–232.

Marshall, L., Molle, M., Hallschmid, M., & Born, J. (2004). Transcranial direct current stimulation during sleep improves declarative memory. *Journal of Neuroscience, 24*(44), 9985–9992.

Martindale, C. (1999). Biological bases of creativity. In R. J. Sternberg (Ed.), *Handbook of creativity* (pp. 137–152). Cambridge, England: Cambridge University Press.

Martindale, C. (2005, October 2). One face, one neuron. *Scientific American, 293,* 22–23.

Martinez, G., Daniels, K., & Chandra, A. (2012, April 12). *Fertility of men and women aged 15–44 years in the United States: National Survey of Family Growth, 2006–2010.* Retrieved November 16, 2013, from http://www.cdc.gov/nchs/data/nhsr/nhsr051.pdf

Maschi, S., Clavenna, A., Campi, R., Schiavetti, B., Bernat, M., & Bonati, M. (2008). Neonatal outcome following pregnancy exposure to antidepressants: A prospective controlled cohort study. *BJOG—An International Journal of Obstetrics and Gynaecology, 115,* 283–289.

Mash, E. J., & Wolf, D. A. (2010). *Abnormal child psychology* (4th ed.). Belmont, CA: Wadsworth.

Mashour, G. A., Walker, E. E., & Martuza, R. L. (2005). Psychosurgery: Past, present, and future. *Brain Research Reviews, 48,* 409–419.

Masling, J. M., & Bornstein, R. F. (2005). *Scoring the Rorschach: Retrospect and prospect.* Mahwah, NJ: Erlbaum.

Maslow, A. (1968). *Toward a psychology of being* (2nd ed.). New York, NY: Van Nostrand.

Maslow, A. (1970). *Motivation and personality* (2nd ed.). New York, NY: Harper & Row.

Mason, J. W. (1971). A re-evaluation of the concept of "non-specificity" in stress theory. *Journal of Psychiatric Research, 8,* 323–333.

Mason, J. W. (1975). A historical view of the stress field. *Journal of Human Stress, 1,* 6–12.

Masten, C. L., Eisenberger, N. I., Borofsky, L. A., Pfeifer, J. H., McNealy, K., Mazziotta, J. C., & Dapretto, M. (2009). Neural correlates of social exclusion during adolescence: Understanding the distress of peer rejection. *Social Cognitive Affective Neuroscience, 4,* 143–157. doi: 10.1093/scan/nsp007.

Masters, J., & Barr, S. (2010). Young children online: E-learning in a social networking context. *Knowledge Management & E-Learning: An International Journal, 1,* 295–304.

Masters, W. H., & Johnson, V. E. (1966). *The human sexual response.* Boston, MA: Little & Brown.

Masters, W. H., Johnson, V. E., & Kolodny, R. C. (1986). *Masters and Johnson on sex and human loving.* Boston, MA: Little & Brown.

Masuda, A., & Wendell, J. W. (2010). Mindfulness mediates the relation between disordered eating–related cognitions and psychological distress. *Eating Behaviors, 11,* 293–296.

Masuda, T., & Nisbett, R. E. (2001). Attending holistically versus analytically: Comparing the context sensitivity of Japanese and Americans. *Journal of Personality and Social Psychology, 81,* 922–934.

Mateo, Y., Budygin, E. A., John, C. E., & Jones, S. R. (2004). Role of serotonin in cocaine effects in mice with reduced dopamine transporter function. *Proceedings of the National Academy of Sciences, 101,* 372–377.

Mathiak, K., & Weber, R. (2006). Toward brain correlates of natural behavior: fMRI during violent video games. *Human Brain Mapping, 27,* 948–956.

Mathias, J. L., & Wheaton, P. (2007). Changes in attention and information-processing speed following severe traumatic brain injury: A meta-analytic review. *Neuropsychology, 21,* 212–223.

Mathiesen, B. B., Förster, P. L. V., & Svendsen, H. A. (2004). Affect regulation and loss of initiative in a case of orbitofrontal injury. *Neuropsychoanalysis, 6,* 47–62.

Maticka-Tyndale, E., Harold, E. S., & Opperman, M. (2003). Casual sex among Australian schoolies. *Journal of Sex Research, 40,* 158–169.

Matson, J. L., & Boisjoli, J. A. (2009). The token economy for children with intellectual disability and/or autism: A review. *Research in Developmental Disabilities, 30,* 240–248.

Matson, J. L., Turygin, N. C., Beighley, J., Rieske, R., Tureck, K., & Matson, M. L. (2012). Applied behavior analysis in autism spectrum disorders: Recent developments, strengths, and pitfalls. *Research in Autism Spectrum Disorders, 6,* 144–150. Retrieved from http://dx.doi.org/10.1016/j.rasd.2011.03.014

Matsumoto, D., & Juang, L. (2004). *Culture and psychology* (3rd ed.). Belmont, CA: Thomson-Wadsworth.

Matsumoto, D., & Willingham, B. (2006). The thrill of victory and the agony of defeat: Spontaneous expressions of medal winners of the 2004 Athens Olympic Games. *Journal of Personality and Social Psychology, 91,* 568–581.

Matsumoto, D., Yoo, S. H., & Fontaine, J. (2008). Mapping expressive differences around the world: The relationship between emotional display rules and invidualism versus collectivism. *Journal of Cross-Cultural Psychology, 39,* 55–74. doi: 10.1177/0022022107311854.

Matthews, K. A., Glass, D. C., Rosenman, R. H., & Bortner, R. W. (1977). Competitive drive, Pattern A, and coronary heart disease: A further analysis of some data from the Western Collaborative Group Study. *Journal of Chronic Diseases, 30,* 489–498.

Mauss, I. B., Levenson, R. W., McCarter, L., Wilhelm, F. H., & Gross, J. J. (2005). The tie that binds? Coherence among emotion experience, behavior, and physiology. *Emotion, 5,* 175–190.

Max, J. E., Levin, H. S., Schachar, R. J., Landis, J., Saunders, A. E., Ewing-Cobbs, L., . . . Dennis, M. (2006). Predictors of personality change due to traumatic brain injury in children and adolescents six to twenty-four months after injury. *Journal of Neuropsychiatry and Clinical Neurosciences, 18,* 21–32. doi: 10.1176/appi.neuropsych.18.1.21.

Max, J. E., Robertson, B. A. M., & Lansing, A. E. (2001). The phenomenology of personality change due to traumatic brain injury in children and adolescents. *Journal of Neuropsychiatry and Clinical Neurosciences, 13,* 161–170.

Maximova, K., McGrath, J. J., Barnett, T., O'Loughlin, J., Paradis, G., & Lambert, M. (2008). Do you see what I see? Weight status misperception and exposure to obesity among children and adolescents. *International Journal of Obesity, 32,* 1008–1015.

May, P. A., & Gossage, J. P. (2001). Estimating the prevalence of fetal alcohol syndrome. A summary. *Alcohol Research & Health, 25,* 159–167.

Mayberg, H. S. (1997). Limbic-cortical dysregulation: A proposed model of depression. *Journal of Neuropsychiatry and Clinical Neuroscience, 9,* 471–481.

Mayberg, H. S. (2003). Modulating dysfunctional limbic-cortical circuits in depression: Towards development of brain-based algorithms for diagnosis and optimized treatment. *British Medical Bulletin, 65,* 193–207.

Mayberg, H. S. (2009). Targeted electrode-based modulation of neural circuits for depression. *Journal of Clinical Investigation, 119,* 717–725.

Mayberg, H. S., Liotti, M., Brannan, S. K., McGinnis, S., Mahurin, R. K., Jerabek, P. A., . . . Fox, P. T. (1999). Reciprocal limbic-cortical function and negative mood: Converging PET findings in depression and normal sadness. *American Journal of Psychiatry, 156,* 675–682.

Mayberg, H. S., Lozano, A. M., Voon, V., McNeely, H. E., Seminowicz, D., Hamani, C., . . . (2005). Deep brain stimulation for treatment-resistant depression. *Neuron, 45,* 651–660.

Mayer, J. D., Salovey, P., Caruso, D. R., & Sitarenios, G. (2003). Measuring emotional intelligence with MSCEIT V.2.0. *Emotion, 3,* 97–105.

Mayer, M. (2004). Structure and function of glutamate receptors in the brain. *Annals of the New York Academy of Sciences, 1038,* 125–130.

McArdle, J. J., & Prindle, J. J. (2008). A latent change score analysis of a randomized clinical trial in reasoning training. *Psychology and Aging, 23,* 702–719.

McCabe, C., & Rolls, E. T. (2007). Umami: A delicious flavor formed by convergence of taste and olfactory pathways in the human brain. *European Journal of Neuroscience, 25,* 1855–1864.

McClain, C. S., Rosenfeld, B., & Breitbart, W. (2003). Effect of spiritual well-being on end-of-life despair in terminally-ill cancer patients. *The Lancet, 361,* 1603–1607.

McClelland, D. C. (1985). How motives, skills, and values determine what people do. *American Psychologist, 40,* 812–825.

McClelland, J. L. (1988). Connectionist models and psychological evidence. *Journal of Memory and Language, 27,* 107–123.

McClelland, J. L., & Rogers, T. (2003). The parallel distributed processing approach to semantic knowledge. *Nature Reviews Neuroscience, 44,* 310–322.

McClelland, J. L., & Rumelhart, D. (1985). Distributed memory and the representation of general and specific information. *Journal of Experimental Psychology: General, 114,* 159–188.

McCrae, R. R. (2002). NEO-PI-R data from 36 cultures: Further intercultural comparisons. In R. R. McCrae & J. Allik (Eds.), *The Five-Factor Model of personality across cultures* (pp. 105–125). New York, NY: Kluwer Academic/Plenum.

McCrae, R. R., & Allik, J. (Eds.). (2002). *The Five-Factor Model of personality across cultures.* New York, NY: Kluwer Academic/Plenum.

McCrae, R. R., & Costa, P. T. (1996). Toward a new generation of personality theories: Theoretical contexts for the Five-Factor Model. In J. S. Wiggins (Ed.), *The Five-Factor Model of personality: Theoretical perspectives* (pp. 51–87). New York, NY: Guilford Press.

McCrae, R. R., & Costa, P. T. (1997). Personality trait structure as a human universal. *American Psychologist, 52,* 509–516.

McCrae, R. R., & Costa, P. T. (1999). A five-factor theory of personality. In L. A. Pervin & O. P. John (Eds.), *Handbook of personality theory and research* (pp. 139–153). New York, NY: Guilford Press.

McCrae, R. R., & Costa, P. T. (2003). *Personality in adulthood: A five-factor theory perspective* (2nd ed.). New York, NY: Guilford.

McCrae, R. R., & Costa, P. T., Jr. (2008). The five-factor theory of personality. In O. P. John, R. W. Robins, & L. A. Pervin (Eds.), *Handbook of personality: Theory and research* (pp. 159–181). New York, NY: Guilford Press.

McCrae, R. R., Terracciano, A., De Fruyt, F., De Bolle, M., Gelfand, M. J., & Costa, P. T., Jr. (2010). The validity and structure of culture-level personality scores: Data from ratings of young adolescents. *Journal of Personality, 78,* 815–838.

McDaniel, M. A. (2005). Big-brained people are smarter: A meta-analysis of the relationship between in vivo brain volume and intelligence. *Intelligence, 33*(4), 337–346. doi: 10.1016/j.intell.2004.11.005.

McEvoy, J. P., Lieberman, J. A., Stroup, T. S., Davis, S. M., Meltzer, H. Y., Rosenheck, R. A., . . . Hsiao, J. K. (2006). Effectiveness of clozapine versus olanzapine, quetiapine, and risperidone in patients with chronic schizophrenia who did not respond to prior atypical antipsychotic treatment. *American Journal of Psychiatry, 163,* 600–610. doi: 10.1176/appi.ajp.163.4.600.

McEwen, B S. (2005). Glucocorticoids, depression, and mood disorders: Structural remodeling in the brain. *Metabolism, 54,* 20–23.

McEwen, B. S., De Kloet, E. R., & Rostene, W. (1986). Adrenal steroid receptors and actions in the nervous system. *Physiological Review, 66,* 1121–1188.

McGaugh, J. L. (2000). Memory—A century of consolidation. *Science, 287,* 248–251.

McGenney, B. E. (2012). Cannabinoids and hallucinogens for headache. *Headache, 53,* 447–458. doi: 10.1111/head.12025.

McGowan, P. O. (2012). Epigenetic clues to the biological embedding of early life adversity. *Biological Psychiatry, 72,* 4–5. doi: 10.1016/j.biopsych.2012.04.017.

McKenna, B. S., Meloy, M. J., Wetherell, L., Stricker, J., & Drummond, S. P. A. (in press). Change in neural networks following total sleep deprivation and recovery sleep. *Sleep.*

McKinley, M., Cairns, M., Denton, D., Egan, G., Mathai, M., Uschakov, A., . . . Oldfield, B. J. (2004). Physiological and pathophysiological influences on thirst. *Physiology & Behavior, 81*(5), 795–803. doi: 10.1016/j.physbeh.2004.04.055.

McLay, R. N, Graap, K., Spira, J., Perlman, K., Johnston, S., Rothbaum, B. O., . . . Rizzo, A. (2012). Development and testing of virtual reality exposure therapy for post-traumatic stress disorder in active duty service members who served in Iraq and Afghanistan. *Military Medicine, 177,* 635–642.

McLay, R. N., McBrien, C., Wiederhold, M. D., & Wiederhold, B. K. (2010). Exposure therapy with and without virtual reality to treat PTSD while in combat theater: A parallel case series. *Cyberpsychology, Behavior, and Social Networking, 13,* 37–42. doi: 10.1089/cyber.2009.0346.

McTiernan, A. (2005). Obesity and cancer: The risks, science, and potential management strategies. *Oncology (Williston Park), 19,* 871–881.

Meaney, M. J. (2010). Epigenetics and the biological definition of gene [H11003] environment interactions. *Child Development, 81,* 41–79.

Mechelli, A., Crinion, J. T., Noppeney, U., O'Doherty, J., Ashburner, J., Frackowiak, R. S., & Price, C. J. (2004). Neurolinguistics: Structural plasticity in the bilingual brain. *Nature, 431,* 757. doi: 10.1038/431757a.

Mechtcheriakov, S., Brenneis, B., Koppelstaetter, F., Schocke, M., & Marksteiner, J. (2007). A widespread distinct pattern of cerebral atrophy in patients with alcohol addiction revealed by voxel-based morphometry. *Journal of Neurology, Neurosurgery, and Psychiatry, 78,* 610–614.

Medina, A. E., & Krahe, T. E. (2008). Neocortical plasticity deficits in fetal alcohol spectrum disorders: Lessons from barrel and visual cortex. *Journal of Neuroscience Research, 86,* 256–263.

Mednick, S. A., & Mednick, M. T. (1967). *Remote Associates Test: Experimenter's manual.* Boston, MA: Houghton Mifflin.

Mednick, S. C., & Ehman, M. (2006). *Take a nap! Change your life.* New York, NY: Workman.

Mednick, S. C., Makovski, T., Cai, D. J., & Jiang, Y. V. (2009). Sleep and rest facilitate implicit memory in a visual search task. *Vision Research, 49,* 2557–2565.

Mednick, S. C., Nakayama, K., & Stickgold, R. (2003). Sleep-dependent learning: A nap is as good as a night. *Nature Neuroscience, 6,* 697–698.

Medvec, V., Madey, S., & Gilovich, T. (1995, October). When less is more: Counterfactual thinking and satisfaction among Olympic medalists. *Journal of Personality and Social Psychology, 69*(4), 603–610.

Megan Fox makes 10 celebrities with OCD. (n.d.). Retrieved from http://abcnews.go.com/Entertainment/Media/celebrities-obsessive-compulsive-disorders-hollywood-stars-ocd/story?id=10689626&page=4

Mehta, M. A., Sahakian, B. J., & Robbins, T. W. (2001). Comparative psychopharmacology of methylphenidate and related drugs in human volunteers, patients with ADHD, and experimental animals. In M.V. Solanto, A.F.T Arnsten, & F.X Castellanos (Eds.), *Stimulant drugs and ADHD: Basic and clinical neuroscience* (pp. 303–311). New York, NY: Oxford University Press.

Mei, L., & Xiong, W.-C. (2008). Neuregulin 1 in neural development, synaptic plasticity and schizophrenia. *Nature Reviews Neuroscience, 9,* 437–452.

Melis, A. P., & Semmann, D. (2010). How is human cooperation different? *Philosophical Transactions of the Royal Society of London B, 365,* 2663–2674.

Mell, J. C., Howard, S. M., & Miller, B. L. (2003). Art and the brain: The influence of frontotemporal dementia on an accomplished artist. *Neurology, 60,* 1707–1710.

Meltzoff, A. N., & Moore, M. K. (1977). Imitation of facial and manual gestures by human neonates. *Science, 198,* 75–78.

Meltzoff, A. N., & Moore, M. K. (1983). Newborn infants imitate adult facial gestures. *Child Development, 54,* 702–709.

Melzack, R., & Wall, P. D. (1965). Pain mechanisms: A new theory. *Science, 150,* 971–979.

Melzack, R., & Wall, P. D. (1988). *The challenge of pain* (rev. ed.). New York, NY: Penguin.

Mendelsohn, A., Furman, O., & Dudai, Y. (2010). Signatures of memory: Brain coactivations during retrieval distinguish correct from incorrect recollection. *Frontiers in Behavioral Neuroscience, 4,* 1–12.

Mennella, J. A., & Beauchamp, G. K. (1996). The early development of human flavor preferences. In E. D. Capaldi (Ed.), *Why we eat what we eat: The psychology of eating* (pp. 83–112). Washington, DC: APA Books.

Mennella, J. A., Johnson, A., & Beauchamp, G. K. (1995). Garlic ingestion by pregnant women alters the odor of amniotic fluid. *Chemical Senses, 20,* 207–209.

Mental health: A report of the surgeon general. (2001). Retrieved from http://www.surgeongeneral.gov/library/mentalhealth/home.html

Merskey, H., & Bogduk, N. (1994). *Classification of chronic pain.* Seattle, WA: International Association for the Study of Pain Press.

Merten, J. (2005). Culture, gender and the recognition of the basic emotions. *Psychologia, 48,* 306–316.

Meunier, M., & Bachevalier, J. (2002). Comparison of emotional responses in monkeys with rhinal cortex or amygdala lesions. *Emotion, 2,* 147–161.

Meyer, D. E., & Kieras, D. E. (1997). A computational theory of executive cognitive processes and multiple-task performance: Part 1. Basic mechanisms. *Psychological Review, 104,* 3–65.

Meyer-Bahlburg, H. F. L., Dolezal, C., Baker, W. W., & New, M. I. (2008). Sexual orientation in women with classical or non-classical congenital adrenal hyperplasia as a function of degree of prenatal androgen excess. *Archives of Sexual Behavior, 37,* 85–99.

Miao, C. F., Lund, D. J., & Evan, K. R. (2009). Reexamining the influence of career stages on salesperson motivation: A cognitive and affective perspective. *Journal of Personal Selling and Sales Management, 29,* 243–255.

Michael, J. (1975). Positive and negative reinforcement, a distinction that is no longer necessary; or a better way to talk about bad things. *Behaviorism, 3,* 33–45.

Miczek, K. A., de Almeida, R. M. M., Kravitz, E. A., & Rissman, E. F. (2007). Neurobiology of escalated aggression and violence. *Journal of Neuroscience, 27,* 11803–11806.

Mikolajczak, M., & Luminet, O. (2008). Trait emotional intelligence and the cognitive appraisal of stressful events: An exploratory study. *Personality and Individual Differences, 44,* 1445–1453.

Milgram, S. (1963). Behavioral study of obedience. *Journal of Abnormal and Social Psychology, 67,* 371–378.

Milgram, S. (1974). *Obedience to authority: An experimental view.* New York, NY: Harper.

Mill, J., & Petronis, A. (2008). Pre- and perinatal environmental risks for attention-deficit hyperactivity disorder (ADHD): The potential role of epigenetic processes in mediating susceptibility. *Journal of Child Psychology and Psychiatry, 49,* 1020–1030.

The millennials: Confident. Connected. Open to change. (2010). Washington, DC: Pew Research Center. Retrieved from http://pewresearch.org/pubs/1501/millennials-new-survey-generational-personality-upbeat-open-new-ideas-technology-bound

Miller, A. (1996). *Insights of genius: Imagery and creativity in science and art.* New York, NY: Springer Verlag.

Miller, A. H., Capuron, L., & Raison, C. L. (2005). Immunologic influences on emotion regulation. *Clinical Neuroscience Research, 4,* 325–333.

Miller, A. S., & Kanazawa, S. (2000). *Order by accident: The origins and consequences of conformity in contemporary Japan.* Boulder, CO: Westview.

Miller, B. L., & Cummings, J. L. (Eds.). (1999). *The human frontal lobes: Functions and disorders.* New York, NY: Guilford Press.

Miller, G. A. (1956). The magical number seven, plus or minus two: Some limits on our capacity for processing information. *Psychological Review, 63,* 81–97.

Miller, G. E., & Chen, E. (2013). The biological residue of childhood poverty. *Child Development Perspectives, 7,* 67–73. doi: 10.1111/cdep.12021.

Miller, G. E., Chen, E., Fok, A. K., Walker, H., Lim, A., Nicholls, E. F., Cole, S., & Kobor, M. S. (2009). Low early-life social class leaves a biological residue manifested by decreased glucocorticoid and increased proinflammatory signaling. *Proceedings of the National Academy of Sciences, 106,* 14716–14721.

Miller, G. F. (2000). *The mating mind: How sexual choice shaped the evolution of human nature.* New York, NY: Doubleday.

Miller, G. F., & Penke, L. (2007). The evolution of human intelligence and the coefficient of additive genetic variance in human brain size. *Intelligence, 35,* 97–114. doi: 10.1016/j.intell.2006.08.008.

Miller, L. A., & Tippett, L. J. (1996). Effects of focal brain lesions on visual problem-solving. *Neuropsychologia, 34,* 387–398.

Miller, N., & Dollard, J. (1941). *Social learning and imitation.* New Haven, CT: Yale University Press.

Miller, S. L., & Maner, J. K. (2010). Scent of a woman: Men's testosterone responses to olfactory ovulation cues. *Psychological Science, 21,* 276–283.

Milner, B. (1962). Les troubles de la mémoire accompagnant des lésions hippocampiques bilatérales. In *Physiologie de l'hippocampe* (pp. 257–272). Paris, France: Centre National de la Recherche Scientifique. English translation: P. M. Milner & S. Glickman (Eds.). (1965). *Cognitive processes and the brain: An enduring problem in psychology. Selected readings* (pp. 97–111). Princeton, NJ: Van Nostrand.

Milner, B., Corkin, S., & Teuber, H. L. (1968). Further analysis of the hippocampal amnesic syndrome: 14-year follow-up study of H. M. *Neuropsychologia, 6,* 215–234.

Min, B.-K., Marzelli, M. J., & Yoo, S.-S. (2010). Neuroimaging-based approaches in the brain-computer interface. *Trends in Biotechnology, 28,* 552–560.

Mirescu, C., & Gould, E. (2006). Stress and adult neurogenesis. *Hippocampus, 16,* 233–238.

Mirescu, C., Peters, J. D., Noiman, L., & Gould, E. (2006). Sleep deprivation inhibits adult neurogenesis in the hippocampus by elevating glucocorticoids. *Proceedings of the National Academy of Sciences, 103,* 19170–19175. doi: 10.1073/pnas.0608644103.

Mirnics, K., Middleton, F. A., Marquez, A., Lewis, D. A., & Levitt, P. (2000). Molecular characterization of schizophrenia viewed by microarray analysis of gene expression in prefrontal cortex. *Neuron, 28,* 53–67.

Mischel, W. (2009). From personality and assessment (1968) to personality science, 2009. *Journal of Research in Personality, 43,* 282–290.

Mischel, W., & Shoda, Y. (1995). A cognitive-affective system theory of personality: Re-conceptualizing situations, dispositions, dynamics, and invariance in personality structure. *Psychological Review, 102,* 246–268.

Mischel, W., & Shoda, Y. (1999). Integrating dispositions and processing dynamics within a unified theory of personality: The cognitive-affective personality system. In L. A. Pervin & O. P. John (Eds.), *Handbook of personality: Theory and research* (pp. 197–218). New York, NY: Guilford Press.

Miyake, A., Friedman, N. P., Emerson, M. J., Witzki, A. H., & Howerter, A. (2000). The unity and diversity of executive functions and their contributions to complex "frontal lobe" tasks: A latent variable approach. *Cognitive Psychology, 41,* 49–100.

Miyashita, T., Kubik, S., Lewandowski, G., & Guzowski, J. F. (2008). Networks of neurons, networks of genes: An integrated view of memory consolidation. *Neurobiology of Learning and Memory, 89,* 269–284.

Mizuno, S., Mihara, T., Miyaoka, T., Inagaki, T., & Horiguchi, J. (2005, March). CSF iron, ferritin and transferrin levels in restless legs syndrome. *Journal of Sleep Research, 14*(1), 43–47.

Moffitt, T. E., Brammer, G. L., Caspi, A., Fawcett, J. P., Raleigh, M., Yuwiler, A., & Silva, P. (1998). Whole blood serotonin relates to violence in an epidemiological study. *Biological Psychiatry, 43,* 446–457.

Moffitt, T. E., Caspi. A., & Rutter, M. (2005). Strategy for investigating interactions between measured genes and measured environments. *Archives of General Psychiatry, 62,* 473–481.

Moffitt, T. E., Caspi, A., Taylor, A., Kokaua, T. J., Milne, B. J., Polanczyk, G., & Poulton, R. (2010). How common are common mental disorders? Evidence that lifetime prevalence rates are doubled by prospective *versus* retrospective ascertainment. *Psychological Medicine, 40,* 899–909. doi: 10.1017/S0033291709991036.

Moghaddam, B. (2003). Bringing order to the glutamate chaos in schizophrenia. *Neuron, 40,* 881–884.

Mokdad, A. H., Serdula, M. K., Dietz, W. H., Bowman, B. A., Marks, J. S., & Koplan, J. P. (1999). The spread of the obesity epidemic in the United States, 1991–1998. *Journal of the American Medical Association, 282,* 1519–1522.

Moller, J., Hallqvist, J., Diderichsen, F., Theorell, T., Reuterwall, C., & Ahblom, A. (1999). Do episodes of anger trigger myocardial infarction? A case-crossover analysis in the Stockholm Heart Epidemiology Program (SHEEP). *Psychosomatic Medicine, 61,* 842–849.

Montague, D. P. F., & Walker-Andrews, A. S. (2001). Peekaboo: A new look at infants perception of emotion. *Developmental Psychology, 37,* 826–838.

Montgomery, G. H., DuHamel, K. N., & Redd, W. H. (2000). A meta-analysis of hypnotically induced analgesia: How effective is hypnosis? *International Journal of Clinical and Experimental Hypnosis, 48,* 138–153.

Moody, E. W., Sunsay, C., & Bouton, M. E. (2006). Priming and trial spacing in extinction: Effects on extinction performance, spontaneous recovery, and reinstatement in appetitive conditioning. *Quarterly Journal of Experimental Psychology, 59,* 809–829.

Moore, E. S., Ward, R. E., Wetherill, L. F., Rogers, J. L., Autti-Rämö, I., Fagerlund, A., . . . Foroud, T. (2007). Unique facial features distinguish fetal alcohol syndrome patients and controls in diverse ethnic populations. *Alcoholism: Clinical and Experimental Research, 31,* 1707–1713. doi: 10.1111/j.1530-0277.2007.00472.x.

Moore, R. Y., & Eichler, V. B. (1972). Loss of a circadian adrenal corticosterone rhythm following suprachiasmatic lesions in the rat. *Brain Research, 42,* 201–206.

Moradi, A. R., Herlihy, J., Yasseri, G., Shahraray, M., Turner, A., & Dalgleish, T. (2008). Specificity of episodic and semantic aspects of autobiographical memory in relation to symptoms of post-traumatic stress disorder (PTSD). *Acta Psychologica, 127,* 645–653.

Morales-Medina, J. C., Dumont, Y., & Quirion, R. (2010). A possible role of neuropeptide Y in depression and stress. *Brain Research, 1314,* 194–205.

Moran, E. M., Snelson, C., & Elison-Bowers, P. (2010). Image and video disclosure of substance use on social media websites. *Computers in Human Behavior, 26,* 1405–1411.

Moray, N. (1959). Attention in dichotic listening: Affective cues and the influence of instructions. *Quarterly Journal of Experimental Psychology, 11,* 56–60.

Moreno, J., Mitsumasa, K., Holloway, T., Lopez, J., Cadagan, R., Martinez-Sobrido, L., Garcia-Sastre, A., & Gonzalez-Maeso, J. (2011). Maternal influenza viral infection causes schizophrenia-like alterations of 5-HT$_{2A}$ and mGlu$_2$ receptors in the adult offspring. *Journal of Neuroscience, 3,* 1863–1872. doi: 10.1523/JNEUROSCI.4230-10.2011.

Moreno, M. A., Jelenchick, L., Cox, E., Young, H., & Christakis, D. A. (2011). Problematic Internet use among US youth: A systematic review. *Archives of Pediatric and Adolescent Medicine, 165,* 797–805. doi: 10.1001/archpediatrics.2011.58.

Morgenstern, N. A., Lombardi, G., & Schinder, A. F. (2008). Newborn granule cells in the ageing dentate gyrus. *Journal of Physiology, 586,* 3751–3757.

Morris, J. S., Frilt, C. D., Perrett, D. I., Rowland, D., Yong, A. N., Calder, A. J., & Dolan, R. J. (1996). A different neural response in the human amygdala in fearful and happy facial expressions. *Nature, 383,* 812–815.

Morris, M. W., & Peng, K. (1994). Culture and cause: American and Chinese attributions for social and physical events. *Journal of Personality and Social Psychology, 67,* 949–971.

Morris, N. M., Udry, J. R., Khandawood, F., & Dawood, M. Y. (1987). Marital sex frequency and midcycle female testosterone. *Archives of Sexual Behavior, 16,* 27–37.

Morris, P. L., Robinson, R. G., Raphael, B., & Hopwood, M. J. (1996). Lesion location and post-stroke depression. *Journal of Neuropsychiatry and Clinical Neurosciences, 8,* 399–403.

Morrison, R. S., Maroney-Galin, C., Kralovec, P. D., & Meier, D. E. (2005). The growth of palliative care programs in United States hospitals. *Journal of Palliative Medicine, 8*(6), 1127–1134.

Morton, F., Lee, P. C., Buchanan-Smith, H. M., Brosnan, S. F., Thierry, B., Paukner, A., . . . Weiss, A. (2013). Personality structure in brown capuchin monkeys (Sapajus apella): Comparisons with chimpanzees (Pan troglodytes), orangutans (Pongo spp.), and rhesus macaques (Macaca mulatta). *Journal of Comparative Psychology, 127*(3), 282–298. doi: 10.1037/a0031723.

Moruzzi, G., & Magoun, H. W. (1949). Brain stem reticular formation and activation of the EEG. *Electroencephalography and Clinical Neurophysiology, 1,* 455–473.

Mosconi, M., Cody-Hazlett, H., Poe, M., Gerig, G., Gimpel-Smith, R., & Piven, J. (2009). Longitudinal study of amygdala volume and joint attention in 2- to 4-year-old children with autism. *Archives of General Psychiatry, 66,* 509–516. doi: 10.1001/archgenpsychiatry.2009.19.

Moscovici, S. (1985). Social influence and conformity. In G. Lindzey & E. Aronson (Eds.), *The handbook of social psychology* (3rd ed., Vol. 2, pp. 347–412). New York, NY: Random House.

Moscovitch, M. (2010). Memory consolidation: Past, present and future. *Journal of Neurology, Neurosurgery, and Psychiatry, 81,* e2. doi: 10.1136/jnnp.2010.217554.4.

Moses-Kolko, E. L., Bogen, D., Perel, J., Bregard, A., Uhl, K., Levin, B., . . . (2005). Neonatal signs after late in utero exposure to serotonin reuptake inhibitors: Literature review and implications for clinical applications. *Journal of the American Medical Association, 293,* 2372–2383.

Moskowitz, J. (2003). Positive affect predicts lower risk of AIDS mortality. *Psychosomatic Medicine, 65,* 620–626.

Moskowitz, J., Folkman, S., Collette, L., & Vittinghoff, E. (1996). Coping and mood during AIDS related caregiving and bereavement. *Annals of Behavioral Medicine, 18,* 49–57.

Moss, M. (2013). *Salt, sugar, fat: How the food giants hooked us.* New York, NY: Random House.

Motluk, A. (2005, January 29). Senses special: The art of seeing without sight. *New Scientist, 2484,* 37. Retrieved from http://www.newscientist.com

Mount, M. K., Barrick, M. R., Scullen, S. M., & Rounds, J. (2005). Higher-order dimensions of the Big Five personality traits and the Big Six vocational interest types. *Personnel Psychology, 58,* 447–478.

Mühlberger, A., Wieser, M. J., Gerdes, A. B. M, Frey, M. C. M., Weyers, P., & Pauli, P. (2011). Stop looking angry and smile, please: Start and stop of the very same facial expression differentially activate threat- and reward-related brain networks. *SCAN, 6,* 321–329.

Müller-Oerlinghausen, B., Berghöfer, A., & Bauer, M. (2002). Bipolar disorder. *The Lancet, 359,* 241–247.

Mulvey, T. A., & Grus, C. L. (2010, August). *What can I do with a degree in psychology?* Paper presented at Annual Convention of American Psychological Association, San Diego, CA. Retrieved from http://www.apa.org/

workforce/presentations/2010-psychology-degree.pdf

Munro, G. D., Lasane, T. P., & Leary, S. P. (2010). Political partisan prejudice: Selective distortion and weighting of evaluative categories in college admissions applications. *Journal of Applied Social Psychology, 40,* 2434–2462.

Munsinger, H. (1975). The adopted child's IQ: A critical review. *Psychological Bulletin, 82,* 623–659.

Murphy, S. E. (2010). Using functional neuroimaging to investigate the mechanisms of action of selective serotonin reuptake inhibitors (SSRIs). *Current Pharmaceutical Design, 16,* 1990–1997.

Murray, H. A. (1938/1962). *Explorations in personality.* New York, NY: Science Editions.

Murray, J. (2009). *Top 10 weight loss tips: Physical activity and healthy eating habits are key to losing weight.* Retrieved from http://weight-loss-methods.suite101.com/article.cfm/top_10_weight_loss_tips

Muscanell, N. L, & Guadagno, R. E. (2012). Make new friends or keep the old: Gender and personality differences in social networking use. *Computers in Human Behavior, 28,* 107–112.

Muthukumaraswamy, S. D., Carhart-Harris, R. L., Moran, R. J., Brookes, M. J., Williams, T. M., Errtizoe, D., . . . Nutt, D. J. (2013). Broadband cortical desynchronization underlies the human psychedelic state. *Journal of Neuroscience, 33,* 15171–15183. doi: 10.1523/JNEUROSCI.2063-13.2013.

Myers, I. B. (1962). *Myers-Briggs Type Indicator manual.* Princeton, NJ: Educational Testing Service.

Nabi, H., Shipley, M. J., Vahtera, J., Hall, M., Korkeila, J., Marmot, M., . . . Singh-Manoux, A. (2010). Effects of depressive symptoms and coronary heart disease and their interactive associations on mortality in middle-aged adults: The Whitehall II cohort study. *Heart, 11,* 1645–1650.

Nacash, N., Foa, E. B., Fostick, L., Polliack, M., Dinstein, Y., Tzur, D., . . . (2007). Prolonged exposure therapy for chronic combat-related PTSD: A case report on five veterans. *CNS Spectrums, 12,* 690–695.

Nadarajah, B., & Parnavelas, J. (2002). Modes of neuronal migration in the developing cerebral cortex. *Nature Reviews Neuroscience, 3,* 423–432.

Nadkarni, A., & Hofmann, S. (2012). Why do people use Facebook? *Personality and Individual Differences, 52,* 243–249.

Nakajima, K., Takeoka, M., Mori, M., Hashimoto, S., Sakurai, A., Nose, H., . . . Taniguchi, S. (2010). Exercise effects on methylation of *ASC* gene. *International*

Journal of Sports Medicine, 31, 671–675. doi: 10.1055/s-0029-1246140.

Naqvi, N. H., Rudrauf, D., Damasio, H., & Bechara, A. (2007). Damage to the insula disrupts addiction to cigarette smoking. *Science, 315,* 531–534.

Nasar, S. (1998). *A beautiful mind.* New York, NY: Touchstone.

Nash, M. R., Hulsey, T. L., Sexton, M. C., Harralson, T. L., Lambert, W., & Lynch, G. V. (1993). *Adult psychopathology associated with a history of childhood sexual abuse: A psychoanalytic perspective.* Washington, DC: American Psychological Association.12National Center for Health Statistics (NCHS). (2000). *Data file documentation, National Health Interview Survey, 1998* (machine readable data file and documentation). Hyattsville, MD: Author.

National Eye Institute. (2002). *Vision problems in the U.S.: Prevalence of adult vision impairment and age-related eye disease in America, 2002.* Retrieved January 20, 2007, from http://www.nei.nih.gov/eyedata/pdf/VPUS.pdf

National Highway Traffic Safety Administration (NHTSA). (2010). *Distracted driving 2009.* Retrieved from http://www-nrd.nhtsa.dot.gov/Pubs/811379.pdf

National Human Genome Research Institute. (2010). *A brief guide to genomics.* Retrieved from http://www.genome.gov/18016863

National Institute of Mental Health (NIMH). (2007). *Schizophrenia.* Washington, DC: NIMH Publication # 06-3517.

National Institute on Alcohol Abuse and Alcoholism. (2005). *Heavy episodic consumption of alcohol.* Retrieved April 4, 2008, from http://www.collegedrinkingprevention.gov/NIAAACollegeMaterials/TaskForce/HeavyEpisodic_00.aspx

National Institute on Deafness and Other Communication Disorders. (2008). *Quick statistics.* Bethesda, MD: U.S. Department of Health and Human Services. Retrieved from http://www.nidcd.nih.gov/health/statistics/quick.htm

National Sleep Foundation. (2008). *2008 Sleep in America poll.* Retrieved April 2, 2008, from http://www.sleepfoundation.org/site/c.huIXKjM0IxF/b.3933533/

Natural born copycats. (2002, December 20). *The Guardian.* Retrieved from http://www.mediaknowall.com/violence/nbk.html

Naumann, R. B., & Dellinger, A. M. (2013, March 15). Mobile device use while driving—United States and seven European countries, 2011. *Morbidity and Mortality Weekly Report, 62,* 177–182. Retrieved November 20, 2013, from http://www.cdc.gov/mmwr/preview/mmwrhtml/mm6210a1.htm?s_cid=mm6210a1_w#fig1

Nauta, W. J. H., & Feirtag, M. (1979). The organization of the brain. *Scientific American, 241,* 88–111.

Nave, K.-A. (2010, November 11). Myelination and support of axonal integrity by glia. *Nature, 468,* 244–252.

Neal, D. T., & Chartrand, T. L. (2011). Embodied emotion perception. *Social Cognition and Personality Science, 2,* 673–678.

Neisser, U., Boodoo, G., Bouchard, T. J., Boykin, A. W., Brody, N., Ceci, S. J., . . . (1996). Intelligence: Knowns and unknowns. *American Psychologist, 51,* 77–101.

Nelson-Gray, R. O., Keane, S. P., Hurst, R. M., Mitchell, J. T., Warburton, J. B., Chok, J. T., . . . (2006). A modified DBT skills training program for oppositional defiant adolescents: Promising preliminary findings. *Behaviour Research and Therapy, 44,* 1811–1820.

Nemeroff, C. B. (2007). The burden of severe depression: A review of diagnostic challenges and treatment alternatives. *Journal of Psychiatric Research, 41,* 189–206.

Nesbit, S. M., Conger, J. C., & Conger, A. J. (2007). A quantitative review of the relationship between anger and aggressive driving. *Aggression and Violent Behavior, 12,* 156–176.

Nettle, D. (2006). The evolution of personality variation in humans and other animals. *American Psychologist, 61,* 622–631.

Nettle, D. (2011). Evolutionary perspectives on the Five-Factor Model of personality. In D. M. Buss & P. H. Hawley (Eds.), *The evolution of personality and individual differences.* (pp. 5–28). New York: Oxford University Press.

Nettle, D., & Clegg, H. (2005). Schizotypy, creativity, and mating success in humans. *Proceedings of the Royal Society (B).* doi: 10.1098/rspb.2005.3349.

Neuberg, S. L., & Cottrell, C. A. (2006). Evolutionary bases of prejudices. In M. Schaller, J. A. Simpson, & D. T. Kenrick (Eds.), *Evolution and social psychology* (pp. 163–187). New York, NY: Psychology Press.

Neuberg, S. L., Kenrick, D. T., & Schaller, M. (2011). Human threat management systems: Self-protection and disease avoidance. *Neuroscience and Biobehavioral Reviews, 35,* 1042–1051.

Neugebauer, R., Hoek, H. W., & Susser, E. (1999). Prenatal exposure to wartime famine and development of antisocial personality disorder in early adulthood. *Journal of the American Medical Association, 282,* 455–462.

Newcomb, T. M. (1961). *The acquaintance process.* Oxford, England: Holt, Rinehart & Winston.

Newcombe, N. S., & Uttal, D. H. (2006). Whorf versus Socrates, round 10. *Trends in Cognitive Sciences, 10,* 394–396.

Newport, E. L. (2003). Language development, critical periods in. In L. Nadel (Ed.), *Encyclopedia of cognitive science* (Vol. 2, pp. 733–740). London, England: Nature Group Press.

Neyens, D. M., & Boyle, L. N. (2007). The effect of distraction on the crash types of teenage drivers. *Accident Analysis and Prevention, 39,* 206–212.

Nickerson, C., Schwarz, N., Diener, E., & Kahneman, D. (2003). Zeroing in on the dark side of the American dream: A closer look at the negative consequences of the goal for financial success. *Psychological Science, 14,* 531–536.

Nicoll, R. A., & Alger, B. E. (2004). The brain's own marijuana. *Scientific American, 291,* 69–75.

Nieman, D. C., Custer, W. F., Butterworth, D. E., Utter, A. C., & Henson, D. A. (2000). Psychological response to exercise and/or energy restriction in obese women. *Journal of Psychosomatic Research, 48*(1), 23–29.

Nikolaus, S., Antke, C., Beu, M., & Muller, H. W. (2010). Cortical GABA, striatal dopamine and midbrain serotonin as the key players in compulsive and anxiety disorders—Results from in vivo imaging studies. *Reviews in the Neurosciences, 21,* 119–139.

Nilsson, L. G. (2003). Memory function in normal aging. *Acta Neurologica Scandinavica Supplementum, 179,* 7–13.

Nisbett, R. E., Peng, K., Choi, I., & Norenzayan, A. (2001). Culture and systems of thought: Holistic versus analytic cognition. *Psychological Review, 108,* 291–301.

Nisbett, R. E., & Wilson, T. D. (1977). Telling more than we can know: Verbal reports on mental processes. *Psychological Review, 84,* 231–259.

Nishida, A., Hisaoka, K., Zensho, H., Uchitomi, Y., Morinobu, S., & Yamawaki, S. (2002). Antidepressant drugs and cytokines in mood disorders. *International Immunopharmacology, 2,* 1619–1626.

Nishimura, E., Granter, S. R., & Fisher, D. E. (2005). Mechanisms of hair graying: Incomplete melanocyte stem cell maintenance in the niche. *Science, 307,* 720–724.

Nishino, S. (2007). Clinical and neurobiological aspects of narcolepsy. *Sleep Medicine, 8,* 373–399.

Nithianantharajah, J., & Hannan, A. (2006). Enriched environments, experience dependent plasticity and disorders of the nervous system. *Nature Reviews Neuroscience, 7,* 697–709.

Nixon, R. D. V., Ellis, A. A., Nehmy, T. J., & Ball, S.-A. (2010). Screening and predicting posttraumatic stress and depression in children following single-incident trauma. *Journal of Clinical Child & Adolescent Psychology, 39,* 588–596.

Nock, M. K., Park, J. M., Finn, C. T., Deliberto, T. L., Dour, H. J., & Banaji, M. R. (2010). Measuring the suicidal mind: Implicit cognition predicts suicidal behavior. *Psychological Science, 21,* 511–517.

Noda, H., Iso, H., Toyoshima, H., Date, C., Yamamoto, A., Kikuchi, S., . . . (2005). Walking and sports participation and mortality from coronary heart disease and stroke. *Journal of the American College of Cardiology, 46,* 1761–1767.

Nolen-Hoeksema, S. (2007). *Abnormal psychology* (4th ed.). New York, NY: McGraw-Hill.

Nolte, C., & Yollin, P. (2006, April 19). Officials salute city's majestic rise from rubble of '06—and the survivors. *San Francisco Chronicle,* pp. A1, A12.

Norcross, J. C., Bike, D., & Evans, K. (2009). The therapist's therapist: A replication and extension 20 years later. *Psychotherapy: Theory, Research, Practice, Training, 46,* 32–41. doi: 10.1037/a0015140.

Norcross, J. C., Karpiak, C. P., & Lister, K. M. (2005). What's an integrationist? A study of self-identified integrative and (occasionally) eclectic psychologists. *Journal of Clinical Psychology, 61,* 1587–1594.

Norcross, J. C., Sayette, M. A., Mayne, T. J., Karg, R. S., & Turkson, M. A. (1998). Selecting a doctoral program in professional psychology: Some comparisons among PhD counseling, PhD clinical, and PsyD clinical psychology programs. *Professional Psychology: Research and Practice, 29,* 609–614.

Norenzayan, A., & Nisbett, R. E. (2000). Culture and causal cognition. *Current Directions in Psychological Science, 9,* 132–135.

Nottebohm, F. (1985). Neuronal replacement in adulthood. *Annals of the New York Academy of Sciences, 457,* 143–161.

Novak, M. A. (2003). Self-injurious behavior in Rhesus monkeys: New insights into its etiology, physiology, and treatment. *American Journal of Primatology, 59,* 3–19.

Nowak, M. A., & Sigmund, K. (2005, October 27). Evolution of indirect reciprocity. *Nature, 437,* 1291–1298.

Nuechterlein, K., & Parasuraman, R. (1983). Visual sustained attention: Image degradation produces rapid sensitivity decrement over time. *Science, 220,* 327–329.

Nusbaum, E. C., & Silvia, P. J. (2011). Are intelligence and creativity really so different? Fluid intelligence, executive processes, and strategy use in divergent thinking.

Intelligence, 39(1), 36–45. doi: 10.1016/
j.intell.2010.11.002.

Oaten, M., Stevenson, R. J., & Case, T. I.
(2009). Disgust as a disease-avoidance mechanism. *Psychological Bulletin, 135*, 303–321.
doi: 10.1037/a001482.

Oatley, K., & Johnson-Laird, P. N. (2011).
Basic emotions in social relationships, reasoning, and psychological illnesses. *Emotion
Review, 3*, 424–433.

Oberlander, T. F. (2012). Fetal serotonin
signaling: Setting pathways for early childhood development and behavior. *Journal of
Adolescent Health, 51*, S9–S16. doi: 10.1016/
j.jadohealth.2012.04.009.

Oberman, L. M., & Ramachandran, V. S.
(2007). The simulating social mind: The role
of mirror neuron system and simulation in
the social and communicative deficits of autism spectrum disorders. *Psychological Bulletin, 133*, 310–327.

**Ochsner, K. N., Bunge, S. A., Gross, J. J.,
& Gabrieli, J. D. E.** (2002). Rethinking feelings: A fMRI study of the cognitive regulation
of emotion. *Journal of Cognitive Neuroscience, 14*, 1215–1229.

**O'Cleirigh, C., Ironson, G., Fletcher,
M. A., & Schneiderman, N.** (2008). Written emotional disclosure and processing of
trauma are associated with protected health
status and immunity in people living with
HIV/AIDS. *British Journal of Health Psychology, 13*, 81–84.

O'Conner, M. J., & Paley, B. (2006). The
relationship of prenatal alcohol exposure and
the postnatal environment of child depressive
symptoms. *Journal of Pediatric Psychology,
31*, 50–64.

**O'Connor, S. S., Whitehill, J. M., King,
K. M., Kernic, M. A., Boyle, L. N., Bresnahan, B. W., . . . Ebel, B. E.** (2013). Compulsive cell phone use and history of motor
vehicle crash. *Journal of Adolescent Health,
53*, 512–519.

O'Craven, K. M., & Kanwisher, N. N.
(2000). Mental imagery of faces and places
activates corresponding stimulus-specific brain regions. *Journal of Cognitive Neuroscience, 12*, 1013–1023. doi:
10.1162/08989290051137549.

The odds of dying from . . . (2010). National Safety Council. Retrieved from http://
www.nsc.org/news_resources/injury_and_
death_ statistics/pages/theoddsofdyingfrom.
aspx

**Oehen, P., Traber, R., Widmer, V.,
& Schnyder, U.** (2013). A randomized, controlled pilot study of MDMA
(±3,4-Methylenedioxymethamphetamine)-
assisted psychotherapy for treatment of resistant, chronic post-traumatic stress disorder
(PTSD). *Journal of Psychopharmacology, 27*,
40–52. doi: 10.1177/0269881112464827.

Öhman, A. (2002). Automaticity and the
amygdala: Nonconscious responses to emotional faces. *Current Directions in Psychological Science, 11*, 62–66.

**Ohnishi, T., Matsuda, H., Asada, T.,
Aruga, M., Hirakata, M., Nishikawa,
M., . . . Imabayashi, E.** (2001). Functional
anatomy of musical perception in musicians.
Cerebral Cortex, 11, 754–760. doi: 10.1093/
cercor/11.8.754.

**Ohno, H., Urushihara, R., Sei, H., &
Morita, Y.** (2002). REM sleep deprivation
suppresses acquisition of classical eyeblink
conditioning. *Sleep, 25*, 38–41.

**Oitzl, M. S., Champagne, D. L., van der
Veen, R., & de Kloet, E. R.** (2010). Brain
development under stress: Hypotheses of
glucocorticoid actions revisited. *Neuroscience & Biobehavioral Reviews, 34*, 853–866.

Olds, J., & Milner, P. (1954). Positive reinforcement produced by electrical stimulation
of septal area and other regions of rat brain.
*Journal of Comparative and Physiological
Psychology, 47*, 419–427.

Oliver, M. B., & Hyde, J. S. (1993). Gender
differences in sexuality: A meta-analysis.
Psychological Bulletin, 114, 29–51.

Olsen, E., Shults, R. A., & Eaton, D. K.
(2013). Texting while driving and other risky
motor vehicle behaviors among U.S. high
school students. *Pediatrics, 131*, e1708. doi:
10.1542/peds.2012-3462.

Olson, J. M., & Zanna, M. P. (1993). Attitudes and attitude change. *Annual Review of
Psychology, 44*, 117–154.

Omark, D., Omark, M., & Edelman, M.
(1973). Formation of dominance hierarchies
in young children. In T. R. Williams (Ed.),
Physical anthropology. The Hague, Netherlands: Mouton.

**O'Neill, J., Pleydell-Bouverie, B., Dupret,
D., & Csicsvari, J.** (2010). Play it again:
Reactivation of waking experience and memory. *Trends in Neurosciences, 33*, 220–229.
doi: 10.1016/j.tins.2010.01.006.

Ong, J. C., Shapiro, S. L., & Manber, R.
(2008). Combining mindfulness meditation
with cognitive-behavior therapy for insomnia: A treatment-development study. *Behavior Therapy, 39*, 171–182.

Onodera, A. (2003). Changes in self-concept
in the transition to parenthood. *Japanese
Journal of Developmental Psychology, 14*,
180–190.

Ophir, E., Nass, C. I., & Wagner, A. D.
(2009). Cognitive control in media multi-taskers. *Proceedings of the National Academy of
Sciences, 106*, 15583–15587.

Orne, M. T. (1959). The nature of hypnosis:
Artifact and essence. *Journal of Abnormal
and Social Psychology, 58*, 277–299.

Orr, E. S., Sisic, M., Ross, C., Simmering, M. G., Arseneault, J. M., & Orr, R.
(2009). The influence of shyness on the use
of Facebook in an undergraduate sample.
Cyberpsychology & Behavior, 12(3), 337–340.
doi:10.1089/cpb.2008.0214.

Ortigosa, A., Carro, R. M., & Quiroga, J.
(2014). Predicting user personality by mining
social interactions in Facebook. *Journal of
Computer & System Sciences, 80*(1), 57–71.
doi: 10.1016/j.jcss.2013.03.008.

Oscar-Berman, M., & Marinkovic, K.
(2003). Alcoholism and the brain: An
overview. *Alcohol Research & Health, 27*,
125–133.

Osherow, N. (1999). Making sense of the
nonsensical: An analysis of Jonestown. In
E. Aronson (Ed.), *Readings about the social
animal* (8th ed., pp. 71–88). New York, NY:
Worth/Freeman.

Ost, J. (2009). Recovered memories. In
R. Bull, T. Valentine, & T. Williamson (Eds.),
*Handbook of psychology of investigative
interviewing: Current developments and future directions* (pp. 181–204). New York, NY:
Wiley-Blackwell.

Oster, H. (2005). The repertoire of infant facial expressions: An ontogenetic perspective.
In J. Nadel & D. Muir (Eds.), *Emotional development* (pp. 261–292). New York, NY: Oxford
University Press.

Osterling, J., & Dawson, G. (1994). Early
recognition of children with autism: A study
of first birthday home videotapes. *Journal
of Autism and Developmental Disorders, 24*,
247–257.

**Ostry, D. J., Darainy, M., Mattar, A. A. G.,
Wong, J., & Gribble, P. L.** (2010). Somatosensory plasticity and motor learning. *Journal of Neuroscience, 30*, 5384–5393.

Ottersen, O. P. (2010). How hardwired is the
brain? Technological advances provide new
insight into brain malleability and neurotransmission. *Nutrition Reviews, 68*, S60–S64. doi:
10.1111/j.1753-4887.2010.00350.x.

**Otto, M. W., McHugh, R. K., & Kantak,
K. M.** (2010). Combined pharmacotherapy
and cognitive-behavioral therapy for anxiety
disorders: Medication effects, glucocorticoids, and attenuated treatment outcomes.
*Clinical Psychology: Science and Practice,
17*, 91–103.

**Ouellet, M.-C., Beaulieu-Bonneau, S., &
Morin, C. M.** (2006). Insomnia in patients
with traumatic brain injury: Frequency, characteristics, and risk factors. *Journal of Head
Trauma Rehabilitation, 21*, 199–212.

Ouellet, M.-C., & Morin, C. M. (2006).
Fatigue following traumatic brain injury: Frequency, characteristics, and associated factors. *Rehabilitation Psychology, 51*, 140–149.

Overgaard, M. (2009). How can we know
if patients in coma, vegetative state or

minimally conscious state are conscious? *Coma Science: Clinical and Ethical Implications, 177,* 11–19.

Owen, A. M. (2013). Detecting consciousness: A unique role for neuroimaging. *Annual Review of Psychology, 64,* 109–133.

Owen, A. M., Coleman, M. R., Boly, M., Davis, M., Laureys, S., & Pickard, J. D. (2006). Detecting awareness in the vegetative state. *Science, 313,* 1402.

Oyama, S. (1976). A sensitive period for the acquisition of a nonnative phonological system. *Journal of Psycholinguistic Research, 5,* 261–283.

Özgüven, N., & Mucan, B. (2013). The relationship between personality traits and social media use. *Social Behavior & Personality: An International Journal, 41*(3), 517–528.

Pace, T. W., Negi, L. T., Adame, D. D., Cole, S. P., Sivilli, T. I., Brown, T. D., Issa, M. J., & Raison, C. L. (2009). Effect of compassion meditation on neuroendocrine, innate immune and behavioral responses to psychosocial stress. *Psychoneuroendocrinology 34,* 87–98.

Pae, C.-U., Lim, H.-K., Han, C., Neena, A., Lee, C., & Patkar, A. A. (2007). Selegiline transdermal system: Current awareness and promise. *Progress in Neuro-Psychopharmacology & Biological Psychiatry, 31,* 1153–1163.

Pajares, F. (2004). *Albert Bandura: Biographical sketch.* Retrieved from http://des.emory.edu/mfp/bandurabio.html

Pan, B. A., Rowe, M. L., Singer, J. D., & Snow, C. E. (2005). Maternal correlates of growth in toddler vocabulary production in low-income families. *Child Development, 76,* 763–946.

Panagopoulou, E., Montgomery, A., & Tarlatzis, B. (2010). Experimental emotional disclosure in women undergoing infertility treatment: Are drop outs better off? *Social Science & Medicine, 69,* 678–681.

Panksepp, J. (1998). *Affective neuroscience: The foundations of human and animal emotions.* Oxford, England: Oxford University Press.

Panksepp, J. (2000). Emotions as natural kinds within the mammalian brain. In M. Lewis & J. M. Haviland-Jones (Eds.), *Handbook of emotions* (2nd ed., pp. 137–156). New York, NY: Guilford Press.

Pantev, C., Engelien, A., Candia, V., & Elbert, T. (2001). Representational cortex in musicians: Plastic alterations in response to musical practice. In R. J. Zatorre & I. Peretz (Eds.), *The biological foundations of music: Annals of the New York Academy of Sciences* (pp. 300–314). New York, NY: New York Academy of Sciences.

Papakostos, G. I., Stahl, S. M., Krishen, A., Seifert, C., Tucker, V. L., Goodale,

E. P., & Faca, M. (2008). Efficacy of bupropion and the selective serotonin reuptake inhibitors in the treatment of major depressive disorder with high levels of anxiety (anxious depression): A pooled analysis of 10 studies. *Journal of Clinical Psychiatry, 69,* 1287–1292.

Parasuraman, R. (1998). *The attentive brain.* Cambridge, MA: MIT Press.

Paris, R., & Helson, R. (2002). Early mothering experience and personality change. *Journal of Family Psychology, 16,* 172–185.

Park, C. L., & Folkman, S. (1997). Meaning in the context of stress and coping. *Review of General Psychology, 1,* 115–144.

Parker, E. S., Cahill, L., & McGaugh, J. L. (2006). A case of unusual autobiographical remembering. *Neurocase, 12,* 35–49.

Parker, S. T., & McKinney, M. L. (1999). *Origins of intelligence: The evolution of cognitive development in monkeys, apes, and humans.* Baltimore, MD: Johns Hopkins University Press.

Parks, E. J. & McCrory, M. A. (2005). When to eat and how often? *American Journal of Nutrition, 81,* 3–4.

Parpura, V., & Verkhratsky, A. (2012). The astrocyte excitability brief: From receptors to gliotransmission. *Neurochemistry International, 61,* 610–621. doi: 10.1016/j.neuint.2011.12.001.

Partanen, E., Kujala, T., Näätänen, R., Liitola, A., Sambeth, A., & Huotilainen, M. (2013). Learning-induced neural plasticity of speech processing before birth. *PNAS Proceedings of The National Academy of Sciences of the United States of America, 110*(37), 15145–15150. doi: 10.1073/pnas.1302159110.

Partanen, E., Kujala, T., Tervaniemi, M., & Huotilainen, M. (2013). Prenatal music exposure induces long-term neural effects. *PLOS/One, 8,* e78946-. doi: 10.1371/journal.pone.0078946.

Participation in education: Undergraduate education. (n.d.). Retrieved from http://nces.ed.gov/programs/coe/2010/section1/indicator07.asp

Pascual-Leone, A. (2001). The brain that plays music and is changed by it. *Annals of the New York Academy of Sciences, 930,* 315–329.

Patchin, J. W., & Hinduja, S. (2006). Bullies move beyond the schoolyard: A preliminary look at cyberbullying. *Youth Violence and Juvenile Justice, 4,* 148–169.

Patihis, L., Frenda, S. J., LePort, A. K. R., Petersen, N., Nichols, R. M., Stark, C. E. L., McGaugh, J. L, & Loftus, E. F. (2013). False memories in highly superior autobiographical memory individuals. *PNAS Early Edition.* Retrieved from http://www.pnas.org/cgi/doi/10.1073/pnas.1314373110

Patil, S. T., Zhang, L., Martenyi, F., Lowe, S. L., Jackson, K. A., Andreev, B. V., . . . Schoepp, D. (2007). Activation of mGlu2/3 receptors as a new approach to treat schizophrenia: A randomized Phase 2 clinical trial. *Nature Medicine, 13,* 1102–1107. doi: 10.1038/nm1632.

Patterson, C. J. (2008). *Child development.* New York, NY: McGraw-Hill.

Patterson, D. R. (2004). Treating pain with hypnosis. *Current Directions in Psychological Science, 13,* 252–255.

Patti, M. E. (2013). Reducing maternal weight improves offspring metabolism and alters (or modulates) methylation. *Proceedings of the National Academy of Sciences, 110,* 12859–12860; published ahead of print July 24, 2013. doi: 10.1073/pnas.1309724110.

Paul, E. S., Harding, E. J., & Mendl, M. (2005). Measuring emotional processes in animals: The utility of a cognitive approach. *Neuroscience and Biobehavioral Reviews, 29,* 469–491.

Paulesu, E., Frith, C. D., & Frackowiak, R. S. J. (1993). The neural correlates of the verbal component of working memory. *Nature, 362,* 342–345.

Paulozzi, L. J. (2006). Opioid analgesia involvement in drug abuse deaths in American metropolitan areas. *American Journal of Public Health, 96,* 1755–1757.

Paus, T., Keshavan, M., & Giedd, J. N. (2008). Why do many psychiatric disorders emerge during adolescence? *Nature Reviews Neuroscience, 9,* 947–957.

Pavlov, I. P. (1906). The scientific investigation of the psychical faculties or processes in the higher animals. *Science, 24,* 613–619.

Pavlov, I. P. (1928). *Lectures on conditioned reflexes: Twenty-five years of objective study of the higher nervous activity (behaviour) of animals* (W. H. Gantt, Trans.). New York, NY: Liveright.

Payne, J. D., & Kensinger, E. A. (2010). Sleep's role in the consolidation of emotional episodic memories. *Current Directions in Psychological Science, 19*(5), 290–295. doi: 10.1177/0963721410383978.

Payne, J. D., & Nadel, L. (2004). Sleep, dreams, and memory consolidation: The role of the stress hormone cortisol. *Learning & Memory, 11,* 671–678.

Pearson, J. D., Morrell, C. H., Gordon-Salant, S., Brant, L. J., Metter, E. J., Klein, L., & Fozard, J. L. (1995). Gender differences in a longitudinal study of age-associated hearing loss. *Journal of the Acoustical Society of America, 97,* 1197–1205. doi: 10.1121/1.412231.

Pearson, N. J., Johnson, L. L., & Nahin, R. L. (2006). Insomnia, trouble sleeping, and complementary and alternative medicine:

Analysis of the 2002 National Health Interview Survey data. *Archives of Internal Medicine, 166,* 1775–1782.

Peckham, P. H., Keith, M. W., Kilgore, K. L., Grill, J. H., Wuolle, K. S., Thrope, G. B., . . . Wiegner, A. (2001). Efficacy of an implanted neuroprosthesis for restoring hand grasp in tetraplegia: A multicenter study. *Archives of Physical Medicine and Rehabilitation, 82,* 1380–1388.

The peculiar institution. (2002). [Editorial]. *Scientific American, 286,* 8.

Pedersen, D. M., & Wheeler, J. (1983). The Müller–Lyer illusion among Navajos. *Journal of Social Psychology, 121,* 3–6.

Peigneux, P., Laureys, S., Fuchs, S., Collette, F., Perrin, F., Reggers, J., . . . Maquet, P. (2004). Are spatial memories strengthened in the human hippocampus during slow wave sleep? *Neuron, 44,* 535–545. doi: 10.1016/j.neuron.2004.10.007.

Pelli, D. G., Farell, B., & Moore, D. C. (2003). The remarkable inefficiency of word recognition. *Nature, 423,* 752–756.

Penfield, W., & Milner, B. (1958). Memory deficit produced by bilateral lesions in the hippocampal zone. *Archives of Neurology & Psychiatry (Chicago), 79,* 475–497.

Pennebaker, J. W. (1995). *Emotion, disclosure, and health.* Washington, DC: American Psychological Association.

Pennebaker, J. W., Kiecolt-Glaser, J. K., & Glaser, R. (1988). Disclosure of traumas and immune function: Implications for psychotherapy. *Journal of Consulting and Clinical Psychology, 56,* 239–245.

Peper, J. S., Schnack, H. G., Brouwer, R. M., Van Baal, G. C. M., . . . Pol, H. E. H. (2009). Heritability of regional and global brain structure at the onset of puberty: A magnetic resonance imaging study in 9-year-old twin pairs. *Human Brain Mapping, 30,* 2184–2196.

Pereira, A. C., Huddleston, D. E., Brickman, A. M., Sosunov, A. A., Hen, R., McKhann, G. M. . . . Small, S. A. (2007). An *in vivo* correlate of exercise induced neurogenesis in the adult dentate gyrus. *Proceedings of the National Academy of Sciences, 104,* 5638–5643.

Perlovsky, L. I., & Ilin, R. (2013). Mirror neurons, language, and embodied cognition. *Neural Networks, 41,* 15–22. doi: 10.1016/j.neunet.2013.01.003.

Perrin, J. S., Leonard, G., Perron, M., Pike, G. B., Pitiot, A., Richer, L., . . . Paus, T. (2009). Sex differences in the growth of white matter during adolescence. *NeuroImage, 45,* 1055–1066.

Perry, B. D. (2002). Childhood experience and the expression of genetic potential: What childhood neglect tells us about nature and nurture. *Brain and Mind, 3,* 79–100.

Perry, R., & Zeki, S. (2000). The neurology of saccades and covert shifts in spatial attention: An event-related fMRI study. *Brain, 123,* 2273–2288.

Persky, H., Dreisbach, L., Miller, W. R., O'Brien, C. P., Khan, M. A., Lief, H. I., . . . Strauss, D. (1982). The relation of plasma androgen levels to sexual behaviors and attitudes of women. *Psychosomatic Medicine, 44,* 305–319.

Persky, H., Lief, H. I., Strauss, D., Miller, W. R., & O'Brien, C. P. (1978). Plasma testosterone level and sexual behavior of couples. *Archives of Sexual Behavior, 7,* 157–173.

Pessoa, L. (2008). On the relationship between emotion and cognition. *Nature Reviews Neuroscience, 9,* 148–158.

Pessoa, L., Padmala, S., & Morland, T. (2005). Fate of unattended fearful faces in the amygdala is determined by both attentional resources and cognitive modulation. *NeuroImage, 28,* 249–255.

Peter, J., Valkenburg, P. M., & Schouten, A. P. (2005). Developing a model of adolescent friendship formation on the Internet. *CyberPsychology & Behavior, 8,* 423–430.

Peters, R. M., Hackeman, E., & Goldreich, D. (2009). Diminutive digits discern delicate details: Fingertip size and the sex difference in tactile spatial acuity. *Journal of Neuroscience, 29,* 15756–15761.

Petersen, J. L., & Hyde, J. S. (2010). A meta-analytic review of research on gender differences in sexuality, 1993–2007. *Psychological Bulletin, 136,* 21–38. doi: 10.1037/a0017504.

Petronis, A. (2004). Schizophrenia, neurodevelopment, and epigenetics. In M. S. Keshavan, J. L. Kennedy, & R. M. Murray (Eds.), *Neurodevelopment and schizophrenia* (pp. 174–190). New York, NY: Cambridge University Press.

Petry, N. M., & O'Brien, C. P. (2013). Internet gaming disorder and the *DSM-5. Addiction, 108,* 1186–1187. doi: 10.1111/add.12162.

Petry, S., Cummings, J. L., Hill, M. A., & Shapiro, J. (1989). Personality alterations in dementia of the Alzheimer type: A three-year follow-up study. *Journal of Geriatric Psychiatry and Neurology, 2,* 203–207.

Petzinger, G. M., Fisher, B. E., McEwen, S., Beeler, J. A., Walsh, J. P., & Jakowec, M. W. (2013). Exercise-enhanced neuroplasticity targeting motor and cognitive circuitry in Parkinson's disease. *The Lancet Neurology, 12*(7), 716–726. doi: 10.1016/S1474-4422(13)70123-6.

Phan, K. L., Wager, T., Taylor, S. F., & Liberzon, I. (2002). Functional neuroanatomy of emotion: A meta-analysis of emotion activation studies in PET and fMRI. *NeuroImage, 16,* 331–348.

Phelps, E. A. (2006). Emotion and cognition: Insights from the study of the human amygdala. *Annual Review of Psychology, 57,* 27–53.

Phelps, E. A., & LeDoux, J. E. (2005). Contributions of the amygdala to emotional processing: From animal models to human behavior. *Neuron, 48,* 175–187.

Phelps, E. A., & Sharot, T. (2008). How (and why) emotion enhances the subjective sense of recollection. *Current Directions in Psychological Science, 17,* 147–152.

Piaget, J. (1954). *The construction of reality in the child.* New York, NY: Basic Books.

Piaget, J. (1962). *Plays, dreams and imitation in childhood.* New York, NY: Norton.

Piaget, J. (1972a). *The child's conception of the world.* Totowa, NJ: Littlefield, Adams.

Piaget, J. (1972b). Intellectual evolution from adolescence to adulthood. *Human Development, 15,* 1–12.

Piaget, J., & Inhelder, B. (1967). *The child's conception of space.* New York, NY: Norton.

Pierce, T. (2009). Social anxiety and technology: Face-to-face communication versus technological communication among teens. *Computers in Human Behavior, 25,* 1367–1372.

Pietrek, C., Elbert, T., Weierstall, R., Müller, O., & Rockstroh, B. (2013). Childhood adversities in relation to psychiatric disorders. *Psychiatry Research, 206,* 103–110. doi: 10.1016/j.psychres.2012.11.003.

Pincus, J. H. (1999). Aggression, criminality, and the frontal lobes. In B. L. Miller & J. L. Cummings (Eds.), *The human frontal lobes: Functions and disorders* (pp. 547–556). New York, NY: Guilford Press.

Pincus, J. H. (2001). *Base instincts: What makes killers kill?* New York, NY: Norton.

Pinker, S. (1994). *The language instinct: How the mind creates language.* New York, NY: HarperPerennial.

Pinker, S. (2002). *The blank slate.* New York, NY: Viking.

Pinker, S. (2004, Fall). Why nature and nurture won't go away. *Daedalus,* 1–13.

Pinsker, H. M., Hening, W. A., Carew, T. J., & Kandel, E. R. (1973). Long-term sensitization of a defensive withdrawal reflex in *Aplysia. Science, 182,* 1039–1042.

Pittman, R. K., Sanders, K. M., Zusman, R. M., Healy, A. R., Cheema, F., Lasko, N. B., Cahill, L., & Orr, S. P. (2002). Pilot study of secondary prevention of posttraumatic stress disorder with propranolol. *Biological Psychiatry, 51,* 189–142.

Platsidou, M. (2010). Trait emotional intelligence of Greek special education teachers in relation to burnout and job satisfaction. *School Psychology International, 31,* 60–76.

Pliner, P. (1982). The effects of mere exposure on liking for edible substances. *Appetite, 3,* 283–290.

Plomin, R., & Caspi, A. (1999). Behavioral genetics and personality. In L. A. Pervin & O. P. John (Eds.), *Handbook of personality theory and research* (pp. 251–276). New York, NY: Guilford Press.

Plomin, R., & Petrill, S. A. (1997). Genetics and intelligence: What's new? *Intelligence, 24,* 53–77.

Plucker, J. A., Beghetto, R. A., & Dow, G. T. (2004). Why isn't creativity more important to educational psychologists? Potentials, pitfalls, and future directions in creativity research. *Educational Psychologist, 39,* 83–96.

Plunkett, K. (1997). Theories of early language acquisition. *Trends in Cognitive Sciences, 1,* 146–153.

Pohlmeyer, E. A., Oby, E. R., Perreault, E. J., Solla, S. A., Kilgore, K. L., Kirsch, R. F., & Miller, L. E. (2009). Toward the restoration of hand use to a paralyzed monkey: Brain-controlled functional electrical stimulation of forearm muscles. *PLoS ONE, 4,* e5924. doi: 10.1371/journal.pone.0005924.

Poldrack, R. A., & Foerde, K. (2008). Category learning and the memory systems debate. *Neuroscience and Biobehavioral Reviews, 32,* 197–205.

Popper, K. (1965). *Conjectures and refutations: The growth of scientific knowledge.* New York, NY: Harper.

Porfeli, E. J., & Skorikov, V. B. (2010). Specific and diversive career exploration during late adolescence. *Journal of Career Assessment, 18,* 46–58.

Posner, M. I., & Rothbart, M. K. (2007). Research on attention networks as a model for the integration of psychological science. *Annual Review of Psychology, 58,* 1–23.

Post, F. (1994). Creativity and psychopathology: A study of 291 world-famous men. *British Journal of Psychiatry, 165,* 22–34.

Post, R. M., Frye, M. A., Denicoff, K. D., Leverich, G. S., Kimbrell, T. A., & Dunn, R. T. (1998). Beyond lithium in the treatment of bipolar illness. *Neuropsychopharmacology, 19,* 206–219.

Potkin, S. G., Saha, A. R., Kujawa, M. J., Carson, W. H., Ali, M., Stock, E., . . . Marder, S. R. (2003). Ariprazole, an antipsychotic with a novel mechanism of action, and risperidone vs. placebo in patients with schizophrenia and schizoaffective disorder. *Archives of General Psychiatry, 60,* 681–690.

Potter, J. W. (1987). Does television viewing hinder academic achievement among adolescents? *Human Communication Research, 14,* 27–46.

Poulin, M. J., Brown, S. L., Dillard, A. J., & Smith, D. M. (2013). Giving to others and the association between stress and mortality. *American Journal of Public Health, 103,* 1649–1655. doi: 10.2105/AJPH. 2012.300876.

Powell, L. H., Kazlauskaite, R., Shima, C., & Appelhans, B. M. (2010). Lifestyle in France and the United States: An American perspective. *Journal of the American Dietetic Association, 10,* 845–847.

Powers, M., Halpern, J., Ferenschak, M., Gillihan, S., & Foa, E. (2010). A meta-analytic review of prolonged exposure for posttraumatic stress disorder. *Clinical Psychology Review, 30,* 635–641. doi: 10.1016/j.cpr.2010.04.007.

Prahbu, V., Sutton, C., & Sauser, W. (2008). Creativity and certain personality traits: Understanding the mediating effect of intrinsic motivation. *Creativity Research Journal, 20,* 53–66.

Preckel, F., Holling, H., & Wiese, M. (2006). Relationship of intelligence and creativity in gifted and non-gifted students: An investigation of threshold theory. *Personality and Individual Differences, 40,* 159–170.

Premack, D. (1971). Language in chimpanzees? *Science, 172,* 808–822.

Price, J. (2008). *The woman who can't forget: A memoir.* New York, NY: Free Press.

Priori, A., Beradelli, A., Rona, S., Accornero, N., & Manfredi, M. (1998). Polarization of the human motor cortex through the scalp. *Neuroreport, 9,* 2257–2260. doi: 10.1097/00001756-199807130-00020.

Prochaska, J. O., & Norcross, J. C. (2007). *Systems of psychotherapy* (6th ed.). Belmont, CA: Wadsworth.

Profet, M. (1992). Pregnancy sickness as adaptation: A deterrent to maternal ingestion of teratogens. In J. Barkow, L. Cosmides, & J. Tooby (Eds.), *The adapted mind* (pp. 327–365). New York, NY: Oxford University Press.

Ptito, M., & Desgent, S. (2006). Sensory input–based adaptation and brain architecture. In P. B. Baltes, P. A. Reuter-Lorenz, & F. Rösler (Eds.), *Lifespan development and the brain: The perspective of biocultural coconstructivism* (pp. 111–133). New York, NY: Cambridge University Press.

Pugh, M. J. V., & Hart, D. (1999). Identity development and peer group participation. In J. A. McLellan & M. J. V. Pugh (Eds.), *The role of peer groups in adolescent social identity: Exploring the importance of stability and change* (pp. 55–70). San Francisco, CA: Jossey-Bass.

Pulver, C. A., & Kelly, K. R. (2008). Incremental validity of the Myers-Briggs Type Indicator in predicting academic major selection of undecided university students. *Journal of Career Assessment, 16,* 441–455.

Purves, D., & Lichtman, J. W. (1985). *Principles of neural development.* Sunderland, MA: Sinauer.

Putnam, F., & McHugh, P. (2005). Issue 3: Is multiple personality disorder a valid diagnosis? In R. P. Halgin (Ed.), *Taking sides: Clashing views on controversial issues in abnormal psychology* (3rd ed., pp. 42–53). New York, NY: McGraw-Hill.

Putnam, F. W. (2006). Dissociative disorders. In D. Cicchetti & D. J. Cohen (Eds.), *Developmental psychopathology: Vol. 3. Risk, disorder, and adaptation* (pp. 657–695). Hoboken, NJ: John Wiley.

Qiu, J., Li, H., Jou, J., Liu, J., Yeujia, L., Feng, T., . . . Zhang, Q. (2010). Neural correlates of the "aha" experiences: Evidence from an fMRI study of insight problem solving. *Cortex, 46,* 397–403.

Quirin, M., Meyer, F., Caciopppo, J., Heise, N., Kuhl, J., Kustermann, E., . . . Cacciopo, J. T. (2013). Neural correlates of social motivation: An fMRI study on power versus affiliation. *International Journal of Psychophysiology, 88,* 289–295.

Quiroga, R. Q., Reddy, L., Kreiman, G., Koch, C., & Fried, I. (2005). Invariant visual representation by single neurons in the human brain. *Nature, 435,* 1102–1107.

Radford, A. (1997). *Syntactic theory and the structure of English: A minimalist approach.* New York, NY: Cambridge University Press.

Raffaele, P. (2006, November). Speaking Bonobo. *Smithsonian.* Retrieved from http://www.smithsonianmagazine.com

Rahman, Q. (2005). The neurodevelopment of human sexual orientation. *Neuroscience and Biobehavioral Reviews, 29,* 1057–1066.

Rahn, E. J., & Hohmann, A. G. (2009). Cannabinoids as pharmacotherapies for neuropathic pain: From the bench to the bedside. *Neurotherapeutics, 6,* 713–737.

Raij, T. T., Numminen, J., Närvänen, S., Hiltunen, J., & Hari, R. (2005). Brain correlates of subjective reality of physically and psychologically induced pain. *Proceedings of the National Academy of Sciences, 102,* 2147–2151.

Raine, A. (2013). *The anatomy of violence: The biological roots of crime.* New York, NY: Pantheon.

Raleigh, M. J., McGuire, M. T., Brammer, G. L., Pollack, D. B., & Yuwiler, A. (1991). Serotonergic mechanisms promote dominance in adult male vervet monkeys. *Brain Research, 559,* 181–190.

Ramachandran, V. S., & Hubbard, E. M. (2003, May). Hearing colors, tasting shapes. *Scientific American, 288,* 52–59.

Ramachandran, V. S., Miller, L., Livingstone, M. S., & Brang, D. (2011). Colored halos around faces and emotion-evoked colors: A new form of synesthesia. *Neurocase: The Neural Basis of Cognition, 18*, 352–358. doi: 10.1080/13554794.2011.608366.

Ramachandran, V. S., & Oberman, L. M. (2006). Broken mirrors: A theory of autism. *Scientific American, 295*, 63–69.

Ramanathan, L., Gulyani, S., Nienhuis, R., & Siegel, J. M. (2002). Sleep deprivation decreases superoxide dismutase activity in rat hippocampus and brainstem. *NeuroReport, 13*, 1387–1390.

Ransdell, S. (2010). Online activity, motivation, and reasoning among adult learners. *Computers in Human Behavior, 26*, 70–73. doi: 10.1016/j.chb.2009.09.002.

Rao, V., Spiro, J. R., Handel, S., & Onyike, C. U. (2008). Clinical correlates of personality changes associated with traumatic brain injury. *Journal of Neuropsychiatry and Clinical Neurosciences, 20*, 118–119.

Rapoport, J., Chavez, A., Greenstein, D., Addington, A., & Gogtay, N. (2009). Autism spectrum disorders and childhood-onset schizophrenia: Clinical and biological contributions to a relation revisited. *Journal of the American Academy of Child & Adolescent Psychiatry, 48*(1), 10–18. doi: 10.1097/CHI.0b013e31818b1c63.

Rashid, T. (2008). Positive psychotherapy. In S. J. Lopez (Ed.), *Positive psychology: Exploring the best in people, Vol. 4: Pursuing human flourishing* (pp. 188–217). Westport, CT: Praeger/Greenwood.

Rathus, J. H., Cavuoto, N., & Passarelli, V. (2006). Dialectical behavior therapy (DBT): A mindfulness-based treatment for intimate partner violence. In R. A. Baer (Ed.), *Mindfulness-based treatment approaches: Clinician's guide to evidence base and applications* (pp. 333–358). San Diego, CA: Elsevier Academic Press.

Rawl, S. M., Skinner, C. S., Perkins, S. M., Springston, J., Wang, H.-L., Russell, K. M., . . . Champion, V. (2012). Computer-delivered tailored intervention improves colon cancer screening knowledge and health beliefs of African-Americans. *Health Education Research, 27*, 868–885. doi: 10.1093/her/cys094.

Raymaekers, L., Smeets, T., Peters, M., & Merckelbach, H. (2010). Autobiographical memory specificity among people with recovered memories of childhood sexual abuse. *Journal of Behavior Therapy and Experimental Psychiatry, 41*, 338–344. doi: 10.1016/j.jbtep.2010.03.004.

Raz, A., Fan, J., & Posner, M. I. (2005). Hypnotic suggestion reduces conflict in the human brain. *Proceedings of the National Academy of Sciences, 102*, 9978–9983.

Raz, A., & Shapiro, T. (2002). Hypnosis and neuroscience. *Archives of General Psychiatry, 59*, 85–90.

Raz, N. (2000). Aging of the brain and its impact on cognitive performance: Integration of structural and functional findings. In F. I. M. Craik & T. A. Salthouse (Eds.), *The handbook of aging and cognition* (pp. 1–90). Mahwah, NJ: Erlbaum.

Read, J. P., Beattie, M., Chamberlain, R., & Merrill, J. E. (2008). Beyond the "binge" threshold: Heavy drinking patterns and their association with alcohol involvement indices in college students. *Addictive Behaviors, 33*, 225–234.

Ready, D. J., Gerardi, R. J., Backscheider, A. G., Mascaro, N., & Rothbaum, B. O. (2010). Comparing virtual reality exposure therapy to present-centered therapy with 11 U. S. Vietnam veterans with PTSD. *Cyberpsychology, Behavior, and Social Networking, 13*, 49–54. doi: 10.1089/cyber.2009.0239.

Reed, C., Novick, D., Gonzalez-Pinto, A., Bertsch, J., & Haro, J. (2009). Observational study designs for bipolar disorder—What can they tell us about treatment in acute mania? *Progress in Neuro-Psychopharmacology & Biological Psychiatry, 33*, 715–721. doi: 10.1016/j.pnpbp.2009.03.024.

Reed, G. M., Kemeny, M. E., Taylor, S. E., Wang, H. Y. J., & Visscher, B. R. (1994). Realistic acceptance as a predictor of decreased survival time in gay men with AIDS. *Health Psychology, 13*, 299–307.

Refinetti, R. (2006). *Circadian physiology* (2nd ed.). Boca Raton, FL: CRC Press.

Regier, T., & Kay, P. (2009). Language, thought, and color: Whorf was half right. *Trends in Cognitive Sciences, 13*, 439–446.

Regier, T., Kay, P., Gilbert, A., & Ivry, R. (2010). Language and thought: Which side are you on, anyway? In B. C. Malt & P. Wolff (Eds.), *Words and the mind: How words capture human experience* (pp. 165–182). New York, NY: Oxford University Press.

Reilly, D., & Neumann, D. L. (2013). Gender-role differences in spatial ability: A meta-analytic review. *Sex Roles, 68*(9–10), 521–535. doi: 10.1007/s11199-013-0269-0.

Reimagining the tragic mulatto. (2010, March 2). [Radio broadcast transcript]. Retrieved from http://www.npr.org/templates/transcript/transcript.php?storyId=124244813

Remafedi, G., Resnick, M., Blum, R., & Harris, L. (1992). Demography of sexual orientation in adolescents. *Pediatrics, 89*, 714–721.

Renaud, S., & de Lorgeril, M. (1992). Wine, alcohol, platelets, and the French paradox for coronary heart disease. *The Lancet, 339*, 1523–1526.

Renshaw, K. D. (2011). Working with the new generation of service members/veterans from Operations Enduring and Iraqi Freedom. *Cognitive and Behavioral Practice, 18*, 82–84. doi: 10.1016/j.cbpra.2010.03.003.

Rentfrow, P. J., & Gosling, S. D. (2003) The do re mi's of everyday life: The structure and personality correlates of music preferences. *Journal of Personality and Social Psychology, 84*, 1236–1256.

Retz, W., Reif, A., Freitag, C., Retz-Junginger, P., & Rösler, M. (2010). Association of a functional variant of neuronal nitric oxide synthase gene with self-reported impulsiveness, venturesomeness and empathy in male offenders. *Journal of Neural Transmission, 117*, 321–324.

Rexrode, K. M., Buring, J. E., & Manson, J. E. (2001). Abdominal and total adiposity and risk of coronary heart disease in men. *International Journal of Obesity, 25*, 1047–1056.

Rexrode, K. M., Carey, V. J., Hennekens, C. H., Walters, E. E., Colditz, G. A., Stampfer, M. J., . . . Manson, J. E. (1998). Abdominal adiposity and coronary heart disease in women. *Journal of the American Medical Association, 280*, 1843–1848. doi: 10.1001/ jama.280.21.1843.

Reynolds, C. R. (2000). Why is psychometric research on bias in mental testing so often ignored? *Psychology, Public Policy, and Law, 6*, 144–150.

Reynolds, S., & Lane, S. J. (2008). Diagnostic validity of sensory over-responsivity: A review of the literature and case reports. *Journal of Autism & Developmental Disorders, 38*, 516–529.

Rhoades, G. K., Stanley, S. M., & Markman, H. J. (2009). The pre-engagement cohabitation effect: A replication and extension of previous findings. *Journal of Family Psychology, 23*, 107–111.

Ricciardelli, L. A. (1992). Creativity and bilingualism. *Journal of Creative Behavior, 26*, 242–254.

Rice, F., Jones, I., & Thapar, A. (2007). The impact of gestational stress and prenatal growth on emotional problems in offspring: A review. *Acta Psychiatrica Scandinavica, 115*(3), 171–183.

Rice, M. L. (1989). Children's language acquisition. *American Psychologist, 44*, 149–156.

Rice, W. R., Friberg, U., & Gavrilets, S. (2012). Homosexuality as a consequence of epigenetically canalized sexual development. *Quarterly Review of Biology, 87*, 343–368.

Richards, J. E., Reynolds, G. D., & Courage, M. L. (2010). The neural basis of infant attention. *Current Directions in Psychological Science, 19*, 41–46.

Richards, R. L. (1994). Creativity and bipolar mood swings: Why the association? In

M. P. Shaw & M. A. Runco (Eds.), *Creativity and affect* (pp. 44–72). Norwood, NJ: Ablex.

Richards, R. L., & Kinney, D. K. (1990). Mood swings and creativity. *Creativity Research Journal, 3,* 202–217.

Richardson, J. D., Huddy, W. P., & Morgan, S. M. (2008). The hostile media effect, biased assimilation, and perceptions of a presidential debate. *Journal of Applied Social Psychology, 38,* 1255–1270. doi: 10.1111/j.1559-1816.2008.00347.x.

Ridley, M. (2003). *Nature via nurture: Genes, experience, and what makes us human.* New York, NY: HarperCollins.

Ries, M., & Marks, W. (2005). Selective attention deficits following severe closed head injury: The role of inhibitory processes. *Neuropsychology, 19,* 476–481.

Rinpoche, S. (1992). *The Tibetan book of living and dying.* New York, NY: HarperCollins.

Risch, N., Herrell, R., Lehner, T., Liang, K.-Y., Eaves, L., Hoh, J., . . . Mirerikangas, K. R. (2009). Interaction between the serotonin transporter gene (*5-HTTLPR*), stressful life events, and risk of depression: A meta-analysis. *Journal of the American Medical Association, 301,* 2462–2471.

Ritschel, L. A., Cheavens, J. S., & Nelson, J. (2012). Dialectical behavior therapy in an intensive outpatient program with a mixed-diagnostic sample. *Journal of Clinical Psychology, 68,* 221–235.

Riva, G. (2009). Virtual reality: An experiential tool for clinical psychology. *British Journal of Guidance & Counselling, 37,* 337–345. doi: 10.1080/03069880902957056.

Rizvi, S., Kennedy, S. H., McNeely, H., Giacobbe, P., Mayberg, H. S., & Lozano, A. M. (2009). Functional outcome after 12 months of deep brain stimulation for treatment resistant major depressive disorder. *European Neuropsychopharmacology, 19,* S388–S389.

Rizzolatti, G., & Arbib, M. A. (1998). Language within our grasp. *Trends in Neuroscience, 21,* 188–194.

Rizzolatti, G., & Craighero, L. (2004). The mirror-neuron system. *Annual Review of Neuroscience, 27,* 169–192.

Rizzolatti, G., Fadiga, L., Gallese, V., & Fogassi, L. (1996). Premotor cortex and the recognition of motor actions. *Brain Research: Cognitive Brain Research, 3,* 131–141.

Roberts, B. W., & Mroczek, D. (2008). Personality trait change in adulthood. *Current Directions in Psychological Science, 17,* 31–35.

Roberts, B. W., Walton, K. E., & Viechtbauer, W. (2006). Patterns of mean-level change in personality traits across the life course: A meta-analysis of longitudinal studies. *Psychological Bulletin, 132,* 1–25.

Robertson, I. (2003). The absent mind: Attention and error. *The Psychologist, 16,* 476–479.

Robinson, D. N. (1995). *An intellectual history of psychology* (3rd ed.). Madison: University of Wisconsin Press.

Robinson, L. A., & Kleseges, R. C. (1997). Ethnic and gender differences in risk factors for smoking onset. *Health Psychology, 16,* 499–505.

Röder, B. (2006). Blindness: A source and case of neuronal plasticity. In P. B. Baltes, P. A. Reuter-Lorenz, & F. Rösler (Eds.), *Lifespan development and the brain* (pp. 134–157). New York, NY: Cambridge University Press.

Rodgers, A. B., Morgan, C. P., Bronson, S. L., Revello, S., & Bale, T. L. (2013). Paternal stress exposure alters sperm microRNA content and reprograms offspring HPA stress axis regulation. *Journal of Neuroscience, 33,* 9003–9012.

Rodrigues, A., Loureiro, M., & Caramelli, P. (2010). Musical training, neuroplasticity and cognition. *Dementia & Neuropsychologia, 4*(4), 277–286.

Roehr, B. (2007). High rate of PTSD in returning Iraq War veterans. *Medscape Medical News.* Retrieved July 5, 2008, from http://www.medscape.com/viewarticle/565407

Roehrs, T., Zorick, F. J., & Roth, T. (2000). Transient and short-term insomnias. In M. H. Kryger, T. Roth, & W. C. Dement (Eds.), *Principles and practice of sleep medicine.* Philadelphia, PA: Saunders.

Rogelberg, S. G., & Gill, P. M. (2006). The growth of industrial and organizational psychology: Quick facts. Retrieved December 6, 2007, from http://www.siop.org/tip/backissues/july04/05rogelberg.aspx

Rogers, C. R. (1951). *Client-centered counseling.* Boston, MA: Houghton Mifflin.

Rogers, C. R. (1959). A theory of therapy, personality, and interpersonal relationships, as developed in the client-centered framework. In S. Koch (Ed.), *Psychology: A study of a science* (Vol. 3). New York, NY: McGraw-Hill.

Rogers, C. R. (1980). *A way of being.* Boston, MA: Houghton Mifflin.

Roid, G. H., & Pomplun, M. (2005). Interpreting the Stanford-Binet Intelligence Scales, fifth edition. In D. P. Flanagan & P. L. Harrison (Eds.), *Contemporary intellectual assessment: Theories, tests, and issues* (pp. 325–343). New York, NY: Guilford Press.

Rolland, J. P. (2002). Cross-cultural generalizability of the Five-Factor Model of personality. In R. R. McCrae & J. Allik (Eds.), *The Five-Factor Model of personality across cultures* (pp. 7–28). New York, NY: Kluwer Academic/Plenum.

Rolls, E. T. (2000). The orbitofrontal cortex and reward. *Cerebral Cortex, 10,* 284–294.

Rolls, E. T. (2004). The functions of the orbitofrontal cortex. *Brain and Cognition, 55,* 11–29.

Rolls, E. T. (2006). Brain mechanisms underlying flavour and appetite. *Philosophical Transactions of the Royal Society of London, 361,* 1123–1136.

Romain, J. (2008). Grand larceny in the first grade: Traumatic brain injury in the school-aged years. In J. N. Apps, R. F. Newby, & L. W. Roberts (Eds.), *Pediatric neuropsychology case studies: From the exceptional to the commonplace* (pp. 23–31). New York: Springer Science.

Ronn, T., Volkov, P., Davega, C., Dayeh, T., Hall, E., Olsson, A. H., . . . Ling, C. (2013). A six months exercise intervention influences the genome-wide DNA methylation pattern in human adipose tissue. *Plos Genetics, 9,* e1003572. doi: 10.1371/journal.pgen.1003572.

Rosch, E. (1973). Natural categories. *Cognitive Psychology, 4,* 328–350.

Rosch, E. (1975). Cognitive representations of semantic categories. *Journal of Experimental Psychology: General, 104,* 192–223.

Rose, A. J., Vegiopoulos, A., & Herzig, S. (2010). Role of glucocorticoids and the glucocorticoid receptor in metabolism: Insights from genetic manipulations. *Journal of Steroid Biochemistry & Molecular Biology, 122,* 10–20.

Rosellini, A. J., Lawrence, A. E., Meyer, J. F., & Brown, T. A. (2010). The effects of extraverted temperament on agoraphobia in panic disorder. *Journal of Abnormal Psychology, 119,* 420–426.

Roseman, I. J. (1984). Cognitive determinants of emotion: A structural theory. *Review of Personality & Social Psychology, 5,* 11–36.

Rosen, L. D., Cheever, N. A., Cummings, C., & Felt, J. (2007). The impact of emotionality and self-disclosure on online dating versus traditional dating. *Computers in Human Behavior, 24,* 2124–2157.

Rosenberg, E. L. (1998). Levels of analysis and the organization of affect. *Review of General Psychology, 2,* 247–270.

Rosenberg, E. L. (2005). The study of spontaneous facial expressions in psychology. In P. Ekman & E. L. Rosenberg (Eds.), *What the face reveals: Basic and applied studies of spontaneous expression using the Facial Action Coding System (FACS)* (2nd ed., pp. 3–17). New York, NY: Oxford University Press.

Rosenberg, E. L., & Ekman, P. (1994). Coherence between expressive and experiential systems in emotion. *Cognition & Emotion, 8*, 201–229.

Rosenberg, E. L., & Ekman, P. (2000). Emotion: Methods of study. In A. Kasdan (Ed.), *Encyclopedia of psychology* (pp. 171–175). Washington, DC: American Psychological Association and Oxford University Press.

Rosenberg, E. L., Ekman, P., Jiang, W., Coleman, R. E., Hanson, M., O'Connor, C., . . . Blumenthal, J. A. (2001). Linkages between facial expressions of anger and transient myocardial ischemia in men with coronary artery disease. *Emotion, 1*, 107–115. doi: 10.1037/1528-3542.1.2.107.

Rosenberger, P. H., Ickovics, J. R., Epel, E., Nadler, E., Jokl, P., Fulkerson, J. P., . . . Dhabhar, F. (2009). Surgery stress-induced immune cell redistribution profiles predict short-term and long-term postsurgical recovery. A prospective study. *Journal of Bone and Joint Surgery, 91*, 2783–2794.

Rosenman, R. H., Brand, J. H., Jenkins, C. D., Friedman, M., Straus, R., & Wurm, M. (1975). Coronary heart disease in the Western Collaborative Group Study: Final follow-up experience of 8.5 years. *Journal of the American Medical Association, 233*, 872–877.

Rosenman, R. H., Friedman, M., Straus, R., Wurm, M., Kositchek, R., Hahn, W., & Werthessen, N. T. (1964). A predictive study of coronary artery disease. *Journal of the American Medical Association, 189*, 113–124.

Rosenquist, J. N., Murabito, J., Fowler, J. H., & Christakis, N. A. (2010). The spread of alcohol consumption behavior in a large social network. *Annals of Internal Medicine, 152*, 426–433.

Rosenthal, R. (1976). *Experimenter effects in behavioral research, enlarged edition.* New York, NY: Irvington.

Rosenthal, R. (1986). Meta-analytic procedures and the nature of replication: The debate. *Journal of Parapsychology, 50*(4), 315–336.

Rosenthal, R. (1994). On being one's own case study: Experimenter effects in behavioral research—30 years later. In W. Shadish & S. Fuller (Eds.), *The social psychology of science* (pp. 214–229). New York, NY: Guilford Press.

Rosenthal, R., & Fode, K. L. (1963). The effect of experimenter bias on the performance of the albino rat. *Behavioral Science, 8*, 183–189.

Rosenthal, R., & Rubin, D. B. (1978). Interpersonal expectancy effects: The first 345 studies. *The Behavioral and Brain Sciences, 3*, 377–386.

Rosenzweig, M. R., & Bennett, E. L. (1969). Effects of differential environments on brain weights and enzyme activities in gerbils, rats and mice. *Developmental Psychobiology, 2*, 87–95.

Rosenzweig, M. R., Krech, D., Bennett, E. L., & Diamond, M. C. (1962). Effects of environmental complexity and training on brain chemistry and anatomy: A replication and extension. *Journal of Comparative and Physiological Psychology, 55*, 429–437.

Ross, L. (1977). The intuitive psychologist and his shortcomings: Distortions in the attribution process. In L. Berkowitz (Ed.), *Advances in experimental social psychology* (Vol. 10, pp. 173–220). New York, NY: Academic Press.

Rossetto, A., Megighian, M., Scorzeto, C., & Montecucco, C. (2013). Botulinum neurotoxins. *Toxicon, 67*, 31–36.

Rothbaum, B. O., Cahill, S. P., Foa, E. B., Davidson, J. R. T., Compton, J., Connor, K. M., . . . Hahn, C.-G. (2006). Augmentation of sertraline with prolonged exposure in the treatment of posttraumatic stress disorder. *Journal of Traumatic Stress, 19*, 625–638. doi: 10.1002/jts.20170.

Rothenberg, D. (2005). *Why birds sing: A journey through the mystery of bird song.* New York, NY: Basic Books.

Rowe, G., Hirsch, J. B., & Anderson, A. K. (2007). Positive affect increases the breadth of attentional selection. *Proceedings of the National Academy of Sciences, 104*, 383–388.

Rowland, N. E., Li, B.-H., & Morien, A. (1996). Brain mechanisms and the physiology of feeding. In E. D. Capaldi (Ed.), *Why we eat what we eat: The psychology of eating* (pp. 173–204). Washington, DC: American Psychological Association.

Roy, M., Piché, M., Chen, J.-I., Peretz, I., & Rainville, P. (2009). Cerebral and spinal modulation of pain by emotions. *Proceedings of the National Academy of Sciences, 106*, 20900–20905.

Rozin, P. (1996). Sociocultural influences on human food selection. In E. D. Capaldi (Ed.), *Why we eat what we eat: The psychology of eating* (pp. 233–263). Washington, DC: American Psychological Association.

Rozin, P., & Fallon, A. E. (1987). Perspectives on disgust. *Psychological Review, 94*, 23–41.

Ruan, J. (2004). Bilingual Chinese/English first-graders developing metacognition about writing. *Literacy, 38*, 106–112.

Ruff, H. (1999). Population-based data and the development of individual children: The case of low to moderate lead levels and intelligence. *Journal of Developmental & Behavioral Pediatrics, 20*(1), 42–49.

Rumbaugh, D. M., Beran, M. J., & Savage-Rumbaugh, S. (2003). Language. In D. Maestripieri (Ed.), *Primate psychology* (pp. 395–423). Cambridge, MA: Harvard University Press.

Runyan, W. M. (1981). Why did Van Gogh cut off his ear? The problem of alternative explanations in psychobiography. *Journal of Personality and Social Psychology, 40*, 1070–1077.

Runyan, W. M. (1982). *Life histories and psychobiography.* New York, NY: Oxford University Press.

Rushton, W. A. H. (1961). Rhodopsin measurement and dark adaptation in a subject deficient in cone vision. *Journal of Physiology, 156*, 193–205.

Rutter, M. (2002). Nature, nurture, and development: From evangelism through science toward policy and practice. *Child Development, 73*, 1–21.

Rutter, M. (2006). *Genes and behavior: Nature-nurture interplay explained.* Malden, MA: Blackwell.

Ruzgis, P. M., & Grigorenko, E. L. (1994). Cultural meaning systems, intelligence and personality. In R. J. Sternberg & P. Ruzgis (Eds.), *Personality and intelligence* (pp. 248–270). New York, NY: Cambridge University Press.

Ryan, G., Baerwald, J., & McGlone, G. (2008). Cognitive mediational deficits and the role of coping styles in pedophile and ephebophile Roman Catholic clergy. *Journal of Clinical Psychology, 64*, 1–16.

Ryan, R. M., Huta, V., & Deci, E. L. (2008). Living well: A self-determination theory perspective on eudaimonia. *Journal of Happiness Studies, 9*, 139–170.

Ryan, T., & Xenos, S. (2011). Who uses Facebook? An investigation into the relationship between the Big Five, shyness, narcissism, loneliness, and Facebook usage. *Computers in Human Behavior, 27*(5), 1658–1664. doi: 10.1016/j.chb.2011.02.004.

Rymer, R. (1993). *Genie: A scientific tragedy.* New York, NY: HarperPerennial.

Saarni, C. (1984). An observational study of children's attempts to monitor their expressive behavior. *Child Development, 55*, 1504–1513.

Saarni, C. (1999). *The development of emotional competence.* New York, NY: Guilford Press.

Sabbagh, L. (2006, August/September). The teen brain, hard at work: No, really. *Scientific American Mind, 17*, 21–25.

Sacco, R. L., Elkind, M., Boden-Albala, B., Lin, I.-F., Kargman, D. E., Hause, W. A., . . . Paik, M. C. (1999). The protective effect of moderate alcohol consumption on ischemic stroke. *Journal of the American Medical Association, 281*, 53–60. doi: 10.1001/jama.281.1.53.

Sackeim, H. A., Greenberg, M. S., Weiman, A. L., Gur, R. C., Hungerbuhler, J. P., & Geschwind, N. (1982). Hemispheric asymmetry in the expression of positive and negative emotions: Neurologic evidence. *Archives in Neurology, 39,* 210–218.

Sagan, C. (1987). The burden of skepticism. *Skeptical Inquirer, 12,* 38–46.

Sahdra, B. K., MacLean, K. A., Ferrer, E., Shaver, P. R., Rosenberg, E. L., Jacobs, T. L., . . . Saron, C. D. (2011). Enhanced response inhibition during intensive meditation training predicts improvements in self-reported adaptive socio-emotional functioning. *Emotion, 11,* 299–312.

Saisan, J., Smith, M., & Segal, J. (2010, May). *Psychotherapy and counseling: Finding a therapist and getting the most out of therapy.* Retrieved September 10, 2010, from http://www.helpguide.org/mental/psychotherapy_therapist_counseling.htm

Sakai, K. (2005). Language acquisition and brain development. *Science, 310,* 815–819.

Salehan, M., & Negahban, A. (2013). Social networking on smartphones: When mobile phones become addictive. *Computers in Human Behavior, 29*(6), 2632–2639.

Sallinen, M., Holm, A., Hiltunen, J., Hirvonen, K., Härmä, M., Koskelo, J., . . . Müller, K. (2008). Recovery of cognitive performance from sleep debt: Do a short rest pause and a single recovery night help? *Chronobiology International, 25,* 279–296. doi: 10.1080/07420520802107106.

Salmerón, J., Manson, J. E., Stampfer, M. J., Colditz, G. A., Wing, A. L., & Willett, W. C. (1997). Dietary fiber, glycemic load, and risk of non-insulin-dependent diabetes mellitus in women. *Journal of the American Medical Association, 277,* 472–477. doi: 10.1001/jama.1997.03540300040031.

Salovey, P., & Mayer, J. D. (1990). Emotional intelligence. *Imagination, Cognition, and Personality, 9,* 185–211.

Salthouse, T. A. (2000). Steps toward the explanation of adult differences in cognition. In T. J. Perfect & E. A. Maylor (Eds.), *Models of cognitive aging* (pp. 19–49). Oxford, England: Oxford University Press.

Salvucci, D. D., & Taatgen, N. A. (2008). Threaded cognition: An integrated theory of concurrent multitasking. *Psychological Review, 115,* 101–130. doi: 10.1037/0033-295X.115.1.101.

Samimi, P., & Alderson, K. G. (2014). Sexting among undergraduates. *Computers in Human Behavior, 31,* 230–241.

Sanders, L. (2009). Single brain cells selectively fire in response to specific thoughts: Thinking about her face activates "Halle Berry" neuron. *Science News, 176,* 9. doi: 10.1002/scin.5591761107.

Santrock, J. W. (2010). *A topical approach to life-span development* (5th ed.). New York, NY: McGraw-Hill.

Sapolsky, R. (1998). *Why zebras don't get ulcers: An updated guide to stress, stress-related disease and coping.* New York, NY: Freeman.

Sarlio-Lähteenkorva, S. (2001). Weight loss and quality of life among obese people. *Social Indicators Research, 54*(3), 329–354.

Sauter, D. A., Eisner, F., Ekman, P., & Scott, S. K. (2010). Cross-cultural recognition of basic emotions through nonverbal emotional vocalizations. *Proceedings of the National Academy of Sciences, 107,* 2408–2412.

Sava, F. A., Yates, B. T., Lupu, V., Szentagotai, A., & David, D. (2009). Cost-effectiveness and cost-utility of cognitive therapy, rational emotive behavioral therapy, and fluoxetine (Prozac) in treating depression: A randomized clinical trial. *Journal of Clinical Psychology, 65,* 36–52.

Savicki, V., Downing-Burnette, R., Heller, L., Binder, F., & Suntinger, W. (2004). Contrasts, changes, and correlates in actual and potential intercultural adjustment. *International Journal of Intercultural Relations, 28*(3–4), 311–329. doi: 10.1016/j.ijintrel.2004.06.001.

Savin-Williams, R. C., & Vrangalova, Z. (2013). Mostly heterosexual as a distinct sexual orientation group: A systematic review of the empirical evidence. *Developmental Review, 33,* 58–88. doi: 10.1016/j.dr.2013.01.001.

Sawyer, R. K. (2006). *Explaining creativity: The science of human innovation.* New York, NY: Oxford University Press.

Scarr, S. (1981). *Race, social class, and individual differences in I.Q.* Hillsdale, NJ: Erlbaum.

Schaal, B., Marlier, L., & Soussignan, R. (2000). Human fetuses learn odors from their pregnant mother's diet. *Chemical Senses, 25,* 729–737.

Schacter, D. L. (2001). *The seven sins of memory.* Boston, MA: Houghton Mifflin.

Schacter, D. L., & Tulving, E. (1994). *Memory systems.* Cambridge, MA: MIT Press.

Schaefer, E. J., Gleason, J. A., & Dansinger, M. L. (2005). The effects of low-fat, high-carbohydrate diets on plasma lipoproteins, weight loss, and heart disease risk reduction. *Current Atherosclerosis Reports, 7,* 421–427.

Schaie, K. W. (1996). *Intellectual development in adulthood: The Seattle Longitudinal Study.* New York, NY: Cambridge University Press.

Schein, E., & Bernstein, P. (2007). *Identical strangers: A memoir of twins separated and reunited.* New York, NY: Random House.

Schellenberg, E. G. (2004). Music lessons enhance IQ. *Psychological Science, 15,* 511–514.

Schellenberg, E. G. (2006). Long-term positive associations between music lessons and IQ. *Journal of Educational Psychology, 98,* 457–468.

Schellenberg, E. G. (2011). Examining the association between music lessons and intelligence. *British Journal of Psychology, 102*(3), 283–302. doi: 10.1111/j.2044-8295.2010.02000.x.

Scherag, S., Hebebrand, J., & Hinney, A. (2010). Eating disorders: The current status of molecular genetic research. *European Child and Adolescent Psychiatry, 19,* 211–226. doi: 10.1007/s00787-009-0085-9.

Scherer, K. R., Banse, R., & Wallbott, H. G. (2001). Emotion inferences from vocal expression correlate across languages and cultures. *Journal of Cross-Cultural Psychology, 32,* 76–92.

Scherer, K. R., Banse, R., Wallbott, H. G., & Goldbeck, T. (1991). Vocal cues in emotion coding and decoding. *Motivation and Emotion, 15,* 123–148.

Scherer, K. R., Dan, E., & Flykt, A. (2006). What determines a feeling's position in affective space? A case for appraisal. *Cognition & Emotion, 20,* 92–113.

Schienle, A., Schäfer, A., & Vaitl, D. (2008). Individual differences in disgust imagery: A functional magnetic resonance imaging study. *NeuroReport, 19,* 527–530.

Schiff, E. R. (1997). Hepatitis C and alcohol. *Hepatology, 26* (Suppl. 1), 39S–42S.

Schipani, D. (2014). Real-life online dating success stories. Retrieved online April 3, 2014 at http://www.womansday.com/sex-relationships/dating-marriage/real-life-online-dating-success-stories-111464

Schlaepfer, T. E. (2013). Neuromodulation of reward circuits with deep brain stimulation in treatment resistant depression. *Biological Psychiatry, 73,* 143s.

Schlaepfer, T. E., Bewernick, B., Kayser, S., Maedler, B., & Coenen, V. E. (2013). Rapid effects of deep brain stimulation for treatment-resistant major depression. *Biological Psychiatry, 73,* 1204–2014. doi: 10.1016/j.biopsych.2013.01.034.

Schlaug, G., Jäncke, L., Huang, Y., Staiger, J. F., & Steinmetz H. (1995). Increased corpus callosum size in musicians. *Neuropsychologia, 33,* 1047–1055.

Schmand, B., Eikelenboom, P., & van Gool, W. A. (2011). Value of neuropsychological tests, neuroimaging, and biomarkers for diagnosing Alzheimer's disease in younger and older age cohorts. *Journal of the American Geriatrics Society, 59*(9), 1705–1710. doi: 10.1111/j.1532-5415.2011.03539.x.

Schmand, B., Smit, J., Lindeboom, J., Smits, C., Hooijer, C., Jonker, C., & Deelman, B. (1997). Low education is a genuine risk factor for accelerated memory decline and dementia. *Journal of Clinical Epidemiology, 50*, 1025–1033.

Schmidt, M. E., & Vandewater, E. A. (2008). Media and attention, cognition, and school achievement. *The Future of Children, 18*, 63–85.

Schmithorst, V. J., Holland, S. K., & Dardzinski, B. J. (2008). Developmental differences in white matter architecture between boys and girls. *Human Brain Mapping, 29*, 696–710.

Schmitt, D. (2003). Universal sex differences in the desire for sexual variety: Tests from 52 nations, 6 continents, and 13 islands. *Journal of Social and Personality Psychology, 85*, 85–104. doi: 10.1037/0022-3514.85.1.85.

Schneider, J. A., Arvanitakis, Z., Bang, W., & Bennett, D. A. (2007). Mixed brain pathologies account for most dementia cases in community-dwelling older persons. *Neurology, 69*, 2197–2204.

Schuldberg, D. (2000–2001). Six subclinical spectrum traits in normal creativity. *Creativity Research Journal, 13*, 5–16.

Schuler, J. L. H., & O' Brien, W. H. (1997). Cardiovascular recovery from stress and hypertension risk factors: A meta-analytic review. *Psychophysiology, 34*, 649–659.

Schulkin, J. (Ed.). (2005). *Allostasis, homeostasis, and the costs of physiological adaptation.* New York, NY: Cambridge University Press.

Schultz, W. T. (2005). *Handbook of psychobiography.* New York, NY: Oxford University Press.

Schutte, C., & Hanks, R. (2010). Impact of the presence of alcohol at the time of injury on acute and one-year cognitive and functional recovery after traumatic brain injury. *International Journal of Neuroscience, 120*, 551–556.

Schutte, N. S., Malouff, J. M., Thorsteinsson, E. B., Bhullar, N., & Rooke, S. E. (2007). A meta-analytic investigation of the relationship between emotional intelligence and health. *Personality and Individual Differences, 42*, 921–933.

Schwartz, G. M., Izard, C. E., & Ansul, S. E. (1985). The 5-month-old's ability to discriminate facial expressions of emotion. *Infant Behavior and Development, 8*, 65–77.

Schwartz, J. H. (2000). Neurotransmitters. In E. R. Kandel, J. M. Schwartz, & T. M. Jessell (Eds.), *Principles of neural science* (4th ed., pp. 280–297). New York, NY: McGraw-Hill.

Schwartz, J. M. (1999a). First steps toward a theory of mental force: PET imaging of systematic cerebral changes after psychological treatment of obsessive-compulsive disorder. In S. R. Hameroff, A. W. Kaszniak, & D. J. Chalmers (Eds.), *Toward a science of consciousness III: The third Tucson discussions and debates.* Boston, MA: MIT Press.

Schwartz, J. M. (1999b). A role for volition and attention in the generation of new brain circuitry: Toward a neurobiology of mental force. *Journal of Consciousness Studies, 6*, 115–142.

Schwerdtfeger, A. (2007). Individual differences in auditory, pain, and motor stimulation. *Journal of Individual Differences, 28*, 165–177.

Scott, J. (2000). Rational choice theory. In G. Browning, A. Halcli, & F. Webster (Eds.), *Understanding contemporary society: Theories of the present* (pp. 126–138). New York, NY: Sage.

Scruggs, J. L., Schmidt, D., & Deutch, A. Y. (2003). The hallucinogen 1-[2,5-dimethoxy-4-iodophenyl]-2-aminopropane (DOI) increases cortical extracellular glutamate levels in rats. *Neuroscience Letters, 346*, 137–140.

Scully, J. A., Tosi, H., & Banning, K. (2000). Life event checklists: Reevaluating the Social Readjustment Rating Scale after 30 years. *Educational and Psychological Measurement, 60*, 864–876.

Sebastian, C., Viding, E., Williams, K. D., & Blakemore, S. (2010). Social brain development and the affective consequences of ostracism in adolescence. *Brain and Cognition, 72*, 134–145.

Segal, N. (1999). *Entwined lives: Twins and what they tell us about human nature.* New York, NY: Plume.

Segal, Z. V., Williams, J. M. G., & Teasdale, J. D. (2002). *Mindfulness-based cognitive therapy for depression.* New York, NY: Guilford Press.

Seifert, K. L., Hoffnung, R. J., & Hoffnung, M. (2000). *Lifespan development* (2nd ed.). Boston, MA: Houghton Mifflin.

Seligman, M. E. P., & Csikszentmihalyi, M. (2000). Positive psychology: An introduction. *American Psychologist, 55*, 5–14. doi: 10.1037/0003-066X.55.1.5.

Seligman, M. E. P., & Hager, J. L. (Eds.). (1972). *The biological boundaries of learning.* New York, NY: Appleton.

Seligman, M. E. P., Rashid, R., & Parks, A. C. (2006). Positive psychotherapy. *American Psychologist, 61*, 774–788.

Seligman, M. E. P., Schulman, P., & Tryon, A. M. (2007). Group prevention of depression and anxiety symptoms. *Behaviour Research and Therapy, 45*, 1111–1126.

Selkoe, D. (2002). Alzheimer's disease is a synaptic failure. *Science, 298*(5594), 789–791.

Sell, R. L. (1997). Defining and measuring sexual orientation: A review. *Archives of Sexual Behavior, 26*, 643–658. doi: 10.1007/978-0-387-31334-4_14.

Selten, J. P., Frissen, A., Lensvelt-Mulder, G., & Morgan, V. A. (2010). Schizophrenia and the 1957 pandemic of influenza:

Meta-analysis. *Schizophrenia Bulletin, 36*, 219–228. doi: 10.1093/schbul/sbp147.

Selye, H. (1946). The general adaptation syndrome and diseases of adaptation. *Journal of Clinical Endocrinology, 6*, 117–230.

Selye, H. (1976). *The stress of life.* New York, NY: McGraw-Hill.

Sen, B., & Swaminathan, S. (2007). Maternal prenatal substance use and behavior problems among children in the U.S. *Journal of Mental Health Policy and Economics, 10*, 189–206.

Sergerstrom, S. C., & Sephton, S. E. (2010). Optimistic expectancies and cell-mediated immunity: The role of positive affect. *Psychological Science, 21*, 448–455. doi: 10.1177/095679761036206.

Serpell, R. (1982). Measures of perception, skills, and intelligence. In W. W. Hartup (Ed.), *Review of child development research* (Vol. 6, pp. 392–440). Chicago, IL: University of Chicago Press.

Serrano-Blanco, A., Palao D. J., Luciano, J. V., Pinto-Meza, A., Lujan, L., Fernandez, A., . . . Haro, J. M. (2010). Prevalence of mental disorders in primary care: Results from the Diagnosis and Treatment of Mental Disorders in Primary Care Study (DASMAP). *Social Psychiatry and Psychiatric Epidemiology, 45*, 201–210. doi: 10.1007/s00127-009-0056-y.

Shank, D. B., & Cotten, S. R. (2014). Does technology empower urban youth? The relationship of technology use to self-efficacy. *Computers & Education, 70*, 184–193.

Shargorodsky, J., Curhan, S. G., Curhan, G. C., & Eavey, R. (2010). Change in prevalence of hearing loss in U.S. adolescents. *Journal of the American Medical Association, 304*, 772–778.

Shastry, B. S. (2005). Bipolar disorder: An update. *Neurochemistry International, 46*, 273–279.

Shaw, P., Greenstein, D., Lerch, J., Clasen, L., Lenroot, R., Gogtay, N., . . . Giedd, J. (2006). Intellectual ability and cortical development in children and adolescents. *Nature, 440*, 676–679.

Shedler, J. (2010). The efficacy of psychodynamic psychotherapy. *American Psychologist, 65*, 98–109.

Shekelle, R. B., Hulley, S. B., Neston, J. D., Billings, J. H., Borboni, N. O., Gerace, T. A., . . . (1985). The MRFIT behavior pattern study: Type A behavior and incidence of coronary heart disease. *American Journal of Epidemiology, 122*, 559–570.

Shen, H., Sabaliauskas, N., Sherpa, A., Fenton, A. A., Stelzer, A., Aoki, C., & Smith, S. S. (2010). A critical role for 4β GABAA receptors in shaping learning deficits at puberty in mice. *Science, 327*, 1515–1518.

Shepard, M. (1995). Kraepelin and modern psychiatry. *European Archives of Psychiatry and Clinical Neuroscience, 245,* 189–195.

Shepard, R., & Metzler, J. (1971). Mental rotation of three-dimensional objects. *Science, 171,* 701–703.

Shergill, S. S., Brammer, M. J., Fukuda, R., Williams, S. C. R., Murray, R. M., & McGuire, P. K. (2003). Engagement of brain areas implicated in processing inner speech in people with auditory hallucinations. *British Journal of Psychiatry, 182,* 525–531.

Shergill, S. S., Brammer, M. J., Williams, S. C. R., Murray, R. M., & McGuire, P. K. (2000). Mapping auditory hallucinations in schizophrenia using functional magnetic resonance imaging. *Archives of General Psychiatry, 57,* 1033–1038.

Shermer, M. (1997). *Why people believe weird things: Pseudoscience, superstition, and other confusions of our time.* New York, NY: W. H. Freeman.

Shermer, M. (2011). *The believing brain: From ghosts and gods to politics and conspiracies—How we construct beliefs and reinforce them as truths.* New York, NY: St. Martin's Griffin.

Shestyuk, A. Y., Deldin, P. J., Brand, J. E., & Deveney, C. M. (2005). Reduced sustained brain activity during processing of positive emotional stimuli in major depression. *Biological Psychiatry, 57,* 1089–1096.

Shomaker, L. B., & Furman, W. (2009). Interpersonal influences on late adolescent girls' and boys' disordered eating. *Eating Behaviors, 10,* 97–106.

Shore, L. M., & Wayne, S. J. (1993). Commitment and employee behavior: Comparison of affective commitment and continuance commitment with perceived organizational support. *Journal of Applied Psychology, 78,* 774–780.

Short, S. J., Lubach, G. R., Karasin, A. I., Olsen, C. W., Styner, M., Knickmeyer, R. C., . . . Coe, C. L. (2010). Maternal influenza infection during pregnancy impacts postnatal brain development in the rhesus monkey. *Biological Psychiatry, 67,* 965–973.

Siegers, K., van Boxtel, M. P. J., & Jolles, J. (2012). Computer use in older adults: Determinants and the relationship with cognitive change over a 6 year episode. *Computers in Human Behavior, 28,* 1–10.

Siegman, A. W., Anderson, R., Herbst, J., Boyle, S., & Wilkinson, J. (1992). Dimensions of anger-hostility and cardiovascular reactivity in provoked and angered men. *Journal of Behavioral Medicine, 15,* 257–272.

Sigman, M., & Hassan, S. (2006). Benefits of long-term group therapy to individuals suffering schizophrenia: A prospective 7-year study. *Bulletin of the Menninger Clinic, 70,* 273–282.

Sigurdsson, T., Doyere, V., Cain, C. K., & LeDoux, J. E. (2007). Long-term potentiation in the amygdala: A cellular mechanism of fear learning and memory. *Neuropharmacology, 52,* 215–227.

Silbersweig, D. A., Stern, E., Frith, C., Cahill, C., Holmes, A., Grootoonk, S., . . . Frackowiak, R. S. J. (1995). A functional neuroanatomy of hallucinations in schizophrenia. *Nature, 378,* 176–179. doi: 10.1038/378176a0.

Silva, L. M., Cignolini, A., Warren, R., Budden, S., & Skowron-Gooch, A. (2007). Improvement in sensory impairment and social interaction in young children with autism following treatment with an original Qigong massage methodology. *American Journal of Chinese Medicine, 35,* 393–406.

Silverman, I., Choi, J., & Peters, M. (2007). The Hunter-Gatherer Theory of sex differences in spatial abilities: Data from 40 countries. *Archives of Sexual Behavior, 36,* 261–268. doi: 10.1007/s10508-006-9168-6.

Silverstein, S. M., Menditto, A. A., & Stuve, P. (2001). Shaping attention span: An operant conditioning procedure to improve neurocognition and functioning in schizophrenia. *Schizophrenia Bulletin, 27,* 247–257.

Silvia, P. J. (2006). *Exploring the psychology of interest.* New York, NY: Oxford University Press.

Silvia, P. J., & Kimbrel, N. A. (2010). A dimensional analysis of creativity and mental illness: Do anxiety and depression symptoms predict creative cognition, creative accomplishments, and creative self-concepts? *Psychology of Aesthetics, Creativity and the Arts, 4,* 2–10.

Sime, J. D. (1983). Affiliative behavior during escape to building exits. *Journal of Environmental Psychology, 3,* 21–41.

Simmons, V. N., Heckman, B. W., Fink, A. C., Small, B. J., & Brandon, T. H. (2013). Efficacy of an experiential, dissonance-based smoking intervention for college students delivered via the internet. *Journal of Consulting and Clinical Psychology, 81,* 810–820. doi: http://dx.doi.org/10.1037/a0032952.

Simner, J., Sagiv, N., Mulvenna, C., Tsakanikos, E., Witherby, S., Fraser, C., . . . Ward, J. (2006). Synesthesia: The prevalence of atypical cross-modal experiences. *Perception, 35,* 1024–1033.

Simon, H. A. (1978). Information-processing theory of human problem solving. In W. K. Estes (Ed.), *Handbook of learning and cognitive processes: Vol. 5. Human information processing* (pp. 271–295). Hillsdale, NJ: Erlbaum.

Simon, N. M., Smoller, J. W., McNamara, K. L., Maser, R. S., Zalta, A. K., Pollack, M. H., . . . Wong, K. K. (2006). Telomere shortening and mood disorders: Preliminary support for a chronic stress model of accelerated aging. *Biological Psychiatry, 60,* 432–435.

Simonds, J., Kieras, J. E., Rueda, M. R., & Rothbart, M. K. (2007). Effortful control, executive attention, and emotional regulation in 7–10-year-old children. *Cognitive Development, 22,* 474–488.

Simons, D. J., & Chabris, C. F. (1999). Gorillas in our midst: Sustained inattentional blindness for dynamic events. *Perception, 28,* 1059–1074.

Simon-Thomas, E. R., Keltner, D. J., Sauter, D., Sinicropi-Yao, L., & Abramson, A. (2009). The voice conveys specific emotions: Evidence from vocal burst displays. *Emotion, 9,* 838–846.

Simonton, D. K. (1999). *Origins of genius.* New York, NY: Oxford University Press.

Simpson, K. (2001). The role of testosterone in aggression. *McGill Journal of Medicine, 6,* 32–40.

Simpson, K. A., & Bloom, S. R. (2010). Appetite and hedonism: Gut hormones and the brain. *Endocrinology Metabolism Clinics of North America,39,* 729–743.

Singer, T., Seymour, B., O'Doherty, J. O., Kaube, H., Dolan, R. J., & Frith, C. D. (2004). Empathy for pain involves the affective but not sensory components of pain. *Science, 303,* 1157–1162.

Sirignono, S. W., & Lachman, M. E. (1985). Personality change during the transition to parenthood: The role of perceived infant temperament. *Developmental Psychology, 21,* 558–567.

Skinner, B. F. (1938). *The behavior of organisms.* New York, NY: Appleton.

Skinner, B. F. (1953). *Science and human behavior.* New York, NY: Free Press.

Skinner, B. F. (1957). *Verbal behavior.* New York, NY: Appleton-Century-Crofts.

Skinner, B. F. (1971). *Beyond freedom and dignity.* New York, NY: Knopf.

Skinner, B. F. (1990). Can psychology be a science of mind? *American Psychologist, 45,* 1206–1210.

Skoe, E., & Kraus, N. (2012). A little goes a long way: How the adult brain is shaped by musical training in childhood. *Journal of Neuroscience, 32*(34), 11507–11510. doi: 10.1523/JNEUROSCI.1949-12.2012.

Slamecka, N. J., & McElree, B. (1983). Normal forgetting of verbal lists as a function of their degree of learning. *Journal of Experimental Psychology: Learning, Memory, & Cognition, 9,* 384–397.

Slater, E., & Meyer, A. (1959). Contributions to a pathography of the musicians:

Robert Schumann. *Confinia Psychiatrica, 2,* 65–94.

Slavich, G. M., O'Donovan, A., Epel, E., & Kemeny, M. (2010). Black sheep get the blues: A psychobiological model of social rejection and depression. *Neurosciences and Biobehavioral Reviews, 35,* 39–45. doi: 10.1016/j.neubiorev.2010.01.003.

Sloan, P., Arsenault, L., & Hilsenroth, M. (2002). *Use of the Rorschach in the assessment of war-related stress in military personnel.* Ashland, OH: Hogrefe & Huber.

Slutske, W. E., Moffitt, T., Poulton, R., & Caspi, A. (2012). Undercontrolled temperament at age 3 predicts disordered gambling at age 32: A longitudinal study of a complete birth cohort. *Psychological Science, 23,* 510–516. doi: 10.1177/0956797611429708.

Small, G. W., Moody, T. D., Siddarth, P., & Bookheimer, S. Y. (2009). Your brain on Google: Patterns of cerebral activation during Internet searching. *American Journal of Geriatric Psychiatry, 17,* 116–126.

Smallwood, P. M., Olveczky, B. P., Williams, G. L., Jacobs, G. H., Reese, B. E., Meister, M., & Nathans, J. (2003). Genetically engineered mice with an additional class of cone photoreceptors: Implications for the evolution of color vision. *Proceedings of the National Academy of Sciences, 100,* 11706–11711. doi: 10.1073/pnas.1934712100.

Smith, B. D. (1998). *Psychology: Science and understanding.* New York, NY: McGraw-Hill.

Smith, C., & MacNeill, C. (1994). Impaired motor memory for a pursuit motor task following Stage 2 sleep loss in college students. *Journal of Sleep Research, 3,* 206–213.

Smith, C. A., & Ellsworth, P. C. (1987). Patterns of appraisal and emotion related to taking an exam. *Journal of Personality and Social Psychology, 52,* 475–488.

Smith, C. T., Aubrey, J. B., & Peters, K. R. (2004). Different roles for REM and Stage 2 sleep in motor learning: A proposed model. *Psychologica Belgica, 44,* 81–104.

Smith, H. R., Comella, C., & Högl, B. (2008). *Sleep medicine.* Cambridge, United Kingdom: Cambridge University Press.

Smith, J. (2009, March 25). *Number of U.S. Facebook users over 35 nearly doubles in last 60 days.* Retrieved from http://www.insidefacebook.com/2009/03/25/number-of-us-facebook-users-over-35-nearly-doubles-in-last-60-days/

Smith, J., Cianflone, K., Biron, S., Hould, F. S., Lebel, S., Marceau, S., Marceau, P. (2009). Effects of maternal surgical weight loss in mothers on intergenerational transmission of obesity. *The Journal of Clinical Endocrinology & Metabolism, 94,* 318–319. doi: 10.1210/jc.2009-0709.

Smith, M., & Glass, G. (1977). Meta-analysis of psychotherapy outcome studies. *American Psychologist, 32,* 752–760.

Smith, M., & Kollock, P. (Eds). (1999). *Communities in cyberspace.* London, England: Routledge.

Smith, N., Young, A., & Lee, C. (2004). Optimism, health-related hardiness and well-being among older Australian women. *Journal of Health Psychology, 9,* 741–752.

Smyth, J. M. (1998). Written emotional expression, effect sizes, outcome types, and moderating variables. *Journal of Consulting & Clinical Psychology, 66,* 174–184.

Snarey, J. R. (1985). Cross-cultural universality of social-moral development: A critical review of Kohlbergian research. *Psychological Bulletin, 97,* 202–232.

Snyderman, M., & Rothman, S. (1987). Survey of expert opinion on intelligence and aptitude testing. *American Psychologist, 42,* 137–144.

Soeter, M., & Kindt, M. (2010). Dissociating response systems: Erasing fear from memory. *Neurobiology of Learning and Memory, 94,* 30–41.

Soler, J., Pascual, J. C., Tiana, T., Cebria, A., Barrachina, J., Campins, M. J., . . . Pérez, V. (2009). Dialectical behaviour therapy skills training compared to standard group therapy in borderline personality disorder: A 3-month randomized controlled clinical trial. *Behaviour Research and Therapy, 47,* 353–358.

Solms, M. (2000). Dreaming and REM sleep are controlled by different brain mechanisms. *Behavioral and Brain Sciences, 23,* 843–850.

Solms, M. (2004). Freud returns. *Scientific American, 290*(5), 82–88.

Solms, M., & Turnbull, O. (2002). *The brain and the inner world: An introduction to the neuroscience of subjective experience.* New York, NY: Other Press.

Song, S. (2006, March 27). Mind over medicine. *Time, 167,* 13.

Soorya, L. V., Carpenter, L. A., & Romanczyk, R. G. (2011). In E. Hollander, A. Kolevzon, & J. T. Coyle (Eds.). *Textbook of autism spectrum disorders* (pp. 525–535). Arlington, VA, US: American Psychiatric Publishing, Inc.

Sorce, J. F., Emde, R. N., Campos, J., & Klinnert, M. D. (1985). Maternal emotional signaling: Its effect on the visual cliff behavior of 1-year-olds. *Developmental Psychology, 21,* 195–200.

Southwick, S. M., Vythilingam, M., & Charney, D. S. (2005). The psychobiology of depression and resilience to stress: Implications for prevention and treatment. *Annual Review of Clinical Psychology, 1,* 255–291.

Sowell, E. R., Thompson, P. M., Tessner, K. D., & Toga, A. W. (2001). Mapping continued brain growth and gray matter density reduction in dorsal frontal cortex: Inverse relationships during postadolescent brain maturation. *Journal of Neuroscience, 21,* 8619–8829.

Spalding, K. L., Arner, E., Westermark, P. O., Bernard, S., Buchholz, B. A., Bergmann, O., . . . (2008, June 5). Dynamics of fat cell turnover in humans. *Nature, 453,* 783–787. doi: 10.1038/nature06902.

Spearman, C. (1904). "General intelligence," objectively determined and measured. *American Journal of Psychology, 15,* 201–292.

Spearman, C. (1923). *The nature of 'intelligence' and the principles of cognition.* London, England: Macmillan.

Spector, F., & Maurer, D. (2009). Synesthesia: A new approach to understanding the development of perception. *Developmental Psychology, 45,* 175–189.

Speisman, R. B., Kumar, A., Rani, A., Pastoriza, J. M., Severance, J. E., Foster, T. C., & Ormerod, B. K. (2013). Environmental enrichment restores neurogenesis and rapid acquisition in aged rats. *Neurobiology of Aging, 34,* 263–274. Retrieved from http://dx.doi.org/10.1016/j.neurobiolaging.2012.05.023

Spelke, E. (2008). Effects of music instruction on developing cognitive systems at the foundations of mathematics and science. *Learning, Arts and the Brain: The Dana Consortium Report on Arts and Cognition.* New York, NY: Dana Press.

pencer, J. P. (2010). The impact of fruit flavonoids on memory and cognition. *British Journal of Nutrition, 104*(Suppl.), S40–S47. doi: 10.1017/S0007114510003934.

Spencer, S. M., & Patrick, J. H. (2009). Social support and personal mastery as protective resources during emerging adulthood. *Journal of Adult Development, 16,* 191–198.

Sperry, R. W., Gazzaniga, M. S., & Bogen, J. E. (1969). Interhemispheric relationships: The neocortical commissures: Syndromes of hemisphere disconnection. In P. J. Vinken & G. W. Bruyn (Eds.), *Handbook of clinical neurology* (pp. 273–290). Amsterdam, Netherlands: North-Holland.

Spiegel, D., Bloom, J. R., Kraemer, H. C., & Gottheil, E. (1989). Effect of psychosocial treatment on survival of patients with metastatic breast cancer. *The Lancet, 8668,* 88–91.

Spinrad, T. L., Eisenberg, N., Cumberland, A., Fabes, R. A., Valiente, C., Shepard, S. A., . . . (2006). Relation of emotion-related regulation to children's social competence: A longitudinal study. *Emotion, 6*, 498–510.

Sproesser, G., Schupp, H. T., & Renner, B. (2014). The bright side of stress-induced eating: Eating more when stressed but less when pleased. Psychological Science, 25, 58–65, first published on October 28, 2013. doi: 10.1177/0956797613494849.

Squire, L. (1987). *Memory and brain.* New York, NY: Oxford University Press.

Squire, L. R. (1977). ECT and memory loss. *American Journal of Psychiatry, 134,* 997–1001.

Squire, L. R. (2009). *The history of neuroscience in autobiography* (Vol. 6). New York, NY: Elsevier.

Staggs, G. D., Larson, L. M., & Borgen, F. H. (2007). Convergence of personality and interests: Meta-analysis of the multidimensional personality questionnaire and the strong interest inventory. *Journal of Career Assessment, 15,* 423–445.

Stanley, J. (1996). In the beginning: The study of mathematically precocious youth. In C. P. Benbow & D. Lubinski (Eds.), *Intellectual talent* (pp. 225–235). Baltimore, MD: Johns Hopkins University Press.

Stanton, A. L., Danoff-Burg, S., Sworowski, L. A., Rodriguez-Hanley, A., Kirk, S. B., & Austenfeld, J. L. (2002). Randomized, controlled trial of written emotional expression and benefit finding in breast cancer patients. *Journal of Clinical Oncology, 20,* 4160–4168.

Starr, C., & Taggart, R. (2004). *Biology: The unity and diversity of life* (10th ed.). Belmont, CA: Thomson-Brooks Cole.

Stefansson, H., Ophoff, R. A., Steinberg, S., Andreassen, O. A., Chicon, S., Rujescu, D., . . . Collier, D. A. (2009). Common variants conferring risks of schizophrenia. *Nature, 460,* 744–747.

Steinberg, L. (2005). Cognitive and affective development in adolescence. *Trends in Cognitive Science, 9,* 69–74.

Steinberg, L. (2010). *Adolescence* (9th ed.). New York, NY: McGraw-Hill.

Steiner, B., Wolf, S., & Kempermann, G. (2006). Adult neurogenesis and neurodegenerative disease. *Regenerative Medicine, 1,* 15–28.

Steinhausen, H., & Spohr, H. (1998). Long-term outcome of children with fetal alcohol syndrome: Psychopathology, behavior, and intelligence. *Alcoholism: Clinical and Experimental Research, 22*(2), 334–338.

Stellar, E. (1954). The physiology of motivation. *Psychological Review, 61,* 5–22.

Stenberg, C. R., Campos, J. J., & Emde, R. (1983). The facial expression of anger in seven-month-old infants. *Child Development, 54,* 178–184.

Stepanski, L. M. (2006). At day's close: Night in times past. *Journal of Popular Culture, 39,* 1111–1113. doi: 10.1111/j.1540-5931.2006.00347.x

Stephane, M., Barton, S., & Boutros, N. N. (2001). Auditory verbal hallucinations and dysfunction of the neural substrates of speech. *Schizophrenia Research, 50,* 61–78.

Stephens, T. (2007). How a Swiss invention hooked the world. http.//www.swissinfo.ch/eng/how-a-swiss-invention-hooked-the-world/5653568.

Sterling, P., & Eyer, J. (1988). Allostasis: A new paradigm to explain arousal pathology. In S. Fisher & H. S. Reason (Eds.), *Handbook of life stress, cognition and health* (pp. 629–649). New York, NY: John Wiley.

Stern, S. A., & Alberini, C. M. (2013). Mechanisms of memory enhancement. *Wiley Interdisciplinary Reviews: Systems Biology and Medicine, 5,* 37–53. doi: 10.1002/wsbm.1196.

Sternberg, R. J. (1985). *Beyond IQ: A triarchic theory of human intelligence.* New York, NY: Cambridge University Press.

Sternberg, R. J. (1986). A triangular theory of love. *Psychological Review, 93,* 119–135.

Sternberg, R. J. (1988). *The triarchic mind: A new theory of human intelligence.* New York: Viking Press.

Sternberg, R. J. (1998). Principles of teaching for successful intelligence. *Educational Psychologist, 55,* 65–72.

Sternberg, R. J. (2000). The concept of intelligence. In R. J. Sternberg (Ed.), *The handbook of intelligence* (pp. 3–15). Cambridge, England: Cambridge University Press.

Sternberg, R. J. (2003). A broad view of intelligence: A theory of successful intelligence. *Consulting Psychology Journal: Practice and Research, 55,* 139–154.

Sternberg, R. J. (Ed.). (2004). *Definitions and conceptions of giftedness.* Thousand Oaks, CA: Corwin Press.

Sternberg, R. J. (2005). The triarchic theory of successful intelligence. In D. P. Flanagan & P. L. Harrison (Eds.), *Contemporary intellectual assessment: Theories, tests, and issues* (pp. 103–119). New York, NY: Guilford Press.

Sternberg, R. J. (2006a). *Cognitive psychology* (4th ed.). Belmont, CA: Thomson-Wadsworth.

Sternberg, R. J. (2006b). The Rainbow Project: Enhancing the SAT through assessments of analytical, practical, and creative skills. *Intelligence, 34,* 321–350.

Sternberg, R. J., & Detterman, D. K. (Eds.). (1986). *What is intelligence? Contemporary viewpoints on its nature and definition.* Norwood, NJ: Ablex.

Sternberg, R. J., Grigorenko, E. L., & Kidd, K. K. (2005). Intelligence, race, and genetics. *American Psychologist, 60,* 46–59.

Stevens, J. S., & Hamann, S. (2012). Sex differences in brain activation to emotional stimuli: A meta-analysis of neuroimaging studies. *Neuropsychologia, 50*(7), 1578–1593. doi: 10.1016/j.neuropsychologia.2012.03.011.

Stevens, S. B., & Morris, T. L. (2007). College dating and social anxiety: Using the Internet as a means of connecting to others. *CyberPsychology & Behavior, 10,* 680–688.

Stephens, T. (2007). How a Swiss invention hooked the world. http://www.swissinfo.ch/eng/how-a-swiss-invention-hooked-the-world/5653568

Stewart, J. H. (2005). Hypnosis in contemporary medicine. *Mayo Clinic Proceedings, 80,* 511–524.

Stewart, R. A., Rule, A. C., & Giordano, D. A. (2007). The effect of fine motor skill activities on kindergarten attention. *Early Childhood Education Journal, 35,* 103–109.

Stewart, V. M. (1973). Tests of the "carpentered world" hypothesis by race and environment in America and Zambia. *International Journal of Psychology, 8,* 83–94.

Stice, E., Shaw, H., Bohon, C., Marti, C. N., & Rhode, P. (2009). A meta-analytic review of depression prevention programs for children and adolescents: Factors that predict magnitude of intervention effects. *Journal of Consulting and Clinical Psychology, 77,* 486–503.

Stickgold, R. (2005). Sleep-dependent memory consolidation. *Nature, 437,* 1272–1278.

Stickgold, R. (2013). Early to bed: How sleep benefits children's memory. *Trends in Cognitive Sciences, 17,* 261–262. Retrieved from http://dx.doi.org/10.1016/j.tics.2013.04.006

Stickgold, R., & Walker, M. P. (2007). Sleep-dependent memory consolidation and reconsolidation. *Sleep Medicine, 8,* 331–343.

Strack, F., Martin, L. L., & Stepper, S. (1988). Inhibiting and facilitating conditions of the human smile: A nonobtrusive test of the facial feedback hypothesis. *Journal of Personality and Social Psychology, 54,* 768–777.

Strange, B. A., & Dolan, R. J. (2006). Anterior medial temporal lobe in human cognition: Memory for fear and the unexpected. *Neuropsychiatry, 11,* 198–218.

Strassman, R. J. (1984). Adverse reactions to psychedelic drugs. A review of the literature. *Journal of Nervous and Mental Disease, 172,* 577–595.

Strauss, M. E., Pasupathi, M., & Chatterjee, A. (1993). Concordance between observers in descriptions of personality change in

Alzheimer's disease. *Psychology and Aging, 8*, 475–480.

Strayer, D. L., & Drews, F. A. (2007a). Cellphone-induced driver distraction. *Current Directions in Psychological Science, 16*, 128–131.

Strayer, D. L., & Drews, F. A. (2007b). Multitasking in the automobile. In A. F. Kramer, D. A. Wiegmann, & A. Kirlik (Eds.), *Attention: From theory to practice* (pp. 121–133). New York, NY: Oxford University Press.

Strayer, D. L., Drews, F. A., & Couch, D. J. (2006). A comparison of the cell phone driver and the drunk driver. *Human Factors, 48*, 381–391.

Streissguth, A., Barr, H., Sampson, P., Darby, B., & Martin, D. (1989). IQ at age 4 in relation to maternal alcohol use and smoking during pregnancy. *Developmental Psychology, 25*(1), 3–11.

Striedter, G. (2005). *Principles of brain evolution.* Sunderland, MA: Sinauer.

Stroodley, C. J., & Schmahmann, J. D. (2009). Functional topography in the human cerebellum: A meta-analysis of neuroimaging studies. *NeuroImage, 44*, 489–501.

Stroop, J. R. (1935). Studies of interference in serial-verbal reaction. *Journal of Experimental Psychology, 18*, 643–662.

Strueber, D., Lueck, M., & Roth, G. (2006–2007). The violent brain. *Scientific American Mind, 17*, 20–27.

Styles, E. A. (2006). *The psychology of attention* (2nd ed.). Hove, England: Psychology Press.

Styron, W. (1990). *Darkness visible: A memoir of madness.* New York, NY: Vintage.

Suarez, E. C., Bates, M. P., & Harralson, T. L. (1998). The relation of hostility to lipids and lipoproteins in women: Evidence for the role of antagonistic hostility. *Annals of Behavioral Medicine, 20*, 59–63.

Suarez, E. C., Harlan, E., Peoples, M. C., & Williams, R. B., Jr. (1993). Cardiovascular reactivity and emotional responses in women: The role of hostility and harassment. *Health Psychology, 12*, 459–468.

Suarez, E. C., & Williams, R. B., Jr. (1989). Situational determinants of cardiovascular and emotional reactivity in high and low hostile men. *Psychosomatic Medicine, 51*, 404–418.

Subrahmanyam, K., & Greenfield, P. (2008). Online communication and adolescent relationships. *The Future of Children, 18*, 119–146.

Subrahmanyam, K., Greenfield, P. M., & Tynes, B. (2004). Constructing sexuality and identity in an online teen chatroom. *Journal of Applied Developmental Psychology, 25*, 651–666.

Subrahmanyam, K., Šmahel, D., & Greenfield, P. M. (2006). Connecting developmental processes to the Internet: Identity presentation and sexual exploration in online teen chatrooms. *Developmental Psychology, 42*, 1–12.

Sullivan, E. V., Harris, R. A., & Pfefferbaum, A. (2010). Alcohol's effects on brain and behavior. *Alcohol Research & Health, 33*, 127–143.

Sullivan, K., Zaitchik, D., & Tager-Flusberg, H. (1994). Preschoolers can attribute second-order beliefs. *Developmental Psychology, 30*, 395–402.

Sullivan, K. M. (2009). *The Bundy murders: A comprehensive history.* Jefferson, NC: McFarland.

Suomi, S. (2005). Genetic and environmental factors influencing the expression of impulsive aggression and serotonergic functioning in rhesus monkeys. In R. E. Tremblay, W. W. Hartup, & J. Archer (Eds.), *Developmental origins of aggression* (pp. 63–82). New York, NY: Guilford Press.

Susskind, J. M., Lee, D. H., Cusi, A., Feiman, R., Grabski, W., & Anderson, A. K. (2008). Expressing fear enhances sensory acquisition. *Nature Neuroscience, 11*, 843–850.

Sutton, J. (2013, October 15). *Two girls arrested in Florida online bullying death.* Retrieved October 17, 2013, from http://www.reuters.com/article/2013/10/15/us-usa-bullying-florida-idUSBRE99E0G820131015

Sweatt, J. D. (2010, May 7). Epigenetics and cognitive aging. *Science, 328*, 701–702. doi: 10.1126/science.1189968.

Swets, J. A. (1964). *Signal detection and recognition by human observers.* New York, NY: Wiley.

Syed, M., & Azmitia, M. (2010). Narrative and ethnic identity exploration: A longitudinal account of emerging adults' ethnicity-related experiences. *Developmental Psychology, 46*, 208–219.

Szaflarski, J. P., Schmithorst, V. J., Altaye, M., Byars, A. W., Ret, J., Plante, E., & Holland, S. K. (2006). A longitudinal functional magnetic resonance imaging study of language development in children 5 to 11 years old. *Annals of Neurology, 59*, 796–807. doi: 10.1002/ana.20817.

Tafti, M., Dauvilliers, Y., & Overeem, S. (2007). Narcolepsy and familial advanced sleep-phase syndrome: Molecular genetics of sleep disorders. *Current Opinion in Genetics & Development, 17*, 222–227.

Takahashi, Y., Yamagata, S., Kijima, N., Shigemasu, K., Ono, Y., & Ando, J. (2007). Continuity and change in behavioral inhibition and activation systems: A longitudinal behavioral genetic study. *Personality and Individual Differences, 43*(6), 1616–1625.

Takeuchi, H., Taki, Y., Sassa, Y., Hashizume, H., Sekiguchi, A., Fukushima, A., & Kawashima, R. (2010). White matter structures associated with creativity: Evidence from diffusion tensor imaging. *NeuroImage, 51*, 11–18.

Talassi, E., Cipriani, G., Bianchetti, A., & Trabucchi, M. (2007). Personality changes in Alzheimer's disease. *Aging & Mental Health, 11*, 526–531.

Talati, A., Bao, Y., Kaufman, J., Shen, L., Schaefer, C. A., & Brown, A. S. (2013). Maternal smoking during pregnancy and bipolar disorder in offspring. *American Journal of Psychiatry, 170*, 1178–1185. doi: 10.1176/appi.ajp.2013.12121500.

Talmi, D., Grady, C. L., Goshen-Gottstein, Y., & Moscovitch, M. (2005). Neuroimaging the serial position curve: A test of single-store versus dual-store models. *Psychological Science, 16*, 717–723.

Tambs, K., Hoffman, H. J., Borchgrevink, H. M., Holmen, J., & Engdahl, B. (2006). Hearing loss induced by occupational and impulse noise: Results on threshold shifts by frequencies, age and gender from the NordTrØndelag Hearing Loss Study. *International Journal of Audiology, 45*, 309–317.

Tammet, D. (2006). *Born on a blue day: A memoir.* New York, NY: Free Press.

Tang, Z., & Orwin, R. G. (2009). Marijuana initiation among American youth and its risks as dynamic processes: Prospective findings from a national longitudinal study. *Substance Use & Misuse, 44*, 195–211.

Tangney, J. P., Stuewig, J., & Mashek, D. J. (2007). Moral emotions and moral behavior. *Annual Review of Psychology, 58*, 345–372.

Tanielian, T., & Jaycox, L. H. (Eds.). (2008). *Invisible wounds of war: Psychological and cognitive injuries, their consequences, and services to assist recovery.* Santa Monica, CA: Rand Corp.

Tardif, T., Gelman, S., & Xu, F. (1999). Putting the "noun bias" in context: A comparison of English and Mandarin. *Developmental Psychology, 70*, 620–635.

Tare, M., & Gelman, S. A. (2010). Can you say it another way? Cognitive factors in bilingual children's pragmatic language skills. *Journal of Cognition and Development, 11*(2), 137–158. doi: 10.1080/15248371003699951.

Tarmann, A. (2002, May/June). Out of the closet and onto the Census long form. *Population Today, 30*, 1, 6.

Tashkin, D. (2006, May 23). *Marijuana smoking not linked to lung cancer.* Paper presented at the annual meeting of the American Thoracic Society, San Diego, CA.

Tashkin, D. R., Baldwin, G. C., Sarafian, T., Dubinett, S., & Roth, M. D. (2002). Respiratory and immunologic consequences of marijuana smoking. *Journal of Clinical Pharmacology, 42,* S71–S81.

Tavris, C. (2013, May 18). How psychiatry went crazy. *The Wall Street Journal,* C5.

Taylor, K. N., Harper, S., & Chadwick, P. (2009). Impact of mindfulness on cognition and affect in voice hearing: Evidence from two case studies. *Behavioral and Cognitive Psychotherapy, 37,* 397–402.

Taylor, S. E. (1989). *Positive illusions: Creative self-deception and the healthy mind.* New York, NY: Basic Books.

Taylor, S. E. (2009). *Health psychology* (7th ed.). New York, NY: McGraw-Hill.

Taylor, S. E., Kemeny, M. E., Reed, G. M., Bower, J. E., & Gruenewald, T. L. (2000). Psychological resources, positive illusions, and health. *American Psychologist, 55,* 99–109.

Teasdale, G., & Jennett, B. (1976). Assessment and prognosis of coma after head injury. *Acta Neurochirurgica, 34,* 45–55.

Teasdale, J. D., Segal, Z., Williams, M. G., Ridgeway, V. A., Soulsby, J. M., & Lau, M. A. (2000). Prevention of relapse/recurrence in major depression by mindfulness-based cognitive therapy. *Journal of Consulting and Clinical Psychology, 68,* 615–623.

Teasdale, J. D., Segal, Z. V., & Williams, J. M. G. (1995). How does cognitive therapy prevent depressive relapse and why should attentional control (mindfulness) training help? *Behaviour Research and Therapy, 33,* 25–39.

Tellegen, A. (2000). *Manual for the multidimensional personality questionnaire.* Minneapolis: University of Minnesota Press.

Tellegen, A., Ben-Porath, Y. S., McNulty, J. L., Arbisi, P. A., Graham, J. R., & Kaemmer, B. (2003). *The MMPI-2 Restructured Clinical Scales: Development, validation, and interpretation.* Minneapolis: University of Minnesota Press.

Tellegen, A., Lykken, D. T., Bouchard, T. J., Wilcox, K. J., Segal, N. L., & Rich, S. (1988). Personality similarity in twins reared apart and together. *Journal of Personality and Social Psychology, 54,* 1031–1039.

Teo, K., Lear, S., Islam, S., Mony, P., Dehghan, M., Li, W., . . . Yusuf, S. (2013). Prevalence of a healthy lifestyle among individuals with cardiovascular disease in high-, middle- and low-income countries: The Prospective Urban Rural Epidemiology (PURE) Study. *Journal of the American Medical Association, 309*(15), 1613–1621. doi: 10.1001/jama.2013.3519.

Terrace, H. S. (1987). *Nim: A chimpanzee who learned sign language.* New York, NY: Columbia University Press.

Thacher, P. V. (2008). University students and "the all-nighter": Correlates and patterns of students' engagement in a single night of total sleep deprivation. *Behavioral Sleep Medicine, 6,* 16–31.

Thagard, P. (2005). *Mind: An introduction to cognitive science* (2nd ed.). Cambridge, MA: MIT Press.

Thapar, A., Langley, K., Asherson, P., & Gill, M. (2007). Gene-environment interplay in attention-deficit hyperactivity disorder and the importance of a developmental perspective. *British Journal of Psychiatry, 190,* 1–3.

Thayer, S. E., & Ray, S. (2006). Online communication preferences across age, gender, and duration of Internet use. *CyberPsychology & Behavior, 9,* 432–440.

Thibaut, J. W., & Kelley, H. H. (1959). *The social psychology of groups.* New York, NY: Wiley.

Thomas, A., & Chess, S. (1977). *Temperament and development.* New York, NY: Brunner/ Mazel.

Thomasius, R., Zapletalova, P., Petersen, K., Buchert, R., Andresen, B., Wartberg, L., . . . Schmoldt, A. (2006). Mood, cognition and serotonin transporter availability in current and former ecstasy (MDMA) users: The longitudinal perspective. *Journal of Psychopharmacology, 20,* 211–225. doi: 10.1177/0269881106059486.

Thompson, P. M., Giedd, J. N., Woods, R. P., MacDonald, D., Evans, A. C., & Toga, A. W. (2000). Growth patterns in the developing brain using continuum mechanical tensor maps. *Nature, 404,* 190–193.

Thompson, R. F., & Madigan, S. A. (2005). *Memory: The key to consciousness.* Washington, DC: Joseph Henry Press.

Thompson, W. L., & Kosslyn, S. M. (2000). Neural systems activated during visual mental imagery. In A. W. Toga & J. C. Mazziotta (Eds.), *Brain mapping: The systems* (pp. 535–560). San Diego, CA: Academic Press.

Thorndike, E. L. (1905). *Elements of psychology.* New York, NY: Seiler.

Thornhill, R., Gangestad, S. W., Miller, R., Scheyd, G., McCollough, J. K., & Franklin, M. (2003). Major histocompatibility complex genes, symmetry, and body scent attractiveness in men and women. *Behavioral Ecology, 14,* 668–678.

Thornton, L. M., Mazzeo, S. E., & Bulik, C. M. (2011). The heritability of eating disorders: Methods and current findings. *Current Topics in Behavioral Neuroscience, 6,* 141–156. doi: 10.1007/7854_2010_91.

Three in four Americans believe in paranormal. (2005, June 16). Retrieved October 11, 2013, from http://www.gallup.com/poll/16915/three-four-americans-believe-paranormal.aspx?version=print

Thune, I., & Furberg, A. S. (2001). Physical activity and cancer risk: Dose-response and cancer, all sites and site specific. *Medicine and Science in Sports and Exercise, 33,* S530–S550.

Titov, N., Andrews, G., Johnston, L., Robinson, E., & Spence, J. (2010). Transdiagnostic Internet treatment for anxiety disorders: A randomized controlled trial. *Behavior Research and Therapy, 48,* 890–899.

Tobe, E. H. (2013). Mitochondrial dysfunction, oxidative stress, and major depressive disorder. *Neuropsychiatric Disease and Treatment, 9,* 567–573. doi: 10.2147/NDT. S44282.

Tobias, S., & Everson, H. T. (2002). *Knowing what you know and what you don't: Further research on metacognitive knowledge monitoring.* New York, NY: College Entrance Examination Board.

Tobin, D. J. (2004). Biology of hair pigmentation. In B. Forslind, M. Lindberg, and L. Norlen (Eds.), *Skin, hair, nails: Structure and function* (pp. 319–363). New York, NY: Marcel Dekker.

Tolin, D. F. (2010). Is cognitive-behavioral therapy more effective than other therapies? A meta-analytic review. *Clinical Psychology Review, 30,* 710–720.

Tolman, E. C., & Honzik, C. H. (1930). Introduction and removal of reward, and maze performance in rats. *University of California Publications in Psychology, 4,* 257–275.

Tomasello, M., & Hermann, E. (2010). Ape and human cognition: What's the difference? *Current Directions in Psychological Science, 19,* 3–8.

Tomiyama, A., O'Donovan, A., Lin, J., Puterman, E., Lazaro, A., Chan, J., . . . Epel, E. (2012). Does cellular aging relate to patterns of allostasis? An examination of basal and stress reactive HPA axis activity and telomere length. *Physiology & Behavior, 106*(1), 40–45. doi: 10.1016/j.physbeh.2011.11.016.

Tomkins, S. S. (1962). *Affect, imagery, consciousness: Vol. 1. The positive affects.* New York, NY: Springer.

Tomkins, S. S. (1981). The quest for primary motives: Biography and autobiography of an idea. *Journal of Personality and Social Psychology, 41,* 306–329.

Tomkins, S. S., & McCarter, R. (1964). What and where are the primary affects? Some evidence for a theory. *Perceptual and Motor Skills, 18,* 119–158.

Tomson, S. N., Narayan, M., Allen, G. I., & Eagleman, D. M. (2013). Neural networks of colored sequence synesthesia. *Journal of Neuroscience, 33,* 14098–14106. doi: 10.1523/JNEUROSCI.5131-12-2013.

Tong, E. M. W., Ellsworth, P. C., & Bishop, G. D. (2009). An S-shaped relationship between changes in appraisal and changes in emotions. *Emotion, 9,* 821–837.

Tooby, J., & Cosmides, L. (1990). The past explains the present: Emotional adaptations and the structure of ancestral environments. *Ethology and Sociobiology, 11,* 375–424.

Tooby, J., & Cosmides, L. (1992). The psychological foundations of culture. In J. H. Barkow, L. Cosmides, & J. Tooby (Eds.), *The adapted mind: Evolutionary psychology and the generation of culture* (pp. 19–136). New York, NY: Oxford University Press.

Tourino, C., Evan-Rothschild, A., & de Lecea, L. (2013). Optogenetics in psychiatric diseases. *Current Opinion in Neurobiology, 23,* 430-435. doi: 10.1016/j.conb,2013.03.007.

Townsend, S. S. M., Markus, H. R., & Bergsieker, H. B. (2009). My choice, your categories: The denial of multiracial identities. *Journal of Social Issues, 65,* 185–204.

Toyota, Y., Ikeda, M., Shinagawa, S., Matsumoto, T., Matsumoto, N., Hokoishi, K., . . . Tanabe, H. (2007). Comparison of behavioral and psychological symptoms in early-onset and late-onset Alzheimer's disease. *International Journal of Geriatric Psychiatry, 22*(9), 896–901. doi: 10.1002/gps.1760.

Tracy, J. L., & Matsumoto, D. M. (2008). The spontaneous display of pride and shame: Evidence for biologically innate nonverbal displays. *Proceedings of the National Academy of Science, 105,* 11655–11660.

Tracy, J. L., & Robins, R. W. (2007). Emerging insights into the nature and function of pride. *Current Directions in Psychological Science, 16,* 147–150.

Tracy, J. L., & Robins, R. W. (2008). The nonverbal expression of pride: Evidence for cross-cultural recognition. *Journal of Personality and Social Psychology, 94,* 516–530.

Tracy, J. L., Robins, R. W., & Tangney, J. P. (2007). *The self-conscious emotions: Theory and research.* New York, NY: Guilford Press.

Tracy, J. L., Shariff, A. F., Zhao, W., & Henrich, J. (2013). Cross-cultural evidence that the nonverbal expression of pride is an automatic status signal. *Journal of Experimental Psychology: General, 142,* 163–180. doi: 10.1037/a0028412.

Transcripts of "Secrets of the Wild Child." (1997). Retrieved from http://www.pbs.org/wgbh/nova/transcripts/2112gchild.html

Treffert, D. A. (2006). *Extraordinary people: Understanding savant syndrome* (Updated Version). Lincoln, NE: iUniverse.

Treffert, D. A., & Christensen, D. D. (2005). Inside the mind of a savant. *Scientific American, 293,* 108–113.

Treisman, A. (1964). Verbal cues, language and meaning in selective attention. *American Journal of Psychology, 77,* 206–209.

Tremblay, K., & Ross, B. (2007). Effects of age and age-related hearing loss on the brain. *Journal of Communication Disorders, 40,* 305–312.

Trentacosta, C. J., & Izard, C. E. (2007). Kindergarten children's emotion competence as a predictor of their academic competence in first grade. *Emotion, 7,* 77–88.

Trepte, S., & Reinecke, L. (2013). The reciprocal effects of social network site use and the disposition for self-disclosure: A longitudinal study. *Computers in Human Behavior, 29,*1102–1112. http://dx.doi.org/10.1016/j.chb.2012.10.002.

Triplett, N. (1898). The dynamogenic factors in pacemaking and competition. *American Journal of Psychology, 9,* 507–533.

Trivers, R. L. (1971). The evolution of reciprocal altruism. *Quarterly Review of Biology, 46,* 35–57.

Trivers, R. L. (1972). Parental investment and sexual selection. In B. Campbell (Ed.), *Sexual selection and the descent of man, 1871–1971* (pp. 136–179). Chicago, IL: Aldine.

Trivers, R. L. (1985). *Social evolution.* Menlo Park, CA: Benjamin/Cummings.

Troisi, A. (2003). Psychopathology. In D. Maestripieri (Ed.), *Primate psychology* (pp. 451–470). Cambridge, MA: Harvard University Press.

Tronick, E., Morelli, G. A., & Ivey, P. K. (1992). The Efe forager infant and toddler's pattern of social relationships: Multiple and simultaneous. *Developmental Psychology, 28,* 568–577.

Trucking stats and FAQ's. (n.d.). Retrieved January 20, 2007, from http://www.geocities.com/TheTropics/1608/stats.htm

True, M., Pisani, L., & Oumar, F. (2001). Infant-mother attachment among the Dogon of Mali. *Child Development, 72,* 1451–1466.

Trugman, J. M. (1998). Tardive dyskinesia: Diagnosis, pathogenesis, and management. *Neurologist, 4,* 180–187.

Tsai, J., & Chentsova-Dutton, Y. (2003). Variation among European Americans in emotional facial expression. *Journal of Cross-Cultural Psychology, 34,* 650–657.

Tsai, J. L., Chentsova-Dutton, Y., Friere-Bebeau, L., & Przymus, D. E. (2002). Emotional expression and physiology in European Americans and Hmong Americans. *Emotion, 2,* 380–397.

Tsai, J. L., Levenson, R. W., & Carstensen, L. L. (2000). Autonomic, expressive, and subjective responses to emotional films in older and younger Chinese American and European American adults. *Psychology and Aging, 15,* 684–693.

Tsakiris, M., Hesse, M. D., Boy, C., Haggard, P., & Fink, G. R. (2007). Neural signatures of body ownership: A sensory network for bodily self-consciousness. *Cerebral Cortex, 17,* 2235–2244.

Tseng, W. S. (1973). The development of psychiatric concepts in traditional Chinese medicine. *Archives of General Psychiatry, 29,* 569–575.

Tucker-Drob, E. M., Rhemtulla, M., Harden, K., Turkheimer, E., & Fask, D. (2011). Emergence of a gene × socioeconomic status interaction on infant mental ability between 10 months and 2 years. *Psychological Science, 22*(1), 125–133. doi: 10.1177/0956797610392926.

Tugade, M. M., & Fredrickson, B. L. (2004). Resilient individuals use positive emotions to bounce back from negative emotional experiences. *Journal of Personality and Social Psychology, 86,* 320–333.

Tulku, T. (1984). *Knowledge of freedom.* Berkeley, CA: Dharma.

Tully, K., & Bolshakov, V. (2010). Emotional enhancement of memory: How norepinephrine enables synaptic plasticity. *Molecular Brain, 3,* 15. doi: 10.1186/1756-6606-3-15.

Tully, P. J., & Cosh, S. M. (2013). Generalized anxiety disorder prevalence and comorbidity with depression in coronary heart disease: A meta-analysis. *Journal of Health Psychology, 18,* 1601–1616. doi: 10.1177/1359105312467390.

Tulving, E. (1972). Episodic and semantic memory. In E. Tulving & W. Donaldson (Eds.), *Organization of memory* (pp. 381– 403). New York, NY: Academic Press.

Tulving, E. (1985). How many memory systems are there? *American Psychologist, 40,* 385–398.

Turati, C., Natale, E., Bolognini, N., Senna, I., Picozzi, M., Longhi, E., & Cassia, V. M. (2013). The early development of human mirror mechanisms: Evidence from electromyographic recordings at 3 and 6 months. *Developmental Science, 16,* 793–800.

Turkheimer, E., & Gottesman, I. (1991). Individual differences and the canalization of human behavior. *Developmental Psychology, 27,* 18–22.

Turner, E. H., Matthews, A. M., Linardatos, E., Tell, R. A., & Rosenthal, R. (2008). Selective publication of antidepressant trials and its influence on apparent efficacy. *New England Journal of Medicine, 358,* 252–260.

Turner-Shea, Y., Bruno, R., & Pridmore, S. (2006). Daily and spaced treatment with transcranial magnetic stimulation in major depression: A pilot study. *Australian and*

New Zealand Journal of Psychiatry, 40, 759–763.

Tversky, A., & Kahneman, D. (1974). Judgment under uncertainty: Heuristics and biases. *Science, 185,* 1124–1131.

Tversky, A., & Kahneman, D. (1983). Extensional versus intuitive reasoning: The conjunction fallacy in probability judgment. *Psychological Review, 90,* 293–315.

20 legal medical marijuana states and DC. (2013, September 16). Retrieved November 20, 2013, from http://medicalmarijuana. procon.org/view.resource. php?resourceID=000881

Twyman, K., Saylor, C., Taylor, L. A., & Comeaux, C. (2009). Comparing children and adolescents engaged in cyberbullying to matched peers. *Cyberpsychology.* doi: 10.1089/cpb.2009.0137.

Tyron, W. W. (2005). Possible mechanisms for why desensitization and exposure therapy work. *Clinical Psychology Review, 25,* 67–95.

Udry, J. R., Morris, N. M., & Waller, L. (1973). Effect of contraceptive pills on sexual activity in the luteal phase of the human menstrual cycle. *Archives of Sexual Behavior, 2,* 205–214.

Uher, J. (2008). Comparative personality research: Methodological approaches. *European Journal of Personality* [serial online], *22*(5), 427–455.

Uher, R., & McGuffin, P. (2010). The moderation by the serotonin transporter gene of environmental adversity in the etiology of depression: 2009 update. *Molecular Psychiatry, 15,* 18–22.

Uhlhaas, P. J., Roux, F., Singer, W., Haenschel, C., Sireteanu, R., & Rodriguez, E. (2009). The development of neural synchrony reflects late maturation and restructuring functional networks in humans. *Proceedings of the National Academy of Sciences, 106,* 9866–9871.

Uhlhaas, P. J., & Singer, W. (2010). Abnormal neural oscillations and synchrony in schizophrenia. *Nature Reviews Neuroscience, 11,* 100–113.

University of Cambridge. (2011, February 10). Extra testosterone reduces your empathy, researchers find. *ScienceDaily.* Retrieved from http://www.sciencedaily.com/ releases/2011/02/110209105556.htm

U.S. Census Bureau. (2009a). *Current population survey.* Retrieved from http://www. census.gov/population/socdemo/hh-fam/ms2. xls

U.S. Census Bureau. (2009b). *Table 4: Annual estimates of the two or more races resident population by sex and age for the United States: April 1, 2000 to July 1, 2008* [Data file]. Retrieved from http:// www.census.gov/popest/national/asrh/NC-EST2008/NC-EST2008-04-TOM.csv

U.S. Department of Health and Human Services (USDHHS). (2004). *The health consequences of smoking: A report of the surgeon general.* Atlanta, GA: Author.

U.S. Department of Health and Human Services. (2006). *The health consequences of involuntary exposure to tobacco smoke: A report of the surgeon general—Executive summary.* Retrieved from http://www. surgeongeneral.gov/library/secondhandsmoke/ report/executivesummary.pdf

U.S. Senate. (2004). *Report of the Select Committee on Intelligence on the U.S. intelligence community's prewar intelligence assessments on Iraq.* Retrieved from http:// www.gpoaccess.gov/serialset/creports/iraq. html

Utz, K. S., Dimova, V., Oppenländer, K., & Kerkhoff, G. (2010). Electrified minds: Transcranial direct current stimulation (tDCS) and galvanic vestibular stimulation (GVS) as methods of non-invasive brain stimulation in neuropsychology—A review of current data and future implications. *Neuropsychologia, 48,* 2789–810. doi: 10.1016/ j.neuropsychologia.2010.06.002.

Utz, S., Tanis, M., & Vermeulen, I. (2012). It is all about being popular: The effects of need for popularity on social network site use. *Cyberpsychology, Behavior, and Social Networking, 15*(1), 37–42. doi: 10.1089/cyber. 2010.0651.

Uylings, H. B. M. (2006). Development of the human cortex and the concept of "critical" or "sensitive" periods. *Language Learning, 56,* 59–90.

Valente, M., Placid, F., Oliveira, A. J., Bigagli, A., Morghen, I., Proietti, R., & Gigli, G. L. (2002). Sleep organization pattern as a prognostic marker at the sub-acute stage of post-traumatic coma. *Clinical Neurophysiology, 113,* 1798–1805.

Valenzuela, M. J., Matthews, F. E., Brayne, C., Ince, P., Halliday, G., Kril, J. J., . . . Sachdev, P.S. (2012). Multiple biological pathways link cognitive lifestyle to protection from dementia. *Biological Psychiatry, 71,* 783–791. doi: 10.1016/j.biopsych.2011.07.036.

Valkenburg, P. M., & Peter, J. (2007a). Preadolescents' and adolescents' online communication and their closeness to friends. *Developmental Psychology, 43,* 267–277.

Valkenburg, P. M., & Peter, J. (2007b). Who visits online dating sites? Exploring some characteristics of online daters. *CyberPsychology & Behavior, 10,* 849–852.

Valkenburg, P. M., & Peter, J. (2009). Social consequences of the Internet for adolescents: A decade of research. *Current Directions in Psychological Science, 18,* 1–5.

Valkenburg, P. M., Peter, J., & Schouten, A. P. (2006). Friend networking sites and their relationship to adolescents' well-being and social self-esteem. *CyberPsychology & Behavior, 9,* 584–590.

Valois, R. F., Zullig, K. J., Huebner, E. S., & Drane, J. W. (2003). Dieting behaviors, weight perceptions, and life satisfaction among public high school adolescents. *Eating Disorders, 11,* 271–288.

Van Gerven, P., Van Boxtel, M., Meijer, W., Willems, D., & Jolles, J. (2007). On the relative role of inhibition in age-related working memory decline. *Aging, Neuropsychology, and Cognition, 14,* 95–107. doi: 10.1080/138255891007038.

van IJzendoorn, M., & Juffer, F. (2005). Adoption is a successful natural intervention enhancing adopted children's IQ and school performance. *Current Directions in Psychological Science, 14,* 326–330.

van IJzendoorn, M., & Sagi, A. (1999). Cross-cultural patterns of attachment: Universal and contextual dimensions. In J. Cassidy & P. Shaver (Eds.), *Handbook of attachment* (pp. 265–286). New York, NY: Guilford Press.

van Leeuwen, T. M., den Ouden, H. M., & Hagoort, P. (2011). Effective connectivity determines the nature of subjective experience in grapheme-color synesthesia. *Journal of Neuroscience, 31*(27), 9879–9884. doi: 10.1523/JNEUROSCI.0569-11.2011.

van Praag, H., Kempermann, G., & Gage, F. H. (1999). Running increases cell proliferation and neurogenesis in the adult mouse dentate gyrus. *Nature Neuroscience, 2,* 266–270.

Van Rooij, A. J., Schoenmakers, T. M., van de Eijnden, R. J. J. M., & van de Mheen, D. (2010). Compulsive Internet use: The role of online gaming and other Internet applications. *Journal of Adolescent Health, 47,* 51–57.

Van Voorhees, B. W., Paunesku, D., Kuwabara, S. A., Basu, A., Gollan, J., Hankin, B. L., & Reinecke, M. (2008). Protective and vulnerability factors predicting new-onset depressive episode in a representative of U.S. adolescents. *Journal of Adolescent Health, 42,* 605–616. doi: 10.1016/ j.jadohealth.2007.11.135.

van Vugt, M. K., & Jha, A. P. (2011). Investigating the impact of mindfulness meditation training on working memory: A mathematical modeling approach. *Cognitive, Affective & Behavioral Neuroscience, 11,* 344–353. doi: 10.3758/s13415-011-0048-8.

Van Wyk, P. H., & Geist, C. S. (1984). Psychosocial development of heterosexual, bisexual and homosexual behavior. *Archives of Sexual Behavior, 13,* 505–544.

Vandewater, E. A., Rideout, V. J., Wartella, E. A., Huang, X., Lee, J. H., & Shim, M. (2007). Digital childhood: Electronic media and technology use among infants, toddlers, and preschoolers. *Pediatrics, 119*, e1006–e1015.

Vandewater, E. A., Shim, M., & Caplovitz, A. G. (2004). Linking obesity and activity level with children's television and video game use. *Journal of Adolescence, 27*, 71–85.

Vanhaudenhuyse, A., Boly, M., Balteau, E., Schnakers, C., Moonen, G., Luxen, A., . . . Faymonville, M. E. (2009). Pain and non-pain processing during hypnosis: A thulium-YAG event-related fMRI study. *NeuroImage, 47*, 1047–1054.

Vanlessen, N., Rossi, V., De Raedt, R., & Pourtois, G. (2013). Positive emotion broadens attention focus through decreased position-specific spatial encoding in early visual cortex: Evidence from ERPs. *Cognitive, Affective & Behavioral Neuroscience, 13*(1), 60–79. doi: 10.3758/s13415-012-0130-x.

Vaswani, M., Linda, F. K., & Ramesh, S. (2003). Role of selective serotonin reuptake inhibitors in psychiatric disorders: A comprehensive review. *Progress in Neuro-Psychopharmacology and Biological Psychiatry, 2*, 85–102.

Vaughan, W. (2009). Painless deprivation. *Science, 324*(5930), 1014.

Veith, I. (1965). *Hysteria: The history of a disease.* Chicago, IL: University of Chicago Press.

Vellas, B., Coley, N., Ouseet, P.-J., Bartigues, J.-F., Dubois, B., Grandjean, H., . . . Andrieu, S. (2012). Long-term use of standardised ginkgo biloba extract for the prevention of Alzheimer's disease (GuidAge): A randomised placebo-controlled trial. *The Lancet Neurology, 11*, 851–859.

Velliste, M., Perel, S., Spalding, M., Whitford, A. S., & Schwartz, A. B. (2008, June 19). Cortical control of a prosthetic arm for self-feeding. *Nature, 453*, 1098–1101. doi: 10.1038/nature06996.

Venning, A., Kettler, L., Eliott, J., & Wilson, A. (2009). The effectiveness of cognitive-behavioural therapy with hopeful elements to prevent the development of depression in young people: A systematic review. *International Journal of Evidence-Based Healthcare, 7*, 15–33. doi: 10.1111/j.1744-1609.2009.00122.x.

Venkatasubramanian, G., & Kalmady, S. V. (2010). Creativity, psychosis, and human evolution: The exemplar case of *neuregulin 1* gene. *Indian Journal of Psychiatry, 52*, 282.

Verkhratsky, A., Rodrıguez, J. J., & Parpura, V. (2012). Neurotransmitters and integration in neuronal-astroglial networks. *Neurochemistry Research, 37*, 2326–2338. doi: 10.1007/s11064-012-0765-6.

Verquer, M. L., Beehr, T. A., & Wagner, S. H. (2003). A meta-analysis of relations between person-organization fit and work attitudes. *Journal of Vocational Behavior, 63*, 473–489.

Vetter, H. J. (1968). New-word coinage in the psychopathological context. *Psychiatric Quarterly, 42*, 298–312.

Villemure, C., & Schweinhardt, P. (2010). Supraspinal pain processing: Distinct roles of emotion and attention. *The Neuroscientist, 16*, 276–284.

Vinson, G. A., Connelly, B. S., & Ones, D. S. (2007). Relationships between personality and organization switching: Implications for utility estimates. *International Journal of Selection and Assessment, 15*, 118–133.

Virués-Ortega, J. (2010). Applied behavior analytic intervention for autism in early childhood: Meta-analysis, meta-regression and dose-response meta-analysis of multiple outcomes. *Clinical Psychology Review, 30*, 387–399.

Von dem Hagen, E. A. H., Beaver, J. D., Ewbank, M. P., Keane, J., Passamonti, L., Lawrence, A. D., & Calder, A. J. (2009). Leaving a bad taste in your mouth but not in my insula. *Social Cognitive and Affective Neurosciences, 4*, 379–386.

Vyas, N. S., Patel, N. H., Nijran, K. S., Al-Nahhas, A., & Puri, B. K. (2010). Insights into schizophrenia using positron emission tomography: Building the evidence and refining the focus. *British Journal of Psychiatry, 197*, 3–4.

Vygotsky, L. S. (1978). *Mind and society: The development of higher psychological processes.* Cambridge, MA: Harvard University Press.

Wadlinger, H. A., & Isaacowitz, D. M. (2006). Positive mood broadens visual attention to positive stimuli. *Motivation & Emotion, 30*, 89–101.

Wagner, A. W., & Linehan, M. M. (2006). Applications of dialectical behavior therapy to posttraumatic stress disorder and related problems. In V. M. Folette & J. I. Ruzek (Eds.), *Cognitive-behavioral therapies for trauma* (2nd ed., pp. 117–145). New York, NY: Guilford Press.

Wagner, T. D., & Ochsner, K. N. (2005). Sex differences in the emotional brain. *NeuroReport, 16*, 85–87.

Wahlbeck, K., Forsen, T., Osmond, C., Barker, D. J. P., & Erikkson, J. G. (2001). Association of schizophrenia with low maternal body mass index, small size at birth, and thinness during childhood. *Archives of General Psychiatry, 58*, 48–55.

Wai, J., Lubinski, D., & Benbow, C. (2009). Spatial ability for STEM domains: Aligning over 50 years of cumulative psychological knowledge solidifies its importance. *Journal of Educational Psychology, 101*, 817–835.

Waite, L. J., Laumann, E. O., Das, A., & Schumm, L. P. (2009). Sexuality: Measures of partnerships, practices, attitudes, and problems in the National Social Life, Health, and Aging Study. *Journal of Gerontology: Social Sciences, 64B*(S1), i56–i66. doi: 10.1093/geronb/gbp038.

Wakimoto, S., & Fujihara, T. (2004). The correlation between intimacy and objective similarity in interpersonal relationships. *Social Behavior and Personality, 32*, 95–102.

Waldinger, M. D., Zwinderman, A. H., Schweitzer, D. H., & Olivier, B. (2004). Relevance of methodological design for the interpretation of efficacy of drug treatment of premature ejaculation: A systematic review and meta-analysis. *International Journal of Impotence Research, 16*, 369–381.

Walhovd, K. B., Fjell, A. M., Brown, T. T., Kuperman, J. M., Chung, Y., Hagler, D. R., . . . Dale, A. M. (2012). Long-term influence of normal variation in neonatal characteristics on human brain development. *Proceedings of the National Academy of Sciences of the United States of America, 109*(49), 20089–20094. doi: 10.1073/pnas.1208180109.

Walker, M. P., Brakefield, T., Morgan, A., Hobson, J. A., & Stickgold, R. (2002). Practice with sleep makes perfect: Sleep-dependent motor skill learning. *Neuron, 35*, 205–211.

Walker, M. P., & Stickgold, R. (2006). Sleep, memory and plasticity. *Annual Review of Psychology, 57*, 139–166. doi: 10.1146/annurev.psych.56091103.070307.

Walker, R. W., Skowronski, J. J., & Thompson, C. P. (2003). Life is pleasant—And memory helps to keep it that way. *Review of General Psychology, 7*, 203–210.

Wallace, B. A. (2006). *The attention revolution: Unlocking the power of the focused mind.* Boston, MA: Wisdom.

Wallas, G. (1926). *The art of thought.* New York, NY: Harcourt & Brace.

Wallhagen, M. I., Strawbridge, W. J., Cohen, R. D., & Kaplan, G. A. (1997). An increasing prevalence of hearing impairment and associated risk factors over three decades of Alameda County Study. *American Journal of Public Health, 87*, 440–442.

Walsh, S. P., White, K. M., & Young, R. M. (2009). The phone connection: A qualitative exploration of how belongingness and social identification relate to mobile phone use amongst Australian youth. *Journal of Community and Applied Social Psychology, 19*, 225–240. doi: 10.1002./casp.983.

Wamsley, E. J., Tucker, M., Payne, J. D., Benavides, J. A., & Stickgold, R. (2010). Dreaming of a learning task is associated with enhanced sleep-dependent memory consolidation. *Current Biology, 20*, 850–855. doi: 10.1016/j.cub.2010.03.027.

Wamsley, E. J., Tucker, M. A., Payne, J. D., & Stickgold, R. (2010). A brief nap is beneficial for human route-learning: The role of navigation experience and EEG spectral power. *Learning & Memory, 17,* 332–336.

Wang, J., Nansel, T. R., & Iannotti, R. J. (2011). Cyber and traditional bullying: Differential association with depression. *Journal of Adolescent Health, 48,* 415–417. doi: 10.1016/j.jadohealth.2010.07.012.

Wang, S., Zhang, Z., Guo, Y., Teng, G., & Chen, B. (2008). Hippocampal neurogenesis and behavioural studies on adult ischemic rat response to chronic mild stress. *Behavioural Brain Research, 189,* 9–16.

Wang, Z., Inslicht, S. S., Metzler, T. J., Henn-Haase, C., McCaslin, S. E., Tong, H., . . . Marmar, C. R. (2010). A prospective study of predictors of depression symptoms in police. *Psychiatry Research, 175,* 211–216.

Ward, J. (2013). Synesthesia. *Annual Review of Psychology, 64,* 49–75. doi: 10.1146/annurev-psych-113011-143840.

Warga, C. (1987). Pain's gatekeeper. *Psychology Today, 21,* 50–59.

Wason, P. C. (1960). On the failure to eliminate hypotheses in a conceptual task. *Quarterly Journal of Experimental Psychology, 12,* 129–140.

Wasserman, J. D., & Tulsky, D. S. (2005). A history of intelligence assessment. In D. P. Flanagan & P. L. Harrison (Eds.), *Contemporary intellectual assessment: Theories, tests, and issues* (pp. 3–38). New York, NY: Guilford Press.

Waterhouse, J. J., Atkinson, G. G., Edwards, B. B., & Reilly, T. T. (2007). The role of a short post-lunch nap in improving cognitive, motor, and sprint performance in participants with partial sleep deprivation. *Journal of Sports Sciences, 25,* 1557–1566.

Waterland, R., & Jirtle, R. L. (2003). Transposable elements: Targets for early nutritional effects on epigenetic gene regulation. *Molecular and Cellular Biology, 23,* 5293–5300.

Watkins, L. R., & Maier, S. F. (2003). When good pain turns bad. *Current Directions in Psychological Science, 12,* 232–236.

Watson, D., & Tellegen, A. (1985). Toward a consensual structure of mood. *Psychological Bulletin, 98,* 219–235.

Watson, J. B. (1925). *Behaviorism.* New York, NY: Norton.

Watson, J. B., & Rayner, R. (1920). Conditioned emotional reactions. *Journal of Experimental Psychology, 3,* 1–14.

Watson, J. M., & Strayer, D. L. (2010). Supertaskers: Profiles in extraordinary multitasking ability. *Psychonomic Bulletin & Review, 17,* 479–485.

Watters, E. (2006, November 22). DNA is not destiny. *Discover.* Retrieved from http://discovermagazine.com

Watters, E. (2010). *Crazy like us: The globalization of the American psyche.* New York, NY: Free Press.

Waxenberg, S. E., Drellich, M. G., & Sutherland, A. M. (1959). The role of hormones in human behavior: I. Changes in female sexuality after adrenalectomy. *Journal of Clinical Endocrinology and Metabolism, 19,* 193–202.

Waxman, J., Van Lieshout, R. J., Saigal, S., Boyle, M. H., & Schmidt, L. A. (2013). Still cautious: Personality characteristics of extremely low birth weight adults in their early 30s. *Personality and Individual Differences, 55*(8), 967–971. doi: 10.1016/j.paid.2013.08.003.

Way, B. M., Taylor, S. E., & Eisenberger, N. I. (2009). Variation in the μ-opioid receptor gene (OPRM1) is associated with dispositional and neural sensitivity to social rejection. *Proceedings of the National Academy of Sciences, 106,* 15079–15084.

Weathers, S. B. (2000). *Left for dead: My journey home from Everest.* New York: Villard Books (Kindle edition).

Weaver, D. (1998). The suprachiasmatic nucleus: A 25-year retrospective. *Journal of Biological Rhythms, 13,* 100–112.

Weaver, I. C. G., Cervoni, N., & Champagne, F. A. (2004). Epigenetic programming by maternal behavior. *Nature Neuroscience, 7,* 847–854.

Weber, J., & Wahl, J. (2006). Neurological aspects of trepanations from Neolithic times. *International Journal of Osteoarchaeology, 16,* 536–545.

Wechsler, D. (1944). *Measurement of adult intelligence* (3rd ed.). Baltimore, MD: Williams & Wilkins.

Wechsler, D. (1958). *The measurement and appraisal of adult intelligence* (4th ed.). Baltimore, MD: Williams & Wilkins.

Wechsler, H. L., Lee, J. E., & Kuo, M. (2002). Trends in college binge drinking during a period of increased prevention efforts. *Journal of American College Health, 50,* 203–217.

Weil, A., & Rosen, W. (1998). *From chocolate to morphine.* Boston, MA: Houghton Mifflin.

Weilund, J. D., & Humayan, M. S. (2008). Visual prosthesis. *Proceedings of the IEEE, 96,* 1076–1084.

Weinberg, R. A. (1989). Intelligence and IQ: Issues and great debates. *American Psychologist, 44,* 98–104.

Weinberg, R. S., & Gould, D. (2007). *Foundations of sport and exercise psychology* (4th ed.). Champaign, IL: Human Kinetics.

Weinberger, D. R., Egan, M. F., Bertolino, A., Callicott, J. H., Mattay, V. S., Lipska, B. K., . . . Goldberg, T. E. (2001). Prefrontal neurons and the genetics of schizophrenia. *Biological Psychiatry, 50,* 825–844.

Weinberger, M., Hiner, S. L., & Tierney, W. M. (1987). In support of hassles as a measure of stress in predicting health outcomes. *Journal of Behavioral Medicine, 10,* 19–31.

Weinstein, A. A., Deuster, P. A., Francis, J. L., Bonsall, R. W., Tracy, R. P., & Kop, W. J. (2010). Neurohormonal and inflammatory hyper-responsiveness to acute mental stress in depression. *Biological Psychology, 84,* 228–234.

Weinstein, T. A., Capitanio, J. P., & Gosling, S. D. (2008). Personality in animals. In O. P. John, R. W. Robins, & L. A. Pervin (Eds.), *Handbook of personality: Theory and research* (pp. 328–348). New York, NY: Guilford Press.

Weisinger, R., Denton, D., McKinley, M., & Miselis, R. (1993, November). Forebrain lesions that disrupt water homeostasis do not eliminate the sodium appetite of sodium deficiency in sheep. *Brain Research, 628*(1), 166–178.

Weitzman, E. D., Fukushima, D., Nogeire, C., Roffwarg, H., Gallagher, T. F., & Hellman, L. (1971). Twenty-four hour pattern of the episodic secretion of cortisol in normal subjects. *Journal of Clinical Endocrinology and Metabolism, 33,* 14–22.

Weller, J. A., Shackleford, C., Dieckmann, N., & Slovic, P. (2013). Possession attachment predicts cell phone use while driving. *Health Psychology, 32*(4), 379–387. doi: 10.1037/a0029265.

Wellisch, D. K., & Cohen, M. (2011). In the midnight hour: Cancer and nightmares. A review of theories and interventions in psycho-oncology. *Palliative and Supportive Care, 9,* 191–200. 2011 1478-9515/11.

Wenden, A. L. (1998). Metacognitive knowledge and language learning. *Applied Linguistics, 19,* 515–537.

Weng, H. Y., Fox, A. S., Shackman, A. J., Stodola, D. E., Caldwell, J. Z. K., Olson, M. C., Rogers, G. M., & Davidson, R. J. (2013). Compassion training alters altruism and neural responses to suffering. *Psychological Science, 24,* 1171–1180. doi: 10.1177/0956797612469537.

Wermke, M., Sorg, C., Wohlschläger, A. M., & Drzega, A. (2008, February 26). A new integrative model of cerebral activation, deactivation and default mode function in Alzheimer's disease. *European Journal of Nuclear Medicine and Molecular Imaging.* Advance online publication. doi: 10.1007/s00259-007-0698-5.

Wertheimer, M. (1959). *Productive thinking.* New York, NY: Harper.

Wessely, S., & Kerwin, R. (2004). Suicide risk and the SSRIs. *Journal of the American Medical Association, 292,* 379–381.

Westen, D., Blagov, P. S., Harenski, K., Kilts, C., & Hamann, S. (2006). Neural bases of motivated reasoning: An fMRI study of emotional constraints on partisan political judgment in the 2004 U.S. presidential election. *Journal of Cognitive Neuroscience, 18,* 1947–1958.

Westen, D., Gabbard, G. O., & Ortigo, K. M. (2008). Psychoanalytic approaches to personality. In O. P. John, R. W. Robins, & L. A. Pervin (Eds.), *Handbook of personality: Theory and research* (pp. 61–113). New York, NY: Guilford Press.

Westlye, L. T., Walhovd, K. B., Dale, A. M., Bjornerud, A., Due-Tonnessen, P., Engvig, A., . . . Fjell, A. M. (2010). Life-span changes of the human brain white matter: Diffusion tensor imaging (DTI) and volumetry. *Cerebral Cortex, 20,* 2055–2068.

Westmaas, J. L., & Silver, R. C. (2006). The role of perceived similarity in supportive responses to victims of negative life events. *Personality and Social Psychology Bulletin, 32,* 1537–1546.

Weston, D. (1998). The scientific legacy of Sigmund Freud: Toward a psychodynamically informed psychological science. *Psychological Bulletin, 124,* 333–371.

Whalen, C. K., & Henker, B. (1998). Attention-deficit/hyperactivity disorder. In T. H. Ollendick & M. Hersen (Eds.), *Handbook of child psychopathology* (pp. 181–212). New York, NY: Plenum Press.

What causes Down syndrome? (2011). National Down Syndrome Society. Retrieved July 20, 2007, from http://www.ndss.org/index.php?option=com_content&view=article&id=60&Itemid=77

What people do and do not believe. (2009, December 15). Retrieved October 11, 2013, from www.harrisineractive.com/vault/Harris_Poll_2009_15_15.pdf

Whitaker, K. L., Jarvis, M. J., Beeken, R. J., Boniface, D., & Wardle, J. (2010). Comparing maternal and paternal intergenerational transmission of obesity risk in a large population based sample. *American Journal of Clinical Nutrition, 91,* 1560–1567.

White, A. M. (2003, Spring). What happened? Alcohol, memory blackouts, and the brain. *Alcohol Research & Health,* 186–196.

White, P. (2006). A background to acupuncture and its use in chronic painful musculoskeletal conditions. *Journal of the Royal Society of Health, 126,* 219–227.

White, R. (1964). *The abnormal personality.* New York, NY: Ronald Press.

White, R. W., & Horvitz, E. (2009). Cyberchondria: Studies of the escalation of medical concerns in Web search. *ACM Transactions on Information Systems (TOIS), 27.* Retrieved from http://doi.acm.org/10.1145/1629096.1629101

Whiten, A., Horner, V., & de Waal, F. B. M. (2005). Conformity to cultural norms of tool use in chimpanzees. *Nature, 437,* 737–740.

Whitfield, C. L., Dube, S. R., Felitti, V. J., & Anda, R. E. (2005). Adverse childhood experiences and hallucinations. *Child Abuse and Neglect, 29,* 797–810.

Whiting, B., & Edwards, C. (1988). *Children of different worlds: The formation of social behavior.* Cambridge, MA: Harvard University Press.

Whitlock, J. R., Heynen, A. J., Shuler, M. G., & Bear, M. F. (2006). Learning induces long-term potentiation in the hippocampus. *Science, 313,* 1093–1097.

Whorf, B. L. (1956). *Language, thought, and reality: Selected writings of Benjamin Lee Whorf* (J. B. Carroll, Ed.). Cambridge, MA: MIT Press.

Wickelgren, I. (2009, September/October). I do not feel your pain. *Scientific American Mind,* 51–57.

Wickens, T. D. (2002). *Elementary signal detection theory.* New York: NY: Oxford University Press.

Wiederhold, B. K., & Wiederhold, M. D. (2005). Specific phobias and social phobia. In B. K. Wiederhold & M. D. Wiederhold (Eds.), *Virtual reality therapy for anxiety disorders: Advances in evaluation and treatment* (pp. 125–138). Washington, DC: American Psychological Association.

Wilensky, A., Schafe, G., Kristensen, M., & LeDoux, J. (2006). Rethinking the fear circuit: The central nucleus of the amygdala is required for the acquisition, consolidation, and expression of Pavlovian fear conditioning. *Journal of Neuroscience, 26*(48), 12387–12396.

Wiley, C. (1997). What motivates employees according to over 40 years of motivation surveys. *International Journal of Manpower, 18*(3), 263–280.

Wilkening, F., & Sodian, B. (2005). Scientific reasoning in young children: An introduction. *Swiss Journal of Psychology, 64,* 137–139.

Wille, B., De Fruyt, F., & Feys, M. (2010). Vocational interests and Big Five traits as predictors of job instability. *Journal of Vocational Behavior, 76,* 547–558.

Williams, G., Cai, X. J., Elliot, J. C., & Harrold, J. A. (2004). Anabolic neuropeptides. *Physiology and Behavior, 81,* 211–222.

Williams, J. H. G., Waiter, G. D., Gilchrist, A., Perrett, D. I., Murray, A. D., & Whiten, A. (2006). Neural mechanisms of imitation and "mirror neuron" functioning in autistic spectrum disorder. *Neuropsychologia, 44,* 610–621.

Williams, K. D., & Zudro, L. (2001). Ostracism: On being ignored, excluded, and rejected. In M. R. Leary (Ed.), *Interpersonal rejection* (pp. 21–53). New York, NY: Oxford University Press.

Williams, P. A., Haertel, E. H., Hartel, G. D., & Walberg, H. J. (1982). The impact of leisure time television on school learning: A research synthesis. *American Educational Research Journal, 19,* 19–50.

Williams, R., Briggs, R., & Coleman, P. (1995). Carer-rated personality changes associated with senile dementia. *International Journal of Geriatric Psychiatry, 10,* 231–236.

Williams, R. B., Jr., Haney, T. L., Lee, K. L., Kong, Y., Blumenthal, J. A., & Whalen, R. (1980). Type A behavior, hostility, coronary atherosclerosis. *Psychosomatic Medicine, 42,* 539–549.

Willis, S. L., Tennstedt, S. L., Marsiske, M., Ball, K., Elias, J., Koepke, K. M., . . . for the ACTIVE Study Group. (2006). Long-term effects of cognitive training on everyday functional outcomes in older adults. *Journal of the American Medical Association, 295,* 2805–2814.

Wilson, J. K., Baran, B., Pace-Schott, E. F., Ivry, R. B., & Spencer, R. M. C. (2012). Sleep modulates word-pair learning but not motor sequence learning in healthy older adults. *Neurobiology of Aging, 33,* 991–1000. Retrieved from http://dx.doi.org/10.1016/j.neurobiolaging.2011.06.029

Wilson, M. A., & McNaughton, B. L. (1994). Reactivation of hippocampal ensemble memories during sleep. *Science, 265,* 676–679.

Wimmer, H., & Perner, J. (1983). Beliefs about beliefs: Representation and constraining function of wrong beliefs in young children's understanding of deception. *Cognition, 13,* 103–128.

Wims, E., Titov, N., Andrews, G., & Choi, I. (2010). Clinician-assisted Internet-based treatment is effective for panic: A randomized controlled trial. *Australian and New Zealand Journal of Psychiatry, 44,* 599–607.

Winawer, J., Witthoft, N., Frank, M. C., Wu, L., Wade, A. R., & Boroditsky, L. (2007). Russian blues reveal effect of language on color discrimination. *Proceedings of the National Academy of Sciences, 104,* 7780–7785.

Wing, J. M. (2008). Computational thinking and thinking about computing. *Philosophical Transactions of the Royal Society A: Mathematical, Physical and Engineering Sciences, 366,* 3717–3725.

Wing, L., & Potter, D. (2002). The epidemiology of autistic spectrum disorders: Is the prevalence rising? *Mental Retardation* and *Mental Disabilities Research Review, 8*, 151–161.

Wing, R., & Jeffery, R. (1999). Benefits of recruiting participants with friends and increasing social support for weight loss and maintenance. *Journal of Consulting and Clinical Psychology, 67*, 132–138.

Witelson, S. F., Kigar, D. L., Scamvougeras, A., Kideckel, D. M., Buck, B., Stanchev, P. L., Bronskill, M., & Black, S. (2008). Corpus callosum anatomy in right-handed homosexual and heterosexual men. *Archives of Sexual Behavior, 37*, 857–863.

Witkin, H. A., & Asch, S. E. (1948). Studies in space orientation. IV. Further experiments on perception of the upright with displaced visual fields. *Journal of Experimental Psychology, 38*, 762–782.

Witte, K., & Allen, M. (2000). A meta-analysis of fear appeals: Implications for effective public health campaigns. *Health Education & Behavior, 27*, 591–615.

Witten, I. B., Lin, S.-C., Brodsky, M., Prakash, R., Diester, I., Anikeeva, P., . . . Deisseroth, K. (2010). Cholinergic interneurons control local circuit activity and cocaine conditioning. *Science, 330*, 1677–1681.

Wolak, J., Mitchell, K., & Finkelhor, D. (2002). Close online relationships in a national sample of adolescents. *Adolescence, 37*, 441–455.

Wölfling, K., Flor, H., & Grüsser, S. M. (2008). Psychophysiological responses to drug-associated stimuli in chronic heavy cannabis use. *European Journal of Neuroscience, 27*, 976–983.

Wolkowitz, O. M., Epel, E. S., Reus, V. I., & Mellon, S. H. (2010). Depression gets old fast: Do stress and depression accelerate cell aging? *Depression and Anxiety, 27*, 327–338.

Wollmer, M. A., Boer, C., Kalak, N., Beck, J., . . . Kruger, T. H. C. (2012). Facing depression with Botulinum toxin: A randomized controlled trial. *Journal of Psychiatric Research, 46*, 574–581.

Wong, C. C. Y., Caspi, A., Williams, B., Craig, I. W., Houts, R., Ambler, A., . . . Mill, J. (2010). A longitudinal study of epigenetic variation in twins. *Epigenetics, 5*, 1–11.

Woodworth, R. S., & Schlosberg, H. (1954). *Experimental psychology* (Rev. ed.). New York, NY: Henry Holt.

Work-related hearing loss. (2001). National Institute for Occupational Safety and Health, NIOSH, Publication No. 2001-103. Retrieved from http://www.cdc.gov/niosh/docs/2001-103/

World Health Organization. (2009). Intervention on diet and physical activity: What works: Summary Report. Retrieved from http://www.who.int/dietphysicalactivity/summary-report-09.pdf

World's greatest living polyglot. (n.d.). Retrieved May 31, 2007, from http://www.spidra.com/fazah.html

Wouters-Adriaens, M., & Westerterp, K. (2006). Basal metabolic rate as a proxy for overnight energy expenditure: The effect of age. *British Journal of Nutrition, 95*, 1166–1170.

Wright, J. S., & Panksepp, J. (2012). An evolutionary framework to understand foraging, wanting, and desire: The neuropsychology of the SEEKING system. *Neuropsychoanalysis, 14*(1), 5–39.

Wu, X., Chen, X., Han, J., Meng, H., Luo, J., . . . (2013). Prevalence and factors of addictive Internet use among adolescents in Wuhan, China: Interactions of parental relationship with age and hyperactivity-impulsivity. *PLoS ONE, 8*, e61782. doi: 10.1371/journal.pone.0061782.

Wurtz, R. H., & Kandel, E. R. (2000a). Central visual pathways. In E. R. Kandel, J. H. Schwartz, & T. M. Jessell. (2000). *Principles of neural science* (4th ed., pp. 523–545). New York, NY: McGraw-Hill.

Wurtz, R. H., & Kandel, E. R. (2000b). Perception of motion, depth, and form. In E. R. Kandel, J. H. Schwartz, & T. M. Jessell (Eds.), *Principles of neural science* (4th ed., pp. 548–571). New York, NY: McGraw-Hill.

Xia, M., Huang, R., Guo, V., Southall, N., Ming-Hsuang, C., Inglese, J., . . . Nirenberg, M. (2009). Identification of compounds that potentiate CREB signaling as possible enhancers of long-term memory. *Proceedings of the National Academy of Sciences, 106*, 2412–2417. doi: 10.1073/pnas.0813020106.

Xiang, J., Shen, H., & Li, J. (2009). Need-pressure trials of borderline personality disorder in Thematic Apperception Test. *Chinese Mental Health Journal, 23*, 340–344.

Xie, L., Kang, H., Xu, Q., Chen, M. J., Liao, Y., Thiyagarajan, M., . . . Nedergaard, M. (2013). Sleep drives metabolite clearance from the adult brain. *Science, 342*, 373–377. doi: 10.1126/science.1241224.

Xu, F., & Garcia, V. (2008). Intuitive statistics by 8-month-old infants. *Proceedings of the National Academy of Sciences, 105*, 5012–5015.

Xu, F., Luk, C., Richard, M. P., Zaidi, W., Farkas, S., Getz, A., . . . Syed, N. I. (2010). Antidepressant fluoxetine suppresses neuronal growth from both vertebrate and invertebrate neurons and perturbs synapse formation between *Lymnaea* neurons. *European Journal of Neuroscience, 31*, 994–1005.

Yaemsiri, S., Slining, M. M., & Agarwal, S. K. T. I. (2011). Perceived weight status, overweight diagnosis, and weight control among US adults: The NHANES 2003–2008 Study. *International Journal of Obesity, 35*, 1063–1070. doi: 10.1038/ijo.2010.229.

Yamada, M., & Yasuhara, H. (2004). Clinical pharmacology of MAO inhibitors: Safety and future. *NeuroToxicology, 25*, 215–221.

Yang, Y., Raine, A., Han, C.-B., Schug, R. A., Toga, A. W., & Narr, K. L. (2010). Reduced hippocampal and parahippocampal volumes in murderers with schizophrenia. *Psychiatry Research: Neuroimaging, 182*, 9–13.

Yang, Y., Raine, A., Narr, K. L., Colletti, P., & Toga, A. W. (2009). Localization of deformations within the amygdala in individuals with psychopathy. *Archives of General Psychiatry, 66*, 966–994. doi: 10.1001. archgenpsychiatry.2009.110.

Yanagisawa, K., Masui, K., Furutani, K., Nomura, M., Ura, M., Yoshida, H. (2011). Does higher general trust serve as a psychosocial buffer against social pain? An NIRS study of social exclusion. *Social Neuroscience, 6*, 190–197. DOI: 10.1080/17470919.2010.506139.

Yao, Y., Kelly, M. T., Sajikumar, S., Serrano, P., Tian, D., Bergold, P. J., . . . Sacktor, T. C. (2008). PKM maintains late long-term potentiation by N-ethylmaleimmide-sensitive factor/GluR2-dependent trafficking of postsynaptic AMPA receptors. *Journal of Neuroscience, 28*, 7820–7827. doi: 10.1523/JNEUROSCI.0223-08.2008.

Ybarra, M. L. (2004). Linkages between youth depressive symptomatology and online harassment. *CyberPsychology & Behavior, 7*, 247–257.

Ybarra, M. L., & Mitchell, K. J. (2004). Youth engaging in online harassment: Associations with caregiver-child relationships, Internet use, and personal characteristics. *Journal of Adolescence, 27*, 319–336.

Ybarra, M. L., & Mitchell, K. J. (2008). How risky are social networking sites? A comparison of places online where youth sexual solicitation and harassment occurs. *Pediatrics, 121*, e350–e357, doi: 10.1542/peds.2007.0693.

Yen, J.-Y., Ko, C.-H., Yen, C.-F., Wu, H.-Y., & Yang, M.-J. (2007). The comorbid psychiatric symptoms of Internet addiction: Attention deficit and hyperactivity disorder (ADHD), depression, social phobia, and hostility. *Journal of Adolescent Health, 41*, 93–98.

Yeragani, V. K., Tancer, M., Chokka, P., & Baker, G. B. (2010). Arvid Carlsson, and the story of dopamine. *Indian Journal of Psychiatry, 52*, 87–88. Retrieved from http://www.indianjpsychiatry.org/text.asp?2010/52/1/87/58907

Yerkes, R. M., & Dodson, J. D. (1908). The relation of strength of stimulus to rapidity of habit-formation. *Journal of Comparative Neurology and Psychology, 18*, 459–482.

Yin, D.-M., Chen, Y.-J., Lu, Y.-S., Bean, J. C., Sathyamurthy, A., Shen, C., . . . Mei, L. (2013). Reversal of behavioral deficits and synaptic dysfunction in mice overexpressing neuregulin 1. *Neuron, 78,* 644–657. doi: 10.1016/j.neuron2013.03.028.

Yin, J. C. P., Del Vecchio, M., Zhou, H., & Tully, T. (1995). CREB as a memory modulator: Induced expression of a dCREB2 activator isoform enhances long-term memory in *Drosophila. Cell, 81,* 107–115.

Yoemans, N. D. (2011). The ulcer sleuths: The search for the cause of peptic ulcers. *Journal of Gastroenterology and Hepatology, 26*(Suppl. s1), 35–41.

Yoon, J., & Thye, S. (2000). Supervisor support in the work place: Legitimacy and positive affectivity. *Journal of Social Psychology, 140,* 295–316.

Young, A. S., Niv, N., Cohen, A. N., Kessler, C., & McNagny, K. (2010). The appropriateness of routine medication treatment for schizophrenia. *Schizophrenia Bulletin, 36,* 732–739.

Young, L. C., Zaun, B. J., & VanderWerf, E. A. (2008). Successful same-sex pairing in Laysan albatross. *Biology Letters, 4,* 323–325.

Yu, A. Y., Tian, S. W., Vogel, D., & Kwok, R. C.-H. (2010). Can learning be virtually boosted? An investigation of online social networking impacts. *Computers & Education, 55,* 1494–1503.

Yuan, H., Liu, T., Szarkowski, R., Rios, C., Ashe, J., & He, B. (2010). Negative co-variation between task-related responses in alpha/beta-band activity and BOLD in human sensorimotor cortex: An EEG and fMRI study of motor imagery and movements. *NeuroImage, 49,* 2596–2606. doi: 10.1016/j.neuroimage.2009.10.028.

Yuen, E. K., Herbert, J. D., Forman, E. M., Comer, R., Bradley, J., Goetter, E. M., & Park, J. A. (2009, November). Virtual therapy for social anxiety disorder using Second Life: Preliminary results. Poster presented at the conference of the Association of Behavioral and Cognitive Therapies, New York, NY.

Zajonc, R. B. (1965). Social facilitation. *Science, 149,* 269–274.

Zajonc, R. B. (1968). Attitudinal effects of mere exposure. *Journal of Personality and Social Psychology, 9,* 1–27.

Zak, P. J., Stanton, A. A., & Ahmadi, S. (2007). Oxytocin increases generosity in humans. *PLoS ONE, 2,* 1–5.

Zametkin, A. J., Nordahl, T. E., Gross, M., King, A. C., Semple, W. E., Rumsey, J., . . . Cohen, R. M. (1990). Cerebral glucose metabolism in adults with hyperactivity of childhood onset. *New England Journal of Medicine, 15,* 1361–1366.

Zang, Y. F., Jin, Z., Weng, X. C., Zhang, L., Zeng, Y. W., Yang, L., . . . Faraone, S. V. (2005). Functional MRI in attention-deficit hyperactivity disorder: Evidence for hypofrontality. *Brain Development, 27,* 544–550. doi: 10.1016/j.braindev.2004.11.009.

Zanna, M. P., Kiesler, C. A., & Pilkonis, P. A. (1970). Positive and negative attitudinal affect established by classical conditioning. *Journal of Personality and Social Psychology, 14,* 321–328.

Zeidan, F., Martucci, K. T., Kraft, R. A., Gordon, N. S., McHaffie, J. G., & Coghill, R. C. (2011). Brain mechanisms supporting the modulation of pain by mindfulness meditation. *Journal of Neuroscience, 31,* 5540–5548.

Zeino, Z., Sisson, G., & Bjarnason, I. (2010). Adverse effects of drugs on small intestine and colon. *Best Practice & Research Clinical Gastroenterology, 24,* 133–141.

Zhang, L. (2010). Do thinking styles contribute to metacognition beyond self-rated abilities? *Educational Psychology, 30,* 481–494. doi: 10.1080/01443411003659986.

Zhang, Y., Jin, X., Shen, X., Zhang, J., & Hoff, E. (2008). Correlates of early language development in Chinese children. *International Journal of Behavioral Development, 32,* 145–151. doi: 10.1177/0165025407087213.

Zhao, Y., Montoro, R., Igartua, K., & Thombs, B. D. (2010). Suicidal ideation and attempt among adolescents reporting "unsure" sexual identity or heterosexual identity plus same-sex attraction or behavior: Forgotten groups? *Journal of the American Academy of Child &*

Adolescent Psychiatry, 49(2), 104–113. doi: 10.1097/00004583-201002000-00004.

Zhou, R., We, C., Patrick Rau, P.-L., & Zhang, W. (2009). Young driving learners' intention to use a handheld or hands-free mobile phone when driving. *Transportation Research Part F: Traffic and Behaviour, 12,* 208–217. doi: 10.1016/j.trf.2008.11.003.

Ziegler, G., Dahnke, R., Winkler, A. D., & Gaser, C. (2013). Partial least squares correlation of multivariate cognitive abilities and local brain structure in children and adolescents. *NeuroImage, 82,* 284–294.

Zigler, E. F., Finn-Stevenson, M., & Hall, N. W. (2002). *The first three years and beyond.* New Haven, CT: Yale University Press.

Zimbardo, P. G. (2007). *The Lucifer effect: Understanding how good people turn evil.* New York, NY: Random House.

Zimmer, C. (2005, March 1). Looking for personality in animals, of all people. *The New York Times.* Retrieved from http://www.nytimes.com

Zimmer, C. (2008, November 11). Now: The rest of the genome. *The New York Times.* Retrieved from http://www.nytimes.com

Zimmer-Gembeck, M. J., & Collins, W. A. (2008). Gender, mature appearance, alcohol use, and dating as correlates of sexual partner accumulation from ages 16–26 years. *Journal of Adolescent Health, 42,* 564–572.

Zimmerman, C. (2007). The development of scientific thinking skills in elementary and middle school. *Developmental Review, 27,* 172–223.

Zimmermann, J., & Neyer, F. J. (2013). Do we become a different person when hitting the road? Personality development of sojourners. *Journal of Personality and Social Psychology, 105*(3), 515–530. doi: 10.1037/a0033019.

Zullig, K., Pun, S., & Huebner, E. (2007). Life satisfaction, dieting behavior, and weight perceptions among college students. *Applied Research in Quality of Life, 2*(1), 17–31.

Name Index

A

Aamodt, M. G., 10, 415, 416
Abbate-Daga, G., 407
Aberg, M. A. L., 195
Abramovitz, A., 609
Abrams, R., 595
Abramson, A., 432
Ackerman, D., 140
Adam, T. C., 468
Adams, D., 594
Adams, L., 489
Adamson, L., 294
Ader, R., 461
Adessi, C., 87
Adler, A., 413, 414, 490
Adler, J., 10, 265, 266
Adolphs, R., 95, 275, 425, 431
Adrian, E. D., 84
Agarwal, S. K. T. I., 402
Aghajanian, G. K., 244
Ahmadi, S., 432
Aichorn, W., 594
Ainsworth, M. D. S., 182, 543
Aitken, J. R., 619
Akaike, A., 200
Akers, J. F., 184
Akinola, M., 585
Aknin, L. B., 438, 538
Alaggia, R., 195
Alam, M., 430
Al-Atiyyat, N. M. H., 153
Alberini, C. M., 266
Alderson, K. G., 205
Aldington, S., 243
Alex, C., 469
Alger, B. E., 242, 243, 401
Allee, W. C., 515
Allemand, M., 506, 507
Allen, D. G., 417
Allen, L., 408
Allen, M., 532
Allergan, Inc., 430
Allik, J., 484
Allison, D. B., 403
Alloway, T., 556
Allport, G. W., 480, 497, 526
Alt, K. W., 11
Alterovitz, S., 206
Altman, J., 104
Alzheimer's Association, 200
Amabile, T. M., 384, 416
Amaral, D., 93
Amedi, A., 113
American Heart Association, 240, 464
American Psychiatric Association, 14, 370,
    405, 551, 552, 555, 556, 558, 563, 565,
    567, 570, 571, 572, 574, 575, 576, 577,
    578, 579, 582
American Psychological Association, 15, 63
Ames, M. A., 411
Amichai-Hamburger, Y., 29, 527
Amin, R., 314
Amsel, E., 37, 189
Amsterdam, J., 608

Anacker, C., 452
Anda, R. F., 565, 573
Anderson, A. K., 420
Anderson, C. A., 310, 534, 535
Anderson, N. D., 221
Anderson, P. L., 609
Andrade, F. C. D., 403
Andreasen, N. C., 560, 585
Aniston, J., 572
Anselmi, P., 529
Anson, K., 245
Ansul, S. E., 425
Anthonisen, N. R., 297, 319
Aouizerate, B., 575
APA Presidential Task Froce, 607
Apsche, J., 524
Arbib, M., 326
Arbib, M. A., 330
Archimedes, 381
Argyle, M., 439
Aristotle, 35
Arling, G. L., 183, 184
Armagan, E., 72, 111, 112, 113
Armstrong, H. E., 613
Armstrong, T., 364
Arnett, J. J., 193, 194, 195, 196
Arnold, M. B., 423
Arseneault, L., 243, 483, 501
Arterberry, M. E., 169
Artola, A., 452
Asch, S. E., 516
Aserinsky, E., 224
Asherson, P., 76
Ashkenazi, S., 310
Ashmore, R. D., 191
Asperger, H., 556
Assouline, M., 505
Atkinson, G., 224
Atkinson, J. W., 414
Atkinson, R. C., 252, 260
Aubrey, J. B., 315
Austin, E. J., 584
Austin, M., 166
Aycicegi, A., 319
Azadfar, P., 508
Azizian, A., 257
Azmitia, M., 195

B

Baan, R., 467
Baars, B. J., 211
Babson, K. A., 230
Bachevalier, J., 95, 557
Bachorowski, J., 428
Bachtiar, V., 389
Baddeley, A. D., 254, 255, 271
Badour, C. L., 230
Baer, R. A., 214, 221, 613
Baerwald, J., 501
Bagwell, C. L., 191
Baier, B., 265, 266
Bailey, M. J., 409, 411, 412
Bailey, N. W., 411

Baillargeon, R., 174, 175
Baime, M. J., 221
Baird, A. A., 194
Baird, B., 223
Baird, J. C., 137
Bakeman, R., 294
Balcetis, E., 122
Baldwin, D. S., 618
Ball, K., 206, 438
Ballanyi, K., 79
Balsis, S., 508
Baltes, P. B., 169, 198, 199
Banaji, M. R., 527, 528, 529
Bandura, A., 306, 307, 308, 309, 317, 415, 534
Banks, M. S., 168
Banks, W. C., 34
Banning, K., 446
Banse, R., 428
Bär, K.-J., 120
Barac, R., 354
Baran, B., 274
Barbaresi, W. J., 556
Barbazanges, A., 483
Barber, L. K., 229
Barbour, K. A., 468
Barch, D. M., 198, 559, 560
Bargh, J. A., 211
Barkham, M., 607
Barlow, D. H., 570, 571
Barlow, J. H., 184
Baron, A., 295
Bar-On, R., 436
Baron, R. A., 534
Baron-Cohen, S., 556, 584
Barr, C. L., 87
Barr, R. F., 203
Barres, B. A., 79
Barrés, R., 469
Barrett, L. F., 423, 435
Barron, F. X., 480
Bartels, M., 375
Barth, J., 466
Bartholow, B. D., 535
Bartlett, F., 18, 19
Barton, S., 561
Basak, C., 199, 206
Basbaum, A. L., 146
Bassett, E. B., 561
Basson, R., 408
Bates, M. P., 465
Batey, M., 388, 389
Batson, C. D., 536, 538
Bauer, F., 143
Bauer, M., 569
Baumeister, R. F., 211, 413, 414
Baumrind, D., 62
Bavelier, D., 103, 203
Beach, F., 408, 409
Beadle-Brown, J., 298, 299
Beauchamp, G. K., 164
Beaulieu-Bonneau, S., 245
Beck, A. T., 604
Beebe, D. W., 314
Beehr, T. A., 505

Beekman, A. T. F., 617
Beeman, M. J., 98, 387
Beever, T. G., 98
Beghetto, R. A., 384
Begley, S., 21, 22, 103, 105, 113
Belisle, P., 537
Bell, A. G., 15
Bell, A. P., 412
Bellack, A. S., 603
Bellesi, M., 226, 228
Belmonte, M. K., 557
Bem, D. H., 196
Bem, D. J., 41
Benavides, J. A., 261
Benbow, C., 372
Benbow, C. P., 372
Benet-Martinez, V., 484
Benjamin, J., 481
Benjamin, L. T., Jr., 9, 15, 16, 18
Benner, E. J., 79
Bennett, C. M., 194
Bennett, E. L., 66, 104, 316
Bennett, P. J., 131
Benson, A., 38
Benson, B. A., 298
Benson, J. W., 619
Beran, M. J., 333, 335
Berenbaum, S. A., 341
Berghöfer, A., 569, 599
Bergsieker, H. B., 195
Berhardt, B. C., 539
Berk, M., 594
Berkman, L. F., 455
Berland, M., 204
Berlin, K. L., 231
Berlyne, D., 400
Berna, C., 146
Bernardi, R. E., 294
Bernat, J., 212, 213
Bernier, A., 314
Bernier, R., 312
Bernstein, P., 160
Berridge, C. W., 267
Berridge, K. C., 398
Berry, C. M., 505
Berthoud, H. R., 401
Bewernick, B. H., 598
Bexton, W. H., 399
Bherer, L., 199, 201, 469
Bialystok, E., 324, 352, 353, 354
Bickerton, D., 325
Bike, D., 611
Binder, E., 468
Binet, A., 365
Birch, L. L., 402
Birdsong, D., 352
Birks, J., 266
Bishop, S. J., 533
Bjarnason, I., 593
Bjork, R. A., 261, 280, 281
Black, D. W., 619
Blackburn, E., 458
Blackburn, E. H., 458
Blair, R. J. R., 432
Blais, A., 122
Blakeslee, M., 144
Blakeslee, S., 144, 557
Blalock, J. E., 462
Blass, T., 519
Bleidorn, W., 484
Bleier, P., 619
Blier, P., 594
Block, J., 506
Block, J. H., 506

Block, J. J., 582
Blonigen, D. M., 506
Bloom, S. R., 401
Blumenthal, J. A., 468
Bocchieri Riccardi, L., 438
Boettger, M. K., 120
Bogduk, N., 145
Bogen, J. E., 100
Boisjoli, J. A., 603
Boland, J., 267
Bollen, E., 407
Bolour, S., 408
Bolshakov, V., 274
Bond, R., 517
Bongartz, W., 234
Bonnet, M., 339
Boone, C., 432
Boorboor, S., 461
Bopp, K., 276
Borgen, F. H., 504
Born, J., 315
Börner, K., 6
Bornstein, R. F., 501
Boroditsky, L., 336, 338
Borst, J. P., 217, 219, 582
Boska, P., 21
Boska, P., 560
Botvinick, M. M., 95
Botwin, M., 541
Bouchard, T. J., 482
Bouchard, T. J., Jr., 375, 483
Bourgeois, S., 202
Bouso, J. C., 242
Bouton, M. E., 291, 571
Boutros, N. N., 561
Bouvard, M., 619
Bowden, C. L., 585
Bowden, E. M., 98, 387
Bower, B., 336
Bowers, A. J., 204
Bowlby, J., 181, 543
Bowman, L. L., 5
Boyack, K. W., 6
Boyd, D., 28
Boyle, L. N., 219
Boysen, G. A., 577
Bradberry, C. W., 87
Bradley, M. M., 419, 437
Bradley, P., 502
Bradley, R. M., 164
Brain, M., 131
Brambilla, P., 611
Brand, B. L., 577
Brand, G., 153
Brand, S., 315
Brandone, A., 327
Brandtzæg, P. B., 526
Branigan, C., 420
Brant, A. M., 173, 375
Brasil-Neto, J. P., 269
Braunstein, G., 408
Braver, T. S., 198
Breer, H., 149
Breitbart, W., 201
Breiter, H. C., 431
Breland, K., 304
Breland, M., 304
Brennan, P. A., 542
Brenner, J., 204, 220
Brent, D., 230
Brepson, L., 525
Breugelmans, S. M., 429
Brewer, M. B., 515
Brickman, A. M., 470

Bridge, J., 230
Bridges, K., 185
Briggs, C., 570
Briggs, R., 508, 509
Brivic, S., 489
Broadbent, D. E., 215
Broca, P., 98
Broekman, B. F. P., 376
Broude, G., 409
Brown, A. S., 21, 166, 560
Brown, K. W., 211, 214, 221
Brown, R., 275
Brown, R. T., 369
Brown, T. S., 401
Bruder, C. E. G., 160
Brunelin, J., 596
Bruner, J. S., 122
Brunetti, M., 94
Bruno, R., 596
Brunwasser, S. M., 617
Bryans, W. A., 104
Buboltz, W. C., 314
Buchanan, J., 609
Buchanan, T. W., 275
Buck, L. B., 148, 149
Buckley, C., 535
Bucy, P., 95
Buka, S. L., 560
Bukh, J., 565
Bukowski, W. M., 191
Bulik, C. M., 406
Bulkeley, K., 224, 225, 226, 231
Bullivant, S. B., 408
Burch, G., 584
Burd, L., 166
Burger, J., 520
Burgess, W., 592
Burguière, E., 614
Buring, J. E., 468
Burnett, G. B., 191
Burney, R., 471
Burnstein, E., 537
Burt, K. B., 195
Burton, C. M., 455
Busch, N., 213
Bushman, B. J., 310, 534, 535
Buss, D. M., 22, 25, 400, 408, 409, 480, 530, 539, 541, 542
Bussing, R., 557
Buxton, O. M., 228

C

Cabeza, R., 274
Cacioppo, J. T., 526
Cahill, L., 250
Cahill, S. P., 611, 612
Caird, J. K., 28, 218
Caldwell, J. A., 315
Calkins, M. W., 16, 19, 256
Calvert, S. L., 203
Cameron, J., 415
Cameron, J. D., 404
Cameron, K., 205
Campbell, A., 432
Campbell, F. A., 378
Campbell, K., 557
Camperio-Ciana, 507
Campos, J., 185
Campos, J. J., 185
Camras, L. A., 185
Cannarella, J., 526
Cannon, W. B., 78, 398, 401, 429
Canter, R. R., 122

Capitanio, J. P., 485
Caplovitz, A. G., 203
Caporael, L. R., 515
Cappuccio, F. P., 228
Capri, M., 452
Capuron, L., 462
Caramanica, K., 576
Caramelli, P., 173
Cardilla, K., 187
Cardno, A. G., 559
Carew, T. J., 286
Carey, B., 252
Carlat, D. J., 567
Carless, S. A., 504
Carlo, G., 483
Carlsson, A., 562
Carlsson, I., 385, 386, 387
Carnagey, N. L., 535
Carney, S. M., 599
Carpenter, B., 508
Carpenter, L. A., 298
Carr, T. S., 533
Carriere, J., 276
Carrion, V. G., 576
Carro, R. M., 502
Carroll, J. B., 359, 361
Carroll, J. L., 180
Carskadon, M. A., 314
Carson, S. H., 584
Carstensen, L. L., 199, 425, 435
Carter, C. S., 95
Caruso, E. M., 122
Carver, C. S., 456
Case, T. I., 418
Casey, B. J., 107
Caspi, A., 20, 26, 76, 88, 187, 196, 481, 482, 483,
    506, 533, 550, 553, 566, 581
Cassidy, T., 155
Castelli, D. M., 170
Castles, A., 203
Catalano, P., 143
Catalino, L. I., 439
Catapano, F., 618
Cattell, R. B., 359, 360
Cavallero, C., 232
Cavuoto, N., 613
CBS News, 535
Ceci, S. J., 341, 378
Centers for Disease Control and Prevention,
    166, 192, 241, 402, 405, 467
Chabris, C. F., 215
Chadwick, P., 612
Chaffee, J., 344
Chaiken, S., 532
Chan, A. S., 173
Chan, C., 327
Chance, P., 344
Chandra, A., 191, 194, 196, 411
Chang, E. C., 456
Chang, H., 557
Chapais, B., 537
Chapman, B. P., 471
Chappell, M., 262
Chaput, J. P., 405
Charil, A., 452
Charmorrow-Premuzic, T., 504
Charney, D. S., 572, 617
Chartrand, T. L., 430, 616
Chatterjee, A., 508, 509
Chaudhari, N., 149
Cheah, C. S. L., 195
Cheavens, J. S., 613
Chechik, G., 170
Cheetham, C. E. J., 399

Chen, D. Y., 266
Chen, E., 464
Chen, H., 469
Chen, S. Y., 605
Chentsova-Dutton, Y., 434
Chepenik, L. G., 569
Chess, S., 181
Cheung, M.-C., 173
Cheyne, J., 276
Chia, E., 197
Chiarello, R. J., 98
Chiesa, A., 611
Chiou, W., 413
Chitins, A., 371
Choi, I., 522
Choi, J., 341
Chomsky, N., 331, 335
Chow, T. W., 385
Chowdhury, M., 298
Choy, Y., 609
Christakis, D., 203
Christakis, N. A., 4, 205, 405, 455, 456, 525, 526
Christensen, D. D., 373
Christensen, K., 438
Chuang, D. M., 594
Cicchetti, D., 171, 172
Cillessen, A. H. N., 186
Cipriani, A., 594
Clancy, P. M., 327
Clark, A. S., 483
Clark, L., 508, 509
Clark, L. A., 565
Clark, R. D., III, 409, 410
Clark, W. R., 74, 75
Clarke, G. N., 617
Clasen, L., 189, 190
Clegg, H., 481, 584
Cobb, J. M., 219
Coe, C. L., 165
Cohen, J., 333, 335
Cohen, J. D., 95, 418
Cohen, K. M., 411, 412
Cohen, M., 230, 231
Cohen, M. S., 37
Cohen, N., 461
Cohen, S., 455, 463, 464
Colcombe, S. J., 199, 201
Cole, S., 452
Coleman, B., 439
Coleman, P., 508, 509
Collignon, O., 435
Collins, A., 262
Collins, L. M., 486
Collins, W. A., 194
Collinson, S. L., 279
Colom, R., 373
Comella, C., 230
Comer, R. J., 569, 576, 577, 604, 605
Comery, T. A., 104
Condon, 539
Conduct Problems Prevention Research
    Group, 436
Conel, J. L., 170
Conger, A. J., 534
Conger, J. C., 534
Connelly, B. S., 505
Connors, B. W., 399
Cook, C. C., 576
Copeland, P., 87, 403, 411, 412, 481, 482, 572
Corkin, S., 265
Cosh, S. M., 466
Cosmides, L., 18, 19, 23, 24, 419
Costa, P. T., 480, 484, 497, 502, 504, 506
Cote, J., 485

Cotman, C. W., 198
Cotten, S. R., 203
Cottrell, C. A., 514, 524, 528, 530
Couch, D., 29
Couch, D. J., 28, 204
Courage, M. L., 172
Courchesne, E., 557
Coyle, J. T., 558, 561, 562, 591, 592, 599, 607
Craft, M. A., 454
Craig, I. W., 566
Craighero, L., 82, 330
Craik, F. I. M., 253, 259, 260, 261, 324, 353
Crain, M. A., 146
Crain, S., 146, 148
Crain, S. M., 146
Crandall, C., 537
Crawford, D., 438
Crawford, S. E., 195
Crews, F., 493
Crook, T. H., 277
Cross, S. E., 484
Cross-Disorder Group of Pyschiatric
    Genomics Consortium, 553
Crouch, R., 469
Crow, S. J., 406
Crump, T., 21, 35
Crystal, J. D., 242
Csikszentmihalyi, M., 17, 19, 214, 399, 400,
    456, 494, 495
Cuijpers, P., 610
Cukor, J., 609
Culvers, J., 405
Cummings, J. H., 467
Cummings, J. L., 96, 189, 271, 385, 432
Cummings, W. C., 141
Cunningham, A. J., 455
Cunningham, W. A., 530
Curci, A., 275
Curley, J. P., 77
Curtiss, S., 328
Cusack, C. L., 170
Cussler, E. C., 468
Cutting, A. L., 186
Cynkar, J., 218
Cyr, M., 404
Cytowic, R. E., 151
Czech, C., 87

D

Dabbs, J. M., Jr., 534
Daee, A., 402
Dale, P. S., 332
Dale, S., 120
Dalgleish, T., 432
Dallaire, D. H., 617
Dallman, M. F., 468
Dalton, A. N., 430
Damasio, A. R., 98, 431, 489
Dan, E., 423
Danesh, J., 580
D'Anglejan, A., 354
Danhauer, J. L., 143
Daniels, K., 196
Daniels, W. M. U., 469
Dansinger, M. L., 467
Danziger, J. N., 5
Dardzinski, B. J., 189
Darley, J., 43
Darley, J. M., 536
Darwin, C., 16, 23, 425, 426, 434
Das, G. D., 104
Dasgupta, N., 528
Daubman, K. A., 420

D'Ausilio, R., 415
Dauvilliers, Y., 230
Davidovitch, M., 556
Davidson, M., 107
Davidson, R. J., 221, 418, 428, 432
Davis, G. C., 454
Davis, J. I., 430, 616
Davis, S. S., 314
Dawkins, R., 536
Dawson, G., 312, 556
Day, H. I., 399
Deacon, T., 326, 335
Deacon, T. W., 334
Deary, I., 378
Deary, I. J., 378
Debener, S., 211
Debes, R., 82
DeCasper, A. J., 172
Deci, E. L., 400, 416, 439
Declerck, C. H., 432
De Fruyt, F., 504, 505
de Graaf-Peters, V. B., 189, 194
Deisseroth, K., 614
DeKeyser, R., 329, 352
De Kloet, E. R., 452
de Lecea, L., 615
Delgado, P. L., 593
DeLisi, M., 533
De Lisi, R., 203
Dellinger, A. M., 218
Dell' Osso, B., 619
DeLongis, A., 446
de Lorgeril, M., 467
Dement, W., 222, 224, 225, 226, 228,
    229, 231, 232
de Mestral, G., 381
Demir, E., 412
De Neys, W., 524
Deoni, S. C. L., 81
Derbyshire, S. W. G., 235
Derry, G., 40
Derryberry, D., 420
DeRubeis, R. J., 607, 608
Descartes, R., 21
Desgent, S., 165
DeSoto, M. C., 341
Després, J. P., 405
Detterman, D. K., 359
Deutch, A. Y., 244
Devilbiss, D. M., 267
Devine, P., 528
DeVos, J., 174, 175
de Waal, F. B. M., 538
DeWall, C., 413
DeWall, C. N., 514
de Win, M. M. L., 88
DeYoung, C., 373
Dhabhar, F. S., 472
Dharap, S. B., 212
Diamond, L. M., 411
Dias, R. G., 274
Dibben, G. R. M., 166
Dickens, C., 120
Dickson, B. J., 412
Diego, M., 184
Diekelmann, S., 315
Diener, E., 437, 438
Dietrich, K., 371, 376
Digman, J. M., 497
Dimberg, U., 430, 616
Dingemanse, N. J., 485, 486
Dinn, W. M., 319
DiPietro, J. A., 162, 166, 483
Dix, D., 13

Dobbs, D., 590, 598
Dockray, S., 457
Dodson, J. D., 399
Doetsch, F., 317
Dolan, R. J., 274, 540
Dolcos, F., 274
Dolinoy, D., 165
Doll, R., 241, 467
Dollard, J., 307
Domes, G., 435
Domhoff, G. W., 245
Dominguez, J. M., 408
Dong, J. Y., 404
Donn, J. E., 205
Doty, R. L., 197
Doucet, E., 404
Doud, A. J., 99
Dow, G. T., 384
Doyon, S., 240
Drabant, E. M., 433
Drellich, M. G., 408
Drevets, W. C., 593, 597
Drews, F. A., 28, 204, 218
Dubai, Y., 261
Duch, H., 203
Duckworth, A., 457
Duckworth, R. A., 480
Dudai, Y., 263
Due, P., 438
Duggan, M., 204
DuHamel, K. N., 234
Dumont, Y., 565
Dunbar, R. I. M., 8, 90, 326, 331
Duncan, J., 373, 374
Duncan, S. C., 192
Duncan, T. E., 192
Duncker, K., 383
Dunn, E. W., 438, 538
Dunn, J., 186
Dunne, M. P., 411
Dunning, D. L., 203
Durazzo, T. C., 239
Durlak, J. A., 436
Durrow, H., 195
Dvir, Y., 592
Dye, M. W. G., 203

E

Eagly, A. H., 532
Eaton, D. K., 218
Eaves, L. J., 403
Eban-Rothschild, A., 615
Ebbeling, C. H., 404
Ebbinghaus, H., 276
Ebstein, R. P., 75, 432, 482
Edelman, M., 186
Edelman, S., 455
Edenfield, T. M., 468
Eder, P., 417
Edinger, J. D., 231
Edmonds, C. V., 455
Edmonds, G. W., 506
Edwards, , J. H., 612
Edwards, C., 186
Edwards, V. J., 560
Egner, T., 432
Ehman, M., 315
Ehsanpour, S., 473
Eichenbaum, H., 264
Eichler, V. B., 224
Eikelenboom, P., 200
Eisenberger, N. I., 146, 432, 514, 525
Eisenberger, R., 413, 415, 417

Ekman, P., 25, 56, 57, 418, 419, 422, 425, 426,
    427, 428, 430, 433, 434, 451, 465, 522, 523
Elbert, T., 172
Elder, G. H., 196
Elias, M., 250
Elison-Bowers, P., 526
Ellason, J. W., 577
Ellenbogen, J. M., 314
Ellickson, P. L., 318, 319
Elliott, J., 556
Elliott, P., 269
Elliott, S., 196
Ellis, E., 411
Ellsworth, P. C., 423, 424
Elman, J. L., 332
Elms, A., 44
Elwood, R. W., 486
Emde, R., 185
Emery, G., 604
Emery, R. A., 504
Emmons, R. A., 602
Empana, J. P., 466
Engel, A. K., 211, 216
Engle, R. W., 254
Enticott, P., 312
Enzinger, C., 198
Epel, E., 458
Epel, E. S., 457, 458, 468
Erdelyi, M., 276
Erickson, K. I., 199, 317, 469
Erikson, E. H., 28, 192, 197, 198, 204
Eriksson, P. S., 105, 317
Eroglu, C., 79
Ervin, F. R., 303
Escher, M. C., 135
Etcoff, N., 541, 542
Etkin, A., 432
Evan, K. R., 416
Evans, A., 190
Evans, K., 611
Evans, L. M., 75
Evans, S., 619
Everett, D. L., 336
Everson, H. T., 354
Exner, J. E., Jr., 501
Eyer, J., 451
Eysenck, H. J., 319, 498, 499, 572, 584

F

Facione, P. A., 344, 346
Fadiga, L., 313
Faith, M. A., 508
Fallgatter, A. J., 562
Fallon, A. E., 418
Famy, C., 568
Fan, J., 234
Fancher, R. E., 15, 288, 377
Fantz, R. L., 169
Farb, N., 611
Farber, N. B., 236
Farell, B., 137
Fargo, J. D., 184
Fazel, S., 580
Fechner, G., 15, 19
Feinberg, M., 421
Feirtag, M., 79, 82
Feist, D., 210, 245, 279, 414
Feist, G., 245
Feist, G. J., 10, 25, 27, 36, 340, 345, 382, 383,
    384, 385, 387, 388, 389, 446, 478, 480
Feist, J., 478
Feldman, D. H., 371

Feldman-Barrett, L., 254
Feldner, M. T., 230
Feng, X., 185
Feng, Z., 241
Fenson, L., 326
Ferguson, C. J., 535
Fergusson, D., 594
Fergusson, L., 559
Fernald, A., 330, 434
Ferrari, P. F., 312
Ferrucci, R., 269
Ferster, C. B., 299
Festinger, L., 530
Fetz, E. E., 99
Feys, M., 505
Fiedorowicz, J., 593
Field, T., 184
Field, T. M., 184
Fields, H. L., 147, 315
Fields, R. D., 81, 171, 189, 271
Fierros, E., 363
Fifer, W., 172
Filimon, F., 312
Finger, S., 12, 96, 100
Fink, A., 584
Fink, M., 595
Finke, R. A., 387
Finkelhor, D., 204
Finnerty, G. T., 399
Finn-Stevenson, M., 166
Fischer, A. H., 434
Fischer, G. G., 212
Fisher, D. E., 458
Fisher, J. A., 402
Fisher, J. E., 584
Fitch, W. T., 335
Fitzgerald, K. D., 575
Fitzgerald, M., 584
Fitzgerald, P. B., 596
Flaherty, M., 341
Flament, M. F., 619
Flammer, E., 234
Flegal, K. M., 402, 403
Flege, J. E., 352
Fleischer, J., 149
Flor, H., 243
Flykt, A., 423
Foa, E., 611
Foa, E. B., 611, 612
Fode, K. L., 54
Fodor, E. M., 585
Foerde, K., 5, 218, 264
Fogassi, L., 312, 313
Fogel, A., 185
Folkman, S., 446, 447, 453, 454, 456, 457
Folley, B. S., 385
Fong-Torres, B., 416
Fontaine, J., 434
Fonteille, V., 95
Ford, C., 408, 409
Ford, D., 368, 377
Forgeard, M., 173
Förster, P. L. V., 508
Foster, S. C., 315
Foulkes, D., 226, 232
Fournier, J. C., 599
Fouts, D. H., 355
Fouts, R. S., 355
Fowler, J. H., 4, 205, 405, 455, 456, 525, 526
Frackowiak, R. S. J., 271
Frady, R. L., 533
Fraga, M. F., 160
Franco, O. H., 468
Frangou, S., 371

Frank, M. C., 338
Frank, M. G., 523
Franklin, M. S., 223
Franklin, S., 211
Fratiglioni, L., 199, 200
Fredrickson, B. L., 420, 425, 439, 456, 457
Freeman, H., 486
Fregni, F., 269, 270
French, S. E., 195
French-Belgian Collaborative Group, 465
Freud, A., 601
Freud, S., 13, 16, 17, 19, 213, 231, 488, 489
Freund, A., 198
Friberg, U., 412
Friederici, A. D., 185
Friedman, J. M., 402
Friedman, M., 465
Friesen, W. V., 57, 425, 426, 427, 428, 433, 434, 451
Frijda, N. H., 425
Frith, C., 8
Frith, C. D., 261, 540
Frith, U., 8
Frokjaer, V. B., 88
Frost, R. O., 550
Fründ, I., 213
Fruntes, V., 21
Fuchs, D. L., 577
Fudala, P. J., 240
Fujihara, T., 539
Fuld, K., 137
Fuller, J. L., 74
Furberg, A. S., 468
Furman, O., 263
Furman, W., 191
Furnham, A., 388, 389
Furster, J. M., 96
Furuichi, T., 537
Furumoto, L., 16
Fuster, J. M., 189
Fyer, A. J., 609

G

Gaab, N., 314
Gabbard, G. O., 493
Gable, P. A., 420
Gabrieli, J. D. E., 199
Gage, F. H., 104, 316, 565
Galanter, E., 120
Gale, A., 498
Galin, D., 213
Galizio, M., 295
Gallagher, A. M., 378
Gallagher, M., 438
Gallagher, R. M., 240
Gallese, V., 313
Gallop, R., 608
Ganasen, K., 610
Ganis, G., 339
Gao, X., 469
Garcia, G. E., 354
Garcia, J., 301, 302, 303, 304, 461
Garcia, V., 173
Garcia-Bailo, B., 149
Garcia-Sierra, A., 353
Gardner, B. T., 333
Gardner, H., 18, 168, 359, 361, 362, 363, 364
Gardner, R. A., 333
Garoff-Eaton, R. J., 274
Garrett, R. K., 5
Gates, M. F., 515
Gathercole, S. E., 203
Gathercole, V. C. M., 329

Gavrilets, S., 412
Gazdzinski, S., 239
Gazzaniga, M. S., 100
Geary, D., 341
Gebicke-Haerter, P. J., 559, 560
Geerlings, S. W., 466
Geesey, M. E., 239
Geist, C. S., 412
Gelman, S., 327
Gelman, S. A., 354
Genovese, K., 43
Georges, E., 454
Georgiadis, J., 408
Georgiadis, J. R., 418
Gershberg, F. B., 271
Geschwind, N., 613
Gibson, E., 169
Gibson, J. J., 132
Giedd, J., 189, 190
Giedd, J. N., 170
Gilbert, S. P., 314
Giles, G. E., 267
Gill, P. M., 10
Gillespie, N. A., 506
Gillham, J. E., 617
Gilovich, T., 423
Giltay, E. J., 456
Giordano, D. A., 168
Gironda, M., 205
Giuliani, N. R., 433
Givón, T., 326, 339
Gjerde, P. F., 187
Glaser, R., 463
Glasper, E. R., 105, 452
Glass, G., 607
Glass, T., 455
Glassman, A., 466
Gleason, J. A., 467
Gleitman, L. R., 332
Glick, I. D., 585
Gluckman, P. D., 77
Gneezy, U., 415
Goel, V., 387, 524
Goff, D. C., 562
Gogtay, N., 190
Goldapple, K., 597
Goldfield, B. A., 327
Goldin, P., 433
Goldman-Rakic, P. S., 560
Goldreich, D., 145
Goldsmith, T. H., 124
Goldstein, E. B., 120, 137, 139, 146, 148, 150, 197
Goldstein, T., 230
Goleman, D. P., 435
Golier, J. A., 576
Gonzalez, V., 218
Goodall, J., 44
Goodwin, G. M., 599
Goodwin, P., 196
Goodwin, P. J., 455
Gopnik, A., 172, 179
Gordon, P., 336
Gore, M. A., 212
Gorenstein, E. E., 604, 605
Gorrindo, T., 610
Gorski, R., 408
Gosling, S. D., 485, 486, 502
Gossage, J. P., 166
Gosselin, F., 95
Goto, H., 327
Gottesman, I., 375
Gottesman, I. I., 559
Gottfredson, L., 377

Gottleib, N. H., 446
Gottlieb, G., 375
Gottman, J. M., 435
Gottschalk, S., 29
Gough, H. G., 502
Gould, D., 10
Gould, E., 105, 170, 197, 198, 317, 452
Gould, S. J., 25
Gow, A., 368
Graepel, T., 502, 503
Graff, J., 77
Grafman, J., 533
Graham, S., 18
Gralewski, J., 391
Grandin, T., 557
Grant, A. M., 538
Grant, B. F., 571
Grant, J. A., 222
Granter, S. R., 458
Gray, J. A., 498
Gray, J. L., 374
Green, D., 121
Green, K. F., 204
Green, L. W., 446
Green, V. A., 186
Greenberg, G., 599
Greenberg, L., 537
Greenberg, M. T., 436
Greenberg, S., 551
Greene, S., 409
Greenemeier, L., 582
Greenfield, P., 28, 205
Greenfield, P. M., 204, 205
Greengross, G., 389
Greenough, W. T., 170
Greenstein, D., 190
Greenwald, A. G., 527, 528, 529
Gregory, R. J., 368, 369
Greiling, H., 480
Griffeth, R. W., 417
Griffiths, R. R., 240, 244
Grigorenko, E., 374, 375
Grigorenko, E. L., 377, 379
Grolnick, W. S., 185
Groome, L., 172
Gross, C. G., 104
Gross, J. J., 422, 423, 424, 432, 433, 435, 454
Grossberg, S., 184
Grossman, A. W., 559
Grossman, D., 120
Grossman, P., 471
Grossman, T., 185
Groves, J. E., 610
Grunstein, M., 74, 75
Grus, C. L., 9
Grüsser, S. M., 243
Guadagno, R. E., 28
Guarnaccia, V., 501
Guarraci, F. A., 38
Guehl, D., 575
Guénard, F., 77
Guilford, J. P., 391
Guillem, K., 89
Guilleminault, C., 230
Guiraud, A., 467
Gunderson, E., 143
Güngör, D., 484, 507
Gupta, S., 161
Gurevich, M., 446
Guthrie, H., 60
Gutteling, B. M., 166
Guzman-Marin, R., 228

H

Habib, R., 619
Hackeman, E., 145
Hadders-Algra, M., 189, 194
Hafetz, J. S., 28, 218
Hager, J., 57
Hager, J. L., 304
Haider, B., 83
Haidt, J., 427
Haier, R. J., 373
Hakuta, K., 352
Halaas, J. L., 402
Hale, B., 339
Hall, G. S., 15, 16, 19
Hall, J. A., 435
Hall, N. W., 166
Halpern, D., 341
Halpern, J. H., 242
Hamann, S., 95, 435
Hamer, D., 75, 87, 403, 411, 412, 481, 482, 572
Hamilton, W. D., 537
Hamlin, J. K., 538
Hammer, A. L., 504
Hammersmith, S. K., 412
Hampson, S. E., 506
Han, J., 148
Haney, C., 34, 55
Hankin, B. L., 565
Hanks, R., 212
Hannan, A., 201
Hannigan, T. P., 153
Hansen, R., 266
Hansen, R. A., 200
Hanson, M. A., 77
Harackiewicz, J. M., 415
Harber, K. D., 54
Harding, E. J., 425
Hare, R. D., 580
Hargrave, G. E., 505
Hargrove, L. J., 99
Hargrove, M. F., 533
Harkins, S. G., 515
Harlow, H., 183, 184
Harlow, H. F., 183
Harmon, D., 228
Harmon-Jones, E., 420, 432
Harold, E. S., 409
Harper, S., 612
Harralson, T. L., 465
Harrington, H., 566
Harris, C. L., 319
Harris, J. R., 186
Harris, M. B., 534
Harris, R. A., 239
Harris, S., 37
Harris Interactive, 28, 29
Harrison, P. J., 559, 560, 562
Hart, B., 329
Hart, D., 191
Hasher, L., 198, 259
Haslam, S. A., 520
Hassan, S., 607
Hatami, N., 613
Hatfield, E., 409, 410
Hauser, M. D., 335
Havas, D. A., 430
Hawley, P. H., 480
Hawton, K., 565
Hayashi, A., 327
Hayes, B. D., 240
Haynes, S. G., 465
Hazan, C., 183, 543

Headey, B., 438
Health and Human Services, 241
Heard, H. L., 613
Heath, R. G., 432
Hebb, D. O., 263, 265
Hebebrand, J., 406
Hecht, M. A., 435
Hedden, T., 199
Hedges, L., 378
Hedges, S. M., 418
Hegelson, V. S., 456
Heider, F., 521
Helmholtz, H. von, 15, 138
Helson, R., 507
Hen, R., 470
Hendriks, A. A. J., 506
Henker, B., 557
Hennenlotter, A., 429
Herbert, A., 21, 72
Herdener, M., 172
Hering, E., 139
Hermann, E., 333
Hernandez-Reif, M., 184
Heron, W., 399
Herrington, J. D., 432
Herrmann, C., 213
Herrmann-Lingen, C., 466
Herrnstein, R. J., 377
Herskind, A. M., 438
Herz, R., 149
Herzig, S., 449
Hesse, E., 183
Hessels, S., 276
Hettema, J. M., 572
Hiatt, D., 505
Hicks, J. A., 439
Hien, D. A., 454
Higgins, D. M., 584
Hilgard, E., 234
Hillman, C. H., 170, 315, 317, 469
Hilsenroth, M., 501
Hinduja, S., 205
Hiner, S. L., 446
Hines, L. M., 239
Hines, M., 341, 408, 411, 412
Hinney, A., 406
Hippocrates, 12, 19
Hirsch, C., 267
Hirsch, J., 122
Hirsch, J. B., 420
Hirshfeld-Becker, D. R., 619
Hitzig, E., 96
Ho, Y.-C., 173
Hobson, J. A., 232
Hochberg, L. R., 99
Hodgetts, W., 143
Hoek, H. W., 165
Hoff, E., 329, 330, 332, 352
Hoffman, D. A., 538
Hoffmann, H., 435
Hoffnung, M., 176, 376
Hoffnung, R. J., 176, 376
Hofman, S. G., 619
Hofmann, S., 29, 413, 414
Hofstede, G., 484
Hogan, M. J., 436
Hogan, T. P., 367, 370
Hogeboom, D. L., 205
Högl, B., 230
Hohmann, A. G., 242, 243, 244
Holden, C., 160
Holder, M., 439
Holland, J. L., 505
Holland, S. K., 189

Holling, H., 391
Hollon, S., 607, 608
Holmes, J., 203, 556
Holmes, T. H., 446
Holstege, G., 408
Hölzel, B. K., 222
Honzik, C. H., 305
Hopfield, J. J., 262
Hopper, L., 486
Hopson, J. L., 164, 165
Horn, J. L., 359, 360
Horne, J. A., 315
Horney, K., 19, 492, 493
Horonton, C., 41
Horvitz, E., 578
Horwood, J., 559
Hosking, S., 219
Hoss, R. A., 542
Hötting, K., 317
Houlihan, A. E., 192
Houlihan, D., 609
Howard, B. V., 404
Howard, K. I., 607
Howard, M. A., 267
Howard, S. M., 385
Howe, D., 556
Howell, A. J., 314
Howes, C., 186
Hu, S.-H., 412
Hua, K., 109
Huang, A. L., 149
Huang, H., 166
Hubbard, E. M., 151, 152
Hubel, D., 127, 128
Huddleston, D. E., 470
Huddy, W. P., 122
Hudson, W., 152, 153
Huebner, E., 438
Huesmann, L. R., 534
Huff, D., 60
Hughes, D. J., 389
Hull, C. L., 397
Hull, E. M., 408
Humphreys, M. S., 262
Hunter, J. E., 369
Hurley, D., 268
Hurvich, L. M., 125
Huston, A. C., 203
Huta, V., 439
Hutchinson, S., 67, 172
Huttenlocher, J., 329
Hyde, J. S., 341, 409, 412
Hyde, K. L., 172
Hyde, T. S., 259, 260, 261
Hyman, S. E., 79
Hysek, C. M., 242

I

Iacoboni, M., 184, 312
Ianotti, R. J., 205
Iarocci, G., 556
Ijichi, C., 486
Ilieva, I., 267
Ilin, R., 324
Inagaki, T. K., 525
Inhelder, B., 175, 177
Ipser, J., 610
Ironson, G., 454
Isaacowitz, D. M., 420
Isacsson, G., 594
Isen, A. M., 420
Itri, J., 224
Iuculano, T., 373
Iversen, L. L., 562

Iversen, S., 94, 253, 258
Iversen, S. D., 562
Ivey, P. K., 44
Izard, C. E., 185, 425, 426, 436

J

Jablensky, A., 13
Jabr, F., 553
Jacklin, C., 19
Jacklin, C. N., 19, 186, 378, 534
Jackson, K. M., 239
Jackson, L. A., 203
Jackson, T., 469
Jacobs, B. L., 565
Jacobs, D. R., Jr., 467
Jacobs, G. H., 123, 124, 139
Jacobs, T. L., 457, 458
Jacobsen, L. K., 318
Jacobson, J., 371, 376
Jacobson, S., 371, 376
Jacoby, L. L., 276
Jahrig, J. C., 314
Jain, S., 212
James, W., 15, 16, 19, 429
Jamison, K. R., 568, 585
Jan, J. E., 228
Jandorf, L., 418
Janeck, A. S., 574
Janis, I. L., 517
Jarema, M., 594
Jauk, E., 390, 391
Javaheri, F., 613
Javitt, D. C., 558, 561, 562, 591, 592, 599, 607
Jaycox, L. H., 576
Jazaieri, H., 539
Jeannerod, M., 99
Jeffery, R., 405
Jenkins, J. J., 260, 261
Jenkins, W. M., 100, 145, 172
Jennett, B., 212
Jensen, A. R., 377
Jerison, H. J., 90, 93
Jessell, T. M., 146
Jha, A. P., 221
Ji, D., 271, 315
Ji, Y. G., 527
Jiang, M., 352
Jimenez, R. T., 354
Jirtle, R. L., 165
Johansen, J. P., 431
Johansson, S., 326
John, O., 435
John, O. P., 424, 454, 485, 486, 497
Johnson, A., 164, 202
Johnson, C., 344
Johnson, D. P., 612
Johnson, E. C., 505
Johnson, K. J., 420
Johnson, L. L., 229
Johnson, M. W., 244
Johnson, R. E., 240
Johnson, V. E., 407
Johnson, W., 482, 483, 506
Johnson-Laird, P. N., 419
Johnston, J. C., 137
Jokela, M., 196, 507
Jolles, J., 206
Jones, D. K., 109
Jones, I., 483
Jones, P. B., 166
Jope, R. S., 594
Jordahl, T., 194
Jordan, C., 605
Josefsson, K., 506

Joseph, R., 431
Joy, S. P., 391
Juang, L., 152, 153, 180, 277
Judd, T., 219, 526
Juffer, F., 374
Juliano, L. M., 240
Jump, V. K., 184
Junco, R., 219
Jung, C. G., 16, 198, 491
Jung, R. E., 221, 373, 385, 391
Jung-Beeman, M., 387
Juraska, J. M., 170
Juricevic, I., 111, 112
Jusczyk, P. W., 327
Jussim, L., 54
Just, M. A., 218
Juster, R.-P., 451

K

Kabat-Zinn, J., 214, 221, 471
Kadosh, R. C., 269
Kagan, J., 187
Kahan, T. L., 226, 232
Kahn, R. S., 557
Kahneman, D., 347, 348, 349, 350
Kahn-Greene, E. T., 229
Kaiser, B., 619
Kaiser Family Foundation, 203
Kalat, J. W., 200
Kales, A., 230
Kaliman, P., 200, 201
Kalish, R., 432
Kalmady, S. V., 584
Kam, C. M., 436
Kaminsky, Z., 77
Kammrath, L. K., 506
Kanarek, R. B., 60
Kanayama, G., 243
Kanazawa, S., 517
Kandel, E. R., 21, 79, 80, 84, 94, 98, 100, 125, 126, 127, 128, 129, 162, 253, 258, 261, 265, 266, 267, 271, 272, 273, 286, 301, 315, 559, 560
Kanner, A. A., 456
Kanner, A. D., 446
Kantak, K. M., 619
Kanwisher, N., 425
Kanwisher, N. N., 108
Karama, S., 94, 95
Karatsoreos, I. A., 451
Kare, M. R., 149
Karkowski, L. M., 565
Karni, A., 228, 314
Karpiak, C. P., 611
Karwowski, M., 391
Kaube, H., 540
Kaufman, A. S., 365, 366, 367
Kaufman, J. C., 378, 384, 391
Kaufman, N. L., 365, 366, 367
Kaufman, S. B., 358
Kaul, P., 221, 230
Kaviani, H., 613
Kawamura, Y., 149
Kay, L. M., 94
Kay, P., 337
Kazemi, A., 473
Keeler, R. F., 165
Keenan, R. M., 241
Kegeles, L. S., 562
Kehle, S., 607
Keller, A., 473
Keller, H., 140
Keller, M. C., 539, 541
Keller, T. A., 218

Kelley, H. H., 521, 537
Kellman, P. J., 169
Kellner, C. H., 600
Kelly, K. R., 504
Keltner, D., 421, 422, 427
Kempermann, G., 104, 198, 201, 316
Kenardy, J., 438
Kendler, K. S., 76, 88, 550, 565, 572
Kendrick, T., 598
Kennedy, G., 526
Kennedy, J. M., 111, 112
Kennedy, S., 597
Kennedy, S. H., 598
Kenrick, D. T., 400, 418
Kensinger, E. A., 233, 274, 314
Keppel, R., 550
Keri, S., 584
Kerig, P., 371
Kerwin, R., 594, 617
Keshavan, M., 189
Kessler, R. C., 553, 554, 556, 569, 583, 614, 617
Keyes, C. L. M., 439
Keyes, S., 506
Khaire, M., 416
Khandaker, G. M., 166
Khatami, M., 452
Kidd, K. K., 377
Kiecolt-Glaser, J. K., 463
Kieras, D. E., 217
Kihlstrom, J. F., 577
Kilburn, J., 535
Kim, B., 612
Kim, E. S., 617
Kim, H. K., 391
Kim, J., 413
Kim, K. H. S., 352, 353
Kim, S., 198
Kim, S.-E., 469
Kim, Y., 526, 557
Kimball, J., 489
Kimbrel, N. A., 585
Kimeldorf, D. J., 301, 461
Kimura, D., 341
Kincses, T. Z., 269
Kindt, M., 266
King, D. E., 239
King, L. A., 438, 439, 455
Kingsbury, R., 525
Kinney, D. K., 584, 585
Kinsey, A. C., 46, 409, 411
Kirby, K. N., 339
Kirk, K. M., 409
Kirkham, T. C., 401
Kirkpatrick, L. A., 181
Kirk-Sanchez, N. J., 469
Kirsch, I., 599
Kirsh, S. J., 534
Kisilevsky, B. S., 162
Kitayama, S., 153, 537
Kiyonari, T., 432
Klahr, D., 189
Klavans, R., 6
Klein, D. A., 298
Klein, J., 318
Klein, R. G., 90
Klein, S., 194
Klein-Schwartz, W., 240
Kleitman, N., 224
Kleseges, R. C., 319
Klocke, U., 218
Kloosterman, K., 118
Klopfer, P. H., 515
Klucharev, V., 517
Klüver, H., 95

Knösche, T. R., 109
Knowlton, B., 5
Knox, R., 143
Kobayashi, M., 153
Koelling, R. A., 301, 303, 461
Koenig, J. I., 166, 560
Koerner, K., 613
Kogan, A., 538
Koh, J. S., 241
Kohlberg, L., 178
Kohn, P. M., 446
Kokko, K., 196
Kolodny, R. C., 407
Komarov, I., 594
Kometer, M., 244
Kopell, B. H., 96
Kopta, S. M., 607
Korkeila, M., 438
Korman, K., 341
Kornell, N., 261, 280, 281
Kornhaber, M. L., 363, 364
Kosinski, M., 502, 503
Koslowski, B., 37, 343
Kosslyn, S., 339
Kosslyn, S. M., 339
Kottke, J. L., 417
Kounios, J., 95
Kovács, A. M., 354
Kraaj, V., 454
Krahe, T. E., 166
Krakauer, J., 396
Kral, J. G., 77
Kramarik, A., 371, 372
Kramer, A. F., 199, 317, 469
Kramer, S. J., 416
Kranczioch, C., 211, 216
Kraus, N., 172
Kremer, S., 197
Kristeller, J. L., 613
Kristjansson, A. L., 191
Kristof-Brown, A. L., 505
Kroeber, A. L., 155
Kröger, C., 613
Krohn, E., 368
Krompinger, J., 221
Krueger, R. F., 482, 483, 506, 565
Krummel, D., 60
Krystal, A. D., 229
Ku, J., 610
Kübler-Ross, E., 201
Kubota, M., 239
Kubzansky, L. D., 456
Kuhl, B., 276
Kuhl, P. K., 179, 327, 330
Kuhn, D., 37, 189, 345, 346
Kujala, T., 162
Kulikov, A., 594
Kunkel, C., 364
Kuo, L. E., 468
Kuo, M., 239
Kupfermann, I., 94, 253, 258
Kuriyama, K., 314
Kurowski, C. O., 185
Kurson, R., 129
Kusché, C. A., 436
Kwon, Y., 189

L

LaBar, K. S., 274
LaBerge, S., 232
Labonte, B., 463
Lachman, M. E., 508

la Fleur, S. E., 468
LaFrance, M., 435
Lafreniere, K., 446
Lagopoulos, J., 107
Lai, C., 565
Laird, B. A., 585
Lamb, R. J., 297
Lambracht-Washington, D., 200
Lamp, R., 368
Lanciano, T., 275
Landry, R. G., 354
Lane, S. J., 556
Lang, E., 234
Lang, P. J., 419, 437
Lange, C., 429
Lange, P. G., 5, 29
Langley, K., 76
Langlois, J. H., 541, 542
Lansing, A. E., 508
La Precious, H., 204
Lapsley, D. K., 180
Larson, L., 504
Larson, L. M., 504
Larson-Hall, J., 329, 352
Larsson, H., 556
Larsson, J., 556
Lasagabaster, D., 354
Lasane, T. P., 122
Laschet, J., 88
Latané, B., 43, 536
Laumann, E., 438
Laureys, S., 211, 212, 213, 245
Lauzon, N. M., 266
Lavelli, M., 185
Lavie, N., 216
Law, A. J., 615
Lawless, H. T., 150
Lawson, A. E., 189
Laxton, A. W., 597
Lazar, S. W., 222
Lazarus, A. A., 609
Lazarus, R. S., 25, 418, 422, 423, 446, 447,
    453, 454, 456
Leary, M., 413, 414
Leary, M. R., 413, 414, 525
Leary, S. P., 122
Le Bars, P. L., 267
LeDoux, J., 431
LeDoux, J. E., 94, 95, 274, 572
LeDuc, P. A., 315
Lee, C., 413, 456, 507
Lee, C. S., 387
Lee, H., 432
Lee, J. E., 239, 413
Lee, K. A., 230
Lemay, E. P., Jr., 191
Lenhart, A., 204, 205
Lenneberg, E., 328
Lennie, P., 139
Lenroot, R., 190
Lepage, J.-F., 184, 312
Lerch, J., 190
Lerner, L., 595
Lesch, K. P., 481
Lethbridge-Cejku, M., 464
Letzring, T. D., 506
Leuner, B., 105, 197, 198, 452
LeVay, S., 411, 412
Levenson, R. W., 418, 419, 422, 424, 425, 430,
    435, 451, 454, 456
Leveroni, C., 341
Levitt, P., 559, 560
Levy, B., 276
Levy, D. M., 221

Lewin, T., 203
Lewis, D., 559, 560
Lewis, G. D., 469
Lewis, K., 543
Li, B.-H., 401
Li, H., 316
Li, J., 501
Liamputtong, P., 29
Lichtenstein, P., 556
Lichtman, J. W., 162, 560
Lidz, J., 332
Liebal, K., 326
Lieberman, J. A., 560, 592, 599
Lieberman, M. D., 514
Liebert, R. M., 534
Liehr, P., 471
Lihoreau, M., 525
Limosin, F., 21
Lin, J., 458
Linda, F. K., 594
Linderholm, T., 507
Lindgren, K. P., 529
Lindsay, D. S., 278
Linehan, M. M., 612, 613, 619
Lipkus, I. M., 319
Lippa, R., 532
Lipsitz, J. D., 609
Lipsman, N., 497
Lipworth, L., 471
Lisetti, C., 29, 609
Lister, K. M., 611
Litt, E., 527
Liu, H., 196
Liu-Ambrose, T., 199, 469
Locke, J., 14, 19, 20
Lockhart, R. S., 260, 261
Lockwood, G. A., 455
Lodi-Smith, J., 506
Loehlin, J. C., 482, 483
Loeser, J. D., 148
Loewenstein, R. J., 577
Loftus, E., 277, 278
Loftus, E. F., 262
Logothetis, N. K., 107
Lohman, B. J., 194
Lombardi, G., 198
Long, M., 352
Lopez, S., 438
Lopez, S. J., 439
Lorenc, Z. P., 430
Lorenz, K., 181, 311
Losada, M. F., 439
Loureiro, M., 173
Lovaas, O. I., 297, 298
Lovell, B., 449
Lovett, R., 240
Low, J. A., 162
Lowery, B. S., 18
Lowry, C. A., 565
Lozano, A. M., 597–598
Lubach, G. R., 165
Lubben, J., 205
Lubinski, D., 372
Luborsky, L., 607
Luchins, A. S., 382
Luchins, E. H., 382
Lüders, M., 526
Ludwig, A. M., 389, 583, 584, 585
Lueck, M., 580
Luminet, O., 436
Lund, D. J., 416
Lupien, S. J., 451
Lutman, M. E., 143
Lutz, A., 221

Luykx, J. J., 569
Lyketsos, C. G., 597
Lynn, R., 374
Lynn, S. J., 577
Lyons, D. E., 312
Lyons, D. M., 452

M

Ma, X., 90
Maas, J., 229
McArdle, J. J., 206
Macaskill, M., 118
McCabe, C., 149
McCarter, R., 426
McClain, C. S., 201
McClelland, D. C., 414
McClelland, J. L., 137, 263, 341, 342
Maccoby, E., 19
Maccoby, E. E., 19, 186, 378, 534
McCrae, R. R., 480, 484, 497, 502, 506
McCrory, M. A., 404
McCullough, M. E., 602
Macdaid, G. P., 504
McDaniel, M. A., 371
MacDonald, G., 480, 525
McDonald, J., 556
McElree, B., 276
McEvoy, J. P., 599
McEwen, B. S., 451, 452, 483
McGaugh, J. L., 250, 261
McGenney, B. E., 244
McGhee, D. E., 528
McGill, B., 196
McGlone, G., 501
McGough, E. L., 469
McGowan, B. A., 304
McGowan, L., 120
McGowan, P. O., 452
McGue, M., 375
McGuffin, P., 550, 565
McGuire, E. J., 339
Machilek, F., 502
McHugh, P., 577
McHugh, R. K., 619
MacKay, I. R. A., 352
McKenna, B. S., 314
McKhann, G. M., 470
McKinley, M., 397
McKinney, M. L., 335
MacKinnon, D. W., 384
MacLane, C. N., 505
McLay, R. N., 609
MacLean, K. A., 221, 244
McMenamy, J. M., 185
Macmillan, M., 97, 508
McNaughton, B. L., 315
MacNeill, C., 314
McTiernan, A., 467
MacWhinney, B., 332
Madden, M., 204, 205
Maddi, S. R., 457
Madey, S., 423
Madigan, S., 256
Madigan, S. A., 253, 255, 257, 261, 273
Maes, H. M. M., 403
Maestripieri, D., 11
Magoun, H. W., 93
Maguire, E. A., 95
Maier, N. R. F., 382
Maier, S. F., 145
Main, M., 183
Mainieri, A. G., 82
Mainous, A. G., III, 239

Malberg, J. E., 565
Malhi, G. S., 594
Malle, B. F., 326
Mamidala, M. P., 556
Manber, R., 230
Maner, J. K., 514, 542
Mangels, J. A., 271
Mangialasche, F., 266
Mann, T., 404
Manson, J. E., 468
Manstead, A. S. R., 434
Mansury, I. M., 77
Mantler, T., 473
Marais, L., 469
Marcus, B., 502
Marczinski, C. A., 267
Marek, G. J., 244
Marin, O., 83
Marinkovic, K., 238
Mark, G., 218
Markman, H. J., 196
Marks, B. L., 315
Marks, R., 149
Marks, W., 245
Markus, H., 153, 484
Markus, H. R., 195
Marlier, L., 164
Marlin, D. W., 402
Maron, E., 572
Marsh, A. A., 432
Marshall, L., 269
Martin, C. E., 46, 411
Martin, L. L., 429
Martin, N. G., 411
Martin, R. A., 389
Martindale, C., 129, 387
Martinez, G., 196
Martuza, R. L., 595
Marzelli, M. J., 99
Maschi, S., 166
Mash, E. J., 371
Mashek, D. J., 418
Mashour, G. A., 595
Masicampo, E. J., 211
Masling, J. M., 501
Maslow, A., 17, 19, 400, 494
Mason, J. W., 451
Masten, A. S., 195
Masten, C. L., 514, 525
Masters, J., 203
Masters, W. H., 407
Masuda, A., 471
Masuda, T., 153, 154
Mateo, Y., 241
Matheson, C. C., 186
Mathiak, K., 204
Mathias, J. L., 245
Mathiesen, B. B., 508
Maticka-Tyndale, E., 409
Matlin, M., 103
Matson, J. L., 299, 603
Matsumoto, D., 152, 153, 180, 277, 434, 435
Matsumoto, D. M., 420
Matsumoto, T., 428
Matthews, K. A., 465
Maurer, D., 151, 152
Mauss, I. B., 419
Max, J. E., 508
Maximova, K., 403
Maxwell, K. W., 242
May, P. A., 166
Mayberg, H., 598
Mayberg, H. S., 26, 37, 597
Mayer, J., 435

Mayer, J. D., 436
Mayer, M., 562
Mazzeo, S. E., 406
Mazziotta, J. C., 184, 312
Mead, N. L., 122
Meaney, M. J., 76, 77
Means, M. K., 231
Mechelli, A., 353
Mechtcheriakov, S., 238
Medina, A. E., 166
Mednick, M. T., 385
Mednick, S. A., 385
Mednick, S. C., 314, 315
Medvec, V., 423
Mehler, J., 354
Mehta, M. A., 267
Mei, L., 559, 615
Meier, E. I., 505
Meier, S., 415
Meilijson, I., 170
Melis, A. P., 515, 528
Mell, J. C., 385
Meltzoff, A. N., 179, 184, 312, 330, 425
Melzack, R., 146, 148
Mendelsohn, A., 263
Mendelsohn, G. A., 206
Mendes, W. B., 585
Menditto, A. A., 298
Mendl, M., 425
Mendoza-Denton, R., 506
Mennella, J. A., 164
Merskey, H., 145
Merten, J., 435
Mesiäinen, P., 196
Metzler, J., 340
Meunier, M., 95
Meyer, A., 584
Meyer, D. E., 217
Meyer, R. G., 551
Meyer-Bahlburg, H. F. L., 411
Meyerhoff, D. J., 239
Meyyappan, A., 279
Miao, C. F., 416
Michael, J., 295
Michela, J. L., 521
Miczek, K. A., 533
Miele, G. M., 454
Mikolajczak, M., 436
Milgram, S., 62, 63, 64, 478, 518, 519, 520
Mill, J., 77
Miller, A., 340, 387
Miller, A. H., 462
Miller, A. L., 298
Miller, A. S., 517
Miller, B. L., 96, 189, 271, 385, 432
Miller, G., 389
Miller, G. A., 254
Miller, G. E., 452, 463, 464
Miller, G. F., 371, 400, 481, 541, 542
Miller, L. A., 387
Miller, N., 307
Miller, S. L., 542
Millot, J.-L., 153
Milner, B., 251, 265
Milner, P., 432
Min, B.-K., 99
Mineka, S., 571
Minturn, A. L., 122
Mirescu, C., 105, 170
Mirnics, K., 560
Mischel, W., 496, 506
Mitchell, K., 204
Mitchell, K. J., 29, 205
Miyake, A., 271, 432

Miyashita, T., 263
Mizuno, S., 230
Moffitt, T. E., 26, 76, 534, 550, 551, 559, 566
Moghaddam, B., 562
Moise-Titus, J., 534
Mokdad, A. H., 403
Molaison, H., 251
Moline, J., 143
Moller, J., 466
Montague, D. P. F., 184
Montgomery, A., 454
Montgomery, G. H., 234
Moody, E. W., 291
Moore, D. C., 137
Moore, E. S., 166
Moore, M. K., 184, 312, 330, 425
Moore, R. Y., 224
Moradi, A. R., 275
Morales-Medina, J. C., 565
Moran, E. M., 526
Moray, N., 215
Morelli, G. A., 44
Moreno, J., 560
Moreno, M., 582
Morgan, S. M., 122
Morgenstern, N. A., 198
Morien, A., 401
Morikawa, H., 330
Morin, C. M., 245
Morland, T., 432
Morris, J. S., 95
Morris, M. W., 522
Morris, N. M., 408
Morris, P. L., 432
Morris, T. L., 29
Morrison, R. S., 202
Morton, F., 485
Moruzzi, G., 93
Mosconi, M., 557
Moscovici, S., 518
Moscovitch, M., 261
Moses-Kolko, E. L., 166
Moskowitz, J., 454, 457, 471
Moskowitz, J. T., 456
Moss, M., 402
Motluk, A., 111, 113
Mount, M. K., 504
Moynihan, J., 471
Mrazek, M. D., 223
Mroczek, D., 478, 506
Mucan, B., 502
Mühlberger, A., 431, 432
Muir, D. W., 162
Müller-Oerlinghausen, B., 569
Mulvey, T. A., 9
Munro, G. D., 122
Munro, M. J., 352
Munsinger, H., 374
Murphy, G., 298
Murphy, S. E., 593
Murray, C., 377
Murray, H. A., 413
Murray, J., 405
Murvielde, I., 504
Muscanell, N. L., 28
Musselman, L., 541
Muthukumaraswamy, S. D., 88
Myers, I. B., 504

N

Näätänen, R., 162
Nabi, H., 466
Nacash, N., 611

Nadarajah, B., 89, 162
Nadel, L., 228, 233, 314
Nadkarni, A., 29, 413, 414
Nahin, R. L., 229
Nakajima, K., 469
Nakayama, K., 314
Nansel, T. R., 205
Naqvi, N. H., 98
Nasar, S., 584
Nash, J. F., Jr., 584
Nash, M. R., 501
Nass, C. I., 204
Nathans, J., 123, 124, 139
National Center for Health (NCHS), 473
National Eye Institute, 348
National Highway Traffic Safety
    Association, 218
National Human Genome Research
    Institute, 78
National Institute on Alcohol Abuse and
    Alcoholism, 239
National Institute on Deafness, 143
National Institute of Mental Health
    (NIMH), 558
National Safety Council, 348
National Sleep Foundation, 229
Naumann, R. B., 218
Nauta, W. J. H., 79, 82
Nave, K.-A., 81
Neal, D. T., 430, 616
Neale, M. C., 403, 572
Negahban, A., 582
Neisser, U., 359
Nekoei-Zahraei, N. S., 473
Nelson, J., 613
Nelson, L., 195
Nelson-Gray, R. O., 613
Nemeroff, C. B., 599
Nesbit, S. M., 534
Nettle, D., 481, 584
Neuberg, S. L., 418, 514, 524, 528, 530
Neugebauer, R., 165
Neumann, D. L., 341, 378
Neville, H., 103
Newbury, J., 469
Newcomb, A. F., 191
Newcomb, T. M., 539
Newcombe, N. S., 336
Newport, E. L., 328
Neyens, D. M., 219
Neyer, F. J., 507
Nickerson. C., 438
Nicoll, R. A., 242, 243, 401
Nieman, D. C., 438
Nikolaus, S., 572
Nilsson, L. G., 199
Nisbett, R. E., 56, 153, 154, 522
Nishida, A., 462
Nishimura, E., 458
Nishino, S., 230
Nithianantharajah, J., 201
Nixon, R. D. V., 576
Nock, M. K., 529
Noda, H., 468
Nolen-Hoeksema, S., 13, 406, 559, 580, 596,
    603, 612
Nolte, C., 257
Norcross, J. C., 10, 611
Norenzayan, A., 522
Norton, M. I., 438, 538
Nottebohm, F., 104
Novak, M. A., 11
Nowak, M. A., 326
Nowell, A., 378

Nowicki, G. P., 420
Nuechterlein, K., 217
Nusbaum, E. C., 391

O

Oaten, M., 418
Oatley, K., 419
Obama, B., 195, 346, 524
Oberlander, T. F., 483
Oberman, L. M., 312, 557
O'Brien, C. P., 582
O' Brien, W. H., 466
Ochsner, K. N., 423, 432, 435
O'Cleirigh, C., 454
O'Conner, M. J., 568
O'Conner, S. S., 28, 218
O'Craven, K. M., 108
Odbert, H. W., 497
O' Doherty, J. O., 540
Oehen, P., 242
O'Hara, R., 256
Öhman, A., 95, 431
Ohnishi, T., 172
Ohno, H., 315
Oishi, S., 484
Oitzl, M. S., 376
Olds, J., 432
Oliver, M. B., 409
Olney, J. W., 236
O'Loughlin, M., 37, 189
Olson, J. M., 529
O'Malley Olsen, E., 218
Omark, D., 186
Omark, M., 186
O'Neill, J., 315
Ones, D. S., 505
Ong, J. C., 230
Onodera, A., 508
Ophir, E., 204
Opperman, M., 409
Orne, M. T., 234
Orr, E. S., 29
Ortigo, K. M., 493
Ortigosa, A., 502
Orwin, R. G., 192
Oscar-Berman, M., 238
Osherow, N., 544
Ost, J., 279
Oster, H., 185
Osterling, J., 556
Ostry, D. J., 145
O'Sullivan, M., 522, 523
Ottersen, O. P., 21, 72
Otto, M. W., 619
Ouellet, M-C., 245
Oumar, F., 182
Overeem, S., 230
Overgaard, M., 213
Owen, A. M., 213
Owen, M., 559, 562
Owren, M. J., 428
Oyama, S., 352
Özgüven, N., 502

P

Pace, T. W., 539
Padmala, S., 432
Pae, C.-U., 593
Pajares, F., 306
Paley, B., 568
Paluk, B. L., 435
Pan, B. A., 329
Panagopoulou, E., 454

Panaitescu, B., 79
Panksepp, J., 146, 431, 493
Pantev, C., 145
Parasuraman, R., 217
Paris, R., 507
Park, C. L., 457
Park, S., 385
Parker, E. S., 250
Parker, S. T., 335
Parks, A. C., 602
Parks, E. J., 404
Parks, R., 180
Parnavelas, J., 89, 162
Parpura, V., 79
Partanen, E., 162
Pascual-Leone, A., 173, 198, 316
Passarelli, V., 613
Pasupathi, M., 508, 509
Patchin, J. W., 205
Patihis, L., 278
Patil, S. T., 599
Patrick, J. H., 194
Patterson, C. J., 161, 168, 176
Patterson, D. R., 234
Patti, M. E., 77
Paul, E. S., 425
Paulesu, E., 271
Paulozzi, L. J., 240
Paulson, R. M., 454
Paus, T., 189, 190
Pavlov, I. P., 288, 289, 291
Payne, J. D., 228, 233, 261, 274, 314
Payne, R., 240
Pearsall, S., 189, 345
Pearson, J. D., 197
Pearson, N. J., 229
Pearson, P. D., 354
Peckham, P. H., 99
Pecoraro, N. C., 468
Pedersen, D. M., 152
Peigneux, P., 228
Pelli, D. G., 137
Penfield, W., 265
Peng, K., 522
Penke, L., 371
Pennebaker, J. W., 454, 455, 463
Peoples, L., 89
Peper, J. S., 170, 171
Perdue, B. M., 335
Pereira, A. C., 315, 316, 469, 470
Perlovsky, L. I., 324
Perner, J., 178, 179
Perrin, J. S., 189
Perry, B. D., 102, 170, 171, 377, 560, 573
Perry, R., 129
Persky, H., 408
Pessoa, L., 432
Peter, J., 29, 204, 205
Peters, K. R., 315
Peters, M., 341
Peters, R. M., 145
Petersen, J. L., 409
Peterson, J. B., 584
Petrie, K. J., 454
Petrill, S. A., 374, 375
Petronis, A., 77, 559
Petry, N. M., 582
Petry, S., 508
Petty, T., 416
Petzinger, G. M., 200, 201
Pfefferbaum, A., 239
Phan, K. L., 432
Phelps, E. A., 95, 274, 418, 431
Phillips, D. T., 223

Piaget, J., 19, 173, 174, 175, 177, 365
Pickrell, J. E., 278
Pierce, T., 205
Pietrek, C., 565
Pika, S., 326
Pincus, J. H., 533, 580
Pine, D. S., 432
Pinel, P., 13
Pinker, S., 20, 21, 25, 98, 100, 328, 331
Pinsker, H. M., 266, 315
Pisani, L., 182
Pittman, R. K., 266
Plato, 14
Platsidou, M., 436
Pliner, P., 402
Plomin, R., 20, 374, 375, 481, 482, 483
Plucker, J. A., 384, 391
Plunkett, K., 327
Podolski, C., 534
Pohlmeyer, E. A., 99
Poldrack, R., 5
Poldrack. R. A., 264
Polich, J., 257
Polkinghorn, C., 618
Pomeroy, W. B., 46, 411
Pomplun, M., 368
Ponsford, J., 245
Popper, K., 38
Porfeli, E. J., 194
Posner, M. I., 203, 234
Post, F., 583
Post, R. M., 594
Potkin, S. G., 592
Potter, J. W., 203
Poulin, M. J., 538
Poulton, R., 566
Powell, L. H., 467
Powell, R. A., 314
Powers, M., 611
Prahbu, V., 389
Preckel, F., 391
Premack, D., 333
Prescott, C. A., 565
Price, J., 250
Pridmore, S., 596
Prindle, J. J., 206
Priori, A., 269
Prochaska, J. O., 611
Profet, M., 148, 165
Ptito, M., 165
Pugh, M. J. V., 191
Pulkkinen, L., 196
Pulver, C. A., 504
Pun, S., 438
Purves, D., 162, 560
Putnam, F., 577
Putnam, F. W., 577

Q

Qiu, J., 95
Quillian-Wolever, R., 613
Quinlivan, E., 414
Quinn, P. D., 457
Quirin, M., 413
Quirion, R., 565
Quiroga, J., 502
Quiroga, R. Q., 129

R

Radford, A., 331
Raffaele, P., 335
Rahe, R. H., 446
Rahman, Q., 411, 412

Rahn, E. J., 244
Raij, T. T., 235
Raine, A., 581
Raison, C. L., 462
Raleigh, M., 534
Ramachandran, V. S., 151, 152, 312, 557
Ramanathan, L., 228
Ramesh, S., 594
Ramey, C. T., 378
Ramón y Cajal, S., 104
Ransdell, S., 346
Rao, V., 508
Rapoport, J., 190
Rapoport, J. L., 170
Rashid, R., 602
Rashid, T., 602
Rathus, J. H., 613
Rawl, S. M., 473
Ray, S., 206
Raymaekers, L., 278, 279
Rayner, R., 291, 292
Raz, A., 233, 234
Raz, N., 198, 206
Read, J. P., 239
Ready, D. J., 609
Redd, W. H., 234
Reed, C., 599
Reed, G. M., 456
Refinetti, R., 224
Regan, M., 219
Regier, T., 337
Reicher, S. D., 520
Reilly, D., 341, 378
Reilly, T., 224
Reinecke, L., 527
Remafedi, G., 192
Renaud, S., 467
Renshaw, K. D., 576
Rentfrow, P. J., 502
Ressler, K. J., 274
Rest, J., 180
Retz, W., 481
Reuter-Lorenz, P. A., 169
Rexrode, K. M., 468
Rey-Biel, P., 415
Reynolds, C. R., 368, 369, 377
Reynolds, G. D., 172
Reynolds, S., 556
Rhoades, G. K., 196
Rhoades, L., 415
Ricciardelli, L. A., 354
Rice, F., 483
Rice, M. L., 330
Rice, W. R., 412
Rich, A., 21, 72
Richards, J. E., 172
Richards, J. M., 424, 454
Richards, R. L., 585
Richardson, J. D., 122
Ridder, E. M., 559
Ridley, M., 21
Rieger, J., 143
Ries, M., 245
Rimm, E. B., 239
Rinpoche, S., 201
Risberg, J., 385, 386
Risch, N., 565
Risley, T. R., 329
Ritschel, L. A., 613
Ritter, J., 198
Riva, G., 609, 619
Rivault, C., 525
Rizvi, S., 598

Rizzolatti, G., 82, 312, 313, 330
Robbins, T. W., 267
Roberts, B. W., 478, 482, 506, 507
Roberts, L. S. E., 399
Roberts, T. A., 478
Robertson, B. A. M., 508
Robertson, I., 276
Robins, R. W., 421
Robinson, D. N., 11, 12
Robinson, L. A., 319
Röder, B., 111, 113, 317
Rodgers, A. B., 78
Rodrigues, A., 173
Rodriguez, J. J., 79
Roehr, B., 576
Roehrs, T., 229
Rogelberg, S. G., 10
Rogers, C. R., 17, 19, 495, 602
Rogers, T., 263, 341, 342
Roggman, L. A., 541
Roid, G. H., 368
Rolland, J. P., 484
Rolls, E. T., 148, 149, 150
Romain, J., 508
Romanczyk, R. G., 298
Ronn, T., 469
Roper, S. D., 149
Rosch, E., 342, 524
Rose, A. J., 449
Rose, D., 314
Rosellini, A. J., 572
Roseman, I. J., 423
Rosen, B., 107
Rosen, L. D., 205
Rosen, W., 152, 236, 239, 241, 244
Rosenberg, E. L., 56, 418, 419, 427, 428, 465,
     466, 480, 523
Rosenberg, R. N., 200
Rosenberger, P. H., 472
Rosenfeld, B., 201
Rosenfeld, J. V., 279
Rosenman, R. H., 465
Rosenquist, J. N., 526
Rosenthal, L. J., 240
Rosenthal, R., 41, 52, 53, 54
Rosenzweig, M. R., 66, 104, 316
Rösler, F., 170
Ross, B., 197
Ross, C. A., 577
Ross, D., 307, 308, 309
Ross, L., 522
Ross, S. A., 307, 308, 309
Rossetto, A., 430
Rostene, W., 452
Roth, G., 533, 580
Roth, T., 229
Rothbart, M. K., 203
Rothbaum, B. O., 611
Rothenberg, D., 333
Rothman, S., 359
Rowe, G., 420
Rowland, N. E., 401
Roy, M., 146
Rozin, P., 402, 418
Ruan, J., 354
Ruangkittisakul, A., 79
Rubin, D. B., 54
Ruff, H., 376
Rule, A. C., 168
Rumbaugh, D. M., 333, 335
Rumelhart, D., 263, 341
Runyan, W. M., 44, 550
Ruppin, E., 170

Rushton, W. A. H., 123
Rutter, M., 21, 26, 74, 76, 481, 483, 550
Ruyak, P. S., 315
Ruzgis, P. M., 378
Ryan, G., 501
Ryan, J., 324
Ryan, R. M., 211, 214, 221, 400, 416, 439
Ryan, T., 413
Rymer, R., 328

S

Saarni, C., 185
Sabbagh, L., 189, 190
Sacco, R. L., 239
Sackeim, H. A., 432, 600
Sackett, P. R., 505
Safiullina, X., 389
Sagan, C., 37
Sagi, A., 182
Sahakian, B. J., 267
Sahdra, B. K., 221
Saisan, J., 615
Sakai, K., 170, 189, 328, 352
Salapatek, P., 168
Salehan, M., 582
Sallinen, M., 315
Salmerón, J., 404
Salomon, R., 608
Salovey, P., 435, 436
Salthouse, T. A., 277
Salvucci, D. D., 218, 219
Samimi, P., 205
Sanders, L., 129
Sansone, C., 415
Santrock, J. W., 197
Sapolsky, R., 451, 460
Sarlio-Lähteenkorva, S., 438
Sauser, W., 389
Sauter, D. A., 434
Sava, F. A., 599
Savage-Rumbaugh, S., 333, 334
Savicki, V., 507
Savin-Williams, R. C., 411
Sawyer, R. K., 383
Scarr, S., 375
Schaal, B., 164
Schacter, D. L., 264, 271, 274, 276, 277
Schaefer, E. J., 467
Schäfer, A., 433
Schaie, K. W., 198, 199
Schaller, M., 418
Scharff, C., 317
Scheier, M. F., 456
Schein, E., 160
Schellenberg, E. G., 173
Scherag, S., 406
Scherer, K. R., 423, 428
Schienle, A., 433, 435
Schiff, E. R., 467
Schinder, A. F., 198
Schipani, D., 4
Schlaepfer, T. E., 598
Schlaug, G., 67, 172
Schmahmann, J. D., 93
Schmand, B., 200, 277
Schmidt, D., 244
Schmidt, F. L., 369
Schmidt, M. E., 203
Schmithorst, V. J., 189
Schmitt, D., 409
Schmitt, D. P., 542
Schneider, J. A., 199

Schneider, M. L., 483
Schoenfeld, D., 335
Schooler, J. W., 223
Schouten, A. P., 205
Schuldberg, D., 584
Schuler, J. L. H., 466
Schulkin, J., 451
Schulman, P., 618
Schultz, W. T., 44
Schumacher, M., 466
Schutte, C., 212
Schutte, N. S., 436
Schütz, A., 502
Schwartz, G. M., 425
Schwartz, J. H., 84
Schwartz, J. L. K., 528
Schwartz, J. M., 575
Schweinhardt, P., 146
Schwerdtfeger, A., 145
Scott, J., 349
Scott, T. H., 399
Scruggs, J. L., 244
Scully, J. A., 446
Sebastian, C., 191
Segal, J., 615
Segal, N., 160
Segal, Z. V., 611, 613
Segerstrom, S. C., 456
Seifert, K. L., 176, 376
Seiser, L., 339
Sekuler, A. B., 131
Sekuler, R., 131
Seligman, M. E. P., 17, 19, 304, 437, 456, 494, 495, 602, 618
Seligson, F., 60
Selkoe, D., 87
Sell, R. L., 411
Selten, J. P., 560
Selye, H., 450, 451, 460
Semin, G. R., 275
Semmann, D., 515, 528
Sen, B., 166
Senate, U.S., 517
Sephton, S. E., 456
Serpell, R., 379
Serrano-Blanco, A., 553
Serretti, A., 611
Sestir, M. A., 535
Seymour, B., 540
Shackelford, T. K., 541
Shank, D. B., 203
Shapiro, P., 466
Shapiro, S. L., 230
Shapiro, T., 233
Sharafinski, C. E., 417
Shargorodsky, J., 143
Sharot, T., 274
Shastry, B. S., 569
Shaver, P., 183, 543
Shaw, P., 189, 190
Shaw, S., 525
Shedler, J., 607
Shekelle, R. B., 465
Shelton, R., 608
Shen, H., 190, 501
Shepard, M., 13
Shepard, R., 340
Shergill, S. S., 561
Sherman, R. C., 205
Sherman, S. M., 94
Shermer, M., 37, 41
Shestyuk, A. Y., 597
Sheth, S. A., 37

Shiffrin, R. M., 252, 260
Shim, M., 203
Shimamura, A. P., 271
Shiner, R. L., 482
Shlik, J., 572
Shoda, Y., 496, 506
Shomaker, L. B., 191
Shore, L. M., 417
Short, S. J., 560
Shults, R. A., 218
Shuman, D. W., 551
Siegers, K., 206
Siegman, A. W., 466
Sigman, M., 607
Sigmund, K., 326
Sigurdsson, T., 274
Silbersweig, D. A., 561
Silva, L. M., 184
Silver, R. C., 539
Silverman, I., 341
Silverstein, S. M., 298
Silvia, P. J., 391, 400, 585
Sime, J. D., 537
Simmons, V. N., 531
Simner, J., 151
Simon, H. A., 379
Simon, N. M., 565
Simon, T., 365
Simonds, J., 186
Simons, D. J., 215
Simon-Thomas, E. R., 428
Simonton, D. K., 383, 389, 391
Simpson, K., 49
Simpson, K. A., 401
Singer, B., 607
Singer, T., 146, 433, 539, 540
Singer, W., 189
Sippola, L. K., 191
Sirignono, S. W., 508
Sisson, G., 593
Skinner, B. F., 17, 19, 292, 294, 296, 299, 301, 305, 330, 415
Skjetne, J. H., 526
Skoe, E., 172
Skorikov, V. B., 194
Skowronski, J. J., 274
Slamecka, N. J., 276
Slater, E., 584
Slavich, G. M., 565
Slining, M. M., 402
Sloan, P., 501
Slutske, W. E., 506
Smahel, D., 205
Small, G. W., 206
Small, S. A., 470
Smallwood, P., 592
Smallwood, P. M., 139
Smilek, D., 276
Smith, A. P., 464
Smith, B. D., 120, 399
Smith, C., 314
Smith, C. A., 424
Smith, C. T., 315
Smith, E. M., 462
Smith, G. S., 597
Smith, H., 230
Smith, J., 77, 199, 205
Smith, J. D., 335
Smith, M., 607, 615
Smith, N., 456
Smith, P. B., 517
Smith, S. M., 387
Smoski, M. J., 428

Smyth, J. M., 454
Snarey, J. R., 180
Snelson, C., 526
Snyderman, M., 359
Söderkvist, S., 430, 616
Sodian, B., 189
Soeter, M., 266
Soler, J., 613
Solms, M., 245, 489, 493
Solomon, J., 183
Solso, S., 557
Song, H., 104
Song, S., 234
Soorya, L. V., 298
Sorce, J. F., 185, 425
Sorenson, E. R., 426
Sosunov, A. A., 470
Soussignan, R., 164
Southwick, S. M., 617
Sowell, E. R., 189
Spalding, K. L., 404
Spanagel, R., 294
Spearman, C., 359
Spechler, J. A., 526
Spector, F., 151, 152
Speigel, D., 577
Speisman, R. B., 316
Spelke, E., 173
Spence, M. J., 172
Spencer, H. S., 143
Spencer, J. P., 267
Spencer, S. M., 194
Sperry, R. W., 100
Spiegel, D., 455
Spiers, H. J., 95
Spinrad, T. L., 185
Spohr, H., 376
Sproesser, G., 468
Squire, L., 258
Squire, L. R., 264, 596
Srivastava, S., 497
Staggs, G. D., 504
Stanley, J., 372
Stanley, S. M., 196
Stanton, A. A., 432
Stanton, A. L., 454
Starr, C., 74
Stefansson, H., 559
Stein, D., 610
Stein, D. J., 469
Steinberg, L., 190, 191
Steiner, B., 201
Steinhausen, H., 376
Steinmetz, C., 504
Steketee, G., 550
Stellar, E., 401
Stenberg, C., 185
Stenberg, C. R., 185
Stepanski, L. M., 229
Stephane, M., 561
Stepper, S., 430, 431
Steptoe, A., 457
Sterling, P., 451
Stern, S. A., 266
Stern, W., 365
Sternberg, R. J., 337, 342, 354, 358, 359, 361, 362, 377, 379, 543
Stevens, E., 327
Stevens, J. S., 435
Stevens, S. B., 29
Stevenson, R. J., 418
Stewart, J. H., 233, 234
Stewart, R. A., 168

Stewart, V. M., 152
Stice, E., 617
Stickgold, R., 228, 261, 314, 315
Stillwell, D., 502, 503
Stoléru, S., 95
Stone, A. A., 418
Storandt, M., 508
Strack, F., 429
Strange, B. A., 274
Strassman, R. J., 244
Strauss, M. E., 508, 509
Strayer, D. L., 28, 204, 218, 220
Streissguth, A., 371, 376
Streissguth, A. P., 568
Striano, T., 185
Striedter, G., 90
Stroodley, C. J., 93
Stroop, J. R., 234
Strotmann, J., 149
Strueber, D., 533, 534, 580, 581
Strycker, L. A., 192
Stuewig, J., 418
Stuve, P., 298
Styles, E. A., 214, 215
Styron, W., 564
Suarez, E. C., 465
Subrahmanyam, K., 28, 204, 205
Suchak, M., 538
Sugden, K., 76, 88, 566
Sullivan, E. V., 239
Sullivan, K., 179
Sullivan, K. M., 550
Sumner, F. C., 16, 19
Sunsay, C., 291
Suomi, S., 88
Susser, E., 165
Susskind, J. M., 434
Sutherland, A. M., 408
Sutton, C., 389
Svendsen, H. A., 508
Swaminathan, S., 166
Swartz, K., 593
Sweatt, J. D., 77
Swets, J., 121
Swets, J. A., 121
Syed, M., 195
Szabo, Y., 7, 8
Szaflarski, J. P., 332, 333
Szaluta, J., 489
Szarko, R., 143

T

Taatgen, N. A., 217, 218, 219, 582
Tafti, M., 230
Tager-Flusberg, H., 179
Taggart, R., 74
Takahashi, Y., 506
Takeuchi, H., 385, 387
Talassi, E., 508
Talati, A., 165
Talmi, D., 257
Tambs, K., 143
Tammet, D., 250, 373
Tang, Z., 192
Tangney, J. P., 418, 420, 421
Tanielian, T., 576
Tanis, M., 413
Tardif, T., 327
Tare, M., 354
Tarlatzis, B., 454
Tarmann, A., 411
Tashkin, D., 243
Tashkin, D. R., 243

Tavris, C., 553
Taylor, A., 566
Taylor, K. N., 612
Taylor, S. E., 236, 456, 514
Teasdale, G., 212
Teasdale, J. D., 221, 610, 611, 613, 618
Tellegen, A., 482, 502, 504
Teo, K., 469
Terman, L., 365
Terrace, H. S., 335
Teuber, H. L., 265
Thacher, P. V., 314
Thagard, P., 339
Thapar, A., 76, 483
Thayer, S. E., 206
"The Millennials," 205
Théoret, H., 184, 312
Therriault, D., 507
Therriault, D. J., 387
Thibaut, J. W., 573
Thiessen, D., 539
Thomas, A., 181
Thomasius, R., 242
Thompson, C. P., 274
Thompson, P., 374
Thompson, P., 374
Thompson, P. M., 65
Thompson, P. O., 141
Thompson, R. F., 253, 255, 257, 261, 273
Thompson, S., 605
Thompson, W., 339
Thompson, W. L., 339
Thompson, W. R., 74
Thorndike, E. L., 292, 293
Thornhill, R., 542
Thornton, L. M., 406
Thune, I., 468
Thurstone, E. L., 359
Thye, S., 417
Tierney, W. M., 446
Tippett, L. J., 387
Titchener, E., 16
Titov, N., 610
Tobe, E. H., 565
Tobias, S., 354
Tobin, D. J., 458
Tolin, D. F., 607, 619
Tolman, E. C., 305
Tomasello, M., 333
Tomiyama, A., 458
Tomkins, S., 425, 429
Tomkins, S. S., 418, 426
Tomson, S. N., 152
Tong, E. M. W., 424
Tooby, J., 18, 19, 23, 24, 419
Tosi, H., 446
Touriño, C., 615
Townsend, S. S. M., 195
Toyota, Y., 279
Tracy, J. L., 419, 420, 421
Tranel, D., 275, 431
Treffert, D. A., 372, 373
Treisman, A., 215
Tremblay, A., 405
Tremblay, K., 197
Trentacosta, C. J., 185
Trepte, S., 527
Trivers, R. L., 409, 537, 542
Troisi, A., 11
Tronick, E., 44
True, M., 182
Trugman, J. M., 592
Tryon, A. M., 618

Tsai, J., 434
Tsai, J. L., 425
Tsakiris, M., 98
Tseng, W. S., 12
Tucker, D. M., 420
Tucker, J. S., 318
Tucker, M., 228, 261
Tucker-Drob, E. M., 375
Tugade, M. M., 254, 457
Tulku, T., 22
Tully, K., 274
Tully, P. J., 466
Tulsky, D. S., 365
Tulving, E., 258, 260, 261, 264
Turati, C., 312
Turkheimer, E., 375
Turnbull, O., 489
Turner, E. H., 599
Turner, R., 109
Turner-Shea, Y., 596
Tversky, A., 347, 348, 349, 350
Twenge, J. M., 414
Twyman, K., 205
Tynes, B., 205
Tyron, W. W., 602, 607, 609
Tyrrell, D. A. J., 464

U

Udry, J. R., 408
Uher, J., 485
Uher, R., 550, 565
Uhlhaas, P. J., 189
Umberson, D., 196
Umphress, Z. R., 533
Unis, A. S., 568
University of Cambridge, 534
U.S. Census Bureau, 195, 196
U.S. Department of Health and Human
    Services, 467
Uttal, D. H., 336
Utz, K. S., 267
Utz, S., 413
Uylings, H. B. M., 166, 328, 352

V

Vaitl, D., 433
Valente, M., 245
Valenzuela, M. J., 469
Valkenburg, P. M., 29, 204, 205
Valois, R. F., 438
VanBergen, A., 577
Van Boxtel, M. P. J., 206
Van Cantfort, T. E., 333
VanderWerf, E. A., 411
Vandewater, E. A., 202, 203
Van Gerven, P., 277
van Gool, W. A., 200
Vanhaudenhuyse, A., 234
van IJzendoorn, M., 182, 374
Van Kleeck, M. H., 339
van Leeuwen, T. M., 152
Vanlessen, N., 420
van Praag, H., 316, 565
Van Rijn, H., 217, 582
Van Voorhees, B. W., 617
van Vugt, M. K., 221
Van Wyk, P. H., 412
Vartanian, O., 387, 524
Vaswani, M., 594
Vaughan, W., 294
Vaughn, M. G., 533
Vaupel, J. W., 438

Veenema, S., 363
Vegiopoulos, A., 449
Veith, I., 12
Vellas, B., 267
Velliste, M., 99
Venkatasubramanian, G., 584
Venning, A., 607
Verkhratsky, A., 79
Vermeulen, I., 413
Verquer, M. L., 505
Vetter, H. J., 559
Vickerie, J., 464
Viechtbauer, W., 506, 507
Villemure, C., 146
Vinitzky, G., 29, 527
Vinson, G. A., 505
Vladusich, T., 184
Vohs, K. D., 211
Volkmar, F. R., 170
Voltaire, 37
Von dem Hagen, E. A. H., 433
von Strauss, E., 199
vos Savant, M., 389
Vrangalova, Z., 411
Vrba, E. S., 25
Vyas, N. S., 559, 560
Vygotsky, L. S., 178
Vythilingam, M., 617

W

Wade, A. R., 338
Wadlinger, H. A., 420
Wagner, A., 276
Wagner, A. D., 204
Wagner, A. W., 619
Wagner, M., 137
Wagner, S. H., 505
Wagner, T. D., 435
Wahl, J., 11
Wahlbeck, K., 165
Wai, J., 372
Waite, L. J., 409
Wakimoto, S., 539
Waldinger, M. D., 594
Walhovd, K. B., 483
Walk, R., 169
Walker, E. E., 595
Walker, M. P., 228, 261, 314, 315
Walker, R. W., 274
Walker-Andrews, A. S., 185
Wall, P. D., 146
Wallace, B. A., 220
Wallace, J., 439
Wallace, P., 401
Wallas, G., 384
Wallbott, H. G., 428
Waller, L., 408
Wallhagen, M. I., 197
Walmsley, P. T., 505
Walsh, S. P., 28, 29
Walton, K. E., 506, 507
Wamsley, E. J., 228, 261
Wang, J., 205
Wang, S., 452
Wang, Z., 565
Ward, J., 151
Ward, T. B., 387
Warga, C., 148
Washburn, A. L., 401
Wason, P. C., 343
Wasserman, J. D., 365
Waterhouse, J., 224
Waterhouse, J. J., 315

Waterland, R., 165
Watkins, L. R., 145
Watson, J. B., 16, 17, 19, 291, 292
Watson, J. M., 220
Watters, E., 553
Waugh, C. E., 420
Waxenberg, S. E., 408
Waxman, J., 483
Way, B. M., 514
Wayne, S. J., 417
Weathers, S. B., 396, 397
Weaver, C. C., 314
Weaver, D., 224
Weber, E., 15, 122
Weber, J., 11
Weber, R., 204
Wechsler, D., 365
Wechsler, H. L., 239
Weil, A., 152, 236, 239, 241, 244
Weinberg, M. S., 412
Weinberg, R. A., 375
Weinberg, R. S., 10
Weinberger, D. R., 559, 560
Weinberger, M., 446
Weinstein, A. A., 565
Weinstein, T. A., 485
Weisinger, R., 397
Weitzman, E. D., 232
Weller, J. A., 218
Wellisch, D. K., 230, 231
Wenar, C., 371
Wendell, J. W., 471
Wenden, A. L., 354
Wendt, P., 385, 386
Weng, H. Y., 539
Wermke, M., 200
Wernicke, C., 98
Wertheimer, M., 17, 19, 134, 340
Wessely, S., 594, 617
Westen, D., 493
Westerterp, K., 228
Westlye, L. T., 170
Westmaas, J. L., 539
Weston, D., 490
Wetherell, M. A., 449
Whalen, C. K., 557
Wheaton, P., 245
Wheeler, J., 152
Whitaker, J. S., 369
Whitaker, K. L., 77
White, A. M., 88
White, K. M., 28
White, P., 147
White, R., 384
White, R. W., 578
Whitfield, C. L., 560
Whiting, B., 186
Whitlock, J. R., 265
Whorf, B. L., 336
Whybrow, P. C., 569
Wickelgren, I., 153
Wickens, T. D., 121
Wiederhold, B. K., 602, 619
Wiederhold, M. D., 602, 619
Wiese, M., 391
Wiesel, T., 127, 128
Wilensky, A., 431
Wiley, C., 415
Wiley, E., 352
Wilhelm, I., 315
Wilkening, F., 189
Wille, B., 505
Willer, R., 421

Williams, G., 401
Williams, J. H. G., 312
Williams, J. M. G., 611, 613
Williams, K. D., 414, 514
Williams, P. A., 203
Williams, R., 508, 509
Williams, R. B., Jr., 465
Williams, S. C. R., 371
Williams, W. M., 341, 378
Willingham, B., 428, 434
Willis, S., 206
Willis, S. L., 199
Wills, T. A., 455, 464
Wilson, A., 469
Wilson, J. K., 315
Wilson, M. A., 271, 315
Wilson, T. D., 56
Wimmer, H., 178, 179
Wims, E., 610
Winawer, J., 337, 338
Winblad, B., 199
Wing, J. M., 204
Wing, L., 298
Wing, R., 405
Witelson, S. F., 412
Witkin, H. A., 516
Witte, K., 532
Witten, I. B., 615
Witthoft, N., 338
Wojciechowski, F. L., 407
Wolak, J., 204
Wolf, D. A., 371
Wolf, S., 201
Wölfling, K., 243
Wolford, J. L., 203
Wolkowitz, O. M., 565
Wollmer, M. A., 430, 616
Wong, C. C. Y., 77
Woodbury, M. A., 13
Woolf, V., 568
Woollett, K., 95
Wouters-Adriaens, M., 228
Wright, J. S., 493
Wu, L., 338
Wu, X., 582
Wundt, W., 15, 16, 19
Wurtz, R. H., 98, 125, 126, 127, 128, 129

X

Xenos, S., 413
Xia, M., 266
Xiang, J., 501
Xie, L., 226, 228
Xiong, W.-C., 559, 615
Xu, F., 173, 327, 599

Y

Yaemsiri, S., 402
Yamada, M., 593
Yanagisawa, K., 514
Yang, Y., 533, 581
Yao, Y., 266
Yasuhara, H., 593
Ybarra, M. L., 29, 205
Yeragani, V. K., 562
Yerkes, R. M., 399
Yin, D.-M., 615
Yin, J. C. P., 266
Yoemans, N. D., 459
Yollin, P., 257
Yoo, S. H., 434
Yoo, S.-S., 99

Yoon, J., 417
Young, A., 456
Young, A. S., 592
Young, K., 219
Young, L. C., 411
Young, P., 608
Young, R. K., 539
Young, R. M., 28
Yu, A. Y., 413, 526
Yu, H. H., 432
Yuan, H., 99
Yuen, E. K., 610
Yuheda, R., 576

Z

Zacks, R. T., 259
Zaitchik, D., 179

Zajonc, R. B., 515, 530, 539
Zak, P. J., 432
Zametkin, A. J., 557
Zang, Y. F., 557
Zanna, M. P., 529
Zaun, B. J., 411
Zeidan, F., 221
Zeino, Z., 593
Zeki, S., 129
Zelazo, P. D., 530
Zhang, L., 354
Zhang, Y., 329
Zhao, Y., 192
Zhou, R., 28
Ziegler, G., 371
Zigler, E. F., 166
Zimbardo, P. G., 34, 64
Zimmer, C., 77, 485, 486

Zimmer-Gembeck, M. J., 194
Zimmerman, C., 37
Zimmerman, J., 507
Zimmerman, R. D., 505
Zimprich, D., 506
Zorick, F. J., 229
Zucker, K. J., 412
Zudro, L., 414
Zuk, M., 411
Zullig, K., 438

Subject Index

Note: Page references followed by "*f*" refer to figures.

A

AA (Alcoholics Anonymous), 606
ABA (applied behavioral analysis), 298–299
absent-mindedness, 276–277
absolute thresholds, 120–121, 120*f*–121*f*
ACC. *See* anterior cingulate cortex
accommodation, 123
ACE (Adverse Childhood Experiences) Study, 573–574
acetylcholine (ACh), 87, 87*f*, 200
  drugs to boost, 266
achievement motivation, 414–415
acquired immunity, 462–463
acquisition, 290*f*
acronyms, in encoding, 261
acrophobia, 12
ACTH (adrenocorticotropic hormone), 449, 449*f*
action potential, 83–85, 84*f*, 89
adaptations, 24
  emotions as, 419–420
  evolution and, 23–25
  to stress, 451
adaptive behavior, 370
Adderall, 267
addiction, 236, 582
ADHD. *See* attention deficit hyperactivity disorder
adolescence, 187
  cognitive development in, 188–190, 190*f*, 204
  depression risk factors in, 617
  personality development in, 192, 192*f*
  physical development in, 188, 188*f*
  sleep in, 227*f*
  social development in, 191–192, 192*f*, 204
  suicide in, 230
  technology use in, 204–205, 204*f*
adoption studies. *See* twin-adoption studies
adrenal glands, 109
  location of, 110*f*
  stress and, 448, 449*f*
adrenaline (epinephrine), 87, 109
adrenal-medullary system, 448, 449*f*
adrenocorticotropic hormone (ACTH), 449, 449*f*
adulthood. *See also* parenting
  death and dying, 201–202
  early, 193–197, 194*f*, 195*f*, 196*f*, 205
  emerging, 193–195, 205
  late, 198–202, 205–206. *See also* late adulthood, middle
  middle, 197–198, 197*f*
  parenthood, 196, 196*f*
  personality development, 197, 198
  sleep in, 227*f*
  technology and, 205–206
  young, 195–197, 195*f*, 196*f*
Adverse Childhood Experiences (ACE) Study, 573–574
Advertising. *See also* media

modeling in, 307
statistics in, 60–61
affective neuroscience, 431
affective traits, 418–419
affiliation, need for, 413–414
African Americans. *See also* race–ethnicity
  implicit bias and, 528–529
  prejudicial attitudes toward, 528, 529
  as psychologists, 16
  smoking by, 319
afterimages, 139, 139*f*
aggression, 533. *See also* anger; hostility; violence
  amygdala and, 95
  hostility vs., 533
  nature and nurture of, 533–535
  serotonin and, 88
  social influences on, 534–535
  social learning theory and, 307–308, 307*f*, 308*f*
  video games and, 534–535
aging. *See also* late adulthood
  chronic stress and, 458
  dementia and, 199–200, 200*f*
  education and, 277
  memory and, 277
  neurogenesis and, 102, 104–105, 197–198
  personality and, 507, 507*f*, 508
agoraphobia, 571–572
agreeableness, 482, 482*f*
AIDS, 243
AIM (activation, input, and mode), 232, 232*f*
alarm stage, 450, 450*f*
alcohol
  binge drinking, 239
  bipolar disorder in offspring, 568
  blood alcohol concentration, 237–238, 238*f*
  brain changes and, 238–239, 238*f*
  driving and, 238, 238*f*
  effects and risks of, 237–239, 238*f*, 467
  GABA and, 88
  operant conditioning and, 296
  in pregnancy, 166, 166*f*, 568
Alcoholics Anonymous (AA), 606
algorithms, 381
alleles, 74
  dominant and recessive, 74
all-or-none principle, 85
allostasis, 451
allostatic load, 451
alpha waves, 225, 226*f*
Alternate Uses test, 388
altruism, 536–538
Alzheimer's disease, 199–200
  acetylcholine in, 87, 200
  caregivers for, 463
  drugs for treatment of, 266
  memory loss in, 279
  personality change in, 508, 509
  signs and symptoms of, 199–200, 200*f*

American Journal of Psychology, 16
American Psychological Society (APA), 63
American Sign Language (ASL), 333–335
Ames room, 133, 133*f*
amnesia, 278
amphetamines, 241–242
amygdala, 95
  aggression and, 533
  emotion and, 273, 274, 275, 429, 431, 431*f*
  functions of, 95
  location of, 94*f*
  long-term memory and, 264, 264*f*, 272*f*, 273
Anafranil, 593
analgesics, 148
analytic intelligence, 362
anger, *See also* hostility
  amygdala and, 431
  bodily sensations of, 429*f*
  facial expression of, 422*f*
  heart disease and, 464–466, 466*f*
  physiological changes with, 425
anima, 492
animal research
  on brain–machine interface, 99
  chronic stressors impact, 463
  on conditioned taste aversion, 301–303, 302*f*
  on emotions and the brain, 431
  ethics in, 64–65, 64*f*
  on immunosuppression, 461
  on imprinting, 311–312
  instinctive drift in, 304
  on neurogenesis, 104
  on personality, 485–486, 486*f*
  on physical contact in infancy, 183–184, 183*f*
  on sexual orientation, 411
  on sign language, 333–335, 334*f*
  on stress, 450–451
  stress or nonstress reaction to cancer, 472
  symptoms of depression, 565
animistic thinking, 175
animus, 492
anorexia nervosa, 405–407, 406*f*
ANS. *See* autonomic nervous system
antecedent event, 422, 423*f*
anterior cingulate cortex (ACC)
  emotion and, 432
  obsessive–compulsive disorder and, 575
  pain and, 146, 147*f*, 432
  violence and, 204
anterograde amnesia, 278
anthropomorphizing, 485
antianxiety medications, 619
antidepressants, 593, 593*f*, 598–599, 618–619
antigens, 461
antipsychotics, 591–592, 599
antisocial personality disorder, 579–580, 579*f*
  maternal nutrition and, 165
anxiety, 492–493, 492*f*

anxiety disorders, 569
agoraphobia, 571–572
drug treatments for, 592–594, 592f, 593f, 618–619
generalized anxiety disorder, 570, 570f
major symptoms, 570f
nature and nurture explanations of, 572–574
obsessive–compulsive disorder. *See* obsessive–compulsive disorder
panic disorder, 570–571
post-traumatic stress disorder. *See* post-traumatic stress disorder
psychotherapeutic treatments for, 619
social phobia, 571
APA (American Psychological Society), 63
apes, sign language and, 333–335, 334f
aphasia, 98, 100
Aplysia (sea slug), 265–267, 266f
apparent motion, 131
applied behavioral analysis (ABA), 298–299
appraisal, 423–424, 432, 446–447
arachnophobia, 572, 603, 603f
arborization, 102
archetypes, 491
Area 25, 597–598, 597f
Aricept, 266
arthropods, 90, 90f
Asch conformity studies, 516–517, 516f
Asian cultures
anorexia nervosa in, 553
attributions in, 522
personality in, 484–485, 484f
social networking sites in, 527
ASL (American Sign Language), 333–335
Asperger's syndrome, 584
association, 262, 286, 287
associative network, 262, 262f
assortative mating, 539
astrology, 40, 41
asylums, 13
Atkinson's model of success, 414–415
atmospheric perspective, 132, 132f
attachment, 181–183, 184f, 543
attention, 214
in cell-phone use while driving, 218–219, 219f
in encoding, 259
frontal lobes and, 96
meditation and, 220, 221
in multitasking, 204, 217–220
selective, 214–216, 215f, 234, 245
sustained, 216–217, 217f
technology use and, 203
attention deficit hyperactivity disorder (ADHD), 555–556, 555f
brain activity, 557
combined drugs and behavioral therapy for, 612
drug treatments for, 593
environmental factors, 556–557
Internet addiction and, 582
norepinephrine and, 87
attitudes, 529
changes in, 530–532, 531f
components of, 529–530
nature and nurture of, 530
attraction, 539, 541–542, 541f
attributions, 521–522
atypical antipsychotics, 592
auditory canal, 142, 142f
auditory cortex, 98, 103
schizophrenia and, 561, 561f

auditory nerve, 142f, 143
Australopithecus, 91f
autism
Asperger's syndrome, 584
creativity and, 583–584
neural synchrony in, 189
operant conditioning and, 298–299
savant syndrome and, 372
synesthesia and, 250–251
touch therapy and, 184
vaccines and, 26, 37f
autism spectrum disorder, 555f, 556, 556f
head size as marker, 557
mirror neurons, 557
autobiographical memory, 274
automatic processing, 259
autonomic nervous system (ANS), 78. *See also* sympathetic nervous system
emotional response and, 424–425
immune system and, 462
stress and, 447–448, 449f
structure of, 78–79, 79f
Autrey, Wesley, 535
availability heuristic, 348–349
avatars, in therapy, 29
avatar therapy, 610, 619
averages, 58
avoidant personality disorder, 579f, 580
awareness, 211, 212f
axons, 81, 81f, 83, 84f, 85

B

babbling, 327
BAC (blood alcohol concentration), 237–238, 238f
backward conditioning, 289
Baddeley's model of short-term memory, 255–256, 255f
bad stress, 472–473
barbiturates, 594
basal ganglia, 94f, 95–96, 561f
basic anxiety, 492–493, 492f
basic emotions, 419, 419f, 421f
basic hostility, 492, 492f
basic tendencies, 497–498
basilar membrane, 142, 142f
A Beautiful Mind, 584
Bedlam, 12
behavior
behavioral thresholds, 480
change of, 530–532, 531f
counterproductive work, 505
evolution of, 22–25, 23f
four Ds of mental disorders, 551
genetics and, 73–78, 77f, 481–483, 482f
observation of, 56–57, 500–501
prosocial, 535–539
sexual, 46, 46f
Type A Behavior Pattern, 465–466, 466f
behavioral geneticists, 481
behavioral genetics, 18, 74
complexity of, 74–75
epigenetics and, 76–78, 77f
gene-by-environment interaction research, 76
personality, 481–483, 482f
polygenic influence, 75
principles of, 74
twin-adoption studies, 75–76
behavioral measures, 55f, 56–57
behavioral neuroscience, 8–9, 18
behavioral thresholds, 480

behavior change, 530–532, 531f
behaviorism, 16–17
behavior modification, 319. *See also* operant conditioning
behavior therapies, 602–603
bell curve, 58f. *See also* normal distribution
The Bell Curve (Herrnstein and Murray), 377
belongingness, 414
beneficence, 63
Benzedrine, 241
benzodiazepines, 594, 619
beta-blockers, 619
beta waves, 225
bias
assumptions about objectivity, 53–54
confirmation, 343
experimenter expectancy effects, 52
fundamental attribution error, 522
implicit, 528
in-group/out-group, 524–525
in IQ tests, 368–369
self-serving, 522
social desirability, 55–56
Big Five model, 497–498, 497f
bilingualism, 352–354, 353f
binge drinking, 239
binocular depth cues, 131
binocular disparity, 131
biological constraint model, 304
biological psychology, 8–9
bipolar disorder, 567
brain and, 568f, 569
causes of, 568–569
creativity and, 584f, 585
drug treatment of, 592f, 594, 599
symptoms of, 567, 567f
birds, neurogenesis in, 104
birth order, 490–491
birth weight, 376
bisexuality, 192. *See also* sexual orientation
blindness
brain reorganization in, 103, 103f, 111
color, 139, 139f
painting and, 72, 72f, 111–113, 111f, 112f
perception and, 112–113
blind spot, 124f, 125, 125f
blocking, 277
blood alcohol concentration (BAC), 237–238, 238f
blood sugar, in digestion, 401
B lymphocytes, 463
BMI (body mass index), 402–403, 403f
Bobo doll studies, 307–308, 307f, 308f, 534
bodily-kinesthetic intelligence, 362, 363f
bodily senses, 144. *See also specific senses*
body image, 403
body mass index (BMI), 402–403, 403f
body temperature, 224f, 398, 398f
borderline personality disorder, 579, 579f, 612, 613
Botox
emotion and, 430
new areas of treatment, 615–616
bottom-up processing, 137
Braille, 113
Brain. *See also specific brain structures*
in adolescence, 188–190, 190f
aggression and, 95, 533
alcohol use and, 238–239, 238f
bipolar disorder and, 569, 569f
blindness or deafness and, 103
cerebral cortex, 96–98, 96f, 100

cerebral hemispheres, 98, 100, 101f, 328, 385, 387
  in childhood, 169–171, 170f, 171f, 560, 560f
  creativity and, 384–387, 387
  depression and, 26, 565, 597–598, 597f
  in early adulthood, 194
  electrical stimulation to enhance memory, 268–269, 270
  emotions and, 431–433, 431f
  empathy and, 539
  environmental influences on, 21, 66–67, 170–171, 171f
  evolution of, 90–91, 91f, 92f
  exercise and, 469, 470
  forebrain, 92f, 93–94
  glutamate and, 88–89
  hearing and, 143–144
  hindbrain, 92f, 93
  in infancy, 169–171, 171f
  intelligence and, 189–190, 190f, 373–374, 374f
  language acquisition and, 332, 333f
  in late adulthood, 198, 206
  learning and, 102–103, 313f, 314–316
  limbic system, 94–98, 94f, 100
  of mammals, 92f
  measurement techniques, 106–109, 106f, 107f, 108f
  meditation and, 221–222, 223, 223f
  memory storage and, 268f, 271, 272f, 273, 274f
  midbrain, 92f, 93
  in middle adulthood, 197–198
  mind and, 21
  musical training and, 66f, 67, 172–173, 198, 316
  myelination in, 171, 171f, 189
  neurons in, 82
  pain and, 146–147, 147f
  painting and, 111–113, 112f
  personality and, 498–499
  plasticity and neurogenesis, 100–103, 102f, 200–201
  prenatal development of, 162, 163f, 163f–164f
  regions of, 92–98, 92f, 94f, 96f, 97f, 100, 101f
  schizophrenia and, 560–561, 560f, 561f
  second-language learning and, 352–353, 353f
  sexual activity and, 408
  sexual orientation and, 412
  sleep and, 224–226, 225f–226f, 226f
  smell and, 148
  social pain and, 514, 525, 525f
  stress and, 451–452
  taste and, 149–150
  technology and development of, 202, 206
  vision and, 125–129, 127f
  visual imagery and, 339
brain–computer interfaces, 99
brain injury
  aggression and, 533
  consciousness and, 210, 212, 245
  frontal lobes, 97, 97f
  memory and, 251–252, 252f, 273
  personality change after, 97, 431, 508
  personality disorders and, 580–581
  sleeping and dreaming and, 245
brain–machine interfaces, 99
brain maps, 145
BrdU, 105
broaden-and-build model, 420

broad intelligence, 361
Broca's area, 98
  language learning and, 326, 326f, 333f
  language production and, 98, 100
  second-language learning and, 353f
Brodmann's Area, 597–598, 598f
buffering hypothesis, 455
bulimia nervosa, 406
Bundy, Ted, 550
buprenorphine, 240
buspirone, 619
by-products, of natural selection, 25
bystander effect, 43, 535–536

C

caffeine, 240, 240f
  memory effects of, 267
California Personality Inventory (CPI), 502, 505
cancer
  alcohol use and, 467
  marijuana smoke and, 243
  stress and nonstress conditions, 472
  tobacco smoke and, 241, 467
Cannabis sativa, 242–244
CANOE acronym, 497, 497f
carbon monoxide, 241
cardiovascular disease
  depression and, 466
  positive emotions and, 456
  psychological risk factors for, 464–466, 466f
  stress and, 460
cardiovascular reactivity (CVR) model, 465–466
cardiovascular system, 460
career identity, 194
carpentered world, 152
case studies, 43–44
casual sex, 409, 410
cataplexy, 230
catecholamines, 109, 448
categories, 341–342
catharsis, 602
Cattell–Horn–Carroll (CHC) model of intelligence, 360–361, 361f, 368
causal inferences, 343
causation, 48–49, 49f
CBT (cognitive–behavioral therapy), 605, 611, 613, 619
Celexa, 593
cell damage, sleep and, 228
cell phones
  driving and, 204, 218–219, 219f
  psychology research on, 28
cells, chromosomes in, 73, 73f
cellular immunity, 463
central executive, 255, 255f, 272f
central nervous system (CNS), 78, 79f
cerebellum, 93
  alcohol use and, 238f
  location of, 92f
  long-term memory and, 264, 264f, 271, 272f
cerebral cortex, 96–98, 96f, 100
cerebral hemispheres
  communication between, 99, 101f
  creativity and, 385, 387
  functions of, 98, 100
  language and, 328
cerebral palsy, 184
cerebrum, 96–98, 96f, 100
certainty effect, 350

chance mutations, 23
CHC (Cattell–Horn–Carroll) model of intelligence, 360–361, 361f, 368
chemotherapy, marijuana and, 243
child abuse
  Adverse Childhood Experiences (ACE) Study, 573–574, 573f
  depression, 565
  language development and, 328–329
  neglect, 170–171, 171f, 560, 560f
  schizophrenia related, 560, 560f
childbirth, cultural differences in, 155
child-directed speech, 330
children. See also child abuse; infancy
  Adverse Childhood Experiences (ACE) Study, 573–574
  adverse experiences, 560, 560f
  attention deficit hyperactivity disorder. See attention deficit hyperactivity disorder
  birth order of, 490–491
  brain development in, 169–171, 171f, 560, 560f
  chronic stress impact, 463–464
  cognitive development in, 171–178, 174f–177f
  in Efe culture, 44–45
  emotional competence of, 185–186
  frontal lobes in, 96
  language development in, 326–328, 327f
  moral reasoning in, 178–180, 180f
  motor development in, 167–168, 167f
  musical training in, 172–173, 316
  nature–nurture debate, 20–21
  neglected, 170–171, 171f, 560, 560f
  peer interaction, 186
  sleep in, 227f
  social networking by, 203–204
  socioemotional development in, 181–187, 184f
  technology and, 202–204, 203f
chimpanzees
  personality traits, 485–486, 486f
  sign language and, 333–335, 334f
Chinese culture, ancient, 11–12
chlorpromazine (Thorazine), 591
chromosomes, 73, 73f
chunking, 255, 261
cigarette smoking. See tobacco use
cilia, 148, 149f
cingulate gyrus, 94f, 95
circadian rhythms, 222, 224, 224f
cirrhosis, 238
civil disobedience, 180
classical conditioning, 288–292
  conditioned taste aversion, 301–303, 302f
  immunosuppression and, 461
  of Little Albert, 291–292, 291f
  operant conditioning vs., 298f
  operation of, 288–292, 288f
  Pavlov's dogs, 288–289, 289f
  smoking and, 317–318, 318f
claustrophobia, 572
client-centered therapy, 601
clinical psychologists, 614
clinical psychology, 9, 11–14, 13f
  on electronic social interaction, 29
closure, 134, 135f
clozapine (Clorazil), 592, 599
CNS (central nervous system), 78, 79f
cocaine, 87, 241
cochlea, 142, 142f, 144f
cocktail party effect, 215, 215f

codeine, 239
cognition, 339. *See also* cognitive development; thinking
    creative thinking and, 387–388
    exercise and, 199, 201, 468–471, 470
cognitive–behavioral therapy (CBT), 605, 611, 613, 619
cognitive development
    in adolescence, 188–190, 190*f*, 204
    fluid vs. crystallized intelligence, 199, 199*f*
    in infants and children, 171–178, 174*f*–177*f*, 202–203
    in late adulthood, 198, 206
    moral reasoning, 178–180, 180*f*
    physical fitness and, 195
    technology and, 202–204, 203*f*, 204*f*, 206
    theory of mind, 178, 179*f*
cognitive dissonance, 530–531, 531*f*, 546
cognitive maps, 305
cognitive psychology, 8, 339
    on electronic social interactions, 28
    mental representation, 339–342, 340*f*, 342*f*
    verbal representation, 341–342, 342*f*
cognitive science, 17–18
cognitive symptoms (of schizophrenia), 559
cognitive theory, on dreaming, 232
cognitive therapy (CT), 603–605, 608, 611–612
cognitivism, 17–18
collective unconscious, 491
collectivist cultures, 484–485, 517
college students
    personality and college major, 504–505
    sleep deprivation in, 229, 314–315, 314*f*
Collyer brothers, 550
color blindness, 139, 139*f*
color vision
    eye structure and, 124, 125*f*
    language and, 337, 338*f*
    perception of color, 138–139, 138*f*, 139*f*
coma, 211, 212, 212*f*
commitment, 543, 543*f*
common cold, stress and, 464
common sense, 35
communication, in scientific method, 38, 39*f*
comorbidity, 553
companionate love, 543, 543*f*
compassion, 539
compensation, 490
complex cells (neurons), 128
compulsions, 574. *See also* obsessive–compulsive disorder
computers and Internet. *See also* social networking
    brain interfaces with, 99, 99*f*
    cognitive development and, 203
    cyberbullying, 205
    Internet addiction, 582
    online dating services, 205
    sexual material on, 205
    video games, 203, 206, 534–535
    virtual reality therapies, 609–610
concentration meditation, 221
concept hierarchy, 341
concepts, 341, 342*f*
concrete operational stage, 174*f*, 177
conditioned response (CR), 289–290, 290*f*
conditioned stimulus (CS), 289–290, 290*f*
conditioned taste aversion, 301–303
    as classical conditioning, 301–303, 302*f*
    immune system and, 461
conditioning. *See also* classical conditioning; operant conditioning
    behavior therapies, 602–603
    classical, 288–292

conditioned taste aversion, 301–303, 302*f*
    defined, 286
    instinctive drift and, 304
    language acquisition and, 330
    latent learning and, 305
cones, 123, 124, 125*f*
confidentiality, 63
confirmation bias, 343
conformity, 515–517, 516*f*, 545–546
confounding variables, 51
conjunction fallacy, 349
conscientiousness
    in animals, 485–486
    chimpanzees, 485–486, 486*f*
    culture and, 484
    nature and nurture in, 482
consciousness, 210. *See also* psychoactive drugs
    brain injury and, 210, 212, 245
    dreaming and, 226, 231–232, 232*f*
    full, 212–213
    as global workspace, 211
    hypnosis and, 233–235, 233*f*
    meditation training, 220–222, 223*f*
    meditation training and, 223
    minimal, 212–213, 212*f*
    moderate, 213
    multitasking, 204, 217–220
    selective attention, 214–216, 215*f*, 234, 245
    sleeping and, 222–231, 224*f*–226*f*, 229*f*, 232*f*
    sustained attention, 216–217, 217*f*
    wakefulness and awareness, 211, 212*f*
conservation, 176–177, 176*f*, 177*f*
consolidation, 261–262
construct validity, 368
continuity, 134, 134*f*
Continuous Performance Test (CPT), 216–217
continuous reinforcement, 299
control, positive emotion and, 456
control group, 50
conventional level, 180, 180*f*
convergent thinking problems, 380
cooing, 327
coping, 453
    dissociative disorders and, 577
    positive psychology and, 456–457
    strategies for, 453–456, 453*f*
cornea, 123, 124*f*
corpus callosum, 98, 100, 101*f*
correct rejection, 121
correlational designs, 47–49, 48*f*, 49*f*
correlation coefficients, 47–48, 49*f*
cortical arousal, 498–499
cortical localization, 96
corticotropin releasing factor (CRF), 449, 449*f*
cortisol, 109, 449
    functions of, 109
    sleep and, 233
    stress and, 449, 449*f*, 452
counseling psychology, 9–10
counselors, 614
counterproductive work behaviors, 505
CPI (California Personality Inventory), 502, 505
CPT (Continuous Performance Test), 216–217
CR (conditioned response), 289–290, 290*f*
creative intelligence, 362
creativity, 384
    brain and, 384–387, 387
    cognitive processes in, 387–388
    creative personality, 388–389
    creative problem-solving stages, 384
    definitions of, 383–384
    employee, 416
    genius, 384–385

genius and intelligence, 389–391, 390*f*
    psychological disorders and, 583–585, 583*f*, 584*f*
    self-actualizing, 494–495
    visual imagery and, 339–340, 386, 387, 387*f*
CREB, 266, 267, 268*f*
CRF (corticotropin releasing factor), 449, 449*f*
critical thinking, 26–27, 344–345, 346
cross-activation, 152
crystallized intelligence, 199, 199*f*, 360
crystal meth, 241
CS (conditioned stimulus), 289–290, 290*f*
CT (cognitive therapy), 603–605, 608, 611–612
cults, 544
cultural test bias hypothesis, 368–369
culture. *See also* race–ethnicity
    attachment styles and, 182
    collectivist and individualist, 484, 517
    death and dying and, 201
    depth perception and, 152–153, 153*f*
    emotional expression and, 433–434
    food preferences and, 402
    intelligence and, 360, 362, 378–379
    intelligence tests and, 368–369
    language and, 335–337
    pain and, 153, 155, 155*f*
    perception and, 152–155, 153*f*, 154*f*
    personality and, 483–485, 484*f*
    prehistoric, 11
    psychological disorders and, 552–553
    recall and, 154
    sensation and perception and, 152–155, 153*f*, 154*f*
    sexual behavior and, 409
    smoking and, 319
    universality of facial expressions in, 425–427, 427*f*
CVR (cardiovascular reactivity) model, 465–466
cyberbullying, 205
cyberchondriacs, 578
cyclothymia, 568
cytokines, 462

D

dark adaptation, 123, 286
Darkness Visible (Styron), 564–565
data. *See* statistics
DBT (dialectical behavior therapy), 612, 613, 619
deafness, brain reorganization in, 103, 103*f*
death and dying, 201–202
debriefing, 63
deception, detecting, 552–553
decibels (dB), 140
decision making. *See also* problem solving
    availability heuristic, 348–349
    economic, 349–350
    nonrational, 349–350
    representativeness heuristic, 347–348
declarative memory, 258, 263, 272*f*, 273
deductive reasoning, 343, 353–354
deep brain stimulation, 597–599, 598*f*
defense mechanisms, 489, 601–602
delta waves, 226
delusions, 559
dementia, 199–200, 200*f*
dementia praecox, 13. *See also* schizophrenia
dendrites, 81, 81*f*, 86*f*, 89, 102
dependent personality disorder, 579*f*, 580
dependent variable, 49, 50*f*
depolarization, 83, 84*f*
depressants, 236–240, 238*f*

depression
    brain and, 26
    cardiovascular disease and, 466
    characteristics of, 567f
    cognitive–behavioral therapy for, 605
    cognitive therapy for, 604–605, 607, 608
    creativity and, 584–585
    drug treatment for, 598–599, 608
    electrical and magnetic therapies for, 595–598, 595f, 596f, 598f
    genetic and environmental influences in, 566, 566f
    inflammation and, 466
    mindfulness-based cognitive therapy for, 611, 613, 613f
    motivation and, 396–397
    nature and nurture explanations for, 565
    prefrontal cortex and, 432
    prevention of, 617–618
    serotonin and, 88, 565, 566
    treatments for, 590
depressive disorders, 563–565
    Botox treatment for, 616
    drug treatment for, 592f, 593f, 592–594
    major depressive disorder, 563
    persistent depressive disorder (PDD), 564
    prevalence of, 563
    symptoms, 563
depressogenic thinking, 605
depth perception, 131–132
    binocular cues for, 131, 131f
    culture and, 152–153, 153f
    illusions in, 136f
    in infancy, 169, 169f
    monocular cues for, 132, 132f
    perceptual constancy and, 132–134, 133f
descriptive designs, 42–46, 43f
descriptive statistics, 58–59, 58f
despair, 201
development. See human development
developmental psychology, 8, 28, 160
deviant behavior, 552
dextroamphetamine (Dexedrine), 241
diabetes, from clozapine, 599
Diagnostic and Statistical Manual
    5th edition (DSM-5), 14, 551
    first publication, 551
dialectical behavior therapy (DBT), 612, 613, 619
diathesis-stress model, 559
    anxiety disorders, 572
    depression, 565
    schizophrenia, 559
dichotic listening task, 215
DID (dissociative identity disorder), 576–577
dieting, weight loss success with, 404–405
difference thresholds, 121–122
difficult child, 181
diffusion of responsibility, 536
diffusion tensor imaging, 109
DIGFAST mnemonic, 567
direct effects hypothesis, 455
direction, sense of, 273
disclosure, in coping, 454
discrimination, 527–528
disease, stress and, 459–460. See also immune system
disgust
    bodily sensations of, 429, 429f
    display rules for, 434
    facial expression of, 427f
    insula and, 433
    physiological changes with, 425

disorders. See psychological disorders; treatment of disorders
display rules, 433–434
dispositional attributions, 521
dissociative disorders, 576–577
dissociative identity disorder (DID), 576–577
distancing, 454
distressing behavior, 552
disturbance from mental disorders, 551–552
divergent thinking problems, 381
divided attention, 276
DNA (deoxyribonucleic acid), 73, 73f, 76–77, 77f
dodo bird verdict, 607
dominant alleles, 74
dopamine, 87
    cocaine and, 241
    discovery of, 561–562
    drug addiction and, 87
    endocrine system and, 109
    functions of, 87, 87f
    LSD and, 244
    phenothiazines and, 591
    schizophrenia and, 561–562
    thrill-seeking behavior and, 482
double-blind studies, 52
Down syndrome, 370–371, 371f
dramatic–emotional personality disorders, 579–580, 579f
DRD4 gene, 482
dream analysis, 601
dreams, 226, 231–233, 232f
drive reduction model, 397–398, 398f
drives, 397
driving
    aggression and, 533, 534
    alcohol and, 238, 238f
    cell phone use while, 204, 218–219, 219f
    sleep debt and, 229
drugs. See drug therapies; prescription drugs; psychoactive drugs
drug therapies
    for anxiety and depressive disorders, 592–594, 593f
    cognitive therapy compared with, 608, 608f
    for depressive and anxiety disorders, 592f
    effectiveness of, 598–600
    for OCD and anxiety disorders, 618–619
    psychotherapy combined with, 610
    for schizophrenia, 591–592, 592f, 599
DSM-5 (Diagnostic and Statistical Manual, 5th edition), 14, 551
dualism, 21–22
Duchenne smile, 428, 428f
dysfunctional behavior, 552
dysthmia. See persistent depressive disorder (PDD)

E

early adulthood, 193–197, 194f, 195f, 196f, 205
early-onset Alzheimer's, 200. See also Alzheimer's disease
ears, 142–143, 142f, 144f
Eastern philosophy, 22
easy child, 181
eating
    biology of, 401–402
    food preferences, 402
    health and, 467–468
    hypothalamus and, 94
    in pregnancy, 165
    psychology of, 402
    stress and, 468

thinness and obesity and, 402–407, 403f
    weight loss success, 404–405
eating disorders, 405–407, 406f
Ebbinghaus's forgetting curve, 276, 276f
echoic memory, 253
echolocation, 118
ecstasy (MDMA), 88, 88f
ECT (electroconvulsive therapy), 595–596, 595f, 599–600
educational psychology, 10
EEG (electroencephalography), 106, 106f
Efe people, 44–45
effect size, 47
effortful processing, 259
ego, 488, 489f
egocentrism, 175–176
egoistic motivation, 538
Egypt
    ancient, 12
    protests, social networking in, 527, 527f
    revolution (2011), 4
Elavil, 593
electrical stimulation, of prefrontal cortex (PFC), 270
electroconvulsive therapy (ECT), 595–596, 595f, 599–600
electroencephalography (EEG), 106, 106f
electromagnetic spectrum, 138, 138f
electronic social interactions. See social networking
embarrassment, 421, 422f
embryo, 162
embryonic stage, 162
emerging adulthood, 193–195, 205
emotion, Botox and, 430
emotional competence, 185–186
emotional disclosure, 454
emotional intelligence, 362, 435, 435–436
Emotional Intelligence (Goleman), 435
emotional memories, 264, 273–275, 274f
emotional response, 424–429, 426f, 428f
emotion-focused coping strategies, 453f, 454–455
emotion recognition, 435
emotion regulation, 424
emotions, 362, 418, 434–436. See also emotional intelligence; socioemotional development
    affect types, 418–419
    affiliation and, 439
    amygdala and, 95
    appraisal in, 423–424, 432
    basic, 419, 419f, 421f
    brain and, 431–433, 431f
    culture and expression of, 433–434
    development of, 185–186
    emotional response, 424–429, 426f, 428f
    as evolutionary adaptations, 419–420
    facial expressions and, 422f, 425–428, 426f, 427f, 428f
    gender and, 434–435
    life satisfaction and, 437–439
    meaning in life and, 439
    memory and, 273–275, 274f
    pain and, 146, 147f
    positive, 456–457, 617
    process of, 422–423, 423f
    regulation of, 424
    self-conscious, 419f, 420–421, 421f, 422f
    stress and, 447f, 449f
    subjective changes in, 429–430, 429f
    vocal expression of, 428, 434
empathic motivation, 538
empathy, 538–539, 540, 540f

empathy–altruism hypothesis, 538
empirical method, 502
empiricism, 14
employment. *See* industrial/organizational
(I/O) psychology; workplace
enactive learning, 306
encoding, 259–261, 260*f*, 261*f*
enculturation, 495
endocannabinoids, 243–244, 401
endocrine system, 109, 110*f*, 448. *See also*
hormones
endorphins, 147–148, 239, 468
environmental deprivation, 371, 375
environmental influences
on aggression, 533
on attitudes, 530
on the brain, 66–67, 170–171, 171*f*
on depression, 565, 566, 566*f*
genes and, 75–76
on intelligence, 374–375, 374*f*, 376*f*
on language acquisition, 329, 331–332
on neurogenesis, 105, 201, 316
on obesity, 403
on sexual orientation, 411, 412
on smoking, 319
twin-adoption studies and, 75–76
environmentalism, 17
enzymatic degradation, 85
enzymes, sleep and, 228
epigenetics, 76–78, 77*f*, 165
twins, 160
epigenome, 77*f*
epilepsy, 88
epinephrine, 87, 87*f*, 88, 109
episodic buffer, 255*f*, 256
episodic memory, 258
EQ-I, 436
ERP (event-related potential), 106
ESP (extrasensory perception), 40
esteem needs, 400
estradiol, 188
ethics in research, 62–66
animal research, 64–65, 64*f*
human research, 62–64
Little Albert conditioning study, 292
Milgram's studies on obedience, 62, 520
ethnic identity, 195
ethnicity. *See* race–ethnicity
ethology, 311
Eureka insights, 381–382
event-related potential (ERP), 106
evidence-based therapies, 607
evolution, 22–23
of altruism, 537
of attitudes, 530
of the brain, 90–91, 91*f*
exaptations, 25
of human behavior, 22–25
natural selection in, 23–25, 23*f*
of personality traits, 480–481
evolutionary model of motivation, 400
evolutionary psychology, 18, 24
exaptations, 25
excitatory neurotransmitters, 85
exercise benefits, 199, 201, 468–471, 470
exhaustion stage, 450*f*, 451
expectations of success, 414
experiment, 49
experimental group, 50
experimental psychologists, 8
experimental studies, 49–52, 51*f*
experimenter expectancy effects, 52
self-fulfilling prophecy, 54
explicit memory, 258, 263, 272*f*, 273

explicit prejudice, 528
*The Expression of the Emotions in Man and
Animals* (Darwin), 425
expressive suppression, 424
extinction, 290, 290*f*, 299
extrasensory perception (ESP), 40
extraversion
anxiety disorders and, 572
college major and, 504
culture and, 484
in Eysenck's personality model, 498, 498*f*
nature and nurture in, 482, 482*f*
extrinsic motivation, 415–416
eyes, 123–1132, 124*f*, 125*f*
eyewitness testimony, 18, 276, 277

F

Facebook, 526–527, *See also* social
networking
face–vase figure, 135, 135*f*
Facial Action Coding System (FACS),
427–428, 428*f*
facial attractiveness, 541–542, 541*f*
facial expressions
emotion and, 422*f*, 427–428, 427*f*, 428*f*
evolution of, 434
universality of, 425–427, 427*f*
facial feedback hypothesis, Botox, 430
facial recognition, 108, 108*f*, 129–130, 130*f*
FACS (Facial Action Coding System),
427–428, 428*f*
failure, uses of, 363
false alarms, 121
false belief task, 179, 179*f*
false memories, 278
familial–cultural retardation, 371
farsightedness, 126, 126*f*
FASD (fetal alcohol spectrum disorder), 166,
166*f*, 371
fat cells, 404
fear, 422, 422*f*. *See also* anxiety disorders
amygdala and, 95, 431
bodily sensations of, 429*f*
evolution and, 25, 434
facial expression of, 422, 422*f*, 425, 427*f*, 434
persuasion and, 532
fear of flying (phobia), 572, 604*f*
feature detectors, 127
fertilization, 161, 161*f*, 162*f*
FES (forearm electrical stimulation), 99, 99*f*
fetal alcohol spectrum disorder (FASD), 166,
166*f*, 371
fetal development. *See* prenatal development
fetal stage, 162
FFA (fusiform face area), 108, 108*f*
fidelity, 192
fight-or-flight response, 78
figure–ground effects, 134–135, 135*f*
fine motor skills, 168
five-factor model, 497–498, 497*f*
fixation, 382
fixed interval (FI) schedule, 300, 300*f*
fixed ratio (FR) schedule, 299–300, 300*f*
flashbacks, 575
flashbulb memories, 274–275
flatworms, 90
flexibility of thought, 388
float test, 12
flooding, 603
flourishers, 439
flow, 214, 399
fluid intelligence, 199, 199*f*, 360
fluoxetine (Prozac), 166, 593, 599

fMRI (functional MRI), 106–107, 107*f*, 108, 108*f*
food. *See* eating
foot-in-the-door technique, 545
forearm electrical stimulation (FES), 99, 99*f*
forebrain, 92*f*, 93–94
foreground–background perception, 154, 154*f*
forensic psychology, 10
forgetting, 276
amnesia, 278
Ebbinghaus's forgetting curve, 276, 276*f*
types of, 276–279, 276*f*
forgetting curve, 276, 276*f*
formal operational stage, 174*f*, 177, 188–189
forward conditioning, 289
fovea, 123, 124*f*
Fragile X syndrome, 371
fraternal twins, 75–76
See also twin-adoption studies
free association, 488, 601
frequency, 41, 58, 144*f*
FR (fixed ratio) schedule, 299–300, 300*f*
friending, 29
frontal lobes
in adolescence, 189
alcohol use and, 238*f*
creativity and, 385
location and function of, 96, 96*f*
schizophrenia and, 561*f*
functional fixedness, 383
functionalism, 16
functional MRI (fMRI), 106–107, 107*f*, 108, 108*f*
fundamental attribution error, 522
fusiform face area (FFA), 108, 108*f*

G

GABA (gamma–aminobutyric acid), 87*f*,
88, 572
GAD (generalized anxiety disorder), 570, 570*f*
Gage, Phineas, brain injury of, 97, 97*f*,
104, 431
ganglion cells, 125
Gardner's multiple intelligences, 362–363,
363*f*, 364
GAS (general adaptation syndrome),
450–451, 450*f*
gate control theory of pain, 146–147
gender differences
in adolescent brain development, 189
in age of first marriage, 195–196, 196*f*
in age-related hearing loss, 197, 197*f*
in drive for casual sex, 409, 410
in emotion, 434–435
in insomnia, 229–230
in intelligence, 378, 378*f*
in mental rotation tasks, 340–341
in pain thresholds, 153, 155
in parenthood, 196, 196*f*
in peer interactions, 186
in personality development, 187
in puberty, 188, 188*f*
in sexual attraction and mate selection, 542
in sexual response cycle, 407–408, 407*f*
in smoking, 318–319
in social network influences, 455–456
in tactile sensitivity, 145
gene-by-environment interaction research, 76
general adaptation syndrome (GAS),
450–451, 450*f*
general intelligence, 359–360. *See also*
intelligence
Carroll's analysis, 361
generalized anxiety disorder (GAD), 570, 570*f*
generativity, 198

genes, 73. *See also* heritability
  behavior and, 73–78, 77*f*
  chance mutations, 23
  environment and, 75–76
  epigenetics, 76–78, 77*f*
  expression of, 76–78, 77*f*
  genetic markers, 76, 481
  in the human genome, 78
  identical twins, 160
  long-term memory and, 267, 268*f*
  neurodevelopmental disorders, 556–557
  polygenic transmission by, 75
  research on regulation of, 615
  structures and mechanisms of, 73–74, 73*f*
genetic influences
  on aggression, 533
  on anxiety disorders, 572
  on attitudes, 530
  on bipolar disorder, 568
  on depression, 566, 566*f*
  environmental forces and, 21, 77*f*
  on intelligence, 374–375, 374*f*, 376*f*
  on language acquisition, 332
  on obesity, 404
  on personality, 481–483, 482*f*,
    498–499, 498*f*
  on schizophrenia, 559, 559–560
  on sexual orientation, 411, 412
  softwiring and, 21
  on stress, 452
  twin-adoption studies and, 75–76
genetic markers, 76, 481
genius, 384–385
genome, 73, 73*f*, 78
genotype, 76
  twin studies, 160
genotypes, identical twins, 160
Genovese, Kitty, 535–536
genius, 389–391
germinal stage, 161
Gestalt laws of grouping, 134–137, 134*f*,
  135*f*, 136*f*
Gestalt psychology, 17, 17–18
g-factor theory of intelligence, 360
ghrelin, 401
giftedness, 371–373, 372*f*
ginkgo biloba, 267
Glasgow Coma Scale, 212
glial cells, 79
glucocorticoids, 448
glucose, 401
glutamate, 88
  functions of, 87*f*, 88–89
  LSD and, 244
  schizophrenia and, 562, 599
good stress, 472
graded potentials, 85
grammar, 325, 331
graphs, misleading, 61, 61*f*
grasping reflex, 168
gratitude training, 602
gray matter, 107, 170
group behavior. *See* social behavior
group therapy, 605–607, 619
groupthink, 517

H

habituation, 286
hair cells, 142*f*, 143, 144*f*
Halle Berry neurons, 129, 130*f*
hallucinations, 558, 561
hallucinogens, 242, 242–244
haloperidol (Haldol), 591

happiness
  basic needs and, 437–438
  bodily sensations of, 429*f*
  facial expression of, 427*f*
  higher needs and, 438
  meaning in life and, 439, 457
  oxytocin and, 432
  positive emotions, 456–457, 617
  world happiness map, 437, 438*f*
Hassles and Uplifts Scale, 446
Head Start, 377, 436
health, changing beliefs about, 473
health behavior approach, 459, 466–467
health psychology, 10, 459
  on electronic social interaction, 29
hearing
  auditory cortex and, 98
  ear and, 142–143, 142*f*, 144*f*
  in middle adulthood, 197, 197*f*
  physics of sound, 140–141, 141*f*
  prenatal, 162, 163*f*
  psychology of, 140–141
  signal detection theory, 120–121
hearing loss, 143
heart disease. *See* cardiovascular disease
Heinz dilemma, 180
hemispheres, cerebral. *See* cerebral
  hemispheres
herbal medications for memory, 267
heritability, 75. *See also* genes; genetic
  influences
  gene-by-environment interaction
    research, 76
  soft inheritance, 77
  twin-adoption studies, 75–76
heroes, 535
heroin, 239
hertz (Hz), 141
heterosexuality, 192. *See also* sexual
  orientation
heuristics, 347, 347–349
hierarchies, 262
hierarchy of needs, 400, 400*f*
hindbrain, 92*f*, 93
hippocampus, 94
  alcohol use and, 238*f*
  emotion and, 273, 431, 431*f*
  exercise and, 469
  functions of, 94–95, 96
  location of, 94*f*
  in long-term memory, 264, 264*f*
  memory and, 251, 252*f*, 271, 272*f*, 273
  post-traumatic stress disorder and, 576
  schizophrenia and, 560, 561*f*
  sleep and, 228
  stress and, 452
Hispanics. *See* race–ethnicity
histrionic personality disorder, 579, 579*f*
HIV/AIDS, 243
Hobson's A-I-M model, 232, 232*f*
homeostasis, 398, 398*f*, 451
Homo erectus, 91*f*
Homo neanderthalensis, 91, 91*f*
homophobia, 489
Homo sapiens, 90–91, 91*f*
homosexuality, 192. *See also* sexual
  orientation
hormones, 109. *See also specific hormones*
  aggression and, 534
  functions of, 109
  hunger and, 401–402
  sex, 109, 188, 341, 408, 534
  stress, 448–452, 449*f*, 452
hospice, 202

hostile aggression, 533
hostility
  aggression vs., 533
  basic, 492, 492*f*
  heart disease and, 465–466, 466*f*
HPA axis. *See* hypothalamic–pituitary-adrenal
  (HPA) axis
human development, 160
  cognitive, in adolescence, 188–190, 190*f*
  cognitive, in infancy and childhood,
    171–180, 174*f*–177*f*, 180*f*, 202–203
  death and dying, 201–202
  in early adulthood, 193–197, 194*f*, 196*f*
  of emotions, 185–186
  of language, 326–329, 326*f*, 327*f*
  in late adulthood, 198–201, 199*f*, 200*f*, 206
  in middle adulthood, 197–198, 197*f*, 205–206
  of moral reasoning, 178–180, 180*f*
  personality, in adolescence, 192, 192*f*
  personality, in early adulthood, 197
  personality, in infancy, 181
  personality, in late adulthood, 201
  personality, in middle adulthood, 198
  physical, in adolescence, 188, 188*f*
  physical, in infancy and childhood,
    167–171, 167*f*–171*f*, 171*f*
  prenatal, 161–165, 161*f*–165*f*
  of sleep over the life span, 226, 227*f*
  social, in adolescence, 191–192, 192*f*
  socioemotional, in infants and children,
    181–187, 184*f*, 203–204
  technology and, 202–206, 203*f*, 204*f*
  of vision, 129
humane treatment, 65
humanistic–positive psychological theories
  Maslow on, 494–495
  Rogers on, 495
  summary of, 499*f*
  in treatment, 601–602
humanistic psychology, 17, 494–495
human language, 325. *See also* language
human research, ethics in, 62–64
hunger
  biology of digestion, 401–402
  food preferences and, 402
  metabolism and, 401
  thinness and obesity and, 402–407, 403*f*
  weight loss success, 404–405
Huntington's disease, 75, 96
hyperactivity, OCD and, 575. *See also*
  attention deficit hyperactivity disorder
hypercomplex cells, 128
hypersomnia, 230, 245
hyperthymestic syndrome, 250
hypnosis, 233–235, 233*f*
hypochondriasis, 577
hypomanic episodes, 567
hypothalamic-pituitary-adrenal (HPA)
  axis, 449
  depression and, 565
  eating and, 468
  stress and, 449, 449*f*
hypothalamus, 94
  aggression and, 533
  alcohol use and, 238*f*
  emotion and, 431, 431*f*
  functions of, 94, 109
  hunger and, 401
  location of, 94*f*, 110*f*
  menstrual cycle and, 109
  sexual behavior and, 408
  sexual orientation and, 412
  stress and, 448, 449*f*
hypothesis, 38

I

IAT (Implicit Associations Test), 528–529
iconic memory, 253
id, 488, 489f
ideational fluency, 388
identical twins, 76. See also twin-adoption
    studies
identity
    career, 194
    dissociative identity disorder, 576–577
    in emerging adulthood, 193–195
    Erikson on, 192, 192f
    ethnic, 195
    peer groups and, 191
    sexual, 194
identity crisis, 192
illness anxiety disorder, 577
imagery, in encoding, 259
imagery rehearsal, 230
imitation, 312, 330
immune system
    conditioned immunosuppression, 461
    overview of, 462–463
    stress and, 450, 460–461, 463–464
immunity, 462–463
immunosuppression, 463
implantation, 161–162, 161f, 162f
Implicit Associations Test (IAT), 528–529
implicit bias, 528
implicit memory, 258
    priming and, 258, 258f
    retrieval from, 263
    storage of, 264, 264f, 272f, 273
implicit prejudice, 528
implosion therapy, 603
imprinting, 181, 311–312
inattentional blindness, 215–216
incentives, 397
incentive value, 414–415
independent variable, 49, 50f
individualist cultures, 484, 517
individuation, 198
inductive reasoning, 343
industrial/organizational (I/O) psychology,
    10. See also workplace
    congruence, 505
    employee motivation, 415–417, 417f
    perceived organizational support, 417
infancy
    attachment in, 181–183
    brain development in, 169–171, 169f, 171f
    cognitive development in, 171–178,
        174f–177f
    emotional development, 185–186
    facial expressions and, 184–185, 425
    imitation in, 312, 330
    language development in, 327
    motor development in, 167–168, 167f
    personality development in, 181
    physical contact in, 183–184, 184f
    sensory development in, 168–169, 168f, 169f
    sleep in, 226, 227f
    social referencing in, 185
    technology and, 202–203, 203f
    touch needs in, 183–184, 184f
inferential statistics, 59–61
inferior colliculus, 144
inferiority complex, 490
inflammation, 462, 466
informational social influence, 515
informed consent, 63
in-group/out-group bias, 524–525
inheritance. See genetic influences; heritability

inhibitory neurotransmitters, 85
innately guided learning, 332
inner ear, 142, 142f
Inquisition, 12
insecure-avoidant attachment, 182
insecure-disorganized/disoriented
    attachment, 183
insecure-resistant attachment, 182
insight solutions, 381–382
insomnia, 229–230
Instagram, 526
instinctive drift, 304
institutional review boards (IRBs), 63–64
instrumental aggression, 533
insula, 98, 146, 147f, 432–433
insulin, 109, 401–402
integrative therapies, 610–611
integrity, 201
intellectual disability, 370–371, 371f
intellectual honesty, 37
intelligence, 358–359. See also IQ tests
    birth weight and, 376
    brain activation and, 373–374, 374f
    brain development and, 189–190, 190f
    cardiovascular fitness and, 195
    Cattell–Horn–Carroll model of, 360–361,
        361f, 368
    definitions of, 359
    emotional, 362, 435–436
    fluid vs. crystallized, 199, 199f, 360
    gender and, 378, 378f
    genetic and environmental factors in,
        374–375, 374f, 376f, 377–378
    genius and, 384–385
    genius, 389–391
    g-factor theory of, 360
    giftedness, 371–373, 372f
    intellectual disability, 370–371, 371f
    IQ tests, 389–391, 390f
    modern measures of, 365–368
    multiple-factor theory of, 360
    multiple intelligences, 362, 363f, 364
    non-Western views of, 378–379
    polygenic transmission of, 75
    race–ethnicity and, 377–378
    test bias, 368–369
    test reliability and validity, 368
    theory summary, 359f
    traditional measures of, 363, 365
    triarchic theory of, 362
intelligence quotient (IQ), 365. See also IQ tests
intelligence ratio, 365
intermittent reinforcement, 299–301, 300f
internal reliability, 368
International Flat Earth Research Society,
    344, 345f
Internet. See computers and Internet; social
    networking
Internet addiction, 582
Internet disorder, 582
Internet gaming disorder, 582
interneurons, 82–83
interpersonal intelligence, 362, 363f
interpersonal relatedness, 484–485
interposition, 132, 132f
interpretation, 38, 39f
The Interpretation of Dreams (Freud), 231
inter-rater reliability, 500
interviews, 45, 54–55, 501
intimacy, 197, 543, 543f
intrapersonal intelligence, 362, 363f
intrinsic motivation, 416, 416f
    well-lived life and, 438–439
introspection, 16

ions, 83, 89
I/O psychology. See industrial/organizational
    (I/O) psychology
iPods, hearing loss and, 143
IQ (intelligence quotient), 365
IQ tests
    bias in, 368–369
    of Binet and Simon, 365
    genius, 389–391, 390f
    Kaufman-Assessment Battery for
        Children, 365–367
    normal distribution of scores,
        369–370, 370f
    reliability and validity of, 368
    Stanford–Binet test, 365
    of Stern, 365
    Wechsler Adult Intelligence Scale, 365,
        366f, 367, 367f, 368
    Wechsler Intelligence Scale for Children,
        365, 367, 367f
IRBs (institutional review boards), 63–64
iris, 123, 124f
iron deficiency, 229

J

James–Lange theory of emotion, 429
Japanese culture
    language acquisition in, 327, 331
    perception in, 153, 154, 154f
jet lag, 224
JND (just noticeable differences), 121–122
jobs. See workplace
joint attention, 556
Jonestown cult, 544–546, 545f
juries, minority opinion in, 517
just noticeable differences (JND), 121–122

K

Kaufman-Assessment Battery for Children
    (K-ABC), 365–367
K-complexes, 226
ketamine, 562
kin selection, 537
Kinsey surveys, 46, 46f
koro, 552–553
Kramarik, Akiane, 371, 372f

L

LAD (language acquisition device), 331
language
    animals and human language,
        333–335, 334f
    bilingualism and, 324
    cerebral hemispheres and, 98, 100,
        101f, 328
    color perception and, 337, 338f
    conditioning and learning theory, 330
    development in individuals, 326–329,
        326f, 327f
    evolution of, 326
    metacognition and, 354
    motherese, 434
    nativist theory, 330–331
    nature of, 325–326
    nature vs. nurture in, 331–333, 333f
    perception and, 338, 338f
    second, 352–354, 353f
    sensitivity period in learning, 328–329, 352
    sociocultural theories, 329–330
    thought and, 335–337
    vocal anatomy and, 334f
language acquisition device (LAD), 331

late adulthood, 198–202. *See also* aging;
  Alzheimer's disease
  dementia in, 199–200, 200*f*
  memory and intelligence in, 198–199, 199*f*
  personality, 201
  personality changes in, 507, 507*f*, 508
  sleep in, 227*f*
  technology and, 206
latent learning, 305
latent level, 231
lateral geniculate nucleus (LGN), 126–127,
  127*f*, 128*f*
laughter, 428
law of closure, 134, 135*f*
law of effect, 292–294
learning. *See also* classical conditioning;
  operant conditioning
  in adolescence, 190
  by association, 286
  association, 286
  brain plasticity and, 102–103, 102*f*
  conditioned taste aversion, 301–303, 303*f*
  enriched environments and, 316–317
  examples of, 286
  flow and, 399–400
  habituation, 286
  hippocampus and, 94–95
  imitation, 312
  imprinting, 311–312
  innately guided, 332
  instinctive drift and, 304
  language, 326*f*, 327, 333*f*
  latent, 305
  by mimicry, 286
  mirror neurons and, 82, 312–313, 313*f*, 330
  neurogenesis and, 104
  observational, 306–310, 307*f*, 308*f*, 309*f*,
    313, 313*f*
  reasons for smoking, 317–319, 318*f*
  second languages, 352–354, 353*f*
  sleep and, 228, 314–315, 314*f*
  social–cognitive, 307, 496, 496*f*, 499*f*
  social learning theory, 306–310, 308*f*, 309*f*,
    317, 330
  socioemotional, 436
  synaptic change during, 313*f*, 314–316
learning disabilities, among famous
  people, 358
lens, 123, 124*f*
leptin, 401–402, 403
lesbian, gay, bisexual, or transgendered
  (LGBT), 194. *See also* sexual orientation
levels of processing, 260, *260*, 261*f*
LGN (lateral geniculate nucleus), 126–127,
  127*f*, 128*f*
lie detectors, 523
Lie to Me, 523
Life Change Units, 446, 446*f*
life expectancy, tobacco use and, 241, 467
life satisfaction, 437–439
light waves, 138, 138*f*
Likert scale, 502
limbic system, 94–98, 94*f*, 100
  schizophrenia and, 561*f*
linear perspective, 132, 132*f*
linguistic determinism hypothesis, 336–337
linguistic intelligence, 362, 363*f*
linguistic relativism, 337
lithium, 594, 599
Little Albert conditioning study, 291–292, 291*f*
liver, alcohol use and, 238
lobes of the brain, 96, 96*f*
lobotomy, prefrontal, 595
logic, in science, 35

logical-mathematical intelligence, 362, 363*f*
long-term memory, 252
  consolidation in, 261–262
  cortex and, 271, 272*f*, 273
  encoding in, 259–261, 260*f*, 261*f*
  genes and, 267, 268*f*
  retrieval from, 263, 273
  sensory cortexes and, 264
  storage in, 262–263, 264*f*, 272*f*, 273
  types of, 257–258, 260*f*
long-term potentiation (LTP), 265
love, 400, 543, 543*f*
love and belongingness needs, 400
loving-kindness meditation, 612
LSD, 244
lust, 543
lymphocytes, 462

M

magnetic resonance imaging (MRI), 106, 107*f*
major depressive disorder, 563, 566*f*
manic episodes, 567
manifest level, 231
MAO (monoamine oxidase) inhibitors,
  592–593, 599
marijuana, 242–244
marriage, 196, 196*f*
marriage and family therapists (MFT),
  614–615
Maslow's hierarchy of needs, 400–401, 400*f*
massage therapy, 184
matchstick problem, 381*f*
matrix reasoning, 360
Mayer–Salovey–Caruso Emotional
  Intelligence Test (MSCEIT), 436
MBCT (mindfulness-based cognitive therapy),
  611–612, 613, 613*f*, 619
MBSR (Mindfulness-Based Stress
  Reduction), 471
MBTI (Myers-Briggs Type Indicator), 504
MDMA (ecstasy), 242
mean, 58
meaning in life, 439, 457
measures, 54–57, 55*f*
mechanisms, 480
mechanoreceptors, 145
media, 310, 534. *See also* advertising; social
  networking; aggression and violence in
  cognitive and brain development and,
    202–203, 203*f*
  persuasion in, 532
  statistics used in, 60–61, 61*f*
medial geniculate nucleus (MGN), 144
medial prefrontal cortex (mPFC), 191
median, 58
meditation, 220
  brain changes with, 221–222, 221*f*
  conscious experience and, 221
  for stress reduction, 471
medulla, 92*f*, 93
melatonin, 224, 224*f*
memory, 252. *See also* long-term memory;
  short-term memory
  acetylcholine and, 87
  aging and, 198–199
  biological memory systems, 264–265, 264*f*
  brain and, 268*f*, 271, 272*f*, 273, 274*f*
  brain injury and, 251–252, 252*f*
  brain stimulation and, 268–269, 270
  cortisol and, 233
  distorted, 277–278
  emotion and, 273–275, 274*f*
  exercise and, 470

extraordinary, 250–251
  forgetting, 276–279, 276*f*
  hippocampus and prefrontal cortex and,
    95, 96, 271, 272*f*, 273
  long-term, 252
  medications for, 266–267
  as personal reconstruction, 18
  sensory, 252, 253, 264
  short-term, 252, 254–257, 255*f*, 257*f*
  sleep and, 228, 261, 274, 274*f*, 314–315, 314*f*
  stress and, 452
  studying tips, 280–281
  three-stage model of, 252, 260*f*–261*f*
  without recollection, 251–252, 253*f*
memory loss, 276–279
menarche, 188
men and boys, 407, 407*f*. *See also* gender
  differences, sexual response cycle in
  spermarche in, 188
menstrual cycle, 109
mental age, 365
mental disorders, "4 Ds" to distinguish,
  551–552
mental representation, 339–342, 340*f*, 342*f*
mental rotation, 340, 340*f*
mental sets, 380*f*, 382
meta-analysis, 46–47
metabolism, 401, 468–469
metacognitive thinking, 345, 345*f*, 354
methamphetamine (meth), 241
MFT (marriage and family therapists), 614–615
MGN (medial geniculate nucleus), 144
midbrain, 92*f*, 93
middle adulthood, 197–198, 197*f*, 205–206
Middle Ages, 12, 12*f*
middle ear, 142*f*
midlevel processing, 260
midlife crisis, 198
Milgram's studies of obedience, 62, 518–520,
  519*f*, 520*f*
mind, 21–22
mind–body dualism, 21–22
mindfulness, 214, 221
mindfulness-based cognitive therapy
  (MBCT), 611–612, 613, 613*f*, 619
Mindfulness-Based Stress Reduction
  (MBSR), 471
mindfulness meditation, 223, 471, 611–612
Minnesota Multiphasic Personality Inventory
  (MMPI), 502
minority social influence, People's Temple, 545
mirror neurons, 82
  animal studies on, 313, 313*f*
  autism spectrum disorder, 557
  language acquisition and, 330
  learning and, 82, 312–313, 330
mitochondria, depression and, 565
MMPI (Minnesota Multiphasic Personality
  Inventory), 502
mnemonic devices, 261, 281
mobile addiction, 582
mode, 58
modeling, 307
money, 415, 438
monoamine oxidase (MAO) inhibitors,
  592–593, 599
monocular depth cues, 132, 132*f*
monogenic transmission, 75
monosodium glutamate (MSG), 149
mood disorders. *See also* depression
  bipolar disorder, 567, 567*f*, 568–569, 569*f*,
    585, 594
  drug treatments for, 593*f*
  psychological treatment for, 607

moods, 418. *See also* emotions
moon illusion, 136–137, 137*f*
moral reasoning, 178–180, 180*f*
moral treatment, 13
morning sickness, 165
morphine, 148, 239
motherese, 434
motion perception, 130–131
motivation, 397
 achievement, 414–415
 egoistic vs. empathic, 538
 emotion and, 396–397
 extrinsic, 415–416
 happiness and, 437–439
 hunger as, 401–407, 403*f*
 intrinsic, 416, 416*f*
 models of, 397–401, 398*f*, 398*f*–399*f*
 needs, drives, and incentives in, 397,
  398*f*–399*f*
 needs to belong and excel, 413–415
 sex as, 407–412, 407*f*
 thinness and obesity, 402–407, 403*f*
 in the workplace, 415–417, 418*f*
motor cortex, 96, 97, 97*f*
motor development, 167–168
motor neurons, 82
movement, brain–computer interfaces and,
 99, 99*f*
MP3 players, hearing loss and, 143
mPFC (medial prefrontal cortex), 191
MPQ (Multidimensional Personality
 Questionnaire), 504
MRI (magnetic resonance imaging), 106, 107*f*
MSCEIT (Mayer–Salovey–Caruso Emotional
 Intelligence Test), 436
MSG (monosodium glutamate), 149
Müller–Lyer illusion, 136, 136*f*, 152
Multidimensional Personality Questionnaire
 (MPQ), 504
multiple-factor theory of intelligence, 360
multiple intelligences, 362, 363*f*, 364
multiple sclerosis, meditation and, 471
multitasking, 204, 217–220
musical intelligence, 362, 363*f*
musical training, brain and, 66*f*, 67, 172–173,
 199, 316
mutations, 23
myelination, 81, 171, 171*f*, 189
myelin sheath, 81, 81*f*
Myers-Briggs Type Indicator (MBTI), 504
MySpace, 526. *See also* social networking

N

narcissistic personality disorder, 579, 579*f*
narcolepsy, 230
narcotics (opioids), 148, 239–240
narrow intelligence, 361
nativist view of language, 330–331
natural immunity, 462
naturalistic intelligence, 362, 363*f*
naturalistic observation, 44–45
natural killer cells, 463
natural selection, 23–25, 23*f*
nature–nurture debate, 310–311
nature through nurture, 21
nausea, marijuana and, 243
Nazi atrocities, obedience in, 518, 518–520
Ndembu culture, 454
Neanderthals, 91, 91*f*
nearsightedness, 126, 126*f*
needs, 397
 for achievement, 414–415
 for affiliation, 413–414

basic and higher, 437–438
 for esteem, 400
 hierarchical model of, 400, 400*f*
 for touch, 183–184, 184*f*
negative punishment, 295, 295*f*
negative reinforcement, 294–295, 295*f*
negative symptoms (of schizophrenia), 559
NEO-Personality Inventory (PI), 484, 502,
 509, 509*f*
nervous system. *See also* autonomic nervous
 system; neurogenesis; sympathetic
 nervous system
 brain–computer interfaces and, 99
 GABA and, 88
 glial cells in, 79
 neural transmission steps, 89
 neurons in, 79–81, 81*f*
 neuroplasticity, 102–103, 102*f*
 organization of, 78–79, 79*f*
neural migration, 162
neural networks, 262–263
neural synchrony, 189
neurocultural theory of emotion, 433–434
neurodevelopmental disorders, 555
 causes, 557–558
 subtypes, 555–556, 555*f*
neuroendocrine system, 448
neurogenesis, 102
 in the adult brain, 104–105
 Alzheimer's and, 200–201
 in deaf and blind people, 103
 exercise and, 469, 470
 in infancy, 170–171, 170*f*
 in middle adulthood, 197–198
neuron doctrine, 104
neurons, 79–81. *See also* neurogenesis
 action potential, 83–85, 84*f*
 environmental influences on, 170, 171*f*,
  316–317
 in infancy, 170, 170*f*
 long-term memory and, 265–267, 268*f*
 mirror, 82, 312–313, 313*f*, 330
 neural plasticity, 274
 neural transmission steps, 89
 neurotransmitters and, 85, 86*f*
 olfactory sensory, 148
 prenatal development of, 162
 sleep and, 228
 structure and types of, 81–83, 81*f*
 synaptic change during learning, 313*f*,
  314–316
 synchronization of, 216
 vision and, 127–130, 128*f*, 130*f*
neuropeptide Y (NPY), 401, 402, 565
neuroplasticity, 102–103, 102*f*
 vision, 129
neuropsychoanalysis, 493–494
neuroses, 619
neuroticism
 anxiety disorders and, 572
 culture and, 484
 depression and, 565
 in Eysenck's personality model, 498, 498*f*
 nature and nurture in, 482, 482*f*
 social networking sites and, 527
neuroticism (anxiety), 479, 479*f*
neurotransmitters, 81. *See also specific*
 neurotransmitters
 depression and, 565
 functions of common, 85, 87–89, 87*f*
 monoamine oxidase inhibitors and, 592
 in neurotransmission, 81, 85, 86*f*, 89
 pain and, 147
 schizophrenia and, 562

newborns. *See* infancy
nicotine. *See also* tobacco use
 effects and risks of, 240–241, 467
 glutamate and, 89
 in pregnancy, 166
night terrors, 230
nine-dot problem, 381*f*, 382
NMDA, 562
nociceptive pain, 146
nociceptors, 146
node, 262
nondeclarative memory, 258. *See also* implicit
 memory
non-REM sleep, 225, 225*f*
norepinephrine, 87
 antidepressants and, 593, 619
 in emotional memories, 274
 in the endocrine system, 109
 functions of, 87, 87*f*, 109
 stress and, 448, 449*f*
normal distribution, 58–59
 of IQ scores, 369–370, 370*f*
 of personality traits, 479
 in statistics, 58–59, 58*f*
normative social influence, 515–516, 516*f*
norms, 515
NPY (neuropeptide Y), 401, 402
nutrition. *See* eating

O

obedience, 518–520, 520*f*
obesity
 BMI definition of, 402–403, 403*f*
 environmental and genetic factors in,
  403–404
 epigenetic research on, 77
 happiness and, 438
 health effects of, 467
 hypothalamus and, 94
 prevalence of, 402–403
 social support and, 405, 455–456
 weight loss success, 404–405
object permanence, 174, 174–175, 175*f*
observation
 behavioral, 55–56, 500–501
 limits of, 35–36
 naturalistic, 44–45
 in the scientific method, 38, 39*f*
observational learning, 306–310, 307*f*, 308*f*,
 309*f*, 313
obsessions, 574
obsessive–compulsive disorder (OCD),
 574–575
 causes of, 575
 cognitive–behavioral therapy for, 605, 607
 combined therapies in, 619
 drug therapy for, 618–619
 optogenetic treatment for, 614
 symptoms of, 574
obsessive–compulsive personality disorder,
 579*f*, 580
occipital lobes, 96*f*, 98, 271, 272*f*
 schizophrenia and, 561*f*
OCD. *See* obsessive–compulsive disorder
OCEAN acronym, 497, 497*f*
odd–eccentric personality disorders,
 578–579, 579*f*
OFC (orbitofrontal cortex), 150
olanzapine, 592
olfaction. *See* smell
olfactory bulb, 148
olfactory sensory neurons, 148
one-word utterances, 327, 328*f*

online dating services, 205
online games, 582
open communication systems, 325
openness, 482, 484
operant conditioning, 293
    applications of, 298–299
    behavior modification, 319
    in behavior therapy, 602–603
    classical conditioning vs., 298*f*
    conditioned taste aversion, 301, 303*f*
    consequences in, 293, 293*f*
    instinctive drift and, 304
    law of effect in, 292–294, 293*f*
    operation of, 296–297, 296*f*, 298*f*, 299*f*
    reinforcement and punishment in,
        294–296, 295*f*
    schedules of reinforcement, 299–301,
        299*f*, 300*f*
    smoking and, 317, 317–319, 318*f*
    used by oneself, 294
opioids, 148, 239–240
opponent-process theory, 139
OPTIC, 39*f*
optic chiasm, 126, 127, 127*f*
optic nerve, 125, 127, 127*f*
optimal arousal model, 398–400, 399*f*
optimism, 456, 617–618
optogenetics, 614–615, 616*f*
orbitofrontal cortex (OFC), 150
organizational psychology. *See* industrial/
    organizational (I/O) psychology
orgasm, 407–408, 407*f*
originality, 388
outer ear, 142, 142*f*
out-group homogeneity, 525
oval window, 142, 142*f*
ovaries, 110*f*
ovulation, sex drive and, 408
oxytocin, 432

P

pain, 145
    anterior cingulate cortex and, 432
    cultural variation in, 153, 155, 155*f*
    empathy with, 539, 540, 540*f*
    hypnosis and, 235
    marijuana and, 243
    opioids and, 240
    perception of, 145–146, 147*f*
    phantom limb, 146
    social, 514, 525, 525*f*
painting
    blindness and, 72, 72*f*, 111–113, 111*f*, 112*f*
    brain and, 111–113, 112*f*
palliative care, 202
pancreas, 109, 110*f*
panic attacks, 570–571
panic disorder, 570–571
papillae, 149
parahippocampal place area (PPA), 108, 108*f*
parallel distributed processing (PDP), 263,
    341, 342*f*
paralysis, computers and, 99, 99*f*
paranoid personality disorder, 578–579, 579*f*
parasympathetic nervous system, 78, 79*f*,
    80*f*, 425
parathyroid gland, 110*f*
parental investment theory, 409, 542
parenting
    decision to become a parent, 196, 196*f*
    infant attachment and, 184
    language acquisition and, 330
    nature–nurture debate and, 20–21

personality changes with, 507–508
parietal lobes, 96*f*, 97, 97*f*
    somatosensory cortex, 271
Parkinson's disease, 93, 96, 562
passion, 543, 543*f*
passionate love, 543, 543*f*
PATHS program, 436
Pavlov's dogs, 288–289, 289*f*
Paxil, 593
PCP, 562
PDP (parallel distributed processing), 263,
    341, 342*f*
Peek, Kim, 373
peers
    interaction with, 186, 191–192
    pressure from, 515–516, 516*f*
    smoking and, 319
Penn Resiliency Program (PRP), 617
People's Temple tragedy, 544–546, 545*f*
perceived organizational support, 417
perception, 119. *See also* hearing; vision
    absolute thresholds of, 120–121, 120*f*–121*f*
    bottom-up and top-down
        processing in, 137
    of color, 138–139, 138*f*, 139*f*
    culture and, 152–155, 153*f*, 154*f*
    of depth, 131–132, 131*f*, 132*f*, 152–153, 153*f*
    difference thresholds in, 121–122
    foreground–background and, 154, 154*f*
    Gestalt laws of grouping, 134–137, 134*f*,
        135*f*, 136*f*
    meditation training and, 221
    of motion, 130–131
    of pain, 145–146, 147*f*
    perceptual constancy, 132–134, 133*f*
    perceptual set, 122, 122*f*
    principles of, 119–120
    signal detection theory, 120–121, 121*f*
    of smell, 148–149, 149*f*
    synesthesia, 151–152, 151*f*
    of taste, 149–150, 150*f*
    of touch, 145
    of visual stimuli, 130–134, 132*f*, 133*f*
    Weber on, 15
perceptual constancy, 132–134, 133*f*
perceptual load model, 216
perceptual set, 122, 122*f*
Percocet, 239
performance, visual imagery and, 339, 340*f*
peripheral hearing, 103
peripheral nervous system, 78, 79*f*
peripheral vision, 103
personality, 166, 478
    Adler on, 490–491
    in adolescence, 192, 192*f*
    Alzheimer's and, 508, 509
    animal research, 485–486
    in animals, 485–486, 486*f*
    anxiety disorders and, 572
    biological theories, 498–499, 498*f*, 499*f*
    brain injury and, 508
    changes across the life span, 506–507, 507*f*
    in children, 186–187
    college major and, 504–505
    consistency of, 506
    creative, 388–389
    culture and, 483–485, 484*f*
    definition of, 478–480
    in early adulthood, 197
    evolution of traits, 480–481
    Eysenck on, 498, 498*f*
    Freud on, 487–490, 489*f*
    frontal lobe injury and, 97, 97*f*
    genetics and, 481–483, 482*f*

    Horney on, 492–493, 492*f*
    in infancy, 181
    job performance and, 505
    Jung on, 491–492
    in late adulthood, 201
    late adulthood, 201
    life circumstance changes and, 507–508
    living abroad and, 507
    Maslow on, 494–495
    measurement of, 500–503
    in middle adulthood, 198
    multiple personality disorder, 576–577
    neuropsychoanalysis, 493–494
    parenthood and, 196
    personality disorders, 578–581, 579*f*
    prenatal environment and, 166, 483
    Rogers on, 495
    smoking and, 319
    social–cognitive learning theories and,
        496, 496*f*
    social network measurement of, 502, 503*f*
    summary of approaches to, 499*f*
    switching jobs, 505
    trait theories, 496–498, 497*f*
    Type A Behavior Pattern, 465–466, 466*f*
personality disorders, 578
    anxious–fearful, 579*f*, 580
    creativity and, 584
    dramatic–emotional, 579–580, 579*f*
    nature and nurture explanations of,
        580–581
    odd–eccentric, 578–579, 579*f*
personality psychology, 9
    on electronic social interaction, 29
personality questionnaires, 501–502
personal unconscious, 491
persuasion, 532
pessimists, 456
PET (positron emission tomography),
    107, 109
phagocytosis, 462
phantom limb pain, 146
phenothiazines, 591
phenotype, 77
pheromones, 542
The Philosophical Baby (Gopnik), 172
phobias, 571
    agoraphobia, 571–572
    cognitive–behavioral therapy for, 605
    fear of flying, 572, 604*f*
    social phobia, 571
    specific, 572
    systematic desensitization and, 603,
        603*f*–604*f*, 609, 619
phonemic processing, 260
phonological loop, 255*f*, 256, 271
photoreceptors, 123, 124*f*
physical dependence, 236
physical development
    in adolescence, 188, 188*f*
    in infancy and childhood, 167–171,
        167*f*–171*f*, 171*f*
physical fitness, cognitive functioning and, 195
physical mechanisms, 480
physiological measures, 55*f*, 57
physiological reactivity model, 459–460, 460*f*
Piaget's stages of cognitive development,
    173–177, 174*f*, 175*f*, 176*f*
pineal gland, 224
Pirahã people, 336, 336*f*
pituitary gland, 109
    hypothalamus and, 94
    location of, 110*f*
    stress and, 448, 449*f*

placebo, 50
plasticity
    in the adult brain, 104–105
    learning and, 102–103, 102f
    neurogenesis and, 100–103, 102, 200–201
pleasure, hypothalamus and, 432
PNI (psychoneuroimmunology), 461–464
polygenic transmission, 75
pons, 92f, 93
pop psychology, 6
population, in research design, 42
positive psychology, 17, 495, 617–618. See
        also humanistic–positive psychological
        theories
positive psychotherapy, 602
positive punishment, 294, 295f
positive reinforcement, 294, 295f
positive symptoms (of schizophrenia), 558
positron emission tomography (PET),
        107, 109
postconventional level, 180, 180f
posthypnotic suggestion, 234–235
postsynaptic neurons, 85, 86f, 89
post-traumatic stress disorder (PTSD),
        575–576
    cognitive–behavioral therapy for, 605
    memory and, 275, 275f
    prolonged exposure therapy for, 611, 612
    symptoms of, 575
potassium ion channels, 83, 84f, 89
PPA (parahippocampal place area),
        108, 108f
practical intelligence, 362
preconscious, 213
preconventional level, 180, 180f
prediction, 38, 39f
predictive validity, 368
prefrontal cortex, 264
    aggression and, 533
    attention and focus, 271
    electrical stimulation to enhance
        memory, 270
    emotion and, 431–432
    IQ tasks and, 373–374, 374f
    memory and, 264–265, 271, 272f, 273
    recall and, 271, 272f, 273
    schizophrenia and, 560
prefrontal lobotomy, 595
pregnancy. See also prenatal development
    alcohol in, 166, 166f, 567
    nutrition during, 165
    parental investment theory and, 409
    schizophrenia and, 21
    tobacco use in, 166
pregnancy sickness, 165
prehistoric cultures, 11
prejudice, 526–528
prenatal development. See also pregnancy
    alcohol and bipolar disorder and, 567
    of brain and sensory system, 162–165,
        163f, 163f–164f
    of intelligence, 376
    maternal nutrition and, 165
    of personality, 166, 483
    schizophrenia and, 560
    stages of, 161–162, 161f, 163f
    of temperament, 483
    teratogens and, 165–166, 166f
prenatal programming, 165
preoperational stage, 175, 176f, 177f
presbyopia, 126
prescription drugs
    for memory improvement, 266–267
    in pregnancy, 166

presynaptic neurons, 85, 86f, 89
prevention programs, 617–618
pride, 420–421, 421f
primacy effect, 256–257, 257f
primary appraisal, 446–447
primary motor cortex, 96, 98
primary olfactory cortex, 149
primary reinforcers, 294
primary visual cortex, 98
primates
    brain evolution in, 91
    human language and, 333–335, 334f
    neurogenesis in, 105, 105f
priming, 258, 258f, 273
privately public, 29
proactive interference, 276
probability level, 59
problem-focused coping strategies,
        453–454, 453f
problem solving, 379–380. See also decision
        making
    brain and, 96, 385, 387
    creative, 384, 386, 388, 388f
    by infants, 177
    obstacles to solutions, 382–383
    solution strategies, 381–382, 381f
    types of problems, 380–381, 381f
procedural memory, 258
prodigies, 371–372, 372f
projection, 489
projective tests, 501
prolonged exposure therapy, 611, 613
propanolol, 619
prosocial behavior, 535–539
prospect theory, 350
protolanguage, 326
prototypes, 342
proximity, 134, 134f
Prozac, 166, 593, 599
PRP (Penn Resiliency Program), 617
pruning, 169–170, 189
pseudoscience, 40–41, 40f
psilocybin, 244
psoriasis, mindfulness training and, 471
psychiatrists, 614
psychiatry, 551
psychoactive drugs, 236, 237f
    alcohol. See alcohol
    amphetamines, 241–242
    caffeine, 240, 240f
    cocaine, 241
    dependence and addiction, 236
    LSD, 244
    marijuana, 242–244
    MDMA (ecstasy), 242
    nicotine, 89, 166, 240–241, 467
    operant conditioning and, 296
    opioids, 148, 239–240
    psilocybin, 244
    sedatives, 239
psychoanalysis, 13
psychoanalytical theory
    Adler on, 490
    on dreams, 231
    Freud on, 487–490, 489f
    Horney on, 492–493, 492f
    Jung on, 491
    neuropsychoanalysis, 493–494
    summary of, 499f
    in treatment of psychological disorders,
        600–602
psychoanalytical therapy, 600–602
psychobiography, 44
psychodynamic therapy, 600

psychological dependence, 236
psychological disorders. See also treatment
        of disorders
    anxiety disorders, 554f, 570f, 571f
    choosing a therapist, 614–615
    classification of, 553–554, 554f
    creativity and, 583–585, 583f, 584f
    defining, 551–555
    Diagnostic and Statistical Manual, 14,
        551–553, 554f
    dissociative disorders, 576–577
    elements necessary, 405
    Internet dependency, 582
    major, 553, 554f, 555
    mood disorders, 566f, 567f
    moral treatment movement, 13
    neurodevelopmental disorders, 555–557
    personality disorders, 578–581, 579f
    prevalence of, 553, 553f
    prevention of, 617–618
    schizophrenia. See schizophrenia
    somatic symptom disorders, 577–578
psychology, 5
    critical thinking in, 26–27
    definition of, 5–6
    history of clinical psychology, 11–14,
        12f, 13f
    history of scientific psychology, 14–19
    mind–body dualism in, 21–22
    nature–nurture debate in, 20–21
    pop, 6
    reasons for study of, 6–8
    subdisciplines of, 8–10, 8f
    timeline of, 19f
psychoneuroimmunology (PNI), 461–464
psychophysics, 14–15, 119
psychosomatic theory, 459
psychosurgery, 595
psychotherapy, 13–14, 602
    for anxiety disorders, 619
    behavioral treatments, 602–603
    choosing a therapist, 614–615
    cognitive and cognitive–behavioral
        treatments, 603–605, 608
    combined with drug therapy, 610
    effectiveness of, 607–609
    group therapy, 605–607, 619
    humanistic–positive therapy, 601–602
    mindfulness training and, 611–612
    psychoanalytic/psychodynamic therapy,
        600–602
    summary of techniques, 606f
psychotic disorders, 558
psychoticism, 498
PTSD. See post-traumatic stress disorder
puberty, 188, 188f
publicly private, 29
punishment, 295–296, 295f
pupil, 123, 124f
purity, of sound waves, 141, 141f

Q

quantitative trail loci (QTL) approach,
        481–482
quasi-experimental design, 67
questioning authority, 37
questionnaires, 55, 55f, 501–502

R

race–ethnicity. See also culture; specific
        ethnic groups
    implicit bias and, 528
    intelligence and, 377–378

racism, 526
Rain Man, 373
random assignment, 50, 51
rapid eye movements (REM), 224–226, 225*f*, 227*f*, 233
rational choice theory, 349–350
rational (face valid) method, 502
Raven's Progressive Matrices Test, 360, 360*f*
reaction formation, 489
reaction range, 375, 376*f*
reappraisal, 424
  in coping strategies, 454
  as copy strategy, 472–473
  prefrontal cortex in, 432
reasoning, 189, 342–344, 353–354
recall, 260–261, 261*f*
recency effect, 256–257, 257*f*
  in language learning, 327
recessive alleles, 74
reciprocal altruism, 537
recovered memories, 278–279
reflexes, 93, 168
refractory period, in neural impulse, 83, 84*f*
rehearsal, 256, 261, 271
  prefrontal cortex, 271
reinforcement. *See also* operant
    conditioning
  positive and negative, 295*f*, 296–297
  primary and secondary reinforcers, 294
  schedules of, 299–301, 299*f*, 300*f*
  in social learning theory, 308
reinforcers, 294–297, 295*f*
rejection, 414, 514, 525
relational view of stress, 445
relationships
  happiness and, 438, 439
  love, 400, 543, 543*f*
  marriage, 195–196, 196*f*
  of self-actualizing individuals, 494–495
relaxation techniques, 603
reliability, 368, 500
Reminyl, 266
remote association word problems, 385, 387
REM (rapid eye movement), 224–226, 225*f*, 227*f*, 233
repetitive transcranial magnetic stimulation, 596–597, 596*f*
replication, 39
  in scientific method, 38
replication, in scientific method, 39*f*
representativeness heuristic, 347–348
representative sample, 45, 45*f*
repression, 277, 489, 602
research. *See also* animal research
  assumptions about objectivity, 53–54
  correlational studies, 47–49, 48*f*, 49*f*
  descriptive studies, 42–46, 43*f*
  design principles, 41–42
  ethics in, 62–66, 292, 520
  experimenter expectancy effects in, 52
  experiments, 49–52, 50*f*
  measures used in, 54–57, 55*f*
  meta-analysis, 46–47
  quasi-experimental design, 67
  scientific method in, 38–39, 39*f*
  statistics in, 47–49, 49*f*, 57–61, 58*f*, 61*f*
research design, 41–42
resilience, 457
resistance stage, 450, 450*f*
response view of stress, 445
resting potential, 83, 84*f*
reticular formation, 93
retina, 123, 124*f*, 127*f*
retrieval, memory, 263, 273

retroactive interference, 276
retrograde amnesia, 278
reuptake, 85
rewards, motivation and, 415–416
rhyming, 261
risperidone, 592
Ritalin, 267
rods, 123, 124*f*
rooting reflex, 168
Rorschach Inkblot Test, 501, 501*f*
rubella, schizophrenia and, 21
Russian language, color perception and, 337, 338*f*

S

sadness, 427*f*, 429, 429*f*
samples, in research design, 42, 45–46, 45*f*
Samurai culture, 433–434
SAT (Scholastic Aptitude Test), 353–354
savant syndrome, 372–373
scatterplots, 49, 49*f*
scent, attraction and, 542
schedules of reinforcement, 299–301, 299*f*, 300*f*
schemas, 262, 523
schizoid personality disorder, 578, 579*f*
schizophrenia, 558
  brain and, 560–561, 560*f*, 561*f*
  cingulate gyrus and, 95
  creativity and, 584
  diathesis-stress model, 559
  dopamine hypothesis, 561–562
  drug treatments for, 591–592, 592*f*, 599
  explanations of, 26
  genetic research on treatments, 615
  group therapy in, 607
  major symptoms of, 558–559, 558*f*
  marijuana and, 243
  maternal infections and, 21, 166, 560
  maternal nutrition and, 166
  meditation-based therapies, 612
  nature and nurture explanations of, 559–562, 561*f*
  neural synchrony in, 189
  prevalence of, 558
schizotypal personality disorder, 578, 579*f*
Scholastic Aptitude Test (SAT), 353–354
school psychology, 10
science. *See also* research
  common sense and logic in, 35
  limits of observation, 35–36
  map of the sciences, 36*f*
  pseudoscience and, 40–41, 40*f*
  questioning authority in, 37
  scientific method, 38–39, 39*f*
  scientific thinking, 36–37
scientific method, 38–39, 39*f*
scientific psychology
  behaviorism, 16–17
  cognitivism, 17–18
  empiricism, 14
  evolutionary psychology and behavioral neuroscience, 18
  Hall and, 15–16
  humanistic and positive, 17
  James and, 15*f*, 16
  psychophysics, 14–15
  structuralism and functionalism, 16
  Wundt and, 15, 15*f*, 16
scientific thinking, 36–37, 346
SCN (suprachiasmatic nucleus), 224
sea slug studies, 265–267, 266*f*
secondary appraisal, 447

secondary olfactory cortex, 149
secondary (or conditioned) reinforcers, 294
secondhand smoke, 467
second languages, 352–354, 353*f*
Second Life, 29, 609–610
secure attachment, 182
sedatives, 239
selective attention, 214–216, 215*f*, 234, 245
selective norepinephrine reuptake inhibitors, 619
selective serotonin reuptake inhibitors (SSRIs), 593–594, 593*f*, 598–599, 618
self-actualization, 400, 400*f*, 494–495
self-conscious emotions, 419*f*, 420–421, 421*f*, 422*f*
self-esteem, social networking and, 205
self-fulfilling prophecy, 54
self-reports, 54–56, 55*f*
self-serving bias, 522
SEL (socioemotional learning), 436
semantic memory, 258
semantic processing, 260
semicircular canals, 142, 142*f*
sensation, 119. *See also* perception; *specific senses*
  age-related decrease in, 197, 197*f*
  culture and, 152–155, 153*f*, 155*f*
  infant development of, 168–169, 168*f*
  prenatal development of, 162–165, 163*f*
  sensory cortexes, 264
sensitivity period
  in language development, 328–329, 352
  in learning, 311
sensorimotor stage, 174, 174*f*
sensory adaptation, 119
sensory cortexes, 264, 269, 271
sensory deprivation, 399
sensory memory, 252, 253, 264
sensory neurons, 82
sentence phase, 327–328, 328*f*
separation anxiety, 181
serial-position effect, 256–257, 257*f*
serotonin, 88
  aggression and, 534
  antidepressants and, 593, 593*f*, 599
  in bipolar disorder, 569
  cocaine and, 241
  depression and, 565, 566
  Ecstasy and, 88, 88*f*
  functions of, 87*f*, 88
  LSD and, 244
  in schizophrenia, 592
serotonin gene and depression, 565, 566
set point, 398, 398*f*
seven-square match problem, 380, 381*f*, 382
sex glands, 109
sex hormones, 109, 188, 341, 408, 534
sexism, 526
sexting, 205
sexual behavior, 407
  in adolescence, 191–192
  age of first intercourse, 191
  arousal, 95, 407–408, 407*f*
  casual sex, 409, 410
  creativity and, 481
  culture and, 409
  in emerging adulthood, 194
  happiness and, 438
  Internet and, 205
  Kinsey surveys on, 46, 46*f*
  sexual orientation, 409, 411–412
  sexual response cycle, 407–408, 407*f*
sexual identity, 194

sexual orientation, 409, 411–412
  adolescence and, 192
  in animals, 411
  as continuum, 409–410, 411
  genetic and environmental factors in,
    411, 412
  Kinsey surveys on, 46
  sexual identity and, 194
sexual response cycle, 407–408, 407*f*
sexual strategies theory, 542
shadow, 491–492, 491*f*
shamans, 11
shape constancy, 133–134, 133*f*
shaping, 17*f*, 297, 297*f*
shock therapy, 595, 595*f*, 599–600
short-term (acute) stress, 472
short-term memory, 252
  capacity of, 254–255
  electrical stimulation to enhance, 270
  hippocampus and prefrontal cortex and,
    271, 272*f*
  operation of, 255–257, 255*f*
  serial position effect, 256–257, 257*f*
  uses of, 254
signal detection theory, 120–121, 121*f*
similarity, 134, 134*f*
simple cells (neurons), 128, 128*f*
single-blind studies, 52
situational attributions, 521
size constancy, 133, 133*f*, 135*f*, 153
skepticism, in science, 37
Skinner box, 296–297, 296*f*
sleep
  brain and, 224–226, 225*f*–226*f*, 226*f*
  brain injury and, 245
  characteristics, 222
  circadian rhythms and, 222, 224, 224*f*
  disorders of, 229–231
  dreaming, 226, 231–233, 232*f*
  function of, 226, 227*f*, 228
  learning and, 314–315, 314*f*
  memory and, 228, 261, 274, 274*f*
  over the life span, 226, 227*f*
  reticular formation and, 93
  sleep deprivation, 228, 228–229, 229*f*
  tips for improving, 229*f*
  weight loss and, 405
sleep debt, 229
sleep spindles, 226
sleepwalking, 230, 231*f*
slow-to-warm-up child, 181
smell
  age-related decrease in, 197
  cultural variation in, 153
  prenatal development of, 164
  sense of, 148–149, 149*f*
smiling, 426*f*, 428
smoking. *See* tobacco use
SMPY (Study for Mathematically Precocious
    Youth), 371–372
social anxiety disorder, 571
  technology-based therapy for, 610
social behavior
  aggression. *See* aggression
  attitudes, 529–532, 531*f*
  attraction, 539, 541–542, 541*f*
  attributions, 521–522
  conformity, 515–517, 516*f*, 545–546
  detecting deception, 522–523
  exclusion and inclusion, 524–525
  groupthink, 517
  in Jonestown cult, 544–546, 545*f*
  love, 543, 543*f*
  minority social influence, 517–518

obedience, 518–520, 520*f*
  prejudice and discrimination, 526–529
  prosocial behavior, 535–539
  schemas, 523
  social facilitation vs. social loafing, 515
  in social networks, 526–527
  social pain, 514, 525, 525*f*
  stereotypes and, 523–524
social capital, 527
social–cognitive learning, 307, 496, 496*f*, 499*f*
social desirability bias, 55–56
social development
  in adolescents, 191–192, 192*f*
  in children, 181–187, 184*f*
  sexual orientation and, 412
social exchange theory, 537–538, 538
social facilitation, 515
Social Learning and Imitation (Miller and
    Dollard), 307
social learning theory, 307
  aggression in, 534
  Bobo doll studies and, 307–308, 307*f*,
    308*f*, 309*f*
  language acquisition and, 330
  modeling in, 308
  smoking and, 317, 318*f*
social loafing, 515
social networking. *See also* computers and
    Internet
  in adolescence, 204–205, 204*f*
  for children, 203–204
  children, 203–204
  in coping, 455–456
  immune system and, 464
  impact of, 4–5
  Internet disorder, 582
  in middle adulthood, 205–206
  payoff in "likes," 527
  psychology subdisciplines on, 28–29
  social psychology of, 526–527
  sustained attention, 219–220
  texting, 204, 218–219
social networking sites (SNS), personality
    measurement through, 502, 503*f*
social networks, 455
  measurement of personality, 502, 503*f*
social norms, 515
social pain, 514, 525, 525*f*
social phobia, 571
social psychology, 9, 514
  on electronic social interactions, 28–29
  on social networks, 526–527
Social Readjustment Rating Scale (SRRS),
    446, 446*f*
social referencing, 185
social support
  in coping, 454, 455–456
  in weight loss, 405
social support strategy, 455–456
social workers, 614
sociocultural theories of language, 329–330
socioemotional development
  in adolescence, 191–192, 192*f*, 204
  attachment in, 181–183, 184*f*
  in infants and children, 181–187, 184*f*,
    203–204
  technology use and, 204–205, 204*f*
socioemotional learning (SEL), 436
sociopaths, 579
sodium ion channels, 83, 84*f*, 89
soft inheritance, 77
softwiring, 21, 95
sojourners, 507
soma, 81, 81*f*

somatic nervous system, 78, 79*f*
somatic symptom disorder, 577–578
somatosensory cortex, 97, 97*f*
sound, physics of, 140–141, 141*f*
sound waves, 141*f*
spatial ability, 340–341
spatial intelligence, 362, 363*f*
speech
  babbling, 327, 328*f*
  brain and, 98, 100
  vocal expression, 425, 428
  word salad, 383–384, 559
speed (Benzedrine), 241
spermarche, 188
spirituality, 244, 439
split-brain research, 100, 101*f. See also*
    cerebral hemispheres
spontaneity, 494
spontaneous recovery, 290–291, 290*f*
sports psychology, 10
SRRS (Social Readjustment Rating Scale),
    446, 446*f*
SSRIs (selective serotonin reuptake
    inhibitors), 593–594, 593*f*, 598–599, 618
stagnation, 198
standard deviation, 58
Stanford–Binet test, 365, 368
Stanford Prison Experiment, 34, 63, 63*f*
statistics, 57
  in advertising, 60–61, 61*f*
  correlation coefficients, 47–48, 49*f*
  descriptive, 58–59, 58*f*
  inferential, 59–61
stereotypes, 18, 523–524
stimulants, 240–242, 240*f*
stimulus discrimination, 289
stimulus generalization, 289
stimulus view of stress, 445–446
storage, memory, 262–263, 264*f*, 272*f*, 273
strange situation, 182
stress, 444–445
  acute versus chronic, 472
  adaptation to, 451
  aging effects from, 458
  beliefs related to illness, 473
  brain and, 451–452
  changing beliefs about, 473
  coping strategies, 453–456, 453*f*, 472–473
  depression and, 466, 565
  eating and, 468
  general adaptation syndrome,
    450–451, 450*f*
  genes and, 452
  good and bad stress, 472
  heart disease and, 464–466, 466*f*
  hormones, 448–452, 449*f*, 452
  immune system and, 450, 460–461,
    463–464
  meaning in life and, 457
  meditation and, 471
  neurogenesis and, 105
  perceived, 464
  perceptions of, 472–473
  physiology of, 447–452, 449*f*
  positive psychology of coping, 456–457
  primary and secondary appraisal and,
    446–447, 447*f*
  psychoneuroimmunology, 461–464
  psychosomatic theory and, 459–460
  as response, 445
  as stimulus, 445–446, 446*f*
  stressors, 445
stressors, 445
striatum, 264, 264*f*, 272*f*, 273

striving for superiority, 490
stroke, 98, 199
Stroop effect, 234–235, 235f
structuralism, 16
structural processing, 260
studying tips, 280–281, 315
Study for Mathematically Precocious Youth (SMPY), 371–372
subjective experience of emotion, 429–430, 429f
subjective well-being, 437–439
sublimation, 489
subsonic sounds, 141
substance abuse, 296. See also psychoactive drugs
    operant conditioning in, 296
    optogenetic treatment for, 614–615, 616f
success, Atkinson's model of, 414–415
successful intelligence, 362
suggestibility, 277
suicide
    antidepressants and, 594
    depression and, 565
    hypersomnia and, 230
    Jonestown cult and, 544–546, 545f
    operant conditioning and, 298
SuperClubsPLUS, 203–204
superego, 488, 489f
support groups, 606
suprachiasmatic nucleus (SCN), 224
surprise, 427f, 429f
surveys, 45–46
sustained attention, 216–217, 217f
swallowing, 93f
symbolic communication systems, 325
sympathetic nervous system, 78
    in emotional response, 425
    stress and, 448–449, 460
    structure of, 78, 79f, 80f
synapse, 81
synaptic cleft, 81, 86f
synaptic pruning, 189
synaptic vesicles, 85, 86f
synaptogenesis, 102
synchronization, 216
syndromes, 551
synesthesia, 151–152, 151f, 251
syntax, 325
systematic desensitization, 603, 603f–604f, 609, 619

T

TABP (Type A Behavior Pattern), 465–466, 466f
tabula rasa, 14
Tactile Dome, San Francisco, 72
Tadrart Acacus of Libya rock painting, 24f
Tammet, Daniel, 373
tardive dyskinesia, 592
taste, 149–150, 150f, 164, 197
taste aversion. See conditioned taste aversion
taste buds, 149
taste receptor cells, 149
taxicab drivers, hippocampi of, 95
tDCS (transcranial direct current stimulation), 269, 269f
technology
    impact of use of, 4–5
    in infancy and toddlerhood, 202–203, 203f
    in therapies, 609–610
technology-based therapies, 609–610
television. See also advertising; media
    aggression and violence on, 310

cognitive and brain development and, 202–203, 203f
telomerase, 458
temperament, 166. See also personality
    in children, 186–187
    prenatal environment and, 483
temporal lobes, 96f, 98, 271, 272f, 273
teratogens, 165–166, 166f
terminal buttons, 81, 81f, 86f
test bias, 369
test fairness, 369
testosterone
    aggression and, 534
    in puberty, 188
    sex drive and, 408
    spatial ability and, 341
test–retest reliability, 368
tetrahydrocannabinol (THC), 242
texting, 204, 218–219
texture gradient, 132, 132f
thalamus, 93–94
    emotion and, 431, 431f
    location of, 94f
    vision and, 126, 127, 127f
THC (tetrahydrocannabinol), 242
theory, 38
theory of mind, 178, 179f
    bilingual children, 354
theta waves, 225, 226f
thinking. See also cognition; cognitive development; cognitive psychology
    critical, 26–27, 344–345, 346
    decision making, 345, 347
    linguistic determinism hypothesis, 336–337
    mental representation, 339–342, 340f, 342f
    metacognition, 345, 345f, 354
    nonrational decision making, 349–350
    reasoning from evidence, 342–344, 353–354
    scientific, 346
thinking outside the box, 382, 382f
Thorazine, 591
threaded cognition theory of multitasking, 218–219
three degrees rule, 526
three-dimensional movies, 131, 131f
three mountains task, 175–176, 176f
three-stage model of memory, 252
thresholds, in action potentials, 85
thyroid gland, 109, 110f
thyroid hormones, bipolar disorder and, 569
timbre, 141
timeline of psychology, 19f
tip-of-the-tongue phenomenon, 213, 277
T lymphocytes, 463
TMS (transcranial magnetic stimulation), 596–597, 596f
tobacco use
    cognitive dissonance and, 531, 531f
    effects and risks of, 240–241
    health effects of, 467
    nicotine, 89, 240–241, 467
    in pregnancy, 166
    reasons for, 317–319, 318f
    secondhand smoke, 467
    social networks and, 526
token economies, 602
tongue, 149, 150f
top-down processing, 137
touch, 145, 183–184, 184f
tracts, 109
traditional antipsychotics, 591
traits, 479

in personality, 479, 496–498, 497f, 499f
    polygenic transmission of, 75
    trait theories, 496–498, 497f, 499f
transcranial direct current stimulation (tDCS), 269, 269f
transcranial magnetic stimulation (TMS), 596–597, 596f
transduction, 119
transference, 601
treatment of disorders
    of anxiety disorders, 618–619
    behavioral treatments, 602–603
    biological treatment effectiveness, 598–600
    choosing a therapist, 614–615
    cognitive and cognitive–behavioral treatments, 603–605, 608
    combined approach effectiveness, 611–612, 613f
    combined drug therapy and psychotherapy, 610
    combined mindfulness training and psychotherapy, 611–612
    drug therapies, 592–594, 592f, 593f, 598–600, 608
    electric and magnetic therapies, 595–598, 596f, 598f, 599–600
    group therapies, 605–607, 619
    humanistic–positive therapies, 601–602
    integrative therapies, 610–611
    major approaches, 591f
    prevention of disorders, 617–618
    psychoanalytic/psychodynamic therapies, 600–602
    psychological treatment effectiveness, 607–609
    psychosurgery, 595
    technology-based therapies, 609–610
trephination, 11, 11f
triangular theory of love, 543, 543f
triarchic theory of intelligence, 362
trichromatic color theory, 138
tricyclic antidepressants, 593, 618–619
triplet puzzle, 343–344
trisomy–21, 370–371
t-test, 59–60
twin-adoption studies, 75–76, 160
    on bipolar disorder, 569
    eating disorders, 406–407
    epigenetics and, 77
    identical twins, 160
    on intelligence, 374, 375f, 377
    on language acquisition, 332
    on personality traits, 482, 482f
    on schizophrenia, 559
    on sexual orientation, 412
twins, identical, 160
Twitter, 526, 527
two-string problem, 380, 380f, 382, 383
two-word utterances, 327, 328f
tympanic membrane, 142f
Type A Behavior Pattern (TABP), 465–466, 466f

U

ultrasonic sounds, 141
umami, 149
unconditional positive regard, 495
unconditioned response (UCR), 288–289, 290f
unconditioned stimulus (UCS), 288–289, 290f
unconscious, 487
universal, definition of, 426
universal grammar, 331, 336

V

vaccines, 26, 37*f*, 463
validity, 368
Van Gogh, Vincent, 550, 551
variable interval (VI) schedule, 300–301, 300*f*
variable ratio (VR) schedule, 300, 300*f*
variables, 41–42, 49
vegetative state, 212*f*, 213
verbal representation, 341–342, 342*f*
verification–elaboration, 384
veterans, PTSD in, 275, 275*f*, 575–576
Vicodin, 239
video games, 203, 206, 534–535
violence, 431. *See also* aggression,
    amygdala and
    sensitivity to, 535
    in video games, 204, 534–535
virtual reality exposure, 603
virtual reality therapies, 609–610
viruses, as teratogens, 166
vision
    absolute thresholds in, 120, 120*f*–121*f*
    bottom-up and top-down
        processing in, 137
    brain and, 125–127, 127*f*
    color, 124, 125*f*, 138–139, 138*f*, 139*f*
    cultural variation in, 152–153, 153*f*, 154*f*
    depth perception, 131–132, 132*f*,
        152–153, 153*f*
    eye and, 123–124, 124*f*, 125*f*
    Gestalt laws of grouping, 134–137, 134*f*,
        135*f*, 136*f*
    infant development of, 168–169, 168*f*, 169*f*
    motion perception, 130–131
    neurons and, 127–130, 128*f*, 130*f*
    night, 120
    perceptual constancy in, 132–134, 133*f*
    prenatal development of, 165
    visual cortex and, 98
    visual representation, 339–340, 340*f*
visual acuity, 123, 168
visual cliff, 169, 169*f*
visual cortex, 98
visual imagery, 339, 387, 387*f*
visual pathways, 125–127, 127*f*
visuospatial sketch pad, 255*f*, 256, 271, 272*f*
VI (variable interval) schedule, 300–301, 300*f*
vividness, 348
vocal expression, emotions and, 425, 428, 434
voltage-dependent channels, 83
VR (variable ratio) schedule, 300, 300*f*

W

WAIS (Wechsler Adult Intelligence Scale), 365,
    366*f*–367*f*, 367, 368
wakefulness, 211–212, 212*f*
water jar problems, 379, 380*f*, 381
Weathers, Beck, 396–397
Weber's law, 122
Wechsler Adult Intelligence Scale (WAIS), 365,
    366*f*–367*f*, 367, 368
Wechsler Intelligence Scale for Children
    (WISC), 365, 367, 367*f*
weight, properties of, 15
weight loss, 404–405, 438
well-being, 437–439
Wernicke's area, 100
    language learning and, 326, 326*f*, 333*f*
    language production and, 100
wet dreams, 188
white matter, 107–108, 170
Whorf-Sapir hypothesis, 336
wilderness survival, 396–397
Willie Horton advertisements, 532
WISC (Wechsler Intelligence Scale for
    Children), 365, 367, 367*f*
wisdom, 199, 201
witch hunts, 11, 12*f*
women and girls. *See also* gender differences;
        pregnancy
    menarche in, 188
    as psychologists, 16
    sexual response cycle in, 407–408, 407*f*
    testosterone in, 408
    thinness and obesity in, 402–403, 405*f*
word salad, 383–384, 559
working memory, 254–257, 367, 367*f*. *See also*
    short-term memory
workplace. *See also* industrial/ organizational
        (I/O) psychology
    career identity, 194
    employee motivation models, 415–417, 417*f*
    hearing loss in, 143, 197
    personality and, 505
work-related hearing loss, 197
world happiness map, 438*f*
writing, as coping strategy, 454–455

Y

Yap people, 153, 155
Yerkes–Dodson law, 399, 399*f*
young adulthood, 195–197, 196*f*

Z

Zoloft, 166, 593
zone of proximal development, 178
zygote, 161